KENNY'S
OUTLINES OF
CRIMINAL LAW

KENNY'S

OUTLINES OF CRIMINAL LAW

EIGHTEENTH EDITION, 1962

BY

J. W. CECIL TURNER
M.C., M.A., LL.B.
of the Middle Temple, Barrister-at-Law,
Fellow of Trinity Hall, Cambridge

CAMBRIDGE
AT THE UNIVERSITY PRESS
1964

CAMBRIDGE UNIVERSITY PRESS
Cambridge, New York, Melbourne, Madrid, Cape Town,
Singapore, São Paulo, Delhi, Mexico City

Cambridge University Press
The Edinburgh Building, Cambridge CB2 8RU, UK

Published in the United States of America by Cambridge University Press, New York

www.cambridge.org
Information on this title: www.cambridge.org/9781107675919

First edition 1902
Second edition 1904
Third edition 1907
Fourth edition 1909
Fifth edition 1911
Sixth edition 1914
Seventh edition 1915
Eighth edition 1917
Ninth edition 1918
Tenth edition 1920
Reprinted 1920
Eleventh edition 1922
Twelfth edition 1926
Thirteenth edition 1929
Fourteenth edition 1933
Fifteenth edition 1936
Reprinted 1942, 1944, 1945, 1946, 1947
Sixteenth edition 1952
Seventeenth edition 1958
Eighteenth edition 1962
Reprinted 1964
First published 1962
First paperback edition 2013

A catalogue record for this publication is available from the British Library

ISBN 978-1-107-67591-9 Paperback

PREFACE TO THE SIXTEENTH EDITION

Kenny's *Outlines of Criminal Law* first appeared in 1902. The author declared that it was his aim to make the study of criminal law attractive to the reader, not only by supplying him with illustrative examples which might give vividness and reality to abstract legal principles, but also by tracing its connexion with the past, so as to explain the historical anomalies with which the law was still encumbered. His further purpose was to suggest the most important controversies, psychological, social and judicial, that the law of crime seemed likely to arouse in the future. Kenny's hopes and prophecies were abundantly fulfilled, and he lived to prepare twelve more editions, the last of which appeared in 1929. The book was founded on the course of lectures which the author had delivered for some twenty-five years before he wrote it and its immediate and enduring success could have been no surprise to anyone who had been his pupil. For Kenny had the faculty not only of looking widely but also of looking forward; he welcomed new ideas but, being a man with great practical experience in the law and possessed of shrewd common sense, he appraised them wisely. This broad and sane outlook, coupled with his remarkable oratorical gift of clear and charming presentation, enabled him to render work on criminal law an educational exercise as well as a vocational training. It was found, moreover, to be an attractive exercise; for it was never Kenny's fate to watch his audience dwindle as the academical year wore on. Yet the outstanding characteristic of Kenny's work which has won its most lasting distinction is that he saw the connexion between criminal law and all the social sciences more clearly than any English legal writer before him had done: he thus laid the foundation for the conception of criminal science as one composite subject of which criminal law is a part. For one who had the good luck as an undergraduate to be taught by Courtney Stanhope Kenny and subsequently, as a colleague, to enjoy his courteous friendsship and wise advice, it is an honour to be entrusted with the preparation of a new edition of his famous book. Since his death there have been so many developments and fresh problems in criminal law that it is no longer satisfactory to splice new material into the old work, and it has become imperative to rewrite a great part of it. I am confident that if he could have lived until now Kenny's lively appreciation of new situations and his desire for progress would have caused him to take this course. The changes which I have made in the general arrangement of the text have been prompted by the experience gained in many years of close association with students: that same experience has led me to the view that the principal part of what is called teaching should consist in stimulating the student to teach himself, and to that end to encourage his critical powers so that he may hope to distinguish the good from the bad, and the better from the good. I have therefore made no attempt to obscure anomalies of legal principle or conflicts of legal interpretation: to recognize that an authoritative decision must be followed is a very different thing from accepting it as necessarily sound or satisfactory.

In conclusion I wish to record my gratitude to my friends, Professor Glanville Williams and Mr A. Ll. Armitage, for their kindness in reading through the page proofs of this book and for the many valuable suggestions which they have made.

J. W. C. TURNER

TRINITY HALL
June 1951

PREFACE TO THE SEVENTEENTH EDITION

This book makes no claim or pretence to be a work on criminal jurisprudence. It is offered as an endeavour to assist students to such an understanding of the rules of criminal law as will enable them to form a clear idea of the practical task which will confront the prosecution and the defence in the trial of a person accused of each specific crime dealt with in its pages. It has been written in the belief that it is impossible to satisfy every reader who may take the trouble of reading it, but also that it is the duty of the author of a text-book for beginners to present the principles of law in the simplest terms, avoiding so far as possible ambiguities of expression; and in particular when a definition has been adopted to adhere strictly to it throughout the subsequent exposition of the subject.

A legal text-book begins to run out of date so soon as it reaches the printer's hands, and in the years since 1951 there have been many new decisions and statutory enactments which have called for references to over four hundred fresh cases and some rewriting of the text. In particular the wording of the Homicide Act, 1957, has created problems which have required the retention, from the last edition, of many pages which clearer thinking on the part of the legislature would have made it possible to relegate to historical treatises and to exclude from a text-book for students who are preparing for examinations in criminal law. The result is that in order to restrict the inflation of the book it has, with regret, been found necessary to sacrifice Professor Kenny's original chapter on the Nature of a Crime, which formed Appendix I of the sixteenth edition. It is to be hoped that this will eventually be reproduced in some collection of legal essays by eminent writers of the past.

I wish to record my gratitude to Mrs E. E. Jansen and to Miss Isobel Gawler, whose skill and painstaking industry have done so much to make this and the previous edition suitable for printing.

J. W. C. TURNER

TRINITY HALL
January 1958

PREFACE TO THE EIGHTEENTH EDITION

Since this book went to press in 1958 there have been new statutes and many new cases of sufficient importance to call for inclusion in the present edition. The judgments in some of the new cases have excited criticism, and in others previously accepted principles have been overridden. The result is that the task of the younger students of criminal law has been rendered more difficult and onerous, and the attempt to describe this situation has compelled some increase in the size of the book.

During the past fifty years there has been developing a movement towards the extension of the sphere of judicial discretion, and towards the elimination of the subjective element in the test of criminal liability. There can also be detected an impulse, probably not consciously appreciated by those who act under its influence, to extend the scope of the law of crime to cover persons previously beyond its reach. These tendencies can be seen in such cases as *D.P.P.* v. *Smith*, *Welham* v. *D.P.P.*, and *Sykes* v. *D.P.P.* The resuscitation of the offence of misprision of felony in the last mentioned case might have interesting consequences, for if it were taken seriously by the general public the guess may safely be hazarded that the total number of crimes in the Metropolitan area alone would rise by certainly not less than ten thousand more larcenies reported to the police in the year.

I am glad once more to be able to express my grateful thanks to Mrs E. E. Jansen and to Miss Isobel Gawler for their invaluable help.

J. W. C. TURNER

TRINITY HALL
February 1962

CONTENTS

BOOK I

GENERAL CONSIDERATIONS

CHAPTER I

CRIME AND CRIMINAL LAW

CHAPTER II

PRINCIPLES OF CRIMINAL LIABILITY

CHAPTER III

VARIATIONS IN LIABILITY

CHAPTER IV

PRELIMINARY CRIMES

CHAPTER V

THE POSSIBLE PARTIES TO A CRIME

CHAPTER VI

THE CLASSIFICATION OF CRIMES

BOOK II

DEFINITIONS OF PARTICULAR CRIMES

CHAPTER VII

HOMICIDE

CHAPTER VIII

OFFENCES AGAINST THE PERSON THAT ARE NOT FATAL

CHAPTER IX

BIGAMY

CHAPTER X

CRIMINAL LIBEL

CHAPTER XI
OFFENCES AGAINST PROPERTY

CHAPTER XII
BURGLARY AND HOUSEBREAKING

CHAPTER XIII
STEALING

CHAPTER XIV

EMBEZZLEMENT

CHAPTER XV

FRAUDULENT CONVERSION

CHAPTER XVI

CHEATS PUNISHABLE AT COMMON LAW

CHAPTER XVII

FALSE PRETENCES

CHAPTER XVIII

RECEIVING STOLEN PROPERTY

CHAPTER XIX

OTHER OFFENCES INVOLVING FRAUD

CHAPTER XX

FORGERY

CHAPTER XXI

OFFENCES AGAINST THE STATE

CHAPTER XXII

CONSPIRACY AND INDUSTRIAL DISPUTES

CHAPTER XXIII

PERJURY AND OTHER OFFENCES AGAINST PUBLIC JUSTICE

CHAPTER XXIV

OFFENCES AGAINST INTERNATIONAL LAW

CHAPTER XXV

OFFENCES OF VAGRANCY

BOOK III

MODES OF JUDICIAL PROOF

CHAPTER XXVI

THE NATURE OF PRESUMPTIONS AND OF EVIDENCE

BOOK IV

CRIMINAL PROCEDURE

CHAPTER XXIX

LIMITATIONS ON CRIMINAL JURISDICTION

CHAPTER XXX
CRIMINAL COURTS

CHAPTER XXXI
SUMMARY PROCEDURE

CHAPTER XXXII

ORDINARY PROCEDURE

I. Preliminary Steps

CHAPTER XXXIII

ORDINARY PROCEDURE

II. From Accusation to Sentence

CHAPTER XXXIV

ORDINARY PROCEDURE

III. DETENTION AND PROBATION

INDEX OF CASES

[Figures in heavy type refer to pages.]

INDEX TO THE PRINCIPAL STATUTES

LIST OF PRINCIPAL BOOKS CITED

AND THE ABBREVIATIONS USED IN THE NOTES

ARCHBOLD, JOHN FREDERICK. *Criminal Pleading, Evidence and Practice.* [Arch.]

BLACKSTONE, SIR WILLIAM. *Commentaries on the Laws of England* (17th ed. by E. Christian, 1830), 4 vols. [Bl. *Comm.*]

COKE, SIR EDWARD. *Institutes of the Laws of England* (1797), 4 vols. [Co. *Inst.*]

EAST, SIR E. H. *A Treatise of the Pleas of the Crown* (1803), 2 vols. [East P.C.]

FOSTER, SIR MICHAEL. *Crown Cases; to which are added Discourses upon a few branches of the Crown Law* (3rd ed. by M. Dodson, 1792). [Foster]

HALE, SIR MATTHEW. *Pleas of the Crown: or, a Methodical Summary of the Principal Matters relating to that Subject* (1682), 2 vols. [Hale P.C.]

HAWKINS, W. *A Treatise of the Pleas of the Crown* (7th ed. by T. Leach, 1795). 4 vols. [Hawk. P.C.]

HOLDSWORTH, SIR WILLIAM. *A History of English Law* (1923–1938), 12 vols. [Holdsworth, *Hist. Eng. Law*]

Journal of Criminal Science, ed. by L. Radzinowicz and J. W. Cecil Turner, vol. I, 1948; vol. II, 1950.

Mental Abnormality and Crime, ed. by L. Radzinowicz and J. W. Cecil Turner, 1949.

Modern Approach to Criminal Law, ed. by L. Radzinowicz and J. W. Cecil Turner, 1948. [*Mod. Appr. Crim. Law*]

POLLOCK, SIR FREDERICK, AND MAITLAND, F. W. *The History of English Law before the Time of Edward I* (2nd ed. 1911), 2 vols. [Pollock and Maitland]

RADZINOWICZ, L. *A History of English Criminal Law*, vol. I (1948), vols. II, III (1956). [Radzinowicz, *Hist. Eng. Crim. Law*]

RUSSELL ON CRIME (11th ed. by J. W. Cecil Turner, 1958), 2 vols. [Russ.]

STEPHEN, SIR JAMES FITZJAMES. *A History of the Criminal Law of England* (1883). [Stephen, *Hist. Crim. Law*]

TURNER, J. W. C. AND ARMITAGE, A. LL. *Cases on Criminal Law* (2nd ed. 1958). [*T.A.C.*]

WILLIAMS, GLANVILLE L. *Criminal Law* (1961).

BOOK I

GENERAL CONSIDERATIONS

Chapter I

CRIME AND CRIMINAL LAW

Section 1. The Nature of a Crime

DIFFICULTY OF DEFINITION

¶ 1. The definition of a crime has always been regarded as a matter of great difficulty. The problem was discussed by Professor Kenny in his first edition of this work, and his exposition ever since has been regarded with careful consideration in any approach to the question. Where the task of definition is difficult it is advisable that a student should not address himself to it until he has acquired some considerable knowledge of the subject-matter to be defined. Professor Kenny's original chapter was therefore reproduced as an appendix in the last edition[1] followed by a brief note of some points of criticism to which it has been subjected. The truth appears to be that no satisfactory definition has yet been achieved, and that it is, indeed, not possible to discover a legal definition of crime which can be of value for English law. The reasons for this are to be found in the history of our common law.

TORT AND CRIME

¶ 2. Writers on English legal history have often mentioned that in early law there was no clear distinction between criminal and civil offences. The two have been called[2] 'a viscous intermixture', and it has been explained[3] that the affinity between tort and crime is not in the least surprising when we remember how late in the history of law there emerged any clear conception of a difference between them; this is, moreover, not a peculiarity of the English system, as was pointed out by Sir Henry Maine.[4] There is indeed no fundamental or inherent difference between a crime and a tort. Any conduct which harms an individual to some extent harms society, since society is made up of individuals; and therefore although it is true to say of crime that it is an offence against society, this does not distinguish crime from tort. The difference is one of degree only, and the early history of the common law shows how words which now suggest a real distinction began rather as symbols of emotion than as terms of scientific classification. Thus the

[1] 16th ed., App. I, p. 530. [2] Winfield, *Province of the Law of Tort* (1931), 190.
[3] Allen, *Legal Duties* (1931), 222. [4] See 16th ed., App. I, p. 554.

word 'felony' originally indicated something cruel, fierce, wicked or base. As Maitland says:[1] 'In general it is as bad a word as you can give to man or thing, and it will stand equally well for many kinds of badness, for ferocity, cowardice, craft.'[2]

CRIME IN THE PRIMITIVE STATE. EARLY ROME

¶ 3. The earliest reference to the word 'crime'[3] puts the date in the fourteenth century, and there is not to be seen any more precision in its meaning than there was originally in that of felony: it conveyed to the mind something disreputable, wicked, or base. Any conduct which a sufficiently powerful section of any given community feels to be destructive of its own interests, as endangering its safety, stability or comfort, it usually regards as especially heinous and seeks to repress with corresponding severity; if possible it secures that the forces which the sovereign power in the State can command shall be utilized to prevent the mischief or to punish anyone who is guilty of it. Offences of this kind are termed crimes and the procedure taken in the courts in respect of them is a 'criminal proceeding'. Of course a variety of factors may operate at the same time to produce this result, and it is rarely possible to identify them clearly: all that can be said is that an offence may become a crime as a result of the combined effect of a number of different social forces. It is easy to see that in a primitive monarchy or an oligarchy when all nominal state power rests in the hands of a personal sovereign, or of a small group of men, anything in the nature of an attempt to displace the governing body will be classed as treason and as criminal in the highest degree; and it will be repressed by all means available to the ruling element. In the early Roman Republic the sovereign power was conceived as being in the senate and people of Rome. Conduct regarded as endangering the safety and good order of the State so constituted was *perduellio* (making war upon the citizens) and *maiestas* (a later term, somewhat vague, meaning 'an infringement of the greatness of the State'[4]). In the first stages of national development there is little or no police organization and the sanctions of crime are freely left to the hands of the ordinary citizen. In early Rome for example the traitor suffered *consecratio capitis* and anyone who slew him was held guiltless; the English law of outlawry was at one time equally severe.[5] In the ancient city states of Europe security depended largely on the strength and construction of the city walls; it is due to this consideration that, for example, it was prohibited to erect private buildings near them since these might hinder the movements of defending troops within, and offer cover to approaching enemies without. The maintenance of the walls in a state of efficiency

[1] Pollock and Maitland, *History of English Law*, II, 465.

[2] The development of the felonies as a special category of crime is discussed below, ¶ 73.

[3] See *Oxford English Dictionary*, *s.v.*

[4] Greenidge, *Roman Public Life*, 100.

[5] Pollock and Maitland, I, 449, citing Bracton's *Caput gerat lupinum*.

was so important that at Rome religious superstition was invoked for their protection and they were classed as *res sanctae*; it was a capital offence to harm them or even to climb over them to enter the city instead of coming through the gates in the proper way.[1]

The advent of a new political regime whether as the result of violent or non-violent revolution is usually followed by the creation of new crimes. For example, it may become a crime to form any new political party, a crime to wear emblems or uniforms which could be mistaken for the insignia of the government, the political police may be placed outside the jurisdiction of any court, and empowered to treat as criminal and to take appropriate action thereon any conduct which they should regard as inimical to the established power; it may be the rule that no legal precedent is allowed to be any longer binding if it be not consistent with the official view of justice and equity,[2] and so on.

Even an autocrat may think not only of himself but also of the welfare of his subjects, and will therefore include in the category of crimes some harms which may be done to large numbers of them, or which cannot be satisfactorily redressed by civil action taken by the victim. Thus the social forces and the impulses which can effect developments in law are of many different kinds. They vary from the legislative power of a dictator to the undefined pressure of what is called public opinion. An illustration is the change in the law of incest made at Rome by the Emperor Claudius for his own private purposes. Desiring to marry Agrippina, the daughter of his brother, he procured a change in the law which permitted a marriage between a niece and her paternal uncle, leaving the law unaltered as to other marriages between uncles and nieces or aunts and nephews, so that these remained incestuous.[3] At the other extreme stands the Misappropriation by Servants Act, 1863,[4] which in effect provided that it should be no larceny for a servant to give to his master's animals, contrary to his orders, food that belonged to the master. Until that time it had been held by the courts that on the law as it then stood such a taking of the food was theft,

[1] Another example of the forces governing criminal policy is to be found in the Norman rules about 'Presentment of Englishry' (Pollock and Maitland, I, 88, 91; II, 487; Stephen, *History of Criminal Law*, III, 30). William the Conqueror enacted that a heavy fine should be paid by the hundred in which a Frenchman was slain unless the slayer were produced. A slaying by a person unknown was termed *murdrum*, hence our word murder. But, more than that, there developed a presumption that every person slain was French unless his Englishry could be proved. Here we see, not the desire to protect Norman-French (because by the reign of Henry I such special protection was out of date, as the two races were now from the constitutional point of view fused), but the desire to increase the royal revenue. The fine itself was also called *murdrum*. (This led in 1348 to a curious mistake as to the old law; Y.B. 21 Ed. III, p. 17*b* (Stephen, *Hist. Crim. Law*, III, 41), a mistake followed by Coke, 2 *Inst.* 148. See Pollock and Maitland, II, 481.)

Presentment of Englishry was abolished in 1340 (14 Ed. III, sect. 1, c. 4) just about the time when there was a period of antagonism between England and France, an antagonism which soon developed into war.

[2] As happened under the Nazi regime in Germany.

[3] Gaius, *Inst.* I, 62.

[4] 26 and 27 Vict. c. 103.

and a felony. As the result of a case which aroused some public feeling the law was changed by the above-mentioned statute.

CRIMES THE CREATIONS OF GOVERNMENT POLICY

¶ 4. Crimes therefore originate in the government policy of the moment;[1] the governing power in society at any given period has made, or accepted, rules of law which forbid a man to bring about certain specified results by his conduct.[2] Since that policy is influenced by many considerations it is not easy to discover in any specific case of new law, what exactly and exclusively are the forces which have produced it; nor, of course, is the policy always followed consistently or logically. It will often be difficult to say why certain kinds of harmful conduct are either not treated as unlawful at all or are left in the category of mere civil offences, while other kinds of apparently less harmful conduct have been selected for inclusion in the list of crimes. Rules of criminal law have often lingered in our legal system long after the changing stream of history has removed the situations which formerly seemed to call so urgently for their creation. Many harms are both crimes and civil wrongs.[3]

Confusion may also be caused by an inconsistency or lack of defined principle as to the methods which a community adopts for dealing with the crimes which it creates. In periods when a police force is non-existent, or only rudimentary, much is still left to the activity of individual citizens. The system of penal actions formerly common in England[4] is an illustration of this, for in such cases the State authority delegates to private individuals the task of putting the law into operation and may bribe them to do it by the award to them of the fines to be paid by the offenders.

Nor do the rules of procedure in English law provide a precise line by which tort and crime can be exclusively separated.[5] Even if these rules were changed by statute[6] so that civil offences and criminal offences could be thereby distinguished, this would not give a scientific definition of the nature of crime, since a thing is not adequately

[1] For example, the Waltham Black Act; Radzinowicz, *History of English Criminal Law*, I, 16, 49–51. And see ¶ 232, *post*.

[2] Such a result, within the field of criminal law, constitutes what is called an 'actus reus'; *post*, ¶¶ 11, 12.

[3] For example, assault, theft and libel.

[4] See Radzinowicz, *op. cit.* II, 14; and Kenny, 16th ed., App. I, p. 533. The Common Informers Act, 1951, removed this procedure from some forty-eight specified statutes (including s. 102 of the Larceny Act, 1861), but did not entirely abolish it from our law. For example the House of Commons (Disqualification) Acts of 1782 and 1801, s. 9, were left unrepealed. As to these Acts see *Forbes* v. *Samuel* [1913] 3 K.B. 706; *Bird* v. *Samuel* (1913) 30 T.L.R. 323; *Burnett* v. *Samuel* [1913] 3 K.B. 706 at p. 742 n.

[5] See Kenny, 16th ed., App. I, p. 536.

[6] Of course the legislature could do this (as suggested in [1956] *Crim. L.R.* 792), although the framing of such an Act would be extremely difficult. But even so the definition would be arbitrary, and would merely give effect to the legislative policy of the moment as to what 'offences' were to be covered by the statute.

defined by the statement of merely one or two of its innumerable characteristics.

So long as crimes continue (as would seem inevitable) to be created by government policy the nature of crime will elude true definition.[1] Nevertheless it is a broadly accurate description to say that nearly every instance of crime presents all of the three following characteristics: (1) that it is a harm, brought about by human conduct, which the sovereign power in the State desires to prevent; (2) that among the measures of prevention selected is the threat of punishment; (3) that legal proceedings of a special kind are employed to decide whether the person accused did in fact cause the harm, and is, according to law, to be held legally punishable for doing so.

Section 2. The Place of Criminal Law in Criminal Science

CRIMINOLOGY, CRIMINAL POLICY, CRIMINAL LAW

¶ 5. Whatever attempt may be made to define crime, it is clear that it is an offence committed by an individual in society. Criminal science is therefore a social study, and its aims are to discover the causes of criminality, to devise the most effective methods of reducing its amount, and to perfect the machinery for dealing with those who have committed crimes. It has three main branches, *criminology*, *criminal policy*, and *criminal law*.[2]

Criminology is concerned with the causes of crime, and comprises (*a*) criminal biology, which investigates causes of criminality which may be found in the mental and physical constitution of the delinquent himself (such as hereditary tendencies and physical defects), and (*b*) criminal sociology, which deals with enquiries into the effects of environment as a cause of criminality.

Criminal policy is the name given to that branch of criminal science which studies the means by which the volume of harmful conduct in society can be limited. It makes use of the information provided by criminology, and its subjects for investigation therefore are (*a*) the appropriate measures of social organization whereby harmful activities may be prevented, and (*b*) the treatment to be accorded to those who have caused harm. Under the last-mentioned heading fall decisions as to which transgressions can be adequately left in the class of torts, to

[1] 'The domain of criminal jurisprudence can only be ascertained by examining what acts at any particular period are declared by the State to be crimes, and the only common nature they will be found to possess is that they are prohibited by the State and that those who commit them are punished'; *Proprietary Articles Trade Assoc. and others* v. *Att.-Gen. of Canada and others* [1931] A.C. 310 *per* Lord Atkin at p. 324. The reference to punishment in this statement cannot be taken as intended to give the distinguishing characteristic of crime: see Kenny, 16th ed., App. I, p. 536.

[2] See Radzinowicz and Turner, 'The meaning and scope of criminal science', *Modern Approach to Criminal Law* (1948), 12 *et seq.*

be redressed by civil actions for compensation brought by the victim, and which need to be dealt with by the special sanctions imposed by criminal law, and further, which of those sanctions are appropriate in each case. These range from the penalty of death, through various degrees of deprivation of liberty down to such measures as medical treatment, supervision on probation, and mere warnings. Since it is criminal policy which must dictate the principles by which harms are to be classed as crimes and criminals are to be detected and treated, it is clear that criminal law, which forms the third branch of criminal science, is the instrument of criminal policy.

Chapter II

PRINCIPLES OF CRIMINAL LIABILITY

Section 1. At Common Law

A. HISTORICAL: NOT EMBODIED IN A CODE

¶ 6. Our system of criminal law is not, as is the case in some countries, contained in a single code promulgated by a legislative body. It is, on the contrary, a conglomerate mass of rules based upon the ancient common law of England as modified and extended by the authoritative decisions of the judges in the long passage of history, and vastly enlarged by the addition of statutory enactments made by parliament from time to time, to meet the needs of the moment. For a proper understanding of our criminal system it is therefore necessary to begin with a study of the common law, for as Blackstone wrote: 'Statutes also are either declaratory of the common law, or remedial of some defects therein.'[1]

THE PERIOD OF STRICT LIABILITY

¶ 7. There is evidence that throughout Europe in the remote past acts which caused serious harm were supposed to bring about the infliction upon the people of some calamitous punishment by the gods. In such circumstances severe sufferings were inflicted upon the offender in order to placate the outraged deity. But combined with this notion, and eventually outliving it, was the idea that the person whose active conduct appeared as the visible cause of the harm should be held responsible for it; indeed, this responsibility was attached to animals[2] and even to inanimate objects,[3] under the crude conception of causation formed by primitive and superstitious minds, which attributed some kind of spiritual personality to lifeless objects with which man himself had brought about a human death.[4] The English law as to 'deodands'

[1] 1 *Comm.* 85–6.

[2] See E. P. Evans, *The Criminal Prosecution and Capital Punishment of Animals* (Heinemann, 1906). Exod. xxi. 28: 'If an ox gore a man or a woman, that they die: then the ox shall be surely stoned, and his flesh shall not be eaten.' In 1386, in Falaise, a sow was sentenced to be maimed and hanged for having torn the face and arms of a child and caused its death (Charange, *Dict. des Titres Originaux*, 1764, II, 72); the official executioner of Falaise received 10 sous and 10 deniers and the cost of a new glove, for his services.

[3] Aeschines, *Against Ctesiph.* CCXLIV: 'When sticks and stones and iron, voiceless and senseless things, fall on any one and kill him, we cast them beyond the borders; and when a man kills himself the hand that did the deed is buried apart from the body.' Pausanias, I, 28, 10: 'The Court in the Prytaneum, as it is called, [is] where they try iron and all similar inanimate things...; leaving the axe where it lay, he went out of the country into exile, and the axe was forthwith tried and acquitted.'

[4] Cf. Pollock and Maitland, II, 474, 'that unreasoning instinct that impels the civilized man to kick, or by voice consign to eternal perdition, the chair over which he has stumbled'.

was a relic of this prehistoric notion; the deodand was any inanimate instrument by which the killing had been effected. In the Anglo-Saxon era it was called *brana*, the slayer,[1] and it was handed over to the family of the man killed in order that they might take vengeance upon it.[2] The old couplet ran

> Whatever moved to do the deed
> Is deodand and forfeited,

but forfeiture was not confined to things that had moved:[3] so once where a small boy fell into a pan full of milk and was drowned, the pan was forfeited.[4] As in many other instances the Church adopted this ancient superstition and harmonized it with the new religion by attaching a rule that the object should be 'given to God' for pious uses. The deodand thus assumed an added character of compensation, and, since the object in many cases formed part of the property of a man who himself was held responsible for the killing, the rule came to be associated with another rule which required that all a felon's goods should be forfeited. Accordingly the deodand was exacted not only where death was due to some natural accident, as in the case of a man falling from a tossing boat and being drowned, or where a man fell under a cart wheel,[5] but also in the case of a man on horseback riding over a man asleep on the highway. The deodand was generally sold by the King, the purchase money, or commutation money, received for it being devoted to pious uses for the soul that had died unabsolved. After the Reformation, the money was usually handed to the poor, or to the relations of the deceased. Thus when in 1716 the coroner's jury of Yarmouth declared a stack of timber which had fallen on a child to be forfeited as a deodand, it was ransomed for 30*s*., which was paid over to the child's father. Deodands were not abolished until 1846.[6] The change was hastened by the advent of the railway. In 1841, after an accident on the Great Western Railway at Sonning, a railway carriage is said to have been taken by the Lord of the Manor as a deodand,[7] and in 1840 the deodand was valued by the jury at £2000 after an accident on the London and Birmingham Railway.[8]

[1] *Munimenta Gildhallae Londoniensis* (Rolls Series), I, 98; Bracton, fo. 116.

[2] Brunner, *Deutsche Rechtsgeschichte*, II, 558. For a startling modern decision which harmonizes with this antiquated superstition see *Kensington Borough Council* v. *Walters* [1959] 3 W.L.R. 945, discussed in [1960] *Crim. L.R.* 89 and 168, *sub tit.* 'Back to the deodand'.

[3] Bracton, fo. 136*b*, thought otherwise.

[4] *Select Coroners' Rolls*, 50.

[5] Jacobs, *Law Dictionary*, 1782, *s.v.* 'deodand': 'As if a man driving a cart falls so as the cart wheel runs over him, and presseth him to death, the cart wheel and horses are forfeited to the lord of the liberty for *omnia quae movent ad mortem sunt deodanda*. But it hath been observed that at this day if a man be killed by the wheels of a cart drawn with horses the jury find that only deodand which was the immediate cause of his death, viz. the wheel...for in the present enlightened age juries are not much pleased with this obsolete law.' And see *Northumberland Assize Rolls*, 96, for the older view.

[6] 9 and 10 Vict. c. 62.

[7] Webb, *Local Government*, II, 75 n. 3.

[8] *Monthly Law Magazine* (1841), X, 15.

EXPIATION OF GUILT BY MONEY PAYMENT

¶ **8.** The seeds of our common law germinated in bygone days when complexities of commercial life were unknown: the kinds of offences which called for criminal sanction were not many, and apart from some cases of treason and religious transgressions they took the form of some physical interference with life, liberty, or tangible property. The rules of criminal liability were also simple. Thus, in Anglo-Saxon times, the law treated all homicides, heinous or innocent, as matters to be expiated by the payment of a pecuniary *wer*. So late as 1118, the compiler of the so-called *Leges Henrici Primi* gives it as still the Wessex rule that for every homicide, whether intentional or even accidental, the *wergild* must be paid[1] to the family of the slain man. The rough-and-ready rule became established that if the deed could be directly traced to a man's acts, then he was held responsible to pay the compensation which the law prescribed. This is what is called 'absolute', or 'strict', liability. The connexion between the acts and the injury was plain, and since in any case the consequential suffering and loss must be borne by someone, it seemed proper that the burden should as far as possible be carried by him whose active conduct had brought about this misfortune. He must accordingly make a pecuniary betterment (*bót*) to the injured party, according to an elaborate tariff which laid down the price of different blows and wounds varying with the rank of the victim.[2] In the case of homicide the compensation to be paid to the family was called *wer*, being the value set upon the man's life.[3] In addition the King exacted a fine called *wíte*.[4] Most crimes became 'emendable' in this way; but the gravest offences remained unemendable and were termed 'bootless',[5] the offender being left to the King's mercy. The exaction of *wíte* made crime a source of royal profit and this became more important as the class of crimes reserved for the King's jurisdiction was enlarged.[6] But for the 'bootless' crimes various kinds of afflictive punishment of a most brutal character were applied, forfeiture of property being incidentally possible. By Norman times the system of emendation was becoming obsolete, being replaced by afflictive punishments, prescribed at the discretion of the King, as a substitute for outlawry. The early

[1] Cap. 70, s. 12. 'Sive autem sponte aut non sponte fiant hec, nichilominus tamen emendetur. *Que enim per inscienciam peccamus, per industriam corrigamus.*' Pollock and Maitland, II, 471, and (for Alfred's quaint thirty-sixth law, as to various accidents caused by carrying a spear) I, 53.

[2] Examples are given in Pollock and Maitland, II, 458 *et seq.*

[3] See Pollock and Maitland, I, 48 and II, 449.

[4] All these fines amounted to a very large payment, according to the value of money in those ages, so great indeed that it is considered that few were able to pay them and in default were outlawed or sold as slaves. See Pollock and Maitland, II, 460.

[5] O.E. *bótleás*.

[6] This is not the place to trace the steady process of encroachment whereby the kings extended their supreme jurisdiction until it eventually covered all crimes and all persons in all places in the realm, and thus made the 'King's peace' universal.

Norman kings varied the penalties at their will between death, various kinds of horrible mutilation, and fines. But gradually the penalty of death prevailed and mutilation became uncommon.[1]

THE MOST SERIOUS CRIMES RECOGNIZED FIRST

¶ 9. The very ancient records are mostly concerned with crimes which in our modern system appear the most serious among a vast number of relatively minor kinds of offences; but in early Norman times, as mentioned above, the list of crimes was short, and our common law developed its principles mainly in dealing with that small group, in which treason, breaches of feudal obligations, homicide and theft were predominant. For although the wide extension of the King's peace nominally brought all minor transgressions within the orbit of the Crown's criminal jurisdiction the practice developed of leaving these less harmful offences to be dealt with by tribunals which awarded damages[2] assessed in accordance with the facts of the case in substitution for the compensatory *bót* of the past ages. This was one of the main factors in the appearance in the thirteenth century of a distinction between crime and tort.

Up to this point the outstanding features of the first period in the historical development of the principles of criminal liability are three in number: (1) The paramount importance of the 'deed'; a man was held strictly accountable for any harmful result traceable to his active conduct.[3] (2) The consequential principle, that a man was not liable when he had done nothing active, even though his omission to act may have been clearly the cause of the harm.[4] (3) The great severity of the penal system when the sanction of compensatory payment was replaced by afflictive punishment, generally that of death.

THE NEED FOR A NEW TEST OF CRIMINAL LIABILITY

¶ 10. In the next stage several factors united to bring about the realization that a new conception of criminal responsibility was required. In accordance with their determination to extend their control and stabilize their supremacy the Norman kings appointed royal officers for the enforcement of law, and this led not only to the growth of legal science but also to the building-up of a machine for the administration of justice which was capable of a more refined assessment of the facts in prosecutions for crime than had previously been possible. There were fiscal considerations[5] also which indirectly assisted the development of discriminatory investigations into criminal charges; for the royal policy of enlargement brought many offences within the purview of the criminal law, and established a practice of exacting fines calculated at the discretion of the judges, in place of the old system of fixed payments.

[1] See Pollock and Maitland, II, 459, 460.

[2] Pollock and Maitland, II, 520.

[3] See the examples in Pollock and Maitland, II, 470.

[4] Even an attempt (if unsuccessful) to commit an offence was no crime in that period; Pollock and Maitland, II, 475, citing Brunner, *Deutsche Rechtsgeschichte*, II, 558–64.

[5] Pollock and Maitland, II, 453.

The term 'felony' also assumed a more precise and technical significance; it came to be used only to mark the class of the more serious offences such as homicide, grievous bodily harm (known as mayhem), arson, rape, false imprisonment, robbery, burglary and larceny. For this class of crime 'emendation' was not possible; the penalty was death or mutilation. The combination of the ancient rule of strict liability and the new system of condign physical punishment produced a situation in which the criminal law appears as a regime of appalling ferocity. Yet even in the pre-Norman age there were devices found whereby in some cases at least the worst cruelties could be evaded, in deference to the moral sense of the time;[1] one illustration which brings this predicament vividly before the modern mind is the rule which lasted for centuries that one who killed another by mere misadventure, or even in reasonable self-defence, must be held guilty of homicide, and could only be saved by a pardon, granted by the King in the exercise of his mercy.[2]

The appreciation of the severity to which the strict rules of law had come had two main consequences. One was that attempts were made to find a working test for the legal limit to be placed on the endless chain of consequences which could be traced from any act. An example of the length to which the ancient conception of causation would go is to be seen in the rule of the *Leges Henrici Primi* that a man accused of homicide must swear that he had done nothing whereby the dead man was 'further from life and nearer to death';[3] this is given as the basis for a decision that where *A* put his spear or sword in a certain place, and *B* knocked it down so that it killed or wounded *C*, then *A* must pay for the harm suffered by *C*. So extensive a range of liability was not, of course, maintained in later times. On the one hand, for those offences which came to be dealt with as civil wrongs, redressable by an action for damages, there gradually emerged the basic principle, now firmly established in our law of tort, that save in special circumstances the liability of a defendant does not run beyond that kind of consequence of his conduct which a reasonable man, placed in his position, could be expected to have foreseen. In the law of crime there is no such authoritative test of remoteness.[4] It was indeed rendered unnecessary by the counterbalancing restriction imposed upon criminal liability by the requirement of *mens rea*,[5] even in its earliest objective form, when it meant little more than an outward manifestation of wicked behaviour.[6] For moral wickedness cannot well be imputed to a man who has

[1] As to this see *post*, ¶ 55, Benefit of clergy.

[2] Pollock and Maitland, II, 479.

[3] *Leg. Hen. Pr.* 90, s. 11; Bracton, fo. 141*b*.

[4] Special difficulties as to remoteness which have arisen in the crime of 'attempt' are discussed below, ¶ 63.

[5] In actions in tort for trespass to person or property a subjective *mens rea* is even now not required; here the test for civil liability has remained objective, so that it is both necessary and enough for the defendant to conduct himself as a reasonable man would have done in the same circumstances. In the law of tort, moreover, there are still relics of strict liability in some cases, e.g. in relation to mistake as a defence.

[6] See ¶ 14. The subject of causation is discussed below, ¶ 13.

behaved as a reasonable man behaves; and a reasonable man does not alter his course of conduct when he has no reason to foresee that any harm will come of it. But there was still lacking any definite rule that a man should not suffer criminal punishment unless it appeared that he himself had realized that the action which he was taking could result in the harmful 'deed' which constituted a crime. In other words, it was not yet established as a rule of law that the tribunal before which he was arraigned should have evidence from which it could be satisfied that when he acted as he did, he was, in his own mind, conscious that he was doing wrong.

None the less it would be a mistake to assume that the Anglo-Saxon and early Norman lawyers were insensible to the moral distinction between harm which a man intended, and harm which he brought about by accident.[1] Such records as we have show that in all ages an appreciation of degrees in moral blame caused men in particular instances to adopt devices whereby the strictness of the law could be in some measure evaded.[2] So also many of the grants of pardon which have been preserved express conditions which vary with the royal view of the amount of blame to be imputed to the suppliant for mercy.

The courts were, however, not possessed of facilities for investigating the working of a man's mind, and were uncertain as to the possibility of assessing it accurately. This difficulty is illustrated even as late as 1477 by a much quoted saying of Brian, C.J.,[3] 'for it is common knowledge that the intention of a man will not be probed, for the Devil does not know man's intention'. In practice the judges seem to have gone on the rough-and-ready assumption that a man must in almost every case have intended to do what he had done, or at least have foreseen that the mischief would follow upon his acts; as Maitland has pointed out, our old law started from a position which could be expressed in a Latin sentence, *factum reputabitur pro voluntate*.[4]

It is true that the common law at this stage displayed in more than its usual measure the defect of clumsiness ameliorated by inconsistency. Its basic rule of strict liability had been suitable enough in the earlier period when, in theory at any rate, the penalty for such an offence as homicide was merely the payment of compensation; it was unfair and inappropriate in an age when criminal policy had substituted cruel punishments for pecuniary atonement.

On the other hand the attitude of the Church was quite different. To the ecclesiastics the working of a man's mind was of paramount

[1] See Raymond, 'The origin and rise of moral liability in Anglo-Saxon criminal law' (1935–6), 15 *Oregon L.R.* 93.

[2] See Pollock and Maitland, II, 469; Winfield, 'The myth of absolute liability' (1926), 42 *L.Q.R.* 37.

[3] Y.B. 17 Ed. IV, fo. 2; a civil action arising out of an agreement for the sale of growing crops, the point in argument being the purchaser's uncommunicated approval of the property sold. The word 'trie' in the Y.B. text has sometimes been mistranslated as triable (instead of 'probed' or 'investigated') which gives a wrong meaning to the Chief Justice's declaration.

[4] Pollock and Maitland, II, 477.

importance, since their aim was to eradicate sin and wickedness, and it was in the mind of man that these grave faults originated and existed; in their view that which called for penance and atonement was the evil intention or motive which had prompted the harmful deed. In their own spiritual courts they not only exercised a considerable jurisdiction over laymen,[1] but they also claimed and established an exclusive right to deal with ordained clerks who were charged with serious crimes,[2] and they admitted no impossibility in the investigation of the mental element in wrongdoing. In this they were assisted by their training in the principles of Roman law which reflected a refined appreciation of the distinctions in mental attitude denoted by the terms *dolus malus*, *culpa lata*, *culpa levis*, and *casus*. The religious doctrine that there must be expiation for sinful deeds was in accord with rules of criminal law as to punishment; but the religious sanctions, although by no means lenient, were varied to match the degree of moral turpitude which could be detected in the offence, and the spiritual courts were therefore primarily concerned with the mental ingredient in the commission of an offence.

THE RECOGNITION OF A MENTAL ELEMENT IN CRIMINAL LIABILITY

¶ 11. Influences of the kind mentioned in the preceding paragraph combined to reinforce the ethical conception that it was not proper to punish a man criminally unless he had known that he was doing wrong. Attention was thus more strongly directed to the mental element in crime, and the moral notion gradually crystallized into a rule of law. This process was assisted by the now more clearly distinguished law of the civil offence, the tort, which, as previously mentioned, retained the ancient rule of strict liability without any objectionable consequences, since condemnation purported to give no more than pecuniary compensation for the harm done.

It happened that long before this period St Augustine had said: *Ream linguam non facit nisi mens rea.*[3] This remark, slightly altered, eventually appeared in the *Leges Henrici Primi*[4] as a test of guilt in the crime of perjury. It was a phrase which was destined to win general application and to become the best known maxim of English criminal law, in the words ultimately used by Coke to express it:[5] *Et actus non facit reum nisi mens sit rea.* In this famous phrase there is a clear distinction between a man's 'deed' (*actus*) and his mental processes (*mens*) at the time when he was engaged in the activity which resulted in the deed.[6] This means that

[1] Including matters relating to marriage, wills, intestate succession, and over transgressions such as adultery and defamation.

[2] See below, Benefit of clergy, ¶ 55.

[3] *Sermones*, no. 180, c. 2; cited in Pollock and Maitland, II, 476 n. 5.

[4] *Leg. Hen. Pr.* 5, s. 28.

[5] 3 *Inst.* 6.

[6] As we have seen (¶ 9), the early common law was almost exclusively concerned with the harmful results of a man's *active* conduct, and it is convenient for brevity to speak of 'deeds' when discussing general principles. But students should remember that the expression '*actus reus*' covers also results caused by omissions to act in those rare circumstances in which the common law imposes a legal duty to take action (*post*, ¶ 12).

the conduct which resulted in the deed was inspired and actuated by his *mens rea*,[1] because in the usual case he intends to produce that result and regulates his conduct in order to produce it. But it will be enough to involve him in criminal liability if he consciously *takes the risk* of the result (i.e. if he is reckless as to that result, *post*, ¶ 24); and in this instance, although his *mens rea* does not actuate his conduct, it accompanies it, or, we may say, is coincident with it, so that he acts with knowledge that the deed may result from his conduct.[2]

This maxim,[3] which has been accepted in our courts for centuries,[4] recognizes that there are two necessary elements in crime, a physical element and a mental element, and it makes plain that at common law no man may be found guilty of crime, and therefore legally punishable, unless in addition to having brought about a harm which the law forbids, he had at the time a legally reprehensible state of mind. It is therefore necessary that the student should attempt to reach an understanding of these two constituent parts of criminal responsibility.

B. *ACTUS REUS*. (*a*) Deed of commission

¶ 12. The word *actus* connotes a 'deed', a physical result of human conduct. When criminal policy regards such a deed as sufficiently harmful it prohibits it and seeks to prevent its occurrence by imposing a penalty for its commission. It has long been the custom of lawyers to describe a deed so prohibited by law in the words *actus reus*. Thus *actus reus* may be defined as 'such result of human conduct[5] as the law[6] seeks to prevent'.

The 'deed' so defined in law may be either (*a*) simple (such as unlawful car-parking); or (*b*) made up of several stated facts. In these latter cases the prosecution must establish against the accused person these legally essential facts, and included amongst them there may be one or more which are personal to the accused man himself, including even his own thoughts. Thus in burglary[7] the prosecution must prove that the prisoner (i) broke and entered, (ii) the dwelling house of another, (iii) in the night, (iv) *with intent to commit a felony therein*. Of these

[1] See *Fowler* v. *Padget* (1798) 7 T.R. 509, *per* Kenyon, C.J.: 'The intent and the act must both concur to constitute the crime.'

[2] See Russ. 60, where the case of *R.* v. *Meli* [1954] 1 W.L.R. 228 is criticized.

[3] The Latin is clumsy: '*reum*' is an adjective in the predicate, with 'hominem' understood as the object, and means 'legally guilty', 'punishable as a criminal'; but the word '*rea*', while it qualifies the noun '*mens*', does not do so in the same subjective sense as the previous '*reum*', for it means 'legally blameworthy', an attitude of mind which the law reprobates. The noun '*actus*' is a general word, in the sense 'whatever the deed a man may have done'.

[4] In *Fowler* v. *Padget* (1798) 7 T.R. 509, Lord Kenyon, C.J., said: 'It is a principle of natural justice, and of our law, that *actus non facit reum nisi mens sit rea*.' And see *Younghusband* v. *Luftig* [1949] 2 K.B. 354, '*actus non facit reum, nisi mens sit rea* is a cardinal doctrine of the criminal law', *per* Lord Goddard, C.J., at p. 370.

[5] The word 'conduct' here covers both acts and omissions.

[6] Basically, of course, it is the sovereign power which, through the law, seeks to prevent the result; *ante*, ¶ 4.

[7] *Post*, Chapter XII.

elements, (ii) and (iii) are objective facts as to which the subjective mental attitude of the prisoner is irrelevant; that is to say, whether or not the prisoner believed it to be a dwelling house, or belonging to another man, or that it was 'in the night' (as defined by law) can make no difference to his liability to conviction if the other necessary facts are established against him. But (iv) is subjective and the prosecution must establish beyond reasonable doubt that he had the specified intention. The student must note, however, that although this is a subjective matter—an attitude of mind—it has nothing to do with the *mens rea* (as defined below, ¶ 14) of the crime of burglary[1] but is simply one of the several facts which together constitute the *actus reus*.[2]

It is important to note that the *actus reus*, which is the result of conduct, and therefore an event,[3] must be distinguished from the conduct which produced the result. For example, in a simple case of murder it is the victim's death (brought about by the conduct of the murderer) which is the *actus reus*; the *mens rea* is the murderer's intention to cause that death. In other words, the crime is constituted by the event, and not by the activity (or in certain cases, as we shall see, by the omission to act) which caused the event.

Again it is only such events as the law has chosen to forbid, that are crimes: a deed may consist of harm and destruction of property and even of life, but it is not a crime unless the circumstances are such that it is legally prohibited.[4]

The law may indeed (*a*) command, or (*b*) permit harm to be inflicted. Accordingly (*a*) no crime is committed when a duly appointed executioner puts to death a condemned criminal; for although he does so with the full intent to kill yet this deed, so far from being forbidden, was commanded by the law: it is therefore not an *actus reus* on his part.[5]

As to (*b*) another instance of harm which is legally justified is found in the operation of the rule which allows a person in certain situations to employ even fatal force in order to prevent another from committing a crime, or in arresting one who has committed a serious offence. Again, hurt of a less serious kind is not forbidden when inflicted in the reasonable chastisement of a child by a parent, or by a schoolmaster to whom the parent has delegated, or is deemed to have delegated, his authority.

There are other instances where the law permits the harm to be done, or risked, provided the person exposed to hurt or risk of hurt has himself consented to what is being done. In such a case there is the consent

[1] It is of course the *mens rea* of the felony which the burglar intends to commit in the house, e.g. murder, rape, arson, larceny, etc. [2] See Russ. 28.

[3] The word 'event' is used here in the sense of a consequential occurrence; it therefore includes not only the result of active conduct (i.e. a deed) but also the result of inactivity.

[4] See *Mod. Appr. Crim. Law*, 197; Russ. 29 *et seq.*

[5] It would be an *actus reus* if the condemned prisoner had been put to death by some unauthorized person; or even by the lawfully appointed executioner if he had used an unlawful method of taking the prisoner's life (Coke, 3 *Inst.* 50). For cases in which, on grounds of humanity, this rule was disregarded see Foster, 268. See Radzinowicz, *op. cit.* I, 212.

of the law accompanied by the consent of the person. Thus no criminal liability arises when hurt is inflicted by a properly skilled person in the course of a surgical or dental operation upon a patient.[1] Those also who consent to take part in proper sports and exercises may receive injuries which do not attract the sanctions of the criminal law.[2] It must be remembered, of course, that the consent of the party must be freely given and not obtained by deceit or fraud.[3]

In all such cases the man who caused the harm is immune, for in criminal proceedings it is incumbent upon the prosecution to establish not merely that the *actus* was brought about by the accused person, but also that in the circumstances of the particular case, that *actus* was forbidden (*reus*).

The plea of 'no *actus reus*' of course covers the usual defence of an accused person who denies that he had anything whatever to do with the crime; but it has often been thought to cover also the more difficult case of the man who pleads that the harm suffered is too remote a consequence of his acts to be, in law, imputable to him.[4]

(*b*) Result of omission

The ancient doctrine that a man should be held responsible for anything which he could be proved to have done, led naturally to the converse idea that a man could incur no liability if harm resulted as the result of his doing nothing at all. This doctrine has persisted to the present day in so far that no one is held criminally responsible, at common law, for the harmful consequences of his omission to act, whether that omission be careless or intentional, unless the prosecution can prove[5] that he was under a legal obligation to take action in the particular circumstances in which he was placed.

It seems that with few exceptions no duty under the common law rests upon a person to take action to protect others unless he has directly or indirectly undertaken so to do.[6] One exception is the duty which rests upon every citizen to aid and assist a police officer in the execution of his duty in order to preserve the peace when reasonably called upon, and reasonably able, to do so. Again, at common law the captain of a British ship is bound to try to rescue any of his own sailors or pas-

[1] See *R.* v. *van Butchell* (1829) 3 C. and P. 629 (*T.A.C.*).

[2] In the Middle Ages a tournament was an unlawful act, or anything in the nature of a gladiatorial combat; but, if the King commanded or permitted such a diversion, death or hurt resulting would only be a case of misadventure, for then the act was lawful; see Hale, 1 P.C. 473; 4 Bl. *Comm.* 183. The legal principles governing cases of consent are further discussed in relation to the specific crimes against the person; see Chapters VII and VIII.

[3] Which of course vitiates the consent and thus deprives the person who practised the fraud from using in his own defence the consent thereby obtained.

[4] *Ante*, ¶ 10; *post*, ¶ 13. Circumstances of the kind illustrated above are sometimes alluded to as 'matters of justification and excuse'. See the discussion of justifiable homicide, *post*, ¶ 94.

[5] *R.* v. *Edwards* (1838) 8 C. and P. 611; *R.* v. *Barrett* (1846) 2 C. and K. 343.

[6] *R.* v. *Brown* (1841) C. and M. 314.

sengers who have fallen overboard.[1] Another exception is that of parents who, by virtue of their parenthood, are automatically under a common law duty to provide for their children and to protect them from harm.[2] Until modern times there was the limitation that a parent who neglected to provide food, clothing and shelter for the child could be excused on proof that he or she was too poor to procure what was needed. But this defence disappeared as the result of modern legislation which provided that parents in poverty could obtain the necessary assistance from the appropriate public authority. And now under the Children and Young Persons Act, 1933,[3] poverty is no longer an excuse for any parent (or any other person legally liable to maintain a child or young person) who fails to provide or to take steps to procure to be provided adequate food, clothing, medical aid or lodging for the child, or young person.

In all other instances it seems that it is only where a person has by his own conduct undertaken the responsibility that he incurs any liability for failing to take steps to assist or save another.

A duty to take action may be directly undertaken, or may be an inherent part of a wider assumption of legal obligation.[4] So any person who is old enough to be subjected to legal responsibility and who has undertaken, whether for reward or not, to care for someone who through age or infirmity is unable to help himself, is under a duty to take all reasonable steps to safeguard his charge.[5] Again, one who has engaged himself upon some work or employment, whether for reward or not, upon the performance of which the safety or life of another may depend, must perform that task with reasonable care and diligence, and must not abandon it without giving adequate and proper warning to anyone who, within his knowledge, may be endangered by its cessation.[6] In all these cases therefore the prosecution is loaded with the burden of convincing the judge that there was the duty to act. But there is often the additional obstacle of difficulty in establishing the causation; for in cases of harm resulting from omission it is frequently hard to prove beyond reasonable doubt that an omission must be held to have caused the harm. This is especially likely to arise in charges of homicide.[7]

CAUSATION

¶ 13. A harm which has been suffered is an event, and it is difficult to imagine any event which is not the product of a plurality of factors. Thus there may be several causes of one event. It is, however, reason-

[1] The Maritime Conventions Act, 1911, s. 6, extends this duty to the rescue of *any person* at sea who is in danger of being lost, even an alien enemy.

[2] *R.* v. *Senior* [1899] 1 Q.B. 283.

[3] 23 Geo. V, c. 12, s. 1.

[4] E.g. the master of an apprentice; *R.* v. *Self* (1776) 1 East P.C. 226; and see cases cited in Russ. 456 *et seq.*, 460 *et seq.*

[5] *R.* v. *Marriott* (1838) 8 C. and P. 425; *R.* v. *Instan* [1893] 1 Q.B. 450.

[6] *R.* v. *Pittwood* (1902) 19 T.L.R. 37; contrast the narrow scope of duty apparently adopted in *R.* v. *Smith* (1869) 11 Cox 210 (*post*, ¶ 131).

[7] Cf. *R.* v. *Pocock* (1851) 17 Q.B. 34. This matter is discussed below in connexion with the felonies of murder and manslaughter.

able to say that an event is caused by one of these factors if it would not have happened without that factor.[1] From this it would follow that a man can be said to have caused the *actus reus* of a crime if that *actus* would not have occurred without his participation in what was done. As we have seen[2] the ancient rule of strict liability required no more than this simple test of causation. Yet to many minds it would seem too severe to hold a man liable to criminal punishment for every harm which could be traced back along the chain of causation to something which he had done, and to obviate such excessive harshness the requirement of the additional element of *mens rea* was especially beneficial. Under the modern conception of *mens rea* no hardship can result from any finely drawn investigation of causes,[3] since the more remote the cause the greater the difficulty of proving that the accused person intended or realized what the effect of it would be. Unfortunately, however, our records contain many reports of cases decided in the transitional period when the doctrine of *mens rea* was changing and its implications were not fully grasped by the courts, which, hampered by the persistence of the ancient rules, sought to avoid unreasonable severity by an unscientific distinction of causes proximate and causes remote. But no clear line has been (or indeed could be) laid down between these two categories.[4] Some account must therefore be given of the attempts which have been made to assess the physical element in criminal liability, and these can be most conveniently examined under the following heads.[5]

(i) Where there is no physical participation

A man may be held fully liable although he has taken no physical part at all in the actual commission of the crime. Thus our law has from very early times attached to one who procures or advises another to commit a crime at least an equal responsibility with that of the actual perpetrator of the deed. The law relating to such situations is dealt with in greater detail under the special heads of principals and accessories,[6] incitement,[7] and conspiracy.[8]

The instigator may well be primarily liable and the person instigated guiltless, as where a man has effected his criminal aim through an innocent agent such as a little child,[9] or a lunatic.[10]

[1] *R.* v. *Towers* (1874) 12 Cox 530 (*T.A.C.*). [2] *Ante*, ¶ 8.

[3] E.g. *Anon.* (1328) Y.B. 2 Edw. III, fo. 34, Hil. pl. 1 (*T.A.C.*); *The Harlot's Case* (1560) Crompt. 24 (*T.A.C.*); *R.* v. *Hickman* (1831) 5 C. and P. 151 (*T.A.C.*); *R.* v. *Coleman* (1920) 84 J.P. 112; *post*, ¶ 85.

[4] E.g. *post*, ¶ 63. In Italy the 'Progetto definitivo di un nuovo codice penale', of Alfredo Rocco, Art. 45, 'solves all these problems by the simple rule that only those supervening causes exclude the relation of causality which are by themselves sufficient to determine the event'; Stallybrass, in *Mod. Appr. Crim. Law*, 400.

[5] In the illustrations selected the reader will frequently detect a confusion between the mental and the physical elements of responsibility.

[6] ¶¶ 66 *et seq.* [7] ¶ 58. [8] ¶ 59.

[9] *R.* v. *Manley* (1844) 1 Cox 104 (*T.A.C.*).

[10] 1 East P.C. 226; 1 Hawk. c. 31, s. 7. Or an animal.

(ii) Where the participation is indirect

The *actus reus* is fully attributed to anyone who has done things which have led or allowed some wholly innocent person to act under mistake so as to cause the harm in question. Simple examples would be where *A* secretly puts poison into a drink which he knows or expects *B* will offer to *C*,[1] or where *A* recklessly leaves machinery or indeed any objects in a position that, as he realizes, they may cause harm to person[2] or to property[3] through being operated or moved inadvertently by someone else, or otherwise.[4] In early times it would have been murder where a man gave perjured evidence against an innocent person accused of a capital crime with intent to bring about his death, if the accused was condemned and executed.[5] This view was not followed, for even in an age when the definition of murder was much wider than now, and when the judges were more pliant to the Crown, the lawyers of James II did not indict Titus Oates, the inventor of the imaginary 'Popish Plot', for the murder of the men whose lives he had sworn away. Yet their desire to see him expiate his guilt by death, if it were legally possible, is sufficiently evident by the sentence passed (and executed) upon him, viz. two floggings of about two thousand lashes each. The opinion that the old common law guilt of murder in such a case was no longer law was supported by Foster in his remarks upon the *Macdaniel Case*.[6] In that case the Attorney-General declined to argue the point of murder, perhaps (as has been suggested)[7] from prudential reasons lest witnesses might be deterred from coming forward to give evidence in capital proceedings. However this may be, it seems now to be established that 'killing by perjury' is not murder.

(iii) Where another person has intervened

Cases frequently arise in which it would seem that the harm could not have occurred but for an act or omission on the part of the prisoner, but in which he has been excused on the ground that some other person intervened and appeared to have been the more immediate and direct cause of the harm; in such circumstances the prisoner has been exonerated, the reason being given that the harm was not the consequence of what the prisoner did, *but was the consequence of what the intervener did.* In *R.* v. *Huggins*[8] the warden of a gaol[9] was held not guilty of the murder of a prisoner whose death had been caused by confinement for forty-four days in a room which was 'very unwholesome and dangerous to

[1] *Anon.* (1633) Kel. 52 (*T.A.C.*).

[2] *R.* v. *Martin* (1881) 8 Q.B.D. 54; *R.* v. *Lowe* (1850) 3 C. and K. 123 (*T.A.C.*).

[3] *R.* v. *Pembliton* (1874) 2 C.C.R. 119 (*T.A.C.*); and see Malicious damage, *post*, ¶ 190.

[4] *R.* v. *Dant* (1865) L. and C. 567 (*T.A.C.*).

[5] Britt. c. 52; Bract. lib. 3, c. 4; 1 Hawk. P.C. c. 31, s. 7.

[6] *R.* v. *Macdaniel* (1754) 1 Leach 44 (*T.A.C.*); Foster, 130.

[7] E.g. 4 Bl. *Comm.* 196, note (g).

[8] (1729) 17 St.Tr. 309; (1730) 2 Ld.Raym. 1574.

[9] Who, under a scandalous practice prevalent at that period, had leased his position (for a money payment) to a deputy. See *R.* v. *Bambridge* (1729) 17 St.Tr. 582 at p. 617.

the life of any person kept therein', since there was not enough evidence to show that he had caused or consented to such confinement of the man.[1] But whenever the above argument for exoneration is advanced the facts must be carefully scrutinized lest a fallacious conclusion[2] be reached. Thus if one person was engaged in beating another with intent to kill him, and had already done him such harm as would shortly have caused his death,[3] and then a stranger, without being requested, were to rush in and add some more blows so that the victim's death was more speedily brought about, both would be guilty of murder and the first man could not be allowed the defence that it was the second assailant's strokes that finally ended the victim's life. In most instances the true defence for a prisoner in these intervention cases, if indeed he can be excused, is to be found in the failure of the prosecution to adduce the necessary evidence of *mens rea*. The problem has most frequently arisen in cases of harm caused by omission. Thus in *R.* v. *Hilton*,[4] on an indictment for manslaughter, it appeared that the prisoner, who was in charge of a steam-engine, had stopped the engine and gone away. During his absence some unauthorized person had set the engine in motion and it had killed the deceased. The judge stopped the case, holding that 'the death was the consequence, not of the act of the prisoner, but of the person who set the engine in motion after the prisoner had gone away'. A sounder reason for acquittal would have been that the prisoner did not expect that any harm would result from his breach of duty, as was really the case of the fireman in the London Fire Brigade who was absent from his post in charge of a fire-escape when the deceased had lost his life in a fire.[5] In contrast to these cases, an engineer who deserted his post at a colliery, leaving in charge of the engine an ignorant boy who declared himself incompetent to manage it, was held guilty of manslaughter of a collier who was killed through the boy's failing to stop the engine properly.[6] In this last case the prisoner clearly knew the danger which his dereliction of duty would create. For reasons stated in the opening passages of this paragraph[7] the older cases which have been reported show some variation of doctrine, and even at the present time it is unfortunate that the principles to be applied in deciding what chain of causation will in law be sufficient to establish criminal liability are far from clear. This is especially difficult in cases

[1] Although he had from time to time been present in the gaol, and had also acted temporarily as warden while his deputy was away. The gaoler, Barnes, who was in direct charge of the prisoner, was declared to be guilty of his murder. See also *Castell* v. *Bambridge* (1729) 2 Str. 854 where it was declared that it would be murder by a gaoler if a prisoner died of smallpox caught by his having been confined by the gaoler in a room occupied by another prisoner who to the gaoler's knowledge was suffering from that disease.

[2] Reasoning of this kind was the cause of the decision in *R.* v. *Saunders and Archer* (1576) 2 Plowden 473, although the decision itself can be defended. See ¶ 69 *post.*

[3] In *Meli* v. *R.* [1954] 1 All E.R. 373 (*post*, p. 53) it appeared doubtful from the evidence whether the blows inflicted on the deceased would have caused his death.

[4] (1838) 2 Lew. 214 (*T.A.C.*).

[5] *R.* v. *Rees* (1886) C.C.C. Sess. Pap. CIV, 171 (*T.A.C.*).

[6] *R.* v. *Lowe* (1850) 3 C. and K. 123 (*T.A.C.*).

[7] ¶ 13, pp. 17–18.

where the effect of medical treatment administered to the victim of an unlawful attack has to be assessed. Thus it has been judicially declared that if a dangerous wound be struck and under the best medical advice a surgical operation be performed which is the immediate cause of death, the striker is criminally responsible.[1] In *R.* v. *Jordan*[2] the appellant had been convicted of murder on evidence that he had stabbed the deceased who subsequently died in hospital from broncho-pneumonia following a penetrating abdominal wound. Application for leave to submit further medical evidence as to the cause of the death was granted in the special circumstances of the case by the Court of Criminal Appeal which, after hearing it, quashed the conviction. The new evidence was to the effect that the death was caused not by the stab wound which was mainly healed but by a mistaken administration of antibiotics and intravenous injection of liquid.[3] The court said:[4]

> We are disposed to accept it as law that death resulting from any normal treatment employed to deal with a felonious injury may be regarded as caused by the felonious injury but we do not think it necessary...to formulate for the assistance of those who have to deal with such matters in the future the correct test...with regard to what is necessary to be proved...to establish causal connexion between the death and the felonious injury...in the end it would have been a question of fact for the jury depending on what evidence they accepted as correct and the view they took on that evidence.

(iv) Where the victim's own conduct has affected the result

Although there is no definite test laid down by authority it would seem that so long as it is reasonably certain that the result charged against the prisoner in the indictment (*a*) would have occurred even if nothing subsequently had been done by the victim, or (*b*) did occur, although it might have been averted if the victim had taken some remedial action, then the prisoner should be convicted. Of course, as always in a criminal trial, if, in the opinion of the jury, there is on the evidence a reasonable doubt, the prisoner must have the benefit of it and be acquitted.

In *R.* v. *Horsey*[5] the prisoner was indicted for murder and it appeared that he had set fire to a stack of straw. While the stack was burning the deceased was seen in the flames and his body was afterwards found in the stack yard. There was no evidence of the identity of the deceased, nor of how he came there, nor that the prisoner had any idea that any one would be there: the prisoner indeed had tried to save the deceased.[6]

[1] *R.* v. *Pym* (1846) 1 Cox 339. See also *R.* v. *McIntyre* (1847) 2 Cox 379, and *R.* v. *Davis* (1883) 15 Cox 174.

[2] (1956) 40 Cr.App.R. 152. Contrast the facts, and the decision, in *R.* v. *Smith* [1959] 2 All E.R. 193; and see comment in [1959] *Crim. L.R.* 443, 444.

[3] The accuracy of this evidence has been subsequently challenged: see *The British Medical Journal*, 22 September and 13 October 1956.

[4] At p. 157.

[5] (1862) 3 F. and F. 287 (*T.A.C.*).

[6] On the authorities as they then stood it was considered to be murder if a man caused another's death even unintentionally while engaged in the commission of a felony (arson, in this case). It would seem that Baron Bramwell's sense of humanity led him to adopt a direction to the jury which would enable them to acquit the prisoner.

Bramwell, B., told the jury that if they were not satisfied that the deceased was in the enclosure at the time the prisoner set fire to the stack, but came in afterwards, then as his own act intervened between the death and the act of the prisoner his death could not be the natural result of the prisoner's act, and that in that view he ought to be acquitted. A case which went the other way was that of Governor Wall.[1] In that case the prisoner was found guilty of murdering a sergeant upon whom he had caused to be inflicted an illegal and brutal flogging from which the man died five days later. There was evidence that in the military hospital in which the deceased had been placed after the flogging a quantity of brandy had been supplied to him in accordance with the medical practice of that establishment, and that but for his drinking this there would have been a chance of his recovery. In addressing the jury the Lord Chief Baron Macdonald said: 'If a man by violence, places another in such a situation that a mortification, for instance, may come on, and is not unlikely to come on by mis-treatment of himself, that shall not be an excuse; and a murder may be committed, though unskilful treatment, or his misusage of himself, may have accelerated the death of the deceased.' A somewhat stronger case was *R.* v. *Holland*[2] in which the prisoner was convicted of the murder of a man whom he had wounded and who refused to follow medical advice and submit to the amputation of a finger, which, according to the evidence, might have saved his life.

In *R.* v. *Martin*[3] the prisoner was charged with manslaughter of a child four years old by giving it gin. It appeared that he had held out a glass to a little boy who snatched the glass and drank nearly the whole of the liquor, which brought about his death shortly after. Vaughan, B., told the jury: 'As it appears clearly that the drinking of the gin in this quantity was the act of the child, the prisoner must be acquitted.' Here again the sounder reason for acquittal would have been that the prisoner did not expect that his action would have the fatal result which followed; for it is plain that if he had not offered the glass the calamity would not have occurred.

(v) Contributory negligence of the victim

That the victim of an offence may himself have contributed to the harm by his own negligence affords no such defence to the accused in criminal proceedings as it may do in a civil action. In *R.* v. *Swindall and Osborne*[4] it appeared that the prisoners were each driving a horse and cart on the public road and encouraging each other to drive at a dangerous pace. In the course of this they ran over and killed a pedestrian.

[1] *R.* v. *Wall* (1802) 28 St.Tr. 51.

[2] (1841) 2 M. and R. 351 (*T.A.C.*); see also *R.* v. *Sawyer* (1887) C.C.C. Sess. Pap. CVI, 301 (*T.A.C.*). In Scots law the corresponding rule does not include the conduct of the deceased nor the mere omissions of third parties.

[3] (1827) 3 C. and P. 211 (*T.A.C.*). And see *R.* v. *Dalloway* (1847), 2 Cox 273 (*T.A.C.*).

[4] (1846) 2 C. and K. 230 (*T.A.C.*).

Pollock, C.B., told the jury that it mattered not whether the deceased was deaf or drunk, or negligent, or in part contributed to his own death. Of course the carelessness of the injured man may have produced a situation in which there is no criminal liability at all in anyone else; for example, where a pedestrian without looking or giving any warning steps off a pavement under the wheels of a passing vehicle. The facts of a particular case may present difficulty in such an assessment of liability.[1]

(vi) Where the participation is superfluous

It must finally be noted that the courts have had no difficulty in holding that an *intentional* participation in a crime is not excused by the fact that it would have taken place irrespective of the co-operation of the accused; in such circumstances a man is involved in responsibility for the *actus reus* though his assistance in it was superfluous, and even though any opposition which he might have offered to it would have been quite ineffective. If two strong men, *A* and *B*, were engaged in beating *C* to death, and *X*, a stranger, rushed in unasked and undesired by them, and administered to the victim some puny blow, he would be held as guilty of his murder as would *A* and *B*, if it appeared that all three foresaw that the death of *C* would be the result of the general attack which was being made upon him.[2]

C. MENS REA. (*a*) The objective standard of morality

¶ 14. That condition of mind which is termed *mens rea* is the second of the two essential constituents of crime at common law. We have already seen why it came about that this was held to be a necessary condition of liability to punishment: but in the courts recognition of the mental element was a gradual process and, as so often happened in our common law, there was to begin with some irregularity in the extent to which different judges were inclined to accept and to interpret the new idea. Therefore the student must expect to find occasional instances of conflict between decisions given in the ancient cases, since some judges were more resistant to change than were others.

It has, however, for long past been firmly established as a cardinal feature of the criminal law.[3]

As already stated it was the idea of moral wickedness interwoven with that of legal crime which was originally taken as the test of guilt.

[1] See *R.* v. *Kew and Jackson* (1872) 12 Cox 355 (*T.A.C.*); *R.* v. *Dant* (1865) L. and C. 567 (*T.A.C.*); *R.* v. *Monks* (1870) C.C.C. Sess. Pap. LXXII, 424 and Quain, J.'s observations in *R.* v. *Arnold* (1873) C.C.C. Sess. Pap. LXXVII, 351, at p. 354; *R.* v. *Stubbs* (1913) 8 Cr.App.R. 238.

[2] Cf. *R.* v. *Macklin* (1838) 2 Lew. 225 (*T.A.C.*). And see the rules as to 'principals in the second degree', *post*, ¶ 68. *R.* v. *Betts and Ridley* (1930) 22 Cr.App.R. 148 (*T.A.C.*); *R.* v. *Short* (1932) 23 Cr.App.R. 170. And note the qualification as to punishment contained in sect. 5 (2) of the Homicide Act, 1957.

[3] As a great criminal judge has said, 'the full definition of every crime contains expressly or by implication a proposition as to a state of mind'; Stephen, J., in *R.* v. *Tolson* (1889) 23 Q.B.D. 168, at p. 187.

This test was at first applied objectively, that is to say, the facts of each case were studied to see whether the prisoner's behaviour did or did not reach the moral standard generally accepted and approved in the period.[1] The question was not whether he himself thought that his conduct had been blameworthy or not; the courts went on the assumption that their own standard of what was right or wrong was the true one,[2] that it must be known to everyone, including the prisoner, and that if facts showed that the prisoner had not conducted himself as a man obedient to the moral code would have been expected to conduct himself, this established his *mens rea*. In this ethical framework a contention on the prisoner's behalf that he held a different criterion of good and evil, within which he had acted, would have been more likely to magnify than to reduce his offence.

(*b*) The emergence of a subjective standard

¶ 15. Although the adoption of the accepted rules of morality as a criterion of *mens rea* in practice meant that the courts appraised the prisoner's conduct objectively, yet a consideration of the actual working of his mind was in some degree necessarily involved. If, for example, a man was honestly mistaken as to the facts upon which he took action[3] or was so insane as not to understand what he was doing, or was compelled by overpowering physical force to be a helpless instrument in another person's misdeed he could not reasonably be regarded as a transgressor of the moral code. In such circumstances criminal guilt was often negatived in the courts by the argument that what had been done was 'not the prisoner's act'.[4] This ambiguous interpretation of the facts had the advantage that it could as well mean that the prisoner had not caused the harm as that there was no *mens rea* on his part, and thus it satisfied both the old and the new canon of responsibility.

Again, it often happened that the *actus reus* and the *mens rea* were not clearly distinguished. One who had duly executed a condemned criminal had effected a homicide which was justifiable; his own innocence of crime stood really on the basis that the *actus* was not forbidden (and therefore was not *reus*) but, under the old view, it could equally well be established by the plea that he had done nothing wicked nor immoral, and therefore had displayed no *mens rea*.

¶ 16. *Advantages of the new doctrine*. Rules of morality are necessarily unstable and nearly always lacking in precision, changing from age to age, since they reflect mankind's emotional reaction to external con-

[1] See *Mod. Appr. Crim. Law*, 201; Russ. 20 *et seq.*

[2] In 1868 an objective standard of morality was adopted by the court, *R.* v. *Hicklin*, L.R. 3 Q.B. 360, a case under the Obscene Publications Act, 1857, now repealed by the Obscene Publications Act, 1959.

[3] For the effects of mistake, see ¶¶ 39, 40 *post*.

[4] In former editions of this book Lord Hewart, C.J., was quoted as saying on 25 May 1922: 'If a man walking in his sleep do something, it is not his act at all.' This is an interesting survival of the ancient method of thought. For what, it is submitted, is the correct analysis of such a situation, see ¶ 18 below.

ditions,[1] and it should not be expected that the legal decisions and writings which have survived from those periods when a transgression of the current code of ethics was a requisite in criminal guilt can yield any precise definitions and distinctions, especially since the more ancient rule of strict accountability had not then, and indeed has not even now, entirely lost its force.

But the moral criterion was a necessary historical preliminary to an ultimate recognition that if crime is to be reduced and prevented criminal policy must direct attention to the personality, mental as well as physical, of the individual delinquent. The very requirement that an allegation of felony must be made in the indictments for grave offences opened the way to the consideration of the actual intention of the prisoner, and therefore to the decision as to the existence of a subjective fact. There was also the advantage that the new doctrine gave the courts a method of circumventing some practical difficulties in the law of homicide caused by the old rule of liability; for as will be seen later, where a man had killed another in self-defence (*se defendendo*) or by misadventure (*per infortunium*) it had previously been necessary that he should be convicted and then that the hardships should be obviated by royal pardon, a troublesome and expensive expedient;[2] whereas now the judge could direct the jury to bring in a verdict of acquittal. Furthermore, under the new doctrine there was built up the system of rules by which honest mistake of fact came to be accepted as a ground of excuse from criminal liability.

MALA IN SE AND *MALA PROHIBITA*[3]

¶ 17. The new conception, however, had some less beneficial consequences. Any emphasis laid upon the wickedness of an offender tends to inflame mass emotion and to stimulate prejudice; it is easily allied with superstitious fears and operates to suggest and justify cruel punishments. The conception also led to an unscientific and fallacious[4] separation of crimes into two classes, which were supposed to be basically different in nature, the one comprising what were called *mala in se* and the other *mala prohibita*. Among the members of any community at a given period, certain offences are by general agreement regarded as especially serious and excite deep moral reprobation, whereas other transgressions are regarded as venial and are more or less condoned, especially when they infringe rules of law which are unpopular. It is indeed inevitable that this apportionment of blame should be made. Yet the vague and fluctuating line which in everyday

[1] The results which can flow from the application of an objective moral test for criminal liability can be seen in the trial and execution of one William Flower, a monk of Ely, who was burned for sacrilege in 1555, described by a contemporary, Henry Machyn. See an article 'Sacrilege at St Margaret's', *The Spectator*, 22 April 1955, p. 496.

[2] See 1 East P.C. 222.

[3] See *Mod. Appr. Crim. Law*, 220.

[4] See Allen, *Legal Duties*, 239. And see *Board of Trade* v. *Owen* [1957] A.C. 602 *per* Lord Tucker.

life is drawn between the one group and the other only marks a variation in degree; it is not a boundary which separates things fundamentally alien in kind. Ethical reprobation of homicide, homosexuality, libel, adultery, bigamy and slave-trading, to take a few examples, is not the same in all countries, and indeed may vary from section to section of the people in the same country.

The unsoundness of the classification which was so uncritically accepted in the past can be seen by a consideration of some of the offences which were placed in the one group or the other by Blackstone, who was a convinced exponent of the arrangement. Amongst the *mala in se*, which he described as 'offences against those rights which God and Nature have established',[1] he included heresy, witchcraft, theft, perjury, breaches of 'natural duties, such as, for instance, the worship of God, the maintenance of children, and the like'. Blackstone did not expressly dissent from Coke's inclusion,[2] in the same list, of mingling defective malt with other good malt and 'putting the same to sale'; 'the selling of such unclean corrupt and mingled spices and drugs used in meats and drinks' ('the penalty of spices not garbled'); and offences against the statute of that time which levied a duty on foreign hops. The *mala prohibita* were said by Blackstone to comprise breaches of 'those laws which enjoin only positive duties, and forbid only such things as are not *mala in se*...without any intermixture of moral guilt'. Examples of these which he gave were exporting wool into foreign countries, exercising a trade without previous service as an apprentice, not burying the dead in woollen, and not performing work on public roads in accordance with statute.

This defective classification of crimes clearly formed an unsound premise from which to draw any jurisprudential conclusion[3] but it has an insidious attraction, and in the form of English phrases such as 'in itself unlawful' it has penetrated into one or two modern judgments with vitiating effects upon the logic and clarity of the argument.[4]

VOLUNTARY CONDUCT

¶ **18.** The first stage in the adoption of a subjective *mens rea* was reached when it was recognized that a man should be held guiltless if he could show that his movements which led to the harm were involuntary. If *X* is holding a knife and then *Y* seizes *X*'s arm and by means of his greater physical strength causes the knife in *X*'s hand to wound *Z*, the

[1] 1 *Comm.* 53.

[2] 4 *Inst.* c. 54.

[3] Cf. *Proprietary Articles Trade Assoc.* v. *Att.-Gen. of Canada* [1931] A.C. 310: 'It appears to their Lordships to be of little value to seek to confine crimes to a category of acts which by their very nature belong to the domain of "criminal jurisprudence"...', *per* Lord Atkin, at p. 324.

[4] E.g. *R.* v. *Donovan* [1934] 2 K.B. 498, at p. 508 (*T.A.C.*); *Andrews* v. *D.P.P.* (1937) 26 Cr.App.R. 34, at p. 50 (*T.A.C.*), 'there is an obvious difference in the law of manslaughter between doing an unlawful act, and doing a lawful act with a degree of carelessness which the Legislature makes criminal'; see *Mod. Appr. Crim. Law*, 221, 222, 239.

wounding would in early law have been held to be 'not the act of *X*',[1] but the real reason would be that *X*'s movement was not voluntary, and was not the result of any mental intention on his part. The defence would be the same if harm resulted from a man's movements in an epileptic seizure, or while suffering from St Vitus's dance, or while sleep-walking, or so drunk as not to know what he was doing. In all these instances an investigation has to be made into the working of the accused man's mind at the appropriate moment, and this is a subjective matter. Nowadays it is essential that the conduct of the accused should have been the result of the exercise of his will in all crimes at common law[2] and indeed in all crimes under statute unless the statute is so worded as necessarily to exclude such a requirement.[3] Since this rule developed from the original conception of *mens rea* as a manifestation of moral wickedness, it is not surprising that the expression *mens rea* should be used in reference to it in modern cases;[4] it must be noted that *mens rea* in this sense relates not to the harm which the man brought about, but to the movements (or omissions) by which he brought it about. In other words it indicates his mental attitude to his conduct and not his mental attitude to the consequences of his conduct (see ¶ 33 *post*).

In cases in which a man is able to show that his conduct, whether in the form of action or of inaction, was involuntary, he must not be held liable for any harmful result produced by it:[5] it is an *actus reus* (a result forbidden by law), but his defence is that he is not legally responsible for this *actus reus*. As above mentioned, cases of this kind would arise where a man, through no fault of his own, falls upon and injures or kills another; or where the like harm results from his walking in his sleep;[6] and in some cases of insanity,[7] or intoxication.[8]

FORESIGHT OF THE CONSEQUENCES

¶ 19. By the end of the Middle Ages the courts had abandoned the notion that the mind of man cannot be investigated. Much later Bowen, L.J., in 1891[9] declared such a principle to be fallacious and said:

[1] Hale P.C. 434.

[2] *R.* v. *Charlson* [1955] 1 W.L.R. 317, *post*, p. 80. See [1958] *Crim. L.R.* 361, 'Automatism and involuntary conduct' by S. Prevezer; and *Bratty* v. *A.-G. for N.I.* [1961] 3 All E.R. 523.

[3] As in *R.* v. *Larsonneur* (1933) 97 J.P. 206, see ¶ 31 *post*; and see Jackson, 'Absolute prohibition in statutory offences', *Mod. Appr. Crim. Law*, 262 *et seq.* This principle must also be applied when a person is charged with crime in respect of some omission to act; see *Harding* v. *Price* [1948] 1 K.B. 695; 1 All E.R. 283 (*T.A.C.*); *Kensington Borough Council* v. *Walters* [1959] 3 W.L.R. 945 and [1960] *Crim. L.R.* 89 and 168.

[4] *R.* v. *Wheat & Stocks* (1921) 15 Cr.App.R. 134, at p. 135 (*T.A.C.*) (see *post*, ¶ 173); *R.* v. *Maughan* (1934) 24 Cr.App.R. 130, at p. 132 (*T.A.C.*); *Cotterill* v. *Penn* [1936] 1 K.B. 53 at p. 61; (1935) 153 L.T. 377, at p. 378 (*T.A.C.*); *Law Society* v. *United Services Bureau* (1933) 98 J.P. 33, at p. 36. See Jackson, *op. cit.* 271.

[5] See, however, the exceptional case (under statute) of *R.* v. *Larsonneur* (1933) 97 J.P. 206.

[6] See *R.* v. *Tolson* (1889) 23 Q.B.D. 168 (*T.A.C.*), *per* Stephen, J., at p. 187.

[7] *R.* v. *Hay* (1911) 22 Cox 268; *R.* v. *Fryer* (1915) 24 Cox 403.

[8] *R.* v. *Moore* (1852) 3 C. and K. 319.

[9] *Angus* v. *Clifford* [1891] 2 Ch. 449, at p. 471.

'So far from saying that you cannot look into a man's mind, you must look into it, if you are going to find fraud against him; and unless you think you see what must have been in his mind, you cannot find him guilty of fraud.' Once it had been admitted that some degree of wickedness was a requisite in criminal guilt, it followed logically that *mens rea* must eventually become a subjective matter of an increasingly subtle kind. It is not enough to be satisfied that an accused person's conduct was voluntary since there may still be no moral blame if voluntary action does result in harm, provided that the harm was not contemplated. Accordingly there has developed in the common law a principle that a man should not be punished unless he had been aware that what he was doing might lead to mischievous results; he must have had foresight of the consequences of his conduct.[1] The nature of the precise circumstances, the foresight of which attracts criminal guilt, is fixed by law and varies from crime to crime. But whatever they may be for the particular crime, foresight of them is the common requirement for all, and it is this subjective element of foresight which nowadays constitutes *mens rea*.[2] Accordingly if he embarks on a course of action the harmful consequences of which he does foresee, he has *mens rea*; and if later he finds (or thinks he has found) that he has achieved these consequences (a result which we will assume constitutes an *actus reus*) his *mens rea* has come to an end, since he no longer intends or foresees that deed, he merely observes and remembers it. Any further activities by him will produce some new deed or deeds, as to which again he may have a *mens rea*; but if so, it will be a new *mens rea* and not a continuance of the previous one. This second *mens rea* cannot in logic be linked with the performance of the first deed; nor can the first *mens rea* in logic be linked with the second deed. Of course the question whether a man has, or thinks he has, achieved the first deed (and therefore has exhausted and ended his first *mens rea*) is a question of fact for a jury to decide on the evidence.[3]

Several of the common law crimes have always required a subjective mental element of a specific kind either from their very nature or from their earliest recorded definitions; such are incitement, conspiracy, attempt, rape, robbery, larceny, perjury, forgery and breaking prison.[4] These have accordingly not given any special difficulty on this particular point. But in the crime of homicide, assault, and false imprisonment there has been, and still is, great doubt and obscurity as to what precisely is the required *mens rea*. As we have already seen, the English system,

[1] This will also depend upon his accurate *knowledge* of the existing facts upon which he decides to take, or abstain from, action; see ¶¶ 39, 40 *post*.

[2] See the discussion of 'malice aforethought' *post*, pp. 142 *et seq*.

[3] This is the basis of the criticism of the judgment in *Meli* v. *R*. [1954] 1 W.L.R. 228; *post*, p. 53. And see now *R*. v. *Chiswibo* 1961, 2 S.A. 714.

[4] They are dealt with individually, under their separate headings, below. In some of them guilt depends upon a specific *intention* on the part of the offender; but this is covered by the term 'foresight', since that which a man intends he must necessarily foresee.

whereby changes in the law are made gradually by the accretion of judicial decisions, has often created the situation in which old and new doctrines have been employed in the courts of the same period, according as the judges inclined one way or the other. Precedents can thus be found for conflicting principles, with puzzling results: unfortunately this state of uncertainty still exists in the law of murder and manslaughter.[1]

It was during the eighteenth century that in the most intellectual circles there arose a movement for the reform of criminal law.[2] The chief criticism was directed against the excessive severity of the prevailing system of punishments but in due course attention was directed to the unsatisfactory state of the law on the principles of liability.

Thus Bentham stated[3] that the factors which should be considered in every transaction which is examined with a view to punishment are 'the act itself; the accompanying circumstances; the intention of the perpetrator; his degree of understanding, or his perceptive faculties, to be inferred from the nature of the act or from circumstances peculiar to it; the particular motive or motives at its root and the general disposition of which it is indicative'.

In the first quarter of the nineteenth century controversies in Parliament on the proposals for reform of the English penal system revealed the chaotic condition of the criminal law in general and a Commission was in due course appointed to consider the situation. This Commission made a series of Reports, and in their investigations its members were led to make certain recommendations on the principles of criminal liability. In their Fourth Report the Commissioners[4] said:

> And so in all cases it is essential to the criminality of the act, both in law and morals, not only that the act should in its own nature under the circumstances be attended with peril to life, but that the offender should be aware of such peril. Where the offender does an act attended with manifest danger to life wilfully, that is with knowledge of the consequences, he may properly be said to have the '*mens mala*, or heart bent upon mischief'; but if he does an act, however dangerous it be in its own nature, without any knowledge or suspicion of its tendency, that is, if he does not wilfully place life in peril, he cannot be said to show *mens mala* or heart bent on mischief.[5]

In these observations can be seen not merely an acceptance of a moral basis of liability but a realization that this necessarily involved a subjective examination of the delinquent's mental process, since in the view of the Commissioners it is essential for criminal guilt that the perpetrator of the harm should be proved to have realized that it would be at least a possible result of the course which he was pursuing.

[1] See below, ¶ 93.

[2] See Radzinowicz, *Hist. Eng. Crim. Law*, I, 399 *et seq.*

[3] *Principles of Morals and Legislation*, 36 *et seq.* On Bentham's great contribution to the development of criminal science see Radzinowicz, *Hist. Eng. Crim. Law*, I, 355–96, III, 472.

[4] 1839 [1687]–XIX–245, p. xxi.

[5] The reference is to Foster, 257.

¶ **20.** *Acceptance by the courts of the requirement of foresight.* It is unnecessary at this point to do more than give one or two dicta from decided cases to show that the new doctrine of liability soon began to win its way into the common law. In a direction to the jury in 1841 the judge said:

> It will be for you, in the present case, to consider whether the prisoner left the child in such a situation that, to all reasonable apprehension, she must have been aware the child must die, or whether there were circumstances that would make it likely that the child would be found by someone else, and its life preserved....[1]

In 1862 Pollock, C.B., said:

> the crimes of murder and manslaughter were in some instances very difficult of distinction. The distinction which seemed most reasonable consisted in the consciousness that the act done was one which would be likely to cause death. No one, however, could commit murder without that consciousness.[2]

At this point it is a depressing necessity to refer to the retrograde judgment of the House of Lords in *D.P.P.* v. *Smith* [1961] A.C. 290, in the course of which their lordships purported to brush aside the explicit words of Pollock, C.B., by stating that 'the real issue in the case was whether, by reason of her age, the accused had the necessary *mens rea*'. To seek in this way the concealment of one element by emphasizing another is an unworthy rhetorical device.

¶ **21.** *The confusion caused by the simultaneous existence of different criteria of liability.* We have more than once noted the uncertainty created when at the same period judicial decisions could be based on either of two diverse canons of guilt, namely, either strict accountability for the deed effected, or the requirement of moral wickedness in the culprit. This position was aggravated when foresight of consequences also came to be a test applied. Sometimes two of the doctrines were relied upon in the same judgment, but it was not always clear whether they were used conjunctively or disjunctively. Thus Martin, B., in 1863, said:[3]

[1] *R.* v. *Walters* (1841) C. and M. 164, at p. 170, *per* Coltman, J.

[2] *R.* v. *Vamplew* (1862) 3 F. and F. 520, at p. 522. The conception of foresight can be seen also in *R.* v. *Bubb* (1851) 4 Cox 457; *R.* v. *Greenwood* (1857) 7 Cox 404; *R.* v. *Horsey* (1862) 3 F. and F. 287; *R.* v. *Street* (1866) 4 F. and F. 931; *R.* v. *Whitmarsh* (1898) 62 J.P. 711; *R.* v. *Bottomley* (1903) 115 L.T. 88; *R.* v. *Lumley* (1911) 22 Cox 635; and see *R.* v. *Gunewardene* [1951] 2 All E.R. 290; *R.* v. *Buck and Buck* [1960] Crim. L.R. 760.

[3] *R.* v. *Townley* (1863) 3 F. and F. 839 (*T.A.C.*), at pp. 846 and 848. This duality can be observed in many judicial pronouncements on *mens rea* in relation to statutory crimes, e.g. *R.* v. *Tolson* (1889) 23 Q.B.D. 168 (*T.A.C.*), at p. 171, 'the guilty intent...must at least be the intention to do something wrong', *per* Wills, J.; and *Sherras* v. *de Rutzen* [1895] 1 Q.B. 918 (*T.A.C.*), at p. 921, 'there is a presumption that *mens rea*, an evil intention, or a knowledge of the wrongfulness of the act, is an essential ingredient in every offence', *per* Wright, J. See also *Younghusband* v. *Luftig* [1949] 2 K.B. 354; 2 All E.R. 72, at p. 80, '...he does not commit an offence if he honestly believes he was within his rights in describing himself as he did.... We can sum up this part of the case by saying that there must be *mens rea* and the presence or absence of that state of mind must be tested on ordinary principles and in the light of common sense. *Actus non facit reum, nisi mens sit rea* is a cardinal doctrine of the criminal law.'

If the jury believe that at the time the act was committed the prisoner was labouring under a delusion and believed he was doing an act...of which he did not know the consequences, he would be excused....Unless they [the jury] were satisfied...that he did not know the consequences of his act, or that it was against the law of God and man...he was guilty of murder.

It was, of course, not necessary that a moral test[1] should be expressly applied when once the test of foresight had been established, and nowadays, as we shall see, in common law crimes it is not necessary, nor indeed relevant, to consider whether there was any moral culpability in the conduct of the accused person, save in two instances, first, where he is under fourteen years of age, and second, where he sets up the defence of insanity.

The doctrine of strict accountability, however, has survived to create a most unsatisfactory obscurity in the law of homicide.[2]

This confused intermingling of three different criteria of responsibility has not only made it a tiresome task to distinguish the true nature and origin of each, but it leads to vagueness and ambiguity in judicial pronouncements and in the works of legal writers.

INTENTION, RECKLESSNESS AND NEGLIGENCE[3]

¶ 22. The complexity has been increased by the use of the words malice aforethought, intention, recklessness, and negligence to indicate the element of *mens rea*. Malice aforethought is the term which came into use during medieval times to indicate the mental element necessary in the felony of murder. It has been the subject of voluminous jurisprudential enquiry and the explanation of it must be postponed until the law of the different kinds of homicide is discussed.[4] It will, indeed, be better understood after the analysis of the other terms now mentioned has been completed.

¶ 23. *Intention.*[5] To intend is to have in mind a fixed purpose to reach a desired objective; the noun 'intention' in the present connexion is

[1] Even as late as 1953 a judge of the High Court, Mr Justice Humphreys, in giving evidence before the Royal Commission on Capital Punishment (*Report of 1953*, Minutes of Evidence, p. 261, question 3282), said 'Probably the words "a wicked mind" are too strong, but I think "wrongful intention" is as near as one can get to the English conception of *mens rea*.'

[2] *Post*, ¶ 78 *et seq.*

[3] These expressions represent very much the same conceptions as do *dolus*, *culpa lata* and *culpa levis* in Roman law.

[4] Chapter VII.

[5] See Austin, *Jurisprudence* (4th ed.), I, 431–42. 'Intention' in this sense must be distinguished from 'motive'. 'Intention' indicates that a man is consciously shaping his conduct so as to bring about a certain event; 'motive' indicates the reason why he desires that event and therefore why he pursues his selected course of conduct so as to achieve it. At common law the *motive* of the accused is not a necessary element of his liability and therefore the prosecution have no need to prove what his motive may have been; but evidence of his motive is of course admissible against him as tending to establish either the *actus reus* or the *mens rea*, or both. In statutory offences, however, it may be otherwise; contrast, e.g., *R.* v. *Steane* [1947] K.B. 997, *post*, p. 66, with *R.* v. *Smith* [1960] 2 W.L.R. 164, *post*, p. 365.

used to denote the state of mind of a man who not only foresees but also wills the possible consequences of his conduct.[1] Thus if one man throws another from a high tower or cuts off his head it would seem plain that he both foresees the victim's death and also desires it: the desire and the foresight will also be the same if a person knowingly leaves a helpless invalid or infant without nourishment or other necessary support until death supervenes. It will be noted that there cannot be intention unless there is also foresight, since a man must decide to his own satisfaction, and accordingly must foresee, that to which his express purpose is directed.

Again, a man cannot intend to do a thing unless he desires to do it. It may well be a thing that he dislikes doing, but he dislikes still more the consequences of his not doing it. That is to say he desires the lesser of two evils, and therefore has made up his mind to bring about that one.

¶ 24. *Recklessness.*[2] Intention cannot exist without foresight, but foresight can exist without intention. For a man may foresee the possible or even probable consequences of his conduct and yet not desire them to occur; none the less if he persists on his course he knowingly runs the risk of bringing about the unwished result.[3] To describe this state of mind the word 'reckless' is the most appropriate.[4] The words 'rash' and 'rashness' have also been used to indicate this same attitude.[5]

A man who is reckless may prefer that the contemplated event shall not happen, or he may not care whether it happens or not; but in either case he does not *desire* it to happen and therefore does not act with the purpose that it shall happen. It is, unfortunately, a very common attitude of mind and is found, for example, in those cases in which dangerous driving of motor vehicles has caused death.[6]

[1] Of course a man may foresee some but not necessarily all the consequences of his conduct. He may be doing things voluntarily (¶ 18) and to that extent intend them, but not foresee the further event to which they are leading. This appears in some of the statutory offences where the liability is strict (¶ 32).

[2] Austin, *op. cit.* 431–42; Stephen, *Hist. Crim. Law*, III, 55, 56.

[3] Cf. Austin, *op. cit.* 441, 'the party *conceives* the future event, and believes that there is a chance of its following his volition or act'.

[4] This word was chosen by the House of Lords in *Andrews* v. *D.P.P.* [1937] A.C. 576, at p. 583. It has, however, been used in more than one meaning: thus, in *R.* v. *Russell* [1953] 1 W.L.R. 77, the C.C.A. approved a dictum of Donovan, J., in *R.* v. *Bates and Russell* [1952] W.N. 506, to the effect that the word 'reckless' in s. 12 (1) of the Prevention of Fraud (Investments) Act, 1939, 'must be left to bear its full meaning, and be construed, therefore, as covering also the case where there was a high degree of negligence without dishonesty'. *R.* v. *Bates and Russell* was discredited in *R.* v. *MacKinnon* [1958] 3 W.L.R. 688 by Salmon, J., at p. 691. And both these cases were, on this point, discredited in *R.* v. *Grunwald* [1960] 3 All E.R. 380 by Paull, J., at p. 384. On this point see *Horabin* v. *British Overseas Airways Corporation* [1952] 2 All E.R. 1016 at pp. 1019–24; and *R.* v. *Cunningham* [1957] 2 All E.R. 412.

[5] Described by Eve, J., in a Chancery action as 'an attitude of mental indifference to obvious risks', *Hudston* v. *Viney* [1921] 1 Ch. 98, at p. 104.

[6] E.g. *R.* v. *Stringer* (1933) 24 Cr.App.R. 30; *Andrews* v. *D.P.P.* [1937] A.C. 576; see *post*, ¶ 134.

To the great confusion of the law it has become the common practice of lawyers to indicate this state of mind by the word 'negligence', qualified by the addition of condemnatory but unprecise adjectives such as 'wicked', 'criminal', 'culpable',[1] 'gross',[2] 'complete', or 'clear'. The ordinary function of an adjective is not to alter entirely the meaning of a noun, but to qualify or restrict its scope by emphasizing a particular characteristic of the thing for which the noun is employed as a symbol. So a judge once said that he could see no difference between negligence and gross negligence—that it was the same thing, with the addition of a vituperative epithet.[3] Sometimes, however, an adjective is combined with a noun so as to create a composite name with a new and special meaning,[4] and, if so, great confusion will be caused unless this special meaning is made known and the composite noun thereafter employed only in that sense. It is necessary therefore in the first place to decide what meaning should be given to the word 'negligence' when it is employed as a legal expression.

¶ **25.** *Negligence.* The use of identical terms in different meanings is a grave defect in any serious exposition of ideas. For if the changes or meaning are not carefully explained the argument will be incomprehensible, while on the other hand repeated explanations are tedious and confusing.[5]

We have seen that a man who intends a result, or is reckless in running the risk of it, must necessarily foresee its possibility; he adverts to the result in question.

Yet a man may bring about an event without having adverted to it at all; he may not have foreseen that his actions would have this consequence and it will come to him as a surprise. The event may be harmless or harmful; if harmful the question arises whether there is

[1] *R.* v. *Roberts* [1942] 1 All E.R. 187, at p. 192 *per* Humphreys, J.

[2] In *Lynch* v. *Nurdin* (1841) 1 Q.B. 29, at p. 38, Denman, C.J., said 'between wilful mischief and gross negligence the boundary line is hard to trace; I should rather say, impossible. The law runs them into each other, considering such a degree of negligence as some proof of malice.' Compare the well-known phrase in Roman law *lata culpa dolo comparabitur*; *Digest*, XI, 6. 1. 1.

[3] Rolfe, B., in *Wilson* v. *Brett* (1843) 11 M. and W. 113, at p. 116.

[4] E.g. 'royal flush', 'tall boy', 'silver fish', 'black guard' (eventually combined into single words 'tallboy', 'silverfish', 'blackguard'), 'hot dog'. Such expressions usually begin as colloquialisms. But in *Kat* v. *Diment* [1951] 1 K.B. 34; [1950] 2 All E.R. 657 a Divisional Court confirmed a finding to the effect that the noun 'vinegar' denotes acetic acid in a diluted form produced by fermentation in a process of brewing, but that this meaning of the noun is not altered by prefixing to it the adjective 'non-brewed', with the intention of denoting diluted acetic acid for table use produced by other methods; see ¶ 33 *post*.

[5] In the words of an eminent French writer: 'The first condition which logic imposes on language is that it must be clear and that it must avoid ambiguity; to that end it is necessary that as far as possible each sign should have only one value, and that each value should have only one sign to represent it; that a word, for example, should have only one meaning, and that each idea should have only one word to express it.' Bally, *Le Langage et la vie* (Paris, 1928), 63.

legal liability for it. In tort (at common law) this is decided by considering whether or not a reasonable man in the same circumstances would have realized the prospect of harm and would have stopped or changed his course so as to avoid it. If a reasonable man would not, then there is no liability and the harm must lie where it falls. But if the reasonable man would have avoided the harm then there is liability and the perpetrator of the harm is said to be guilty of negligence. The word 'negligence' denotes, and should be used only to denote, such blameworthy inadvertence; and the man who through his negligence has brought harm upon another is under a legal obligation to make reparation for it to the victim of the injury who may sue him in tort for damages.[1] But it should now be recognized that at common law[2] there is no *criminal* liability for harm thus caused by inadvertence. This has been laid down authoritatively for manslaughter again and again.[3] There are only two states of mind which constitute *mens rea*, and they are *intention* and *recklessness*. The difference between recklessness and negligence is the difference between advertence and inadvertence: they are opposed and it is a logical fallacy to suggest that recklessness is a degree of negligence.[4] The common habit of lawyers to qualify the word 'negligence' with some moral epithet such as 'wicked', 'gross', or 'culpable' has been most unfortunate since it has inevitably led to great confusion of thought and of principle. It is equally misleading to speak of criminal negligence since this is merely to use an expression to explain itself.[5]

Nor indeed can there be degrees of inadvertence when that word is

[1] Provided there is a legal duty. See Winfield, *Law of Tort* (1948), 5; Lawson, 'The duty of care in negligence', 22 *Tulane L.R.* no. 1, 111.

[2] Save, perhaps, in nuisance and for certain cases of libel; see ¶¶ 28, 184. The position under statute may be different; see ¶¶ 31–35.

[3] 'Mere negligence will not do...you must be of opinion that the prisoner had a wicked mind, in the sense that she was reckless and careless whether the creature died or not', *R.* v. *Nicholls* (1874) 13 Cox, at p. 76. 'But if there was only the kind of forgetfulness which is common to everybody...any injury which resulted might furnish a ground for claiming civil damages, but it would be wrong to proceed against a man criminally in respect of such injury', *R.* v. *Doherty* (1887) 16 Cox, at p. 309. 'Simple lack of care such as will constitute civil liability is not enough', *Andrews* v. *D.P.P.* [1937] A.C., at p. 583 (*T.A.C.*). 'Negligence, everybody agrees, in the sense of mere want of ordinary care, is not enough to justify conviction by a jury on a charge of manslaughter', *R.* v. *Bonnyman* (1942) 28 Cr.App.R., at p. 134. 'Simple negligence, in the sense of ordinary carelessness, is not enough', *The People* v. *Dunleavy* [1948] 2 I.R. 95 (*T.A.C.*); and see Russ. 47. *R.* v. *Burdee* (1916) 12 Cr.App.R. 153 is a case in which, even as late as 1916, the court were looking backward to the ancient doctrine of strict liability (see ¶¶ 19, 21, 131), no reference being made to such cases as *R.* v. *Nicholls* and *R.* v. *Doherty*; see *post*, ¶ 135.

[4] It is the mistake of confusing cause with effect. Both recklessness and negligence cause blame and legal liability to arise; there are degrees of blame and degrees of legal liability but it is a *non sequitur* to say that therefore the one *cause* is a degree of the other.

[5] 'Criminal negligence means no more than the negligence that would amount to a crime, but whether it does or not is still the thing in question', *per* O'Brien, J., in *R.* v. *Elliott* (1889) 16 Cox 710, at p. 714. 'The word "criminal" in any attempt to define a crime is perhaps not the most helpful', *per* Lord Atkin in *Andrews* v. *D.P.P.* [1937] A.C., at p. 582.

used to denote a state of mind, since it means that in the man's mind there has been a complete absence of a particular thought, a nullity; and of nullity there can be no degrees.

To make one mistake is to incur the danger of making another; students should therefore guard against being led astray by the rule that in criminal proceedings there exists a presumption[1] that a man has intended (and therefore foreseen) the natural consequences of his acts.[2] According to this rule so soon as the prosecution has established the *actus reus* there arises this presumption (which is, of course, a presumption of *mens rea*) and this puts upon the prisoner the burden of establishing in the minds of the jury at least a reasonable doubt as to his foresight in the matter.[3] The truth may be that he did not foresee the consequences as a reasonable man would have done, and that he was negligent in the true sense of the word, and therefore civilly, although not criminally, liable. Yet the prisoner may be unfortunate in not being able to convince the jury that this is so, and they may convict him, being of opinion on the evidence that he did foresee the consequences of his conduct.[4] In these circumstances, therefore, a negligent man will in fact have been convicted, but to say that he has been convicted *because* he was negligent is to make two grave errors which a student should be careful to avoid, the first logical, that of confusing cause with effect, and the second legal, that of confusing evidence with law.

Negligence must also be carefully distinguished from neglect.[5] This word 'neglect' does not indicate a specific attitude of mind, but states a matter of objective fact, which may be produced either by intention or by negligence. Thus a man who has neglected to feed his animal may have done so (*a*) consciously and purposely because, for example, he did not want to take the trouble; or on the other hand (*b*) negligently, in that he simply forgot to feed it. Again, if a man, being aware that the

[1] A presumption which can be rebutted (*Woolmington* v. *D.P.P.* [1935] A.C. 462), notwithstanding dicta to the contrary effect in *D.P.P.* v. *Smith* [1960] 3 W.L.R. 546.

[2] See *post*, ¶ 499. This use of the word 'natural', although hallowed by tradition, is not happy; for all consequences must be 'natural'. What is really meant is consequences which an average man, placed in the same circumstances, would be expected to foresee. Cf. Russ. 49.

[3] *Woolmington* v. *D.P.P.* [1935] A.C. 462 (*T.A.C.*) as qualified in *Mancini* v. *D.P.P.* [1942] A.C. 1 (*T.A.C.*); *R.* v. *Jackson* (1936) 80 S.J. 977. Cf. Russ. 38. And see *R.* v. *Lobell* [1957] 2 W.L.R. 524, confirming *Chan Kau* v. *R.* [1955] A.C. 206 and disapproving, on this point, *R.* v. *Smith* (1837) 8 C. and P. 160.

[4] In *Hosegood* v. *Hosegood* (1950) 66 T.L.R. 735 Denning, L.J., said 'The presumption of intention is not a proposition of law but a proposition of ordinary good sense. It means this: that a man is usually able to foresee what are the natural consequences of his acts, so it is, as a rule, reasonable to infer that he did foresee them and intend them. But, while that is an inference which may be drawn, it is not one which must be drawn. If on all the facts of the case it is not the correct inference, then it should not be drawn.' And note the cases in which a specific intent is required by law, such as *R.* v. *Stearne* [1947] K.B. 997; *R.* v. *Foley* [1959] Crim.L.R. 286, *post*, ¶ 499. A man's denial is not always worthy of belief; see *Taylor* v. *Kenyon* [1952] 2 All E.R. 726.

[5] Note the unhappy confusion of 'neglect' and 'negligence' by Patterson, J., in *R.* v. *Marriott* (1838) 8 C. and P. 425 (*T.A.C.*).

brakes or wheels of his motor car are defective, yet takes it on the road well knowing that with it in that condition he may cause injury to some person, and if such injury is thereby caused, then this will be a case of harm brought about not by his negligence but by his wilful neglect and recklessness.[1]

WHERE THE CONSEQUENCES ARE DIFFERENT FROM THOSE FORESEEN

¶ 26. It can often happen that a man has directed his actions to the achievement of one particular aim, but that the result turns out to be different from what he had anticipated would follow. It is necessary to consider various sets of circumstances in which this may arise.

(*a*) It is easy to see that where his intended aim was harmless, then the unexpected result of his conduct, since it was not foreseen by him, cannot, at common law, bring criminal liability upon a man, however harmful it may be, for he had no *mens rea*, since he did not foresee the harm. A simple example would be where *A*, intending to give *B* a drink of water, innocently hands him a liquid into which some other person has put poison.

(*b*) Where the intended aim was harmful but not unlawful (i.e. not an *actus reus*). In this case the deed done was legally different from the one intended and there will be no liability. For example if *C* had been sentenced to death then it would not be an *actus reus* for *A*, the duly appointed executioner, to kill him. But if there is produced to *A* a man *B*, whom *A* reasonably believes to be *C*, and *A* executes *B*, then *A* is not guilty of the felonious homicide of *B*, notwithstanding that he intended to kill. It will be a case of death by misadventure so far as *A* is concerned.[2]

(*c*) Where the intended aim is an *actus reus*, and a different *actus reus* of the same kind is committed. In this case the liability is the same as if the intended harm had been inflicted, provided the *mens rea* is the same for each. Thus, if *A*, intending to kill *B*, shoots at him but misses and happens to kill *C* whom he did not know to be near, and whom he did not wish to kill, then *A* is guilty of the murder of *C*, for he intended an unlawful killing, and he was inspired by an intention to kill (malice aforethought).[3]

(*d*) Where the intended aim is an *actus reus* and an *actus reus* of a different kind is committed. In these circumstances the two cases must be considered separately. Thus if *A*, intending to kill *B*, shoots at

[1] A misdemeanour under the Offences against the Person Act, 1861, s. 35. *Post*, ¶ 163*a*. And see *Gibbins and Proctor* (1918) 13 Cr.App.R. 134.

[2] He would have the defence of 'mistake of fact'; *post*, ¶ 39. Those responsible for producing *B* instead of *C* may perhaps be liable. And see ¶¶ 15 and 98.

[3] *R.* v. *Hopwood* (1913) 8 Cr.App.R. 143; *Commonwealth* v. *Mink* (1877) 9 Lathrop 422 (*T.A.C.*). Note the vagueness of the conception of malice aforethought in the old case of *R.* v. *Salisbury* (1553) 1 Plowd. 100 (*T.A.C.*). See 1 Hale 436; Foster, 261, 262. The acquittal of Archer in *R.* v. *Saunders and Archer* (1576) 2 Plowd. 473 is discussed below, ¶ 69.

him, but misses and happens to kill an animal; in this case *A* will be guilty of attempting to murder *B*, but his liability for the killing of the animal will depend, (1) on whether it is a crime to kill such an animal (for example a dog as contrasted with a fox) and (2) whether *A* realized that an animal of that kind was likely to be killed if he fired.[1]

When the cases are thus considered separately sometimes the criminal liability will be found to be less[2] than it would have been if the intended crime had been achieved, and sometimes it will be greater. It will be greater if an unlawful harm, but not fatal harm, against the person be intended and unfortunately death is caused, for here the felony of manslaughter will have been committed,[3] whereas perhaps only a minor assault and battery was intended.

Again, on the authorities as they stood before the Homicide Act, 1957, there were two situations in which a death unintentionally caused was held to be murder.[4]

MENS REA ALONE NOT ENOUGH

¶ 27. In law an *actus reus* is always required, although in ethics a guilty mind alone may be held sufficient to constitute guilt. Hence[5] on Garrick's declaring that whenever he acted Richard III he felt like a murderer, Dr Johnson retorted, 'Then he ought to be hanged whenever he acts it'. But there is no such searching severity in the rules of law. They, whether civil or even criminal, never inflict penalties upon mere internal feeling, when it has produced no result in external conduct. So a merely mental condition—Shakespeare's 'wicked meaning in a lawful deed'—is not the proper subject for a crime.[6] It is true that there appears at first sight to be an important exception to this principle, in that form of high treason called 'compassing the King's death'.[7] But the exception is only apparent; for the Statute of Treasons goes on to make it essential to a conviction that some 'overt act' should have been committed towards accomplishing the end contemplated. In another apparent exception, the misdemeanour of conspiracy,[8] it is true that the conspiracy itself is purely a mental state—the mere agreement of two men's minds—and that here, unlike treason, it is not

[1] Compare the cases of *R.* v. *Pembliton* (1874) 2 C.C.R. 119 (*T.A.C.*) and *R.* v. *Latimer* (1886) 17 Q.B.D. 359 (*T.A.C.*), *post*, ¶ 159.

[2] See *The Abby* (1804) 5 C. Rob., 254 where a man shot at an Englishman and killed an alien enemy.

[3] *Post*, ¶¶ 131 *et seq.*

[4] Where it was caused in resistance to lawful arrest or 'in the course of a felony of violence'; *post*, ¶¶ 109, 111.

[5] Boswell, *anno* 1783. Dr Johnson's remark was not a serious argument but a neat *jeu d'esprit*. For the actor, when on the stage, was a mere simulacrum of a man long since dead and gone, and the feeling was against another such lifeless creature; any moral censure therefore could only be levelled against the character portrayed.

[6] The well-known dictum of Brian, C.J. (Y.B. 17 Ed. IV, fo. 2; *ante*, p. 12), did not refer to this point, as has often been mistakenly supposed owing to an incorrect translation of the word 'trie'.

[7] *Post*, ¶ 402; Russ. 220.

[8] *Post*, ¶ 59.

necessary to a conviction that any act should have been done towards carrying out the agreement; but it would be impossible for two men to come to an agreement without communicating to each other their common intentions by speech or gesture, and thus even in conspiracy a physical act is always present. Hence conspiracies are amongst the commonest instances of the 'overt acts' relied upon in charges of treason.

A still greater divergence from ethics will be remarked if we turn from the criminal to the non-criminal branches of law; for they often inflict their sanctions on mere external conduct, which is not the result of any blamable state of mind. Thus,

(1) In breaches of contract, the mental and moral condition of the defaulter has no effect upon the question of his liability or non-liability, unless the very language of the contract implies that it can only be broken by some act which is wilful. Thus a wife's covenant in a separation deed 'not to molest' her husband, is held not to be broken by anything but an intentional annoying of him. And, similarly, if the defaulter be liable, the wilfulness or wickedness of his conduct will not affect the amount of the damages to be recovered from him (except in the case of a breach of promise to marry).

(2) And in torts the mental condition of the wrongdoer is ignored very largely. But not so universally as in the law of contract;[1] for there are a few classes of tort (e.g. malicious prosecution) in which it is an indispensable element of liability; and in very many (if not, indeed, in all[2]) of the remaining classes, namely the torts in which liability can exist without it, it still may be taken into account in estimating the amount of the damages.

VICARIOUS LIABILITY AT COMMON LAW

¶ 28. We have seen that a man will be held liable at common law for another's misdeed not only if he gives some assistance in its performance but also if he merely advised or procured that other to commit the offence. In all cases so far considered, he must foresee the consequences of the particular course of conduct in which he is thus participating. This is indeed the rule for all ordinary offences at *common* law[3] and a purely vicarious liability for them is not recognized. In them the law does not, for example, regard a master as having any such connexion with acts done by his servants as will involve him in any *criminal* liability for them (whatever may be his liability in a *civil* action of tort or contract), unless he has himself actually authorized them[4] or aided and abetted them.[5] And to render him liable criminally this authoriza-

[1] So in divorce proceedings a wife who has been ravished is not treated as an adulteress, *Long.* v. *Long* (1890) 15 P.D. 218; 'there cannot be an *innocent* "adultery"'. And see *S.* v. *S. and O. and B.* [1961] 3 All E.R. 133.

[2] Halsbury, *Laws of England* (Hailsham ed.), x, 88.

[3] It is not necessarily the rule in *statutory* offences; see *post*, ¶¶ 32, 35.

[4] See *Harvard Law Review*, XLIII, 689.

[5] See ¶ 68 *post.* In the case of a master, mere presence without remonstrance may, it is submitted, amount to aiding and abetting, and acquiescence may sometimes amount to

tion must have been given either expressly or else by a general authority couched in terms so wide as to imply permission to execute it even criminally.[1] Thus, if a bargeman steers his barge carelessly and so sinks a skiff and drowns the oarsman, or a chemist's shopman carelessly puts a poison into the medicine he makes up, this negligence of his may involve his master in a civil liability, but not in any criminal one.

So fundamental is this rule that the common law seems to have departed from it in only one or two instances.[2] At common law the proprietor of a newspaper was liable criminally as well as civilly for libels published by his servants in conducting his newspaper even though he had not authorized their publication;[3] but since the Libel Act, 1843,[4] he may show that the libel was published without his authority and with no lack of care on his part. But it is a misdemeanour at common law to publish, exhibit, or represent any matter which is 'calculated' (whether intended to do so or not) to interfere with the fair trial of a legal proceeding pending in any court of justice,[5] and the Libel Act, 1843, gives no defence to this charge; *mens rea* thus being in no way material except as to penalty. Another instance is an anomalous offence where often the prosecution is criminal merely in form, and in substance and effect is only a civil proceeding, its object usually being not punishment but simply the cessation of the offence. The offence in question is that of a public nuisance.[6] A public nuisance is an act which obstructs, or causes inconvenience or damage to, the public in the exercise of rights common to all the Queen's subjects.[7] In the case of any *private* nuisance, as the remedy is by a civil action, the master is liable, under the ordinary civil rule, for all the acts of his servant done in the course of his employment, even though they may have been done without the master's knowledge and contrary to his general orders. For public nuisances, on the other hand, a civil action can usually[8] not be brought, but only an indictment. There would therefore often be much

authorization. Cf. *Moreland* v. *The State* (1927) 139 S.E. 77; *Gough* v. *Rees* (1929) 46 T.L.R. 103; *Newman* v. *Overington* (1929) 93 J.P. 46; and *Ferguson* v. *Weaving* [1951] 1 All E.R. 412 (*T.A.C.*), in which it was held that the licence-holder was not guilty of aiding and abetting the consumption of intoxicating liquor by visitors to her premises who had been allowed by her servants (contrary to her orders and in her absence from the room) to drink there after the permitted hours.

[1] *R.* v. *Huggins* (1730) 2 Ld. Raym. 1574 (*T.A.C.*); *Hardcastle* v. *Bielby* [1892] 1 Q.B. 709; *Newman* v. *Jones* (1886) 17 Q.B.D. 132.

[2] See 18 *Modern Law Rev.* 385.

[3] *R.* v. *Walter* (1799) 3 Esp. 21.

[4] 6 and 7 Vict. c. 96, s. 7, a defence now extended by the Administration of Justice Act, 1960, to publications in contempt of court.

[5] *R.* v. *Williams* (1823) 2 L.J. (o.s.) K.B. 30; intention is irrelevant and lack of knowledge that criminal proceedings had been begun is not material except as to penalty. See *R.* v. *Evening Standard* [1954] 1 Q.B. 578, following *R.* v. *Payne* [1896] 1 Q.B. 577 and followed by *R.* v. *Odhams Press Ltd.* [1956] 3 W.L.R. 796; *R.* v. *Griffiths* [1957] 2 All E.R. 379.

[6] See *post*, ¶ 447*a*.

[7] *R.* v. *Price* (1884), 12 Q.B.D. 247, 256. Thus see its exceptional position as to pardon, Kenny, 16th ed., App. I, p. 539.

[8] See Winfield, *Law of Tort* (6th ed.), 540.

greater difficulty in obtaining effectual redress for them than for the more trivial class of nuisances, were not the master's liability for his servant's conduct made as general as in the case of mere private nuisance. It accordingly is made so.[1] This rule has the further justification that the master, by the very fact of setting a servant upon work that may result in a nuisance, has brought about a state of things which he ought at his peril to prevent from actually producing that criminal result. Hence, instead of, as in ordinary offences, being liable only if he had authorized the servant's crime, he will, in the case of nuisance, be liable even though he had actually forbidden it. For here he ought, at his peril, to have seen his prohibition obeyed.

GENERAL PRINCIPLES OF LIABILITY AT COMMON LAW. CONCLUSIONS

¶ 29. Rules of law must in the first instance be stated as they apply to what may be termed the legally normal person, who for English criminal law is one in whom the following characteristics are united. He must be a person of the male sex, of full age, of sound mind, and living within the jurisdiction of the Crown of England, and must have committed the offence within that jurisdiction. For such a person we may deduce from the preceding paragraphs the following rules of criminal responsibility in offences at common law. The prosecution must establish

(1) that his conduct contributed either directly or indirectly to the *actus reus*;
(2) that this conduct on his part was voluntary;
(3) that he foresaw at the time that his acts or omissions might produce or help to produce certain consequences. The nature of these consequences is fixed by law for each specific crime.[2]

SECTION 2. IN STATUTORY OFFENCES

A. *ACTUS REUS* IN STATUTORY OFFENCES

¶ 30. In deciding what matter is prohibited by statute little difficulty need be found, since the ordinary rules of interpretation of statutes are of course to be applied; it has been judicially laid down that a penal enactment is to be construed, like any other instrument, according to the fair common-sense meaning of the language used; and the court is not to find or make any doubt or ambiguity in the language of a penal statute where such doubt or ambiguity would clearly not be found or made in the same language in any other instrument.[3]

The fundamental rule is that the words of the statute make the law,

[1] *R.* v. *Stephens* (1866) L.R. 1 Q.B. 702.

[2] As above mentioned the expression '*mens rea*' has often been used in the courts to denote both (2) and (3). For the effects of mistake as to the existing facts upon which a man decides to take, or abstain from, action, see ¶¶ 39, 40 *post*. The doubts raised by the judgment of the House of Lords in *D.P.P.* v. *Smith* [1960] 3 W.L.R. 546 are discussed *post*, ¶ 116*b*.

[3] *The Gauntlet* (1871) 4 P.C. 184, at p. 191.

that they are to be taken in their ordinary meaning as given in the standard dictionaries, and that so long as that meaning is plain it must be accepted as representing the intention of the legislature, and cannot be varied by any evidence that the legislature meant otherwise.

B. *MENS REA* IN STATUTORY OFFENCES[1]

¶ 31. In former times it was frequently maintained that the legislature was not competent to override the established rules of the common law. That view is now quite abandoned and there can be no doubt that in modern law the authority of statute is paramount. Yet it has been laid down that a statute must be interpreted to conform with the common law except where and so far as the words of the statute show plainly that it is intended to alter the course of the common law or cannot in their plain meaning be otherwise construed.[2] From the last mentioned qualification it should follow that in any crime created by statute there should *prima facie* be a presumption that *mens rea* as understood in the common law is a necessary ingredient. This rule of interpretation has been applied, but in varying degrees, so that the reports contain judicial references to *mens rea* which it is not always easy to reconcile. These pronouncements as to *mens rea* in statutory crimes can, however, be better understood if it be remembered that in modern times the term *mens rea* has been used by the courts in two different senses: (1) to denote the accused person's attitude of mind to what he was doing, from which can be decided the question whether his conduct was or was not voluntary;[3] and (2) to denote the accused person's foresight of the consequences of what he was doing. Now in all crimes, whether at common law or under statute,[4] the prosecution must establish the first of the above points, namely that the accused knew what he was doing, and that he was a free agent in so acting. But this topic can better be illustrated and explained after the question of foresight has been discussed.

FORESIGHT OF CONSEQUENCES IN STATUTORY OFFENCES

¶ 32. The general proposition that *mens rea* must be presumed to be a necessity in any crime created by statute was at one time so fully accepted that it used commonly to be stated that nothing but express words or a very strong implication in the statute itself could rebut the presumption.[5] But in the latter half of the nineteenth century the policy of the legislature moved towards a more minute regulation of

[1] On this topic see Jackson, 'Absolute prohibition in statutory offences', *Mod. Appr. Crim. Law*, 262; Stallybrass, 'The eclipse of *mens rea*', 52 *L.Q.R.* 65.

[2] See Craies on Statute Law (4th ed.), ch. IV; *R.* v. *Morris* (1867) 1 C.C.R. 90, Byles, J., at p. 95.

[3] *Ante*, ¶¶ 18, 29.

[4] Unless of course the statute be so worded in a particular case as to deprive the citizen of even this protection: *R.* v. *Larsonneur* (1933) 97 J.P. 206; see ¶ 18.

[5] *Fowler* v. *Padget* (1798) 7 T.R. 509 at p. 514; *R.* v. *Sleep* (1861) L. and C. 44 at p. 52; *R.* v. *Prince* (1875) L.R. 2 C.C.R. 154, *per* Brett, J., at p. 163; *Hobbs* v. *Winchester Corporation* [1910] 2 K.B. 46, at p. 55; Kenny, 1st ed. 86.

social life by the creation of many non-indictable offences carrying a relatively light punishment, and defined in the statutes with greater exactitude than had formerly been the practice. The result was that the courts were more inclined to have regard solely to the words of the statute without importing the common law requirement of *mens rea*. This development became more marked after the case of *R.* v. *Prince*[1] in which the accused, reasonably believing her to be over the age of sixteen years, had taken a girl, who was in fact below that age, out of the possession and against the will of her father contrary to the words of 24 and 25 Vict. c. 100, s. 55. His conviction was upheld by all the judges save one of the Court for Crown Cases Reserved; the words of the statute were plain and made no reference to *mens rea* and it was not necessary to read into the section any such words as 'with knowledge that she is under sixteen'. In *Bond* v. *Evans*,[2] where a licensee had been charged with permitting gaming to be carried on upon the licensed premises,[3] Stephen, J., said: 'I think the meaning is that the landlord of licensed premises must prevent that which the Act prohibits from being done on his premises, and if he does not prevent it so much the worse for him.'[4]

In 1899 a man was held liable for selling adulterated milk although the adulteration had been effected by a dishonest stranger, against whose acts he had no means of protecting himself.[5] Similarly in a modern case[6] the divisional court, in upholding the conviction of a dairy farmer whose milk was adulterated by a stranger after it had passed out of his control, said: 'It is said in this case, and in my opinion it is true, that it is a great hardship upon the dairy farmer, the position being that he is obliged to enter into a contract[7] whether he agrees or not with the terms of it. He may be made responsible in law for the watering of milk although

[1] (1875) 2 C.C.R. 154 (*T.A.C.*); for a criticism of some judgments delivered in which general dicta as to *mens rea* were pronounced, see *Mod. Appr. Crim. Law*, 218, 219, 265.

[2] (1888) 21 Q.B.D. 249.

[3] Contrary to the Licensing Act, 1910, s. 79. 'Gaming' consists in the playing for money or money's worth at any game, even though a lawful one.

[4] See also the remarks of Channell, J., in *Pearks, Gunsten and Tee Ltd.* v. *Ward* [1902] 2 K.B. 1, at p. 11: 'The Legislature has thought it so important to prevent the particular act from being committed that it absolutely forbids it to be done, and if it is done the offender is liable to a penalty whether he had any *mens rea* or not, and whether or not he intended to commit a breach of the law.' See also *Provincial Motor Cab Co.* v. *Dunning* [1909] 2 K.B. 599; *Griffiths* v. *Studebakers Ltd* [1924] 1 K.B. 102; *Mousell Bros.* v. *London and North Western Rly. Co.* [1917] 2 K.B. 836.

[5] *Parker* v. *Alder* [1899] 1 Q.B. 20. Contrast *Brooks* v. *Mason* [1902] 2 K.B. 743, with *Emary* v. *Nolloth* [1903] 2 K.B. 264; showing that the law holds a publican liable for selling liquor in an unsealed vessel to a child under fourteen, although he honestly believed (mistakenly) that it was sealed; yet the law does *not* go so far as to hold him liable for its being similarly sold by his barman who is authorized to sell (unless this barman has the general control of the inn). Either seller's reasonable though mistaken belief that the child is over fourteen *would* excuse him. Cf. *R. C. Hammett* v. *L.C.C.* (1933) 49 T.L.R. 209, where the master was a limited company.

[6] *Watson* v. *Coupland* [1945] 1 All E.R. 217, *per* Humphreys, J., at p. 219; and see *Lamb* v. *Sunderland and District Creamery, Ltd* [1951] 1 All E.R. 923.

[7] Under regulations made by the Milk Marketing Board.

in point of fact he may be perfectly innocent morally of any such offence at all.' Other instances of this kind of criminal liability are:

(*a*) An undischarged bankrupt's obtaining credit for £10 or upwards without disclosing that he is an undischarged bankrupt; even though he had directed his agent to disclose it, and had reasonable grounds for believing that the agent had done so.[1]

(*b*) Keeping two or more lunatics without a licence; though without knowing the persons to be lunatics.[2]

(*c*) Possessing, for sale, unsound meat; though without knowing it to be unsound.[3]

(*d*) Selling an adulterated article of food; though without knowing it to be adulterated.[4]

(*e*) Selling or permitting to be sold intoxicating liquor to a drunken person; though without noticing that he was drunk.[5]

Again, a man who shot at a bird, which he thought to be a wild pigeon but which turned out to be a house-pigeon, was convicted of shooting it contrary to section 23 of the Larceny Act, 1861.[6] Several instances of absolute prohibition were given by Humphreys, J., in *Harding* v. *Price*.[7]

¶ 33. *References by the courts to* mens rea *as a necessity in statutory offences.* We have seen that by the end of the nineteenth century the courts had become ready to adopt a strict interpretation of the words of the statute which would exclude *mens rea*. A study of the cases, however, will reveal that this new principle was not applied to the extent of contravening the well-recognized rule that the legislature is not to be supposed to have intended to encroach upon the rights of the subject if a more lenient interpretation be possible. Moreover, of two possible interpretations the more reasonable is to be preferred. Indeed, so many are the considerations which the court has to reconcile in this matter[8] that it cannot be expected that the judgments in reported cases can yield any simple formula. Strict interpretation of statutory language has

[1] *R.* v. *Duke of Leinster* [1924] 1 K.B. 311. Cf. *R.* v. *Dyson* (1894) 18 Cox 1.

[2] *R.* v. *Bishop* (1879) 5 Q.B.D. 259.

[3] *Hobbs* v. *Corporation of Winchester* [1910] 2 K.B. 46.

[4] *Betts* v. *Armstead* (1888) 20 Q.B.D. 771; *Goulder* v. *Rook* [1901] 2 K.B. 290. Contrast *Derbyshire* v. *Houliston* [1897] 1 Q.B. 772.

[5] *Cundy* v. *Lecocq* (1884) 13 Q.B.D. 207.

[6] *Cotterill* v. *Penn* (1935) 153 L.T. 377 (*T.A.C.*), following *Horton* v. *Gwynne* [1921] 2 K.B. 661.

[7] [1948] 1 All E.R. 283, at p. 285. And see *Armstrong* v. *Clark* [1957] 2 W.L.R. 400 where a man held guilty under s. 15 (1) of the Road Traffic Act 1930 of driving while under the influence of drugs was a diabetic who had been unexpectedly overcome by a normal injection of insulin taken two and a half hours previously; and *Strong* v. *Dawtrey* [1961] 1 All E.R. 926, in which a motorist was convicted for leaving his car in a parking bay for two minutes while obtaining change with which to pay.

[8] See *Mousell Bros. Ltd.* v. *L. & N.W. Rly.* [1917] 2 K.B. 836, *per* Atkin, J., at p. 845.

been used at one time to mitigate the severity of the law[1] and (much more rarely) at another time to increase it.[2] In some quite modern cases there have been judicial utterances which suggest a tendency to revert to the older view that the need for *mens rea* was to be presumed.[3] Thus it has been said:[4] 'It is of the utmost importance for the protection of the liberty of the subject that a Court should always bear in mind that, unless a statute either clearly or by necessary implication rules out *mens rea*, as a constituent part of a crime, the Court should not find a man guilty of an offence against the criminal law unless he has a guilty mind.'[5] And again:[6] 'Of late years the Courts have been so accustomed to dealing with a host of offences created by regulations and orders independent of guilty intention that it is desirable to emphasize that such cases should be regarded as exceptions to the rule that a person cannot be convicted of a crime unless it is shown not only that he has committed a forbidden act or default but also that a wrongful intention or blameworthy condition of mind can be imputed to him.'[7] As

[1] See Radzinowicz, *Hist. Eng. Crim. Law*, I, 83 *et seq.*; *Remington* v. *Larchin* [1921] 3 K.B. 404 *per* Bankes, L.J., at p. 40. For a modern instance see *Rogerson* v. *Stephens* [1950] 2 All E.R. 144 in which it was held in effect that although it is an offence to use a motor car in the manner charged in the information against the accused, yet it is not an offence known to the law to use a motor car and trailer in that manner. See also *R.* v. *Parkin* (1949) 34 Cr.App.R. 1 (*post*, ¶ 217); *Baxter* v. *Keldon* [1955] 1 W.L.R. 84.

[2] Radzinowicz, *op. cit.* I, 51.

[3] The fluctuation will be seen in some of the cases of bigamy, e.g. *R.* v. *Tolson* (1889) 23 Q.B.D. 168; *R.* v. *Thomson* (1905) 70 J.P. 6; *R.* v. *Cunliffe* (1913) 57 S.J. 345; *R.* v. *Connatty* (1919) 83 J.P. 292; *R.* v. *Wheat and Stocks* [1921] 2 K.B. 119; 15 Cr.App.R. 134 (*T.A.C.*); *R.* v. *Kircaldy* (1928) 167 L.T.Jo. 46; *Evans* v. *Dell* [1937] 1 All E.R. 349; *R.* v. *Weiwow* (1945), Notts. Summer Ass. (Arch. p. 1424); *R.* v. *Dolman* [1949] 1 All E.R. 813, Leeds Ass.

[4] *Brend* v. *Wood* (1946) 62 T.L.R. 462 *per* Lord Goddard, L.J., at p. 463; see also *Harding* v. *Price* [1948] 1 K.B. 695, and the Australian case, *McCrae* v. *Downey* [1947] A.L.R. 157 and *In re Mahmoud and Ispahani* [1921] 2 K.B. 716.

[5] In *Kay* v. *Butterworth* (1945) 89 S.J. 381, the driver of a motor car, who while returning home in the morning after working all night had become overpowered by sleep, was held guilty under sects. 11 and 12 of the Road Traffic Act, 1930, the Divisional Court stating that he 'must have known that drowsiness was overtaking him'. The court added, however, that a person who through no fault of his own became unconscious while driving, for example, by being struck by a stone or by illness, ought not to be liable at criminal law.

[6] *Younghusband* v. *Luftig* [1949] 2 K.B. 354; 2 All E.R. 72, at p. 80.

[7] It should perhaps be mentioned that in *Brend* v. *Wood* the accused was charged under a statutory regulation with the offence of 'having in his possession with intent to deceive' certain forged petrol coupons. Since it was found that he did not know the coupons were forged, and believed that he was doing nothing wrong in handing them over in return for petrol supplied to him, it would seem that a strict interpretation of the words of the statute should ensure his acquittal and that it was not really necessary to call in aid the common law doctrine of *mens rea*. The position in *Younghusband* v. *Luftig* was similar, for the charge was that the accused had 'wilfully and falsely' pretended to be a doctor of medicine, and to be registered under the Medical Act, 1858, whereas the justices had found as a fact that he did not use the title of doctor of medicine wilfully and falsely, and that his name-plate did not imply that he was registered under the Act. See *Wilson* v. *Inyang* [1951] 2 All E.R. 237, and *Taylor's Central Garages* (*Exeter*) v. *Roper* (1951) 115 J.P. 445. Contrast *Hill* v. *Baxter* [1958] 1 Q.B. 277 (*T.A.C.*).

mentioned above[1] the topic has been complicated by the use of the term *mens rea* to indicate not foresight of consequences, but the other mental element in crime, namely the free and conscious undertaking of the course of conduct which resulted in the harm done. Save in the rarest of cases where the words of the statute compel the opposite interpretation it will be found that *mens rea*, in this last and perhaps less proper[2] sense of the phrase, is always essential. It was in this sense that it was used in *R.* v. *Wheat and Stocks* by Shearman, J.,[3] in *R.* v. *Maughan*[4] by Avory, J., and in *Cotterill* v. *Penn*[5] by Lord Hewart, C.J.[6] This is also the only sense in which the term *mens rea* can be applied in such cases as *Nichols* v. *Hall*[7] and *Harding* v. *Price*.[8] In the former the defendant had been charged with failing to give notice that his animals were infected with disease.[9] It was found as a fact that he did not know they were infected and Keating, J., said: 'I cannot understand how, on any reasonable construction of these words, it can be said that a man can neglect to give notice...without knowledge of the fact of which he is to give notice.' In the latter case the defendant was charged with failing to give notice of a collision between a trailer attached to his motor lorry and a stationary motor car which his lorry had passed. He was able to prove that he had no knowledge that the collision had taken place, and a divisional court held that the justices were right in acquitting him.

In *Harding* v. *Price* the court said:[10] 'If the duty be to report, he cannot report something of which he has no knowledge.' In *James & Son Ltd.* v. *Smee*[11] it was stated that the word 'permit' in the phrase 'permit to be used', in a statute 'imports a state of mind', whereas in the same statute the word 'use' is employed in an offence which is absolutely prohibited.[12] The words 'cause to be acted' were held to exclude from statutory liability[13] the licensee of a theatre in which an actor without authority had introduced into a play some lines not previously approved by the Lord Chamberlain.[14]

The student should guard against the confusion to which the use of the expression *mens rea* in two different senses may give rise in his mind.

[1] ¶ 31.

[2] See *Allard* v. *Selfridge & Co.* [1925] 1 K.B. 129, *per* Shearman, J., at p. 137.

[3] (1921) 15 Cr.App.R. 134 at p. 135 (*T.A.C.*).

[4] (1934) 24 Cr.App.R. 130 at p. 132 (*T.A.C.*): 'Was not the real ground of the decision that the prisoner had done the thing which was forbidden by the statute, and that it was not necessary to prove any further *mens rea*?'

[5] [1936] 1 K.B. 53 (*T.A.C.*): 'The element of *mens rea* is not required beyond the point that the facts must show an intention on the part of the person accused to do the act forbidden.'

[6] At p. 61.

[7] (1873) L.R. 8 C.P. 322.

[8] [1948] 1 K.B. 695; 1 All E.R. 283.

[9] Contagious Diseases (Animals) Act, 1869.

[10] [1948] 1 All E.R. at p. 285. Here the statute was interpreted on the exact meaning of its words, and the reference in the judgment to *mens rea* as an element of liability was otiose.

[11] [1954] 3 W.L.R. 631 at p. 638.

[12] *Green* v. *Barnett* [1954] 3 W.L.R. 631 at p. 640; Slade, J., dissenting.

[13] Under s. 15 of the Theatres Act, 1843.

[14] *Lovelace* v. *D.P.P.* [1954] 1 W.L.R. 1468.

Thus in *Kat* v. *Diment*[1] the appellant had been convicted[2] of having applied the false trade description of 'non-brewed vinegar' to a synthetic but wholesome product, although this name had long been used and recognized in the trade and by the Ministry of Food. The provision (subsect. (1) of sect. 2) of the statute under which he was prosecuted contains the words 'unless he proves that he acted without intent to defraud'. The divisional court dismissed his appeal, Lord Goddard, C.J.,[3] saying: 'Where a statute forbids the doing of a certain act, the doing of it in itself supplies *mens rea*....By throwing an onus on the defendant of proving that he acted without intent to defraud, it seems to me that the statute assumes that the doing of the act alone implies an intent to defraud, but the person charged can escape if he shows that he did not do the act intentionally.' This judgment interprets the statute as embodying an absolute prohibition, and the allusion to *mens rea* merely means that the defendant knew the constituents of the liquid to which he applied the description 'non-brewed' vinegar and knew that he had applied that description to it; it also in effect states that for the purposes of this Act there is no difference between saying that a person acted without intent to defraud and that he acted mistakenly. It has thus been held that for the purposes of subsect. (1) an accused person can have an 'intent to defraud'[4] although he had no idea of cheating or defrauding any person in the ordinary meaning of these words.[5]

[1] [1951] 1 K.B. 34; [1950] 2 All E.R. 657.

[2] Under the Merchandise Marks Act, 1887, s. 2 (1) (*d*).

[3] At p. 661, basing the decision on the following cases: *Starey* v. *Chilworth Gunpowder Company* (1889) 24 Q.B.D. 90, in which the defendant company being under contract to supply to the Government gunpowder manufactured by themselves had put their own name on barrels which they had filled with gunpowder imported from abroad; *Wood* v. *Burgess* (1889) 24 Q.B.D. 162, where the charge was brought not under subsect. (1) but under subsect. (2) of sect. 2 (in which there is no mention of intent to defraud, but a defence is allowed if the accused can prove that he 'acted innocently') and the court held that an intent to defraud was not a necessary ingredient of the offence charged; *Stone* v. *Burn* [1911] 1 K.B. 927, where also the conviction was under subsect. (2) and upheld on the grounds (i) that the facts brought the case within sect. 5 (i), and (ii) that the words 'acted innocently' point to some misapprehension of fact; *Allard* v. *Selfridge & Co.* [1925] 1 K.B. 129, another case under subsect. (2), and decided on the points (i) that the innocence contemplated by the Act can only exist where the infraction was committed by inadvertence or mistake of fact, which was not what the respondent company had done, and (ii) that the evidence failed to establish that they had taken all reasonable precautions so as to bring themselves within the protection of para. (*a*) of the subsection; *Mercer* v. *Pyramid Sand & Gravel Co.* (1944) 109 J.P. 54, a case under the same subsection and decided on the same points as *Allard* v. *Selfridge & Co.* And see *Slatcher* v. *George Mence Smith Ltd.* [1951] 2 All E.R. 388, where the accused had taken all reasonable precautions.

[4] See *Sayce* v. *Coupe* [1952] 2 All E.R. 715, 'Perhaps they [the justices] thought that he did not realize that he was defrauding the revenue. That, however, is not an answer to the charge. If people are dealing in this way with uncustomed goods, they defraud the revenue and that is enough', *per* Lord Goddard, C.J., at p. 717.

[5] But the doer of an innocent act is not brought within the liability for transgression of an absolute prohibition by his act's being rendered unlawful through the intervention of a stranger; *Reynolds* v. *Austin & Sons, Ltd.* [1951] 1 All E.R. 606; *Roper* v. *Taylor's*

In some statutory provisions there appears the requirement that the accused should have acted 'wilfully' or 'knowingly'. The interpretation of these words by the courts has not been consistent and the result is that each such provision has to be considered separately. Some instances will be examined below[1] when the crime of malicious damage is discussed.

NEGLIGENCE IN STATUTORY OFFENCES

¶ 34. In such circumstances as those given above it is quite irrelevant to the question of guilt or innocence that the defendant may or may not have been negligent. The prohibition is absolute and the defendant must be found guilty if he has done the forbidden thing. It is no excuse for him to show that he had taken all reasonable precautions[2] to avoid committing any offence, or to show that there were no precautions that he could have taken to avoid what was done. It may well be true in any particular case that the defendant, had he been reasonably prudent, would have been able to discover the true state of affairs and have saved himself from transgressing the law, so that in one sense he could be said to have brought the misfortune of a conviction upon himself; that fact however would not be the *ratio decidendi* of the conviction. The essential in all cases is to discover what the statute requires the prosecution to establish, on the evidence, in order to obtain a conviction, and whether or not the statute also allows the defendant to escape by proving some other facts by way of exoneration.[3] A good illustration is to be found in the cases and statutory provisions relating to the sale of fertilizers and feeding stuffs. In *Laird* v. *Dobell*[4] a vendor of feeding meal had taken the precaution of previously having a sample analysed and had then proceeded to sell the meal under an invoice which stated that it contained a rather lower percentage of oil and albumenoids than the percentage certified in the analyst's report. It was, however, found by the appropriate officer of the Board of Agriculture and

Central Garage Ltd. [1951] 2 T.L.R. 284. But it was held in *Browning* v. *Watson Ltd.* [1953] 2 All E.R. 775 that ignorance was no excuse where the accused had innocently carried in their coach strangers who had improperly insinuated themselves as members of a 'private party' (they were in fact 'agents provocateurs') since they ought to have taken measures to prevent this.

[1] ¶¶ 186 *et seq.* For 'intent to deceive' see *R.* v. *Greenberg* (1942) 28 Cr.App.R. 160. For 'knowingly' see *R.* v. *Hallam* [1957] 1 Q.B. 596; *R.* v. *Stewart and Harris* (1960) 44 Cr.App.R. 29 in which it was held that, for the purpose of the Explosive Substances Act, 1883, sect. 4 (1), the prosecution must prove (i) that the prisoner knew he had the substance in his possession or under his control and also (ii) that he knew it was an explosive substance.

[2] Save, of course, where the statute expressly allows such a defence, as e.g. the Merchandise Marks Act, 1887, s. 2 (2) (*a*). See *Trickers Ltd.* v. *Barnes* [1955] 1 All E.R. 803.

[3] Thus the Larceny Act, 1916, s. 28 (2) makes it an offence for any person to be found by night 'having in his possession without lawful excuse (the proof whereof shall lie on such person) any...implement of housebreaking'. As to the extent of the burden of proof see *R.* v. *Ward* [1915] 3 K.B. 696, *post*, ¶¶ 217 (3), 596. See *Wong Pooh Yin* v. *D.P.P.* [1954] 3 W.L.R. 471, for 'lawful excuse' within the Malay Emergency Regulations, 1951, reg. 4 (1).

[4] [1906] 1 K.B. 131, following *Korten* v. *W. Sussex C.C.* (1903) 67 J.P. 167.

Fisheries to contain a still lower percentage of these elements, and the vendor was convicted of selling with a false description to the prejudice of the purchaser under the statutory provision then in operation. The hardship of this particular class of cases was thereafter corrected by the legislature, which in succeeding statutes in effect allowed it to be a defence if the person accused proves that he did not know and could not with reasonable care have ascertained that the invoice or description was false.[1] Another such special defence is allowed by the Sexual Offences Act, 1956, s. 6 (3), where a man, being under the age of twenty-four is charged with having unlawful sexual intercourse (or attempting to do so) with a girl not under the age of thirteen but under the age of sixteen; for in such a case it is a defence if the offender can show that he believed and had reasonable cause to believe that the girl was over sixteen. It was, however, decided in 1923[2] that this defence was not available when the offender was charged under section 52 of the Offences against the Person Act, 1861,[3] with *indecent assault* upon the female even though the indecent assault in question consisted of carnal knowledge; the court said:[4] 'The result of this legislation is that a boy who is tempted and induced to have carnal knowledge of a girl who misrepresents herself to be over sixteen, and who appears to be so, has no possible answer if he is charged with indecent assault and not with the full offence.'[5]

VICARIOUS LIABILITY IN STATUTORY OFFENCES

¶ 35. Since, as we have seen, statutes frequently create crimes for which the liability is absolute, it is quite common under their provisions for a man to be held criminally responsible for acts of his servant which he has not authorized, and indeed which he has forbidden, provided that the servant when committing the offence was acting within the general scope of his employment.[6] Instances can be found in cases under the Licensing (Consolidation) Act, 1910. Under this Act a publican is held liable if his servants permit drunkenness or sell intoxicating liquor to a drunken person,[7] or knowingly permit prostitutes to meet in the premises,[8] or supply liquor or refreshment to a constable on duty,[9] or

[1] Fertilizers and Feeding Stuffs Act, 1906, s. 6 (1); *ibid.* 1926, s. 7 (1).

[2] *R.* v. *Forde* [1923] 2 K.B. 400, followed in *R.* v. *Maughan* (1934) 24 Cr.App.R. 130 (*T.A.C.*).

[3] Now repealed by the Sexual Offences Act, 1956, s. 51, and replaced by s. 14 (1).

[4] At p. 404.

[5] Further instances of these special defences will be found in the next paragraph.

[6] *Barker* v. *Levinson* [1950] 2 All E.R. 825 (*T.A.C.*); 66 T.L.R. Pt 2, 717; *Slatcher* v. *George Mence Smith Ltd.* [1951] 2 All E.R. 388.

[7] Sect. 75. *Worth* v. *Brown* (1898) 62 J.P. 658; *Cundy* v. *Lecocq* (1884) 13 Q.B.D. 207. Contrast *Ferguson* v. *Weaving* [1951] 1 All E.R. 412, in which it was held that sect. 4 (*b*) of the Licensing Act, 1921, does not impose a vicarious liability on the licence-holder whose servants, in his absence and contrary to his express orders, fail to prevent visitors to the licensed house from continuing to consume, after the permitted hours have ended, intoxicating liquor previously supplied to them within the permitted hours. See ¶ 28 *ante*.

[8] Sect. 76. *Allen* v. *Whitehead* [1930] 1 K.B. 211.

[9] Sect. 78.

allow 'gaming' to be carried on upon the premises.[1] Similarly a master has been convicted of using a motor vehicle without a licence when his servant had used the vehicle contrary to his express orders.[2] But in *Wilson* v. *Murphy*[3] the Court of Criminal Appeal, on the ground that there had been no delegation of authority, quashed the conviction of an employer in a credit betting business, whose employee had, contrary to his express instructions, taken money and thereby in effect had published coupons of ready-money betting. When a statute requires guilty knowledge there must be such knowledge at least on the part of the servant.[4] The Pharmacy and Poisons Act, 1933,[5] in effect provides that in proceedings arising out of the unlawful sale of poisons by an employee (*a*) it shall not be a defence that the employee acted without the authority of the employer, and (*b*) any material fact known to the employee shall be deemed to have been known by the employer. The Dogs (Protection of Livestock) Act, 1953 (*post*, ¶ 198*a*), imposes upon the owner vicarious liability for the misdeeds of his dog.

¶ 35*a*. Another, although different, form of vicarious liability is to be found in the Children and Young Persons Act, 1933,[6] which in effect provides that where an offence for which a fine, damages, or costs may be awarded has been committed by a child or young person then the court if the offender be a child shall (or if a young person, may) order that the fine, etc., be paid by the parent or guardian of the offender unless the court is satisfied that he has not conduced to the commission of the offence by neglecting to exercise due care of the child or young person. Other instances of vicarious liability arise under the now numerous statutory provisions which impose criminal liability on corporations, and make directors and officers liable unless they can exonerate themselves.[7]

MENS REA AS AFFECTING THE MEASURE OF PUNISHMENT

¶ 36. It should be noted that in cases where *mens rea* is irrelevant in point of law to the question of the offender's guilt or innocence of the crime charged, it may yet be taken into account by the tribunal in assessing the *punishment* to be inflicted. Thus in *Cundy* v. *Lecocq*,[8] in upholding the conviction of a licensee who had been convicted of serving alcohol to a man who was drunk although neither he nor his assistant had noticed the condition of the customer, who had in fact behaved in a very quiet and orderly way, it was said that the absence of

[1] Sect. 79. *Redgate* v. *Haynes* (1876) 1 Q.B.D. 89; *Bond* v. *Evans* (1890) 21 Q.B.D. 249.

[2] *Griffiths* v. *Studebakers Ltd.* [1924] 1 K.B. 102. And see *Provincial Motors* v. *Dunning* [1909] 2 K.B. 599.

[3] [1937] 1 All E.R. 315. And see *Melias Ltd.* v. *Preston* [1957] 3 W.L.R. 42 for the definition of the words 'actual offender' in sect. 12 (5) of the Weights and Measures Act, 1926.

[4] *Allen* v. *Whitehead* [1930] 1 K.B. 211.

[5] Sect. 24 (2).

[6] Sect. 55. By the Criminal Justice Act, 1961, s. 8, this liability is extended to payment of compensation to the victim.

[7] E.g. the Prevention of Fraud (Investments) Act, 1939, s. 17. See Lieck, 'The administration of criminal justice', *Penal Reform in England* (2nd ed.), 52.

[8] (1884) 13 Q.B.D. 207; 48 J.P. 599.

mens rea was a matter 'for mitigation of the penalties'. Similarly Lord Russell, C.J., said:[1] 'If the magistrate was convinced that the respondent honestly intended to carry out the law he would take that into account and impose only a small fine, and would also abstain from ordering the conviction to be endorsed on the licence.'[2]

MENS REA IN STATUTORY OFFENCES. CONCLUSIONS

¶ 37. From the preceding paragraphs it is to be observed that it is not possible to formulate any general principle by which to decide to what extent *mens rea* is a constituent in statutory offences. Students must remember that the first essential is to examine carefully the words of the statute itself, and then if no guidance can be obtained from authoritative interpretations of them given by the courts, they should employ the ordinary principles of construction,[3] remembering first that there is a strong presumption that there is no liability for the consequences of *involuntary* conduct, and second, that there is still a presumption, although a weaker one, that common law *mens rea* is required. Indeed so much weaker is this last presumption that it is often held to be rebutted by straightforward words of prohibition alone where no obvious injustice would thereby result. One or two cases may now be considered as examples of the difficulty of this topic.[4] The crime of bigamy is defined in sect. 57 of the Offences against the Person Act, 1861.[5] As will be seen, when this felony is discussed, the section makes no reference to any mental ingredient in the offence, but does include certain provisos which give sets of circumstances which exclude liability. One of these in effect is where the original wife or husband has been continuously absent from the accused husband or wife during seven years preceding the second marriage and has during that time not been known by the accused to be living. In *R.* v. *Tolson*[6] the Court for Crown Cases Reserved held that a reasonable belief that the missing spouse was dead before the seven years had elapsed would excuse a second marriage. From certain references made by the judges in that case to *mens rea* it was often thought that the section must be construed as impliedly requiring common law *mens rea* throughout, since that

[1] *Commissioners of Police* v. *Cartman* [1896] 1 Q.B. 655.

[2] Nominal punishments were so imposed in *R.* v. *Forde*, *R.* v. *Maughan* and *R.* v. *Larsonneur*. And see *Melias Ltd.* v. *Preston* [1957] 3 W.L.R. 42 in which a distinction is drawn between conviction alone (where no intention to contravene the statute can be seen), and conviction plus punishment; and in which *Wakeling Ltd.* v. *Robinson* (1930) 46 T.L.R. 151 was explained away.

[3] See *Pendar* v. *Smith* [1959] 2 All E.R. 360 as to the strictness of the rules for interpretation of statutes, and *R.* v. *Oakes* [1959] 2 W.L.R. 694 as to when a statute may be interpreted *against* the subject.

[4] Cp. the *ratio decidendi* of *Fisher* v. *Barrett and Pomeroy* [1954] 1 W.L.R. 351 (a cigarette end in a bread-roll) with that of *Miller Ltd.* v. *Battersea Borough Council* [1956] 1 Q.B. 43 (a piece of metal in a bun), both charges under sect. 9 of the Food and Drugs Act, 1938 (rep.). It may be suggested, however, that a cigarette would taint the whole of the bread-roll, whereas the metal was not regarded as tainting the bun.

[5] *Post*, ¶ 170.

[6] (1889) 23 Q.B.D. 168 (*T.A.C.*). See Russ. 83.

element was not expressly or necessarily excluded. Such was not the view of the Court of Criminal Appeal in 1921[1] in a case in which the defence relied upon another proviso relating to the termination of the first marriage by divorce. The court held that the judgments in *Tolson's Case* did not go further than deciding that the words of the particular proviso must be read as meaning that a reasonable belief in the spouse's death would be an excuse, the reference to seven years' absence being given as only one example of facts which could ground such belief, whereas the proviso relating to the termination of the first marriage by divorce did not admit of such a construction and must be taken to exclude *mens rea*. It was therefore held that the prisoner's erroneous but honest belief that his divorce had been made absolute was no defence.[2] It has been held, however, that a genuine belief that he was not already married[3] affords a defence to a charge of bigamy if he marries again. Again it would seem that the prisoner must have acted voluntarily in doing what he did, so that ignorance of the fact that he was going through a ceremony of marriage should afford a defence.[4]

Another instance of contrast is between *Sherras* v. *de Rutzen* and *Cundy* v. *Lecocq*.[5] In the former it was held, in effect, that a publican who served drink to a policeman who was on duty should be excused if he could prove that he believed the officer not to be on duty from the fact that he was not wearing his armlet: whereas in the latter case it was held that, on a charge of supplying drink to a man who was drunk, it was no defence to prove a belief that the customer was sober. Perhaps an adequate justification for the difference in the interpretation of the statutory provisions in these two cases may be suggested. In the former the publican had no reasonable means of discovering whether the policeman was on duty except by looking to see if he was wearing the armlet. The police authorities alone had certain means of information on this point, namely, the record of the appropriate officer at the police station. But in the latter case the customer's drunkenness could be ascertained just as well by the publican (or his representative) as it could be by any police witness who observed the man's condition at the material time in the public house.

[1] *R.* v. *Wheat and Stocks* (1921) 15 Cr.App.R. 134; *post*, ¶ 174.

[2] Some writers have suggested that *R.* v. *Wheat and Stocks* was wrongly decided, and others have tried to explain it by distinctions between mistakes of fact and mistakes of law, or by importing some idea of negligence (see Stallybrass, *Mod. Appr. Crim. Law*, 458 *et seq.*). See 51 *L.Q.R.* 286 and 52 *L.Q.R.* 65. It is submitted that it is neither necessary nor profitable to go into such questions and that the case is simply one of strict interpretation of the words of the statute. See Edwards, '*Mens rea* and bigamy', 2 *Current Law Problems*, 47.

[3] *R.* v. *Connatty* (1919) 83 J.P. 292; *R.* v. *Weiwow* (1945) Notts. Summer Ass. (Arch. 1352); *R.* v. *Dolman* [1949] 1 All E.R. 813, Leeds Ass. See also *R.* v. *Taylor* [1950] 2 K.B. 368; *post*, p. 206.

[4] *Kelly (Hyams)* v. *Kelly* (1932) 49 T.L.R. 99; 148 L.T. 143

[5] [1895] 1 Q.B. 918; (1884) 13 Q.B.D. 207.

Chapter III

VARIATIONS IN LIABILITY

SECTION 1. INTRODUCTORY

¶ 38. In this chapter will be considered the chief instances in which criminal guilt is lessened or entirely excluded owing to special circumstances or to something peculiar to the person who has brought about the *actus* of a crime. As previously mentioned[1] rules of law are in the first instance stated for what we have termed the legally normal individual. We have now to consider the situation in criminal law of persons who are not, in this sense, normal. It will also be convenient to consider some sets of circumstances in which even the normal person's liability is modified, although upon examination it will be found that these modifications are really no more than applications of the general principles of responsibility which have already been discussed, and logically should have been dealt with in the last chapter. To have done so, however, would have overloaded the exposition of the main features of this branch of the law and would have tended to distract the student's attention from them. They can be grouped under the headings of Mistake, Intoxication and Compulsion.

SECTION 2. MISTAKE

MISTAKE AS A DEFENCE AT COMMON LAW

¶ 39. It is plain that if mistake is to be held to excuse a harmful deed the law is allowing an examination into a subjective mental element, namely the operation of the accused person's mind.[2] This examination will only be made at the instance of the accused on whom will rest the burden of producing evidence that he was mistaken and that his conduct in the matter was due to his mistake. In this way the accused raises the defence either that he had no *mens rea* or, where the facts so warrant, that he should be treated as though his harmful deed had not been an *actus reus*. This in effect means, in simple language, that the man can claim that his present trial shall proceed on the fiction that the facts were as he had mistakenly believed them to be, and not as they really were.[3] But if this defence is to be successful, the law requires that the following conditions shall be fulfilled.

[1] *Ante*, ¶ 29.

[2] 1 Hale P.C. 42, 'but in some cases *ignorantia facti* doth excuse, for such an ignorance many times makes the act itself morally involuntary'. See *ante*, ¶¶ 14 and 15; and Russ. 75.

[3] 'I think it may be laid down as a general rule that an alleged offender is deemed to have acted under that state of facts which he...believed to exist when he did the act alleged to be an offence'; *per* Stephen, J., in *R.* v. *Tolson* (1889) 23 Q.B.D. 168 at p. 188. See *post*, ¶ 175.

(1) The first condition is that the mistake must be of such a character that, had the supposed circumstances been real, they would have prevented the alleged liability from attaching to the person in doing what he did. Therefore it is no defence for a burglar, who breaks into no. 5, to show that he mistook that house for no. 6,[1] or that he did not know that nine o'clock had struck.[2] For in these instances the *actus reus* and *mens rea* would still have existed even in the circumstances supposed. On the other hand, it will be no offence to lay violent hands upon a person, whom you reasonably, though mistakenly, suppose to be committing a burglary.[3] In this case the defence is that if things had been as they were supposed to be the man's *actus* would not have been *reus* since it was permissible (and indeed formerly a duty) to kill one who was engaged in the felony of burglary.[4] Accordingly it would not be murder if an executioner whose duty it was to put to death a condemned prisoner *X* (whom he did not know) were to kill *Y* who was produced to him in circumstances which were such as to make him believe he was executing the right victim: in the language used in the earlier cases the killing of *Y* could 'not be imputed to him'. Certainly he intended to kill the individual under his hands, but if the facts had been as he supposed his *actus* would not have been *reus*.[5] Similarly, in an American case,[6] where a constable was charged with arresting a man unlawfully, it was stated that if it appeared that the man had fallen down in the street in a fit,[7] and his friends had first tried to revive him by administering whisky, and then had gone away to seek help, the constable should be acquitted; for the fact that the man smelt of whisky would afford reasonable ground for supposing his insensibility to be due to intoxication (a lawful ground for arrest).[8]

Mostly, however, mistake negatives *mens rea* rather than *actus reus*. A good example is mentioned by Sir Michael Foster.[9] A man, before

[1] Providing, of course, that no. 5 is 'the dwelling house of another'.

[2] For this, and the preceding, fact is an objective part of the *actus reus*; *ante*, ¶ 12. *R.* v. *Forbes and Webb* (1865) 10 Cox 362, and *R.* v. *Maxwell and Clanchy* (1909) 73 J.P. 176, in which it was held that, on an indictment under sect. 38 of the Offences against the Person Act, 1861, for assaulting a constable 'in discharge of his duty', it was no defence that the assailants did not know of his official character, were cases decided upon a strict interpretation of the words of the statute.

[3] *R.* v. *Levett* (1638) Cro. Car. 538 (*T.A.C.*); *R.* v. *Dennis* (1905) 69 J.P. 256. The subjective mental element in these cases relates to the man's *belief* in the facts upon which he takes action. *Post*, ¶ 96.

[4] See 4 Bl. *Comm.* 27: 'As if a man, intending to kill a thief or housebreaker in his own house, by mistake kills one of his own family. This is no criminal action.'

[5] Another example would be that of a boxer who, being dazed, struck the referee, mistaking him for his opponent.

[6] *Commonwealth* v. *Presby* (1859) 14 Gray 65.

[7] To distinguish epilepsy from intoxication is a difficult task; the police have been sometimes censured most unjustly for failing to achieve it.

[8] As to the killing of a supposed dead man by one who imagines himself to have *already* murdered him, see two Indian cases where it was held not to be murder; 36 *L.Q.R.* 6–8. And see the criticism of *Meli* v. *R.* [1954] 1 W.L.R. 228, in Russell at p. 60.

[9] Foster, 265 (*T.A.C.*).

going to church, fired off his gun, and left it empty. But during his absence some person went out shooting with the gun and, on returning, left it loaded. The owner, late in the same day, took up the gun again and, in doing this, touched the trigger. The gun went off, and killed his wife, who was in the room. Foster held that the man had reasonable grounds to believe that the weapon was not loaded. In reading these early cases it must be remembered that the rules of criminal liability and the conception of *mens rea* were different from what they have since become with the passage of time.[1] Nowadays the acquittal would be based on the absence of *mens rea* in a man who clearly had no idea that the gun might go off when he picked it up.

(2) A further condition is that the mistake must be a reasonable one. Examination of the cases will reveal that this rule is fundamentally a matter of evidence. Since the defence of mistake raises an essentially subjective point as to what the prisoner really believed, the objective question of reasonableness is strictly irrelevant; for, as we shall see, an insane person may be held criminally irresponsible for his deeds when through disease of his mind he has acted under the most unreasonable of delusions. The truth of the matter is this, that the prisoner must himself plead the defence of mistake, and in support he must either produce evidence or draw attention to evidence already produced which goes reasonably to show that he may well be telling the truth when he alleges that he did make the mistake,[2] and if (without pleading insanity) he sets up facts which would not have deceived an ordinary man, the tribunal will probably reject the prisoner's contention that he was deceived: a description of this rejection as based on the fact that the prisoner's mistake was not reasonable, really means that the tribunal does not believe that he is telling the truth when he says he made a mistake.[3] It must be admitted, however, that in this matter the language of the authorities is not always clear. Thus Professor Kenny thought that no belief which has now come to be currently regarded as an obsolete superstition can be treated as a mistake sufficiently reasonable to excuse a crime. In 1880, at Clonmel, a woman who had placed a child naked on a hot shovel, in the honest belief that it was a deformed fairy sent as a substitute for the real child (who would be restored if the changeling were thus imperilled), was convicted and sentenced. So, in 1895, again

[1] See Russ. 34 *et seq.*

[2] The burden thus resting on the accused is not so heavy that he has to *prove* his mistake; for, as we have seen, it is a basic rule of the common law that it is enough for the accused to raise a reasonable doubt as to the prosecution's having discharged its clear duty to prove his guilt; see *Woolmington* v. *D.P.P.*; *ante*, ¶ 25.

[3] Cf. the citation from *Hosegood* v. *Hosegood* (1950) 66 T.L.R. 735 in ¶ 25 *ante*. And see *Wilson* v. *Inyang* [1951] 2 All E.R. 237. See *R.* v. *MacKinnon* [1958] 3 All E.R. 657 in which it was stated: 'In any event, once it is proved that the forecast is misleading, false or deceptive, and that there were no reasonable grounds for believing it, there exists powerful evidence that the accused who made the forecast for some purpose of his own either must have known that it was untrue or had no reasonable belief in its truth'; *per* Salmon, J., at p. 660.

at Clonmel, were men who had caused the death of the wife of one of them by holding her over a fire and searing her with a red hot poker, in the honest expectation of thereby exorcizing a demon that was supposed to possess her.[1] And even people who break the law in consequence of a belief that they are obeying a divine command, have been regarded as actuated by a mistake which is 'unreasonable'.[2] Illustrations are afforded in America by the prosecutions of Mormons for polygamy;[3] and in England by the prosecutions of the 'Peculiar People' for withholding medical aid from their sick children. It would be more satisfactory if these instances of fantastic superstitious belief could be approached as insane delusions and treated in accordance with the rules applicable thereto,[4] for some religious delusions are of so extreme a character as to be plain evidence of insanity, and have been held to afford a defence upon that ground;[5] others would fall within the M'Naghten Answer IV (Insane Delusions); others again would come within Answers II and III (*post*, pp. 77 *et seq*). Some delusions would be found to lie outside the Answers, and among these religious belief would afford no defence, since it would be a mistake of law, i.e. that divine command overrides ordinary law, as in *Reynolds* v. *United States*, *supra*. It may ultimately be found that section 2 of the Homicide Act, 1957, which has introduced the defence of 'diminished responsibility' has opened up an avenue to special treatment of some difficult cases of strange beliefs.

(3) The final condition is that the mistake, however reasonable, must not relate to matters of law but to matters of fact. For a mistake of law, even though inevitable, is not allowed in England to afford any excuse for crime. *Ignorantia juris neminem excusat.*[6] The utmost effect it can ever have is that it may occasionally, like drunkenness, rebut the existence of the peculiar form of *mens rea* which some particular kind of

[1] In 1894 an Indian sentinel in Canada who had killed a man under the belief of his being an evil spirit that would attack human beings was convicted of manslaughter; *R.* v. *Machekequonabe* (1897) 28 Ontario 309. The report of the case does not indicate whether the court explained the principles of liability upon which the decision rested. See the *Hammersmith Ghost Case* (*R.* v. *Smith*, 1804), 4 Bl. *Comm.* 201, n; *post*, ¶ 96 n. 3. And cf. *R.* v. *Dhlamini* (1955) (1) S.A. 120; [1955] Curr. Law 75, where the prisoner who, half awake after a nightmare, had stabbed the deceased who was by his bed, was held not guilty of murder. For instances of belief in the supernatural in Africa see [1959] *Crim. L.R.* 71.

[2] E.g. *R.* v. *Senior* [1899] 1 Q.B. 283. See the discussion of this case in Russ. 81.

[3] *Reynolds* v. *United States* (1878), 98 U.S. 145 (*T.A.C.*).

[4] Under the M'Naghten answers, *post*, ¶ 53. See *R.* v. *Codère* (1916) 12 Cr.App.R. 21.

[5] E.g. *R.* v. *Hadfield* (1800), 27 St.Tr. 1281; *R.* v. *Allen* (1911) C.C.C. Sess. Pap. CLIV, 357.

[6] For a discussion of the justifications that may be offered for this severe rule, see Austin's *Jurisprudence*, Lect. XXV, Markby's *Elements of Law*, sects. 269, 270, and C. K. Allen's *Legal Duties*, 195 and 196. Perhaps after considering them all, the student may still feel compelled, with the late Prof. Henry Sidgwick, to regard the rule as 'not a realization of ideal justice, but an exercise of Society's right of self-preservation'. For the milder principles adopted in Roman law see Justinian's *Digest*, XXII, 6, and Lindley's *Jurisprudence*, 24 and App. xix. And see Winfield, 'Mistake of law' (1943), 59 *L.Q.R.* 327, on the difficulty of distinguishing mistake of law and mistake of fact.

crime may require. Thus larceny even at common law[1] could only be committed when a thing is stolen without even the appearance of right to take it; and, accordingly, a *bona fide* and reasonable mistake, even though it be of law—like that of a woman who gleans corn in a village where it is the practice to do so (¶ 281 *post*)—will afford a sufficient defence. Similarly a mortgagor who, under an invalid but *bona fide* claim of right, damages the fixtures in the house which he has mortgaged, will not be guilty of 'malicious' damage.[2] Apart, however, from such exceptional offences, the rule which ignores mistakes of law is applied with rigour. A sailor has been convicted of an offence that had been forbidden only by an Act of Parliament of which he could not possibly know, since it was enacted when he was far away at sea, and the offence was committed before the news of its enactment could reach him.[3] Frenchmen, who had acted as seconds in a fatal duel here, have similarly been committed for trial on a charge of murder, although their own land practised duelling and they did not know the English law forbade it.[4] A husband may be guilty of wilfully neglecting to maintain his wife, even though he *bona fide*, though mistakenly, believes that he is not legally liable to maintain her.[5] Italians have been punished in London for keeping lotteries, in spite of their urging that in Italy every little village possessed a lottery sanctioned by the State, and that they had no idea that the English law could be different. It is therefore easy to see that a veterinary surgeon's mistaken belief that an operation, which he knows to be painful and purposeless, is nevertheless unpunishable legally, will afford him no defence for performing it.

These mistakes are reasonable enough; yet they afford no excuse. Nor would they do so, even if the prisoner could show that he had taken pains to obtain a lawyer's advice and had been misled by it. Still less, therefore, can any excuse be conferred by legal errors that are unreasonable. Such are apt to occur in connexion with the crime of bigamy. In a trial for it at the Central Criminal Court in 1883,[6] not only the prisoner himself, but also his first wife and all her family, had believed his marriage with her to be void, because the wedding-ring was only of brass and not of gold.[7]

But although mistakes of law, unreasonable or even reasonable, thus leave the offender punishable for the crime which he has blundered

[1] The rule is now contained in s. 1. of the Larceny Act, 1916. See ¶ 222.

[2] *R.* v. *Croft* (1889) C.C.C. Sess. Pap. CXI, 202. Cf. *R.* v. *Twose* (1879) 14 Cox 327 (*T.A.C.*); and see *Solle* v. *Butcher* [1949] 2 All E.R. 1107. This topic is dealt with in greater detail below, ¶¶ 186 *et seq.*

[3] *R.* v. *Bailey* (1800) R. and R. 1 (*T.A.C.*).

[4] *Re Barronet* (1853) 1 E. and B. 1.

[5] *Biggs* v. *Burridge* (1925) 89 J.P. 75.

[6] Which Professor Kenny himself witnessed.

[7] One female bigamist, tried in 1920, had been assured, by the authorities of the asylum, in which her incurably insane husband had been confined for eleven years past, that his incurableness had set her legally free to marry again; a man, tried also in 1920, had honestly believed that his wife's elopement with an adulterer had *ipso facto* dissolved the marriage. A frequent error is the belief that a mere decree *nisi* effects an immediate dissolution; cf. ¶ 174 *post.*

into, they may of course afford good grounds for inflicting on him a milder punishment.[1]

MISTAKE AS A DEFENCE IN STATUTORY OFFENCES

¶ 40. As we have seen, in all questions relating to statutory offences it is necessary to have careful regard to the words of the statute which may expressly, or by implication, excuse the results of mistake. *R.* v. *Tolson*, *Sherras* v. *de Rutzen* and other cases discussed above[2] afford examples. Conversely a statute may expressly, or by implication, exclude the defence of mistake: examples of this can also be found among the cases previously discussed.[3] And certainly a statute may be so framed as to admit a mistake (even unreasonable) of law as a defence.[4] Subject however to the essential qualification that the words of the statute are paramount, it may be said that the rules under which mistake may excuse are the same for statutory offences as for those at common law.

SECTION 3. INTOXICATION

¶ 41. The older law[5] regarded intoxication as aggravating[6] the guilt of any crimes whose predisposing cause it was, and in no way affording an excuse for the commission of a criminal deed; for unlike insanity, it had been produced voluntarily, and to produce it was wrong, both morally and also legally.[7] But at the present day the effects of drunkenness upon criminal liability must be considered in the light of the ordinary rules as to *actus reus* and *mens rea*, in the same way as the effects of illness produced by any other kind of poison. Thus actual insanity produced by drunken habits (as in some cases of *delirium tremens*) exempts from criminal responsibility to the same extent as if it had originated from less reprobated causes. And where a man is intoxicated through no fault of his own—for example, as the result of medical treatment or the fraud of malicious companions[8]—this was, even under the older law, regarded as carrying the full exemptive effect. There seems nowadays to be no reason, on principle, why there should be retained any idea that because a man has voluntarily indulged in

[1] Cf. *R.* v. *Esop* (1836) 7 C. and P. 456.

[2] *Ante*, ¶ 37. [3] *Ante*, ¶ 35.

[4] *R.* v. *Rutter* (1908) 1 Cr.App.R. 174; *R.* v. *Bernhard* [1938] 2 K.B. 264; *R.* v. *Day* (1844) 8 J.P. 186.

[5] 4 Co. *Inst.* 125*a*. Both Coke and Hale term it *dementia affectata* (acquired madness).

[6] Though not on the principle of Lord Cockburn's convivial Scottish judge who argued, 'If he remains so bad even when drunk, what must he be when sober?'

[7] Until 1872 it was a criminal offence, under 4 Jac. I, c. 5, s. 2; and even now a conspiracy to produce drunkenness might be criminal, and a contract for it would be void. See *Reniger* v. *Fogossa* (1550) 1 Plowd. 1, 19. For a curious proposal for a means of measuring by a mathematical calculation the criminal liability of a man who had committed an offence while under the influence of alcohol see Paley, *Moral Philosophy*, B. 4, c. 2, cited in a footnote to *R.* v. *Pearson* (1835) 2 Lew. 144. For an attempt to deal with the evils resulting from habitual drunkenness, see the Inebriates Act, 1898, *post*, ¶ 787.

[8] *Pearson's Case* (1835) 2 Lew. 144.

intoxicating liquor he should be held fully liable for any consequences which may follow, without regard to the question of his mental ability when under the influence of the alcohol which he has consumed. On the other hand it is clear that in law he cannot be allowed any excuse because the alcohol may have inflamed his passions[1] or increased his audacity or reduced his self-control. Medical research has established that a common effect of alcohol upon a man is to produce in him a much exaggerated notion of his abilities while at the same time it in fact reduces them, so that a position is created in which he is prone to take excessive risks. At common law, a man who consciously takes risks of causing harm is acting with *mens rea* and will be criminally responsible if he does such harm, however confidently he may have expected that his skill would enable him to avoid it.[2] Nevertheless, it is submitted that if he can establish that the effect of the alcohol upon his mind was to make him unable to appreciate that he was taking any risk at all, that fact should negative a finding of *mens rea* on his part. In the cases where the measure of intoxication is held not to excuse from conviction the point may then arise as to whether or not it should mitigate punishment;[3] different views may be held on this question, which, it is apprehended, falls rather within the province of ethics than of law.

INTOXICATION RELEVANT IN ESTABLISHING MISTAKE, LACK OF INTENT, ETC.

¶ **42.** If the ordinary criteria of liability are observed it will be found that drunkenness may be relevant:

(1) To establish mistake. Intoxication may cause—on grounds slighter than could be expected to lead a sober man to the same erroneous conclusion—such a mistake of fact as is incompatible with criminal liability,[4] thus a drunken man may fancy someone else's umbrella to be his own, or think an innocent gesture to be an assault, and hit back in supposed self-defence.[5]

(2) To negative the existence of any intent at all. In *R.* v. *Cruse*[6] Patteson, J., said 'although drunkenness is no excuse for any crime whatever, yet it is often of very great importance in cases where it is

[1] *D.P.P.* v. *Beard* [1920] A.C. 479, at p. 502 (*T.A.C.*).

[2] *R.* v. *Doherty* (1887) 16 Cox 306, 309; *James* v. *British General Insurance Co.* [1927] 2 K.B. 311, 325.

[3] *R.* v. *Morton* (1908) 1 Cr.App.R. 255; *R.* v. *Nuttall* (1908) 25 T.L.R. 76.

[4] At a baby's christening party, its nurse, having got so drunk as to be 'quite stupid and senseless', put the infant on the fire by mistake for a log of wood. The magistrates discharged her (*Gent. Mag.* 1748, 570). This mistake would nowadays enable the accused to establish that her *actus* was not to be treated as *reus* (see ¶ 39 *ante*); also, since she was said to be 'senseless', that she was incapable of forming any malice aforethought (*post*, ¶ 103).

[5] *R.* v. *Gamlen* (1858) 1 F. and F. 90. Cf. 31 T.L.R. 361; and (1917) 12 Cr.App.R. 221. It has been held in America that drunkenness may negative knowledge, e.g. in receiving stolen goods, *U.S.* v. *Roudenbosh* (1832) Baldwin 514; *The People* v. *Harris* (1866) 29 Cal. 678.

[6] (1838) 8 C. and P. 541, at p. 546.

a question of intention'. A person may be so drunk 'as to be utterly unable to form any intention at all'. So it was held to be no crime when an apparent suicide jumped into a well when 'so drunk as not to know what she was about'.[1]

(3) To negative the existence of some specific intent. It was held by the Court of Criminal Appeal in *R.* v. *Meade*,[2] that if a man were so drunk as to be 'incapable of knowing that what he was doing was dangerous, i.e. likely to inflict serious injury,' this would rebut the presumption that he *intended* the natural consequences of his act. A few years later the judgment in *R.* v. *Meade* came under consideration in *Director of Public Prosecutions* v. *Beard*[3] and it was laid down that evidence of such drunkenness as 'renders the accused incapable of forming the specific intent, essential to constitute the crime, should be taken into consideration, with the other facts proved, in order to determine whether or not he had this intent'. In such a case the drunkenness, if it negatives the existence of the indispensable mental element of the crime 'negatives the commission of that crime'. Thus a drunken man's inability to form an intention to kill, or to do grievous bodily harm[4] involving the risk of killing, at the time of committing a homicide, may reduce his offence from murder[5] to manslaughter (which latter crime requires no more than a realization that some bodily harm may be caused).[6] Drunkenness may likewise show that a supposed burglar had no intention of stealing,[7] or that wounds were inflicted without any 'intent to do grievous bodily harm',[8] or that a false pretence was made with no 'intent to defraud'.[9] But it must be remembered that a man may be so drunk as not to form an intention to kill or do grievous bodily harm while yet in sufficient control of his senses to be able to contemplate some harm and so to be guilty of manslaughter or of an unlawful wounding. The question whether the effect of alcohol on the mind could produce a state of diminished responsibility within sect. 2 of the Homicide Act, 1957, is mentioned below.[10]

(4) When it is a constituent part of the offence. There are statutory provisions, too numerous to recount here, under which intoxication is

[1] *R.* v. *Moore* (1852) 3 C. and K. 319. See *R.* v. *Mathieson* (1906) 25 New Zealand L.R. 879.

[2] [1909] 1 K.B. 895.

[3] [1920] A.C. 479; ¶ 112 *post*. For a criticism of the dicta in this case see 'Defence of drunkenness in criminal law', by R. V. Singh, 49 *L.Q.R.* 528.

[4] *H.M. Advocate* v. *Campbell* (1921) S.C. (J.) 1 (Scotland).

[5] *R.* v. *Monkhouse* (1849) 4 Cox 55. In *R.* v. *Meakin* (1836) 7 C. and P. 297 the court was influenced by the ancient doctrine of strict liability, and it took the view that when a dangerous instrument is used drunkenness can have no effect on the consideration of malicious intent; in contrast, see *R.* v. *Doherty* (1887) 16 Cox 306, for the more modern doctrine.

[6] See ¶ 136 *post*.

[7] *The State* v. *Bell* (1870) 20 Stiles 316. See also *Ruse* v. *Read* [1949] 1 All E.R. 398 (*T.A.C.*).

[8] *R.* v. *Meakin* (1836) 7 C. and P. 297.

[9] *A.G. for N. Ireland* v. *Gallagher* [1961] H.L. 3 W.L.R. 619, Ld Denning at p. 640 on the general principle as to drunkenness as a defence.

[10] *R.* v. *Di Duca* (1959) 43 Cr.App.R. 167; *post*, p. 85 n. 4.

itself part of the offence created. These include drunkenness when in charge of a child under seven,[1] or of a horse, when in possession of firearms, when in a public place or on licensed premises[2] and so on. In particular under the Road Traffic Act, 1960,[3] it is an indictable offence[4] to drive or attempt to drive a motor-vehicle on a road or other public place when under the influence of drink or a drug to such an extent as to be incapable of having proper control of the vehicle;[5] one who is unfit, as above, and is in charge of the vehicle, but *not* driving it, also commits an offence[6] less severely punishable. The offender is, unless the court otherwise orders, disqualified from holding a licence for twelve months, and a longer period of disqualification may be imposed.[7] The Act also makes it an offence[8] for a pedal cyclist to ride while unfit as above.

It must finally be noted that the question 'Was he drunk?' is often answered too definitely, as if there existed some single standard of sobriety. Intoxication is a question of degree, ranging from mere exhilaration down to unconsciousness. The man may be too drunk to do this act properly, yet sober enough to do some other.[9] Our earliest legal standard of sobriety was over-lenient, regarding a man as not intoxicated unless 'the same legs which carry him into the house cannot bring him out again'.[10]

(5) In certain cases of provocation. This is a topic on which the law is unfortunately still not quite clear. It will be discussed in more detail later,[11] and it will suffice to state here that it has long been the law that an intentional homicide will be reduced from murder to manslaughter if it appears that the accused had killed someone in a sudden fit of passion caused by a sufficient act of provocation committed by the dead man. It has often been laid down by the courts that the test to be applied in these cases is an objective one, namely that the jury are to say whether in

[1] Licensing Act, 1902, s. 2 (1). [2] Licensing Act, 1872, s. 12.

[3] Which has in some sections been modified by the Road Traffic Improvement Act, 1960. [4] Sect. 6 (1), (6).

[5] Punishment, fine, or imprisonment up to two years: on summary conviction maximum fine £100, imprisonment for four months, or both. *R.* v. *Hawkes* (1931) 22 Cr. App.R. 172; *Armstrong* v. *Clark* [1957] 2 W.L.R. 400.

[6] Sect. 6 (2).

[7] Sect. 104, sched. 11. For a ruling as to the exercise of the court's discretion see *Whittall* v. *Kirby* [1947] K.B. 194; *Jowett-Shooter* v. *Franklin* [1949] 2 All E.R. 730; *Aichroth* v. *Cottee* [1954] 1 W.L.R. 1214 (driving whilst disqualified); as to 'special reasons', see *R.* v. *Wickins* [1958] 42 Cr.App.R. 236.

[8] Sect. 6 (2); punishable on summary conviction with a fine up to £30; for a subsequent offence the like fine or imprisonment up to three months.

[9] We may add that an accused man may sometimes be helped towards acquittal by the fact of his having been drunk even on some occasion *subsequent* to the date of the crime in question. For it may afford an innocent explanation of conduct that otherwise would suggest a consciousness of guilt; as where, on being arrested, he has made untrue statements or has refused to make any statement at all. The Inebriates Act, 1898, made special provision for dealing with habitual drunkards convicted of offences committed when under the influence of drink, or to which drunkenness contributed.

[10] Dalton's *Country Justice* (1635), 27. [11] ¶ 117 *post*.

their opinion the provocation offered was such as to cause 'a reasonable man' to lose control of himself so that he took the life in an irresistible burst of resentment, without any premeditation. There are cases in which it has been held that a man, who is peculiarly sensitive and less able to control his temper than the average man, is not to be allowed the defence of provocation if he has killed in an instant reaction to some attack which would not have been likely so to arouse the average man, notwithstanding the fact that owing to his special circumstances the accused was completely overwhelmed by passion.[1] Yet there are other cases in which the temporary effect of alcohol in rendering a man more inflammable than an ordinary sober man would be, has been taken into consideration as admitting the defence of provocation in his favour.[2] Such uncertainty is a defect in any branch of a legal system. But now the Homicide Act, 1957, has made some changes; see *post*, ¶ 108 *a*.

SECTION 4. COMPULSION

¶ 43. In the old authorities statements[3] are to be found to the effect that there may be circumstances in which a man may be excused for deeds which he has done not of his own free volition but under compulsion exercised upon him by another. A simple example can be imagined of a powerful man who, seizing the hand of one much weaker than himself and overcoming his resistance by sheer strength, forces the hand to strike someone else. The defence, if it be admitted, must be that the mental element of 'volition' is absent—the accused, in other words, pleads that his conduct was not voluntary.[4] Compulsion can take other forms than physical force; but in whatever form it appears the courts have been indisposed to admit that it can be a defence for any crime committed through yielding to it and the law of the matter is both meagre and vague. It can best be considered under the heads of obedience to orders, marital coercion, duress *per minas*, and necessity.

OBEDIENCE TO ORDERS

¶ 44. This rarely affords any defence in English law, though there are, of course, deeds which are legal when done lawfully for the advancement of justice but which would otherwise be illegal,[5] e.g. the execution of the lawful sentence of a court,[6] deeds done for the prevention of forcible crimes and breaches of the peace,[7] or to secure the arrest of criminals.[8] Any deed so done, of course, does not constitute an *actus reus*. Though the King can do no wrong, either civilly or even criminally—and also *because* the King can do no wrong—his subordinates must be held strictly accountable for any wrongs they may commit on his behalf.

[1] E.g. *R.* v. *Alexander* (1913) 9 Cr.App.R. 139; *R.* v. *Lesbini* (1914) 3 K.B. 1116.

[2] E.g. *R.* v. *Hopper* (1915) 2 K.B. 431; *R.* v. *Letenock* (1917) 12 Cr.App.R. 221. But see now *R.* v. *McCarthy* [1954] 2 Q.B. 105, *post*, ¶ 121; Russ. 602.

[3] 1 Hale P.C. 43; 4 Bl. *Comm.* 27. [4] See ¶ 18, and [1960] *Crim. L.R.* 89, 168.

[5] See in particular in relation to homicide ¶ 94 *post*.

[6] ¶ 95 *post*. [7] ¶ 96 *post*. [8] ¶ 695 *post*.

Hence, if a soldier or sailor or constable unlawfully does violence to any one, he cannot plead as a defence merely that he was acting under orders from his superior officer, or even from the King himself.[1]

Of course such orders, when not *obviously* unlawful, may be relevant to his defence under some more general rule of law. They may give him such a 'claim of right'[2] as renders it no larceny for him to appropriate another man's goods, or such grounds for supposing the immediate circumstances to justify his conduct as will render this mistake of fact[3] a valid defence, or negative a particular intent[4] or excuse apparent recklessness.[5]

And, more than this, it is said that a mistake even of law may afford a defence to a public servant who has obeyed unlawful orders under a reasonable (though mistaken) belief that they were lawful. Thus when force is exercised by a gaoler or hangman in carrying out an invalid sentence, then, if the court which passed the sentence had jurisdiction over the offence, and the sentence had all reasonable appearance of validity, the man's mistake affords him immunity.[6]

Cases of this kind illustrate the point that fundamentally it is impossible to distinguish a mistake of law from a mistake of fact.[7] They are further complicated by the use of language which suggests that the defence is based upon the obligation of an inferior officer to obey the directions of his superior;[8] this, it is suggested, is a misconception, the real point being that the inferior officer was led to suppose that the man before him was, for example, a condemned criminal (whose execution could not have been an *actus reus*), or (as in *R.* v. *Trainer*) that the signal given on the railway meant that it was safe to proceed (so that he had no *mens rea*, since he did not foresee any risk of the collision). Persons in the naval, military, and air forces of the Crown may find themselves in a difficult position if superior orders are given to them to carry out something which seems contrary to the ordinary criminal law of the land. There is no conclusive English authority which extends immunity to such a person if, in obedience to discipline, he carries out the order and thus commits what proves to be a crime. He can, of course, rest his defence upon the rules as to mistake when the facts are appropriate. Thus a marine who, thinking to obey orders, shot a boatman who insisted on rowing up to the ship, was held[9] guilty of murder; the court

[1] *Post,* ¶ 49; cf. Winfield, *Tort,* 6th ed., ch. 3, para. 23. See Hallam's *Constitutional History,* ch. 1, 3, as to this peculiarly English check upon royal authority. The dangers of allowing such a defence are in effect recognized in the *British Manual of Military Law.*

[2] *Post,* ¶¶ 189, 281.

[3] *Ante,* ¶ 39.

[4] *R.* v. *James* (1837) 8 C. and P. 131.

[5] *R.* v. *Trainer* (1864) 4 F. and F. 104.

[6] 9 Coke 68; 1 Hale 496; 1 Hawk., c. 28; 1 East P.C. 331. See the authorities cited in *Marks* v. *Frogley* [1898] 1 Q.B. 396, 404. Cf. 3 C. and K. 199.

[7] See ¶ 39 (3) *ante.*

[8] See the observations of Willes, J., in *R.* v. *Trainer* (1864) 4 F. and F. 104, at pp. 105, 111. Cf. 4 F. and F. at p. 805 and *R.* v. *Hutchinson* (1864) 9 Cox 555.

[9] *R.* v. *Thomas* (1816) MS. of Bayley, J., the court indicated that this was a proper case for a royal pardon. (Russ. 93; *T.A.C.*); R. v. *Smith* (1899) 17 Cape of Good Hope 561 (*T.A.C.*); and see Stephen's *Hist. Crim. Law,* 1, 205.

pointed out that the homicide would have been justifiable 'if the act had been necessary for the preservation of the ship; as, for instance, if the deceased had been stirring up a mutiny'. But the courts of the United States have repeatedly refused to recognize any such excuse at all; and insist that a soldier or sailor cannot plead his commander's orders as a defence unless they not merely seemed to be legal but actually were so.[1] This extreme American doctrine has been ridiculed by French jurists as 'la théorie des baïonettes intelligentes'. The difficulty in which a member of the armed forces of the Crown may find himself when ordered to do something which contravenes the civil law of the land has long been recognized, but so far neither the legislature nor the courts[2] have been able to enunciate any principles by which it may be removed. It seems indeed to be an insoluble dilemma since it rests upon the inevitable conflict between military necessity and civic liberty which must arise from time to time in moments of national peril. In this predicament it would seem best to make no change either in military or in civil law, so that a tribunal (military or civil) should proceed to a decision within its jurisdiction, leaving each case to be subsequently reviewed, if necessary, on its merits for the exercise of the royal prerogative of mercy.

MARITAL COERCION

¶ 45. *Private* civil subjection has been of more frequent importance than *public*, as a defence. It never afforded exemption to servants or children who committed crimes at the instigation of a master or a parent. Only in the case of conjugal subjection did it ever amount to a defence. For if a wife[3] committed an ordinary felony in her husband's actual presence, the common law raised a *prima facie* presumption that she had committed it under such a compulsion as to entitle her to be acquitted, even though there were no proof of any actual intimidation by him. (Yet for any crime committed by her when he was not actually present, his previous orders or threats would afford her no more excuse than those of any other instigator[4] would do.) This presumption of coercion never applied in non-indictable offences. But it extended (so the majority of writers[5] assert) to all misdemeanours, except those that are connected with the management of the house (for in that matter the wife is assumed to be the person chiefly active). And it extended to most felonies,[6] e.g. to burglary, larceny, forgery, but not to felonies of extreme gravity, such as treason and murder. Still, as we have said, this presumption of subjection was only a *prima facie* one, rebuttable by

[1] See *United States* v. *Jones* (1813) 3 Washington 218; and *United States* v. *Carr* (1872) 1 Woods 480.

[2] See the cases discussed in Russ. 93 *et seq.*

[3] Not a concubine, *R.* v. *Court* (1912) 7 Cr.App.R. 127.

[4] Cf. ¶ 58 *post.*

[5] And so Lord Birkenhead's committee of 1922 reported. Cf. *R.* v. *Torpey* (1871) 12 Cox 45; *R.* v. *Smith* (1916) 12 Cr.App.R. 42.

[6] Kel. 31 (*T.A.C.*). In 1891 Cave, J., allowed it in arson.

proof that the wife took so active a part in the crime as to show that her will acted independently of her husband's.[1]

The singular privilege thus accorded to the wife, yet denied to the child, has an obscure history. It was suggested by Sir James Stephen[2] that it was due to the rule that for a long period our common law gave to a man who could read the right known as 'benefit of clergy'[3] whereby he could escape capital punishment for felony. This relaxation was not allowed to women[4] with the result that when a man and his wife were charged with jointly committing a felony, the man, if he could make a semblance of reading, would get off lightly, whilst his wife, even though the less guilty of the two, would be sentenced to death. Stephen thought that this comparative injustice led to the doctrine of marital coercion, because the judges wished to give to married women 'some sort of rough equivalent for the benefit of clergy enjoyed by their husbands'. This, however, appears rather to have been a relatively late justification for retaining the rule than the original reason for its existence.[5] It seems very likely that it really depended upon the ancient notion that the wife was entirely subservient to her husband and that while he was alive she had legally no will of her own.[6] Bracton[7] mentions the case of Roger de Fanborne and Agnes his wife who were charged with uttering a forged writ of right; Roger was hanged but his wife was liberated irrespective of whether she was a party to the offence or not, because she was under the rod of her husband (*sub virga viri sui*).

Whatever the origin and however unreasonable the rule, it was applied by our courts up to 1925.[8] In that year, largely as the result of public comment following upon a case in which the rule was applied,[9] the Criminal Justice Act, 1925 (sect. 47), abolished the presumption although, strangely enough, it retained the defence. The statutory provision was as follows:

> Any presumption of law that an offence committed by a wife in the presence of her husband is committed under the coercion of the husband is hereby abolished, but on a charge against a wife, for any offence other than treason or murder it shall be a good defence to prove that the offence was committed in the presence of, and under the coercion of, the husband.

[1] *R.* v. *Cruse* (1838) 2 Moody 53.

[2] *Hist. Crim. Law*, II, 105.

[3] *Post*, ¶ 55.

[4] Maitland (Pollock and Maitland, I, 445) found some traces of the privilege's being allowed to nuns and perhaps some other women in very early times. In 1692 benefit of clergy was allowed to all women; see *post*, ¶ 55.

[5] See Hale 1 P.C. 45: 'this being the modern practice and *in favorem vitae* is fitted to be followed; and the rather, because otherwise for the same felony the husband may be saved by the benefit of clergy, and the wife be hanged..., tho' I confess the reason is but of small value.' See also *Anon.* (1604) Moore K.B. 754, cited in *R.* v. *Alison* (1838) 8 C. and P. 418.

[6] See Pollock and Maitland, II, 409.

[7] Fo. 413*b*.

[8] It was in effect repudiated by a judge in 1912, but the old rule was fully accepted by the Court of Criminal Appeal who quashed the conviction; *R.* v. *Caroubi* (1912) 66 J.P. 262.

[9] *R.* v. *Peel and Wife* (1922), *The Times*, 15 March.

The result of this hesitant legislation is that the burden of proof has now been shifted to the wife, who must affirmatively establish 'coercion' by her husband. A clear definition of what this marital coercion is has not yet been judicially laid down in a reported case.[1] Presumably it is something less than such duress as would operate as a defence[2] to someone other than the wife who participated in the man's crime, since otherwise there would be no point in the statute's express declaration of the defence for her. *R.* v. *Bourne*[3] is unhelpful because, although counsel took the point that the wife had acted under 'marital coercion', the court spoke only of 'duress' without considering whether there might not be a difference of meaning between these two expressions.

It may perhaps be convenient, though not strictly relevant, to mention here that there are a few cases in which even an act itself, otherwise criminal, that has been done by a wife, will fail to be *reus* because of its connexion with the relations between her and her husband. Thus, if a husband who has committed a crime is received and sheltered by his wife, she (see ¶ 70 *post*) is not regarded by the law as becoming by such 'bare reception' an accessory after the fact; for she is bound to receive him. Again, in consequence of the conjugal unity by which the married pair are—for some purposes—treated in law as though they constituted only a single person,[4] no criminal agreement to which they are the only parties can amount to the crime of conspiracy (¶ 59 *post*); for a conspiracy needs at least two conspirators. And, similarly, a libel published against a husband by his wife, or one against a wife published by her husband, constitutes no offence.[5] Nor (see ¶ 254 *post*) can a husband or wife normally be guilty of stealing each other's property.

DURESS *PER MINAS*

¶ 46. Duress *per minas* is a very rare defence; so rare that Sir James Stephen, in his long forensic experience, never saw a case in which it was raised. It has, however, been thought that threats of the immediate infliction of death, or even of grievous bodily harm, will excuse *some* crimes that have been committed under the influence of such threats. Yet it has been found impossible to say with precision for what crimes the defence will be allowed to avail. It certainly will not excuse murder.[6]

[1] It was mentioned, but not affirmatively declared, in *R.* v. *Pierce* (1941) 5 Jo. Crim. Law 124. In this connexion see *R.* v. *Watson and Watson* Manchester Ass. 5 March 1959; [1959] Crim. L.R. 111.

[2] If indeed duress really can be set up as a defence; see *post*, ¶ 46.

[3] (1952) 36 Cr.App.R. 125. On this point see Russ. 143. The judgment included dicta as to the effect of the compulsion in fact exercised in this case on the existence of *mens rea* in the wife: these dicta have been criticized; see articles in 69 *L.Q.R.* 226 and 354; Williams, *Cr. Law*, 1, para. 129; Russ. 145.

[4] See the observations of Maule, J., in *Wenman* v. *Ash* (1853) 13 C.B. 936, at p. 1844; Glanville Williams, 'The legal unity of husband and wife' (1947) 10 *Mod. L.R.* 16.

[5] *R.* v. *Lord Mayor of London* (1866) 16 Q.B.D. 772.

[6] 1 Hale P.C. 434; 1 East P.C. 225.

Perhaps it may excuse the still graver offence of treason, though only in its minor forms: as where a prisoner shows that under pain of death, or of some physical injury falling little short of death, he was forced into giving some subordinate assistance in a rebellion. But he must show that the compulsion continued throughout the whole time that he was assisting, and that he did no more than he was obliged to do, and that he desisted at the earliest possible opportunity.[1] Moreover, according to Sir James Stephen, this defence is admissible only where the prisoner has been threatened by a body of rebels or rioters. Yet it would seem, on principle, that two persons may differ so much in strength, or in weapons, that a degree of compulsion sufficient to exempt may have been exercised by one of them over the other, although there was but this single threatener. It has been held in Ireland, upon a charge of receiving stolen property,[2] that acts otherwise criminal may be excused if they were performed under threats, by one person, of immediate death or personal violence so terrifying as to overcome ordinary human resistance at the very time when the acts were committed. It has always been clear that if after the threats have been made there is time and opportunity for the person threatened to assert his will then no excuse can be allowed.

The law as to duress was discussed by the Court of Criminal Appeal in *R.* v. *Steane*,[3] and its obscurity was recognized: the court, however, decided that duress could, in appropriate circumstances, operate to negative an allegation that a prisoner acted with the particular intent specified in the statute,[4] on the argument that where one, being subjected to the complete control of another (especially if he be a brutal enemy), obeys his orders under threats of violence, it is impossible to say that an inference that he intended the natural consequences of his acts must be drawn merely from the fact that he did them.[5]

Fears of some lesser degree of violence, insufficient to excuse a crime, may nevertheless mitigate its punishment. Wherever there are two criminals, one of them is often to some extent in terror of the other. In such a case the timid rogue may deserve a less severe punishment than his masterful associate.

NECESSITY

¶ 47. The fact that a man who has inflicted harm upon another's person or property, did so for the purpose of saving himself or others from a much greater harm, has from early times been recognized as a defence in civil actions, brought to recover compensation for the harm thus

[1] *R.* v. *M'Growther* (1746) Foster 13 (*T.A.C.*). M'Growther was convicted but not executed. *R.* v. *Crutchley* (1831) 5 C. and P. 133.

[2] *Att.-Gen.* v. *Whelan* [1934] Ir.R. 518.

[3] [1947] K.B. 997; 1 All E.R. 813; 32 Cr.App.R. 61. And see *R.* v. *Foley* [1959] Crim. L.R. 286 for the position where a specific intent is required by statute.

[4] Defence (General) Regulations, 1939, 2A. See *Subramaniam* v. *P.P.* [1956] 1 W.L.R. 965, duress recognized as a defence under the Malayan Penal Code, *post*, p. 485.

[5] And see *Hosegood* v. *Hosegood* (1950) 66 T.L.R. 735; *ante*, ¶ 25.

inflicted.[1] It is admittedly no tort to pull down houses to prevent a fire from spreading,[2] or to enter a person's house to put out a fire. It would therefore seem natural that such prospect of greater harm should be still more readily admissible as a defence to criminal proceedings. For in them the main object is not to compensate loss but to punish actual guilt (which here seems almost or altogether absent); and punishment itself must fail to attain its great object, that of deterrence, in those cases of so-called necessity where the evil it threatens is less than the evil which would have been suffered if the crime had not warded it off. So a person who commits some trivial offence, for the purpose of saving life —who goes at night, shall we say, on a lampless bicycle to fetch the fire-engine—might seem to have a valid legal excuse. Yet, though theoretical writers have been willing to accept this ground of defence, there is no English case in which the defence has been actually raised with success; however, Lord Mansfield gave an obiter dictum that even an act of treason, like the deposition of a colonial governor by his council, might, in some circumstances of public danger, be justified by its necessity.[3] The word 'necessity' which is often used to indicate these predicaments, is somewhat misleading. Strictly speaking there is no necessity in the sense that the thing is inevitable or unavoidable. For if it were, then there would be the legal defence that the accused's act was not voluntary. In reality the position is that the person (perhaps with very good reason) much prefers to do the thing which he does rather than something else, which would be more unpleasant.

It has often been thought that if provisions run short during a voyage, the captain of the ship commits no larceny by breaking into the cargo to feed his crew. In *Gregson* v. *Gilbert* (1783),[4] which was an action on a policy of marine insurance to recover the value of a hundred and fifty slaves, who had been thrown overboard during a voyage because the casks of water were running short and a hundred slaves had already died of thirst, no doubt was suggested, either by the court or even at the bar, as to extreme urgency being capable of excusing even so awful an act as this. But there the question of criminal liability did not directly arise; and now, since *R.* v. *Dudley and Stephens* (1884),[5] it seems that the criminal law would concede no exemption, on the ground of necessity, for such an act of homicide.

Clearly no such defence can be accepted in any case (1) where the evil averted was a lesser evil than the offence committed to avert it, or (2) where the evil could have been averted by anything short of the commission of that offence, or (3) where more harm was done than was necessary for averting the evil. Hence it is scarcely safe to lay down

[1] For necessity as a civil defence, see Winfield, *Law of Tort*, 6th ed., 64. For self-defence in cases of offences against the person, see ¶ 97 *post*. And see Williams, 'The defence of necessity', in 6 *Current Law Problems*. [2] 1 Dyer 36*b*.

[3] *R.* v. *Stratton* (1779) 21 St.Tr. 1222. The correctness of this dictum was conceded by Lord Coleridge in *R.* v. *Dudley and Stephens*, *post*.

[4] 3 Douglas 232. [5] 14 Q.B.D. 273.

any more definite rule than that suggested by Sir James Stephen, viz. that 'It is just possible to imagine cases in which the expediency of breaking the law is so overwhelmingly great that people may be justified in breaking it; but these cases cannot be defined beforehand'.[1]

In the only reported English case where this defence has been expressly raised, it failed.[2] Three men and a boy escaped in an open boat from the shipwreck of the yacht *Mignonette*. After having passed eight days without food, the men killed the boy in order to eat his body. Four days later, they were rescued by a passing ship. On their arrival in England, two of the men were tried for the murder of the boy. Lord Bacon had suggested (*Maxims*, v) that if two shipwrecked men were clinging to a plank which was only sufficient to support one, and one of them pushed the other off, he would be exempt from any criminal liability, because his conduct was necessary to save his life.[3] But the Court of Queen's Bench declared emphatically that there is no general principle of law which entitles a man to take the life of an innocent person in order to preserve his own. The court appears to have been willing, if necessary, even to overrule Lord Bacon's dictum about the plank; but Sir James Stephen considers that their actual decision does not go so far as to overrule it. For, as he points out, the accused man does no direct bodily harm to the other, but leaves him still the chance of getting another plank,[4] whereas in the *Mignonette Case* the boy was actually killed, moreover by men who did it for the sake of avoiding a starvation which the jury only found to have been otherwise '*probable*', not otherwise '*inevitable*'.

The defence of necessity, however, can only be important where, as in capital offences, there is a prescribed minimum of punishment. For in all others an English judge would probably take the extremity of the offender's situation into account, by reducing the sentence to a nominal penalty.[5]

[1] *Hist. Crim. Law*, II, 109. [2] *R.* v. *Dudley and Stephens* (1884) 14 Q.B.D. 273.

[3] 1 Hale P.C. 54. Much legal controversy was aroused in France in 1898 by a judgment at Amiens which adopted Bacon's lenient principle; for Hale's view is more generally adopted by French judges. And see the Offences against the Person Act, 1861, s. 17, which in effect provides that it shall be a felony to prevent or impede anyone who is endeavouring to escape from a wreck.

[4] A point which might be described as unrealistic. Stephen maintained that the circumstances of *R.* v. *Dudley and Stephens* distinguish it from many cases in which there is a choice of evils; for instance, where an accoucheur finds it necessary to destroy a child at the approach of birth in order to save the mother (an act that is not considered to be the subject of a prosecution). See *R.* v. *Bourne* [1939] 1 K.B. 687. We may add that it is clearly distinguishable from those in which the question is not which one shall live, but whether any shall live; as where three mountaineers are roped together, but two of them slip, and the third cuts the rope to save himself from being dragged to death with them. In such a case the defence should be that there was no *actus reus*, for the survivor had not caused the others' death (since nothing could save them) but had merely severed the rope to prevent them from pulling him over also. See Plowden 13 for a prisoner's escape from a burning gaol, *to save his life*.

[5] But in Continental countries (where a minimum is frequently set to punishments) the necessity of averting grave bodily harm is often raised as a defence.

Yet where immediate death is the inevitable consequence of abstaining from committing a prohibited act, it seems futile for the law to continue the prohibition, if the object of punishment be only to deter. For it must be useless to threaten any punishment the threat of which cannot have the effect of deterring.[1] Hence, perhaps, it is that in the United States the defence of necessity seems to be viewed with favour.[2]

SECTION 5. LEGALLY ABNORMAL PERSONS

¶ 48. We have considered the instances in which a legally normal person, owing to the peculiarity of the circumstances in which he was placed, may be excused from liability for the harmful consequences which his conduct has brought about. We must now turn to the position of those persons who, owing to some peculiarity in themselves, are not invested with the same responsibility for their acts as are those whom we term legally normal. They are the Sovereign, corporations, children, insane persons, and clerks in holy orders.

(*a*) The Sovereign

¶ 49. Influenced by the fact that the cases in which excuse from criminal liability mostly depends upon an absence of the necessary *mens rea*, and by the conception of *mens rea* as moral wickedness, Blackstone, by a totally unnecessary legal fiction, ascribed[3] the King's unquestionable immunity to an imaginary 'perfection' in his will, which he supposed rendered the Sovereign incapable of *mens rea*. But it is clear that our law does not really regard the King as incapable of committing crime; inasmuch as, though it will never punish him, it would readily punish, as an accessory before the fact, any evil counsellor who might prompt him to a crime. The King himself has indeed an exemption from liability; but it is sufficiently explained by the absence, in our constitution, of any tribunal possessed of jurisdiction to try him. It is thus a matter of adjective law; and not the result of any fiction in our substantive law.

But, whichever be the proper branch of law to class it under, the exemption itself is a matter of recognized policy. Almost every nation has considered it necessary to clothe its chief magistrate with this immunity. (It is true that in the United States the personal responsibility of the President for any crimes he may commit is fully recognized;[4] but the particular circumstances in which the States framed their

[1] At a court martial held in consequence of a collision (*The Times*, 28 July 1893), it was shown that naval discipline regards even disobedience to an admiral's orders as being excusable by necessity, e.g. the paramount necessity of not endangering the safety of a ship.

[2] *Commonwealth* v. *Brooks* (1868) 99 Mass. 434; *The State* v. *Wray* (1875) 72 N.C. 253. In *Rice* v. *Georgia* (1899) 34 S.E.R. 202, a man prosecuted for breach of a statute, that forbade taking alcoholic liquor to church, pleaded that it was necessary for his wife's life that she should always have alcohol at hand. But the defence was disallowed, on the ground that it was not necessary for the wife to go to church.

[3] I *Comm.* c. vii, 246; IV, c. ii, 32.

[4] Constitution of U.S.A., art. II, s. 4. Cf. *The Federalist*, no. 69.

constitution sufficiently account for this unusual liability.) At the trial of Charles I, even the Parliament's counsel admitted[1] the correctness of a judicial dictum, of Henry VII's time, that 'If the King should, in passion, kill a man, this would be no felony for which to take away the King's life.'

The like immunity conceded by the comity of nations to every foreign sovereign[2] and to ambassadors and their suites, whilst resident in this country, must be remembered.[3] In some modern cases of the unlawful driving of motor cars, it has had practical results.

Further, an Act of State[4] cannot be examined into by the courts of the state which does the act.[5]

(b) Corporations

¶ 50. Corporations formerly lay quite outside the criminal law. If a crime were committed by a corporation's orders, criminal proceedings, for having thus instigated the offence, could only be taken against the separate members, in their personal capacities, and not against the corporation as itself a guilty person.[6] This was a consequence of the technical rule that criminal courts expected prisoners to stand at their bar, and did not permit 'appearance by attorney'.[7] But it was further supported also by more scientific considerations, which Roman law had anticipated and accepted.[8] It was urged that a corporation, as it had no actual existence, could have no will, and therefore could have no guilty will.[9] And it was further urged that, even if the legal fiction which gives to a corporation an imaginary existence may be stretched so far as to give it also an imaginary will, yet the only activities that could consistently be ascribed to the fictitious will thus created, must be such as are connected with the purposes which it was created to accomplish.

[1] 4 St.Tr. 1034.

[2] Unless they are deposed, exiled or fugitive in England, when the immunity ceases (*R.* v. *Mary Queen of Scots* (1586) 1 St.Tr. 1161).

[3] They must not even be subpœnaed as witnesses. In 1913 a secretary of the Danish embassy was drowned in the Thames; and the embassy claimed (with success) that no inquest could be held on his body. See Oppenheim, *International Law*, 7th ed., I, 174 n. 2, as to the kidnapping in 1896 of Sun Yat Sen (afterwards twice President of the Republic of China) in the London residence of the Chinese Imperial Legation. See *Engelke* v. *Musmann* [1928] A.C. 433 for the *conclusiveness* of a certificate from our Foreign Office as to a person's possessing diplomatic privilege. As to semi-sovereign rulers, as were the Indian princes, see *Statham* v. *Statham* [1912] P. 92.

[4] See Wade and Phillips, *Constitutional Law*, 6th ed., 249 *et seq.*

[5] Stephen, *Hist. Crim. Law*, II, 61.

[6] Cf. Pollock and Maitland, I, 473, 661.

[7] A corporation may now appear by a representative, see Criminal Justice Act, 1925, s. 33 and Magistrates' Courts Act, 1952, schedule 2.

[8] Yet the theory of Germanic law inclined the other way, as our English institution of frankpledge (Stubbs, *Constitutional History*, I, 618) may serve to remind us. Cf. Maitland's *Political Theories*, 39.

[9] Hence, even in civil actions, doubts were long entertained as to the possibility of holding a corporation liable for those torts in which 'express malice' is necessary. Contrast *Abrath* v. *N.E. Rly. Co.* (1886) 11 App. Cas. 247, with *Chuter* v. *Freeth* [1911] 2 K.B. 832.

If so, it could not compass a crime; for any crime would be necessarily *ultra vires*. Moreover a corporation is devoid not only of mind, but also of body, and therefore incapable of the usual criminal punishments. 'What? must they hang up the common seal?' asked an advocate in 1682.[1]

But under the commercial development which the last few generations have witnessed, corporations have become so numerous that there would have been grave public danger in continuing to permit them to enjoy this immunity.[2] The various theoretical difficulties have therefore been brushed aside; and it is now settled law that corporations may, in an appropriate court, be indicted by the corporate name, and that fines may be consequently inflicted upon the corporate property. The innovation was introduced at first by drawing a distinction between offences of *non*-feasance and those of *mis*feasance, on the ground that, whilst in the case of a criminal misfeasance the servant or agent who actually did the criminal act could always be himself indicted, no such indictment would be available in the case of a non-feasance; for the omission would not be imputable to any individual agent but solely to the corporation itself. Hence, in 1840, an indictment for non-feasance, in omitting to repair a highway, was allowed against a corporation, in *R.* v. *Birmingham and Gloucester Ry. Co.*[3] Soon afterwards, in the case of *R.* v. *The Great North of England Ry. Co.* (1846),[4] an indictment was similarly allowed even for a misfeasance, that of actually obstructing a highway. And the principle has received legislative approval. For the Interpretation Act, 1889,[5] provides that in the construction of every statutory enactment relating to an offence, whether punishable on indictment or on summary conviction, the expression 'person' shall, *unless a contrary intention appears*, include a body corporate. The gravity, or the nature, of an offence may be sufficient to show that the framers of the enactment against it could not have had any intention of regarding bodies corporate as capable of committing it.

It has been generally held that the impossibility of hanging or imprisoning[6] a corporation sets a limit to the range of its criminal liability. On this view a corporation can only be prosecuted, as such, for offences which can be punished by a fine, and it was thought that though manslaughter was formerly finable, a corporation could not be indicted for it, nor for any other crime that involves personal violence (e.g. assault or riot) or that is a felony (*R.* v. *Cory Bros.* [1927] 1 K.B. 810). Thus, whilst it can be indicted and fined for a libel published by

[1] *R.* v. *City of London* (1682) 8 St.Tr. 1039 at p. 1138.

[2] On this subject see Burrows, 'The responsibility of corporations under criminal law', in *Journal of Criminal Science* (1948), 1, 1; Welsh, 'The criminal liability of corporations', 62 *L.Q.R.* 345.

[3] (1840) 2 Q.B. 47.

[4] 9 Q.B. 315.

[5] 52 and 53 Vict. c. 63, s. 2. *Pearks* v. *Ward* [1902] 2 K.B. 1.

[6] Or 'committing' for trial, *Daily Mirror Newspapers Ltd.* v. *Glover* (1922) 16 Cr.App.R. 131; so the Criminal Justice Act, 1925, s. 33 (1), substituted an order empowering the prosecutor to prefer a bill of indictment.

its order,[1] it was doubted if it could be indicted for a burglary, or any other offence which was too grave to admit of being visited by a merely pecuniary penalty.[2] Clearly if any such crime be committed by the orders of a corporation, the various persons by whom it was ordered can be indicted individually in their own names, and punished in their own persons. It must be remembered that they are also liable to be thus individually indicted, even in the case of those less heinous offences for which their corporation might itself be indicted; for *it* becomes indictable only through the fact that a wrong has been instigated by *them*.

The extension of the criminal responsibility of corporations was for some time largely effected by importing into criminal law something of the notion of the vicarious liability of a master for the acts of his servants which was developed in the law of tort, but this aspect of the matter has not been found sufficient and the courts have moved with some hesitation in the direction of making the corporation directly responsible, by the fiction that the elements of criminal liability present in the responsible agent of the corporation can be 'imputed' to the corporation itself.[3] But in recent times the judges have been more ready to enlarge the field of the criminal responsibility of corporations and it has been judicially stated that this is a branch of the law to which the attitude of the courts has in the passage of time undergone a process of development.[4] In *Director of Public Prosecutions* v. *Kent & Sussex Contractors Ltd.*[5] a divisional court held that it was erroneous to suppose that a body corporate could not be guilty of offences charged on the ground that there was implicit in their commission an act of will or state of mind which could not be imputed to a corporation. The offences in this case were prosecuted under a regulation which had the effect of a statute, but in a subsequent case *R.* v. *I.C.R. Haulage Ltd.*[6] the Court of Criminal Appeal held that a limited liability company can be indicted at common law for a conspiracy to defraud. In this last case the court referred to *R.* v. *Cory Bros.*[7] in which an indictment preferred against a limited company with two counts, one alleging manslaughter and the other an offence involving personal violence punishable with penal servitude, had been quashed on the argument that such crimes could not be committed by a corporation. The court now said of *R.* v. *Cory Bros.*: 'It is sufficient in our judgment to say that, inasmuch as that case was decided before the decision in *Director of Public Prosecutions* v. *Kent & Sussex Contractors Ltd.* and that *Chuter* v. *Freeth & Pocock Ltd.*[8] was not

[1] See 5 App. Cas. 857, 870, *per* Lord Blackburn.

[2] But see now Criminal Justice Act, 1948, s. 13.

[3] See Burrows, 'The responsibility of corporations under criminal law' in *Journal of Criminal Science* (1948), 1, 1 *et seq.*

[4] 30 Cr.App.R., at p. 37.

[5] [1944] 1 K.B. 146.

[6] [1944] 1 K.B. 551; 1 All E.R. 691; 30 Cr.App.R. 31 (*T.A.C.*).

[7] [1927] 1 K.B. 810.

[8] [1911] 2 K.B. 832.

cited at all, if the matter comes before the court to-day, the result might well be different.'[1]

The formulation of clear principles of criminal liability for corporations is urgently needed. Our common law long ago recognized the need for regulating the business relations of individual men, and its adaptation to the circumstances of the modern world, in which transactions of all kinds are increasingly carried out by large associations of a corporate character cannot satisfactorily be effected by disconnected decisions.[2]

(c) Infants

¶ 51. If an ethical basis be sought for a legal doctrine of absolute liability the most appropriate is the assumption that the average man realizes and intends the consequences of his acts. Whether or not that was consciously adopted in the earliest period of our law it became obvious, after the notion was accepted that moral delinquency was a prerequisite of criminal guilt, that a realization of consequences could not in every case be imputed to very young children; but there was much uncertainty how it should be decided whether the child should be held fully responsible.[3] To begin with it was held that a child could not be guilty of crime unless it had reached the age of twelve.[4] Later, however, the law became more severe and the age for the termination of immunity was fixed at seven years. Until that age no evidence of precocity would avail for it was an irrebuttable presumption of law that the child had no adequate discretion or understanding.[5] But now infants are divided into three classes.

(i) Those under eight[6] years of age. There is a conclusive presumption that a child so young cannot be *doli capax*.[7] Nothing, therefore, that he does can make him liable to be punished by a criminal court; so a child of six, who was arrested for crime, obtained damages from

[1] 30 Cr.App.R. at pp. 36, 37. In *Moore* v. *Bresler* [1944] 2 All E.R. 515, a company was held liable for a criminal act committed by its responsible agent even though his purpose was to defraud the company. In *Bolton (Engineering) Co.* v. *Graham and Sons* [1956] 3 W.L.R. 804, where Denning, L.J., citing with approval *R.* v. *I.C.R. Haulage Ltd.* (1 K.B. 559), said 'Where in any particular case there is evidence to go to a jury that the criminal act of an agent, including his state of mind, intention, knowledge or belief is the act of the company...whether the jury are satisfied...must depend on the nature of the charge, the relative position of the officer or agent, and the other relevant facts... of the case', and (at p. 813): 'So here the intention of the company can be derived from the intention of its officers and agents.'

[2] See articles in *Justice of the Peace*, LXXXVIII, 198, and CIII, 780, by A. H. Lieck.

[3] See Kean, 'The criminal liability of children', 53 *L.Q.R.* (1937) 364; and 'The criminal responsibility of children' by G. L. Williams, [1954] *Crim. L.R.* 493.

[4] See Wilkinson, *Leges Anglo-Saxonicae*, 65 *et seq.* Under Athelstan no child under fifteen could be executed unless he had resisted or fled.

[5] 1 Hale P.C. 27, 28.

[6] The age of immunity was raised from seven (as at common law) to eight by the Children and Young Persons Act, 1933 (23 Geo. V, c. 12), s. 50.

[7] This exclusion is a rule of law, and, properly speaking, not a *presumption* at all, since it cannot be rebutted, see ¶ 491.

the arrester.[1] But it is not illegal for parents to administer domestic punishment to such children, if they have in fact become old enough to understand it.[2]

(ii) Between eight[3] and fourteen.[4] Even at this age an 'infant' is still presumed to be *doli incapax*; but the presumption is no longer conclusive, it may be rebutted by evidence. Yet the mere commission of a criminal act is not, as it would be in the case of an adult, sufficient *prima facie* proof of *mens rea*. The presumption of innocence is so strong in the case of a child under fourteen that some clearer proof of the mental condition is necessary. For this purpose a necessity for special proof of a 'mischievous discretion' is impressed upon the jury who try such an infant, by their being asked not only the ordinary question, 'Did he do it?' but also the additional one, 'Had he a guilty knowledge that he was doing wrong?'[5] As with adults the 'guilty mind' requisite varies with different crimes, but where the accused is a 'child' it must probably be shown, even in the case of crimes involving absolute liability (see ¶ 8 *ante*), that as in the case of insane persons he had knowledge that he was doing wrong. A boy under fourteen cannot be guilty of rape nor of some other sexual offences.[6]

This guilty knowledge may be shown by the fact of the offender's having previously committed some earlier offence of the same kind,[7] especially if he had been convicted of it; or even by the circumstances of the present offence itself, for they may afford distinct proof of a wicked mind.[8] Thus a boy of eight was hanged in 1629 for burning two barns, 'it appearing that he had malice, revenge, craft and cunning'.[9] In 1959

[1] *Marsh* v. *Loader* (1863) 14 C.B. (n.s.) 535. See *Walters* v. *Lunt* [1951] 2 All E.R. 645 (*T.A.C.*) *post*, ¶ 359.

[2] *R.* v. *Griffin* (1869) 11 Cox 402; *Cleary* v. *Booth* [1893] 1 Q.B. 465; *R.* v. *Woods* (1921) 85 J.P. 272. Children and Young Persons Act, 1933, s. 1 (7). See ¶ 152 *post*.

[3] The age of immunity was raised from seven (as at common law) to eight by the Children and Young Persons Act, 1933 (23 Geo. V, c. 12), s. 50.

[4] Modern statutory terms (23 Geo. V, c. 12, s. 107) are: up to fourteen, a 'child'; from fourteen to seventeen, a 'young person'; from seventeen to twenty-one, a 'juvenile adult'.

[5] *R.* v. *Owen* (1830) 4 C. and P. 236 (*T.A.C.*). This is an instance of the retention of the ancient objective standard of morality, mentioned above in ¶ 14. In *R.* v. *Vamplew* (1862) 3 F. and F. 520, after stating the requirements for guilt of murder (*ante* ¶ 20), Pollock, C.B., told the jury that they must be satisfied that the accused 'had arrived at that maturity of intellect which was a necessary condition of the crime charged'.

[6] *R.* v. *Tatam* (1921) 15 Cr.App.R. 132.

[7] The evidence of this should only be admitted within the principles laid down in *Makin* v. *Att.-Gen. of N.S.W.* [1894] A.C. 57 (*T.A.C.*) and *Harris* v. *D.P.P.* [1952] A.C. 694 (*T.A.C.*); *post*, p. 608.

[8] There must be 'mischievous discretion', *R.* v. *Gorrie* (1918) 83 J.P. 136. By the 'Lübeck apple proof', if a child was convicted of homicide, he was offered an apple and a penny. If he chose the penny, capacity was held to be established (see Stallybrass, *Mod. Appr. Crim. Law*, 414).

[9] 1 Hale P.C. 25. Michael Hammond and his sister, aged *seven* and eleven, were hanged at Lynn for felony in 1708; Richard's *King's Lynn*, p. 888. A boy of twelve and a half was hanged in New Jersey in 1828; 18 American Decisions 404.

it was stated by the Q.B. Divisional Court, in a case of a child of eight years, that the evidence of the home background and of all the circumstances of the accused was highly material to the question whether he knew that he was doing wrong, and that it should be admitted in spite of the risk that it might disclose information highly prejudicial to him.[1]

(iii) Between fourteen and twenty-one. A child may know right from wrong long before he knows how to make a prudent speculation or a wise will.[2]

Hence at fourteen a person comes under full criminal responsibility. But it is in effect provided by section 9 (3) of the Homicide Act, 1957, in substitution for the Children and Young Persons Act, 1933, s. 53 (1), and the Criminal Justice Act, 1948, s. 16, that sentence of death shall not be pronounced on any person who appears to the court to have been under the age of eighteen years at the time when the offence was committed, nor shall any such person be sentenced to imprisonment for life under section 9 of the Homicide Act, 1957; but in lieu thereof the court shall (notwithstanding anything in this or any other Act) sentence him to be detained during Her Majesty's pleasure, and if so sentenced he shall be liable to be detained in such place and under such conditions as the Secretary of State may direct. And by virtue of the Criminal Justice Act, 1948, s. 17, no person under seventeen may be sentenced to imprisonment by a court of summary jurisdiction, or by a court of assize or quarter sessions if he be under fifteen.[3] Further, no court is to impose imprisonment on any person under twenty-one unless the court is of opinion that no other method of dealing with him is appropriate. And where the child or young person is convicted on indictment of an attempt to murder, or of manslaughter, or of wounding with intent to do grievous bodily harm, he is to be detained in such place and under such conditions as the Secretary of State may direct.

(*d*) Insane persons

¶ 52. The difficulty which, as we have seen, the courts encountered in finding a test by which to decide the line between the immunity and liability of children in criminal law was greater in the case of persons whose minds were affected by disease, whether in the form of a temporary delirium or of a permanent insanity, while the need for distinction was no less.

So long as the doctrine of absolute liability prevailed any defence of insanity was correspondingly kept within narrow limits. For lunatics are in most cases capable of being influenced by some ordinary motives and often seem to plan their misdeeds with care, and take means to

[1] *R.* v. *Padwick* [1959] Crim. L.R. 439; this principle of evidence was applied in *B.* v. *R.* (1960) 44 Cr.App.R. 1, 'a child who has had apparently every opportunity in life, coming from a respectable family and properly brought up'.

[2] A person under twenty-one (an 'infant') can be adjudicated bankrupt; and certain criminal questions may arise in such circumstances; see *In re A Debtor* [1950] 1 Ch. 282.

[3] Now modified by the Criminal Justice Act, 1961, *post*, ¶¶ 758, 762*a*, 763.

avoid detection, so that to the untrained observer their conduct may appear to be due rather to a controlled intention of great malignity than to the workings of a mind crippled by disease, and to afford 'plain indications of an heart regardless of social duty and fatally bent on mischief'.[1] But in comparatively recent years great advances have been made in medical knowledge of the human mind, and mental variations have been subjected to scientific classification.[2]

Yet English law, even in its harshest days,[3] recognized insanity as a possible defence. On the other hand, it never held that the mere existence of any insanity whatever would suffice to exempt the insane person from criminal responsibility.[4] Only insanity of a particular and appropriate kind was regarded as enough to produce exemption.[5]

Careful observation of insane patients, in various countries throughout many years, has now thrown much light upon the mental processes of the insane. The world, it is now recognized, contains many 'warped' men and women, in whom there exists some taint of insanity, but who nevertheless are in most respects influenced by the ordinary hopes and fears that control the conduct of ordinary people. To place such persons beyond the reach of such curative and deterrent methods of treatment as are now available to the courts would not only be to violate the logical consistency of our theory of crime, but would also be a cause of actual danger to the lives and property of their neighbours. And now English law, so far as the crime of murder is concerned, has moved to a new position[6] by the passing of the Homicide Act, 1957, which in section 2 recognizes the defence of 'diminished responsibility' (discussed below ¶ 53 *a*).

Our law in this matter was, however, for many centuries crude in the extreme. Thus as late as 1724 a judge declared that no mentally affected prisoner should escape unless it should appear that he 'is totally deprived of his understanding and memory, and doth not know what he is doing, no more than an infant, than a brute, or a wild beast'.[7] But at

[1] Foster, 257.

[2] See *Mental Abnormality and Crime* (English Studies in Criminal Science Series). For a general discussion of insanity in law see Hall, 'Mental disease and crime', 45 *Columbia L.R.* (1945), 677.

[3] Cf. (1313) *Eyre of Kent*, I, 81 (Seld. Soc. Y.B. Series, v): 'demens et furiosus, non per feloniam.'

[4] Thus a man who had an insane delusion that his wife had committed adultery with *A*, *B* and *C* was nevertheless sentenced to death for killing *Z*; *The Times*, 29 Oct. 1909.

[5] Similarly in civil matters, the will of a man who carried on his business intelligently has been held valid although he was so insane as to believe that his farm and animals were impregnated with sulphur, *Jenkins* v. *Morris* (1880) 14 Ch.D. 674. For the question of liability in tort when the point of insanity arises, see *Robins* v. *Robins* [1960] 3 All E.R. 66, following *Astle* v. *Astle* [1939] 3 All E.R. 967. See also *Morriss* v. *Marsden* [1952] 1 All E.R. at p. 928.

[6] A position already reached in Scots law by a doctrine developed in the Scottish courts on the basis of the direction to the jury in the case of *Dingwall* (Irvine 466) in 1867, and confirmed in the case of *Savage* (1923) J.C. 49.

[7] *Arnold's Case* (1724) 16 St.Tr. 695, *per* Tracey, J., at p. 765.

the end of that century largely as a result of the eloquence of defending counsel[1] in the case of *R.* v. *Hadfield*,[2] the attitude of the courts towards mentally afflicted prisoners was radically altered.

¶ 53. *The M'Naghten answers.* In 1843 an authoritative pronouncement was made with a degree of precision unusual for any common law doctrine, through its formulation in an abstract shape by a set of answers delivered by the judges in reply to questions propounded to them by the House of Lords. One Daniel M'Naghten[3] had aroused public excitement by the murder of a Mr Drummond, the private secretary of Sir Robert Peel in mistake for that statesman. The acquittal of M'Naghten on the ground of insanity provoked such widespread dissatisfaction that it became the subject of debate in the House of Lords (though the case never came before that House in its judicial capacity). In consequence of the debate, the Lords submitted to the judges certain abstract questions respecting persons afflicted with insane delusions.[4] The replies given by the judges may be summed up thus:

(i) Every man is presumed[5] to be sane, and to possess a sufficient degree of reason to be responsible for his crimes, until the contrary be proved to the satisfaction of a jury.

(ii) To establish a defence on the ground of insanity, it must be clearly proved that, at the time of committing the act, the party accused was labouring under such a defect of reason, from disease of the mind, as not to know the nature and quality[6] of the act he was doing, or, if he did know it, that he did not know[7] he was doing what was wrong.[8]

(iii) As to his knowledge of the wrongfulness of the act, the judges said: 'If the accused was conscious that the act was one which he ought not to do and if that act was at the same time contrary to the law of the land, he is punishable.'[9]

(iv) Where a person under an insane delusion as to existing facts commits an offence in consequence thereof, the judges indicated that the answer must depend on the nature of the delusion; but making the assumption that he labours under partial delusion only, and is not in other respects insane, he must be considered in the same situation as to responsibility as if the facts with respect

[1] Erskine, afterwards Lord Chancellor Erskine. [2] (1800) 27 St.Tr. 1281.

[3] The name is spelt variously.

[4] *R.* v. *M'Naghten* (1843) 10 Cl. and F. 200 (*T.A.C.*). [5] Cf. Ch. XXVI *post.*

[6] These two words are synonyms (though medical witnesses have often treated their meanings as dissimilar). They refer to the '*physical* nature of the act, as distinguished from moral' (see *R.* v. *Codère*, below) e.g. the madman who cut a woman's throat under the idea that he was cutting a loaf of bread.

[7] Stephen thought that inability 'calmly and rationally' to *consider* its wrongness suffices to disprove this knowledge.

[8] E.g. he fancied, like Hadfield, that he had received a divine command to kill.

[9] Thus the test is the power of distinguishing between right and wrong, not, as was once supposed, in the abstract, but in regard to the particular act committed.

> to which the delusion exists were real. For example, if, under the influence of his delusions, he supposes another man to be in the act of attempting to take away his life, and he kills that man, as he supposes, in self-defence,[1] he would be exempt from punishment. If his delusion was that the deceased had inflicted a serious injury to his character and fortune, and killed him in revenge for such supposed injury, he would be liable to punishment.

It should be added that, for a defence of insane delusion, the deed must be connected with the delusion directly. That is to say, the accused's conduct while committing the particular *actus reus* in question must have been actuated by his insane delusion. An instance of such connexion (though the delusion was due not to insanity but to sleep) may be cited from Scotland where a man, dreaming that he was struggling with a wild beast, killed his baby.[2] On the other hand, a man has been convicted of obtaining money by false pretences notwithstanding his insanity, when his delusion was only that he was the lawful son of a well-known prince.[3]

Since the M'Naghten answers were promulgated the courts have adopted the rules, (*a*) that where insanity is pleaded the onus of proof (but only to the extent of raising reasonable doubt) of the insanity rests upon the defence;[4] and (*b*) that even where insanity is not pleaded by the defence (perhaps) it is open for the prosecution to argue that the evidence before the court does establish insanity within the M'Naghten rules;[5] and (*c*) that where in a charge of murder the defence plead and submit evidence of diminished responsibility the prosecution may call evidence in order to establish insanity;[6] and (*d*) that when the prosecution do so lead insanity they must prove it beyond reasonable doubt;[7] and (*e*) that where the defence lead insanity it is open to the prosecution to call rebutting evidence whereby to establish diminished responsibility;[8] and (*f*) that, apart from the special instances mentioned above, the prosecution may not lead insanity against the accused.[9]

[1] Or if he killed under the delusion that he was an executioner lawfully carrying out a judicial sentence; in both these situations the killing would have been a justifiable homicide if the facts had really been as he supposed.

[2] *H.M. Advocate* v. *Fraser* (1878) 4 Couper 70. He was discharged.

[3] I.e. he did not think that *because* he was the prince's son he was lawfully entitled to obtain the money, nor did his insane belief make him think that his false statement was a true one.

[4] E.g. *R.* v. *Smith* (1910) 6 Cr.App.R. 19; *Hill* v. *Baxter* (1958) 42 Cr.App.R. 51, *per* Devlin, J. (*T.A.C.*); *R.* v. *Bentley* [1960] Crim. L.R. 777; 24 Jo. Crim. Law 314, a case in which insanity was not pleaded, and the C.C.A. said: 'The summing-up... was almost tearing in two the golden thread which could be said to run right through the criminal law that the burden of proof rested on the prosecution.'

[5] *R.* v. *Kemp* [1957] 1 Q.B. 399 (*T.A.C.*).

[6] *R.* v. *Bastian* [1958] 1 All E.R. 568 (*T.A.C.*); *post*, ¶ 53 *a*.

[7] *R.* v. *Grant* Liverpool Ass. Feb. 1960; [1960] Crim. L.R. 424. See *post*, ¶ 596.

[8] *R.* v. *Nott* (1959) 43 Cr.App.R. 8.

[9] *R.* v. *Dixon* [1961] 1 W.L.R. 337. And see [1960] *Crim. L.R.* 453, an article by H. A. Samuels. The doctrine of *Bastian*, *Grant*, and *Nott* was questioned in *R.* v. *Morris*

The M'Naghten rules are still received in the courts as the binding authority on the defence of insanity. Since they were first promulgated they have been many times criticized and defended by members of both the medical and legal professions.[1] In 1916 their meaning was explained by the Court of Criminal Appeal in the case of *R.* v. *Codère*;[2] in that case the court refused to admit that the question should be decided by the standard of the accused person himself. In thus rejecting a contention that the test was subjective the court added: 'The standard to be applied is whether according to the ordinary standard adopted by reasonable men the act was right or wrong...once it is clear that the appellant knew that the act was wrong in law, then he was conscious that it was an act which he ought not to do, and, as it was against the law, it was punishable by law; assuming therefore that he knew the nature and quality of the act, he was guilty of murder.' Briefly, it may be said that *R.* v. *Codère* lays down (i) that an objective moral test must be applied in cases where insanity is pleaded, the test being 'the ordinary standard adopted by reasonable men'; (ii) that an act is 'wrong' according to that standard if it is punishable by law; (iii) that the accused must be deemed 'to know he was doing what was wrong' if he was aware that the act was one which was so punishable; and (iv) that the words 'nature and quality' do not refer to the moral aspects of what the offender was doing but solely to the physical facts. Since it would seem reasonable to suppose that the court in *R.* v. *Codère* did not consider that a person suffering from a defect of reason should be put in a worse position legally than that of a normal man, it would seem proper to add that the jury, before they can find the accused guilty, must also be satisfied (*a*) that his conduct was voluntary, and (*b*) that he realized the probable consequences of his conduct.[3]

This objective moral test was applied in *R.* v. *Windle*[4] following the principles to be extracted from *R.* v. *Codère*; it was said:[5] 'A man may be suffering from defect of reason, but, if he knows that what he is doing is wrong—and by "wrong" is meant contrary to law—he is

[1961] 2 W.L.R. 986, a case where the trial judge had refused to allow the prosecution to call evidence of insanity in rebuttal of the defence of diminished responsibility. See especially the remarks of Lawton, J., at p. 990.

[1] Stephen, *Hist. Crim. Law*, II, 156 *et seq.*; Stallybrass, 'Comparison of criminal law', *Mod. Appr. Crim. Law*, ch. 20, p. 415 *et seq.*; Hall, 'Mental disease and crime', 45 *Columbia L.R.* (1945), 679; Ellenbogen, *Journal of Criminal Science* (1948), I, 178 *et seq.*; Maudsley, *Responsibility in Mental Diseases*; Sullivan, *Crime and Insanity*; Meredith, 'Insanity as a criminal defence', 25 *Can. Bar Review* (1947), 251. The Royal Commission on Capital Punishment in their Report (1953, Cmd. 8932) reviewed the history of this topic, and (with one dissentient) agreed 'that the test of responsibility laid down by the M'Naghten Rules is so defective that the law on the subject ought to be changed'.

[2] (1916) 12 Cr.App.R. 21.

[3] For a review of the leading cases in which insanity was pleaded see Russ. 112 *et seq.*

[4] [1952] 2 Q.B. 826.

[5] At p. 832, *per* Lord Goddard, C.J.

responsible....Courts of law can only distinguish between that which is in accordance with law and that which is contrary to law.'[1]

¶ 53*a*. *Defect of reason through disease of the mind.* The determination of the exact meaning to be given to the words, 'disease of the mind' (in ¶ 53 (ii) above) does not appear to have exercised the courts for over 100 years. This may well have been because the word 'disease' has been a recognized medical term both in professional and lay circles to indicate some pathological variation (a defective condition) from the normal and healthy in the tissues of the living body whereby physical functions are disturbed or deranged. For the present purposes it is the brain that must be particularly considered, i.e. the convolutions of nervous tissue situated in the cranium. Medical science in the past century has made great advances in discovering the way in which this organ, the brain, operates by the generation of power, in the course of its functional processes, activities denoted by the common words, 'thought', 'memory', 'reason', 'imagination', 'intention', 'purpose', and conceived as taking place in the 'mind'. 'Mind' is an abstraction which cannot have any *material* existence at all. Therefore it cannot suffer from any 'disease', unless the term 'disease' be used in a purely figurative sense, to indicate either (*a*), that a person's thoughts or intentions etc. are objectionable; or (*b*), that they are the output of a '*brain*' which is abnormal either congenitally or through damage caused by contusion or disease. Notwithstanding these basic distinctions the words 'mind' and 'brain' have often been used synonymously when precision of speech is not important.

Two modern cases present difficulties; but students should be careful to note that the defence of 'diminished responsibility' has no application to the facts of either of them, since (*a*) they occurred before the enactment of the Homicide Act, 1957 (which created that offence in section 2), and (*b*) that defence is only available when the prisoner is charged with murder.

In the first case[2] the indictment contained three counts charging the prisoner under sections 11, 18 and 20 respectively of the Offences against the Person Act, 1861, by inflicting grievous bodily harm upon his son, aged 10, whom he had hit on the head with a mallet and thrown out of the window into a river below. Evidence that he was a kind and indulgent father and that there was no disagreement or ill feeling, even temporary, between them, was accepted. Also medical evidence was accepted that there was a history of ill health both in the prisoner and in members of his family, and that it was suspected that he might be suffering from a cerebral tumour, the effect of which would be to make him liable to an outburst of impulsive violence over

[1] The High Court of Australia in *Stapleton* v. *The Queen* (1952) 86 Commonwealth Law Reports 358, has refused to follow the doctrine of *R.* v. *Windle*; see [1954] *Crim. L.R.* 276; 16 *Mod. L.R.* 435; 103 *L.J.* 148.

[2] *R.* v. *Charlson* [1955] 1 W.L.R. 317; 1 All E.R. 859.

which he would have no control. The prisoner did not raise the defence of insanity[1] but pleaded that his act was not his conscious act, or one over which he had control. He was found not guilty on all three charges.

In the second case[2] the prisoner was charged with causing grievous bodily harm to his wife, whom he had struck on the head with a hammer during the night. It appeared that the prisoner, K., suffered from arteriosclerosis. He was an elderly man of excellent character, and he and his wife were reputed to be a devoted couple. His explanation was that he was entirely unconscious at the time, and it was accepted by the prosecution that he did not know what he was doing. Since the reports of the case show that counsel for the defence argued throughout that the prisoner was not insane within the M'Naghten rules it is clear that a defence of insanity was never set up, and that *R.* v. *Charlson* was relied upon in the submission that the prisoner should be found not guilty.

The facts in *R.* v. *Kemp* were on all fours with the facts in *R.* v. *Charlson*; and the defence in each case was basically the same, viz. that neither man had the intention required by the statute, and that the movements whereby the harm was caused were not voluntary in either of the two cases. In neither case did the defence set up insanity. Before *R.* v. *Kemp* it had generally been considered that the language of the M'Naghten answers II and III indicated that 'insanity' is a defence and that it has to be set up by the accused person.[3] The question arises, therefore, how the M'Naghten rules came into this case. This will be discussed below.

In *R.* v. *Kemp* all the doctors agreed that K. struck his wife 'not knowing anything about it, and not having any real memory of it',[4] and, according to the judge,[5] that he 'was not conscious that he picked up the hammer or that he was striking his wife with it'. But in the course of their evidence two of them (one called for the prosecution and one for the defence) said that the arteriosclerosis led to a congestion of blood in the brain which caused a temporary loss of consciousness as a result of which the patient acted 'irrationally and irresponsibly' but that there was not, in the present case, 'such a degeneration of the accused's brain cells as to amount to disease of the mind'. A third medical witness for the prosecution gave it as his opinion that the arteriosclerosis induced 'a condition of melancholia' as a result of which the accused committed the act; and that melancholia was 'a disease of the mind'. The reports do not disclose any agreement as to, or even discussion of, the exact concepts indicated by the two words 'brain' and 'mind' whereby the conflicting conclusions to which the medical witnesses came could be appraised and contrasted; their language, as reported, is both confused and confusing.

[1] Indeed the medical officer of the prison, in the course of his evidence, stated that Charlson was not insane, and was not suffering from 'disease of the mind'.

[2] *R.* v. *Kemp* [1957] 1 Q.B. 399; (1956) 40 Cr.App.R. 121, before Devlin, J.

[3] See Russ. 123 and *R.* v. *Charlson* [1955] 1 All E.R. at p. 860 B, *per* Barry, J.; *R.* v. *Dixon* [1961] 1 W.L.R. 337.

[4] Presumably this clumsy sentence alluded to his mental attitude at the time of the striking and his mental attitude later on when he had come to his senses; the latter of which was, of course, irrelevant.

[5] 40 Cr.App.R. at p. 123.

Faced with this situation the judge in effect set aside the evidence of the doctors, and distinguished *R.* v. *Charlson* on the ground that there the doctors were in agreement; and he said 'the sole question that I have to determine, which was not considered in that case [*R.* v. *Charlson*] is what is meant by "disease of the mind" within the meaning of the M'Naghten Rules'. Without expressly mentioning the standard interpretation of these rules as applying solely to the case where insanity was pleaded as a defence, his lordship turned to section 2(1) of the Trial of Lunatics Act, 1883, of which, he said, the material words were 'Where...it is given in evidence on the trial of such person for that offence that he was insane, so as not to be responsible, according to law, for his actions at the time when the act was done'.

With all respect it must be submitted that these words in section 2(1) are not strong enough, and had never been treated as strong enough, to negative the established doctrine that the M'Naghten rules are to be applied only *where the defence has pleaded insanity*; the words 'it is given in evidence that' require an allegation, supported by adequate evidence, that the accused was insane. The accused certainly did not lead evidence to that effect, and the precedents (up to the time of *R.* v. *Kemp*) were to the effect that it was not open to the prosecution to do so. This point has nothing to do with the definition of insanity but solely with the question, which party can plead insanity. It may be asked what there is in the Act of 1883 to give the prosecution the right to allege (moreover, without previous warning) that the accused was insane when he did the forbidden thing. The words of the section, 'where it is given in evidence', should not be read as 'where it appears from the evidence'.[1]

Turning to the meaning of 'disease of the mind' his lordship's judgment proceeded on the basis that the words 'brain' and 'mind' were not synonymous, saying 'the law is not in any way concerned with the brain but with the mind in the sense in which the term is ordinarily used in speaking of the mental faculties of reasoning, memory and understanding'. This is a strange proposition; the adjective 'mental' means either (*a*) 'of the mind' or (*b*) 'of the brain'. To adopt (*a*) makes the statement futile, for it purports to define mind as a faculty of itself. To adopt (*b*) makes 'brain' and 'mind' synonymous, and reveals a true distinction, between the brain and its faculties (i.e. what it can do); and this harmonizes with the words of the M'Naghten Rules '*defect* of reason through *disease* of the mind'. The words of the judge, 'If one read for "disease of the mind" "disease of the brain" it would follow that in many cases pleas of insanity would not be established because it would not be established that the brain had been affected either by degeneration of the cells *or in any other way*', followed by the statement

[1] It would seem extraordinary if the prosecution could, in effect, charge a man with being not guilty (see *Felstead* v. *R.*, *post*, p. 89). It is respectfully submitted that the dictum, 'The old notion that only the defence can raise a defence of insanity is now gone', *per* Lord Denning in *Bratty* v. *A.-G. for N.I.* [1961] 3 All E.R. at p. 534, is unsound and should not be followed.

'the condition of the brain is irrelevant', seem to take the defence of insanity out of the limitations of the M'Naghten Rules altogether.[1]

It would seem, therefore, that K. should not have been found insane (within the M'Naghten rules) unless (i) the defence had set up insanity; and (ii) that the evidence established that his brain (the physical organ) was diseased; and (iii), even if melancholia could rightly be classed as a disease of the brain, that K.'s melancholia caused him not only to become unconscious, but also caused him, while he was unconscious, to pick up the hammer and to strike his wife with it.

¶ 53*b*. *Diminished Responsibility*. The questions put to the judges in reference to M'Naghten's case were directed, as we have seen, only to the effect of insane delusions and insane ignorance. But insanity affects not only men's beliefs, but also (and indeed more frequently) their emotions and their wills. Hence since 1843 much discussion has taken place as to the effect of these latter forms of insanity in conferring immunity from criminal responsibility. The result has been that, though the doctrines laid down after M'Naghten's trial remain theoretically unaltered,[2] the practical administration of them affords a wider immunity than their language would at first sight seem to recognize. For many forms of insanity, which do not in themselves constitute those particular defects of reason which the judges recognized as conferring exemption from responsibility, have often been treated as sufficient evidence to show that one or other of those exemptive defects was also actually present. A man who, after killing his child, goes forthwith to the police station to surrender himself, and gives a lucid account of what he has done, would certainly seem to know the nature and quality of the act committed, and to know that in doing it he did wrong. Yet if he had previously shown some symptoms of madness, and had killed his child with no discoverable motive and no attempt at concealment, a judge on the modern practice might encourage a jury to regard these facts as evidence of his labouring under such insanity as would render him irresponsible.[3] The mere fact that a crime has been committed without any apparent motive is, of course, not sufficient of itself to establish any

[1] And incidentally out of the limitations of diminished responsibility as provided in sect. 2 of the Homicide Act, 1957 (especially the limitation to charges of murder). Contrast this judgment of Devlin, J., in *R.* v. *Kemp* with that of the C.C.A. in *R.* v. *Bentley* [1960] Crim. L.R. 777 where also the accused (*a*) did not set up insanity and (*b*) pleaded that he was temporarily incapable of knowing what he was doing, owing to an overdose of medicine.

[2] Cf. *R.* v. *Perry* (1919) 14 Cr.App.R. 48 at p. 54; *R.* v. *Holt* (1920) 15 Cr.App.R. 10, at p. 12; and especially *R.* v. *True* (1922) 16 Cr.App.R. 164. The courts are concerned not with insanity as such but with criminal responsibility, see A. L. Goodhart, *Essays in Jurisprudence*, 46–7.

[3] Cf. the case (*The Times*, 29 July 1901) of Hannah Cox, a devoted mother, who, under pressure of poverty, drowned two of her infants, 'as it was the best thing she could do for them'. Though she had shown no other symptoms of insanity, either before or after this act, Bigham, J., advised the jury to declare her irresponsibly insane.

similar immunity.[1] It should be noted that, as was declared in 1950, it is for the jury, and not for medical men of whatever eminence, to determine the issue of insanity.[2]

But now, for the crime of murder, a profound change has been introduced by the legislature, namely, the defence of diminished responsibility. Such a defence has for many years been recognized in Scotland,[3] and the Scottish cases have been cited as persuasive authority in the English courts.[4]

By the Homicide Act, 1957, section 2,

(1) Where a person kills or is a party to the killing of another, he shall not be convicted of murder if he was suffering from such abnormality of mind (whether arising from a condition of arrested or retarded development of mind or any inherent causes or induced by disease or injury) as substantially impaired his mental responsibility for his acts and omissions in doing or being a party to the killing.

(2) On a charge of murder, it shall be for the defence to prove[5] that the person charged is by virtue of this section not liable to be convicted of murder.

(3) A person who but for this section would be liable, whether as principal or as accessory, to be convicted of murder shall be liable instead to be convicted of manslaughter.

(4) The fact that one party to a killing is by virtue of this section not liable to be convicted of murder shall not affect the question whether the killing amounted to murder in the case of any other party to it.

The interpretation put upon this section by the courts has been much as was anticipated in the last edition of this book. First, in *R.* v. *Spriggs*[6] the interpretation of the terms 'abnormality of mind' and 'mental

[1] *R.* v. *Haynes* (1859) 1 F. and F. 666 (*T.A.C.*).

[2] *R.* v. *Rivett* (1950) 34 Cr.App.R. 87. For a criticism of this case see Norval Morris, 'Insanity and responsibility', 13 *Mod. L.R.* 372. And see the letter of 12 June 1879 from Cockburn, C.J., to the Attorney-General, *Parl. Pap.*, Accounts and Papers 18, 1878–9, LIX, 233, at p. 247. In *R.* v. *Holmes* [1953] 1 W.L.R. 686, it was held that a doctor may be asked and may answer whether in his opinion the accused man's conduct immediately after the homicide (described by another witness) would indicate that he knew (1) the nature of the act he was committing, or (2) that his act was contrary to law. But as to this the question may be asked if the man's conduct *after* the deed is a very cogent guide to his attitude of mind at the time when he was committing it. And see *R.* v. *Wilkinson* [1953] 12 Curr. Law 512.

[3] See the *Report of the Royal Commission on Capital Punishment*, 1953, Cmd. 8932, p. 131, paras. 377–83.

[4] E.g. *Dingwall* 1867 Irvine 466; *Savage* 1923 J.C. 49; *Braithwaite* 1945 J.C. 55; *Carraher* 1946 J.C. 108. See *R.* v. *Dunbar* [1957] 3 W.L.R. 330; [1958] 1 Q.B. 36.

[5] Following the principle of *Woolmington* v. *D.P.P.* [1935] A.C. 462 and *R.* v. *Carr-Briant* [1943] K.B. 607, it has been said in *R.* v. *Dunbar* [1957] 3 W.L.R. 330, that these words in the Homicide Act do not lay as heavy a burden on the defence as rests on the prosecution to prove its case beyond reasonable doubt; and that the burden on the defence is discharged if the evidence justifies the conclusion that the balance of probabilities is in favour of the accused person.

[6] [1958] 1 Q.B. 270.

responsibility' was left to the jury. Then, in *R.* v. *Walden*,[1] it was laid down by the Court of Criminal Appeal that *R.* v. *Spriggs* must not be taken to mean that a judge is limited to bringing before the jury the exact words of the section; and that, on the contrary, it is open to him to point out to the jury the sort of things which they can look for in order to decide whether, on the facts, the case comes within the section; and therefore it was not improper for the judge at the trial of Walden to refer to the definition of insanity in the M'Naghten answers and to say to the jury: 'There are some cases, you may think, where a man... is wandering on the borderline between being sane and insane, where you can say to yourself...he is not fully responsible for what he has done', since these remarks, in the view of the court, were only giving an illustration of the kind of thing which the jury might consider. A year later in *R.* v. *Byrne*[2] the reference to 'borderline of insanity' was repeated; but in 1961[3] the Judicial Committee of the Privy Council stated that a reference to the borderline of insanity was 'not always helpful', especially when linked to insanity as defined in the M'Naghten rules, since that would be 'an undue limitation of the wide words of the section'. The Judicial Committee however expressed their agreement with other statements of the Court of Criminal Appeal in *R.* v. *Byrne* that the words 'abnormality of mind' in the section appeared to be 'wide enough to cover the mind's activities in all its aspects',[4] including 'the ability to exercise will-power to control physical acts in accordance with rational judgment'. Furthermore, it was stated in *R.* v. *Byrne* that the interpretation of the words 'substantially impaired' is for the jury, and is a matter on which they may 'quite legitimately differ from doctors'.[5]

It seems therefore a fair conclusion from the above declarations that section 2 of the Homicide Act permits the jury in a trial for murder to take into account evidence of irresistible impulse in deciding whether the prisoner's mental responsibility for his acts and omissions in doing, or being a party to, the killing had been substantially impaired. Students must note that these new rules of diminished responsibility apply solely where murder is charged. Therefore an irresistible impulse to commit any other crime, e.g. grievous bodily harm or larceny, has no more relevance since the Act than it had before it.[6]

¶ 54. *Irresistible impulse.* As the law at present stands, apart from the above special provisions of the Homicide Act, an irresistible impulse to do an act is merely evidence of exculpative insanity and does not *in itself* affect criminal responsibility. It seems to have been generally overlooked that from very early times the common law has recognized

[1] [1959] 3 All E.R. 203.

[2] [1960] 3 All E.R. 1, at p. 5, c.

[3] *Rose* v. *Reginam* [1961] 1 All E.R. 859; *R.* v. *Terry* [1961] 2 All E.R. 569.

[4] Yet in *R.* v. *Di Duca* (1959) 43 Cr.App.R. 167 the toxic effect of drink was held not to constitute such abnormality.

[5] And see *R.* v. *Jennion* [1962] 1 All E.R. 689.

[6] But see the remarks on *R.* v. *Kemp*, *ante*, p. 81.

an irresistible impulse of a temporary character as a ground of partial excuse in the case of homicide committed under the emotional stress of provocation (see *post*, ¶ 117). In the United States both the Supreme Court and the courts of some of the States recognize irresistible impulse as being a sufficient defence; even when accompanied by a knowledge that the act was wrong. In England there are judicial dicta[1] supporting the view that an impulse should be admitted as a defence if really irresistible (not merely unresisted), because then the act done would not be a 'voluntary' act at all; and in 1924 Lord Atkin's Committee reported[2] in favour of a change in the law to admit the defence of irresistible impulse, but when the judges were consulted on the point ten out of twelve advised against its recognition. The defence was repudiated by the Court of Criminal Appeal in 1925.[3] Yet if a man can prove that he was unable to control his actions through any other cause than mental defect, he will be excused. There is, however, little doubt that in practice juries more often than not accept the defence of insanity in cases of irresistible impulse.[4] It is perhaps worthy of consideration whether a ground of exculpation might be found by regarding an impulse of overpowering effect as establishing that the acts which it stimulated were not 'voluntary' (*ante*, ¶ 18). The difficulty is, of course, to distinguish, on the evidence, between uncontrolled and uncontrollable impulse.[5]

There is one form of impulse, that of kleptomania, which is sometimes put forward, with or without evidence, by well-to-do persons accused of trivial acts of theft. That an impulse to steal does sometimes arise from actual insanity seems to be established by the fact that it is often limited to special times (e.g. that of pregnancy) or to some special class of objects (e.g. hats, boots, tablecloths) which are accumulated in numbers not at all needed by the thief. Naturally, it was chiefly in courts of petty sessions that these unimportant charges were preferred; in such courts a plea of insanity used formerly to be the safer to raise because they did not possess the power, enjoyed by higher tribunals, of ordering an accused person, who established this plea, 'to be kept in custody as a criminal lunatic'.[6] But now by virtue of the Mental Health Act, 1959, a court of summary jurisdiction may, under the conditions stated in section 60, make an order directing the

[1] *R.* v. *Hay* (1911) 22 Cox 268; *R.* v. *Fryer* (1915) 24 Cox 403; *R.* v. *Jolly* (1919) 83 J.P. 296. Sir James Stephen so interpreted the M'Naghten answers, *Hist. Crim. Law*, II, 167.

[2] Cmd. 2005, p. 8.

[3] *R.* v. *Kopsch* (1925) 19 Cr.App.R. 50, following the cases of *Brough* (1854) 2 F. and F. 838 n. (*a*), *Haynes* (1859) 1 F. and F. at p. 667, *Barton* (1863) 3 F. and F. at p. 780, *Quarmby* (1921) 15 Cr.App.R. 163, *True* (1922) 16 Cr.App.R. 164, and followed by *Flavell* (1926) 19 Cr.App.R. 141, and *Sodeman* [1936] 2 All E.R. 1138 (*T.A.C.*). See Goodhart, 'Recent tendencies in English jurisprudence', 7 *Can. Bar Review*, 289; Seaborne Davies, 'Irresistible impulse in English law', 17 *Can. Bar Review*, 147; Stallybrass, 'Comparison of criminal law', *Mod. Appr. Crim. Law*, 417.

[4] 159 *L.T. Jo.* 436.

[5] A. L. Goodhart, *Essays in Jurisprudence*, 46–7.

[6] Trial of Lunatics Act, 1883, s. 2.

accused person to be received and detained in such institution for persons of unsound mind as may be named in the order. It had been provided[1] that the expression 'criminal lunatic' should cease to be used, and that there should be substituted for it wherever it occurred in any enactment the expression 'Broadmoor patient' (s. 62(2)). But this expression has now in its turn been eliminated by the Mental Health Act which uses the word 'patient' for a person 'suffering or appearing to be suffering from mental disorder'.

The defence of insane impulses is now rarer than that of unconscious automatism,[2] as in epilepsy or sleep-walking.[3] But our courts, unlike Continental tribunals, have not yet become familiar with the plea that a crime was committed under the influence of post-hypnotic 'suggestion' exercised by some designing person who had induced hypnotic sleep in the offender. It remains to be seen what exemptive effect will ever be accorded in England to such 'suggestions', or to those affections which (like hysteromania and neurasthenia) have been called the borderland of insanity. Such questions have become of great practical importance, now that modern science has come to recognize so clearly, in addition to the ordinary 'intellectual' insanity which impairs a man's judgment, a 'conative' form which affects his will, whether by weakening his natural impulses to action, or by inspiring abnormal impulses, and an 'affective' insanity which disturbs his emotions of love or hatred.[4]

(i) *Classification of the mentally abnormal.* Moreover, there are many persons, who, whilst not so insane as to be exempt from criminal responsibility, or perhaps even to require restraint, are nevertheless mentally abnormal. Such afflicted persons, under a classification made by the Royal Commission in 1908, were dealt with in a series of Mental Deficiency Acts which have now been repealed by the Mental Health Act, 1959, which discards the term 'mental deficiency', replacing it by 'mental disorder', defined in section 4 as follows:

4. (1) In this Act 'mental disorder' means mental illness, arrested or incomplete development of mind, psychopathic disorder, and any other disorder or disability of mind; and 'mentally disordered' shall be construed accordingly.

(2) In this Act 'severe subnormality' means a state of arrested or incomplete development of mind which includes subnormality of intelligence and is of such a nature or degree that the patient is incapable of living an

[1] By the Criminal Justice Act, 1948; *post*, p. 89.

[2] Which is covered by the M'Naghten rules; *R.* v. *Perry* (1919) 14 Cr.App.R. 48, at p. 55.

[3] See *R.* v. *Tolson* (1889) 23 Q.B.D. 168, 'simply because he would not know what he is doing', *per* Stephen, J., at p. 187.

[4] The *temporary* disturbance of a sane mind by intense grief was considered in *R.* v. *Beadon*, where a sane woman was indicted for poisoning her child at a time when she was sane, but was distressed by the death of her husband. Shearman, J., told the jury that, if they thought she was 'so distraught that she did not know it was a dangerous thing to administer poison', they might find her guilty of only a manslaughter. But he admitted his ruling to be 'an innovation' (*Daily Telegraph*, 12 Sept. 1924).

independent life or of guarding himself against serious exploitation, or will be so incapable when of an age to do so.

(3) In this Act 'subnormality' means a state of arrested or incomplete development of mind (not amounting to severe subnormality) which includes subnormality of intelligence and is of a nature or degree which requires or is susceptible to medical treatment or other special care or training of the patient.

(4) In this Act 'psychopathic disorder' means a persistent disorder or disability of mind (whether or not including subnormality of intelligence) which results in abnormally aggressive or seriously irresponsible conduct on the part of the patient, and requires or is susceptible to medical treatment.

(5) Nothing in this section shall be construed as implying that a person may be dealt with under this Act as suffering from mental disorder, or from any form of mental disorder described in this section, by reason only of promiscuity or other immoral conduct.

The Act makes no special provision for dealing with persons suffering from such mental disturbance as does not amount to 'mental disorder', but leaves them to be dealt with by the provisions of the Criminal Justice Act, 1948, sect. 4.[1] Where 'mental disorder' is established, by the Act of 1959,[2] the court of trial before which the person is convicted (save where the offence is one for which the sentence is fixed by law[3]) is given power to order admission[4] to and detention in a 'special hospital'.

In the United States, in France and in Scotland a degree of mental affliction that is too slight to confer complete exemption from responsibility has been recognized as a circumstance that may mitigate the offender's punishment.[5] This view is defended on the ground that every form of insanity weakens the power of self-control, so that the offender's moral guilt is proportionately lessened, and therefore, on the retributive theory, his punishment ought to be the less. In English practice the lessened capacity of self-control is often treated as a mitigating circumstance; for instance, when sunstroke or sleepy sickness has left a man with a will-power permanently so weakened that he pursues any passing pleasure with little regard for consequences. The modern view is that a non-exemptive insanity instead of merely lessening the punishment should modify it, by giving it a curative form.

In the near future attempts may perhaps be made to induce the legislature to extend the new principle of diminished responsibility to other crimes than murder; but in view of the provisions of the Criminal Justice Act, 1948, and of the Mental Health Act, 1959, relating to medical reports and the courts' powers to bring offenders within the scope of remedial treatment it may be doubted if any such movement will develop sufficient weight to succeed.

[1] In which, by its seventh and eighth schedules, it also makes certain consequential amendments.

[2] Section 60.

[3] E.g. murder.

[4] Called a 'hospital order'.

[5] Cf. infanticide, ¶ 138 *post*.

(ii) *Special hospitals.* In cases where a defence of insanity had been accepted[1] by a jury,[2] the form of their verdict used to be 'not guilty, on the ground of insanity'. But under the Trial of Lunatics Act, 1883 (46 and 47 Vict. c. 38), it was changed to 'guilty of the act (or omission), but so insane as not to be responsible, according to law, for his actions at the time when the act was done (or the omission made)'.[3] Thereupon, under the Criminal Justice Act, 1948, s. 62, the court used to order the prisoner to be kept in custody in a 'Broadmoor Institution' (previously called a criminal lunatic asylum) as a 'Broadmoor patient', till Her Majesty's pleasure should be known. This, however, has now been altered by the Act of 1959, which, as we have seen, brings insanity within the category of 'mental disorder', repeals the above section 62 of the Act of 1948, and vests the Broadmoor institutions (and some others) in the Minister of Health who has to provide the same accommodation in what are henceforth to be termed 'special hospitals'.[4] Elaborate regulations are set out in the Act for determining the period of detention in these hospitals.

It may be added that insanity is sometimes important in criminal law, even apart from its bearing on criminal responsibility. For if a man become insane[5] after committing a crime, he cannot be tried until his

[1] English law (*ante*, ¶ 53) presumes an accused person to be sane. Hence the prisoner must give 'clear' proof (10 Cl. and F. at p. 210) of insanity. The burden of proof, however, is not higher than that which rests upon a plaintiff or defendant in civil proceedings; *Sodeman* v. *R.* [1936] 2 All E.R. 1138 (*T.A.C.*). Moreover the present practice is that the Crown hands to the judge and to the accused all its information as to the latter's state of mind, e.g. the prison-surgeon's report. An undefended prisoner may fail to raise the defence of insanity; hence, if a prisoner has no counsel, the Crown counsel will expressly ask whether the judge thinks it desirable for him to call the medical witnesses. A medical witness who has not seen the accused before trial must not be asked whether on the evidence he thinks the accused was insane.

[2] Justices of the peace can accept the defence when trying an offender *summarily*; but not when examining for commitment to a higher court.

[3] This 1883 form was devised by Queen Victoria, to emphasize, somewhat illogically, a 'guilt' which the law denies. Her life had once or twice been threatened by insane assailants. See the remarks of Lord Atkin in addressing the Medico-legal Society in (1925), 159 *L.T.Jo.* 436. An unusually minute picture of the practical working of a trial where this defence is raised may be seen in *The Times* of 20 April 1882. This special verdict has been held in *Felstead* v. *R.* [1914] A.C. 554, to be a verdict of acquittal, against which no appeal lies; the injustice which this may cause has been commented on by the Court of Criminal Appeal in *R.* v. *Duke* [1961] 3 All E.R. 737, the court suggesting that corrective legislation is needed. See also *R.* v. *Kemp* [1956] 3 W.L.R. 724 at p. 727, where Devlin, J., calls it a 'qualified' as distinguished from an 'absolute' acquittal; the judge considered that the Act of 1883 altered 'the common law position that if a man is not responsible for his actions he is entitled to be acquitted by the ordinary form of acquittal, and it matters not whether his lack of responsibility was due to insanity or to any other cause'. In Australia the form of verdict is 'Not guilty on the grounds of insanity'; see [1954] *Crim. L.R.* 277.

[4] Sect. 97. Sect. 60 gives the court discretionary power (*R.* v. *Higginbotham* [1961] 1 W.L.R. 1277); and sect. 65 gives higher courts power to restrict discharge from hospital where this is necessary for the protection of the public.

[5] Even certifiable insanity, not covered by the M'Naghten rules.

recovery, any more than can a foreigner, or deaf mute, for whom no interpreter is available. Where such a man is certified insane the Secretary of State may order his detention in a special hospital until remittal to prison or discharge,[1] or the court before whom he is brought may upon a jury's verdict that he is unfit to plead order him to be kept in custody during the royal pleasure.[2] Again, if after conviction a prisoner become insane,[3] he cannot be hanged until his recovery. The origin and reason for this rule are obscure. It has been suggested that the reason for it is that the condemned man might have some plea which, if sane, he could urge in stay of execution; but there seems to be no real authority for this view.[4] The thorough inquiry made by doctors in such cases does not in law reverse a jury's verdict if it has been against a prisoner.[5] No prisoner, however, has since 1840 been executed after a certificate of insanity has been given; and the Court of Criminal Appeal is reluctant to allow a long term of imprisonment to follow upon detention in an asylum.[6]

(*e*) Clerks in holy orders. Benefit of clergy

¶ 55. Benefit of clergy was a remarkable privilege[7] which, although now abolished, was for centuries of great importance in criminal law.

[1] Mental Health Act, 1959, s. 73. And see R. M. Jackson, 'A note on Broadmoor patients' (1951) 11 *Cambridge L.J.* 57.

[2] Criminal Lunatics Act, 1800; with the like consequences, under the Mental Health Act, 1959, s. 71.

[3] In *any* form of certifiable insanity, even though not such as the M'Naghten rules would cover.

[4] Blackstone (4 *Comm.* 25) followed Hale (1 P.C. 35) in stating this as the reason; but Coke (3 *Inst.* c. 1, p. 4) said 'If a man commit treason or felony...if after judgment he become *de non sane memorie*, he shall not be executed, for it cannot be an example to others'. (The meaning of the word 'memorie' here and in Hale was discussed in *R.* v. *Podola* [1959] 3 All E.R. 418 at p. 430.) On the other hand Sir John Hawles, in his remarks on *R.* v. *Bateman* (1685) 4 St.Tr. 162 at p. 205, supported the rule for the reason that to make examples of the insane was inconsistent with humanity and with religion, as being 'against Christian charity to send a great offender quick, as it is stil'd, into another world when he is not of a capacity to fit himself for it'.

[5] The modern practice has been for the sentence of death to be respited 'until further signification of Her Majesty's Pleasure', and for the prisoner then to be removed to Broadmoor by a warrant issued under section 2 (1) of the Criminal Lunatics Act, 1884, which is now repealed by the Mental Health Act, 1959. The sentence of death could not be executed so long as the respite subsisted, but it was not formally commuted to imprisonment for life, either before or after the transfer to Broadmoor. If the prisoner later recovered his sanity difficulties of a technical character arose. See the *Report of the Royal Commission on Capital Punishment*, 1953 (Cmd. 8932), para. 460 wherein it is stated (at p. 158): 'it is unthinkable that the sentence should ever be carried out in the event of his recovery.' The Commissioners recommended that the older (pre-1879) practice be restored and that a conditional pardon should be granted commuting the sentence to imprisonment for life, before the prisoner was removed to Broadmoor. The situation is not expressly dealt with by the Mental Health Act, 1959, although it has repealed the Act of 1884; the procedure now to be followed seems to be uncertain.

[6] *R.* v. *Kenneally* (1930) 22 Cr.App.R. 52.

[7] See Pollock and Maitland, I, 441 *et seq.*: Holdsworth, *History of English Law*, I, 615, III, 293. Abolished by the Criminal Law Act, 1827, s. 6.

Some knowledge of it is even now essential for a proper understanding of common law crimes. After William the Conqueror separated the ecclesiastical from the secular courts, the clergy put forward the claim that all persons in holy orders should be exempt from secular jurisdiction in all proceedings, civil or criminal. Eventually the rule was established that 'clerks' of all kinds, who committed any of the serious crimes termed felonies, could be tried only in an ecclesiastical court, and therefore were only amenable to such punishments as that court could inflict. Any clerk[1] accused of such crime was accordingly passed over to the bishop's court. He was there tried before a jury of clerks by the oaths of twelve compurgators; a mode of trial which usually ensured him an acquittal. But even if he were convicted, the court could not inflict death, but could only degrade him and imprison him. About 1300, however, a change was made, by surrendering no accused clerks to the bishop until after they had undergone conviction in the secular court, and had thereby forfeited their chattels. And it was also settled that the clergy had no such 'benefit' in civil cases, or in misdemeanours.[2] But, on the other hand, the benefit was extended to all persons eligible for ordination, although not actually ordained. In the time of Henry III it had become available to all males who could read; which soon came to mean those who could learn a few words by heart.[3] But in 1487 it was enacted that these laymen should have the benefit only once, and should be branded on the thumb to show that they had had it. Under Henry VIII[4] benefit of clergy was removed from 'wilful murder of malice aforethought' (*post*, ¶ 104). Under Elizabeth I all surrenders to the bishop, and all distinctions between ordained clerks and laymen, were abolished; and henceforth every person who obtained the benefit became liable to be kept in gaol for a year. Under William III[5] the benefit was extended to women, and independently of their being able to read; and under Anne reading was made unnecessary for men also. On the other hand, successive statutes took away the benefit from the more heinous crimes, until in Blackstone's time there were one hundred and sixty felonies in which it could not be claimed, i.e. which

[1] By 25 Edw. III, st. 3, c. 4, 'Pro clero', in 1350, the privilege was extended to monks, secular clerks and other persons in religious employment. There are some indications that at a very early period nuns were similarly privileged, although later all women were debarred. See 2 Hale P.C. 373; Pollock and Maitland, I, 445.

[2] Stephen (*Hist. Crim. Law*, I, 464) follows Hale (2 P.C. 350) in holding that treason was from the first excluded.

[3] The so-called 'neck verse' was usually the first verse of Psalm li, which consisted solely of the three words 'Miserere mei, Deus', which could be learned by heart in advance, yet we read that many delinquents failed. This choice seems not to have been binding on the judge, who had jurisdiction to test the prisoner's scholastic attainments further, for Kelyng, J., reports (pp. 50, 51) that in a case which he tried, having noticed that the prisoner did not really look at the book, he called him forward and ordered him to read a passage, whereupon the wretched man confessed that he could not read.

[4] 23 Hen. VIII, c. 1.

[5] 3 Will. and Mary, c. 9. A partial extension to women had been made in 1622 by 21 Jac. I, c. 6.

were really capital. In the course of its history benefit of clergy had become an institution with technical rules which led to many difficulties.[1] Although in later centuries it was gradually whittled away (and finally abolished in 1827[2]) its effects are still to be seen, for example, in some of the unnecessary distinctions which exist even now in the law of larceny, and in the complexities of the peculiar arrangement of our criminal law.[3] It survived longer in parts of the United States, and was successfully claimed in South Carolina at least so recently as 1855 (*The State* v. *Bosse* (1855), 42 S.C. 276; cf. 35, 372).

[1] See *R.* v. *Gogerly* (1818) R. and R. 343; *R.* v. *Byford* (1823) R. and R. 521.

[2] 7 and 8 Geo. IV, c. 28.

[3] E.g. *post*, ¶ 66.

Chapter IV

PRELIMINARY CRIMES

Section I. Introductory

¶ 56. In all crimes, other than those brought about by omission to perform a legal duty, some active conduct, whether brief or prolonged, on the part of the offender must precede his attainment of the *actus reus*. This preparatory activity consists in a series of steps taken in furtherance of his ultimate aim, and any one of these steps may be (although none need be) in itself an independent, completed, crime. Thus a man, having formed the intention to murder another, may commit the misdemeanour of malicious damage to property by breaking open a cupboard, the felony of larceny by taking from it a revolver and ammunition, an offence under the Road Traffic Act, 1930, by driving off another's motor vehicle to reach his victim, and the felony of attempt to murder by firing a shot at him which misses. Of the crimes thus committed three are independent and complete, for any one of the three might have been committed as an end in itself. But the crime of attempt is preparatory in its nature for it can have no existence except as part of a larger purpose. Attempt therefore may be classed as one of the three crimes which are essentially preliminary, the other two being incitement and conspiracy. For each of these crimes is effected as a means of reaching a desired end. High treason is the one crime (in its chief classes) to which none of these three offences can be ancillary, for acts which would constitute either an incitement or a conspiracy or an attempt to commit treason are treated as overt acts of treason and are therefore prosecuted as treason. These preliminary crimes have sometimes been erroneously described as 'inchoate' offences.[1] This is misleading because the word 'inchoate' connotes something which is not yet completed, and it is therefore not accurately used to denote something which is itself complete, even though it be a link in a chain of events leading to some object which is not yet attained. The offence of incitement is fully performed even though the person incited immediately repudiates the suggested deed, a conspiracy is committed although the conspirators have not yet moved to execute their purposed crime, and the performance of a criminal attempt must always have been reached before the end is gained. In all these instances it is the ultimate crime which is inchoate and not the preliminary crime, the position indeed being just the same as in the example imagined above of a man who stole a revolver and committed other crimes in order to effect his purpose of murder. There the murder was inchoate, but the larceny and other crimes (including the attempt) were completed.[2]

[1] Stephen, *Hist. Crim. Law*, II, 229.

[2] Russ. ch. 6, Sect. I (ii).

¶ 57. *Their original interconnexion.* The history of the preliminary crimes shows that in origin they were closely interconnected: they were all developments of the early law of principal and accessory.[1] Very early in our law it was a rule that one who had instigated another to commit a felony became himself also guilty of the felony so soon as it was effected. It is, however, not clear whether at that period he was held guilty of an offence at common law if the felony was not committed, unless the facts showed a conspiracy between the two men, for there was an early doctrine[2] that 'no accessory can be convicted or suffer any punishment where the principal is not attainted or hath the benefit of clergy'.[3] Again, in the early cases no clear line of demarcation was drawn between an incitement and attempt.[4] This close association of the three offences will appear when the history of each is examined.[5]

SECTION 2. INCITEMENT

¶ 58. This takes the form of soliciting some other person to commit a crime. The desired crime (except in a few statutory cases) must be an *indictable* one. To 'counsel or procure' the commission of a non-indictable crime is not an offence at all if the offence counselled is not committed,[6] but if it be actually committed then the inciter is held equally guilty of it. Incitement is a misdemeanour, punishable with fine or imprisonment, even though the ultimate indictable crime is not performed; but if it is, then the inciter's liability increases, for he will become an accessory before the fact if the suggested crime be a felony and liable as a principal offender if it be a misdemeanour.[7]

SECTION 3. CRIMINAL CONSPIRACY

¶ 59. The first form in which this crime appeared in the common law was as an agreement of persons who combined to carry on legal proceedings in a vexatious or improper manner.[8] It was mostly treated as a civil wrong but it could also be punished on indictment. The criminal side of such a combination was emphasized by the Star Chamber, which recognized its possibilities as an engine of government and moulded it into a substantive offence of wide scope, whose attractions were such that its principles were gradually adopted in the common law courts, into which it was insinuated by way of the law of

[1] ¶¶ 66–71 *post*. [2] Quoted by Stephen, *Hist. Crim. Law*, II, 232.

[3] But nowadays a person who 'counsels' etc. a felony may be indicted for the substantive felony whether or not the principal shall have been previously convicted (Accessories and Abettors Act, 1861, s. 2).

[4] *R.* v. *Johnson* (1678) 2 Show. 1; an attempt to induce a witness to come foward to give evidence.

[5] See Hudson, 'A treatise on the Court of Star Chamber', *Collect. Jurid.* II, 5, p. 87; Spedding, *Letters and Life of Bacon*, IV, 399–409; Holdsworth, *Hist. Eng. Law*, V, 200; Russ. 184.

[6] See Williams, *Criminal Law*, 466.

[7] It must be within the sphere of the incitement, *post*, ¶ 69; see *R.* v. *Smith* [1961] Curr. Law (Nov.) 327. [8] Stephen, *Hist. Crim. Law*, II, 228.

principals and accessories. It was also closely associated with attempts[1] and often treated as a form of attempt to commit a wrong.[2] But so far as the law of the present day is concerned the House of Lords has declared (*a*) that the gist of conspiracy is the agreement, whether or not the object is attained; and (*b*) that the purpose of making such agreements punishable is to prevent the commission of the substantive offence before it has even reached the stage of attempt, and (*c*) that it is all part and parcel of the preservation of the Queen's peace within the realm.[3] In the hands of the common law judges conspiracy was maintained as a vague offence capable of almost indefinite extension.[4] The variety of facts which it has been held to cover, and the considerations of criminal policy which are involved in it, make it advisable to postpone the discussion of it in more detail to a later place among the independent crimes.[5]

SECTION 4. ATTEMPT

¶ **60.** This is the most common of the preliminary crimes. At common law it consists of steps taken in furtherance of an indictable offence[6] which the person attempting intends to carry out if he can. As we have seen there can be a long chain of such steps and it is necessary to have some test by which to decide that the particular link in the chain has been reached at which the crime of attempt has been achieved; that link will represent the *actus reus* of attempt, and the test for ascertaining it is suggested below (¶ 63).

HISTORY OF THE CRIME OF ATTEMPT

¶ **61.** The earliest record of the official repression of attempts as an exercise of criminal policy[7] is to be found in the measures adopted by the Star Chamber to suppress the practice of duelling. This practice constituted a manifestation of self-help and a disregard of the Crown's machinery of justice, and the royal judges were alive to its possible implications. The common law at that time could deal adequately with the principal parties (or the survivor of them) and their accessories if the duel actually took place; but this was felt to be insufficient. Accordingly the Star Chamber exercised its arbitrary jurisdiction and punished with fine or imprisonment any person proved to have participated in the preliminary arrangements for a duel even if the contest never took place.[8] In the language used in the early cases there can be seen that intermingling of attempt, conspiracy and incitement to

[1] Stephen, *ibid.* 227.
[2] Holdsworth, *op. cit.* v, 201.
[3] *Board of Trade* v. *Owen* [1957] 2 W.L.R. 351 at p. 357.
[4] For a modern revival of this judicial discretion see *Shaw* v. *D.P.P.* [1961] 2 All E.R. 446 at pp. 464–7; but *contra, per* Lord Reid, at p. 457.
[5] ¶ 448 *post.*
[6] In some statutory offences which are indictable and some which are not indictable, the statute provides expressly that an attempt to do the forbidden thing or even, in some instances, a mere act of preparation (as for example under reg. 90 (1) of the Defence (General) Regulations, 1939; see *Gardner* v. *Ackeroyd* [1952] 2 All E.R. 306 (*T.A.C.*), *post* p. 91) itself constitutes an offence.
[7] *Ante*, ¶ 5.
[8] Holdsworth, *op. cit.* v, 200.

which reference has already been made.[1] Indeed, it was not until about the end of the eighteenth century that incitement, conspiracy, and attempt broke off into distinct and separate crimes.

In the offence of attempt the gravamen is measured by the kind of crime intended, and this means that the essence of attempt lies in the intention rather than in the acts done in furtherance thereof. In other words the criminality is constituted more by the *mens rea* than by the *actus reus*. Yet since *mens rea* alone is not a crime the courts required a physical element also; but in this case only as much was necessary as could establish the *mens rea*.[2] In this can be observed a strong resemblance to the crime of treason, which in the form of 'compassing the King's death' as we shall see,[3] consists mainly in the rebellious and evil thought of the traitor which needs only the physical support that the person accused 'be thereof proveably attainted of open deed'.

In 1784 Lord Mansfield, in *R.* v. *Scofield*,[4] said: 'When an act is done, the law judges, not only of the act done, but of the intent with which it is done: and, if it is coupled with an unlawful and malicious intent, though the act itself would otherwise have been innocent, the intent being criminal, the act becomes criminal and punishable.'

The first case in which it was clearly decided that an attempt to commit a crime is at common law[5] itself a crime was *R.* v. *Higgins* in 1801.[6] Yet the language used in *R.* v. *Higgins* still showed a disinclination to distinguish clearly incitement from attempt.[7] However, since *R.* v. *Higgins* it has become established beyond doubt that at common law it is now an indictable misdemeanour to attempt to commit any felony,[8] or any misdemeanour, whether such felony or misdemeanour is an offence at common law or by statute.[9]

ELEMENTS OF LIABILITY IN ATTEMPT

¶ 62. As mentioned above, to constitute attempt at common law, there must be evidence of some overt act[10] as well as evidence of *mens rea*. The

[1] ¶ 56 *ante*.

[2] Cf. *R.* v. *Sutton* (1736) 2 Str. 1074, 'here the intent is the offence, and the having in his custody, an act that is evidence of his intent'. This case was overruled later on the ground that 'having in his possession' could not be regarded as an act, and that an intent without an act was not a misdemeanour; *R.* v. *Heath* (1810) R. and R. 184.

[3] ¶ 402 *post*.

[4] (1784) Cald. 397, in rejecting a contention that an attempt to commit a misdemeanour was not a misdemeanour.

[5] Statute had in several instances declared that an attempt to commit a felony was a crime; e.g. 3 Geo. IV, c. 114.

[6] (1801) 2 East 5 (*T.A.C.*).

[7] Counsel on either side alluded to incitement as an attempt to procure the commission of a felony by another person.

[8] As stated by Parke, B., in *R.* v. *Roderick* (1837) 7 C. and P. 795. Including suicide; *R.* v. *Doody* (1854) 6 Cox 463; *R.* v. *Burgess* (1862) L. and C. 258.

[9] In some cases the attempt to commit an offence is made punishable by statute in the same manner as the completed offence, or is specially punishable as a substantive felony or misdemeanour; e.g. Sexual Offences Act, 1956, s. 10.

[10] *R.* v. *Linneker* [1906] 2 K.B. 99 (*T.A.C.*).

burden is therefore on the prosecution to show (i) the *actus reus*, that the accused had done something which in point of law marked the commission of the offence, and (ii) the *mens rea*, that in taking this step he was inspired by the intention to go on to reach a definite objective[1] which would constitute a specific felony or misdemeanour.

It has already been pointed out[2] that in cases of absolute liability under statute it may well be that a man must be found guilty of the offence committed although he had no idea that it was being committed. This will happen in certain cases where the offence is the result of the intervention of a stranger,[3] or where there is vicarious liability for the acts of a servant. Yet it seems clear that in such offences it is impossible for a man properly to be found guilty of *attempting* to commit the crime unless he in fact did consciously intend its commission.[4]

To decide on what constitutes the *mens rea* in attempt has not been a matter of difficulty since it is nothing more than a clear intention to perform the *actus reus* of some other crime. It should be noted that considerations of the mental attitude which we have described above as 'recklessness'[5] have no place in the crime of attempt; still less is it relevant to discuss negligence. For whatever a man attempts to do he must *intend* to achieve if he is able to do so. A man may be doubtful of his powers or of his chances of success, yet it is clear that the word 'attempt' cannot be correctly used to denote his actions unless he intends thereby to reach the mark at which he is aiming, if it be possible for him.[6]

ACTUS REUS IN ATTEMPT

¶ 63. Statute of course may define, and often has expressly defined, the *actus reus* of any particular statutory crime.[7] But it has repeatedly been declared difficult, if not impossible, to establish a principle by which to decide, for the purposes of *common law*, at what stage in the preparation for a crime the *actus reus* of the offence of attempt has been reached. Suggested definitions by the courts and by the writers have been too vague to be of any practical use.[8]

[1] *R.* v. *Whybrow* (1951) 35 Cr.App.R. 141, where it was held that on an indictment for attempt to murder it is essential to prove an intent to cause death, and that it was a misdirection to tell the jury that they could find the prisoner guilty if they were of opinion that his intention was to cause grievous bodily harm.

[2] *Ante*, ¶ 32.

[3] E.g. *Parker* v. *Alder* [1899] 1 Q.B. 20.

[4] See *Gardner* v. *Ackeroyd* [1952] 2 All E.R. 306 (*T.A.C.*).

[5] *Ante*, ¶ 24.

[6] A man may go through certain motions in an apparent attempt when he is convinced that he cannot succeed; this is, however, no real attempt at all, since his intention is not to succeed but to demonstrate his incapacity to do so. If, on the other hand, although without hope, he honestly tries, then he makes a real attempt.

[7] E.g. the Offences against the Person Act, 1861, s. 18; ¶ 159 *post*.

[8] E.g. 'Acts remotely leading to the commission of the offence are not to be considered as attempts to commit it, but acts immediately connected with it are'; *R.* v. *Robinson* (1915) 11 Cr.App.R. 124, at p. 129 citing Parke, B., in *R.* v. *Eagleton* (1855) Dearsly 515. This was followed in *Hope* v. *Brown* [1954] 1 W.L.R. 250, a case which is critically examined in Russ. 190, where it is submitted that Parke, B.'s dictum is not, and was not intended to be, a definition of the *actus reus* of attempt. Contrast Coleridge, J., in

The solution of this problem, however, is not difficult if one or two fundamental points are kept in mind. These are that in all crimes an *actus reus* must consist in a deed (i.e. a result of human conduct; *ante*, ¶ 12), and in attempt the deed must be one performed *in actual furtherance of the crime intended*. And, in addition, that deed must be such that it raises a presumption that the accused was aiming at the crime in question. In other words the accused must have actually done things which are steps intentionally taken in furtherance[1] of some specific aim, and which themselves are enough to suggest clearly what that specific aim was. This is the position in most of the cases of criminal attempts which come before the courts, since the accused person usually denies any criminal aim at all (i.e. he denies *mens rea*), and if convicted is convicted solely on the evidence of what he did, which the tribunal regards as enough to establish his guilty intention. It is true that the criminality of the attempt lies in the intention, the *mens rea*, but this *mens rea* must be evidenced by what the accused has *actually done towards the attainment of his ultimate objective*. Thus the *actus reus* of attempt is reached in *such act of performance* as first gives clear *prima facie* evidence of the *mens rea*.[2] It must be noted that a man may well desire to produce more than one result by his adopted course of action; but provided he has done enough to make manifest his purpose to achieve the particular result which the prosecution has chosen as the basis of the charge brought against him, this is enough; and so long as his course of action *does clearly indicate this one* it is immaterial that his conduct points to another aim also. Other evidence of *mens rea* (such as a confession by the accused), *not* yielded by some act done in furtherance of the ultimate crime, must be disregarded as irrelevant to the question whether the *actus reus* has been reached. The case of *R.* v. *Robinson*[3] gives a good illustration of this point. In that case R., a jeweller, had insured his stock against burglary and theft. He subsequently hid some jewellery under his safe and, after binding himself up with cords, called for assistance. A police officer entered the shop and R. stated that he had locked all his jewellery in the safe and was going upstairs when he was attacked from behind by a stranger who had tied him up and rifled the safe, which was seen by the officer to be open and empty. The officer was suspicious of the story, took R. to the police station to make a statement, and in his absence the shop was searched and the jewellery discovered under the safe. When R. was told this he confessed that his story was a lie and that his intention had been to obtain from the underwriters the amount for which the jewellery had been insured. He was charged with attempting to obtain the money

Dugdale v. *R.* (1853) 1 E. and B. at p. 439, to the effect that 'the first step towards the committing of the misdemeanour' would be sufficient. See Russ. 189 *et seq.*

[1] For the meaning to be given to the word 'furtherance', see ¶ 114 *post.*

[2] See Archbold, 33rd ed. 1954, 1489. Wightman, J., observed in *R.* v. *Roberts* (1855) Dearsly 539, at p. 551, 'In truth the prisoner could have had no other object than to commit the offence'. This of course, as indicated above, was too narrow to form a general definition, although quite true of the evidence in the case before his lordship.

[3] [1915] 2 K.B. 342; 11 Cr.App.R. 124 (*T.A.C.*).

by false pretences and convicted, but his conviction was quashed by the Court of Criminal Appeal on the ground that his acts of preparation had not reached the point which the law requires. The court, however, did not enunciate any clear guiding principle which should be applied to decide this point. But on the test submitted above it is clear that the confession, not being a step taken by R. in furtherance of his end, was irrelevant to the question of *actus reus*, and if he had not made the confession his acts would not have suggested beyond reasonable doubt that he intended the specific crime alleged in the indictment, namely the defrauding of the underwriters. Doubtless they showed some reprehensible intention or other, but no one offence with sufficient clearness to support a charge of criminal attempt to commit that offence.[1] If R. had gone so far as to fill in a form of claim against the underwriters or to have written a letter to them telling his false story (even though he had not yet posted it), this would have been part of his performance of the ultimate crime, which would have clearly raised a *prima facie* presumption of his *mens rea*.[2]

Again, if a man were to tell a friend beforehand that he intended to murder *X*, evidence that he then procured a knife and took the train to the place where *X* lived would not be enough to establish the *actus reus* of attempt to murder, since the statement of his intention was not part of the performance of that intention, and without the knowledge of the man's statement it would not have been reasonable to suppose that the discovery of a man at a railway station in possession of a knife was *prima facie* evidence of his intention to murder *X*, or indeed anyone else. If, however, a man on returning home late at night found that he had lost his house key and, not wishing to disturb the household, were trying to climb in through a window, his conduct would raise a *prima facie* presumption that he was a wrongdoer whose intention was to commit burglary, that is to say he would have performed the *actus reus* of attempted burglary. He would of course be able to rebut the presumption of *mens rea* by proving his identity and true purpose.[3]

The test suggested above was in effect adopted in *R.* v. *Miskell* in 1954.[4]

Miskell, the appellant, had been convicted of attempting to procure an act of gross indecency with a male person.[5] In dismissing the appeal the Courts Martial Appeal Court said: 'The conduct of the appellant immediately

[1] See also *R.* v. *Woods* (1930) 22 Cr.App.R. 41. There was evidence that Robinson had insured his stock a little over one month before he put his plan into operation. It may perhaps be thought that this fact, taken with the rest of his acts, might be just enough to raise the necessary presumption against him; but there is nothing in the report to suggest that the prosecution or the court applied their minds to this point at all.

[2] On the same facts as those in *R.* v. *Robinson*, an offender could now be convicted of public mischief; see ¶ 445 *post*.

[3] For a fuller discussion of the *actus reus* in attempt see *Mod. Appr. Crim. Law*, 278, and Russ. ch. 6.

[4] 1 W.L.R. 438; 1 All E.R. 137; see Russ. 196.

[5] Contrary to sect. 11 of the Criminal Law Amendment Act, 1885 (now repealed, and replaced by sect. 13 of the Sexual Offences Act, 1956).

before and at the time of the invitation, in our view, manifested his purpose in inviting the boy to meet him the next evening.... That conduct made manifest the purpose of the invitation and the meeting and the suggestion of another walk.'[1]

R. v. *Miskell* was approved and followed in *R.* v. *Gammon*,[2] as a case in which 'the acts were such as to make it perfectly clear that an immoral purpose was in mind'.

ATTEMPTS TO DO THAT WHICH IS IMPOSSIBLE

¶ 64. As we have seen, attempt as a distinct crime at common law is relatively modern, and this may account for some of the obscurities as to its principles. Thus it was for some time supposed that it would be no crime if a man attempted to do that which in fact it was impossible to perform. This fallacy was due to a misunderstanding of a case tried in 1857.[3] However, it is now established[4] that impossibility of performance does not *per se* render the attempt guiltless; thus it is a criminal attempt to steal when a man, with that intention, puts his hand into a pocket which is empty. It has been suggested, however, that it would not be a criminal attempt to murder if a man fired a gun at a wooden post under the belief that it was his living enemy,[5] and even that a distinction can be drawn between what is impossible and what is 'absolutely impossible'. These doubts are illusory, for there can be no degrees of impossibility: it is no less impossible for any one to steal from an empty pocket than it is to kill a man already dead or to kill a man by shooting at a post when he is not near. The supposed difficulty is due to a failure to appreciate the true test for attempt. In all cases the prosecution must prove the *actus reus* and the *mens rea*, and the point is really one of evidence. The picture of a man shooting at a post by itself does not suggest an attempt to murder: if, however, there was further evidence that a living man was standing near the post the conclusion to be drawn might well be different.[6]

MERGER OF ATTEMPT WHEN THE CRIME INTENDED IS COMPLETED

¶ 65. It was an early common law rule that a man who had instigated another to commit a felony became himself guilty of the felony[7] as

[1] See *R.* v. *Spicer* (1955) 39 Cr.App.R. 189.

[2] (1959) 43 Cr.App.R. 155.

[3] *R.* v. *M'Pherson* (1857) 1 D. and B. 197; 7 Cox 281. See *Mod. Appr. Crim. Law*, 286.

[4] Since the decisions in *R.* v. *Brown* (1889) L.J.M.C. 47; (1890) 24 Q.B.D. 357; and *R.* v. *Ring* (1892) L.J.M.C. 116; 17 Cox 491; *R.* v. *Brown and others* (1899) 63 J.P. 790. In *Munah Binti Ali* v. *Public Prosecutor* (1958) 24 M.L.J. 159, the Court of Appeal in Malaya held that one who acted with intent to cause a miscarriage could be found guilty of attempt, notwithstanding that the woman was not pregnant.

[5] *R.* v. *Osborn* (1919) 84 J.P. 63, 'It is not a question of impossibility, the man is never on the thing at all', *per* Rowlatt, J.

[6] For a fuller discussion of attempts to do what is impossible see *Mod. Appr. Crim. Law*, 285 *et seq.*, and Russ. 197 *et seq.* And note the curious case of *R.* v. *Moran* (1952 36 Cr.App.R. 10, discussed in Russ. 994.

[7] *Post*, ¶ 69.

accessory before the fact, if the felony was actually committed. When the law came to recognize that the instigation was a misdemeanour if the crime instigated was not effected, the position was reached in which it could be said that the misdemeanour merged in the felony if the crime was committed. This led to the establishment of a like rule for attempts and it was laid down in decided cases that if the attempt were successful the preliminary offence of attempt disappeared since the misdemeanour merged in the felony.[1] A consideration of the authorities leads to the conclusion that this rule that attempt merges in the completed crime was not due to any peculiarity in the nature of an attempt but was merely a fortuitous doctrine of the common law.[2] It only applied when the attempt was a misdemeanour and the intended crime a felony. If both the attempt and the ultimate crime were felonies[3] or both were misdemeanours[4] there would be no merger. In *Rogers* v. *Arnott*[5] the Queen's Bench Divisional Court upheld an acquittal on a charge of attempted larceny where the evidence disclosed a completed larceny. But in *R.* v. *Males*[6] the Court of Criminal Appeal distinguished *Rogers* v. *Arnott* as a case 'where the matter under consideration was a decision of justices', and held that the Criminal Procedure Act, 1851, in effect abolished the doctrine of merger of attempt in the completed crime since it provides (s. 12)[7] that if, upon the trial of any person for any misdemeanour, it shall appear that the facts given in evidence amount in law to a felony, such person shall not by reason thereof be entitled to be acquitted of such misdemeanour.

[1] *Harmwood's Case* (1787) Winchester Sp. Assizes, cited 1 East P.C. 411. Also *R.* v. *Simpson & Kerrison* (1851) 3 C. and K. 207 and *R.* v. *Nicholls* (1847) 2 Cox 182. And see *R.* v. *Welham* (1845) 1 Cox 192, a considered opinion of Parke, B., and Patteson, J., on the merger doctrine in the particular instance of incitement.

[2] See Russ. 206. It seems not to apply to conspiracy; ¶ 448 *post*.

[3] E.g. attempt to murder is a statutory felony.

[4] E.g. in several cases of malicious damage (Malicious Damage Act, 1861). Though not decided on the point of merger, the case of *R.* v. *Percy Dalton (London)* (1949) 65 T.L.R. 326, is interesting in this connexion.

[5] [1960] 2 All E.R. 417.

[6] [1961] 3 All E.R. 705.

[7] It could have been argued that the purpose of the Act of 1851 was purely procedural, to obviate the rigidity of difference in form of the indictment for felony from that for misdemeanour (eventually cured by the Indictments Act, 1915) and not to alter the substantive law. The cases cited are inconclusive; *R.* v. *Evans* (1833) turned on the point of statutory interpretation (*post*, ¶ 398); in *R.* v. *Garland* (1909) 22 Cox 292 the point of appeal was that the indictment was on its face defective since it was framed for the misdemeanour of receiving property alleged therein to have been feloniously stolen, and not with feloniously receiving it. The Court of Criminal Appeal held the indictment to be good by virtue of s. 12 of the Crim. Procedure Act, 1851, adding that it was not necessary to decide the point that, as contended by the prosecution, this common law misdemeanour would not merge in the statutory felony (under s. 91 of the Larceny Act, 1861) on the submitted principle that 'offences created by statute are cumulative upon and not in substitution for offences at common law', although the court expressed an inclination to think that suggestion to be a right one. Nor is *R.* v. *Loughlin* [1959] Crim. L.R. 518 decisive since the accused had pleaded guilty to the misdemeanour and his conviction of the felony was quashed, the question of merger not being argued, so far as can be seen.

It is in effect provided by section 9 of the above Act that on the trial of any person for felony or misdemeanour if it appears to the jury that the accused did not complete the offence charged but that he was guilty of an attempt to do so the jury may find the accused not guilty of the offence charged but guilty of an attempt to commit the same.[1]

An attempt at common law is a common law misdemeanour and the court is not limited in the amount of imprisonment to which it may sentence the person guilty of it;[2] but the Court of Criminal Appeal have stated[3] that the term ought not to exceed the maximum which could be ordered for the completed offence.

[1] From *R.* v. *White* [1910] 2 K.B. 124 it seems that this section applies whether an attempt to commit the particular crime be a misdemeanour or a felony.

[2] *R.* v. *Morris* [1951] 1 K.B. 394.

[3] *R.* v. *Pearce* [1952] 2 All E.R. 718.

Chapter V

THE POSSIBLE PARTIES TO A CRIME

Section I. Introductory

¶ 66. Crimes are often grouped by English lawyers into three classes—treasons, felonies and misdemeanours. In the gravest, and also in the least grave, of these three, no legal distinction, either of substance or even of form, is drawn between the various recognized modes of taking part in the commission of them. For the guilt of even the slightest share in any treason is regarded as being so heinous that it is needless to distinguish it from still deeper shades of guilt. And, on the other hand, no activity in a misdemeanour is considered heinous enough to make it worth while to draw a *formal* distinction between it and any less prominent mode of taking part in the offence.[1] Hence if a crime belongs to either of these two opposite extremes, all persons who are concerned in it in any way—whether by actually committing it, or only by keeping near in order to assist whilst it is being committed, or merely by suggesting its commission—are indiscriminately classed together by the law as being alike 'principals' in the offence.

But in the intermediate group of crimes, viz. felonies, the rules of the common law were more complicated,[2] and formal notice was taken of gradations of participation in them. Thus it was an ancient principle of the common law that no accessory could be convicted or suffer any punishment where the principal offender was not attainted, or had the benefit of his clergy (*ante*, ¶ 55). As the result of this, if the principal fled the country, or died, or had his clergy, or was pardoned, the accessory went free. In the interests of the Crown, however, the courts held that any kind of participation in treason made the participant a principal. Treason, of course, was never clergyable. These old difficulties have now been removed by a series of legislative enactments, but the gradations of guilt which arise from the various ways in which a man may be concerned in a single crime are still distinguished, though their practical importance has now almost entirely disappeared. An accurate comprehension of the distinctions is, however, still of great value to the student[3] as enabling him, not merely in felonies but also in treasons and misdemeanours, to trace with precision the lines at which the law ceases to take notice of participation in a crime—the stages, in other words, where complicity ends and immunity begins. Four several categories of guilty association with a felony are recognized: (1) a principal

[1] *Gould and Co. Ltd.* v. *Houghton* [1921] 1 K.B. 509.

[2] See Stephen, *Hist. Crim. Law*, II, 221–41; Pollock and Maitland, II, 507–9.

[3] It is indeed essential for the proper understanding of many old cases which are frequently cited in argument at the present day.

in the first degree, (2) a principal in the second degree (often called an 'aider and abettor'[1]), (3) an accessory before the fact, (4) an accessory after the fact.[2]

Students should at the outset note carefully that for the purposes of the law of principals and accessories there is one crime only,[3] although more than one person may be held criminally responsible for its commission. When, therefore, two or more persons have engaged in a crime there arises the question into which of the above classes of participator is each to be placed.[4] It must also be remembered that in *statutory* offences the statute may be sometimes so worded as to create a variation in liability in any of the categories of participation; therefore the words of the statute, and their interpretation by the courts, must always be carefully studied.[5]

It must also be observed that the somewhat subtle distinctions drawn between the different categories of participation in a *crime* have no proper relevance in our civil law of contract and tort, in which field the basic rule, *qui facit per alium facit per se*, is all that is needed. If this be borne in mind difficulties that at first sight may seem to arise in such civil proceedings as *Saqui and Lawrence* v. *Stearns* [1911] 1 K.B. 426, will be found to disappear.[6]

Again there must be remembered the change introduced, in cases of participation in felonious homicides, by the Homicide Act, 1957, under which by virtue of section 2 a person suffering from 'diminished responsibility'[7] who has been a party to the killing of another shall not be liable (irrespective of what may be the liability of any other party to the homicide) to be convicted of murder (subsect. 1) but shall be liable to be convicted of manslaughter (subsect. 3); and by virtue of section 4 (1) a party to a 'suicide pact'[8] shall not be guilty of murder, but of manslaughter, if he kills the other or was a party to the other's being killed. And by virtue of section 5 (2) in cases of capital murder within subsection (1) where more than one person is guilty of the murder it is not a capital murder in any of them who did not by his own act cause the death, or inflict or attempt to inflict grievous bodily harm on the victim, or himself use force on the victim in the course or furtherance of an attack on him.

[1] Styled 'accessory at the fact' by ancient writers; Foster 347.

[2] Whose offence is a distinct and different crime although dependent on the 'fact' of the felony; *Mahadeo* v. *R.* [1936] 2 All E.R. 813; *post,* ¶ 71.

[3] *Surujpaul v. R.* [1958] 1 W.L.R. 1050 at p. 1053.

[4] See Russ. ch. 5. Of course one who advises or instigates another to commit a felony is himself at once guilty of the common law misdemeanour of incitement (*ante,* ¶ 58) of which he may be convicted if the felony be not carried out; but incitement is a different offence from the crime solicited and it is only if and after the latter crime has been committed that the law of principal and accessory comes into operation. Modern examples are *Morris* v. *Tolman* [1923] 1 K.B. 166 and *Thornton* v. *Mitchell* [1940] 1 All E.R. 339.

[5] See Foster 355 *et seq.*

[6] See the discussion of this case in Russ. 11th ed. 149 *et seq.*

[7] *Ante,* ¶ 53*a.*

[8] *Post,* ¶ 127.

Furthermore we must note the curiously anomalous position created by section (1) of the Suicide Act, 1961, whereby it is made a substantive offence[1] by any person who 'aids, abets, counsels or procures' the suicide of another, although the Act, in section 1, makes it no crime for a person to commit suicide.[2]

Section 2. Principals in the First Degree

¶ 67. By a principal in the first degree, we mean the actual offender—the man in whose guilty mind lay the latest blamable mental cause of the criminal act. Almost always, of course, he will be the man by whom this act itself was done. But occasionally this will not be so; for the felony may have been committed by the hand of an innocent agent who, having no blamable intentions in what he did, incurred no criminal liability by doing it. In such a case the man who instigates this agent is the real offender; his was the last *mens rea* that preceded the crime, though it did not cause it immediately but mediately. Thus, if a physician provides a poisonous draught and tells a nurse that it is the medicine to be administered to her patient, and then by her administration of it the patient is killed, the murderous physician—and not the innocent nurse—is the 'principal in the first degree'.[3] Similarly, if a man sends a six-year-old child[4] into a shop to steal something out of it for him, the man himself will be the principal in the first degree in this theft. Thus if you hand in to your master's book-keeper a lying statement of money matters, and he believes it and makes entry of it, you are yourself indictable for the offence of 'falsifying' the master's account-books in which the untrue statement was so entered.[5] Even an animal may be employed as an 'innocent agent'. For, just as anyone who sets a dog upon people is himself guilty of assaulting them, so any one who should send his trained retriever to purloin meat from a butcher's stall might be convicted of the larceny of the meat, as a principal in the first degree; and this, even though he were out of sight when the dog took it.

There may, of course, be more than one principal in the first degree. Thus if a dishonest servant in the night time unlocks the door of his master's house and admits a confederate who enters in order to steal therein, both men are guilty of burglary as principals in the first degree.[6] So both the father and the mother of a little child may have together concurred in starving it; or one man may hold the victim in order that another may cut his throat, as Bramwell, B., said.[7] And persons may be

[1] Punishable with a maximum of fourteen years' imprisonment, but not a felony.

[2] *Post*, ¶ 127.

[3] Kel. 52 (*T.A.C.*); *R.* v. *Saunders and Archer* (1576) 2 Plowden 473, *post*, p. 112.

[4] *R.* v. *Manley* (1844) 1 Cox 104 (*T.A.C.*).

[5] *R.* v. *Butt* (1884) 15 Cox 564. *Post*, ¶ 323.

[6] And so in stealing, *R.* v. *Hornby* (1844) 1 C. and K. 305; *R.* v. *Kelly* (1847) 2 C. and K. 379; and manslaughter, *R.* v. *Haines* (1847) 2 C. and K. 368.

[7] In *R.* v. *Jackson* (1857) 7 Cox 357.

thus joint principals in the first degree, even though one of them commits his share of the crime in one town whilst his colleague commits his in another.[1]

It should be remembered that a person who takes part in a treason,[2] or a misdemeanour,[3] or a summary offence,[4] is liable, and is charged, in exactly the same way whether he instigated or himself committed, or aided and abetted the crime.

Section 3. Principals in the Second Degree: Aiders and Abettors

¶ 68. A person can aid and abet another in the perpetration of a crime of any category, and at common law has always been equally punishable with the actual doer of the deed. In ancient times the writers on our law regarded and referred to a person who was present and who encouraged or assisted in any way the man who effected the crime, simply as an 'accessory at the fact'. But in those days the strict rule that any accessory, whether before, at, or after the fact, could not be brought to justice until that fact had been established by the conviction or outlawry of the principal offender often led to the accessory's going free as the result of the principal's death, pardon, successful evasion of apprehension, or having his clergy.[5] From this predicament the judges extricated the administration of justice by a gradual change of terminology whereby the mischievous expression 'accessory at the fact' was replaced by 'principal in the second degree'. Even then there was also a wider rule that had to be carefully observed, namely, that the indictment must always state exactly the offence charged, so that the category of participation had to be declared in it; and from this no variance was allowed, the result being that the prosecution must fail unless the evidence clearly established the kind of participation alleged.[6] The awkwardness of this situation was reduced little by little by the legislature,[7] and was finally removed by the Accessories and Abettors Act,

[1] *R.* v. *Bingley* (1821) R. and R. 446; *R.* v. *Kirkwood* (1831) 1 Moo. 304.

[2] Foster 341; Stephen, *Hist. Crim. Law*, II, 233.

[3] *R.* v. *Burton* (1875) 39 J.P. 532.

[4] *Benford* v. *Sims* [1898] 2 Q.B. 641. See Magistrates' Courts Act, 1952, s. 35.

[5] 40 Ass. 25; 40 Ed. II, c. 42*a*. See Stephen, *Hist. Crim. Law*, I, 458 *et seq.* and II, 235.

[6] *Heydon's Case* (1585) 4 Co. Rep. 42*b*; *R.* v. *Gordon* (1789) 1 Leach 515; *R.* v. *Stewart* (1818) R. and R. 363. This is the explanation of the judge's ruling in *R.* v. *Brown* (1878) 14 Cox 144, directing the acquittal of the accused who had been *charged in the indictment* as accessory before the fact, whereas the evidence adduced by the prosecution merely showed that she was actually present at the time of the deed, in which case she participated as principal in the second degree. This result would, it is submitted, follow at the present day if the prosecution made a similar mistake; see Russ. 166, and *R.* v. *Adair*, *infra*.

[7] See Stephen, *Hist. Crim. Law*, II, 235. Cases decided during this transitional period must be carefully read, since many of them turned on rules of law and the interpretation of statutes now obsolete: see for example *R.* v. *Murphy* (1853) 6 Cox 340 (on 7 Will. IV and 1 Vict. c. 86); *R.* v. *Gogerly* (1818) R. and R. 343 and *R.* v. *Byford* (1823) R. and R. 521 were cases on the ouster of benefit of clergy.

1861,[1] which deals solely[2] with the rules of procedure, and in effect allows the prosecution the option of indicting an accessory before the fact as if he were a principal felon, and an accessory after the fact (of felony) as a felon, in each instance whether or not the actual doer of the felonious deed has been previously convicted or is amenable to justice.[3] But in each case it must be established that the alleged felony *has been committed*.

A principal in the second degree is one by whom the actual perpetrator of the felony is aided and abetted at the very time when it is committed; for instance, a car-owner sitting beside the chauffeur or other person driving the car[4] who kills someone by over-fast driving, or a passenger on a clandestine joy-riding expedition which results in manslaughter;[5] or a bigamist's second 'spouse' if he or she knows the true facts. It is important to note that, for the purpose of the rules relating to evidence given by an accomplice (*post*, ¶ 602), receivers of stolen goods are treated as accomplices of the thieves from whom they have received them,[6] although a receiver as such is neither an aider and abettor, nor an accessory after the fact. But the thief himself is regarded as the aider and abettor of the guilty receiver to whom he passes the stolen property;[7] as is also that receiver, if and when he passes on the stolen property to a second guilty receiver.

This subordinate principal may or may not be actually present at the scene of the crime; the essential point is that *while the crime is being committed* the accomplice should be rendering aid, assistance, or encouragement. Thus he may be keeping watch and ward near at hand, or can be aiding by distracting someone's attention a long distance away. Accordingly when *A* is inside a house, committing a burglary, *B* and *C* may be waiting outside it, ready to help him in carrying off the plunder or

[1] Space does not permit the reproduction of the provisions of this important statute, but they may be seen in Russ. 167.

[2] See *R.* v. *Adair* [1958] 2 All E.R. 629, in which the Court of Criminal Appeal quashed the conviction of the appellant, A., who had been found guilty as accessory before the fact to a burglary on a count in the indictment which charged him simply with burglary, there being however no evidence before the jury of his having done anything which would have constituted him an accessory before the fact.

[3] The Act also, by section 8, renders anyone who shall aid, abet, counsel, or procure the commission of any misdemeanour (whether at common law or under statute) liable to be tried, indicted, and punished as a principal offender. And see, as to summary offences, the Magistrates' Courts Act, 1952, s. 35.

[4] *Du Cros* v. *Lambourne* [1901] 1 K.B. 40; *Rubie* v. *Faulkner* [1940] 1 K.B. 571.

[5] *R.* v. *Baldessare* (1930) 22 Cr.App.R. 70; 144 L.T. 185. And see *R.* v. *Swindall and Osborne* (1846) 2 C. and K. 230 (*T.A.C.*); contrast *R.* v. *Mastin* (1834) 6 C. and P. 396. See *R.* v. *Coney* (1882) 8 Q.B.D. 534 at p. 536: 'The surgeon who attends a duel, to *save* the lives imperilled, attends it as a criminal.' But sitting on the pillion seat of a motorcycle is not *per se* enough evidence to establish a joint enterprise, *R.* v. *Parsons* [1960] 1 W.L.R. 797.

[6] See *Davies* v. *D.P.P.* [1954] A.C. 378. A receiver was declared by the Larceny Act, 1827 (now repealed), to be an accessory after the fact to the thief.

[7] *R.* v. *Norris* (1916) 12 Cr.App.R. 156; *Carter Paterson & Pickford's* v. *Wessel* [1947] K.B. 849.

to protect him by giving warning of the approach of the police.[1] A prize-fight used often to have sentinels thus on the alert. In a case in Ohio, a man who invited a shopkeeper to accompany him to a convivial gathering, and took care to keep him agreeably occupied at it while some accomplices broke into his shop, was held to have been giving, even at the moment of the burglary, a sufficiently effective assistance in it to render him a principal in the second degree.[2]

Yet, to be guilty of aiding and abetting, a person must at the critical time either render effective aid to the principal offender or else must be present and in some way lend encouragement to him in what he is doing;[3] but an encouraging acquiescence sufficient to constitute the offence may be established by evidence of the accused person's motive and of his *subsequent* conduct.[4]

It follows that the aider and abettor must have knowledge of what is afoot; as was stated in a modern case 'before a person can be convicted of aiding and abetting the commission of an offence, he must at least know the essential matters which constitute the offence'.[5] On the other hand a man who does something which he knows will assist a crime which is going on is liable as an aider and abettor even though the main offender is unaware of this support, or even objects to it.[6]

If, however, there is no evidence of encouragement by him, a man's presence at the scene of the crime will not suffice to render him liable as an aider and abettor.[7] The encouragement must be intentional.[8]

The principal in the first degree and the aider and abettor must have a common purpose existing at the time when the felony is being committed;[9] but it is not essential that there should have been between them any agreement as to what the principal in the first degree should

[1] 1 Hale P.C. 439; Foster, 350. Cf. *R.* v. *Griffith* (1553) 1 Plowden 97 (*T.A.C.*); *R.* v. *Jordan and Sullivan* (1836) 7 C. and P. 432; *R.* v. *Betts and Ridley* (1930) 144 L.T. 526; 22 Cr.App.R. 148.

[2] *Breese* v. *The State* (1861) 12 Ohio 146.

[3] In *R.* v. *Craig and Bentley* (1952) *The Times*, 10–13 December, the prisoner Bentley was held guilty of murder in aiding and abetting Craig by encouraging him to shoot a policeman after he himself had been seized by another officer, who thus held him under arrest. See now sect. 5 (2) of the Homicide Act, 1957; *post*, p. 148.

[4] *Wilcox* v. *Jeffery* [1951] 1 All E.R. 464. In *National Coal Board* v. *Gamble* [1958] 3 All E.R. 203, completing a sale of goods loaded on a lorry, with knowledge that the lorry had been overloaded and would be illegally driven on the road, was held to be an aiding and abetting of the unlawful use of the lorry.

[5] *Per* Lord Goddard, C.J., in *Johnson* v. *Youden* [1950] 1 K.B. 544, cited in *Ferguson* v. *Weaving* [1951] 1 All E.R. 412 at p. 414; see also *Thomas* v. *Lindop* [1953] 1 All E.R. 966; *Davis, Turner & Co.* v. *Brodie* [1954] 1 W.L.R. 1364 at p. 1368; *Poultry World* v. *Conder* [1957] Crim. L.R. 803.

[6] See *R.* v. *Kupferberg* (1918) 13 Cr.App.R. 166.

[7] *R.* v. *Kelly* (1820) R. and R. 421; *R.* v. *Coney* (1882) 8 Q.B.D. 534 at p. 539. Cf. *R.* v. *Gray* (1917) 12 Cr.App.R. at p. 246.

[8] 'A man may unwittingly encourage another in fact by his presence, by misinterpreted words, or by his silence, or non-interference; or he may encourage intentionally by expression, gestures or actions intended to signify approval. In the latter case he aids and abets, in the former he does not.' *Per* Hawkins, J., in *R.* v. *Coney* (1882) 8 Q.B.D at p. 557.

[9] *R.* v. *Hilton* (1858) 1 Bell 20; *R.* v. *Short* (1932) 23 Cr.App.R. 170.

do, still less, that an agreement in express terms should have been made.[1] In certain cases of suicide pact[2] the evidence may not establish the incitement of the one party by the other, but merely that knowledge of their respective intentions operated as a mutual encouragement so as to make each the abettor of the other's suicide.[3]

It is not necessary that there should have been any such previous agreement as would constitute a conspiracy,[4] although, of course, there will very often be such a conspiratorial agreement. Where the parties are proved in fact to have been conspirators then the purely inactive presence of one may, and usually will, operate as encouragement and thus make him guilty of abetting:[5] but, as in all cases of aiding and abetting, it is a question of fact for the jury.

A person who is incapable of being a principal in the first degree in the crime committed may yet be a principal in the second degree; such will be the position in a case of rape[6] if a boy under fourteen,[7] or a woman,[8] has aided and abetted this felony.[9] A man may support and encourage (and thereby 'abet') a principal in the latter's course of action without necessarily intending the same consequences as the principal, that is to say, the *mens rea* of each may be different, and if so the respective guilt of the two men may also be different.[10]

SECTION 4. ACCESSORIES BEFORE THE FACT

¶ 69. An accessory before the fact[11] is a person who 'being absent at the time of the felony committed, doth yet procure, counsel, commend, or abet to commit a felony'.[12] From the old authorities[13] the essential elements[14] which made a man an accessory before the fact were (*a*) that he

[1] *Sissinghurst House Case* (1673) 1 Hale 462; *R.* v. *Pridmore* (1913) 8 Cr.App.R. 198, explained in *R.* v. *Appleby* (1940) 28 Cr.App.R. 1.

[2] *Post*, ¶ 127.

[3] *Anon.* (1604) Moore K.B. 754; *R.* v. *Dyson* (1823) R. and R. 523.

[4] *R.* v. *Kupferberg* (1918) 13 Cr.App.R. 166.

[5] Foster, 350–2; see *R.* v. *Plummer* (1701) Kel. (J.) 109.

[6] *Post*, ¶ 143.

[7] 1 Hale P.C. 636; *R.* v. *Eldershaw* (1828) 3 C. and P. 396. The cases on sodomy present difficulties; see the discussion of *R.* v. *Cratchley* (1913) 9 Cr.App.R. 232 and *R.* v. *Tatam* (1921) 15 Cr.App.R. 132, in Russ. 143 *et seq.*

[8] *R.* v. *Lord Baltimore* (1768) 4 Burr. 2179; *R.* v. *Ram* (1893) 17 Cox 609.

[9] Difficult questions as to the effect of consent in various kinds of sexual offences are discussed in Russ. 140 *et seq.*; see especially p. 143, where *R.* v. *Bourne* (1952) 36 Cr.App.R. 125 is examined.

[10] 1 East P.C. 350: 'Several persons present at the death of a man may be charged with different degrees of homicide..., as one with murder, another with manslaughter. For if there be no malice in the party striking but malice in the abettor, it will be murder in the latter, though only manslaughter in the former.' See also *R.* v. *Murtagh and Kennedy* (1955) *The Times*, 22 March, for the converse case; 39 Cr.App.R. 72.

[11] See Coke's explanation of the Statute of Westminster I, c. 14, discussed in Russ. 159 *et seq.* And see Pollock and Maitland, II, 509; and Sayre, 'Criminal responsibility for the acts of another', 43 *Harvard L.R.* 689.

[12] 1 Hale P.C. 615; Hawk. 2 P.C., c. 29, sect. 16.

[13] Coke, Hale, Foster and Hawkins; see Russ. 160.

[14] In most cases, of course, the accessory does more than the bare minimum.

must have known the particular deed contemplated; (*b*) that he assented to or approved of it; (*c*) that his view of it was expressed in some form which operated to encourage the principal to perform the deed; and (*d*) that those first three elements came into existence before the time when the offence was being committed.[1]

Some cases have been thought to raise a little difficulty.

In *R.* v. *Taylor*[2] the prisoner had held the stakes for a prize-fight in the course of which one of the pugilists was killed. Cockburn, C.J., said: 'At first I was struck with the view that the stakes were something essential to the fight and that the prisoner by holding the stakes might be said to participate in the fight. But I do not think that mere consent to hold the stakes can be said to be such a participation as is necessary to support the conviction.'

This dictum certainly seems to cut down the scope of liability laid down by all the earlier authorities.[3]

Here again mere knowledge, without evidence of encouragement, will not be enough;[4] and the encouragement must be intentional as in the case of an aider and abettor.[5]

In *R.* v. *Lomas*[6] it appeared that the accused man was bailee of a burglar's jemmy which he handed to the bailor, *K*, at his request, knowing that *K* wanted it for some burglary or other but not knowing or seeking to know on what particular house, or when, *K* was going to make his attack. Since the case went up to the Court of Criminal Appeal on a special verdict of the jury as to the facts, the court could not look outside the words of that verdict, the material part being '*L*...handed the jemmy to *K* with the knowledge that it was wanted for a burglary. He did not know that it was wanted for this burglary.' The court held that the question of law before them was whether on this finding by the jury the appellant was accessory before the fact to this burglary, and quashed the conviction because in their view on the facts so found the case was not within the definition as counsel for the prosecution had framed it, a definition upon which they did not wish to express any opinion as to whether it was right or wrong.

[1] If, as may well often happen, the accessory before the fact goes further and lends help or encouragement while the crime is taking place, then he adds to his participation by becoming also an accessory at the fact, an aider and abettor; and he could be charged with that participation in a second count of the indictment. Now, of course, this is unnecessary (and would be unwise) since the prosecution would take advantage of the provisions of the Accessories and Abettors Act, 1861; *ante*, p. 107. On the question of wording the charge, see *Pope* v. *Minton* [1954] Crim. L.R. 711.

[2] (1875) L.R. 2 C.C.R. 147.

[3] And see Stephen, *Hist. Crim. Law*, III, 8, for a similar narrowness of view, unless his remarks mean that the messenger of bad news had studiously avoided any suggestion as to what the hearer should do.

[4] Hale 1 P.C. 616; Hawk. 2 P.C., c. 29, s. 23; *R.* v. *Fretwell* (1862) L. and C. 161 (it would seem that Fretwell might have been successfully charged under section 59 of the Offences against the Person Act, 1861).

[5] *Ante*, ¶ 68.

[6] (1913) 9 Cr.App.R. 220.

Since the court was bound by the words of the special verdict, which showed that *L* had no exact knowledge of any specific burglary and did not indicate any approval or encouragement by him, it is difficult to see what other decision their lordships could have reached. In *R.* v. *Bullock*,[1] the appellant *B* had been convicted as accessory before the fact by supplying the burglars with a motor car (which he had hired) on each of two occasions to effect a burglary.

In delivering the judgment dismissing his appeal Devlin, J., said:

> In the circumstances of this case once it was plain that the appellant had hired the car and had control of it, it was equally plain, if he knew that it was being used, that he must also have permitted it to be used. He must formally or informally have lent it for that purpose and that was enough...; it must have been borrowed, if borrowed at all, for a specific purpose.

This judgment does not state expressly what is needed in addition to knowledge but it may be suggested that since the jury appear to have been satisfied that *B* did lend the car with knowledge of the use to which it was to be put all the ancient essentials of the crime were really present since the loan of the car was both an aid to its commission and an encouraging approval of it.[2]

The fact that a crime has been committed in a manner different from the mode which the accessory had advised will not excuse him from liability for it. Accordingly if *A* hires *B* to poison *C*, but *B* instead kills *C* by shooting him, *A* is none the less liable as accessory before the fact to *C*'s murder. But a man who has counselled a crime does not become liable as accessory if, instead of any form of the crime suggested, an entirely different offence is committed.[3] Yet where the principal in the first degree who has been instigated makes some mistake in the performance of their common aim, this mistake will not excuse the accessory before the fact unless it will also excuse the principal; so if *A* has hired *B* to murder *C*, and *B* by mistake kills *C*'s twin brother *D* instead, *A* may be convicted as an accessory to *D*'s murder.

It is not always easy to decide whether or not the crime actually committed comes within the terms of the incitement so as to make the inciter legally responsible for it. The courts in some of the older cases tended to take a strict view of the facts.[4] A good illustration is *R.* v.

[1] [1955] 1 W.L.R. 1; the cases of *Lomas* and *Bullock* were elaborately discussed in *Nat. Coal Board* v. *Gamble* [1958] 3 All E.R. 203.

[2] In *R.* v. *Bainbridge* [1959] 3 All E.R. 200, a case of office-breaking, it was held necessary to prove that the accused knew the type of crime that was intended and that the equipment (provided by him) was bought with that in view; but that it was not necessary that he should know the particular premises or the date for the attack. Cf. *R.* v. *Smith* [1961] Curr. Law (Nov.) 327, where S. knew a knife was carried.

[3] Therefore there can be no accessory before the fact in '*voluntary* manslaughter' (i.e. intentional homicide, but committed under sudden provocation and not premeditated). See ¶ 117 *post*. An accessory may argue that no crime has been committed, even though the principal may have pleaded guilty; *Mahadeo* v. *R.* [1936] 2 All E.R. 813. And see *R.* v. *Rowley* [1948] 1 All E.R. 570.

[4] See the cases discussed in Russ. 151 *et seq.*

Saunders and Archer in 1576;[1] Saunders, desiring to kill his wife in order that he might marry another woman, consulted Archer, who advised him to put certain poison in an apple which was then to be given to the wife. Saunders did so (Archer not being present), but the wife after taking a bite from the apple handed it to their child who died of the poison, Saunders, who 'dearly loved' the child, refraining from preventing its eating the apple for fear of discovery. The court, after a little hesitation, agreed that Saunders could be convicted of murder since he 'gave the poison with intent to kill a person and in the giving of it he intended that death should follow'. But they held that Archer could not be convicted as accessory to the murder of the child since his offence 'was the aid and advice which he gave to Saunders, and that was only to kill his wife, and no other...and though by the consequences which followed from the giving of the poison by Saunders, the principal, it so happened that the daughter was killed, yet Archer did not...advise him to kill her...for the poisoning of the daughter is a distinct thing from that to which he was privy'. This decision was well thought out, for the facts, although near the line, are of the same order as if Saunders had changed his mind and on a later occasion had used such poison as Archer had named, in order to murder some quite different person of whom Archer had never heard.

The student should notice that in criminal law the word 'principal' suggests the very converse of the idea which it represents in mercantile law. In the former, as we have seen, an accessory proposes an act, and the 'principal' carries it out.[2] But in the law of contract, and in that of tort, the 'principal' only authorizes an act, and the 'agent' carries it out. Where the same transaction is both a tort and a crime, this double use of the word may cause confusion. For example, if, by an innkeeper's directions, his chamber-maid steals jewels out of a guest's portmanteau, the maid is the 'principal' in a *crime*, wherein her master is an accessory before the fact; whilst she is also the agent in a *tort*, wherein her master is the 'principal'.

It has been long ago declared that if a man had commanded or encouraged another to commit a felony, but had subsequently withdrawn and expressly countermanded his order and support, he would not be liable as an accessory should the principal disregard the cancellation and proceed to commit the felony.[3]

As we have already seen, to participate in a treason (in most cases) or a misdemeanour in either the second or the third of the modes now enumerated would be not only an act of crime but an act which the law does not distinguish (as in the case of felonies) from that of the 'principal in the first degree'; it is immaterial, for technical purposes, whether a misdemeanant was accessory 'at the fact'[4] or before the fact.

[1] 2 Plowden 473.

[2] In *R.* v. *Gunewardine* [1951] 2 All E.R. 290, the words 'an accessory before the fact and, therefore, a principal in the second degree' must be taken to have been uttered *per incuriam*.

[3] 1 Hale 618.

[4] Foster 347.

SECTION 5. ACCESSORIES AFTER THE FACT

¶ 70. The accessory after the fact stands in a fourth and remoter degree of complicity, which in the case of misdemeanours[1] involves no criminal responsibility at all. An accessory of this species is a person who, knowing that a felony has been committed, subsequently shelters or relieves one of the felons (even one who was only an accessory) in such a way as to enable him to elude justice.[2] He may do this, for instance, by concealing a fugitive murderer in his house or supplying him with the means of escape,[3] or by helping a convicted murderer to get out of prison. There must be *mens rea*, an intention to assist the felon.[4] Active assistance to the felon is necessary.[5] Hence merely abstaining (however wilfully) from arresting a known felon, and so leaving him to make his escape, is not enough[6] to make the sympathizer guilty, as an accessory, of the felony itself. But it does make him guilty of the specific misdemeanour of a misprision of felony.[7] Similar passive connivance in a treason would, in like manner, be a misprision of treason. For crimes so grave as felonies or treasons ought to be disclosed to the police authorities by everyone who knows of them. But in the case of misdemeanours there is no such duty. It should be noted that, since it is a wife's duty to aid her husband and to keep his secrets, she incurs no[8] liability (save under special statutory provision[9]), if, after he has committed an offence, even treason, she hides him from justice. But a husband enjoys no similar exemption when he assists a felonious wife; he becomes accessory to her felony. But if the wife, acting alone, receives and assists a felon, her husband being ignorant of the fact, then she is the accessory, and not the husband.[10]

[1] Or of the petty offences punishable summarily.

[2] Concerning an 'accessory by receiptment' within the Statute of Westminster I, Coke (1 *Inst.* 182) says: 'This is understood after the fact done, that is, when one knowing the felonie doth receive the felon, and not only conceale his offence, but favour and aid him that he be not knowne.' Note the words 'and thus evade the justice of the country' in *R.* v. *Butterfield* (1843) 1 Cox 39, which indicate that it is a question of evidence; see [1959] Crim. L.R. at p. 46. See *Sykes,* v. *D.P.P.* [1961] 3 W.L.R. 371 at p. 382.

[3] Or destroying dangerous evidence, *R.* v. *Levy* (1912) 7 Cr.App.R. 61.

[4] *R.* v. *Revuelta* [1959] Crim. L.R. 777; cf. *R.* v. *Matthews* [1950] 1 All E.R. 137.

[5] *R.* v. *Chapple* (1840) 9 C. and P. 355. But it need not be to him *personally*, as *R.* v. *Levy* shows. And a person may be convicted as accessory after the fact though the help he gave was intended directly to assist another such accessory and only *indirectly* to assist the felon; *R.* v. *McKenna and Busby* (1960) 44 Cr.App.R. 63.

[6] 1 Hale P.C. 618–19. *R.* v. *Jones* [1949] 1 K.B. 194 (*T.A.C.*); *R.* v. *Powell* [1956] Crim. L.R. 255. But in Roman-Dutch law it is enough if the accessory associates himself with the principal's offence by merely passive conduct, provided that the intention of the inactivity is to assist the principal to escape, *Nkau Majara* v. *R.* [1954] 2 W.L.R. 771.

[7] If he does not report it; *post,* ¶ 421.

[8] *Ante,* ¶ 45; 1 Hawk. P.C. c. 50, s. 10.

[9] E.g. if he is a deserter from the army; *R.* v. *Davis* (1945), 9 *Journal of Crim. Law,* 81; Army Act, 1955, s. 192; Air Force Act, 1955, s. 192; Naval Discipline Act, 1957, s. 97 (i) (E).

[10] 1 Hale P.C. 621.

SECTION 6. ACCOMPLICES

¶ 71. Even in felonies but little practical importance in substantive law now attaches to the distinctions between the first three of these four classes of 'accomplices'—a term which the law applies to all the *participes criminis*, whatever their degree of 'complicity' in the offence, though popular use generally limits it to those who take only a minor part. For the maximum punishment prescribed for any given crime is the same in the case of all three classes. And, as we have seen, the mischievous rule of the old common law, that the accessories to a crime could not be convicted until their principal was convicted (though he perhaps might be acquitted utterly unjustly or might die before he could be arrested), was abolished by statute in 1861; so that now all accessories whether before or after the fact may be indicted even though the principal felon has not yet been convicted, or even is not amenable to justice.[1] Moreover, as we have also observed, by virtue of the same statute an accessory before the fact and also an aider and abettor may be indicted and convicted as himself a principal. So far as the *indictment* is concerned these provisions are no more than permissive. It is still open to the prosecutor to indict a prisoner expressly as an accessory of one or the other sort; but if he does so he saddles himself with the task of proving that the accused man's participation in crime fell within the category so stated in the indictment.[2] In the converse case, however, i.e. if a principal is indicted as an accessory, he cannot be convicted, for the statute does not touch that situation.

In modern times a much more lenient punishment is awarded to the man who is only an accessory *after* the fact. Instead of being, like accessories before the fact, liable to the same heavy maximum of sentence as the principal, he is punishable with nothing more than two years' imprisonment (except in the case of murder, where the maximum punishment for an accessory after the fact is imprisonment for life).

In the law of procedure, however, and in the law of evidence, the distinction between principals and accessories still claims attention. Thus it must be observed that the Accessories and Abettors Act, 1861, does not permit an accessory *after the fact* to be indicted as a principal. And although that Act abolished (sect. 5) the old rule that an accessory after the fact could not be convicted or punished until after the principal had first been brought to justice and convicted, yet it has been decided that it is improper to accept a plea of guilty from a person so charged until after the guilt of the alleged principal has been established.[3] And since the crime of the principal and that of the offender are different, it is open to the alleged accessory after the fact to plead that the felony in question

[1] Accessories and Abettors Act, 1861.

[2] *R.* v. *Brown* (1878) 14 Cox 144; *ante*, p. 106.

[3] *Surujpaul* v. *R.* [1958] 1 W.L.R. 1050, approving the decision of the C.C.A. in *R.* v. *Rowley* [1948] 1 All E.R. 570 and strongly disapproving *R.* v. *Hughes* (1860) Bell 242; 1 L.T. 450.

was not in fact committed (even though the man accused of it had pleaded guilty and been convicted).[1] Again, the rules relating to corroboration of the evidence of accomplices[2] can give rise to difficulties in certain cases of participation in unlawful sexual conduct and intercourse.[3]

It is scarcely necessary to say that a man may be an accomplice in more than one way to the same act of crime; and thus he may be convicted on one count as an accessory before the fact, and on another count as an accessory after the fact.[4] For that famous and still mysterious crime, the murder of Sir Edmondbury Godfrey in 1678, Atkins (the secretary of Pepys the diarist) was indicted both as an accessory before the fact and also as a principal.[5]

¶ 71 *a*. By the Prison Act, 1952, s. 39,

> Any person who aids any prisoner in escaping or attempting to escape from a prison or who, with intent to facilitate the escape of any prisoner conveys anything into a prison or to a prisoner, or places anything anywhere outside a prison with a view to its coming into the possession of a prisoner, shall be guilty and liable to imprisonment for a term not exceeding two years.[6]

[1] *Mahadeo* v. *R.* [1936] 2 All E.R. 813.

[2] *Post*, ¶¶ 602, 603.

[3] See Russ. 141 *et seq.*

[4] *R.* v. *Blackson and Walker* (1837) 8 C. and P. 43. But evidence that he is merely an accessory after the fact does not support a charge that he is an accessory before the fact, or a principal, *R.* v. *Fitzpatrick* (1926) 19 Cr.App.R. 91.

[5] 6 St.Tr. 1491.

[6] For offences in connexion with prison breaking see Russ. chapters 19, 20, 21.

Chapter VI

THE CLASSIFICATION OF CRIMES

SECTION I. INDICTABLE AND PETTY OFFENCES

¶ 72. Public wrongs, pleas of the crown, or—to use a word more familiar but more ambiguous—crimes, may be arranged, according to their technical degrees of importance, in the following groups.

(*a*) Indictable offences, i.e. those which admit of trial by jury:

(i) treasons,
(ii) (other[1]) felonies,
(iii) misdemeanours.

(*b*) Petty offences, i.e. those which can only be tried summarily, by justices of the peace sitting without a jury.[2]

The word 'crime' is properly applicable to all these; and thus, for instance, in the Judicature Acts[3] the expression 'criminal cause or matter' includes them all. But sometimes more restricted senses have been adopted: as when Serjeant Stephen, in rewriting Blackstone's *Commentaries*, limited crime to 'offences that are indictable'; or when Blackstone himself went still further, and limited it to indictable offences that are graver than misdemeanours.[4]

The two groups, indictable and non-indictable, were originally quite exclusive of each other; but now they overlap to some extent. For, under the Magistrates' Courts Act, 1952, sections 19 and 20,[5] some common indictable offences *may* under certain circumstances be tried summarily instead, whilst all such of the petty offences as are heinous enough to admit of a sentence of imprisonment for over three months *may* instead be tried on indictment.[6]

HISTORICAL

¶ 73. The discussion of the distinction between indictable and non-indictable offences may conveniently be postponed until we reach the subject of procedure. But the mode in which indictable offences themselves are subdivided springs from so noteworthy a historical

[1] For 'felony' *properly* includes treasons. *Post*, ¶ 73.

[2] Commonly, and sometimes even officially, styled 'summary offences'. 'Misdemeanour' in a wide sense includes these as 'petty misdemeanours', and means any offence below felony (*Pickup* v. *Dental Board of U.K.* [1928] 2 K.B. 459); Blackstone (IV. I. 5) recognized it as having also a third sense, synonymous with 'crime', and so including even felonies.

[3] 36 and 37 Vict. c. 66, s. 47. Now 15 and 16 Geo. V, c. 49, s. 31.

[4] 4 Bl. *Comm.* I.

[5] 15 and 16 Geo. VI and I Eliz. II, c. 55. *Post*, Ch. XXXI. A very high proportion of all the indictable offences prosecuted *are* so tried. See Lieck, 'Administration of criminal justice', in *Penal Reform in England* (1946), ch. III, 33.

[6] Sect. 25 (¶ 679, *post*).

origin,[1] and produces so many important consequences, as to deserve immediate consideration.

Amongst indictable crimes, the common law singled out some as being so conspicuously heinous that a man adjudged guilty of any of them incurred—not as any express part of his sentence but as a consequence that necessarily ensued upon it—a forfeiture of property,[2] whether of his lands or of his goods or of both (in the case of treason). Such crimes came to be called 'felonies'. The other, and lesser, crimes were known as 'transgressions' or 'trespasses', and did not obtain their present name of misdemeanours until a much later date. A felony is, therefore, a crime which either involved by common law such a forfeiture, or else has been placed by statute on the footing of those crimes which did involve it. (This definition, it will be seen, includes treason; and, accordingly, the Statute of Treasons[3] speaks of 'treason or other felony'. But the differences of procedure between cases of treason and those of other felonies were so numerous and important that treasons have usually had to be discussed apart; hence, for brevity's sake, the term 'felony' is commonly employed as exclusive of them.)

The very word 'felony' has been said[4] to contain a reference to the forfeiture which the crime entailed, and to be derived from the words *fee*, i.e. feudal holding, and *lon*, i.e. price; felony thus being such a crime as 'costs you your property'. But according to the Dictionary of Professor Skeat the word is derived from a Celtic root, meaning 'evil' (or, according to the *Oxford English Dictionary*, from the Latin *fel*, 'venom'); and at any rate it is akin to our English adjective 'fell', as in Shakespeare's 'fell and cruel hounds'.[5] Moreover, excusable homicides[6] (*per infortunium* and *se defendendo*) were not felonies and yet they did involve forfeiture,[7] until in 1828 it was provided by 9 Geo. IV, c. 31, s. 10 (re-enacted by s. 7 of the Offences against the Person Act, 1861) that 'no punishment or forfeiture shall be incurred by any person who shall kill another by misfortune, or in his own defence, or in any other manner without felony'.

SECTION 2. FELONIES AND MISDEMEANOURS

SOME DISTINCTIONS ABOLISHED

¶ 74. Familiar instances of felonies are murder, manslaughter, burglary, housebreaking, larceny, bigamy, rape; whilst the most conspicuous instances of misdemeanours are perjury, conspiracy, false pretences, libel, riot, assault. The differences between felonies and misdemeanours are no

[1] See Pollock and Maitland, I, 284–6, II, 463–8, 509.

[2] Now abolished. See *infra*, and ¶ 420 *post*.

[3] 25 Edw. III, st. 5, c. 2. Cf. Maitland's *Collected Papers*, I, 316.

[4] 4 Bl. *Comm.* 95. It occurs in French before 1066, but only as the name of one specific offence—the breach of a vassal's fealty to his lord, naturally involving the loss of his feudal land.

[5] Pollock and Maitland, II, 465. *Ante*, ¶ 10.

[6] *Post*, ¶ 98.

[7] 1 Hawk. P.C. c. 28.

longer so numerous as they once were. Amongst those, however, that have now disappeared there are some whose historical importance requires notice.

(1) Originally, as we have seen, every felony tacitly produced a forfeiture; whilst no misdemeanour did, and in extremely few misdemeanours could forfeiture be imposed even as an express part of the sentence. But all forfeitures for felony and treason were abolished by the Forfeiture Act, 1870 (33 and 34 Vict. c. 23, s. 1).

(2) Originally all felonies (except petty larceny) were punished with death, whilst no misdemeanour was.[1] Hence the idea of capital punishment became so closely connected with that of felony that any statute making a crime a felony made it capital by silent implication, whilst in an enactment which created a misdemeanour even the widest general words could not suffice to make it capital,[2] and nothing but the most express language would suffice.

(3) Originally, a felon could not, at his trial, call any witnesses in his defence,[3] or have any counsel to defend him[4] (except for the argument of strict points of law), whereas a misdemeanant, like a defendant in a civil case, could have both. These disabilities were removed in 1702 and in 1836 respectively.

But some of the ancient differences between felonies and misdemeanours still exist in the law of the present day. The discussion of most of these may be postponed until we reach the general subject of procedure, when we can more appropriately discuss[5] those which relate to such matters as the mode of accusation, the procedure at the trial,[6] and the disqualifications produced by a conviction.

REMAINING DISTINCTIONS

¶ 75. There are some differences which can more conveniently be considered now.

(1) It is, as we have already seen,[7] only in felonies that the distinction between the four classes of *participes criminis* is technically drawn, or the fourth class made criminal.

(2) When the Act of 1870[8] put an end, as we have seen, to the forfeitures which were formerly created by a conviction for treason or any other felony, it did not restore the offender's property free of all lia-

[1] Heresy (though never a felony) was punishable with death; but it was an ecclesiastical offence not triable in temporal courts.

[2] Hence the statute of Anne (7 Anne, c. 12) which, in consequence of the unfortunate arrest of the Russian ambassador, subjects those who violate an ambassador's privileges to 'such pains, penalties, and corporal punishment *as the court shall think fit*' did not make it possible to punish this offence with death: though its framers may have hoped that 'his Czarish Majesty', whom they avowedly were attempting to appease, would be unaware that its language would be construed thus restrictively. 1 Bl. *Comm.* 255.

[3] *R.* v. *Throckmorton* (1554) 1 St.Tr. 869 at p. 885; *R.* v. *Udall* (1590) 1 St.Tr. 1277 at pp. 1281, 1304.

[4] Y.B. 30 and 31 Edw. I, app. II, p. 529.

[5] *Post*, Chs. XXXI and XXXII.

[6] *Ibid.*

[7] *Ante*, ¶ 65.

[8] 33 and 34 Vict. c. 23.

bilities, but justly saddled him with certain burdens which the crime itself had brought about. Thus, section 4 of the Forfeiture Act enables the court before which any person is convicted of felony—but not of treason—to order that he shall pay damages, not exceeding £100, for any 'loss of property' which the felony has occasioned (as where cash has been given for a forged cheque).[1] And under the Criminal Justice Act, 1948, s. 11, a court[2] may order an offender to pay such damages for injury or compensation for loss as the court thinks reasonable; but if the court be a court of summary jurisdiction such damages and compensation together must not exceed £100; the provisions of this section are not limited to felonies.

But for these enactments, the person who had suffered the loss would have had to incur the trouble and expense of bringing an action in some civil court to obtain compensation. French procedure has long permitted the intervention, in criminal proceedings, of a *partie civile*, so as to save expense and trouble by enabling one litigation to do the work of two.

¶ 76. (3) As felonies at common law were always heinous offences (and resulted in forfeiture), the law regarded it as of great moment that the offender should be brought to justice. Hence whenever a felony has been committed, anyone who, on reasonable grounds, suspects any person of being the offender, is permitted to arrest him forthwith. And anyone who actually sees a felony committed is not only permitted, but required, to do his best forthwith to arrest the felon, and may use any degree of violence that may be reasonably needed to attain that object. But in the case of misdemeanours the common law never permitted (and it is only in particular cases that modern statutes[3] now permit) even the eyewitnesses of the offence to arrest the offender without first obtaining a magistrate's warrant to enable them to do so. Hence a man who steals a penny may be seized on the spot, since he is a felon. But a man who has obtained a herd of cattle by false pretences is only a misdemeanant; accordingly, under the old common law rule, the farmer had to let him go.[4] On the same principle, the justices of the peace who committed a felon for trial have always had authority to insist, if they thought fit, on his remaining in prison until the trial took place, though a person committed for trial for misdemeanour could, at common law, insist on being released on bail if he found sufficient

[1] This power is extended to magistrates' courts by the Magistrates' Courts Act, 1952, s. 34. The Forfeiture Act also empowered the court which convicted a person of felony or of treason to charge him with the *costs* of the prosecution. But by the Costs in Criminal Cases Act, 1952 (for cases tried on indictment), and by the Magistrates' Courts Act, 1952 (for cases tried summarily), wide powers are given to the court to order the costs either of the prosecution or of a successful defence to be paid out of public funds, or by the prosecutor or by the accused person, as the merits of the case may be.

[2] On making a probation order etc., as provided elsewhere in the Act, see ¶ 711 *post*.

[3] *Post*, ¶ 695.

[4] But now by virtue of s. 41 of the Larceny Act, 1916, he may be arrested.

sureties. By modern legislation, however, the discretion which justices possess in felonies has been extended—first to many—now to all misdemeanours.[1] The anxiety of the law to secure the punishment of felons (perhaps not unconnected with the desire to secure the resulting forfeiture to the Crown of the felon's property) led to the further rule that no person injured by a felony could bring a civil action[2] against the felon, to recover compensation for his loss, until *after* a criminal prosecution had either taken place or (as by the death or the pardon of the offender) had been rendered impossible. In misdemeanours, on the other hand, either the civil or the criminal remedy may be taken first; or indeed, in theory, both may be pursued simultaneously,[3] though in practice such a course would never be prudent.[4] But it should be added that, even in the case of felonies, it is not altogether easy for a defendant to defeat a civil action by raising this defence that he has not yet been prosecuted for the wrong which is complained of. So audacious an attempt to 'take advantage of his wrong' is not allowed by the courts to be raised in the form of an ordinary defence. But the defence does certainly exist; see *Smith* v. *Selwyn*.[5] A defendant can set it up by a summons at chambers to stay the action; or the court itself may spontaneously refuse to hold the trial. The objection, however, was never regarded as applying to actions, even though connected with the felony, in which the defendant was not the felon himself, or in which the plaintiff was not the injured party himself.[6]

¶ 77. (4) The heinousness of felonies is vividly shown by the legal disqualifications which arise from the infamy of being convicted of one. The convicted felon[7] loses any office or pension;[8] and he cannot vote at an election for or sit in Parliament, or hold military or civil or ecclesiastical office, until after he either has been pardoned or has worked out his sentence.[9] These disqualifications are not entailed by any misdemeanour, but conviction and imprisonment for more than three months without the option of a fine either within five years before election or after election entails disqualification for local government office,[10] and a member of Parliament who commits a misdemeanour may be expelled.[11]

[1] See now the Magistrates' Courts Act, 1952, s. 7; and *post*, ¶ 706.

[2] The matter must be very clear for the court to stop the proceedings at the outset; *Jack Clark (Rainham) Ltd.* v. *Clark* [1946] 2 All E.R. 683.

[3] *Jones* v. *Clay* (1798) 1 B. and P. 191; *Ex parte Edgar* (1913) 29 T.L.R. 278.

[4] Cf. *R.* v. *Mahon* (1826) 4 A. and E. 575.

[5] (1914) 3 K.B. 98. Felonies of *homicide* are made an exception by the Fatal Accidents Act, 1846.

[6] *Appleby* v. *Franklin* (1885) 17 Q.B.D. 93.

[7] Unless sentenced merely to imprisonment for twelve months or less, or (23 Geo. V, c. 12, s. 51) unless convicted when younger than seventeen.

[8] But in practice the pensioning authorities now deal with each case on its merits, and note any favourable report from the judge.

[9] Forfeiture Act, 1870, s. 2.

[10] Local Government Act, 1933 (23 and 24 Geo. V, c. 51), s. 59, as amended by the Crim. Justice Act, 1948, and the Costs in Crim. Cases Act, 1952.

[11] Wade and Phillips, *Constitutional Law*, 6th ed. 104.

The existence of so many differences,[1] some of them still so important, between felonies and misdemeanours naturally suggests that crimes in the former class are marked by some special gravity. Yet it is not easy to discover on what principle the separation has been made between the crimes which are allotted to the one class or to the other. It cannot depend—like the French classification into *crimes*, *délits*, and *contraventions*—upon the degree of dignity of the tribunal before which the offender is to be tried. For a man may be tried for larceny, which is a felony, before a magistrate, and yet for misdemeanours he may, in theory, be impeached before the House of Lords. Nor, again, can it depend upon the amount of evil actually caused by the offence. For perjury, though it may cause the death of an innocent person, is only a misdemeanour, whilst keeping a horse-slaughterer's yard without licence is a felony.[2] Nor, thirdly, can it depend upon the gravity of the punishment. For simple larceny, which is a felony, and false pretences, which is a misdemeanour, are punishable alike, while fraudulent conversion, another misdemeanour, is punishable more severely. And the misdemeanour of conspiracy to murder is punishable with ten years' imprisonment;[3] yet the felony of stealing mineral ores is only punishable with two years' imprisonment (Larceny Act, 1916, s. 11). An arrangement which produces such anomalies as these, can only be explained by considerations purely historical. It probably may be traced back to ancient times when particular offences were first found to be of such frequency and gravity as to render it no longer safe to leave them to the chance of a prosecution by the injured, in the forms of ordinary litigation. The public safety demanded a periodical public investigation by the Crown, through a jury of accusation provided for the purpose, into the question whether any offences of this deep dye had been committed. Hence arose[4] 'Grand Juries'. To facilitate their operations it became necessary to frame a precise legal definition of each of the offences about which they were to report.[5] To such offences the name of 'felonies' became[6] limited; and the procedure concerning them gradually acquired its peculiar characteristics. But offences less grave, or less common, were for a long time left very loosely defined (as some of them still are, e.g. conspiracy), and were never prosecuted in this 'inquisitorial' mode, but were left as before to the 'litigious' action of private persons (though in later days that action would usually

[1] See ¶ 744, *post*.

[2] 26 Geo. III, c. 71. The object was to prevent stolen horses from being easily disposed of.

[3] Offences against the Person Act, 1861, s. 4, as amended by the Criminal Justice Act, 1948, s. 1. In the period when rape was only a misdemeanour it nevertheless was punished by the loss of the offender's eyes and testicles; 1 Hawk. P.C. c. 4, s. 7. A threat, by letter or in writing, to murder, is a felony under the Offences against the Person Act, 1861, s. 16.

[4] See *post*, ¶ 718.

[5] Cf. (1313) *Eyre of Kent*, I, 52, 57 (Seld. Soc. Y.B. Series, V).

[6] For an earlier and wider meaning (i.e. an 'appealable' crime) see Pollock and Maitland, II, 466.

be nominally taken on behalf of the Crown). These latter offences (except where statutory enactment has since erected any of them into felonies) constitute our modern misdemeanours. They, said Bracton six hundred years ago, are tried like civil actions ('civiliter intentantur'); and even now, as Sir James Stephen said, a prosecution for misdemeanour is akin to an action for tort in which the Crown is plaintiff and which aims at punishment and not at damages. Thus, in a trial for misdemeanour, the juryman's oath used to be to 'truly try the *issue* joined between our sovereign Lord the King and the *defendant*'. But in a felony it was to 'true *deliverance*[1] make between our sovereign Lord the King and the *prisoner* at the bar'. Hence it is easy to understand why, in so many respects, the older law assimilated the idea of misdemeanours rather to that of civil wrongs than to that of felony; as in the conspicuous instance of its requiring a peer to be tried by the House of Lords if the charge were one of felony,[2] but by a jury of mere commoners if it is one of misdemeanour. In the course of time, the analogies of civil procedure have gradually caused the litigious type of procedure to supersede the inquisitorial, even in the case of felonies.[3] The influence of the old inquisitorial theory, however, still survives in the conduct of all public prosecutions. Thus, in cases of homicide, every person present at the killing is usually called by the Crown as a witness, if he seem honest, even though he be manifestly hostile to the Crown. In a case of poisoning, all the chemists who have made analyses for the Crown, alike those who thought they found poison and those who did not, will be called. It is the view of English law that the Crown counsel are not 'litigants' battling with the prisoner, but a royal commission of 'inquirers' dispassionately investigating the truth.[4]

We may add that in 1870, long before the abolition of forfeitures for felony, they had ceased to be of any financial importance. The annual amounts received between 1848 and 1870 ranged only from £253 to £1317. Most felons were poor; and the rich ones disposed of their wealth between arrest and conviction. The time had come for this change.

It is quite possible that, in a perfect criminal code, crimes would

[1] It is uncertain whether this referred to (1) the deliverance of the verdict, or (2) the deliverance of the prisoner (who is said to 'stand on his deliverance') from custody, or (3) the jury's *deliberation* on the evidence. The juryman's oath since 1949, whether the offence is felony or misdemeanour, is 'that I will well and truly try the several issues joined between our Sovereign Lady the Queen and the prisoner(s) at the bar, and a true verdict give according to the evidence'.

[2] Now abolished by the Criminal Justice Act, 1948, s. 30 (1).

[3] But coroners still proceed inquisitorially; they obtain all the evidence they can get, whichever way it may tell. See ¶ 665 *post*.

[4] Similarly the judge in all criminal trials can, if necessary, call a witness whom neither party wishes to be called (though the 'litigious' nature of civil trials forbids him thus to interpose in them). See *R.* v. *Stroner* (1845) 1 C. and K. 650. And the prosecuting counsel is only a 'minister of justice'; *post*, ¶ 749.

In trials for felony, the curious proclamation, inviting other charges against the prisoner, was a survival from 'inquisitorial' procedure.

continue to be separated into two great divisions according to their greater or lesser heinousness, and that particular incidents both of procedure and punishment would attach to the graver class. But, in English law, great objection may be taken, as we have seen, both to the illogical manner in which particular crimes have been placed in the one class or the other, and also to some of the incidents attached to one or other of the classes. Hence the Criminal Code Bill,[1] in its earlier form, abolished altogether the distinction between felonies and misdemeanours, and though the last draft, that of 1880, retained the distinction, yet it removed nearly all its importance. For it proposed that some incidents then attached to felonies should be attached only to such crimes as were punishable with death or penal servitude; whilst a few of the other incidents were to be extended to all crimes, and other incidents, again, were to be wholly abolished. The view has often been expressed that, of all parts of our criminal law, none is in greater need of a thorough reconstruction than that which concerns the classification into felonies and misdemeanours.

[1] [C. 2345] 1879. See pp. 11 and 14–15 of the Report of the Commissioners.

BOOK II

DEFINITIONS OF PARTICULAR CRIMES

Chapter VII

HOMICIDE

Section i. Introductory

¶ 78. Writers for centuries past have found it convenient to classify crimes by reference to the various kinds of interests which the respective offences violate. Of the arrangements of the subject-matter which have been made upon this basis the clearest is that of Blackstone's later editor, Serjeant Stephen, who divided them simply into (1) offences against the persons of individuals, (2) offences against the property of individuals, (3) offences against public rights.

Following this last arrangement, our list of crimes must begin with those which affect the security of men's persons—employing here that much abused word, not in its ancient technical legal sense of 'a subject of rights and duties',[1] but in the modern meaning of 'the living body of a human being'.[2] Of all such offences homicide attracts the most attention and, to every student of criminal law, is a crime peculiarly instructive. For it is, as we have seen, in connexion with homicide that *mens rea*, the basic element of responsibility in our modern system, has been developed.

CLASSIFICATION

¶ 79. We have already had occasion to indicate the uncertainty which besets most important principles at the present time in the law of homicide, owing, as we have observed, to a variety of factors which have operated during the peculiar growth of the common law.[3] In all periods English law has regarded the killing of a human being as a deed of the utmost gravity; but many, if gradual, changes have occurred since the early days when the simple fact that a death could be traced to a man's active conduct involved him in a liability of which no degrees were

[1] See Holland's *Jurisprudence*, ch. viii.

[2] This sense perhaps was brought into English law by Sir Matthew Hale, who has the grotesque phrase, 'the interest which a *person* has in the safety of his own *person*'. (*Analysis of the Law*, s. 1.)

[3] See Ch. ii. A great deal of information on this matter is to be found in 'A rationale of the law of homicide', by Wechsler and Michael in 37 *Columbia L.R.* (1937), 701 and 1261.

recognized and for which hardly any excuses were admitted. Nowadays it is the subjective element of *mens rea* which is of the first importance, imperfectly defined though it still is, and this has brought about the division of homicide into several grades, which must be described and defined separately. These are justifiable homicide, excusable homicide, murder, suicide, manslaughter, infanticide, child destruction.

It is to the working of the social conscience of the English people that all these modifications are due. The first five were produced through the common law system in which changes can only be effected by an indirect and very gradual pressure. Infanticide and child destruction, however, were created by statute a short time ago, in an era when public opinion was becoming more conscious of its strength, and the legislature correspondingly sensitive to it. It may incidentally be noted that the governing principles in these last two instances are free from the doubts and obscurities which surround the common law homicides.

ACTUS REUS IN HOMICIDE

¶ 80. Before turning to the discussion of the different grades of homicide it is necessary to consider some matters which arise in connexion with the *actus reus*. The first point to note is that the *actus* is the same in each of the several kinds of homicide. In homicide the particular physical result of human conduct which constitutes the *actus* is the deed of having caused the death of a human being, which for simplicity of language we may call the death. As we shall see, not every homicide is criminal. But if the death can be traced to the act (or omission, where there is a legal duty to act) of some person, and provided that a death in the particular circumstances of the case is one which the law seeks to prevent by threat of punishment, then that death constitutes the *actus reus* of a criminal homicide committed by that person.

DEFINITION

¶ 81. In the antique phraseology which has been repeated since the time of Lord Coke[1] the *actus reus* of murder (and therefore of any criminal homicide)[2] was declared to be unlawfully killing a reasonable person who is in being and under the King's peace, the death following within a year and a day. In this sentence the word 'reasonable' does not mean 'sane', but 'human'. In criminal law a lunatic is a *persona* for all purposes of protection, even when not so treated for the assessment of liability.

THE KING'S PEACE

¶ 82. The crime of homicide may be committed upon any human being who is within the King's peace. Accordingly if even an alien enemy, being within the realm, is killed otherwise than in the actual

[1] 3 *Inst.* 47.

[2] Except child destruction, which is restricted to the killing of a child before it has an existence independent of its mother.

course of an operation of war the killing may be as much murder (or manslaughter) as the killing of an Englishman.[1]

'The King's majesty is, by his office and dignity royal, the principal conservator of the peace within all his dominions.'[2] Yet in our Anglo-Saxon period the King's peace was only partial in its operation, and merely supplemented that national peace which it finally supplanted. The national peace, which apparently had its origin in the sanctity of the homestead, was protected only in the local courts; and these were weak. The King's peace, on the other hand, was enforced with vigour by royal officers of justice. At first it applied only in certain holy seasons, or to persons to whom it was specially granted by the King, or to places which were under the King's special protection (such as the precincts of his house and the four great roads).[3] These limits, however, soon became indefinitely extended. 'The interests of the King and of the subject conspired to the same end.'[4] The King profited in the way of fees, and the subject was anxious to appeal to the one authority which could not anywhere be lightly disobeyed. Accordingly, 'after the Conquest, the various forms in which the King's special protection had been given disappear, or rather merge in his general protection and authority'.[5] But even then the King's peace did not arise throughout the nation at large until he proclaimed it; and it lasted only till his death. So on the death of Henry I, the chronicler tells us, 'There was seen tribulation in the land; for every man that could forthwith robbed another'. Finally, as Edward I was away in Palestine when his father died, the magnates themselves proclaimed the King's peace, in spite of his absence, to avoid the confusion which would otherwise have arisen. Thenceforward even the King's death was never regarded as suspending the royal peace.

A man attainted of praemunire was not under the King's peace; and, therefore, until 5 Eliz. I, c. 1, it was not murder to kill him.[6] On the other hand, to kill an outlaw was murder;[7] and, in addition to an alien enemy, even a savage[8] or a condemned criminal[9] is under the King's peace. As above mentioned an alien enemy cannot lawfully be killed except in the actual course of true war.[10] In such he, of course, may be; so, if the captured crew, on board a prize brought into British waters, should endeavour to release themselves from their British captors, and

[1] 1 Hale P.C. 433. *Maria* v. *Hall* (1807) 1 Taunt. 33, at p. 36. See *post*, ¶ 137*a*.

[2] 4 Bl. *Comm*. 350.

[3] Cf. Maitland's *Collected Papers*, II, 290–7.

[4] Pollock, *Oxford Essays* ('The King's peace'), 83.

[5] *Ibid*. p. 87.

[6] Brooke's Abridgment, *tit*. Corone, 196.

[7] 1 Hale P.C. 433.

[8] See p. 146 n. 1, *post*.

[9] 1 Hale P.C. 433; *Commonwealth* v. *Bowen* (1816) 13 Mass. 356.

[10] Hence in 1902 four Zeerust natives were sentenced to death by the criminal court at Pretoria for having killed a Boer in the war of 1900 *outside* their frontier, when their chief's only commission from the British authorities was to defend his own territory. Similarly in the Transvaal, van Aan was executed for having shot an English officer approaching under a flag of truce.

in the consequent struggle one of the prisoners should be killed by one of the captors, the homicide[1] would not be felonious.

The law (as we are often told) is no respecter of persons. Without being universally true, this is a principle which has always applied with special force to the law of homicide. Thus the villein could not be killed by his lord with impunity. Nor could the slave, even in Anglo-Saxon times, be killed by his master; for the laws of Alfred inflicted a fine on the master who murdered his slave, and this at a time when most homicides admitted of being atoned for as lightly. The King's peace was powerful to protect both villein and slave from the extremity of tyranny. It is instructive to notice that, even in much more recent times, a West Indian legislature imposed on masters no severer responsibility than Anglo-Saxon legislation had done in their dealings with the lives of their slaves. Thus one of the Acts of Barbados ran as follows: 'If any slave under punishment by his master, for running away or any other misdemeanour towards his master, unfortunately shall suffer in life or member, no person whatsoever shall be liable to a fine. But if any man out of wantonness or cruel intention shall wilfully kill a slave of his own, he shall pay into the public treasury £15 sterling.'

'IN BEING': CHILD DESTRUCTION

¶ 83. The intentional killing of one not 'in being', i.e. an unborn child, was until 1929[2] punishable neither as murder nor as infanticide.[3] There can be no murder nor manslaughter[4] of a child which dies before being born or even whilst being born, only of one that has been born and, moreover, been born alive. For purposes of criminal law—and also for those of property law, e.g. to become a holder of property and so transmit it again to new heirs, or to enable the father to obtain curtesy of his wife's lands—*birth* consists in extrusion from the mother's body, i.e. in having 'come into the world'. If but a foot be unextricated, there can be no murder, the extrusion must be complete, the whole body of the infant must have been brought into the world.[5] But it is not necessary that the umbilical cord should have been severed.[6] And to be born alive the child must have been still in a living state after having wholly quitted the body of the mother. Hence that life still existed must be actually proved, and this may be done by giving evidence of any cry, or breathing, or pulsation, or movement, after extrusion. But it is not necessary that the child should have continued

[1] *Per* James, L.J., in *Dyke* v. *Elliott* (1872) L.R. 4 P.C. 184.

[2] When the felony of child destruction was created; *post*, ¶ 138.

[3] *Post*, ¶ 138.

[4] By statute (24 and 25 Vict. c. 100, s. 58) to use means to procure abortion is a felony punishable with imprisonment for life.

[5] *R.* v. *Poulton* (1832) 5 C. and P. 330.

[6] *R.* v. *Reeves* (1839) 9 C. and P. 25. The ambiguous phrases, 'separate existence' and 'independent circulation', differently understood by different doctors, should be avoided, as more easily uttered than explained (20 *L.Q.R.* 142–5).

to live until it was severed from the mother, or even until it could breathe,[1] for a child may perhaps not breathe until some time after full extrusion (though, on the other hand, infants sometimes breathe, and even cry, before they are fully extricated). A parliamentary committee of 1893 recorded the sapient verdict of a coroner's jury upon 'a child found dead, *aged about three months*: but no evidence as to whether or not it had been born alive'. Thus to constitute murder the birth must precede the death; but it need not also precede the injury. Thus an act which causes a child to be born much earlier than in the natural course, so that the child is rendered much less capable of living when born and accordingly soon dies, may itself amount to murder.

THE TIME OF DEATH

¶ 84. It has long been the rule that no one can be convicted of the murder or manslaughter[2] of another person who does not die within a year and a day of the blow received or other cause of death.

'Day' was here added merely to indicate that the 365th day after that of the injury must be included. Such an indication was rendered necessary by an old rule (now obsolete) that, in *criminal* law, in reckoning a period 'from' the doing of any act, the period was (in favour of prisoners) to be taken as beginning on the very day when this act was done.[3]

The doctrine that a charge of homicide could not be sustained unless the death ensued within a limited period after the injury that caused it, was a wise precaution in view of the defectiveness of medical science in medieval days. In Holland, indeed, so brief a period as six weeks was adopted; but the modern Roman-Dutch law of South Africa, in view of the present advanced state of forensic medicine, recognizes no time-limit (Nathan, s. 2605). Nor is any recognized in Scots law (Hume, 1, 186); nor in the Indian Penal Code. But in England the common-law rule is still retained.

CAUSATION

¶ 85. It is in cases of homicide that the most difficult questions of causation have arisen, especially when it is alleged that the death was brought about by the prisoner's omission to perform some legal duty. The main rules as to harm due to omissions, and as to causation generally, have already been discussed[4] and need not be repeated here.[5] In particular regard to the present topic, however, it should be observed

[1] *R.* v. *Brain* (1834) 6 C. and P. 349. Nor is it necessary that it should be capable of *continued* life. In 1812, at York summer assizes, a midwife was convicted of murder for drowning a new-born child which, from the absence of part of the skull, could not have lived many hours. Bayley, J., however, recommended commutation of her sentence, because she had sincerely believed her act to be lawful (*Annual Register* for 1812, p. 96).

[2] *R.* v. *Dyson* [1908] 2 K.B. 454.

[3] *Norris* v. *Hundred of Gawtry* (1617) Hob. 139. But now see *Radcliffe* v. *Bartholomew* [1892] 1 Q.B. 161.

[4] ¶¶ 12 (*b*), 13 *ante*.

[5] For a fuller account and a discussion of cases see Russ. 466.

that homicide may be committed in many ways,[1] by striking, poisoning, drowning, starving and so on.[2] Indeed, as already suggested,[3] now that the requirement of *mens rea* is so firmly established there seems to be no reason for hesitating to accept a lengthy line of causation in this matter. It was different in early law, for when liability was felt to depend upon causation rather than upon intention a method of avoiding injustice was to refuse to regard the death as sufficiently proximate to the accused person's acts. Hale,[4] however, seems to have inclined to the view that it would be an *actus reus* of homicide if a person suffering from plague went about and infected another with fatal results. In his day the doctrine of strict liability still had some force and he felt it necessary to give reasons why this would not be murder,[5] unless the accused had gone abroad with intent to infect another in which case, he says 'whether this be not murder by the common law must be a question'. Since it would nowadays almost certainly be held to be murder if it could be proved that one man with intent to kill had brought about another's death by tainting his food with some deadly bacillus, or by conveying the like lethal agent through the dressing of a cut or sore, there would seem on principle to be no reason why he should not equally be held responsible if, with the same murderous intention, he were to pass a fatal infection from his own person to that of his victim. On this argument, too, it would seem that if the intention were to hurt but not to kill, then if death were not foreseen as a possibility but were caused in one of these ways the crime would be manslaughter.[6] It used formerly to be thought that killing by a *mental* shock could not be murder, but such a cause of death is no longer considered too remote for the law to trace.[7]

¶ 86. *Killing by perjury.* It was in early times maintained[8] that bringing about the conviction (and resulting execution) of a man by giving false evidence in his trial for a capital offence would be murder: but it seems now to be established that killing a man by perjury is not murder. The

[1] 1 Hale P.C. 432, '*moriendi mille figurae*'.

[2] E.g. *The Harlot's Case*, 1 Hawk. P.C. c. 31, s. 6; *R.* v. *Huggins* (1729) 17 St.Tr. 309 and cases given in 1 East P.C. 226; ¶ 13 (i) *ante*.

[3] ¶ 13 *ante*.

[4] 1 P.C. 432.

[5] (*a*) Because it was difficult to prove that the illness was contracted from the accused, for if 'from the contagion of the air, it is God's arrow'; (*b*) because 'mutual conversation' is a necessity for mankind; and (*c*) because contagions are common among mankind by visitation of God, and the extension of capital punishments should be avoided.

[6] Unless, under the doctrine of the House of Lords in *D.P.P.* v. *Smith* [1961] A.C. 290, it would be held to be murder.

[7] *R.* v. *Hayward* (1908) 21 Cox 692, death from fear caused by threats of violence; *R.* v. *Towers* (1874) 12 Cox 530; *Wilkinson* v. *Downton* [1897] 2 Q.B. 57. Contrast Hale's view (1 P.C. 429) that if a man by working upon another's fancy or by harsh or unkind usage puts him into such grief or fear that he dies suddenly, or contracts some fatal disease, this cannot, *in foro humano*, come under the judgment of felony, because no external act of violence was offered whereof the common law can take notice, and secret things belong to God; citing the need for the Witchcraft Act, 1603.

[8] Britt. c. 52; Brac. lib. 3, c. 4; 3 Co. *Inst.* 48; 1 Hawk. P.C. c. 31, s. 7.

failure to indict Titus Oates for murder in 1685[1] may in some measure have been due to the atmosphere of public panic and uncertainty which prevailed at that time. For the evidence on which the victims of the perjury by Oates and his associates were convicted (and executed) did not in substance differ from that which secured the conviction of the perjurors themselves and enabled Jeffreys, L.C.J., to say 'There does not remain the least doubt, but that Oates is the blackest and most perjured villain that ever appeared upon the face of the earth.'[2] In 1692 a bill was introduced into Parliament to make it a capital offence to commit (or to suborn) perjury in a capital case, but this did not pass into law, and the modern rule depends on the result of the last prosecution for murder by perjury, in 1756.[3] In that case the prisoners were convicted, but judgment was respited so that the point of law could be further argued: the Attorney-General, however, declined to argue the point, perhaps (as suggested[4]) lest witnesses might be deterred from giving evidence in capital prosecution if it must be at the peril of their own lives.

HOMICIDE BY OMISSION TO ACT

¶ 87. Although the outline of the rules as to liability for the results of an omission has already been given, it will be useful to consider some of the instances which have arisen of death caused by failure to perform some active duty. The first question which always has to be decided is whether or not the accused was under a duty to act. This is a question of law for the judge and the burden of proving the facts, on which the judge can find the duty, rests upon the prosecution in each case.[5] The few positions in which the common law has automatically imposed a duty to take action have been mentioned already.[6] Of the many which arise from the voluntary assumption of duty the following examples may now be given.

¶ 88. *Neglect of apprentices and servants.* There are many reports of old cases in which the death of an apprentice or servant living in the household of the accused was alleged to be due not merely to ill treatment but also to neglect to supply nourishment or aid in sickness. Such situations are not likely to arise under modern social conditions and the cases now are only of importance in so far as they reveal the principles to be applied when the point to be decided is whether the deceased was helpless or in some way necessarily dependent upon the care of the head of the house. The law in this category of circumstances therefore merges in that to be discussed in the next paragraph. As it was put in 1865,[7] 'It is undisputed law that if a person who has the custody of

[1] (1685) 10 St.Tr. 1079; *ante*, ¶ 13.
[2] (1685) 10 St.Tr. 1226; Stephen, *Hist. Crim. Law*, I, 383 *et seq.*
[3] *R.* v. *Macdaniel* (1755) 19 St.Tr. 745; Foster, 121 (*T.A.C.*).
[4] 4 Bl. *Comm.* 196, note (g).
[5] *R.* v. *Edwards* (1838) 8 C. and P. 611; *R.* v. *Barrett* (1846) 2 C. and K. 343.
[6] ¶ 12 (*b*) *ante*.
[7] *R.* v. *Smith*, 34 L.J.M.C. 153 *per* Erle, C.J., at p. 162.

another who is helpless, leaves that other with insufficient food, and so causes his death, he is criminally responsible. But it is also clear that if a person, having the exercise of free will, chooses to stay in a place where he receives insufficient food and his health is injured, and death supervenes, the master is not criminally responsible.'[1]

¶ 89. *Neglect of the helpless or infirm.* Anyone who undertakes the care of another who is by reason of age or sickness incapable of providing necessaries for himself will be held criminally responsible if through his conscious neglect[2] to perform the duty which he has undertaken the death of the invalid is caused.[3]

¶ 90. *Neglect of members of the family.* At common law the parent is under a duty to provide food, medical aid and shelter for the child and there have been many cases in which a child's death caused by its parent's neglect has been held to constitute a criminal homicide.[4] A guardian *in loco parentis* is under the same responsibility.[5] Between other relatives there is no such duty based merely on the relationship alone; but the courts have not been reluctant to see in the circumstances, where appropriate, the assumption of a duty of care which will invest with responsibility the person in control of the household in which the helpless relative was included. A modern case is *R.* v. *Bonnyman*,[6] in which the prisoner, who was a medical man, was convicted of the manslaughter of his wife, a drug addict, whom he had himself neglected and refused to allow to be moved elsewhere. In dismissing his appeal the Court of Criminal Appeal stated that it was clear that the deceased was as helpless as a human being could be, and that the plain duty of the appellant was to have given her aid and treatment, which he withheld.

[1] In certain circumstances the crime *could* be manslaughter. See *R.* v. *Senior* [1899] 1 Q.B. 283, and ¶ 89, n. 2, *post*.

[2] 'Neglect' is not the same thing as 'negligence'. In the present connexion the word 'neglect' indicates, as a purely objective fact, that a person has not done that which it was his duty to do; it does not indicate the *reason* for this failure. 'Negligence', on the other hand, is a subjective state of mind, and it indicates a particular reason why the man has failed to do his duty, namely because he has not kept the performance of the duty in his mind as he ought to have done. A man can 'neglect' his duty either intentionally or negligently, see *ante*, p. 35.

[3] *R.* v. *Marriott* (1838) 8 C. and P. 425 (note the judge's unfortunate use of the word 'negligence' when dealing with a case of *neglect*, in this case); *R.* v. *Instan* [1893] 1 Q.B. 450; *R.* v. *Chattaway* (1922) 17 Cr.App.R. 7; it will be murder if the neglect to act was deliberate, with the intention that death should result, or even with the realization that his omission involved the risk of the loss of life (¶ 107 *post*). It will be manslaughter if the accused did not realize that death might occur, but did realize that some physical harm would be caused (¶ 136 *post*).

[4] E.g. *R.* v. *Middleship* (1851) 5 Cox 275; *R.* v. *Walters* (1841) C. and M. 164; and see *R.* v. *Senior* [1899] 1 Q.B. 283; *R.* v. *Izod* (1904) 20 Cox 690; *R.* v. *Handley* (1874) 13 Cox 79; *R.* v. *Gibbins and Proctor* (1918) 13 Cr.App.R. 134. In *R.* v. *Watson and Watson* (1959) Cr.App.R. 111, the wife, although she was living with her husband, was held guilty of the manslaughter of her child by wilful neglect to provide food or medical aid.

[5] *R.* v. *Bubb* (1851) 4 Cox 457.

[6] (1942) 28 Cr.App.R. 131.

¶ 91. *Neglect of a duty of employment.* Men's lives often depend upon the due performance of the tasks which a workman is employed to perform. Thus deaths in a mine resulting from an explosion of gas which accumulated because the man employed to keep in operation an engine by which the passage of pure air should have been maintained[1] did not keep the engine working, or through failure to take other steps to prevent the accumulation of gas,[2] or to prevent objects falling down the mine shaft on to men working below,[3] or to attend to the proper working of machinery,[4] have been imputed to the neglectful employee. So also workers upon a railway may be criminally responsible for deaths caused by their not carrying out their duties.[5]

MENS REA IN HOMICIDE

¶ 92. We have seen that the *actus reus* is the same in all cases of homicide for which the killer is held criminally liable. This is so even in the modern crimes of child destruction and infanticide.[6] It should be noted that a justifiable homicide[7] is not criminal, since it is a killing which the law has either commanded or permitted: the *actus* in such a case is not legally punishable, and therefore we may perhaps say that it is an *actus* of killing which is not *reus*. As we shall see in most cases of justifiable homicide the killing is intentional, and therefore the mental element in criminal responsibility is clearly present: but there is no crime committed since there is no *actus reus*.

Accordingly, since the *actus reus* is the same in all instances of criminal homicide it follows that the different kinds of such homicides are distinguishable solely by the variations in the *mens rea* required for each. We must therefore examine each class of homicide separately, including justifiable homicide, but some preliminary remarks must first be made.

¶ 93. *Homicide. Preliminary survey.* Since the history of the general principles of criminal liability at common law is also largely the history of the crimes of homicide, a good deal has already been said about the latter.[8] But the uncertainty of this branch of the law is still so great that attention must again be directed to certain points even though this entails some repetition. In reading the paragraphs which follow students should bear in mind that the history begins with the period when liability for homicide was strict, so that, generally speaking, every killing, where it was not legally justified, involved the killer in liability. The justifiable homicides were few, and there was no

[1] *R.* v. *Barrett* (1846) 2 C. and K. 343. [2] *R.* v. *Haines* (1847) 2 C. and K. 368.

[3] *R.* v. *Hughes* (1857) Dears. and B. 248.

[4] *R.* v. *Lowe* (1850) 3 C. and K. 123 (*T.A.C.*). See *R.* v. *Hilton* (1838) 2 Lew. 214 (*T.A.C.*); *ante*, p. 20.

[5] *R.* v. *Benge* (1865) 4 F. and F. 504; *R.* v. *Pittwood* (1902) 19 T.L.R. 37.

[6] Although child destruction is limited to the killing of a child before it has an independent existence, and infanticide to the killing of her child by the mother before it is twelve months old. [7] *Post*, ¶ 94. [8] Ch. II.

criminality at all in them. In them the mental attitude of the killer has never been legally relevant: it is true that in most of the cases of justifiable homicide (e.g. the execution of duly sentenced criminals) the executioner is inspired by the most deliberate and complete intention to kill, but this is of no legal importance. Therefore if a homicide be held to be in fact justified in law there is no further question to be investigated. Now in early times the only avenue of escape from all penalties for one who had killed another was to establish that the killing was justified; for at that period homicide committed in self-defence, or by misadventure, involved the payment of compensatory penalties just as did an intentional murder. But later the punishments accorded to homicide became more severe, and there accordingly developed a movement to differentiate between different sets of circumstances in which the killing occurred. Killing in defence of oneself, or of a member of one's household would be justified if done in opposing any *felonious* attack which was itself a capital offence, but even here there are signs that in early times a royal pardon was needed, although given as a matter of course. Again our old law recognized that a sudden physical attack, even though not so serious as to amount to felony, could so provoke[1] an ordinary man that he would lose his self-control and might well strike and kill his assailant on the spur of the moment. A blow so struck is not always easy to distinguish from a blow struck in self-defence, and a study of the early cases reveals a considerable measure of identification of the two ideas. But homicides due to misadventure could not be worked into the same principle. Since 'misadventure' included many cases of harm for which at the present day we recognize that damages should be recoverable in a civil action, no serious hardship would seem to be caused when the rule was that the killer merely had to pay compensation; but when later the punishment for homicide became afflictive and harsh, then a difficulty arose. At that stage, as Maitland says, 'What to do with cases of misadventure, the law did not see'.[2] From the complicated story to be collected from the old records it emerges that homicides in self-defence and by misadventure were treated as excusable and not classed as felonies, and that in both cases the punishment of imprisonment was avoided by the grant of pardon by the Crown; but even so there was liability to forfeiture of goods. Forfeiture indeed fell into desuetude, but was not formally abolished until 1828.[3] Justifiable homicide, murder, manslaughter, homicide under provocation, in self-defence and by misadventure were all sadly confused. In this tangle the conception of *mens rea* germinated and grew. The requirement of a mental element in guilt rendered it more easy to divide homicide into different grades but it brought further complication into the law. The old strict test of liability which did not look beyond the *actus reus* was expressly negatived by the

[1] Provocation is discussed below, ¶ 117. [2] Pollock and Maitland, II, 483.

[3] 9 Geo. IV, c. 31, s. 10, abolished forfeitures for killing without felony. See also the Forfeiture Act, 1870.

maxim *actus non facit reum nisi mens sit rea* and logically should have been entirely abandoned. But it was allowed to linger on, and relics of it exist even now. In their presentation of the law the judges varied, some taking the old view, some the new, some indeed basing their decisions on more than one view at a time. Our system of precedents has led to the preservation of old cases, decided on principles now obsolete, which are from time to time cited without appreciation of their ancient meaning or modern inapplicability. In the result the law of homicide now resembles a heap of interesting but mostly useless objects jumbled together in a curiosity shop. An authoritative re-statement of the law of homicide is long overdue.

SECTION 2. JUSTIFIABLE HOMICIDE

¶ 94. The homicides classed as strictly justifiable have never involved any legal penalty; they were not felonies, and they never caused forfeiture of the killer's property.[1] In them the act is either enjoined or permitted by the law (the slayer thus being treated as acting on behalf of the State), and it is an ancient principle of the common law that what the law requires it also justifies.[2] A homicide is justifiable in the following circumstances.

(i) The execution of public justice[3]

¶ 95. The hangman who carries out[4] the sentence of a competent court incurs no criminal liability. The sheriff who burnt the martyrs Latimer and Ridley at the stake was accordingly in no danger, either under Mary or even under Elizabeth, of being himself convicted of murder for having so done. His immunity was due—not, as Blackstone (IV, 28) ascribes it, to the absence of *mens rea* (because his act was extorted by a compulsion of official duty which overbore his own reluctance to commit it)—but to the entire absence of an *actus reus*. It was not a crime for him to carry out the sentence; indeed, it would have been a crime (though it might have been an act of moral heroism) for him to refuse to carry it out. For some instances of technical 'murder' committed by a merciful deviation from a sentence to a horrible death, see ¶ 419 *post*.

(ii) The advancement of public justice

¶ 96. Life may be taken with impunity, if it be necessary and reasonable for arresting a felon,[5] or suppressing a felonious riot,[6] or preventing a crime of a 'forcible or atrocious' character.[7] The old books in speaking of 'atrocious and violent crimes' referred to felonious attacks; for in the old days these were capital.[8] There was accordingly a temptation for

[1] 1 Hawk. P.C. 28.
[2] 5 Co. Rep. 115*b*.
[3] 1 Hale P.C. 496; Foster, 267; 4 Bl. *Comm.* 178.
[4] If with precision; e.g. no change of day or of form of death.
[5] 3 Co. *Inst.* 56; 1 Hale P.C. 494; 1 Hawk. P.C. c. 28; Foster, 270; 4 Bl. *Comm.* 179. *Post*, ¶ 698.
[6] Riot Act, 1714, s. 3; *post*, ¶ 438.
[7] 4 Bl. *Comm.* 180
[8] 4 Bl. *Comm.* 182.

wrongdoers to use any violence in order to evade arrest, and since there was in that period no such network of police organization with its scientific equipment for pursuit and for proof of their connexion with the crime as exists nowadays, they had good hope of getting safely away and escaping ultimate detection. It was therefore regarded as reasonable and necessary for officers of justice, and for private citizens also, to take any steps which might be effective to prevent the escape of persons who had committed such offences or who were resisting arrest. But in modern times the test of what is reasonable must restrict very much the limits within which either private persons or police officers can use deadly measures to prevent crimes or to arrest delinquents. The reports of the old cases should therefore be read subject to this reservation.[1] As long ago as 1879 it was stated in the Report of the Criminal Code Bill Commission:[2] 'We take one great principle of the common law to be that, though it sanctions the defence of a man's person, liberty and property against illegal violence, and permits the use of force to prevent crimes, to preserve the public peace, and to bring offenders to justice, yet all this is subject to the restriction that the force used is necessary; that is, that the mischief sought to be prevented could not be prevented by less violent means; and that the mischief done by, or which might reasonably be anticipated from, the force used is not disproportionate to the injury or mischief which it is intended to prevent.'[3]

With regard to the arrest of wrongdoers it should be observed that in modern law an arrest without warrant, whether made by a police officer or by a private person, is not lawful (save as otherwise provided by statute[4]) and therefore cannot be justified unless the charge against the wrongdoer has first been made known to him, save where the situation is such that he must obviously know what in substance is the misdeed for which he is being apprehended. Of course he cannot be heard to complain if by his own conduct (e.g. where he has attacked the officer, or has run away) he has made it impracticable to inform him of the charge. For every citizen has the right to know for what crime, or on suspicion for what crime, he is being arrested, and if he is seized without having been so informed then the person seizing him, whether private person or policeman, is (except in special cases provided for by the law) liable for assault and for false imprisonment.[5] A homicide caused in effecting an *unlawful* arrest of course cannot be justified. It may be repeated here that in our very early law when

[1] As to officers' indemnification for firing on aircraft that fly illegally, see 2 and 3 Geo. V, c. 22, s. 2.

[2] [C. 2345], p. 11.

[3] See *R.* v. *Scully* (1824) 1 C. and P. 319. In 1804 it was held that one who had shot a man who had gone about at night dressed in white as a ghost in order to alarm the neighbourhood (the 'Hammersmith Ghost') was not legally justified and was guilty of murder since the masquerade thus terminated was not a violent crime but merely the misdemeanour of 'nuisance'. He was eventually respited (*R.* v. *Smith*, 4 Bl. *Comm.* 201 n.). See Glanville Williams, 'Homicide and the supernatural' (1949), 65 *L.Q.R.* 491.

[4] E.g. the Metropolitan Police Act, 1839. See *Gelberg* v. *Miller* [1961] 1 W.L.R. 153.

[5] *Christie* v. *Leachinsky* [1947] A.C. 573. See Arrest, *post*, ¶ 692.

liability for homicide was 'strict', the man who had killed another 'justifiably' suffered no punishment and did not have to pay compensation to the family of the victim; but the field of justifiable homicide was narrow.[1]

SELF-DEFENCE

¶ **97.** It has often been stated in the past that a death inflicted by a man in self-defence against an unlawful assailant would be a case of justifiable homicide. But Blackstone[2] pointed out that this was too wide and based upon misconception; for such a homicide could only be justified when the attack resisted was itself a felonious one[3] and therefore the cases must be classed with those above discussed, as homicides justified by the fact that they were effected in order to prevent a capital felony.[4] This is historically sound, for in early law a homicide committed *se defendendo* was only 'excusable' and not 'justifiable'.[5] Homicide in self-defence was therefore caught by the ancient rule of strict liability and the killer could only be saved by the King's mercy. The High Court of Justiciary in Scotland has declared that to justify a plea of homicide in self-defence it is essential that the fatal resistance should have been made to save the accused's life.[6]

Finally, it should be noted that the burden of proof, where self-defence is raised, is on the prosecution;[7] *post*, ¶ 99.

SECTION 3. EXCUSABLE HOMICIDE

¶ **98.** It may seem strange to modern minds that for centuries it was a rule of our law that a man who killed another either by misadventure (*per infortunium*) or in reasonable self-defence (against an attack not itself felonious), although he did not commit a felony, must yet be held guilty of unlawful homicide and require the King's pardon if he were to escape punishment, and even if granted pardon would still be liable to suffer forfeiture of his property;[8] and that he was exposed to

[1] Pollock and Maitland, II, 479.

[2] 4 *Comm.* 180.

[3] Maitland doubted if in the thirteenth century a homicide in self-defence would have been justifiable, even though it was perpetrated in the endeavour to prevent a felony; Pollock and Maitland, II, 479 n. 2.

[4] *Howel's Case* (1221) Maitland's Select Pleas 94 (*T.A.C.*). In 1811 Mr Purcell, of Co. Cork, a septuagenarian, was knighted for killing four burglars with a carving knife.

[5] At p. 183 he writes: 'This species of self defence [*se defendendo*] must be distinguished from that just now mentioned as calculated to hinder the perpetration of a capital crime; which is not only a matter of excuse but of justification.'

[6] *McCluskey* v. *H.M. Advocate* (1959) S.L.T. 26.

[7] *Chan Kau* v. *R.* [1955] A.C. 206; *R.* v. *Lobell* [1957] 1 All E.R. 734; *R.* v. *Porritt* [1961] 3 All E.R. 463.

[8] 1 Hawk. P.C. c. 28; Pollock and Maitland, II, 481. It is significant to note that it required a statute to secure an alleviation of this severity, to meet a group of especially hard cases; 24 Hen. VIII, c. 5, 'For the Declaration of...Ambiguity and Doubt', in effect provided that persons killing those who were attempting to rob or murder, or to

claims for compensation from the family of the deceased.[1] But so it was, and this rule of antiquity which, as we have seen,[2] was not too severe when it involved little more than compensation to be paid, lingered on for centuries after changes in the law of punishment rendered it brutally harsh; as time went on the severities were considerably alleviated by various devices but the law of this matter was complicated and unsatisfactory.[3] One unfortunate result of this complexity was that an artificial distinction existed between cases of justifiable homicide on the one hand and of homicide in self-defence and by misadventure on the other, which the writers endeavoured to explain, not by a true historical analysis, but by purporting to find some blameworthy element in the latter two instances.[4] Since forfeitures have been abolished, homicide by misadventure and excusable homicide have ceased to be distinguishable from justifiable homicide by their consequences to the slayer and this has increased the tendency to confuse the three. In their nature, of course, even the first two are quite dissimilar but since through the narrowness of early law each was without legal excuse they were commonly dealt with together.[5] There is, however, still one important point in which a homicide committed in self-defence differs from a justifiable homicide. If a felonious attack is made upon a man he has the legal right to stand his ground and to resist, and if he kills his assailant the homicide will be justifiable, provided, nowadays, that the measures of resistance which he takes are reasonable in the circumstances. But if the assault is not felonious, then the person attacked must if safely possible retreat, and must not use force against his assailant unless he is placed in such a position that he cannot otherwise evade the attack:[6] as it used to be said, he must flee until he is driven to the wall.

RESISTANCE TO ILLEGAL ARREST

¶ 99. The policy of early law was to accord the maximum protection to officers of justice, and so long as they were acting legally it was

commit burglary were not to suffer any forfeiture of goods etc., but were to be fully acquitted. This enactment was repealed by 9 Geo. IV, c. 31 which also abolished (sect. 10) forfeitures in cases of homicide by misadventure or in self-defence. The words of the statute of Henry VIII show that there was doubt whether or not even justifiable homicide in some cases might not involve forfeiture.

[1] Pollock and Maitland, II, 480.

[2] *Ante*, ¶ 8.

[3] 4 Bl. *Comm.* 188 says that the 'delinquent' had a pardon and writ of restitution of his goods, but had to pay for suing out the same, an expense which was evaded by the judge's usually permitting a general verdict of acquittal.

[4] E.g. 4 Bl. *Comm.* 186, 'for the law sets so high a value upon the life of a man, that it always intends some misbehaviour in the person who takes it away, unless by the command or express permission of the law. In the case of misadventure it presumes...at least a want of sufficient caution in him who was so unfortunate as to commit it; who therefore is not altogether faultless. And as to the necessity which excuses a man who kills another *se defendendo*...the law intends that the quarrel or assault arose from some unknown wrong or provocation either in word or deed.'

[5] For a fuller discussion of this topic see Russ. 511.

[6] 4 Bl. *Comm.* 184.

justifiable for them to adopt the most severe measures to effect the arrest of persons guilty or suspected of crimes. But the law was also jealous of the honest citizen's right to go about unmolested by any other person whether private or official. Accordingly unless the officer attempting an arrest was acting in an entirely legal manner the private citizen attacked by him was allowed to resist by force, and in the older cases particularly it can be seen that the courts were often ready to interpret the facts so far as possible in favour of the victim of the unlawful arrest.[1]

As the law now stands, however, it would seem that although a citizen need not submit to unlawful arrest he must be careful to use no more force than in all the circumstances is reasonable;[2] he certainly will not be justified in maiming or killing the illegal arrester unless the attempted arrest took the form of an attack of a deadly character,[3] in which circumstances, of course, the resistance could as well be regarded as self-defence against a murderous assault. Further, the fact that an arrest is illegal will not of itself cause it to amount to such provocation[4] as will reduce the killing of the arrester from murder to manslaughter (as used to be argued in the ancient cases).

As to burden of proof it has been stated:

> in cases where the evidence discloses a possible defence of self-defence the onus remains throughout on the prosecution to establish that the accused is guilty of the crime of murder and the onus is never upon the accused to establish this defence...; the rule with regard to onus of proof in cases of murder and manslaughter is of general application and permits of no exceptions save only in the case of insanity which is not strictly a defence.[5]

CHANCE MEDLEY

¶ 100. From early times a physical attack upon a harmless man which has so provoked him as to cause him to retaliate immediately with fatal effect has been held to be such provocation as would reduce the killing of the assailant from murder to manslaughter.[6] But, as we have seen, if the original attack were felonious then the victim of it could be held entirely guiltless if he killed his assailant to prevent the commission of the threatened felony upon himself. Between these cases lay that of a man who had been assaulted in some sudden brawl or quarrel (in respect of which he himself was regarded as not entirely without blame) and then, before serious harm was done, had declined further

[1] *R.* v. *Tooley* (1710) 2 Ld. Raym. 1301; Foster, 312 *et seq.*; *R.* v. *Thompson* (1825) 1 Moo. 80; *R.* v. *Walker* (1854) Dearsly 358. The subject is discussed in Russ. 500. But sympathizers are not excused if they use force; *R.* v. *Allen* (1867) 17 L.T. (n.s.) 222.

[2] *R.* v. *Wilson* [1955] 1 W.L.R. 493; *Gelberg* v. *Miller* [1961] 1 W.L.R. 153.

[3] *The People* (*A.-G.*) v. *White* [1947] Ir.R. 247, discussed in 45 *Journal of Criminal Law* (1948), 82 *et seq.*

[4] But see *R.* v. *Cobbett* (1940) 28 Cr.App.R. 11, and ¶ 117 *post.*

[5] *Chan Kau* v. *R.* [1955] A.C. 206. See *R.* v. *Lobell* [1957] 2 W.L.R. 524.

[6] *Post,* ¶ 117.

combat and withdrawn; if, after that, his adversary were to launch upon him a fresh and unprovoked attack, against which in necessary self-defence he killed the attacker, the law held that although he could not be treated as quite guiltless (since he had been in some degree to blame in the first instance) yet his offence could be reduced from murder to excusable homicide, which only involved forfeiture of goods. For such an affair the legal term was chance medley,[1] or casual affray. From the old books it can be seen that the boundaries between chance medley and homicide under provocation were indistinct. Now, however, the old law of chance medley has become quite obsolete. The Offences against the Person Act, 1828, s. 10 abolished punishment and forfeiture in any case of killing without felony[2] and thus removed a difference which had till then distinguished in practice (if not in theory) chance medley from the other cases of excusable homicide, and it has now been declared[3] that the old doctrine of chance medley is no longer valid in the law of homicide. Any such facts as would formerly have been within it must now be considered under the established principles of justifiable homicide, self-defence, or provocation as the case may be.

EXCUSABLE HOMICIDE BY MISADVENTURE

¶ 101. Before 1200 many kinds of intentional killing had been withdrawn from the category of offences which were emendable,[4] and they had become punishable by death or mutilation. But as above mentioned the law for the case of a man who killed another by misadventure (*per infortunium*) was not clear; the position for a long time seems to have been that however blameless he might be the man who caused the death must pay the fines; but in time the rules as to payment of fines broke down, and homicides by misadventure were treated in the same way as those in self-defence, and a pardon was sued for. Forfeiture, however, continued unless the court adopted the device of directing the jury to acquit the prisoner.[5] All this is a thing of the past, and homicide by misadventure now carries no criminal penalties at all, since the killer's defence is absence of *mens rea*. It therefore may now be defined as a homicide brought about by one who neither intended to cause unlawful bodily hurt to anyone nor foresaw that such hurt might result from the action or omission on his part which in fact caused the death;[6] and it is classed as an excusable homicide.

¶ 102. *Homicide in the course of an unlawful act.* It has frequently been stated that a death, however unforeseen, which has been brought about by a man engaged on any unlawful course of conduct will be at the least

[1] *Chaude mêlée*, an affray in the heat of blood; Foster, 275; 4 Bl. *Comm.* 184.

[2] The Forfeiture Act, 1870, abolished all forfeitures for felony or treason.

[3] By the Court of Criminal Appeal in *R.* v. *Semini* [1949] 1 All E.R. 233.

[4] That is, which could be expiated by payment of *wer* and *wite*; see ¶ 8 *ante*.

[5] 1 East P.C. 219; *ante*, ¶ 98.

[6] Subject to the further interpretation of the strange dicta of the House of Lords in *D.P.P.* v. *Smith* [1960] 3 All E.R. 161.

manslaughter, and that it cannot be treated as a case of excusable homicide. However, it is submitted that, for modern law, this is an error. The point will be dealt with in greater detail below[1] but it may be briefly repeated here that the question whether a homicide is excusable or not depends upon the mental processes of the killer at the time when he was pursuing the particular line of conduct which caused the death; it cannot be murder unless that attitude of mind amounted to malice aforethought, and it cannot be manslaughter unless he had that *mens rea* which consists in foresight of possible physical harm less than *fatal* harm.[2] Subject to these conditions it matters not at all that the man may have been engaged in some unlawful proceeding. The reader may also be reminded once more that there are many situations in life in which the law *permits* a certain measure of harm to be inflicted or risked,[3] so that if in any such case, a man, acting within the limits so allowed, unfortunately causes another's death, he will be free from the guilt of felonious homicide.

Section 4. Murder

¶ 103. In early Norman times murder and manslaughter were not distinguished. Every homicide was felonious, unless it was justified, or, within the limits described above, excusable. Among the Germanic peoples on the Continent a distinction had been drawn between an open killing which was emendable[4] and a secret killing which was not. Cases of secret killing were classed as *morth* and it is from this that our word 'murder' has come. Under the law of William the Conqueror if a Norman was slain[5] and the slayer was not produced, the district (the hundred) had to pay a fine, and the name *murdrum* was given both to the homicide and to the fine in such a case.[6] But in the twelfth century every homicide that was grave, whether secret or not, became unemendable, and the term *murdrum* gradually came to be used to describe a homicide of the most heinous kind.[7] But it is in connexion with the ancient view that a secret and treacherous killing (especially when it was effected by lying in ambush for the victim)[8] was unemendable that, as it would seem, the allegation that the homicide was done with *malice aforethought*, or *malice prepense* had its origin.[9] For in proceedings by way of appeal the appellor had to make an allegation of *assultus praemeditatus*; this expression eventually came to be a mere formal declaration and in later centuries was replaced by the words

[1] ¶¶ 111, 132. [2] *Post*, ¶ 135.

[3] E.g. in medical operations and in normal sports and pastimes: see assault and battery (*post*, ¶ 164). [4] Perhaps because it partook of the nature of a fair combat.

[5] Pollock and Maitland, II, 487.

[6] The dead man was presumed to be a Norman unless there was 'express presentment of Englishry'.

[7] In 1340 the fine was abolished by 14 Edw. III, st. 1, c. 4.

[8] The old English *forsteal*, Norman French *aguet purpense* (mod. *guet-apens*).

[9] *Malitia excogitata, malitia praecogitata.*

per malitiam praecogitatam. At this period *malitia* signified general wrong-doing[1] and did not indicate any state of mind on the part of the slayer, while *praecogitata* was a term of art used to indicate that the offence was of the most serious class. The allegation was eventually rendered into English in the well-known words 'malice aforethought'. This development was assisted by the policy of the courts in quite early times of tempering the severity of the law for a man who, inflamed by the sting of a sudden provocation,[2] had forthwith slain his attacker. It should accordingly be remembered that at the time when the word *malitia* began to be used it meant rather the wrongful act intended than the intention itself: it certainly did not have any special reference to the feeling of ill will or hatred, which the word malice now popularly denotes.

Murder then is the most grave kind of felonious homicide. Its essential elements have never been defined by statute, but it is traditionally[3] said to be 'when a person, of sound memory and discretion, unlawfully killeth any reasonable creature in being, and under the King's peace, with malice aforethought, either express or implied'.

In so far as this description deals with the essential elements of the *actus reus*, it has already been discussed,[4] as also have the main questions of causation,[5] and it is unnecessary to add anything here on these topics. But since murder is a crime at common law *mens rea* is required, and this calls for careful consideration.

MENS REA IN MURDER. MALICE AFORETHOUGHT

¶ 104. Malice aforethought is the archaic and now misleading phrase which tradition has fixed in the definition of murder to indicate the *mens rea* of this crime. As stated in the last paragraph the term *malitia praecogitata* or *excogitata* (often rendered as malice aforethought) ultimately came to be a necessary allegation in a charge of the most serious kind of homicide. It served to separate those killings for which no pardon could be expected from those done in self-defence or by misadventure. It also was the basis upon which was built the doctrine that in certain circumstances provocation[6] could be accepted as a defence which would save an intentional killer from the penalty of death. In the discussion of general principles in the earlier part of this book we saw that in broad outline three stages of development could be discerned in the history of criminal responsibility, namely:

(1) The stage of absolute or strict liability in which the law looked to the *consequences* of a man's conduct.
(2) The stage in which medieval law applied an objective moral test to the *conduct* leading to these consequences.
(3) The stage, stretching into the nineteenth century, when the law came to adopt a subjective test; that is to say, it now looked

[1] See Pollock and Maitland, II, 469. [2] *Post*, ¶ 117.
[3] 3 Co. *Inst.* 47; 4 Bl. *Comm.* 198. [4] *Ante*, ¶ 80. [5] *Ante*, ¶¶ 13, 85.
[6] *Post*, ¶ 117. This led to the distinction between murder and manslaughter, ¶ 129 *post*.

primarily at the *attitude of the defendant's mind* which inspired his conduct.

Throughout the same long period of legal growth, changes in penal policy also were taking place and these too can be seen to fall into a series of main chapters, which, however, do not coincide at all closely with the above mentioned stages in the development of the principles of responsibility. They might be grouped according to the penalties imposed.

(1) The penalty for homicide was outlawry and the blood feud; which gave way to

(2) The penalty of pecuniary compensation and fine. These penalties in turn were replaced[1] by

(3) The penalty of capital punishment and mutilation.

The severity of the penal law[2] in this last stage (for the position was reached in which not merely murder but also theft in its various forms and some other felonies were capital offences) stimulated a change of view as to the essentials of responsibility and also led to various devices by which the cruelties of the penal system[3] might be evaded, of which one of the most remarkable was the use which was made of the old ecclesiastical privilege known as benefit of clergy. We have seen[4] that this was extended to cover any layman who could pass a simple test of being able to read; but the technicalities of this legal institution and the repeated changes made from time to time in its rules caused great complications and absurdities.[5] Under 23 Henry VIII, c. 1 benefit of clergy was largely taken from the homicides then described as 'murder with malice aforethought', and thereafter the term 'murder' soon became limited, as it now is, to the form of homicide dealt with by that statute.

Malice aforethought, then, indicates the necessary mental element in the crime of murder.

¶ 105. *Changes of meaning in malice aforethought.* The alterations in the principles of criminal responsibility which were woven into the common law have almost entirely consisted of alterations in the conception of what the mental element should be. Consequently the one phrase, malice aforethought, having been retained unaltered, has had different meanings at different periods. This has more than once been mentioned in previous paragraphs but the matter is so important that the student's attention must be repeatedly directed to it. *Malitia* to begin with indeed connoted not so much an attitude of mind as a secret or treacherous

[1] As Maitland said, 'under cover of charges of felony, *guet-apens* (ambush), and breach of the King's peace, the old rule of *wer* and *wite* was devoured'.

[2] Hume, *History of England*, II, 230; Pike, *History of Crime*, II, 619; Stephen, *Hist. Crim. Law*, I, 466. On this topic see Radzinowicz, *Hist. Eng. Crim. Law*, I, c. 5.

[3] *Ibid.* c. 3.

[4] *Ante*, ¶ 55.

[5] See Stephen, *Hist. Crim. Law*, I, 463. The criminal policy of the Tudors was very harsh, and it moved towards complete abolition of the privilege of clergy, but in later reigns there was a reaction and the law entered on a period of bewildering confusion in which 'clergy' was first allowed and then removed or modified and restored once more.

killing. Next it indicated an objective wickedness in the acts of the accused when freely done without the compulsion of force, fear, or madness. And thirdly, in the nineteenth century, it came to be interpreted as meaning not merely that the accused must have acted voluntarily[1] but also must have foreseen that this course of conduct would, or at least might, bring about a person's death.[2]

¶ 106. The changes just mentioned were a matter of gradual development; the new idea did not at one stroke destroy the earlier. The tree of the common law grows slowly and often puts out new leaves before the old have fallen. There are numbers of cases reported in which, at the same period, one judge has applied the old principle and another the new. Often the judgment calls both in aid in the same case. Still more confusing is the fact that there remain two situations in which the law, as authoritatively declared in the courts, will be found on careful analysis to have retained the principle of strict liability; that is to say, cases of homicide held to be murder despite the fact that the prisoner neither intended to kill nor foresaw that any risk of death was attendant on what he was doing at the time. In neither the one nor the other of these two instances of murder will any of the definitions or explanations of malice aforethought apply: they are indeed anomalous,[3] and, it has been submitted, ought to be, and could safely be, expunged from our law. The objection to them is fundamentally one of ethics as was plainly stated over a hundred years ago by Bentham,[4] and by H.M. Commissioners on Criminal Law who said:[5]

> Impediments to the formation of a uniform and consistent system of criminal statute law sometimes result from the retention of doctrines founded upon ancient notions which are totally incongruous with general principles of our jurisprudence.

And again:[6]

> The proper test of guilt...is that of knowledge and consciousness on the part of the malefactor that hurt or damage is likely to result or will probably result from what he does: his criminality consists in the wilfully incurring the risk of causing loss or suffering to others.... The principle of exemption from criminal responsibility in respect of a hurtful consequence is that of

[1] *Ante*, ¶ 18.

[2] *Ante*, ¶¶ 19, 20.

[3] They are where a death is brought about (*a*) in resisting lawful arrest, and (*b*) 'in the course of, or in furtherance of, a felony of violence'. They are dealt with in more detail below, ¶ 111.

[4] See ¶ 19, *ante*.

[5] *First Report* (1834) [537] XXVI—117 at p. 149.

[6] *Seventh Report* (1843) [448]—XIX-1 at p. 23; see also the Second Report of the Commissioners of 1845, (1846) [709]—XXIV-107, which, at p. 17, quotes with approval statements to the same effect made by the Indian Law Commissioners (cited in Russ. 530).

bona fide ignorance of the connection existing between the mere mechanical act and its consequences.

A step towards their abolition was thought to have been taken by the enactment of the Homicide Act, 1957, but any hopes that this would be the case have been largely frustrated by the decisions of the courts before whom the interpretation of this statute has come. It is discussed below, ¶ 108*a*.

¶ 107. *Suggested definition of malice aforethought.* If these two anomalous cases were removed, the mental ingredient in the crime of murder, to which the name 'malice aforethought' might, in deference to antiquity, still be applied, could be defined simply as the freely formed intention of a man to pursue a course of conduct which he realizes will or may bring about the death of some person. Such a definition will cover all of the following attitudes of mind, each of which has been stated[1] as an example of malice aforethought.

(1) Intention to kill the particular person, who, in fact, was killed. This of course is the most common case of murder.

(2) Intention to kill a particular person, but not the one who actually was killed.[2]

If *A* shoots at *B* with the intention of killing him, but misses and kills *C*, a person whose life he had no intention to take, then the death of *C* is in law treated not as a homicide by misadventure, but as murder.[3] It will make no difference whether *A* thought it probable that he would hit *C*, or thought it improbable, or did not even know that *C* was there; for *A* had the intention to kill (*mens rea*) and he has actually killed (*actus reus*).[4]

(3) Intention to kill, but without selecting any particular individual as the victim.

This has been called 'universal malice'. It is exemplified by the case, put by Blackstone, of a man who resolves to kill the next man he meets and does kill him;[5] and by the occasional case of Malays who from a sudden psychological complex of inferiority are driven to kill indiscriminately in order to assert themselves; and by that of the miscreant who, about 1890, placed an explosive machine on board an Atlantic liner about to sail from Bremerhaven, in order to get the money for which he had insured part of the cargo. It is also exemplified by such atrocities as those attributed to the early settlers in Queensland, who are said to have

[1] In the previous editions of this book.

[2] *R.* v. *Salisbury* (1553) 1 Plowd. 100 (*T.A.C.*). Contrast *R.* v. *Saunders and Archer* (1576) 2 Plowd. 473, which is discussed *ante*, ¶ 69. On 14 January 1858 Orsini attempted to assassinate Napoleon III in Paris by throwing three bombs. The emperor escaped unhurt but 10 spectators were killed and 156 wounded.

[3] Or manslaughter if there was such provocation (see *post*, ¶ 117) as would have reduced the killing of *B* to manslaughter; *R.* v. *Gross* (1913) 23 Cox 455.

[4] Similarly it would be murder if a man intending to commit suicide adopted measures which failed to take his own life but happened to kill another person; *R.* v. *Hopwood* (1913) 8 Cr.App.R. 143; cf. *Commonwealth* v. *Mink* (1877) 9 Lathrop 422. *Post*, ¶ 137.

[5] 4 Bl. *Comm.* 200.

rubbed poison into carcases of sheep or into masses of flour, and then placed them in the bush in hopes of their being eaten by the aborigines.[1]

(4) Intention only to hurt—and not to kill—but to hurt by means of an act which the prisoner realized was likely to kill someone.

The prisoner foresaw that his course of conduct might bring about someone's death (*mens rea*) but none the less he continued it. There are some old cases in which the facts would clearly fall within this principle, but students must remember that, as it is above worded, it is a relatively modern principle, which has been gradually developed in the common law, and cannot be said to have existed at the period when those cases were decided. Thus in *R.* v. *Grey* (1666),[2] where a blacksmith was charged with the murder of his apprentice by striking him on the head with a bar of iron, it was held that the use of so dangerous an instrument 'is all one as if he had run him through with a sword'. And, similarly, a mother who had punished her child by stamping on its body, and had thereby killed it, was held guilty of murder.[3] *R.* v. *Halloway*[4] in 1628 is not, as has sometimes been supposed, a good illustration; it was a case of 'implied malice'.[5] In the early seventeenth century the ancient doctrine of strict liability had still persisted to the extent that death caused by any 'unlawful act' was held to be murder.[6]

(5) Intention to do an act which the prisoner realized was likely to kill, although he had no purpose of thereby inflicting any hurt.

Here again there are many apparent, but not real examples of the application of this principle to be found in the old reports.[7] In modern times some sections of public opinion have felt that to treat this attitude of mind as murderous malice is too severe a standard. Others, however, have thought that the person who for his own purposes is prepared to risk[8] the taking of another's life should rightly incur the guilt of murder if he does so take it; for there is a much greater number of persons whose ruthless selfishness exposes the peaceful citizen to danger than

[1] Haydon's *Trooper-Police of Australia*, 304. On 15 December 1838, seven settlers were hanged in New South Wales for the unprovoked massacre of thirty natives, although they had pleaded: 'It has been so common that we had no idea it was against the law.' Cf. the case of Christiana Edmunds, who in 1872 used wilfully to supply a confectioner's shop with chocolate-creams poisoned with strychnine.

[2] Kel. 64 (*T.A.C.*).

[3] *Ibid.*

[4] (1628) Cro. Car. 131 (*T.A.C.*).

[5] *Post*, ¶ 108.

[6] See Coke's dictum in 3 *Inst.* 56, 'if he had shot...at any tame fowl of another man's, and the arrow by mischance had killed a man, this had been murder, for the act was unlawful'; discussed in *Mod. Appr. Crim. Law*, 213; Russ. 529.

[7] E.g. Y.B. 2 Edw. III, fo. 34, Hil. pl. 1 (*T.A.C.*); *R.* v. *Hull* (1664) Kel. 40 (*T.A.C.*). If these cases are read with a due appreciation of the historical development of malice aforethought they will be seen to have been decided at a time when the judges were exercised as to how to reconcile the old strictness of the law with the new, and imperfectly defined, conception of *mens rea* which was establishing itself in their period. This conflict of principle, exemplified in the statements of Lord Coke, Holt, and Sir Michael Foster, is discussed in *Mod. Appr. Crim. Law*, 212 *et seq.* and Russ. 527 *et seq.*

[8] E.g. as in *R.* v. *Hedley* (1945) 31 Cr.App.R. 35. Some foreign systems of criminal law do place this category of offender in a lower grade of liability.

there is of those who are likely to kill him intentionally. The judgment of the Court of Criminal Appeal[1] quashing the conviction of J. Smith in 1960[2] was fully in harmony with this point of view; but it came as a startling surprise to many lawyers to learn that the judges[3] in the House of Lords could uphold a standard more archaic than either of these two principles, as they did when this case came before them on the fiat of the Attorney General.[4] As previously suggested criminal policy rests upon an ethical basis[5] and in matters of ethics the judiciary can claim no monopoly of decision; the House of Lords can lay down the law but they have no power to dictate the moral conclusions to be reached by free people. It is therefore not a matter of wonder that this judgment has attracted an impressive mass of criticism.[6]

IMPLIED MALICE

¶ 108. The five variations in mental attitude discussed in the last paragraph have been universally accepted as amounting to true malice aforethought in modern law since Professor Kenny propounded them in the first edition of this book. We have seen that a definition of malice aforethought based upon foresight of consequences, which is offered in this edition, comprises them all. But the common law of homicide has always been encumbered with a relic of the archaic system which obtained before any requirement of *mens rea* figured in the law, a hard fragment which has resisted destruction throughout all the changes which have taken place in social views as to the principles which should govern liability to criminal punishment.

It could hardly be expected that those who administered and expounded a law based upon precedent would be over eager to relinquish an old doctrine and welcome a new one, especially when some reason of public policy could be advanced for its retention. So it is that there remained until recently judicial authority for the continued existence, in two instances, of the old doctrine that a homicide is murder even though there is no malice aforethought, that is to say, two situations in which the prisoner had no intention to kill and no realization that his acts might have any fatal result. These were: (1) a death caused by a man in resisting lawful arrest by an officer of justice; and (2) a death caused by

[1] Byrne, Sachs and Winn, JJ.

[2] *R.* v. *Smith* [1960] 2 All E.R. 450.

[3] Lords Kilmuir, Goddard, Tucker, Denning and Parker of Waddington.

[4] *D.P.P.* v. *Smith* [1960] 3 W.L.R. 546.

[5] Cf. the old cases of 'pious perjury' described in Radzinowicz, *Hist. Eng. Crim. Law*, I, 94 *et seq.* See Holmes, *The Common Law* (1887), 35–6: 'Every important principle which is developed by litigation is in fact...the unconscious result of instinctive preferences and inarticulate convictions, but none the less traceable to views of public policy in the last analysis.' An interesting example of this benevolent rigidity when applied to the interpretation of indictments is *R.* v. *Waters* (1835) 1 Moo. 457. See the case of *Taylor* (1800), described by Radzinowicz, *op. cit.* I, 100. Cf. p. 44, n. 1 *ante*.

[6] E.g. 23 *M.L.R.* (G. L. Williams); [1960] *Crim. L.R.* 728 (R. Cross); [1960] *Crim. L.R.* 766 (J. C. Smith). This topic is dealt with more fully below, ¶ 116*b*.

a man in the course of or in furtherance of a felony of violence. In these instances there never has been any real malice aforethought; but, in an attempt to achieve an appearance of conforming with the doctrine *actus non facit reum nisi mens sit rea* while in fact disregarding it, the old writers declared that the law 'implied' malice in these cases. The more modern semantic device, which, by its suggestion of something positive the better conceals the truth, has been to call it 'constructive'[1] malice. This was the position which the legislature purported to revise by the passing of the Homicide Act, 1957, section 1, *infra*.

¶ 108*a*. *The Homicide Act, 1957.* By the Homicide Act, 1957:

1.–(1) Where a person kills another in the course or furtherance of some other offence, the killing shall not amount to murder unless done with the same malice aforethought (express or implied) as is required for a killing to amount to murder when not done in the course or furtherance of another offence.

(2) For the purposes of the foregoing subsection, a killing done in the course or for the purpose of resisting an officer of justice, or of resisting or avoiding or preventing a lawful arrest, or of effecting or assisting an escape or rescue from legal custody, shall be treated as a killing in the course or furtherance of an offence.

The printed marginal note to section 1 reads 'Abolition of "constructive malice"'.

5.–(1) Subject to subsection (2) of this section, the following murders shall be capital murders, that is to say,

(*a*) any murder done in the course or furtherance of theft;[2]

(*b*) any murder by shooting or by causing an explosion;

(*c*) any murder done in the course or for the purpose of resisting or avoiding or preventing a lawful arrest, or of effecting or assisting an escape or rescue from legal custody;

(*d*) any murder of a police officer acting in the execution of his duty or of a person assisting a police officer so acting;

(*e*) in the case of a person who was a prisoner at the time when he did or was a party to the murder, any murder of a prison officer acting in the execution of his duty or of a person assisting a prison officer so acting.

(2) If, in the case of any murder falling within the foregoing subsection, two or more persons are guilty of the murder, it shall be capital murder in the case of any of them who by his own act caused the death of, or inflicted or attempted to inflict grievous bodily harm on, the person murdered, or who himself used force on that person in the

[1] 'These "constructive" doctrines always lead to trouble'; *per* Denning, L.J., in *Hosegood* v. *Hosegood* (1950) 66 T.L.R. 735.

[2] 'Theft' includes any offence which involves stealing or is done with intent to steal; s. 5 (5) (*e*).

course of furtherance of an attack on him; but the murder shall not be capital murder in the case of any other of the persons guilty of it.[1]

. . . .

(4) In this Act "capital murder" means capital murder within subsections (1) and (2) of this section.

It will thus be seen that the Act, while indicating in the marginal note that constructive malice is abolished, yet retains implied malice aforethought in the text, and gives no explanation of what is the difference between these two expressions.[2] We do not find the term 'constructive malice' in the ancient writers from Lambard to East, but they do speak of malice implied, or imputed,[3] and the contexts in which they do so suggest that basically they were considering a matter of evidence, namely, that they were searching in the circumstances of each case for some facts which would establish that the prisoner had been inspired by that attitude of mind towards his acts which constituted 'malice', as that word was understood by the lawyers of the particular writer's own period.[4] The term 'constructive malice' made its appearance as a synonym for implied malice during the past 100 years or so.[5] Since the new Act plainly aims at removing from the crime of murder some cases (*a*) of killing done in the course or furtherance of some other offence, and (*b*) of killing while resisting arrest, it seemed to follow that the courts would have to achieve some clear definition, and presumably a new one, of implied malice. In a number of past cases it has often been stated that it is murder when a death is caused not with definite intention to kill (which would be 'express malice'), but with intention to cause grievous bodily harm[6] (which has been termed at one time 'implied malice aforethought' and at another 'constructive malice aforethought'). This was the situation which faced the Court of Criminal Appeal in *R.* v. *Vickers*;[7] the judgment in that case,[8] however, has created problems which unhappily compel us to continue to grapple with the complexity and uncertainty of this topic.

DEATH CAUSED IN RESISTING ARREST

¶ 109. It was natural that those charged with the maintenance of law and order should feel that every possible measure of protection should be given to officers of justice in the performance of their arduous duties,

[1] Subsection (3) of this section deals with the indictment and the punishment for capital murder.

[2] No distinction between them is recorded in the *Report of the Royal Commission 1949–1953*, Cmd. 8932.

[3] See Russ. 539.

[4] We have seen that 'malitia' or 'malice' is a word which has acquired somewhat different meanings in the course of its long life.

[5] *R.* v. *Greenwood* (1857) 7 Cox 404.

[6] The Act itself in section 5 (2) uses the words 'inflicted or attempted to inflict grievous bodily harm...or used force...'.

[7] [1957] 3 W.L.R. 326.

[8] Discussed below, pp. 162 *et seq.*

and for this purpose that they should aim at striking terror into the mind of a malefactor by the prospect of condign punishment for any harm done in resistance to them.[1] The courts and the early writers therefore did not feel it necessary to apologize[2] for holding that the law would, if necessary, imply malice in any case where the death of such an officer had been caused in resisting arrest by him, however unlikely and unexpected such a fatality had been.[3] The imperfection of this part of the law of homicide was noted by the Commissioners in 1839.[4] To exonerate officers of justice from the old strictness of criminal responsibility when, in due discharge of their duty, they were compelled to take measures which resulted in the death of the person resisting them was seen to be necessary; but this is not the same thing as holding that the person resisting must necessarily be guilty of murder in every case in which he brings about the death of the officer. If, however, it were decided as a matter of policy that this strict rule must be preserved then it would be preferable, in the view of the Commissioners, that this should be made a distinct crime, and should not be drawn by presumptions and fictions into the general class of murder. But even so they thought that the purpose of securing obedience and preventing resistance would be better effected by making the punishment of *resistance* more severe than it then was, where death did *not* result from resistance, and by relaxing its severity where death did accidentally result. For the real evil to be prevented was the unlawful resistance. It must be remembered that if the resister kills the officer intentionally, or by measures which he realizes involve the risk of killing him, then there is no difficulty of principle, for in that case there would really be malice aforethought, as defined in ¶ 107 above. The Commissioners of 1839 were against the old rule and would have required that there should be a real and not an implied malice aforethought to constitute murder in these cases. In 1873 Brett, J., gave to the jury a direction which went some way, at least, towards a recognition of the Commissioners' view.[5] The prisoner had kicked a man who was assisting a policeman to arrest him, and although it did not at the time appear that any serious hurt had been done, the man died two or three days later. The judge said that the question for the jury was whether the prisoner inflicted the kick wilfully, and intending to inflict grievous injury or to resist arrest in which case it would be murder, or whether the kick was accidental, in the course of a wild struggle, in which case it would be manslaughter. The principle to be extracted from this direction is that it is not any death brought about by resistance to arrest (even in a 'wild struggle') which will constitute murder, but only a death brought about by a blow intentionally given.

[1] Foster, 270; 4 Bl. *Comm.* 200. For a more detailed discussion of this topic see Russ. 543.

[2] E.g. 1 Hale P.C. 457, 460; Foster, 308. Blackstone, *ubi supra*.

[3] Much of the early law on this subject is collected in 1 East P.C. 295.

[4] *Fourth Report (1839) on Criminal Law*, [168]–xix–235 at p. x, Art. 54, note (p).

[5] *R.* v. *Porter* (1873) 12 Cox 444.

The doctrine of 'implied' malice was criticized by Sir James Stephen,[1] and in the Draft Code of 1879[2] the killing of a man in resisting lawful apprehension was declared to be murder only when the killer meant to kill or to inflict grievous bodily injury for the purpose of facilitating his escape. This trend towards a more logical development of the law received a check in 1925 as the result of the decision of an Irish court which adopted the earlier doctrine of Hale and Foster without modification and in despite of the views of the Commissioners of 1839, the direction of the court in *R.* v. *Porter*, and the learned opinion of Sir James Stephen. The case was *State* v. *M'Mullen*.[3] A modification of the ancient doctrine was marked by the case of *Appleby* in 1940.[4] This was an appeal against a conviction of murder by a prisoner who had been indicted as a principal in the second degree to the shooting of a police officer, the evidence being that he had used words of encouragement to his companion who had fired the fatal shot. It was argued for the appellant that the jury ought to have been told by the judge that it must be found to their satisfaction that the two men had a common design to use such violence as would be likely to kill or at least to do grievous bodily harm. The court stated[5] that this argument was founded on a fallacy and that 'a much less degree of violence may be sufficient to justify a verdict of guilty of murder in the case of a police officer who is killed in the execution of his duty...than would suffice in the case of another person....The word used here is "violence".' This judgment therefore moved away from the strict liability of the older cases to the extent of requiring 'violence', but violence of lesser degree than that contemplated by the words 'violence likely to do grievous bodily harm'. It may be thought that the Homicide Act, 1957,[6] has gone one step further than *R.* v. *Appleby*, and has at least brought the liability down to 'such violence as would be likely to do grievous bodily harm'; but it may be noted that the word 'violence' does not appear anywhere in the Act. Since, however, it may be introduced again in arguments or judgments, it is as well to consider some of the difficulties that have always been inherent in the word.

¶ **110.** *The meaning of 'violence'*. The word 'violence', as employed in this connexion, has not been precisely defined.[7] In ordinary speech it may denote the exercise of physical force so as to inflict injury on, or cause damage to, person or property.[8] If that were all it would be diffi-

[1] *Hist. Crim. Law*, III, 60–87 (published in 1883). He does not use, nor refer to, the term 'constructive malice'.

[2] Of which he was really the author.

[3] [1925] 2 Ch. and C.L., I.R. 9. For a fuller account of this case see Russ. 10th ed. 546. This Irish decision was, of course, never of more than persuasive authority in the English courts.

[4] (1940) 28 Cr.App.R. 1.

[5] At p. 4.

[6] As interpreted in *R.* v. *Vickers* [1957] 3 W.L.R. 326, *post*, p. 162.

[7] In an attempt to define it in *R.* v. *Appleby*, the court was reduced to the statement 'in other words, violence means violence'.

[8] *Oxford English Dictionary* (1933), XII, p. 221.

cult to see why a death *accidentally* caused in a struggle should not be due to such 'less degree' of violence 'as would suffice to make the killing of the officer murder'. The word is also used to mean 'great force, severity, or vehemence'.[1] But even to adopt this meaning will not solve the difficulty. For a man may employ great force to dislodge a block of stone from its position and if he does so without any intent to harm anyone, and without any knowledge that it may harm someone, it would not seem apt to describe it as a killing by violence if the stone were unfortunately to fall upon and kill a child who, unknown to him, happened to be there. On the other hand, if by the expenditure of only a fraction of such strength he had intentionally struck the child upon the head with a hammer and thus killed it, the crime would, presumably, be correctly described as a crime of violence. The conclusion to which, it is submitted, we must come is that if the introduction of the word 'violence'[2] is to have any effect at all and therefore is to be taken as in some way qualifying the strictness of the ancient doctrine, then it must indeed connote a subjective mental attitude on the part of the killer: that is to say, it must be a vague and indirect indication that *mens rea* is required. But now, in *D.P.P.* v. *Smith*, the House of Lords have eliminated the necessity to establish any foresight of fatality, or even of grievous bodily harm, as a subjective mental element[3] in the guilt of murder; so that, at any rate for the time being, the question of felony or of violence is unimportant and we are back in the primitive position which was deprecated by such eminent jurists as Sir Michael Foster in the eighteenth century and Sir James Stephen in the nineteenth.[4]

DEATH CAUSED BY AN ACT OF VIOLENCE DONE IN THE COURSE OF OR IN FURTHERANCE OF A FELONY INVOLVING VIOLENCE

¶ III. This is the second instance of the survival—although in a modified form—of the ancient doctrine of strict liability under which a subjective mental ingredient was not essential to guilt. Coke's[5] alleviation of its severity by the requirement that the death at least should result from an *unlawful* act, and Foster's[6] further qualification that the act must be felonious, were both regarded by Sir James Stephen as 'monstrous'. In another passage[7] Stephen called the doctrine amazing, but added that it had been repeated so often that he amongst others had accepted and acted upon it, though with regret. Indeed the

[1] *Ibid.* 222.

[2] It was not used by Hale or Foster in the passages selected for approval by the court in *State* v. *M'Mullen.*

[3] Indeed the only subjective element now required is that contained in the words 'voluntarily doing something to someone', in [1961] A.C. at p. 327.

[4] See *post*, ¶ III, and Stephen, *Hist. Crim. Law* III, 57.

[5] 3 *Inst.* 36.

[6] Foster, 258. See *Mod. Appr. Crim. Law*, 213, and Russ. 10th ed. 534 *et seq.*

[7] *Hist. Crim. Law*, III, 57.

severity of the rule had previously led to its being doubted. Thus as early as 1773, in *R.* v. *Lad*,[1] the judges hesitated to say whether it would be murder to cause a child's death by a rape.

¶ 112. *Director of Public Prosecutions* v. *Beard*.[2] In this case the prisoner (who was to some extent under the influence of intoxicating liquor) while raping a girl of thirteen years had, in order to overcome her struggles, placed his hand over her mouth and pressed his thumb on her throat, thereby causing her death by suffocation and shock. He was convicted of murder but on appeal to the Court of Criminal Appeal a verdict of manslaughter was substituted, the court holding itself bound by previous decisions of its own as to the test to be applied when drunkenness was set up as a defence, and being of opinion that if a proper direction had been given to the jury by the trial judge, the verdict might perhaps have been different. A second line of defence was that the jury should have been told that, if they were of opinion that the violent act which caused the girl's death was accidental, then they should return a verdict of manslaughter. This was, however, rejected by the Court of Criminal Appeal. On the ground that the case involved an important point of law it was taken to the House of Lords[3] who restored the conviction for murder.

There were two main points of law to be considered: (*a*) as to the effects of drunkenness upon criminal liability, and (*b*) as to the continued validity of the ancient rule that death caused by a felonious act would be murder even though the prisoner did not intend to kill nor realize that he might kill. The law with regard to drunkenness has been dealt with earlier in this book (¶ 42). As to (*b*) their Lordships accepted the pronouncement of the Court of Criminal Appeal that the evidence established that the prisoner killed the child by an act of violence done in the course of, or in furtherance of, the crime of rape, a felony involving violence,[4] and that by the law of England such an act was murder. Their Lordships said that 'in Beard's case it was only necessary to prove that the violent act causing death was done in furtherance of the felony of rape'; their conclusion was that drunkenness could be no defence unless it could be established that Beard at the time of

[1] 1 Leach 96; and study *R.* v. *Horsey* (1862) 3 F. and F. 287 (*T.A.C.*); *ante*, ¶ 13 (iv). See also Sir James Stephen's judgment in *R.* v. *Serné* (1887) 16 Cox 311 (*T.A.C.*) and the judgments in such cases as *Whitmarsh*, *Bottomley*, *Lumley*, *Bubb* (abortion operations which proved fatal), cited *ante*, ¶ 20, which led Professor Kenny to formulate a restatement of the 'felony murder' rule as limited to 'such felonious acts as involve violence against an unwilling victim'. This was in effect (but without acknowledgment) accepted in *D.P.P.* v. *Beard*, *post*, ¶ 112.

[2] [1920] A.C. 479 (*T.A.C.*). For a detailed discussion of this important case see *Mod. Appr. Crim. Law*, 254 *et seq.*, and Russ. 550 *et seq.*

[3] Prior to the hearing the Home Secretary had intimated that in no case would the death sentence be carried out.

[4] As to the meaning now given to 'involving' by the Court of Criminal Appeal, see *R.* v. *Grant and Gilbert* (1954) 38 Cr.App.R. 107, and the comment thereon in Russ. 565.

committing the rape was so drunk that he was incapable of forming the intent to commit it.

¶ 113. '*In the course or in the furtherance of*'. The expression 'in the course or furtherance of' calls for explanation since it occurs in sections 1 and 5 of the Homicide Act, 1957. It cannot be said for certain if the words 'in furtherance of' were intended to be a mode of expression merely alternative to the words 'in the course' of; or if, on the other hand, the two phrases were used disjunctively to indicate different situations. Up to the present there has been no authoritative declaration in the courts on this point. Assuming, however, that each phrase does refer to a different situation then it is suggested that both must relate to what is done *before* the felony has been completed. The reasons are (*a*) that once a felony has been committed it is automatically completed and becomes a past event; hence its 'course of commission' is also at an end; and (*b*) that the word 'furtherance' means 'the action of helping forward'[1] and points to something which aids the attainment of some objective. Presumably it may be taken as a restatement of Foster's proposition,[2] 'if it be done in prosecution of a felonious intention it will be murder'. Therefore nothing which is done *after* the felony has once been committed can properly be said to be done in furtherance of the felony. The felon may do many things to further his escape or to further the concealment of the crime, but these do not further its commission.

¶ 114. Assuming therefore that the phrases mean something different it is suggested that an act may be said to have been done in furtherance of the felony only when it was a step intentionally taken for the purpose of achieving the felony which was the offender's ultimate aim. For example, if a man who intends to commit a burglary takes a ladder and goes towards the house, he is doing things in furtherance of the felony. But if, as he goes along, he slips, or turns suddenly, and happens to break a window, this is merely coincidental, and it cannot be said that he has broken the window in furtherance of the felony. If, however, he had purposely thrust the ladder at the window in order to break the glass and to facilitate his entry, it would have been done in furtherance of the felony. As we have already observed[3] the mere fact that a man is seen carrying a ladder will not be enough to constitute the *actus reus* of attempt to commit burglary, even though there may be other evidence[4] of his *mens rea*, i.e. of his intention to commit the burglary. It will, however, none the less be a thing done in furtherance of the felony at which he is aiming; on this analysis it appears that things may be done in furtherance of the objective which are not yet sufficient to constitute the *crime* of attempt to reach that objective.

[1] See *Oxford English Dictionary* (1933), IV, 619.

[2] Foster, 258.

[3] *Ante*, ¶ 63.

[4] E.g. a confession by him.

When the acts of preparation do reach the point when attempt is constituted, then also, it is suggested, we can say that the offender begins the stage when he is 'in the course of committing' the offence. This stage will end when the offence has been committed.

¶ 115. *In the course or furtherance of theft.* Any murder done 'in the course or furtherance of theft' is made a capital murder by section 5 (1) (*a*) of the Homicide Act, 1957; the penalty for this is death.[1] In this section 'theft' includes any offence which 'involves stealing or is done with intent to steal'.[2] There is nothing in the Act to decide whether or not a non-felonious theft (e.g. of a dog or a ferret) is covered by these words.[3] The question of the interpretation of the words 'in the course or furtherance' soon arose in *R.* v. *Stokes*,[4] but, following what seems to be developing into a modern tendency, the judge left the words to the jury, making it plain to them that his remarks must not be regarded as judicial directions as to their interpretation. But in the following year the question came before the Court of Criminal Appeal in *R.* v. *Jones*.[5]

It appeared that late one evening Jones had broken into a co-operative society's stores, and gone upstairs to a room containing a safe which the manager had carelessly left open while he went downstairs. Jones took money from the safe and put it into his pocket and was about to descend the stairs when he heard the manager coming up from below. When the manager approached the top Jones emerged from behind some sacks and struck him on the head so severely that his skull was fractured in five places, as a result of which he died. Jones appealed against his conviction of capital murder on two grounds, (*a*) that he did not intend either to kill or to do grievous bodily harm in that the injuries were caused by the deceased's falling downstairs after being pushed, so that his offence was no more than manslaughter; (*b*) that even if it were held to be murder it would not be capital since the fatal attack was made after the theft had been committed and not in the course or furtherance of it.

In dismissing the appeal Lord Parker, C.J., said there was ample evidence on which the jury could come to the decision that this was murder and not manslaughter. With regard to the defence that it could not be regarded as in the course or furtherance of theft since the theft had been fully completed, Lord Parker said: 'It does not seem to this court that the argument is sound that if a man has committed a theft the offence is complete for all purposes, so that, if thereafter, in an attempt to avoid detection he strikes somebody and commits murder, it is not capital murder. This was a case where the appellant was caught, if one may use the expression, red-handed, and in order to avoid detection, and while still on the scene of his theft, he committed murder. It

[1] Sect. 6 (1).
[2] Sect. 5 (5) (*e*).
[3] If it should be so held, then our law has become more fierce than ever before, since, albeit indirectly, it would be the stealing or even attempted stealing of the dog which would render the offence capital.
[4] [1958] Crim. L.R. 688.
[5] [1959] 1 All E.R. 411; 43 Cr.App.R. 94.

is difficult to see why that should not be within the words "in the course... of theft".'

With regard to this judgment it must, with all respect, be submitted that the reasoning is open to the following objections. (*a*) It is a basic rule that the interpretation of statutory words should begin with their dictionary meaning, and the above phrase 'in the course of' quite plainly does not include things done *after* the theft has been effected[1] and done for another purpose, namely, to escape detection and to avoid arrest; and one may pray leave to see no difficulty in this.[2] (*b*) If the legislature had intended to include what might be done after the theft, why did it not follow the lines of section (23) (1) (*b*) of the Larceny Act, 1916, i.e. 'robs...and, at the time of or immediately before or immediately after such robbery, uses any personal violence to any person'? (*c*) No explanation is given as to where the limit of 'in the course' is to be drawn. Supposing Jones had just reached the street and had been accosted by the manager who asked what he had been doing; or had returned to his lodgings and had been disturbed by someone (whom he could not trust) while emptying his pockets, would the blows struck still be in the course of the theft? Or were the words 'and while still on the scene of his theft' intended to be a statement of essential fact?[3] (*d*) The meaning of the words 'or furtherance of theft' was not explained but was expressly left 'for another occasion'. This seems to be treating them disjunctively; if so we are faced with a proposition containing two members, correlated but different, and it is not easy to imagine what meaning the Court of Criminal Appeal will devise for the word 'furtherance'.

There is, however, the further point that the court cited as persuasive authority a passage from the judgment of Lord Sorn in a Scottish case,[4] prefaced by the statement, 'The facts do not matter'. With all respect it must be objected that the facts of that case do matter, since without knowledge of them it is easy to misunderstand the point with which Lord Sorn was dealing.

Graham was trying to break into a public house with intent to steal, when the door was opened and he was confronted by the publican *X*. G. then used words amounting to an admission of his purpose but also indicating that he now abandoned it: *X* then struck G. who thereupon drew a knife and wounded *X*. On these facts G. was charged with unlawful wounding, but this charge was dropped since *X* subsequently died of the wounds, and G. was charged with capital murder. The defence set up provocation and self-defence, and alternatively pleaded that if it were murder then it would not be

[1] I.e. so as to satisfy sect. 1 of the Larceny Act, 1916.

[2] See [1960] *Crim. L.R.* at p. 12.

[3] If so, although the scope is narrowed, yet there will still be doubts such as those which the Roman jurists experienced in trying to define the point at which a *furtum* ceased to be *manifestum* and became *nec manifestum*.

[4] *H.M. Advocate* v. *Graham*, 1958 Sc.L.T. 167.

capital murder because G. had made it plain, before *X* assaulted him, that he had given up his plan of stealing so that his use of the knife was not 'in the course of theft'. It was in answer to this last submission for the defence that Lord Sorn was speaking in the cited passage.

We are not here concerned with the merits or demerits of Lord Sorn's dictum; but when it is examined carefully it will be seen that it is *not* authority, even persuasive, for the conclusion reached in *R.* v. *Jones.* For Lord Sorn's interpretation of the words is:

> that the course of theft is begun when perpetration is begun; that it covers the period of attempt as well as the period of completion; the attempt as well as the crime; and I say that if a burglar is interrupted in that course, the course of perpetration, and he murders even in order to get away, and not with the idea of going on, but with the idea of getting away, it is still murder done in the course of theft.

This clearly indicates that his lordship was envisaging the 'course' of theft as *beginning with attempt* and *ending with perpetration.* His further remarks are referring to things done *within the period* of 'course of' as laid down earlier in the passage:

> It would, I think, be somewhat ridiculous to suppose that Parliament has said: 'We will make it murder if the householder who wakes up and goes to interfere with a burglar gets killed by the burglar who kills him to go on with his stealing, but we won't make it capital murder if the burglar murders him in order to run away.' I think it does not matter what he was going to do afterwards; or what he did afterwards; if he was in the course of theft and he did the killing it is 'in course of' within the meaning of section 5 of the Homicide Act.

The conclusion to which we must come is that the judgment in *R.* v. *Jones* stands alone and that it has interpreted the statute as though the words 'in the course or furtherance of theft' were equivalent to 'by any action in connexion with theft before or after its commission'.

Some constitutional lawyers might regard this as a judicial usurpation of the function of the legislature.

¶ 116. *R.* v. *Betts and Ridley*; *R.* v. *Stone.* The judgment of the House of Lords in *Beard's Case* was followed ten years later in the case of *R.* v. *Betts and Ridley.*[1] The two men had agreed that Betts should waylay one Andrews while he was taking money to a bank, and should push him down and rob him of the money, while Ridley waited in a motor car in a nearby street. Betts did intercept Andrews and struck him to the ground with a severe blow on the head, from which attack he died. The jury were directed that if they thought Betts had done an act which was 'calculated in the judgment of ordinary people to cause death' they might properly find him guilty of murder, which they did. The Court

[1] (1930) 22 Cr.App.R. 148 (*T.A.C.*).

of Criminal Appeal dismissed his appeal against this conviction on the ground that the direction was if anything too favourable to him since he was committing a felonious act of violence against the person. On this ground also they dismissed the appeal of Ridley since he was a principal in the second degree and anticipated that Andrews would at least be pushed down. That the court did, however, feel that Ridley's part in this homicide was less reprehensible may be seen from a hint at the end of the judgment that the prerogative of mercy might be exercised in favour of Ridley, as in fact it was. But now by virtue of section 5 (2) of the Homicide Act, 1957, this would not be a 'capital' murder by Ridley.

The same principle was approved in the case of *Stone*[1] in 1937. The prisoner had accidentally caused the death of a woman during an unsuccessful attempt to rape her; and in answer to a question by the jury, 'If as a result of an intention to commit rape a girl is killed, although there was no intention to kill her, is the man guilty of murder?' the Lord Chief Justice had answered 'Yes, undoubtedly'. The Court of Criminal Appeal dismissed Stone's appeal against conviction of murder, the abortion cases being distinguished as instances where there was 'no intention to do any harm or anything against the wish of the person hurt'.[2] It was thought that by virtue of section 1 (1) of the Homicide Act such a case as *Stone* would now be no more than manslaughter but here again *D.P.P.* v. *Smith* has rendered this doubtful.[3] The same may be said of *R.* v. *Jarmain*,[4] in which it was stated that 'the use of a loaded firearm in order to frighten the person victimized into submission is a violent measure'.

GRIEVOUS BODILY HARM

¶ 116*a*. The term 'grievous bodily harm'[5] has very often been used in connexion with homicide cases without any precise definition. In regard to crimes involving non-fatal harm to the person it occurred in two statutes of 1803 and 1828,[6] and has been repeated in several sections of the Offences against the Person Act, 1861, also without definition.[7] For the purposes of these statutes it has been laid down in the decided cases that the bodily harm may be external or internal, and that it need not be dangerous to life[8] nor be permanent in its effects; but that it is not

[1] *R.* v. *Stone* (1937) 53 T.L.R. 1046. This case was criticized in a note in 54 *L.Q.R.* 22.

[2] This distinction has perhaps disappeared since the judgment in *D.P.P.* v. *Smith*, so that the deaths resulting from a felonious abortion operation may in future be cases of murder.

[3] Unless a dictum in *R.* v. *Vickers* [1957] 3 W.L.R. at p. 328 is to be taken to imply that an intention to commit rape would not be enough, even if the man 'used a moderate or even small degree of violence'.

[4] [1946] K.B. 74 (*T.A.C.*). See the criticism of this case in Russ., 10th ed. 561. Jarmain was not executed.

[5] See the discussion of this topic in Russ., ch. 29.

[6] 43 Geo. III, c. 58 and 9 Geo. IV, c. 31 (both repealed).

[7] It appears in section 5 (2) of the Homicide Act, 1957, with the added words 'or himself used force'.

[8] *R.* v. *Cox* (1818) R. and R. 362.

'grievous' unless it seriously interferes with health or comfort,[1] even though for no longer than a limited period of time. The Act of 1861, however, provides for a higher maximum penalty in cases where the harm is intended. The foregoing are all instances of non-fatal harm; but where a death has been caused and the question of liability arises, both writers and judges have, during the past hundred years or so, frequently spoken of an 'intention to do grievous bodily harm' as a sufficiently heinous attitude of mind to fix the guilt of murder on the man who has killed, and this can only mean that it constitutes the necessary 'malice aforethought'. But never did those who used this expression define with precision what 'grievous bodily harm' was; yet it does seem that none would have gone so far as to use it for murder in the wide sense given to it in the cases of bodily harm mentioned above. Indeed it is submitted that when the various statements on this point are studied it will be found that behind most of them there lay (undeclared and perhaps not always realized by those who made them) the notion of what we have called recklessness;[2] that is to say, although it was not the man's desire and intention to cause death yet he was well aware that what he was doing might have fatal consequences, and none the less went on to take that risk.

It must, however, be remembered that intentionally to do grievous bodily harm was (and still is) a felony, so that the cases in question fell within the old doctrine of constructive (implied) malice aforethought. The mental confusion engendered by failure to appreciate this point is to be seen, for example, in one of the answers given by a judicial witness to the Royal Commission of 1949–53. When asked 'If he inflicts grievous bodily harm, he must know that death is likely to ensue?', the witness answered:

> Yes, but then he may say 'I did not intend to inflict grievous bodily harm, I only intended to inflict a small degree of harm', and of course, in certain cases that might be perfectly true. A man might throw a stone at somebody which he thought was only going to hit him in a fleshy part of the body, but which put out his eye, and that might lead to death; but nowadays I do not think it would be in accordance with right feeling that it should be regarded as murder.[3]

If that is so, then the principle emerges that what the prosecution has to establish is the subjective fact that the prisoner foresaw that his conduct might cause death; and this recklessness, or readiness to *risk*

[1] *R.* v. *Ashman* (1858) 1 F. and F. 88, *per* Wilkes, J. But now the C.C.A. in *R.* v. *Metharam* [1961] 3 All E.R. 200, have declared that, as a result of the decision in *D.P.P.* v. *Smith* [1961] A.C. 290, it is a misdirection of the jury to adopt the old formula (of *R.* v. *Ashman*) if the only intent established is one to interfere seriously with health and comfort; see ¶ 159 *post*. [2] *Ante*, ¶ 24.

[3] *Report of the Royal Commission*, 1953, Cmd. 8932, Minutes of Evidence, p. 252, Question 3164, Lord Goddard, C.J. And see the Questions and Answers quoted in Russ. 558 *et seq.* to the same effect. As to the effect of a dictum in *R.* v. *Vickers* [1957] 3 W.L.R. 326 (*T.A.C.*), see *post*, p. 163.

inflicting fatal harm may be ascertained by the jury to their satisfaction, from evidence as to the particular hurt which the man *intended* to inflict upon the deceased.[1] It is indeed fundamentally a question of evidence and not a question of law. This, most unfortunately, is constantly being overlooked, with the confusing result that evidence pointing to the facts to which a legal principle will apply is treated as though it were the definition of that same principle. Of course it is necessary for a judge to put to the jury what their task is in language which they can understand, for the purposes of the particular case before them; but it is for the jury, and not for the judge, to decide questions of fact; and although the judge may himself conclude from the serious nature of the attack made by the prisoner that he contemplated (there being no special evidence to the contrary) the likelihood of its causing death, the judge should still leave that conclusion for the jury to draw. To put it to the jury as a point of *law* is to deprive the prisoner of the *chance* (however slender) that the jury might have a reasonable doubt as to his being guilty of murder.[2] Consider the mixture of thought in the following passage:[3]

> In murder the jury is told—and it has always been the law—that if a person...attacks another intending to kill or intending to do grievous bodily harm, and the person attacked dies, that is murder, the reason being that the requisite malice aforethought, which is a term of art, is satisfied if the attacker intends to do grievous bodily harm.... But if the charge is one of attempted murder..., in that particular case the intent is the essence of the crime while, where the death of another is caused, the necessity is to prove malice aforethought which is supplied in law by proving intent to do grievous bodily harm.

There is no word in the above declaration to suggest that what the prisoner himself had in mind as to the *risk of his killing* the deceased is of any importance at all, whereas, according to what is here put forward as the true principle, the question for the jury should be: 'Did the prisoner, or did he not, realize that his conduct was such as to endanger life?' When such words as those in *R.* v. *Whybrow* are used, a jury will not regard the direction to them as a guide in assessing evidence, and then such verdicts as occurred in *R.* v. *Grant and Gilbert*,[4] *R.* v. *Ward*,[5] and *R.* v. *Smith*[6] must be expected to follow.

In *R.* v. *Ward* the appellant was a man of subnormal intelligence[7] who

[1] As the Commissioners of 1839 said: 'And so in all cases it is essential...not only that that act should...be attended with peril to life, but hat the offender should be aware of such peril' [168]–xix–235.

[2] For the duty of the judge to make sure that any defence legally available to the accused person should be submitted to the jury see, e.g., *Kwaku Mensah* v. *R.* [1946] A.C. 83; *Chan Kau* v. *R.* [1955] A.C. 206; *Bullard* v. *R.* [1957] A.C. 635.

[3] *R.* v. *Whybrow* (1951) 35 Cr.App.R. 141 at p. 146.

[4] *Ante*, p. 153.

[5] [1956] 1 Q.B. 351.

[6] [1960] 2 All E.R. 450, later in the H.L. as *D.P.P.* v. *Smith* [1960] 3 All E.R. 161.

[7] Such as could now possibly come within sect. 2 of the Homicide Act, 1957, as a case of 'diminished responsibility'; *ante*, ¶ 53*a*.

suffered from gastric ulcers. He was cohabiting with a woman who had a backward child of eighteen months by another man and there was evidence that he had treated the child kindly. It appeared that on returning home one evening after his day's work, he was asked to mend the bed while the mother went out for some purpose, and while he was so engaged the child was continually crying, which so irritated him that, as he said, he lost his temper and picked up the child and shook her 'with full force', but that he did not want her to die and had no intention of killing or hurting her and only thought of making her be quiet. But when he put her down he found her to be dead. The mother and he took the body of the child and buried it in a heap of some 200,000 tons of slag or shale where it remained for about twenty months; during this period the shale shifted owing to the weather and the police had to dig twelve to fifteen feet into the mass to get at the body, which was found in an advanced stage of decomposition. The skull was there until it was moved, after which it disintegrated; but it was seen to be fractured in two places. A medical witness spoke of two dents and a crack in the bone of the skull which he thought were not caused by the pressure of the shale, and by themselves would not have caused death but might have been due to a man's grip on the child while pressing its face into the mattress for a few seconds, so as to bring about death by asphyxia accelerated by the fractures. In cross-examination this witness said 'You really cannot say how it died', and that the destruction of the vital organs had prevented him from ascertaining the exact cause of death.[1] Pilcher, J., directed the jury that 'If, when he did the act which he did do, he must as a reasonable man have contemplated that death or grievous bodily harm was likely to result to the child as the result of what he did, then...if you are satisfied about that he is guilty of murder. If on the other hand he could not, as a reasonable man, have contemplated that death would result in consequence of what he did, then he is guilty of manslaughter.' Here clearly the jury were directed to apply an objective test, and moreover one which excluded the benefit of doubt by the words 'If he could not, as a reasonable man, have contemplated that death would result, he would be guilty of manslaughter', which were tantamount to telling the jury that they must convict of murder unless they were sure that no reasonable man could have foreseen that death might result. The case for the appellant was carefully and fully argued by counsel but their lordships did not call upon counsel for the Crown to reply. In dismissing the appeal Lord Goddard, C.J., said[2] that the judge's summing-up was 'unimpeachable', and added 'The objection which Mr Lyon takes to that is that it brings in the test of a reasonable man, and you have to say what that particular man knew. Of course the test must be applied to all alike and the only measure that can be brought to bear in these matters is what a reasonable man would or would not contemplate...; if the jury come to the conclusion that any reasonable person, that is to say, a person who cannot set up a plea of insanity, must have known that what he

[1] See the reports in the *Yorkshire Evening Post* and the *Yorkshire Evening News*, 13 December 1955.

[2] [1956] 1 Q.B. at p. 356.

was doing would cause at least grievous bodily harm, and the death is the result of that grievous bodily harm, then that amounts to murder in law.'[1]

As to this judgment it will be observed (*a*) that, in repudiating a subjective test, it in effect adopted the ancient doctrine of constructive malice in a death caused in the course of commission of another offence (in *Ward's Case* causing grievous bodily harm);[2] (*b*) that it offered no definition of grievous bodily harm; and (*c*) that, if a 'reasonable man' is one who 'cannot set up a plea of insanity', then either the jury are expected to assess the foresight of a person, for example, who is classed as mentally defective, or else they are to decide as a fact what the particular prisoner before them did foresee, which would be to apply the subjective test contended for by counsel for the appellant, and rejected by the court, thus constituting a self-contradiction in the judgment. It is submitted that all this puzzling confusion arose from treating as a matter of law that which is essentially a matter of evidence.

Thus in *R.* v. *Vickers*[3] the Court of Criminal Appeal declared[4] that the words of the statute '"where a person kills another in the course or furtherance of some other offence" cannot, in our opinion, be referred to the infliction of the grievous bodily harm if the case which is made against the accused is that he killed a person by having assaulted the person with intent to do grievous bodily harm, and from the bodily harm he inflicted that person dies'. As to the intention of the prisoner the court said:[5] 'If a person does an act which amounts to the infliction of grievous bodily harm he cannot say that he only intended to cause a certain degree of harm.'[6] The court also stated that the summing-up of the trial judge, Hinchcliffe, J., was quite impeccable, and cited from it the following passages:

> If you are in doubt whether the accused man had the intention to inflict grievous bodily harm upon Miss Duckett, it is right that in these circumstances the accused would be guilty of manslaughter.... If...you come to the conclusion that the accused killed Miss Duckett without any malice, that is, without intending her any harm, or only trifling harm,[7] then your verdict will be one of guilty of manslaughter.... Murder is with the intention to

[1] Much public attention was aroused by this case and Ward's sentence was commuted a few days before the date fixed for his execution. For criticisms of the judgment see Prevezer, 'Murder by mistake' in [1956] *Crim. L.R.* 375; Denny, 'Objectivity in murder', 19 *Mod. L.R.* 44; Russ. 566 *et seq.*

[2] The effect now of section 1 (1) of the Homicide Act, 1957, in such circumstances as those in *Ward's Case* was discussed in *R.* v. *Vickers* [1957] 3 W.L.R. 326, *infra.* For a detailed criticism of this case see [1958] *Crim. L.R.* 15, 'Malice implied and constructive' by the present editor, who has seen no need to modify what is therein expressed through anything contained in an anonymous reply to it in [1958] *Crim. L.R.* 714.

[3] [1957] 3 W.L.R. 326; 2 All E.R. 741 (*T.A.C.*).

[4] At pp. 328, 329.

[5] At p. 328, line 39.

[6] This statement must presumably be taken to override the answer to question 3164 given before the Royal Commission on Capital Punishment; *ante*, p. 159 n. 3.

[7] These words were explained in the Court of Criminal Appeal (at p. 330) as 'for instance, a push to get her out of the way'.

kill or to do grievous bodily harm; manslaughter is an unlawful killing, but without any[1] intention....Malice will be implied, if the victim was killed by a voluntary act of the accused...done with the intention either to kill or to do some grievous bodily harm. The grievous bodily harm need not be permanent, but it must be serious, and it is serious or grievous if it is such as seriously and grievously to interfere with the health or comfort of the victim.

The salient points which emerge from this judgment seem to be:

(i) that, if the sole intention of the accused was to commit an assault and battery (within the provisions of the Offences against the Person Act, 1861) on the deceased, that offence may not be regarded as 'some other offence' within the meaning of section 1 (1) of the Homicide Act;

(ii) that for the purposes of this Act the terms 'grievous' or 'serious' are synonymous;

(iii) that the expression 'grievous bodily harm' comprises any harm which 'is such as seriously and grievously to interfere with the comfort of the victim', and that it 'need not be permanent';[2] and

(iv) that if such harm as falls within (iii) above, does in fact occur and death ensues therefrom, the prisoner cannot escape conviction of murder on the argument that he only intended to cause a less degree of harm; so that the requirement of intention to do grievous bodily harm is purely objective, i.e. the prisoner is legally held to have intended grievous bodily harm if grievous bodily harm resulted from his conduct.[3]

On the face of all the dicta contained in the *Vickers* judgment it was difficult to resist the conclusion that the law of murder with implied malice (which has sometimes, perhaps more lucidly, been called 'implied murder')[4] had in effect been rendered more severe than it was before the Act, since it was most unlikely that before the Act a 'constructive malice'[5] killer would have been put to death;[6] while for others in whom there was not proved to have existed a clear intention to kill there was a reasonable hope of escaping the extreme penalty. It seemed probable that after the interpretation in the *Vickers* judgment the prerogative of mercy would be more sparingly exercised.[7] More-

[1] It would seem that these words could hardly have been intended as a definition of the felony of manslaughter, but that the learned judge must have meant 'any such intention as I have mentioned'.

[2] It seemed therefore to have the same scope as it had been held, in decided cases, to have for the purpose of the Acts dealing with offences against the person, e.g. *R.* v. *Cox* (1818) R. and R. 362; *R.* v. *Ashman* (1858) 1 F. and F. 88, *post,* ¶ 159. But see the remarks of the House of Lords in *D.P.P.* v. *Smith, infra* ¶ 116*b*, as interpreted in *R.* v. *Metharam* [1961] 3 All E.R. 200.

[3] *Ex hypothesi*, death must have been caused, otherwise the question of murder could not arise; and death must be the most grievous possible harm. Can the court have meant to return to the archaic rule of absolute liability in homicide in this way?

[4] *R.* v. *Vamplew* (1862) 3 F. and F. 520; *R.* v. *Skeet* (1866) 4 F. and F. 931.

[5] As defined in the *Vickers* judgment.

[6] See e.g. *R.* v. *Jarmain* [1946] K.B. 74, in which the prisoner was sentenced to death but was reprieved.

[7] As was envisaged in the debate in the House of Lords on the Homicide Bill, *Weekly Hansard*, 21 Feb. 1957, 1197–1200.

over the law of manslaughter was made even more obscure than it was before. The judgement is yet one more example of the jurisprudential evil and, indeed, practical mischief[1] which arise when the courts allow and encourage the transmutation of matters of evidence into matters of law.

Earlier in 1957[2] the Court of Criminal Appeal[3] approved the proposition that, not only for the purposes of section 18 of the Offences against the Person Act, 1861, but also in any statutory definition of a crime, 'malice' must be taken as requiring either (i) an actual intention to do the particular kind of harm that in fact was done, or (ii) recklessness as to whether such harm might occur or not; and declared: 'In our opinion "maliciously" in a statutory crime postulates "foresight of consequences".' The principle so laid down extended[4] to felonies consisting of serious, but not fatal, attacks on the person for which the penalty could be as much as imprisonment for life. Is there any sensible reason why it should not also be applied to cases of murder, where the fixed penalty must be either life-imprisonment, or death?[5] And yet the House of Lords in *D.P.P.* v. *Smith* not only refused to apply this principle to cases of murder, but, it seemed, incidentally ruled that it is not to apply to cases falling within section 18 of the above Act of 1861.[6]

¶ 116*b*. *D.P.P.* v. *Smith.* Space does not permit a detailed examination of this important decision by the House of Lords.[7] Some criticisms have already been mentioned and it must suffice here merely to bring together the main points which emerge from the judgment, without testing the soundness of the reasoning on which they were based. They are: (*a*) An emphatic repudiation of the subjective principle of liability in the crime of murder. The judgment states: 'It matters not what the accused in fact contemplated, or whether he ever contemplated at all, provided he was in law responsible and accountable for his actions, i.e. was a man capable of forming an intent, not insane within the M'Naghten Rules, and not suffering from diminished responsibility.' (*b*) A declaration that it is not a rebuttable presumption, but a rule of law, that an accused person is held to intend the natural and probable consequences of his acts. (*c*) That the only test for deciding the question whether 'the unlawful and voluntary' act of the accused was of such a kind that grievous bodily harm was the natural and probable result was 'what the ordinary, responsible man, in all the circumstances of the case, would have contemplated as the natural and probable result'. (*d*) That the same test of liability to conviction of murder was the

[1] For results so often follow which offend the ethical feelings of the general community.

[2] *R.* v. *Cunningham* [1957] 2 Q.B. 396; *post,* ¶ 158.

[3] Byrne, Slade and Barry, JJ.

[4] E.g. in the Offences against the Person Act, 1861.

[5] Where section 5 of the Homicide Act applies.

[6] See, however, *R.* v. *Metharam* [1961] 3 All E.R. 200; *post,* ¶ 159.

[7] But see now the interpretation of this judgment adopted by the C.C.A. in *R.* v. *Metharam* [1961] 3 All E.R. 200; *post,* ¶ 159.

test to be applied to liability to conviction of unlawfully and maliciously causing grievous bodily harm within section 18 of the Offences against the Person Act, 1861.[1] (*e*) A declaration that it is 'unnecessary and, I would add, inadvisable, to add anything to the expression "grievous bodily harm" in its ordinary and natural meaning'; and that 'in the vital direction given just before the jury retired he [the trial judge] referred to "serious hurt" or "serious harm"'; and that 'it is quite impossible to say that the harm, which the respondent [Smith] must be taken to have contemplated, could be anything but of a very serious nature coming well within the term "grievous bodily harm"'.

PROVOCATION, VOLUNTARY MANSLAUGHTER

¶ 117. For many centuries past the common law has recognized one situation[2] in which criminal liability may be reduced, although not entirely removed, namely, if it be proved that the misdeed was done under the influence of an irresistible impulse.[3] This sole case is that of an intentional homicide committed when the slayer has been so provoked by an attack made upon him that he has suddenly and temporarily lost his self-control and has killed another in the ungovernable passion of the moment. Thus Coke drew a distinction between an intentional killing in hot blood and an intentional killing when the blood was cool (a killing *sedato animo*),[4] speaking of the latter[5] as covering a case where 'one killeth another without any provocation on the part of him that is slain'. The writers of authority who succeeded Coke continued to treat an intentional killing in hot blood as a less heinous kind of homicide than one done by a man who was in possession of his self-control.[6] It was only in the ancient period, when *malice aforethought* was an expression used to denote a calmly premeditated killing, that it would be true to say that provocation negatived malice aforethought.[7] The cases in which it has been held that provocation may reduce a homicide from murder to manslaughter have throughout the ages been those in which the killing was intentional but done by the prisoner when so inflamed by passion that he was for the moment not the master of his mind.[8] This kind of homicide has been traditionally termed 'voluntary manslaughter'.

[1] *Post*, ¶ 159.

[2] And relative to only one charge, viz., a charge of murder. In no other crime is provocation a *defence*, although it may be taken into account when assessment of punishment has to be made. See *R.* v. *Cunningham* [1958] 3 All E.R. 711.

[3] *Ante*, ¶ 54.

[4] 3 *Inst.* 50, 55. Students must remember that in Coke's day the expression 'malice forethought' (or 'malice prepense', *malitia praecogitata*) indicated the latter kind, namely a killing which had been planned beforehand, as by waiting in ambush, or by poisoning. See Maitland, *Collected Papers*, I, 308 *et seq.*

[5] At p. 51.

[6] E.g. 1 Hale P.C. 451; Foster, 290; 1 East P.C. 232.

[7] Notwithstanding, it is submitted, the dictum in the judgment of Viscount Simon in *Holmes* v. *D.P.P.* [1946] A.C. (*T.A.C.*) at p. 598, which is contradicted by *A.-G. of Ceylon* v. *Kumarasinghege Don John Perera* [1953] 2 W.L.R. 238. See Russ. 585.

[8] See *R.* v. *Hopper* [1915] 2 K.B. 431; *Kwaku Mensah* v. *The King* [1946] A.C. 83.

'UNDER PROVOCATION' EASILY CONFUSED WITH 'IN SELF-DEFENCE'

¶ 118. When provocation takes the form of physical assault of such a nature as would be expected to arouse overwhelming passion in the person attacked, the victim's immediate retaliation will not always be easy to distinguish from a resistance by way of self-defence. It is therefore not surprising that the early authorities did not always keep homicide under provocation separate from homicide in self-defence.[1] In their time the consequences were much the same in either case, but nowadays of course a homicide in reasonable self-defence does not involve the killer in any legal liability; whereas one committed under provocation will be, as it used to be, the felony of manslaughter (punishable now with a maximum of imprisonment for life). Yet it has always been common knowledge that a light physical attack which by itself could not be regarded as enough to arouse murderous feelings in an ordinary man, may do so when it is accompanied by insulting words or gestures. Moreover, insulting words alone can of themselves, especially in certain circumstances, have the like effect. Nevertheless the old authorities were in substantial agreement that words alone, however grossly insulting, could not be regarded in law as provocation sufficient to reduce the homicide to manslaughter.[2] The law on this point however is now settled by the Homicide Act, 1957, which provides by section 3:

> Where on a charge of murder there is evidence on which the jury can find that the person charged was provoked (whether by things done or by things said or by both together) to lose his self-control, the question whether the provocation was enough to make a reasonable man do as he did shall be left to be determined by the jury; and in determining that question the jury shall take into account everything both done and said according to the effect which, in their opinion, it would have on a reasonable man.

¶ 119. *Provocation formerly a matter of law.* Until relatively modern times the question whether in any particular case the provocation actually given should be regarded as excusing a man for the loss of his self-control was decided by the judges as a matter of law,[3] and in such a position it is not surprising to find that in the old cases there was some variation of view from one judge to another. The principle upon which their decision had to be taken was simple—it was that the law's benignity would only operate when the provocation had been such that human frailty could not withstand it. Human frailty must be measured by the general average standard of ordinary men. The average man would not

[1] As recently as 1917, there was a judgment of the Court of Criminal Appeal which did not clearly distinguish the two; *R.* v. *Letenock* (1917) 12 Cr.App.R. 221. And see *R.* v. *Cobbett* (1940) 28 Cr.App.R. 11.

[2] 1 Hale P.C. 456; Foster, 290; *R.* v. *Taylor* (1771) 5 Burr. at p. 2796 *per* Lord Mansfield. Nor gestures, Foster, 290; 1 Hawk. P.C. c. 31, s. 33; *Watts* v. *Brains* (1600) Cro. Eliz. 778.

[3] E.g. *R.* v. *Carroll* (1835) 7 C. and P. 145 at p. 146; *R.* v. *Fisher* (1837) 8 C. and P. 182 at p. 186.

be so disturbed by a light attack as to be immediately overcome by a desire to murder his assailant; but he might be angered to the point of retaliation in kind, returning the like blow for the blow received. Accordingly it was not unusual for the judge to declare[1] that it was not every slight provocation even by a blow which would suffice to reduce the homicide to manslaughter, and sometimes to add that the retaliation must bear some relationship to the provocation given. This last statement may have been partly due to the ancient confusion of homicide under provocation with homicide in self-defence to which reference has already been made. But it can hardly have meant that the blows on either side must be equal, for if that were so, then the defence of provocation would not be needed at all, as nothing less than a felonious assault could be a balance to a return consisting of a stroke intended to kill—and in those circumstances it could be better pleaded that the homicide was justified (in which case there would be no criminal liability at all and the verdict 'not guilty'),[2] rather than provoked (when it would be 'voluntary manslaughter' carrying the punishment of imprisonment for any period up to life). It is therefore submitted that the reappearance of the statement that 'the mode of resentment must bear a reasonable relationship to the provocation', which is found in *Mancini* v. *D.P.P.*,[3] can only make sense if it be taken not as intended to declare an equality of force or of weapon to be essential, but as indicating a point of evidence which the jury should bear in mind. In the detailed review of the law as to provocation which is given in the judgment of the House of Lords in *Holmes* v. *D.P.P.*[4] this seems to be the interpretation placed upon the passage in question. If this were not so the 'reasonable retaliation' doctrine would conflict with a whole line of cases[5] and would be absurd in a case of discovering in adultery or of provocation by words alone.[6] None the less the courts in recent cases have continued to repeat this 'reasonable relation' cliché[7] and since the Homicide Act is silent on the matter they may perhaps continue to do so.

[1] E.g. *Stedman's Case* (1704) Foster 292; 1 East P.C. 234. *R.* v. *Lynch* (1832) 5 C. and P. 324; *R.* v. *Sherwood* (1844) 1 C. and K. 556.

[2] Indeed the origin of the idea that the mode of attack and the mode of retaliation must balance may perhaps lie in the ancient cases where the plea was 'not guilty' on the grounds of justifiable self-defence against a murderous attack.

[3] [1942] A.C. 1 at p. 9 (*T.A.C.*) and repeated in *R.* v. *Gauthier* (1943) 29 Cr.App.R. 113, and *R.* v. *Duffy* [1949] 1 All E.R. 932. The evidence showed that Mancini was expecting some attack and had armed himself with a knife before going to interview the other man whom he killed.

[4] [1946] A.C. 588, at p. 598 (*T.A.C.*). *R.* v. *Duffy* seems to go too far on this point.

[5] E.g. *R.* v. *Lynch* (1832) 5 C. and P. 324; *R.* v. *Thomas* (1837) 7 C. and P. 817; *R.* v. *Sherwood* (1844) 1 C. and K. 556; *R.* v. *Smith* (1865) 4 F. and F. 1066; *R.* v. *Hopper* [1915] 2 K.B. 431; *R.* v. *Larkin* [1943] K.B. 174.

[6] Under the Homicide Act, s. 3 *ante*.

[7] E.g. *R.* v. *McCarthy* [1954] 2 Q.B. 105: 'It is undoubted law that the violence used must have some reasonable relation to the provocation' at p. 109; and 'this provocation ... could not have justified the infliction of such injuries as to cause three or four fractures of the skull and the beating of the man's head on a stony road' at p. 110. See Russ. 602. *et seq.*

¶ **120.** *Now a matter of fact.* In the last paragraph it was stated that the question, whether the provocation received was enough to reduce the homicide to manslaughter, was originally decided by the judge. Gradually, however, the judges developed the practice, which became the established rule and has now been confirmed in section 3 of the Homicide Act, 1957 (*ante*, ¶ 118), that they should leave it to the jury to decide as a matter of fact whether there was sufficient provocation or not.[1]

STANDARD OF A 'REASONABLE MAN'

¶ **121.** Primarily it has always been for the defence to raise the plea that the prisoner was overwhelmed by the provocation he had received.[2] When the question was left to the jury they had to scrutinize the evidence to see whether it was reasonable to believe the contention of the defence,[3] and in practice they could only reach a conclusion by considering how they, or the people whom they knew or had observed in everyday life, would react to such a situation as that described to them. The judges gradually developed a practice of steering the jury on these lines by directing them that they should decide whether the provocative acts were in their opinion enough to cause an ordinary 'reasonable' man to lose his mastery over his passions. This was, however, to begin with, merely a guide as to how the jury should marshal the evidence in their minds in order to decide a subjective point, namely, whether or not the prisoner had indeed been made to lose his power of self-control.[4] But here again, as has so often happened, what began as a matter of evidence crystallized into a rule of law[5] and became an objective legal test of liability. This objective test has been repeatedly applied in modern cases, the jury being told that whether the proved acts of provocation could be expected to overcome the self-control of the particular individual himself against whom they were directed is *not* the question which they have to consider. And[6] now the Homicide Act,

[1] But the judge must decide if there is enough evidence of this to be left to the jury.

[2] In modern times it has been laid down that it is the duty of the judge to draw the jury's attention to matters in evidence which might establish provocation, even though the defending counsel may not have found it practicable to do so. See *R.* v. *Hopper* [1915] 2 K.B. 431; *Mancini* v. *D.P.P.* [1942] A.C. 1; *Kwaku Mensah* v. *R.* [1946] A.C. 83; *R.* v. *Bullard* [1957] A.C. 635; *Bharat* v. *R.* [1959] 3 All E.R. 292; *R.* v. *Porritt* [1961] 3 All E.R. 463; see *post*, ¶ 136.

[3] It must be remembered that it was not until the end of the nineteenth century that a prisoner could give evidence on his own behalf.

[4] The ancient basic fact upon which the doctrine of provocation had depended.

[5] That it was a modern development can be seen from some of the earlier cases in which no such rule was enunciated, e.g. *R.* v. *Lynch* (1832) 5 C. and P. 324; *R.* v. *Hayward* (1833) 6 C. and P. 157. See Russ. 596 *et seq.*

[6] *R.* v. *Alexander* (1913) 9 Cr.App.R. 139; *R.* v. *Lesbini* [1914] 3 K.B. 1116, at p. 1119. 'There must exist such an amount of provocation as would be excited by the circumstances in the mind of a reasonable man'; *Mancini* v. *D.P.P.* [1942] A.C. at p. 9 (*T.A.C.*). *R.* v. *Gauthier* (1943) 29 Cr.App.R. 113: 'Further, the law provides that the test to be applied is...the effect of the alleged provocation, whatever it is, upon a reasonable man.'

1957, s. 3, lays down that in determining the question of provocation the jury shall take into account everything both said and done according to the effect which, in their opinion, it would have on the reasonable man.[1] The Act does not give any definition of 'a reasonable man', and it has been stated:[2] 'No court has ever given, nor do we think ever can give, a definition of what constitutes a reasonable man, or an average man. That must be left to the collective good sense of the jury.'

As a practical method of assessing the truth of the prisoner's assertion that he was overwhelmed by the provocation, a comparison of his reaction with that which each of the twelve jurymen would expect from an ordinary person such as he considers himself to be[3] is a sensible approach to the question, and its vagueness can do no harm since it leaves it to the defence to point to any special circumstances affecting his own case, with the benefit of any reasonable doubt in his favour. But applied as a rule of law it can yield results which are not only inconsistent with the basic justification for allowing provocation to be taken into account at all, but also seem unfair to many who themselves claim to be 'reasonable' or 'average' people in their sense of what is true equality of treatment.[4] An illustration of this can be found in the case of *Bedder* v. *D.P.P.*,[5] where the defence of provocation, on a charge of murder, was rejected.

The appellant *B*, a youth of eighteen who was sexually impotent, was convicted of murder committed in a courtyard of a public street by stabbing

And see Criminal Code (Laws of the Gold Coast (1936), 1, c. 9), s. 234, accepted by the Judicial Committee of the Privy Council as reproducing the common law of England on the subject, in *Kwaku Mensah* v. *The King* [1946] A.C. at p. 93. See also *Bedder* v. *D.P.P.* [1954] 1 W.L.R. 1119, discussed *infra*. In such cases, of course, the prerogative of mercy can be exercised and the sentence commuted.

[1] Of course in many instances the prisoner's mental variation may be so serious that he can rely upon the more exculpatory defence of insanity, or now, perhaps, of diminished responsibility (*ante*, ¶¶ 52, 53 *a*). A question which one day may have to be considered is what the position would be if a man deliberately irritated another whom he knew to be constitutionally liable to lose control of himself for certain small causes, with the consequence that the unfortunate object of his provocation retaliated immediately by killing him. None of the authorities, whether ancient or modern, seems to have expressed the view that the reason for allowing the defence of provocation was in any way due to the idea that the man slain had brought the disaster upon himself.

[2] *R.* v. *McCarthy* [1954] 2 Q.B. at p. 112; *R.* v. *Spriggs* [1958] 1 Q.B. 270; cp. the dicta in *D.P.P.* v. *Smith* discussed in ¶ 116*b*, *ante*.

[3] It would seem proper that the standard of what is reasonable should be the standard of the general community of which the accused is a member, e.g. an African standard for Africans: see the clear and cogent argument in the judgment delivered by H.M. High Court of Tanganyika in *Chacha s/o Wamburu* v. *Regina*, 1953 C.S. case 25, Crim. App. no. 208. For the application of this criterion in cases of killing by aborigines in Australia, see [1961] *Crim. L.R.* 41, 'What colour is the Reasonable Man?' by C. Howard.

[4] They may feel that if a 'normal' man is excused because his natural powers of self-control were not strong enough then a man so unfortunate as to have been born with subnormal powers of self-control ought also to be excused if in his natural weakness he has been unable to resist a surge of passion.

[5] [1954] 1 W.L.R. 1119.

a prostitute who had jeered at him because of his weakness, and in addition had assaulted him in a disgusting and painful manner.

Counsel for the appellant argued that the hypothetical reasonable man should be invested with the peculiar physical qualities of the accused, as in the present case with the characteristic of impotence, and that the question should be asked what would be the reaction of the impotent reasonable man in the circumstances? The House of Lords refused to accept the argument on the grounds, (*a*) that 'it would be plainly illogical not to recognize an unusually excitable or pugnacious temperament...as a matter to be taken into account but yet to recognize for that purpose some unusual physical characteristic, be it impotence or another'; and (*b*) that it would make nonsense of the traditional test,[1] for 'if the reasonable man is then deprived in whole or in part of his reason or the normal man endowed with abnormal characteristics, the test ceases to have any value'. The appeal was accordingly dismissed.

This judgment has excited the comment of writers who have felt that the situation created by it is both puzzling and disturbing.[2] The unsatisfactory operation of the test of the reasonable man was stressed by some of the witnesses who gave evidence to the Royal Commission of 1949–53; the suggestion for its abrogation was, however, opposed by the judges, one of whom gave as a reason that if it were changed 'there might be circumstances in which a bad-tempered man would be acquitted[3] and a good-tempered man would be hanged, which, of course, is neither law nor sense'. This argument affected the Commissioners so much[4] that they decided to recommend that the law on this point should remain unaltered. But it must be respectfully submitted that the argument is quite without value. If the comparison of a good-tempered man with a bad-tempered man[5] must be made then it is logically essential that the facts of the imagined provocation must be exactly the same for each man. Now on the basis of the present law if the facts so postulated constitute a provocation sufficient to cause the good-tempered man to lose his self-control, and so to excuse him, they must also cause the bad-tempered man to lose his self-control and so by the existing test excuse him, with the result that neither man will be convicted of murder. On the other hand, if the facts of the provocation are not enough to cause the imaginary 'good-tempered' man to lose his self-control, he will not kill his attacker and therefore will not be convicted of homicide at all, still less hanged. It is plain then that, whether under the present law the bad-tempered man must be convicted of

[1] As to this it may be thought by some that the traditional test established by judicial dicta is itself illogical and unsound.

[2] See Russ. 605 *et seq.*; (1954) *Cam. L.J.* 165; 70 *L.Q.R.* 442; 33 *Can. Bar Rev.* 93; [1954] *Crim. L.R.* 84.

[3] This overlooks the fact that a successful plea of provocation does not result in acquittal but in conviction of manslaughter with a possible punishment of life imprisonment.

[4] *Report of the Royal Commission*, 1953, Cmd. 8932, para. 143.

[5] Whatever may be the canon for the distinction between the two.

murder, or whether, under the suggested change of the law, he would be convicted of manslaughter, the good-tempered man's position is quite unaffected; to him the fate, one way or the other, of the bad-tempered man is a matter of indifference, while his own fate will depend solely upon the amount of provocation which he himself has received and his own reaction to it.

Space does not permit a more detailed criticism here of the argument in *Bedder's Case*;[1] but, since the Court of Criminal Appeal has spoken of 'any reasonable person, that is to say, a person who cannot set up a plea of insanity', the question arises whether a prisoner such as Bedder who, according to evidence accepted by the court, had been assailed both by insulting words and by an indecent and painful blow,[2] could not now be regarded as a 'reasonable person' (since plainly he could not plead insanity) who in the circumstances in which he was placed, was 'provoked ...to lose his self-control'.[3]

On some occasions when the defence of provocation has been raised by a prisoner accused of murder,[4] the fact that a man who is to some extent the worse for drink is more liable to lose control of himself when irritated has been admitted by the courts as a matter which could be taken into account; but this has been repudiated in *R.* v. *McCarthy*,[5] in which it was declared:

> We see no distinction between a person who by temperament is unusually excitable or pugnacious and one who is temporarily made excitable or pugnacious by self-induced intoxication. It may be that an excitable, pugnacious or intoxicated person may be more easily provoked than a man of quiet or phlegmatic disposition, but the former cannot rely upon his excitable state of mind if the violence used is beyond that which a reasonable, or perhaps we should say an average, person would use to repel an act which can in law be regarded as provocation.

LOSS OF SELF-CONTROL

¶ 122. There is, however, one point in which the actual mental attitude of the prisoner has to be considered, for it has always[6] been the rule that

[1] The student should refer to Russ. 605 *et seq.*

[2] See sect. 3 of the Homicide Act 'whether by things done or by things said or by both together'.

[3] Homicide Act, s. 3.

[4] E.g. *R.* v. *Hopper* [1915] 2 K.B. 431; *R.* v. *Letenock* (1917) 12 Cr.App.R. 221. The argument that drunkenness could be taken into account had been repudiated in *R.* v. *Carroll* (1835) 7 C. and P. 145, and doubted in *R.* v. *Mason* (1912) 8 Cr.App.R. 121.

[5] [1954] 2 Q.B. 105. See *R.* v. *Wardrope* [1960] Crim. L.R. 770 (C.C.C. 13 Oct. 1959), a charge of murder to which the defences of provocation, self-defence, drunkenness and mistake were pleaded concurrently, the judge, *inter alia*, directing the jury that drunkenness might be considered in so far as it might have caused a mistake as to the prisoner's being attacked and as to the gravity of that supposed attack.

[6] 1 Hale P.C. 453; Foster, 290 *et seq.*; 1 East P.C. 233; *R.* v. *Thomas* (1837) 7 C. and P. 817; *Mancini* v. *D.P.P.* [1942] A.C. 1 (*T.A.C.*); *Holmes* v. *D.P.P.* [1946] A.C. at p. 597 (*T.A.C.*); *R.* v. *Duffy* [1949] 1 All E.R. 932.

the killing can only be reduced from murder to manslaughter if the evidence establishes that in fact the prisoner did lose control of himself as the result of the provocation. It may happen that a man is abnormally cool under gross provocation but none the less extremely resentful of any kind of personal affront; if he were to kill at once, but in cold blood, he cannot be excused by the fact that the acts of provocation would have been expected to cause an ordinary man to lose his self-control.

LAPSE OF TIME BETWEEN PROVOCATION AND DEED

¶ 123. It has never been doubted that the defence of provocation can only avail when the homicide attributed to it has been committed in hot blood, while the prisoner was still in the grip of his ungovernable fury. It is true that some of the early writers contemplated a surprisingly long period during which this state of passion might continue,[1] but in modern times at any rate it has been repeatedly declared that juries must take careful account of any opportunity which the prisoner had for cooling off.[2] It is really a question of fact, for the evidence may establish that the prisoner's conduct during a very short interval elapsing between the provocation and the fatal retaliation was so calm as to show that he had recovered his control. In another case it may be plain that he did remain beside himself for a relatively long time; but here the jury will have to decide whether an ordinary man could be expected to have been influenced for so long.

PROVOCATION BY AN ATTACK UPON A THIRD PERSON

¶ 124. There is some authority for the view that the defence of provocation is available to one who has killed someone who was making an attack upon a third person.[3] Thus it was suggested[4] that a father might be so provoked if he found a man committing an unnatural offence upon his son; and *R.* v. *Harrington*[5] was a conviction for manslaughter of a man who had killed his daughter's husband whom he saw beating her.

HUSBAND AND ADULTERER

¶ 125. Contrary to the general rule there has been from very early times one kind of provocation which the law has regarded as sufficiently gross to produce an ungovernable passion which will reduce the homicide to manslaughter although it does not take the form of a

[1] E.g. where on a quarrel the two men go away to fetch weapons, and return to fight it out, 1 Hale P.C. 453.

[2] *R.* v. *Lynch* (1832) 5 C. and P. 324; *Mancini* v. *D.P.P.* [1942] A.C. at p. 9; *Holmes* v. *D.P.P.* [1946] A.C. at p. 597. See *R.* v. *Ayes* (1810) R. and R. 166.

[3] The two cases of the men playing bowls, 12 Co. Rep. 87, and *R.* v. *Rowley*, Cro. Jac. 296 (Foster, 294), are doubtful, since it is not certain that they were not really cases of homicide by misadventure.

[4] *R.* v. *Fisher* (1837) 8 C. and P. at p. 185.

[5] (1866) 10 Cox 370.

physical attack upon the slayer. This arises in the case where a husband detects a man in the act[1] of adultery with his wife, and kills one or other of the guilty parties on the spot.[2] It has been emphatically stated that this concession to outraged feelings is only made where the man and woman are lawfully man and wife and could not be made where they are merely an engaged couple,[3] nor where they are living together although not married.[4] Nevertheless there are several cases in which this restriction has not been taken into account,[5] although to have done so would have rendered the decision of some of them much easier; and now perhaps the restriction has disappeared as the result of the wide terms in which section 3 of the Homicide Act, 1957, has been expressed.

¶ 126. *Confession of adultery not sufficient provocation.* It was formerly thought that a confession of past adultery made unexpectedly by a wife to her husband could be treated as sufficient provocation to reduce his immediate killing of her to manslaughter.[6] This supposed rule was expressly repudiated by the House of Lords in *Holmes* v. *D.P.P.*[7] It would seem, however, that as a result of section 3 of the Homicide Act the judges will decide that confessions of adultery may be taken into account by the jury.[8]

¶ 126*a*. Finally it should be noted that if the evidence before the court shows a possibility that there was sufficient provocation to afford a defence to the prisoner, then, even if counsel for the defence does not

[1] Speaking of the words 'finding in the act of adultery', the High Court of Tanganyika said: 'We are not satisfied that they require that the wife and the adulterer should be caught during the actual period of intercourse. If they are found together in circumstances from which immediately recent intercourse is, and can safely and correctly be inferred, we think they may be found in the act of adultery within the meaning of the rule.' *Chacha s/o Wamburu* v. *Regina*, 1953 C.S. case 25, Crim. App. no. 208.

[2] *R.* v. *Maddy* (1672) 1 Ventris 158 (also reported as *R.* v. *Manning* in T. Raym. 212). The rule was confirmed in *Holmes* v. *D.P.P.* [1946] A.C. 588, at p. 598; and the view was expressed that it would apply in the converse case of a wife killing her husband or his paramour.

[3] *R.* v. *Palmer* [1913] 2 K.B. 29.

[4] *R.* v. *Greening* [1913] 3 K.B. 846.

[5] *R.* v. *Kelly* (1848) 2 C. and K. 814; *R.* v. *Alexander* (1913) 9 Cr.App.R. 139; *R.* v. *Gauthier* (1943) 29 Cr.App.R. 113; *R.* v. *Larkin* [1943] K.B. 174.

[6] *R.* v. *Rothwell* (1871) 12 Cox 145; *R.* v. *Jones* (1908) 72 J.P. 215. But a wife's confession that she *intended* to commit adultery did not suffice; *R.* v. *Ellor* (1921) 15 Cr.App.R. 41.

[7] [1946] A.C. 588.

[8] *R.* v. *Larkin* [1943] K.B. 174, was a case in which the man and woman were not married, nor was there either discovery in the act of intercourse or any evidence of confession of it; yet the man's belief that it was going to take place was treated as sufficient provocation to constitute his killing of the woman a manslaughter. And see *R.* v. *Millward* (1931) 23 Cr.App.R. 119. In *R.* v. *Fantle* [1959] Crim. L.R. 584 (C.C.C.) the defence of provocation succeeded. The prisoner, carrying a loaded revolver, went to interview the deceased to persuade him to discontinue association with the prisoner's wife, and shot him dead upon his refusal to do so and his announcement that he had slept with her the night before.

set up provocation (which, for example, it would be embarrassing for him to do if his instructions were to plead accidental killing) it is none the less the duty of the judge himself to draw the attention of the jury to such evidence and to direct them upon it just as if the defence of provocation had been raised by counsel.[1] It should be remembered that where the defence of provocation is set up it is for the prosecution to establish beyond reasonable doubt that the legal requirements for that defence are not present.[2]

SECTION 5. SUICIDE

¶ 127. (*a*) *History*. Murder consists in the unlawful taking of a human life: it was therefore always a felony even though the life which the man took was his own, the malice aforethought in such case being in the usual case the intention of the man to bring his own existence to an end (*felonia de se*), which led to the crime's being often called self-murder.[3] But it occurred also when the intention was to kill another, e.g. where a duellist was killed by the bursting of his own pistol. It must be remembered that in the days when it was held to be murder if a man killed another unintentionally but in the course of an 'unlawful' (or at least 'felonious'[4]) act, it would follow that where he accidentally killed himself in the same circumstances, he should be adjudged a *felo de se*,[5] as some writers have maintained.[6]

Since suicide was a felony an attempt to commit it was an attempt to commit a felony,[7] although the attempt itself was not a felonious attempt to murder within the meaning of the Offences against the Person Act, 1861,[8] but only a misdemeanour.[9]

(*b*) *Modern legislation: Suicide no longer a crime*. Another consequence of the criminality of suicide used to be that if two persons agreed to die together, but only one succeeded in putting an end to his life, the survivor was guilty of murder.[10] But the Homicide Act, 1957, section 4, provides:

[1] *Kwaku Mensah* v. *R.* [1946] A.C. 83; *Chan Kau* v. *R.* [1955] 1 All E.R. 266; *R.* v. *McPherson* (1957) 41 Cr.App.R. 213; *R.* v. *Porritt* [1961] 3 All E.R. 463; and *post*, ¶ 594.

[2] See *Chan Kau* v. *R.* [1955] A.C. 206.

[3] 4 Bl. *Comm.* 188; *R.* v. *Russell* (1832) 1 Moo. 356; *R.* v. *Gaylor* (1857) D. and B. 288; Stephen, *Hist. Crim. Law*, III, 104. The cases of *Russell* and of *Gaylor* turned upon the ancient conceptions of malice aforethought; in *R.* v. *Russell* a woman had taken a drug in order to procure her own miscarriage and this poisoned her to death; since she was committing a felonious act (abortion) her death was held to be self-murder, although she did not intend to take her own life. See Russ., 10th ed. 605, 608.

[4] See ¶ 111 *ante*.

[5] *Felo de se* does *not* mean the felony, but the felon himself.

[6] 4 Bl. *Comm.* 189; cf. Coroner's Rules, 1927 (S.R. and O. 1927, no. 344), sch. para. 3. See Jervis, *Coroners*, 8th ed. (1946), 148, 'There is no authority for making any division of self-destruction that is comparable to murder and manslaughter:...'

[7] *R.* v. *Burgess* (1862) 2 L. and C. 258.

[8] Sects. 11–15.

[9] *R.* v. *Mann* (1914) 10 Cr.App.R. at p. 32.

[10] 1 Hawk. P.C. c. 27, s. 6; *R.* v. *Dyson* (1823) R. and R. 523; *R.* v. *Alison* (1838) 8 C. and P. 418; unless he has previously and expressly countermanded or revoked the pact, *R.* v. *Croft* [1944] 1 K.B. 295.

(1) It shall be manslaughter, and shall not be murder, for a person acting in pursuance of a suicide pact between him and another to kill the other or be a party to the other [killing himself or][1] being killed by a third person.

(2) Where it is shown that a person charged with the murder of another killed the other or was a party to his [killing himself or][1] being killed, it shall be for the defence to prove that the person charged was acting in pursuance of a suicide pact between him and the other.

(3) For the purposes of this section 'suicide pact' means a common agreement between two or more persons having for its object the death of all of them, whether or not each is to take his own life, but nothing done by a person who enters into a suicide pact shall be treated as done by him in pursuance of the pact unless it is done while he has the settled intention of dying in pursuance of the pact.

And now suicide has ceased to be a crime. The Suicide Act, 1961, provides:

1. The rule of law whereby it is a crime for a person to commit suicide is hereby abrogated.

2.—(1) A person who aids, abets, counsels or procures the suicide of another, or an attempt by another to commit suicide, shall be liable on conviction on indictment to imprisonment for a term not exceeding fourteen years.

(2) If on the trial of an indictment for murder or manslaughter it is proved that the accused aided, abetted, counselled or procured the suicide of the person in question, the jury may find him guilty of that offence.[2]

In the past it was settled that, if a man in the course of an unsuccessful effort to take his own life accidentally killed someone else, then this would be murder.[3] The new Act of 1961 does not deal with this situation, so that it may be expected that the courts will apply the ordinary tests for homicide without the complications involved in the consideration of death caused in the course of a felony involving violence; or in the doctrine of *D.P.P.* v. *Smith*, since the would-be suicide no longer 'intends to do something unlawful to someone'.

¶ 128. *Former consequences of suicide.* The common law endeavoured to deter men from this crime by the threat of degradations to be inflicted upon the suicide's corpse, and also by threatening the forfeiture of his

[1] These words are repealed by the Suicide Act, 1961, s. 3 (2).

[2] In subsects. (3) and (4) of sect. 2, and in sect. 3, the Act makes consequential amendments and repeals (in part) the Coroners (Amendment) Act, 1926; the Children and Young Persons Act, 1933; the Extradition Act, 1870; the Visiting Forces Act, 1952; the Army Act, 1955; the Air Force Act, 1955; the Naval Discipline Act, 1957; the Forfeiture Act, 1870; the Interments Act, 1882; the Magistrates' Courts Act, 1952; the Homicide Act, 1957.

[3] *R.* v. *Hopwood* (1913) 8 Cr.App.R. 143; *R.* v. *Spence* (1957) 41 Cr.App.R. 80.

goods. Thus the man who feloniously took his own life was at one time buried in the highway, with a stake through his body; and his goods were forfeited. In 1824 this mode was replaced by the practice of burial between the hours of nine and twelve at night, without any service. The Forfeiture Act, 1870, abolished confiscation of the goods of suicides in the general abolition of forfeitures for felony. And in 1882, the statute 45 and 46 Vict. c. 19 (rep.) removed every penalty, except the purely ecclesiastical one that the interment must not be solemnized by a burial service in the full ordinary Anglican form.[1] Even before the common law penalties of *felonia de se* were legally abolished, the popular disapprobation of them had gone very far in reducing the number of cases in which they were actually inflicted. For it rendered coroners' juries eager to avail themselves of the slightest grounds for pronouncing an act of suicide to have been committed during a fit of insanity, and consequently to have involved no felonious guilt. This practice of 'pious perjury'—to borrow a phrase of Blackstone's—became so inveterate that it survived the abolition of those penalties which were its cause and its excuse. A verdict of insanity is nowadays unpopular since it may throw upon the family of the deceased an undeserved stigma, gravely affecting their social or matrimonial or commercial prospects. A Departmental Committee on Coroners (1936) recommended[2] that the verdict of *felo de se* be abolished, and that there should be no reference in the verdict to the deceased's state of mind, but that the verdict should simply be that the deceased died by his own hand. But pending any such reform it became the common practice to adopt the form of words (recommended by the Council of the Coroners' Society in 1937) 'while the balance of his mind was disturbed'.[3]

Section 6. Manslaughter

¶ 129. No clear-cut definition of manslaughter is to be found in any of the old authorities.[4] They all dealt with this crime in a negative way, as being a homicide which for one reason or another (e.g. provocation) did not amount to murder.[5] Throughout its history the law has not been brought within any precisely expressed principle, and even at the present day such is the confusion in which the law of homicide stands

[1] For the present practice see Mayfield, *The Church of England*, 1958, p. 63.

[2] Cmd. 5070. This recommendation does not imply that suicide may not be self-murder in law. It affects only the duties of a coroner.

[3] On this see the observations of Singleton, L.J., in *R.* v. *Horner* [1956] Crim. L.R. 482, cited in [1956] Crim. L.R. 551.

[4] An intentional homicide committed as the result of provocation (*ante*, ¶ 117), and thereby reduced from murder to manslaughter, is traditionally termed 'voluntary manslaughter'; but to this there must now be added, under the Homicide Act, 1957, a killing by a person suffering from 'diminished responsibility' (sect. 2 (3)) and a killing by a survivor in a suicide pact (sect. 4 (1)). For 'involuntary manslaughter' see ¶ 131.

[5] See Russ. 622 *et seq.* where the views as to manslaughter expressed by Coke, Hale, Hawkins, Foster, Blackstone and East are discussed.

that it is not possible to give an authoritative definition of manslaughter in plain terms. Up to the nineteenth century it was discussed as a residuary category of homicide, into which fell all killings which were not justified, excusable, or murderous. It has always been a felony, but more than any other kind of homicide its legal nature was obscured not only by the historical variations of meaning in the concept of *mens rea*, but also by the relics of the archaic rule of strict liability which knew no requirement of a mental element in criminal responsibility. For although, being a crime at common law, manslaughter must be governed by the maxim *actus non facit reum nisi mens sit rea*, yet the *mens rea* required for manslaughter has not been defined in clear terms, and in innumerable instances has never even been referred to.

ACTUS REUS IN MANSLAUGHTER

¶ 130. Of the *actus reus* in manslaughter little need here be said, since it is the same as in murder and the other kinds of homicide[1] and has already been discussed (¶¶ 80–91). As in murder, so also in manslaughter, a death may be unexpectedly caused by the infliction of some harm which can be justified: for example, in the course of the lawful arrest of a criminal, in the carrying out of a lawful sentence upon a convicted person, in self-defence, in reasonable chastisement of a child by its parent and so on.[2] It should be remembered that in each of these instances the harm inflicted can only be justified if the requirements of the law have been observed; thus the punishment inflicted upon a criminal must be in strict accordance with his sentence, or if upon a child by a master or parent it must be moderate and reasonable in all the circumstances, while in the case of surgical operations and in games and sports the true consent of the patient[3] to undergo the operation, or of the player to take part in the game, is an essential condition.

In the case of sports and games there is no hard and fast line drawn. Very many of the recognized sports and games involve the risk and indeed the certainty that some bodily hurt will be suffered by the participants and the law does not prohibit them if they are carried on without rancour and without what the ethical feeling of the period would regard as brutality. The same considerations have affected the question whether the exercise itself is unlawful or not. Thus an armed tournament was unlawful in medieval times, and a knight who killed another in such a contest would usually be guilty of criminal homicide. Yet it was otherwise if the King had commanded the particular tournament in question. In a struggle so legalized by royal order the death of any of the combatants was not an *actus reus* and the homicide ranked as merely one of misadventure. At the present day such

[1] Except child destruction.

[2] *Ante*, ¶¶ 12, 96–100.

[3] Save, of course, where the sufferer is physically unable to give it and delay would endanger his life. Fraud may vitiate an apparent consent; see *post*, ¶¶ 156, 247.

engagements with naked swords or spears would be illegal[1] as would any dangerous or morally offensive activity[2] of which public opinion disapproved. But ordinary fencing, wrestling, football[3] and the like are lawful games if carried on with due care, as also is boxing[4] (but not prize-fighting). In all of them the law allows a person to consent to receive or to risk receiving a certain amount of bodily harm. But no one is allowed to consent to receive serious bodily harm such for example as would amount to 'maiming'[5] him: so that if he does take part in a dangerous contest and is killed his consenting affords no legal excuse to the killer. Such a contest would indeed constitute a breach of the peace and all concerned would be guilty of an offence. For both these reasons prize-fighting has always been held to be illegal; in former days as tending to arouse disorder, the combatants being regarded as careless what hurt might be given and only concerned to obtain notoriety and the promised reward.[6] It is, however, not easy to say what precisely is the difference between a prize-fight and a boxing contest for a money prize,[7] the answer seems to depend on the ruling public opinion of the moment in the area in which the contest is staged. Even a permitted game will become unlawful if anger and a 'manifest' intention to do harm are imported into it, and the immunity from criminal liability will consequently at once disappear.[8]

MENS REA IN MANSLAUGHTER

¶ 131. It must here be repeated that the persistence of the ancient principle of strict liability has led to many cases being decided by reference to the circumstances and to the conduct of the prisoner without either attaching any importance to or attempting any precise analysis of his attitude of mind in the matter. We have seen that Coke thought that an unforeseen (and certainly unintended) death brought

[1] Unless authorized by the legislature (i.e. the King in Parliament) by way of a special enactment.

[2] *R.* v. *Donovan* [1934] 2 K.B. 498 (*T.A.C.*), a case of indecent physical force.

[3] *R.* v. *Bradshaw* (1878) 14 Cox 83 (*T.A.C.*).

[4] *R.* v. *Coney* (1882) 8 Q.B.D. 534. See *post*, ¶ 156.

[5] *Post*, ¶ 159.

[6] *Ward's Case* (1789) 1 East P.C. 270.

[7] The fact that the boxers are contesting for money does not necessarily make it a prize-fight; on the other hand the wearing of gloves does not necessarily prevent its being one. Nor do the rules of the contest decide the matter, as they may permit the use of dangerous force or the fight to be prolonged unduly.

[8] *R.* v. *Canniff* (1840) 9 C. and P. 359. The fact that the prisoner was playing in strict accordance with the established rules of the game will help towards showing that he was not actuated by anger and, again, towards showing that the way in which he was playing was not so obviously perilous as to be illegal. Hence, for either of these purposes, these rules may be admissible evidence on behalf of the prisoner. But, on the other hand, if the prisoner was playing in violation of the rules, they are not thereby rendered admissible evidence against him. For it is not criminal, and not necessarily either dangerous or malicious, to break them. On this point the case of *R.* v. *Bradshaw* (1878) 14 Cox 82 may be compared with that of *R.* v. *Moore* (1898) 14 T.L.R. 229, where, in a game of association football, the prisoner had killed a man by charging him from behind, in defiance of the rules.

about by a man engaged in any unlawful act was murder. Holt, C.J., and Hale, and Foster would not accept this severity: they all, however, agreed that it was manslaughter and were constrained to leave the matter at that, without considering wherein, even for manslaughter, lay the *mens rea*,[1] which accordingly was never defined. The resultant legal position was that the old writers either gave to manslaughter but slight and superficial treatment, or else set out numbers of individual cases without succeeding in bringing them within any sound and scientific classification.[2] From them the modern reader can extract little more that is definite than (*a*) that manslaughter was in those days a less heinous form of felonious homicide than murder, in that it was not committed with malice aforethought[3] (express or implied), (*b*) that an intentional killing under provocation was manslaughter, and (*c*) that, within the limitation in (*a*), manslaughter consisted in causing a death in the course of some unlawful act or omission. The term 'manslaughter' being thus indefinite meant little more than 'killing',[4] and it has often been the practice to divide the crime into (i) voluntary manslaughter,[5] which used to comprise only those homicides which are reduced from murder to manslaughter owing to provocation,[6] but now, since the passing of the Homicide Act, 1957, will also include a killing by a person suffering from 'diminished responsibility' (s. 2 (1)) and a killing by a person acting in pursuance of a suicide pact with the person killed (s. 4(1)[7]), and (ii) involuntary manslaughter, which includes all other cases. It is in respect of (ii) that there has persisted the antiquated dictum that a death caused in the course of doing any unlawful act will be at least manslaughter.[8] Consistently with this archaism the reports show that the common law requirement of *mens rea* has been repeatedly overlooked or disregarded and cases have again and again been decided by reference to the circumstances and to the acts of the prisoner without either attaching any importance to, or attempting any precise analysis of, his attitude of mind in the matter. So in *R.* v. *Smith*,[9] where a watchman who was employed to stand at a point where a tramway privately owned by a colliery crossed a main road, and to give warning to passengers that a truck was approaching, absented himself from his post with the result that a man passing along the road was run over and

[1] Through the operation of benefit of clergy (*ante*, ¶ 55) the consequences for the prisoner were little different from what they would have been if the homicide had been held to be *per infortunium*. See Stephen, *Hist. Crim. Law*, I, 463 *et seq.*

[2] See for example the criticism of Hale's attempt at classification made by Sir James Stephen (*op. cit.* III, 61); Russ. 631.

[3] This originally denoted that the killing was deliberately planned, and did not include, as in modern times, an intention to kill, however short the interval of time between its formation and its being put into effect.

[4] Foster, 302–3.

[5] It will be observed that this expression was appropriate so long as 'manslaughter' merely meant 'the killing of a man'.

[6] *Ante*, ¶ 117 *et seq.*

[7] As modified by the Suicide Act, 1961, s. 3.

[8] Repudiated in *The State* v. *Van der Mescht* 1962 1 S. A. 521.

[9] *R.* v. *Smith* (1869) 11 Cox 210.

killed, it was held not to be manslaughter because the watchman was merely the private servant of the owner of the colliery, and (apparently) because he owed no active duty to anyone but his employer. Yet in *R.* v. *Pittwood*[1] where a gatekeeper on the level crossing of a railway forgot to close the gate before going off for luncheon, and soon afterwards a train killed a man who was crossing, it was held to be manslaughter. If the cases are correctly reported it would seem that Smith might have been convicted, since he must have well known that in going away he was exposing to risk any passenger who might come along the highway; whereas if Pittwood was to be believed he suffered a mental lapse, a loss of memory, which meant that he was not aware that he was exposing anyone to risk. Such variations must arise when the principles are not clearly settled. It may be asked, for example, what principle underlies the dicta (obiter) in *A.-G. for N.I.* v. *Gallagher*,[2] 'In each of these cases it would not be murder. But it would be manslaughter'; and in *Shoukatallie* v. *R.*,[3] 'M.A. thought he was dead..., in that event M.A. would not have been guilty of murder.... He would have been guilty of manslaughter'.

INVOLUNTARY MANSLAUGHTER

¶ 132. Changes in the law of benefit of clergy, and its complete abolition in 1827, led to a conviction for manslaughter becoming a more serious matter than it formerly had been and there arose a greater need for precision than before. As the authorities then stood there was good support for the dictum that an accidental death caused in the course of doing an unlawful act would be manslaughter, and we find the rule so stated as late as 1830 in *R.* v. *Fenton*.[4] But during the next fifty years there developed an increasing dislike of any rule which imposed criminal liability upon one who had not intended to do harm, so that when the same point arose in 1883 the principle enunciated in the case of *Fenton* was, although not expressly discarded, at any rate evaded, in *R.* v. *Franklin*.[5] The prisoner Franklin, who was charged with manslaughter, had purloined a wooden box from a refreshment stall on the pier at Brighton and thrown it into the sea. Undoubtedly this was an unlawful thing to do[6] and as the box had unfortunately fallen upon and killed a person bathing in the sea, the prosecution relied upon *R.* v. *Fenton* and argued that apart from any question of negligence this homicide must be manslaughter. For the prisoner, defending counsel submitted that the prosecution must prove criminal negligence on the part of Franklin, maintaining that there was no proof of criminal,

[1] (1902) 19 T.L.R. 37. See also *R.* v. *Benge* (1865) 4 F. and F. 504, where the foreman of a gang on the railway line misread the time-table supplied to him and therefore did not allow sufficient time to complete work before a train arrived.

[2] [1961] 3 All E.R. 299 at p. 313, para. G.

[3] [1961] 3 All E.R. 996 at p. 998, para. D.

[4] *R.* v. *Fenton* (1830) 1 Lew. 179.

[5] *R.* v. *Franklin* (1883) 15 Cox 163 (*T.A.C.*); Franklin was sentenced to two months' imprisonment for manslaughter, 'upon the broad ground of negligence'.

[6] The question whether it was the felony of larceny so to take the box was not discussed.

as distinct from ordinary, negligence.[1] The judge (Field, J.) said:[2] 'I have a great abhorrence of constructive crime. We do not think that the case cited by counsel for the prosecution is binding upon us in the facts of this case, and, therefore, the civil wrong against the refreshment-stall keeper is immaterial to this charge of manslaughter.'

OBJECTIONS TO CONSTRUCTIVE MANSLAUGHTER

¶ **133**. The objection to constructive crime taken in *R.* v. *Franklin* was no new thing. In 1839 H.M. Commissioners on Criminal Law had recommended,[3] in effect, that manslaughter, being an involuntary homicide, should comprise cases where death results from conduct which was neither intended to cause nor to risk causing death, but which the killer *did* intend to cause, or to risk causing, physical harm to some person. In the past hundred years the courts have not expressly repudiated the old doctrine of 'constructive manslaughter' as no longer law: nor have they enunciated any positive rule on the lines envisaged by the Commissioners of 1839.[4] Yet in practice it is hard to find any case of the conviction for manslaughter of a man who did not intend some personal harm, or at least did not realize that some personal harm might result from what he was doing.[5] Since motor vehicles first became common on the roads there have been a very large number of cases in the courts in which it has appeared that a driver while committing some breach of traffic regulations has unintentionally caused someone's death, yet in very few of these has he been even charged with manslaughter. Again, where a charge of manslaughter and a charge for the traffic offence have both been joined in the same indictment, in the great majority of instances the accused has been acquitted of manslaughter although found guilty of the lesser crime.

¶ **134**. *R.* v. *Stringer*.[6] A striking example of this was *R.* v. *Stringer*, in which the prisoner, who was charged both with manslaughter and with dangerous driving,[7] was proved to have driven a lorry at speed round a blind corner, passing a warning notice and a red flag, and paying no heed to the signals of two men who tried to stop him, with the result that he ran into and killed one of a party of men engaged in road work. He was found not guilty of manslaughter but guilty of dangerous driving. If the old principle[8] were still operative in the law then the jury's finding that Stringer was not guilty of manslaughter

[1] As to this conception see ¶ 25 *ante*. [2] After consultation with another judge.

[3] *Fourth Report* (1839) [168]–XIX–235, p. xlii, arts. 65–71.

[4] A case in which the old doctrine was applied was *R.* v. *Sullivan* (1836) 7 C. and P. 641.

[5] Even in *R.* v. *Sullivan* (1836) 7 C. and P. 641 it could be argued that the boy who as a practical joke took out the trap-stick of a cart (which accordingly tipped and caused the carman to fall with fatal results) must have expected that the deceased would suffer at least some slight physical hurt.

[6] (1933) 24 Cr.App.R. 30.

[7] Under sect. 11 of the Road Traffic Act, 1930.

[8] I.e. that manslaughter was death caused in doing an unlawful act of any kind.

necessarily involved a finding that he was not guilty of dangerous driving, but this argument was rejected both at the trial and in the Court of Criminal Appeal.[1] A nearer approach to an express repudiation of the old doctrine was made by the House of Lords in *Andrews* v. *D.P.P.*,[2] in which it was stated that there was a passage in the judge's direction to the jury which was open to objection in that 'he began with the statement that if a man kills another in the course of an unlawful act he is guilty of manslaughter, and then proceeded to ascertain what the unlawful act was by considering Section 11 of the Road Traffic Act, 1930'.

Unfortunately the judgment in *Andrews* v. *D.P.P.* while in effect demolishing the ancient doctrine did not replace it by any precise principle. It certainly made it plain that in the law of manslaughter it makes no difference whether the death is caused[3] by the use of a motor car or by any other means. It also confirms the rule that 'simple lack of care such as will constitute civil liability is not enough'.[4] But it failed to state affirmatively what exactly is the *mens rea* in manslaughter, and oscillated in a puzzling way between the adoption of an objective and a subjective test of liability in discussing whether or not a death caused by 'dangerous' driving[5] must or could be manslaughter, and in using the same word 'negligence' at one time to indicate the offender's conduct, and at another to indicate his attitude of mind.[6] It also added to the difficulty of eliciting a clear principle of liability by stating: 'There is an obvious difference in the law of manslaughter between doing an unlawful act and doing a lawful act with a degree of carelessness which the Legislature makes criminal.'[7] The confusion and obscurity of principle which this kind of language engenders is not alleviated by the judgment in *R.* v. *Cashmore*,[8] which speaks of 'in the course of conduct which was unlawful and dangerous' and lays it down that if the accused 'had fired the rifle accidentally' he was 'none the less guilty of manslaughter'.

[1] For a closer examination of this case see *Mod. Appr. Crim. Law*, 232 *et seq.* And see *R.* v. *Leach* [1937] 1 All E.R. 319. Contrast with it *R.* v. *Gylee* (1908) 1 Cr.App.R. 242; *R.* v. *Dalloz* (1908) 1 Cr.App.R. 258; and *R.* v. *Thirgood* (1899) 63 J.P. 442, death caused by a cyclist.

[2] [1937] A.C. 576 (*T.A.C.*). See *R.* v. *Large* (1939) 27 Cr.App.R. 65 in which the Court of Criminal Appeal disapproved a direction to the jury which in substance was based upon the old doctrine. For the case of *Andrews* see *Mod. Appr. Crim. Law*, 237 *et seq.*; and Russ. 657 *et seq.*; this case was severely criticized in 53 *L.Q.R.* (1937) 380, 'Manslaughter and dangerous driving', by P. H. Dean.

[3] The death must be *caused by* the driving; see *R.* v. *Dalloway* (1847) 2 Cox 273 (*T.A.C.*).

[4] I.e. negligence sufficient to establish liability in a civil action in tort by which damages are claimed.

[5] Under sect. 11 of the Road Traffic Act, 1930.

[6] On this point see ¶ 25 *ante*.

[7] It is submitted that in fact there is no difference. For a critical analysis of the statement see *Mod. Appr. Crim. Law*, 238–40. There is the like misleading confusion of expression in *R.* v. *Larkin* [1943] 1 All E.R. 217.

[8] [1959] Crim. L.R. 850 (Cts.-Ml. A.C., Hilbery, Havers and Thesiger, JJ.).

¶ 135. *Negligence*. The greater part of the confusion in the modern law of manslaughter is due to the ambiguous use of the word 'negligence' in connexion with it. The one meaning in which it should be used in English criminal law has been suggested earlier in this book.[1] That meaning is 'inadvertence', the state of mind of one who does not foresee the consequences of his conduct to the same extent as the imaginary 'reasonable man' would foresee them. Such inadvertence, if the unforeseen consequences cause a legally recognized harm, will involve the inadvertent individual in *civil*, but not in *criminal*, liability at common law. This has repeatedly been laid down by the courts,[2] and is now beyond all question. But as already indicated the courts have not yet taken the constructive step of stating what precisely is the *mens rea* in manslaughter.[3]

¶ 136. *Foresight of harm*. For many years past it has been the practice at trials for manslaughter to speak of the necessity to establish against the prisoner what is unfortunately described as 'criminal negligence' and to assume that there can be degrees of negligence. The House of Lords went some way towards improving the position by saying in *Andrews* v. *D.P.P.* that the word 'reckless' most nearly covers the case.[4] Even so there was still no exact definition of the *mens rea* required for manslaughter which was of binding authority. Since then this depressing situation has deteriorated and it seems fruitless even to hope for any remedial intervention by the judiciary. For the law of manslaughter was rendered still more obscure by the judgment of the Court of Criminal Appeal in *R.* v. *Vickers*,[5] where it is stated: 'If a person does an act which amounts to the infliction of grievous bodily harm he cannot say that he only intended to cause a certain degree of harm';[6] and 'manslaughter is an unlawful killing, but without any

[1] ¶ 25 *ante*.

[2] E.g. in the cases of *Markuss* (1864) 4 F. and F. 358; *Noakes* (1866) 4 F. and F. 920; *Finney* (1874) 12 Cox 625 (*T.A.C.*); *Nicholls* (1874) 13 Cox 75; *Doherty* (1887) 16 Cox 306; *Elliott* (1889) 16 Cox 710; *Andrews* [1937] A.C. 576 at p. 583 (*T.A.C.*); *Dabholkar* v. *R.* [1948] A.C. 221.

[3] The much cited direction to juries recommended in *R.* v. *Bateman* (1925) 19 Cr.App.R. 8, at p. 11 (*T.A.C.*), by Lord Hewart, C.J., is: 'In explaining to juries the test which they should apply to determine whether the negligence, in the particular case, amounted or did not amount to a crime, judges have used many epithets, such as "culpable", "criminal", "gross", "wicked", "clear", "complete". But, whatever epithet be used and whether an epithet be used or not, in order to establish criminal liability the facts must be such that, in the opinion of the jury, the negligence of the accused went beyond a mere matter of compensation between subjects and showed such disregard for the life and safety of others as to amount to a crime against the State, and conduct deserving punishment.' It presented many difficulties (see *Mod. Appr. Crim. Law*, 210, 211). Now, however, it may be regarded as carrying little authority since the House of Lords (in *Andrews* v. *D.P.P.* at p. 796) stated that the expressions used in it 'are not, indeed they probably were not intended to be, a precise definition of the crime'; and see *The People* v. *Dunleavy* [1948] 2 I.R. 95 (*T.A.C.*).

[4] At p. 583; followed in *R.* v. *Bonnyman* (1942) 28 Cr.App.R. 131, at p. 134. See Russ. 658.

[5] [1957] 3 W.L.R. 326; *ante*, p. 152.

[6] At p. 328.

intention'.[1] And now the disintegration of principle has been accelerated by the dicta of the House of Lords in *D.P.P.* v. *Smith* (*ante*, ¶116*b*). Only the legislature can cure this malady, and it is therefore once more submitted that the law should be clarified by a statutory provision which should in effect settle that *it shall be the crime of involuntary manslaughter when a man who has caused the death of another did so in a course of conduct which he realized*[2] *would or might cause someone a physical harm but not a fatal harm, provided that he had no lawful justification or excuse for inflicting or for risking the infliction of the physical harm which he foresaw*. The question whether there was any justification or excuse for the harm foreseen would be for the judge to settle, as it is at present.

This would cover many cases of death on the roads for which, under the obscure directions as to 'criminal negligence' usually given to juries, convictions of manslaughter cannot usually be obtained. For it is a mistake to suppose that the driver of a motor-car cannot envisage that a non-fatal hurt to some person may result from the way in which he is driving. Year by year the published statistics show that of the total number of collisions on the roads involving personal injuries the vast majority were not fatal, and of these only about twenty-five per cent were serious.[3] But quite often the evidence would show that the driver of the car knew quite well that he was taking the risk of causing some bodily hurt. It is submitted that the reason for the deplored[4] reluctance of juries to convict a motorist for manslaughter is to be found in the failure of the prosecution and the courts to enunciate the law of manslaughter in simple language which a jury can understand. An attempt has been made by the legislature to remedy the unsatisfactory position into which lack of clear definition has brought the law relating to manslaughter by the enactment of section 8 in the Road Traffic Act, 1956 (now replaced by section 1 of the Road Traffic Act, 1960), whereby it is in effect provided that any person who causes death by dangerous driving (as now defined in the Road Traffic Act, 1960, s. 2) shall be liable on conviction on indictment to imprisonment for a period not exceeding five years. It is still open to the prosecution to indict the accused for manslaughter but nothing is said in the Act as to what, if any, difference there is in the essential elements of this new crime from those in manslaughter. So far this seems to have resulted in some courts' sentencing to periods of imprisonment

[1] At p. 330.

[2] This is a *subjective* matter, and the question for the jury would be whether they were satisfied that the prisoner in fact *did* realize this. It would *not* be enough if all that they could be satisfied about was that he ought to have realized it.

[3] E.g. see *Road Accidents, 1952* (1954), Min. of Transport and Civil Aviation, H.M.S.O.

[4] E.g. *R.* v. *Beresford* (1952) 36 Cr.App.R. 1: 'It is disturbing to find that the police have been content to prefer a charge of dangerous driving in a case in which a coroner's jury arrived at a verdict of manslaughter...; speaking generally, when dangerous driving results in death, there is likely to be, at any rate, a *prima facie* case of manslaughter.' The limitation indicated by the words '*prima facie*' was explained in *R.* v. *Nuneaton ex p. Parker* [1954] 3 All E.R. 251.

motorists who have had the misfortune to be involved in a fatal collision when driving in such a manner as in other courts would be regarded as no more than careless driving: on the other hand there are indications that it may be operated in such a way as to diminish the already small number of cases in which a motorist, who has caused a death, however reckless his driving may have been, is charged with manslaughter, to the point that in effect the maximum punishment which 'motor manslaughter' can be expected to attract will be imprisonment for five years.

Finally, it must be noted that every man on trial for murder has the right to have the issue of manslaughter left to the jury if there is any evidence upon which such a verdict can be given.[1]

SECTION 7. PUNISHMENT FOR FELONIOUS HOMICIDE AT COMMON LAW

¶ 137. The maximum punishment for manslaughter is imprisonment for life.[2] The punishment for murder was death.[3] Until 1828 those murders which constituted an act of petit-treason[4] (e.g. where a person was murdered by his wife or servant, or a bishop by one of his clergy) received an enhanced punishment. The offender, if a male, instead of being taken in a cart to the scaffold, was dragged thither on a hurdle; and, if a woman, she was not hanged, but burned,[5] as in the case of Catherine Hayes, in 1726, familiar to readers of Thackeray. By the Capital Punishment Amendment Act, 1868 (as amended by section 11 of the Homicide Act, 1957), every execution for murder must take place within the prison walls, before such persons only as the sheriff may admit.

CAPITAL MURDER

¶ 137*a*. But now by virtue of Part II of the Homicide Act, 1957, liability to the death penalty[6] is limited by section 7 to the cases set out in section 5 (*ante*, ¶ 108*a*) (which are now to be called 'capital murders'), and to cases within section 6 (1) which provides:

[1] *Bullard* v. *R.* [1957] A.C. 635; confirmed in *R.* v. *Porritt* [1961] 3 All E.R. 463. See *ante*, ¶ 121.

[2] Offences against the Person Act, 1861, s. 5, as amended by the Criminal Justice Act, 1948, s. 1 and sch. x.

[3] Except for a murderer who was under the age of eighteen years at the time when the offence was committed; instead the court must sentence him to be 'detained during Her Majesty's pleasure'; Criminal Justice Act, 1948, s. 16.

[4] Petit-treason was abolished in 1828.

[5] See Radzinowicz, *Hist. Eng. Crim. Law*, I, 209, *et seq.*

[6] By section 9 (3) (as amended by the Mental Health Act, 1959), 'Sentence of death shall not be pronounced on or recorded against a person convicted of an offence who appears to the court to have been under the age of eighteen years at the time the offence was committed, nor shall any such person be sentenced to imprisonment for life under section nine of the Homicide Act, 1957; but in lieu thereof the court shall issue an order for his detention in a special hospital.' See *ante*, ¶ 54.

A person convicted of murder shall be liable to the same punishment as heretofore, if before conviction of that murder he has, whether before or after the commencement of this Act, been convicted of another murder done on a different occasion (both murders having been done in Great Britain).

Further, by section 7 no person shall be liable to suffer death for murder in any case not falling within sections 5 or 6 of this Act; and by section 9 (1) where a court (including a court martial) is precluded by this part of this Act from passing sentence of death, the sentence shall be one of imprisonment for life. And by schedule 1 of the Act, Part 1, 1 (1), on an indictment charging a person with capital murder, he may be found not guilty of capital murder but guilty of murder.

As murder is so heinous an offence, the legislature has enacted severe penalties for even incipient approaches to it. Thus any conspiracy to murder, though it still remains only a misdemeanour, is by statute punishable with ten years' imprisonment,[1] a far higher maximum of punishment than is allowed in the case of many felonies. And every attempt to commit a murder is now made by statute[2] a felony, and is punishable with imprisonment for life. It is also a felony punishable with ten years' imprisonment to send a letter threatening to murder[3] (or to destroy property).[4]

¶ 137*b*. *No limit of territorial jurisdiction in murder and manslaughter.* In concluding this subject, it may be added that murder affords a noteworthy exception to the general legal rule that 'criminal jurisdiction is territorial'.[5] Every nation tries and punishes all crimes committed in its own territory (or in its own ships), whether committed by its own subjects or by foreigners. Conversely, on the same principle, a nation usually does not concern itself with crimes committed anywhere else, even though committed by its own subjects. But to this latter branch of the rule, homicide has been made an exception in English law, by a succession of statutes commencing as far back as Henry VIII.[6] The enactment now in force is 24 and 25 Vict. c. 100, s. 9, under which the courts of any part of the United Kingdom may try a British subject for *murder or manslaughter* committed by him on land anywhere outside the United Kingdom, whether within or without the Commonwealth. The power thus does not extend to homicides committed in a foreign ship. It is immaterial whether the person killed were a British subject or not.[7] (It may be convenient to add here that similarly bigamy, when committed by a British subject, even in a foreign country, may, by virtue of s. 57 of the same statute, be tried in the United Kingdom.)

[1] 24 and 25 Vict. c. 100, s. 4, as amended by the Criminal Justice Act, 1948, s. 1.

[2] *Ibid.* ss. 11–15.

[3] *Ibid.* s. 16.

[4] 24 and 25 Vict. c. 97, s. 50.

[5] *Post*, ¶ 641. *Macleod* v. *Att.-Gen. of N.S.W.* [1891] A.C. 455.

[6] 33 Hen. VIII, c. 23; and see *R.* v. *Sawyer* (1815) R. and R. 294; *R.* v. *Serva* (1845) 2 C. and K. 53 at p. 101.

[7] *Ante*, ¶ 82; see *R.* v. *Page* [1954] 1 Q.B. 170 for a sketch of the history.

As regards the effect of felonious homicide upon rights of property, it should be noted that both murder and manslaughter debar a sane killer from receiving any benefit under his victim's will.[1] It was formerly suggested that it might be otherwise under an intestacy, as the Statute of Distributions spoke imperatively;[2] but the contrary view is now established.[3] A policy of insurance on the life of the victim, effected by the killer with a view to the killing, is invalid, as a fraud.[4]

SECTION 8. INFANTICIDE

¶ 138. This modern felony is the creation of statute. During the seventeen years 1905–21 sixty women were sentenced to death for infanticide, but in fifty-nine of these cases the sentence was commuted. To remove this divergence between theory and practice an Act[5] was passed in 1922 which in effect provided that if a woman had wilfully caused the death of her 'newly born' child, but at the time the balance of her mind was disturbed from the effect of giving birth to the child, she should be guilty of the felony of infanticide and might be punished as if guilty of manslaughter. The Act gave no definition of 'newly born' and difficulties of interpretation of this expression arose.[6] To dispose of these difficulties the Infanticide Act, 1938,[7] repealed the Act of 1922 and provided:[8]

> Where a woman by any wilful act or omission causes the death of her child being a child under the age of twelve months, but at the time of the act or omission the balance of her mind was disturbed by reason of her not having fully recovered from the effect of giving birth to the child or by reason of the effect of lactation consequent upon the birth of the child, then, notwithstanding that the circumstances were such that but for this Act the offence would have amounted to murder, she shall be guilty of felony, to wit of infanticide, and may for such offence be dealt with and punished as if she had been guilty of the offence of manslaughter of the child.

The Act also contains a provision whereby a woman who is charged with the murder of her child may, subject to the same facts as above being proved, be found guilty of infanticide although but for the

[1] *Re Crippen* [1911] P. 108; *Re Hall* [1914] P. 1; not where the killer is insane, *In re Pitts* [1931] 1 Ch. 546.

[2] *In re Houghton* [1915] 2 Ch. 173.

[3] *In re Pitts* [1931] 1 Ch. 546; *Re Sigsworth* (1934) 152 L.T. 328.

[4] 25 Beav. 605. As to a policy of insurance effected by a suicide on his own life, see *Beresford* v. *Royal Insurance Co. Ltd.* [1936] 2 All E.R. 1052.

[5] Infanticide Act, 1922 (12 and 13 Geo. V, c. 18).

[6] See 'Child-killing in English law' by D. Seaborne Davies, in *Mod. Appr. Crim. Law*, 301.

[7] 1 and 2 Geo. VI, c. 36.

[8] Sect. 1 (1). Thus giving exemptive effect to a form of insanity not amounting to irresistible impulse (¶ 54, *ante*) nor within the M'Naghten rules (¶ 53, *ante*). The Act gives her no such exemption if while so mentally affected she happens to kill one of her other children; but the circumstances might be such as to admit the defence of diminished responsibility.

provisions of the Act she might have been found guilty of murder. The Act still leaves it open to the jury, upon an indictment of the mother for murder of the child, to return a verdict of manslaughter, or of guilty but insane, or of concealment of birth,[1] if the evidence so warrants. And on an indictment for infanticide she may be found guilty of child destruction,[2] or concealment of birth[3] or (if she has attained the age of sixteen) of cruelty.[4]

SECTION 9. CHILD DESTRUCTION[5]

¶ **139.** As previously stated[6] the killing of a person not 'in being', i.e. an unborn child, was until 1929 not punishable as murder nor as infanticide.

A great encouragement to infanticide was afforded by the rule that, for a charge of it, *partial* extrusion was not sufficient. There was therefore passed in 1929 the Infant Life (Preservation) Act (19 and 20 Geo. V, c. 34). By this Act[7] any person who, with intent to destroy the life of a child capable of being born alive, by any wilful act causes a child to die before it has an existence independent of its mother, shall be guilty of the felony of child destruction, and shall be liable to imprisonment for life. Evidence that a woman has been pregnant for twenty-eight weeks or more is *prima facie* proof that she was at that time pregnant of a child capable of being born alive. Before anyone can be convicted of this felony it must be proved that the act which caused the death of the child was not done in good faith for the purpose only of preserving the life of the mother. Upon a trial for the murder or manslaughter of any child, or for infanticide, or for using means to procure an abortion, the jury may acquit of the crime charged and, if they find that the facts prove the felony of child destruction, may convict of that felony without the necessity of a fresh trial or indictment. Similarly upon a trial of child destruction the jury may convict of using means to procure an abortion.

CONCEALMENT OF BIRTH

¶ **140.** It is also convenient here to mention the offence of concealment of birth. Concealment from the world in general must be intended; it is no crime to conceal a birth merely from some particular individual alone; 'there would be a hardship in punishing a girl for concealment from her master, if there had been no concealment from her mother'.[8] But there may be sufficient concealment although the birth is already

[1] *Post*, ¶ 140. [2] *Post*, ¶ 139.

[3] *Post*, ¶ 140.

[4] Under sect. 1 (4) of the Children and Young Persons Act, 1933.

[5] Although this offence, strictly speaking, does not come within the established definition of homicide, yet it is convenient to deal with it here.

[6] *Ante*, ¶ 83.

[7] As amended by the Criminal Justice Act, 1948.

[8] Mr Justice Wright, *Draft Criminal Code for Jamaica*, 108.

made known to some persons pledged to secrecy. Where evidence of concealment is slight a prosecution is sometimes brought for the common law misdemeanour of preventing a coroner from holding an inquest when he ought to hold one,[1] but there must be shown both a duty to hold an inquest and an intention to prevent its being held.[2]

Section 60 of the Offences against the Person Act, 1861,[3] in effect provides that where a woman has been delivered of a child it shall be a misdemeanour punishable with imprisonment not exceeding two years if any person by any secret disposition[4] of the dead[5] body of the said child (whether it died before, at, or after its birth) endeavours to conceal its birth.[6] And further, that if any person tried for the murder of a child should be acquitted of that crime, the jury may, if the evidence so warrants, find that the child had been recently born and that the accused had endeavoured to conceal its birth as above stated, and may convict him of the misdemeanour, although he had not been so charged in the indictment.

PROCURING OR ATTEMPTING ABORTION

¶ 141. Closely allied to the crimes last discussed is the statutory offence of procuring or attempting to procure abortion.[7] Although at common law, as we have seen, it was not murder to cause the death of an infant not yet born, yet according to Coke[8] it was 'a great misprision'. But now the offence is regulated by the Offences against the Person Act, 1861,[9] which provides in effect that it shall be a felony punishable with imprisonment for life if a woman is with child, and any person (including the woman herself) unlawfully administers to her any noxious drug or unlawfully uses any instrument or other means whatsoever with intent to procure her miscarriage. It is also a misdemeanour punishable with imprisonment for five years for any person to supply any such noxious drug or instrument knowing that it is to be unlawfully used with the same intent, whether or not the woman is with child.[10] Acts done in the course of proper medical treatment in the

[1] *R.* v. *Price* (1884) 12 Q.B.D. 247; *R.* v. *Stephenson* (1884) 13 Q.B.D. 331.

[2] *R.* v. *Purcy* (1933) 24 Cr.App.R. 70; 149 L.T. 432.

[3] Repealing former enactments on the subject.

[4] E.g. throwing into a pond, or burning. Thus mere *denial* is not a sufficient concealment. See Russ. I, ch. 32.

[5] There is no offence under this statute in concealing the birth of a child that is still alive.

[6] 'An imaginary crime, consistent with perfect [moral] innocence'; Pollock, B. (*Life of Lord Bramwell*, 37). 'I always regarded its moral guilt as altogether unworthy of punishment'; Lord Brampton (*Reminiscences*, ch. XXXII).

[7] See Russ. I, ch. 32; Glanville Williams, 'The law of abortion', (1952) *Curr. Legal Problems*, 128.

[8] *Inst.* III, 50; 1 Hawk. P.C. c. 31, s. 16.

[9] Sect. 58, as amended by the Criminal Justice Act, 1948, s. 1. If a woman with intent to procure abortion takes something which she believes to be noxious but which is harmless, she may be convicted of an attempt to commit an offence within sect. 58.

[10] Sect. 59.

interest of the life or health of the woman are not within these sections, being excluded by the word 'unlawfully'. So where it appeared that a girl of fourteen years had been violently raped in circumstances likely to terrify any woman, by a man who was subsequently convicted of that crime, and in consequence of the rape the girl became pregnant and the defendant, a properly qualified obstetric surgeon, had with the consent of her parents performed the operation, it was held that this was not unlawfully done, since upon the evidence the continuance of the pregnancy would probably have caused serious injury to the girl, and the consequence of giving birth to the child was likely to be that she would become a nervous wreck.[1]

[1] *R.* v. *Bourne* [1939] 1 K.B. 687 (*T.A.C.*). See Seaborne Davies, 'The law of abortion and necessity', *Mod. L.R.* (1938–9), II, 126; and 54 *L.Q.R.* 472 n.

Chapter VIII

OFFENCES AGAINST THE PERSON THAT ARE NOT FATAL

Section 1. Introductory

¶ 142. Crimes of this class are of two main types, the sexual and the non-sexual. For a long period the former were dealt with as offences against morals and religion by the ecclesiastical courts who imposed their own punitive sanctions; this jurisdiction, though long obsolete in practice,[1] has never been formally abolished.[2] But the common law had no penal prohibitions of similar comprehensiveness, its criminal rules taking cognizance only of those grosser breaches of sexual morality that were rendered peculiarly odious, either by the abnormality of the form they took, or by the violence with which they were accompanied; aggravations to which the legislature subsequently added that of the tender age of the female concerned in them, or of her near consanguinity. Hence, the voluntary illicit intercourse of the sexes, even though it take the form of mercenary prostitution or of an adulterous violation of marital legal rights, furnishes no ground for a criminal indictment. Since a substantial proportion of all offences against the person which come before the courts consists of sexual crimes it is necessary that some account of these be given in this book, although it will not be possible to treat any of them in detail.

Section 2. Sexual Offences

RAPE

¶ 143. At common law the crime of rape consists in having carnal knowledge of a woman without her consent. Although the offence is usually effected by violence, it has been decided that rape can be committed without the use of any violence, the essential point being that the woman's free and conscious permission has not been obtained. This crime seems to have been originally punishable by death (the punishment was later varied to mutilation[3]) and then was reduced to a trespass[4] punishable with only two years' imprisonment; but soon afterwards it was again made a capital felony. Subsequent statutory modifications have been replaced by the Sexual Offences Act, 1956, s. 1 (1), which makes the crime a felony punishable with imprisonment for life.[5] It is an irrebuttable presumption that a boy under the age of fourteen years

[1] See *Blunt* v. *Park Lane Hotel Ltd.* [1942] 2 K.B. 253, at p. 257 *per* Goddard, L.J.

[2] Stephen, *Hist. Crim. Law*, II, 396–429; *Phillimore* v. *Machon* (1876) 1 P.D. 481.

[3] Bract. lib. III, c. 28; 4 Bl. *Comm.* 211.

[4] Statute of Westminster I, c. 13 (3 Edw. I).

[5] Section 37.

is incapable of committing rape,[1] irrespective of evidence as to his physical ability. But such an infant can be a principal in the second degree, aiding and assisting in the offence, if his *mens rea* can be proved.[2]

It has been stated[3] that as a general rule of law a husband cannot be guilty of rape on his wife because, upon marriage, the wife gives a consent (which she cannot retract) to the husband's exercising a right of intercourse with her. On this principle there is a general matrimonial obligation imposed on the wife by reason of the marriage, so long as the ordinary relations created by the marriage subsist between the spouses.[4] The court may, however, intervene to terminate those relations, by an order that the wife be no longer bound to cohabit with the husband, and if it does so then the husband is not entitled to have intercourse with her without her consent, and thus could be guilty of rape on her.[5]

For rape to be constituted there must be proof of penetration although very slight penetration is sufficient; but the completion of the sexual act need not have occurred.[6] As it is of the essence of rape that the woman did not consent, the offence is committed when a man has had connexion with a woman when she was asleep, or after personating her husband,[7] or has forced her to consent by threats,[8] or by false representation that he was performing a surgical operation.[9] If a female is mentally defective or is under sixteen she may yet consent in fact and if she does the man is not guilty of rape but may be guilty of other statutory offences.[10] But where a female is mentally so defective that she is incapable of expressing either assent or dissent it has been held to be rape to have connexion with her.[11] Any person, even another woman, who aids and abets the

[1] And therefore cannot be found guilty of committing it (*R.* v. *Groombridge* (1836) 7 C. and P. 582), nor of an assault with intent to commit it (*R.* v. *Eldershaw* (1828) 3 C. and P. 396).

[2] 1 Hale P.C. 630; on the same facts as would suffice to convict an older person he can be convicted of indecent assault (*R.* v. *Williams* [1893] 1 Q.B. 320) or common assault (*R.* v. *Angus* (1907) 27 N.Z.L.R. 948).

[3] 1 Hale P.C. 629.

[4] *R.* v. *Miller* [1954] 2 W.L.R. 138; but in the circumstances of the force used in this case the prisoner was held guilty of common assault under the Offences against the Person Act, 1861, s. 47.

[5] *R.* v. *Clarke* [1949] 2 All E.R. 448; 33 Cr.App.R. 216.

[6] Sexual Offences Act, 1956, s. 44; *R.* v. *Cox* (1832) 1 Lew. 292.

[7] Sexual Offences Act, 1956, s. 1 (2). A false representation by the man as to his physical condition was held, by a majority of the judges in *R.* v. *Clarence* (1888) 22 Q.B.D. 23, not to warrant the inference that she did not consent to the act.

[8] *R.* v. *Jones* (1861) 4 L.T. (n.s.) 154; unless it be held now to fall within sect. 2 (1) of the Sexual Offences Act, 1956, which declares it to be an offence (punishable with imprisonment for two years) to procure a woman, by threats or intimidation, to have unlawful sexual intercourse in any part of the world; but see *R.* v. *Williams* [1923] 1 K.B. 340.

[9] *R.* v. *Flattery* (1877) 2 Q.B.D. 414; *R.* v. *Williams* [1923] 1 K.B. 340.

[10] *Post*, ¶¶ 144, 145. *R.* v. *Harling* [1938] 1 All E.R. 307.

[11] *R.* v. *Fletcher* (1859) Bell 63, at p. 70; *R.* v. *Ryan* (1846) 2 Cox 115; *R.* v. *Pressy* (1867) 10 Cox 635; *R.* v. *Barratt* (1873) L.R. 2 C.C.R. 81.

commission of rape may be indicted and convicted as a principal offender.[1] An attempt to commit rape is now by statute[2] made punishable with imprisonment for seven years. On indictment for rape it is possible for the jury to find, on the evidence, that one of a number of lesser offences has been committed.[3]

¶ 144. *Unlawful sexual intercourse with mental defectives.* There may be evidence of consent (even consisting of the reaction of a mere animal instinct) by persons who are mentally afflicted; for the better protection of such females the Sexual Offences Act, 1956,[4] as amended by the Mental Health Act, 1959, section 127, in effect provides that it shall be a misdemeanour (punishable with two years' imprisonment) to have or to attempt to have unlawful sexual intercourse with a woman who is a defective (and known or suspected by the prisoner to be such) under circumstances not amounting to rape, or to procure such a woman to have intercourse. 'Defective' is defined as 'a person suffering from severe subnormality'; and 'severe subnormality' is defined as:

> a state of arrested or incomplete development of mind which includes subnormality of intelligence and is of such a nature or degree that the patient is incapable of living an independent life or of guarding himself against serious exploitation, or will be so incapable when of an age to do so.

A similar liability is imposed[5] upon any person who is a member of the staff of any institution for mentally disordered persons,[6] who has, or attempts to have, unlawful sexual intercourse with any female patient who is under the care or treatment of the institution or of himself; and there is provision that no consent or alleged consent shall be any defence to an indictment or prosecution for such offence.

¶ 145. *Unlawful sexual intercourse with young girls.* Analogous to the above mentioned special statutory protection given to the mentally afflicted were the provisions contained in the various Criminal Law Amendment Acts from 1885 to 1928, now repealed and replaced by the Sexual Offences Act, 1956, whereby young girls of normal intelligence are protected even against the consequences of their actual consent,[7] which is thus rendered legally ineffective to constitute any defence to the person accused of the offences which these statutes create.

(1) *Girls under thirteen.* It is a felony[8] to have unlawful sexual inter-

[1] *R.* v. *Ram* (1893) 17 Cox 609.

[2] Sexual Offences Act, 1956, s. 37, sched. 2, pt. 1.

[3] Sect. 37 and Sched. II (1) (*a*); and note *R.* v. *Touhey* (1960) 45 Cr.App.R. 23.

[4] Sects. 7–9.

[5] Mental Health Act, sect. 128.

[6] Or who has the care or charge of, or is an attendant of, any single patient. And see *R.* v. *Cook* [1954] 1 W.L.R. 125; *R.* v. *Balderstone* (1955) 39 Cr.App.R. 97.

[7] These provisions do not in any way modify the law of rape where the girl has not in fact consented.

[8] Sect. 5; punishable with imprisonment for life.

course with a girl below the age of thirteen and a misdemeanour[1] to attempt to do so; in either case her consent is no defence.[2] On an indictment for the felony (or, it seems, for the misdemeanour) the accused, if the evidence so warrants, may be convicted of indecent[3] assault.[4]

(2) *Girls of thirteen or over, but under sixteen.* Having, or attempting to have, unlawful sexual intercourse with any girl in this age group is a misdemeanour.[5] By the Sexual Offences Act, 1956, s. 6 (3), on a charge for this offence, a reasonable belief that the girl is over the age of sixteen is not a valid defence except to a defendant[6] who is under the age of twenty-four. But if the accused is also charged or indicted for indecent assault[7] it has been held that the same belief that the girl was over sixteen will *not* be a defence, even though the only indecent assault which can be proved against him is the very same act of carnal knowledge.[8] It may be noted that although a marriage between persons, being either of them under sixteen, was declared void by the Age of Marriage Act, 1929 (a provision now repeated in sect. 2 of the Marriage Act, 1949), yet under the Sexual Offences Act, 1956, s. 6 (2), it is a valid defence to anyone charged with unlawful intercourse or indecent assault[9] to prove that at the time of the alleged offence he had reasonable cause to believe that the girl was his wife.[10]

INDECENT ASSAULT

¶ 146. By the Sexual Offences Act, 1956, an indecent assault upon a female[11] (of any age) is made a misdemeanour[12] and on a charge for indecent assault upon a child or young person under the age of sixteen it is no defence that she (or he) consented to the act of indecency.[13] The

[1] Punishable with imprisonment for two years.

[2] Evidence by a child of tender years under the Children and Young Persons Act, 1933, s. 38, must be corroborated, see ¶ 600 *post*. And apart from the provisions of this section where evidence is given by young girls on oath the jury should be cautioned to be careful in acting upon it alone.

[3] But not of common assault.

[4] Punishable with imprisonment for two years.

[5] Sect. 6; punishable with imprisonment for two years.

[6] *R.* v. *Chapman* [1931] 2 K.B. 606. But only on the *first* occasion on which he is charged with such an offence. As to the meaning of 'charged' see *R.* v. *Rider* [1954] 1 All E.R. 5; 37 Cr.App.R. 209.

[7] *Post*, ¶ 146.

[8] *R.* v. *Forde* [1923] 2 K.B. 400; *R.* v. *Maughan* (1934) 24 Cr.App.R. 130 (*T.A.C.*). An illogicality due to the wording of the statute. *R.* v. *Laws* (1929) 21 Cr.App.R. 45.

[9] *Post*, ¶ 146.

[10] The Act does not provide the defence if the supposed husband is charged with abduction (*post*, ¶ 147).

[11] By s. 15 of the same Act an indecent assault upon a *male* person whether by another male or by a female is a misdemeanour punishable with ten years' imprisonment. The word 'assault' is understood in its strict legal meaning (*post*, ¶ 164) as distinct from 'battery', and it is the indecency which has to be corroborated and not the act of assaulting, *R.* v. *Rolfe* (1952) 36 Cr.App.R. 4.

[12] Sect. 37; punishable with imprisonment for two years.

[13] Sect. 14 (2), and the same applies (by subs. (4)) to a woman of any age who is a 'defective'. A question has arisen which has caused differences of opinion: is an indecent

special defence created by the Age of Marriage Act, 1929 (rep.) has been mentioned in the preceding paragraph. An assault becomes indecent only if it is accompanied by circumstances of indecency towards the person assaulted.[1]

ABDUCTION OF FEMALES

¶ 147. By the Sexual Offences Act, 1956, it is a misdemeanour[2] without lawful authority or excuse to take out of the possession and against the will of any person having the lawful care of her[3] an unmarried girl being under the age of sixteen.[4] It has been held that this enactment must be strictly construed and therefore that it is no defence that the defendant honestly believed the girl to be over sixteen,[5] or that she appeared to be, or had told him that she was, over that age. Furthermore it is not necessary that the girl should have been taken away for any immoral or improper purpose, so that it is no defence to prove that there was no such corrupt or improper intent or motive.[6] Nor need the taking be by force or any kind of mental pressure; and it seems[7] that it is immaterial that the girl may have consented or even herself have made the suggestion. But where, without any inducement by the man, the girl of her own initiative went to the man, the case is not within the statute.[8] And it was held in *R.* v. *Hibbert*[9] that a conviction under the

act essential to this offence, or does it suffice that an assault, decent in itself, was committed with an indecent *aim*? The former view was taken by the Supreme Court of New South Wales (*R.* v. *Culgan* (1898) 19 N.S.W. 160), who held it not sufficient that the accused had 'tried to drag' the prosecutrix to a place where he could have intercourse with her; and by that of South Africa (*R.* v. *Abrahams* [1918] C.G.H. 590). But the contrary view was adopted by the Supreme Court of Ontario (*R.* v. *Chong* (1915) 32 Ontario 66), who held that 'an indecent assault is an assault which has in it *an element* of indecency', even a merely mental one. Lord Esher (then Brett, J.) in the case of Col. Valentine Baker (*The Times*, 30 July and 3 Aug. 1875) took the latter view, by instructing the grand jury that 'If a man kisses a young woman against her will, and with feelings of carnal passion and with a view to gratify his passions or to excite hers, that would be an indecent assault. The kisses of young people in seasons of universal gaiety are not indecent, but kisses given by a man under the influence of carnal passion are indecent.' In *Beal* v. *Kelley* [1951] 2 All E.R. 763, *Fairclough* v. *Whipp* [1951] 2 All E.R. 834 and *D.P.P.* v. *Rogers* [1953] 1 W.L.R. 1017, it was held that there must be a hostile act as well as indecent conduct by the prisoner, but this has been enlarged by the Indecency with Children Act, 1960.

1 *R.* v. *George*, Lincoln Ass. 3 Nov. 1955; [1956] Crim. L.R. 52. And see *R.* v. *Coombes* [1961] Crim. L.R. 54, in which it seems to have been assumed that a light touch with the hand on a woman's back was an indecent assault; perhaps because it accompanied words which suggested a request for sexual intercourse. *Contra*, *R.* v. *Abrahams*, *supra*.

2 Sect. 20; punishable with imprisonment for two years.

3 Normally, her parent or guardian.

4 If under sixteen she must, by virtue of the Age of Marriage Act, 1929, be unmarried.

5 *R.* v. *Prince* (1875) L.R. 2 C.C.R. 154 (*T.A.C.*); see *Mod. Appr. Crim. Law* (1948), 218, 219. See also *R.* v. *Booth* (1872) 12 Cox 231; *R.* v. *Mycock* (1871) 12 Cox 28.

6 *R.* v. *Tinkler* (1859) 1 F. and F. 513. And see *R.* v. *Baillie* (1859), 8 Cox 238.

7 From cases decided under previous enactments, replaced by the Offences against the Person Act.

8 *R.* v. *Jarvis* (1903) 20 Cox 249; *R.* v. *Alexander* (1912) 76 J.P. 215.

9 (1869) L.R. 1 C.C.R. 184.

section should be quashed on the ground that there was no evidence that the prisoner knew, or had reasonable cause to know, that the girl was under the charge of her father or mother or other lawful guardian.

¶ 148. By section 19 of the same Act to take any unmarried girl under eighteen out of the possession and against the will of her lawful guardian, with intent that she shall have unlawful sexual intercourse with men or a particular man, is a misdemeanour,[1] unless the defendant had reasonable cause to believe the girl was over eighteen. Yet here too the willingness of the girl to go away with the defendant does not give him a defence.[2] The word 'unlawful' has been held to be equivalent to 'illicit' in the sense of 'outside lawful wedlock'.[3]

¶ 149. *Statutory offences against females.* It is beyond the scope or purpose of this volume to enumerate all the offences of this character which have been created by statute for the protection of females. Details may be obtained from the larger books for practitioners. Examples are: permitting the defilement of girls under sixteen,[4] procuration by threat, fraud, or drugs,[5] detention in brothels,[6] allowing a child or young person to be in a brothel[7], trading in prostitution.[8] And for the allied offence of importuning by prostitutes see the Public Health Amendment Act, 1907, s. 81, and the Street Offences Act, 1959; and by men, section 32 of the Sexual Offences Act, 1956.[9]

INCEST

¶ 150. This crime consists in sexual intercourse between persons within certain prohibited degrees of relationship as stated in the Sexual Offences Act, 1956, s. 10.[10] It is a defence that the male person did not know of the relationship but it is no defence that the female consented. However, if she is of the age of sixteen or over, and does consent, with

[1] Punishable with imprisonment for two years.

[2] By virtue of s. 17 it is a felony (punishable with imprisonment for fourteen years) for any person to take away or detain a woman of any age, against her will, with the intention that she shall marry or have unlawful sexual intercourse with that or any other person, if she is so taken away or detained either by force or for the sake of her property or expectations of property; and if she be under twenty-one it is the like felony fraudulently to take or detain her out of the possession and against the will of her parent or guardian, for the same purposes, if she has property or expectations of property.

[3] *R.* v. *Chapman* [1958] 3 All E.R. 143; 3 W.L.R. 401.

[4] Sexual Offences Act, 1956, s. 28.

[5] Sects. 2, 3 and 4.

[6] Sect. 24.

[7] Sects. 25 and 26.

[8] Sects. 30 and 31. See *Calvert* v. *Mayes* [1954] 1 All E.R. 41; *R.* v. *Silver* [1956] 1 All E.R. 716; *R.* v. *Thomas* [1957] 1 W.L.R. 747; *Smith* v. *Hughes* [1960] 2 All E.R. 859; *Shaw* v. *D.P.P.* [1961] 2 W.L.R. 897.

[9] *Burge* v. *D.P.P.* [1962] 1 W.L.R. 265.

[10] These are: a man and his granddaughter, daughter, sister (including half-sister), or mother. It is immaterial that the relationship is not traced through lawful wedlock.

knowledge of the relationship, she too is guilty. The crime is a misdemeanour punishable with imprisonment for seven years.[1]

SODOMY

¶ 151. This offence is dealt with by the Sexual Offences Act, 1956, which provides in effect that to commit the crime is a felony punishable with imprisonment for life: an attempt to commit the crime is a misdemeanour punishable with imprisonment for ten years.[2] The offence consists in penetration *per anum*, and it can be committed by a man with a man, or with a woman, or with an animal.[3] Any person (if old enough to be criminally responsible) who consents to the commission of this offence is himself or herself liable as a principal.[4] It is a misdemeanour[5] for any male person whether in public or private to take part in or attempt[6] to procure the commission by any male person of any act of gross indecency.

SECTION 3. NON-SEXUAL OFFENCES

¶ 152. *Classification.* We turn now to those offences against the person, of a non-fatal character, which are not sexual. These fall roughly into two classes, (*a*) those which occasion actual bodily harm, and (*b*) those in which actual bodily harm is not essential. As in the case of homicide, so in the case of non-fatal hurt, it must be remembered that an *actus reus* is essential and that there are many instances in which to use force against, or even to hurt, another person does not constitute an *actus reus.* For it may be commanded by the law, e.g. in the execution of sentence on a convicted offender, in preventing a breach of the peace, in arresting[7] a felon, or forcibly feeding a hunger-striking prisoner;[8] or it may be permitted[9] as an act of self-defence (in which circumstances the harm inflicted is justified);[10] or it may be legally permitted as in surgical operations,[11] in the correction of your children or the scholars or

[1] But for life if the offence is committed with a girl under thirteen, and it is so charged in the indictment; the penalty for attempt is seven years' imprisonment, Indecency with Children Act, 1960.

[2] Sects. 12 and 37, sch. II. The same punishment is provided for any indecent assault upon a male person (whether committed by another male or by a female).

[3] See Russ. ch. 42. And see *R.* v. *Bourne* (1952) 36 Cr.App.R. 152, *ante*, ¶ 45.

[4] And being an accomplice requires corroboration.

[5] Punishable with two years' imprisonment, under the Sexual Offences Act, 1956, sect. 13. Actual physical contact is not essential, *R.* v. *Hornby and Peaple* [1946] 2 All E.R. 487; 32 Cr.App.R. 1; this case is explained in *R.* v. *Pearce* [1951] 1 All E.R. 493. See also *R.* v. *Hunt and Another* [1950] 2 All E.R. 291; 34 Cr.App.R. 135.

[6] Even by letter; *R.* v. *Bentley* [1923] 1 K.B. 403. And see *R.* v. *Miskell* [1954] 1 W.L.R. 438; 37 Cr.App.R. 214; *R.* v. *Gammon* (1959) 43 Cr.App.R. 155.

[7] But any *unnecessary* handcuffing would be an assault; *Wright* v. *Court* (1825) 3 D. and R. (M.C.), 299.

[8] *Leigh* v. *Gladstone* (1909) 26 T.L.R. 139.

[9] An instance of the exercise of lawful force is where the stewards of a public meeting remove persons who persist in disturbing it; see ¶ 155 *post*.

[10] See ¶¶ 94–7 *ante*, and Russ. 490.

[11] ¶¶ 12, 99 *ante*; and see Russ. 29.

apprentices who have been placed under your authority,[1] and in recognized sports and pastimes (in which circumstances it is excusable).[2] It is true that the old authorities seem to approve the most drastic action in certain instances, such as in the prevention of felonies (even those which are not in themselves an attack on human life), in the apprehension of felons, and in self-defence against unlawful arrest. But in modern times it is certain that it is unlawful to go further than is reasonable in the circumstances of the particular situation. Nowadays the police authorities have such widespread and efficient machinery for the detection of crime and the apprehension of offenders that the immediate and deadly steps which a private person would have been praised for taking in the less organized conditions of bygone days[3] would now be regarded as excessive, and themselves outside legal excuse.

SELF-DEFENCE, LAWFUL FORCE

¶ 153. It is natural that a man who is attacked should resist, and his resistance, as such, will not be unlawful. It is not necessary that he should wait to be actually struck, before striking in self-defence. If one party raise up a threatening hand, then the other may strike. Nor is the right of defence limited to the particular person assailed; it includes all who are under any obligation, even though merely social and not legal, to protect him. The old authorities exemplify this by the cases of a husband defending his wife, a child his parent,[4] a master his servant, or a servant his master (and perhaps the courts would now take a still more general view of this duty of the strong to protect the weak).[5]

UNLAWFUL FORCE

¶ 154. But the justification covers only blows struck in sheer self-defence and not in revenge.[6] Accordingly if, when all the danger is over and no more blows are really needed for defence, the defender nevertheless strikes one, he commits an assault and battery.[7] The numerous decisions that have been given as to the kind of weapons that may lawfully be used to repel an assailant, are merely applications of this simple principle. Thus, as we have already seen,[8] where a person is attacked in such a way that his life is in danger he is justified in even killing his assailant to prevent the felony. But an ordinary assault must not be thus met by the use of fire-arms or other deadly weapons.[9] And, similarly, a knife is not usually a reasonable instrument of self-defence,

[1] *McGee* v. *Robinson* (*The Times*, 30 Nov. 1910). [2] See Russ. 661.

[3] Cf. the case of Mr Purcell, mentioned *ante*, ¶ 97 n. 4.

[4] *R.* v. *Rose* (1884) 15 Cox 540 (*T.A.C.*).

[5] Cf. 2 C.C.R. 178; 11 Mod. 242; 1 East P.C. 292; 1 Hawk. P.C. c. 31, ss. 56 and 57.

[6] On self-defence see Dicey, *Law of the Constitution*, 8th ed., app. note IV.

[7] *R.* v. *Driscoll* (1841) C. and M. 214 (*T.A.C.*). For the precise meaning of these two words 'assault' and 'battery' see ¶ 164 *post*. The term 'assault' is quite commonly used to connote what should, more strictly, be called a 'battery'. [8] *Ante*, ¶ 97.

[9] *Osborn* v. *Veitch* (1858) 1 F. and F. 317; *McCluskey* v. *H.M. Advocate* (1959) S.L.T. (N.R.D.) 26; [1959] Crim. L.R. 453.

although it may be used where serious bodily danger is apprehended, or where a robbery (i.e. a theft *by violence*) is to be prevented.[1] Hence its use could rarely be justified where the attack is made with a leather strap.[2] It should, however, be noted that where more force than was needful has been used for self-defence, the case is not necessarily to be treated as if all the force employed had been illegal; for the evidence, considered as a whole, may establish that a charge of 'wounding with intent to do grievous bodily harm' should be reduced to one of unlawful wounding.

DEFENCE OF PROPERTY LAWFUL

¶ 155. The right of self-defence extends, as we have said, to the defence not only of your person but also of your property. Thus reasonable force may lawfully be used in expelling anyone who is trespassing in your house,[3] or on your land (or even on a railway-carriage *reserved* for you), if no milder mode of getting rid of him would avail. If his entry had itself been effected forcibly, as by a burglary or even by breaking open a gate, you may at once use force to expel him.[4] But in the case of an ordinary peaceful trespasser, it will not be until you have first requested him to depart, and he has failed to comply with the request, that you will be justified in ejecting him by the strong hand. Disturbance of an easement is a wrong in the nature of a trespass, and therefore force may similarly be used to prevent it.[5]

A similar right exists in the case of movable property. Force may accordingly be used to resist anyone who attempts to take away your goods from you.[6] And there is modern authority[7] for saying that force may even be used to *recapture* your goods, after they have been actually taken out of your possession. In the case of real property this right to recover by force certainly does not exist. Under an Act of Richard II (5 Ric. II, st. 1, c. 8) a landlord commits an indictable offence by 'forcibly entering' a house, although it is his own, if any full (though unlawful) possessor is excluding him.[8] Real property, unlike personal, is in no danger of being meanwhile destroyed, or lost, if the owner waits to sue at law for it.

EFFECT OF CONSENT

¶ 156. There is, again, a presumption that those who go about in public consent to receive the trifling degree of force involved in those

[1] *R.* v. *Hewlett* (1858) 1 F. and F. 91.

[2] Or the use of a razor to repel an attack by the fist; *R.* v. *Morse* (1910) 4 Cr.App.R. 51

[3] *R.* v. *Hussey* (1924) 18 Cr.App.R. 160 (*T.A.C.*); cf. *Hurst* v. *Picture Theatres Ltd.* [1915] 1 K.B. 1. As to what is 'reasonable' see *R.* v. *Taylor*, 1952, *The Times*, 28 Nov.

[4] *Green* v. *Goddard* (1704) 2 Salk 641 (*T.A.C.*).

[5] To defend one's precedence in a procession does not justify a battery, e.g. a contest between a D.D.'s wife and a J.P.'s wife, *Ashton* v. *Jennings* (1675) 2 Levinz 133.

[6] *Bird* v. *Jones* (1845) 7 Q.B. 742.

[7] In *Blades* v. *Higgs* (1865) 11 H.L.C. 621, the House of Lords seems to have tacitly accepted this doctrine. But see Pollock, *Law of Torts* 15th ed., 282.

[8] *Newton* v. *Harland* (1840) 1 Scott, N.R. 474; cf. 17 Ch.D. at p. 188.

petty instances of contact which inevitably arise in the ordinary social intercourse of everyday life; such as tapping a friend's shoulder to attract his attention,[1] or jostling past one's neighbour in a crowd. Of course, in appropriate circumstances, a man may make it plain that he does not consent to be touched, and then it will be an offence intentionally to touch him in the way prohibited. Even apart from any express prohibition, the acts of contact must be done *bona fide*, and with no unusual vehemence, for no one is presumed to consent to be treated in such fashion.

In all cases consent, express or implied, is the gist of the matter; for if consent be given there is no *actus reus*. Hence seduction is no assault,[2] either in the law of crime or in that of tort.

But the consent must be given freely (i.e. without force, fear or fraud), and by a sane and sober person, so situated as to be able to form a reasonable opinion upon the matter to which consent is given.[3] 'Fraud vitiates consent' is a well-known legal maxim, but it must be interpreted cautiously. As Stephen, J., said,[4] 'the proposition that fraud vitiates consent in criminal matters is not true if taken to apply in the fullest sense of the word and without qualification. It is too short to be true as a mathematical formula is true'. The fraud must relate to a fundamental fact,[5] i.e. the identity of the deceiver, or the nature of the assault.[6] Accordingly an impostor, who, by pretending to be a named surgeon, induces an invalid to submit to be operated upon by him, will be guilty of assault (and battery),[7] notwithstanding the consent which was nominally given. As regards the mental capacity to consent, it may be repeated that, in the case of indecent assaults, the legislature has established a definite rule as to age, by enacting that consent given by a child of either sex under sixteen years of age shall not constitute a defence.[8] And, again, even the most complete consent, by the most competent person, will not suffice to legalize an assault which there are public grounds for prohibiting. Thus consent is no defence, criminally,[9] for any

[1] A man was indicted at the Central Criminal Court in 1925 (18 June) for an assault on his former fiancée, though her utmost charge was 'He caught hold of my coat and said he wanted a few words with me'. Sankey, J., left it to the jury; but only as 'a very, very small matter'. They acquitted.

[2] In the paragraphs which follow, the word 'assault' is used in the comprehensive meaning of 'assault and battery'; see *post*, ¶ 164.

[3] For a submission is not always a permission.

[4] In *R.* v. *Clarence* (1888) 22 Q.B.D. at p. 43 (*T.A.C.*).

[5] But error as to a matter of law does not vitiate consent. And although fraud may *vitiate* consent, so as to deprive the wrong-doer of that defence, yet it does not *negative* consent, as is sometimes erroneously thought; see *post*, ¶ 234.

[6] *R.* v. *Clarence* (1888) 22 Q.B.D. 23 (*T.A.C.*) *per* Stephen, J.; *R.* v. *Williams* [1923] 1 K.B. 340.

[7] Or if he merely pretended to be a qualified medical man.

[8] *Ante*, ¶¶ 145, 146. And compare *D.P.P.* v. *Rogers* [1953] 1 Q.B. 311 with *Beal* v. *Kelley* (1951) 35 Cr.App.R. 128.

[9] *R.* v. *Coney* (1882) 8 Q.B.D. 534. The difference between civil and criminal law in this matter lies in the fact that in the civil action of tort the plaintiff is a 'party' to the

assault that involves some extreme and causeless injury to life, limb, or health; or even one that constitutes a mere breach of the peace; nor for any assault likely to cause bodily harm (whether extreme or not) and not justified by any good reason, e.g. sport, lawful chastisement, etc.[1] If, therefore, one of the parties to a duel is injured, his consent is no excuse. Yet it is uncertain at what degree of danger the law thus denies a man's right to consent to be placed in situations of peril[2] (as, for instance, by allowing himself to be wheeled in a barrow along a tight-rope).[3] As already explained, in the case of a surgical operation carried out by a competent surgeon, however great be the risk, there will usually be adequate cause for running it; and so the patient's consent will be full justification for what would otherwise be an aggravated battery.

TORTIOUS ASSAULT AND CRIMINAL ASSAULT

¶ 157. These rules as to the amount of violence which constitutes an assault, and as to the circumstances which will excuse that violence, hold equally good in the law of tort and in the law of crime. But those two branches of law differ in their rules as to the state of mind which will render a man liable for the exercise of such violence as has been shown to be a forbidden act. In actions of tort, either intention or even negligence[4] (as where a waiter clumsily upsets over a customer a boiling teapot) will suffice to render the wrongdoer liable to damages. But an assault will not render a man liable to criminal punishment unless it were committed with actual intention,[5] or at least with recklessness.

A. *OFFENCES WHERE ACTUAL BODILY INJURY IS ESSENTIAL*

¶ 158. The present law regarding this aggravated class of crimes is entirely the creation of statutes.[6] Wounding and maiming did, in early times, entitle the sufferer to bring an 'appeal' of felony; and if the appeal were successful the wrongdoer forfeited life and member. But these appeals seldom proved successful, as they were usually quashed for some technical informality; and if the appellee were then arraigned at the King's suit he received no heavier punishment than that for a misdemeanour—imprisonment or fine. Appeals for wounding consequently died out, though the injured parties, if unwilling to indict the

proceedings, which are an issue between himself and the defendant; whereas in the criminal prosecution the prosecutor is not a 'party', for here the issue is between the Crown and the accused person, and only the Crown (i.e. the law) can effectively consent. Cf. the case of the tournament in medieval times, when held by command or permission of the king. If the law does consent then there is no *actus reus*. See Hale, 1 P.C. ch. VII, sect. 1; *ante*, ¶ 12.

[1] E.g. *R.* v. *Donovan* [1934] 2 K.B. 498.

[2] See Winfield, *Law of Tort*, 6th ed., 26.

[3] But as to *juvenile* acrobats, see Children and Young Persons Act, 1933, part II.

[4] *Weaver* v. *Ward* (1627) Hobart 134; yet see Bigelow on Torts, 7th ed., s. 374.

[5] *Ackroyd* v. *Barett* (1895) 11 T.L.R. 115. Cf. *Commonwealth* v. *Adams* (1873) 114 Mass. 323. In India, in the United States (Wharton's *Criminal Law*, bk. IV, ch. VIII), and in Scotland (Macdonald's *Criminal Law*, 154), negligence is similarly held to be not sufficient to make assaults criminal.

[6] See Stephen, *Hist. Crim. Law*, III, 108–20.

offender for an assault, had still the alternative of a civil remedy by way of an action of trespass[1] to recover pecuniary damages. But subsequently, by various statutes, offences of this class have again been made to carry a more adequate punishment. The present law on the subject is, however, as Mr Justice Wright has said, 'singularly fragmentary and unsystematic'.[2] It is mainly to be found in the Offences against the Person Act, 1861 (consolidating earlier enactments), which makes the graver offences felonies, the others ranking as misdemeanours. In this statute[3] we are confronted with the expression 'malice' which has caused much trouble in our jurisprudence, and has in the past been used in conflicting senses.

¶ 158*a*. *Malice*. The malice required in the present connexion is narrower than that vague general idea of a wicked state of mind which the word in early times denoted at common law, as in the phrase 'mute of malice'. But so many have been the variations of meaning in which during the course of centuries the words 'malice' and 'maliciously' have been employed in the law[4] that it used to be as difficult in the crime of malicious damage as we have seen it to be in the crimes of felonious homicide, to find judicial authority for an exact definition of the word 'maliciously' where it occurs in the statutes relating to this offence. In an endeavour to bring clarity into this matter Professor Kenny in the first edition of this book[5] propounded a principle which held its position without any successful attack ever since, and was in 1957 approved by the Court of Criminal Appeal in *R.* v. *Cunningham*.[6] The principle is that in any statutory definition of a crime 'malice' must be taken not in the old vague sense of wickedness in general, but as requiring either (1) an actual intention to do the particular *kind* of harm that in fact was done, or (2) recklessness as to whether such harm should occur or not (i.e. the accused has foreseen that the particular kind of harm might be done, and yet has gone on to take the risk[7] of it). It is neither limited to, nor does it indeed require, any ill will towards the person injured.[8] The principle is well illustrated by the case of *R.* v. *Pembliton*.[9] This was a successful appeal against conviction under sect. 51 of the Act for unlawfully and maliciously breaking a window. The appellant had been concerned in a quarrel at night in a public house, and after the whole party had been ejected the fight continued in the street; the appellant broke away and from the other side of the street threw at his opponents a stone which missed them and broke the window of the public house. The jury found as a fact that he did not

[1] Pollock and Maitland, II, 489. [2] *Draft Criminal Code for Jamaica*, p. 106.

[3] And in the contemporaneous enactment, the Malicious Damage Act; *post*, Ch. XI.

[4] *Ante*, ¶¶ 14, 103, 105; *post*, ¶ 737; and cf. *R.* v. *Oneby* (1727) 2 Ld. Raym. 1485.

[5] 1902. [6] [1957] 2 All E.R. 412.

[7] *R.* v. *Welch* (1875) 1 Q.B.D. 23. But a specific intent may be a requirement expressed by a particular statute; see *R.* v. *Steane* [1947] K.B. 997, *ante*, ¶ 46.

[8] Sect. 58 of the Malicious Damage Act, 1861.

[9] (1874) 2 C.C.R. 119 (*T.A.C.*); see *R.* v. *Lockhead* [1955] Crim. L.R. 573.

intend to break the window, but nevertheless convicted him. In quashing the conviction the Court for Crown Cases Reserved said: 'The jury might perhaps have found on this evidence that...he was reckless whether he did it or not; but the jury have not so found.'[1] But so long as the particular *kind* of harm intended or risked was in fact done, it makes no difference that it fell upon a different object or person than that on which it was expected to fall.[2] An Irish case, which was decided upon the footing that the prisoner did not foresee that what he was doing might result in the kind of harm which he in fact brought about, was *R.* v. *Faulkner.*[3] The man was a sailor who, while concentrating on a theft of rum from a cask in the hold of his ship, held in his hand a lighted match, which ignited the rum and so caused the destruction of the ship. The Court for Crown Cases Reserved in Ireland quashed his conviction, following *R.* v. *Pembliton.*

It was generally believed that the clearly expressed judgment by the Court of Criminal Appeal in *R.* v. *Cunningham* had finally settled the meaning of 'malice' in these statutory provisions. But in 1960 the House of Lords took the opportunity, as it would seem, to discredit this judgment without alluding directly to it and without argument, in the course of their much criticized pronouncements in *D.P.P.* v. *Smith.*[4] In what appears to have been their desire to eliminate any subjective mental element from criminal liability they declared that the appeal of the Director of Public Prosecutions involved an important question, 'raising, as it does, the question what is the proper direction to be given to a jury in regard to the necessary intent which has to be proved in cases of murder, and also in cases under s. 18 of the Offences against the Person Act, 1861.'

That this declaration,[5] without more, should have the effect of overruling a case which was not under appeal before their lordships, and was not argued, would have been regarded as beyond belief, were it not for the summary fashion in which their lordships' judgment brushed aside the arguments and disregarded authorities not according with their views, in the case of *Smith* itself, with which they were immediately concerned. It remained therefore to be seen whether this further havoc of legal principles would be held to follow.[6]

(*a*) Felonies

¶ 159. (i) It is a felony, punishable with imprisonment for life, unlawfully and maliciously to wound or cause any grievous bodily harm to anyone—or shoot (or even attempt to shoot) at him—*with intent* to

[1] *Per* Blackburn, J.

[2] E.g. *R.* v. *Latimer* (1886) 17 Q.B.D. 359 (*T.A.C.*); *post,* ¶ 159.

[3] (1877) 13 Cox 550 (*T.A.C.*).

[4] [1960] 3 All E.R. 161; 3 W.L.R. 546; [1961] A.C. 290.

[5] Startling, in that, on the face of it, it disregards the words of the section, 'with intent to maim...or to do some other grievous bodily harm...'.

[6] See ¶ 159, *post.*

maim, disfigure, disable, or do any other grievous bodily harm, or prevent an arrest.[1]

Some of the phrases here used are so technical as to need explanation. Thus, to constitute a 'wound' the continuity of the skin must be broken, i.e. that of both[2] skins, *cutis vera* as well as epidermis.[3] Hence a scratch in the latter is not a wound; nor will it even suffice that bones have been fractured if the skin is not broken also. Harm may be 'caused' without personal contact; so, if *A* suffers 'a cut eye and some bleeding' by jumping out of a window to avoid *B*'s threatened attack, *B* is indictable for 'causing' this injury.[4]

Bodily harm becomes 'grievous' whenever it seriously interferes with health or even with comfort. It is not necessary that its effects should be dangerous, nor that they should be permanent.[5] The rather vague question whether, in any particular case, the harm done was serious enough to be classed as grievous is for the jury to determine. The obscurity surrounding this phrase 'grievous bodily harm' has been intensified rather than relieved by the judgment of the House of Lords in *D.P.P.* v. *Smith*.[6] Their lordships cited without disapproval a dictum of the trial judge, Donovan, J., wherein he equated 'grievous bodily harm' with 'some harm which would seriously interfere at least for a time with health or comfort', a dictum which they stated was based on 'the well-known direction of Willes J., in *R.* v. *Ashman* (1858) 1 F. and F. 88'. Yet the Lord Chancellor said: 'I can find no warrant for giving the words "grievous bodily harm" a meaning other than that which the words convey in their ordinary and natural meaning ... grievous means no more and no less than "really serious",'[7] later adding 'it is unnecessary, and I would add inadvisable to add anything to the expression "grievous bodily harm" in its ordinary and natural meaning'.

[1] 24 and 25 Vict. c. 100, s. 18, as amended by the Criminal Justice Act, 1948, s. 1. To make or attempt to make use of a firearm or imitation firearm with intent to resist or prevent the lawful apprehension of the offender or any other person is a felony punishable with fourteen years' imprisonment. The penalty for any offence, lawful apprehension for which is resisted, may be imposed in addition. Possession of the forbidden implement at the time of the commission of certain specified offences renders the possessor liable to seven years' imprisonment in addition to the penalty for the offence in question, unless he shows that he had possession for a lawful object (Firearms Act, 1937, 1 Edw. VIII and 1 Geo. VI, c. 12, s. 23). And see the Prevention of Crime Act, 1953 (Russ. ch. 35), and the Restriction of Offensive Weapons Act, 1959; *Fisher* v. *Bell* [1960] 3 All E.R. 731.

[2] The 'three skins' of the older anatomists. Internal skin, e.g. in the mouth, suffices.

[3] So no injury can be a wound unless it bleeds. Thus a burn is not a 'wound', nor is a kick that causes internal haemorrhage but breaks no skin.

[4] *R.* v. *Parker* (1864) C.C.C. Sess. Pap. LIX, 392.

[5] Merely that 'the shoulder was very much bruised' was held insufficient (*R.* v. *Bolter* (1875) C.C.C. Sess. Pap. LXXXI, 440). 'Any bullet-wound, in any part of the body', even a finger, suffices (Avory, J.). Any injury sufficient to confine the party wounded to his bed for even a week, and though life be not endangered thereby, was stated to be enough in *R.* v. *M'Neill and Bleakley* (1839) 1 Craw. and Dix, Ir. Circ. Cases, 80 at p. 82.

[6] [1961] A.C. 290.

[7] The word 'really' did not occur in the *Ashman* direction.

Further on, however, the Lord Chancellor spoke of harm 'of a very serious nature coming well within the term grievous bodily harm', a statement which suggests that 'grievous' is *wider* than 'really serious'. But now in *R.* v. *Metharam*[1] the Court of Criminal Appeal have interpreted the judgment in *D.P.P.* v. *Smith* as ruling that it is a misdirection to invite a jury to find a man accused of wounding with intent to do grievous bodily harm guilty 'if the only intent established is one to interfere seriously with health or comfort'.[2] Their lordships did not, however, state what precise meaning is to be given to the expression 'grievous bodily harm' for the purposes of the statute. But that they were applying a *subjective* test of liability seems to be inherent throughout their judgment, and indeed to be expressed in their statement, 'The issue before the jury was the intent in the mind of the accused when he inflicted the wounds on her'.

To 'maim' is to do such a hurt to any part of a man's body that he is rendered less capable, in fighting, either of defending himself or of annoying his adversary.

The *statutory* 'attempt' to shoot at a person is not made until some decisive step is taken; as, for instance, that of drawing the trigger; cf. p. 97, n. 7 *ante*. Hence merely to point a pistol, even if loaded, at a man (though it may amount to an 'assault' on him[3]) will not suffice for the crime we are now considering. But to pull the trigger, even though the discharge fails through a defect in the cartridge (or barely to put your finger on the trigger with the intention of pulling it, even though you be interrupted before you actually pull it), does suffice to constitute the *actus reus* of an attempt to shoot, within the statute.[4]

In this crime the Crown must prove the intent. But the act itself *may* afford sufficient proof. Thus, to fire intentionally a loaded pistol at short range must be evidence of this 'intent of doing grievous bodily harm' (and it may well show an intent to murder). Students should note carefully that, since this section 18 *specifically requires intent* to be proved, it thereby necessarily cuts down the meaning of the word 'maliciously' (in its overall significance as laid down in *R. v. Cunningham, ante*), so as to exclude the mental element of 'recklessness'.

The wording of the statute does not make it necessary that the person whom it was intended to harm should be the one actually harmed.

[1] [1961] 3 All E.R. 200.

[2] Thus inferentially discrediting *R.* v. *Ashman*.

[3] *Post*, ¶ 164.

[4] The courts were much exercised as to the meaning to be given to the word 'loaded' in this and the earlier statutes, and the student must read the reported cases with great care on this point. See Russ. 685 for a discussion of *R.* v. *St George* (1840) 9 C. and P. 483; *R.* v. *Lewis* (1840) 9 C. and P. 523; *R.* v. *James* (1844) 1 C. and K. 530; *R.* v. *Brown* (1883) 10 Q.B.D. 381; *R.* v. *Duckworth* [1892] 2 Q.B. 83; *R.* v. *Jones* (1877) 36 L.J. (Newsp.) 650; *R.* v. *Jackson* (1890) 17 Cox 104; *R.* v. *Linneker* [1906] 2 K.B. 99 (*T.A.C.*); failure to realize that these cases throughout were concerned with the interpretation of the statutory wording may lead to erroneous conclusions as to the legal principles involved.

Thus where a soldier aimed a blow at another man with his belt but the belt glanced off and the heavy buckle at the end of it (with which it was the soldier's intention to strike the man) cut open the face of a woman who was standing near, he was held guilty of maliciously wounding her.[1]

(ii) It is a felony, punishable with imprisonment for life, to administer or attempt to administer chloroform, laudanum, or other stupefying or overpowering matter in order to procure the commission of an indictable crime.[2]

(iii) It is a felony, punishable with imprisonment for ten years, unlawfully and maliciously to administer any poison or other noxious thing to anyone so as thereby to endanger his life or inflict upon him grievous bodily harm.[3]

(*b*) Misdemeanours

(i) Unlawfully and maliciously wounding

¶ 160. Unlawfully and maliciously wounding, or inflicting any grievous bodily harm upon, any person is the first of three statutory misdemeanours punishable with five years' imprisonment.[4]

This misdemeanour under section 20 must be studied in conjunction with the felony under section 18, discussed above. It will be observed that, since grievous bodily harm done *intentionally* is the essence of the felony in section 18 (so that recklessness is not enough), therefore the word 'maliciously' in section 20 must be *restricted* to recklessness, for otherwise there would be a mutual contradiction between the two sections.

¶ 161. *Malice and intention.* Once more students must be warned that in reading old cases they must bear in mind the history of the principles[5] involved, and seek to discover what were the prevailing legal conceptions at the date when each case was decided. They should remember also that many changes in our law have been effected gradually, often producing the confusing situation in which a judgment was phrased so as to pay deference to the older principle while giving recognition to the newer which, as we can see now, was destined to replace it.[6] Contrast, for example, *R.* v. *Smith and York* (1902) 37 L.J. (Newsp.) 89 with *R.* v. *Baverstock* [1954] Crim. L.R. 625.

[1] *R.* v. *Latimer* (1886) 17 Q.B.D. 359 (*T.A.C.*); *ante* ¶ 158*a*.

[2] Sect. 22.

[3] *Ibid.* s. 23. See also s. 21 (attempting to choke etc. in order to commit any indictable offence); ss. 28 and 29 (causing bodily injury by explosives); s. 17 (impeding escape from wreck).

[4] Sect. 20, s. 24 (*post*, ¶ 163), and s. 47 (*post*, ¶ 162), as amended by the Penal Servitude Act, 1891, and by the Criminal Justice Act, 1948.

[5] See Russell, 11th ed., appendix 3, 'Malice in statutory offences'.

[6] See the cases of *Farrington* (1811) R. and R. 207; *Philp* (1830) 1 Moo. 263; *Newill* (1836) 1 Moo. 458; *Davies* (1858) 1 F. and F. 69; *Ward* (1872) 1 C.C.R. 356; *Matthews* (1877) 14 Cox 5; *Martin* (1881) 8 Q.B.D. 54.

(ii) Occasioning actual bodily harm by an assault[1]

¶ 162. The reason of the framers of the Act of 1861 for separating this offence from that described above (in ¶ 160) is not obvious, especially as they both entail the same punishment. Indeed, 'occasioning actual bodily harm by an assault' would seem a description wide enough to include all the acts covered by (i); unless 'inflict' be taken to have been used by the legislature as a wider word than 'assault', and as capable of including the production of harm by some indirect and protracted chain of causation, e.g. by poisoning (see ¶ 163), or infecting with disease. Arguments of great force have been used in favour of this wide construction.[2] And we may add to them that in *R.* v. *Halliday* (1889),[3] the Court for Crown Cases Reserved held that grievous bodily harm had been 'inflicted', where the defendant had frightened a woman so that she jumped from a window and was hurt; and this frightening, though an 'assault' in the old technical meaning of that word, was no assault in the modern sense of a 'battery'. In *R.* v. *Coleman* (1920),[4] in similar circumstances a husband was convicted of an assault occasioning actual bodily harm. But in *R.* v. *Clarence* (1888),[5] when the majority of the court held that the communication of venereal disease by a husband (even though he knew of it) to his wife (even though she did not know of it) was no assault, inasmuch as there was consent to the contact, they decided that it consequently was not an '*inflicting* of grievous bodily harm', on the ground that they considered that an 'inflicting' must be by assault and battery[6] and requires a direct and immediate causing of the harm.

(iii) Unlawfully and maliciously administering poison

¶ 163. Unlawfully and maliciously administering to anyone any poison or other noxious thing with intent to injure, aggrieve, or annoy him.[7]

If the thing administered be a recognized 'poison', it seems probable that the offence would be committed by giving even a quantity so small as to be incapable of doing harm.[8] But if it be not a poison, and be 'noxious' only when taken in large quantities (as, for example, castor-oil or ardent spirits), the offence will not be committed by giving a person only a small dose of it.

(iv) Occasioning bodily harm by furious driving

¶ 163*a*. A misdemeanour less severely punishable (viz. only by two years' imprisonment) is committed when any person having the charge of any carriage or vehicle (for instance, a bicycle) causes bodily harm

[1] Sect. 47.

[2] See *per* Hawkins, J., in *R.* v. *Clarence* (1888) 22 Q.B.D. at p. 49.

[3] 61 L.T. 701. Cf. *R.* v. *Beech* (1912) 7 Cr.App.R. 197; and *R.* v. *Martin* (1881) 8 Q.B.D. 54.

[4] 84 J.P. 112.

[5] 22 Q.B.D. 23. Cf. *Hegarty* v. *Shine* (1878) 14 Cox 145.

[6] Wills, J., at p. 37; Stephen, J., at p. 41; Pollock, B., at p. 62.

[7] Sect. 24.

[8] See *per* Field, J., and Stephen, J., in *R.* v. *Cramp* (1880) 5 Q.B.D. 307, a case arising upon similar words in a different statute.

to any one by wanton or furious driving, or racing, or other wilful misconduct, or by wilful *neglect.*[1]

¶ 163 *b*. In general it appears that, upon an indictment which charges an aggravated assault (such as using *excessive* force in resisting an arrest which, owing to a technicality, was not a lawful apprehension), it is open to the jury to convict of the lesser offence of common assault and battery; *R.* v. *Wilson* [1955] 1 W.L.R. 493.

B. *OFFENCES WHERE ACTUAL BODILY HARM IS NOT ESSENTIAL*

(*a*) Assault and battery

¶ 164. An assault is a crime at common law. Although, as mentioned above, the word 'assault' is quite commonly and conveniently used to include actual physical force used against the person of another man yet that is, strictly speaking, too wide; for the actual application of force to the person is properly termed a 'battery'. Assault in the narrow sense goes no further than a *threat* to inflict unlawful force (however slight or great) upon another man.[2] The *actus reus* of the crime at common law is constituted when the threatener has made some movement which has caused the other person *to believe that this unlawful physical contact is imminent.* In other words the *actus reus* consists of the *effect on the victim's mind* which the threat creates.[3]

The *mens rea* is constituted by the threatener's intention to produce that expectation in the victim's mind. It is thus irrelevant that the threatener had no intention or even no ability to inflict the contact which he had induced the victim to expect.

The contact may be, but need not be, hurtful; for a movement made to kiss or caress another would be the *actus reus* of assault if such contacts would, in the circumstances (e.g. if the other person does not consent), be unlawful.

A battery consists in the actual application of unlawful force, and it can be committed on a person who does not expect it; for example

[1] Sect. 35. But to cause injury by reckless cycling is not an assault and battery *at common law*; *Ackroyd* v. *Barett* (1895) 11 T.L.R. 115. Students must be careful to note that 'neglect' is not 'negligence'; see *ante*, ¶ 25. '"Wilfully" means deliberately, not by inadvertence'; Lord Russell, C.J., *R.* v. *Senior* (1899) 47 W.R. 367 at p. 369.

[2] 'The offence of assault is often confused with the offence of battery. An assault can be committed without touching the person.' *R.* v. *Rolfe* (1952) 36 Cr.App.R. 4, *per* Lord Goddard, C.J., at p. 6. See also *Beal* v. *Kelley* [1951] 2 All E.R. 763; *Fairclough* v. *Whipp* [1952] 1 All E.R. 834; *D.P.P.* v. *Rogers* [1953] 1 W.L.R. 1017.

[3] *Smith* v. *Newsam* (1673) 3 Keble 283. See *Mod. Appr. Crim. Law*, 346 *et seq.* Cf. Comyns, *Digest* (5th ed. 1822), II, 275. 'In the case of an assault the *damage* consists in the inconvenience produced by the fear which the act impresses upon the plaintiff's mind.' See especially the remarks of Baron Parke in *R.* v. *St George* (1840) 9 C. and P. 483 at pp. 490, 493; Baron Parke was there speaking of assault *at common law*; the actual charge against St George was different, for he was indicted for the *statutory* felony under 7 Will. IV and 1 Vict. c. 85 (repealed by 24 and 25 Vict. c. 95, s. 1) which by s. 11 created a special statutory assault.

because his back is turned, or he is asleep.[1] Not so an assault, since the gist of assault is the *expectation* of the contact. Mostly, of course, both offences are committed in rapid succession, the expected blow following immediately upon the threat to inflict it; the whole affair is then in proper legal phraseology termed 'an assault and battery'. Save in special circumstances a victim of assault alone is rarely disposed to initiate a prosecution since he has suffered no actual hurt. Accordingly in the current speech even of lawyers the word 'assault' is habitually used as if it included 'battery'. Even in a battery no actual harm need be done. The slightest force will suffice, if it be exercised intentionally; thus merely spitting on a person may amount to an indictable battery. The force applied need not involve immediate contact with the body of the victim. Thus it is sufficient if the contact is made with his clothes without touching the skin.[2] It has been held that a battery can be effected even indirectly,[3] as by striking a horse and thereby making it throw its rider,[4] or by breaking the ice just in front of a skater.[5]

To deprive another person of his liberty will usually involve touching or threatening to touch him; and thus the crime of false imprisonment[6] usually involves an obvious assault, if not also a battery.[7] Some bodily *movement*, however, is essential to an assault or battery;[8] so that supposing you only offer motionless obstruction, acting as if you were 'a door or a wall'[9]—as where a cyclist is brought down by collision with a person who only stands still, however wilfully, in front of him—no proceedings can be taken for assault. Similarly, words alone, however threatening, can never make an assault.[10] Yet they may *un*make an assault; as in a case where a man laid his hand menacingly on his sword, but at the same time said, '*If it were not assize time*, I would not take such language from you'.[11]

[1] Or is a newly born baby; see *R.* v. *Renshaw* (1847) 2 Cox 285; *R.* v. *March* (1844) 1 C. and K. 496.

[2] *R.* v. *Day* (1845) 1 Cox 207. Similarly a threat so to attack the clothes will constitute an assault.

[3] *Hopper* v. *Reeve* (1817) 7 Taunt. 698; *Scott* v. *Shepherd* (1773) 2 W.Bl. 892; *Short* v. *Lovejoy* (1752) Bull (N.P.) 16.

[4] *Dodwell* v. *Burford* (1670) 1 Mod. 24.

[5] In *R.* v. *Jolly* (S.A. Law Reports, 1923, 176) the Supreme Court of South Africa held that a 'battery' had been committed when J. so tampered with a railway line as to secure the derailment of the next train, several hours later, and a consequent hurt to the engine-driver.

[6] *Post*, ¶ 169.

[7] But this is not essential, e.g. where an accoucheur was locked into the patient's room, lest he should depart before her child was born; *R.* v. *Linsberg* (1905) 69 J.P. 107, *post*, ¶ 169.

[8] The movement need not be made in the direction of the victim; an upraised fist, for instance, or a movement away from him towards the release of some object which might fall upon him, might be sufficient to create in his mind the necessary expectation.

[9] *Innes* v. *Wylie* (1844) 1 C. and K. at p. 263.

[10] Thus the alarming utterance which caused 'weeks of physical suffering' in *Wilkinson* v. *Downton* [1897] 2 Q.B. 57, was no assault.

[11] *Tuberville* v. *Savage* (1669) 1 Mod. 3; *Dause* v. *Luce* (1665) 1 Keble 921.

¶ 165. *Expectation essential.* As stated above expectation[1] is essential to an assault. Hence to threaten to strike another who is obviously so far off or so placed that the menace cannot be put into effect can hardly be proved to be an assault since the other person will find it almost impossible to establish (*a*) that he thought the blow was about to fall upon him, and (*b*) that the threatener intended (*mens rea*) that he should so anticipate it (*actus reus*). Failure to appreciate the true nature of the *actus reus* of assault has led to the erroneous[2] view that there must in all cases be the means of carrying the threat into effect.[3] This is not necessary: therefore it is an assault to point a pistol at another in such a way as to make him believe that he is about to be shot[4] and with intent that he should so believe, whether or not the pistol be loaded, and whether or not the threatener knows it to be loaded or unloaded; the essential points are that the victim should expect to be shot, and that the threatener should intend to create that impression on his mind.

¶ 166. *Poisoning usually not a battery.* Poisoning, where the poison (as is usually the case) is taken by the sufferer's own hand, does not constitute a battery.[5] A contrary view was at one time taken here, and has been favoured in America.[6] But it is essential to a battery that there should be a personal exertion of force by the assailant. If therefore the actual taking up of the glass was the act of the person poisoned, there is no battery,[7] even though he took it in consequence of the poisoner's false representation that it was harmless.

¶ 167. *Penalty for common assault or battery.* The penalty for common assault or battery is, by virtue of the Offences against the Person Act, 1861,[8] imprisonment for not more than two months or a fine (with costs, if ordered) not exceeding £5 where the proceedings are by

[1] The expectation is often one of alarm or fear but this is not essential.

[2] See *Mod. Appr. Crim. Law*, 351 *et seq.*

[3] Apparently based upon a remark of Tindal, C.J., in the civil action of *Stephens* v. *Myers* (1830) 4 C. and P. 349, in which the plaintiff succeeded although it was plain on the facts that the defendant could not have committed the threatened battery; the error was increased by a misunderstanding of *R.* v. *James* (1844) 1 C. and K. 530 which, like *R.* v. *St George* (*ante*, p. 208 n. 3), was a prosecution not for assault at common law, but for an offence under 1 Vict. c. 85 (now repealed) which expressly required that the firearm with which the assault was committed should be *loaded*. In *R.* v. *James* there were five counts all alleging felonies. There was no count for common assault (nor could there have been since the indictment was framed for felony and not for misdemeanour). Hence the *only* assault of which the judge was speaking was necessarily the assault under sect. 11 (of 1 Vict. c. 85). And see *R.* v. *Baker* (1843) 1 Cox 45. See *Mod. Appr. Crim. Law*, pp. 351–5.

[4] See *Kwaku Mensah* v. *R.* [1946] A.C. 83, at p. 91.

[5] See *R.* v. *Clarence* (1888) 22 Q.B.D. at p. 42 (*T.A.C.*).

[6] *Commonwealth* v. *Stratton* (1873) 114 Mass. 303.

[7] But there will be a statutory offence (see ¶ 163, *ante*) of 'administering poison'.

[8] Sect. 42.

complaint heard in the magistrates' court of summary jurisdiction.[1] Alternatively, the proceedings may be by way of indictment,[2] and if so, the accused may be imprisoned for not more than one year[3] (or fined[4]).

(*b*) Statutory assaults

¶ 168. Many assaults and batteries of an aggravated character have been dealt with by statute; the following are misdemeanours, punishable with imprisonment for two years:

(*a*) Under the Offences against the Person Act, 1861, s. 38
Assault with intent to commit a felony;
Assault upon a constable in the execution of his duty, or upon any person acting in aid of such constable;
Assault with intent to prevent the lawful apprehension either of the assailant himself or of any other person;[5]

(*b*) Under other statutes
Obstructing a police officer in the execution of his duty;[6]
Indecent assault upon a female.[7]

The person assaulted has usually also the option of prosecuting the offender summarily before a magistrates' court. For though an assault must be dealt with by indictment if it either (i) involves the title to lands,[8] or (ii) is accompanied by an attempt to commit a felony, yet in ordinary cases of assault, the offender may be summarily convicted, without a jury, before two justices of the peace.[9] Still the maximum penalties that such a court can inflict are only:

(1) Nine months' imprisonment; for assaulting a constable in the execution of his duty, after having been recently convicted of a similar assault.[10]

[1] Sect. 47.

[2] Under s. 45 a person summarily convicted under any of ss. 42, 43 or 44 may, after satisfaction of his sentence, obtain a certificate to that effect which will bar any further proceedings whether criminal or civil, brought against him 'for the same cause'. For a discussion of this section see [1958] *Crim. L.R.* 33.

[3] And if he had a real or imitation firearm in his possession an additional seven years under the Firearms Act, 1937, s. 23 (2), unless he can prove that he had the weapon for a lawful object. And see the Prevention of Crime Act, 1953.

[4] See *post*, ¶ 766, for extension of the power to fine an offender convicted on indictment.

[5] In the first two cases there is an additional penalty of seven years' imprisonment if a real or imitation firearm is found in the offender's possession unless he can prove he had it for a lawful object; in the third case there is an additional penalty of fourteen years if he used or attempted to use such a weapon; Firearms Act, 1937, s. 23 (4) and (2).

[6] Prevention of Crimes Amendment Act, 1885; *Betts* v. *Stevens* [1910] 1 K.B. 1; *Hinchcliffe* v. *Sheldon* [1955] 1 W.L.R. 1207. 'Police officer' includes proctors' constables in the Universities of Oxford and Cambridge, appointed under 6 Geo. IV, c. 97.

[7] Under the Sexual Offences Act, 1956, s. 14. *Ante*, ¶ 146. But an indecent assault on a male, although it is only a misdemeanour, can be punished by ten years' imprisonment (Sexual Offences Act, 1956, s. 37, sch. II).

[8] Offences against the Person Act, 1861, s. 46. See ¶¶ 188, 684, *post*.

[9] *Ibid.* s. 42.

[10] 34 and 35 Vict. c. 112, s. 12.

(2) Six months' imprisonment, or a fine

i. of £20 for assaulting a constable in the execution of his duty,[1]

ii. of £50[2] for assaulting a boy under fourteen, or any female, if the assault is of an aggravated nature.[3]

(3) Two months' imprisonment, or a fine of £5, for a common assault. The justices in this instance can summarily convict only when the complaint has been made by (or, as in the case of children assaulted, on behalf of) the party aggrieved and not merely by the police.[4] For a resort to this summary procedure takes away the aggrieved party's right of civil action.[5]

By the Summary Jurisdiction (Married Women) Act, 1895, any court which convicts a husband (either summarily or not) of an aggravated assault on his wife may, if satisfied that her future safety is in peril, make an order that she shall no longer be bound to cohabit with him, and may also make an order for her maintenance. The first-mentioned order will have the effect[6] of a judicial separation.[7] The word 'aggravated', in this enactment, is not limited to the various statutory aggravations of assaults.

(c) False imprisonment

¶ 169. False imprisonment is a specific crime at common law[8] although its frequent association with assault and battery has tended to obscure this fact, so that some writers have mistakenly treated it as a special instance of assault. It has, however, been an indictable misdemeanour from the earliest times.[9] The confusion of false imprisonment with assault has produced statements which have the effect of treating false imprisonment as amounting to 'constructive assault' when in fact no

[1] *Ibid.* Even though not knowing him to be a constable; 73 J.P. 176.

[2] Under the Criminal Justice Act, 1925, s. 39. By this Act the offender, in (2) ii and in (3), may be also bound over.

[3] Aggravated by its violence; Offences against the Person Act, 1861, s. 43. An *indecent* assault upon a male person is punishable with a maximum of ten years' imprisonment (Sexual Offences Act, 1956, s. 37, sch. II).

[4] But in proceedings under s. 43 for 'aggravated' assaults on females or boys, the right of prosecution is not thus limited. The legislature had wife-beaters in view, and realized that injured wives are often unwilling to prosecute.

In Cambridge the proctors and their men enjoy exemption from all summary jurisdiction of justices, in respect of assaults committed by them 'in the exercise of the authority of the Proctor', though the person assaulted may still proceed by indictment or by civil action; Cambridge Award Act, 1856, 19 Vict. c. 17, s. 7. This enactment arose from fines having been imposed upon a proctor and two of his men by the borough justices on 3 December 1850.

[5] *Ante*, ¶ 167. Railway companies in 1932 agreed not to prosecute for assaults committed upon their employees until the employee assaulted had had an opportunity to sue for damages.

[6] *R.* v. *Clarke* [1950] 1 All E.R. 546.

[7] But not of a divorce; neither party can marry anyone else.

[8] See *Mod. Appr. Crim. Law*, 349, 350.

[9] 2 Co. *Inst.* 55 refers it to Magna Carta. And see Comyns, *Digest* (5th ed.), 480. Blackstone does not identify it with assault.

assault or battery has taken place (as in *R.* v. *Linsberg*,[1] where an accoucheur was locked in a room with his patient so that he could not leave her, although he was neither threatened with any force nor touched); or statements that 'every false imprisonment includes an assault'.[2] Of course in very many cases of arrest and imprisonment the arresting officer has plainly intimated that he is about to take the prisoner by force, and this is sufficient to constitute assault by the ordinary principles even if the man goes quietly without in fact being touched.

[1] (1905) 69 J.P. 107. And see *Arrowsmith* v. *Le Mesurier* (1806) 2 Bos. and Pul. (N.R.), 221, where Mansfield, C.J., ruled there could be an arrest without any physical touch.

[2] As in *Pocock* v. *Moore* (1825) Ry. and M. 321, a case in which *Arrowsmith* v. *Le Mesurier* was not cited.

Chapter IX

BIGAMY[1]

SECTION I. DEFINITION

¶ 170. It seems appropriate to discuss bigamy in close association with the offences contained in the preceding chapter, for although bigamy was originally an ecclesiastical offence based upon the broad ground of its 'involving an outrage upon public decency by the profanation of a solemn ceremony'[2] and was first made a felony by an Act of 1603[3] which seems to have similarly regarded it, yet at the present day the substantial justification for retaining it as a serious crime is that in many cases it may cause great suffering to an innocent party to the bigamous marriage.[4] It is now governed by the Offences against the Person Act, 1861, s. 57. The word 'bigamy' properly means being married *twice*[5] but in the crime as now existing,[6] it is employed as synonymous with polygamy, or having a plurality of wives at one time.

The offence is committed when a person

(*a*) being married

(*b*) goes through a legally recognized ceremony of marriage with another person

(*c*) whilst the original wife or husband is still living;

(*d*) unless

(i) the second marriage is contracted elsewhere than in England and Ireland by any other than a subject of the Crown; or

(ii) the first marriage has been legally dissolved by divorce; or

(iii) the first marriage has been declared void by a competent court; or

(iv) the original husband or wife has been continually absent, for the space of seven years then last past, from the person marrying a second time and shall not have been known by such person to be living within that time.

[1] The law of bigamy is intricate and difficult; only an outline of its main features is given in this chapter.

[2] Professor Kenny's words in former editions of this book. Blackstone (*Comm.* IV, 163) said the reason for making it a felony was because it was 'so great a violation of the public oeconomy and decency of a well-ordered state'.

[3] 1 Jac. I, c. 11. The preamble speaks of the crime as being 'to the great Dishonour of God and the utter undoing of divers honest Men's Children, and others'.

[4] See 61 *L.Q.R.* 76–8, where the principles for its treatment as a crime are discussed by Professor Glanville Williams.

[5] It was so regarded by the canonists, who included the case of a man once marrying a widow.

[6] Offences against the Person Act, 1861, s. 57.

(*a*) The first marriage[1]

¶ 171. To sustain an indictment for bigamy the first marriage[2] must have been valid according to the law of the domicile of the parties, so far as concerns their personal capacity to marry;[3] and according to the law of the place of celebration, so far as concerns the ceremonial form.

The first marriage must be *proved* to the satisfaction of the jury; a presumption is not enough.[4]

Amongst possible causes of voidness may be mentioned the fact of either party's being an idiot at the time of marriage, or the fact of the parties' being within the prohibited degrees of relationship (as upon a man's marriage with his niece).[5] So too, if the prisoner's first alleged spouse had been actually the wife or husband of someone else at the time of that alleged marriage, that marriage would necessarily be void. Consequently for him or her to proceed to marry some other person, though apparently a bigamy, will be really no crime.[6] Similarly if *X* marries first *A*, and secondly *B*, and then thirdly, after *A*'s death, marries *C*, this marriage between *X* and *C* will not be indictable as a bigamy, inasmuch as the marriage with *B* was null,[7] although bigamous.

But besides those invalid marriages which are actually void (in which case they may be treated as null by any court where evidence is given of the circumstances that invalidate them), there are others which are only voidable, i.e. the cause of their invalidity is merely one for which a court of matrimonial jurisdiction may set aside the marriage, if called upon to do so, whilst both the parties are still alive. But, until thus set aside, such a marriage must be treated by all courts as valid. Hence even a voidable marriage,[8] as where either party to the marriage is sexually impotent, has always been regarded as sufficient to fix the wife's nationality and domicile, and to render any second marriage bigamous.

[1] As to the proof of this, see ¶ 177 *post*.

[2] *R.* v. *Moscovitch* (1924) 44 T.L.R. 4. A marriage under polygamous law will suffice; *Srini Vasan* v. *Srini Vasan* [1945] 2 All E.R. 21; *Baindail* v. *Baindail* [1945] 2 All E.R. 374, cases which, it would seem, dispose of the doubts expressed by Avory, J., in *R.* v. *Naguib* [1917] 1 K.B. 359. See also *Sowa* v. *Sowa* [1960] 3 W.L.R. 733.

[3] Dicey's *Conflict of Laws*, 5th ed., 734. But see *ibid.* 921 *et seq.* as to the growing tendency to test 'capacity' by the same rule as 'form'.

[4] *R.* v. *Morrison* [1938] 3 All E.R. 787; *R.* v. *Willshire* (1881) 6 Q.B.D. 366 (*T.A.C.*). But the presumption may be decisive in *civil* proceedings; see *In re Taylor* [1961] 1 W.L.R. 9.

[5] And see the Marriage Act, 1949, s. 2 (*ante*, ¶ 145), which declares void a marriage between persons either of whom is under the age of sixteen.

[6] Lord Euston in 1871 married *A*. Afterwards, on finding that *B*, whom *A* had married in 1863, was still alive, he sued for nullity of marriage. But her successful defence was that in 1863 *B* was already married to *C*, who lived till 1867.

[7] A petitioner has a right *ex debito justitiae* to a decree of nullity where the respondent's husband, or wife, was alive at the time of the second marriage, and the court has no discretion to withhold relief; Latey on Divorce, 13th ed. (1945), 173.

[8] See *post*, ¶ 630: *R.* v. *Algar* [1954] 1 Q.B. 279.

(*b*) Legally recognized ceremony

¶ 172. Bigamy, like homicide, forms one of the rare exceptions to the principle that criminal jurisdiction is purely territorial, For, if the person accused be a British subject, it is immaterial in what territory (even though it be outside the British dominions altogether)[1] the second marriage took place; and he may be tried in any part of the United Kingdom where he may be in custody. But a person who is not a subject of Her Majesty cannot thus be tried here for a bigamy committed outside the United Kingdom.

The second marriage (the alleged crime) must have been in a form recognized by the law of the place where it was celebrated.[2] But any form, legally recognized there, is sufficient. It is enough that it would have been good on some occasions; notwithstanding its being one which could not have been effectual on that particular occasion, even had the guilty person not been already married. Thus it is no defence for a man, accused of bigamy, to show that he is a Christian, and that the form of marriage which he went through at his second wedding was one that is valid for Jews alone. Nor is it any defence to show that the parties were too near akin to be able to contract a valid marriage.

(*c*) Original spouse still living

¶ 173. The prosecution must establish the fact that the prisoner's original husband or wife was still living at the time of the second marriage. Still it is not necessary that this should be shown by the direct evidence of someone who can speak to having seen that person alive at that date. It may be sufficiently established by probable inference from circumstances; e.g. from the fact that the prisoner's first wife was alive and well a few days before his second marriage. But the fact of her having been alive merely within the often cited period of 'seven years' before that marriage, will frequently be utterly insufficient to justify an inference that she was still alive when it was solemnized. For the effect of showing that she was alive at some time within these seven years is merely to neutralize the presumption[3] of her death, not to reverse it and so throw back the burden of proof upon the prisoner. It simply releases the jury from any technical presumption, and sets them free to look to the circumstances of the particular case.[4] From the woman's age and health, the climate of the country in which she resided, the period which has elapsed since she was heard of, and

[1] *Earl Russell's Case* [1901] A.C. 446. Cf. ¶ 130 *ante*.

[2] *R.* v. *Allen* (1872) 1 C.C.R. 367 (*T.A.C.*). In India, where the first marriage was under monogamous law, a second marriage even under a polygamous law was held to be a criminal bigamy; *The Emperor* v. *Lazar* (1907) 30 Madras 551. Contrast the presumption of cohabitation where bigamy is not in question, *In re Taylor* [1961] 1 W.L.R. 9, *post*, ¶ 495.

[3] *Post*, ¶ 494.

[4] I.e. the *law* makes no presumption either way; *R.* v. *Lumley* (1869) L.R. 1 C.C.R. 196.

similar circumstances, they must draw an inference as to whether she did or did not survive until the time when her husband married again. Any[1] presumption of continuance of life that there may be is a presumption of fact, not of law; and where no statute lays down another rule, the issue whether a person is to be presumed dead is also a presumption of fact; with the following exception, that where due inquiries have been made and a person has not been traced as the result of them there is a presumption of law that, if he has not been heard of during seven years by those who would have been likely to hear of him if he had been alive, he has died within the seven years.

(*d*) Not divorced

¶ 174. It will be a good defence to a charge of bigamy, if the prisoner proves that the first marriage had been validly dissolved[2] (or judicially declared to have always been void), before the celebration of the second marriage. In *R.* v. *Wheat and Stocks*[3] it appeared that the prisoner Wheat was a man of little education to whom, as a poor person, solicitors had been assigned to conduct proceedings for divorce against his wife. A delay occurred and a year later the solicitors wrote that they would lose no time over his petition, and some three months later, in response to a telegram from him they replied that they hoped 'to send you papers for your signature in the course of a day or two'. Believing that he was then divorced, three weeks later Wheat married the other prisoner Stocks, and both were subsequently convicted of bigamy. In dismissing their appeal the Court of Criminal Appeal decided that the proviso must be strictly construed and that the words do not admit of any qualification, the only defence admitted by them being that the accused has in fact been divorced from the bond of the first marriage; if not, then at the time of the second marriage he is a person who, being married, intends to do the act[4] forbidden by the statute, namely to marry during the life of the former wife, and that there is no indication in the words of this particular proviso in the statute that any *presumption or belief* that he had been divorced can afford any defence.

The divorce must be a legal one; legal, that is, by the law of the country where the divorced parties were domiciled at the time.[5] If it

[1] *Chard* v. *Chard* [1955] 3 All E.R. 721 at pp. 726, 728. But the *accused*, in appropriate circumstances, can make use of this presumption to raise a reasonable doubt in his favour, as in *R.* v. *Willshire* (1881) 6 Q.B.D. 366.

[2] A decree *nisi* is *not* enough, a point too often overlooked.

[3] [1921] 2 K.B. 119 (*T.A.C.*). This case is discussed by G. W. Paton, 'Bigamy and *mens rea*', 17 *Can. Bar Review* (1939), 94.

[4] *Ante*, ¶ 18. And see *Current Legal Problems* (1949), '*Mens rea* and bigamy' by J. L. J. Edwards.

[5] *Le Mesurier* v. *Le Mesurier* [1895] A.C. 517. It may be convenient to note here that by the Administration of Justice Act, 1920, s. 15, questions of even a *foreign* law must now be decided by the judge himself, instead of being submitted, as formerly, to the jury, as questions of fact.

were not thus valid, the fact that, by an error of law, they honestly though mistakenly supposed it to be valid, will not prevent the second marriage of either of them from being criminal. But if valid under that country's law, a divorce will be effectual here as a defence to a charge of bigamy, even though the ground on which it was granted was one that would not have enabled the parties to obtain a divorce in this country, had they then been domiciled here.

(*e*) Not absent for seven years

¶ 175. It is provided by the statute[1] that it shall be a conclusive defence to show that the prisoner's original spouse (1) has been continuously absent from the prisoner (even though by his wilful desertion) during the seven years preceding the second marriage, and (2) had never been heard of by the prisoner meanwhile. It is not necessary that the prisoner should give express proof of both the elements requisite to this defence. For if his wife's continuous absence for seven years be proved, this will suffice to raise a *prima facie* presumption of her not having been heard of throughout that period.[2] But of course the prosecution may rebut this presumption, by showing that within the seven years the fact of her being alive had become known to the prisoner.

It has been held in effect by the Court of Criminal Appeal[3] that the proper interpretation of this proviso in s. 57 is that it affords a defence if the accused can show that he or she had a reasonable belief that the former wife or husband was dead at the time of the second marriage, and that the reference to seven years' absence means that such mere separation for seven years has the effect which reasonable belief of death caused by other evidence would have at any other time. If this view of the meaning of the proviso is to be accepted as authoritative and binding, there is no difficulty in regarding the decision in the well-known case of *R.* v. *Tolson*[4] as based solely upon the words of the statute.[5] In that case the prisoner, Mrs Tolson, had been deserted by her husband in 1881; she made inquiries and was told by his elder brother and others that he had been lost in a vessel bound for America which went down with all hands on board. Believing that she was a widow she went through a form of marriage with another man in 1887, telling him and everyone else the story of Tolson as she believed it to be. Tolson shortly afterwards returned from America. Her conviction for bigamy was quashed by the Court for Crown Cases Reserved.[6] Some of the judges in that case laid great emphasis upon the maxim *actus non facit reum nisi mens sit rea*[7] in language which, it was afterwards argued,

[1] Sect. 57; cf. 1 Jac. I, c. 11, s. 2.

[2] *R.* v. *Curgerwen* (1865) 1 C.C.R. 1 (*T.A.C.*).

[3] In *R.* v. *Wheat and Stocks* [1921] 2 K.B. 119, referring particularly to the judgment of Stephen, J., in *R.* v. *Tolson* (1889) 23 Q.B.D. 168, at p. 192.

[4] (1889) 23 Q.B.D. 168 (*T.A.C.*). [5] *Ante*, ¶¶ 31, 33.

[6] But of course her 'second marriage' was not thereby rendered a valid marriage.

[7] Especially Cave, J., at p. 181.

meant that the maxim applied in all statutory offences *unless they were excluded expressly or by necessary implication.* The Court of Criminal Appeal in *R.* v. *Wheat and Stocks* declared that such a principle would be too wide, and if it was intended to be laid down in *Tolson's Case* as of general application the court could not agree with it.[1] The case of *R.* v. *Wheat and Stocks*, in which this declaration of the meaning of the proviso was made, has been discussed in ¶ 174 *ante*.

¶ 175 *a*. *R.* v. *Treanor; R.* v. *Taylor.* In *R.* v. *Treanor*[2] it appeared that the prisoner had married B.L. in 1916 and had deserted her in 1918. In 1930 he went through a form of marriage with L.A. and he deserted her in 1937. In 1938 he went through a form of marriage with K.D. The prosecution produced no evidence that at any time after 1918 he knew that his first wife B.L. was alive. The prisoner relied on the proviso in s. 57 relating to seven years' absence, but was convicted on the ground that the proviso spoke expressly of *second* marriage, whereas the bigamous marriage with which he was charged was his third. His appeal to the Court of Criminal Appeal was dismissed, Lord Hewart, C.J., saying 'The proviso means precisely what it says, nothing more or less—any second marriage, and not second or subsequent marriage'. This was a harsh interpretation of the proviso and would produce strange results if applied to other passages in the statute where the words 'second marriage' occur.[3] It has accordingly been disapproved by the Court of Criminal Appeal in *R.* v. *Taylor*,[4] in which the words 'second marriage' were held to refer to the second marriage *charged in the indictment* and no other.

SECTION 2. MISTAKE AS TO FIRST MARRIAGE

¶ 176. It was formerly uncertain whether or not any excuse was afforded by a mistaken belief that the former marriage was to a married person and therefore void. This defence was rejected by Humphreys, J., in *R.* v. *Kircaldy*,[5] again (as in the case of *Wheat and Stocks*) in reliance upon the terms of the statute. But now it appears settled that a belief that the first marriage was void (and perhaps ignorance that the ceremony was a ceremony of marriage[6]) is a defence, since it was held in the unreported case of *R.* v. *Weiwow*[7] that where a prisoner believed on reasonable grounds that his first marriage was null and void because of a previous subsisting marriage it was a good defence to a charge of bigamy. This was followed in *R.* v. *Dolman* in 1949.[8]

[1] *Per* Avory, J., at p. 126. See *ante*, ¶ 31.

[2] [1939] 1 All E.R. 330.

[3] See 58 *Law Notes* (1939), 80.

[4] [1950] 2 K.B. 368; 2 All E.R. 170 (*T.A.C.*); see Glanville Williams, 'Bigamy and the third marriage', 13 *Mod. L.R.* 417.

[5] (1928) 167 *L.T. Jo.* 46 not following *R.* v. *Connatty* (1919) 83 J.P. 292, which had followed dicta in *R.* v. *Thomson* (1905) 70 J.P. 6.

[6] *Kelly* v. *Kelly* (1933) 148 L.T. 143.

[7] Notts. Summer Assizes 1945; Macnaghten, J. (Arch. 1352).

[8] Leeds Assizes; [1949] 1 All E.R. 813; Streatfeild, J.

SECTION 3. EVIDENCE, PUNISHMENT AND DEGREES OF GUILT

¶ 177. As regards the evidence[1] which will be available at the trial, it should be noted that, although the husbands or wives of accused persons were excluded by the common law from giving evidence at the trial of the accusation, Parliament has greatly relaxed this exclusion. The Criminal Evidence Act, 1898,[2] now admits the husband or wife to give evidence *for* a prisoner; and, if the accusation be one of bigamy, by the Criminal Justice Administration Act, 1914, the husband or wife may also be called even for the prosecution, and without the consent of the person accused.[3]

Bigamy is a felony, punishable with imprisonment for not more than seven years. It is, like manslaughter, a peculiarly 'elastic' crime:[4] the degrees of guilt varying—according to the degree of deceit practised and the sex of the person wronged—from an offence closely approximating in heinousness to a rape,[5] down to cases in which the parties' only guilt consists in their having misused a legal ceremonial for the purpose of giving a decent appearance to intercourse which they knew to be illicit. Indeed there may even be cases of an undoubtedly criminal bigamy where there is no moral guilt at all. For both parties may have been misled by some very natural misapprehension of law. The great dissimilarity between the matrimonial laws of civilized nations has made it but too easy for a man and woman to be husband and wife in one country and yet not so in another.

The other party to the bigamous marriage, if at the time aware of its criminal character, became guilty of aiding and abetting the crime; and accordingly may be indicted for bigamy as a principal in the second degree. On the other hand, when a woman, who reasonably believes her husband to be dead, marries a man who knows (but conceals) the fact of his being still alive, this man will escape all punishment; for the woman committed no crime, so he cannot be treated as an accessory.[6]

[1] See Norval Morris, 'Burden of proof in bigamy', 18 *Mod. L.R.* 452.

[2] *Post*, ¶ 621.

[3] Sect. 28; but is not himself or herself a compellable witness, see ¶ 631 *post*.

[4] During the one year 1920 the sentences inflicted for it by one very experienced judge ranged from four years' penal servitude down to a single day's imprisonment.

[5] Hence when the guilty party is the man, the judge, before passing sentence, sometimes inquires from the 'wife' whether sexual intercourse has taken place between them before the 'marriage'. If it has *not*, his offence is considered to be more heinous.

[6] *Draft Criminal Code for Jamaica*, p. 112.

Chapter X

CRIMINAL LIBEL

Section 1. Private Libel usually treated as a Tort

¶ **178.** A libel[1] is such a writing or picture as either defames an individual ('private' libel) or injures religion, government[2] or morals ('public' libel).

We have already seen[3] that most crimes are also torts. But the most conspicuous illustration of this is afforded by the defamatory, or private, libel. It is a crime which not only is a tort, but is constantly treated as such in actual practice. For it is only a misdemeanour, and accordingly not affected by the rule which delayed, and therefore usually frustrated, civil proceedings for crimes that were of the degree of felonies. And again, it is a crime which, unlike most others, is often committed by persons whose pecuniary means are large enough to enable them to pay whatever compensation a civil court may award. Hence libels are much more frequently followed up by civil than by criminal proceedings. And the judges have desired to see *indictments* for defamation restricted to those cases in which the libel is sufficiently aggravated, either by its intrinsic gravity or its public nature (e.g. libels on persons in a public position, or tending to defame persons of influence in foreign countries so as to interfere with pacific relations[4]) or where the offensive statements are repeated by numbers of persons of small means, so that a civil action would not afford their victim any adequate remedy or means of terminating the mischief. A prosecution should not be employed in a mere squabble between two individuals. It is not however, incumbent on the prosecution to prove that the libel would have been unusually likely to provoke the wrath of the person defamed.[5]

Section 2. Fundamental Principles Common to the Civil and Criminal Law

¶ **179.** It is sufficient for the purposes of the present volume to indicate briefly the fundamental principles which are common to both the civil and the criminal law of libel, and then explain the distinguishing

[1] The *Oxford English Dictionary* states that the original meaning, 'a little book' (*libellus*), had been narrowed to the present meaning of an unlawful book at least as early as 1631.

[2] E.g. *R.* v. *Horsley* (1909) C.C.C. Sess. Pap. CLI, 459.

[3] *Ante*, ¶ 2.

[4] *R.* v. *Peltier* (1803) 28 St.Tr. 589.

[5] *R.* v. *Wicks* (1936) 52 T.L.R. 253.

features of the latter aspect of this wrong.[1] The following principles are common to both its aspects:

(I) Anyone who publishes a defamatory document[2] concerning another person, so as to tend to bring him into hatred,[3] contempt, or ridicule,[4] or in any way to diminish the good opinion that other persons have of him, is guilty of 'publishing a defamatory libel'.[5] This 'document' may consist of either a written or a pictorial[6] composition; e.g. even of an effigy suspended from a mock gibbet.

(II) The publication need not be 'malicious' in the popular sense of that word (i.e. it need not be due to spite, or, as it is called, 'express malice'), nor even in the statutory one discussed in ¶ 161 *ante*. A printer's purely accidental omission of a 'not' will suffice. It is true that the Libel Act, 1843, when dealing with criminal libel, does in terms restrict the offence to 'malicious publication'. But the meaning seems to be that from the mere fact of publishing such matter, without any of the recognized legal grounds of excuse, the law draws a presumption that the publication was intentional. Hence it is now settled[7] that it is not even necessary for the prosecutor or plaintiff to make in his pleadings any formal allegation that the libel was published maliciously. The law of libel has thus, at last, worked itself free from entanglement with the old fictions of a 'constructive malice', which sometimes (as in the case of ardent social or political reformers) was—in Lord Macaulay's words—'only a technical name for benevolence'.[8]

(III) The unlawful meaning which the document is alleged to have conveyed must be one which it was reasonably capable of conveying to ordinary people of the class addressed.[9]

(IV) Everyone who circulates, or authorizes the circulation of, a libel is *prima facie* regarded as publishing it. But if he can be shown to have been a mere unconscious instrument (as, for instance, is generally the case with a newsboy), this will be a sufficient defence,[10] some mental element being necessary to constitute such an act of 'publication' as will render the doer responsible for it.

[1] See Stephen, *Hist. Crim. Law*, II, 298–395.

[2] In the wide and now obsolete sense of an admonition or declaration in a permanent form.

[3] Even amongst a narrow circle of associates, e.g. a little coterie of anarchists; *R.* v. *Malatesta* (1912) 7 Cr.App.R. 273.

[4] In one of the United States, it has thus been held libellous to describe a man as a 'Tory'. With emphatic rhetoric the Supreme Court of Georgia thus ruled the point: 'When the name of Washington shall grow cold to the ear of the patriot, when the poles of the earth shall be swung round to a coincidence with the equator, then and not till then will it cease to be a libel' to call a man a Tory; *Giles* v. *The State* (1849) 6 Cobb 284.

[5] *R.* v. *Munslow* [1895] 1 Q.B. 758 (*T.A.C.*).

[6] *Monson* v. *Tussauds* [1894] 1 Q.B. 671.

[7] *R.* v. *Munslow, ubi supra.*

[8] *Misc. Works*, IV, 189.

[9] *Capital and Counties Bank* v. *Henty* (1880) 7 A.C. at p. 776; *Cassidy* v. *Daily Mirror Newspapers* [1929] 2 K.B. 331; *Hough* v. *London Express Newspaper Ltd.* [1940] 2 K.B. 507.

[10] *Emmens* v. *Pottle* (1885) 16 Q.B.D. 354.

(V) There are certain occasions upon which the publication of (what would on ordinary occasions be) a libel becomes privileged.[1] Such a privilege may be:

(*a*) *Absolute*; e.g. for publication in a House of Parliament,[2] or by its order; and also for publication in a court of justice.[3]

(*b*) *Qualified*; i.e. arising *prima facie*, but ceasing if the prosecution show that the publication was made with a spiteful motive, or, in other words, that there was 'express' malice on the part of the defendant. A privilege of this qualified character is conceded to matter that is published under a legal or even a social duty; or (formerly[4]) as a fair comment upon a subject of public concern; or for the protection of the interests of the person to whom it is published, provided the person publishing it has also an interest in the matter communicated or is under a duty to communicate it;[5] and to fair and accurate reports of parliamentary or judicial proceedings;[6] and also, by statute,[7] to such fair and accurate reports of public meetings, or of open sittings of public bodies, as are published in a 'newspaper' and relate to some matter of public concern.

(VI) It is the function of the judge to decide (i) whether the document is reasonably capable of bearing the alleged defamatory meaning, e.g. a banker's note on a cheque 'Refer to drawer' is *not* defamatory;[8] (ii) whether the occasion was privileged; and—where there exists a qualified privilege—(iii) whether there is *any* evidence of express malice. All other matters, including now even the fundamental question whether the document is or is not a libel,[9] are left to the jury. For the crime lies not in the document itself but in the act of publishing it; and the guilt or innocence of that act lies in the immediate circumstances (of which the jury alone are the judges).

[1] As to libels in conjugal life, see ¶ 45.

[2] *R.* v. *Lord Abingdon* (1794) 1 Esp. 225.

[3] *Watson* v. *Jones* [1905] A.C. 480. This covers communications made to a solicitor or constable, even when legal proceedings are as yet only in contemplation, by a person who may (or may not) become a witness in the case; see *Beresford* v. *White* (1914) 30 T.L.R. 591, contrast *ibid.* 596.

[4] See *Thomas* v. *Bradbury* [1906] 2 K.B. 627. As to whether the defence of fair comment is now to be properly regarded as a species of qualified privilege, see Winfield, *Law of Tort*, 6th ed., 332.

[5] *Watt* v. *Longsdon* [1930] 1 K.B. 130.

[6] *Usill* v. *Hales* (1878) 3 C.P.D. 319. See now the Defamation Act, 1952, sched. pt. 1.

[7] Defamation Act, 1952. But s. 17 (2) provides that nothing in this Act affects the law relating to criminal libel.

[8] *Plunkett* v. *Barclays Bank Ltd.* (1936) 52 T.L.R. 353.

[9] See Lord Campbell's *Lives of the Lord Chancellors*, ch. CLXXVIII, and May's *Constitutional History*, II, 253–63, as to the historic controversy, during 1752–91, on this important constitutional question, ultimately settled by Mr Fox's Libel Act, 32 Geo. III, c. 60.

Section 3. Minor Differences

¶ 180. But though the criminal and the civil rules as to cases of libel are, fundamentally, thus similar, they differ as regards some few minor points. These are the following:

(*a*) Publication to a third person necessary in tort

No civil action will lie for a libel unless it has been published to some *third* person; since the sole object of such an action is to secure to the plaintiff compensation for the wrongful loss of that esteem in which other people formerly held him.[1] Hence a defamatory letter sent to the very person defamed will not, in the ordinary course, become actionable; though a defamatory post-card addressed to him will be.[2] But the reason for the criminal prohibition against libels is, on the other hand, stated to be their tendency to provoke the libelled person into committing a breach of the peace; and this tendency is still present when it is directly to himself that the defamation is addressed. Accordingly a publication to the actual person defamed is quite sufficient to support an indictment.[3]

(*b*) Truth of statement, a justification in tort

¶ 181. The *truth* of the matter complained of—even though the jury find it to have been published 'maliciously'—has long been a good defence in a civil action for libel. For it 'justifies' the words, by showing that the plaintiff has no right to that reputation for the deprivation of which he claims compensation. But the common law did not regard this as being any defence to criminal[4] proceedings; hence in criminal courts it used even to be a maxim that 'the greater the truth, the greater the libel'. This seems due to the fact that the crime of libel first became important in the Star Chamber as a political offence against the King and great men of the State which tended to promote public disorder. It was closely associated with sedition. In such circumstances the defence that the statements were true could not be admitted. And when the law of libel was extended to written blame of private persons truth was still held to be no defence; then crept in the explanation of the rule that even if true a defamatory statement would be likely to provoke the person defamed to commit a breach of the peace. It was further suggested that a scoundrel when exposed would be more likely to become violent than would an honest man when falsely vilified.[5]

[1] *Barrow* v. *Lewellin* (1615) Hobart 62 (*T.A.C.*). [2] *Post*, ¶ 496.

[3] *Clutterbuck* v. *Chaffers* (1816) 1 Starkie 471 (*T.A.C.*). Cf. 4 Bl. *Comm.* 150. It is often said that when the publication is only to the person libelled the indictment must expressly allege an intent to cause a breach of the peace. But it would seem that this is not really necessary; for in *R.* v. *Adams* (1887) 22 Q.B.D. 66 the count contained no such allegation. And see *R.* v. *Wicks* (1936) 52 T.L.R. 253.

[4] *Lake* v. *Hatton* (1619) Hobart 252; *Want's Case* (1601) Moore 627; *Case de libellis famosis* (1605) 5 Co. Rep. 125.

[5] A suggestion which everyday experience hardly confirms.

But this difference between civil and criminal rules has been almost wholly removed by Lord Campbell's Act (6 and 7 Vict. c. 96), which permits the truth—the substantial truth, even with errors of detail—of a *private*[1] libel to be a valid defence to criminal proceedings for it. This permission to 'justify' the defamation is, however, subject to a proviso that the defendant must further allege expressly, and prove to the satisfaction of the jury, that it was for the public benefit that the matter in question should be made known. The existence of this proviso makes it possible to repress the publication of statements which, though quite true, are objectionable, whether on grounds of decency, or as being disclosures of state secrets, or as being painful and needless intrusions into the privacy of domestic life. It may be for the public benefit to make it known that a man is suffering from an infectious fever; but not that he is suffering from heart-disease, or from some carefully concealed deformity (like that club-foot, the consciousness of which embittered the whole life of Byron).

(*c*) Libel against a class of persons, no tort

¶ 182. There is no civil action for libelling a *class* of persons, if, as must usually be the case, its members are too numerous and unascertainable to join as plaintiffs in a litigation. But since, technically speaking, it is not by the persons injured, but by the Queen, that criminal proceedings are carried on, an indictment will lie, provided only that the class defamed be not an indefinite (e.g. 'the men of science', 'the Socialists') but a definite one (e.g. 'the clergy of the diocese of Durham',[2] 'the justices of the peace for the county of Middlesex').

(*d*) Libel upon a deceased person, no tort

¶ 183. No civil action for a libel upon a person *deceased* has ever been brought by his representatives;[3] for the dead have no legal rights and can suffer no legal wrongs. But in those extreme cases where the libel, under the guise of attacking the dead man, attacks living ones by bringing his posterity into contempt or hatred, they—like any other class of persons who are injured by a libel—may obtain protection from the criminal law.[4] Yet to extend that protection to the case of ordinary attacks upon the reputation of persons deceased would be to impose an intolerable restraint upon the literary freedom of every writer of

[1] Hence Mylius, who accused the King of bigamy, was prosecuted, not for a seditious libel, but for a private one, thus enabling him to plead truth, and thereby allowing the King to disprove it (*The Times*, 2 February 1911).

[2] *R.* v. *Williams* (1822) 5 B. and Ald. 595. Cf. 2 Swanston 503.

[3] *R.* v. *Labouchère* (1884) 12 Q.B.D. at p. 324. The Law Reform (Misc. Prov.) Act, 1934, s. 1 excepts defamation from its provision which preserves for the benefit of, or against the estate of, a deceased person all causes of action subsisting vested in or against him at the time of his death.

[4] See *R.* v. *Topham* (1791) 4 T.R. 126; *R.* v. *Ensor* (1887) 3 T.L.R. 366; *R.* v. *Hunt* (1820) 2 St.Tr. (n.s.) 69, for libelling George III in George IV's reign. As to blackmailing by threats to libel the dead, see Larceny Act, 1916, s. 31; *post*, ¶ 311.

modern history;[1] especially as the lapse of time might have rendered it impossible for him to obtain *legal* proof of the truth of his statements, and as that truth, moreover, even if proved, might not be of sufficient public moment to constitute a statutory defence to criminal proceedings. Historical criticism may, no doubt, cause much pain to the descendants of the person criticized; but mental suffering never suffices, by itself, to render an act wrongful.

(*e*) Master liable in tort but not in crime. Slander no crime

¶ 184. In civil actions, a master is liable for *all* libels published by his servants in the course of their employment. But in criminal cases of libel in newspapers, it is a good defence if he can prove that the libel was published neither by his authority nor through his negligence.[2]

Besides differing thus in their treatment of libellous writings the two systems also differ in their treatment of the cognate subject of unlawful *oral* utterances.[3] These never create, as a defamatory libel does, a twofold liability, at once civil and criminal. For if the spoken words are merely slander, i.e. if they only defame private persons, a civil action may lie but an indictment will not lie[4] (except in those rare instances where the words tend quite directly to a breach of the peace,[5] as when they convey a challenge to fight).

¶ 184*a*. (*a*) *Obscene libels*; (*b*) *Blasphemous libels.* (*a*) At common law it was a misdemeanour[6] to make any public display which the judges considered to be offensive, disgusting or indecent so as to injure public morals and corrupt the mind and destroy the love of morality and good order.[7] This loosely defined and unlimited judicial discretion has been thought to be derived from the control originally exercised by the ecclesiastical courts, usurped later by the Court of Star Chamber and, after the abolition of that court, confiscated by the Court of King's Bench, which thus claimed to be '*custos morum*'.[8] In the vague field of moral tenets which vary between individuals and constantly shift with changes in social organization and advances in scientific knowledge, the past history of decided cases shows such variation in the views

[1] In 1916, at Tacoma, U.S.A., a man was convicted as a libeller for having written that George Washington was 'a slaveholder and an inveterate drinker'; Parmelee's *Criminology*, 460.

[2] 6 and 7 Vict. c. 96, s. 7. See ¶ 28 *ante*.

[3] If I dictate to my secretary a defamatory letter, it is an open question whether this (if not privileged) is libel or slander; *Osborn* v. *Boulter* [1930] 2 K.B. 226.

[4] But the Indian Penal Code, 1872 (s. 499), allowed criminal proceedings. Yet unwisely; for oral utterances are heard by few, are transient, are often hasty, and are always apt to be misapprehended.

[5] *R.* v. *Langley* (1704) 6 Mod. 125 (*T.A.C.*). In *London*, 2 and 3 Vict. c. 47 makes such words, if uttered 'in a public place', punishable at petty sessions; cf. *R.* v. *Burford* (1669) 1 Ventr. 16 (*T.A.C.*).

[6] Punishable, at the discretion of the judge, with imprisonment for any period of time.

[7] *R.* v. *Grey* (1864) 4 F. and F. 73.

[8] *Sedley's Case* (1663) 1 Keb. 620; see *R.* v. *Davies* [1906] 1 K.B. 32. There are indications in some old cases that the claim extended to cover the dialogue in stage plays.

adopted by the courts that the doctrine of judicia precedent cannot be expected to be very satisfactory for the solution of a modern case: and in the present book there is no space for a review of these.[1] At common law the prosecution had to prove the publication (as in the case of defamatory libel) and also the obscenity. The publication could take any visible form, e.g. writing, printing, signs, pictures, effigies, *tableaux vivants* or (presumably) pictorial arrangements of inanimate objects. The test of obscenity seems now to be 'whether the tendency of any publication... is to corrupt and deprave those whose minds today are open to immoral influences and into whose hands the publication may fall at the time when it is published or in the future.'[2] It was held[3] in 1955 to be a good defence for the sole effective director of a company which printed the libels that he was absent at the time when the order to print was given and had no knowledge of the books in question. But the defences of privilege, fair comment, and justification are not available in the case of obscene libel at common law. A considerable change in the law was made by the Obscene Publications Act, 1959, of which section 1 (1) in effect provides that an article shall be deemed to be obscene if its effect (or if composite, the effect of any one of its items) is, if taken as a whole, such as to deprave or corrupt persons likely to read, see, or hear the contents of it. 'Article' is explained as 'any description of article containing or embodying matter to be read or looked at or both, any sound record or any film or other record by a picture or pictures'.[4] Section 1 (3) in effect defines what amounts to publication. Section 2 decrees the penalty for the offence of publishing an obscene libel[5] and in effect[6] confirms the defence admitted in *R.* v. *Love* (*ante*). This section also provides (subs. (4)) 'that a person publishing an article shall not be proceeded against for an offence at common law consisting of the publication of any matter contained or embodied in the article where it is of the essence of the offence that the matter is obscene'. Section 4 in effect provides that a person shall not be convicted of the statutory offence in section 2 if it is proved that the publication of the article in question is justified as being for the public good on the ground that it is in the interests of science, literature, art or learning, or of other objects of general concern; and that the opinion of experts as to the literary, artistic, scientific or other merits of an article may be admitted in any proceedings under this Act either to establish or to negative the said ground. The statute also provides for the issue of warrants to search premises and for the seizure and forfeiture (but not

[1] Students will find an outline in Russell on Crime and Archbold, *Criminal Pleading, Evidence and Practice.*

[2] *R.* v. *Martin Secker Warburg, Ltd. and others* [1954] 2 All E.R. 683.

[3] *R.* v. *Love* (1955) 39 Cr.App.R. 30, following *R.* v. *Allison* (1888) 59 L.T. 933.

[4] Section 1 (2).

[5] A maximum fine of £100 or six months' imprisonment on summary conviction; a fine and or imprisonment up to three years on conviction on indictment.

[6] Subsect. (5).

destruction) of obscene articles, substantially on the same lines as laid down in the Obscene Publications Act, 1857, which the present statute repeals. It may be noted that a submission that section 2(4) read in connexion with section 1 (2) would exclude a prosecution for a common law conspiracy against persons who agree to publish material which, in the opinion of the judge would, if published, 'tend to corrupt and deprave' (perhaps within the terms laid down in *R.* v. *Martin Secker Warburg*,[1]) was rejected by the Court of Criminal Appeal in 1960[2] on the short ground that the offence at common law, namely, conspiracy to corrupt public morals, did not 'consist of the publication of the booklet'. Since in very many cases the facts will be that a group of two or more persons are concerned in the publication of any article, it is to be expected that in future the prosecuting authority will seize this opportunity of evading the Obscene Publications Act entirely.[3]

(*b*) Blasphemous libel at common law is an indictable misdemeanour, which originally consisted in almost any attack on the Christian religion (but no other). It is immaterial whether the publication is oral or written or in any other visible form. But nowadays it is apprehended that it is perhaps limited to attacks which take the form of scurrility or vilification of such a kind as might outrage public feelings or tend to cause a breach of the peace. So that it may be said to consist in the manner of the attack rather than in the attack *per se*.[4]

SECTION 4. PUNISHMENT

¶ 185. Libel is a misdemeanour, punishable with fine and imprisonment.[5] In the case of seditious, blasphemous, and other public libels there is no limit to the period of imprisonment;[6] and similar words uttered orally are punishable similarly. But in the case of defamatory libels, the term has been restricted by statute to two years, when the libel was published with a knowledge of its being false, and, in all other cases of defamatory libels, to a single year.[7]

[1] *Ubi supra.*

[2] *R.* v. *Shaw* reported in *Shaw* v. *D.P.P.* [1961] 2 W.L.R. 897, *per* Ashworth, J., at p. 910. See ¶¶ 445, 452 *post.*

[3] As was anticipated earlier in some quarters.

[4] *R.* v. *Ramsay* (1883) 15 Cox 231; *R.* v. *Boulter* (1908) 72 J.P. 188; *Bowman* v. *Secular Society Ltd* [1917] A.C. 406. For a further discussion see Russ., ch. 105. Cf. 1 *Cam. L.J.* 127.

[5] For a libel in a '*newspaper*' a judge's order is needed before taking criminal proceedings against the proprietor or editor (51 and 52 Vict. c. 64, s. 8).

[6] Since they are misdemeanours at common law; see *R.* v. *Morris* [1950] 2 All E.R. 965, *post*, ¶ 758.

[7] Libel Act, 1843, ss. 4, 5.

Chapter XI

OFFENCES AGAINST PROPERTY

Section I. Malicious Damage

GENERAL PRINCIPLES. 'UNLAWFULLY AND MALICIOUSLY'

¶ 186. In early English law attacks upon property which were not made for purposes of gain to the offender but which were inspired by feelings of vindictiveness,[1] or even by a reckless impulse to do damage, were almost entirely left to be remedied by the civil action of trespass. So that, at common law, the only kind of damage to property to rank as a criminal offence was arson,[2] which consisted of the wilful and malicious burning of a dwelling-house. This crime was extended by early statutes to the burning of other buildings and things, and thereafter the legislature by a series of enactments steadily widened the protection which the criminal law could give to property of a great variety of kinds.[3] During this development the draftsmen of the statutes in question formed the practice of describing the criminal damage mostly as having been done 'unlawfully and maliciously', but sometimes 'wilfully or maliciously'. It is necessary therefore, if possible, to ascertain what precise meaning is to be attached to these words.

¶ 187. (*a*) '*Unlawfully.*' This word suggests that there may be cases in which it is not unlawful to damage another person's property, i.e. in which the damage can be justified. Of course if a man can show that he has a legal right to do the harm complained of, there is no *actus reus* and therefore no criminal liability. But it has been suggested that there will be no liability if he was acting in good faith under a *supposed* right, i.e. where the defendant honestly believed he had a legal right which in fact he did not possess.[4]

Mistake of law is but rarely admitted as a defence in criminal proceedings,[5] although it may be expressly so provided by statute. The phrase 'unlawfully and maliciously' was used in most of the sections of the first statute to consolidate the law of injuries to property;[6] which, save in one section,[7] gave no indication that a *bona fide* claim of right could constitute any defence. Yet it was not long before the courts

[1] Whether against the owner or against the property itself (e.g. an animal).

[2] So called from Latin *ardere*, to burn. *Post*, ¶ 200.

[3] Now for the most part comprised in the Malicious Damage Act, 1861 (24 and 25 Vict. c. 97).

[4] See ¶ 281 *post*, and *R.* v. *Nundah* (1915) 16 N.S.W. 482 for the like defence on charges of stealing.

[5] *Ante*, ¶ 39 (3); *post*, ¶ 224.

[6] (1827) 7 and 8 Geo. IV, c. 30 (now repealed).

[7] Sect. 24.

began to interpret[1] other sections of that Act in a way which has led to the view mentioned above. A strong case was *R.* v. *Day*[2] in which it appeared that the prisoner had impounded some sheep which had strayed into his land and, when their owner refused to pay the amount he claimed as damages, had deliberately maimed the sheep; he was acquitted, on a direction by the judge that it was no offence within the statute[3] for a man to do an act which he conceived himself, however erroneously, to be justified by his rights in carrying into execution. The same defence was allowed in *R.* v. *Twose*[4] where the prisoner was indicted for having set fire to furze growing on a common.[5] It would seem therefore that there is judicial authority for the view that a claim of right in good faith is a valid defence to charges of malicious damage. Moreover (notwithstanding certain dicta to the contrary[6]), it makes no difference that the accused has conceived himself to possess a right of a kind unknown to the law. The dicta to the contrary would seem to have been due to the misunderstanding of certain special rules as to the ouster of the jurisdiction of justices of the peace when the case before them would necessitate their deciding a question of title to land. These rules must therefore be briefly described.

¶ **188.** *Ouster of the jurisdiction of justices of the peace.* In crimes of damage to property misunderstanding and difficulty have been caused by a certain confusion as to the meaning and scope of a long-standing rule that a court of summary jurisdiction[7] is not competent to try cases which involve the investigation of title to land. This topic is too technical for detailed discussion here,[8] and it must suffice to state that at least as early as 1700[9] the judges of the royal courts held that justices of the peace had no jurisdiction to decide questions of title to real property, and that if the case before them should *prima facie* depend upon such a question, their jurisdiction was ousted and they must hold their hands. This rule is still operative, although its limitations have not always been fully appreciated. In particular two important points have sometimes been overlooked, (1) that the rule is restricted to a dispute as to private title

[1] E.g. *R.* v. *James* (1837) 8 C. and P. 131, Lord Abinger, C.B. And see *James* v. *Phelps* (1840) 11 Ad. and E. 483, in which Lord Denman, C.J., said, at p. 488, 'the principles of the common law prevent the act from being felonious where there is no malice in the intention'. See Russ., chapter 79.

[2] (1844) 8 J.P. 186.

[3] The Malicious Damage Act, 1827.

[4] (1879) 14 Cox 327 (*T.A.C.*).

[5] See also *Watkins* v. *Major* (1878) 44 L.J.M.C. 164, at p. 168, where Lord Coleridge, C.J., said 'where there must be *mens rea* to constitute an offence, an honest claim of right, however absurd, would frustrate a summary conviction'.

[6] E.g. by the trial judge in *R.* v. *Bernhard* [1938] 2 K.B. 264, and in the Court of Criminal Appeal in *Gott* v. *Measures* [1947] 2 All E.R. 609, two cases which are discussed below in ¶ 310 and ¶ 199 respectively.

[7] *Post*, ¶ 671.

[8] A fuller account will be found in Russ., appendix 2.

[9] *R.* v. *Speed* (1700) 1 Ld. Raym. 583.

to *real* property,[1] and (2) since the justices have to decide whether a dispute as to title to land *is* involved, the defendant must do something more than *merely allege* that it is involved. He must state affirmatively the precise legal right in real property which he claims to possess, and which will be in dispute. The interests which any person can have in real property are fixed by law and are limited in number. Accordingly if the alleged interest which the defendant states that he possesses in the land is one which does not exist in law, his contention that the jurisdiction is ousted must fail, because, however honest his belief,[2] there cannot be any legal dispute as to his having in the land a right which no one can have.[3] In such a situation the true reason why the jurisdiction is not ousted is because there is *no dispute* as to title to land, and *not* because the right alleged does not exist in law. It is therefore very misleading and incorrect to state, as a general proposition of law applicable in *all* cases, that no one can have a *bona fide* belief in a right which is unknown to the law.[4]

¶ **189.** *Claims of right expressly recognized by statute.* It must be remembered that, apart from any defence of a claim of right allowed by common law or under some special statutory provision, there are circumstances, such as the protection of one's own property and the abatement of a nuisance, in which a man can justify the use of the force which has damaged the property of someone else; even in such a case he must still not do any more harm than is reasonably necessary for the protection of his own interest; any excess of this will be unlawful.[5] The defence in these cases, however, is the *existence* of a right of self-protection, and not the *belief* that one has that right. Nevertheless, statute has in some instances expressly allowed such a belief to be a defence by way of *excuse*: plainly in these instances the belief must be erroneous, for if the defendant *has* the right he can *justify* his action and does not need a statutory *excuse* for it. If he has the right, then belief is just as irrelevant as it is in the case of a man who intended to break his enemy's window but by mistake broke his own. He had

[1] Accordingly the justices can try a case which involves the question whether the place in question was a public highway (*R.* v. *Critchlow* (1878) 26 W.R. 681). And see *White* v. *Fox* (1880) 49 L.J.M.C. 60 *per* Lord Coleridge, C.J. Nor is a contractual claim to enter the land within the rule, *Lucan* v. *Barrett* (1915) 79 J.P. 463.

[2] And even if the right alleged is one which really does exist in law, yet it is none the less essential that the defendant should honestly believe that *he* is entitled to it; *R.* v. *Dodson* (1839) 9 Ad. and E. 704.

[3] In other words the right alleged by the defendant must be such that it would afford him a good defence to a *civil* action brought in the appropriate court.

[4] E.g. as was said in *R.* v. *Bernhard* (*post*, ¶ 310) and *Gott* v. *Measures* (*post*, ¶ 199).

[5] *R.* v. *Clemens* [1898] 1 Q.B. 556 (*T.A.C.*); and see *Cope* v. *Sharpe* [1912] 1 K.B. 496, discussed in Russ., chapter 89, and the line of cases in which dogs and other animals have been attacked by occupants of land on to which they have trespassed; e.g. *Reynell* v. *Champernoon* (1631) Cro. Car. 228; *Vere* v. *Lord Cawdor* (1809) 11 East 569; *Miles* v. *Hutchings* [1903] 2 K.B. 714; *Cresswell* v. *Sirl* [1948] 1 K.B. 241; *Goodway* v. *Becher* [1951] 2 All E.R. 349; *Workman* v. *Cowper* [1961] 1 All E.R. 683.

mens rea, but he committed no crime of malicious damage because the *actus* was not *reus*. An example of such a statutory defence was in section 52 of the Malicious Damage Act, 1861,[1] now repealed and replaced by section 14 of the Criminal Justice Administration Act, 1914. The combined effect of this legislation was to provide in general terms for the punishment of persons who should do such acts of damage as did not fall within the other sections of the statute; and it expressly states that the section shall not apply 'where the alleged offender acted under a fair and reasonable supposition that he had a right to do the act complained of'. Much difficulty has been caused by the manner in which this provision has been interpreted by the courts[2] but the topic is too complicated for examination in the space available here.[3]

¶ 190. (*b*) '*Maliciously*.' We have already discussed the meaning of this word (*ante*, ¶ 158 *a*) and there should be no need to say anything more about it were it not for the doubts which the judgment of the House of Lords in *D.P.P.* v. *Smith* has raised. We have already mentioned the cases since *R.* v. *Pembliton*[4] (which was followed in the Irish case of *R.* v. *Faulkner*[5]) which have for many years been regarded as the established foundation of the principle that in this statute this word is used subjectively, and requires that, for a verdict of guilty, the jury must be satisfied that the accused either intended to cause the particular *kind* of harm forbidden by the section under which he is charged, or that he was reckless as to whether such harm should occur or not, i.e. that he foresaw that such harm might be done, and yet went on to take the risk of it.[6] The charge in *Smith's* case was murder, an offence against the person; but seeking support for the conclusion to which their lordships had come the five judges in the House of Lords turned to the Irish case of *Faulkner* and selected from it a passage from the judgment of Palles, C.B., in which the Chief Baron said:

> In my judgment the law imputes to a person who wilfully commits a criminal act an intention to do everything which is the probable consequence of the act constituting the *corpus delicti* which actually ensues. In my opinion this inference arises irrespective of the particular consequence which ensued being or not being foreseen by the criminal, and whether his conduct is reckless or the reverse.

[1] Which replaced sect. 24 of the Malicious Damage Act, 1827.

[2] E.g. *R.* v. *Cheshire JJ.* (1850) 23 J.P. 724; *Hanway* v. *Boultbee* (1830) 1 M. and Rob. 14; *White* v. *Feast* (1872) L.R. 7 Q.B. 353; *R.* v. *French* (1873) 37 J.P. 404; *Denny* v. *Thwaites* (1876) 35 L.T. 628; *Leyson* v. *Williams* (1890) 54 J.P. 631; *Heard* v. *Coles* (1891) 56 J.P. 119; *R.* v. *Clemens* [1898] 1 Q.B. 556; *Heaven* v. *Crutchley* (1904) 68 J.P. 53. The cases are discussed in Russ. ch. 79.

[3] For a detailed discussion of the interpretation put upon these provisions by the courts see Russ. ch. 79.

[4] (1874) 2 C.C.R. 119 (*T.A.C.*).

[5] (1877) 13 Cox 550 (*T.A.C.*).

[6] *R.* v. *Cunningham* [1957] 2 Q.B. 396.

As we have noted, the judgment, as delivered, inaccurately stated the result of this appeal as being an affirmation of the conviction of Faulkner, whereas in fact the Irish court quashed his conviction. Moreover, the House of Lords did not mention that, of the ten Irish judges in that case, nine were in favour of quashing the conviction; three following *R.* v. *Pembliton* and four expressing tacit agreement.[1] After the judgment in *Smith's* case was delivered and reproduced in the reports,[2] a corrective alteration was officially issued.[3] This stated that the conviction was quashed 'on grounds immaterial to this case'.[4] It remains to be seen whether these last words are to be interpreted as intended to leave the subjective principle of *R.* v. *Pembliton*[5] intact (in which case the dictum of Palles, C.B., must be taken to be wrong in respect of the very case to which he was applying it) or as demolishing that principle, by the implied overruling of the seven judges who followed and certainly approved it[6] (which would be strange in the face of the words of the alteration 'on grounds immaterial to this case'). Unless and until this point is cleared up it must with all respect be said that the House of Lords have placed in a predicament those who have to apply this Act.[7]

¶ 191. *Particularity of early statutes.* The Malicious Damage Act, 1861, contains many provisions in which damage to different kinds of property is repressed by varying punishments, in a policy of legislative particularity which was much approved in that period,[8] but which to modern minds seems unnecessarily complicated. It is not possible here to enter on any detailed enumeration of all the sections.

OFFENCES UNDER THE MALICIOUS DAMAGE ACT, 1861

¶ 192. Apart from arson and cattle-maiming which will be treated separately below,[9] the offences under the Act may be described comprehensively as ranging from felonies, such as damaging or destroying textiles[10] for which the punishment may be imprisonment for life,[11] and

[1] The one dissentient, Keogh, J., held in effect that it was a basic rule that any man engaged in the commission of any felony (here, larceny of rum) must take the full consequences of any result that followed (i.e. that malice, whether statutory or not, was 'implied'). Palles, C.B., and Fitzgerald, B., while accepting Keogh's proposition, held that the conviction should be quashed because the question of fact (whether the burning of the ships was the 'reasonable consequence') had not been left to the jury.

[2] [1960] 3 All E.R. 161; 3 W.L.R. 546. [3] [1960] 3 W.L.R. prefacing p. 1.

[4] I.e. *D.P.P.* v. *Smith*; and declaring 'Palles, C.B., stated the law as follows', thereby implying that all the judges were in agreement with his view.

[5] And other cases such as *R.* v. *Child* (1871) 1 C.C.R. 307, and *R.* v. *Nattrass* (1882) 15 Cox 73. [6] And see *Re Borrowes* [1900] 2 I.R. 593.

[7] On this point see *R.* v. *Metharam* [1961] 3 All E.R. 200, *ante* ¶ 159.

[8] See *Mod. Appr. Crim. Law* 41–3; especially 41 n. 2. [9] ¶¶ 200, 196.

[10] Sect. 14. Other felonies are damaging mines and mining machinery (ss. 28, 29); sea banks, canal walls, bridges, or railways (ss. 30, 31, 33, 35, 36); sending letters threatening to burn or destroy (s. 50).

[11] Criminal Justice Act, 1948; formerly penal servitude.

misdemeanours, such as damaging or destroying any book or work of art[1] (with which are included any railing or fence surrounding a statue or monument) for which the maximum penalty is imprisonment for six months (or, in contrast, damaging a fishpond, for which the penalty may be imprisonment for seven years[2]), down to offences punishable on summary conviction, such as damaging growing trees,[3] fruit or vegetable productions in a garden[4] or cultivated elsewhere for food or medicine.[5] And to damage any kind of real or personal property not specifically mentioned in the Act is a misdemeanour or a petty offence according to the amount of the damage.[6]

¶ 193. Finally there were two sections which were residuary; section 51 created a misdemeanour punishable with imprisonment for two years[7] for any person 'unlawfully and maliciously' to damage (to an amount exceeding £5) any real or personal property whatsoever[8] for which no punishment was specified in previous sections. This section has been modified by section 14 of the Criminal Justice Administration Act, 1914, which allows, alternatively, summary proceedings for damage[9] 'wilfully or maliciously' done up to the amount of twenty pounds, subject to the proviso that 'This provision shall not apply where the alleged offender acted under a fair and reasonable supposition that he had a right to do the act complained of'. The difficulties which have arisen in deciding upon the scope and meaning of the words 'a fair and reasonable supposition' etc. have been alluded to above, ¶ 189. The other residuary provision in the Act of 1861 was section 52 but this was repealed by the above mentioned section 14 of the Act of 1914; until that repeal, however, the interpretation of this section also exercised the courts, particularly since it reproduced the phrase 'wilfully *or* maliciously' from the old enactment[10] which it replaced. An examination of these difficulties would be too lengthy for the present volume[11] but two cases which have attracted special attention[12] must now be explained.

[1] Sect. 39. [2] Sect. 32.

[3] Sect. 22; imprisonment for three months or a fine.

[4] Sect. 23; imprisonment for six months or a fine.

[5] Sect. 24; imprisonment for one month or a fine. An intent to destroy must be proved, *Eley* v. *Lytle* (1885) 50 J.P. 308.

[6] Sect. 51, and Criminal Justice Administration Act, 1914, s. 14.

[7] If by day; but if the offence be committed by night (i.e. between 9 p.m. and 6 a.m.) five years. In either case the court may impose a fine instead of, or in addition to, imprisonment (s. 73).

[8] E.g. where a milk roundsman waters his employer's milk so that he may have more fluid to sell than he has to account for; *Roper* v. *Knott* [1898] 1 Q.B. 868, a prosecution under sect. 52 of the Act.

[9] And in addition to imprisonment authorizes the justices to impose a fine to be paid to the aggrieved party as compensation.

[10] Sect. 24 of the Malicious Damage Act, 1827.

[11] See Russ. ch. 79, where the cases are discussed.

[12] E.g. in previous editions of this book (15th ed., p. 193).

¶ 194. *Gardner* v. *Mansbridge*[1] was decided on the interpretation of sections 52 and 53[2] of the Malicious Damage Act, 1861. It was an appeal to the divisional court by way of case stated from a decision of justices who had acquitted the respondent on a charge (under section 52) of wilfully or maliciously committing damage to real property in gathering mushrooms which were growing wild in the appellant's field, to the value of two shillings. The justices held that these mushrooms were not 'cultivated roots or plants' within the meaning of section 24 of the Act and that the facts did not bring the case within section 52. The divisional court expressed themselves as unable to give a reason for the use of the phraseology 'wilfully *or* maliciously' instead of the words 'unlawfully *and* maliciously' used in other sections,[3] but gave judgment for the respondent, holding that section 53 showed that the intention of the legislature was to restrict the operation of section 52 to damage done to the realty itself as distinct from the natural products of the realty;[4] and furthermore that since the maximum penalty under section 24 of the Act for damaging *cultivated* plants was imprisonment for one month, it was inconceivable that the legislature should have intended that for gathering such wild products as mushrooms growing naturally in a field a person should be liable to two months' imprisonment.[5]

¶ 195. *Hamilton* v. *Bone*[6] was decided on the question whether the accused had done the damage 'under a fair and reasonable supposition that he had a right to do the act complained of'. This was another case stated to the divisional court who upheld the appellant's conviction under section 53 of the Act, for cutting certain blossoms from the respondent's chestnut tree. It appeared that the parties lived on opposite sides of the road, and that the tree on the respondent's land had grown out over the roadway to within a few feet of the appellant's house, but not so as to overhang his boundary. The appellant regarded the tree as a nuisance to him because it cut off light and air from his building and because boys used to stand in the road and throw at the blossoms with stones, some of which fell on his premises and broke his glass. He had therefore cut off some of the blossoms, contending that he had a legal right to abate a nuisance in this manner. The justices had held that he had not acted under a fair and reasonable supposition of right, and the divisional court confirmed their view, Wills, J., saying 'One cannot

[1] (1887) 19 Q.B.D. 217.

[2] Repealed by s. 14 of the Criminal Justice Administration Act, 1914.

[3] The attention of the court was not directed to the judgment of Blackburn, J., in *White* v. *Feast* (1872) L.R. 7 Q.B. 353, at p. 359, which purports to give the explanation.

[4] This construction of the statute has not been judicially repudiated; it was at least curious, in face of the words of the section, which are 'any damage, injury, or spoil to or upon any real or personal property whatsoever'. And see *Gayford* v. *Chouler* [1898] 1 Q.B. 316.

[5] This argument of the divisional court loses its cogency if the explanation given by Blackburn, J., in *White* v. *Feast* (*supra*) was correct.

[6] (1888) 16 Cox 437.

say that the justices were wrong in finding that the appellant did not act upon a fair and reasonable supposition of right'. Field, J., said: 'The evidence only supports the untenable argument that because the boys threw stones, therefore, the appellant was entitled to injure his neighbour's property, and negatives the contention that he acted under a fair and reasonable claim of right.'

It will be seen therefore that the two cases of *Gardner* v. *Mansbridge* and *Hamilton* v. *Bone* do not need any effort of reconciliation. The respective courts went on this distinction, viz. that section 52 did not cover mushrooms, and would not have covered trees, and therefore Mansbridge was not guilty; whereas trees were expressly mentioned in sections 22 and 53 and therefore Hamilton was guilty.

MALICIOUS DAMAGE TO ANIMALS. CATTLE

¶ 196. Under section 40 of the Malicious Damage Act, 1861, it is a felony, punishable with imprisonment for fourteen years, unlawfully and maliciously to kill, maim or wound any cattle. The statute does not define cattle but the term seems to include horses, mares, colts, asses, sheep and pigs[1] in addition to the ordinary bovine animals. The word 'maliciously' must bear the same meaning here as elsewhere in the Act and is satisfied when the act is proved to have been done either intentionally or recklessly,[2] so that there must be a realization that hurt will or may be done[3] although it is irrelevant whether there is or is not any ill-will or spite against the owner or the animal.[4] Except in so far as they have incorporated the rare instances in which damage to property was a crime at common law the successive statutes prohibiting such damage have aimed at providing criminal sanctions for offences for which otherwise there would only be a remedy by civil proceedings: their purpose was not, for example, merely to prevent cruelty to animals. Doubts have accordingly been felt as to the correctness of the decision in *R.* v. *Parry*[5] where the prisoner was convicted on a charge under section 40 for kicking and stabbing with a fork his own horse, since there can be no question that, apart from the point of cruelty, it is not unlawful for a man to do what damage he likes to his own property. Cruel treatment of any animal, whether his own or another's, inflicted by a man is now dealt with under the Protection of Animals Act, 1911.[6]

ANIMALS OTHER THAN CATTLE

¶ 197. Section 41 of the same Act makes it an offence punishable with six months' imprisonment on summary conviction for any one unlawfully and maliciously to kill, maim or wound any dog, bird, beast or

[1] Perhaps also mules and goats, by virtue of the definition in the Dogs Act, 1906.

[2] *Ante*, ¶ 190.

[3] *R.* v. *Mogg* (1830) 4 C. and P. 364.

[4] *R.* v. *Welch* (1875) 1 Q.B.D. 23.

[5] *The Times*, 27 July 1900.

[6] 1 and 2 Geo. V, c. 27; the penalties were altered by an Amendment Act, 1912. And see the Cruelty to Animals Act, 1876 (39 and 40 Vict. c. 77), which regulates the use of animals for scientific experiments.

other animal not being cattle; but limited by the requirement that the creature shall either be one that is the subject of larceny at common law,[1] or is being ordinarily kept in a state of confinement or for any domestic purpose. It is not necessary to prove that the particular creature ill-treated was at the time being kept in confinement so long as it is one of a class which are ordinarily so kept; nor is it necessary to prove the ownership of the creature.[2]

TRESPASSING ANIMALS

¶ 198. Mention has already been made of a line of cases[3] in which trespassing dogs have been killed or hurt by the occupant of the land; these cases have established that the common law right of defence of a man's property extends to the use of force to keep out of or to expel from his land any such trespassing creatures, and to protect from them any of his property on the land which they are damaging or threatening to damage.[4] But in any such case he must not do more harm to the creature than is necessary in the circumstances;[5] and it is only in defence of his own (or his master's) interests that he may justify his action. Two questions therefore have always to be considered: (1) Had the defendant a sufficient interest to protect? and (2) Was the action which he took reasonable in the circumstances?

¶ 198*a*. A noteworthy instance of vicarious liability has been created by the Dogs (Protection of Livestock) Act, 1953, which in effect provides that it shall be a summary offence[6] by the owner of a dog (and also in addition by any other person who may be in charge of the dog)[7] which worries[8] livestock[9] on any agricultural land.[10] It would seem, from the wording of the Act, that it is irrelevant whether or not the person charged had any knowledge of the dog's harmful activity or of its proclivity to act in that way. But the Act does not apply if at the material time the livestock attacked are trespassing on land occupied by

[1] *Post*, ¶ 264. Thus it will include poultry.

[2] *Nye* v. *Niblet* [1918] 1 K.B. 23, in which a presumption of ownership in *someone* was accepted as within the section.

[3] ¶ 189 n. 5.

[4] Thus long ago it was held that a warrener could justify killing a dog, which had entered his warren, to prevent its destroying the rabbits (*Wadhurst* v. *Damme* (1604) Cro. Jac. 45). A man was also held to be justified in killing two greyhounds which he caught *after* they had killed a deer in his park (*Barrington* v. *Turner* (1681) 3 Lev. 28).

[5] *Miles* v. *Hutchings* [1903] 2 K.B. 714; *Cresswell* v. *Sirl* [1948] 1 K.B. 241; *Goodway* v. *Becher* [1951] 2 All E.R. 349; contrast *Barnard* v. *Evans* [1925] 2 K.B. 794 (a charge of cruelty).

[6] Punishable by a fine up to £10 for a first conviction, and up to £50 for a subsequent conviction in respect of the same dog.

[7] But he alone and not the owner will be liable if he is a person whom the owner of the dog reasonably believed to be fit and proper to have charge of the dog, s. 1 (4).

[8] By attacking or chasing the creatures in such a way as may reasonably be expected to cause injury, suffering or loss or diminution of their produce.

[9] Widely defined in s. 3 (1).

[10] As defined in s. 3 (1).

the owner or person in charge of the dog, unless he causes the dog to attack the livestock.[1]

PROPERTY IN WILD CREATURES

¶ 199. Most of the cases in which trespassing animals have been killed or wounded have depended upon the point as to whether the force used exceeded what was reasonable. That was, it is submitted, the only point which called for consideration in the case of *Gott* v. *Measures*, a case stated to the divisional court in 1947.[2] The justices had given judgment in favour of the respondent on a charge[3] of shooting a dog. The respondent owned the sporting rights over the land on which the dog had often trespassed in spite of warnings given to its owner, and while it was chasing a pregnant hare he had shot the dog, which he had shortly before seen tearing a pheasant to pieces. The divisional court, however, allowed the appeal and sent the case back to the justices with an intimation that the offence was proved. In the course of their judgments the court, while declaring that a man may be justified in shooting a dog 'if he honestly believes that it is necessary as being the only way in which he can protect his property', yet held that neither a person owning the sporting rights over land nor the owner of land has any property in a pheasant or other wild game until he has reduced it into possession. This legal proposition conflicts with a whole line of cases running from the *Bishop of London's Case* in the reign of Henry VIII[4] to *Cope* v. *Sharpe* in 1912. On the basis, however, of this novel doctrine which they had propounded the court proceeded to state:[5] 'it cannot be said that the respondent could have reasonably believed that he was entitled to shoot the dog in protection of his property, because that would be a belief in something which the law does not recognize. Just as one cannot have a *bona fide* claim of right if the right is one which the law does not recognize, one cannot, in my opinion, honestly believe that it is necessary to shoot a dog to protect one's property when one has no property to protect.' As we have seen above[6] the question of reasonable belief in a right not recognized by law is only relevant when a defendant claims that the jurisdiction of the justices is ousted, and no such claim has been made by the respondent; that as a matter of fact he did honestly believe he had the right to shoot was beyond question and he had a long line of cases to support his contention. But even if the law

[1] For a special case under sect. 54 (2) of the Metropolitan Police Act, 1839, see *Ross* v. *Evans* [1959] 2 W.L.R. 699.

[2] [1947] 2 All E.R. 609.

[3] Under s. 41 of the Malicious Damage Act, 1861.

[4] (1523) 14 Hen. VIII, fo. 1; and including the *Case of Swans* (1592) 7 Co. Rep. 15*b*, 17*b*; *Sutton* v. *Moody* (1697) 1 Ld. Raym. 250; *Keble* v. *Hickringill* (1706) 11 Mod. 75; *Vere* v. *Lord Cawdor* (1809) 11 East 569; *Deane* v. *Clayton* (1817) 7 Taunt. 489; *Graham* v. *Ewart* (1855) 11 Exch. 326 at p. 346; *Earl of Lonsdale* v. *Rigg* (1856) 11 Exch. 654 at p. 671; *Blades* v. *Higgs* (1865) 10 C.B. (n.s.) at pp. 222, 223, 226; *Armstrong* v. *Mitchell* (1903) 67 J.P. 329, and *Cope* v. *Sharpe* [1912] 1 K.B. 496. These cases are discussed in Russ. ch. 89.

[5] *Per* Lord Goddard, C.J., at p. 611.

[6] ¶ 188.

had not recognized such a right he was, it is submitted, entitled to acquittal, under the common law rule recognized in several cases.[1] It would seem therefore that the principles advanced in *Gott* v. *Measures* need reconsideration.[2]

Section 2. Arson

¶ **200.** *Historical.* In early English law a dwelling-house was regarded as being its occupier's 'castle and fortress, as well for his defence against injury and violence, as for his repose. *Domus sua cuique est tutissimum refugium*'.[3] Hence to set fire wilfully to the humblest cottage is still a heinous felony; though to set fire equally wilfully to some unique picture or some priceless tapestry is at most a misdemeanour, and at common law was no crime at all. Indeed arson[4] was at common law the only case in which *damage* to property was a criminal offence. Therefore to destroy a house by any other means than by fire was not criminally punishable; the legislature, however, supplied the omission by making it a felony *riotously* to demolish a house[5] and a misdemeanour *riotously* to damage[6] one; and more generally, apart from any riot, by rendering the doing of malicious injury to any property, whether a house or not, a crime. That crime is punishable as we have seen in the previous paragraphs as an indictable offence in some cases and in others as a petty offence, according to the amount of damage done.

ARSON AT COMMON LAW

¶ **201.** Arson at common law was defined as 'the malicious and wilful burning of the house or outhouse of another man'. The requirement of wilfulness suggests that arson was one of the earliest crimes in which the mental element was emphasized. 'At a very early time, men must distinguish between fires that are, and fires that are not, intended.'[7] So far back as the days of Bracton[8] it was already settled that 'Incendia fortuita, vel per negligentiam facta, et non mala conscientia, capitali sententia non sic puniuntur, quia civiliter agitur contra tales'.

In limiting the crime to the burning of the house of 'another man', attention was concentrated on the interference with the rights, not of the owner, but of the immediate occupier. Hence, if a tenant were actually in lawful possession of a house, even though his tenancy was to last no longer than for the single day, he would commit no arson by burning the house down.[9] And, on the other hand, his landlord

[1] *R.* v. *James* (1837) 8 C. and P. 131; *R.* v. *Day* (1844) 8 J.P. 186; *R.* v. *Twose* (1879) 14 Cox 327; *Watkins* v. *Major* (1878) 44 L.J.M.C. 164; *R.* v. *Bernhard* [1938] 2 K.B. 264. And see *R.* v. *Rutter* (1908) 1 Cr.App.R. 174.

[2] On this case see Russ. ch. 89.

[3] *Semayne's Case* (1604) 5 Co. Rep. 91.

[4] It was at one time punished with the terrible retaliation of death by burning; Britton, I, 41.

[5] Malicious Damage Act, 1861 (24 and 25 Vict. c. 97), s. 11.

[6] *Ibid.* s. 12.

[7] Pollock and Maitland, II, 492.

[8] Fo. 146*b*.

[9] *Breeme's Case* (1780) 2 East P.C. 1026.

(though the owner of the house) would commit arson if he burned it whilst it was still in the occupation of the tenant.

¶ **202.** '*Malicious.*' The common law definition did not include the word 'unlawful'. A burning, for example, of an unwanted outhouse of another man at his request would not be unlawful and could not conceivably be a crime at common law; accordingly the requirement of unlawfulness must be implied in the word 'malicious', which, it must be remembered, was in early times a wide and vague term which could well connote unlawful or wrongful conduct. To burn one's own house was not a crime at common law, unless the house was in a town, or so near to other houses that its burning might endanger them, in which circumstances it was a misdemeanour.[1] But, if a man burnt his own house and the flames spread to his neighbour's, this would be a felony;[2] and to burn another's barn in a field, if filled with hay or corn, was also a felony at common law.[3]

ARSON UNDER STATUTES

¶ **203.** The common law is now superseded by the various statutes dealing with arson: these were mostly consolidated by the Malicious Damage Act, 1861,[4] which in all cases requires that the property in question shall have been 'unlawfully' and 'maliciously' 'set fire to'. These three phrases will be commented on below, ¶¶ 204, 205 and 206. The possible punishments are death in the rare case of setting fire to the ships or marine stores of the Crown, or the dockyards housing the same,[5] and imprisonment[6] for life in the case of a dwelling-house when any person is therein,[7] also in the case of any dwelling-house (and many other kinds of buildings) if with intent to injure or defraud any person,[8] in the case of a church of other place of divine worship,[9] of a railway station or building,[10] of stacks,[11] coal mine,[12] and a ship.[13] For arson of other buildings than those specified in the first five sections of the Act or for attempting to set fire to goods in a protected building or to the building itself, or to crops and plantations, the penalty is imprisonment for fourteen years; and for attempting to set fire to standing crops or plantations, imprisonment for seven years. All are felonies.

¶ **204.** '*Unlawfully.*' This word, as we have seen, did not appear in the common law definition. Its insertion in the statutes marks the recogni-

[1] 1 Hale P.C. 568; 2 East P.C. 1027. [2] 4 Bl. *Comm.* 221.

[3] Or a stack in the open, 3 Co. *Inst.* 67.

[4] Sects. 1–8 (buildings); 16–18 (crops, etc.); 26, 27 (mines); 42–4 (ships).

[5] Dockyards etc. Protection Act, 1772, s. 1, and the Naval Discipline Act, 1866, s. 34. Students should observe that the Homicide Act, 1957, does not purport to deal with convictions under these two statutes.

[6] Criminal Justice Act, 1948, s. 1; formerly penal servitude.

[7] Sect. 2. Coleridge, C.J., in *R.* v. *Pardoe* (1894) 17 Cox 715, held it to be enough that the prisoner himself was in the house when he set fire to it.

[8] Sect. 3. [9] Sect. 1. [10] Sect. 4. [11] Sect. 17.

[12] Sect. 26. [13] Sect. 42.

tion that 'malice' was coming to have a more precise definition than in the past, and to refer to the attitude of mind of the prisoner rather than to the general unlawfulness of his conduct. It means 'without lawful justification (e.g. the justification that the property is his own) or excuse (e.g. mistake).' It will be seen that section 3 makes it a felony (now punishable with imprisonment for life) for a person (*a*) unlawfully and maliciously (*b*) to set fire to (*c*) any house or any of a stated list of other buildings down to a hovel, shed or fold, (*d*) with intent to injure or defraud any person. Since each of these elements is expressly required by the statute it would be illogical to read the section as though the unlawfulness required by (*a*) were supplied by (*d*), for if that were so (*d*) would thereby become at best merely an illustration of (*a*) and not the necessary fourth ingredient of liability which the wording of the section plainly indicates it to be. Moreover it would be strange if the legislature intended that a man who, desiring to destroy some shed or hovel, adopted the method of burning it, with the additional dishonest intention of claiming its value from his insurance company on a pretence that the fire was accidental, should be guilty of felony and exposed to a sentence of imprisonment for many years whereas if with the same intention he had burned his motor-car or other valuable chattel, the criminal law would provide no other punishment than that under section 32 of the Larceny Act, 1916.[1] The point however, does not seem to have been taken in the courts.[2] A similar difficulty is created by the inclusion of the word 'unlawfully' in section 2 of the Act.[3]

¶ 205. '*Maliciously.*' Burning a house by negligence is no crime. Even the fact that this negligence occurred in the course of the commission of a felonious act will not suffice to render the consequent burning-down indictable as an arson. For in any statutory definition of a crime, 'malice' must, as we have already seen,[4] be taken, not in its vague common law sense as a 'wickedness' in general, but as requiring an actual intention to do the particular kind of harm that in fact was done (or a recklessness as to doing it).[5] Consequently, if a criminal, when engaged in committing some burglary or other felony, negligently sets fire to a house, he usually will not be guilty of arson.[6] He would, how-

[1] A misdemeanour carrying a maximum punishment of imprisonment for five years. Within this section the case of the man who burned his own hovel as above described would already fall.

[2] It was not taken in *R.* v. *Fitzaucher* [1956] Crim. L.R. 118, the accused being acquitted, but exactly on what grounds the report does not state.

[3] It is likely, however, that if the point were taken in respect to either of the two sections the courts would brush aside the argument and would hold that the word 'unlawfully' is surplusage, and must be disregarded, the sections being treated as unhappily worded.

[4] *R.* v. *Pembliton* (1874) 2 C.C.R. 119 (*T.A.C.*). Unless the law has been altered by the judgment of the House of Lords in *D.P.P.* v. *Smith*; *ante*, ¶ 190.

[5] On the other hand it is not limited to, nor does it require, any ill will to the person injured; cf. ¶ 190, *ante*.

[6] *R.* v. *Faulkner* (1877) 13 Cox 550 (*T.A.C.*).

ever, be so in those rarer cases where the original crime he was engaged in was itself an act of burning, such as he would know to be likely to result in producing an arson; for he had foreseen the possibility. Thus if a man by wilfully burning his own house (although with no intention to defraud or injure anyone) happened to burn the closely adjacent house of a neighbour, he might be guilty of arson; since in such a case the law would raise a *prima facie* presumption of his foresight of the consequences from the manifest obviousness of the danger. But it must not be supposed that everyone who has maliciously set fire to some article, which it is not arson to burn, will necessarily become guilty of arson if the fire should happen to spread to an 'arsonable' building. For if a man mischievously tries to burn some chattels inside a house, and sets fire to the house thereby, this is not an arson of the *house*[1] if (as will, of course, rarely be the case) it appears from the evidence that he neither intended, nor foresaw the possibility of the house's catching fire. For it is essential to arson that the incendiary either should have intended the building to take fire, or, at least, should have recognized the probability of its taking fire and have been reckless as to whether or not it did so. The cases emphasize that this test of liability is subjective.[2]

¶ 206. '*Setting fire to.*' The statute speaks of 'setting fire to' houses, where the common law required a 'burning'. But this appears to be a distinction without a difference; since 'set fire to' is regarded as meaning not merely 'place fire against', but actually 'set on fire'. It will be sufficient if any part of the woodwork of the building has been charred by being raised to a red heat, even without any blaze;[3] for some kinds of wood will burn away completely without ever blazing at all. But it has been held not to be sufficient that the action of the fire has scorched some of the wood to blackness, if no part of it has been actually 'consumed'. Yet even a mere blackening of wood would seem to show that the chemical constitution of its cell-walls has (as in the case of charcoal) undergone a change, and that there must consequently have been a 'decomposition' with a consequent actual loss in weight; and therefore, in fact, a 'consumption' of part of the wood, though this appears to have been denied in *R.* v. *Russell* (1842).[4]

[1] Not of the house; and not even of the chattels burned, for, though s. 7 does make it a felony to set fire to '*any* matter or thing' in (or against) a building, it does so only where the incendiary knows and disregards the danger to *the building*. *R.* v. *Child* (1871) 1 C.C.R. 307; *R.* v. *Nattrass* (1882) 15 Cox 73 (*T.A.C.*); *R.* v. *Batstone* (1864) 10 Cox 20. But he will be liable for the *misdemeanour* of malicious damage to the chattels.

[2] *R.* v. *Harris* (1882) 15 Cox 75 (*T.A.C.*). So where a man, indicted (under the Offences against the Person, Act 1861) for maliciously obstructing a railway line with intent to endanger the safety of persons travelling thereon, was found by the jury to be 'guilty of the act, but with an intent, not of causing injury, but only of gaining favour with his employers by professing to discover the obstruction', this was held to amount to a verdict of not guilty (*The Times*, 29 July 1901).

[3] *R.* v. *Parker* (1839) 9 C. and P. 45.

[4] C. and M. 541.

¶ 207. *The Firearms Act, 1937.* It only remains to mention that under the Firearms Act, 1937,[1] if any person at the time of his committing, or at the time of his apprehension for, any offence under specified sections of the Malicious Damage Act, 1861,[2] has in his possession any firearm or imitation firearm, he shall, unless he shows that he had it in his possession for a lawful object, be liable on indictment to a term of imprisonment not exceeding seven years in addition to any penalty to which he may be sentenced for the first-mentioned offence.[3]

[1] Sect. 23 and sch. III, as amended by the Criminal Justice Act, 1948.

[2] Viz. sects. 1–12, 14, 15, 26–9, 33–8 and 54.

[3] See also the Prevention of Crime Act, 1953, which deals with the unlawful carrying of weapons of various kinds. And the Restriction of Offensive Weapons Acts, 1959 and 1961.

Chapter XII

BURGLARY AND HOUSEBREAKING

SECTION I. BURGLARY

AT COMMON LAW A CAPITAL OFFENCE

¶ 208. It seems that according to the ancient authors burglary consisted in breaking into houses, churches, or the walls or gates of a town,[1] by night.[2] Later, however, it came to be defined at common law as breaking and entering the dwelling-house of another in the night, with intent to commit some felony therein, whether such felony be actually committed or not.[3]

It should be remembered that up to the early part of the nineteenth century the felony of burglary was capital. It was excluded from benefit of clergy[4] in 1575[5] but in the latter part of the eighteenth century execution could be respited and transportation substituted at the discretion of the judge.[6] But the Larceny Act of 1827[7] made burglary a capital offence without the alternative of transportation.[8] This severity of punishment tended to lead persons to hesitate to initiate prosecutions in many cases, and in others to temper their evidence in favour of the prisoner. If the cases are examined in their historical sequence it will be observed that in the earlier ones the courts took a much stricter view of the necessity to observe all the technical distinctions in the definition of burglary[9] than was done in the more modern cases after the penalties had been reduced.

UNDER THE LARCENY ACT, 1916

¶ 209. The law relating to burglary is now consolidated by the Larceny Act, 1916,[10] s. 25, which reads:

[1] So 1 Hawk. P.C. c. 38, s. 17. And see Stephen, *Hist. Crim. Law*, I, 56 and III, 150; Pollock and Maitland, II, 493. That towns should be so protected will not surprise anyone who is familiar with the Roman treatment of city-walls as *res sanctae*; or who has learned from a visit to Berwick, or York, or Chester, the importance of the defence, against private as well as public violence, which a medieval town derived from its circumvallation. The original importance of this form of the crime is illustrated by the fact that the earliest English name of the crime was *burgh-breche*. Its Latin name (A.D. 1200) was *burgaria*. See *Oxford English Dictionary*, *s.v.*

[2] In Anglo-Saxon times the crime was termed *hamsocna* and, it would seem, could be committed by day as well as by night. It was a *bót*-less offence, the punishment being death or mutilation.

[3] 3 Co. *Inst.* 63; 1 Hale P.C. 549.

[4] ¶ 55.

[5] 18 Eliz. I, c. 7.

[6] See Radzinowicz, *Hist. Eng. Crim. Law*, I, 110–12 and 328–30.

[7] 7 and 8 Geo. IV, c. 29, s. 11.

[8] Capital punishment was soon afterwards removed from this crime by 7 Will. IV and 1 Vict. c. 86, s. 3.

[9] And of larceny, ¶ 221 *post*. On this tendency see Radzinowicz, *op. cit.* I, 94–7.

[10] 6 and 7 Geo. V, c. 50, as amended by the Criminal Justice Act, 1948, s. 1.

Every person who in the night

(1) breaks and enters the dwelling-house of another with intent to commit any felony therein; or

(2) breaks out of the dwelling-house of another, having

(*a*) entered the said dwelling-house with intent to commit any felony therein; or

(*b*) committed any felony in the said dwelling-house;

shall be guilty of felony called burglary, and on conviction thereof liable to imprisonment for life.

THE PLACE

¶ 210. By the close of the medieval era it came to be settled that this must be a dwelling-house.[1]

Much technicality has arisen in determining what buildings are to be regarded as 'houses', and when a house is to be regarded as being 'dwelt' in. Clearly a house must be something more than a movable caravan or tent or booth, it must be a permanent structure. But it is not necessary that it should consist of the whole of such a structure. Thus one building may contain several dwelling-houses; each single set of chambers, or even each single room, in it may be a separate dwelling-house.[2] The test of separateness is whether or not there is internal communication between this part of the building and the rest of it.[3] If any one occupier's part has no internal communication with other parts, it becomes a separate house. Conversely, a house is regarded as including its accessory buildings that stand outside its own walls, if only they (*a*) stand in the same curtilage[4] with the house, and (*b*) are occupied along with it, and (*c*) communicate with it either directly or at least by a covered and enclosed passage.[5] So to 'break' an area gate, for the purpose of gaining admittance to the house through a door in the area, is not a breaking of the house itself.[6]

But a building, although it be a 'house', is not to be regarded, as being 'dwelt' in unless some person habitually sleeps there,[7] and sleeps in it as his *home*. He must thus be a member of the household that occupies it[8]—whether as himself the possessor[9] of the house or only as one of that possessor's family or servants—and not a mere temporary licensee whose home the place is not. But though he must sleep there habitually, he need not do so invariably, i.e. his residence may at intervals be inter-

[1] The ancient protection of churches continued, and the verbal justification for this retention was offered that 'a church is the dwelling-house of God'; 3 Co. *Inst.* 64.

[2] As in colleges; 3 Co. *Inst.* 65.

[3] *R.* v. *Egginton* (1801) 2 B. and P. 508.

[4] The 'curtilage' is the ground immediately round the house, such as passes upon a grant of the messuage without being expressly mentioned.

[5] Larceny Act, 1916, s. 46 (2). Would an underground passage suffice?

[6] *R.* v. *Davis* (1817) R. and R. 322.

[7] *R.* v. *Martin* (1806) R. and R. 108.

[8] *R.* v. *Harris* (1795) 2 Leach 701.

[9] Even a tenancy at will suffices; *R.* v. *Bridges* (1845) 1 Cox 261.

rupted. For if a householder goes away from home, but with an *animus revertendi*, his house is still considered to be a dwelling, although not a single person remains in it.[1]

THE BREAKING

¶ **211.** This may be either actual or constructive. It is considered as 'actual' whenever the intruder displaces any part of the building or of its closed fastenings. It is therefore not necessary that there should be an actual fracture of anything. Drawing a bolt, or turning a key, or even lifting a latch will suffice. And, similarly, if a 'cat burglar' climb up a rain-pipe and open a closed bedroom window, even though its sash be kept in position by nothing but its own weight, his raising the sash will amount to a 'breaking'.[2] So, too, will the raising of a cellar flap even though it be held down by nothing more than its intrinsic weight, or the turning of a swing window. Yet if a window or fanlight or door be already partly open, it will not be a 'breaking' to open it still further[3] and gain admittance thereby. The reason has been suggested for this that when a householder leaves a window or a door partly open, he gives, as it were, a visible invitation to enter; but the fact of his having left it merely unbolted is not thus conspicuous to the passers-by.

¶ **212.** *Constructive breaking.* (*a*) Besides these actual breakings, in which the intruder himself displaces the fastenings of the house, the definition of burglary has long been interpreted as covering cases in which the breaking is in reality non-existent, and is therefore, for legal purposes, designated a 'constructive' breaking. This occurs where the burglar comes into the house by some aperture which, by actual necessity, is permanently left open. There is thus a sufficient 'breaking' if the thief comes down into the house by the chimney,[4] though there would be no breaking if he came in through a window which the builders had not yet filled with glass. These cases of constructive breaking are not extensions of the law made to cover circumstances not originally envisaged; they are relics of the more strict rule of archaic law which treated as a capital offence *any* coming to a house with intent to commit a felony therein.[5]

[1] *R.* v. *Nutbrown* (1750) Foster 76.

[2] *R.* v. *Haines* (1821) R. and R. 451. In *R.* v. *Lackey* [1954] Crim. L.R. 57, it was held by Cassels, J., that a casement window, partly open, but secured there by a catch, was sufficiently 'closed', so that it would be a breaking if the accused had opened the window further, saying 'if something is secured, and that security is broken, that is a breaking'. It is, however, not easy to see the difference in principle between a window held in place by the counterweights in the ordinary window-sash box, and a window held by a casement bar lowered on to a fixed metal pin, unless it be that in the former case the window can be moved by a simple push whereas in the latter the retaining bar must first be released.

[3] *R.* v. *Smith* (1827) 1 Moo. 178.

[4] *R.* v. *Brice* (1821) R. and R. 450. Cf. the case tried at Cambridge by Sir Matthew Hale, 1 P.C. 552; and an American case (*The State* v. *Donohoe* (1860) 36 Alabama 271). In the latter, the chimney proved to be of such inadequate dimensions that the burglar stuck fast in it, and it had to be pulled down to extricate him.

[5] See 1 Hale P.C. 551.

(*b*) By a false analogy the term 'constructive breaking' has been traditionally employed to indicate also an *actual* breaking, yet one effected not by the burglar himself but by some innocent person at his instigation. Such a case, of course, is one which properly falls within the maxim '*qui facit per alium facit per se*'; so that it is inaccurate and may be misleading to call it a 'constructive breaking'. Thus if an intending burglar gains admittance to the house by threats of violence, which put the inmates into such fear that they open the door to him, there is a breaking for which he is legally responsible. Or, again, if, as is more common, he rings the bell like an ordinary visitor, and then, when the door is accordingly opened to him, he comes in on pretence of wanting to speak to some member of the household, or on pretence of being a representative of some authority or business firm whose duty it is to inspect or repair something inside the house,[1] this is held to be as true a breaking by him as if he had himself opened the door.[2] But if a pretence thus attempted should fail to deceive (so that, though the door be opened to the evil-doer, it is opened solely for the purpose of entrapping him), the law does not regard such an opening as being in any way *his* act, and therefore does not hold it to be, even 'constructively', a breaking.[3]

¶ 213. *Internal breaking. Breaking out.* It should be added that 'breaking', whether actual or constructive, need not be committed upon the external parts of the house; it will be sufficient, for instance, if an inner door be 'broken'. And therefore if a robber gain admittance to a house by means of an open window or door, but then, when inside, proceed to unlock a parlour-door and enter the parlour, he from that moment becomes guilty of burglary.[4] The same principle holds good, of course, in the case of a servant or guest who, whilst resident in the house, opens and enters any of the rooms for a felonious purpose. But whether this is to be extended to the opening of the door of a cupboard in the wall is very doubtful. There is certainly no burglarious 'breaking' in opening the door of a piece of movable furniture, like a sideboard or bureau.

At common law, to break *out of* a house did not amount to a burglarious breaking. But by statute[5] it has been provided that if a person who has committed a felony in a dwelling-house—or even has entered a dwelling-house with the intention of committing a felony—shall proceed to break out[6] of this dwelling-house by night,

[1] *R.* v. *Boyle* (1954) 38 Cr.App.R. 111.

[2] *Le Mott's Case* (166–), Kel. 42; *R.* v. *Cassy* (1666) Kel. 62.

[3] *R.* v. *Johnson* (1841) C. and M. 218 (*T.A.C.*). Contrast with this case *R.* v. *Chandler* [1913] 1 K.B. 125.

[4] Cresswell, J., held it no *burglary* if, having thus entered only by an open door, he do not enter the inner room which he 'breaks'; C.C.C. Sess. Pap. XI, 706. But it is an indictable nocturnal entering; *post*, ¶ 217.

[5] Larceny Act, 1916, s. 25. *Ante*, ¶ 209.

[6] In *R.* v. *Lawrence* (1830) 4 C. and P. 231, Bollond, B., held that leaving a house by pushing up a heavy trap-door over a cellar which was merely kept in place by its own weight, without any catch or bolt, was not breaking; this is of doubtful authority.

he is to be held guilty of a burglary. Thus while both a breaking and an entering are still necessary, either of them may now precede the other.

THE ENTERING

¶ **214**. The entry may be sufficiently made by the insertion of any part of the intruder's own body, however small that part be. Thus a finger, or even a part of a finger,[1] will suffice. And there may even be a sufficient entry—without any part whatever of the man himself having come into the house—by his inserting some instrument which he is holding. But in this case, a subtle distinction is drawn. The insertion of an instrument, unlike that of a limb, is not regarded by law as constituting an entry, unless it were thus inserted for the purpose (not merely of entering or of breaking but) of accomplishing that ulterior felony for the sake of which the house is being broken into. Thus if a man pushes a bar through a window for the simple purpose of making a hole in the shutter, there is only a breaking, but no entry.[2] Yet if he had pushed the bar through the window for the purpose of drawing towards him a spoon which he was going to steal, there would have been both a breaking and also an entry.[3] So, again, it would be no entry to push a pistol through a window, merely in order to make an aperture through which to get in. But if after having broken a window, he were to thrust a pistol through the hole, in order to shoot one of the persons in the room, this would be a sufficient entry.[4] Perhaps the best justification that can be given for this very technical distinction as to entry by instruments is that if the insertion of an instrument were always to be sufficient to constitute an 'entry' most of the common acts of breaking would of themselves include an entry, whereas the definition of burglary evidently supposes the two things to be quite distinct.

THE TIME

¶ **215**. In the earliest law, burglary might be committed in the day-time as well as at night.[5] But afterwards it became essential that it should take place at night. By 'night' was then understood the period between sunset and sunrise. Later, however, it was held not to be night if there was even sufficient sunlight to tell a man's face. This test again was discarded, and night was defined as the period between 9 p.m. and 6 a.m.[6] As to the precise instant when that period begins and ends, it should

[1] *R.* v. *Davis* (1823) R. and R. 499 (*T.A.C.*). Contrast the interpretation put upon sect. 28 (4) of the Larceny Act, 1916 (*post*, ¶ 217) in *R.* v. *Parkin* (1949) 34 Cr.App.R. 1, where it was held that the accused was not 'found *in* the building' when he was discovered with one of his hands through the window for the purpose of pulling himself into the building. And see *R.* v. *Lumsden* [1951] 1 All E.R. 1101, *post*, ¶ 217.

[2] *R.* v. *Rust and Ford* (1828) 1 Moo. 183.

[3] *R.* v. *Hughes* (1785) 1 Leach 406 (*T.A.C.*).

[4] *Anon.* (1584) 1 Anderson 114.

[5] Pollock and Maitland, II, 492.

[6] See now the Larceny Act, 1916, s. 46.

be noted that here (as always when a reference to time occurs in an Act of Parliament or other legal instrument), without the expression of a contrary mode of reckoning, it is to be understood to be *Greenwich* mean time.[1]

To constitute a burglary, then, the breaking must always take place during this statutory night-time. And if, as is usually the case, the breaking precedes the entering, both must take place at night, though not necessarily on the same night.[2] But if the entry precedes the breaking, i.e. if the latter is not a breaking-in but a breaking-*out*, the entry need not be at night.[3]

THE INTENT TO COMMIT A FELONY THEREIN

¶ 216. There must be an intention to commit some felony in the building[4] (e.g. to kill, or to commit a rape; most commonly it is an intention to steal). But it is not necessary that the felony should actually be accomplished. Moreover this intention must exist at the time of the breaking and the entering, and not arise merely after he is in the house.[5] Hence if people break open the front door of a house illegally, but only for some honest purpose (e.g. constables acting with an invalid search warrant), and then are so tempted by the sight of something inside that they steal it, they will not be guilty of any burglary.[6]

Accordingly if only a tort, or even a misdemeanour, be intended—as, for instance, to get a night's shelter,[7] or to commit an adultery or an assault—the breaking and entering for such a purpose will not be burglary, but either a civil trespass and no crime at all, or, if a crime, only an attempt to commit a misdemeanour. Thus, in 1770, where a man broke into a stable and cut the sinews of a horse's fore-leg in such a manner that it died, but it was shown that his intention had not been to kill the horse (which would have been even then a felonious act) but only to maim[8] it, so as to prevent it from running in a race, he was

[1] Except in months when the Summer Time Act prescribes sixty minutes earlier. In Ireland, *Dublin* mean time. But 'sunset' and 'sunrise', for lighting up vehicles, refer to local time.

[2] 1 Hale P.C. 551; *R.* v. *Smith* (1820) R. and R. 417.

[3] Larceny Act, 1916, s. 25.

[4] See *ante*, ¶ 12 (*a*) (iv).

[5] But if he break *out* after actually committing a felony inside, felonious intent at the time of entry is not necessary.

[6] *R.* v. *Gardiner* (1665) Kel. 46 (*T.A.C.*). But it may be housebreaking, which by s. 26 only requires that the accused breaks and enters *and* commits a felony therein.

[7] For a case where the intruder declined to quit the agreeable shelter, see *R.* v. *Pearson* (1910) 4 Cr.App.R. 40; his refusal to depart was held to confirm his contention that he had not entered for a felonious purpose but only to rest. In 1922 a charge was dismissed because the only purpose of the supposed burglars had been to see the apparitions by which the house was reputed to be haunted. See *R.* v. *Curtiss* (1925) 18 Cr.App.R. 174, as to a *bona fide* claim of right.

[8] *R.* v. *Dobbs* (1770) 2 East P.C. 513. The stable was part of a dwelling-house. See now the Malicious Damage Act, 1861, s. 40, which makes maiming of 'cattle' a felony; *ante*, ¶ 196.

held not to have committed a burglary. For in 1770, although killing a horse had already been made a statutory felony, any lesser injury to the animal was merely a tort. At the present time it is a felony not only to kill, but even to maim, a horse.[1]

The fact that the burglar actually committed some felony in the house is excellent evidence that he broke and entered it with an intention of committing this felony. Thus if he drank some wine which he found in the dining-room, this theft would be evidence, though certainly only weak evidence, that he entered the house with intent to steal. But the question is not always an easy one to answer, and it often has to be determined by a somewhat weak chain of inference. Thus in 1899 a boy broke into a house while the family were away, but contented himself with winding up all the clocks and setting them going. Had he been detected before he had undertaken this comparatively innocent course of action, he might have found it difficult to rebut the inference that he had broken into the house for purposes of theft.

PUNISHMENT

¶ 217. Under the Larceny Act, 1916, s. 25,[2] the maximum punishment for burglary is imprisonment for life. The same enactment deals also with some statutory nocturnal offences, which are approximations to burglary. We may mention the following:

(1) Entering (i.e. without breaking) a dwelling-house by night, with intent to commit felony therein, is a felony. It is punishable with seven years' imprisonment.[3]

(2) Being found by night in[4] any building (i.e. although the entry may have been effected only in the day-time), with intent to commit felony therein, is a misdemeanour. It is punishable with five years' imprisonment.[5]

(3) Being found by night in possession[6] of housebreaking imple-

[1] Malicious Damage Act, 1861, s. 40.

[2] As amended by the Criminal Justice Act, 1948, s. 1.

[3] Sect. 27 (1). But such an entry in the day-time is not indictable at all, though there may, under the Vagrancy Act, be the petty offence mentioned in note 5 *infra*.

[4] It is not enough that the accused is found with his hand through the window for the purpose of pulling himself into the building; *R.* v. *Parkin* (1949) 34 Cr.App.R. 1. But it is not necessary that he should be *apprehended* in the building nor that the finder should be in it as well as he, so long as there is clear and unmistakable evidence that he was found there: *R.* v. *Lumsden* [1951] 2 K.B. 513.

[5] Sect. 28 (4). Even in the day-time it is a petty offence, punishable with three months' imprisonment, under the Vagrancy Act, to be found in a house or an enclosed garden, for *any* criminal purpose (5 Geo. IV, c. 83, s. 4). See ¶ 485 *post.*

[6] Sect. 28 (2). Both the possession and finding must be by night, and the possession must be before arrest, *R.* v. *Harris* (1924) 18 Cr.App.R. 157; 41 T.L.R. 205; to be in possession of house-breaking tools with intent to commit a felony, irrespective of time, is an offence under the Vagrancy Act, 1824, s. 4. For the meaning of 'in possession' see *R.* v. *Lester and Byast* (1955) 39 Cr.App.R. 157, and *R.* v. *Harris* [1961] Crim. L.R. 256.

ments without lawful excuse, the proof whereof lies on the accused,[1] is a misdemeanour. It is punishable with five years' imprisonment.[2] A brick has been held to be an implement of housebreaking.[3] Contrast the South African case, *R.* v. *Poza*,[4] in which a screwdriver and some socks were held not sufficient to warrant conviction since they were not 'in their very nature proper and usually used for housebreaking'. Cf. ¶ 531 *post.* Similarly punishable are the misdemeanours of (*a*) being by night armed with a dangerous or offensive weapon or instrument with intent to break in or enter any building and to commit a felony therein and (*b*) of having the face blackened or disguised by night with intent to commit a felony.[5]

Under the Firearms Act, 1937,[6] if any person, at the time of his committing or at the time of his apprehension for any offence under sections 24–7, and 28, paras. (2) (3) and (4), has in his possession any firearm or imitation firearm, he shall, unless he shows that he had it in his possession for a lawful object, be liable to imprisonment for seven years in addition to any penalty to which he may be sentenced for the first mentioned offence.

SECTION 2. HOUSEBREAKING

¶ 218. We have seen that burglary is essentially a nocturnal offence. To do in the day-time what it would be a burglary to do at night was at common law a misdemeanour. It was known as housebreaking. But statutory enactment has now erected it into a felony. It is identical with burglary so far as concerns the breaking, the entry, and the intention that it requires. But in some points it differs from burglary. Thus (1) it is not limited to any particular hours. An indictment for burglary must state that the offence was committed at night; but an indictment for housebreaking omits all reference to time. (2) The felonious intent *need* not exist at the time of the breaking and entering, provided that a felony is actually committed in the building.[7] (3) It extends to a wider range of buildings, including shops, warehouses, etc., besides dwelling-houses. (4) It admits of different maxima of punishment according as the ulterior felony intended is actually committed or not. For it is punishable with imprisonment (i) for fourteen years, if any ulterior felony is actually committed, but (ii) only for seven years, where nothing more is proved than that the breaking and entering

[1] But although the word 'proof' is used in the section it is decided that he need do no more than raise a reasonable doubt; *R.* v. *Ward* [1915] 3 K.B. 696, a case criticized in [1961] Crim. L.R. 257 and in *R.* v. *Patterson* [1962] 1 All E.R. 340. Hence the prosecution may anticipate a possible defence of innocent possession by adducing evidence to rebut it, *R.* v. *Hodges* (1957) 41 Cr.App.R. 218. See ¶ 596, *post*, and App. II, B.

[2] Sect. 28 (2). Even in the day-time such a possession, if *with the intention of housebreaking*, would be a petty offence, similarly punishable under the Vagrancy Act.

[3] *R.* v. *Loney* [1956] Crim. L.R. 494.

[4] 1954 (4) S.A. 137.

[5] Larceny Act, 1916, s. 28 (1) and (3).

[6] Sect. 23 and sch. III as amended by the Criminal Justice Act, 1948, s. 1.

[7] Larceny Act, 1916, s. 26.

were effected *with the intent* to commit some felony.[1] A breaking-*out* will suffice in the first of these two forms, but not in the latter.[2]

Section 3. Sacrilege

¶ 219. The old idea of burglary included a sacrilegious form, in which the place broken into at night was a church. Modern enactments have replaced this by a statutory crime of sacrilege, which differs from that just now mentioned, (1) in being irrespective of the hour of the day, and (2) in extending to other places of worship besides those of the established religion. For, under provisions that are now consolidated in the Larceny Act, 1916, it is the felony of sacrilege, punishable with imprisonment for life,[3] to break and enter and commit a felony in—or to enter and commit a felony in and then to break out of—'any place of Divine worship'. And it is the felony of housebreaking, but punishable with only seven years' imprisonment, to break and enter such a place with the intention of committing a felony, though without accomplishing that intention.[4]

[1] *Ibid.* s. 27.

[2] The definitions of burglary and housebreaking are wide enough to cover acts of a very trivial character. In 1801, Andrew Branning, a boy of thirteen (to whom three witnesses gave a good character), was sentenced to death for burglary, for having, after sunset but before closing-time, broken a pane of glass in a shop window and put his hand through the hole, and stolen a spoon. See *R.* v. *Burrell* (1873) C.C.C. Sess. Pap. LXXVIII, 103.

[3] Sect. 24. As amended by the Criminal Justice Act, 1948.

[4] Sect. 27 (2).

Chapter XIII

STEALING

Section 1. Historical Outline

COMMON LAW DEFINITION

¶ 220. The distinctive feature of the crimes so far discussed has been the physical or material harm they cause to their victims, rather than any economic advantage they bring to the offender. But we now pass to offences of dishonesty, in which the main purpose is the unlawful enrichment of the perpetrators without necessarily doing any physical hurt to person or to property. Of these the most ancient in English law and the most common at the present day is theft, or larceny.[1] The first comprehensive definition[2] of theft for English law was given by Bracton[3] (who borrowed it, with some modification, from Roman law[4]) as *contrectatio rei alienae fraudulenta, cum animo furandi, invito illo domino cuius res illa fuerit* ('The fraudulent handling of another man's thing, without his agreement, and with the intention of stealing it'). The Latin word *fraudulenta* had a wide meaning in Roman law and covered dishonest dealing of many subtle kinds involving deceit and trickery; but in the days when our common law crimes were first defined the economic relations of men were simple and the main need of society was for legal protection against crimes of physical force rather than against deceit.[5] The crime of theft, or larceny, began as a trespass *vi et armis*, and the purpose was no more than to punish such dishonest dealing as took 'the violent and unmistakable form of a change of possession'.[6] The actual taking and carrying away of the material object itself has remained to the present day as an essential requirement in the crime of stealing. No one can commit larceny of anything incorporeal such as a copyright, or a debt, or the *value* of anything.[7]

NARROW CONCEPTION OF THEFT IN EARLY LAW

¶ 221. The ancient conception of theft was subsequently narrowed still further by various subtleties which were introduced by judicial decision. Some of these limitations would seem to us unaccountable, if we did not know that they had been inspired by motives of humanity. The desire of avoiding capital punishment (and in later times the desire of restricting the number of offences in which, by the old procedure in trials for felony, the accused person was denied the support of counsel

[1] *Latrocinium.*

[2] See Stephen, *Hist. Crim. Law*, III, 129, 130.

[3] Lib. 3, c. 32, fo. 150*b*.

[4] Just. *Inst.* IV, 1; *Dig.* XLVII, 2. 1. 3.

[5] Pollock and Maitland, II, 498, 'There can, we think, be little doubt that the "taking and carrying away", upon which our later law insists, had been from the first the very core of the English idea of theft'.

[6] *Ibid.*

[7] *Post*, ¶ 259.

and witnesses)[1] led our medieval judges to invent ingenious reasons for depriving many acts, that seemed naturally to fall within the definition of larceny, of all larcenous character. For so severe was the law of larceny that it exacted death as the penalty for stealing, except when the thing stolen did not exceed the value of twelve pence; see ¶ 296, *post*. This severity was ultimately tempered by two active forces. One was that which Blackstone[2] leniently terms 'a kind of pious perjury' on the part of juries, who repeatedly assessed the value of stolen articles at much below their real value.[3] The other force which similarly opposed putting men to death for thefts was that ingenious judicial interpretation which we have mentioned above.[4]

SECTION 2. STATUTORY DEFINITION

¶ 222. The first statutory definition of stealing (but *not* a definition of larceny) was given in the Larceny Act, 1916,[5] but this did not purport to make any change in the common law of larceny as it was then understood to be.[6] It runs as follows:

For the purposes of this Act

(1) a person steals who, without the consent of the owner, fraudulently and without a claim of right made in good faith, takes and carries away anything capable of being stolen with intent, at the time of such taking, permanently to deprive the owner thereof:

Provided that a person may be guilty of stealing any such thing notwithstanding that he has lawful possession thereof, if, being a bailee or part owner thereof, he fraudulently converts the same to his own use or the use of any person other than the owner:

(2) (i) the expression 'takes' includes obtaining the possession

(*a*) by any trick;

(*b*) by intimidation;

[1] *Ante*, ¶ 74. [2] 4 Bl. *Comm*. 239.

[3] Thus in 1808, to avoid convicting a woman for the capital offence of 'stealing in a dwelling-house to the value of forty shillings', a jury went so far as to find on their oaths that a £10 Bank of England note was worth only 39*s*.; *R*. v. *Macallister* (1808) C.C.C. Sess. Pap. LXXXVI, 18. Sir S. Romilly mentioned another case, in 1732, where a woman had stolen two guineas and two half-guineas, yet the jury pronounced the total value of the four coins to be 'under 40*s*.' In 1823, in an indictment for stealing a guinea and a sovereign, their value was prudently placed at *ten pence*, in order to make a conviction more probable (*The Times*, 21 Oct. 1823). See Radzinowicz, *Hist. Eng. Crim. Law*, I, 94 *et seq*.

[4] For examples see ¶ 270, *post*. [5] 6 and 7 Geo. V, c. 50, s. 1.

[6] When introducing the Bill in the House of Lords the Lord Chancellor said: 'The Bill...is nothing but a careful compilation of all the existing law relating to larceny and kindred offences... This Bill has faithfully consolidated the existing law and not imposed anything new.' The words 'existing law' must be taken to mean both common law and statute law (e.g. embezzlement, fraudulent conversion, stealing dogs, etc.). The Act only deals with larceny triable on indictment and kindred offences. Some thefts that are punishable only on summary conviction, such as the first offence of stealing a dog, are dealt with in unrepealed sections of the Larceny Act, 1861.

(*c*) under a mistake on the part of the owner with knowledge on the part of the taker that possession has been so obtained;

(*d*) by finding, where at the time of the finding the finder believes that the owner can be discovered by taking reasonable steps;

(ii) the expression 'carried away' includes any removal of anything from the place which it occupies, but in the case of a thing attached, only if it has been completely detached;

(iii) the expression 'owner' includes any part owner, or person having possession or control of, or a special property in, anything capable of being stolen.

On this basis, a definition of the narrower crime of simple larceny is established in section 2, which[1] declares that 'stealing for which no special[2] punishment is provided under this Act or any other Act[3] for the time being in force shall be simple larceny and a felony punishable with [imprisonment] for any term not exceeding five years.'[4] The Act also recognizes a variety of other forms of felonious stealing that are punishable with periods of long detention varying up to imprisonment for life. Some of the graver of these had, before the Act, been classed together as 'compound', or 'aggravated', or 'grand' larceny; but, none of these antitheses to 'simple' appears in the Act. No definition of 'larceny', in the abstract, is given; perhaps it must now be 'felonious stealing'. The marginal notes of sections 5, 11 and 16 (*b*) of the Act apply the term 'larceny' to species of stealing which do have 'special punishments', and moreover are less severely punishable than simple larceny; but the modern view is that marginal notes are not part of the statute.[5]

ACTUS REUS IN LARCENY

¶ 223. The *actus reus* in the early common law was simple. It is abundantly clear that it comprised only three facts and was constituted when a man (1) without the consent of the owner (*invito domino*), (2) seized a thing (*cepit*) and (3) carried (or drove) it away (*asportavit*).[6] These essentials still exist, as is to be seen in the definition given in

[1] As modified by the Criminal Justice Act, 1948.

[2] Even the words 'to be punished as in the case of simple larceny' constitute a 'special punishment'; cf. s. 37 (2). Cf. *R.* v. *Millar* (1837) 7 C. and P. 665; *R.* v. *Gooch* (1838) 8 C. and P. 293.

[3] E.g. the Army Act, 1955, s. 70, and the Naval Discipline Act, 1957, s. 42.

[4] As to the question whether this provision creates a specific crime of 'simple larceny', see *post*, ¶ 297, and *R.* v. *Bryant* [1955] 1 W.L.R. 715; 39 Cr.App.R. 59 (*post*, ¶ 297); Russ. 1165.

[5] *Nixon* v. *A.-G.* [1930] 1 Ch. 566, at pp. 593, 594. Halsbury's *Laws of England* (1938), XXXI, 464.

[6] Students should note that the suggestion in *R.* v. *Turvey* [1946] 2 All E.R. 60 that the word *asportavit* indicated the absence of the owner's consent must be regarded as an unfortunate slip made *per incuriam*.

section 1 of the Act of 1916. It was essential at common law to allege and prove both the taking and the carrying away: as Coke said,[1] 'an indictment *quod felonice abduxit equum* is not good, because it wanteth *cepit*'.

THE TAKING

¶ 224. Notwithstanding Bracton's adoption, in his definition, of the Latin word *contrectatio*[2] the English law of larceny extended only to such wrongful dealing with movable property as consisted in an actual physical change of control, i.e. the plain act of seizing hold of the thing, and taking it away.[3] The taking must be a seizing of the thing *acquisitively*. It is not enough merely to touch the thing, or to move it, or even to pick it up if these actions are no more than *inquisitive* in order to ascertain what the thing is. What is needed is a *taking into possession*. See *post*, ¶¶ 227, 253, 358. Hence the words of sect. 1 (2) (i) must be carefully considered: '*the expression "takes" includes obtaining the possession* . . .'. These words and those which follow explain the scope of subsection (1) by amplifying the meaning of the one word 'takes' which figures therein: but they do not remove or affect in any way any other part of subsection (1); for example the words 'without the consent of the owner' remain as an essential element in the definition of the offence of stealing, and they dominate and govern the whole of section 1 of the Act.[4]

Hence the words 'by any trick' do not relieve the prosecution of the necessity of proving that the owner did not consent to the prisoner's taking the thing acquisitively into his possession. If the trick employed by the accused deceives the owner into consenting, then, although the consent is vitiated it is not negatived[5] and therefore there is no larceny.[6] The words 'by intimidation' merely confirm the well-established rule that no one is allowed to set up in his own defence any surrender which he has forced from another by threats of harm.[7] The words 'under a mistake' are explained below, ¶ 251, and the words 'by finding' are considered in ¶ 253.

[1] 3 *Inst.* 107.

[2] Which in Roman law connoted almost any kind of dishonest dealing with the thing, although in that system also the whole of the thing had to be moved.

[3] *Anon.* (1584) Crompton 35*a* (*T.A.C.*). Stephen, *Hist. Crim. Law*, III, 133, conjectured that this narrowness in early law was favoured because the only available proceedings for the owner were (*a*) appeal, in which he might lose his life in trial by combat, or (*b*) indictment in which, although successful, he would not be able to recover his property, which would be forfeited to the Crown. But by *civil* proceedings for trespass he would not have the hazard of battle and could be awarded compensation.

[4] See *Moynes* v. *Coopper* [1956] 1 Q.B. 439; *post*, ¶ 251.

[5] But see *post*, ¶¶ 247, 248, 249.

[6] There may, of course, be some other crime, e.g. the misdemeanour of false pretences under sect. 32 of the Act. On 'larceny by trick' see *Oppenheimer* v. *Frazer* [1907] 2 K.B. 50 at p. 77, *post*, ¶ 235, note 4; and *R.* v. *Fisher* (1910) 5 Cr.App.R. 102 at p. 107, *post*, ¶ 238.

[7] ¶ 250 *post*.

THE SEIZING, A TRESPASS

¶ 225. A strict distinction was made between the seizing of the thing, which could be effected by laying hands upon it without moving it, and the carrying of it away, for which it was necessary that the whole of the thing should be *moved from its place*. Simply to lay hands on a man's thing without his permission would be a trespass, therefore it was held that there could be no larceny without trespass: the converse, however, is not true, because for larceny in addition to the trespass by seizing (*cepit*) there must always be the *moving* away of the thing (*asportavit*) also. But the taking and carrying away need not be by the hand of the prisoner; it is enough if he procures some innocent person (or even an animal, such as a dog) to take the thing for him.[1]

THE ASPORTATION

¶ 226. The slightest removal of the whole thing will suffice and the crime is then complete even though the thief at once abandon the thing,[2] or subsequently change his mind and return it. The test seems to be: Has every atom left the place in which that particular atom was before? Thus there may be a sufficient asportation even though part of the thing still occupies the place which some other part of it previously did; e.g. by half-drawing a sword from its scabbard, or pushing a bag part-way out of the boot of a coach,[3] or pulling a pocket-book not quite out of a man's pocket.[4] But if the thing is attached either to the land or to a person it must be entirely detached therefrom (see ¶ 278 *post*).

SECTION 3. POSSESSION

¶ 227. Larceny was always conceived as an offence against possession,[5] and naturally so, since English law has never recognized in a subject of the realm any absolute right of ownership of chattels, our 'owner' being merely the person who has the best right to possess the thing. It follows therefore that a man can be guilty of larceny by stealing a thing from another who had himself stolen that thing from someone else, for a thief holds possession (albeit *mala fide*) of what he has stolen. Moreover it must be remembered that even a child of tender years[6] may have

[1] E.g. getting an ostler at an inn to saddle another person's horse by pretending that it is your own; *R.* v. *Pitman* (1826) 2 C. and P. 423 (*T.A.C.*).

[2] E.g. to take plate out of a chest and lay it on the floor, *R.* v. *Simson* (1664) Kel. 31; to shift a bale from the back to the front of a cart, *R.* v. *Coslet* (1782) 1 Leach 236 (but not so where the prisoner had raised up and slit open one end only of a long parcel of cloth, *R.* v. *Cherry* (1781) 1 Leach 236 (*T.A.C.*)); also pulling an ear-ring from a woman's ear, even though it were then caught by and remained in her hair, *R.* v. *Lapier* (1784) 1 Leach 320 (*T.A.C.*).

[3] *R.* v. *Walsh* (1824) 1 Moo. 14.

[4] *R.* v. *Taylor* [1911] 1 K.B. 674.

[5] A thief, must 'take possession'. If therefore a thing happens to be already in a man's possession he cannot thereafter 'take it' so as to become guilty of the felony of stealing it (unless he be bailee); see *post*, ¶ 290.

[6] *Haynes' Case* (1614) 12 Co. Rep. 113.

legal possession of property. It was failure to appreciate this point that led to the basic fallacy in the severely criticized[1] dictum in *Walters* v. *Lunt*[2] to the effect that the parents would be guilty of larceny by finding when they received from their child, aged seven, property which the child had dishonestly purloined and brought home. That a child of that age could not be guilty of crime is irrelevant to the present point; for the thing, whether stolen or not, was *in the possession of the child* and therefore could not be 'found' by the parents within the meaning of the rule as to 'larceny by finding', which is discussed below, ¶ 253. In a somewhat similar case, *McGregor* v. *Benyon*,[3] a magistrates' court avoided following the principle of *Walters* v. *Lunt* by distinguishing the facts, and acquitted the accused parent of larceny by finding; but on a case stated the Queen's Bench Divisional Court reversed the magistrate and, as reported, simply declared that the dictum in *Walters* v. *Lunt* was not obiter, and was binding on the court below, and that the mother 'had adopted her daughter's acts',[4] so that 'it was as though she had found the handbag herself and she could not rely upon the child's defence of infancy'. This judgment was even more strongly criticized[5] than the original dictum had been and it certainly appears contrary to principle and to authority. On such facts of the case as are stated in the report it would seem that the mother might properly have been prosecuted for an offence contrary to section 32 of the Larceny Act.

Turning to the nature of the concept 'possession', it must be noted that, to begin with, in the common law there were none of the modern difficulties in fixing its precise meaning[6] which in those days denoted *actual control* as understood in everyday life; the word had no technical, legal meaning. If a man had a thing in such a place and in such conditions as the ordinary English owner usually kept it, then he controlled it sufficiently to make it a felony dishonestly to take it away without his consent. Thus for the purposes of the law of larceny a man held in his possession all his goods in all parts of his house, all his domestic animals

[1] E.g. in 68 *L.Q.R.* 167, 15 *Mod. L.R.* 222, and [1957] *Crim. L.R.* 252 and 609. The dictum indeed must be regarded as one of the unfortunate manifestations of the modern tendency of the higher courts to usurp the functions of the legislature at the cost of the confounding of legal principle.

[2] [1951] 2 All E.R. 645.

[3] [1957] Crim. L.R. 250.

[4] The precise significance of this curious expression (which, it may be remembered, was used, ineffectually, in a case of receiving in 1857, *R.* v. *Dring*, 7 Cox 382) was not explained.

[5] [1957] Crim. L.R. 609.

[6] Which Erle, C.J., in *R.* v. *Smith* (1853) 6 Cox 554 called 'that vaguest of all vague questions'. Note the bewildering variability of meaning apparently given to 'possession' by the Q.B. Divisional Court in *Towers & Co. Ltd* v. *Gray* [1961] 2 All E.R. 68, by a judgment which, *inter alia*, states that its meaning 'depends on the context in which it is used', and that 'you should give the word its popular and common-sense meaning in the particular context'; but does not make it clear whether the judge or the jury are to settle what is the 'popular meaning'. In such a situation of authoritative uncertainty, ignorance of the law seems to have become an inevitable misfortune.

in his stables and fields, the fish in his fishpond, the bees in his hive, and so on. But strictly speaking he did not, in this simple conception, 'possess' such of his things as another person, e.g. his servant or his guest, might, while on his premises, be holding at any given moment, although (in the normal case) they had taken up, or received, these things into their hands with his consent. From this it followed, in the most ancient period of our law, that they would not commit the felony if they proceeded dishonestly to make away with the things, because the words *invito domino* of the definition applied *both* to the seizing (*cepit*) *and* to the carrying away (*asportavit*).

LEGAL POSSESSION

¶ 228. Quite early, however, the desire of property owners to enjoy the protection which the fierce sanctions of the criminal law of felony could give them against the dishonesty of their servants or guests led the judges to create the artificial doctrine of 'legal'[1] possession as distinguished from actual physical control. Under this fiction the owner was treated as retaining 'legal' possession notwithstanding that he allowed the actual physical control of the thing to pass into the hands of his servant or of his guest.[2]

Servants

¶ 229. At first the master only retained legal possession so long as the servant was given the control of the thing whilst still on the master's premises or land. If the master had permitted the servant to take it away from his land and he then dishonestly appropriated it this was no felony.[3] There was also a doubt as to whether it would be felony if a servant purloined from the house itself property such as jewels in a casket which had been *expressly* committed to his charge.[4] But further extensions by interpretation and by statute were made until it was finally established that a servant never has *legal* possession of such of his master's property as he controls by virtue of his position as servant. And this rule is confirmed in the Larceny Act, 1916, s. 17, which thus distinguishes the servant from the ordinary bailee who is expressly mentioned in sect. 1. Of course if the servant is at the time not acting in that capacity (e.g. if he is on holiday) then he could in certain circumstances become a bailee of a thing entrusted to him by his master. Where, however, a thing which is *not already in the master's possession* comes into the hands of the servant *for* the master from some outside source, then it has never been larceny if the servant, having thus acquired control of

[1] Or 'constructive' as it came to be called in modern times. See ¶ 290 *post*.

[2] 'Guest' includes a customer at an inn: see (1353) 27 Libr.Ass. 39 (*T.A.C.*) and (1473) Y.B. 13 Edw. IV, Pasch. pl. 5.

[3] (1506) Y.B. 21 Hen. VII, Hil. fo. 14, pl. 21, 'if I deliver a horse to my servant to ride to the market, and he flees with it, it is not felony, for he comes legally by the horse through delivery'.

[4] Such doubts were removed by statute in 1529 (21 Hen. VIII, c. 7).

it, should proceed dishonestly to appropriate it before it reaches the legal possession of the master.

Here again criminal policy eventually came to the aid of the owner and by a statute of 1799[1] the legislature elevated this situation into the list of felonies, under the name of embezzlement.[2] Nowadays therefore the distinction may be briefly stated thus: the dishonest servant commits larceny of the chattel which he takes *out* of his master's possession, but embezzlement of the chattel which he intercepts *before* it has reached his master's possession.[3]

Guests and others

¶ 230. This conception of an imaginary legal possession continuing after actual physical control is parted with led to further extensions of criminal liability, so that in addition to the early cases of the guest in the house using his host's table-ware, and the visitor or lodger in an inn and the like, it has long been held that legal possession is not lost when, for example, a shopkeeper allows a customer to handle goods the better to inspect them[4] or where the owner of a suit-case hands it to someone to carry to his hotel and walks by his side to that destination. Similarly where at a railway station a woman handed to a man, who was nearer than she to the booking office window, a sovereign with which to buy a ticket for her and he ran off with it, his offence was held to be larceny.[5] And a passenger's luggage on the outside of the cab in which he is riding is, even at common law, still in his legal possession.[6]

SECTION 4. BAILMENT

STEALING BY BAILEES

¶ 231. When the servant and the guest had been deprived of the immunity from the guilt of larceny which their permitted control of the owner's chattel had given them, there still remained the problem of the ordinary bailee to whom the chattel had been entrusted, and into whose possession it had passed. Since he took into his possession and carried away the thing with the consent of the owner it was within the clear principle of the common law that a subsequent appropriation by him, however dishonest, could not be a felony.[7]

[1] 39 Geo. III, c. 85. Before this statute it was not a crime at all.

[2] Now contained in s. 17 (1) (*b*) of the Larceny Act, 1916. See ¶ 318 *post*.

[3] Or such other destination as the master has expressly or impliedly ordered.

[4] *R.* v. *Chisser* (1678) T. Raym. 275 (*T.A.C.*). Sometimes erroneously treated as a case of bailment; see Russ. 1041. Cf. *R.* v. *Williams* (1834) 6 C. and P. 390 (*T.A.C.*).

[5] *R.* v. *Thompson* (1862) L. and C. 225.

[6] And see *R.* v. *Smith* (1852) 2 Den. 449.

[7] (1462) Y.B. 2 Edw. IV, Pasch. pl. 9; (1481) Y.B. 21 Edw. IV, Hil. 9.

In *Raven's Case* (1660) Kel. 24 it was held that a *tenant* (not a *lodger*) of a furnished apartment, who had absconded with the bed-clothes, was not guilty of felony. For he was, under his contract, a hirer and therefore a possessor, as bailee, of the chattels. The predicament of landlords was remedied thirty years later by 3 Will. and M. c. 9, s. 5

Indeed it seems that in the vague early law of bailment the bailee was in some ways placed in a stronger position than the owner himself.[1]

¶ 232. *The Carrier's Case.* A noteworthy disregard of the immunity of the bailee was displayed by the judges in 1473,[2] as the result of the insistence of the King.[3] In that year there came before the Star Chamber the case of a carrier to whom a foreign merchant had entrusted bales of merchandise to carry to Southampton; the carrier dishonestly took them to another place where he broke into the bales and took therefrom the goods, which he made away with. Since up to that time there was no doubt that under the common law a bailee could not commit larceny the judges were in a difficulty to see how this particular case of gross dishonesty could be dealt with. After much discussion they differed and came to no conclusion.[4] But finally,[5] without giving their reasons, they reported to the Lord Chancellor that in the opinion of the majority it was felony.[6]

THE RULE AS TO 'BREAKING BULK'

¶ 233. For a long time after *The Carrier's Case* was decided we do not find anything in the records to show that it was taken as establishing any general rule whereby dishonest bailees could be brought within the criminal law. Yet it is plain that owners of property were handicapped by the immunity which the common law gave to their bailees. Their need compelled attention, so that eventually (although long after the date of *The Carrier's Case*) we find the judges accepting as a principle of law the proposition that if a bailee should 'break bulk' (i.e. break into the unit of property entrusted to him) he brought the bailment to an end, and, by some mysterious process of reasoning, was held thereby to have lost possession of the property which had been bailed to him. As authority for this strange argument, *The Carrier's Case* was cited, although an examination of the report of that case does not support this contention.[7] In truth the new rule was arbitrary and rested on no sound principle at all.[8] It covered adequately many instances of

which made such conduct larceny; this enactment, for this special case, in effect created a special crime of larceny by bailees of this one kind; now Larceny Act, 1916, s. 16.

[1] (1322) Y.B. 16 Edw. II, fo. 490. See Pollock and Maitland, II, 176 *et seq.*

[2] *The Carrier's Case*, Y.B. 13 Edw. IV, fo. 9, Pasch, pl. 5 (*T.A.C.*).

[3] At that period the King was deriving revenue by the granting of licences to foreign merchants to enable them to trade in England. On this case see Stephen, *Hist. Crim. Law*, III, 139, and Hall, *Theft, Law, and Society* (1935).

[4] Even at a second hearing when the case was brought before them in the Exchequer Chamber.

[5] Doubtless under the instructions of the King.

[6] An 'extraordinary decision', as Stephen calls it.

[7] The nearest approach to it was made by Choke, J., who suggested that it was the bale and not its contents that might be regarded as the chattel bailed. This absurdly artificial suggestion was not accepted by Brian, C.J., and was not supported by any other of the judges. See Russ. 1037 *et seq.*

[8] As East says (2 P.C. 695), 'This principle...seems to stand more upon positive law, not now to be questioned, than upon sound reasoning'.

dishonest pilfering by bailees, but there were doubts about its application to the facts of particular cases.[1] However, the position was cleared by a straightforward statutory provision in 1857,[2] now contained in almost the same words in the Larceny Act, 1916, s. 1, which rendered unnecessary the absurd reasoning of the common law invention by making it a felonious theft whenever a bailee dishonestly converts[3] to his own or another's use the thing which had been bailed to him.[4] But before this statutory change was made the judges had once more distorted legal principle in order to bring into the class of felons some at least of the bailees who misappropriated the *whole* of the chattel which had been bailed to them. This they did by devising a new felony which came to be called 'larceny by a trick'.

LARCENY BY A TRICK

¶ 234. *R.* v. *Pear*. The crime of 'larceny by a trick' was created in 1779 to effect the conviction of a man named Pear who had hired a horse with the intention of selling it and absconding with the proceeds, an intention which he in fact fulfilled.[5] It was clear that he was a bailee of the horse and as there could be no question of breaking bulk he could not, as the law then stood, be guilty of larceny.[6] He had entered into a perfectly good contract of bailment, and even if this was vitiated by his fraudulent intention it was not, under the law of contract, rendered *void* thereby.[7] The real reason why, under the original common law rule, the bailee could not commit larceny was because he had received the thing *with the consent of the owner*, and not because he was a bailee. The judges, however, resolved to uphold his conviction and, disregarding the civil law of contract, propounded a doctrine which runs to the following effect: 'If a man who has from the beginning the intent to misappropriate another's chattel induces that other to pass the possession of it to him under an agreement for its bailment and then proceeds to

[1] E.g. one consignment consisting of a number of kegs, *R.* v. *Madox* (1805) R. and R. 92; a package of articles which it was the bailee's duty to sell separately, *R.* v. *Poyser* (1851) 2 Den. 233; a cartload of coal, *R.* v. *Cornish* (1854) Dearsly 425. See Russ. 1040 *et seq.*

[2] 20 and 21 Vict. c. 54, s. 4.

[3] See ¶ 245 *post.*

[4] Whether the whole thing or only part of it, since breaking of bulk, if it is done, is enough to constitute a conversion of the whole thing to his use. By these measures the legislature created the crime of larceny by bailee (see *R.* v. *Bryant* [1955] 2 All E.R. 406 at p. 407, *per* Lord Goddard, C.J.), which thus became a distinct offence long before the misdemeanour of fraudulent conversion was created in 1901 by 1 Ed. VII, c. 10; this latter crime does not touch the dishonest bailee as such, see ¶ 327 *post.*

[5] *R.* v. *Pear* (1779) 1 Leach 212 (*T.A.C.*).

[6] See 3 Co. *Inst.* 107; 1 Hale P.C. 504.

[7] Although it was *voidable* at the option of the bailor; Salmond and Williams, *Contracts* (1945); Hamson, 'The effect of a secret fraudulent intent', 51 *L.Q.R.* 653. But even the avoidance of the contract by the bailor would not eliminate his previous *consent* to allow the bailee to take possession of the horse. As Scrutton, L.J., said in *Folkes* v. *King* [1923] 1 K.B. at p. 305, 'I do not quite understand the view that...if there is no contract there is no consent. There may be consent to a state of facts without any contract at all'. This dictum was approved in *Pearson* v. *Rose & Young Ltd.* [1950] 2 All E.R. 1027.

make away with it, this is larceny.' The reason given was that the secret fraudulent intention on one side negatived any real and *bona fide* contract so that there was no bailment and therefore there was 'on the whole a taking against the will of the owner'.[1] This decision has been vigorously criticized[2] but the opportunity it gave to secure the conviction of dishonest bailees caused it to be followed constantly.[3] It is important to note that the judges were careful to indicate that where a fraudulent intent of an identical kind had inspired the offender when he induced his victim to enter into a contract for the transfer of the *ownership* of the chattel to him, and to transfer it thereunder, then it would *not* negative the owner's consent so as to make the offender guilty of larceny. Logically, however, the secret fraud of the offender ought in this latter case also to have the same effect as the judges held it to have in the case before them where possession only had been obtained. In truth neither principle nor logic were allowed to prevail against the desire to convict the prisoner Pear who had perpetrated what must at that time have been a common and most annoying depredation on other people's property.[4] However, as we have seen, the anomalies of *Pear's Case* were superseded when the legislature in 1857 rendered it a felony for a bailee to misappropriate the object bailed. From that time onwards the prosecution has never needed to discharge what was sometimes the difficult burden of proving that the prisoner had from the very beginning been inspired by an intention to steal. For it was always agreed that if the bailee's dishonest plan had been formed *after* he had obtained possession then the doctrine of *Pear's Case* would not apply.[5]

THE CONFIDENCE TRICK

¶ 235. The rule thus created in *R.* v. *Pear* was freely applied by the courts to secure the conviction of dishonest bailees such as those who effected a fraudulent transaction known in modern times as 'the confidence trick', whereby they were enabled to decamp with money or goods which they had induced their victims to deposit with them as a guarantee of mutual good faith. Examples of this fraud are 'ring-dropping' and 'purse-dropping'. In these a worthless ring or a purse containing some imitation jewellery or false securities is placed on the ground in some public place by a confederate while the prisoner approaches by the side of some stranger whom he has selected as his dupe. On nearing the object on the ground the prisoner rushes forward, picks it up, and after showing it to the stranger, agrees to share

[1] *Per* Eyre, B., in *R.* v. *Pear.*

[2] E.g. Beale, 'The borderland of larceny' (1892), 6 *Harvard L.R.* at p. 305. See Russ. 1043 *et seq.*, and 2 East P.C. 685.

[3] E.g. *R.* v *Russett* [1892] 2 Q.B. 312 (*T.A.C.*) *per* Lord Coleridge, C.J., at p. 314. See ¶ 237 *post.*

[4] For a full discussion of *R.* v. *Pear* see Russ. 1043 *et seq.* And see *Du Jardin* v. *Beadman Bros.* [1952] 2 Q.B. 710, at p. 718.

[5] This was declared by Ashhurst, J., in *Pear's Case* itself; *Oppenheimer* v. *Frazer* [1907] 2 K.B. 50; *Heap* v. *Motor Advisory Agency* [1923] 1 K.B. 577.

the proceeds with him if he will take it to sell, meanwhile depositing something of value of his own as security. If the prosecutor does so the prisoner decamps with the security leaving the prosecutor to discover that the contents of the purse are valueless.[1] The arbitrary doctrine of *Pear's Case* thus had a practical value in bringing within the criminal law some acts of dishonesty which otherwise could not have been dealt with. Sometimes a strained interpretation of the facts of a case was made in order to enable the doctrine to be applied. Thus in *R.* v. *Rodway*[2] the prisoner was convicted of larceny of a receipt which had not been bailed to him but which had been passed over before the whole of the money due as rent had been paid, although in evidence the prosecutor said that when he put it into the prisoner's hands he did not expect or want to have it back again, but wanted his rent to be paid. But after the statute of 1857[3] had made it larceny for a bailee dishonestly to convert to his own use the whole or part of the property bailed there was no longer any need to retain this uncouth legal anomaly.[4] For by virtue of the statute it is irrelevant whether or not the bailee had formed the *animus furandi* previously to the moment when he converts the property. If he has indeed been fraudulent from the very beginning,[5] then he commits the common law felony so soon as he succeeds in inducing the owner to pass the thing into his hands, for he thereby both becomes bailee and converts to his own use.[6]

¶ 236. *R.* v. *Buckmaster.*[7] Unfortunately the courts from time to time have sought to make use of the old conception of 'larceny by a trick', partly from a desire to convict obviously dishonest men who might otherwise have escaped, and partly, it would seem, from a misunderstanding of the doctrine itself. In the result some very unsatisfactory cases are recorded which reveal inconsistencies in principle and strange views of fact. One difficulty was that for a long time after 1857 where the indictment was for larceny only, there could be no conviction if the evidence established that the offence was not that felony but was the misdemeanour of obtaining the ownership of the goods by false pretences.[8]

Again in some instances a man may have obtained the *ownership* of goods

[1] *R.* v. *Patch* (1782) 1 Leach 238; *R.* v. *Moore* (1784) 1 Leach 314; *R.* v. *Watson* (1793) 2 Leach 640. See Russ. 1055 *et seq.* There are of course many variations in the details of this type of fraud.

[2] (1841) 9 C. and P. 784.

[3] 20 and 21 Vict. c. 54, s. 4.

[4] Thus in *Oppenheimer* v. *Frazer* [1907] 2 K.B. 50, at p. 77, Kennedy, C.J., said: 'The expression "larceny by a trick" is not really a legal expression indicating a distinct kind of larceny. It is merely...an inconvenient mode of describing certain cases of larceny in which the goods have neither been taken by force, nor clandestinely without the knowledge of the owner. The cases so described are none the less cases of stealing.'

[5] A fact which, of course, in most cases it is difficult to prove.

[6] That such was the fact can only be shown by his subsequent conduct in relation to the thing bailed to him.

[7] (1887) 20 Q.B.D. 182 (*T.A.C.*).

[8] This difficulty is now overcome by s. 44 (3) of the Larceny Act, 1916, which replaced s. 39 (2) of the Criminal Justice Administration Act, 1914.

or money by entering into a contract which he does not intend to perform; yet he may not have made any such false pretence as would constitute the misdemeanour of thereby obtaining the property.[1] In order to circumvent this difficulty and to justify the conviction of a dishonest man, in *R.* v. *Buckmaster* the Court for Crown Cases Reserved took a strange view of the evidence and in effect held as a fact that when a man on a race-course made a bet with a bookmaker and handed over in cash the amount of his bet, receiving in return the usual betting card, he did not part with his ownership of the coins but merely deposited them by way of bailment with the bookmaker; notwithstanding that in his evidence the prosecutor had made it plain[2] that he never expected or desired to have back the same particular coins which he had handed to the bookmaker.[3]

At the date when *R.* v. *Buckmaster* was heard the crime of fraudulent conversion (¶ 324, *post*) was not available. If, however, the welshing bookmaker is not to be regarded simply as a man who has committed a dishonest breach of an illegal contract, but as one who must be dealt with as a criminal then, it is suggested, the crime of fraudulent conversion might at the present day offer a better charge to bring against him. For it could be argued that the bookmaker has been entrusted with the ownership of the money on the understanding that if the horse should win he must return to the backer at least the same amount of money (i.e. the 'proceeds'[4] of the coins he received) as that which had been handed to him when the bet was made.[5]

¶ 237. *R.* v. *Russett.* Another unsatisfactory case was *R.* v. *Russett*[6] in which it was proved that the prosecutor at a fair had made an unconditional purchase of a horse from the prisoner, paying £8 down by way of part payment, the horse to be delivered on payment by him of the balance which he expected to obtain very soon, the transaction being recorded in writing. The prisoner, without waiting for the balance to be paid, kept the £8 and caused the horse to be removed from the fair in circumstances which led the jury to decide that he did not intend to deliver it. The prisoner was convicted of larceny of the £8 although in evidence the prosecutor had stated that when he paid over the money he never expected to see it again, but did expect to have the horse. The conviction was upheld by the Court for Crown Cases Reserved who went so far as to hold, contrary to his own evidence on the point, that the

[1] Larceny Act, 1916, s. 32, *post*, ¶ 340.

[2] As must surely be obvious to any person who has ever placed a bet in such circumstances. Moreover, it was not clear on the evidence that Buckmaster *at the time the money was first handed to him* (an essential element in the *Pear* doctrine of larceny by a trick) intended to welsh; an intention to do so can seldom arise until the bookmaker finds that his commitments are such that if a particular horse wins he will not have enough money to pay those who backed it.

[3] The arguments by which the court supported their decision are patently unsound; see the criticism of this case in Russ. 1059 *et seq.*

[4] ¶ 330 *post.*

[5] Save in the rare case of a dead heat by an odds-on favourite.

[6] [1892] 2 Q.B.D. 312 (*T.A.C.*). The judgment in this case was strongly criticized in (1892), 6 *Harvard L.R.* 244 by Beale, 'The borderland of larceny', at p. 256. And see Russ. 1062 *et seq.*

prosecutor did not intend to pass ownership of the money but only the possession of it.

¶ 238. *R.* v. *Jones.* Another case which must be read with great care is *R.* v. *Jones.*[1] This was an appeal against sentence by a man who had pleaded guilty to fraudulent conversion of a sum of £3. The appellant was a jobbing painter who had contracted with a woman to decorate a room in her house for a fixed sum. He asked for and obtained from her a payment of £3 in advance, to be set against the contract price, stating that he had not enough money available to purchase the paint needed. He failed to do any of the promised decoration, in circumstances which strongly suggested that he was dishonest and had never intended to do the work at all. The indictment contained five counts, some charging him with larceny of the money he had received and some with fraudulent conversion of it. His plea of not guilty to the charges of larceny was accepted and on his plea of guilty to the charges of conversion he was sentenced to eighteen months' imprisonment. On the principles explained earlier in the present book it is plain that he could not be guilty of larceny of the £3 since the owner of it had transferred it voluntarily into his ownership by way of prepayment of part of the contract price. He was therefore in no sense a bailee of the money, and since he had obtained ownership of it, he could not possibly be guilty of the ancient crime of larceny by a trick under the doctrine of *R.* v. *Pear.*[2] He had not been charged with obtaining the money by false pretences. Even if he had been so charged there was no evidence that his statement that he had not got enough money to buy paint was untrue; moreover, his promise to do the work related to the future.[3] Finally, the money was paid as part of the contract price and there was nothing whatever to establish or even to suggest that it was 'entrusted' to him for any particular and understood purpose. If, for example, he had used the money to pay an outstanding debt for paint previously bought by him for other work and because of this he had been allowed to take on credit the paint now required, there could have been no objection taken by the prosecutor. In truth all that Jones had committed, dishonest as he may have been, was a breach of contract.

Having pleaded guilty, all that he could appeal against was his sentence, but for that purpose the facts of the case came before the Court of Criminal Appeal who were incidentally forced to consider the conviction itself. This they quashed, on the grounds that there was no case whatever of fraudulent conversion since there was no fiduciary relationship.[4] Unfortunately, however, the court let fall certain declarations of principle which it must be respectfully maintained were unguarded and misleading. Thus at p. 13 it was said, 'It cannot be said that the money remained the money of the persons who gave it to the appellant, and he could not therefore be guilty of fraudulently converting it to his own use.' In regard to this remark it may be pointed out that the fact that the ownership of the money had completely passed to Jones

[1] (1948) 33 Cr.App.R. 11. [2] *Ante,* ¶ 234. [3] *Post,* ¶ 346.

[4] *Post,* ¶ 329. *R.* v. *Bryce* (1956) 40 Cr.App.R. 62 follows *R.* v. *Jones* on the point that a fiduciary element is necessary.

so far from making it impossible that he could be guilty of fraudulently converting it to his own use was indeed a fact which would be essential to the success of a prosecution under the charge of fraudulent conversion made in the indictment (i.e. the misdemeanour constituted by the Larceny Act, 1916, sect. 20 (1) (iv));[1] the sole reason why Jones was not guilty was because the money was not 'entrusted' to him within the meaning of the Act, so as to create a fiduciary relationship between him and the prosecutor. The court also expressed the view that 'the appellant might very well have been convicted of larceny by a trick', and later said (at p. 13), 'The appellant is in exactly the same position as a welshing bookmaker.[2] Why the welshing bookmaker is held guilty of larceny is that when he receives the punter's stake he does not intend to pay out if he loses, but simply to appropriate the money and run away with it.' With all due respect it must be pointed out that these statements do not accord with authority. Notwithstanding the anomalies of the crime of larceny by a trick invented by the judges in the case of *R.* v. *Pear*, it was always made clear beyond question not only by those same judges, but also in all the later cases in which the Court for Crown Cases Reserved considered the matter, that this crime could not arise when *ownership*[3] of the property had been obtained by the prisoner. Therefore Jones could not possibly be guilty of larceny by a trick.[4] Secondly his case could not be the same as that of the welshing bookmaker as held in *R.* v. *Buckmaster* since in that case the bookmaker was expressly treated[5] as a person who did *not* acquire ownership of the punter's money but merely took it by way of deposit from the punter.

Students should also note that the declarations above quoted were *obiter*, since the question of larceny was not one which was before the court in this appeal, nor was it argued by counsel. Furthermore, if they were to be accepted as a correct statement of law it would follow that section 32 of the Larceny Act, 1916 (which covers the misdemeanour of obtaining property by false pretences) would seem to be superseded.[6] For if under the doctrine of larceny by a trick an *unexpressed* deceit negatives the owner's consent to transfer ownership of the property with the result that the deceiver commits larceny as soon as the property reaches him, it could hardly be contended that an *expressed* deceit (i.e. the false pretences proved) would not have the same effect.

[1] *Post*, ¶ 326.

[2] On such cases see *ante*, ¶ 236, and Russ. 1059 *et seq.*

[3] E.g. *per* Manisty, J., in *R.* v. *Buckmaster* (1887) 20 Q.B.D. 182, at p. 187 (*T.A.C.*).

[4] It would seem possible that Jones could properly have been convicted of obtaining credit by fraud (*post*, ¶ 365 and Appendix I) if he had been charged with that offence.

[5] Although, as argued *ante*, ¶ 236, contrary to the facts as recognized by those who are accustomed to back horses on the course. In *R.* v. *Dent* [1955] 2 Q.B. 590 at p. 593, Lord Goddard, speaking of *R.* v. *Jones*, said: 'dicta of mine as to the case being one of larceny by a trick when comparing it to the case of a welshing bookmaker were clearly wrong, as I have felt ever since I saw the case reported.'

[6] See *R.* v. *Fisher* (1910) 5 Cr.App.R. 102: 'If you are right there is no distinction between larceny by a trick and false pretences'; *per* Darling, J., at p. 107.

THE PURSE TRICK

¶ 239. Another device which involves the question of the owner's consent is that known as 'the purse trick', which is an example of sleight of hand. In its most common form a man appears in some place where people congregate (such as a race-course) and displays a purse and two silver coins. After apparently placing the coins into the purse he throws it on the ground and offers to sell it with its contents for a smaller sum than he appears to have put into it, but making no promise that it contains any particular amount. After one purse is sold he proceeds to offer another and so on. Some of the purses when bought and opened are found to contain the two silver coins, but many more of them are found to contain only two copper coins. Since no person of even moderate intelligence could expect that there is any promise that the purse shall contain the higher sum it follows that in truth the transaction is a gamble in which the purchaser thinks that his eye is quick enough to detect the rare occasion on which the silver coins have been put into the purse. What is agreed is that the purchaser shall in any event lose the purchase price and in any event gain a purse with whatever it may contain. That being so there can be no larceny on the part of the vendor since the purchaser consents to pass ownership in the money paid, and no obtaining by false pretences since the vendor, on a true interpretation of the facts, does not make any false pretences; for he plainly indicates that his sleight of hand may be too much for the purchaser. Therefore it would seem that the Court for Crown Cases Reserved in *R.* v. *Solomons*[1] were wrong in stating that the prisoner (whose conviction for larceny they quashed) might have been successfully charged with obtaining the money by false pretences.[2]

BAILMENTS IN MODERN LAW

¶ 240. As already explained,[3] in order to obtain the conviction of a dishonest bailee it is no longer necessary to prove either that he broke bulk or that he obtained the bailment by deception. The requisites for the offence nowadays are (*a*) that the owner passed the *possession* of the thing (but *not* the ownership) to the prisoner for some time limited expressly or impliedly; (*b*) that at the expiration of that time the identical thing was to be returned to the owner or delivered to someone else; (*c*) that the prisoner had fraudulently appropriated the property (either for his own benefit or that of someone else) with intent thereby permanently to deprive the owner thereof; (*d*) that this was done without a claim of right to do so, made in good faith. This, for the

[1] (1890) 17 Cox 93.

[2] The real offence would seem to be under the Vagrant Act Amendment Act, 1873, s. 3, which makes both men guilty, as rogues and vagabonds, for gambling in a place to which the public have access, as was stated in the later case of *R.* v. *Ward* (1900) 64 J.P. 776.

[3] *Ante*, ¶ 233.

special case of the bailee, is a statutory contradiction of the ancient rule[1] of the common law, that if a man has first obtained *legal*[2] possession of the thing with the consent of its owner, then he cannot by a subsequent dishonest appropriation of it become guilty of felony.

LARCENY BY BAILEE

¶ 241. Even after the ancient immunity of the dishonest bailee had been removed by the legislature in 1857 there still remained instances of fraudulent breach of confidence which the criminal law did not reach. It often happens that a man is entrusted with property which he has to deal with on behalf either of the person who gives it to him or on behalf of someone else, but where it is *not* required that he should deliver up the identical thing handed to him; in such a case he becomes owner of the thing and is not the bailee of it.[3] The commonest instance is where the property consists of money. For such a case a strained interpretation of the facts was sometimes made by the courts in order that they could hold that there was a bailment[4] and so be able to secure the conviction of the dishonest agent under the new legislation of 1857.

¶ 242. *R.* v. *Bunkall*, etc. Instances of this approach to the facts can be seen in the following cases:

R. v. *Bunkall* (1864) L. and C. 371.[5] Here the Court for Crown Cases Reserved laid down the proposition that since an agent employed to purchase goods for his principal can entrust them to a carrier to be conveyed to the principal so as to make the carrier the principal's bailee, it can make no difference if the agent himself acts as carrier of the goods, his conduct showing that he constituted himself the bailee of them. The interesting feature of *R.* v. *Bunkall*, however, is that on the evidence it would seem that the prisoner's conduct in taking his own sack into which he instructed the coal merchant to put the coal which he was charged with stealing, showed plainly that he did *not* constitute himself a bailee of it.[6]

R. v. *De Banks* (1884) 13 Q.B.D. 29. The prisoner was convicted of larceny as a bailee of money which he had received from the purchaser of a horse which the prosecutor had entrusted to him to sell at a fair. The money (£15) had been paid to him in a public house after the sale had been negotiated. The prosecutor's wife, who from some distance away had witnessed the selling

[1] Which still prevails for other cases than that of bailment.

[2] I.e. not the mere 'detention' which is attributed to a servant or a guest; *ante*, ¶¶ 229 and 230.

[3] *R.* v. *Hoare* (1859) 1 F. and F. 647. Since the Larceny Act, 1901 (now replaced by section 20 of the Act of 1916), in such a situation the culprit's crime would be the misdemeanour of fraudulent conversion, *post* chapter XV.

[4] There can of course be a bailment of money in a case where there is a clear obligation on the recipient to return the identical coins, e.g where they are lent for display in an exhibition.

[5] *T.A.C.*

[6] On this case see Russ. 1083 *et seq.*

of the horse but did not know the price, shortly afterwards asked the prisoner for the money but he pretended that the price was £13 and that he had been paid by a cheque. He showed her a cheque but would not give it to her when she asked him for it, and said he would have to cash it himself. It was proved that the purchaser had paid the prisoner £15 for the horse. Subsequently the prisoner had run away and never paid the prosecutor anything. Taking a distorted view of the evidence the majority of the Court for Crown Cases Reserved (although not without some hesitation) held that De Banks became a bailee so soon as the woman asked him for the cheque and he refused to give it to her, and upheld his conviction. In a dissenting judgment Stephen, J., dealt with the facts in their true significance, saying: 'My view is that the man...was not the bailee of the money. I think he received the money with no obligation to return the identical coins, and that the present case is governed by *R.* v. *Hassall.*[1]...Was this man bound to return the precise coins he received? As I read the evidence such supposition is expressly negatived.'

R. v. *Aden* (1873) 12 Cox 512. The prisoner Aden was a bargeman who had contracted with the prosecutor to purchase coal for him from time to time as he required it, and to deliver it to him by barge. On the occasion of each order the prosecutor handed Aden a fixed sum of money out of which he was to pay for coal, retaining any balance to be carried forward for the next journey. After one such order Aden did not bring back any coal but falsely stated he had been robbed of the money on the canal bank. On appeal the Court for Crown Cases Reserved upheld Aden's conviction for larceny on the ground that he was a bailee of the coins handed to him.[2]

R. v. *Holloway, ex p. George* (1897) 66 L.J.Q.B. 830. The prisoner had been entrusted with a bond with authority and instructions to obtain a loan of money upon it. He obtained the loan but fraudulently appropriated to his own use the money handed to him. The court held that he was bailee of the money and guilty of larceny in appropriating it. This was a stronger case than *De Banks's*, but it is doubtful if now it would be treated as a bailment since the statutory offence of fraudulent conversion has been established.[3]

¶ 243. *R.* v. *Hassall.* But more often the courts found it impossible to construct a bailment out of the evidence, and the accused man escaped.[4] The leading case was *R.* v. *Hassall*,[5] in which the prisoner as treasurer of a money club received and accumulated the weekly contributions of the members so as to form a fund of club-money out of which he had authority to lend sums at interest to such members as from time to time needed a loan. At the end of each year the total fund,

[1] See below, ¶ 243.

[2] The general course of business between the principal and his agent in this case seems really to have been such that ownership, and not mere possession, was passed on each occasion when the money was handed over, so that there would be no bailment.

[3] In 1901. See now Larceny Act, 1916, s. 20; *post*, ¶¶ 243 and 324.

[4] *R.* v. *Garrett* (1860) 8 Cox 368; *R.* v. *Hunt* (1861) 8 Cox 495.

[5] (1861) L. and C. 58 (*T.A.C.*).

less certain agreed deductions, was to be distributed among the members. He misappropriated part of the fund and was convicted of larceny as a bailee. His conviction was quashed on appeal, Cockburn, C.J., saying: 'The word bailment must...be understood in its legal acceptance, viz. a deposit of something to be returned in specie, and does not apply to the receipt of money with an obligation to return the amount where there is no obligation to return the identical coin.' Further illustrations of this situation are where an auctioneer sells an article (of which of course he *is* a bailee) and absconds with the money which he receives from the purchaser; or where a land agent who collects rent absconds with the rent-money (save in the unusual case where it is required that he shall keep such money separate from his own and hand it over in specie to his principal or to his principal's bank).

Of course if the agent is a clerk or servant of his principal then it may be more easy to establish that he has the duty to place all money or goods received into the legal possession of the principal, in some such circumstances as those of a shop-assistant or an omnibus conductor who is required to place all takings into the till or into the leather wallet which he carries. Should the servant appropriate the takings *before* passing them into his employer's possession he commits the felony of embezzlement.[1] Where, however, he was not under the duty to put the specific property into the possession of his employer or of someone else, he used to escape criminal punishment until the mischief was attacked by the legislature in 1901,[2] which, as we have noted above, created the special misdemeanour known as fraudulent conversion.[3]

THE NATURE OF BAILMENT

¶ 244. The traditional definition[4] of bailment is that it is a delivery of goods on a condition, express or implied, that they shall be restored[5] by the bailee to the bailor, or according to his directions[6] as soon as the purpose for which they were bailed shall be answered. Bailment most commonly arises from a contract, and there have been doubts expressed as to whether it can arise without contract,[7] but such a contention was repudiated in *R.* v. *Macdonald*.[8] It is well settled that there can be no bailment where *ownership* of the goods is passed to the agent, and therefore that in all cases of bailment the bailee must be under the duty

[1] *Post*, ¶ 318. If he takes money *out* of the till he commits larceny (Larceny Act, 1916, s. 17 (1) (*a*)).

[2] 1 Edw. VII, c. 10. Now replaced by the Larceny Act, 1916, s. 20 (1) (iv).

[3] *Post*, ¶ 324.

[4] Jones, *Treatise on the Law of Bailment* (1781).

[5] In many of the criminal cases the word 'returned' is used.

[6] E.g. to someone else, such as a parcel bailed by *A* to a carrier for him to deliver it to *B*.

[7] E.g. *R.* v. *Robson* (1861) L. and C. 93.

[8] (1885) 15 Q.B.D. 323, *per* Lord Coleridge, C.J., where an infant, who in the circumstances was incapable in law of making such a contract, hired furniture and was held to have committed larceny by selling it.

to deliver either to the owner or to the person designated[1] by the owner *the same identical* goods which have been bailed to him.[2]

CONVERSION BY THE BAILEE CONSTITUTES LARCENY

¶ 245. Exactly what amounts to the 'conversion', which involves the bailee in the felonious guilt of stealing, has now been authoritatively stated.[3] The prisoner must have possession of the goods, otherwise he would not be bailee, and then, as it would seem, any conduct on his part which shows that he assumes either the full title of ownership in the goods,[4] or asserts a right to pass the full title of ownership,[5] will amount to such conversion as will render him guilty of stealing them within the statute. This assertion or assumption of title may be expressed; or it may be implied by the bailee's conduct, for example, if he uses the thing in such a way as to show that he is setting up ownership in himself to the exclusion of the bailor,

Only some act that is quite inconsistent with the bailor's title can constitute sufficient appropriation. Clearly if silver forks be bailed for use, melting them down, or selling them, or dishonestly refusing to return them would amount to conversion.[6] The pawning of the article bailed, although it may create *prima facie* a presumption of conversion, will not be conclusive: for the bailee may be able to raise sufficient doubt as to his guilt by evidence that he honestly intended to redeem it, and that there was a reasonable prospect of his being able to do so; or that he had pawned it in order to secure its safe custody.[7]

Yet although there can in such a case be no conviction for larceny there may well have been committed the minor offence of unlawful pawning,[8] and the abandonment of control may be an actionable breach of the contract.

Once the article has been returned or delivered according to the bailor's instructions, so that the bailment has terminated, then no promises or contracts made about it by the ex-bailee can amount to a conversion.[9]

It must be observed that there does not exist, as seems sometimes to be supposed, a specific offence entitled 'larceny by a bailee'. The statute

[1] E.g. a buyer of the thing from the bailor, *R.* v. *Richmond* (1873) 12 Cox 495; or a bill which the bailee is to get discounted for the bailor, *R.* v. *Oxenham* (1877) 13 Cox 349.

[2] As Cockburn, C.J., said in *R.* v. *Hassall* (1861) L. and C. 58, 'a deposit of something to be returned in specie'.

[3] *Rogers* v. *Arnott* [1960] 2 All E.R. 417 at p. 419.

[4] But his conduct must be clearly inconsistent with the bailment; *R.* v. *Jackson* (1864) 9 Cox 505 (*T.A.C.*).

[5] E.g. by offering them for sale to someone.

[6] *R.* v. *Wakeman* (1912) 8 Cr.App.R. 18; or pawning them, if the prisoner can show no reasonable chance or intention of redeeming them. *R.* v. *Trebilcock* (1858) D. and B. 453; *R.* v. *Medland* (1851) 5 Cox 292 (*T.A.C.*).

[7] As where a solicitor, to whom a client had entrusted a valuable watch, pawned it for that purpose; *R.* v. *Pentland* (1906) C.C.C. Sess. Pap. CXLV, 419, at p. 420.

[8] Pawnbrokers Act, 1872, s. 33. Punishable by fine on summary conviction.

[9] *R.* v. *Jones* (1842) C. and M. 611 (*T.A.C.*).

places conversion by a bailee on the same footing as stealing by any person by 'taking and carrying away', etc.; so that an indictment for it need not even contain the word 'bailee'.

SECTION 5. CONSENT

WHERE THERE IS NO BAILMENT

¶ 246. The Act of 1916[1] preserves the common law rule[2] that a thing is not stolen unless taken 'without the consent of the owner', or of his duly authorized agent. Upon this point a question of practical importance often arises in consequence of the plans laid by the police for the detection of a suspected thief. If, for mere purposes of detection, the owner of goods acquiesces in a thief's carrying them off, does such a consent suffice to prevent the thief's act from being a larceny? The rule is the same as in burglary, where an entry permitted, after an *unsuccessful* attempt to deceive, does not amount to a constructive breaking. Similarly in larceny, if the owner, either himself or through another person, should suggest to the thief the perpetration of the theft, his action would constitute a sufficient consent to render the taking no larceny, although his sole object was to secure the detection of the offender. Yet if he went no further than to facilitate the commission of the theft (e.g. by not preventing one of his servants from assisting the thief),[3] such conduct would no more amount to a consent than if a man, knowing of the intention of burglars to break into his house, were to leave one of the bolts on the front door unfastened.

FACTS WHICH NEGATIVE AN APPARENT CONSENT: (*a*) Deceit

¶ 247. We have already discussed fully the anomalous crime of 'larceny by a trick' which was devised by the judges in *R.* v. *Pear*.[4] Quite apart from that fictitious doctrine, under which the actual consent of the owner has been treated as if it were non-existent, a wrongdoer may make such a complete misrepresentation of fundamental facts as to create a mistake on the part of his victim so profound that when the details are examined it appears that in truth he was consenting to an imagined situation quite different from that which actually existed. The student must be careful to distinguish such a case as this, where the mistake induced is as to a matter so fundamental that there is in truth no consent at all, from the more common position in which there is consent, but it is a consent which is legally regarded as *vitiated* by the deceit of the other party.[5]

[1] Sect. 1 (1). And see *R.* v. *Stewart and wife* (1845) 1 Cox 174 (*T.A.C.*); *R.* v. *Caslin* [1961] 1 W.L.R. 59.

[2] 'It is of the essence of robbery and larceny, that the goods be taken against the will of the owner'; Foster, 123. *R.* v. *Macdaniel* (1755) Foster 121 (*T.A.C.*); *R.* v. *Turvey* [1946] 2 All E.R. 60 (on this case see above, p. 255 n. 6).

[3] As distinct from giving the servant instructions or authority to assist the thief; *R.* v. *Egginton* (1801) 2 Leach 913.

[4] *Ante*, ¶ 234.

[5] See *ante*, ¶ 156.

¶ **248.** *Cundy* v. *Lindsay.* It is a situation of this kind which is covered in the Larceny Act, 1916,[1] by the provision that in the definition of stealing 'the expression "takes" includes obtaining the possession by any trick'. For if the phrase 'obtains the possession by any trick' be substituted for the word 'takes' in that definition, it still remains necessary for the prosecution to prove that the owner did not consent.

Such was the position in *Cundy* v. *Lindsay*,[2] where it appeared that a man, A. Blenkarn, occupied a room in a house, part of which looked into Wood Street in which (at no. 123) were the premises of W. Blenkiron & Co., a firm whose good repute (although not the exact street-number of its house) was well known to Lindsay. Giving the address '37 Wood Street', Blenkarn conducted some correspondence with, and ordered goods on credit from Lindsay, by letters signed in such a way as to resemble the name 'Blenkiron & Co'. Lindsay's replies, and the goods, were all addressed to W. Blenkiron and Co., 37 Wood Street, and were taken in there by Blenkarn, who, being fraudulent throughout, sold the goods in question to an innocent purchaser Cundy, who then disposed of them in the ordinary way of his business. It was decided in effect by the House of Lords that the evidence showed that Lindsay could not be held to have contracted with Blenkarn nor to have intended to pass ownership of the goods to him.[3] On this view of the facts Blenkarn could pass no title in the goods to Cundy; and he must himself have been guilty of larceny of them from Lindsay.[4]

¶ **249.** *Ringing the changes.* Again, it may happen that the deceit practised produces a complicated situation and such mental confusion in the victim that although from his actions there would seem to be a consent by him to transfer the ownership of the property, yet on examination of all the circumstances it is plain that in fact he did not give any such consent. Of this kind is the fraud known as 'ringing the changes', which, in broad outline, consists in the offender's producing in a shop a coin or note of large denomination in proposed payment for some small purchase so as to cause the seller to place on the counter the amount of change which would be due. Thereupon, by a series of manœuvres such as asking for some further article of little value, or for smaller change for some of the money on the counter, with pretended changes of mind, so that the money is moved about, a confused situation

[1] Sect. 1 (2) (i) (*a*); *ante*, ¶ 222. [2] (1878) 3 App. Cas. 459.

[3] 'Of him they knew nothing, and of him they never thought. With him they never intended to deal. Their minds never, even for an instant of time, rested upon him, and as between him and them there was no *consensus* of mind which could lead to any agreement or contract whatever.' *Per* Lord Cairns, L.C., at p. 465.

[4] Contrast the case of *Phillips* v. *Brooks* [1919] 2 K.B. 243 in which it was held that the ownership did pass to a purchaser, who, present in person, assumed the name of a reputable man and purported to pay for them by a cheque which he signed in the name of that man. On the difficult question of the distinction between this case and *Cundy* v. *Lindsay* see Glanville Williams, 'Mistake as to party in the law of contract' (1945), 23 *Can. Bar Review*, 271. *Phillips* v. *Brookes* was approved in *Dennant* v. *Skinner and Collom* [1948] 2 K.B. 164.

is created which enables the offender to pick up much more of the money than is really his due.[1] A dishonest manœuvre for which the name 'trick' would seem particularly appropriate is where a person extracts something[2] from an automatic machine by inserting a worthless metal disk instead of the proper coin. The property is plainly taken *invito domino* just as completely as if the machine had been broken open, or unlocked by a skeleton key, since the owner has indicated that he only consents to pass the ownership of the contents of his machine if the correct money is first put into it.

(*b*) Intimidation

¶ 250. To be effective the owner's consent must be full and free. It may be that the owner has expressed his consent but only under the compulsion of threats made by a wrongdoer to harm him if he does not allow the goods to be taken. The courts have always refused to regard a consent so enforced as a real consent, and therefore they have held that notwithstanding it the taking of the goods is larceny, as for example where the keepers of an auction-room forced a woman to pay for some lots for which she had not made a bid, by threatening that she should not leave the place until she had so paid.[3]

(*c*) Mistake

¶ 251. The Larceny Act, 1916, further provides[4] that in the definition of stealing the expression 'takes' shall include 'obtaining the possession under a mistake on the part of the owner with knowledge on the part of the taker that possession has been so obtained'. Here again the substitution of these words for the word 'takes' in the definition leaves unaffected the requirement that the owner shall not have consented.

Thus in *Moynes* v. *Coopper*,[5] the appeal committee of quarter sessions, in stating a special case to the divisional court, expressed their opinion[6] that in the Larceny Act, 1916, the words 'without the consent of the owner' dominated and governed the whole definition of larceny in section 1 (1) of the Act; and that the special meaning given by subsection (2) to the word 'takes' did not dispense with the necessity of a larceny being an obtaining without the consent of the owner. No objection to this proposition was enunciated by the court, and in delivering his judgment in favour of the prisoner Lord Goddard, C.J., said:[7]

> This Act was not intended to alter the law and...it has not done so....

[1] *R.* v. *McKale* (1868) 1 C.C.R. 125; contrast *R.* v. *Williams* (1857) 7 Cox 355 in which consent was given and the offence was obtaining by false pretences; and see *R.* v. *Hollis* (1883) 12 Q.B.D. 25 and the criticism thereof in Russ. 1078. *R.* v. *Thomas* (1841) 9 C. and P. 741 was not an example of ringing the changes but a plain case of conversion by a bailee, which at that date was not a felony.

[2] E.g. matches, stamps, or gas from a gas-meter; *R.* v. *Hands* (1887) 16 Cox 188.

[3] Larceny Act, 1916, s. 1 (2) (i) (*b*). *R.* v. *McGrath* (1869) 1 C.C.R. 205 (*T.A.C.*); *R.* v. *Lovell* (1881) 8 Q.B.D. 185. And see *R.* v. *Hilliard* (1914) 9 Cr.App.R. 171.

[4] Sect. 1 (2) (i) (*c*).

[5] [1956] 1 Q.B. 439; *post*, ¶ 294*a*. [6] At p. 441. [7] At pp. 444, 445.

Section 1 (2) (i)...provides 'the expression "takes" includes obtaining the possession...(*c*) under a mistake on the part of the owner with knowledge on the part of the taker that possession has been so obtained'. This in our opinion is affirming the common law that the taker must have *animus furandi* at the time when he takes the property. In *Middleton's Case*[1] the wrong amount of money was paid by the post-office clerk before the prisoner who picked it up knowing of the clerk's mistake and so took it *animo furandi*.'[2]

An example of the kind of situation covered by the words of the statute would be where a shopkeeper, intending to pass over a specific package to the prisoner, has put it in a certain place in the shop, and, unknown to him but to the knowledge of the prisoner, one of his assistants has innocently moved it elsewhere and set down in its place another package of greater value. The prisoner then asks the shopkeeper (whose attention is directed elsewhere) where his package is, and if he may take it; whereupon the shopkeeper tells the prisoner to go to the original spot and take the package which he will find there.

¶ 252. *R.* v. *Middleton*. In practice, however, the courts have included, under the head of mistake, transactions in which, although certainly enough the owner has been in some measure mistaken, he has yet undoubtedly consented to transfer ownership in the property to the prisoner. This is due to the assumption that the words of the Act were intended to confirm the decision given by the Court for Crown Cases Reserved in the much discussed appeal of *Middleton* in 1873.[3]

A post-office clerk, when about to pay out money to Middleton, a savings-bank depositor, consulted by mistake the wrong letter of advice, and without properly checking the sum against the figures in the man's deposit book and withdrawal warrant, placed on the counter for him a £5 note and a number of coins to the total amount of £8. 16*s*. 10*d*., instead of the amount really due, which was only ten shillings. Realizing that there was a mistake the prisoner nevertheless took the money. His conviction was upheld by a numerical majority of eleven[4] judges against four. The legal arguments adopted by seven judges against the prisoner were (*a*) that the clerk had *authority* to transfer ownership in the money but that his mistake was such that he did not intend to do so, (*b*) that even if he did so intend yet the prisoner's intent to steal in some way negatived that intention.[5] Three more of the eleven judges while not agreeing with these arguments yet were in favour of upholding the conviction on the ground that the clerk did not have authority to transfer

[1] (1873) 2 C.C.R. 38, *infra*.

[2] On this interpretation it would seem possible to read subs. (2) (i) (*c*) as intended to confirm the common law doctrine of *R.* v. *Pear*, *ante*, ¶ 234; but the dictum does not meet the point of the owner's consent in *Middleton's Case*.

[3] *R.* v. *Middleton* (1873) 2 C.C.R. 38 (*T.A.C.*).

[4] Some of these simply concurred in the judgments delivered by others, so that in fact only four judgments were delivered against Middleton , and one of these (by Pigott, B.) rested upon a special and strange view of the facts and not upon a legal point.

[5] This was a misunderstanding of the doctrine laid down in *R.* v. *Pear*, *ante*, ¶ 234.

ownership in the money and therefore did not transfer it. One judge, differing from all the others, held that in fact the placing of the money upon the counter for Middleton to pick up was not a delivery of the coins to him. But this was really irrelevant, for the guilt of larceny does not depend upon there being no delivery by the owner but upon the prisoner's *taking* the thing without the owner's consent; and since the clerk watched Middleton pick up and take away the cash, and was clearly willing that he should do so, it was obvious that the taking was not *invito domino*. What was overlooked by most of the judges who affirmed the conviction was that the clerk made no mistake whatever as to the transfer of the money: he was quite well aware of what he was doing. His mistake related to his *reason* for doing it.[1] This can hardly be the kind of mistake contemplated by the Act, for if it were so, then difficulties would arise in distinguishing the felony of larceny under sect. 1 from the misdemeanour of obtaining by false pretences under sect. 32;[2] it would also make it a felony for a skilled collector of antiques to purchase an object which an ignorant owner had consented to sell at a price below its real value.

Therefore at the least it must be submitted that, whether the conviction of Middleton was or was not wrong, the facts of that case are not covered by the words of sect. 1 of the Larceny Act, 1916.

CONSENT OF THE OWNER IMPLIED WHEN LOST GOODS ARE FOUND

¶ 253. The early law as to the rights and liabilities of a man who finds and picks up an article which its owner has lost is not clearly recorded.[3] Trespass to goods is declared to be an offence against the owner's possession, by wrongfully handling or damaging another's thing; and yet it was held to be trespass to touch the thing even when it had been lost by the owner and was therefore no longer in his possession. But the handling of the thing will not be wrongful if the owner consents;[4] and so it came to be established[5] that where an *honest* finder takes into his control *lost* goods which are in danger, in order to preserve them for their owner, then the owner's consent to such unsolicited assistance must be presumed, and the taking will be no trespass. Here it is important to note, as previously mentioned,[6] that a merely inquisitive movement of the thing when found, in order to ascertain what it is, does not constitute such a 'taking' as would suffice to invest the finder

[1] This was plainly indicated by Bramwell, B., who in a vigorous judgment held that Middleton's conviction should be quashed. For a detailed examination of this case see *Mod. Appr. Crim. Law*, 356–74.

[2] See Darling, J.'s remarks in *R.* v. *Fisher* (1910) 5 Cr.App.R. 102, cited *ante*, p. 267 n. 6.

[3] Pollock and Wright, *Possession in the Common Law*, 173 *et seq.* On the topic of 'larceny by finding' see Russ. 1141 *et seq.*

[4] But if his consent has not been obtained (or necessarily implied) the good intentions or motive of the trespasser will not excuse him; (1505) Y.B. 21 Hen. VII, 27, pl. 5.

[5] (1467) Y.B. 7 Edw. IV, 3, pl. 9, *per* Nedham (J.); *Isaack* v. *Clark* (1615) 2 Bulstr. at p. 312, *per* Coke, C.J.

[6] *Ante*, ¶ 224.

with legal possession of the thing.[1] What the common law envisaged was a situation where the owner has lost his possession of the thing so that it lies for the time being in no one's possession. Then the person who discovers its presence (i.e. 'finds' it) *takes it into his own possession.* The critical moment is that at which the thing passes into the finder's possession and it is his mental attitude to it at that moment which establishes whether or not he is guilty of felony. Strictly, however, the question of trespass or no trespass is an incidental and not an essential matter in the criminal law of larceny, for that crime is constituted by the *taking and carrying away 'invito domino'*, inspired and accompanied by the *animus furandi.*[2] Accordingly there are two reasons why the honest finder, who thinks the owner can be discovered, does not commit larceny; (1) because the owner consents to his taking the thing, and (2) because he has no intent permanently to deprive the owner of it. If, however, the finder believes that the owner cannot be discovered by taking reasonable steps and therefore resolves to keep the thing permanently for himself he does not necessarily have the owner's consent,[3] but he is saved from the guilt of larceny by his belief in his own claim of right.[4] It is, however, not essential that at the time of the taking the finder should have an honest intention *to seek* the owner; nor is it enough that after taking the thing he later discovered who the owner was but nevertheless proceeded dishonestly to convert it to his own use,[5] nor that it was, in fact, easy to find the owner.[6] It is well to note at this point that if the finder does take possession of the thing he does not thereby constitute himself a bailee of it.[7]

[1] See Stephen, J.'s remarks in *R.* v. *Ashwell* (1885) 16 Q.B.D. at p. 216. That the material moment is when the thing is first 'taken' rather than when it is 'found' can be seen from Cockburn, C.J.'s observation in *R.* v. *Glyde* (1868) 37 L.J.M.C. 107 at p. 111. And see *Feist* v. *Bonython* (1944) S.A.S.R. 176.

[2] As previously emphasized, there can be no larceny without trespass but there can be trespass without larceny (even when committed *animo furandi*; e.g. where the wrongdoer unsuccessfully uses force to detach a bicycle which is chained to the railing of a house, or a watch from the chain which attaches it to its owner's clothing). Furthermore, an owner of land has a 'qualified property' (*propter impotentiam*) in such creatures *ferae naturae* (*post*, ¶ 264) as are too young to fly or run away, and may maintain a civil action of trespass against anyone who without his permission takes them off the land, although such taking is not larceny.

[3] In certain circumstances the owner may in fact have decided to abandon all his rights since he considers that a search would not be worth while.

[4] *R.* v. *Reed* (1842) C. and M. 306; *Williams* v. *Phillips* (1957) 41 Cr.App.R. 5. It is not a felony to steal a dog (*post* ¶ 271), but by the Dogs Act, 1906, s. 4, anyone who takes control of a stray dog must either return it to its owner or notify the police, with details, of the fact that he has it.

[5] *R.* v. *Glyde* (1868) 1 C.C.R. 139; *R.* v. *Deaves* (1869) 11 Cox 227.

[6] *R.* v. *Knight* (1871) 12 Cox 102, where five judges unanimously quashed the conviction of a dishonest finder of a banknote because the jury were wrongly directed that the question for them was whether he 'could within a reasonable time have found the owner', whereas the proper question was 'What was the mind of the prisoner when the banknote first came into his possession?'

[7] *R.* v. *Matthews* (1873) 12 Cox 489; *R.* v. *Ashwell* (1885) 16 Q.B.D. 190, *per* Stephen, J., at p. 215. If indeed the finder did become bailee, then *R.* v. *Thurborn* (1849) 1 Den.

If the goods have not in fact been lost, but an honest person who lights upon them (i.e. 'finds them') thinks they have been lost and acts accordingly, then again although there cannot be even an implied consent by the owner, yet there will still be no larceny, since the finder has no *animus furandi*.

It appears therefore that section 1 (2) (i) (*d*) of the Act is unhappily worded, in that (*a*) it uses the word 'finding'[1] as meaning 'taking after having found', and (*b*) it unnecessarily indicates what will make a dishonest taker of the discovered thing guilty instead of indicating the less obvious circumstances in which a man is free from guilt when he appropriates for himself a thing which he has found.[2] Most of the cases in which the criminal liability of a finder has been discussed are concerned with the position where the finder has in the first instance taken the thing with the honest intention of seeking the loser but later on succumbs to the temptation dishonestly to keep the thing for himself. It is well settled that in such case he does not commit larceny[3] since the common law rule requires that the *animus furandi* must exist at the very time when the thing is *first* taken.[4]

THE PROPERTY OF HUSBAND AND WIFE

¶ 254. As there can be no larceny when the owner consents to the taking, it is obvious that a man cannot be guilty of stealing from himself.[5] Since in many situations the law treated the consequences of acts done by either spouse as though they had been the acts of the other, so that in effect the husband and the wife were for these purposes regarded as one person, it became common to employ the loose (and in modern times misleading) and exaggerated expression 'in law husband and wife are held to be one person'.[6] Of course the absurdity of taking such a statement strictly, as an accepted principle of law, will plainly

387, *R.* v. *Preston* (1851) 2 Den. 353, and all the later cases founded thereon, must have been wrongly decided. A dictum let fall without argument in *Walters* v. *Lunt* [1951] 2 All E.R. 645, to the effect that the parents would become bailees of property which their child aged seven had dishonestly brought home, has been vigorously attacked by critics in 68 *L.Q.R.* 167, 15 *Mod. L.R.* 222 and [1957] *Crim. L.R.* 251 and must be regarded as wrong in principle and unsupported by authority.

[1] A man 'finds' a thing when he discovers exactly where it is, even though he does not move or even touch it, still less 'take and carry it away'.

[2] See *Mod. Appr. Crim. Law*, 372, 373.

[3] *R.* v. *Thurborn* (1849) 1 Den. 387 (*T.A.C.*), *per* Parke, B.; *R.* v. *Thristle* (1849) 1 Den. 502; *R.* v. *Moore* (1861) L. and C. 1; *R.* v. *Matthews* [1950] 1 All E.R. 137 (*T.A.C.*) *per* Lord Goddard, C.J.

[4] This fundamental and long-established rule was emphasized in *R.* v. *Flowers* (1886) 16 Q.B.D. 643, and in *Moynes* v. *Coopper* [1956] 1 Q.B. 439. It is expressly confirmed in s. 1 of the Larceny Act, 1916; but it has been arbitrarily overriden by the judiciary in the cases of *R.* v. *Riley* (1853) Dearsly 149 (*T.A.C.*), *Ruse* v. *Read* [1949] 1 All E.R. 398 (*T.A.C.*) and *R.* v. *Kindon* (1957) 41 Cr.App.R. 208; *post*, ¶ 288.

[5] E.g. when he takes, intending to steal it, an umbrella which turns out to be his own; though the evidence *might* establish the crime of attempting to steal an umbrella belonging to someone else; *ante*, ¶ 62.

[6] Described by Maitland as 'this impossible dogma'; Pollock and Maitland, II, 532.

appear if an attempt be made to apply it to the facts of one spouse killing or wounding the other. The true extent of the rule can be expressed by saying that 'in certain circumstances specially distinguished by the law,[1] husband and wife are treated as though they are one person'.

This principle harmonized well with the old doctrine of the common law that the goods and chattels of a married woman belonged to her husband and were held to be equally in the possession of both. From this developed the rule that an appropriation of his goods by her would not constitute a change of possession, and therefore (at common law) did not constitute a larceny.[2] Nor did even adultery put an end to this. So if a wife went away with money of her husband's, and then met her adulterer and gave him this money, he could not be convicted of receiving stolen goods; for they had not been 'stolen'.[3] Yet if the adulterer had instead assisted her in the original taking of the goods, he could have been convicted of a larceny of them;[4] for then he would have taken them out of the actual possession of the husband himself. But since the Married Woman's Property Act, 1882,[5] husband and wife are criminally liable for stealing each other's property, if (*a*) they were not living together[6] at the date of the offence, or if (*b*) the property was appropriated with a view to their ceasing to live together. But when they once again are living together no prosecution can take place. Therefore one spouse, so long as he or she has no intention of ceasing to cohabit with the other, retains even under the Act of 1916 immunity for committing thefts of the other's property.[7] And even if the wife, for example, were to abscond from the husband temporarily and to take away with her some of his property, but in the expectation of ultimately returning to him and bringing it back with her, then she would commit no larceny. For she would not satisfy the final clause of the definition of the word *stealing*; since she does not intend to deprive him of the property 'permanently'.

SECTION 6. A THING 'CAPABLE OF BEING STOLEN'

¶ 255. The words 'capable of being stolen' in section 1 of the Act refer to a thing the stealing of which is *felonious* (i.e. larceny). At the outset it is important to note that there is a difference between (*a*) a thing which is owned but nevertheless by a rule of law is not the subject of larceny, and (*b*) a thing which is the subject of larceny but which is

[1] Such as in the crime of conspiracy, and in the publication by one to the other of defamatory statements about a third person.

[2] *R.* v. *Harrison* (1756) 1 Leach 47 (*T.A.C.*); Statham, *tit.* Corone, 39.

[3] *R.* v. *Streeter* [1900] 2 Q.B. 601.

[4] *R.* v. *Featherstone* (1854) Dearsly 369 (*T.A.C.*).

[5] Replaced now by s. 36 of the Larceny Act, 1916.

[6] They may 'live together' though geographically apart; 14 Cr.App.R. 19.

[7] Sect. 36. *R.* v. *Creamer* [1919] 1 K.B. 564. Hence a wife's paramour, receiving it from her *then*, does not receive 'stolen goods'. Cf. *Walters* v. *Lunt* [1951] 2 All E.R. 645, property taken by a child under eight; *McGregor* v. *Benyon* [1957] Crim. L.R. 250.

not at the moment owned by anyone, and therefore cannot be taken *invito domino*. It is true to say that it cannot be larceny to take either (*a*) or (*b*); but although not entirely inaccurate it is confusing to say that both (*a*) and (*b*) are things 'not capable of being stolen'. Ambiguity is avoided if the rule be stated affirmatively by indicating the characteristics which render a thing capable of being stolen.

¶ 256. Everything in the universe is made up of a total of attributes or characteristics, and it has no existence at all apart from these characteristics.[1] The number of characteristics which a thing has is so great that they may be regarded as innumerable. That fact, however, presents no practical difficulty, since whenever we have need to contemplate that thing we are only concerned to consider such limited number of its characteristics as are important for the circumstances in which we are for the moment envisaging the thing; all its other characteristics are a matter of indifference and no attention or even thought is given to them. Those characteristics which are essential for the purpose in hand may be indicated in positive or in negative language according to preference and convenience. Thus if a piece of steel is needed for shaving we may say that it must have an edge which is sharp, or one which is not blunt. A piece of paper for writing a letter must be clean (or not dirty), adequately smooth (or not too rough), light enough in colour (or not too dark) and so on; but such attributes are irrelevant if the paper is needed for burning, a purpose which calls for any paper which is readily combustible and therefore dry (or not wet).

CHARACTERISTICS OF SUCH THINGS A MATTER OF LAW

¶ 257. That which makes a thing 'capable of being stolen' is a matter of law, since it is law which lays down the characteristics which such a thing must have and also those characteristics which it is essential that the thing must be without. Students must therefore be careful to note that what the owner, or the taker, may think *on this point* is irrelevant.

At common law the list of attributes which a larcenable object must *not* possess was substantially large; but statutory provisions have gradually brought within the protection of this branch of the criminal law many things which the common law had excluded.

DEFINITION IN THE LARCENY ACT, 1916

¶ 258. Thus a comprehensive provision in the Larceny Act, 1916,[2] declares:

Section 1 (3):

Everything which has value and is the property of any person, and if

[1] Jesperson, *The Philosophy of Grammar* (1924), 75. Cf. Glanville Williams, 'Mistake as to party in the law of contract' (1945), 23 *Can. Bar Review*, 271.

[2] Which purported 'to consolidate and simplify the law relating to larceny...and kindred offences'.

adhering to the realty then after severance therefrom, shall be capable of being stolen:

Provided that

(*a*) save as hereinafter expressly provided with respect to fixtures, growing things, and ore from mines, anything attached to or forming part of the realty shall not be capable of being stolen by the person who severs the same from the realty, unless after severance he has abandoned possession thereof; and

(*b*) the carcase of a creature wild by nature and not reduced into possession while living shall not be capable of being stolen by the person who has killed such creature, unless after killing it he has abandoned possession of the carcase.

Yet for the better understanding of the law as it now stands some reference must be made to the old rules of the common law, as will appear in the following list of the characteristics which at the present time render a thing capable of being stolen.

THE THING MUST BE TANGIBLE

¶ 259. It was essential at common law that the thing must be perceptible by the sense of touch. There can be no larceny of a thing which has no physical substance, such as a debt, a copyright,[1] the plot of a play, the value of an object, a balance of accounts, a difference in price, or any other incorporeal conception. Yet the physical substance may be of very slight density; thus it has been held that gas is larcenable at common law.[2] Any difficulty which might have been encountered in an endeavour to bring electric current within the common law protection was obviated by statute[3] under which it is a felony maliciously or fraudulently to abstract or cause to be wasted or diverted, or to consume or use any electricity.

THE THING MUST BE MOVABLE

¶ 260. This means that the thing must be completely disconnected from the land. As in Roman law it has always been held that land, in the usual legal meaning of the word, cannot be stolen. But the common law went further, in the rule which came to be established that certain movable things, so particularly associated with the land that they could be said to 'savour of the realty', were also excluded from the felony of larceny. More will be said of this in ¶ 273 below.

[1] *R.* v. *Kidd* (1907) 72 J.P. 104.

[2] *R.* v. *White* (1853) Dearsly 203; *R.* v. *Firth* (1869) 1 C.C.R. 172. Under the Gas Act, 1948, 3rd sched. 29 (1), it is in effect made an offence punishable on summary conviction with a fine up to £5 wilfully, fraudulently or by culpable negligence to injure any pipe, meter, or other fitting belonging to the Area Board, or to tamper with a gas meter or fraudulently to abstract or use the gas; all without prejudice to any other right or remedy whether civil or criminal for dealing with the offender.

[3] Larceny Act, 1916, s. 10, re-enacting 45 and 46 Vict. c. 56, s. 23. E.g. the current consumed by making telephone calls fraudulently without paying the call fee, *R.* v. *Scotting and Rasjke* [1957] Crim. L.R. 241.

It must here be noted that statutes in modern times have made provisions whereby in certain specified circumstances it is a felony dishonestly to remove fixtures[1] from buildings, trees, bushes[2] (or portions thereof), plants, etc., growing in gardens and the like places,[3] or ore and other specified minerals from mines[4] (*post*, ¶ 303).

THE THING MUST HAVE AN OWNER

¶ 261. As we have already seen ownership for this purpose originally consisted of an actual physical possession of the thing, larceny being regarded as the forcible (*vi et armis*) removal of the thing from the control of its owner. But the needs of society gradually compelled the acceptance of a notion of 'legal possession' as something different from a simple physical control, and thereafter in the general conception of larceny there ensued an increase in the importance attached to the offender's dishonesty of purpose and a diminution in the attention paid to the amount of force which he employed. Consistently with this tendency the meaning of the term 'owner' was extended so as to bring more persons within the law's protection.[5] At common law, however, it was and still remains, necessary that the 'owner' either has, or previously had, such actual possession of the thing as would have entitled him to sue for the writ of trespass committed against it.[6]

Since the Larceny Act, 1916, does not purport to change, but only to consolidate and simplify the law of larceny as it then existed, it would seem that this requirement as to possession still remains, notwithstanding the wide and vague words of the Larceny Act which provides:[7]

> the expression 'owner' includes any part owner, or person having possession or control of, or a special property in, anything capable of being stolen.

It will be seen that this provision protects, amongst others, a bailee, a finder of lost property,[8] and a servant,[9] in their holding of the property.

[1] Larceny Act, 1916, s. 8 (1).
[2] Sect. 8 (2).
[3] Sect. 8 (3).
[4] Sect. 11.
[5] The Postmaster-General has been held to be a bailee of 'Button B' pennies in a telephone call-box, *R.* v. *Goodchild, The Times*, 23 Jan. 1947. And see *Martin* v. *Marsh* [1955] Crim. L.R. 781, where it was held larceny to extract money from an electricity meter, the money having passed into the ownership of the electricity authority when placed therein.
[6] *R.* v. *Smith* (1852) 2 Den. 449; *R.* v. *Townley* (1871) 1 C.C.R. 315 (*T.A.C.*); *R.* v. *Kidd* (1907) 72 J.P. 104. It has been held that provisions supplied to the crew of a merchant vessel for consumption on the ship do not pass into the ownership of the men, who will therefore be guilty of larceny if they save them and carry them away for their families; *Morgan v. Caldwell* (1919) 35 T.L.R. 381 (in which the conviction was quashed by the divisional court for lack of *mens rea*). The same rule applies where rations are supplied to interned prisoners; *R.* v. *Immer* (1917) 13 Cr.App.R. 22.
[7] Sect. 1 (2) (iii).
[8] See *R.* v. *Swinson* (1900) 64 J.P. 73; ¶¶ 290, 344. There was a count in the indictment of larceny from the loser, and another in which a charge was made of larceny from the wife of the finder, to whom he had entrusted the property for safe keeping, under which latter count the jury found the prisoner guilty.
[9] *R.* v. *Harding* (1929) 21 Cr.App.R. 166; *post*, ¶ 268 n. 1.

Nothing in the above statutory definition alters the common law rule that there is no larceny of creatures *ferae naturae*[1] living at large in their natural state, notwithstanding the ancient and undoubted law that the landowner has a 'qualified property' (*ratione soli*) which gives him the exclusive right to hunt, take, kill, or protect[2] them while they are there;[3] this qualified property also exists *ratione privilegii* in any person to whom the sporting rights have been granted.[4] It also exists in the landowner over such creatures as *propter impotentiam* are too young to run or fly away, so that he may maintain a civil action of trespass[5] against any unauthorized person who takes any of them from the land,[6] although so to take them is not larceny.

¶ 262. *I.e. the thing must be subject to human ownership.* It follows from the preceding paragraph that there can be no larceny of a thing which is not subject to human ownership. An example is a human corpse; thus the 'resurrection men', who, before the passing of the Anatomy Act,[7] used to disinter bodies from churchyards in order to supply the laboratories with subjects, could only commit larceny if they took either coffin or grave-clothes (since these remained the property of the executors who had provided them[8]). It is not entirely certain whether the rule must be taken to be 'once a corpse, always a corpse';[9] if so the protection of the criminal law would perhaps not extend even to skeletons and similar anatomical preparations on which great labour has been expended[10] or to ethnological collections of skulls or mummies—a conclusion which does not seem reasonable.

Other such things are those common to the enjoyment of all, such as the open air, and the water in the sea. Yet a man acquires ownership of sea water which he has taken into a container, and of air which he has pumped into a cylinder, and accordingly on principle such collected water or air (which is a 'gas'[11]) may be stolen.

¶ 263. *Derelict things have no owner.* Again there may be things which are capable of ownership but which at the moment are not owned by anyone. Such are things which an owner has thrown away or has other-

[1] *Post*, ¶ 264.

[2] *Ante*, ¶ 199.

[3] *Blades* v. *Higgs* (1865) 11 H.L.C. 621 at p. 631.

[4] *Ante*, ¶ 199. As in the case of a free warren on another's soil (*Keble* v. *Hickringill* (1706) 11 Mod. Rep. 74, 75), or a licence or grant of shooting or sporting rights.

[5] Halsbury, *Laws of England*, 1, 533.

[6] *Case of Swans* (1592) 7 Co. Rep. 15*b*, 17*b*; Fitzh. *Nat. Brev.* 86 and 89K.

[7] 2 and 3 Will. IV, c. 75.

[8] *R.* v. *Haynes* (1613) 12 Co. Rep. 113.

[9] *Doodward* v. *Spence* (1908) 9 N.S.W. 107. The Judicial Committee refused leave to appeal against the decision which recognized ownership.

[10] But any metal inserted, such as wiring, would of course be larcenable.

[11] *Quaere*, therefore, whether a man who maliciously releases the air from another person's motor tyres can be convicted of larceny of this 'gas'.

wise abandoned;[1] these are not easily distinguishable from things which an owner has placed at the disposal of anyone who cares to take them, as where a man throws coins into a crowd or into the sea for boys to dive after. In all these cases it could be argued that there is no larceny for the reason that they are not taken *invito domino*. In this category fall abandoned wrecks[2] and treasure trove[3] whose present owner cannot be ascertained.

ANIMALS *FERAE NATURAE*

¶ 264. *Contrasted with domestic animals.* Animals *ferae naturae*,[4] straying at large, form the most important of all the classes of things which have no owner. Even the (so-called) property *per privilegium*, which the lord who has a chartered park or forest is regarded by law as having over certain of the wild creatures in it, is not a sufficient ownership to sustain an indictment for larceny,[5] since it is not so much an ownership as a peculiar right to obtain ownership. For the general principle of law is that all true ownership of living things depends upon actual control over them. On the other hand, domestic animals (such as horses, oxen, sheep), or domestic fowls (such as hens, ducks, geese), are definitely owned and can be stolen even though they may be, at the moment, straying beyond their owner's boundaries.[6] Their eggs and other produce will equally be larcenable; and this even when the produce is stolen directly from the living animals themselves (as by milking cows, or plucking wool from the backs of sheep), before the true owner has ever had possession of it as a separate thing. But over animals that are of a *fera natura* there is usually no control, and therefore no ownership. Ownership over them whilst uncontrolled, if it were to exist, could exist only in the owner of the land where at any moment they were; and it would be futile to recognize any such mutable ownership, which the animal itself might vary from hour to hour.[7] But a sufficient control may of course be created, either *per industriam*, by their being killed, or caught, or tamed,[8] or *propter impotentiam*, by their being too young to

[1] E.g. small amounts of coal or farm produce which have fallen from a cart and which the owner does not trouble to pick up. See *R.* v. *Peters* (1843) 1 C. and K. 245 (*T.A.C.*). Justinian, *Digest*, XLVII, 2, 43. 5.

[2] *The Crystal* [1894] A.C. 508, at p. 532. Whales cast ashore are treated as 'wreck'.

[3] 22 Libr. Ass. 95, 99.

[4] *Ferae*, here, is of course an adjective. Yet people talk about 'hunting our *ferae naturae*' and both Sir Walter Scott (*Antiquary*, ch. XXII) and Sir W. H. Rattigan (*Jurisprudence*, 138) have fallen into like error.

[5] 7 Co. Rep. 17*b*.

[6] In which case they rank as things which their owner has lost; *ante*, ¶ 253.

[7] On this account, it is not larceny for anglers to take earthworms out of another man's land, though it is larceny to take them after he has collected them into a pot for sale; Christian's *Game Laws*, 79. It is larceny to take oysters from an oyster-bed actually owned and controlled by another person, oysters having neither will nor power to stray from it. Cf. the Sea Fisheries Act, 1868, s. 51, and other statutes cited in Stone's *Justices' Manual*, 88th ed. p. 2197.

[8] *R.* v. *Rough* (1779) 2 East P.C. 607 (*T.A.C.*).

be able to get away.[1] Consequently larceny may be committed of pheasants which have been shot, or deer which have been so enclosed in a park that they may be taken at pleasure;[2] or of fish in a tank, or even at large in a mere or pond, though not when at large in a running stream.[3] Again, partridge eggs under a barndoor fowl and partridge chicks not yet old enough to leave her protection[4] are the subjects of a true ownership, and so are larcenable.[5]

¶ 265. *Ownership of them is a matter of physical control.* The degree of physical control which is necessary to establish ownership will vary with the habits of the particular species concerned. Creatures may be subjects of ownership although they are not closely confined but are allowed to wander away from home, provided they have a settled habit of returning thither; and this will be so although they are not shut up even at night.[6] Peacocks readily acquire this *animus revertendi*, unlike pheasants and partridges. This rule, that the taking of ownerless things[7] cannot be a larceny, still holds good; but the modern statute law has created many offences of dishonesty which it has not erected into larcenies. And thus deer-stealing,[8] the taking of hares or rabbits in warrens in the night-time,[9] and the taking of fish from private waters[10] have been made offences; but they vary greatly in their degrees of heinousness as well as in their punishments.[11]

¶ 266. *Trespasser can become owner of wild creatures.* It is important to notice that larceny requires not only an ownership, but an ownership which already existed before the act of taking. A proprietorship that was created only by that very act will not suffice. Thus, although rabbits or wild pigeons, on being killed by a trespasser, become the property of the owner of the land where they are killed,[12] yet if this trespasser who kills them should proceed to carry them away, he will not[13] commit larceny thereby. For the *ownership* which he infringes did not exist

[1] Although here too there must be some evidence that the landowner had asserted control over them.

[2] 1 Hale P.C. 511.

[3] *Ibid.* At Cambridge in 1627, before Harvey, J., two men were convicted of larceny for taking fish out of a net lying in the river.

[4] *R.* v. *Shickle* (1868) 1 C.C.R. 159 (*T.A.C.*). But the young, or the eggs, in a *wild* bird's nest are not in the landowner's possession; and so, though he has a 'special property' in them, they are not larcenable; *R.* v. *Stride* [1908] 1 K.B. 617, overruling Lambard, fo. 274. Cf. *R.* v. *Clinton* (1869) 4 Ir.C.L. 6, as to seaweed washed ashore.

[5] (1478) Y.B. 18 Edw. IV, fo. 8, pl. 7 (*T.A.C.*). Cf. 7 Co. Rep. 17. *Ante*, ¶ 261.

[6] *R.* v. *Cheafor* (1851) 2 Den. 361.

[7] Larceny Act, 1916, s. 1 (3). Cf. *The Case of Peacocks* (1526) Y.B. 18 Hen. VIII, fol. 11 (*T.A.C.*).

[8] Larceny Act, 1861 (24 and 25 Vict. c. 96), ss. 12–16.

[9] *Ibid.* s. 17.

[10] Larceny Act, 1861, s. 24.

[11] *Post*, ¶ 304.

[12] *Blades* v. *Higgs* (1865) 11 H.L.C. 621. Previously, as we have seen, he had only a 'qualified property' in the creatures.

[13] *R.* v. *Townley* (1871) 1 C.C.R. 315 (*T.A.C.*); ¶ 273.

before he killed the creatures. (The Larceny Act, 1916, s. 1 (3) *b*, preserves this common law doctrine that 'The carcase of a creature wild by nature, and not reduced into possession while living, shall not be capable of being stolen by the person who has killed such creature; unless, after killing it, he has abandoned possession of the carcase'.) But if, after killing them, he should go away and leave them on the land, with the idea of abandoning them altogether, he would thereby cease to be their possessor, and they would pass into the legal possession of the owner of the soil.[1] So if the trespasser should afterwards change his mind and come back and seize them again, this would be an entirely new act of taking. And, as the things had now got an owner, it would be a larceny. Where a man, employed to trap rabbits, put some into a bag in order to appropriate them, and a keeper (suspecting him) nicked them during his absence, for purposes of identification, it was held that the nicking was not sufficient to reduce them into the possession of the keeper or of his master. Hence the trapper did not become guilty of larceny by carrying them away, even when thus nicked.[2]

POSSESSION IS EVIDENCE OF OWNERSHIP

¶ 267. It should be noted that the owner may be unknown or quite untraceable, as in the case of brass plates being stolen from very old coffins in a vault, or shrouds from disinterred corpses.[3] It must of course in such cases always be proved that the other essentials of larceny were present; and in many cases it will be found that it is impossible to show how and with what intent the suspected person acquired the goods. The man himself cannot be compelled to give an account of how he came to be in possession of property,[4] however suspicious the circumstances may appear. Even if a tramp be found to have, say, six gold watches in his pocket, this by itself is not enough to raise the legal presumption that he has stolen them. His possession indeed is *prima facie* evidence of his ownership of them (*post*, ¶ 497) and his silence, or even his giving an unsatisfactory account, does not reverse this presumption so as to justify his conviction for theft.

POSSESSION OF CO-OWNERS, BAILEES, SERVANTS

¶ 268. But though there can only be a larceny where the thing (at the time of being stolen) already 'belonged' to some other person, it is not necessary that this person should be a sole owner, or even a full owner. (*a*) He may, for instance, be merely a joint-owner with the thief himself. At common law, as every co-owner is lawfully entitled to the possession of the whole thing, he could not commit larceny by taking it. But now, by the Larceny Act, 1916, s. 1 (1), a part-owner may be guilty of stealing a thing 'notwithstanding that he has lawful posses-

[1] Cf. *R.* v. *Foley* (1889) 26 Ir.C.L. 299 (*T.A.C.*).

[2] *R.* v. *Petch* (1878) 14 Cox 116.

[3] *Haynes' Case* (1613) 12 Co. Rep. 113; 1 Hawk P.C. c. 33, s. 29.

[4] Unless it be first *proved* that the property was *recently* stolen; see *post*, ¶ 492.

sions thereof'; cf. s. 40 (3). (*b*) And by s. 1 (2) iii, the person stolen from may be one who is even less than a co-owner, merely some 'person having possession or control of, or a special property[1] in', the thing stolen, e.g. a bailee (or even a thief who himself had stolen it; see 10 Cushing 397).

Consequently, paradoxical as it may seem, a man may commit larceny by stealing his own property. For when an owner of goods has delivered them to anyone on a bailment[2] (e.g. of pawn or of hire) which entitles the bailee to exclude him from possession, that owner may become guilty of larceny, even at common law, if he carries them off from this bailee with any intention to defraud him. He might, for instance, aim at defrauding him by making him chargeable for the loss; or by depriving him of an interest which he had in retaining his possession, such as the lien of a cobbler, upon the boots which he has mended, for the cost of the mending. Possibly it will suffice even though the intention was to defraud (not the bailee but) some other person; as where the owner of goods, which are in a bonded warehouse, surreptitiously takes them out, in order to cheat the Crown of the customs duty payable on them.[3] An old illustration was that[4] of a man who sent his servant on a journey in charge of some valuables, and then disguised himself as a highwayman and robbed the servant of these things, in order to claim their value from the inhabitants of the hundred (under its ancient liability to make good the loss sustained by a crime of violence committed within its boundaries). It must, however, be remembered in this connexion that anciently a servant (certainly when away from his master's premises) *did* have possession of such of his master's goods as he had in his charge (*ante*, ¶ 229).[5]

THE THING MUST HAVE SOME VALUE

¶ 269. For the purpose of the law of larceny only economic value (and not, for example, sentimental or artistic value) is taken into account. The common law was indifferent whether the value of the thing was great or small so long as it had *some* actual money value[6] for *some* person or persons. Since the *measure* of the value was of no legal importance it follows that a mistake by the owner, or by the taker, as to the real value of the thing is equally irrelevant. As we have seen, the law of larceny was always and is still concerned with the physical appropriation of the tangible thing itself and although it had

[1] See *R.* v. *Harding* (1929) 21 Cr.App.R. 166, in which a conviction was upheld for robbing a servant of her master's mackintosh, on the ground that the servant had a 'special property' in the mackintosh. For a criticism of this case see 46 *L.Q.R.* 135.

[2] *Rose* v. *Matt* [1951] 1 K.B. 810 (*T.A.C.*).

[3] *R.* v. *Wilkinson and Marsden* (1821) R. and R. 470.

[4] *Anon.* (1698) 2 East P.C. 654.

[5] *Anon.* (1429) Y.B. 7 Hen. VI, fo. 43, pl. 18. And see Pollock and Wright, *Possession in the Common Law*, 165, 228. Cf. Bishop's *Criminal Law of U.S.A.*, 8th ed., II, s. 790.

[6] For the fiction that certain things (e.g. documents relating to choses in action) had no value, see ¶ 276 *post*.

to have some value (for otherwise the courts should not be troubled with the investigation nor the taker's life or liberty imperilled) it was not '*value*' but the *thing* which was stolen.[1] An appreciation of this point will help in the elucidation of the difficulties presented by the much cited case of *R.* v. *Ashwell.*[2]

It also follows that the smallness of the intrinsic value[3] of a thing is irrelevant: accordingly convictions have taken place for the larceny of proof-sheets,[4] of cancelled bank-notes,[5] of a worthless cheque,[6] and of a small slip with memoranda pencilled on it,[7] and of pigs buried as being unfit for consumption.[8]

¶ 270. *Vagueness of the common law in the matter of value.* The common law's indifference and consequent vagueness in the matter of value had a beneficial effect. Since at common law the exact measure of value was never fixed scope was given for the humane ingenuity of judges, counsel, prosecutors, and juries, in an age when larceny was in the majority of instances a capital felony without benefit of clergy. So fictions were developed and deliberate disregard paid to obvious facts whereby many things in which a legal property existed, and which were of such appraisable importance that damages could have been recovered in a civil action for taking them away, were held to be below the minimum of value that was necessary[9] to support a conviction for capital felony[10] (and in some cases for any felony of larceny at all). At

[1] Of course if the owner thought it had *no* value at all, this fact, if proved, would be some evidence to support the contention that he must have consented to anyone's taking the article; while if the taker could be proved to have thought it had no value, then equally this would go to support his contention that he had taken it under a claim of right made in good faith.

[2] (1885) 16 Q.B.D. 190 (*T.A.C.*), discussed in ¶ 291 *post.*

[3] E.g. 'A hundredth part of a farthing', *R.* v. *Morris* (1840) 9 C. and P. 349 *per* Parke, B.; 'a pin', *R.* v. *Clarence* (1888) 22 Q.B.D. 23 (*T.A.C.*) at p. 52 *per* Hawkins, J.; the electricity used in a fraudulent telephone call, *R.* v. *Scotting and Rasjke* [1957] Crim. L.R. 241.

[4] A proof-sheet containing secret information (e.g. a telegraphic cipher code, or the forthcoming annual report of the directors of a company) might have a very great pecuniary value to certain persons. See *R.* v. *Guernsey* (1858) C.C.C. Sess. Pap. XLIX, 179, a trial for stealing from the Colonial Office a despatch, premature publication of which by the thief rendered futile Mr Gladstone's mission as Lord High Commissioner to the Ionian Islands (Morley's *Gladstone*, bk. IV, ch. X). Still greater political confusion was caused in 1878 when a Foreign Office copyist disclosed to the *Globe* the secret Anglo-Russian agreement which Lord Salisbury had signed. Still the copyist had not 'taken' the documents but had merely copied one and memorized the other. This was no offence, as the Official Secrets Acts (¶ 428 *post*) had not been passed then (*Annual Register*, 1878, 67).

[5] *R.* v. *Clark* (1810) R. and R. 181; a telegram, *R.* v. *Newman* (1910) C.C.C. Sess. Pap. CLIII, 451.

[6] *R.* v. *Perry* (1845) 1 C. and K. 725 (*T.A.C.*).

[7] *R.* v. *Bingley* (1833) 5 C. and P. 602.

[8] *R.* v. *Edwards* (1877) 13 Cox 384.

[9] Under statutory provisions which operated at that period.

[10] Examples are given in Radzinowicz, *Hist. Eng. Crim. Law*, I, 94 *et seq.* In one case the judge (Lord Mansfield) advised the jury to value a gold ornament at less than forty shillings; in another, where a woman was found guilty of stealing a large number of articles clearly worth several pounds, the prosecutor said 'God forbid I should take her life! I value them at 8*s*.'; in a third, where a woman had stolen seven guineas and thirty-

one time it was stated to be doubtful whether even diamonds and other precious stones, if unset, had any such intrinsic worth as to be larcenable 'because they be not of price with all men; howsoever some do hold them dear and precious'.[1]

¶ **271.** *Some domestic animals not larcenable at common law.* There was some ancient precedent for such fictions since from early times it was settled that the law of larceny afforded no protection for the owner of such domestic animals as dogs and cats and also of such wild animals as are kept in captivity yet do not serve either for draught or for food, such as bears, lions, monkeys and ferrets;[2] and birds such as parrots, canaries, and nightingales.[3] Yet captive or tamed pheasants[4] and swans and the like which though wild by nature yet serve for food, were larcenable.[5] Bees, however, though themselves inedible, are a source of food and are therefore held[6] to be larcenable. And the law protected the hawk, when tamed, 'in respect of the nobleness of its nature, and its use for princes and great men'.[7]

¶ **272.** *Statutory protection was given later.* But now statutory protection has been given to any animal or bird ordinarily kept in confinement (such as a canary) or kept for any domestic purpose (such as a cat), not being the subject of larceny at common law.[8] And it is an offence punishable on summary conviction[9] to steal a dog; after previous conviction for stealing a dog it becomes an indictable misdemeanour to steal another.[10]

CHARACTERISTICS WHICH RENDERED THE THING NOT LARCENABLE AT COMMON LAW

(*a*) The thing must not savour of the realty

¶ **273.** As we have seen, to be a subject of larceny, a thing must be

four shillings in a dwelling-house, the jury found her guilty but declared the value of the 'things stolen' to be only thirty-nine shillings.

[1] Hales, J., in 1553; cited by Lambard, *Eirenarcha*, 275.

[2] *R.* v. *Searing* (1818) R. and R. 350 (*T.A.C.*).

[3] For doubts in the case of peacocks, see *Case of Peacocks* (1526) Y.B. 18 Hen. VIII, fo. 11 (*T.A.C.*).

[4] *R.* v. *Rough* (1779) 2 East P.C. 607 (*T.A.C.*).

[5] 1 Hale P.C. 512. Yet for taking a dog damages could be recovered in a civil action even in very early days, (1520) Y.B. 12 Hen. VIII, pl. 3; and see Manwood, *Lawes of the Forest* (1598 ed.), 99. And it has never been denied that stealing the dog's collar, or the dressed skin of a dead dog, would be larceny.

[6] *Hannam* v. *Mockett* (1824) 2 B. and C. at p. 944. A swarm from my hive remains mine until I abandon its pursuit.

[7] 1 Hale P.C. 512. A striking instance of the forces which mould criminal policy.

[8] Larceny Act, 1861, s. 21, which makes it an offence punishable on summary conviction with six months' imprisonment or payment of not more than £20 above the value of the creature.

[9] Larceny Act, 1861, s. 18; six months' imprisonment or a fine over and above the dog's value, up to £20.

[10] Larceny Act, 1916, s. 5.

movable; and therefore in English law land has never been capable of being stolen. Moreover the thing must be movable before the act of theft, and it is not enough that it was made movable by that act. Thus it is no larceny at common law to take mould from a garden or sand from a pit; or to pull down a wall[1] and carry away the bricks. Nor was it larceny to strip woodwork, glass or other fixtures from a house, or to cut down a tree;[2] but these acts have now been made specific statutory offences.[3] Hence if a man demolishes someone else's house and sells the materials, he may be proceeded against in respect of the fixtures. The Larceny Act, 1916, s. 1 (3) *a*, preserves the rule that (with some exceptions as to fixtures, growing plants, and mineral ores) 'anything attached to or forming part of the realty shall not be capable of being stolen by the person who severs the same from the realty, unless, after severance, he has abandoned possession thereof'.[4] For, even at common law, there would be a larceny if, after the severance had once been fully completed, the thing were abandoned by the thief but he afterwards changed his mind and returned and carried it away. On this point *Townley's Case* (1871)[5] may again be referred to, as showing how a poacher who shot rabbits and hid them in a ditch, and then went away, nevertheless retained 'possession', during that interval of personal absence, by mere continuousness of intention. It will be instructive to a student to compare this decision with the case of *R.* v. *Foley* (1889).[6] In the latter case a trespasser mowed some grass, but left it where it fell; then, after two days, he returned and took it away. It was held by the Irish Court for Crown Cases Reserved that, even if he had a continuous intention, there was not a continuous possession; and, therefore, that his ultimate removal of the grass constituted a larceny. If this case be regarded as at variance with that of *Townley*, the latter is of course the one to be followed by English courts. But the two may be reconciled if it be thought right to lay stress on the distinction that Foley, before leaving the hay, had not performed any unequivocal act of taking possession of it, such as Townley performed by hiding the rabbits.

¶ **274.** *Crops.* It may seem strange that land, by far the most important form of wealth in the Middle Ages, should have been left unprotected

[1] This would of course be the crime of malicious damage; *ante*, ¶ 186.

[2] *The Forester's Case* (1338) Y.B. 11 and 12 Edw. III, 641 (*T.A.C.*). Cf. *R.* v. *Pinchbeck* (1896) C.C.C. Sess. Pap. CXXIII, 205 (*T.A.C.*).

[3] Larceny Act, 1916, s. 8. Sometimes *felonies*. See ¶ 304 *post*. And see Malicious Damage Act, 1861, s. 51, and Criminal Justice Administration Act, 1914, s. 14 (*ante*, ¶ 192); Russ. ch. 79.

[4] In *Billing* v. *Pill* [1954] 1 Q.B. 70 it was held that an army hut bolted to a concrete base is not 'attached to...the realty' within the proviso to the section, and is accordingly capable of being stolen *simpliciter*; see a criticism of this case in [1955] *Crim. L.R.* 404, and contrast *R.* v. *Skujins* [1956] Crim. L.R. 266.

[5] 1 C.C.R. 315 (*T.A.C.*). *Ante*, ¶ 266.

[6] 26 Ir.C.L. 299 (*T.A.C.*).

by our early criminal law.[1] The omission, however, is rendered more intelligible by the fact that taking dishonest possession of land cannot involve its complete destruction or disappearance; moreover, to do so will in most cases be impossible without resort to some act which is in itself criminal, such as forcible entry or assault.[2] But a dislike of capital punishment was probably the reason why the judges went still further, and excluded from the scope of larceny even things that really were movable and had only a technical connexion with the land; as when they held it to be no crime to carry off dung which had been spread upon a field.[3] Moreover, even standing corn and similar growing crops, although the law of property gives them to a deceased owner's executors as chattels personal, were held in criminal law to 'savour' so far of the realty as not to be larcenable.[4] Yet, on the other hand, some things which do not thus go to the executor, but to the heir, are larcenable, e.g. some species of heirlooms. It has similarly been held in an American case[5] that though, by a very reasonable rule of law, the keys of a house always pass along with it on any alienation (whether by death or by conveyance), this legal identification of them with the realty does not go so far as to prevent its being a larceny to steal them.

¶ 275. *Title-deeds.* In general, however, the rule of immobility extends to all things which any legal fiction identifies with the land,[6] even though they be physically movable. It was the case, for instance, with title-deeds;[7] they would not pass under a grant of 'all my goods and chattels': so they were not larcenable. And a sealed-up box, enclosing such deeds, was once held to be so identified with them as itself to become not larcenable.[8] (An additional reason has been given for this non-larcenability of title-deeds, namely, that their value is so indefinite that it was impossible to say whether or not they were worth more than 12*d.*; cf. ¶ 296 *post.* For another reason—identification with the right they evidence—see ¶ 276 *post.*) But now under s. 7 (1) of the Larceny Act, 1916, it has been made a statutory felony to steal documents of title to land,[9] thus abolishing the fiction.

It may here be convenient, if not strictly relevant, to repeat that, even at common law, gas is larcenable,[10] and that it is a statutory felony[11]

[1] Hence water in a pond—often carried off copiously by roadmen for steam-rollers—is not larcenable; but it would become so after having been severed, as by being pumped into a cart. In 1900 the East London Waterworks prosecuted a man for stealing 900,000 gallons of their water. And see *Ferens* v. *O'Brien* (1883) 11 Q.B.D. 21 (water in pipes).

[2] See Stephen, *Hist. Crim. Law*, III, 126.

[3] *Carver* v. *Pierce* (1648) Style 66.

[4] 3 Co. *Inst.* 109.

[5] *Hoskins* v. *Tarrance* (1840) 5 Blackford 417.

[6] Thus a villein was so identified; and consequently, though salable, he was not larcenable; 3 Co. *Inst.* 109.

[7] 1 Hale P.C. 510; Stephen, *Hist. Crim. Law*, III, 138.

[8] (1470) Y.B. 10 Edw. IV, fo. 14, pl. 9, 10; Dalton, c. 156, s. 8.

[9] As it also is one to *destroy* them; 24 and 25 Vict. c. 96, s. 28.

[10] *R.* v. *Firth* (1869) 1 C.C.R. 172.

[11] Larceny Act, 1916, s. 10.

'maliciously or fraudulently' to 'abstract, cause to be wasted or diverted, consume, or use, any electricity'.

(*b*) The thing must not be a document relating to a chose in action

¶ 276. The fiction which, as mentioned in the last paragraph, treated a document of title to land as incapable of being stolen because it 'savoured of the realty' was extended to apply to any document which related to a right, on the artificial principle that the documentary evidence of a right must be identified with the right itself—'the accessory must follow its principal'. Accordingly it was held that if the subject of the right could not be stolen then equally the document could not be stolen. Thus documents or instruments which were evidence of the right to a chose in action[1] (such as a promissory note, or a contract for the sale of unascertained goods) were held at common law not to be larcenable, their character as pieces of paper being treated as 'absorbed' or 'converted';[2] the reason for this was sometimes said to be that the documents did not import any property as being in the possession of the prosecutor, and sometimes that they had no intrinsic value.[3]

¶ 277. *Changes made by statute.* It will be convenient here to note briefly that in modern times the legislature has given wide protection to documents and records of all kinds. Thus the Larceny Act, 1916,[4] s. 7, makes it a felony to steal the whole or any part not only of a document of title to lands, but also of a long list of records, official papers and other documents; and the Larceny Act, 1861,[5] makes it a felony to destroy, obliterate or cancel (for any fraudulent purpose) documents of title, records, choses in action, or wills.

(*c*) The thing must not be materially attached to the land, or to a person

¶ 278. We have already noted that a thing to be larcenable must be entirely disconnected from that which is either not larcenable or not moved. Thus it is no larceny to move (with intent to steal) an article which is connected by a cord to a house-railing or shop-counter[6] or take from a man's pocket his watch which is on a chain still buttoned at the other end into his clothing.[7] Nor would it be a larceny if the offender pulled at the watch so hard as to drag its owner along. But if one article be attached to another it would be larceny of both if both be moved, but no larceny[8] of either if only one of them be moved.[9]

1 Dalton, 501; but see now Larceny Act, 1861, s. 27 (damage to valuable securities).
2 *R.* v. *Watts* (1854) Dearsly 326, at p. 334.
3 1 Hawk. c. 33, s. 35; 4 Bl. *Comm.* 234; 2 East P.C. 597. See ¶ 269 *ante*.
4 Repeating provisions from the repealed portions of the Larceny Act, 1861.
5 Sects. 27, 28, 29, 30.
6 *Anon.* 2 East P.C. 556.
7 *R.* v. *Wilkinson* (1598) 1 Hale P.C. 508; 2 East P.C. 536.
8 It would of course be an *attempt* to steal in all these cases.
9 *R.* v. *Newman* in Talfourd, *Guide to Quarter Sessions* (Dickinson's ed.), 216.

SECTION 7. *MENS REA* IN LARCENY

¶ 279. The mental element required by the common law in this crime[1] is indicated in the statutory definition of stealing given in sect. 1 of the Larceny Act, 1916, by the following words:

> (1) A person steals who, without the consent of the owner, fraudulently and without a claim of right made in good faith, takes and carries away anything capable of being stolen with intent, at the time of such taking, permanently to deprive the owner thereof.

This must be examined in detail.

'FRAUDULENTLY'

¶ 280. There seems to be no real need for the inclusion of the word 'fraudulently' in the definition. The Act does not assign any precise meaning to the word and its use in the old cases is no more definite. As it cannot be found to connote anything more than dishonesty, it is unnecessary; since, where there is no claim of right, made in good faith, to take the thing, the taking must be done dishonestly and therefore 'fraudulently'. The word appears to be a relic of the Roman definition (*contrectatio fraudulosa*)[2] which Bracton followed (changing the adjective to *fraudulenta*); but in his definition also it was unnecessary, since he added '*cum animo furandi*'.[3] Originally[4] the word 'feloniously'[5] had to be included in the indictment, but it is now[6] enough to state that the offender is charged with larceny contrary to a specified section of the Act. And yet in *R.* v. *Williams*[7] it was stated:[8]

> The Court thinks that the word 'fraudulently' does add, and is intended to add, something to the words 'without a claim of right' and that it means (though I am not saying that the words I am about to use will fit every case,

[1] See Russ. ch. 51 for a fuller historical account of the mental element in larceny than can be given here.

[2] Justinian, *Inst.* 4. 1.

[3] Emphasizing that a mental element was a necessary part of this crime Bracton continued: 'cum animo dico, quia *sine animo furandi non committitur*.' That the word '*fraudulenta*' was surplusage was the view of Sir James Stephen who (*Hist. Crim. Law* III, 131) said 'Tautologous, though if construed as excluding from the definition of theft the case of taking under a claim of right they are by no means superfluous. They are in the spirit of the Roman law which...attached a full share of importance to the intention of the agent' (citing Paul, in *Digest* 47. 2. 53). Since the Larceny Act, 1916, now expressly includes the words 'without a claim of right etc.' Stephen's view would seem to support the contention that 'fraudulently' is merely an obtuse repetition of the old '*fraudulenta*' of Bracton's definition.

[4] See Y.B. 6 Ric. II, pl. 8 (Fitz. Enditement, 26) where the omission of '*felonice*' was held to be covered by the inclusion of the word *furatus*.

[5] This word also was not precisely defined; see Russ. 1117 *et seq.*

[6] Since the Indictments Act, 1915, has removed the old technical strictness of the law relating to the framing of indictments.

[7] [1953] 1 Q.B. 660.

[8] *Per* Lord Goddard, C.J., at p. 666.

but they certainly will fit this particular case) that the taking must be intentional and deliberate, that is to say, without mistake.... We think that the word 'fraudulently' in section 1 must mean that the taking is done intentionally, under no mistake and with knowledge that the thing taken is the property of another person.

Even so, it is still respectfully submitted that if this is the meaning to be given to 'fraudulently', the word is unnecessary, and therefore superfluous.[1] For the later words of the definition in section 1, 'with intent, at the time of such taking, permanently to deprive the owner thereof', plainly show the necessity for proof of intention, while the same words are quite sufficient to indicate that the taker must act 'with knowledge that the thing taken is the property of another person'; moreover if a taker honestly thinks that it is his own property which he is taking or thinks that he has the consent (whether express or implied) of the owner, even then the omission of 'fraudulently' would not injuriously affect him since he would still have the defence of 'claim of right made in good faith'.[2]

¶ 281. *Claim of right.* There must be an honest belief by the taker that he has the right to *take* the thing and keep it. If property is taken by a true legal right, obviously no criminal wrong is committed by taking it.[3] But immunity is carried further, because the common law has always[4] admitted that a man's honest, though erroneous or unreasonable,[5] *belief* that he had a legal right to take the thing should negative criminal guilt. This clearly covers a mistake of law[6] and it is incorrect to state that a belief in a right which has no existence in law will not suffice.[7] Of course if the accused person sets up a belief in an alleged legal right which the ordinary man would think impossible or absurd it may be difficult for him to satisfy the jury[8] that he himself really so believed. But as long ago as a hundred and fifty years it was stated:[9] 'If there be

[1] See *R.* v. *Bryant* [1955] 1 W.L.R. 715, in which the Courts-Martial Appeal Court, *per* Lord Goddard, ruled in effect that the word 'simple' in section 2 of the Larceny Act had no special meaning and could be disregarded.

[2] It would also be inadmissible to argue that 'fraudulently' carries the meaning of 'deceit', since an element of deceit is not a legal *requirement* for larceny; it would, for example, be absurd to suggest that a man who openly snatches up my bag and runs off with it is not a thief. For a more detailed exposition of the point here contended for see Russ. 1129.

[3] See 1 Hale P.C. 513; 2 East P.C. 659.

[4] See the comments in Russ. 1119, on (1307) Y.B. 33–5 Edw. I.

[5] *Ante*, ¶ 187; and see *R.* v. *Nundah* (1915) 16 N.S.W. 482.

[6] E.g. *R.* v. *Hall* (1828) 3 C. and P. 409 (*T.A.C.*); *R.* v. *Clayton* (1920) 15 Cr.App.R. 45.

[7] *R.* v. *Bernhard* [1938] 2 K.B. 264 (*T.A.C.*); *R.* v. *Reed* (1842) C. and M. 306, a mistake as to the rights of a finder; and see ¶ 187 where the same defence to charges of malicious damage to property is discussed.

[8] It is a question of fact, for the jury, whether the belief was or was not honestly held by the accused; *R.* v. *Daniels* (1915) 11 Cr.App.R. 101.

[9] 2 East P.C. 659.

any fair pretence of property or right in the prisoner or if it be brought into doubt at all, the court will direct an acquittal.' It is always regarded as good evidence that there was actually a sincere belief in his right if the prisoner took the goods quite openly.[1] On the other hand, although a surreptitious taking, or a subsequent denial of the taking, or a concealment of the goods, is strong *prima facie* evidence of the existence of a felonious intent from the beginning, it is not *necessarily* fatal to the prisoner, for he *may* be successful in explaining that it was for some other reason (not criminal) that he had acted in such a suspicious way.[2] The following instances may be mentioned in which the carrying off of someone else's goods may be unpunishable, on account of their being appropriated under a *bona fide* claim of right.

(1) Where something is seized by a landlord in a distress for rent under a mistaken idea that some rent is due, or in ignorance that the article seized is one which is privileged by law from being distrained on.

(2) Where corn is taken by a gleaner, honestly and openly, in a locality where gleaning is customary,[3] although not lawful.

(3) Where the taker believes that the owner has abandoned the thing; or that what he is taking is his own property;[4] or that it is something which he has a right to take,[5] whether as an equivalent for his own property[6] or with a view to mere temporary detention (e.g. by way of lien).

It is important to note that the defence indicated only arises where the taker believes he is legally justified in *taking* the thing in the circumstances and in the way in which he in fact takes it. It is not sufficient of itself that he honestly believes himself to be the *owner*; thus, if I pawn my watch and hand it over into the possession of the pawnbroker, I still own it, but I have no right to take it back from the pawnbroker without his consent; and if I did so, I would be guilty of larceny unless I could establish that I honestly believed I might legally so take it.[7]

It is under the head of a claim of right that there will come the case of one who takes the thing with the consent of another whom he believes (however mistakenly) to be duly authorized by the owner of it; for example, one who is, or seems to be, the servant or wife of the owner.[8] Yet in this last case a careful distinction must be made: if the accused is the wife's adulterer, it may appear on the evidence that he actually was a co-principal in the taking from the husband, appreciating

[1] *R.* v. *Curtiss* (1925) 18 Cr.App.R. 174; *Causey* v. *The State* (1887) 79 Georgia 564.

[2] E.g. that he thought it was his own property which he was recovering from a wrong-doer who might prove violent if the thing were demanded or taken openly.

[3] Russ. 1159.

[4] *R.* v. *Hall* (1828) 3 C. and P. 409 (*T.A.C.*); cf. *R.* v. *Clay* (1909) 3 Cr.App.R. 92.

[5] Even claims under a reprehensible practice, if it be commonly prevalent, may suffice; e.g. where sergeants, in weighing out the regimental meat, used to appropriate a certain percentage of it, *R.* v. *Daniels* (1915) 11 Cr.App.R. 101.

[6] *R.* v. *Boden* (1844) 1 C. and K. 395 (*T.A.C.*).

[7] Obviously it would be a matter of difficulty to prove this; *Rose* v. *Matt* [1951] 1 K.B. 810 (*T.A.C.*).

[8] *R.* v. *Harrison* (1756) 1 Leach 47 (*T.A.C.*).

that the husband did not consent; and if so he is guilty of stealing;[1] although the wife would not be,[2] unless she intended to elope with him.[3] But if the wife alone, not intending to elope, had taken them, the adulterer could not be guilty of the offence of *receiving* the goods knowing them to have been *stolen*.[4]

¶ 282. *Exchange of equal value made, no defence.* It is now well settled that a taking against the will of the owner is not deprived of criminality by the mere fact that money or property of equal value has been left by way of exchange for that which has been taken.[5] In such circumstances the prisoner's only hope nowadays will be to persuade the jury (*a*) that he believed that the owner did consent (i.e. mistake of fact), or (*b*) that he believed that he had a right to take the thing notwithstanding the refusal of the owner (i.e. claim of right).

¶ 283. *Taking* lucri causa. It was for one period thought that to constitute the crime of larceny it was necessary to establish that the prisoner had taken the thing for the purpose of personal gain (*lucrum*) to himself. This doctrine seems to have originated in a faulty interpretation of a statement by Blackstone[6] which, intended merely as a comparative illustration,[7] was taken as a declaration of a necessary ingredient in the crime. From this time onwards for about seventy years it was often argued on behalf of the prisoner that it was incumbent on the prosecution to establish that he had stolen the thing with a view to his own profit. This was indeed rejected in 1815 by a majority of the judges (although not without some hesitation), who upheld a conviction for larceny of a man who took away and destroyed a horse solely in order to protect (as he supposed) his friend who was being charged with the theft of it.[8] The argument was still used, however, especially for cases occurring from time to time in which a servant was prosecuted for larceny of his master's fodder, which, contrary to the master's orders, he took to give to the master's own horses which he thought needed more food than the master allowed them. To harmonize the law with public opinion on these cases the legislature in 1863 intervened by a

[1] *R.* v. *Featherstone* (1854) Dearsly 369 (*T.A.C.*), as explained in *R.* v. *Kenny* (1877) 2 Q.B.D. 307.

[2] *R.* v. *Creamer* [1919] 1 K.B. 564; 14 Cr.App.R. 19.

[3] Larceny Act, 1916, s. 36 (2); *ante*, ¶ 254.

[4] *R.* v. *Streeter* [1900] 2 Q.B. 601.

[5] There was long ago some suggestion that to take goods which were on sale but which the seller did not wish to sell to the taker would not be a felony; see Crompt. 31*b*; Lamb. 269; 1 Hawk. P.C. c. 34, s. 7, p. 149; 2 East P.C. 661, the case of a man who, in the reign of Queen Elizabeth I, took some fish by force from the owner who was on his way to market to sell the fish, but had refused to sell it to him, and after taking the fish left money in excess of its value.

[6] *Comm.* IV, ch. 17, s. 1 (p. 232), 'This taking, and carrying away, must also be felonious; that is, done *animo furandi*: or, as the civil law expresses it, *lucri causa*'.

[7] See (1942), 4 *Toronto L.J.* no. 2, 296; Russ. 1122.

[8] *R.* v. *Cabbage* (1815) R. and R. 292.

statute[1] which provided in effect that such conduct should only be a petty offence, with power to the justices to dismiss the charge, even if proved, without proceeding to conviction. After this enactment the doctrine with regard to *lucrum* became obsolete, and since it does not appear either directly or by implication in the Larceny Act, 1916, it must be taken not to be the law now, even if indeed it ever had been.

THE INTENT PERMANENTLY TO DEPRIVE THE OWNER (*ANIMUS FURANDI*)

¶ 284. Although from the earliest times it appears certain that an intent wholly to deprive the owner of the property was inherent in the phrase *animus furandi*,[2] yet any explicit declaration to that effect is difficult to find in cases earlier than that of *R.* v. *Cabbage*[3] in 1815. It is plainly enunciated in *R.* v. *Holloway*[4] in 1848 and is seen above in the definition given in Part I of the Larceny Act, 1916. Note here the distinction which must be made between a completely inscribed cheque and the material paper of the cheque form, which paper passes through the hands of the bankers concerned back into the possession of the drawer.[5]

¶ 285. *Trespass yet no larceny.* From what has been said above it can be seen that there can be a wrongful handling of another's property which will not constitute larceny, although it may amount to a trespass for which a civil action for damages would lie. Thus, as we have seen, the thing may be wrongfully touched, seized, or even moved (so long as not detached); or again taken under a *bona fide* claim of right; or, as in the case now to be considered, taken for no more than a temporary use.[6] As examples of this last sort Hale instanced the unauthorized borrowing of a neighbour's plough or horse.[7] It will be so even if the taker does not return the thing when he has finished with it,[8] so long as it does not appear that he abandoned it in such circumstances

[1] Misappropriation by Servants Act, 26 and 27 Vict. c. 103.

[2] E.g. *Anon.* (1698) 2 East P.C. 662 (*T.A.C.*).

[3] *Ante*, ¶ 283, n. 4.

[4] 3 Cox 241, 'with regard to the definition of larceny, we have of late years said that there must be an intention to deprive the owner permanently of his property', *per* Denman, C.J., at p. 244.

[5] See *post*, ¶ 343.

[6] But where the facts raise the presumption that permanent appropriation was intended, a vague hope or possibility of ultimate return will not be a defence; *R.* v. *Trebilcock* (1858) D. and B. 453.

[7] 1 Hale P.C. 509. But note that it is now a statutory offence under the Road Traffic Act, 1930, s. 28 (although not larceny) to take and drive away a motor vehicle without the consent of the owner or other lawful authority, although it will be a defence if the accused can show he had a reasonable belief in the existence of lawful authority so to do, or that the owner would have given his consent, if asked. And see *Mowe* v. *Perraton* [1952] 1 All E.R. 423.

[8] *R.* v. *Phillips* (1801) 2 East P.C. 662; *R.* v. *Crump* (1825) 1 C. and P. 658 (*T.A.C.*); *R.* v. *Addis* (1884) 1 Cox 78.

(e.g. remote distance, or dangerous surroundings) that he must have doubted whether it could be recovered by the owner.[1]

So also it is no more than a tort to seize your debtor's property wrongfully, if it is seized only for the purpose of inconveniencing him by detaining it until he pays the debt. Nor is it larceny for the finder of an article to refuse to give it up when asked, if in truth he is delaying in the hope that a reward may be offered. To take a key without the intention of keeping it but in order to unlock a safe, even though with the object of stealing the contents, is no larceny.[2] Nor is it a felonious taking when a man removes another person's goods so that he may bring them back and defraud him by the false pretence of having meanwhile done work upon them and earned payment thereby.[3]

¶ **286**. *Intent to treat the property as one's own.* From the cases last mentioned care should be taken to distinguish those in which the facts show that the taker really meant to treat the property *as his own* (even though for a limited period of time). It can readily be seen that if *X* dishonestly purloins a specific article and sells it to an unsuspecting person who in turn innocently sells it to its real owner who also does not recognize it, then *X*'s guilt of larceny is not eliminated by the fact that the article has in fact returned into the possession of its owner. But although it may not be so easy to appreciate it at first sight, the same result follows, and for the same reason, if *X* having taken the thing, forthwith deceives the owner into thinking that the article was a different one which did not already belong to him, and thereby induces him to buy it. Thus in *R.* v. *Manning*,[4] it was held to be larceny when *M*, the prosecutor's servant, took some of his master's potato bags and placed them at the door so that a confederate *S*, a bag-maker (who had previously sold these same bags to the prosecutor) was enabled to bring them in and, under the pretence that they were new ones, sell them again to the prosecutor.[5]

'AT THE TIME OF SUCH TAKING'

¶ **287**. In the statutory definition[6] it is plainly and explicitly stated that the guilty intention (*animus furandi*) must exist at the very moment

[1] *R.* v. *Oliver* [1921] Transvaal 120; *R.* v. *Laforte* [1922] Cape 487 as to motor cars. Even an intention to reimburse the value will not excuse a *permanent* appropriation, *R.* v. *Williams* [1953] 1 Q.B. 660; *ante*, p. 277.

[2] *R.* v. *Haslam* (1867) C.C.C. Sess. Pap. LXVII, 65. In May 1914 at the porch of the Central Criminal Court a banker's ledger was taken, by deceit, from a witness; but only for temporary detention, to prevent its being used as evidence in a pending trial.

[3] *R.* v. *Holloway* (1848) 1 Den. 370 (*T.A.C.*); *R.* v. *Poole* (1857) D. and B. 345. Contrast the facts in *R.* v. *Richards* (1844) 1 C. and K. 532.

[4] (1852) Dearsly 21. And see *R.* v. *Richards* (*supra*).

[5] An exactly similar case was *R.* v. *Hall* (1848) 1 Den. 381, where a servant of a candle-maker brought out from the store a quantity of fat so that a butcher could sell it back to his master as new fat. See also *R.* v. *Beecham* (1851) 5 Cox 181, where the prisoner was convicted of larceny in taking some railway tickets from the office notwithstanding that, when used for the journeys for which they were taken, they would have to be handed to the ticket-collector.

[6] *Ante*, ¶ 279.

when the thing was first taken.[1] This merely states and confirms what has been the undoubted rule of the common law from the earliest period of its history. It was this principle which rendered it originally impossible to secure the conviction of a bailee who yielded to temptation and dishonestly appropriated the article bailed; we have seen how the courts by specious and unsound reasoning contrived to establish the doctrines of 'breaking bulk'[2] and 'larceny by a trick'[3] which brought some delinquent bailees within the reach of the law, and how eventually this particular matter was put on a firm basis by statutory provisions now contained in section 1 of the Larceny Act, 1916. The old rule, however, even to the present day applies to the case of finders,[4] who when they first take possession of the lost article have no *animus furandi*; for they are not guilty of larceny should they later give way to temptation and determine to appropriate the article.

Once again it must be noted that in the present connexion the word 'take' means 'take into possession', so that where a man moves a thing solely for the purpose of examining it, he does not thereby 'take' it into his possession, nor will he take it into his *possession* (but only into temporary control) even if the owner has consented to his so moving it, or even has handed it to him for inspection.[5]

WHERE THE ORIGINAL TAKING IS A TRESPASS

¶ 288. Although the rule that the *animus furandi* must exist at the time of taking was so ancient and so clear, an attempt to undermine it was made by the Court for Crown Cases Reserved in the case of *R.* v. *Riley* in 1853.[6]

The prisoner, on a dark morning, had taken his flock of lambs from a field in which he had left them for the night, and drove them along the road to a farm where he sold the whole flock to the farmer. Unknown to him an extra lamb belonging to someone else had joined his flock in the field, and when the farmer pointed out that there was one more in the flock than Riley had stated, Riley at once formed the dishonest intent to obtain the farmer's money for that one also and sold it to him. He could clearly have been found guilty of obtaining the farmer's money by false pretences,[7] but he was charged, not with that offence, but with the larceny of the lamb; he was convicted of this at the trial and on appeal his conviction was upheld. In a judgment which took a strange view both of principle and of facts,[8] the court held (*a*) that Riley committed a trespass against the strange lamb when he drove off his flock

[1] *R.* v. *Holloway* (1833) 5 C. and P. 525 (*T.A.C.*); emphatically affirmed in *Moynes* v. *Coopper* [1956] 1 Q.B. 439.

[2] *Ante*, ¶ 233.

[3] *Ante*, ¶ 234.

[4] *Ante*, ¶ 253.

[5] See *R.* v. *Chisser* (1678) T. Raym. 275. This point is of great importance in the situation where lost goods are found; *ante*, ¶ 253.

[6] *R.* v. *Riley* (1853) Dearsly 149 (*T.A.C.*).

[7] *Post*, ¶ 340. In 1853 the statutory provision was 7 and 8 Geo. IV, c. 29, s. 53.

[8] For a criticism of the case see *Mod. Appr. Crim. Law*, 374 *et seq.*; Russ. 1137 *et seq.*

in ignorance that it was amongst them,[1] and (*b*) that because of the trespass, his subsequent *animus furandi* would make the original taking a felony.[2]

No authority was given for this entirely novel proposition, and the correctness of the decision has accordingly been questioned. It was, however, confirmed in a recent case, *Ruse* v. *Read*,[3] by a divisional court and must be accepted as one more instance of the modern exercise of indirect legislative power by the judges, even to the extent of overriding the express words of a statute. The position has been rendered more peculiar by the later case of *Rose* v. *Matt*[4] in which Lord Goddard, C.J., said:

> The Larceny Act, 1916, is entitled: 'An Act to consolidate and simplify the law relating to larceny triable on indictment and kindred offences.' We have now only to look at that Act to find what amounts to larceny. The old cases may be of assistance in the construction of the Act, but, if the words of the Larceny Act, 1916, are clear, that Act governs the decisions which this court must give.[5]

It should be noted that the facts of *Ruse* v. *Read* differed substantially from those of *R.* v. *Riley*, since it was plain on the evidence that Read saw the bicycle before he took it, and it was found as a fact by the justices that, when he thereupon took it to ride it, he did not have an intention permanently to deprive the owner of it. There is, however, the further point that in *R.* v. *Riley* it was assumed, without discussion or argument, that R. had committed a trespass to the white-faced ewe in the first instance when he drove off his flock without knowing that she had got amongst the others. Is it so certain that he did?[6] It was

1 A doubtful proposition, for which no authority was cited.

2 That the court felt some doubt about this is suggested by the statement (made by Pollock, C.B.), 'Here the taking of the lamb from the field was a trespass; or if it be said that there was no taking at that time, then the moment he finds the lamb he appropriates it to his own use'. Here there is not only a confusion of 'taking' with 'trespass', but also a failure to observe that, so far as appears from the reports, it was the farmer who found the lamb after it had passed into his possession with the others (since the universal practice for checking the number of sheep for purchase is to pass them through a narrow gateway or gap), so that Riley never took it or moved it after he first learned that it was there. Parke, B., advanced a doctrine of 'continuing trespass' to chattels, which seems to have had no basis in authority, and now appears to have been incidentally negatived in *R.* v. *Stally* [1959] 3 All E.R. 814 and *R.* v. *Parsons* [1960] 1 W.L.R. 797. See the comment on *R.* v. *Pearce* in [1961] *Crim.L.R.* 123.

3 *Ruse* v. *Read* [1949] 1 All E.R. 398; the prisoner, who had been drinking, mounted a stranger's bicycle and, after riding it about, had dealt with it in a highly suspicious manner. Contrast *R.* v. *Holloway* (1833) 5 C. and P. 525 (*T.A.C.*). And see *R.* v. *Matthews* [1950] 1 All E.R. 137.

4 [1951] 1 K.B. 810; 1 All E.R. 361 (*T.A.C.*).

5 Cf. *R.* v. *Moah* (1856) Dearsly 626 where Martin, B., said (at p. 639): 'I protest against the idea that when an Act of Parliament is made as clear as words can make it, you are to cite as authorities as to its construction, and as a guide to us in its interpretation, cases decided years and years before upon another statute'.

6 It is, of course, clear that Read committed a trespass to the bicycle when he first moved it. Note the difference in the facts of *R.* v. *Thomas* (1953) 37 Cr.App.R. 169.

accepted that he did not know she was there, and did not intend to take her; nor was any evidence of negligence on his part given.[1] In *R.* v. *Kindon*[2] the decision purported to rest on both *R.* v. *Riley* and *Ruse* v. *Read*, but the report does not make it clear whether the jury in deciding that the prisoner was so drunk and affected by a drug that she 'was incapable of forming any intention' included in this the intention to force open the desk and take the total sum of money out of it. If they did, then how could she have committed a trespass? There is nothing in the report to show that they disbelieved her statement that she could recollect nothing about the matter until another woman produced and showed her the money, and handed her £150 of it.[3]

INNOCENT POSSESSION

¶ 289. Under the ancient principle a taking could not be larceny if the intention to steal was not formed until later; so that to call such a taking 'innocent' means no more than 'unaccompanied by *animus furandi*'.[4] Since possession originally connoted physical control, an innocent taking could be called an innocent acquisition of possession; but after the distinction was established between physical control[5] and 'legal possession'[6] only an innocent taking which created a legal possession seemed to come within the doctrine. Thus the law of larceny has been entangled in the vexed question of what constitutes legal possession.[7]

LEGAL POSSESSION

¶ 290. A few examples will show the inconsistencies revealed in the cases. In *Cartwright* v. *Green*[8] the proceedings went on the footing (although the point was not in issue) that the purchaser at an auction of a bureau which (unknown both to the vendor and to the purchaser) contained money in a secret drawer, obtained legal possession of the money. About forty years later in another case, *Merry* v. *Green and Dewes*,[9] in circumstances in all material particulars the same as *Cartwright* v. *Green*,[10] a purchaser at an auction of a bureau was treated as *not*

[1] See the argument and cases cited in *Fowler* v. *Lanny* [1959] 1 All E.R. 290 (a case of trespass to the person, in which the general topic of trespass was discussed).

[2] (1957) 41 Cr.App.R. 208.

[3] It is in keeping with the judicial policy of modern times that the C.C.A. held that the prisoner had a joint possession of all the money with other women up to the time when one of them handed the £150 portion of it to her. How does this harmonize with the dictum in *Russell* v. *Smith* (1957) 41 Cr.App.R. at p. 205 ('I do not think a man can take a thing into his possession or come into possession of a thing of which he has no knowledge')?

[4] It does not mean 'a taking which is no trespass', for there would be a trespass, although no larceny, when a thing is borrowed without its owner's consent.

[5] The *possessio naturalis* of Roman law, often called *detentio*.

[6] *Ante*, ¶ 228.

[7] See *Hibbert* v. *McKiernan* [1948] 1 All E.R. 860 (*T.A.C.*), Lord Goddard, C.J., at pp. 861, 862.

[8] (1802) 8 Ves. 405. A bill in chancery praying a discovery.

[9] (1841) 10 L.J.M.C. 154.

[10] *Cartwright* v. *Green* was cited with approval in this case, without, as it would seem, this point being noticed.

acquiring possession of the money discovered in a secret drawer. In *R.* v. *Rowe*[1] the prisoner had found on the bed of a canal some metal which had been lost from an unknown barge, and it was held that he did not acquire lawful possession of it; whereas on the contrary in *Bridges* v. *Hawkesworth*[2] the finder of a wallet which some unknown customer had dropped on the floor of a shop was held to have lawful possession of, and a good title to, the bank-notes which it contained, as against the shop-keeper. In *R.* v. *Ashwell*[3] the prisoner was said by some of the judges not to have acquired lawful possession of a coin which the prosecutor had put into his hand, because in the darkness both of them believed it to be a silver coin whereas it was a gold one; one of these judges[4] said 'a man has not possession of that, of the existence of which he is unaware'.[5] It is obvious that the recipient of a letter or parcel delivered by post to him intends to possess the contents before he opens the package; accordingly in *R.* v. *Mucklow*,[6] *R.* v. *Davies*[7] and *R.* v. *Fish*[8] it was held that, when a letter, contained in a sealed envelope, was received by the man to whom it appeared to have been correctly addressed, he obtained lawful possession of the letter before he opened the envelope. Yet the two former cases were said by the same judge in *R.* v. *Ashwell* to be irreconcilable with *Cartwright* v. *Green* and *Merry* v. *Green and Dewes*, and therefore wrongly decided.[9] This rejects the idea that the intent of the recipient affects the question of possession: and yet in *Hibbert* v. *McKiernan*[10] it was said[11] that the members of a golf

[1] (1859) Bell 93.

[2] (1851) 15 Jur. 1079; approved and followed in *Hannah* v. *Peel* [1945] K.B. 509.

[3] (1885) 16 Q.B.D. 190; *post*, ¶ 291.

[4] Cave, J., who referred with approval to *Cartwright* v. *Green* as though that established his proposition, which, of course, it did not.

[5] A proposition which would have justified an acquittal in *R.* v. *Rowe* (*supra*).

[6] (1827) 1 Moo. 160. See Post Office Act, 1953, s. 55.

[7] (1856) Dearsly 640.

[8] (1900) 64 J.P. 137.

[9] A view also adopted in *R.* v. *Hudson* [1943] 1 K.B. 458; 1 All E.R. 642 (*T.A.C.*); *post*, ¶ 295.

[10] [1948] 1 All E.R. 860.

[11] At p. 863. See the illustration given by Lord Goddard, C.J., at p. 862: '*A*, meaning to give his neighbour *B* a present of game, takes a brace of pheasants to the latter's house. Finding the door open he leaves them in the hall, and thereby abandons both his property in and possession of them. *B* has at the moment gone out to post a letter, so does not know of *A*'s gift. *C*, who has seen *A*'s action, enters the house before *B* returns and takes the game. Can it be doubted that *C* is guilty of larceny and that the property can rightly be laid in *B*?' Compare this with the statement also made by Lord Goddard in *Russell* v. *Smith* [1957] 2 All E.R. 796 at p. 799: 'I do not think a man can take a thing into his possession, or come into possession of a thing, of which he has no knowledge. If somebody leaves something in my house and I do not know that he has left it, it does not seem to me that it can be said that I am in possession of the property.' See an article on this last case by R. Cross in [1958] *Crim. L.R.* 529. *Russell* v. *Smith* was really a case of simple larceny by Smith (under sect. 2 of the Larceny Act) from the owner of the property, and also larceny by Smith as servant (under sect. 17 (1) (*a*)) from his master who was the bailee of the property. The prisoner never had any possession of the property on the lorry of which he was the driver until the moment when he finally removed it from the lorry for his own dishonest purposes. See Russ. pp. 1114–15.

club had possession of golf balls lost and abandoned in the rough on the golf course by unknown persons, because they had an intention to exclude other people from the place where the balls lay although they did not know that the balls were there. And we have already observed that it was held in *R.* v. *Riley*[1] that the prisoner had taken possession (and committed trespass thereby) of a lamb which he did not know had joined his flock.

In *R.* v. *Swinson*[2] an owner who had lost a pocket book containing a bank-note, owing to its having fallen from her carriage as she was being driven along a street, was held to be in 'constructive possession'[3] of the bank-note even after it had been picked up by a finder.

Running through this conflict in the cases from about 1850 onwards it seems that there has been a tendency, inspired by moral disapproval of obviously dishonest conduct, to adopt whatever theory of possession will enable the conviction of the accused person to be upheld.[4]

Viewing the matter from this angle the student may feel less bewildered by the following well-known cases.

¶ 291. *R.* v. *Ashwell.*[5] Intending to lend Ashwell a shilling the prosecutor *K* handed to him in the dark a coin which both men believed to be a shilling but which was a sovereign. *A* spent it and when subsequently interrogated denied that he had ever received it and made other false statements. He was convicted of larceny at the assizes, but the case was remitted to the Court for Crown Cases Reserved. In that court seven[6] of the fourteen judges were in favour of quashing the conviction, but the other seven[7] were in favour of upholding it; as the judges were, in numbers, equally divided, the conviction of Ashwell stood unaltered, by a rule *praesumitur pro negante* which that court had adopted. Since in this appeal no decision was reached, the judgments delivered can be no more than persuasive. In that situation it would seem to be the proper course to apply the test of legal principle and logic to each of the judgments in order to see which are the better. By this test it can be seen that the four delivered in favour of Ashwell's acquittal by far excel the three which were delivered in favour of his conviction. When the facts are care-

[1] *Ante*, ¶ 288.

[2] (1900) 64 J.P. 73; see ¶ 261 *ante* and ¶ 344 *post*. In fact the jury found S. guilty under the third count in the indictment which laid the property in the wife of the finder (who had handed it to her for safe keeping): but the judge approved an argument on the first count which laid the property in the loser, and let both counts go to the jury.

[3] This would more aptly have been termed 'constructive control'.

[4] For the conflict of views on this matter see Kerr, 'The time of criminal intent in larceny', 66 *L.Q.R.* 174; Cross, 'Larceny *de lege lata*', *ibid.* 497; Edwards, 'Possession and larceny', 3 *Current Legal Problems*, 127; Carter, 'Taking and acquisition of possession in larceny', 14 *Mod. L.R.* 27.

[5] (1885) 16 Q.B.D. 190 (*T.A.C.*). On this case see Russ., app. 1.

[6] Stephen, Smith, Matthew, Manisty, Field, Day and Wills, JJ., of whom each of the four first-named delivered a considered judgment. Their view was approved by Lord Loreburn in the Report of the Committee on the Larceny Bill, p. 21.

[7] Cave, J., Denman, J., Lord Coleridge, C.J., Hawkins, Grove, Pollock and Huddleston, JJ., of whom each of the three first-named delivered a considered judgment.

fully considered it will be found that the sole point in issue was whether in a case of larceny it makes any difference if the owner and the taker are mistaken as to the value of the article alleged to have been stolen. The only mistake which the two men had made was that each thought that the metal disk which was passed by the one to the other was worth 12*d.* when in reality it was worth 240*d.*[1] As we have seen,[2] that mistake was irrelevant and, on the principles explained with singular scholarship and lucidity by Stephen, J., Ashwell ought to have been acquitted.[3]

¶ **292.** *R.* v. *Jacobs.*[4] It is appropriate to note that the attention of the court in *R.* v. *Ashwell* was not directed to the previously decided case of *R.* v. *Jacobs,* who had been indicted for stealing half a sovereign which the prosecutor had passed over to him in mistake for a sixpenny piece, when paying for an article sold to him for one penny. To the argument that the prosecutor, intending to give one coin, gave another, and did not intend to pass to the prisoner the property in the gold, the judge replied, 'Not so. He intended to give the prisoner the particular piece of coin he held between his fingers, although he was mistaken as to the nature of that coin', and after taking the opinion of the assistant judge, ruled that there was no larceny.

¶ **293.** *R.* v. *Flowers.*[5] Within twelve months of the abortive proceedings in *R.* v. *Ashwell,* the Court for Crown Cases Reserved were called upon to consider the case of Flowers,[6] who appealed against a conviction for larceny. It appeared that the prisoner had received from the foreman at his place of employment a paper bag containing his wages; he took out the contents, and finding that the money was threepence too little, returned the empty bag to the cashier's clerk, asking for the balance due to him. The clerk gave him threepence and, picking up what he mistakenly thought to be the prisoner's empty bag, handed it to him. The bag, however, contained money intended for another workman. Flowers took it, and afterwards opened it and appropriated its contents, knowing well from the name written on the bag that the money was not meant for him. The jury found as a fact that he received the bag and its contents innocently, and afterwards fraudulently appropriated the money to his own use. Following *Ashwell's Case* the recorder directed a verdict of guilty to be entered. It is plain that the facts in *Flowers's Case* were more unfavourable to the prisoner than the facts in *R.* v. *Ashwell* were to Ashwell: they were indeed closely parallel to those in *Merry* v. *Green and Dewes.*[7]

Notwithstanding this, the court[8] were unanimous in quashing Flowers's conviction, Lord Coleridge saying of *R.* v. *Ashwell*: 'In that case the judges who were in favour of upholding the conviction did not intend to question

[1] As stated by Smith, J., at p. 197.

[2] *Ante,* ¶ 269.

[3] Since *Moynes* v. *Coopper* [1956] 1 Q.B. 439, *post,* p. 288, it is difficult to see how the conviction of Ashwell can any longer be supported.

[4] (1872), 12 Cox 151, Midd. Sess.

[5] (1886) 16 Q.B.D. 643 (*T.A.C.*).

[6] See Russ., app. 1.

[7] *Ante,* ¶ 290. In his judgment against Ashwell, Lord Coleridge had relied upon *Merry* v. *Green.*

[8] Lord Coleridge, C.J., Manisty, Hawkins, Day and Grantham, JJ.

the ancient doctrine that an innocent receipt of a chattel and its subsequent fraudulent appropriation do not constitute larceny...there is a most substantial difference between that case and the present....'

As above indicated the undoubted difference of fact between the two cases did not justify his lordship's conclusion; for if Ashwell was guilty then *a fortiori* Flowers should also have been convicted.

¶ 294. *R.* v. *Hehir.*[1] The fallacies contained in the remarks of those judges who supported the conviction of Ashwell were vigorously exposed[2] some ten years later in judgments delivered in this Irish appeal. The facts in this case were almost identical with those in *R.* v. *Ashwell*, the prosecutor having handed to the prisoner a £10 bank-note which both believed to be a £1 note. His conviction was quashed by five judges against four. One passage is particularly striking: 'No doubt he would not have given the particular chattel if he knew it was a £10 note; but the very fact of his mistaken belief that it was only a £1 note, made him give the note without any condition or reservation whatever. He manually transferred the chattel...not involuntarily, not accidentally, but on purpose.'[3]

¶ 294 *a*. *Moynes* v. *Coopper.*[4] The facts as found were that C. an employee of a firm of contractors, had been handed, by the wages clerk of the firm, a packet which contained more money than was in fact due to him, the clerk mistakenly thinking that the whole sum in the packet was due to C. and intending that C. should receive that sum. When C. thus received the packet he did not know that it contained more than was due to him; but he discovered its contents later when he opened the packet in his own home, and then, realizing the mistake, he dishonestly appropriated to his own use all the money. In their statement of the case the appeals committee, citing as supporting authority *R.* v. *Prince*,[5] expressed the opinion[6] that *R.* v. *Middleton*[7] was distinguishable in that here the wages clerk (unlike the post-office clerk in *R.* v. *Middleton*) had authority to pass the ownership of the packet and all its contents, and intended to do so, making no mistake as to the identity of the packet, of its contents, or of the recipient; and that the words 'without the consent of the owner' dominated and governed the whole definition of larceny in section 1 (1) of the Larceny Act, 1916; and that the special meaning given by subsection (2) to the word 'takes' did not dispense with the necessity of larceny being an obtaining without the consent of the owner; and

[1] [1895] 2 I.R. 709; an Irish decision of persuasive, but not *binding*, authority in English courts.

[2] Especially by Palles, C.B., and O'Brian, J.

[3] Sir P. O'Brian, L.C.J., at p. 760.

[4] [1956] 1 Q.B. 439, an appeal by way of case stated from a decision of the West Kent quarter sessions' appeal committee, who had quashed the conviction of the respondent C. for larceny.

[5] (1868) L.R. 1 C.C.R. 150.

[6] At p. 441.

[7] (1873) L.R. 2 C.C.R. 38, *ante*, ¶ 252.

that C. had committed no trespass[1], and was not guilty of larceny. The Court of Criminal Appeal, in upholding the decision of the appeals committee, declared[2] that the Larceny Act, 1916, affirmed the common law that the taker must have *animus furandi* at the time when he takes the property, and based their decision on that ground. The result of this decision is that *R.* v. *Flowers*[3] is supported and *R.* v. *Ashwell*[4] still further discredited.

¶ 295. *R.* v. *Hudson.*[5] This was an appeal against conviction of larceny. A sum of money in payment for pigs was due from the Ministry of Food to one Hutson; the appropriate department of the Ministry by mistake made out and despatched a cheque for the amount to 'Mr Hudson'. It happened that the prisoner, whose name was Hudson, kept a farm quite close to Hutson's premises; the postman accordingly delivered the letter containing the cheque to the prisoner, who sent back the cheque to the Ministry with a note, stating merely that he had received it, that there were no initials to the name, and that his name was 'J. Hudson'. The Ministry officials altered the cheque by adding the initial 'J', and returned it to the prisoner with a covering note which stated that the cheque had been so altered, and apologized for any trouble caused to him. Some ten days later the prisoner paid in the cheque to his bank account.[6] The prisoner was convicted of larceny of the cheque at the moment when he read it on taking it from its envelope on the first occasion when it was delivered by the postman to him. In dismissing his appeal the Court of Criminal Appeal relied upon dicta in *R.* v. *Ashwell*,[7] and repudiated the cases of *R.* v. *Mucklow* and *R.* v. *Davies.*[8] It is not easy to see how the facts could be held to establish that Hudson had any *animus furandi* at the moment when he first saw the cheque. His attitude of mind *then* could only be proved by his subsequent dealing with the cheque; and since what he proceeded to do was to send back the cheque to the Ministry with an intimation that there was *some* mistake, his conduct can hardly be regarded as showing beyond reasonable doubt that he had instantly formed an *animus furandi* at the critical moment. For it would have been just as easy for him to have endorsed and cashed the cheque then as it was after the alteration to it had been made. If, on receipt of the cheque when returned by Hudson, the Ministry had made a reasonable investigation of their records they would have discovered their mistake and would never have altered and sent back the cheque to Hudson. Had they retained it, and proceeded to pay their real creditor, Hutson, it could hardly have been possible for the prisoner Hudson to have been convicted on a charge of larceny of it; and it is equally hard to see how his later conduct in negotiating the

[1] This finding excluded the principle of *R.* v. *Riley* as declared in *Ruse* v. *Read*, *ante*, ¶ 288.

[2] At p. 445.

[3] (1886) 16 Q.B.D. 643.

[4] (1885) 16 Q.B.D. 190.

[5] [1943] 1 K.B. 458 (*T.A.C.*).

[6] His endorsement of this cheque was held to be a forgery; see ¶ 389 *post*, and see ¶ 343 on the question of his guilt of the crime of false pretences.

[7] Including one from the judgment of Stephen, J., in which that judge in reality was referring to an entirely different set of facts. See Russ., app. 1.

[8] *Supra*, ¶ 290.

cheque after it had been sent to him a second time in its altered state can have made any relevant difference.[1]

SECTION 8. PUNISHMENT

¶ 296. As regards its punishment, larceny presented some anomaly at common law; for, though a felony, it was not invariably a capital offence. A distinction was made according to the pecuniary value of the thing stolen. If it were worth only twelve pence[2] or less, the offence was merely a 'petty' larceny; and, although a felony, it was not punishable with death. If the thing were worth more than 12*d*., the crime was a 'grand' larceny;[3] and at least as early as the time of Edward I—probably indeed by the legislation of the stern 'Lion of Justice', Henry I[4]—it became punishable capitally.

The law was greatly complicated by the rules of 'benefit of clergy' (*ante*, ¶ 55). This privilege, after becoming general, was taken away from a large number of crimes during the eighteenth century, when many changes were made by statute.[5] The severities to which this policy led were to some extent moderated by an Act of 1768[6] which gave to judges of assize the discretion to order that all persons convicted of crimes without benefit of clergy should be transported (for any term which they thought suitable, or for fourteen years if no term were ordered). During the first half of the nineteenth century capital punishment was progressively removed from all kinds of stealing, and the phrases 'petty', 'grand' have become obsolete since the abolition in 1827 of the distinction between them.[7] But larceny still admitted a division into two forms, 'simple' and 'aggravated'.

SIMPLE LARCENY

¶ 297. Simple larceny, as defined by the Larceny Act, 1916,[8] is now punishable with imprisonment for not more than five years, or with a fine, or with both imprisonment and fine.[9] A person convicted of simple larceny, after having been previously convicted of any felony whatever, may be sentenced to ten years' imprisonment.[10]

Notwithstanding the express words of section 2 of the Larceny Act,

[1] In the course of his judgment delivered in *Moynes* v. *Coopper* (*supra*) Lord Goddard, C.J., mentioned that *R.* v. *Hudson* had been the subject of a good deal of criticism as to whether the charge ought not to have been for obtaining an altered cheque by false pretences adding 'the appellant had certainly been guilty of some crime'.

[2] See the Laws of Athelstane (v. 1). Under Edward I the 12*d*. was reckoned to be eight days' wages of a man.

[3] Cf. Bolland's *General Eyre*, 66.

[4] Pollock and Maitland, II, 496. 'If two or three jointly steal goods to the value of twelvepence halfpenny, they shall *severally* have judgment of life and limb'; (1313) *Eyre of Kent* (Seld. Soc. Y.B. Series, v), I, 90.

[5] Stephen, *Hist. Crim. Law*, I, 459 *et seq.*

[6] 8 Geo. III, c. 15.

[7] 7 and 8 Geo. IV, c. 28, s. 2.

[8] Sect. 2. *Ante*, ¶ 223. As modified by the Criminal Justice Act, 1948, s. 1.

[9] Criminal Justice Act, 1948, s. 13; see ¶ 766 *post*.

[10] Sect. 37 (1).

1916, 'shall be simple larceny and a felony', it has been judicially stated:

> The first thing to be noted is that section 2 of the Larceny Act does not create an offence. Larceny was always an offence at common law. Section 2 of the Larceny Act, 1916, is a section solely concerned with punishment.... If a person is charged with simple larceny, he is charged with a common law offence and not an offence against a particular Statute.[1]

AGGRAVATED LARCENY

¶ 298. Aggravated larceny is punishable by various long periods of imprisonment ranging from the offender's life down to seven years, or a fine.[2] It consists of several kinds which may be roughly grouped according to the grounds of aggravation, which are (*a*) the place where it is committed, (*b*) its association with an attack upon the person, (*c*) the special position occupied by the offender, (*d*) the thing which is stolen.[3]

¶ 299. (*a*) *The place.* Larcenies are aggravated when committed in a ship, dock, wharf, or wreck,[4] or (if the stolen property be worth not less than £5) a dwelling house. In this last case the goods must be under the protection of the house, deposited there for safe custody, and not merely under the protection of a person who happens to be in the house.[5] The maximum punishment in each of these five cases is fourteen years' imprisonment.

¶ 300. (*b*) *Larceny from the person. Robbery.* If the property is stolen without force from the person (e.g. by picking his pocket) the maximum punishment is fourteen years' imprisonment.[6] If the property is not only stolen from the person of someone but taken from him by force (snapping a watch-chain suffices[7])—or if he is led to give it up by being put in fear of force being used, the offence obtains the name of robbery.[8] The force need not be great.[9] Yet obtaining money from a

[1] *R.* v. *Bryant* [1955] 1 W.L.R. 715 (Courts-Martial Appeal Case), *per* Lord Goddard, C.J., at p. 717. See *R.* v. *Bryant* (No. 2) (Practice Note) [1956] 1 W.L.R. 133. On this case see 119 *J.P.Jo.* 474; *Cam.L.J.* (1955) 146; [1955] *Crim. L.R.* 696; Russ. 1165.

[2] Criminal Justice Act, 1948, s. 13; see ¶ 766 *post.*

[3] All the references to the Larceny Act, 1916, which follow, must be read in conjunction with the provisions of the Criminal Justice Act, 1948, which abolished penal servitude, hard labour, and flogging (s. 1); and allows the infliction of a fine in all cases (s. 13).

[4] Sect. 15.

[5] Sect. 13. *R.* v. *Owen* (1792) 2 East P.C. 645; *R.* v. *Carroll* (1825) 1 Moo. 89; and see cases cited in Russ. 948 *et seq.*

[6] Sect. 14. Complete severance of anything attached to the person is necessary; *R.* v. *Thompson* (1825) 1 Moo. 78; *R.* v. *Taylor* [1911] 1 K.B. 674. ¶ 278 *ante.*

[7] *R.* v. *Mason* (1820) R. and R. 419.

[8] Sect 23 (2). Fortescue (L.C.J., 1442–60) preferred the many English robbers to the many French thieves since 'there is more spirit and a better heart in a robber than in a thief' (*Monarchy*, c. 12).

[9] Catching hold of an arm suffices. The gentle application of a chloroformed rag, producing a mere momentary unconsciousness, was held sufficient by the Court of

solitary woman in a lonely place by a threat, not to use force, but merely to accuse her of being there for evil purposes, would not be robbery; though it would, as we shall shortly see (¶ 310), constitute a statutory offence. And even actual force, if it does not begin until after the taking, will not make a larceny become a robbery.[1]

The maximum punishment of these offences is again fourteen years' imprisonment. But for robberies that are further aggravated in certain specified ways (as by the robber's being armed, or having a companion, or using any personal violence), the maximum punishment rises to imprisonment for life.[2] Even if no article be actually taken, and so no robbery be effected, the mere assault with intent to rob is a felony, and punishable with five years' imprisonment.[3]

¶ 301. (*c*) *The position occupied by the offender.* In the case of larceny by a clerk or servant or by one employed in the public service of Her Majesty or in the police of any place whatsoever the maximum punishment is raised to fourteen years' imprisonment,[4] owing to the opportunities of dishonesty which are necessarily placed within the reach of all persons thus employed, and to the breach of confidence which is involved in taking advantage of them. The discussion of the difficult question 'Who is a clerk or servant?' may be deferred until the subject of embezzlement is dealt with.[5]

¶ 302. (*d*) *The thing which is stolen.* The larceny of cattle, or of ten shillings' worth of textile goods exposed in process of manufacture,[6] is punishable with imprisonment for fourteen years. (But maliciously destroying such textile goods is punishable with imprisonment for life.[7]) To kill an animal with intent to steal the carcase or skin is a felony punishable with the same punishment as if the animal had been stolen, provided that stealing the animal would have amounted to felony.[8] Again, for stealing letters from a post office, or from a postman, or for stealing a will,[9] the maximum punishment is imprisonment for life.[10] And yet, curiously enough, a more complex and apparently more heinous offence, viz. the stealing of a post-letter by a person who is

Criminal Appeal, since 'it was all the violence that was necessary for the purpose', *R.* v. *Carney*, 18 Dec. 1922 (unreported). In fact *any* violence suffices, *R.* v. *Harrison* (1930) 22 Cr.App.R. 82. See ¶ 110 *ante*.

[1] *R.* v. *Gnosil* (1824) 1 C. and P. 304, but under the Larceny Act, 1916 (s. 23 (1)), the use of personal violence immediately after a robbery involves the same punishment as the use of personal violence immediately before or at the time of such robbery. At common law cases of extortion by threats to accuse of sodomitical practices were often treated as sufficient to constitute robbery (see Russ., ch. 50), but it would seem that now such cases fall properly within sect. 29 (1) (iii) of the Larceny Act, 1916, *post*, ¶ 308.

[2] Larceny Act, 1916, s. 23.

[3] *Ibid.* s. 23 (3).

[4] *Ibid.* s. 17.

[5] *Post*, ¶ 318.

[6] Larceny Act, 1916, ss. 2, 9.

[7] 24 and 25 Vict. c. 97, s. 14 (¶ 192 *ante*).

[8] Larceny Act, 1916, s. 4.

[9] *Ibid.* s. 6.

[10] *Ibid.* s. 12.

himself an employee of the post office, is punishable only with seven years' imprisonment[1] (unless the letter contain some chattel or money or valuable security, in which case the maximum punishment is imprisonment for life).

QUASI-LARCENIES

¶ 303. In the foregoing account of larceny mention has been made of various articles which, though movable, were not within the old law of larceny.[2] By modern statutes, it has been made a crime to steal almost any of these. But such thefts are not always made 'larcenies'; and some are not even made felonies, but only indictable misdemeanours or offences punishable on summary conviction. The Larceny Act, 1916, contains several instances of these statute-made thefts, but its omission (see ¶ 222 *ante*) to define larceny prevents our ascertaining which of them are properly to be termed larcenies.[3] Such thefts, however, are construed by all the other common law rules about larceny, e.g. rules as to what will constitute a taking[4] or a carrying away, or an intent to steal. It may consequently be convenient if, for want of any recognized name, we call them for the moment 'quasi-larcenies', or, in Lord Loreburn's phrase, 'auxiliary larcenies'.

Common instances

¶ 304. The cases of hares and of fish have already been mentioned. We may add some more common instances.

(1) The theft of any valuable security[5] is felony, and punishable in the same manner as if the thief had stolen a chattel of like value. Similarly punishable is the fraudulent destruction or obliteration of a valuable security.[6]

(2) To steal trees of the value of £1[7] or more, if growing in a park or garden, or of the value of more than £5 in any place whatsoever or of the value of one shilling after two previous summary convictions of such offence, or to steal fixtures[8] or the title-deeds of land[9] or certain court documents is a felony punishable (like simple larceny) with five years' imprisonment.

(3) To steal wild deer in *enclosed* land (24 and 25 Vict. c. 96, s. 13), and to steal mineral ore from a mine,[10] are felonies, but punishable with no higher penalty than two years' imprisonment.

[1] *Ibid.* s. 18. This lessening of punishment was perhaps due to the influence of the ancient rule that embezzlement was no crime.

[2] *Ante*, ¶ 260.

[3] See *R.* v. *Millar* (1837) 7 C. and P. 667 n.; cf. *R.* v. *Gooch* (1838) 8 C. and P. 293. The marginal note to s. 5 of the Larceny Act, 1916, creates further confusion as to this word.

[4] But see *Farey* v. *Welch* [1929] 1 K.B. 388, and n. 6, p. 312 *post*.

[5] Larceny Act, 1916, s. 46 (1).

[6] Larceny Act, 1861, s. 27.

[7] Larceny Act, 1916, s. 8 (2).

[8] *Ibid.* s. 8 (1). The stealing of chattels or fixtures by tenants and lodgers is punishable with seven years' imprisonment if the value exceeds £5, and with two years' imprisonment if the value is less than £5, *ibid.* s. 16.

[9] *Ibid.* s. 7.

[10] *Ibid.* s. 11.

(4) And it is a petty offence punishable, on summary conviction, with six months' imprisonment (for a *first* commission of the crime), to steal[1] any plant, fruit or other vegetable production growing in a garden or orchard,[2] or any *cultivated* root or plant—*fruit* is not included—growing elsewhere,[3] or to steal a dog,[4] or indeed to steal any bird, beast or other animal ordinarily[5] kept in confinement (e.g. a canary) or for any domestic purpose (e.g. a cat) and not larcenable at common law.[6]

It is a misdemeanour punishable with eighteen months' imprisonment to steal a dog after being previously summarily convicted for dog-stealing; or corruptly to take any money or reward to aid in the recovery of a stolen dog; or knowingly to possess a stolen dog or its skin after a previous summary conviction of such offence (Larceny Act, 1916, s. 5).

Section 9. Menaces with Intent to Extort

¶ 305. With extortion by threats of violence (robbery) we have already dealt (*ante*, ¶ 300). In this section we are concerned with a group of offences defined in three sections of the Larceny Act, 1916 (ss. 29–31), which concern menaces of a somewhat different character. These crimes are popularly termed 'blackmail',[7] though the word is untechnical and vague. To utter, knowing the contents thereof, a letter or writing demanding of any person with menaces,[8] and without any reasonable or probable cause, any property or valuable thing is a felony punishable with imprisonment for life.[9] What the accused person has to justify is

[1] These offences are distinct from simple larceny. Where the facts show larceny at common law there can be no conviction under s. 36 of the Larceny Act, 1861; *R.* v. *Friend* (1930) 22 Cr.App.R. 130, where the jury were directed that it was immaterial whether fruit was growing or severed at the material time and the conviction was quashed.

[2] Larceny Act, 1861, s. 36. [3] *Ibid.* s. 37. [4] *Ibid.* s. 18.

[5] It suffices that the individual has been so kept, though those of its species are not confined ordinarily.

[6] *Ibid.* s. 21. Cf. ¶ 271 *ante*. Sect. 23 punishes the unlawful and wilful killing, wounding or taking of any house dove or pigeon under such circumstances as shall not amount to larceny at common law. Belief that the bird was a wild one is no defence to a charge of shooting a pigeon, *Horton* v. *Gwynne* [1921] 2 K.B. 661, *Cotterill* v. *Penn* (1935) 51 T.L.R. 459 (*T.A.C.*). Where the accused fires because of actual though not merely apprehended danger to crops, he is not guilty of an offence, *Taylor* v. *Newman* (1863) 4 B. and S. 89; *Horton* v. *Gwynne* (*supra*). For the meaning of 'take' see *Farey* v. *Welch* [1929] 1 K.B. 388. For a discussion of these scarcely reconcilable cases see 'The eclipse of *mens rea*', W. T. S. Stallybrass, 52 *L.Q.R.* 60; and see *ante*, ¶ 32. And note the possibility of a prosecution for malicious damage (*ante*, Ch. XI).

[7] In such cases it has universally been allowed of late that the prosecutor may, for the purpose of the trial, be anonymous. As to blackmail see Glanville Williams, in [1954] *Crim. L.R.* 79, 162, 240.

[8] The word 'menaces' in this section is not restricted to threats of violence and injury to person or property but covers also threats of other kinds, even of acts which the threatener has a perfect right to do; *Thorne* v. *Motor Trade Association* [1937] A.C. 797 (*T.A.C.*), *per* Lord Atkin at p. 806. See Campbell, 'The anomalies of blackmail', 55 *L.Q.R.* 382.

[9] Larceny Act, 1916, s. 29 (1) (i).

not the threat but the demand of money.[1] The presence or absence of reasonable or probable cause to demand the money is a question of fact for the jury.[2] And it has been said[3] that the belief of the accused affords no defence; in other words, there must be in fact a cause and not merely a genuine belief in a cause. This last statement has, however, been doubted in the House of Lords, where Lord Atkin said:[4] 'This seems to me to have been incautiously expressed: and I do not think that doubt should exist upon a well established proposition in criminal law that normally a genuine belief in the existence of facts, as apart from law, which if they existed would constitute a defence, is itself a sufficient defence.'

¶ **306.** *R.* v. *Denyer.* Section 29 of the Larceny Act has given rise to an unusual difference of judicial opinion. In *R.* v. *Denyer* [1926] 2 K.B. 258, the stop list superintendent of a trade protection society was convicted of this felony for uttering a letter threatening to place upon the stop list of the society the name of a trader who had sold goods at prices lower than the protected prices of the trade, unless he paid a sum of money to the indemnity fund of the society. The Court of Appeal had held in the civil case of *Ware and De Freville Ltd.* v. *Motor Trade Association* [1921] 3 K.B. 40, that there was nothing illegal in placing the name of a trader upon a stop list in order to protect prices, but the Court of Criminal Appeal upheld Denyer's conviction, and the Lord Chief Justice said that there was not the remotest nexus or relationship between the right to put a name upon a stop list and the right to demand a sum of money as the price of abstaining from that course. Relying upon this decision an attempt was made in a subsequent civil action, *Hardie and Lane Ltd.* v. *Chilton and others* [1928] 2 K.B. 306, to recover money that had been paid to the same society in order to avoid inclusion in the stop list. Avory, J., who was himself a member of the court which upheld the conviction in *R.* v. *Denyer*, allowed the claim, but the Court of Appeal overruled his decision and expressed the opinion that *R.* v. *Denyer* was wrongly decided. The Court of Criminal Appeal, however, stated that unless and until the decision in *R.* v. *Denyer* is reversed by the House of Lords it is binding and will be enforced for the purposes of the administration of the criminal law.

¶ **307.** *Thorne* v. *Motor Trade Association.* The point was in fact brought before the House of Lords in the case of *Thorne* v. *Motor Trade Association*[5] in 1937. This was an action claiming a declaration (and an injunction) that a rule of the defendant Association, whereby they might impose fines in lieu of placing a member on the stop list, was illegal and *ultra vires.* At the trial and in the Court of Appeal the action was dismissed on the ground that the point was decided by *Hardie and Lane*

[1] *Thorne* v. *Motor Trade Association* [1937] A.C. 797 (*T.A.C.*) *per* Lord Atkin, at p. 806.
[2] *Ibid.* at p. 808.
[3] *R.* v. *Dymond* [1920] 2 K.B. 260.
[4] *Thorne* v. *Motor Trade Association*, at p. 809.
[5] *Ubi supra.*

Ltd. v. *Chilton and others.*[1] With this view the House of Lords concurred, expressing their disapproval of *R.* v. *Denyer* so far as in principle it conflicted with *Hardie and Lane Ltd.* v. *Chilton*. Lord Russell of Killowen[2] said: 'I am of opinion... that *Denyer's* appeal should have been allowed'; and Lord Wright said:[3] 'The decision in *R.* v. *Denyer* was in my opinion wrong.' Whether these strong expressions of disapproval will in some future case be regarded by the Court of Criminal Appeal as overruling *R.* v. *Denyer* remains to be seen.[4]

THREATS TO ACCUSE ANOTHER OF CRIME

¶ 308. By virtue of sect. 29 (1) (ii) (iii) of the Larceny Act it is a felony (punishable with imprisonment for life) if any person, with intent to extort or gain any property or valuable thing from any other person, either (i) accuses or threatens to accuse that person or any other person (whether living or dead) of any of certain specified crimes, or (ii) utters, knowing the contents thereof, any letter or writing accusing or threatening to accuse any other person (whether living or dead) of any such crime.[5]

COMPELLING THE EXECUTION OR ALTERATION OF VALUABLE SECURITIES

¶ 309. The same section[6] in effect provides that it shall be a felony punishable with imprisonment for life if any person, with intent to defraud or injure another, either (i) by unlawful violence to or restraint of the person of another, or (ii) by accusing or threatening to accuse of crime (as in the above mentioned subsections) or of any felony, compels or induces anyone to execute, accept, endorse, alter or destroy the whole or part of any valuable security or to write or alter any name or corporate seal on any paper etc. in order that it may afterwards be used as a valuable security.

DEMANDING WITH MENACES

¶ 310. By section 30 it is a felony, punishable with imprisonment for five years, to demand with menaces or by force anything capable of being stolen with intent to steal the same. To constitute a menace the threat need not be one of injury to the person or property. It is sufficient

[1] [1928] 2 K.B. 306.
[2] At p. 811.
[3] At p. 821.
[4] In *Hill* v. *Wm. Hill Ltd* [1949] 2 All E.R. 452 at p. 462, Lord Simon (speaking of *Hyams* v. *Stuart King* [1908] 2 K.B. 696) said: 'Farwell, L.J.'s judgment... regards "the gist of the case" as concerned with the question whether threatening to post a defaulter for failure to pay a lost bet could properly be described as blackmail. I should agree that in ordinary circumstances it would not amount to a criminal offence.' On this topic see Russ. 997 *et seq.*
[5] The crimes specified are any crime punishable with death, or imprisonment for not less than seven years, any assault with intent to commit rape, attempted rape, and any solicitation or threat offered to any person to commit or permit an unnatural offence.
[6] By subsect. (2).

that it should produce in an ordinary man such a degree of fear or alarm as would unsettle his mind, and this definition will be construed liberally.[1] It is not necessary that any express threat should be made, nor that there should be an express demand for money in words. It is enough if the jury are satisfied on the evidence that the demeanour of the accused and circumstances of the case were such that an ordinary reasonable man could understand that a demand for money was being made upon him and that that demand was accompanied by menaces—not perhaps direct but veiled menaces—so that his ordinary balance of mind was upset.[2] The word 'steal' in this section is defined by sect. 1 of the Act. Accordingly a claim of right made in good faith is a defence.[3]

THREATS TO PUBLISH

¶ 311. Section 31 in effect provides that it is a misdemeanour, punishable with imprisonment for two years,

(i) to publish or threaten to publish, or
(ii) to propose, either directly or indirectly, to abstain from or to prevent the printing or publishing of any matter or thing touching any other person (whether living or dead), with intent,
  (*a*) to extort any valuable thing from any person, or
  (*b*) to induce any person to confer or procure for anyone an appointment or office of profit or trust.

It is to be noted that in section 31 the words 'without reasonable or probable cause' do not appear (as they do in section 29 (1)). It has therefore been argued that this omission was intentional, so that it would be no defence that the accused believed the thing demanded to be due to him, or even that in fact it was due to him. The point does not seem to have been decided; it was not expressly considered in *Thorne* v. *Motor Trade Association*.[4] Nor does there seem to be any clear authority for regarding the word 'extort' as implying that there is neither a right to demand the property, nor an honest belief in the existence of such a right.

SECTION 10. RESTITUTION OF THE STOLEN PROPERTY

¶ 312. The thief, as we have seen, aims at depriving the true owner of all the benefits of his ownership. But of the ownership itself he cannot deprive him. It is important for the student to avoid the misapprehensions on this point which are apt to arise from the ambiguity of the word 'property'. That term may mean[5] either the physical object

[1] *R.* v. *Boyle and Merchant* [1914] 3 K.B. 339.

[2] *Per* Pilcher, J., in the trial of *R.* v. *Collister and Warhurst* (1955) 39 Cr.App.R. 100 affirming *R.* v. *Jackson and Randall* (1783) 1 Leach 267; and see the curious case of *R.* v. *Moran* (1952) 36 Cr.App.R. 10, discussed in Russ. 994.

[3] *R.* v. *Bernhard* [1938] 2 K.B. 264 (*T.A.C.*); see ¶ 40 *ante*.

[4] *Ante*, ¶ 307; although Lord Atkin at p. 805 said that an amendment had been allowed in order to raise the effect of the section. And see *Burden* v. *Harris* (1937) 54 T.L.R. 86.

[5] Austin's *Jurisprudence*, lect. XLVII.

which is owned (e.g. 'This umbrella is part of my *property*'), or the legal right which the owner has over it (e.g. 'The finder of a lost umbrella acquires a special *property* in it'). It is only in the former sense that we can ever speak of 'lost property' or of 'stolen property'. For property in the second sense (i.e. the intangible right of ownership) cannot be stolen or mislaid. A theft, then, leaves unaltered the ownership in the goods stolen,[1] so that the owner is still entitled to seize the thing, or to bring a civil action to recover it from the thief. There is an apparent exception to this where the thief has gone on to destroy the thing, or even to alter its essence irrecoverably by making out of it an entirely new kind of thing. In the latter case, as when *A* takes *B*'s barley and makes it into malt, he acquires title, by *specificatio*,[2] in the new thing thus created. For, just as if *A* had fed pigs with the barley, *B*'s ownership is utterly gone;[3] and, consequently, his civil remedy is an action for damages alone. Yet even here there is no real exception to the principle we laid down. For it was not by the theft, but by further conduct, posterior to the theft, that *B*'s ownership was extinguished.[4]

A THIEF CANNOT CONFER OWNERSHIP

¶ 313. Since a thief does not become owner, he cannot confer ownership upon anyone else; for *non dat qui non habet*. Hence the original owner may sue the thief, or anyone to whom the thief has given or

[1] It is often said that even the *possession* remains, constructively, in the owner (1 Hale P.C. 507); but see Pollock and Wright, *Possession in the Common Law*, 157, as to whether this should not be understood only as the *right* to possession.

[2] See Justinian, *Inst.* II, 25–9.

[3] Y.B. 5 Hen. VII, fo. 15, pl. 6. The test for English law is not the same as that adopted for Roman law by Justinian. For our law the question of ownership depends upon whether the property can be identified as the major part of the new thing which has been made; the old cases are, however, not easily to be reconciled with any single clear principle. See *Sandeman & Sons* v. *Tyzack & Branfoot S.S. Co. Ltd.* [1913] A.C. 680, at p. 695.

[4] If *A* had dealt with the materials in a less drastic manner, so that the law would regard their identity as still continuing and as being still traceable—as where leather is made into shoes, cloth into a dress, or a log into planks (*Betts* v. *Lee* (1810) 5 Johnson, New York, 348)—ownership would not have been changed; and *B* might lawfully have seized the whole of the manufactured product.

Indeed, *A*'s misconduct will sometimes have even the result of actually enriching *B*. For if *A* mingles *B*'s goods with his own, not in an easily separable combination (like a heap of chairs) but so as to mix them indistinguishably (as in a heap of corn), then the law confers upon *B* the ownership of the whole mass. *B* therefore becomes entitled also to that part which, before the theft, did not belong to him at all providing he is in possession of the whole mass; see *Anon.* (1594) Popham 38, Property 2 (mixing hay) and *Warde* v. *Aeyre* (1615) 2 Bulstr. 323 (mixing coins). Similarly in *accessio*, if *A* take *B*'s dressing-gown and embroider it with his own thread, *B*, as owner of the 'principal', can retake the garment and, along with it, the 'accessory' embroidery (1 Hale P.C. 513). Nor does the English law require him in any of these cases to pay compensation for the advantage he obtains. Roman law made some provision for this; see Prof. Buckland's *Text-Book*, 210–11.

It should be added, however, that in those cases of *confusio* where the commingled articles are identical not only in kind but even in quality, quantity and value, it is doubtful whether the general rule would not be modified, by making *A* and *B* joint owners of the total mass; see *Lupton* v. *White* (1808) 15 Vesey 432 at p. 442.

sold the stolen article, in a civil action to recover it or its value. Moreover, to save owners the trouble and expense of this fresh litigation, it has been enacted that an order for restitution[1] of stolen property may be made by the criminal court (even though it be a court of summary jurisdiction)[2] before which any person is convicted[3] under the Larceny Act, 1916, of larceny or embezzlement or conversion or theft in any form, or even false pretences.[4] But it should only cover such stolen property as has been mentioned in the indictment and has been produced and identified at the trial.[5]

But it must now be added that upon this general principle, *non dat qui non habet*, the common law soon engrafted two exceptions, which the necessities of trade had shown to be indispensable for the security of purchasers. One depends upon a peculiarity in the stolen property itself; the other upon a peculiarity in the place where the purchaser buys it. A man who, in all ignorance of the theft, gives the thief valuable consideration in exchange for the stolen property may, in spite of its having been stolen, acquire a good title to it, if either this stolen property consisted of money or of a negotiable security, or if it was transferred to him in a 'market overt'.

EXCEPTIONS. (*a*) Money and negotiable instruments

¶ 314. To secure the free circulation of current coin,[6] the law treats as indefeasible the title to money which is paid away (i) for value and (ii) to an innocent recipient, and this even though the particular coins may chance to be still identifiable. Yet even a coin can be claimed back by its original owner from a beggar to whom the thief has generously flung it, or from a companion to whom he has paid it in discharge of a bet, or, again, from shopkeepers who have sold goods to him for it, but in full knowledge that he had no lawful right to the coins he was paying them. And it has been held that if the coins were dealt with, not as currency but as chattels, the privilege does not apply. Thus, where a stolen Jubilee £5 piece had been acquired by an innocent purchaser for value, as a curiosity, the original owner was held to be entitled to recover it or its worth.[7] The distinction is perhaps to be regretted, as making a *bona fide* receiver's title depend upon a question so uncertain, even possibly to himself, as that of his intentions about his future treatment of the coin.

[1] Larceny Act, 1916, s. 45 (1), (2). [2] Magistrates' Courts Act, 1952, s. 33.

[3] But *before* conviction no such order can be made. Hence until then the police must exercise discretion about handing to the owner any goods they have rescued from a thief; e.g. about posting to the addressees the letters he has stolen from a pillar-box.

[4] But see ¶ 356 *post*.

[5] It ought to be made only in very clear cases; for the dispossessed third party has no power of appeal (except in a case where the conviction itself is appealed against).

[6] 'Nec secta...de denariis foret acceptanda, propter eorum consimilitudinem qui sunt ejusdem fabrice per totum regnum'; (1313) *Eyre of Kent* (Seld. Soc. Y.B. Series, v), 1, 78. Hence experienced thieves prefer to steal money or bills rather than chattels; for coin is hard to identify, and bills fetch a better price than chattels because the receiver gets a safer title.

[7] *Moss* v. *Hancock* [1899] 2 Q.B. 110.

Similarly a good title is acquired by anyone who takes *bona fide* and for value a negotiable instrument (e.g. a bill of exchange or a promissory note).[1] Hence the honest finder of a lost bill, though he obtains no title to it, can give a title.

(*b*) In market overt

¶ 315. Fairs and markets brought together men from places so distant that, in medieval days, the purchaser had little means of knowledge about the vendor he dealt with there, and consequently he needed the protection of some legal privilege.[2] Hence it became settled that even the most ordinary chattels might be effectually alienated by a thief, if he sold them for value to a *bona fide* purchaser on a market day, in such a place as was a lawfully established market for the particular kind of goods concerned—e.g. cattle, or corn, or cloth. A sale by a tradesman in a shop in the City of London in which goods are publicly displayed is a sale in market overt except on Sundays and holidays; but this does not apply to a sale to another tradesman.[3] And the publicity and rarity of the privileged occasions made this exceptional rule work comparatively little injury in the way of encouraging thieves. But modern facilities of intercourse have lessened the need for this protection; and, accordingly, modern legislation has restricted its completeness. For now, even when the ownership of goods has been divested by a sale in market overt, it will be revested in the old proprietor if the thief, or the guilty receiver, be convicted of the stealing or receiving;[4] a rule intended to stimulate owners to activity in prosecuting. (The court which convicts may itself issue an order for restitution (¶ 313 *ante*), and so save the trouble of a civil action.[5] Such an order does not create any new right; the mere conviction has upset the effect of the sale in market overt.[6]) But a conviction does not revest the ownership retrospectively. Accordingly, though the present holder must give up the article to the old owner, yet if the former were not the original purchaser in market

[1] The holder of a negotiable instrument is normally presumed to have taken it *bona fide* and for value, but this presumption does not apply where it is shown that before reaching the hands of the holder the instrument has been obtained by theft or fraud. It has been held in Australia that, in an action to recover stolen *money* from a thief's payee, the owner must prove that the payee's title is defective (*Freedman* v. *Black* (1911) 12 Commonwealth 105).

[2] Cf. Pollock and Maitland, II, 154, 164.

[3] *Ardath Tobacco Co. Ltd.* v. *Ocker* (1930) 47 T.L.R. 177. For what amounts to sale 'in market overt according to the usage of the market', see *Bishopsgate Motor Finance Corpn.* v. *Transport Brakes* [1949] 1 K.B. 322.

[4] Larceny Act, 1916, s. 45 (1). This rule as to larcenies does not extend to the misdemeanours of false pretences or of fraudulent conversion; in these the offender himself obtains ownership, *post*, ¶¶ 328, 344.

[5] But if notice be given of an appeal against the conviction, both the revesting and the restitution order are thereby suspended and, whether notice of appeal is given or not, the question of a restitution and revesting order is suspended for ten days unless the convicting court otherwise orders, Criminal Appeal Act, 1907, s. 6.

[6] *Scattergood* v. *Sylvester* (1850) 15 Q.B. 506.

overt, the owner will have no right of action in 'trover' against that original purchaser, or against any intermediate holders.

OWNER MAY SUE FOR RESTITUTION

¶ 316. Hence after a conviction for larceny the owner may sue for restitution, except in the case of money or a negotiable security.[1] And even in this excepted case, if the thief has spent the proceeds of the theft in buying some article, the court may order it to be handed over,[2] since in the Larceny Act,[3] 1916, the word 'property' includes not only the property originally possessed, but also any property into or for which it has been converted or exchanged.[4] An innocent purchaser,[5] against whom a restitution order is made, may ask the court to compensate him by returning him, out of any moneys that have been taken from the prisoner on his apprehension, the amount of the price which he had paid.[6]

POLICE PROPERTY ACT, 1897

¶ 317. It will be seen that the rules which we have explained do not include any provisions for cases (1) where a thief, though really guilty, has been acquitted, or (2) where further property is claimed as stolen but has not been included in the indictment, or (3) where stolen property has been recovered by the police, but the thief has not been arrested. Accordingly the Police Property Act, 1897 (60 and 61 Vict. c. 30), has given more extensive powers, by enabling courts of summary jurisdiction to order the delivery of any property, which has come into the possession of the police 'in connexion with any criminal charge', to anyone who appears to be the owner. After six months from the date of such an order, this person will become indefeasible owner.[7]

[1] Under the Factors Act, 1889 (52 and 53 Vict. c. 45), a mercantile agent in possession of goods with the consent of the owner (when the owner is dealing with him in his capacity as a mercantile agent; *Pearson* v. *Rose & Young Ltd.* [1950] 2 All E.R. 1027) is able, by a disposition to a *bona fide* purchaser, to give as good a title as the owner can give. Even though the mercantile agent has obtained the goods dishonestly, he would probably, for the purposes of this Act, be held to be in possession with the owner's consent, *Folkes* v. *King* [1923] 1 K.B. 282 *per* Bankes and Scrutton, L.JJ.; *London Jewellers Ltd.* v. *Attenborough* [1934] 2 K.B. 206, but see also *per* Atkin, L.J. in *Lake v. Simmons* [1926] 2 K.B. 51, 72; contrast the difference of facts in *Rigby* v. *Reliance Marine Insce.* [1956] 3 W.L.R. 407.

[2] *R.* v. *Justices of Central Criminal Court* (1886) 17 Q.B.D. 598.

[3] Sect. 46 (1).

[4] *D'Andrea* v. *Woods* [1953] 1 W.L.R. 1307. But after a conviction for the theft of a blank *cheque-form*, an order cannot be made for the restitution of the money which the thief obtained by forging thereon a *cheque* and cashing it; for the cheque was not *bought* by the bank.

[5] *Ibid.* s. 45 (3).

[6] In the case of a pawnbroker with whom the stolen goods have been pledged for not more than £10, the convicting court may make the restitution order *conditional* upon the owner's repaying the loan, or part of it, to the pawnbroker. (If the owner sued the pawnbroker in a civil court, no such condition could be imposed *there.*) The court will consider whether there has been carelessness on the part either of pawnbroker or of owner; Pawnbrokers Act, 1872, s. 30. But there is no such general power where the loan on the individual pledge exceeds ten pounds; *ibid.* s. 10. See also *post,* ¶¶ 771, 797, as to compensation.

[7] The police should always make an application to the court when there are conflicting claims to property, *Betts* v. *The Receiver for the Metropolitan Police District* [1932] 2 K.B. 595.

Chapter XIV

EMBEZZLEMENT

Section 1. History and Definition

¶ 318. As already mentioned,[1] the criminal liability of servants was extended in 1529 (21 Hen. VIII, c. 7) to cases in which their master had delivered (not into their mere custody but) into their full 'legal' possession any valuable goods to be kept by them as bailees for him. The 'imbezilment' of such goods by them was made a felony. But where money or goods were received by a servant into his own legal possession on his master's account, not from that master himself but from some third person, who intended to part with the ownership of them (either to go to the man's known master or to such person as might be entitled to receive it)[2] the statute did not apply. In such a case the deliveror has ceased to have any possession of the goods, while, on the other hand, they have not yet reached the possession of the master; and they are thus for the time being in the servant's own possession. There they will continue until he puts them into his master's possession or otherwise disposes of them in accordance with the instructions to him by his master. Until then he accordingly cannot commit larceny of them. (Yet, inconsistently, it is held by our civil courts that this delivery to a servant by a stranger gives the master such a possession, as against *third* parties, as entitles him to sue anyone for damages who commits a trespass to the goods, even whilst they are still in the servant's hands.[3]) Accordingly if, for example, a bank cashier, or a shop assistant, on receiving money into his hands from a customer, does not put it into the till, but pockets it and uses it for his own purposes, he commits no larceny. It has not reached the possession of the master; he therefore cannot legally be said to have 'taken' it from the master. That a servant who acted dishonestly in this particular way committed no felony was a defect in the legal system which exposed employers to great risks; accordingly, so soon as the case of *R.* v. *Bazeley*[4] in 1799 focused attention on this unsatisfactory position, Parliament took action. A statute[5]

[1] *Ante*, ¶ 229.

[2] It would make no difference whether the transferor did or did not know that the recipient had a master to whom, in the circumstances of the case, it was his duty to pass the identical property he then received; *R.* v. *Gale* (1876) 2 Q.B.D. 141 (*T.A.C.*). If, however, the circumstances were such as to show definitely that the *ownership* as distinct, from the *possession*, of the money or the goods passed at once to the servant, then the servant cannot, even now, commit the crime of embezzlement of the property so received. He may, however, so behave as to become guilty of the misdemeanour of fraudulent conversion under section 20 (1) (iv) of the Larceny Act, 1916; *post*, Ch. xv.

[3] Pollock and Wright, *Possession in the Common Law*, 130; 1 Hale P.C. 668.

[4] 2 Leach 835 (*T.A.C.*). [5] 39 Geo. III, c. 85. Stephen, *Hist. Crim. Law*, III, 152.

was passed, which made it felony for any servant or clerk to embezzle money or goods thus received into his possession for his employer, although they had not reached the employer's own actual possession. (The words *embezzle* (or *imbezil*) and *bezzle* had been in use since at least the fourteenth century, as meaning 'to make away with', usually connoting some degree of clandestinity.[1]) The enactment now in force as to this crime[2] provides that:

> Every person who, being a clerk or servant,[3] or person employed in the capacity of a clerk or servant...(*b*), fraudulently embezzles the whole or any part of any chattel, money, or valuable security, delivered to, or received or taken into possession by, him for, or in the name of, or on the account of, his master or employer...shall be guilty of felony.[4]

As he occupies a position of confidence he is liable to a higher punishment than that of simple larceny. He may be sentenced to imprisonment for any term not exceeding fourteen years.

The crime of embezzlement presents three points for consideration: (*a*) the persons who can commit the offence; (*b*) the property on which it can be committed; and (*c*) the mode of commission.

(*a*) The persons who can commit the offence

¶ 319. The question, who is a clerk or servant,[5] often presents great difficulty in practice. If *A* is employed by *B* to do work for him he will not necessarily be *B*'s servant, but may only be an 'independent contractor' with *B*.[6] Indeed *A* will not be *B*'s 'servant' unless the agreement between himself and *B* puts him so completely under *B*'s control that he must obey all lawful orders that *B* may from time to time give him in connexion with the employment;[7] i.e. *B* can tell him not only

[1] The derivation is uncertain. Dr Murray traces it to the French *besillier*, to ravage. The legal use of the term is almost exclusively limited, at the present day, to the statutory felony explained in this paragraph. For its use in 1353, see *T.A.C.*, *Anon.* 27 Lib. Ass.

[2] Larceny Act, 1916, s. 17 (1) (*b*).

[3] With clerks and servants there have now been included both a co-partner and a co-owner (by 31 and 32 Vict., c. 116, now repeated in s. 40 (4) of the Larceny Act, 1916) who can be guilty of embezzlement when also employed as clerk or servant of the firm or co-partner (as in *R.* v. *Taffs* (1850) 4 Cox 169, and *R.* v. *Diprose* (1868) 11 Cox 185); and perhaps also even if he is not so employed. See Russ. ch. 61.

[4] The same section, in subsect. (2) (*b*), makes it similarly a felony for anyone employed in the public service or in the police to embezzle, or fraudulently apply, any chattel, money or valuable security that has been entrusted to, or received or taken into possession by, him in his employment. Embezzlement by officers or servants of the Bank of England of bank notes or warrants is a felony punishable with imprisonment for life (Larceny Act, 1916, s. 19).

[5] In the present connexion the term 'servant' includes 'clerk' and hereafter will alone be used in this chapter.

[6] Thus, in *R.* v. *Hoare* (1859) 1 F. and F. 647, it was held that the accused was not a servant, when he was re-employed to collect rents after his contract of service had terminated. See Winfield, *Law of Tort*, 6th ed., 139.

[7] *R.* v. *Negus* (1873) 2 C.C.R. 34 (*T.A.C.*); *Short* v. *J. W. Henderson Ltd.* (1946) 62 T.L.R. 427, *per* Lord Thankerton at p. 429; *Mersey Docks, etc.* v. *Coggins, etc.* [1947] A.C. 1.

what to do, but also how to do it. To ascertain whether or not the contract between the parties did create so complete a right of control, it must first be ascertained if its terms were embodied in a written document. If they were, it will be for the court to determine whether or not they did establish this right of control. But if the contract was an oral one, then it is a question of mixed law and fact, so that the jury must find what were the *facts* of the agreement but the judge must settle what are the legal consequences of these facts. What facts are relevant for this purpose have not been found easy to define since the agreements between the parties are seldom exhaustively detailed, and the usually understood terms of the particular kind of employment may have to be considered. Thus a commercial traveller is often a servant, while an insurance collector or debt collector usually is not.[1] It is not essential, although it is suggestive, that *A* should give the whole of his working time to *B*; for one who is truly a servant may yet also work for himself or for other masters. A man may be a servant for one solitary transaction, and the agreement may not bind the servant to go on any longer than he likes.[2]

¶ 319*a*. *The servant must be acting as such.* Even when it is established that the man is a servant it must yet be remembered that for the purposes of the law of embezzlement one thing has always been essential; and that is that the embezzlement can only be committed by the servant *while he is engaged in the performance of his duties as a servant.*[3] The *criminal liability* of the accused depends not upon his general contractual relationship with his master but upon the fact that on the occasion in question he was performing some task which his contract with his master either expressly or by implication required him to perform. It follows from this that a person who cannot be held to be employed under a regular contract of service with a master can yet consent to act, and can be acting, as servant on some particular occasion. In short, there can be situations where a regular servant is not acting as a servant,[4] and on the other hand situations where a person who is not a regular servant is yet acting as such.[5]

Students should observe that, for the purposes of the law of tort as

[1] *R.* v. *Hoare* (1859) 1 F. and F. 647; *ante*, p. 321. As to taxicab-drivers, see *Smith* v. *G.M.C.C. Ltd.* [1911] A.C. 188. In London they are sometimes not servants but pay the cabowner a percentage of the takings. In any case it is almost invariable that the money paid to them for fares passes at once into their ownership, so that they cannot commit larceny or embezzlement of it; they may, however, be guilty of fraudulent conversion; *post*, ¶ 324.

[2] *R.* v. *Foulkes* (1875) 2 C.C.R. 150 (*T.A.C.*).

[3] For a detailed examination of this essential fact see [1956] *Crim. L.R.* 591–603.

[4] E.g. *R.* v. *Wilson* (1839) 9 C. and P. 27 (*T.A.C.*); *R.* v. *Harris* (1854) Dearsly 344; *R.* v. *Cullum* (1873) 2 C.C.R. 28 (*T.A.C.*); *R.* v. *Read* (1878) 3 Q.B.D. 131; *Cheshire* v. *Bailey* [1905] 1 K.B. 237, at p. 241; *Barker* v. *Levinson* [1951] 1 K.B. 28.

[5] *R.* v. *Spencer* (1815) R. and R. 299; *R.* v. *Hughes* (1832) 1 Moo. 370; *R.* v. *Beaumont* (1854) Dearsly 270; *R.* v. *Foulkes* (1875) 2 C.C.R. 150 (*T.A.C.*); *R.* v. *Gibson* (1861) 8 Cox 436.

to employers' *civil* liability, a decision upon the scope of a servant's authority to act has to be reached in order to ascertain whether some third party who has been injured by the servant's conduct has the right to recover damages from the employer.[1] In the crime of embezzlement, however, the aim is different: for here what has to be assessed is the *criminal* liability of the *servant*; and for this purpose the investigation must be restricted to examining the express and implied terms of the contract of service between the master and the man, so as to discover what is comprised in the man's duty.

¶ 320. *The course of the servant's duty.* The Larceny Act limits the offence to the appropriation of such articles as have been received by the prisoner 'for, or in the name of, or on the account of, his master or employer'. Thus a servant can commit an embezzlement only of things that he has received *as* servant. A shopman who sells such goods as he is authorized to sell—or a workman who executes for his master's customer, and with his master's tools, work which he is authorized to execute and receive payment for—will be guilty of embezzlement if he appropriates the money paid by the customer, *before* it reaches the possession of his master (or such other destination as the master may have directly or impliedly prescribed).[2] But a servant cannot embezzle anything obtained by doing an act outside the authorized scope of his employment.[3] Hence if a coachman proceeds without permission to ply for hire with his master's carriage, and spends the coins so earned, he does not commit embezzlement of them.[4] So, generally, it may be stated that a servant cannot be said to have received money or goods for or on account of his master when he obtained the property by an act done contrary to the duties of his employment.[5] Similarly, if a servant forges a cheque in the name of his master, and cashes it, he does not receive the coins in his capacity of servant,[6] and therefore does not commit embezzlement by making off with them. It is not necessary that the person paying money to a servant should pay it on account of the master, or even that he should know of the master's existence. It is sufficient that the servant receives the money *in his capacity as servant* on account of his master,[7] and that he should be under the duty to pass over

[1] This has led the courts into a different course of legal development, such as the establishment of a doctrine of 'ostensible authority'; see Winfield, *Law of Tort*, 6th ed. 146 *et seq.*

[2] *R.* v. *Hoggins* (1809) R. and R. 145 (*T.A.C.*); *R.* v. *Aston* (1847) 2 C. and K. 413.

[3] See *Barker* v. *Levinson* [1950] 2 All E.R. 825 (in which the question of *embezzlement* did not arise).

[4] *Per* Blackburn, J., in *R.* v. *Cullum* (1873) 2 C.C.R. 28 (*T.A.C.*); and see *R.* v. *Harris* (1854) Dearsly 344.

[5] This principle was applied in *R.* v. *Wilson* (1839) 9 C. and P. 27 (*T.A.C.*), although on the facts of this case it would seem that the decision should have gone against the prisoner; see the discussion of *R.* v. *Wilson* in its relation to *R.* v. *Aston*, *R.* v. *Cullum* (*supra*) and *R.* v. *Read* (1878) 3 Q.B.D. 131, in [1956] *Crim. L.R.* 593 *et seq.*

[6] *R.* v. *Aitken* (1883) C.C.C. Sess. Pap. XCVII, 336.

[7] *R.* v. *Gale*, *infra*.

the *identical* property which he receives into the master's possession (e.g. the till in the shop) or deliver it to such other destination as the master may have ordered.

In *R.* v. *Gale*[1] the servant was a company's office manager who had the duty of opening all letters and of receiving remittances coming to the office, whether in cash or in cheques, which he was then to hand to the cashier of the company after endorsing such cheques as were made payable to his order. On the material occasion he received two such cheques (totalling £600) which he dishonestly kept back and, endorsing them, passed to friends of his own who gave him the amount in cash and paid the cheques into their own banks. Gale handed the £600 cash to the company's cashier to be set against the amount by which he had overdrawn his salary, thereby recovering his I.O.U.'s from the cashier who acted innocently throughout. All this was discovered some months later after Gale had left the company's service and become bankrupt. Gale was convicted of embezzling the £600 and his conviction was affirmed by the Court for Crown Cases Reserved, since it was his duty to pay over the proceeds of the cheques at once in whatever way he received them. As to this it is clear (*a*) that there was no forgery by Gale since he had authority to endorse incoming cheques; and (*b*) that the court had evidence on which they felt they could hold that he had authority to change such cheques into cash, with the over-all duty to pass all cheques and/or cash over to his masters' cashier for transmission to their bank for the benefit of their account: he was thus held to have received the £600 cash 'on account of his masters'.

In *R.* v. *Davenport*[2] the prisoner was secretary and servant of a company, whose bankers were instructed to honour the company's cheques when signed by two directors and in addition countersigned by Davenport. It appeared that some cheque forms were signed in blank by two directors and handed to Davenport with instructions that in due course he should complete them, as and when needed, by filling in the names of creditors of the company, and the correct amounts due to them, adding his own signature in each case. Some of these cheques he dishonestly completed by inserting the amounts due from himself to certain private creditors of his own, and the names of their bankers as payees, thus settling his own personal debts. In certain counts of the indictment D. was charged with (and convicted thereunder of) larceny of the amounts of money stated in these cheques; but his conviction thereof was quashed by the Court of Criminal Appeal since there was no 'taking and carrying away' of any money at all, as alleged.[3] But there were another three of the incomplete cheque forms which D. countersigned and completed by inserting as payee the name of the bank of a friend S. and sums of money to a total which S., on receiving these cheques, met by giving D. in return cash and some open cheques of his own. These latter cheques D.

[1] (1876) 2 Q.B.D. 141 (*T.A.C.*); on this case see [1956] *Crim.L.R.* 600 *et seq.*; [1957] *Crim.L.R.* 640 *et seq.*

[2] [1954] 1 W.L.R. 569; 38 Cr.App.R. 37.

[3] It is submitted that if D. had been charged (*a*) with larceny from his masters (the company) of the blank cheque forms and (*b*) with forgery of the same, he could well have been convicted on each charge.

cashed, and kept for himself the total money which he thus amassed. In the indictment D. was charged with stealing this last mentioned sum of money, and convicted. At the appeal D.'s counsel objected to the conviction for larceny but, strangely, admitted[1] that a verdict of embezzlement might have been possible, thus restricting his appeal to the submission that the Court of Criminal Appeal ought not to substitute a conviction of embezzlement[2] since such a verdict had not been considered by the jury. There was little in this submission and the court, having no hesitation in rejecting it, made the substitution and affirmed the conviction in that form, identifying the facts of the case with those in *R.* v. *Gale*, of which it was said:[3] 'In our opinion that case entirely covers this case so far as the Samuel cheques are concerned.' This decision was unconsidered and was reached without argument on an assumption by both parties and the court that the accused must have been guilty of embezzlement. The facts of *Davenport's Case*, however, were materially different from those of *Gale's*. Nothing that D. did with the cheque forms was done in the exercise of his duty. These forms were put into his charge for no other purpose than to use them for the payment of the company's creditors alone, and not to obtain cash by means of them for any purpose (even for the company's expenses or the like). It would be absurd to suggest that D. was acting in the course of his employment when he stole and forged the cheque forms; the commission of a crime against the master cannot be at the same time the performance of a duty owed to the master. As to the money and cheques which he received from his friend S., it is clear that these were owned by S. and were intended by S. to pass, and did pass, into D.'s ownership for his own use. It is submitted, therefore, that this property coming from S. was not received by D. for or on account of his master;[4] and accordingly that this case should be regarded as wrongly decided. Its retention as an authority would necessarily involve, by implication, the repudiation of such cases as *R.* v. *Wilson*[5] and *R.* v. *Aitken*[6] which have for many years past been cited as establishing the principle that a servant's criminal deeds committed against his master cannot constitute a performance of his duties of service.

(*b*) The property on which the offence can be committed

¶ 320a. '*Chattel, money or valuable security.*' Ever since embezzlement was first created as a crime by the Act of 1799 which stated that the offender 'shall be deemed to have feloniously stolen the same from his master', the courts have held that the words 'chattel, money or valuable security' mean nothing more than 'a thing capable of being stolen' as defined for the purpose of simple larceny.[7] Accordingly, whether the servant is charged under (*a*) or (*b*) of section 17 (1) of the Larceny Act, 1916, it is incumbent on the prosecution to establish that the prisoner

[1] 38 Cr.App.R. at pp. 38, 39.

[2] Under the power conferred by s. 44 (2) of the Larceny Act, 1916, and s. 5 (2) of the Criminal Appeal Act, 1907.

[3] *Per* Lord Goddard, C.J., at pp. 42–3.

[4] For further argument in support of this submission, for which there is here not sufficient space, see [1956] *Crim. L.R.* 660 *et seq.*, and Russ. ch. 61.

[5] (1839) 9 C. and P. 27.

[6] (1883) C.C.C. Sess. Pap. XCVII, 336.

[7] *Ante*, ¶ 297.

has appropriated some specified tangible object or objects. Moreover the words 'or any part of' in the section refer to any *material* part of the property delivered to or received by the servant, and *not* to a part of the *value* of the property. Thus if *X* hands to *A*, who is a servant of *B*, a pound note to be carried by *A* to his master, and *A* dishonestly keeps that note and instead of it gives to *B* a ten-shilling note, then *A* embezzles the pound note and *not* the difference in value between the two notes. To begin with, the courts gave a very strict interpretation to the words of the statute of 1799[1] and insisted upon a specific statement, in the indictment, of at least some one article of the property alleged to have been embezzled. The necessity for such particularity was, however, somewhat modified by the Larceny Act, 1827, s. 48, and this elasticity has been extended by subsequent statutes.[2] But even at the present day it has still remained essential for the prosecution to prove that some tangible object or objects of property (in the case of money, some actual notes or coins) were intercepted by the servant and dishonestly retained or disposed of by him before they passed into the possession of the master or to such other destination as the master had enjoined. Suppose for example that *X* hands to *A*, the servant of *B*, a one-pound note with instructions to take it to a bank or shop and get it changed for coins of which *A* is to bring back five shillings to *X* and then carry the remaining fifteen shillings to his master; and then *A*, after giving five shillings to *X*, dishonestly retains the remaining fifteen shillings, it would seem that, by virtue of section 40 (2), *A* could be charged in the indictment ('so far as regards the description of the property') with having embezzled the one-pound note. Difficulties have arisen through misunderstandings of the points of decision in a line of cases in which many references were made to 'balance of account', 'deficiency', 'difference' and the like terms, from 1835 to 1925.[3] An analysis of this sequence would take up more space than is available in a text-book for students[4] and it must here suffice to submit comprehensively that the major question which exercised the courts throughout was the interpretation of the words of the various statutory provisions under which each prosecution was brought, and that running

[1] See *R.* v. *Furneaux* (1817) R. and R. 335; *R.* v. *Tyers* (1819) R. and R. 402.

[2] The Larceny Act, 1861, s. 71, and the Larceny Act, 1916, s. 40 (2), the latter of which reads: 'An allegation in an indictment that money or banknotes have been embezzled... can, so far as regards the description of the property, be sustained by proof that the offender embezzled or obtained any piece of coin or any banknote or any portion of the value thereof, although such piece of coin or banknote may have been delivered to him in order that some part of the value thereof should be returned to any person and such part has been returned accordingly.' For details of this development, see Russ. ch. 61.

[3] *R.* v. *Grove* (1835) 7 C. and P. 635; 1 Moo. 447; *R.* v. *Jones* (1837) 7 C. and P. 833, 834; *R.* v. *Lloyd-Jones* (1838) 8 C. and P. 288; *R.* v. *Chapman* (1843) 1 C. and K. 119; *R.* v. *Lambert* (1847) 2 Cox 309; *R.* v. *Baxter* (1851) 5 Cox 302; *R.* v. *Moah* (1856) Dearsly 626; *R.* v. *Wright* (1858) 7 Cox 413; *R.* v. *Wolstenholme* (1869) 11 Cox 313; *R.* v. *Balls* (1871) L.R. 1 C.C.R. 328; *R.* v. *Sheaf* (1925) 19 Cr.App.R. 46.

[4] A discussion of the cases will be found in Russ. ch. 61.

through all the cases can be detected the real point that, so far as the crime of embezzlement is concerned, it is not sufficient merely to charge the embezzlement of a general deficiency;[1] *a man cannot embezzle*[2] *a balance of account, nor a difference in value*; but he can embezzle a definite amount of tangible cash which, on the evidence, he has intercepted, and which *represents* a balance or difference disclosed by the figures in his master's accounts.

Failure to bring before the court a clear picture of the above principle vitiated to some extent the decision in *R.* v. *Tomlin*:[3]

The appellant T. was employed to manage a shoe-shop. In March 1953 his employer, suspecting some deficiency, caused a careful check of stock and accounts to be taken, and in the following September made another lengthy examination which revealed that between the two stock-takings goods to the value of over £400 had gone, and that proceeds to cover these goods had never been paid over to the employer nor were then held available in his servant's hands. The appellant, denying dishonesty but admitting the deficiency, subsequently made monetary restitution but did not suggest that the deficiency shown on the accounts was due either to faulty stock-taking or to some loss of stock due to accident or to theft by a third party. He was indicted on charges of embezzlement of the sum of money shown on the books to be due to the firm but not accounted for, and in other counts of the indictment with false accounting. T. appealed against conviction for embezzlement, on the grounds that the charge was bad in law as alleging embezzlement of a lump sum or general deficiency arising from the misappropriation of small unidentifiable sums over a number of months. But counsel for the appellant did not seem to distinguish between (*a*) a lump sum of money proved to have been received little by little and not handed over, and (*b*) a discrepancy (i.e. a difference, or balance) in the figures shown in the firm's books.[4] The former situation was clearly covered by the various statutory provisions applicable in the old reported cases, while the latter was as clearly excluded.[5] That T. must have appropriated the actual total sum of money was proved to the satisfaction of the jury and therefore the contention of the appellant as to the impropriety in law of charging the embezzlement of a 'general deficiency' was misconceived.

It is not easy, however, to see the relevance of the case of *R.* v. *Lawson*[6] which was relied upon by counsel for the Crown;[7] for this case was a prosecution for an entirely different crime, namely, the misdemeanour of fraudulent conversion under section 20 (1) (iv) (*b*) of the Larceny Act, 1916, an offence which did not exist in our law before

[1] *Per* Avory, J., in *R.* v. *Sheaf* (1925) 19 Cr.App.R. 46 at p. 49.

[2] Nor, of course, can he *steal.*

[3] [1954] 2 All E.R. 272; 38 Cr.App.R. 82.

[4] The unhappy misconceptions which can arise from the ambiguity of the expressions 'general balance' and 'general deficiency' can be observed in *R.* v. *Morris* (1933) 24 Cr.App.R. 105. See Russ. ch. 61. And see *R.* v. *West and others* [1948] 1 K.B. 709, *per* Humphries, J., at p. 720.

[5] As was made clear by Brett, J., in *R.* v. *Wolstenholme* (1869) 11 Cox 313.

[6] [1952] 1 All E.R. 804; 36 Cr.App.R. 30.

[7] 38 Cr.App.R. at p. 84.

1901 and therefore is not in point when the old cases of embezzlement (which turned on the wording of other statutes) are under consideration.[1] It may, however, be pointed out that the weakness (if any) in *R.* v. *Tomlin* was that on all sides the evidence was accepted without question as establishing that T. had intercepted all the money, in its various sums accumulated over the months, before any of it had reached the till in the shop: for unless he had done so his crime could not have been embezzlement. It would seem almost impossible for him to have done this. Indeed it is likely that in fact he must have purloined it from the till after his assistants had departed and when he applied himself to the task of falsifying the accounts (to which last offence he confessed), and that he should have been found guilty of larceny under section 17 (1) (*a*) of the Larceny Act.

¶ **321.** *Larceny and embezzlement distinguished.* A servant, as we have already said, can only embezzle what he has received *for* his master. It is not an embezzlement, but a larceny, for him to appropriate money which he has received *from* his master; and this even though it did not come to him from the master directly,[2] but only through the hands of some fellow-servant.[3] Yet if, through the same fellow-servant, he had received money remitted for their master by some stranger, he can commit embezzlement of this money; for it has not yet reached his master's possession, but is stopped by him whilst on its way to the master.[4] But if once he had put this money into his master's till,[5] his subsequently taking it out again and appropriating it would be a larceny and not an embezzlement. So would the conduct of a person who should remove a load of straw after once he had delivered it on his master's premises[6] or even had merely put it into a cart, or a barge,[7] that belonged to (or was possessed by) his master. But larceny and embezzlement have one important element in common, namely, that they concern only specific tangible objects. Just as a man cannot steal a debt or a balance of accounts,[8] so also he cannot embezzle such things. And for embezzlement it is essential that the offender should have the duty to hand in to his master's possession[9] the identical object which he received.[10]

[1] E.g. *R.* v. *Balls* (1871) L.R. 1 C.C.R. 328; *R.* v. *Wright* (1858) 7 Cox 413.

[2] *R.* v. *Hawkins* (1850) 1 Den. 584. [3] *R.* v. *Murray* (1830) 1 Moo. 276 (*T.A.C.*).

[4] *R.* v. *Masters* (1848) 1 Den. 332 (*T.A.C.*); *R.* v. *Sullens* (1826) 1 Moo. 129 (*T.A.C.*).

[5] *R.* v. *Wright* (1858) *ubi supra.*

[6] *R.* v. *Hayward* (1844) 1 C. and K. 518 (*T.A.C.*).

[7] *R.* v. *Reed* (1854) Dearsly 168, 257; *R.* v. *Harding* (1807) R. and R. 125.

[8] *Ante*, ¶ 259.

[9] Or deal with it otherwise, as instructed by his master. For example, the master, *M*, might tell *S*, the servant, to collect a ten-shilling note from *X* and then to hand that same note over to *Y*. It would be embezzlement if *S*, having collected the note, were to detain it dishonestly for himself, and use it for his own purposes.

[10] This statement is not contradicted by s. 40 (2) of the Larceny Act, 1916, for that provision is aimed at such a situation as where, for example, a shop-assistant gives change to a customer for a bank-note which he then appropriates instead of putting it into the till, whether the change which he gave came out of the till or out of his own pocket.

The above illustrations show how fine a line often has to be drawn in determining whether it is a larceny or an embezzlement of which a servant has been guilty. The doctrine of possession is so subtle and technical that it is frequently hard to say for which of the two offences a man should be indicted, and failures of justice used often to arise in consequence; but they are now rare, since the absolute necessity of accuracy on this point is removed, so far as the indictment is concerned. The Larceny Act, 1916, provides, by s. 44 (2), that if, on a charge of stealing, the actual crime committed prove to have been an embezzlement (or vice versa), the jury may convict of the crime actually proved, instead of the crime originally charged. But this still leaves the difficult duty of establishing which one *was* proved.[1]

(*c*) The mode of committing the offence

¶ 322. As embezzlement is committed without the servant's making any change of the possession which he has received, the fact of a 'fraudulent' appropriation by him is often hard to prove. It may be shown by his absconding with the money,[2] or by his denials of having ever received it, or by any really wilful omission to pay it over. But the mere fact of omission, as it may have been due to pure carelessness, does not suffice to show an appropriation.[3] Still less, as we have already had occasion to mention, does the simple fact of there being a deficiency in the servant's accounts, i.e. his not having actually credited to himself, in his books, disbursements sufficient to exhaust all the cash he has received. For he may have lost it by negligence; and negligence, however reprehensible, is not a criminal dishonesty.[4] And even if he has spent it, there is nothing to show that he did not spend it on his master's account. Moreover, when it is proved that there must have been some really dishonest appropriation, this proof will not be enough so long as the misconduct is only shown to have produced a 'general deficiency'.[5] There must further be evidence that the particular amount specified in the indictment was appropriated, and at the particular date or dates (or during a particular period of time) and at the particular place also there specified. For otherwise the prisoner would have no means of securing himself the protection of the plea of 'autrefois convict' or 'autrefois acquit',[6] in case of his being prosecuted a second time for this same charge.

SECTION 2. FALSE ACCOUNTING

¶ 323. It is easy to understand that dishonest clerks often escaped on indictments for embezzlement, because of the difficulty of thus proving

[1] *R.* v. *Gorbutt* (1856) D. and B. 166; and see the Criminal Appeal Act, 1907, s. 5 (2).

[2] *R.* v. *Williams* (1836) 7 C. and P. 338.

[3] *R.* v. *Jones* (1837) 7 C. and P. 833 (*T.A.C.*). So, besides proving non-payment, there should also be proved non-entry in his accounts.

[4] *Lanier* v. *R.* (1914) 24 Cox 53. See ¶ 25.

[5] *R.* v. *Lloyd Jones* (1838) 8 C. and P. 288, and cf. ¶ 330. See *R.* v. *Jones* (1837) 7 C. and P. 833; *R.* v. *Wolstenholme* (1869) 11 Cox 313.

[6] *Post*, ¶ 743.

an actual appropriation, even where it was clear that money had been received by them, and detained without their making any entry or other acknowledgment of the receipt. Hence in 1875, by a measure introduced by Sir John Lubbock but commonly known as Lopes' Act,[1] it was made a misdemeanour, punishable with seven years' penal servitude (now imprisonment), for a clerk or servant wilfully, and with intent to defraud, to alter, or make a false entry[2] in, or omit a material particular from, any account of his master. An indictment for this offence of false accounting is often useful where a clerk to whom a customer has paid money is suspected of misappropriating it, but no more can be actually proved than that he has never credited the customer with the amount. If, however, his books show correctly the sum which he ought to have in hand, the fact of his not really having that amount ready to hand over does not render the entry a 'false' one within this statute.

[1] 38 and 39 Vict. c. 24.

[2] E.g. even by not adjusting or by maladjusting a taximeter-flag, so that the meter fails to record; *R.* v. *Solomons* [1909] 2 K.B. 980. It is also enough if he causes an honest fellow-servant innocently to make the false entry or omission. See *R.* v. *Butt* (1884) 15 Cox 564.

Chapter XV

FRAUDULENT CONVERSION

Section I. Fiduciary Obligations ignored by the Common Law

¶ 324. The statutory crime of embezzlement was added to the ancient development of the common law whereby, as was previously described,[1] servants (including clerks) were deprived of 'legal' possession of their master's property and thus brought within the reach of the law of larceny, so that in the result they could no longer commit with impunity most of the acts of dishonesty for which their confidential position gave them special opportunities. But there still remained the more rare circumstances in which the servant may acquire not merely physical control but also full ownership in money or goods which it is his plain duty to pass over to his master, or at least to expend in his master's interests. In such a position the servant may hold the property, not under an express trust recognized as such in equity, but yet in a fiduciary position which to his knowledge puts him under a very clear moral obligation. The common law did not meet this situation; indeed, it tended to ignore the existence of trusts, even for civil purposes, not regarding a breach of trust as creating any debt.[2] Still less did it attach any criminal liability to acts done by one whose fiduciary duty was less well defined than that of a recognized trustee.

NO STATUTORY PROTECTION ORIGINALLY

¶ 325. Yet servants and clerks are far from being the only persons whose confidential position renders it easy for them to behave fraudulently. We have already alluded[3] to the case of an employer's being defrauded by some agent whose engagement has not placed him under such a control as would render him a 'servant',[4] and thus bring him within the law of embezzlement; so that what was needed was some statutory enactment which would cover both servants and independent agents *who have acquired either the ownership of the property for themselves, or the control*[5] *of the ownership* of property, which it is their fiduciary duty to use, either wholly or in part, for the benefit of some other person.

[1] *Ante*, ¶¶ 228 *et seq.*

[2] In certain circumstances a quasi-contractual claim for money had and received might be enforceable by action *in personam*. See *Sinclair* v. *Brougham* [1914] A.C. 398 at p. 419, and Hanbury, *Modern Equity*, 6th ed. 710. See [1956] *Crim. L.R.* 672.

[3] *Ante*, ¶ 319.

[4] E.g. *R.* v. *Hoare* (1859) 1 F. and F. 647; *ante*, p. 321. And see [1956] *Crim. L.R.* 607.

[5] As in *some* cases of property purchased on 'sale or return' contracts; contrast *Whitehorn Bros.* v. *Davison* [1911] 1 K.B. 463, where, however, there was no fiduciary duty, and therefore no crime of fraudulent conversion. See *post*, ¶¶ 342, 344.

The fiduciary element[1] may rest on one or both of two foundations. First, it may arise from the terms on which the transferor of the property passes it into the ownership of the recipient; an example of this would be when *A* who owes five shillings to each of *B* and *C* gives a ten-shilling note to *B* on an agreement with *B* that *B* will give the balance of five shillings to *C* when he meets him later on. Here *B* becomes owner of the note, being entrusted with it subject to the fiduciary duty[2] to pay half the proceeds of the note to *C*. It will make no difference if the recipient's instructions are that he is to pass the whole of the proceeds to someone else,[3] as, for example, when a man collects money from people who give it to him for the benefit of a specified charity or club, on the understanding that he is to use for his own purposes the actual cash received but to keep an account of it and to hand over to the charity or club an equivalent sum in due course.[4]

Secondly, the fiduciary element may arise from the legal relationship existing between the recipient and the person on whose account he has received the property; an example of this would be when the ownership of property is received by a clerk or servant[5] or by an independent agent[6] from someone who may indeed have no knowledge[7] of the relationship existing between him and his master or principal.

SECTION 2. LARCENY ACT, 1916, SECTION 20

¶ 326. To meet this need, some very limited provisions were introduced in 1811,[8] and something more was done in 1861;[9] but the matter was not adequately dealt with before the Larceny Act, 1901. And now the law is contained in sect. 20 of the Larceny Act, 1916:[10]

(1) Every person who
(i) being entrusted either solely or jointly with any other person with any power of attorney for the sale or transfer of any property,

[1] The fiduciary element is indicated by the word 'entrusted' in s. 20 (i) (iv) (*a*) of the Larceny Act, 1916, *infra*; and it is submitted that this also supports the view that the accused must become *owner* and not *bailee* of property which comes into his hands.

[2] It is the transfer *sub modo* of Roman law.

[3] Or to return the proceeds to the transferor; *R.* v. *Smith* [1924] 2 K.B. 194. See the remarks on *R.* v. *Buckmaster* in ¶ 236 *ante*.

[4] *R.* v. *Hassall* (1861) L. and C. 58 (*T.A.C.*), a case decided before the crime of fraudulent conversion, as it now exists, had been created.

[5] *R.* v. *Solomons* [1909] 2 K.B. 980. It must be repeated that if the servant's duty is to pass the *identical* property into the possession of the master (e.g. an omnibus conductor should put all cash takings into the leather wallet which his employers provide for him to carry) then the *ownership* does not reach the servant and a dishonest interception by him of the property will be embezzlement; *ante*, ¶ 320.

[6] *R.* v. *Lord* (1905) 69 J.P. 467.

[7] *R.* v. *Messer* (1913) 82 L.J.K.B. 913. The case of *R.* v. *South* (1907) 71 J.P. 191 seems to have been wrongly decided.

[8] 51 Geo. III, c. 38, applicable to clerks and servants in Ireland. Also the Larceny Act, 1827, s. 49, in effect re-enacting the Embezzlement by Bankers, etc., Act, 1812. See Stephen, *Hist. Crim. Law* III, pp. 155–6.

[9] Larceny Act, 1861, ss. 75 and 76.

[10] As modified by the Criminal Justice Act, 1948, s. 1

fraudulently sells, transfers, or otherwise converts the property or any part thereof to his own use or benefit, or the use of any person other than the person by whom he was so entrusted; or

(ii) being a director, member or officer[1] of any body corporate or public company,[2] fraudulently takes or applies for his own use or benefit, or for any use or purposes other than the use or purposes of such body corporate or public company, any of the property of such body corporate or public company;[3] or

(iii) being authorized to receive money to arise from the sale of any annuities or securities purchased, or transferred under the provisions of Part V of the Municipal Corporations Act, 1882, or under any Act repealed by that Act, or under the Municipal Corporation Mortgages, etc., Act, 1860, or any dividends thereon, or any other such money as is referred to in the said Acts, appropriates the same otherwise than as directed by the said Acts or by the Local Government Board or the Treasury (as the case may be) in pursuance thereof; or

(iv) (*a*) being entrusted either solely or jointly with any other person with any property in order that he may retain in safe custody or apply, pay, or deliver, for any purpose or to any person, the property or any part thereof or any proceeds thereof; or

(*b*) having either solely or jointly with any other person received any property for or on account of any other person;

fraudulently converts to his own use or benefit, or the use or benefit of any other person, the property or any part thereof or any proceeds thereof;

shall be guilty of a misdemeanour and on conviction thereof liable to imprisonment for any term not exceeding seven years.

(2) Nothing in paragraph (iv) of subsection (1) of this section shall apply to or affect any trustee under any express trust created by a deed or will, or any mortgagee of any property, real or personal, in respect of any act done by the trustee or mortgagee in relation to the property comprised in or affected by any such trust or mortgage.

¶ **327**. *The facts covered by the section.* It will be observed that the words employed in section 20 (1) (iv) are in themselves wide and, standing alone, could be taken as intended to include cases in which possession

[1] In *R.* v. *Shacter* [1960] 2 W.L.R. 258 it was held that for the purposes of the Companies Act, 1948, and of the Larceny Act, 1861 (sects. 83 and 84), an auditor appointed from year to year to fill an office of the company was an officer, whereas an auditor *ad hoc* for a limited purpose was not.

[2] For the purposes of this subsection 'public company' means any company incorporated under the Companies Act, 1948, even though some companies so incorporated rank as private companies; see *R.* v. *Davies* [1954] 3 W.L.R. 664; also *R.* v. *Shacter, ubi supra*, at p. 259.

[3] This would cover the case where the director holds *all* the shares in the company. False accounting and false statements by directors are punishable under the Larceny Act, 1861, ss. 82–4; *R.* v. *Kylsant* [1932] 1 K.B. 442; *R.* v. *Bishirgian* (1936) 52 T.L.R. 361. But the words 'any of the property' will not cover the transfer to himself of a debt or the cancellation of a debt owed by him to the company; *R.* v. *Davies* [1954] 3 W.L.R. 664.

only was given to the offender (as in bailments) and even those in which nothing more than simple physical control was given (as in the case of servants). But the Act must be read as a whole, and since the bailee is expressly included in section 1, where a conversion by him[1] is declared to be a felony, and the servant is expressly dealt with in section 17, under which a dishonest appropriation by him is also a felony, it follows that these persons are excluded from the general words of section 20.[2] Moreover section 20 creates a misdemeanour and it would not be reasonable to suppose that in the same Act the legislature would offer alternative grades of crime (carrying different maxima of punishment) for one and the same deed.[3] It is also plain both from the content of the first three paragraphs of subsection (1) and also from the words of subsection (2), that the section, regarded as a whole, contemplates cases where something more than mere legal possession was given to the offender, accompanied by a duty bordering upon, but yet falling short of an express trust.[4] In practice where e.g. *A* employs *B* to sell *A*'s car for him and *B* disposes of the car and absconds, the charge is usually laid in the alternatives, (i) larceny by bailee of the car, and (ii) fraudulent conversion of the cash which *B* received for it. But it cannot be *both*; and so, if the evidence establishes that *B* took the car and sold it as his own, he stole the car, in which case the money he received was for himself and there was no fiduciary element to bring the case within s. 20 (1) (iv) (*a*); conversely, if he merely carried out his instructions in selling the car as *A*'s employee to the purchaser, this could not be larceny of the car by him; but the money then would be received with the fiduciary duty, arising from his contract with *A*, to transmit that money or its equivalent to *A*, and this would constitute the misdemeanour under s. 20 (1) (iv) (*b*).

THE SCOPE OF THE CRIME OF FRAUDULENT CONVERSION

¶ 328. The only kind of situation therefore which will fit the words of subsection (1) (iv) is one in which *ownership*[5] is handed over, since there

[1] See *R.* v. *Hastings* [1958] Crim. L.R. 128 where the C.C.A. quashed the conviction of H. for larceny as bailee on the grounds that the evidence disclosed that there was no bailment but that there was fraudulent conversion within section 20 (an offence not charged against the prisoner).

[2] Of course the master may, in a particular instance, make his servant *owner* of the property which he hands to him, and then, if a fiduciary duty be attached, the case would be within section 20.

[3] See the argument of counsel (Muir) for the appellant in *R.* v. *Scranton* (1920) 15 Cr.App.R. at p. 105, who 'contended that it could not be a felonious conversion and a conversion which was the subject of misdemeanour by the same statute'. See also *Att., Gen.* v. *Sillem* (1863) 2 H. and C. 431, *per* Pollock, B., at p. 515; *Colquhoun* v. *Brooks* (1889) 14 A.C. 493, *per* Lord Herschell at p. 506; *Canada Sugar Refining Co.* v. *R.* [1898] A.C. 735, *per* Lord Davey at p. 741; and *Goulder* v. *Rook* [1901] 2 K.B. 290, at p. 296, in respect of a statute in which two sections overlap but do not coincide.

[4] For a more detailed discussion of this topic see Russ. ch. 63.

[5] This does not *necessarily* mean that the ownership must be *vested in* the recipient. It is enough that he is given the power to dispose of the ownership as he wishes; as in the cases of *Hassall*, and *Lord* (*ante*, ¶ 325).

is no available intermediate position between legal possession and ownership.

Under this interpretation the crime of fraudulent conversion exactly fills the gap in the law which previously existed, since it completes the net around the dishonest servant, and reaches the dishonest agent.[1] (For special instances of dishonesty by a factor or mercantile agent in respect of the property placed in his possession, section 22 expressly creates a misdemeanour with the same maximum penalty of seven years' imprisonment.) But it does not touch a mortgagee of any real or personal property and it leaves the dishonest trustee to be dealt with separately, under special rules, in section 21 (see ¶ 333 *post*).

It remains to note that subsection (1) (iv) does not include the more unusual case where it is by means of a false pretence that a fiduciary ownership was obtained by the offender. Such a case falls within section 32 of the Act, and therefore, on the principle first discussed in the preceding paragraph, is excluded from section 20.

The crime of obtaining by false pretences contrary to section 32, is described below, ¶ 338.

¶ 329. *The meaning of 'entrusted'.* There must always be a fiduciary element in the transaction under which the offender obtained the property and where only a debt is contracted there can be no criminal liability under section 20. Thus in *R.* v. *Hotine*[2] the accused had required persons joining his service as clerks and travellers to deposit money with him as security for their honesty during the service, promising to repay the amounts so deposited when their employment ceased.[3] He failed to repay the money but this was held not to be within the statute[4] since the accused received the money merely on credit, to do as he liked with it, and not upon custody or trust. Such cases, however, have been said to depend upon the facts, so that it is for the jury to decide what is the true nature of the transaction.[5]

It is clear that a man may be 'entrusted' with property, within the meaning of the section, even though the owner has not delivered it to him directly, and even though the owner did not know of his existence; it is enough that he has obtained or assumed the ownership of another person's property in circumstances whereby he in fact becomes entrusted with it for a known purpose.[6] In like manner a man can receive property

[1] E.g. such a person as the accused in *R.* v. *Hoare* (*ante*, p. 321) would now be guilty of the misdemeanour of fraudulent conversion.

[2] (1904) 68 J.P. 143; and see *R.* v. *Sheaf* (1925) 19 Cr.App.R. 46, and *R.* v. *Jones* (1948) 33 Cr.App.R. 11, *ante*, ¶ 238.

[3] To some of the employees he gave a promissory note payable on the depositor's leaving his service.

[4] Larceny Act, 1901.

[5] *R.* v. *Smith* [1924] 2 K.B. 194 (*T.A.C.*); a doctrine which comes very near to leaving a question of law to the jury; it would seem that Smith (and perhaps Hotine) could well have been convicted of obtaining credit by fraud (*post*, ¶ 365).

[6] *R.* v. *Grubb* [1915] 2 K.B. 683 (*T.A.C.*). G. was the sole owner of the shares and sole controller of the assets of a 'one-man' company; only through him could the company

'for or on account of any other person' even though the person who transfers the property to him has no knowledge of the individual on whose account he receives it, or has no interest in knowing what may be the recipient's duty to do with the property. For example, a payment to a motor taxicab driver (which may include a gratuity to him) passes into his ownership, because, unlike an omnibus conductor, he is not provided by his employers with a wallet into which he must put all takings, but can do what he likes with the cash paid to him by his passengers, being merely required in due course to account properly to them in accordance with the record of the taximeter. In most cases the passenger who pays him neither knows nor cares whether the driver is an employed person or is himself the owner or hirer of the cab. Yet if the driver is in fact not the owner of the cab, nor the hirer of it, then he commits fraudulent conversion of such sums as he dishonestly fails to account for and to pay to his employers.[1]

The charge against the accused must make it plain whether he is being prosecuted under paragraph (*a*) or (*b*) of section 20 (1) (iv), and of course the jury must be satisfied on the evidence relating to that charge.[2]

¶ 330. *The meaning of 'proceeds'*. It has been said[3] that the word 'proceeds' in section 20 (1) (iv) means money which is realized from property which is not money, but this definition is probably to be taken as intended to apply only to the facts of the particular case before the court, for otherwise it would seem unduly narrow. Yet there can be no conviction under an indictment which, charging an offence under section 20, in effect alleges on the face of it no more than the non-payment of a balance which some statement of accounts shows to have been due to the prosecutor;[4] such words show no more than a failure to pay a debt. Where, however, there is evidence that sums of money totalling up to an ascertained amount must have passed into the ownership of the defendant, it is (and always has been) a good charge that he misappropriated that total amount of money.[5]

operate at all; he therefore had the ownership of the company's property entirely in his own hands and discretion. He did not deny the fraudulent conversion of the clients' property but contended that the company was a legal entity entirely distinct from himself, so that the offence was the company's and not his. This defence was rightly rejected; but even if this could have been the company's crime this could not have provided a defence for G., since then he could have been properly indicted as principal jointly with the company. For the company (at that date) was regarded as having no mind and incapable therefore of converting anything 'fraudulently', so that the crime (which, it must be remembered was not committed against the company but against the company's clients) could only be effected by the direct action of G. himself. *R.* v. *Cuffin* (1922) 16 Cr.App.R. 179; *R.* v. *Bottomley* (1922) 16 Cr.App.R. 184; *R.* v. *Morter* (1927) 20 Cr.App.R. 53; for a discussion of this last case see Russ. 1268.

[1] *R.* v. *Solomons* [1909] 2 K.B. 980; *R.* v. *Messer* (1913) 82 L.J.K.B. 913.

[2] See *R.* v. *Pilkington* (1958) 42 Cr.App.R. 233.

[3] *R.* v. *Hotine* (1904) 68 J.P. 143.

[4] *R.* v. *Morris* (1933) 24 Cr.App.R. 105; *R.* v. *Sheaf* (1925) 89 J.P. 207.

[5] *R.* v. *Lawson* (1952) 36 Cr.App.R. 30.

MENS REA IN FRAUDULENT CONVERSION

¶ 331. It is essential to establish that the delinquent intended to appropriate some economic benefit (either by depriving the prosecutor of it, or by denying it to him) to which he knew the prosecutor was entitled. Pure carelessness, however great, will therefore not be enough; so that there is no crime committed by an agent who has negligently lost the property or who has made mistakes in keeping his accounts or has deducted more than is due to him by way of commission and so on; in every case the jury must be satisfied that there was an intent to defraud.[1]

SECTION 3. LARCENY AND FRAUDULENT CONVERSION DISTINGUISHED

¶ 332. It may be useful to repeat that where the facts of the case show that property has been put into a man's possession in circumstances which constitute him a bailee of it, then a dishonest conversion of it by him will be the felony of larceny (Larceny Act, s. 1 (1)) and not the misdemeanour of fraudulent conversion (s. 20 (1) (iv)).[2] If the wrongdoer received the property from his master *while acting in the capacity of a servant*,[3] then he does not acquire legal possession of it and cannot be a bailee; but if he dishonestly takes and carries away the property he commits a felony by virtue of section 17 of the Act. Yet although he does not acquire *possession* of his master's property he can acquire *ownership* if his master gives it to him; and in such a position, if the property was 'entrusted' to him within the meaning of section 20 (1) (iv), any fraudulent misappropriation of it by him will render him guilty of the misdemeanour. Such would be the case if, for example, the master happened to owe his servant, say, fifteen shillings, and not having the exact amount in cash, were to give the servant a pound note and tell him to expend the five shillings due as change in paying a bill for that amount owed by the master at some shop, or in some similar way. If, however, the wrongdoer, whether or not he be a servant, obtained the ownership in the property by means of some false pretence which he had made with intent to defraud, then his crime is the misdemeanour of obtaining by false pretences under section 32 of the Act. Students should therefore guard against being confused by the dicta in *R.* v. *Jones*.[4]

[1] *R.* v. *Hignett* (C.C.A.), *The Times*, 22 February 1950.

[2] And vice-versa; see *R.* v. *Hastings* [1958] Crim. L.R. 128, where the difference between the felony of conversion by a bailee in section 1 and the misdemeanour of fraudulent conversion in section 20 is brought out.

[3] See the criticism of *R.* v. *Davenport* [1954] 1 W.L.R. 569, *ante*, p. 324. It would be otherwise if, for example, the master were to lend the servant some article to take away with him to use while on his holiday; for then a bailment would be created, since the loan would be made solely for the purposes of the man as an independent person, and would have nothing to do with the performance of a servant's duties.

[4] (1948) 33 Cr.App.R. 11; *ante*, ¶ 238.

Section 4. Fraudulent Trustees

¶ **333.** As above stated,[1] section 20 does not extend to trustees 'under any express trust created by a deed or will'. Equitable owners in such cases must thus rely upon other provisions,[2] under which a trustee of either real or personal property is punishable with seven years' imprisonment if, with intent to defraud, he converts or appropriates to any other purpose than that of his trust any property which has been given to him on an express trust *created in writing*. This extension of the criminal law to the protection of equitable ownership was originally an experiment so novel that it had to be restricted closely. Hence no trustee[3] can be thus prosecuted without the leave of the Attorney-General, and if proceedings have already been begun in any civil court in respect of the breach of trust, the person who has taken them must also obtain the leave of that court before beginning a criminal prosecution. Moreover, the criminal liability thus created is not to prejudice any agreement which the trustee may have entered into for making good the loss caused by his dishonesty.[4] So that even a bargain by him, to make restitution in consideration of not being prosecuted, would appear to be rendered enforceable, in spite of the ordinary rules as to contracts that are against public policy, and also unindictable, in spite of the ordinary rule against 'compounding' a misdemeanour.[5] A noteworthy clause in the Larceny Act of 1861 (s. 85), applying not only to trustees but also to agents and many other similar fiduciary misdemeanants, exempts them from criminal prosecution if the misdemeanour was first disclosed by them in the course of civil proceedings instituted against them by the person defrauded; but it removes their privilege of refusing to incriminate themselves when examined in these civil proceedings. Similarly, the offenders' disclosures in bankruptcy proceedings are inadmissible as evidence against them on prosecutions for this peculiar group of misdemeanours (4 and 5 Geo. V, c. 59, s. 166); cf. section 43 (3) of the Larceny Act, 1916.

[1] ¶ 328.
[2] Larceny Act, 1916, ss. 21 and 46 (1); following the Larceny Act, 1861.
[3] Sect. 21 (*a*) and (*b*).
[4] Larceny Act, 1861, s. 86.
[5] See ¶ 422 *post*.

Chapter XVI

CHEATS PUNISHABLE AT COMMON LAW

SECTION 1. FRAUDS

(*a*) Practised upon the individual

¶ 334. As we have seen, the common law, in giving its protection to the private citizen as such, regarded as felonious those acts of dishonesty which took the form of a physical interference with the property itself, against the will of its owner. For frauds of a personal character whereby a man was induced by deceit or lies to part with his ownership of money or of other property the common law provided no criminal punishment; as, for example, where a man tricked another by some sleight of hand or by some false statement about the material or quality of some article which he was selling. Thus, when *A* was charged with obtaining money from *B* by falsely stating that *C* had sent him to receive it for his use,[1] Holt, C.J., said: 'Shall we indict one for making a fool of another?' and bade the prosecutor to have recourse to a civil action.

(*b*) Practised upon the public

¶ 335. Where, however, the dishonest activity was of a sort which aimed at defrauding such members of the public as a whole who might come within its reach, then because of its generally injurious character it was treated by the common law as a crime (although only in the degree of a misdemeanour), in any instance in which any particular member of the public suffered by it. False statements without more were held not to be enough, and some misleading device in a permanent form was needed, such as false weights, measures,[2] trade-marks,[3] loaded dice, marked playing cards or even unwholesome food.[4] Thus in the case mentioned in the preceding paragraph[5] the court stated that it was 'not indictable unless he came with false tokens; playing with false dice is, for that is such a cheat as a person of ordinary capacity[6] cannot discover'. In R. v. *Hudson*[7] the Court of Criminal Appeal upheld the conviction of the appellant on a charge of making false statements to the prejudice of the Crown and the public revenue with intent to defraud by causing

[1] R. v. *Jones* (1703) 2 Ld. Raym. 1013; see also R. v. *Hannan* (1704) 6 Moo. 31; R. v. *Nehruff* (1706) Salk. 151; R. v. *Wheatley* (1761) 1 W.Bl. 273.

[2] R. v. *Wheatley* (1761) 1 W.Bl. 273.

[3] R. v. *Edwards* (1683) Trem. P.C. 103; see Russ. ch. 70.

[4] R. v. *Dixon* (1814) 3 M. and S. 11; R. v. *Treeve* (1796) 2 East P.C. 821. See also R. v. *Closs* (1858) D. and B. 460 (*T.A.C.*); *post*, ¶ 382.

[5] R. v. *Jones*, *ubi supra*.

[6] This reference to the capacity of the victim is discussed further in ¶ 339 *post*.

[7] [1956] 2 W.L.R. 914; 1 All E.R. 814; see 'Revenue fraud at common law', 106 *L.J.* 388; and Russ., ch. 101.

to be submitted to an inspector of income tax with intent to defraud a false certificate of disclosure: the court held that a fraud on the Sovereign or the public (which were synonymous terms) was an indictable misdemeanour at common law.

SECTION 2. DECEIT INJURIOUSLY AFFECTING PUBLIC JUSTICE

¶ 336. False statements which tend to pervert, hinder or discredit the operation of public justice, such as the performance of judicial acts without authority, or conduct aimed at misleading a judicial tribunal were indictable at common law.[1] When two or more persons act together in any such deceit, their agreement constitutes an indictable conspiracy,[2] as being an agreement to create a public mischief.[3]

¶ 337. Numerous cases which were formerly treated as common law cheats are now more conveniently dealt with under more specific heads owing to developments in the law by statute[4] or by an increased particularity in the common law itself, for example by the development of the law of forgery.[5]

SECTION 3. FALSE PRETENCES MADE TO PRIVATE INDIVIDUALS

COMMON LAW TESTS

¶ 338. At common law, then, the position was that the defrauding of a private individual by a false representation or by a bare lie did not constitute an indictable offence. To be punishable at common law it was necessary that the cheat should (*a*) be effected by some false token or device of a tangible character, and (*b*) be one against which common prudence would not have guarded.

This narrowness in the common law was increasingly felt to be a defect as the diversity and complexity of commercial activity developed in the eighteenth century, so that at length the legislature moved in 1757[6] to close the gap by statutory provisions which with some modification are now to be found in section 32 of the Larceny Act, 1916.

TEST OF 'COMMON PRUDENCE' NOT REQUIRED BY STATUTE

¶ 339. For some time, however, the courts were uncertain whether the statutory misdemeanour, thus created to repress private deceit (whether made by mechanical devices or by mere lies), required, as

[1] *R.* v. *Mawbey* (1796) 6 T.R. 619, 635; *O'Mealy* v. *Newell* (1807) 8 East 364; *R.* v. *Fawcett* (1793) 2 East P.C. 862, 952; *R.* v. *Vreones* [1891] 1 Q.B. 360.

[2] *Ante*, ¶ 59; *post*, ¶ 448. *R.* v. *Brailsford* [1905] 2 K.B. 730, 745.

[3] *Post*, ¶ 445. And see cases cited in Russ. ch. 91.

[4] E.g. the Weights and Measures Acts, 1878–1936; the Merchandise Marks Acts, 1887–1953; the Fine Arts Copyright Act, 1861; the Larceny Act, 1916, s. 32.

[5] *R.* v. *Ward* (1727) 2 Ld. Raym. 1461; see *post*, ¶ 373.

[6] 30 Geo. II, c. 24, s. 1.

did the old common law cheat, that the false representation must be one which 'common prudence' would not have guarded against. This would of course have been an unsatisfactory restriction since a fraudulent individual naturally looks for a victim whom it is most easy to dupe; and further, it would introduce an element of uncertainty which might enable many a highly dishonest man to escape. Finally it was decided that the statutory crime did not require any particular degree of care or intelligence on the part of the prosecutor; it was sufficient if it was proved that he was in fact deceived by the false pretence made to him.[1]

[1] See *R.* v. *Woolley* (1850) 1 Den. 559; *R.* v. *Lee* (1863) L. and C. 309.

Chapter XVII

FALSE PRETENCES

Section 1. The Larceny Act, 1916, Section 32

¶ **340.** Section 32 of the Larceny Act[1] provides that:

Every person who by any false pretence

(1) with intent to defraud, obtains from any other person any chattel, money, or valuable security, or causes or procures any money to be paid, or any chattel or valuable security to be delivered, to himself or to any other person for the use or benefit or on account of himself or any other person; or

(2) with intent to defraud or injure any other person, fraudulently causes or induces any other person

(*a*) to execute, make, accept, endorse, or destroy the whole or any part of any valuable security; or

(*b*) to write, impress, or affix his name or the name of any other person, or the seal of any body corporate or society, upon any paper or parchment in order that the same may be afterwards made or converted into, or used or dealt with as, a valuable security;

shall be guilty of a misdemeanour and on conviction thereof liable to imprisonment for any term not exceeding five years.

Under this provision five points arise for consideration: (*a*) the subject-matter of the crime, (*b*) the right obtained over that thing, (*c*) the pretence, (*d*) its effect, and (*e*) the intent.

(*a*) THE SUBJECT-MATTER

¶ **341.** Although the statutes which have regulated this crime have nowhere so stated, it has always been held that the words 'chattel, money, or valuable security' do not include things which at common law were not the subject of larceny.[2] Thus since, as we have seen, a 'difference in value' as such cannot be stolen, it cannot be obtained by false pretences.[3] Accordingly the section does not cover a fraudulent obtaining of real property, or of anything 'savouring of the realty',[4] or of a dog[5] (however valuable). Yet it has been held that a railway ticket, although it is evidence of a chose in action,[6] may be the subject

[1] As modified by the Criminal Justice Act, 1948, s. 1.

[2] Stephen, *Hist. Crim. Law*, III, 162. See *ante*, ¶ 273 *et seq.*

[3] Therefore if *A* by false pretences induces *B* to pay a higher price for some article than he would have paid had he known the truth, *A* obtains the whole of the payment by false pretences and not merely the difference in value (e.g. if a half-crown instead of a two shilling piece is paid).

[4] *R.* v. *Pinchbeck* (1896) C.C.C. Sess. Pap. CXXIII, 205 (*T.A.C.*).

[5] *R.* v. *Robinson* (1859) Bell 34; or a ferret, *R.* v. *Searing* (1818) R. and R. 350 (*T.A.C.*).

[6] *Post*, ¶ 343.

of an indictment for obtaining it by false pretences since it is a chattel. Plainly if what was obtained were not a tangible object at all, as for example accommodation in lodgings[1] or an act of service, the offence is not committed; such as where a man secures a ride in a train by falsely saying 'I am a season-ticket holder'.[2]

But it should be noted that section 32 (2) of the Act reaches anyone who by false pretences, with intent to defraud or injure any other person, procures the execution of any valuable security.

(*b*) THE RIGHT OBTAINED

¶ 342. For the purposes of section 32 the word 'obtains' means that the offender has induced the prosecutor to transfer not merely the article itself but also the full ownership of the article. It may well be that the prosecutor contemplated that the recipient would be retaining the thing for his own use and benefit: this, however, is not essential, and it will be enough that the recipient obtains the power to pass the ownership to someone else if he does not wish to take it for himself. Such a position is obvious when goods are supplied by a wholesale merchant to a shopkeeper; but the same principle applies when a purchaser obtains an article on sale or return by representing that he himself has a customer for that specific thing.[3]

Difficulties have arisen in cases where the deceit practised has related to matters so fundamental as to raise the question whether it can be said that there never was any real transfer of ownership to the offender.[4] Where there has been no transfer of ownership (or, in some cases, even of possession) then the crime will be larceny.

¶ 343. *A bailment is not enough.* If a bailment is obtained by false pretences this misdemeanour is not committed;[5] an example is where the prisoner by false pretences obtained from a livery stable keeper a horse on hire for a third person, and rode it himself for the period of the hire, after which he returned it to the stables.[6] What the prisoner had obtained was the ride and not ownership of the horse.

[1] *R.* v. *Bayley* (1923) 17 Cr.App.R. 162.

[2] Yet for fraudulently travelling on a railway with intent to avoid payment of his fare such a person is punishable on summary conviction under the Regulation of Railways Act, 1889, s. 5; and under the London Cab Act, 1896, it is an offence, punishable on summary conviction, to hire a cab in *London* with intent to avoid payment of the lawful fare. And see the regulations for the use of public service vehicles, S.R. and O. 1936, no. 619, part III.

[3] As in *Whitehorn Brothers* v. *Davison* [1911] 1 K.B. 463 (*T.A.C.*); see also *Folkes* v. *King* [1923] 1 K.B. 282; *Lawther* v. *Harris* [1927] 1 K.B. 393; *London Jewellers* v. *Attenborough* [1934] 2 K.B. 206; and the discussion of *Heap* v. *Motorists A.A.* [1923] 1 K.B. 577 in Russ. 1068.

[4] As in *Cundy* v. *Lindsay* (1878) 3 App. Cas. 459; *ante*, ¶ 248. See Russ. 1068.

[5] Indeed it will be no crime at all unless the bailee permanently appropriates the thing, when it will be larceny, under s. 1 of the Larceny Act, 1916. See *R.* v. *Schweller* (1924) 18 Cr.App.R. 52.

[6] *R.* v. *Kilham* (1870) 1 C.C.R. 261 (*T.A.C.*).

Yet in *R.* v. *Boulton*[1] the prisoner was convicted[2] of obtaining by false pretences from a servant of the railway company a railway ticket for a journey by one of their trains; Pollock, C.B., said that the ticket, while in the hands of the party using it, was an article of value entitling him to travel without further payment, and the fact that it was to be returned at the end of the journey did not affect the question.

This judgment did not explain how the facts showed that the prisoner obtained the ownership of the ticket; and although it has been followed the decision has been doubted,[3] since it is plain that the real intent was to obtain the ride without paying for it.

Where a cheque has been obtained by false pretences it would seem that the misdemeanour has been committed notwithstanding that the cheque form, which is the physical object obtained, will circulate back to the prosecutor through the bank or banks by which it has been cleared. This view rests upon the fact that when drawn the cheque is more than a piece of paper, since it is a valid order for the payment of money; when, however, it is accepted by a bank it is cancelled and thus destroyed as a cheque;[4] and, since the offender did obtain the right so to destroy it, he obtained the whole of the drawer's interest in the cheque as such.

¶ 344. *Essential that ownership be obtained.* It was stated in 1838[5] that it might be a misdemeanour[6] if a man were by false pretences to obtain his own goods from a carrier in whose possession they were, in order to defraud the carrier, since 'the possession would make them the carrier's goods'. But these statements were *obiter* and there seems to be no reported case in which such a doctrine has been applied. It is difficult to see a justification for it. It has been repeatedly laid down that in this crime it is essential that ownership be obtained and that possession alone[7] is not enough; and since the utmost legal interest that

[1] (1849) 1 Den. 508. [2] Under 7 and 8 Geo. IV, c. 29, s. 53.

[3] E.g. in *R.* v. *Chapman* (1910) 4 Cr.App.R. 276; and see the remarks of the editor of the 3rd and 4th editions of Russell on Crime (C. S. Greaves, Q.C.) cited Russ. ch. 70. Contrast the facts in *R.* v. *Potter*, *infra.*

[4] Which is transformed into a record of the transaction by the bank. This, it is suggested, is an offence of which the prisoner was guilty in *R.* v. *Hudson* [1943] 1 K.B. 458; *ante*, ¶ 295.

[5] *R.* v. *Martin* (1838) 8 Ad. and E. 481 *per* Denman, L.C.J., at p. 485, and *per* Patteson, J., at p. 488. This case turned on the wording of the indictment, which was held to be bad because it had failed to state that the goods obtained were the property of any person, and on the face of it therefore the goods might have been the prisoner's own goods. [6] Under 7 and 8 Geo. IV, c. 29, s. 53.

[7] *R.* v. *Ball* (1951) 35 Cr.App.R. 24 at p. 27: 'There is no doubt that "obtains" means obtaining the property and not merely possession', *per* Lord Goddard, C.J.; followed in *R.* v. *Lurie* [1951] 2 All E.R. 704. In face of these declarations by the C.C.A., confirming the established doctrine, the assizes case of *R.* v. *Potter* (1958) 42 Cr.App.R. 168 must be taken as deciding on the facts of the case that ownership of a certificate of competence to drive a motor vehicle passes to the candidate although he will have to surrender it in order to obtain a driving licence. See also *R.* v. *Pople* [1951] 1 K.B. 53;

the carrier has, he being a bailee, is possession, it follows that no more than possession can be obtained from him. Certainly his status of bailee cannot be obtained from him at all,[1] since it rests upon his contract with the bailor, and even if he had authority to employ another as bailee that would be a new bailment. It is indeed not easy to envisage facts of any precise deceit which could enable the owner to cause his own bailee to *transfer* a bailee's rights (whatever they may be) to him. If, however, a person who is *not* the owner of the goods obtains them from a bailee with intent to appropriate them to himself, he could be properly charged with larceny of them from their owner.[2]

An honest finder of a lost article has a special interest in it and a legal position in respect of it, since he has the chance of receiving a reward for its return and the right to retain it for himself if its owner cannot be discovered. It would seem that he could transfer the whole of this interest to another person: accordingly (if indeed it be the law that for the crime of false pretences it is enough that the offender shall have obtained the *whole* of the prosecutor's interest, whatever it may be), it would perhaps be within section 32 of the Larceny Act if a man by false pretences induced a finder to transfer to him the finder's position with its advantageous prospects. But, as above stated, this point does not seem to have been authoritatively decided.[3]

It should finally be noted that if the false pretence secures the payment of a greater sum than the amount really due (e.g. more than the true price for goods sold) then the *whole* of the sum so paid is obtained within the meaning of the section.

(c) THE PRETENCE

¶ 345. The false representation may be made expressly in words (either written[4] or spoken); but it is quite sufficient that it can be even implied from them, or from silent conduct.[5] But the words or the conduct

Gardiner v. *Fudge* [1954] Crim. L.R. 210. Possession, with the power, in addition, to dispose of the ownership, so as to give a good title, would be sufficient; see *Whitehorn Brothers* v. *Davison, ante,* ¶ 342.

[1] That a bailee cannot transfer the bailment to another person without the bailor's consent appears from *Blount* v. *War Office* [1953] 1 All E.R. 1071.

[2] *R.* v. *Swinson* (1900) 64 J.P. 73; *ante,* ¶¶ 261, 290. But not from the bailee, since the bailee had been induced to *consent* to letting him take them; in *R.* v. *Swinson,* the woman from whom the prisoner took the banknote did not consent to his having possession of it, she was merely allowing him to inspect it (as in *R.* v. *Chisser, ante,* ¶ 230).

[3] In a Canadian case, *R.* v. *Sector* (1920) 14 Sask. L.R. 83, the accused was held guilty of obtaining his own motor-car from a garage proprietor, who had a lien on it for payment of his account for repairs to it, by false pretences consisting in his having handed over a post-dated cheque which he knew would be refused by the bank, his purpose, as he alleged, being to force the prosecutor to settle an outstanding contra-account in respect of a previous transaction of a different kind. It seems to have been assumed without argument that the abandonment of a lien would be sufficient to bring the case within s. 405 of the Criminal Code.

[4] Even *written* words must be construed by the jury, not the judge.

[5] For pretence by omissions see *R.* v. *Kylsant (Lord)* [1932] 1 K.B. 442; *R.* v. *Bishirgian* (1936) 52 T.L.R. 361. The pretence can be made abroad, see §§ 647–8.

must be fairly capable of conveying the false meaning; and must moreover have been intended[1] to convey it. (Yet in a *commercial* court it would be no defence to say 'I never meant that construction to be put on my words'.) Thus for a huckster to give an order for goods, to an extent so great that only a man in a very large way of business could require them, may amount to a false pretence; and so may the packing up of goods made by yourself in wrappers closely resembling those used by some well-known firm of manufacturers.[2] Again, without any deceptive words at all, the mere act of wearing a cap and gown in a university town may be enough to constitute a representation that you are a member of its university.[3] Similarly, quite apart from the use of any words asserting the genuineness of the article, there would be a false representation in passing a note of a wound-up bank, or, again, in offering for sale a sparrow painted as a canary (such as the late Lord Justice Mathew described to be a 'gaol-bird').[4]

The statement must refer to the past or present

¶ 346. The pretence must relate to some fact that is either past or present. A statement purely affecting the future will not suffice. For all future events are obviously matters of conjecture, upon which every person should exercise his own judgment. If the buyer says, 'Send me the meat and I will pay to-morrow', it is for the butcher to determine whether he will part with the meat on the strength of this promise. If, therefore, the customer fails to fulfil his promise, the butcher cannot prosecute him for obtaining the meat by false pretences, but can only sue him in a civil action to recover the price of it.[5] In like manner, to borrow money under the pretence that you will use it in paying your rent, is not an obtaining by such a false pretence as will come within the statute. This distinction between present and future is, however, now to some extent undermined by the principle that representations which do not expressly mention anything but the future, may nevertheless imply a representation about the present; viz. a representation that the existing state of affairs is such that, in the ordinary course of events, the future occurrence mentioned will take place. Thus it has been held that sending the half of a bank-note, along with an order for goods, is not only a promise that on a later occasion the other half shall be sent,

[1] As where a hawker of rings announces them as 'all marked' meaning his hearers to understand 'hall-marked'. Or where a man at Tottenham, who had served three terms of penal servitude, set up as a builder, and (with literal truth yet with intentional deceit) headed his letter-paper: 'Employed fourteen years in Government work.'

[2] To use a false name in order to defraud by denying your identity is indictable; but not if used merely to *conceal* identity, e.g. a trade name or stage name.

[3] *R.* v. *Barnard* (1837) 7 C. and P. 784 (*T.A.C.*).

[4] Or in offering, for sale, stolen goods, *Re Pinter* (1891) 17 Cox 497. Cf. *Eichholz* v. *Bannister* (1864) 17 C.B. (n.s.) 708 at p. 723. But none in merely overcharging, where there is no false representation of fact as to the price, *R.* v. *Summerskill* (1918) 13 Cr.App.R. 170.

[5] *R.* v. *Goodhall* (1821) R. and R. 461; *R.* v. *Burrows* (1869) 11 Cox 258; *R.* v. *Lee* (1863) L. and C. 309 (*T.A.C.*). And see the Summary Jurisdiction Act, 1899, s. 3.

but implies also a representation that at the present time the sender already possesses that other half.[1] Similarly the familiar act of drawing a cheque (a document which on the face of it is only a command of a future act) is held[2] to imply at least three statements about the present:

(1) that the drawer has an account with that bank;

(2) that he has authority to draw on it for that amount;

(3) that the cheque, as drawn, is a valid order for the payment of that amount (i.e. that the present state of affairs is such that, in the ordinary course of events, the cheque will on its future presentment be duly honoured).

It may be well to point out, however, that it does not imply any representation that the drawer now has money in this bank to the amount drawn for, inasmuch as he may well have authority to overdraw, or may intend to pay in (before the cheque can be presented) sufficient money to meet it.

A statement of intention about future conduct, whether or not it is a statement of existing fact, is not such a statement as would amount to a false pretence at criminal law. A promise as to future conduct not intended to be kept is not by itself a false pretence for the present purposes.[3]

It has sometimes been suggested that when a man orders a meal at a restaurant he impliedly makes a representation as to his present ability, and present intention, to pay for it. But to treat every order for goods as if it impliedly contained the words, 'I can pay', would render it dangerously easy for disappointed creditors to call in the law of false pretences to the assistance of the law of debt. Accordingly it is now settled[4] that the man who orders and eats a meal at a restaurant does not thereby make any implied false statement about the present. But though his deceit relates only to the future, it is enough to constitute an 'obtaining credit by fraud in incurring a liability' (which is a specific statutory misdemeanour under the Debtors Act, 1869[5]), although the credit given by the innkeeper was to last only until the end of the meal.

¶ 347. Where it is by the joint operation of several representations that the prisoner has induced the owner to part with his property, the offence may be committed, even though some of them were mere promises about the future, if any one representation was as to a present fact. In

[1] *R.* v. *Murphy* (1876) 10 Ir. C.L. 508. 'I will deliver the article' *may* thus involve representations that 'I am now in a position to be then able to deliver it', and that 'I now intend to deliver it'. Cf. *Aaron's Reefs* v. *Twiss* [1896] A.C. at p. 284.

[2] *R.* v. *Hazelton* (1874) 2 C.C.R. 134 (*T.A.C.*). The doctrine probably applies even to *post-dated* cheques. See the Australian cases, *R.* v. *Miller* (1868) 7 N.S.W. S.C.R. 185; *R.* v. *Muston* (1874) 12 N.S.W. S.C.R. 357; *R.* v. *Hattam* (1913) S.R. N.S.W. 410.

[3] *R.* v. *Dent* [1955] 2 Q.B. 590 (*T.A.C.*). See *R.* v. *Caslin* [1961] 1 W.L.R. 246, where a somewhat curious view of fact was taken to avoid a point of futurity.

[4] *R.* v. *Jones* [1898] 1 Q.B. 119 (*T.A.C.*).

[5] 32 and 33 Vict. c. 62, s. 13. See *post*, ¶ 365. Its maximum punishment is only a year's imprisonment. This enactment is useful where there is either (1) a 'fraud' which is not a 'false pretence', as in *R.* v. *Jones*, or (2) 'credit' not on alienation, but on a bailment, or for services or lodgings.

other words, it is sufficient that the false representation of present fact was essential to the transaction, even though it alone would not have been enough to induce the owner to part with his property. Thus if a married man represents himself as unmarried, and proposes marriage to a woman, and thereupon obtains money from her for the pretended purpose of furnishing their house, it has been held that he may be convicted of obtaining this money by false pretences.[1]

It must misrepresent fact, not merely express opinion

¶ 348. Again, even in the case of statements which clearly relate only to the present, it is often hard to say whether they are statements as to actual facts or merely as to matters of opinion, as in the case of a vendor's exaggerated eulogies of his wares. For in English law, as in Roman,[2] the licence of trade has established as to 'dealers' talk' the lax rule that *simplex commendatio non obligat.* In all bargaining there is usually a conflict between the two parties, in commercial skill and general experience; and it would be perilous to employ the criminal law to regulate this conflict. For a man to represent himself as having 'a good business', when he carries on no business at all, is clearly a false statement of a definite fact. But a similar representation made by a man who has a business, however poor a one, will generally be a mere matter of opinion.[3] A seller's misrepresentation of the weight of a sack of corn, if expressed to be merely his opinion, will not constitute the offence if the sale is for a lump sum. In the same way, falsely to represent an article as being silver—or to represent a chain as being of 15-carat gold, when it is really only 6-carat[4]—is a false pretence of fact, the real article being different in *substance* from the pretended article. Yet to represent plated spoons as being 'equal to Elkington's *A*', has been held to be only exaggerated praise, a mere puffing, inasmuch as the person deceived did get plated spoons, differing only in *value* from what he had been led to expect.[5]

It has sometimes been thought[6] that even states of mind may perhaps

[1] *R.* v. *Jennison* (1862) L. and C. 157 (*T.A.C.*).

[2] Justinian, *Digest*, IV, 3. 37; cf. Benjamin on Sale, 8th ed., 661.

[3] *R.* v. *Williamson* (1869) 11 Cox 328; contrast *R.* v. *Cooper* (1877) 2 Q.B.D. 510 (*T.A.C.*).

[4] *R.* v. *Ardley* (1871) 1 C.C.R. 301 (*T.A.C.*).

[5] *R.* v. *Bryan* (1857) D. and B. 265 (*T.A.C.*).

[6] Cf. *R.* v. *Bancroft* (1909) 3 Cr.App.R. 16. In *Hunt* v. *Battersby* (*The Times*, 16 April 1920), a railway servant obtained, 'falsely stating that it was for his wife', a privilege-ticket to which he was entitled for his wife but not for anyone else. A divisional court held that there was a criminal false pretence. Lord Reading, C.J., said that the man had 'the intention in his mind, at that time, to use the ticket for a person other than his wife. It was a false statement that he wanted the ticket for his wife.' Avory, J., said: 'The false pretence was a pretence that the man *bona fide* required the ticket for his wife. Leaving out any intention, that was the false pretence of an existing fact.' The case can, however, better be brought within accepted principle by stating the false pretence as a representation that he was entitled to a privilege-ticket, which he was not. See Craymer, 'Intention' in [1955] *Crim. L.R.* 556.

be regarded as 'facts' within the definition of the offence; so that an indictment might lie against a man for obtaining goods by a false statement of his present intention to do a given future act. In *R.* v. *Gordon* (1889),[1] Mr Justice Wills inclined to think that such a merely mental fact would suffice. But if such expressions of intention were to be recognized as sufficient pretences, it would often be hard to distinguish between them and promises, which (as we have seen[2]) are not sufficient.

It must be remembered that the prosecution must establish not only (1) that the prisoner made a statement which he did not believe to be true, but also (2) that the statement was really false.[3]

(*d*) THE EFFECT

¶ 349. The change of ownership must not merely have been preceded by a false pretence, but also have been actually *caused* by it, wholly or at any rate[4] in material part. The counsel for the Crown should not omit to put an express (but not a leading) question as to this.[5] But proof need not in every case be afforded by the direct evidence of a witness, if the facts are such that the alleged false pretence is the only reason which could be suggested as having been the operative inducement.[6] When a shopkeeper is actually delivering goods on credit to *A*, no offence is created if *A* should *then* say falsely, 'I am the Earl of *Z*'. Nor if the buyer of a sham gem relied, not on the seller's false assurance, but on the (incorrect) report of a jeweller whom he consulted. Similarly, if a false representation had been actually made by the prisoner to the prosecutor's agents, but the agents never communicated it to the principal before he parted with his goods (so that it was not by it that he was led to act), there must be an acquittal. The same principle applies wherever the pretence did not in fact deceive the person to whom it was made; as in the frequent instances where, on the advice of the police, the recipients of a begging letter send money to the writer of it, in order to expose him. (In such cases, however, the prisoner may nevertheless be guilty of an attempt to obtain by false pretences—which is (*ante*, ¶ 61) a common law misdemeanour.[7]) If, however, the person was in fact actuated by the false pretence, it does not matter how credulous or how careless he may have been in accepting it; as where the defrauder professed to have the magical power of bringing back a missing person 'over hedges and ditches'.[8]

It should be noted that nowadays it makes no difference whether the

[1] 23 Q.B.D. 354 (*T.A.C.*).

[2] *R.* v. *Dent* [1955] 2 Q.B. 590; *ante*, ¶ 346.

[3] *R.* v. *Flint* (1821) R. and R. 460; *R.* v. *Evans* (1859) Bell 187.

[4] *R.* v. *West* (1858) D. and B. 575.

[5] *R.* v. *Sullivan* (1945) 30 Cr.App.R. 132; *R.* v. *Grail* (1944) 30 Cr.App.R. 81. For the actuation should be proved by direct evidence, not by mere inference from business ways, *R.* v. *Dargue* (1911) 6 Cr.App.R. 261.

[6] *R.* v. *Sullivan* (1945) 30 Cr.App.R. 132.

[7] *R.* v. *Light* (1915) 11 Cr.App.R. 111.

[8] *R.* v. *Giles* (1865) L. and C. 502.

prosecutor was induced to transfer the property to the accused person himself or whether it was transferred to some other person as the result of the false pretence. But the indictment must allege specifically that the accused obtained the property for some other person, if that is the fact, otherwise a conviction will be quashed.[1] Under the old statutes,[2] however, no provision was made for the case where the prosecutor had been induced to transfer the property to some other person than the false pretender himself.[3]

Express request for the article not essential

¶ 350. Even if there was no express request for the article yet the offender's general behaviour may be such as to warrant the jury's finding that there was an implied one.

It is a question of fact and it may be that the causal connexion is too remote to satisfy a jury beyond reasonable doubt. But lapse of time alone does not necessarily render the obtaining too remote. Moreover, if it is clear that the delivery of the article obtained was made *because of* the false pretence (and was the object and aim of the false pretence, *post*, ¶ 353) it is sufficient, even though other advantages were also obtained. And it is immaterial that the thing ultimately delivered was not in existence at the time of the request.[4]

¶ 351. *R.* v. *Button* and *R.* v. *Clucas.* Difficulty has been caused by failure to observe that the article must have been transferred because of the false pretence, in the sense that the person responsible for the transfer of the ownership must have had in his mind the false pretence as a reason for the transfer.[5] Thus it may well be that if a competitor in a foot-race obtains an undue allowance in a handicap by making a false statement as to his previous performances, and thereby is enabled to win the race and obtain the prize, he can properly be convicted of obtaining it by false pretences. But the indictment should be carefully worded. It is for this reason that the case of *R.* v. *Button*[6] should be read with caution. Button, who was a good and successful runner, entered for two races (for each of which a prize of ten guineas was offered) at a sports meeting, but filled in the entry forms in the name of one Sims and stated therein the results of the last four races in which Sims had run and also that he had never won a race. These statements were true of Sims, but Sims had not signed them and knew nothing of them. In consequence of these statements he was allowed a considerable start in each race, which he won easily. The handicapper was suspicious

[1] *R.* v. *Lurie* [1951] 2 All E.R. 704.

[2] 7 and 8 Geo. IV, c. 29, s. 53, and the Larceny Act, 1861, s. 88.

[3] Students should therefore not allow themselves to be confused by such old cases as *R.* v. *Martin* (1859) 1 F. and F. 501, which was decided under the old law. A similar case was *R.* v. *Wavell* (1829) 1 Moo. 224.

[4] *R.* v. *Martin* (1867) 1 C.C.R. 56 (*T.A.C.*).

[5] See *Guggenheim* v. *Ladbroke & Co.*, *The Times*, 3 Feb. 1950.

[6] [1900] 2 Q.B. 597 (*T.A.C.*); cf. *R.* v. *Dickenson*, *The Times*, 25 July 1879.

after the first race and questioned Button, who still maintained that he was Sims and had never won a race before. However, Button neither applied for the prizes, nor received them. His conviction for attempt to obtain the money by false pretences was upheld by the Court for Crown Cases Reserved, who decided the case by reference to Button's intentions alone, without considering what would have been in the mind of the persons who would have paid over to him the prizes if he had come forward for them. Button's defence was wrongly framed and this last point does not appear to have been argued, but it is submitted that it was really the gist of the matter. His false statement, in effect, was that he was a poor runner who had never won a race. What he obtained thereby was not money but an undeserved advantage in running.[1] But whoever presents the prize at a sports meeting does so not because the successful competitor did not win on some previous occasion but because he *has* won in this particular event. Since Button was charged with attempt, it was perhaps natural that the minds of those taking part in the trial were directed entirely to the question of his intentions. Moreover he had repeated his false statements in response to a direct question *after* the race had been won. But in the ordinary case where the runner has actually received the prize it would seem that the indictment should allege that the accused obtained the prize by falsely pretending that he had won the race fairly and honestly. This he did not do, since he had secured an unfair start by making untrue statements.[2]

In *R.* v. *Clucas*[3] the accused (together with another man) had induced bookmakers to bet with them by falsely representing that they were commission agents acting on behalf of a number of other men. Some of the bets they won and in respect thereof they received the money from the bookmakers, and it was this money that they were found guilty of obtaining by false pretences. In quashing the conviction the Court of Criminal Appeal said: 'No doubt the bookmaker might never have opened an account with these men if he had known the true facts, but we must distinguish between a contributory cause and the effective cause which led the bookmaker to pay the money, namely, the fact that these men had backed a winning horse.'

When the effect is too remote

¶ 352. Again, a person who obtains an appointment by some false representation does not necessarily thereby obtain the salary paid to him in due course; for the salary is paid to him for the services he has rendered and not because of his false statements, which merely gave

[1] That this is so was inherent in a reference to *R.* v. *Button* made by the court in *R.* v. *Clucas* (n. 3 *infra*) at p. 42: 'By the false pretence he obtained for himself a winning chance which otherwise he would not have had and thereby enabled himself to win the race.' And see *R.* v. *Leon*, and *R.* v. *Clucas and O'Rourke*, ¶ 367 *post*.

[2] Therefore on the actual indictment in the case of *R.* v. *Larner* (1880) 14 Cox 497, the accused seems to have been properly acquitted.

[3] [1949] 2 All E.R. 40.

him the opportunity to earn the money.[1] On the other hand the *intervention* of a contract does not *necessarily* prevent a conviction for false pretences since the facts may be such as to make it plain that although a contract is secured it is merely incidental to the main purpose of the false pretence which is to obtain the property without paying for it. Within this principle were *R.* v. *Kenrick*,[2] where the accused succeeded in selling two horses by making absolutely false statements of fact about them, and *R.* v. *Martin*,[3] where the accused induced the prosecutor to make and deliver a van under a contract of sale. On the other side of the line was *R.* v. *Gardner*[4] where the accused secured lodgings by false pretences, and after some time arranged with his landlady to give him food; whereas in *R.* v. *Burton*[5] and *R.* v. *Moreton*[6] it was held as a fact that the food, in similar circumstances, *was* obtained by the false pretence.

(*e*) THE INTENT

¶ **353**. It is not enough that the false pretence obtained the thing, it must have been made with the purpose of obtaining, and of obtaining by defrauding[7] (e.g. not simply to rescue your own chattel from a wrongful possessor, or to get it as a joke and then promptly return it, or to hold it as security for a genuine debt). And it must, moreover, have been made, not by honest mistake, but with knowledge of (or *perhaps*[8] recklessness about) its falsity;[9] e.g. not merely by carelessly signing a paper without reading it. The offender's intention, ultimately to make good the loss *if* he can, does not displace fraud. Accordingly the offence is committed where the false pretence procures a loan of money; for in such a transaction the ownership of the money lent is transferred to the borrower[10] and the crime is complete even though the borrower should repay it afterwards.[11]

It is expressly provided by the Larceny Act[12] that it is not necessary

[1] *R.* v. *Lewis*, Somerset Assizes, Jan. 1922.

[2] (1843) 5 Q.B. 49. In fact the counts for false pretences in this case were bad and the accused were convicted of conspiracy. But the general principle stated above was firmly enunciated by Denman, L.C.J.; *R.* v. *Sanders* [1919] 1 K.B. 550.

[3] (1867) 1 C.C.R. 56 (*T.A.C.*).

[4] (1856) D. and B. 40; and see *R.* v. *Bryan* (1861) 2 F. and F. 567, and *R.* v. *Bagley* (1923) 17 Cr.App.R. 162.

[5] (1886) 16 Cox 62.

[6] (1913) 8 Cr.App.R. 214.

[7] *R.* v. *Weeks* (1928) 20 Cr.App.R. 188; but as to direction to jury see *R.* v. *Moss* (1931) 23 Cr.App.R. 132.

[8] In a civil action of deceit recklessness suffices; see *Reese River Co.* v. *Smith* (1869) L.R. 4 H.L. 64 at p. 79, and *Derry* v. *Peek* (1889) 14 A.C. 337 at p. 368. Cf. *R.* v. *Bishirgian* (1936) 52 T.L.R. 361.

[9] Such knowledge is *prima facie* evidence of intent to defraud.

[10] It is the Roman contract of *mutuum*.

[11] *R.* v. *Crossley* (1825) 2 M. and R. 17; *R.* v. *Burgon* (1856) D. and B. 11; *R.* v. *Carpenter* (1911) 76 J.P. 158; *R.* v. *Kritz* [1949] 2 All E.R. 406 (*T.A.C.*); and see the remarks of Darling, J., in *R.* v. *Brown* (1899) 63 J.P. 790.

[12] Sect. 40 (1).

to prove an intent to defraud any particular person, but that it is enough to prove that the person accused did the act charged with intent to defraud.

Since, as we have seen, the subject matter of false pretences is some physical tangible object capable of being stolen,[1] the word to 'defraud'[2] means by deceit to deprive the prosecutor of something of economic value.

The confusion of principle which, sooner or later, is inevitably engendered by illogical thinking is well illustrated in the situation produced by the judgment of the Court of Criminal Appeal in the case of *R.* v. *Wright*,[3] where the court is stated to have said that it was an essential ingredient of this offence (under section 32) that the action must have been done with intent to defraud, 'which, as has been said in this court over and over again, was really synonymous with dishonesty'. Unless this dictum is to conflict with the principle enunciated in such cases as *R.* v. *Ball* (*ante*, ¶ 344) it must be read as dealing solely with the point that the question whether the accused really had the required intent is one of fact for the jury, and not for the judge.[4]

Section 2. Punishment

¶ 354. Although the statutory offence of obtaining by false pretences is only a misdemeanour, it is punishable as severely as simple larceny, viz. with imprisonment for not more than five years or with a fine.[5]

Section 3. Larceny and False Pretences Distinguished

¶ 355. The distinction between larceny and false pretences can be stated clearly enough, but it has often happened in the past that the evidence given at the trial was somewhat different from what was expected, so that it might appear, for example, that the prosecutor, where larceny was charged, had really been induced to give his consent to passing the ownership of the goods charged to have been stolen.[6] In olden times it was impossible to guard against this by alternative counts, since felonies and misdemeanours could not be joined in the same indictment.

[1] *Ante*, ¶ 341.

[2] This was, in effect, the definition of 'defraud' given by Buckley, J., in *Re London and Globe Finance Corporation* [1903] 1 Ch. 728. This definition has sometimes been misunderstood, see *R.* v. *Bassey* (1931) 22 Cr.App.R. 160; *post*, ¶ 377.

[3] As reported and discussed in [1960] *Crim. L.R.* 366.

[4] On the whole question of the meaning of the word 'defraud' see 'Intent to defraud reconsidered' by G. H. L. Fridman in [1960] *Crim. L.R.* 530. Not to confine to the crime of forgery the doctrine of the House of Lords in *Welham* v. *D.P.P.*, *post*, ¶ 377, would be to open the way for the future harm, which must be expected in relation to that crime, to flow into other branches of law also.

[5] Larceny Act, 1916, ss. 32, 37 (5) (*a*).

[6] See *R.* v. *Caslin* (*ante*, ¶ 346) where a conviction of larceny was quashed and a conviction of false pretences substituted, the objection of futurity being obviated by a special view of the facts adopted by the C.C.A.

But in modern times these difficulties have been overcome by statute and now the Larceny Act, 1916, provides in section 44:

(3) If on the trial of any indictment for stealing it is proved that the defendant took any chattel, money, or valuable security in question in any such manner as would amount in law to obtaining it by false pretences with intent to defraud, the jury may acquit the defendant of stealing and find him guilty of obtaining the chattel, money, or valuable security by false pretences, and thereupon he shall be liable to be punished accordingly.

(4) If on the trial of any indictment for obtaining any chattel, money, or valuable security by false pretences it is proved that the defendant stole the property in question, he shall not by reason thereof be entitled to be acquitted of obtaining such property by false pretences.

But students should remember that in every such case as is envisaged by the above statutory provisions the evidence must, at the trial, clearly establish which of the two crimes has in fact been committed.[1] If the indictment is for *attempted* larceny the accused cannot, under section 44 (3), be convicted of attempting to obtain by false pretences.[2]

SECTION 4. RESTITUTION ORDER

¶ 356. A restitution order[3] may be had against the actual offender, or his *mala fide* sub-purchaser, by any prosecutor who has actually become again the owner, i.e. who has legally rescinded the transfer. But the Sale of Goods Act, 1893 (56 and 57 Vict. c. 71, s. 24), provides that conviction for frauds not amounting to larceny shall not[4] by itself produce such a revesting as to defeat intermediate *bona fide* sales. Hence the courts are chary of granting restitution orders in cases of false pretences, for fear there may have been such a sale. Where, however, the former owner may lawfully disaffirm the transaction, a restitution order may be made.[5]

[1] *R.* v. *Fisher (Edward)* (1910) 5 Cr.App.R. 102; *R.* v. *Fisher* (1921) 16 Cr.App.R. 53; *R.* v. *Fisher (Grace)* (1926) 19 Cr.App.R. 166.

[2] *R.* v. *Gallagher* (1929) 21 Cr.App.R. 172.

[3] *Ante*, ¶ 313 *et seq.*

[4] Cf. Larceny Act, 1916, s. 45 (2). But if, though the conviction were for false pretences, yet the evidence establishes larceny, the ownership revests, *R.* v. *George* (1901) 65 J.P. 729; accordingly a restitution order can be made. An order can be made by a court of summary jurisdiction under s. 33 of the Magistrates' Courts Act, 1952. And see the Police Property Act, 1897, which deals with property coming into the possession of the police in connexion with any criminal charge: *ante*, ¶ 317.

[5] *R.* v. *George*, *ubi supra.*

Chapter XVIII

RECEIVING STOLEN PROPERTY

Section 1. At Common Law and by Statute

¶ **357.** At common law the receiving of stolen goods with knowledge that they had been stolen was a misdemeanour. It was necessary that a larceny of the goods should have been committed; yet the receiver was not indictable at common law[1] as an accessory after the fact to this larceny (unless the receiving in some way assisted the thief's escape from justice), because it was not the thief, but only the goods, that he received. Subsequently, however, by various statutes (whose provisions are now comprised in the Larceny Act, 1916, s. 33 (1)), the scope of the offence was greatly widened, by extending it to cases where the original act of dishonesty was a stealing or obtaining of the property 'in any way whatsoever under circumstances which amounted to felony or misdemeanour'.[2] As to receiving the proceeds of a *non*-indictable theft, see the Act of 1861, *post*, ¶ 363.

The offence thus consists in 'receiving[3] stolen goods, knowing them to have been stolen'. This involves three points for consideration: (*a*) the receiving, (*b*) the thing received, (*c*) the guilty knowledge.

(*a*) The receiving

¶ **358.** There must have been some act of 'receiving', which involves a change of possession. It must therefore be shown that the prisoner took the goods into his possession, actual or constructive.[4] This cannot be the case so long as the original thief retains exclusive possession of them (though there may well be an amicable joint possession by a receiver and a thief together).[5] But, as in all cases of possession, a person may 'receive' without himself taking part in any physical act of receipt. Accordingly if stolen goods are delivered to the prisoner's servant, or

[1] Under the Larceny Act, 1827 (rep.), he was declared so to be; the resulting rule as to corroboration if he should give evidence is stated in *Davies* v. *D.P.P.* [1954] A.C. 378; *post*, ¶ 602.

[2] If an article has been sold and delivered on credit, and the *credit* has been obtained by fraud contrary to s. 13 of the Debtors Act, 1869, it was doubted, as the result of *R.* v. *Schweller* (1924) 18 Cr.App.R. 52, whether it would be an offence within sect. 33 (1) to receive the article, knowing of the fraud. But it has since been held, in *R.* v. *New* (1957) 41 Cr.App.R. 207, that *Schweller's* case turned purely on the procedural point that the counts upon which his convictions were quashed did not, on their face, disclose any offence known to the law.

[3] For any purpose, even temporary custody or carrying. But an *innocent aim* excuses; e.g. to restore the goods to the owner (see *R.* v. *Matthews* [1950], *post*, ¶ 361), or to entrap the thief. As to goods stolen abroad, see ¶ 362 *post*.

[4] *R.* v. *Wiley* (1850) 2 Den. 37; *R.* v. *Berger* (1915) 11 Cr.App.R. 72; *Hawes* v. *Edwards* (1949) 113 J.P. 303.

[5] *R.* v. *Pearson* (1908) 1 Cr.App.R. 77 and 79.

wife,[1] in his absence, but he afterwards does some act that implies an acceptance of the goods—as by removing them to some other part of his premises, or by striking a bargain about them with the thief[2]—he will then (though not till then) become himself a 'receiver' of them. But handling the goods does not necessarily amount to receiving since there may be a picking-up without any taking into possession.[3] The fact that stolen jewels are in a man's house does not make his wife a constructive possessor of them; it is not as if she were wearing them.[4] The question of the prisoner's possession is one of fact and it must be left to the jury.[5]

(*b*) The thing received

¶ 359. There must be proof that the goods received had been stolen antecedently to the act of receiving;[6] but the circumstances in which an accused person has received the goods may of themselves be sufficient proof that they have been stolen,[7] and, further, may prove that he knew this when he received them.[8] It is often not easy to say, before trial, whether a man is a thief or a receiver of stolen property.[9] Moreover, the character of being 'stolen goods' is only a temporary one. For if, after being stolen, the goods happen to return into the possession (actual or even constructive) of their owner, such a return will deprive them of the character of stolen property, so that there will not be any crime in subsequently receiving them.[10] This rule often defeats measures which have been taken by an owner, after detecting a theft, in hopes of entrapping and punishing some expected receiver.

[1] *R.* v. *Dring* (1857) D. and B. 329.

[2] *R.* v. *Woodward* (1862) L. and C. 122 (*T.A.C.*); *R.* v. *Pritchard* (1913) 9 Cr.App.R. 210.

[3] *Hobson* v. *Impett* [1957] Crim. L.R. 476; and see *ante*, ¶ 224.

[4] See *Sonkin and others* (1908) C.C.C. Sess. Pap. CL, 288 at p. 295. The test of receipt is control, *R.* v. *Gleed* (1916) 12 Cr.App.R. 32; *R.* v. *Watson* (1916) 12 Cr.App.R. 62; *Hobson* v. *Impett, ubi supra*; *R.* v. *Harris* [1961] Crim. L.R. 256.

[5] *R.* v. *Crane* (1912) 7 Cr.App.R. 113; *R.* v. *Flatman* (1913) 8 Cr.App.R. 256; *R.* v. *Freedman* (1930) 22 Cr.App.R. 133; *R.* v. *Brooker* [1956] Crim. L.R. 489. A border-line case is *R.* v. *Cavendish* [1961] 2 All E.R. 856.

[6] *Gruncell and Hopkinson* (1839) 9 C. and P. 365 (*T.A.C.*); goods taken by a child under eight are not stolen and therefore cannot be 'received', *Walters* v. *Lunt* [1951] 2 All E.R. 645; a dictum to the effect that the parents might have been treated as bailees has been strongly criticized in 68 *L.Q.R.* 167 and 15 *Mod.L.R.* 222. The dictum can hardly be correct in face of *R.* v. *Matthews* (1873) 12 Cox 489; *ante*, p. 278. See also *Macgregor* v. *Benyon* [1957] Crim. L.R. 250; *R.* v. *Dickson and Gray* [1955] Crim. L.R. 435; Curr.L. 648.

[7] *R.* v. *Sbarra* (1918) 13 Cr.App.R. 118.

[8] *R.* v. *Fuschillo* [1940] 2 All E.R. 489; for the unsatisfactory case of *Carter Paterson & Pickford's Carriers Ltd.* v. *Wessel* [1947] 1 K.B. 849, see 10 *Cambridge L.J.* (1948), 112.

[9] Hence, where the evidence is *prima facie* consistent with either offence the indictment should carry a count for each; and the jury should be left to decide which (if either) it is, after receiving a warning that a man cannot receive from himself; then if the jury decide on one they should be discharged from giving a verdict on the other. *R.* v. *Christ* [1951] 2 All E.R. 254; *R.* v. *Loughlin* (1951) 35 Cr.App.R. 69; *R.* v. *Seymour* (1954) 38 Cr.App.R. 68.

[10] *R.* v. *Villensky* [1892] 2 Q.B. 597 (*T.A.C.*). Contrast *R.* v. *King* [1938] 2 All E.R. 662 (*T.A.C.*).

(c) The knowledge

¶ **360.** The prisoner must have received the stolen goods with knowledge *then*[1] of their having been stolen (not knowledge obtained merely after taking possession). Such knowledge may be presumed, *prima facie* if he knew of circumstances so suspicious as to convince any reasonable man that the goods had been stolen—e.g. when an unlikely vendor offers them for an unlikely price at an unlikely hour.[2] His subsequent conduct may be evidence of such knowledge; e.g. his hiding the goods, or selling them surreptitiously and over-cheaply, or making no written entry of having bought them.

The indictment must allege knowledge of the *category* of the crime, but knowledge of the specific crime within that category need not be so stated; to allege 'knowing the property to have been obtained "by dishonest means" is not sufficient'.[3]

MENS REA

¶ **361.** There must also be *mens rea* in the sense that the receiver intends to appropriate the goods to his own use or to the use of some other person than the true owner. Thus it has been said: 'The court cannot possibly accept the argument which has been addressed to it on behalf of the prosecution, that a person, who intends at once to hand to the police, or its true owner, stolen property which has come into his possession, is nevertheless guilty of the felony of receiving stolen property'.[4] It will be remembered that in the crime of larceny it is necessary at common law that the *animus furandi* be proved to have existed at the time when the thing was first 'taken and carried away'.[5] But, for the crime of receiving stolen property, section 33 does not contain any reference to a similar requirement that the dishonest purpose of the receiver must exist at the time when he first receives the property. It might therefore have been thought that the legislature did not intend that the old common law rule for larceny[6] should be applied also to receivers; especially since it is difficult to see why a person who takes in property which he knows to have been stolen should be in a position of greater immunity than a bailee of it would be. However, the Court of Criminal Appeal have decided that the same requirement

[1] *R.* v. *Johnson* (1911) 6 Cr.App.R. 218. Retaining is not receiving.

[2] Actual *certainty* is not necessary, *R.* v. *White* (1859) 1 F. and F. 665. But negligence (or even recklessness) in not realizing their having been stolen will not create guilt; he must have shut his eyes *wilfully* to facts from which ordinary men would realize it clearly; *R.* v. *Havard* (1914) 11 Cr.App.R. 2, and *R.* v. *Sporton and Hawkins* (1907) C.C.C. Sess. Pap. XCVIII at p. 232. See ¶¶ 500 and 550 *post* as to statutory evidence of knowledge.

[3] *R.* v. *Nieser* [1958] 3 All E.R. 662.

[4] *R.* v. *Matthews* [1950] 1 All E.R. 137 (*T.A.C.*) at p. 138; *R.* v. *Revuelta* [1959] Crim. L.R. 777.

[5] Larceny Act, 1916, s. 1 (1).

[6] Which the courts have indeed done their best to avoid, e.g. *R.* v. *Riley* (1853) Dearsly 149, *ante*, ¶ 288; and *R.* v. *Ashwell* (1885) 16 Q.B.D. 190, *ante*, ¶ 290.

exists for receiving as for larceny and have stated: 'If, when the property is received, the receipt is innocent, the fact that the receiver changes his mind and later misappropriates the property does not turn the receipt into a felony.'[1]

SECTION 2. PROPERTY STOLEN ABROAD

¶ 362. The Larceny Act also provides in section 33 (4) that

> Every person who, without lawful excuse, knowing the same to have been stolen or obtained in any way whatsoever under such circumstances that if the act had been committed in the United Kingdom the person committing it would have been guilty of felony or misdemeanour, receives or has in his possession any property so stolen or obtained outside the United Kingdom, shall be guilty of an offence of the like degree (whether felony or misdemeanour) and on conviction thereof liable to imprisonment for any term not exceeding seven years.

SECTION 3. PUNISHMENT

¶ 363. The main rules as to punishment of receivers in the Larceny Acts, 1861 and 1916,[2] are as follows:

(1) If the original stealing or obtaining was a felony, the receiver is guilty of a felony. The maximum punishment is fourteen years' imprisonment. (Sect. 33 (1) of the Larceny Act, 1916.)

(2) If the original stealing or obtaining was a misdemeanour (e.g. if the goods had been obtained by false pretences), the receiving is a misdemeanour, and punishable with a maximum punishment of seven years' imprisonment. (Sect. 33 (1) of the Larceny Act, 1916.)

(3) If the original stealing was, by the Larceny Act of 1861, a petty offence punishable on summary conviction (e.g. if the thing stolen were only a dog), the receiving is only a similar offence, and is punishable just as the stealing itself is. (Sect. 97 of the Larceny Act, 1861.)

[1] R. v. *Matthews* [1950] 1 All E.R. 137.

[2] As amended by the Criminal Justice Act, 1948.

Chapter XIX

OTHER OFFENCES INVOLVING FRAUD

Section I. Statutory Frauds

CORRUPT REWARDS

¶ 364. By section 34 of the Larceny Act, 1916,

> Every person who corruptly takes any money or reward, directly or indirectly, under pretence or upon account of helping any person to recover any property which has, under circumstances which amount to felony or misdemeanour, been stolen or obtained in any way whatsoever, or received, shall (unless he has used all due diligence to cause the offender to be brought to trial for the same) be guilty of felony and on conviction thereof liable to [imprisonment] for any term not exceeding seven years.

The rule contained in this section is derived from earlier statutes and is said to have originated as a result of the activities of a celebrated criminal in the eighteenth century, Jonathan Wild, who carried on a notorious trade in the collection of such rewards.[1]

Any person who publicly advertises a reward for the return of any property which has been stolen or lost with an intimation, direct or indirect, that no questions will be asked (or publishes such an advertisement) is liable on summary conviction to a fine not exceeding one hundred pounds.[2]

OBTAINING CREDIT BY FRAUD

¶ 365. By virtue of the Debtors Act, 1869, any person who in incurring any debt or liability has obtained credit under false pretences, or by means of any other fraud, is guilty of a misdemeanour and liable to be imprisoned for any time not exceeding one year. As we have seen[3] this provision reaches some cases of dishonesty which cannot be brought within section 32 of the Larceny Act, 1916, for example because the false representation may relate to the future. It has been decided that

[1] See Radzinowicz, *Hist. Eng. Crim. Law*, I, 667, 683; 4 Bl. *Comm.* 132; *R.* v. *Wild* (1725) 1 Leach 17 (n).

[2] Larceny Act, 1861, s. 102, as amended by the Common Informers Act, 1951. In the case of publication by a newspaper the proceedings must be brought within six months; Larceny (Advertisements) Act, 1870, s. 3. Formerly there were many statutes under which any member of the general public was invited to denounce an offender and institute proceedings for the recovery of a fine, being rewarded by the whole, or part, of the fine so exacted; such a person was called 'a common informer'. For an account of this example of criminal policy see Radzinowicz, *op. cit.* vol. II, ch. 6; and Appendix I of the 16th ed. of the present book; cf. *Att.-Gen.* v. *Exeter Corpn.* [1911] 1 K.B. 1092 at p. 1099.

[3] *R.* v. *Jones* [1898] 1 Q.B. 119 (*T.A.C.*). Note that in *R.* v. *Dent* [1955] 2 Q.B. 590 (*T.A.C.*) (*ante*, p. 329) there was no charge of obtaining credit by fraud, contrary to s. 13 of the Debtors Act, 1869. *Ante*, ¶ 346.

'debt' means a debt which can be recovered by civil action, and therefore a betting debt, since it is void under the Gaming Act, 1845, is not within this section.[1] The credit must have been obtained for the offender himself and it is not enough that he has obtained it for some other person.[2] The meaning of the word 'credit' in this connexion is discussed in Appendix I, *post*. In *R.* v. *Mitchell*[3] the appellant (against sentence) had stolen (as bailee) a motor cycle and given it to the prosecutor in part exchange for another machine, at the agreed value of £65. He had pleaded guilty to a charge in one count of the indictment of obtaining credit to the amount of £65 by false pretence. But as this was not a *debt* from him to the prosecutor the facts as charged in the indictment did not satisfy the statute and the conviction was quashed. It is not certain that he could not have been convicted on a more correctly worded charge alleging an obtaining of credit in respect of the unpaid balance of the purchase price of the machine.

FRAUDS BY BANKRUPTS

¶ 366. The various statutes on bankruptcy have rendered criminal many acts done by persons adjudged bankrupt, in order to protect other persons who may deal with them in ignorance of their insolvency.[4] Only a very brief indication of this branch of the law can be given here. The bankrupt must honestly and fully reveal all his assets, books, and accounts; he must not abscond with any of his property to the amount of twenty pounds or more; he must not engage in trade or business under any other name without disclosing to all persons with whom he deals the name under which he was adjudicated bankrupt. And if he obtains credit to the extent of ten pounds or upwards from anyone without informing him that he is an undischarged bankrupt he is guilty of a misdemeanour,[5] punishable with two years' imprisonment. A person adjudged bankrupt, or against whom a receiving order has been made, commits a misdemeanour (similarly punishable) if, irrespective of non-disclosure of his position, in incurring a debt or other liability he obtains credit by fraud, or disposes of or conceals any of his property with intent to defraud his creditors.[6]

FRAUD IN GAMING

¶ 367. By section 17 of the Gaming Act, 1845,[7]

> And be it enacted, That every Person who shall, by any Fraud or unlawful

[1] *R.* v. *Leon* [1945] 1 All E.R. 14.

[2] *R.* v. *Bryant* (1899) 63 J.P. 376; *R.* v. *Steel* (1910) 5 Cr.App.R. 289.

[3] [1955] 3 All E.R. 263. For a case clearly within s. 13 of this Act, see *R.* v. *Ingram* [1956] 2 Q.B. 424 (*T.A.C.*).

[4] See the Bankruptcy Act, 1914.

[5] Bankruptcy Act, 1914, s. 155. Under this section non-disclosure is the gist of the offence; any question of fraud by the bankrupt is irrelevant. This was the offence with which the respondent in *Osborn* v. *Barton* (1950) 66 T.L.R. 115, had been charged. See the discussion of this case, on the question of what constitutes 'credit', in Appendix I, *post*.

[6] Bankruptcy Act, 1914, s. 156.

[7] Based on 9 Anne, c. 14; see Hawk. 1 P.C. 345.

Device or ill Practice in playing at or with Cards, Dice, Tables, or other Game, or in bearing a Part in the Stakes, Wagers, or Adventures, or in betting on the Sides or Hands of them that do play, or in wagering on the Event of any Game, Sport, Pastime, or Exercise, win from any other Person to himself, or any other or others, any Sum of Money or valuable Thing, shall be deemed guilty of obtaining such Money or valuable Thing from such other Person by a false Pretence, with Intent to cheat or defraud such Person of the same, and, being convicted thereof, shall be punished accordingly.

The language of the section makes it plain that it is an offence for anyone to win to himself (or to others) any money or valuable thing from another person by any fraud or unlawful device or ill practice in any one of a stated series of alternative situations. There may, of course, be deceit and fraud whereby a person is induced to take part in any one of these situations; but it is, for the purposes of this section, immaterial whether the game, sport, pastime or exercise is itself unlawful or lawful: the gist of the offence is in the fraud or unlawful device[1] which deprives the other players of a fair chance of winning, and the same point applies in the other activities specified, namely, 'bearing part' in the stakes etc., or betting on the hands of the players, or wagering on the result of the game, sport, or pastime. It has been held that tossing with coins for wagers is a pastime[2] within this section. The cheating must occur during the playing of the game, so that inducing a person to play by deceit does not of itself constitute the offence;[3] but it might amount to a conspiracy to cheat.[4]

In *R.* v. *Leon*[5] the appellant had by false statements induced a bookmaker to accept him as a backer of race-horses. He was successful in backing some winning horses to begin with and received the winnings from the bookmaker, but later, when he lost, he made default. He had been convicted under section 17 of the Gaming Act and his appeal against this conviction was dismissed. That the accused by dishonest misrepresentations had induced the bookmaker to enter into the agreement whereby he consented to receive him as a credit backer was established to the satisfaction of the jury; and they were further satisfied that from the beginning he intended to take what he might receive as his balance of winnings and not pay any balance of his losses. It was abundantly clear that the accused was fraudulent *in* the wagering but it is also clear that he did not *win by* his fraudulence; his misrepresentations related to his own financial position and it was by them that he induced the bookmaker to deal with him; but they had nothing to do with his *winning* the money. Since the attention of the court does not seem to have been properly directed to this requirement of the section, it

[1] Even bending up a corner of a card to make the prosecutor believe that *he* would win unfairly in betting on the three-card trick, *R.* v. *Moore* (1914) 10 Cr.App.R. 54.

[2] *R.* v. *O'Connor* (1881) 15 Cox 3.

[3] *R.* v. *Governor of Brixton Prison* [1912] 3 K.B. 568.

[4] *R.* v. *Bailey* (1850) 4 Cox 390.

[5] [1945] 1 All E.R. 14.

appeared that the decision, in point of law, was unsatisfactory. An analysis of facts, similar to the above, was indeed made in 1949 in a case of obtaining by false pretences,[1] the Court of Criminal Appeal quashing the conviction on the ground that the accused, who had clearly made false statements as to his position whereby he had induced a bookmaker to accept his bets, had not *obtained* his winnings by his false pretences but by the fact that he had selected the horses which won the races. Nevertheless in a later case[2] where, by precisely the same kind of pretence by (what was presumably) the same man, a bookmaker had been induced to accept him as a backer and had paid over money in respect of winning horses, but the charge was laid under section 17 of the Gaming Act, the Court of Criminal Appeal followed *R.* v. *Leon* and upheld the conviction, without, it must be submitted with respect, meeting the argument indicated, but overruling and putting it aside on the footing that there was 'fraud in wagering'. This, again with all respect, was not an answer to, but an evasion of, the point submitted for the defence. But the present position is, therefore, that on authoritative decisions of the Court of Criminal Appeal the accused would not have *obtained* by his fraud if charged under section 32 of the Larceny Act, 1916, but would have *won* by his fraud if charged under section 17 of the Gaming Act, 1845.

FALSE PERSONATION

¶ 368. At common law it was not a special offence to impersonate another person for some fraudulent purpose. Such conduct was indictable only as a cheat (or when carried on in concert with another person it could be dealt with as a conspiracy), and it has often been linked with a forgery.[3] It has, however, been held to be a misdemeanour to personate a juryman, even without any corrupt motive.[4] But the legislature has made it a specific felony to personate a member of the armed forces of the Crown in order to obtain service pay or prize money.[5] And it has been made an offence to personate, for like purposes, police officers,[6] inland revenue officers,[7] or school teachers.[8] It has also been made a felony fraudulently to personate owners of stocks and shares.[9] After the famous *Tichborne Case* an Act[10] was passed making

[1] *R.* v. *Clucas* [1949] 2 All E.R. 40.

[2] *R.* v. *Clucas* [1959] 1 All E.R. 438.

[3] 2 East P.C. 1010.

[4] *R.* v. *Clark* (1918) 82 J.P. 295.

[5] Army Prize Money Act, 1832, s. 49; Admiralty Powers Act, 1865, s. 6; Army Act, 1881, s. 142, replaced each year by the latest Army Act; Chelsea and Kilmarnham Hospitals Act, 1826, s. 38.

[6] Police Pensions Act, 1921, s. 16.

[7] Inland Revenue Act, 1890, s. 12.

[8] Elementary School Teachers (Superannuation) Act, 1898, s. 10; School Teachers (Superannuation) Act, 1918, s. 11.

[9] E.g. Forgery Act, 1861, s. 3; Forgery Act, 1870, s. 4; Government Annuities Act, 1929, s. 34; Companies Act, 1948, s. 84. And see the Representation of the People Act, 1949, s. 47, for the offence of personation of voters.

[10] The False Personation Act, 1874 (37 and 38 Vict. c. 36).

it a felony, punishable (now) with imprisonment for life, falsely and deceitfully to personate any person, or the heir, executor, or administrator, wife, widow, next of kin, or relation of any person, with intent fraudulently to obtain any property, whether real or personal. The offence under this Act is to be distinguished from an attempt to obtain by false pretences, contrary to section 32 of the Larceny Act, 1916; for here the offender must represent that he or she is a particular person to whom some specifically alleged property is legally due.

WITCHCRAFT AND FORTUNE-TELLING

¶ 369. The law on this matter is now substantially governed by the Fraudulent Mediums Act, 1951, which repealed the Witchcraft Act, 1735,[1] and in effect provides that any person who with intent to deceive and for reward[2] purports to act as a spiritualistic medium or to exercise any powers of telepathy, clairvoyance or other similar powers, or in purporting so to act or exercise such powers, uses any fraudulent device, is guilty of an offence.[3] The Act also repeals section 4 of the Vagrancy Act[4] in so far as it extends to persons purporting to act as above described or who in purporting so to act use fraudulent devices.

OTHER STATUTORY FRAUDS

¶ 370. Statutes have created other crimes in connexion with business or trade activities which cannot be dealt with here. Such are the Prevention of Fraud (Investments) Act, 1958, which regulates dealing in securities; the concealment or falsification of matters affecting transfers of real property;[5] fraud in dealing in investments;[6] misconduct in carrying on the business of money lending;[7] the false use of trade marks or trade descriptions;[8] and offences by directors and officials of limited liability companies.[9]

[1] Which by s. 4 had in effect declared it to be an offence punishable with imprisonment for one year to pretend to exercise any kind of witchcraft, sorcery or conjuration, or to pretend to tell fortunes or by occult or crafty science to discover lost property.

[2] Whether money or other valuable thing given to him or any other person.

[3] Punishable on summary conviction by a fine up to fifty pounds and/or imprisonment for up to four months; and on conviction on indictment to a fine up to five hundred pounds and/or imprisonment for up to two years.

[4] Which makes punishable as a rogue and vagabond every person professing to tell fortunes 'to deceive or impose upon' any persons. Any intent to deceive must be proved; *Penny* v. *Hanson* (1887) 18 Q.B.D. 478; *Davis* v. *Curry* [1918] 1 K.B. 109; *R.* v. *Entwistle* [1899] 1 Q.B. 846; *Stonehouse* v. *Masson* [1921] 2 K.B. 818.

[5] Law of Property Act, 1925, s. 183; and see Declaration of Title Act, 1862, s. 44.

[6] Prevention of Fraud (Investments) Act, 1939.

[7] Money Lenders Act, 1900, s. 4.

[8] Merchandise Marks Acts, 1887, 1926 and 1953.

[9] Companies Act, 1948.

SECTION 2. BRIBERY AND CORRUPTION

¶ 371. It is a common law misdemeanour to bribe or offer to bribe a judge or for a judge to accept a bribe,[1] or to bribe or offer to bribe any public officer to omit to do his duty or act contrary to his duty.[2] To attempt to influence a juryman improperly constitutes the misdemeanour of embracery.[3] To sell or purchase, or receive or give any reward in respect of the sale or purchase of, a public office is a misdemeanour punishable with a fine and imprisonment, forfeiture of the office, and absolute disqualification for holding it again.[4]

The offering to or receiving by a member or officer of any local or public body[5] of a reward for doing or forbearing to do any act in connexion with the work of such body is a misdemeanour punishable with two years' imprisonment and/or a fine of £500; or if the offer relates to a contract with any government department or public body with seven years' imprisonment. The offender is also liable to pay to the body whose member or officer he bribes or attempts to bribe the value of the reward. In addition he is liable to be adjudged disqualified for seven years from election or appointment to any public office and, if an officer or servant of a public body, is liable in the discretion of the court to forfeit any rights or claims to compensation or pension. A second offence involves perpetual disqualification for public office and seven years' disqualification for voting at parliamentary or local government elections.[6] Where it is proved that any money or gift has been paid to or received by any person in the employment of the Crown or any public body from any person holding or seeking to obtain a contract, there is deemed to have been corruption, unless the contrary is proved.[7]

By the Prevention of Corruption Act, 1906, it is a misdemeanour punishable with two years' imprisonment and/or a fine of £500 to offer to an agent, or for an agent to accept or attempt to obtain, any gift or consideration as an inducement to do or forbear to do anything in relation to his principal's affairs or business, or for showing or forbearing to show favour or disfavour to any person in relation to his principal's affairs or business. An 'agent' includes any person employed by or acting for another. It is similarly punishable knowingly to give to any agent, or for an agent knowingly to use, any receipt, account or other document in respect of which the principal is interested, and which contains any statement which is false in any material particular and which is intended to mislead the principal. It is not necessary for the

[1] 1 Hawk. P.C. 414, 415.

[2] *R.* v. *Vaughan* (1769) Burr. 2494 and cf. *R.* v. *Whitaker* [1916] 3 K.B. 1283. See Russ., ch. 34.

[3] Winfield, *History of Conspiracy*, ch. VII; Russ., ch. 23, sect. VI.

[4] 49 Geo. III, c. 126.

[5] 6 and 7 Geo. V, c. 64, s. 2.

[6] 52 and 53 Vict. c. 69, ss. 1, 2.

[7] 6 and 7 Geo. V, c. 64, s. 2.

prosecution to prove that the person bribed did in fact do that for which the bribe was given or offered (e.g. to show favour).[1]

Corruption and personation at elections are punishable under the Corrupt Practices Prevention Act, 1854, the Corrupt and Illegal Practices Act, 1883, the Representation of the People Act, 1949, and other statutes.[2] Corruption in connexion with the sale of honours is punishable under the Honours (Prevention of Abuses) Act, 1925.[3]

[1] *R.* v. *Carr* [1957] 1 W.L.R. 165; 40 Cr.App.R. 188. The *motive* of the defendant in offering the bribe is irrelevant; *R.* v. *Smith* [1960] 1 All E.R. 256. No guilt attaches to the receiver of a bribe if he takes it innocently; but the giver may still be guilty of the offence; *R.* v. *Millroy Window Cleaning Co.* [1962] Crim. L.R. 99. And see *R.* v. *Newbould* [1962] 2 W.L.R. 648.

[2] See Russ., ch. 27. For personation to obtain property see *ibid.*, ch. 78, and ¶ 368 *ante.*

[3] And see the National Health Service Act, 1952, s. 2 (false representation).

Chapter XX

FORGERY

Section I. History

ROYAL SEALS AND CHARTERS FIRST PROTECTED

¶ 372. The verb 'to forge', which originally meant simply 'to make', acquired, even before the time of Shakespeare, the special sense of making deceitfully.[1] Yet the crime of forging ordinary (as distinct from sealed, or official) writings is not very ancient in England.[2] In this country the felony of forgery first appeared in connexion with the falsification of royal seals, and it was closely linked with coinage offences and with treason; it was indeed at first regarded as a species of treason.[3] When, however, at an early period[4] not only royal charters but also private charters came to be protected, forgery could be regarded as a distinct crime although it did not yet cover ordinary writings which were not under seal.

Unsealed writings of a private sort did not in those days create the important legal interests which the much later expansion of commerce has made common, so that there was little need for a wider law.[5] At the beginning of the fifteenth century a statute[6] gave a *civil* remedy to persons who had been defrauded through the falsification of deeds relating to real property. This law was extended in 1562;[7] but still the protected writings had, in all cases save that of testaments, to be under seal. Coke made no allusion to a crime of forging ordinary writings, and Hale[8] said nothing of the existence of forgery at common law either as a felony or a misdemeanour.

PROTECTION EXTENDED TO PRIVATE UNSEALED WRITINGS

¶ 373. The law of forgery as it is now understood seems indeed to have begun in 1727[9] when the judges, by a bold interpretation, declared that

[1] The cognate verb 'to fabricate' has passed through a similar development.

[2] At Rome the *lex Cornelia de falsis* (*c.* 81 B.C.) dealt with falsifications, but principally with those relating to testamentary dispositions.

[3] For an outline of the early development of forgery see 32 *Virginia L.R.* (1946), no. 5, 939, *et seq.*

[4] According to Glanvill, under the general head of *crimen laesae maiestatis* was included a *crimen falsi* which covered falsification of money and of charters both royal (*cartae regiae*) and (with lower penalties) private (*cartae privatae*), Lib. I, c. 2 and Lib. XIV, c. 7.

[5] As Maitland said (Pollock and Maitland, II, 539), 'once the royal lawyers have brought the counterfeiting of the king's seal or the king's money within the compass of high treason, they apparently think they have done almost enough'.

[6] 1 Hen. V, c. 3.

[7] 5 Eliz. I, c. 14 which covered the forging of 'false and untrue Charters, Evidences, Deeds and Writings'.

[8] Writing late in the seventeenth century.

[9] *R.* v. *Ward* (1727) 2 Ld. Raym. 1461.

the use of the word 'writings' in the preamble of the above mentioned statute of Elizabeth[1] covered the forging of a writing which was not sealed; and they stated that such a falsification was indictable as a forgery at common law, even before the enactment of Elizabeth. Yet, so much as fifty years later, Hawkins discussed the law of this matter in hesitating terms.[2] He was clear that the falsification of any 'authentick matter of a public nature'[3] would be criminal (whether any third person were actually injured thereby or not); but he doubted if the counterfeiting of other writings 'of an inferior nature' would be a forgery 'unless some one receive a prejudice from it'. This distinction which Hawkins drew between documents of a public character and those of a private character became established in the common law development of this crime[4] and it is now incorporated in the operative statute which has consolidated the law of forgery, viz. the Forgery Act of 1913.[5]

SECTION 2. DEFINITION

SECTION 1 OF THE FORGERY ACT, 1913

¶ 374. That statute by section 1 (1) enacts:

> For the purposes of this Act, forgery is the making of a false document in order that it may be used as genuine, and in the case of the seals and dies mentioned in this Act the counterfeiting of a seal or die, and forgery with intent to defraud or deceive, as the case may be, is punishable as in this Act provided.

It will be observed that the above subsection of section 1 defines 'forgery' but does *not* define 'false document', and it was not doubted that the test of what constituted a false document was left as it had previously been held to be at common law and for the purposes of the Forgery Act, 1861.[6] In the next subsection the Act sets out a number of instances[7] of false documents, every one of which satisfies what, at the date of the statute, was universally held to be the definitive element in the term '*false document*' for the purpose of the law of forgery. The language, however, of subsection (2) was capable of being interpreted as exclusive rather than illustrative, and from time to time in the courts this interpretation was contended for by defending counsel (mostly, it would seem, without success). Eventually the legislature declared[8]

> For the purpose of removing doubts it is hereby declared that a document may be a false document for the purposes of the Forgery Act, 1913, notwithstanding that it is not false in such a manner as is described in subsection (2) of section 1 of that Act.

[1] 5 Eliz. I, c. 14.

[2] 1 P.C. c. 70, s. 11.

[3] Amongst which he included wills.

[4] *Post*, ¶ 376.

[5] 3 and 4 Geo. V, c. 27, s. 4. See *post*, ¶ 376.

[6] See ¶ 387 *post*.

[7] Each of which can be found to enshrine some authoritative decision in a reported case in the past.

[8] Criminal Justice Act, 1925, s. 35 (1).

It was on all sides generally considered that this provision was intended to be read into subsection (2) of section 1 of the Act of 1913, as an addition in the nature of an *eiusdem generis* clause, and not as in any way altering the accepted definition of 'false document'.[1]

SECTIONS 2, 3 AND 5: PRIVATE AND OFFICIAL DOCUMENTS, SEALS AND DIES

¶ 375. Section 2 of the Forgery Act, 1913,[2] makes it a felony punishable with imprisonment for life to forge testamentary documents, deeds, bonds or bank-notes, and a felony punishable with imprisonment for fourteen years to forge valuable securities, documents of title[3] to property, powers of attorney and certain other writings of the like importance. In all the cases within this section it is necessary to prove an intent to defraud.

Section 3 of the Act deals with a number of official documents (the forging of which, with intent *either to defraud or to deceive*, is made a felony), arranged in three groups carrying the punishment of imprisonment for life, for fourteen years and for seven years respectively.

Section 5 deals with the forgery of certain seals and dies. These again are arranged in three classes, with the same three grades of punishment as in section 3.

SECTION 4 STATES THE COMMON LAW

¶ 376. Section 4 of the Act confirms the common law as follows:

(1) Forgery of any document, which is not made felony under this or any other statute for the time being in force, if committed with intent to defraud, shall be a misdemeanour and punishable with imprisonment for any term not exceeding two years.

(2) Forgery of any public document which is not made felony under this or any other statute for the time being in force, if committed with intent to defraud or deceive, shall be a misdemeanour and punishable with imprisonment for any term not exceeding two years.

It will be observed that this section preserves the common law rule (first adumbrated by Hawkins)[4] which requires no more than deceit where public documents are forged, but insists upon an intention to defraud in the case of documents of a private character.[5]

The meaning of 'defraud' and 'deceive'

¶ 377. For nearly two hundred years it appears that the courts administered the law of forgery of private documents without finding it

[1] But see *R.* v. *Hopkins and Collins*, *post*, ¶ 387.

[2] As amended by the Criminal Justice Act, 1948, s. 1.

[3] See Scott, 'Forgery of a log book', [1954] *Crim.L.R.* 604. It is not decided whether a motor registration book is a document of title, *Joblin* v. *Watkins and Roseveare* (1948) 64 T.L.R. 464; see Vehicles (Excise) Act, 1949, s. 21 (*b*).

[4] *Ante*, ¶ 373.

[5] See *post*, ¶ 393.

necessary to define the verb 'to defraud'. The reported cases show that it was treated as meaning 'to cause economic loss[1] to some person by means of deceit'. In 1903, however, it became necessary in proceedings[2] (which had nothing whatever to do with forgery) in the Chancery Division to decide (on a question of costs) whether, *prima facie*, a false statement had been made with intent to deceive or defraud.[3] For the purpose of the case before him the judge said:

> To deceive is, I apprehend, to induce a man to believe that a thing is true which is false, and which the person practising the deceit knows or believes to be false. To defraud is to deprive by deceit; it is by deceit to induce a man to act to his injury. More tersely it may be put, that to deceive is by falsehood to induce a state of mind; to defraud is by deceit to induce a course of action.

This statement has been much quoted in relation to cases of forgery but it has not always been interpreted in accordance with the laws of logic.[4] The careful reader will see that the definition proper of 'defraud' is wholly contained in the words, 'to defraud is to deprive by deceit'. The words which follow merely indicate the general class in which defrauding is placed, namely, the causing of injuries; and the judge's statement goes on to give an even wider classification by indicating that defrauding is in that genus of conduct which deceitfully induces a course of action. It would, however, be a logical error of an elementary kind[5] to reverse such a statement and to say 'deceitfully to induce a course of action is to defraud'. It is obvious that the genus contains many other species besides defrauding; for example to make a false statement which causes a man to touch something which gives him a painful electric shock would be by deceit to induce a course of action, but it would not be 'to deprive' him of anything. It is for this reason that the judgment of the Court of Criminal Appeal in *R.* v. *Bassey*[6] seemed open to objection in so far as it upheld the prisoner's conviction on the charge of forgery by the fabrication of false documents to establish his educational qualification to be admitted as a student of the Inner Temple. It was argued on his behalf that there was at most an intention to deceive, and no defrauding in the matter, since the Benchers of the Inn had not been deprived of anything.[7] But the court swept this point aside, declaring 'the jury might properly say that...the appellant intended to defraud, because he intended to induce the Benchers to act

[1] In the particular and narrow sense of the loss of some right *in rem*. Thus a person who supplies an article on sale suffers the loss of the ownership of the thing notwithstanding that he is paid an adequate price for it.

[2] *Re London and Globe Finance Corporation* [1903] 1 Ch. 728.

[3] Under ss. 83 and 84 of the Larceny Act, 1861, and s. 160 of the Companies Act, 1862.

[4] *R.* v. *Wines* [1953] 2 All E.R. 1497; 37 Cr.App.R. 197.

[5] The fallacy often termed an 'illegitimate antistrophe'. All dogs may be said to be animals, but it is erroneous to say that all animals are dogs.

[6] (1931) 22 Cr.App.R. 160.

[7] Indeed the Inn would receive his fees.

to their injury in admitting as a student a person whom...it was... their duty to exclude'.[1]

The logical difficulty indicated above has now been avoided by the House of Lords in the case of *Welham* v. *D.P.P.*[2] Of the two judgments delivered, one treated the dictum in *Re London and Globe* as definitely obiter,[3] but none the less valuable in that it pointed the contrast between deceiving, the essence of which is to bring about a state of mind, and defrauding, the essence of which is to bring about a course of action, whether doing something or refraining from doing something. In the other judgment[4] it was in effect said[5] that the import of the phrase 'with intent to defraud' was more doubtful the more it was considered; and that it appeared to be used in contrast to the phrase 'with intent to deceive', but that it was extremely difficult to say where one intent ends and the other begins. This uncertainty is manifested throughout the judgment, which finally returns to the common law position adumbrated by Hawkins and accepted by East (as the result of *R.* v. *Ward*), viz., that 'the counterfeiting of any writing with a fraudulent intent whereby another may be prejudiced is forgery'. The judgment gives no clearer definition than this of the word 'defraud'; and the distinction between a public document and a document of a private nature is blurred. So now the law of forgery has been made very wide in scope. But students should understand that the judgment in *Welham's* case does not affect the question, what constitutes a 'false document' (see ¶ 387 *post*).

It should be noted, however, that so long as there is the purpose of depriving by deceit it is none the less an intention to defraud even though the prisoner may have desired to obtain thereby something that was legally due to him, or may have intended to make arrangements whereby the victim of the deceit should ultimately suffer no loss (e.g. by himself meeting a bill of exchange which he had forged); see ¶ 394 *post*.

SECTION 3. THE DOCUMENT

¶ 378. The word 'document' has not so far been defined, either judicially or by statute. In the older books and cases the word usually employed was 'writing', and it seems both impossible on the authorities and unnecessary on principle to attempt to distinguish between the words 'writing' and 'document'. During the eighteenth century commercial activities grew increasingly complex and mercantile custom introduced into the business world written instruments of many kinds which represented valuable economic rights and assets. This social development called for greater scope and subtlety in the common law

[1] The illogical blunder was continued in *R.* v. *Fowler* [1956] Crim. L.R. 330.

[2] [1961] A.C. 103.

[3] By Lord Radcliffe at p. 126.

[4] With which Lord Radcliffe and the other judges expressed agreement.

[5] By Lord Denning at p. 131.

of crime which in early times was only concerned to give protection against the more crude kinds of physical attack upon person or property, because crimes were now becoming more intellectual. To meet the new need the crimes of false pretences[1] and embezzlement[2] were created by statute while judicial interpretation produced 'larceny by a trick'[3] and forgery of unsealed documents.[4]

THE LAW INFLUENCED BY GROWTH OF COMMERCE

¶ 379. But forgery at common law was felt to be still somewhat vague,[5] and it had the further defect that it was only a misdemeanour and therefore did not carry a sufficiently drastic penalty to satisfy the directors of commerce who, under the accepted penal policy of that period, regarded the prospect of condign punishment as the most certain deterrent to criminality. Accordingly the legislature produced a large number of enactments[6] specifying in detail many kinds of writings which it would be a capital felony (mostly without benefit of clergy) to forge. The law of forgery consequently became a matter of minute and sometimes complicated interpretations of statutory provisions,[7] in which there was no need for a general definition of 'writing' or 'document'.

DEFINITION OF A 'DOCUMENT'

¶ 380. Now, however, the Forgery Act, 1913, has declared forgery to be the making of a false document in order that it may be used as genuine; it is therefore desirable that a precise meaning should be given to the word 'document' and in the absence of any statutory or judicial definition the following is suggested:

For the purposes of the law of forgery a document is writing in any form, on any material, which communicates to some person or persons a human statement, whether of fact or fiction.

As we have seen, a document for our present purpose is a writing. Writing is human speech expressed in a more permanent form than sound, and reaching the mind of the person to whom it is addressed by another sense[8] than that of hearing. Therefore a document is a human statement, that is to say, a message proceeding or purporting to proceed from the human mind. Accordingly a merely mechanical register such as the 'reading' on a thermometer or a weighing machine or a gas-

[1] *Ante*, ¶ 338.
[2] *Ante*, ¶ 318.
[3] *Ante*, ¶ 234.
[4] *Ante*, ¶ 373.
[5] As noted by East in his discussion of this crime, 2 P.C. 840 *et seq.*
[6] See Hammond, *The Criminal Code. Forgery* (1826).
[7] Students should be careful to remember this when reading any of the old cases, e.g. *Mitchell* (1754) Foster 119; *Lewis* (1754) Foster 116.
[8] A blind man must read by the sense of touch.

meter is not a subject for the crime of forgery.[1] Secondly the writing must convey the same message of the spoken word to all persons able to read it. Accordingly a drawing or a painting, as works of art, are not documents since such effect as they may create in the mind of the onlooker is emotional and will not necessarily be the same to all who view them. Of course symbols in picture form may be used as a code and then they are a writing, just as are the words written in the recognized shapes of the ordinary alphabets. Thirdly, it is immaterial on what base or how the writing is made; it may be painted or limned on anything capable of retaining the colour or marks; it may be carved into stone[2] or embossed in paper; it may be transient[3] or lasting.

SIGNATURE OF AN ARTIST ON HIS WORK IS A DOCUMENT

¶ 381. Although a picture, as a work of art,[4] is not a document, yet any words written on a picture can be one. Accordingly if *XY*, a painter, writes upon his picture words which are intended to inform the viewer 'I, *XY*, painted this picture', such writing is a document, just as clearly as if the man had written the same statement on a piece of paper and pasted it on the bottom of the picture. Some early painters had the practice of declaring their work by writing words such as '*Hoc feci*', or the like, followed by their names. Indeed, it is commonly understood by painters and those who view pictures, that the painter's signature alone constitutes a declaration that he had painted the picture.

¶ 382. *R.* v. *Closs.* That was, however, not the conclusion to which the Court for Crown Cases Reserved came in *R.* v. *Closs.*[5] In that case the appellant had been convicted of uttering a forgery by offering and exposing for sale as genuine a picture which purported to be painted by J. Linnell, and bore that signature, although he well knew that both painting and signature were false, and only a copy of the original.[6] The indictment had stated that the picture was forged and did not clearly aver that the *signature*

[1] Although it may constitute an 'account', as in the case of the meter on a taxicab; *R.* v. *Solomons* [1909] 2 K.B. 980, *ante*, ¶ 329. The reading on a meter is not a message from the maker of the meter. It would, for example, be absurd to maintain that when a watch made by '*X* & Co.' stopped through not having been wound up, or that when it became out of adjustment and so gained or lost, the direction of the hands was a statement by *X* & Co. of the time. The fullest extent to which (if at all) the machine may be said to convey a message is that the maker's name upon it announces: 'This machine was made by us, *X* & Co., and, when it left our hands, it was in good order.'

[2] Even a notch on a wooden tally; see *Rowland* v. *Burton* (1837) 2 Harr. (Del.) 288; *Kendall* v. *Field* (1836) 14 Me. 30.

[3] E.g. smoke-writing in the sky.

[4] But special drawings may be a substitute for words, and understood to be so, e.g. a surveyor's plan in a conveyance, an engineer's blue-print, or a picture-cipher.

[5] (1858) 27 L.J.M.C. 54; D. and B. 460 (*T.A.C.*).

[6] The appellant had also been convicted on another count in the indictment which charged him with a cheat at common law; *ante*, ¶ 335. While holding that the evidence established this charge the court nevertheless quashed the conviction because of a technical fault in the wording of the count. See also the Fine Arts Copyright Act, 1862, ss. 7 and 8.

was forged, and therefore the Court of Appeal might have quashed the conviction on that ground. They did not, however, take that point and instead quashed the conviction on the ground that 'the name of Linnell in this case can only be regarded as an arbitrary mark put upon the picture by the painter to enable him to recognize his own work'.[1]

It is not easy to see how the court could come to this conclusion, since no evidence had been given as to the meaning which ordinary people, both painters and viewers, attach to the signature on a painting. Certainly Closs must have intended that the signature should be read as proof that the real J. Linnell had painted the picture, just as fully as if he had prefixed the words '*Ego feci*', or the like, in the ancient manner.

¶ 383. *R.* v. *Smith.* A contrasting case is *R.* v. *Smith.*[2] The prisoner had procured a printer to copy the printed wrappers used by George Borwick, a manufacturer of baking powder. These copies were exactly the same as Borwick's, save only that the printed facsimile of Borwick's signature (which appeared on the genuine wrappers) was omitted from them. Smith then wrapped up powder made by himself in the wrappers, with the obvious intention of deceiving the purchasers into thinking that they were buying powder made by Borwick. He was convicted of forgery and of uttering, but his conviction was quashed by the Court for Crown Cases Reserved. Two of the judges did not think that the printed wrappers were documents which could be forged, but Bramwell, B., held that they were documents, but that they were not *false*.[3] There was nothing on these printed labels which made the representation that they were printed by any other person than the man who printed them.

NOT ALL WRITING, PRINTING OR SIGNING IS A DOCUMENT

¶ 384. Yet not all written or printed words will make a document. The purpose for which the writing was made must always be considered, to see whether it really constitutes a message. For just as a drawing can (although rarely) amount to a document,[4] so it may sometimes happen that a writing is made solely as an example of penmanship or of printing-type, without any intention of inscribing a message to the reader. Again the script written by a candidate in an examination is not a document for the purposes of the law of forgery, since his answers are not messages but are merely demonstrations of his knowledge and ability, just the same as, for example, solutions of mathematical problems, or the drawings made by a candidate in an examination in architecture. But the *signature* of the candidate in all these cases does constitute a document, since it is a declaration that the script (or the drawing) is the work of the person whose name is signed.

[1] 7 Cox at p. 497. In 6 W.R. 109, at p. 110, the report reads 'Linnell's name in this case must be looked at merely as in the nature of an arbitrary mark made by the master to identify his own work'. For a criticism of this decision see Russ. ch. 72.

[2] (1858) 27 L.J.M.C. 225; D. and B. 566 (*T.A.C.*).

[3] See ¶ 387 *post.*

[4] E.g. when it is a cipher, or a technical substitute for words, *ante*, ¶ 381 n. 4.

Would a man's signature, and no more, in an autograph book constitute a document? The point has never been decided but it would seem on principle that it should do so, since it is generally read (and indeed intended by the writer to be read) as a declaration made by the signatory that he had written his name there. But a signature cut out from its context (for example from a letter) and kept in a collection could hardly be regarded as conveying a message of any kind.

Section 4. Seals, Dies, etc.

¶ 385. Since a seal formerly served the purpose now usually achieved by a man's written signature, naturally the fabrication of such marks of authentication is preserved as a forgery in the Forgery Act, section 5. The falsification of postage stamps would in most instances come within the Forgery Act, 1913,[1] but it is also dealt with in other statutes which repress various kinds of dishonesty in connexion with the activities of the Post Office.[2]

Section 5. The Falsity

its materiality

¶ 386. The document must be false in some material particular; but this is usually a simple matter to establish since the essence of the crime of forgery is an intent to deceive or defraud, as the case may be, and if the fault in the document be not material it is difficult to see how it could be thought to effect the dishonest purpose, or indeed attract any notice which would lead to the making of any criminal charge. But it is not necessary that the document, as falsified, should be such that if it were genuine it would have any effect. Thus the offence of forgery may be complete even if the document, when forged, is incomplete; or is not, or does not purport to be, such a document as would be binding in law,[3] e.g. an unstamped promissory note. And if the falsity was material at the time when it was made the fact that it may subsequently become immaterial has no relevance to its materiality at the time in question.[4]

the falsity is of purport, not of contents

¶ 387. A writing is not a forgery when it merely *contains* statements which are false, but only when it falsely purports to *be* itself that which it is not. Thus in *Re Windsor*[5] it was declared: 'Forgery is the false making of an instrument purporting to be that which it is not, it is not

[1] Thus it would be a forgery to fabricate a postage stamp for use as new, or to erase a post-mark for the same purpose; but perhaps it would not be a common law forgery to make a stamp look as though it had passed through the post, in order to sell it to a collector; but to do so is an offence under the Stamp Duties Management Act, 1891; *R.* v. *Lowden* (1913) 9 Cr.App.R. 195.

[2] E.g. the Stamp Duties Management Act, 1891, and the Post Office Act, 1953.

[3] Forgery Act, 1913, s. 1 (3) (*b*).

[4] *R.* v. *Wells* [1939] 2 All E.R. 169.

[5] (1865) 10 Cox 118 at p. 123 *per* Blackburn, J.; this definition was accepted in *R.* v. *Ritson* (1869) 1 C.C.R. 200 (*T.A.C.*) and followed in *Re Arton* (1896) 18 Cox 118. See Gooderson, 'When is a document false in the law of forgery?', 15 *Mod.L.R.* 11.

the making of an instrument which purports to be what it really is, but which contains false statements. Telling a lie does not become a forgery because it is reduced into writing.' The simplest and the most effective phrase by which to express this rule is to state that for the purposes of the law of forgery the writing *must tell a lie about itself.* Hence a conveyance which contains false recitals or states incorrectly the price paid is not thereby 'false'. And a letter or telegram sent to a newspaper containing false news is not a forged document;[1] although it would be if it were sent falsely in the name of one (e.g. the official reporter) who did not send or authorize the sending of it, for in such a case it would purport to be *his* message, which it is not. So also if a cashier or foreman makes out a paysheet so as to receive a greater amount of money from his employer than he has to disburse to subordinate members of the staff,[2] this is no forgery, for although it tells lies about the men, it does not tell a lie about itself, since it *is* the pay-sheet which that man has prepared and rendered.

In *R.* v. *Hopkins and Collins*,[3] however, the Court of Criminal Appeal said: 'We are only concerned now with the Forgery Act, 1913, as amended by the Criminal Justice Act, 1925, because forgery is a statutory offence. Parliament has laid down in the clearest possible way what amounts to forgery. The Act starts in section 1 by saying: "(1) For the purposes of this Act, forgery is the making of a false document in order that it may be used as genuine." I think the prevalent opinion of the court is that if a man has a cash book and proceeds to make false entries in it so that it does not represent the truth and does not represent what he received and what he paid out, that book is a false document and it is made false by the person who keeps it.' The judgment went on to recite the words of section 35 (1) of the Criminal Justice Act, 1925,[4] and then continued: '*But I do not think it is necessary to have recourse to that Act for the purpose of this case.... Now that we have seen the books, the difficulties which the court felt have been cleared up, because one can see in the plainest way that totals and individual items have been altered, with the result that that document gives a wholly false impression of the amount that ought to have been in the hands of the appellants....For these reasons...the court has come to the conclusion that the facts which were proved here and which must have been accepted by the jury clearly fall within the words of the Forgery Act, 1913.*'[5]

On this judgment it is with great respect submitted that the statement to the effect that the mere fact of a man's making false entries in his cash book thereby constitutes that book as a 'false document' within section 1 of the Act, is a non-sequitur on the words of the section stated immediately before (which define 'forgery' but not 'false document') and for the reasons already set out above[6] is not within an admissible

[1] *R.* v. *Horner* (1910) 74 J.P. 216.
[2] *R.* v. *Witchell* (1798) 2 East P.C. 830; *R.* v. *Cooke* (1871) 1 C.C.R. 295; *Arton* (2), *re*, [1896] 1 Q.B. 509.
[3] (1957) 41 Cr.App.R. 231; criticized in [1957] *Crim. L.R.* 809.
[4] *Ante*, ¶ 374.
[5] The italics are the editor's.
[6] *Ante*, ¶ 374.

interpretation of the effect of the provision in the Act of 1925. It is also submitted that this part of the judgment should be regarded, in any event, as obiter, since the words in italic show that the court were unanimous in agreeing that the original entries in the cash book had been altered on dates subsequent to those on which they had originally been made and thus the book did satisfy the doctrine established not only before but also since the Forgery Act, 1913, was enacted, that the entries when so altered represented themselves to be that which they were not, i.e. entries made on the original dates.

FICTITIOUS NAME WILL NOT MAKE A FORGERY

¶ 388. But, in order to ascertain what in fact the document itself purports to be, it is not always enough merely to read it: often external factors also must be taken into account. So it was held not to be a forgery where the prisoner, proposing to give his own cheque in payment for goods bought, went into an inn with the vendor, produced from his pocket a cheque book, and in the presence of the vendor filled up a printed form from this book with the name of the vendor as payee and then signed it, but in the name 'William Martin' whereas his own name was 'Robert Martin'. He thereupon handed the cheque to the vendor who put it in his pocket without looking at the signature. The cheque was refused at the bank, the prisoner's account there, in his proper name of Robert M., having been closed some time before. In quashing his conviction the Court for Crown Cases Reserved said that 'in all forgeries the instrument supposed to be forged must be a false instrument in itself; and that if a person give a note entirely as his own, his subscribing it by a fictitious name will not make it a forgery'.[1] But it will be a forgery if it purports to be made by a *fictitious person.*[2]

SIGNATURE BY A MAN OF HIS OWN NAME MAY BE FORGERY

¶ 389. So if a man named David Jones signs a cheque in that name it is not *prima facie* a forgery, however many other men of exactly the same name there may be. But if he does so in order to represent that the cheque was signed by *another* man of the same name then this false representation makes the cheque a false document. Thus to sign your own name as endorser of a cheque, which (to your knowledge) is drawn in favour of another man who has the same name as yourself, is a forgery.[3] Or to procure another man (who knows nothing of the dishonest purpose) to sign his name so that you can use the document as emanating from a third person will make it a false document.[4] Yet on the other hand you may sign in a name which is that of another person (whether real or non-existent) and yet not necessarily thereby make a false document, for a man is free to adopt a pseudonym if he wishes.

[1] *R.* v. *Martin* (1879) 5 Q.B.D. 34 (*T.A.C.*), following *R.* v. *Dunn* (1765) 1 Leach 57.

[2] Forgery Act 1913, s. 1 (2) (*b*). *R.* v. *Butler* (1954) 38 Cr.App.R. 57.

[3] *Mead* v. *Young* (1790) 4 T.R. 28 (*T.A.C.*); *R.* v. *Parkes* (1797) 2 Leach 775; *Re Cooper* (1882) 20 Ch.D. 611; *R.* v. *Hudson* [1943] 1 K.B. 458; *ante*, ¶ 295.

[4] *R.* v. *Mitchell* (1847) 1 Den. 282; *R.* v. *Blenkinsop* (1847) 1 Den. 276.

FORGING A DOCUMENT THROUGH AN INNOCENT AGENT

¶ 390. A man may be guilty of forging a document even though no part of it was written by him. Thus the written manuscript of a telegraphic message, made out at the arrival office, is made by the hand of an innocent agent, the post office clerk; but the sender of the telegram is as much responsible for it as if he had written it with his own hand.[1] Yet it is not forgery merely to use fraud (however gross) to procure the execution of a valuable security e.g. to get a man to sign it by misrepresenting to him its contents.[2] Such conduct is, however, a misdemeanour[3] punishable with five years' imprisonment. Although the point has not been decided it may be argued that, in those cases where the deceived person—as where he is blind or illiterate[4]—is entitled to repudiate the document as not being his genuine act, the fraudulent author of this document is guilty of forgery through an innocent agent.

OMISSIONS BEFORE AND AFTER SIGNING

¶ 391. Omissions made in a document will not necessarily make it 'false'. The test is to see whether the omission has been made before or after the document has been signed. If *before*, the omission will not render the document a forgery,[5] however dishonest may be the intention which inspired the omission and however greatly the signer be deceived as to the statements contained in the document, or as to their purport; for the document as produced *is* the document which the victim signed.[6] If, however, the omission is made after the signature the document will be false: such a case could arise, for example, if a man signs his name at the foot of a sheet of note paper, leaving it for his secretary to type in a message previously dictated and the secretary intentionally omits some material words of it. For then the letter would not be the signatory's real message.

¶ 392. *Instances of false documents.* Instances of documents false in accordance with the above mentioned principles are as follows. To misstate the time or place of making a document will render it 'false' if that time or place be material[7] to its operation, as in the case of the fraudulent antedating of a cheque. So if a telegraph clerk, after learning the result of a race, states falsely in a telegram backing the winning horse that it was handed in at the post office before the race was run (i.e. in time to make a genuine bet with the bookmaker), he commits a forgery.[8] It can also be forgery if a person, to whom a limited authority

[1] *R.* v. *Riley* [1896] 1 Q.B. 309 (*T.A.C.*).

[2] *R.* v. *Chadwick* (1844) 2 M. and R. 545.

[3] Larceny Act, 1916, s. 32 (2). All instruments of title, either to land or goods, are here included as 'valuable securities' (see s. 46).

[4] *Howatson* v. *Webb* [1908] 1 Ch. 1; *Carlisle Banking Co.* v. *Bragg* [1911] 1 K.B. 489.

[5] *R.* v. *Collins* (1843) 2 M. and R. 461; *R.* v. *Chadwick* (1844) 2 M. and R. 545.

[6] It might, however, be a misdemeanour under the Larceny Act, 1916, s. 32 (2); *ante*, ¶ 340.

[7] E.g. a railway ticket.

[8] *R.* v. *Riley* [1896] 1 Q.B. 309 (*T.A.C.*).

to complete a document has been given, exceeds that authority. Thus if a clerk receives from his employer a cheque in his own favour, duly signed but with the amount left blank, and is told to fill it up for the amount due to himself as wages, he will be guilty of forgery if he fills it up for a greater amount. But so long as the agent keeps within his authority in completing a document given to him it is of course no forgery, even if he should afterwards misappropriate the document or its proceeds.[1]

MENS REA NECESSARY

¶ 393. At common law it was necessary that the forger should have a guilty intent. As we have seen[2] in the falsification of writings of a public character it was enough that the forger had an intent to deceive.[3] Examples of this are the falsification of a summons in the county court (*R.* v. *Collier*),[4] and an order from a magistrate to a gaoler to discharge a prisoner (*R.* v. *Harris*).[5] The case of *R.* v. *Barrett and Creager*[6] is sometimes wrongly cited as an exception;[7] this was not a charge of forgery but of conspiracy to forge, the two defendants having fabricated a letter purporting to have been sent by a solicitor giving his authority for them as his clerks to interview a prisoner in gaol, as a person whom he had been instructed to defend. For the crime of conspiracy so to invade the prison no intent to defraud was needed; but if a charge of forgery had been made it would seem that an intent to defraud could have been alleged and established, since it was plain that the aim of the two men was to obtain money for their bogus services.

But in the case of writings of a private character an intention to defraud[8] had always to be proved. Thus in *R.* v. *Toshack*[9] the prisoner was desirous of obtaining from the Corporation of Trinity House a certificate of fitness to act as master of ships. In order to gain admittance as a candidate for the examination as to his fitness, he forged a letter which purported to have come from a captain under whom he had served, telling of his good conduct and sobriety; but the prosecution were careful in the indictment to allege that the prisoner made the forged statement in order to obtain from the examiners a piece of paper of the value of one penny, i.e. the certificate of fitness which he hoped to obtain. So also *R.* v. *Sharman*[10] was decided on the footing that it was a criminal forgery for a person applying for a post of schoolmaster to

[1] *R.* v. *Bateman* (1845) 1 Cox 186 (*T.A.C.*). See s. 1 (2) of the Forgery Act, 1913, for the position when a person, not having authority, purports to sign as another's agent.

[2] *Ante*, ¶ 373. See Russ. ch. 72.

[3] *A fortiori*, if he had also the intent to defraud.

[4] (1831) 5 C. and P. 160.

[5] (1834) 1 Moo. 393.

[6] (1899) C.C.C. Sess. Pap. cxxx, 797.

[7] E.g. Arch. 34th ed. 2142.

[8] *R.* v. *Boult* (1848) 2 C. and K. 604. For the meaning of defraud see *ante*, ¶ 377.

[9] (1849) 1 Den. 492. But the point was dismissed in *Welham* v. *D.P.P.*, *ante*, p. 370.

[10] (1854) 23 L.J.M.C. 51; it was contended for the defence that the words of the indictment which alleged an intent 'to injure, prejudice, and deceive' did not adequately state the necessary intent to defraud, but the judges ruled that the indictment was good, since its words conveyed that meaning. See also *R.* v. *Moah* (1858) D. and B. 550.

support his application by a forged letter of recommendation with intent to obtain the emoluments of the situation. As already mentioned the common law distinction between public and private documents has been incorporated in the Forgery Act, s. 4.

FORGERY AND FALSE PRETENCES DISTINGUISHED

¶ 394. It is not necessary to allege in the indictment, or to prove, an intent to defraud or deceive any particular person; all that is necessary is to prove that the defendant did the act charged with intent to defraud.[1] Students should observe the difference on this point between forgery and obtaining by false pretences. In the former crime all that is necessary is to prove that the accused intended to deprive by deceit, whereas in the crime of false pretences it is necessary to show in addition that the prosecutor was influenced by that deceit at the time when he parted with his property.[2] It makes no difference that there was no intention to cause unjust pecuniary loss, so long as something of value was to be obtained by the forged document: accordingly a letter to a man who really owed money to the forger, falsely purporting to be written by his employer and urging him to pay promptly has been held sufficient.[3] And so is a forged application for a passport, although the proper fee for the passport was paid.[4] And a man may be guilty of forging an acceptance of a bill, although he may from the outset have truly intended to take it up before it should fall due[5] and although the money which he aimed at getting by the forgery was really due to him.[6] Nor does it matter that in fact the forger could not defraud his victim.[7]

HONEST BELIEF IN A RIGHT TO MAKE OR ALTER A DOCUMENT IS A GOOD DEFENCE

¶ 395. There is no crime where the writing or alteration is made under the honest belief that the person making it had the right to do so, even though in fact he had no such right. Thus he may have mistakenly believed that he had another man's authority to sign his name, or do some other act in connexion with the document which rendered it false.[8] And evidence which tends to show that the accused might have had such reasonable belief is clearly admissible.[9] In all cases the accused must at least have supposed (however mistakenly) that someone or other might possibly be defrauded. Hence it is no crime for a man

[1] Or to deceive, in the case of public documents; Forgery Act, 1913, s. 17 (2), *R.* v. *Mazagora* (1815) R. and R. 291.

[2] *Ante*, ¶ 351.

[3] *R.* v. *Parker* (1910) 74 J.P. 208.

[4] *R.* v. *Barrow* (1884) C.C.C. Sess. Pap. C, 641.

[5] *R.* v. *Forbes* (1835) 7 C. and P. 224; *R.* v. *Beard* (1837) 8 C. and P. 143; *R.* v. *Hill* (1838) 2 Moo. 30.

[6] *R.* v. *Wilson* (1847) 2 C. and K. 527 (*T.A.C.*); *R.* v. *Smith* (1919) 14 Cr.App.R. 101.

[7] *R.* v. *Holden* (1809) R. and R. 154.

[8] *R.* v. *Parish* (1837) 8 C. and P. 94; and see *R.* v. *Forbes* (1835) 7 C. and P. 224.

[9] *R.* v. *Clifford* (1845) 2 C. and K. 202.

who is himself the sole payee of a bond to alter it by lessening its amount.[1]

By the Criminal Justice Act, 1925, s. 38, it is an offence, however innocent the intent, to make or cause to be made or to use any document so nearly resembling a banknote or currency note as to be calculated to deceive. The mere appearance of a person's name upon such a document is *prima facie* evidence that that person caused the document to be made.

Section 6. Uttering

¶ 396. The offence of forgery consists in 'making' the document. But it is also an offence[2] to 'utter' a forged document, carrying whatever punishment a forgery of that particular document would have involved, and being a felony or misdemeanour according as that forgery would be. A person is regarded as 'uttering' when he 'uses, offers, publishes, delivers, disposes of, tenders in payment or in exchange...tenders in evidence, or puts off' a forgery, knowing it to be forged, and having the same intent (whether to defraud or to deceive) that the law requires, in the case of that particular thing, to constitute the offence of forging it.[3]

Section 7. Special Offences of Forgery[4]

¶ 397. The Criminal Justice Act, 1925, s. 36, made the forging of a passport—and similarly the deliberate making of any untrue statement for the purpose of procuring a passport (whether for the offender himself or for any other person)—a misdemeanour punishable with imprisonment for two years and/or a fine of £100.

It is an offence for anyone with intent to deceive to forge or alter or use or lend to or allow to be used by any other person a licence or certificate of insurance under the Road Traffic Act, 1960, or to make or have in one's possession any document so closely resembling such a licence or certificate as to be calculated to deceive.[5]

¶ 398. *Obtaining by forged instruments.* Section 7 (*a*) of the Forgery Act, 1913, re-enacts a provision of the Act of 1861[6] whereby it is a felony if anyone with intent to defraud demands, receives or obtains or causes to be delivered[7] any money, security for money, or other property under, upon, or by virtue of any forged instrument whatsoever, knowing the same to have been forged.

[1] *Blake* v. *Allen* (1600) Moore 619. In fact by so doing he loses all, since the bond thereby becomes wholly void.

[2] Forgery Act, 1913, s. 6 (1).

[3] *Ibid.* s. 6 (2). See *R.* v. *Shukard* (1811) R. and R. 200 at p. 202, and the explanation of the case by C. S. Greaves in his note on *R.* v. *Ion* (1852) 3 Den. 475 in Russ. ch. 75.

[4] For an account of the offences which arise in connexion with the falsification of registers of births and marriages, of judicial and public documents and other special documents, seals, etc. see Russ. chs. 73 and 74.

[5] Punishable on indictment with imprisonment for a term not exceeding two years and on summary conviction with imprisonment for a term not exceeding four months and/or with a fine not exceeding £100.

[6] Sect. 38.

[7] Or even attempts to do any of these things.

The use of the word 'instrument' in this section, in distinction from the rest of the statute in which the word used is 'document', might have been expected to be regarded as intentional and to denote only such documents as are themselves, in some sense at least, orders for the payment or delivery of money or property,[1] such for example as a cheque or a bill of lading. But the judges have interpreted the word more widely, and in *R.* v. *Riley*[2] refused to quash a conviction of felony[3] where the forged writing was a telegram making a bet with a bookmaker which the prisoner had falsely entered as having been handed in at a time before the race had been run.[4] It is clear that the telegram was in no way a demand nor an order, nor even a request for the payment of money: all it asked for was a betting contract. However, the decision was taken and has been followed since.[5] The result would seem to be that if money, security for money, or other property, real or personal, be obtained by false pretences which consist in a forged document of any kind, the offender cannot properly be charged with a misdemeanour under section 32 of the Larceny Act, 1916, but must be charged with felony under section 7 of the Forgery Act, 1913, since it is hardly to be supposed that the legislature intended to create alternative offences for exactly the same conduct.

Thus in *R.* v. *Evans*[6] the court ruled that since by section 10 of 1 Will. IV, c. 66 (repealed) it was a felony to forge, utter, put off, etc. a 'request for the delivery of goods', an indictment for the misdemeanour of obtaining goods by false pretences, when the pretence was such request, was bad since it was a felony so to do and not this misdemeanour.

Section 8. Punishment

¶ 399. The punishments of forgeries vary considerably. All that have been made felonies by statute have maxima of punishment ranging from imprisonment for life to imprisonment for seven years. But any forgery which is a misdemeanour is punishable only by imprisonment for two years, and fine, and binding over, or by merely one of these.[7]

[1] See Russ. ch. 76.

[2] *R.* v. *Riley* [1896] 1 Q.B. 309. But see the dissenting dicta of Vaughan Williams, J., at pp. 322–5.

[3] Under s. 38 of the Act of 1861.

[4] See ¶ 392 *ante*.

[5] *R.* v. *Howse* (1912) 7 Cr.App.R. 103; *R.* v. *Cade* [1914] 2 K.B. 209; 10 Cr.App.R. 23.

[6] (1833) 5 C. and P. 553, followed in *R.* v. *Anderson* (1843) 2 M. and Rob. 469; see *Michell* v. *Brown* (1858) 2 E. and E. 267 ('Where a later statute again describes an offence which had been previously created by a former statute..., the later enactment must be taken as operating by way of substitution (and implied repeal) and not cumulatively', *per* Campbell, L.C.J.); *Henderson* v. *Sherborne* (1837) 2 M. and W. 236; *R.* v. *Cross* (1701) 1 Ld. Raym. 711; *R.* v. *Davis* (1783) 1 Leach 271. See also *R.* v. *Gregory* (1866) 1 C.C.R. 77 and *R.* v. *Payne* [1906] 1 K.B. 97 at p. 101. The point does not, however, seem to have been taken in *R.* v. *Nicoloudis* (1954) 38 Cr.App.R. 118.

[7] Forgery Act, 1913 (as amended by the Criminal Justice Act, 1948), ss. 4, 12 (2 (*a*) (*c*)). There are a few statutory misdemeanours of forgery which may be prosecuted either by indictment or even summarily at petty sessions. In the latter case their maximum punishments are reduced, e.g. forged trade-marks, four months' imprisonment or £20 fine; forged telegrams, a £10 fine. See s. 19 (2) of the Forgery Act, 1913.

Chapter XXI

OFFENCES AGAINST THE STATE

SECTION I. TREASON

¶ 400. *Definition.* The most heinous of crimes in a feudal system must naturally be a breach of allegiance to an overlord, and the greatest of overlords was the Lord Paramount, the King; such a crime was called treason,[1] a word derived from the French *trahir* and the Latin *tradere* and denoting a perfidious betrayal. At common law treason was of two kinds, high treason which was a breach of faith due to the King from his subjects, and petit treason which was committed when one subject of the Crown killed another who was his superior. The latter was therefore really a murder, made more atrocious by the duty of allegiance which the murderer owed to his victim: as when a feudal vassal slew his lord, a priest his bishop, or a wife her husband.[2]

THE STATUTE OF TREASONS

¶ 401. *History.* An indictment for high treason was in medieval times a most powerful weapon for the Crown to wield against its two great rivals, the Church and the baronage. For a 'clerk' who was accused of this crime could not claim benefit of clergy;[3] and if any feudal vassal was convicted of it, his lands passed to the Crown instead of to his immediate lord. Hence the King's judges, attentive to their master's interests, expanded the definition of high treason until it became a most comprehensive offence, including any kind of injury to the King's rights, e.g. even the hunting of deer in his forests. At last a reaction was provoked. In the reign of Edward III one John Gerberge of Royston laid hands on one William of Bottisford and would not release him until he made a payment of £90. This act of unlawful imprisonment was construed as an act of treason, on the plea of its being an 'accroaching' (i.e. appropriating) of royal power. At this the barons forthwith took action;[4] and succeeded in confining the law of treason within definite limits by the enactment, in 1351, of the Statute of Treasons (25 Edw. III, st. 5, c. 2). This measure is remarkable, both for the constitutional securities directly conferred by it,[5] and also from

[1] Pollock and Maitland, II, 500; Stephen, *Hist. Crim. Law*, II, 241.

[2] The distinction between petit treason and ordinary murder was abolished in 1828 by 9 Geo. IV, c. 31, s. 2.

[3] *Ante*, ¶ 55. Pollock and Maitland, I, 446; II, 501 and 503 (for the sacrificial element in the traitor's death). [4] Stephen, *Hist. Crim. Law*, II, 246; 1 Hale P.C. 80.

[5] 'No people enjoy a free constitution unless adequate security is furnished by their laws against the discretion of judges in a matter so closely connected [as the law of treason is] with the relation between the Government and its subjects'; Hallam's *Constitutional History*, ch. XV, 203–26 (a passage which should be noted and remembered).

its affording, at so early a date, what is still almost[1] the only instance in which any statutory definition of an important crime has entirely superseded the common law with regard to it. It limited high treason to seven possible forms (two of which have since been reduced to felonies). The seven[2] were:

(i) Compassing the death of the King, Queen or heir

¶ 402. When a man doth compass[3] or imagine the death of our lord the King, or our lady his Queen, or of their eldest son and heir.

So far as these words go, the crime seems to consist in no more than a state of mind. But an *actus reus* is made necessary by words in a subsequent part of the statute, which require the person accused to 'be thereof proveably attainted of *open deed*'.[4] It was for this incipient offence of 'compassing the death' of the King that the regicides of Charles I were indicted; the ultimate act of taking off his head being treated as one of the open deeds which made manifest that compassing.[5]

That in treason, just as in all common law crimes, a *mens rea* will not constitute guilt without an *actus reus* is well illustrated by a transatlantic decision that an American citizen who meant to join the hostile British forces, but found that he had by mistake attached himself to a party of the United States troops, could not be convicted of treason.[6]

¶ 403. *Overt act necessary.* An 'open deed', or 'overt act', has been defined by Alderson, B., as 'any act, measure, course, or means whatever done, taken, used, or assented to, for the purpose of effecting a traitorous intention';[7] and, more tersely, by Lord Tenterden[8] as 'any act manifesting the criminal intention and tending towards the accomplishment of the criminal object'. Thus even so commonplace an event as hiring a boat at a riverside wharf may amount to such an act.[9] And the collecting of information for the use of the King's enemies, though it never be actually sent to them, clearly amounts to one.[10] And even a conspiracy, though going no further than the oral conversation, constitutes a sufficient overt act.[11] But spoken words, however

[1] Cf. ¶¶ 200–7 *ante* as to arson.

[2] As stated by 1 Hale P.C. 89–90.

[3] See Austin's *Jurisprudence*, lect. XXI.

[4] See *post*, ¶ 410. These words do not occur in the statute until the conclusion of the fourth species of treason. But the judges, in construing the statute, did not limit them to that species, and ruled that, in indictments for any form of treason, a definite overt act must be alleged. The first species, being the only one which is purely mental, is the case in which this rule assumes its chief importance. See Foster 220; and 1 Hale P.C. 108.

[5] *R.* v. *Twenty-nine Regicides* (1660) 5 St.Tr. 947 at p. 982.

[6] *Commonwealth* v. *Malin* (1790) 1 Dallas 33.

[7] *Shirley* v. *Fagg* (1675) 6 St.Tr. 1121 at p. 1133.

[8] *R.* v. *Thistlewood* (1820) 33 St.Tr. 681, 684.

[9] *Lord Preston's Case* (1691) 12 St.Tr. 646 (*T.A.C.*).

[10] *R.* v. *Delamotte* (1781) 22 St.Tr. 808.

[11] See *R. v. Langhorn* (1679) 7 St.Tr. (n.s.) 417 at p. 463. A conspiracy to depose the King is held to be an overt act of compassing his death.

seditious and violent, are not as a general rule an overt act.[1] Yet they may become one if they are not simply 'loose words, spoken without relation to any act or project' but help to carry forward, or are connected with conduct which carries forward, the intention which they express.[2] Thus words inciting someone to kill the King are an overt act of high treason. Indeed spoken words, uttered with an intent to confirm men in the prosecution of measures for a deposing of the King by force of arms, 'are in their very nature and essence the clearest and most absolute overt acts of high treason'.[3]

¶ 404. *Is publication essential for written words?* But the publication of *written* words, since they are in a more permanent form, and have usually been composed with more deliberation than mere spoken ones, may be a sufficient overt act of treason, even when it is unconnected with any plan for further conduct of a treasonable character. Yet, whilst published writing may clearly be thus an overt act, it is quite uncertain how far, if at all, the mere writing of a document, without ever publishing it, can be an overt act. In 1615, Edward Peacham[4] was convicted of treason on account of certain passages in a sermon found in his study, which had never been preached. But he was never executed; and died in prison. Algernon Sidney,[5] again, was similarly convicted of treason in 1683, on account of an old unpublished manuscript treatise on sovereignty found in his house. He was executed; but his conviction was subsequently reversed by Parliament. Hence neither of these two cases is of weight as a precedent. Had Sidney's papers been, on the other hand, plainly referable to some definite project of insurrection, they might of course have constituted an overt act.[6]

(ii) Violation of the King's consort, eldest daughter or heir's wife

¶ 405. Or if a man do violate the King's companion [i.e. consort] or the King's eldest daughter unmarried, or the wife of the King's son and heir.[7]

Professor Kenny stated that it seemed illogical to bring in the daughter, since the wives of younger sons are omitted; and that all reference to her was therefore left out in the Draft Criminal Code of Lord Beaconsfield's administration.[8]

[1] Foster, 200; *Pyne's Case* (1628) Cro. Car. 117 (*T.A.C.*).

[2] *R.* v. *Charnock* (1694) 2 Salk. 633 (*T.A.C.*).

[3] *Per* Lord Ellenborough in *R.* v. *Despard* (1803) 28 St.Tr. at p. 487.

[4] (1615) 2 St. Tr. 869. Hallam, *Constitutional History*, ch. VI.

[5] 9 St.Tr. 818; Foster, 198. See also *Lord Preston's Case* (1691) 12 St.Tr. 646 (*T.A.C.*).

[6] ¶ 427 *post*.

[7] *Quaere* whether the male consort of a reigning Queen (e.g. Philip of Spain, the husband of Queen Mary) is within this provision of the statute; see *Coke*, 3 *Inst.* c. 1, pp. 7 *et seq.*

[8] 1879, [C. 2345]. But see Coke, 3 *Inst.* c. 1, p. 9, where, explaining this, he says: '(That is) eldest daughter not married at the time of the violation; albeit that there had been an elder daughter than she, who is dead without issue.... And the reason that the eldest only is here mentioned, is, for that for default of issue male she only is inheritable to the crowne.'

A sufficient 'violating' may take place even by consent. And the executions, in Henry VIII's reign, of two queens, Anne Boleyn and Catherine Howard, serve to show that the royal lady, who consents to her paramour's addresses, shares the full guilt of his treason.

(iii) Levying war against the King in his realm

¶ 406. Or if a man do levy war against our lord the King in his realm.

'War', here, is not limited to the true 'war' of international law, but will include any forcible disturbance that is produced by a considerable number of persons, and is directed at some purpose which is not of a private but of a 'general' character, e.g. to release the prisoners in *all* the gaols. It is not essential that the offenders should be in military array or be armed with military weapons.[1] It is quite sufficient if there be assembled a large body of men who intend to debar the Government from the free exercise of its lawful powers and are ready to resist with violence any opposition.[2]

This kind of treason is therefore distinguishable from a riot by nothing but the 'generality' of the object which is aimed at by those taking part in it. Thus the Edinburgh rioters in the *Porteous Case* of 1736,[3] rendered familiar to English readers by Scott's *Heart of Midlothian*, were, after mature consideration, prosecuted only for riot, and not for treason; inasmuch as, though they sought to interfere with the Crown's prerogative of mercy, they resisted only its being exercised in the particular case of the detested Captain Porteous, and not the general exercise of it. 'It is neither the numbers concerned, nor the force employed, but the object which the people have in view, that determines the character of their crime; which will be a riot or a treason, according as this object is of a private and local or of a public and general character.'[4] Thus in *Damaree's Case* (1709),[5] in Queen Anne's reign, a riotous tumult with the object of demolishing all accessible Nonconformist meeting-houses was held to amount to a treason, on the ground that it was to be regarded as a public resistance to the Toleration Act (which had legalized such meetings) and an attempt to render it ineffectual by numbers and open force. Hence, although the rioters were strong partisans of the Queen and imagined themselves to be serving her interests and advancing her policy, they were, by construction of law, guilty of treason against her.

It will be noticed that the levying of war must be 'in the realm'; so that enlisting men, even within the realm, to go to the aid of the King's

[1] *R.* v. *Dowling* (1848) 7 St. Tr. (n.s.) at p. 460; cf. 32 St. Tr. 3.

[2] Nor need the body be large; three men with dynamite have been held sufficient. *R.* v. *Gallagher and others* (1883) C.C.C. Sess. Pap. XCVIII, 248.

[3] 17 St. Tr. 993; Lord Stanhope's *History of England*, ch. XVII.

[4] *R.* v. *Hardie* (1821) 1 St. Tr. (n.s.) at p. 624. Cf. *R.* v. *Frost* (1839) 4 St. Tr. (n.s.) 85 (*T.A.C.*).

[5] Foster, 213; 15 St. Tr. 521.

enemies in military operations that are to be carried on abroad, will not be punishable under this section.[1] It is, however, punishable under both species (i) and (iv).

(iv) Being adherent to the King's enemies in his realm

¶ 407. Or be adherent to the King's enemies in his realm,[2] giving them aid and comfort[3] in the realm or elsewhere,[4] and thereof be proveably attainted in open deed by the people of their condition.

The words 'giving aid and comfort to the King's enemies' are to be construed in apposition. They explain what is meant by 'adhering to', so that a man may be adherent to the King's enemies in his realm by giving to them aid and comfort in his realm or he may be adherent to the King's enemies elsewhere by giving them aid and comfort elsewhere.[2]

'Enemies', here (unlike 'war' in species (iii)), is to be taken in the strict sense which international law puts upon the word; and accordingly includes none but true public belligerents. Hence to assist mere rebels against the King, or pirates, does not constitute any offence under this section; though if the assistance were rendered within the realm it would be a sufficient 'levying of war' under species (iii).[5]

(v) Counterfeiting the King's seal or money. (vi) Bringing counterfeit money into his realm

¶ 408. And if a man counterfeit the King's great or privy seal, or his money; And if a man bring false money into this realm counterfeit to the money of England...knowing the money to be false, to merchandise or make payment in deceit of our Lord the King and of his people.[6]

(vii) Slaying the chancellor, treasurer or one of the justices

¶ 409. And if a man slay the chancellor, treasurer, or the King's justices of the one bench or the other, justices in eyre, or justices of assizes, and all other justices assigned to hear and determine, being in their places doing their offices.

[1] 'Even the actual enlistment of men to serve against the Government, does not amount to levying of war. To constitute it, there must be an actual *assembling* of men for a treasonable purpose'; 4 Cranch (U.S.A.) 126.

[2] *R.* v. *Lynch* [1903] 1 K.B. 444; *R.* v. *Casement* [1917] 1 K.B. 98; *Joyce* v. *D.P.P.* [1946] A.C. 347 (*T.A.C.*).

[3] E.g. by subscribing to their war loan.

[4] As to aid rendered under compulsion, e.g. when supplies are requisitioned by an occupying enemy's army, see ¶ 43 *ante*.

[5] In Natal it was held in 1901 that by serving the Boer forces even as a cook a man gave them 'aid and comfort'.

[6] These offences were reduced to felony by the following statutes: 2 and 3 Will. IV, c. 123; 2 Will. IV, c. 34, s. 1; 3 and 4 Geo. V, c. 27; Coinage Act, 1936 (26 Geo. V and 1 Edw. VIII, c. 16).

¶ **409a.** To the above forms of treason others were added by later statutes but of them only two have survived, namely:

(*a*) To attempt by overt act to prevent the succession to the Crown of such person as by virtue of the Act of Settlement is entitled to succeed thereto.[1]

(*b*) To maintain in writing or in printing that any other than the person entitled under the Act of Settlement has any right to succeed to the Crown.[2]

OVERT ACT NECESSARY FOR ALL SEVEN FORMS

¶ **410.** The ancient deference of the judges to the King, their lord and master, which expanded by interpretation the common law of treason until it provoked the agitation which produced the Statute of Treasons, was repeated by the courts in the seventeenth and eighteenth centuries so that an extraordinary extension of the scope of that statute was made by interpretations put upon the simple language of the Parliament of Edward III. One of these interpretations was, however, restrictive and salutary; for (as mentioned in ¶ 402 *ante*) it was held that the words in the fourth form of treason, which required proof by 'open deed' should be read as applying to every head. Accordingly to 'compass or imagine' the death of the specified members of the Royal Family needs an *actus reus* established by 'open deed'.

The other interpretations, however, went to the enlargement of the scope of treason and in many cases exceeded all reasonable bounds.[3]

BENEFIT OF KING'S PROTECTION DRAWS DUTY OF ALLEGIANCE

¶ **411.** The original idea of treason was therefore that of a breach of the personal loyalty due to the lord paramount of the realm from each of his vassals. Thus an alien, who had never been even resident in our realm, could not commit treason; for clearly he was under no duty of allegiance. Hence when a charge of adultery was made, in Parliament, against the Queen of George IV, it was pointed out that it did not amount, as in the case of Henry VIII's wives, to a charge of participation in treason. For the acts alleged against Queen Caroline were supposed to have been committed abroad with a paramour (Signor Bergami) who was an alien and had never resided in British territory.

And this rule still remains in force. No alien falls within the law of treason unless, by coming into this realm under the King's permission (express or tacit), and so obtaining the benefit of the King's protection, he has placed himself under the consequent obligation of rendering

[1] 1 Anne, st. 2, c. 21 (17), s. 3.

[2] 6 Anne, c. 41, s. 1. Under s. 2 to maintain the invalidity of the line of succession by spoken words is an offence of praemunire. See ¶ 423 *post*.

[3] As was maintained by Hale who wrote: 'How dangerous it is by construction and analogy to make treasons, when the letter of the law has not done it; for such a method admits of no limits or bounds, but runs as far as the wit and invention of accusers, and the odiousness and detestation of persons accused will carry men.' 1 P.C. 83–7. Words which men in modern times would do well to reflect upon.

him an allegiance, though only a temporary allegiance.[1] And even then, as his duty—unlike the lifelong obligation of the King's own subjects—is only temporary, it has sometimes been urged that it does not necessarily continue throughout the whole of his residence, but only for so long as the King's protection continues to be actually effective. Hence, when British territory, where a Boer had for ten years resided, passed into the military occupation of his own state's forces, and he thereupon took service with them, it was argued that the withdrawal of the British troops had dissolved his British allegiance and that his subsequent conduct was therefore no treason against the King. But the Judicial Committee[2] overruled this contention, pointing out that, so soon as the invaders were expelled, the King's courts gave redress for any wrongs sustained during the hostile occupation, and that the King's protection was therefore a continuous one.

¶ 412. *Joyce* v. *Director of Public Prosecutions.* Normally the duty of allegiance owed by an alien subsists only so long as the alien remains within the realm where he accepts and obtains British protection. But in *Joyce* v. *Director of Public Prosecutions*[3] the House of Lords held that where an alien, by representing himself to be a British subject, had obtained a British passport, then upon the issue of the passport the Crown had assumed the burden of protection and the holder of it the corresponding duty of allegiance and loyalty, a duty which continued even though the holder were an alien. Accordingly the alien holder could be liable for treason even though the acts in question were committed by him outside the realm. The alien who holds a British passport can of course terminate his allegiance upon leaving the realm, by surrendering the passport or in some other way, before he does any act which would be a breach of the allegiance which he had assumed; but whether or not he has so withdrawn his allegiance is a question of fact for the jury.

CONSTRUCTIVE TREASONS OF JUDICIAL INTERPRETATION

¶ 413. The historical development of our nation tended steadily, century after century, to make a consciousness of the importance of the

[1] 4 Bl. *Comm.* 457; Foster 183; *R.* v. *Maclane* (1797) 26 St. Tr. 721. This temporary allegiance by domicile, insisted on in many South African trials, seems to be due (Forsyth's *Cases and Opinions*, 200) from every subject of a friendly state who enters our dominions, even though he avowedly come for hostile purposes alone. See *R.* v. *Lynch* [1903] 1 K.B. 444, for the converse case, that of the Englishman naturalized in a hostile state; his naturalization, if effected during the war, would be in itself a treasonable 'adherence'. Cf. *Johnstone* v. *Pedlar* [1921] 2 A.C. 262, for the rights of an alien.

[2] *De Jager* v. *Att.-Gen. of Natal* [1907] A.C. 326.

[3] [1946] A.C. 347 (*T.A.C.*). On this much discussed case see 62 *L.Q.R.* 105; Biggs, 'Treason and the trial of William Joyce', 7 *Toronto L.J.* (1947), 162; Glanville Williams, 'The correlation of allegiance and protection', 10 *Cambridge L.J.* (1948), 54. It is permissible to wonder if Joyce used his passport to lead the enemy authorities to believe he was really a British subject and therefore of greater value to them for their purpose of propaganda.

stability of public order—rather than the feudal feeling of mere personal loyalty to a prince—become the binding force of the body politic. The criminal law had to begin to take cognizance of politicians who, whilst devoted to the reigning King, were nevertheless disturbing the order of the realm, though possibly only by assailing those institutions whereby the constitution had set a check upon the King's powers. Accordingly the judges became active and transformed the feudal conception of treason, as a breach of personal faith, into the modern one, which regards it as 'armed resistance, made on political grounds, to the public order of the realm'.[1] This new idea they evolved out of Edward III's statute by forced interpretations of the language of forms (i) and (iii). Thus a compassing of the death of the King was held to be sufficiently evidenced by the overt act of imprisoning him, because, as Machiavelli had observed, 'between the prisons and the graves of princes the distance is very small'.[2] And an attempt to raise a rebellion against the King's power, in even a remote colony, was similarly held to show a compassing of his death, though he were thousands of miles away from the scene of all the disturbances.[3] So, again, the overt act of inciting foreigners to invade the kingdom, i.e. of compassing the levying of war, an offence which the statute does not mention, was held to constitute an overt act towards compassing the King's death.[4] Similarly, as we have seen, a levying of war against any general class of the King's subjects was held—by a construction which Hallam[5] pronounces to be 'repugnant to the understandings of mankind in general and of most lawyers'—to be a levying of war against the King himself; as in the case of riots for the purpose of pulling down all public houses or all enclosures of commons, or of forcing all the employers in a particular trade to raise the rate of wages.[6] Yet men may be breakers of the King's peace without being enemies to the King's government.

¶ 414. *Constructive treasons now recognized by statute.* These interpretations were often violently artificial, almost setting the statute of Edward aside by their forced constructions,[7] and accordingly they were viewed with jealousy by the public at large—a jealousy which found expression in the verdicts of jurymen.[8] Thus when, for his share in the No Popery riots of 1780, Lord George Gordon was indicted for the treason of constructively 'levying war',[9] the acquittal which he secured, whilst fully justified by the facts of the case, was facilitated by the popular dislike of strained interpretations of the law.[10] Not long afterwards, Hardy, Horne Tooke and Thelwall were in 1794 indicted for a construc-

[1] Stephen's *General View of the Criminal Law*, 1st ed., 36.

[2] Foster, 196.

[3] *R.* v. *Maclane* (1797) 26 St. Tr. 721.

[4] But if their nation be at peace with us, it is not an adhering 'to the King's enemies'.

[5] *Constitutional History*, ch. XV.

[6] Foster, 211.

[7] Attention was drawn to the dangers of this course by Hale, 1 P.C. 83 *et seq.*

[8] An excellent account of constructive treason will be found in chs. CLXXVI and CLXXX of Lord Campbell's *Lives of the Lord Chancellors*.

[9] 21 St. Tr. 485.

[10] Campbell's *Lives of the Chief Justices*, ch. XXXVIII.

tive compassing of the King's death.[1] The doctrine which was laid down at these trials, as to constructive treasons, was of an extreme character, carrying its 'construction' of Edward III's statute to a length (in Hallam's opinion) 'at which we lost sight of the plain meaning of words'.[2] The verdicts of acquittal showed that such judicial legislation would serve only to defeat its own end. Direct legislation had obviously become necessary. Accordingly the Parliament at once enacted, in 1795, a statute expressly recognizing as treason the most important of the constructive treasons.[3]

TREASON-FELONIES

¶ **415.** After the Irish agitation of 1848, a further statute,[4] extending to Ireland, was passed, which reduced those constructive treasons dealt with in George III's statute (except some which really affected the person of the Sovereign) to felonies, so far as regarded the operation of the Act of 1795. They have no statutory name; but are commonly known as 'treasonable felonies' or 'treason-felonies'. They include all deliberate expression, by overt act, of any intention to depose the King, or to incite an invasion of the realm, or to levy war to constrain either House of Parliament to change its policy. The maximum punishment for them is now imprisonment for life. This change in the punishment rendered it much easier to prosecute these crimes with success.[5] For juries, naturally, are extremely reluctant to convict persons of good character for offences which, however gravely injurious to the community, may involve no ethical guilt and yet are punished with death.

¶ **416.** *Statute of Treasons still in force.* But it is important to notice that these Acts of 1795 and 1848 left untouched the statute of Edward III and the judicial constructions of it, and that, consequently, it is still open to the Crown in such cases to proceed against the offender for a constructive treason instead of on the lighter charge of a treason-felony. That precisely the same action should thus occupy, simultaneously, two different grades in the scale of crime is indeed a singular juridical anomaly.

INNOVATIONS IN TRIALS FOR TREASON, 1695

¶ **417.** As treason was, of all crimes, that in which the Crown had the strongest direct interest in securing the conviction of an accused person, it was the one in which a public prosecutor or a subservient judge had most temptation to conduct the trial so as to press harshly upon the prisoner. The reigns of the Stuarts afforded so many instances of this

[1] 24 St. Tr. 199; 25 St. Tr. 1, 748.

[2] *Constitutional History*, ch. xv.

[3] 36 Geo. III, c. 7. See Russ. 222.

[4] 11 and 12 Vict. c. 12, ss. 6, 7. See 54 and 55 Vict. c. 67, abrogating the merely oral treason-felonies. An account of the subsidiary treason-felonies is given in Russ. 222.

[5] There can be accessories to these treason-felonies, although there cannot be to treasons; see ¶ 66, *ante*.

harshness that, after the Revolution of 1688, the legislature in 1695 introduced great innovations into the course of criminal procedure so far as trials for treason were concerned. By this legislation[1] it was provided that a prisoner accused of high treason should have a right to receive (1) a list of the intended jurors,[2] (2) a copy of the indictment; and to make defence (3) by counsel learned in the law, and (4) by witnesses. Another clause (re-enacting and strengthening an enactment of Edward VI[3]) made necessary (5) a technical minimum of proof, by providing that the prisoner should not be convicted unless either he voluntarily confessed in open court or his guilt were established by *two* witnesses, deposing either to the same overt act, or at least to separate overt acts of the same kind of treason. And (6) it was provided that treason can only be prosecuted within three years from its commission; unless it be committed abroad, or consist of an actual plot to assassinate the Sovereign (not a mere technical 'compassing the death').

TREASON ACT, 1945, NOW REGULATES PROCEDURE

¶ 418. But now all these special rules of procedure in prosecutions for treason have been abolished, save (6) above; for the Treason Act, 1945, has assimilated the procedure in all cases of treason and misprision of treason to the procedure in cases of murder[4] and has accordingly repealed[5] the relevant parts of the earlier statutes.

PUNISHMENT OF DEATH

¶ 419. Treason, like all felonies, was punished with death. But the execution of a traitor was accompanied with special circumstances of horror, to mark the supreme heinousness of his crime.[6] Instead of being taken in a cart to the scaffold, he was drawn to it on a hurdle,[7] hanged only partially, cut down alive[8] and then disembowelled, beheaded and quartered. The head and quarters were permanently exposed in some

[1] 7 and 8 Will. III, c. 3.

[2] To which 7 Anne, c. 21, s. 14 adds a list of the intended Crown witnesses.

[3] 1 Edw. VI, c. 12, s. 22. Hence when a treason had been committed, but the Crown could obtain only a single witness, the only mode of punishing the offender was either to prosecute him for the misdemeanour of sedition—as in the case of *Hampden* (1684), who took part in the Rye House Plot (9 St. Tr. 1054), a grandson of the great opponent of illegal taxation—or to attaint him by an *ex post facto* Act of Parliament, as in the case of *Fenwick* (1696) (13 St. Tr. 538), who plotted the assassination of William III.

[4] Sect. 2 (1) and schedule.

[5] By extending the Treason Act, 1800, to all cases.

[6] See Stephen, *Hist. Crim. Law*, I, 476–7; Pollock and Maitland, II, 500; Radzinowicz, *Hist. Eng. Crim. Law*, I, 220–7.

[7] He was so drawn, and *then* hanged. Avoid the popular sequence 'hanged, drawn and quartered', which suggests that 'drawn' is here used in the culinary sense of disembowelling. The traitor was dragged prostrate to the scaffold, originally with nothing under him (as in the picture of A.D. 1242 in the library of C.C. Coll. Camb.). But in later years a hurdle was allowed.

[8] The regicide Harrison rose and struck the executioner *after* his body was opened. *Trials of the Twenty-nine Regicides* (1660), 5 St. Tr. at p. 1237.

conspicuous place,[1] after being boiled in salt to prevent putrefaction, and in cummin seed to prevent birds pecking at them. But the form of sentence in treason was not quite invariable,[2] and the King often remitted everything excepting the beheading. In later times, even where there was no such remission, the executioner usually took it upon himself to make the strangulation fatal (technically an act of murder, *ante*, ¶ 94). At last it was enacted, in 1814,[3] that the beheading and quartering should not take place till after the prisoner had been put to death by the hanging. (Women were never beheaded or quartered, but were burned.[4]) And finally in 1870 by the Forfeiture Act[5] all the exceptional features of execution for treason were abolished, except in cases where quartering or beheading may be ordered by royal warrant. For by the Act of 1814[6] the Crown has still power to order, by warrant under the sign manual, that any male who has been sentenced to be hanged for treason shall be beheaded. The judge, however, cannot appoint any mode of death[7] but hanging. In treason (as in all capital crimes except murder), the common law rule which permits executions to take place in public still holds.

¶ 420. *Forfeiture of estates to Crown.* A penalty which was entailed at common law by all capital crimes, and which sometimes was more dreaded than that of death, was the loss of all the offender's property, and the consequent ruin of the fortunes of his family. But in treasons his landed estate was not disposed of in the same way as in felonies. For in cases of treason, as we have already seen, not only the personal but also the real estate was forfeited to the Crown absolutely.[8] But in case of felonies, the realty was forfeited to the Crown for no longer than the offender's life and a year afterwards; after which period his estate (if in fee simple and not of gavelkind tenure) escheated at common law to the lord from whom it was held.

SECTION 2. MISPRISION

DEFINITION AND PUNISHMENT

¶ 421. In the account of the law of principal and accessory[9] we saw that, when a treason has been committed, anyone who knowingly receives or assists the traitor, so as to aid him in escaping from justice,

[1] Dr Pusey's mother, who survived until 1858, could remember seeing on Temple Bar the head of one of the rebels of 1745.

[2] The grossest may be seen in 3 Hargrave's State Trials, 340, 409.

[3] 54 Geo. III, c. 146.

[4] Till 1790; 30 Geo. III, c. 48. Here again in later years, by a merciful illegality, a fatal hanging usually preceded the burning.

[5] 33 and 34 Vict. c. 23.

[6] 54 Geo. III, c. 146, s. 2.

[7] As to infants under eighteen, see ¶ 51 *ante*. All sentences on even adult traitors after 1820 were commuted till Casement's in 1916.

[8] Forfeitures for treason and felony were abolished in 1870. See ¶¶ 73 and 74 *ante*.

[9] *Ante*, ¶ 66.

becomes himself guilty of complicity in the past act of treason. And, in the case of felonies,[1] a corresponding rule renders a similar harbourer an 'accessory after the fact' to the original felony. Even where no active assistance is thus given to the person who has committed a treason or a felony, anyone who knows of his guilt, and can give information that might lead to his arrest, will commit an offence if he omits to communicate that information to some justice of the peace.[2] The 'misprision' (i.e. high misdemeanour) of thus concealing a treason, or a felony, is usually termed briefly 'misprision of treason' or 'misprision of felony'.[3] There is some authority[4] for saying that a misprision may also be committed in the case of a treason or felony that is merely being planned, if anyone who knows of the design refrains (however much he may disapprove of the project) from disclosing it to a justice of the peace in order to prevent its accomplishment.[5] If he go so far as to give actual assent and encouragement to the plot, he may of course become guilty (not of this misdemeanour but) as an accomplice in the felony or treason itself, should the design be ultimately carried into effect.

Calling particular attention to the remarks of Lord Westbury[6] the Court of Criminal Appeal in a recent case[7] said: 'If in any future case it is thought necessary or desirable to include in an indictment a count for misprision of felony, great care should be taken to see what—at any rate according to more modern authorities—are the constituents of the offence....It may be that the court will have carefully to consider whether it is necessary to show a concealment for the benefit of the person charged.'

But now in *Sykes* v. *D.P.P.*[8] the House of Lords have laid down a much wider rule.

The essential ingredients of the offence were stated by Lord Denning to the following effect.

(1) The accused must know that a felony has been committed by someone else.

(2) He must have concealed or kept secret his knowledge: he need not have

[1] Including treason-felonies.

[2] In *Williams* v. *Bayley* (1866) L.R. 1 H.L. 200, Lord Westbury said (at p. 220) that misprision of felony was when a man, instead of performing his public duty and giving information to the public authorities of a crime that he was aware of, concealed his knowledge and, further, converted it into a source of emolument to himself.

[3] The word 'misprision' was formerly in use as a general name for any of the more heinous kinds of misdemeanours (4 Bl. *Comm.* 119); but it has become obsolete except in the two offences now mentioned, where it perhaps means 'undervaluing' the crime concealed. In French 'mépriser'. On misprision of felony see 8 *Chicago L.R.* (1941), no. 2, 338.

[4] 2 Hawk. P.C. c. 29, s. 23.

[5] For the wider duty imposed in India, including that of answering questions put by the police, see Indian Penal Code, s. 44.

[6] In *Williams* v. *Bayley*, *ubi supra*.

[7] *R.* v. *Aberg* [1948] 1 All E.R. 601, *per* Lord Goddard, C.J., at p. 602.

[8] [1961] 3 W.L.R. 371. See the criticism of the case when before the C.C.A. in [1961] *Crim. L.R.* 484. Also by G. L. Williams in 1961 *Cambridge L. J.* 142.

done anything active, but it is his duty by law to disclose to proper authority all material facts of which he has knowledge.

(3) If he fails or refuses to perform this duty when there is reasonable opportunity available to him to do so, he is guilty of misprision which is itself a misdemeanour with no other limit on the period of imprisonment than that the sentence 'must not be inordinately heavy'.

(4) But a claim of right made in good faith[1] would be a defence in the cases of lawyer and client, doctor and patient, clergyman and parishioner, each of whom 'might in good faith claim that he was under a duty to keep it confidential'. The judgment continued: 'There are other relationships which may give rise to a claim in good faith that it is in the public interest not to disclose it. For instance, if an employer discovers that his servant has been stealing from the till, he might well be justified in giving him another chance rather than reporting him to the police. Likewise with the master of a college and a student. But close family or personal ties will not suffice where the offence is of so serious a character that it ought to be reported.'

The judgment did not explain whether or not the lawyer, doctor and clergyman *are* under a duty (or privilege?) 'to keep it confidential', nor how the *public interest* is or could be thought to be served by the concealment of the felonies of stealing by an employee or a collegian, but not, apparently, by a member of the family. But further limitations were envisaged by the reference to the judges' ability 'further to define the just limitations to misprision'.[2]

A misprision of felony is punishable with imprisonment and fine,[3] but a misprision of treason[4] (which is not affected by the Forfeiture Act, 1870) with imprisonment for life and the forfeiture of the offender's goods absolutely and of his lands for so long as he lives. In the case of misdemeanours there is no similar crime in omitting to disclose them.

SECTION 3. COMPOUNDING

MERCY SHOULD BE SHOWN, NOT SOLD

¶ 422. It is a misdemeanour at common law to 'compound' a felony (and perhaps also to compound a misdemeanour[5]); i.e. to bargain, *for*

[1] The question whether it would be a crime of misprision not to report a *contemplated* felony was left open.

[2] That the test might be whether 'a reasonable man would consider it his duty to inform the police of it' was expressly repudiated by Lord Morton. This is another indication that the courts are prepared to accept the objective test of the 'reasonable man' when it operates against the accused, but not when it would be in his favour. See *R.* v. *McBride* [1961] 3 All E.R. 6; *post*, ¶ 444.

[3] For many years before 1948 prosecutions for it had been unknown, but Lord Wensleydale had tried two; *The Times*, 18 March 1852. In 1914 a prosecution for it was commenced in County Clare, but was abandoned on the six defendants' agreeing to give evidence against the murderer.

[4] Cf. ¶ 70 *ante*.

[5] Probably as a 'conspiracy to pervert the course of justice'. Cf. ¶ 473 *post*. But as to it in 'quasi-private' crimes, see Anson, *Law of Contracts*, 17th ed., II, vii, s. 1. The numerous authorities on the whole question are collected in Arch. ch. 15, sect. 7. See, too, Winfield, *Abuse of Legal Procedure*, 146–54.

value, to abstain from prosecuting the offender who has committed a crime.[1] You commit this offence if you promise a thief not to prosecute him if only he will return the goods he stole from you; but you may lawfully take them back if you make no such promise. You may show mercy, but must not sell mercy. This offence of compounding is committed by the bare act of agreement; even though the compounder afterwards breaks his agreement and prosecutes the criminal. And inasmuch as the law permits not merely the person injured by a crime, but also all other members of the community, to prosecute, it is criminal for anyone to make such a composition; even though he suffered no injury and indeed has no concern with the crime.

SECTION 4. PRAEMUNIRE

HISTORY AND PUNISHMENT

¶ 423. Akin in nature to treason, though far less heinous in degree, are the miscellaneous offences which have become grouped together under the name of praemunire. Under this head are comprised a variety of crimes whose chief connexion lies in their having the same punishment. But all the earlier offences so punished were, as some of the later also are, acts tending to introduce into the realm some foreign power (usually that of the Pope), to the diminution of the King's authority. The word 'praemunire' was the name of the writ which commenced the proceedings against a person guilty of such an offence; but afterwards it was also applied to any statute that created an offence for which this writ was to be issued; and, still later, it came to be applied to the punishment appointed for such offences, and even to the offences themselves.[2]

Voluminous as are the collections of our State trials, they contain only one English instance of any proceedings under any statute of praemunire, viz. that of some Quakers who refused to swear allegiance to Charles II.[3] The principal offences of praemunire still recognized in our criminal law are the following.

(1) By 25 Hen. VIII, c. 20, the refusal of a dean and chapter to elect to a bishopric the clergyman nominated to them by the King.

(2) By the Habeas Corpus Act, 1679 (31 Car. II, c. 2), the unlawful sending of any prisoner outside the realm, so that he would be beyond the protection of the writ of habeas corpus.

Not only is this offence made a praemunire, but even the Crown's power to pardon it is taken away.[4]

(3) By 6 Anne, c. 23, s. 9, if the Scottish peers, having met to elect their representative peers to the House of Lords, discharge any further business they commit a praemunire.

[1] But one *may* so bargain for not taking divorce proceedings, since they are civil.

[2] 4 Bl. *Comm.* ch. VIII.

[3] *R.* v. *Crook* (1662) 6 St. Tr. 201. There is also one Irish case, *R.* v. *Lalor* (1607) 2 St. Tr. 553.

[4] See Kenny, 16th ed., Appendix I, p. 539.

(4) By 12 Geo. III, c. 11, Royal Marriages Act, 1772, to assist knowingly and wilfully at a marriage or the making of a matrimonial contract forbidden by the Act.

(5) To maintain by spoken words the invalidity of the line of succession to the Crown.[1]

The offence of praemunire is only a misdemeanour; yet it is punished more severely than most felonies. For the offender (*a*) is placed out of the King's protection, e.g. he cannot sue; (*b*) he is imprisoned for life; and (*c*) he forfeits to the Crown all his property, real as well as personal, absolutely. This forfeiture is pronounced expressly as a part of the sentence. Consequently it does not render the offence a felony,[2] and it is not removed by the Forfeiture Act, 1870.

SECTION 5. TREACHERY

CREATED A CRIME IN 1940

¶ 424. The state of emergency in which the country found itself in 1940 led the legislature to make an addition to the number of capital offences by creating the crime of treachery, by the Treachery Act.[3] Although by section 6 it was provided that no person should be guilty of an offence under the Act by reason of anything done after such day as His Majesty should by Order in Council declare to be the date on which the emergency which was the occasion of the passing of the Act came to an end, it may be useful to record section 1 of the Act, as follows:

> If, with intent[4] to help the enemy, any person does, or attempts or conspires with any other person to do, any act which is designed or likely to give assistance to the naval, military or air operations of the enemy, to impede such operations of His Majesty's forces, or to endanger life, he shall be guilty of felony and shall on conviction suffer death.

SECTION 6. ATTEMPTS TO INJURE OR ALARM THE SOVEREIGN

LESS SERIOUS ACTION THAN CONSTITUTES TREASON

¶ 425. To make attacks upon, or to cause annoyance to, the Sovereign by conduct less serious than would amount to treason was made a misdemeanour in 1842[5] (punishable with seven years' penal servitude and whipping[6]). The acts amounting to such conduct, as set out in the statute, include discharging or pointing any kind of firearm (whether

[1] See ¶ 72 *ante*.
[2] *Ante*, ¶ 74.
[3] 3 and 4 Geo. VI, c. 21.
[4] *R.* v. *O'Grady* (1941) 28 Cr.App.R. 33.
[5] Treason Act, 1842 (5 and 6 Vict. c. 51), s. 2. Enacted after a case in which a youth had been sentenced to eighteen months' imprisonment for a common law misdemeanour in displaying an old pistol, not properly loaded, in a crowd as the royal coach drove by; *R.* v. *Bean* (1842) 4 St. Tr. (n.s.) 1382; *post*, ¶ 445.
[6] Imprisonment is now substituted for penal servitude and whipping abolished by the Criminal Justice Act, 1948, s. 1.

loaded or not) near the Sovereign, or striking at the Sovereign with any kind of weapon, or throwing or attempting to throw any substance or thing at the Sovereign.

SECTION 7. SEDITION AND OTHER OFFENCES AGAINST THE STATE

STEPHEN'S DEFINITION OF SEDITION

¶ 426. The law of sedition relates to the uttering of seditious words, the publication of seditious libels, and conspiracies to do an act for the furtherance of a seditious intention. Sedition, whether by words spoken or written, or by conduct, is a misdemeanour at common law punishable by fine and imprisonment. Sir James Stephen[1] defined a seditious intention as 'an intention to bring into hatred or contempt, or to excite disaffection against the person of, His Majesty, his heirs or successors, or the government and constitution of the United Kingdom by law established, or either House of Parliament, or the administration of justice, or to excite His Majesty's subjects to attempt otherwise than by lawful means, the alteration of any matter in Church or State by law established,...or to raise discontent or disaffection amongst His Majesty's subjects, or to promote feelings of ill-will and hostility between different classes of such subjects'. But 'an intention[2] to show that His Majesty has been misled or mistaken in his measures, to point out errors or defects in the government or constitution, as by law established, with a view to their reformation, or to excite His Majesty's subjects to attempt by lawful means the alteration of any matter in Church or State by law established, or to point out, in order to their removal, matters which are producing, or have a tendency to produce, feelings of hatred and ill will between classes of His Majesty's subjects, is not a seditious intention'. It is the right of every citizen to discuss public affairs fully and freely, but such discussions must not be directed to the incitement of unlawful acts or calculated to excite disaffection.[3] In a twentieth-century prosecution for sedition the judge told the jury that they could take into account the state of public feeling.[4]

In *Joshua* v. *R.*,[5] it appeared that the accused had been charged as follows: (*a*) that he had made a seditious speech and (*b*) that he had effected a public mischief by making the said speech. This was declared to be 'highly undesirable'.[6]

[1] *Digest of Criminal Law*, 8th ed., art. 114.

[2] *Ibid.* art. 95.

[3] For illustrations of sedition, see Arch. ch. 13, sect. 7; Russ. 229 *et seq.*; *R.* v. *Burns* (1886) 16 Cox 355.

[4] *R.* v. *Aldred* (1909) 22 Cox 1. And see *R.* v. *Caunt* (1947) reported in *An Editor on Trial* (Morcambe Press, Ltd.) (*T.A.C.*).

[5] [1955] 2 W.L.R. 8; 1 All E.R. 22. On this case see 119 *J.P.Jo.* 196; 18 *Mod.L.R.* 291.

[6] By the Judicial Committee [1955] 2 W.L.R. 8; the jury had found the appellant not guilty of sedition but guilty of public mischief.

¶ 427. *Other statutory offences.* There are several statutes that relate to offences against the state, but cannot be discussed in detail in this volume. The Unlawful Drilling Act, 1819,[1] prohibits unauthorized drilling. The Unlawful Oaths Act, 1797,[2] prohibits unlawful oaths. Tumultuous petitioning to the King or Parliament is prohibited by a statute of Charles II.[3] The Incitement to Mutiny Act, 1797,[4] makes it a felony punishable with penal servitude for life maliciously and advisedly to endeavour to seduce any person or persons serving in His Majesty's forces by sea or land from his or their duty and allegiance to His Majesty, or to make or endeavour to make any mutinous assembly, or to commit any treasonable or mutinous practice whatsoever. Under the Incitement to Disaffection Act, 1934,[5] which contains special provisions for the prevention and detection of offences,[6] it is an offence, triable either on indictment or summarily, maliciously and advisedly to endeavour to seduce any member of His Majesty's forces from his duty or allegiance to His Majesty. The punishment on conviction on indictment is imprisonment for a term not exceeding two years and/or a fine not exceeding £200,[5] and on summary conviction the punishment is imprisonment for a term not exceeding four months and/or a fine not exceeding £20. If any person with intent to commit or aid, abet, counsel or procure the offence of endeavouring to seduce from duty or allegiance has in his possession any document of such a nature that its dissemination would constitute such an endeavour to seduce he is guilty of an offence under this Act.[7] By the Police Act, 1919,[8] it is a misdemeanour punishable with two years' imprisonment to cause or do any act calculated to cause disaffection among the members of any police force, or to induce any member of such a force to commit breaches of discipline.

THE OFFICIAL SECRETS ACTS, 1911 AND 1920[9]

¶ 428. These enactments are directed to the punishment of spies and the prevention of the disclosure of state secrets. They deal with numerous offences including the wrongful approach to prohibited places;[10] the wrongful communication, for a purpose prejudicial to the safety of the state, of documents or information calculated to be useful to an enemy,[11] the wrongful communication of documents or informa-

60 Geo. III and 1 Geo. IV, c. 1. [2] 37 Geo. III, c. 123.

[3] 13 Car. II, st. 1, c. 5.

[4] 37 Geo. III, c. 70. Extended to the Air Force under 7 and 8 Geo. V, c. 51, s. 13.

[5] 24 and 25 Geo. V, c. 56, ss. 1 and 3. [6] See ¶ 692, *post*.

[7] 24 and 25 Geo. V, c. 56, s. 2. See also the Unlawful Oaths Acts of 1797 (37 Geo. III, c. 123) and 1812 (52 Geo. III, c. 104). [8] 9 and 10 Geo. V, c. 46, s. 3.

[9] 1 and 2 Geo. V, c. 28 and 10 and 11 Geo. V, c. 75.

[10] For the full provisions of these Acts, see Arch. ch. 13, sect. 13.

[11] 'Enemy' includes 'a potential enemy with whom we might some day be at war', *R.* v. *Parrott* (1913) 8 Cr.App.R. 186.

tion obtained in confidence from one holding office under His Majesty; the wrongful communication of information received by reason of holding office under His Majesty; failure to take reasonable care of secret official documents; the wrongful receiving of information obtained in contravention of the Acts; the harbouring of spies; the wrongful use of official uniforms; personation or the making of false statements in order to gain admission to prohibited places. By an unusual provision the conduct or known character of the accused is admissible as evidence that his purpose was a purpose prejudicial to the safety or interests of the State. The Acts apply to acts committed by anyone in any part of His Majesty's dominions, or by British officers or subjects anywhere.

SECTION 8. OFFENCES AGAINST THE PUBLIC PEACE

¶ 429. *Early weakness of parish constabulary.* In reviewing the law of treason, we have seen[1] that the extension of that crime by judicial constructions has enlarged its scope so as to include many acts which would seem to fall more naturally under the head of the much less heinous offence of rioting. This offence itself is also one of a very wide and elastic character. This comprehensiveness is probably due (like the vagueness of the law of conspiracy[2]) to the weakness which characterized our constitutional provisions for the prevention of crime throughout the long period that elapsed, after the decay of the old system of corporate responsibility by frankpledge,[3] before the establishment by Sir Robert Peel of our modern force of borough and county police. Throughout these intervening centuries, the common law felt its parish constabulary to be comparatively powerless to prevent any offence that involved the presence of a plurality of offenders. It consequently attempted to supply the defect by very comprehensive prohibitions of all such crimes. Sir William Holdsworth has pointed out[4] that the severity of the law relating to offences against the public peace may be justified as well as explained. 'Unlimited tolerance undermines all those fundamental principles upon which the stability of the state and, therefore, of civilization itself, depends.'

(a) UNLAWFUL ASSEMBLY

¶ 430. Hence it was laid down that whenever so many as three persons meet together to support each other, even against opposition, in carrying out a purpose which is likely to involve violence or to produce in the minds of rational and firm men any reasonable apprehensions of violence, then even though they ultimately depart without doing anything whatever towards carrying out their design, the mere fact of their having thus met will constitute a crime. It will be the indictable

[1] *Ante*, ¶ 413. [2] *Post*, ¶ 452.

[3] Pollock and Maitland, I, 564, 568; Stephen, *Hist. Crim. Law*, I, 65.

[4] *History of English Law*, VIII, 331–3.

misdemeanour of unlawful assembly. The alarm must not be merely such as would frighten any foolish or timid person, but must be such as would alarm persons of reasonable firmness and courage.[1] Such an offence will therefore be committed as soon as three persons collect with a view to attending service in the village church and protesting turbulently against the mode in which it is conducted, even though they never actually start on their expedition. Similarly, a group of people who have come together to see a prize-fight constitute an unlawful assembly, even though the fight never takes place.[2] The offence was sometimes defined so widely as to include all cases where three or more persons were assembled for any unlawful purpose whatever, even one that could cause no fears of violence.[3] But this comprehensive definition, long ago called in question,[4] was set aside by the case of *Field* v. *The Receiver of Metropolitan Police* (which should also be studied for its definition of the offence of riot).[5] Accordingly, when three boys meet to go and gamble at pitch-and-toss on a common, or when three costermongers go into a street on Sunday morning to sell their vegetables contrary to the Sunday Observance Act, they do not constitute an unlawful assembly (though they may be guilty of an indictable conspiracy).[6]

The unlawfulness depends upon behaviour

¶ 431. In the offence of unlawful assembly, as in all others, the law regards persons as responsible for the natural consequences of their conduct. Consequently if people have assembled together under such circumstances as are in fact likely to cause alarm to bystanders of ordinary courage, the assembly will be an unlawful one, even though the original purpose for which it came together involved neither violence nor any other illegality. 'You must look not only to the purpose for which they meet, but also to the manner in which they come, and to the means which they are using' (Bayley, J.).[7] Accordingly the idea of an unlawful assembly is not restricted to gatherings met together for the commission of some crime (like the poachers or prize-fighters already mentioned), or for arousing seditious feelings, or for inciting to some breach of the law (such as the non-payment of rents). For however innocent[8] may be the object for which a meeting is convened—e.g. to support some parliamentary measure by strictly constitutional means—it will nevertheless become an unlawful assembly

[1] *Per* Alderson, B., in *R.* v. *Vincent* (1839) 3 St. Tr. (n.s.) 1037 at p. 1082.

[2] *R.* v. *Brodribb* (1816) 6 C. and P. 571; cf. *R.* v. *Coney* (1882) 8 Q.B.D. 534.

[3] For the law relating to disturbances in churchyards or places of public worship see Russ. ch. 105.

[4] Cf. *Beatty* v. *Gillbanks* (1882) 9 Q.B.D. 308 (*T.A.C.*).

[5] [1907] 2 K.B. 853 (*T.A.C.*). Cf. *Ford* v. *Receiver for the Metropolitan Police District* [1921] 2 K.B. 344.

[6] *Post*, ¶ 451.

[7] *R.* v. *Hunt* (1820) 1 St. Tr. (n.s.) 171 (*T.A.C.*).

[8] The seriousness of possible risks was well illustrated in 1908 when the Battersea Borough Council were told by the Commissioner of Police that they must either remove the 'Battersea Brown Dog' with its provocative anti-vivisectionist inscription or pay £700 a year for special police protection.

if the persons who take part in it act in such a way as to give firm and rational men a reasonable ground for fearing that they will commit or actively provoke some violent breach of the peace.[1] Numbers alone, it is true, will not suffice to make an assembly unlawful; but they are a circumstance to be considered. It is important to notice that, if persons meet together for a purpose not unlawful and are quite peaceable[2] in act and intent, the fact of their being aware that other people, less scrupulous, are likely to disturb them unlawfully and thereby to create a breach of the peace does not render their assembly an unlawful one. A man cannot be convicted for doing a lawful act, *merely* because his doing it may cause someone else to do an unlawful act.[3] But to do this intrinsically lawful act (e.g. to wear a party badge), with the desire of thereby irritating others into a breach of the peace, would render it unlawful. Some authorities go so far as to hold that an act will be rendered unlawful if done by a person who knows, although he does not desire, that it may provoke others to commit a breach of the peace, unless there be some reasonable occasion for doing the act.[4]

In *Humphries* v. *Connor*,[5] an Irish court decided that it was within the due execution of a police officer's duty to remove by force from a lady's dress an orange lily emblem which she was wearing in the public street to the anger of the populace who seemed to be threatening to attack her. On very much the same principle an English divisional court in 1936[6] went further and held that, if a police officer formed the opinion that, should a person *X* address a gathering of some thirty people in a public street, the result of the address might be that certain persons might subsequently create some disturbance on private property not far away, then it would be within the execution of his duty to call upon her not to address the people there (informing her that she might hold the meeting in another street about 175 yards away), and, upon her refusal to obey, to arrest her on the charge of unlawfully and wilfully obstructing a police officer in the execution of his duty.[7]

[1] *R.* v. *Vincent* (1839) 9 C. and P. 91. E.g. if speeches provocative of violence are made.

[2] As to the necessity of this qualification, see *Wise* v. *Dunning* [1902] 1 K.B. 167; Dicey's *Law of the Constitution*, 9th ed., 276.

[3] *Beatty* v. *Gillbanks* (1882) 9 Q.B.D. 308 (*T.A.C.*); cf. 51 L.T. 304, and *McClenaghan* v. *Waters* (*The Times*, 18 July 1882). Yet it seems clear in (at any rate) Irish law, that constables are justified in *removing* such innocent persons to a safer place, if it be the only means of avoiding an *imminent* breach of the peace, *Coyne* v. *Tweedy* [1898] 2 I.R. 167. So too a meeting with a lawful object may be dispersed where dispersal is necessary for the preservation of the peace and persons may be required to find sureties to keep the peace, who might yet be found innocent if charged with taking part in an unlawful assembly, *Wise* v. *Dunning* (*supra*), *O'Kelly* v. *Harvey* (1883) 14 L.R. Ir. 105, *Duncan* v. *Jones* (1935) 52 T.L.R. 26, and see ¶ 796 *post*. Refusal to disperse when lawfully required to do so will render an assembly unlawful, *Humphries* v. *Connor* (1864) 17 Ir. C.L. 1.

[4] *R.* v. *Clarkson* (1892) 17 Cox 483. And see the Draft Code of 1879.

[5] *Ubi supra.*

[6] *Duncan* v. *Jones* [1936] 1 K.B. 218.

[7] This case was criticized by Professor E. C. S. Wade in 6 *Cambridge L.J.* 175, 'Police powers and public meetings'.

¶ 432. *Assemblies forbidden by statute.* The common law was reinforced from time to time by statutes which can only be briefly mentioned here. In 1662[1] it was made an offence (designated 'tumultuous petitioning') punishable with a fine of £100 and imprisonment for three months if any person should 'repair to His Majesty or both or either House of Parliament upon pretence of presenting or delivering any petition... accompanied with...above the number of ten persons'.

By the Seditious Meetings Act, 1817,[2] it is an unlawful assembly if more than fifty persons meet within a mile of Westminster Hall during sittings of Parliament for the purpose or on the pretext of considering or preferring a petition, complaint, remonstrance or address to the King or either House of Parliament for alteration of matters in Church or State. This act is a relic of the legislative restraint inspired by the French Revolution. Of the same era is the Unlawful Societies Act, 1799,[3] which prohibits secret societies and all societies composed of different divisions or branches other than certain excepted societies and societies formed for religious or charitable purposes only.[4]

The Unlawful Drilling Act of 1819 forbade any persons to meet or assemble (save with royal authority[5]) for the purpose of military drilling, training, or exercises, the penalty being imprisonment[6] for seven years.

¶ 433. *Unlawful wearing of uniforms.* In modern times serious disturbances and acts of violence have occurred when persons, wearing uniforms intended to denote their membership of associations with a political object, paraded in public in formations of a military character. In consequence of this the Public Order Act, 1936,[7] made it an offence[8] for any person in any public place or at any public meeting to wear uniform signifying his association with any political organization or with the promotion of any political object. The chief officer of police of the district may in special circumstances give permission to wear such uniforms for some particular occasion, and the same officer is given wide powers for the preservation of public order when a procession is proposed to be held and may impose conditions on persons organizing or taking part in it, even to the extent of applying to the local authority for an order to prohibit the procession entirely.

[1] 13 Car. II, st. 1, c. 5 (amended by the Statute Law Revision Act, 1948).

[2] 57 Geo. III, c. 19, s. 25.

[3] 39 Geo. III, c. 79, amended by 57 Geo. III, c. 19.

[4] These Acts are not applicable to trade unions, see Halsbury, *Laws of England* (Hailsham ed.), IX.

[5] Which may now be given by a Secretary of State (Firearms Act, 1920, s. 16).

[6] Under the Criminal Justice Act, 1948; originally transportation, and later penal servitude.

[7] 1 Edw. VIII and 1 Geo. VI, c. 6.

[8] Punishable on summary conviction with three months' imprisonment and a fine of £50. By s. 2 it is a more serious offence to take part in the control or management of any such association if organized to enable the members to usurp the functions of the police or armed forces of the Crown, punishable with two years' imprisonment and a fine of £500.

Disturbance of public meetings

¶ **434.** Under the Public Meetings Acts of 1908 and 1936 any person who at a lawful public meeting acts in a disorderly manner for the purpose of preventing the transaction of the business of the meeting is made liable to a fine of £5 or imprisonment for one month.[1]

Dispersal of an unlawful assembly may be forcible

¶ **435.** The alarm with which the common law viewed unlawful assemblies naturally led to the establishment of the rule that they may be dispersed forcibly, even by private persons acting on their own initiative.[2] The particular degree of force which such persons will be lawfully justified in using must be determined by the necessities of each individual case. But an unlawful assembly—even when accompanied by such further circumstances as aggravate it into a common-law riot—only amounts to a misdemeanour; and therefore, although blows with fists or with sticks may be struck when necessary to suppress it, it will be unlawful to kill any of the rioters or to employ deadly weapons. If, however, the rioters go beyond their misdemeanour and proceed to the length of some felonious violence, then even the infliction of death will be permissible in resisting such violence or in dispersing or arresting the rioters, and the act of killing will be a justifiable homicide. Indeed, so long as those engaged in suppressing the felonious violence act with due care, the accidental killing of even an innocent bystander by the means lawfully employed for the suppression will amount only to a case of homicide by misadventure.

(*b*) ROUT

¶ **436.** Closely akin to the offence of unlawful assembly are some other crimes of tumultuous disorder which are technically distinguished from it. Thus an unlawful assembly develops into a rout as soon as the persons concerned have done some act towards carrying out the illegal purpose which has made their assembly unlawful, although they have not so far begun to execute that illegal act. The offence is an indictable misdemeanour, punishable with fine and imprisonment.

(*c*) RIOT

¶ **437.** According to the definition given in the year 1907,[3] there are five necessary elements in a riot: (i) there must be at least three persons;[4] (ii) they must have a common purpose; (iii) there must be execution

[1] With power to a constable (if required by the chairman of the meeting) to require the name and address of anyone whom he reasonably suspects of committing the offence.

[2] When an anti-scientist crowd, on 2 December 1833, attacked the Anatomical School at Cambridge the undergraduates aided in its defence.

[3] *Field* v. *The Receiver of Metropolitan Police* [1907] 2 K.B. 853 (*T.A.C.*). See also *Ford* v. *Receiver for the Metropolitan Police District* [1921] 2 K.B. 344.

[4] *R.* v. *Beach* (1909) 2 Cr.App.R. 189. Cf. the offence of affray, *post*, ¶ 447*b*, and Russ. 302 *et seq.*

or inception of the common purpose; (iv) there must be an intent to help one another by force if necessary against any person who may oppose them in the execution of their common purpose; (v) there must be force or violence, not merely used in demolishing, but displayed in such a manner as to alarm at least one person of reasonable firmness and courage.[1] Thus it has been held to be a riot where a crowd, unable to gain admission to a football ground, entered the plaintiff's garden and proceeded to intimidate and assault members of his household in order to obtain a view of the match.[2] It has, however, been stated (obiter) in the Court of Criminal Appeal[3] that 'a riot may involve no noise or disturbance of the neighbours[4] though there must be some force or violence', and that, contrary to the fifth element of riot ('which may require reconsideration at some future time') as laid down in *Field* v. *Receiver of Metropolitan Police* (*supra*), it would not be necessary to call a witness who could say 'I was terrified', but it would be enough for a witness to say that persons appeared to be alarmed. Riot is a common law misdemeanour, as is rout, punishable by fine and imprisonment.

The Riot Act

¶ 438. In consequence of the riots in many towns that followed the accession of George I in 1714 there was enacted the Riot Act of 1714.[5] That statute establishes a wiser mode of prosecuting grave tumults than by treating them as treasonable 'levyings of war'.[6] Under its provisions,[7] whenever an unlawful assembly of *twelve* or more persons do not disperse within an hour after a justice of the peace has read, or has endeavoured to read, to them a proclamation[8] (set out in the Act) calling upon them to disperse, they cease to be misdemeanants and become guilty of a felony, punishable with imprisonment for life. But, by a departure from the general rule of criminal procedure (see ¶ 640 *post*), no prosecution for this felony can be commenced after the lapse of twelve months from its commission.

¶ 439. *Every citizen's right and duty.* The Riot Act contains an express clause[9] indemnifying any persons who, after the expiration of the

[1] *R.* v. *Langford* (1842) C. and M. 602 (same case, *R.* v. *Phillips* (1842) 2 Moo. 252).

[2] *Munday* v. *Metropolitan Police District Receiver* [1949] 1 All E.R. 337.

[3] *R.* v. *Sharp and Johnson* [1957] 2 W.L.R. 472 at pp. 475, 476.

[4] Citing *City of London Fire Insce Co.* v. *Bolands* [1924] A.C. 836.

[5] 1 Geo. I, st. 2, c. 5. This statute contains (s. 7) the remarkable provision that its contents must be 'openly read at every quarter sessions and at every court leet'; a provision disobeyed probably everywhere except at the annual court leet of Southwark.

[6] *Ante*, ¶ 406.

[7] As modified by the Criminal Justice Act, 1948.

[8] The exact words of the proclamation must be read; e.g. it is insufficient if the final words 'God save the King' are omitted, *R.* v. *Child* (1830), 4 C. and P. 442.

[9] Sect. 3.

statutory hour, may have to use violence for dispersing or arresting the rioters and in doing so may hurt or kill someone. Indeed, such an indemnity was already implied in the provision that, after the lapse of the hour, the rioters' offence should become aggravated into a felony;[1] for this rendered justifiable the employment of any amount of force necessary to suppress this tumultuous felony, e.g. even the infliction of death, as by troops firing upon the crowd. But even whilst the hour is still unexpired the common law right of dispersion[2] still exists, unaffected by the Riot Act and by the justice's proclamation. Consequently a moderate degree of force may be lawfully used even then. And if the rioters should proceed to commit any felonious violence, they may be checked with the same extreme measures of force as if the statutory hour were over. But a misapprehension that the Riot Act had somehow impliedly modified the common law right did at one time prevail, and sometimes led to grave disorder being allowed to rage unchecked. In 1780, for instance, in consequence of this misapprehension, London was abandoned to pillage for three days during the disturbances initiated by Lord George Gordon.[3] Neither the citizens nor the soldiers dared to fire upon the plundering incendiaries who had become masters of the metropolis, because no magistrate was present to 'read the Riot Act'. Their timidity was doubtless enhanced by the verdict of murder which had been given at Edinburgh in 1736 against Captain Porteous,[4] and by the indictments which had been found in 1768 against the soldiers who fired upon the Wilkite rioters in London.[5] But the result of the Gordon riots was to make it clear, beyond doubt, that every citizen—and the armed soldier, no less than any other—has by common law the right and the duty of using even deadly violence, whenever it is indispensable for the purpose of protecting person and property against a felonious mob of rioters. For, in Lord Mansfield's phrase, 'whether the citizen's coat be a brown one or a red' it is equally his duty to aid the law.[6] This principle is fully recognized in the present Army Regulations, which (whilst providing that, if a magistrate be present, the officer in command of the troops should not fire without the magistrate's orders)[7] direct that if no magistrate be present, the officer need not wait for one

[1] *Ante*, ¶ 76.

[2] *Ante*, ¶ 435.

[3] For a full account see Hibbert, *King Mob*, 1959; Dickens's *Barnaby Rudge*, chs. LXIII–LXVII. Cf. the Dublin riots in 1913 in which 196 policemen were injured.

[4] *Ante*, ¶ 406.

[5] Of those Wilkites, a certain stout-hearted Mr Green, with the help of his equally courageous maidservant, slew no fewer than eighteen, when they attacked the little alehouse which he kept. He was tried for murder, and acquitted; but seven of his antagonists were hanged (Knight's *Popular History of England*, VI, 291).

[6] During the Littleport riots of 1816 the heads of the Cambridge colleges passed a resolution 'to arm the undergraduates if necessary'.

[7] And even those orders will not absolve the officer from the duty of exercising his own discretion before proceeding to fire.

before taking active steps to prevent outrage upon persons or property.[1]

¶ 440. *Duty to assist police officers.* The matter, indeed, is not merely one of right but of duty. It is an indictable misdemeanour at common law to refuse to aid or assist a constable in the exercise of his duty, in order to preserve the peace. It must be proved that the constable saw the breach of the peace committed, that it was reasonable in the circumstances for him to call for the assistance of the accused, and that the accused when duly called upon to assist refused to do so without lawful excuse or physical inability, whether or not such aid as the accused could have given would have been effective.

¶ 441. *The duty of the justice of the peace.* In 1360 the Justices of the Peace Act[2] created the office of justice of the peace and gave the holders the power and duty 'to restrain rioters and all other barrators, and to pursue, arrest, take and chastise them according to their trespass and offence, and to cause them to be imprisoned and duly punished...and to take of all them that be not of good fame...surety and mainprise of their good behaviour'.[3] This has been interpreted as authorizing a single justice to act; and since the royal judges are justices of the peace for every county, they too can exercise the powers granted by the Act.[4] And the duty of the justice of the peace goes further. It is incumbent on him to proceed to the scene of a riot, and to read the statutory proclamation if the riot be such as to require it, and to take whatever subsequent steps are necessary to disperse the rioters.[5] If he fail to do this, he is guilty of a criminal neglect of duty, unless he can show that he has at least done all that a man of firm and constant mind would have done under the circumstances. In the vast majority of cases the mere arrival of troops suffices to quell the disturbance.[6]

[1] An admirable account of the law as to the suppression of riots will be found in the Report (drafted by Lord Bowen) upon the Featherstone riots of 1893, when 2000 miners, about to destroy a colliery, were faced by twenty-eight soldiers; see *The Times* of 8 December 1893, and Dicey's *Law of the Constitution*, 9th ed., App. *s.v.* Cf. the Report of the Royal Commission of 1914 on the landing of arms at Howth.

[2] 34 Ed. III, c. 1.

[3] Against such an order made by a magistrates' court binding over the person to be of good behaviour there can now, by virtue of the Magistrates' Courts Act, 1956, be an appeal to quarter sessions.

[4] *R.* v. *Sharp and Johnson* [1957] 2 W.L.R. 472.

[5] *R.* v. *Kennett* (1781) 5 C. and P. 283 (*T.A.C.*); *R.* v. *Pinney* (1832) 3 St. Tr. (n.s.) 11; *R.* v. *Neale* (1839) 9 C. and P. 431 (*T.A.C.*). Neglect of duty or misconduct in the performance of duty by a public officer is an indictable misdemeanour at common law, see Russ. ch. 24.

[6] The law of riot includes a remarkable instance of a vicarious liability—that thrown upon the inhabitants of any locality where rioters (even mere misdemeanants) have done damage to 'buildings', to make good that damage. The particular locality assigned as the unit for this purpose was the hundred. It is now the district—whether a borough or a section of a county—which maintains the local police force; and the liability is discharged out of the local police rate (the county or borough rate). See the Riot (Damages) Act, 1886 (49 and 50 Vict. c. 38). It protects not only the building but also the premises appurtenant to it, and the property within.

(*d*) MISUSE OF THE HIGHWAY

¶ **442.** As many road offences affect the public it may be convenient briefly to mention two of them at this point. A misdemeanour[1] is committed under the Offences against the Person Act, 1861,[2] when a person having charge of any carriage or vehicle[3] by wanton or furious driving, or racing or other wilful misconduct or by wilful neglect,[4] does or causes to be done any bodily harm to any person whatsoever.

¶ **443.** *Control of motor vehicles.* The Road Traffic Acts[5] were enacted to reduce the dangers of uncontrolled motor traffic on the roads. Accordingly they have made it an offence[6] punishable summarily with a fine not exceeding £40 (and in the case of a subsequent conviction with a fine not exceeding £80 or with up to three months' imprisonment or with both such fine and imprisonment) to drive a motor vehicle without due care or reasonable consideration for others.[7] But to drive recklessly or at a speed or in a manner dangerous to the public is punishable[8] on conviction or indictment with two years' imprisonment and/or a fine; and on summary conviction[9] with a fine not exceeding £100 or four months' imprisonment and on any subsequent conviction with the like fine and/or with six months' imprisonment. On a conviction under any one of sections 1,[10] 2 or 3 of the Road Traffic Act of 1960 the court *may* disqualify the offender from holding a driving licence for such a period as is provided in the Act,[11] and in certain cases *must* do so unless there is some special reason to the contrary.[12]

¶ **444.** *R.* v. *Stringer.* In *R.* v. *Stringer*,[13] the Court of Criminal Appeal upheld a conviction for dangerous driving though on the same facts the accused had been acquitted by the same jury on a charge of manslaughter. The court, in this unsatisfactory decision, did not point out in

[1] Punishable by two years' imprisonment.

[2] Sect. 35.

[3] E.g. a bicycle.

[4] Neglect is not the same thing as negligence; see *ante*, ¶ 25.

[5] From 1930 onwards. See now the Road Traffic Act, and the Road Traffic Improvement Act, of 1960.

[6] Sect. 3 of the Road Traffic Act of 1960.

[7] Contrast *Thompson* v. *Wigley* [1956] Crim. L.R. 205 with *Baker* v. *Williams* [1956] 54 L.G.R. 197. There are also provisions for disqualifying the driver from holding a driving licence for a period of time; see s. 5 of the Act of 1934, and sch. 8 of the Act of 1956.

[8] Under s. 2 of the Road Traffic Act of 1960.

[9] See Ch. XXXI *post*.

[10] *Ante*, ¶ 42 (4).

[11] Sect. 104 and sched. 11.

[12] To find special reasons for not disqualifying a convicted person from holding a driving licence, the facts said to constitute special reasons must be special to the offence and not to the offender. That it would cause great hardship to the offender, e.g. financial or business hardship, or that he had never been convicted before is not a ground which can be regarded as affording 'special reasons'; *Jowett-Shooter* v. *Franklin* [1949] 2 All E.R. 730 confirming *Whittall* v. *Kirby* [1946] 2 All E.R. 552, which was also affirmed and explained in *Richroth* v. *Cottee* [1954] 2 All E.R. 856.

[13] [1933] 1 K.B. 704.

what respect the *mens rea* required to establish a charge of dangerous driving differs from that required in manslaughter.[1]

For the effect of section 1 of the Road Traffic Act, 1960 (replacing section 8 of the Act of 1956), which created a new offence of killing by dangerous driving, see *ante*, p. 184. It has, however, since been laid down that the test for 'dangerous driving' is purely objective, so that *mens rea* is, for this statutory crime, eliminated, the jury being instructed to consider whether an imaginary onlooker would say that the accused was driving dangerously.[2] On this principle the accused cannot set up any special personal circumstances by way of defence; but, it would seem, the prosecution can use his actual subjective situation *against* him, this *volte-face* being justified by treating, e.g., the intake of alcohol by him as part of 'the circumstances relevant to the issue'.[3]

(*e*) PUBLIC MISCHIEF

¶ 445. The history of our common law shows that the judiciary have not merely expanded it by interpretation of long-established rules, but also from time to time, when the facts of a case before them seemed to be such that it would appear proper for them to give rein to their personal feelings of indignation, have gone so far as to enlarge it by decisions which created new crimes for which there was neither previous precedent nor statutory authority.[4] Thus Lord Abinger, in addressing a youthful prisoner who from his place in a crowd had pointed an old pistol in the direction of the carriage of Queen Victoria which was proceeding at a rapid pace far out of range of the weapon (which indeed was not properly loaded), said: 'That your attempt is highly criminal, and that you have been guilty of an abominable crime, no man can doubt.'[5] Holding that the offence was short of high treason his lordship declared that all the court could do was to pass 'that sentence which the common law justifies',[6] and sentenced Bean to

[1] For a discussion and criticism of this case see *Mod. Appr. Crim. Law*, 232 *et seq.*; and ¶ 134 *ante*. The difficulty created by treating 'dangerous' driving as an objective matter is seen in *R.* v. *Parker* (1957) 41 Cr.App.R. 134; *R.* v. *Curphey* (1957) 41 Cr.App.R. 78 ('a momentary act of negligence').

[2] See *Hill* v. *Baxter* [1958] 1 Q.B. 277; *R.* v. *McBride* [1961] 3 All E.R. 6 at p. 9.

[3] *R.* v. *McBride*, *ubi supra*. Again with the proviso as to the exercise of discretion by the judge, see *post*, ¶ 547*a*.

[4] The Star Chamber, of course, had always adopted the practice of issuing arbitrary orders, a practice which ultimately enriched the common law, since many of their rules proved salutary and were eventually incorporated into the common law. See ¶ 460 *post*.

[5] *R.* v. *Bean* (1842) 4 St. Tr. (n.s.) 1382. From the evidence it appeared that most of the bystanders regarded the affair as a joke, and two policemen refused to take the youth in charge. However, since the man who had taken the pistol from him was afterwards mistakenly supposed to have been himself about to commit some offence, Bean was subsequently arrested and charged.

[6] Adding 'if any desperate character should follow your example, he may, if not convicted of high treason, by which his life would be forfeited, gain another species of notoriety by being publicly whipped at a cart's tail through any street in the metropolis',

eighteen months' imprisonment.[1] Another example is *R.* v. *Higgins*[2] where Lawrence, J., stated 'all offences of a public nature, that is, such acts or attempts as tend to the prejudice of the community' are indictable. This case formed the basis of the modern law of criminal attempts, as has already been mentioned.[3] The dangers inherent in such legislative activity by the courts have often been indicated.[4] On the other hand it may be argued that where an obviously harmful act has been deliberately and dishonestly done, the bold intervention of the judiciary, without waiting for the possible working of the slow machinery of the legislature has sometimes been salutary.

¶ 446. *Vagueness and uncertainty of definition.* There can, however, be no question that it is a defect in any system of law that it should be vague and uncertain, especially in its definition of crime. And from that point of view it has been objected that the Court of Criminal Appeal went further than was necessary in giving a general confirmation to the above cited dictum of Lawrence, J., in *R.* v. *Higgins*, when the case of *R.* v. *Manley*[5] came before them in 1933.[6] The defendant was a woman who by false statements had led policemen to waste their time in investigation of her false allegation that she had been the victim of a robbery. The conviction might have been justified on the ground that her deceit interfered with the administration of justice, but the judgment went on the wider and more vague basis of the old dictum and has thus extended the element of uncertainty which already existed in cases of conspiracy[7] to cases where there is no combination, creating the new crime known as 'public mischief'. The question whether the particular act does or does not constitute a public mischief seems to rest with the judge,[8] the function of the jury being confined to the decision whether the prisoner did the acts with which he is charged.

¶ 447. *Its recent development.* In addition to cases like *R.* v. *Manley* in which the services of the police have been misdirected,[9] it has been

[1] A few days after this case Sir Robert Peel introduced the measure which became law as 5 and 6 Vict. c. 51 (*ante*, ¶ 425), a course which suggests that some doubt was felt as to the soundness of the law expounded by Lord Abinger.

[2] (1801) 2 East 4 (*T.A.C.*), at p. 21.

[3] *Ante*, ¶ 61. And see *Mod. Appr. Crim. Law*, 273 *et seq.*

[4] E.g. by Fitzjames Stephen (himself a distinguished judge), *Hist. Crim. Law*, III, 359; Stallybrass, 'Public mischief', 49 *L.Q.R.* 183; see also note on *R.* v. *Manley* on p. 153 of 49 *L.Q.R.*; and Jackson, 'Common law misdemeanours', *Mod. Appr. Crim. Law*, 292. And note *R.* v. *Johnson* (1678) 2 Show. 1 and the reporter's comment thereon. And see the claims made in the House of Lords in *Shaw* v. *D.P.P.* [1961] 2 W.L.R. 897 particularly at pp. 917 and 918, and the contrary view expressed by Lord Reid at pp. 921 *et seq.*

[5] [1933] 1 K.B. 529 (*T.A.C.*).

[6] Indeed in delivering judgment Lord Hewart, C.J., laid it down that 'all such acts or attempts as tend to the prejudice of the community are indictable', a sweeping statement which opens wide the door to an indefinite multiplication by the judiciary of criminal offences. Cf. C. K. Allen, *Legal Duties*, 245–6.

[7] *Post*, ¶ 448.

[8] Contrast the Libel Act of 1792 (32 Geo. III, c. 60).

[9] E.g. *R.* v. *Rose* (Westminster Police Court, 24 Feb. 1937), *Journal of Criminal Law* I, 172.

held to be a public mischief (although not on a direct charge of that offence, but on a charge of *conspiring* to effect it) where a clerk of works had falsely given progress reports of the proper erection of air-raid shelters whereas in fact the shelters were not built in accordance with the architect's specifications and were therefore ineffective and unsafe.[1] Again in 1936 it was held to be a public mischief to print and publish scandalous and libellous statements regarding His Majesty's Jewish subjects.[2] It is worthy of note that two years before *R.* v. *Manley* the Court of Criminal Appeal held (on a charge of conspiracy) that it was a public mischief to procure and use forged certificates of educational qualification in order to obtain admission as a student to one of the Inns of Court.[3]

But in 1953 doubts as to the soundness of the doctrine in *R.* v. *Manley* were voiced by the Court of Criminal Appeal in *R.* v. *Newland and others*[4] where it was stated:[5]

> It may be that *Manley's Case* will some day be considered by the House of Lords and in any case we venture to think that it would be a useful reform if such conduct as was there disclosed were made a summary offence by the legislature. We need not further enlarge upon it...except to say that in our considered opinion the safe course is no longer to follow it.

In *Police* v. *Brown*,[6] the defendant who had wasted the time of the police by sending a false telegram was successfully charged under section 66 of the Post Office Act, 1953. And in the Court of Appeal of Northern Ireland, in the case of a man who had knowingly made a false confession to the police implicating himself and two others in a murder, it was held that the appellant's acts were prejudicial to the administration of justice and constituted an indictable misdemeanour.[7]

(*f*) PUBLIC NUISANCE

¶ 447*a*. It is a misdemeanour at common law either by act or omission to cause substantial annoyance to the subjects of the Crown in general by exposing to danger or in other ways affecting injuriously their lives, health, property or even morals,[8] or by obstructing them in the exercise of the rights common to all subjects of the realm. The gist of the offence lies in the inconvenience[9] created, and not in the intention or even knowledge of the person held responsible, for example, as owner

[1] *R.* v. *Young* (1944) 30 Cr.App.R. 57.

[2] *R.* v. *Leese and Whitehead* (Sept. 1936, Central Criminal Court), 82 *Law Journal* (Newsp.) 310.

[3] *R.* v. *Bassey* (1931) 22 Cr.App.R. 160 (*T.A.C.*); *ante*, ¶ 377.

[4] (1953) 37 Cr.App.R. 154.

[5] At p. 167. See also the doubt expressed in *Joshua* v. *R.* [1955] A.C. 121 at p. 129.

[6] [1956] Crim. L.R. 568.

[7] *R.* v. *Bailey* [1956] N.I. 15 (*T.A.C.*). The judgment in this case should be carefully read by all students.

[8] *R.* v. *Quinn* [1961] 3 All E.R. 88.

[9] Which may be caused by smells, noise, vibration, pollution, distributing unwholesome food or drink, exposing men or animals to the risk of infectious diseases, the unlawful treatment of dead bodies, and so on.

or occupier of the land or premises from which the nuisance emanates. Owing to the wide range of offensive conduct covered by the common law under this head, and to the number of the statutes which have been enacted in addition in order to repress particular instances of interference with public health, morals and amenities, the law of public nuisance is too extensive a subject for convenient inclusion in a book for students who should therefore turn to the larger works[1] on criminal law for further information.

(g) AFFRAY

¶ 447b. Affray has been stated[2] to be the fighting of two or more persons in a public place, to the terror of the subjects of the Crown, and is a misdemeanour at common law; 'public place' seeming to mean a highway or other place where the public may be or pass as of right. Affray differs from riot in that it may be committed by as few as two persons; on the other hand an affray may fail to amount to riot even when many persons take part in it, for example, if general fighting breaks out in a crowd without there having been any concerted plan between them so to do. An affray may be aggravated by the special circumstances of the case[3] such as a deliberately staged duel or a forcible interference with officers of justice or when committed in the Queen's courts:[4] but in these cases the offence will probably fall within the law relating to aggravated assaults already discussed.[5] It has also been considered that an affray can be committed without actual violence, as by appearing armed with dangerous and strange weapons such as may naturally cause terror to the people.[6] In R. v. *Sharp and Johnson*[7] it was laid down that it is enough that the disturbance was proved to be such as might very well intimidate or frighten reasonable people and that it was not necessary to produce a witness who could state that he personally was terrified, so long as it was established that persons appeared to be alarmed. An affray is a disturbance but a disturbance is not *necessarily* an affray.[8]

[1] E.g. Halsbury's *Laws of England*, Russell on Crime, Archbold's *Criminal Pleading, Evidence and Practice*.

[2] 3 Co. *Inst.* 158; 4 Bl. *Com.* 144.

[3] See 1 Hawk. c. 63.

[4] An offence severely punishable; 1 Hawk. c. 21, ss. 6, 10. See also 3 Co. *Inst.* 140; 4 Bl. *Com.* 125; and Russ. 344.

[5] *Ante*, ¶ 168.

[6] 1 Hawk. c. 63, ss. 2, 4. See now the Prevention of Crime Act, 1953. Note also the Statute of Northampton (2 Ed. III, c. 3) which in effect forbids unauthorized display of force and arms before the Sovereign or his ministers or judges, or riding armed in fairs or markets etc.

[7] [1957] 2 W.L.R. 472.

[8] *R.* v. *Woodrow and others* (1959) 43 Cr.App.R. 105; disturbance is the genus, affray the species.

Chapter XXII

CONSPIRACY AND INDUSTRIAL DISPUTES

Section 1. Conspiracy

DEFINITION

¶ 448. In English law conspiracy first began as an agreement of persons who combined to carry on legal proceedings in a vexatious or improper way.[1] It was for a long time closely allied to attempts and was indeed often regarded as one form of attempt to commit a wrong. However, in modern times conspiracy has become a separate crime and is defined as the agreement of two or more persons to effect any unlawful purpose, whether as their ultimate aim or only as a means to it. This definition presents four points for notice: (*a*) the *actus reus*, (*b*) the persons agreeing, (*c*) the purpose agreed upon, (*d*) the *mens rea*.

(*a*) *Actus reus*. Agreement

¶ 449. It must not be supposed that conspiracy is a purely mental crime, consisting in the concurrence of the intentions of the parties. Here as everywhere in our law, bare intention is no crime. 'Agreement', as Lord Chelmsford puts it clearly, 'is an act in advancement of the intention which each person has conceived in his mind.'[2] It is not mere intention, but the announcement and acceptance of intentions. A distinction is to be drawn between the conspiracy and the overt acts which may be given as evidence of the conspiracy.[3] Bodily movement, by word or gesture, is indispensable to effect it. In order of time, this precedes the act agreed upon. But the fact of the parties having come to such an arrangement suffices to constitute a conspiracy.[4] Hence it is not necessary to show that they went on to commit some overt act towards carrying it out, though this (and also some consequent damage) would be necessary in an action of tort for conspiracy.[5] It follows that a person may be convicted of a conspiracy as soon as it has been formed, and before any overt act to carry out the agreed purpose has been committed. The offence is complete as soon as the parties have agreed as to their unlawful purpose, although nothing has yet been settled as to the means and devices to be employed for effecting it. Thus if two lovers

[1] See Stephen, *Hist. Crim. Law*, II, 228; Russ. ch. 100. As to the nature of conspiracy see 216 *L.T.* 552.

[2] *Mulcahy* v. *The Queen* (1868) L.R. 3 H.L. at p. 328.

[3] *R.* v. *Hammersley and others* (1958) 42 Cr.App.R. 207.

[4] *R.* v. *Gill* (1818) 2 B. and Ald. 204 (*T.A.C.*).

[5] *Mogul Steamship Co.* v. *McGregor, Gow & Co.* (1888) 21 Q.B.D., *per* Lord Coleridge, C.J., at p. 549; *Sorrell* v. *Smith* [1925] A.C. 700, 725–6.

agree to commit suicide together, but promptly think better of it, they nevertheless are liable to an indictment for conspiracy.[1] On the other hand, the actual accomplishment of the crime agreed upon will not cause the original offence of conspiracy to become 'merged' in it.[2] Hence it would be technically possible to bring an indictment for a conspiracy to commit some grave crime, and then support it by evidence that tends to show an actual consummation of the crime; but judges discourage such a course as unfair to the accused.[3]

Conversely it has been held that if a man is indicted for conspiracy to steal, and in another count for the completed crime of larceny, then if the jury find the accused not guilty of the larceny (i.e. not guilty of doing the things which he was charged with conspiring to do) but, on the same evidence, guilty of conspiracy, the conviction must be quashed on the ground that the jury's verdict of guilty of conspiracy as a specific offence under the first count was unreasonable.[4] This judgment must be read with care, and as applicable only to the facts of the case before the court, which, on the evidence (which the jury had refused to believe), showed only that the prisoners had completed their agreed purpose.

It is not necessary that the intended victims should be persons already ascertained. An indictment may charge a conspiracy to defraud 'such persons as might thereafter be induced to deal with' the conspirators.

(*b*) Two or more persons

¶ 450. The very name of the crime indicates that it is essentially one of combination; a man cannot by himself *con*-spire.[5] Moreover, the law applies here the old doctrine that for certain purposes husband and wife can be counted as one person, so that an unlawful combination by him and her alone does not amount to a conspiracy, even in a polygamous marriage.[6] But though there must be a plurality of conspirators, it is

[1] The question has been raised whether there is an indictable conspiracy when one of the parties has no intention to carry it out, and aims merely at getting money from the other under pretence of conspiring; but this would seem to be the common law misdemeanour of attempt to conspire. The question is critically discussed by Fridman, '*Mens rea* in conspiracy', 19 *Mod. L.R.* 276.

[2] As attempts *are* sometimes merged; see *ante*, ¶ 65, and Russ. ch. 6.

[3] See *R.* v. *Luberg* (1927) 19 Cr.App.R. at p. 137; 135 L.T. 414; *R.* v. *Boulton* (1871) 12 Cox 87, at p. 93; *R.* v. *West and others* [1948] 1 All E.R. 718, at p. 720 *et seq.*, where it was declared that a tendency to charge persons with criminal conspiracy rather than with the specific offences which the evidence shows them to have committed is not to be encouraged.

[4] *R.* v. *Cooper and Compton* [1947] 2 All E.R. 701 (*T.A.C.*), in which it was also stated that to clog a perfectly simple case of stealing in one or more instances with a count for conspiracy is not a proper course to adopt. The difficulties facing the court and jury (e.g. in *R.* v. *Sweetland* (1958) 42 Cr.App.R. 62) and the procedure to be followed, were indicated in *R.* v. *Dawson and Wenlock* [1960] 1 W.L.R. 163.

[5] So, on indictment of *A* and *B* for conspiring together, if *A* be acquitted, *B* cannot be convicted; *R.* v. *Plummer* [1902] 2 K.B. 339; *post*, ¶¶ 639, 736.

[6] *Mawji* v. *R.* [1957] 2 W.L.R. 277. See ¶ 45 *ante*, and Glanville Williams, 'Legal unity of husband and wife', 10 *Mod. L.R.* (1947), 16. But either spouse may be convicted of *inciting* the other to commit a crime if such be proved.

not necessary that all should be brought to trial together. One person may be indicted, alone, for conspiring with other persons who are not in custody, or who are even unknown to the indictors. Indeed, some of the conspirators may be unknown to the rest, provided all be acting under the directions of one leader. There need not be communication between each conspirator and every other, provided there be a design common to all.[1]

A conspirator who is also present at the time and scene of the crime will not necessarily be guilty of aiding and abetting in it; it depends on whether he renders assistance or, alternatively, if his presence of itself lends support and encouragement to the principal offender[2] and is intended so to do.

(*c*) An unlawful purpose

¶ 451. The term 'unlawful' is here used in a sense which is unique;[3] and, unhappily, it has never yet been defined precisely. The purposes which it comprises appear to be of the following species.

(i) Agreements to commit a substantive crime; e.g. a conspiracy to steal, or even merely to incite someone else to steal. This extends to all cases where it would be criminal for any of the conspirators to commit the act agreed upon, even though there be in the gang other persons in whom it would be no offence to commit it; and to all 'crimes', even non-indictable ones,[4] e.g. non-payment of poor rates.

(ii) Agreements to commit any tort that is malicious[5] or fraudulent. Some say that agreements to commit any tort, of whatever kind, are indictable as conspiracies. But the weight of authority[6] seems to be in favour of limiting the rule to torts of fraud or malice, thus excluding, for instance, a trespass committed *bona fide* by persons eager to assert their supposed right of way.

(iii) Agreements to commit a breach of contract under circumstances that are peculiarly injurious to the public.[7]

(iv) Agreements to do certain other acts, which (unlike all those hitherto mentioned) are not breaches of law at all, but which nevertheless are outrageously immoral or else are, in some way, extremely injurious to the public. We may quote, as instances,[8] agreements to facilitate the seduction of a woman;[9] or to run slackly in a race so as to

[1] *R.* v. *Meyrick and Ribuffi* (1929) 21 Cr.App.R. 94 (*T.A.C.*).

[2] See *ante*, ¶ 68.

[3] Contrast its sense in the Vagrancy Act; *post*, ¶ 485.

[4] *R.* v. *Whitchurch* (1890) 24 Q.B.D. 420. Cf. ¶ 430 *ante*; and Lord Campbell's 'If two men agree to blow their noses together during Divine Service so as to disturb the congregation, they may be indicted for conspiracy' (*Hansard*, 1 March 1859).

[5] Wright's *Criminal Conspiracy*, 40; e.g. to pirate a copyright book.

[6] The conflicting authorities are well collected in Harrison on Conspiracy, 91–6. See also 'Criminal conspiracy', 35 *Harvard L.R.* 393.

[7] *Vertue* v. *Lord Clive* (1779) 4 Burr. 2472 (*T.A.C.*). Cf. ¶ 456 *post*.

[8] And see the cases of public mischief discussed in ¶¶ 445–7 *ante*.

[9] *R.* v. *Howell* (1864) 4 F. and F. 160.

enable a confederate to win his bets;[1] or to hiss a play unfairly;[2] or to defraud a shipowner by secretly putting stowaways on board. Similar criminality would arise in agreements to raise by false reports the price of the Funds[3] or of any other vendible commodity;[4] or so to carry on trade as to diminish the revenue;[5] or to persuade a prosecutor not to appear at the trial; or to give false information to the police;[6] or to indemnify a prisoner's bail.[7] On the other hand, it is doubtful whether an agreement to make loud noises for the purpose of disturbing an invalid neighbour would be indictable as a conspiracy.[8] And a thrifty combination of poor-law authorities to marry a female pauper to a pauper of another parish, in order to relieve the ratepayers of the woman's parish, is not a conspiracy.[9] Yet some combinations for procurement of marriage will amount to conspiracy; e.g. taking a young woman of property from the custody of her relations in order to marry her to one of the conspirators.[10] And although some combinations 'in restraint of trade' may be so far illegal as to be unenforceable,[11] it is now settled that they do not necessarily constitute a criminal offence.[12] As to the question whether a conspiracy formed in England to effect some unlawful purpose abroad would be indictable here, the House of Lords[13] has laid it down that a conspiracy to commit a crime abroad is not indictable in this country unless the contemplated crime is one for which an indictment would lie here, and that a conspiracy to attain a lawful object by unlawful means, rather than to commit a crime, is not triable here when the unlawful means and the ultimate object are both outside the jurisdiction.[14]

¶ 452. *Vagueness of the word 'unlawful'*. The vagueness of the definition of this fourth class of 'unlawful' purposes—to say nothing of the minor uncertainties hanging over the second and third classes—is historically intelligible. For in days when our police system was ineffective, the law felt itself dangerously threatened by any concert amongst evildoers; and consequently, in the seventeenth and eighteenth centuries, indictments against conspirators were held good very readily. 'A con-

[1] *R.* v. *Orbell* (1704) 6 Mod. 42.

[2] *Gregory* v. *Duke of Brunswick* (1843) 6 Man. and Gr. 205.

[3] *R.* v. *De Berenger* (1814) 3 M. and S. 67 (*T.A.C.*) (the trial of Lord Cochrane).

[4] *R.* v. *Aspinall* (1876) 1 Q.B.D. 730 at p. 743, and 2 Q.B.D. 48 at p. 59.

[5] *R.* v. *Starling* (1663) 1 Sid. 174 (*T.A.C.*).

[6] *R.* v. *Barrett and Creager* (1899) C.C.C. Sess. Pap. CXXX. 797.

[7] *R.* v. *Porter* [1910] 1 K.B. 369; ¶ 706 *post.*

[8] Contrast *R.* v. *Lloyd* (1803) 4 Esp. 200, with *R.* v. *Levy* (1819) 2 Starkie 458.

[9] *R.* v. *Seward* (1834) 1 A. and E. 706 (*T.A.C.*). At Meldreth (Cambs.) in 1724 a widow who cost the ratepayers 70*s*. a year was thus got rid of for only 50*s*. 8*d*.

[10] *R.* v. *Wakefield* (1827) 2 Lew. 1; cf. *R.* v. *Thorp* (1696) 5 Mod. 221.

[11] *Mogul Steamship Co.* v. *McGregor, Gow & Co.* [1892] A.C. 25. [12] See ¶ 455 *post.*

[13] *Board of Trade* v. *Owen* [1957] 2 W.L.R. 351, *per* Lord Tucker at p. 366; 41 Cr.App.R. 11. And see *R.* v. *Naylor* [1961] 2 All E.R. 932.

[14] *R.* v. *Martin and others* [1956] 2 W.L.R. 975, where the indictment was quashed; see ¶ 739 *post.*

spiracy', said Holt, C.J., 'is odious in the law.'[1] But this vagueness renders it possible for judges to treat all combinations to effect any purpose which happens to be distasteful to them as indictable crimes, by declaring this purpose to be 'unlawful'.[2] Owing to this elasticity in the definition of the crime, and also to the unusually wide range of evidence by which (as we shall see) indictments for it may be supported, there was felt to be much justification for the language used by Fitzgerald, J., in reference to it, in the Irish State Trials of 1867: 'The law of conspiracy is a branch of our jurisprudence to be narrowly watched, to be jealously regarded, and never to be pressed beyond its true limits.' For, in the prudent words of one of the greatest of American judges: 'It is more safe that punishment should be ordained by general laws, formed upon deliberation, under the influence of no resentments, and without knowing on whom they are to operate, than that it should be inflicted under the influence of those passions which a trial seldom fails to excite, and which a flexible definition of the crime, or a construction that would render it flexible, might bring into operation.'[3] Now, however, in a recent case[4] before the House of Lords, a majority of judges manifested an attitude which could be regarded as inconsonant with the doctrine of the above citations, so that some may prefer the dissenting judgment (on the point of conspiracy) delivered by Lord Reith.[5]

(*d*) *Mens rea*

¶ 453. Since conspiracy is a crime at common law it follows that *mens rea* must be an essential element in it.[6] Yet perhaps because of the vagueness of 'unlawful purpose' the decisions of the courts do not seem to have laid down exactly what it is that the accused person must have intended or foreseen. In this connexion a statement made by the Court of Criminal Appeal in *R.* v. *Sorsky*[7] must be read with caution. The case before the court turned upon the interpretation of a statutory provision.[8] The court expressly alluded to 'the statement...that it is a good answer to a charge of having committed a misdemeanour at common law to show that the accused acted under a belief in the existence of a state of facts which, if true, would have exonerated him', and added 'We are in no way controverting that general proposition of law'.

It may be, however, that in the crime of conspiracy a claim of right is of no avail, in the same sense in which that claim is understood to provide a defence to a charge of malicious damage[9] or of larceny;[10] for

[1] 5 Mod. 407. [2] E.g. see *Shaw* v. *D.P.P.* [1961] 2 W.L.R. 897, *infra*.

[3] *Per* Marshall, C.J., in *Ex parte Bollman* (1807) 4 Cranch (U.S.A.) 127. The modern tendency was for the courts to require greater particularity in charges of conspiracy: e.g. *R.* v. *West and others* [1948] 1 All E.R. 718. And see now *Board of Trade* v. *Owen* [1957] 41 Cr.App.R. 11 at p. 54. [4] *Shaw* v. *D.P.P.* [1961] 2 W.L.R. 897.

[5] At pp. 921–9. [6] *Ante*, ¶ 11.

[7] 'A criminal conspiracy consists in the agreement to do an unlawful act without reference to the knowledge on the part of the accused of its illegality', [1944] 2 All E.R. 333, at p. 336D. [8] Prices of Goods Act, 1939; *R.* v. *Jacobs* [1944] K.B. 417.

[9] *Ante*, ¶ 187. [10] *Ante*, ¶ 281.

in *R.* v. *Sorsky* it was also stated:[1] 'It follows that, if Sorsky did act under any mistake at all, it was a mistake of law and not of fact, and ignorance of the law affords no excuse.'

WIDE RANGE OF EVIDENCE

¶ 454. As to the evidence admissible, the principles are just the same for conspiracy as for other crimes. But, owing to two peculiarities in the circumstances to which those principles are here applied, it often seems as if there were an unusual laxity in the modes of giving proof of an accusation of conspiracy.[2] For (*a*) it rarely happens that the actual fact of the conspiring can be proved by direct evidence, since such agreements are usually entered into both swiftly and secretly. Hence they ordinarily can be proved only by an inference from the subsequent conduct of the parties, in committing some overt acts which tend so obviously towards the alleged unlawful result as to suggest that they must have arisen from an agreement to bring it about.[3] Upon each of several isolated doings a conjectural interpretation is put; and from the aggregate of these interpretations an inference is drawn. The circumstantial evidence thus rendered necessary will often embrace a very wide range of acts, committed at widely different times and in widely different places.[4] The range of admissible evidence is still further widened (*b*) by the fact that each of the parties has, by entering into the agreement, adopted all his confederates as agents to assist him in carrying it out. Consequently, by the general doctrine as to principal and agent, any act done[5] subsequently for that purpose[6] by any of them will be admissible as evidence against him;[7] unless, before it was done, he had given them notice that he *withdrew* from the conspiracy. Just the same doctrine is, of course, applicable to any crime where a plurality of offenders are concerned, and so is not peculiar to trials for conspiracy. But in them it assumes unusual prominence, because in cases of conspiracy an unusually long interval often elapses—with consequently an

[1] At p. 337.

[2] See *R.* v. *Hunt* (1820) 1 St. Tr. (n.s.) 171 at p. 437; cf. *R.* v. *Langhorn* (1679) 7 St Tr. (n.s.) 417 at pp. 472–5.

[3] *R.* v. *Parnell* (1881) 14 Cox 505 (*T.A.C.*), *R.* v. *Parsons* (1762) 1 W.Bl. 391. For acts *not* obvious enough, see *R.* v. *Connolly* (1909) 3 Cr.App.R. 27 at pp. 31, 32.

[4] *R.* v. *Hammond and Webb* (1799) 2 Esp. 718 (*T.A.C.*).

[5] But not simply an *admission* uttered; see *post*, ¶ 618. The cobbler is the burglar's agent for mending the noiseless shoes, but not for uttering a remark as to the use they have been put to (though he can, of course, give evidence as to such a remark having been made by the burglar).

[6] But not acts that go beyond that purpose; e.g. where the purpose was only theft, yet murder was committed. Nor acts done after the purpose has been accomplished; e.g. the disposal of his share of the proceeds of the theft.

[7] Hence in trials for conspiracy a difficulty is apt to arise in determining at what stage the judge will pronounce the evidence to have given sufficient *prima facie* proof of a conspiracy, and of the defendant's being a party in it, to render it now permissible to give against him evidence of the conduct of his colleagues (furthering it) when he was *absent* from them.

unusually long series of acts—between the time when the common criminal purpose is formed and the time when it is carried out or is frustrated by arrest.

Moreover there is often, just as on every other protracted trial of a plurality of defendants, the danger that the jury may—even despite judicial warning—be influenced against one of the accused by evidence that is legally admissible only against another of them. Thirteen days were occupied at Birmingham in 1925 by the trial of a group of nineteen men for a conspiracy to defraud. To prevent any misapplication of evidence by the jury, the judge found it desirable to sum up against each prisoner separately, and took the verdict upon him before passing to the next man's case.

Conspiracy is a misdemeanour, punishable with fine and imprisonment, to which no limit is affixed. A conspiracy to murder is punishable with imprisonment for ten years, though it still remains only a misdemeanour (Offences against the Person Act, 1861, s. 4 as amended by the Criminal Justice Act, 1948).

SECTION 2. INDUSTRIAL DISPUTES

THE RIGHT TO STRIKE

¶ 455. It is now only of historical interest to consider how far combinations of employees to raise wages or improve conditions were criminal conspiracies at common law as being in restraint of trade or as designed to 'molest, ignore, or impoverish an individual, or to prevent him from carrying on his business.'[1] The right to strike was established beyond doubt by the Conspiracy and Protection of Property Act, 1875 (38 and 39 Vict. c. 86), which enacted (section 3) that 'An agreement or combination by two or more persons to do or procure to be done any act in contemplation or furtherance of a trade dispute between employers and workmen shall not be indictable as a conspiracy if such act committed by one person would not be punishable as a crime'. An individual who withholds his labour does not commit a crime. A strike which is in itself legal may, however, be accompanied by violence or other illegalities and the same section provides that 'Nothing in this section shall exempt from punishment any persons guilty of a conspiracy for which a punishment is awarded by any Act of Parliament' and that 'Nothing in this section shall affect the law relating to riot, unlawful assembly, breach of the peace, or sedition, or any offence against the State or the Sovereign'.

WHEN BREACHES OF CONTRACT MAY BE CRIMINAL

¶ 456. A strike may, though it need not, involve breaches of contract; but for an individual to break a contract is not ordinarily a crime, and

[1] Contrast *R.* v. *Bunn* (1872) 12 Cox 316 with the speech of Lord Bramwell in *Mogul Steamship Co.* v. *McGregor, Gow & Co.* [1892] A.C. 25, at p. 47. See Wright, *Criminal Conspiracy*, for the history.

a strike which involves broken contracts does not for that reason become a criminal conspiracy. But in the public interest certain breaches of contract have been made criminal. By the above Act of 1875 it is a crime punishable by a fine of £20 or imprisonment for not more than three months for any person employed by suppliers of gas or water (whether municipal authorities or private contractors) wilfully and maliciously to break a contract of service knowing or having reasonable cause to believe that the probable consequences of his so doing, either alone or in combination with others, will be to deprive the inhabitants of any place wholly or partly of their supply of gas or water. These provisions were extended by the Electricity (Supply) Act, 1919,[1] to electricity undertakings. Similar penalties are also imposed by the Act of 1875 on any person who wilfully or maliciously breaks any contract of service knowing or having reasonable cause to believe that the probable consequences of so doing, either alone or in combination with others, will be to endanger human life, or cause serious bodily injury, or to expose valuable property to destruction or serious injury.

INTIMIDATION AND MOLESTATION OF FELLOW-WORKMEN

¶ 457. While, apart from breaches of contract, a man is free to withhold his labour as he wills, he is not free to coerce others into withholding theirs. The right to work is as important as the right to strike. It is impossible for the law to interfere with the pressure of the opinions of a man's fellow-workmen, but the law will not allow pressure to take the form of intimidation or molestation. By the Conspiracy and Protection of Property Act, 1875, s. 7, it is an offence, subject to a penalty of a fine of £20 or imprisonment for not more than three months, wrongfully and without legal authority, with a view to compelling any other person to abstain from doing or to do any act which such other person has a legal right to do or abstain from doing,

(1) to use violence to or to intimidate[2] such other person or his wife or children, or to injure his property,

(2) persistently to follow such other person about from place to place,

(3) to hide any tools, clothes or other property owned or used by such other person, or to deprive him of, or to hinder him in, the use thereof,

(4) to watch or beset[3] the house or other place where such other person resides, or works, or carries on business, or happens to be, or the approach to such house or place,

(5) to follow such other person with two or more other persons in a disorderly manner in or through any street or road.

By the Trade Disputes Act, 1906 (6 Edw. VII, c. 47, s. 2), it was declared lawful for 'one or more persons, acting on their own behalf or on behalf of a trade union or of an individual employer or firm in

[1] As modified by the Electricity Act, 1947, sch. IV.

[2] For the meaning of 'intimidate' see the cases given in Arch. 3729.

[3] For the meaning of these words see the cases given in Arch. 3731.

contemplation or furtherance of a trade dispute, to attend at or near a house or place where a person resides or works or carries on business or happens to be, if they so attend merely for the purpose of peacefully obtaining or communicating information, or of peacefully persuading any person to work or abstain from working'.

TRADE DISPUTES ACT, 1906

¶ 458. The protection against the common law of conspiracy given by section 3 of the Act of 1875 (*ante*, ¶ 455) extends only to acts 'in furtherance of a trade dispute'. By the Trade Disputes Act, 1906, protection was given against civil liability for certain acts done in contemplation or furtherance of a trade dispute, and by section 5 (3) of that Act the expression 'trade dispute' was defined as follows for the purposes of both that Act and the Act of 1875:

> The expression 'trade dispute' means any dispute between employers and workmen, or between workmen and workmen, which is connected with the employment or non-employment, or the terms of employment, or with the conditions of labour, of any person, and the expression 'workmen' means all persons employed in trade or industry, whether or not in the employment of the employer with whom a trade dispute arises.[1]

It is clear that this definition is wide enough to cover 'sympathetic strikes' and that the protection given cannot be confined to acts done by parties to a dispute. It was, however, contended[2] that the General Strike of 1926 was not in furtherance of a trade dispute and was illegal as being designed to bring pressure not upon employers but upon the Government.

[1] The words 'between employers and workmen' in s. 3 of the Act of 1875 were expressly repealed.

[2] And it was so decided by Astbury, J., in *National Sailors' and Firemen's Union* v. *Reed* [1926] Ch. 536; but for a powerful argument to the contrary see Prof. A. L. Goodhart's 'The legality of the General Strike in England' in *Essays in Jurisprudence and the Common Law*, ch. XI.

Chapter XXIII

PERJURY AND OTHER OFFENCES AGAINST PUBLIC JUSTICE

SECTION I. PERJURY

HISTORY

¶ 459. *Early limitations.* In Anglo-Saxon legal procedure, judicial oaths played a very important part, being taken both by jurors and by compurgators. Both these classes were punishable for any perjuries they uttered. But the functions of the modern witness had not yet been differentiated from those of the juror; and perjury by witnesses was consequently an unknown crime.[1] And when, in the fourteenth century, witnesses began to be brought in to inform the jury, perjury by them was not made a punishable offence. Hence it became a maxim that the law regarded every witness's oath as true. Even the ecclesiastical courts, though treating breaches of faith in general as matters within their jurisdiction, took no notice of the grave breach of faith involved in giving false witness. But, before the end of the fifteenth century, the Star Chamber sometimes interposed to punish perjuries. And, in the sixteenth century, Parliament itself began to interfere with the immunity of witnesses, dealing in 1540[2] with subornation of perjury, and in 1562[3] with perjury itself. But for each of these offences it imposed only a pecuniary penalty, recoverable civilly by a penal action. Finally, however, the Star Chamber, in 1613, declared perjury by a witness to be punishable at common law.[4]

¶ 460. *Subsequent extension.* The offence thus created was one which could only be committed in a judicial proceeding,[5] and by a witness who gave false evidence on oath. But the law gradually came to assume a far more complicated form. Parliament specified various matters which were not judicial proceedings, yet in which the telling a falsehood upon oath was to be a perjury. Again, some classes of witnesses came to be allowed by statute to give evidence in judicial proceedings on mere affirmation, without any oath; and falsehood by them, though no perjury, was made as severely punishable as if it were one. Moreover, the judges proceeded to declare that, in any matter wherein the law required an oath to be taken, the taking it falsely—if it were not judicial, and so not a perjury—would be at least a common law

[1] See Pollock and Maitland, II, 542; Stephen, *Hist. Crim. Law*, III, 240.

[2] 32 Hen. VIII, c. 9, s. 3.

[3] 5 Eliz. I c. 9.

[4] *R.* v. *Rowland ap Eliza* (1613) 3 Co. *Inst.* 164.

[5] *The Keepers of the Liberties* v. *Gwinn* (1652) Style 336.

misdemeanour,[1] punishable with fine and imprisonment, though not with the penalties of perjury.

THE PERJURY ACT, 1911

¶ **461.** The multifarious rules on these subjects have now been reduced to a comparatively simple and logical form. The task of codifying our criminal law, a task attempted by the statesmen of a few generations ago[2] on a comprehensive scale but with no practical result, was resumed in 1910 by Lord Loreburn in a more fragmentary manner but with legislative success. For he carried the Perjury Act, 1911 (1 and 2 Geo. V, c. 6), which modifies not only the common law but also the provisions of upwards of a hundred and thirty Acts of Parliament.

It creates, or continues, numerous offences of false public statement. All, however severely punishable, are only misdemeanours. In each of them the offence lies in the breach of the oath or affirmation or declaration; that breach constituting only one single crime, however many be the lies that falsify the evidence. A fresh lie does not create a fresh perjury, but is merely a fresh proof of the one general perjury; or, in technical phrase, 'matter for a new *assignment* of perjury'. 'Assertory' oaths, not 'promissory' ones, are concerned.

CLASSIFICATION AND DEFINITION

Grade A. (i) Falsehood in judicial proceedings

¶ **462.** The statute[3] classifies the offences into three grades, A, B and C.

Grade A, the most heinous, consists of the offences punishable with seven years' imprisonment, or with a fine, or both. Of these offences there are several.

'Perjury' is a term which henceforth is restricted, as it was originally, to the case of *forensic* false evidence. It is defined—section 1 (1)—as the crime committed when a person, lawfully 'sworn'[4] as a witness (or an interpreter) in a *judicial* proceeding wilfully makes a statement, material in that proceeding, which he knows to be false or which he does not believe to be true. The expression 'sworn' is here not limited to religious oaths, but includes also the taking of a legal affirmation or declaration—section 15 (2). Under the Children and Young Persons Act, 1933,[5] if a child of tender years, who is allowed by the court to give unsworn evidence,[6] wilfully gives false evidence in such circumstances that, if the evidence had been given on oath, he would have been guilty of perjury, he may on summary conviction be dealt with as if he had been summarily convicted of an indictable offence punishable in the case of an adult with imprisonment.[7]

[1] *R.* v. *Foster* (1821) R. and R. 459.

[2] In the Criminal Code Bill of 1879; [C. 2345].

[3] As amended by the Criminal Justice Act, 1948.

[4] See *R.* v. *Singh* (1958) 42 Cr.App.R. 44; ¶ 584 *post.*

[5] Sect. 38.

[6] *R.* v. *Clark* [1962] 1 W.L.R. 180; *Post,* ¶ 583.

[7] For the punishments available in the case of children, see ¶¶ 758 and 763 *post.*

¶ 463. *Meaning of 'judicial'*. The term 'judicial' is employed here in a wide sense which will cover not only inferior courts, like petty sessions, or courts outside the common law, like a court martial, but even many matters of administrative business. For it is to include—section 1 (2)—all proceedings 'before any court, tribunal, or person, having by law the power to hear, receive, and examine evidence on oath'.[1] An action brought against a non-existent person has been held to be a judicial proceeding.[2] Yet clearly the offence will not be committed unless the evidence be actually taken before a person who has legal power to take it. Thus when a registrar in bankruptcy, who was presiding over the examination of a debtor, left the room to discharge other duties but bade the solicitor go on questioning the debtor, false answers given after his leaving were held to be no perjury.[3] And when justices of the peace held an informal preliminary meeting, at which they took evidence, in order to lighten the labour of their statutory licensing session, a witness who swore falsely at this unauthorized meeting was held to have committed no offence.[4]

(ii) False oaths in non-judicial proceedings

¶ 464. Similar conduct when committed, outside all judicial proceedings, by a person who has been 'required or authorized by law to make any statement on "oath" [including, by section 15, affirmation or declaration] for any purpose'; section 2 (1).

In these two crimes of grade A, in which, whether in a judicial or a non-judicial proceeding, the offender has been 'sworn', it is not necessary that his statement should be false at all. The man becomes punishable simply through uttering an assertion, false or true, which he does not positively 'believe to be true'; section 1 (1), section 2 (1). For a man who tells the truth quite unintentionally is morally a liar. Bracton (fo. 289) enforces this principle by the grotesque illustration of a Jewish juryman who, by concurring in a verdict that Christ was born of a virgin, committed a perjury, whilst his Christian colleagues of course committed none.[5] Conversely, false swearing is no crime when it is not wilful, but simply inadvertent (see ¶ 469).

¶ 465. *The statement must be material.* On the other hand, a rule of leniency[6] is borrowed by the Act from the older law, for these two important offences in grade A and also for one—viz. B—of those that

[1] Difficulties as to the common law 'territoriality' of criminal jurisdiction (*post*, ¶ 641) the Act obviates by treating as perjuries punishable in this country not only such as are committed here for the purposes of a judicial proceeding in colonial or foreign territory (s. 1 (4)), but also (s. 1 (5)) all that are committed for the purposes of an English judicial proceeding, though committed in other parts of the Queen's dominions or (if before a British functionary) even in some foreign country.

[2] *R.* v. *Castiglione* (1912) 106 L.T. 1023. [3] *R.* v. *Lloyd* (1887) 19 Q.B.D. 213.

[4] *R.* v. *Shaw* (1911) 6 Cr.App.R. 103.

[5] Falsity as to a *mental* fact suffices, e.g. the witness's belief, or his 'I cannot remember'; *R.* v. *Schlesinger* (1847) 10 Q.B. 670.

[6] The Indian and Canadian Penal Codes show no such leniency.

are less heinous. For in these three crimes no guilt is incurred by a wilful false statement unless it be 'material'[1] to the proceeding, or the purpose, for which it was made. However, the judges construe the rule very narrowly. Thus they have held that the evidence need not be material to the actual issue of the litigation—a lie about his solvency by a man who merely offers himself as bail is sufficiently material to a criminal prosecution. Again, evidence may be sufficiently 'material' even though it were material, not intrinsically, but only by its facilitating the jury's acceptance of other testimony which had an intrinsic materiality,[2] so that trivial details, mentioned by a witness in giving his account of a transaction, may become important by their leading the jury to believe that his knowledge of the transaction is complete, and his evidence therefore likely to be accurate. On the same ground, all statements made by a witness as to matters that affect his credibility are material,[3] e.g. his denial of having been convicted of a crime. And even if the false evidence were legally inadmissible, yet this need not prevent its being regarded as 'material' enough to form the subject of an indictment for perjury. There is, for instance, a rule that when a witness answers questions that relate merely to his own credibility,[4] his answers are to be taken as final, so that no other witness can legally be brought to contradict them. Yet if, by a breach of this rule, some second witness be permitted to give this contradiction, and he give it falsely, he may be indicted for perjury; for, so soon as the contradiction was admitted, it did affect the credit given to the previous witness, and so became 'material'.[5]

The long-disputed question whether it is for the judge or for the jury to say if a statement was or was not 'material', is determined by the Act in favour of the judge; section 1 (6).

(iii) False affidavits

¶ 466. The wilful use of a false affidavit for the purposes of the Bills of Sale Act, 1878;[6] section 2 (2).

This first grade of crimes includes the following two offences which may be committed even when no formal oath or affirmation has been taken.[7]

False statements, declarations, etc., whether they be 'sworn' to or not,

[1] I.e. such as might actually affect the mind of the tribunal. Materiality as to the *sentence* suffices, *R.* v. *Wheeler* [1917] 1 K.B. 283.

[2] 'A witness's statements as to his identity—his name, abode, position in life—are material. For they affect the degree of trust which the jury will give him.' *Per* Darling, J., at C.C.C., 12 Jan. 1923.

[3] *R.* v. *Baker* [1895] 1 Q.B. 797 (*T.A.C.*). The point was not accepted in *R.* v. *Holden* (1872) 12 Cox 167 (*T.A.C.*).

[4] *Post*, ¶ 557.

[5] *R.* v. *Gibbon* (1862) L. and C. 109.

[6] 41 and 42 Vict. c. 31.

[7] The Criminal Justice Act, 1925 (s. 28), allows in *both* these two offences the alternative of trial at petty sessions; but in that case the utmost punishment for either would be a fine of £50.

made with reference to the celebration or registration of a marriage; section 3 (1).[1]

False statements, sworn to or not, with reference to the registration of a birth or of a death; section 4 (1).

Grade B. Statutory declarations

¶ 467. A group of less serious offences consists of some that are punishable only with two years' imprisonment, or a fine, or both (section 5).

In these no oath has been taken. They are committed when statements, wilfully false in a *material* particular, are made in a 'statutory declaration',[2] or in some document which the offender was authorized or required to make, or some oral declaration or answer which he was required to make, by a public general Act of Parliament.[3]

Grade C. Registration of practitioners

¶ 468. The least heinous grade is that of the offences for which the punishment is imprisonment for a year with or without a fine, or a fine alone. These offences arise when a man makes (either in writing or orally) a representation 'which he knows to be false or fraudulent' for the purpose of getting himself registered, or of procuring a certificate of someone's being registered, on the statutory roll of persons legally qualified to practise a particular calling—e.g. medicine or dentistry (section 6).[4]

¶ 469. *Wilfulness essential.* In all these various offences, from perjury downwards, wilfulness is an element essential to guilt. The man who makes an untrue assertion, but with an honest belief that it is true, commits no crime. His clerk made out the account, or his solicitor prepared the affidavit; and then he, on reading it over, felt no doubt of its correctness. Though due to inadvertence or forgetfulness or even careless and stupid mistake, his untrue words were not due to wilfulness. It is therefore not sufficient evidence that the accused had made, on oath, two contradictory statements, since he might have been honestly mistaken on the one occasion and had tried to correct his mistake on the other—or had honestly suffered from a lapse of memory.[5]

[1] The entry of the word 'bachelor' by a man previously divorced was held not to be a false statement within this section, *R.* v. *Peters* [1955] Crim. L.R. 712; and in *R.* v. *Frickey* [1956] Crim.L.R. 421 a document recording a parent's consent was held not to be mandatory, and therefore the forgery of it is not within the section.

[2] See the Statutory Declaration Acts, 1835 (5 and 6 Will. IV, c. 62). For details of the alternative of trial at petty sessions see the Magistrates' Courts Act, 1952 *post*, ¶ 679 *et seq.*

[3] As when a voter is questioned by the returning officer at a general election.

[4] The Act is so comprehensively framed that perhaps no form of public statement is omitted. But what of false statements given orally, and not on oath, by a witness at a local government public inquiry? For false statements made to procure motor licences, etc., see Road Traffic Act, 1960, s. 235.

[5] *R.* v. *Jackson* (1823) 1 Lew. 270 (*T.A.C.*).

The case would be different if, instead of an actual belief that his assertion was true, he had had no belief either way;[1] for, by making the assertion, he pledged himself that his mind was not a blank with regard to it, so he lied 'wilfully'. It may, however, be doubted whether such non-belief would support a conviction for those offences which the Act requires to be committed not only wilfully but *knowingly*.

SUBORNATION

¶ **470.** If anyone incites a person to commit either perjury or any other offence against the Act, he commits, of course (*ante*, ¶ 58), a misdemeanour for which he may be fined and imprisoned. But if his incitement prove so successful that the other man does commit the offence, there is then an actual subornation; and for this the suborner may be visited with as severe a punishment as for the perjury, or other offence, itself (section 7).

THE AMOUNT OF EVIDENCE NEEDED

¶ **471.** For all the above-mentioned offences a time-honoured precaution, which the common law of evidence imposed in prosecutions for perjury, is perpetuated. By section 13, a person shall not be liable to be convicted of *any offence* against this Act (or of any offence declared by any other Act to be, or to be punishable as, perjury or subornation of perjury) solely upon the evidence of one witness as to the falsity of any statement alleged to be false. Otherwise there would but be one man's oath against another's—the statement originally sworn to by the defendant and, on the other hand, the contradiction of it now sworn to by the witness for the prosecution. (See *post*, ¶ 598.) But it is sufficient if this one direct witness be corroborated by some admission which the prisoner has made, or by circumstantial evidence.[2]

SECTION 2. OTHER OFFENCES AGAINST PUBLIC JUSTICE

FALSE INFORMATION

¶ **472.** A number of modern statutes have made it an offence to give false information regarding the various matters with which they deal. It is outside the scope and purpose of the present book to do more than state that they include the Sugar Industry (Reorganization) Act, 1936, the Cotton Spinning Industry Act, 1936, the Liabilities (War-Time Adjustment) Act, 1941, the Coal Industry Nationalization Act, 1946.

FABRICATION OF EVIDENCE

¶ **473.** It is held to be an indictable misdemeanour at common law to do an act which shows a tendency and is intended to pervert the administration of public justice, and this includes the fabrication of

[1] See *Smith* v. *Chadwick* (1884) 9 A.C. 187 at p. 203.

[2] Cf. *R.* v. *Saldanha* (1921) 85 J.P. 47; *R.* v. *Hook* (1858) D. and B. 606 (*T.A.C.*).

false evidence even if it is never used.[1] Similarly it is a misdemeanour to persuade a witness to give at the trial an account different from that given at the police court.[2]

CONTEMPT OF COURT

¶ 473a. Properly speaking contempt of court is a common law offence which was held to consist in 'scandalising the court'[3] by uttering in court disparaging or offensive words to the judge in court, or by uttering such disparaging remarks out of court concerning judges of the superior courts, in relation to their office or otherwise.[4] The term, however, is commonly used in a wider sense to cover any representation[5] intended or calculated to interfere with the fair trial of a legal proceeding pending in any court of justice. The offence is regarded objectively and it is immaterial that there was no intention to affect the course of justice or that there was no moral blame in reporter, editor, or proprietor of the enterprise[6] concerned, the responsibility being either direct or vicarious.[7]

MAINTENANCE

¶ 474. It is a common law misdemeanour to procure, without lawful justification, any person to institute, carry on, or defend civil proceedings.[8] It is not essential that money should be provided by the accused; for it is maintenance where there is any wanton and officious intermeddling with the disputes of others in which the defendant has no interest whatever, and where the assistance he renders to one or the other party is without justification or excuse.[9] A legitimate interest extends as far as a bare contingency[10] and even kinship,[11] and a gift of money can be justified if it is made by way of pure charity.[12]

CHAMPERTY

¶ 475. Champerty is the name[13] given to the special instance of maintenance where a plaintiff or defendant agrees with someone (the

[1] *R.* v. *Vreones* [1891] 1 Q.B. 360, *per* Pollock, B.; followed in *R.* v. *Smalley* [1959] Crim. L.R. 587.

[2] *R.* v. *Greenburg* (1919) 121 L.T. 288. Cf. 'Depositions', *post*, ¶ 709.

[3] *Re Read and Hugginson* (1742) 2 Atk. 469.

[4] But see now *Macleod* v. *St. Aubyn* [1899] A.C. 549 at p. 550 and Russ. ch. 17.

[5] *R.* v. *Jolliffe* (1791) 4 T.R. 285, dissemination of exculpatory statements; *R.* v. *Williams* (1823) 2 L.J. (o.s.) K.B. 30; *R.* v. *Tibbits* [1902] 1 K.B. 77, publication of results of private investigator into the crime charged. *Att.-Gen.'s Application, in re,* [1962] 2 W.L.R. 70.

[6] Not confined to newspapers.

[7] *R.* v. *Evening Standard Co.* [1954] 1 Q.B. 578.

[8] See Russ. ch. 23.

[9] *British Cash etc.* v. *Lamson Store Co.* [1908] 1 K.B. at 1014; *Neville* v. *London Express Newspaper Ltd.* [1919] A.C. 368. See Winfield, *Abuse of Procedure*, chs. III–V.

[10] See Russ. 392.

[11] But only near relatives may lawfully spend money on the cause.

[12] See *Harris* v. *Brisco* (1886) 17 Q.B.D. 504, at p. 512.

[13] Derived from *champ* and *partir*.

champertor) in return for his support to divide with him the land or other property sued for, if they are successful in the proceedings.[1] So if strangers put up money to maintain litigation for recovery of property on the understanding that they are to be repaid out of the property if recovered, they are guilty of both maintenance and champerty.[2] It is an offence at common law although some ancient statutes expressly dealt with certain cases of it.[3]

BARRATRY

¶ 476. Another form of unlawful traffic in litigious quarrels is barratry, which is defined as habitually to move, excite, or maintain suits or quarrels in the courts. The indictment must charge the accused with being 'a common barrator', and therefore to prove no more than one act of this kind will not be enough. This crime is now rare and the last recorded case appears to have occurred in 1889.[4]

[1] See *Haseldine* v. *Hosken* [1933] 1 K.B. 822.

[2] See *Sprye* v. *Porter* (1856), 7 E. and B. 58.

[3] (1275), 3 Edw. I, c. 25; (1285), 13 Edw. I, c. 49; (1300), 28 Edw. I, c. 11; (1305), 33 Edw. I, *Diffinitio de conspiratoribus*.

[4] *R.* v. *Bellgrave*, 1889, Guildford assizes; Arch. (26th ed.), 1195.

Chapter XXIV

OFFENCES AGAINST INTERNATIONAL LAW

¶ 477. *Three main divisions.* In order to discharge the duties to other nations (of so-called civilized mankind) which are imposed alike by political prudence and by international law, English criminal law has made provision for the punishment of persons who (1) commit acts of piracy or (2) commit certain breaches of the neutrality due to belligerent nations, or (3) infringe the established privileges of ambassadors sent to us by foreign governments.

SECTION 1. PIRACY

¶ 478. It has been said[1] that piracy *jure gentium* is only a sea term for robbery, piracy being robbery within the jurisdiction of the Admiralty. 'If the mariners of any ship shall violently dispossess the master, and shall afterwards carry away the ship itself or any of the goods...with a felonious intention...this is robbery and piracy....' This statement, however, is not sufficiently precise for a definition, and indeed there has not so far been given an authoritative definition of this crime.[2] A piratical robbery is not quite the same as actual robbery; moreover, an unsuccessful attempt to commit a piratical robbery is as much piracy *jure gentium* as if the robbery had been actually effected.[3] Violence is certainly essential, and therefore mere larceny will not suffice. Perhaps the best approach to a correct definition is: Any armed violence at sea which is not a lawful act of war;[4] e.g. by mutineers on board. For a pirate must be one who may be taken to be a source of danger to the vessels of all nations; and therefore those who act solely against a particular belligerent and in the interests of the Power that is at war with it are not pirates, even though they go beyond their commission.[5] Nor will they be, even though their action be spontaneous and without any commission at all from the Power (whether a recognized State or not)

[1] *R.* v. *Dawson* (1696) 13 St. Tr. 454; and see *Att.-Gen. of Hong Kong* v. *Kwok-a-Sing* (1873) L.R. 5 P.C. 199; *China Navigation Co. Ltd.* v. *Att.-Gen.* [1932] 2 K.B. at p. 222.

[2] Stephen, *Hist. Crim. Law*, II, 27.

[3] *In re Piracy jure gentium* [1934] A.C. 586 (*T.A.C.*).

[4] Of this definition the Privy Council said, *ibid.*, 'Possibly the definition of piracy which comes nearest to accuracy coupled with brevity is that given by Kenny in *Outlines of Criminal Law* when he said: "Piracy is armed violence at sea which is not a lawful act of war", though even that would include a shooting affray between two passengers on a liner, which could not be held to be piracy.'

[5] 'Enemies not of the human race, but solely of a particular State'; for the essence of piracy 'consists in the pursuit of private, as contrasted with public, ends'; see *Republic of Bolivia* v. *Indemnity Co. Ltd.* [1909] 1 K.B. 785.

whose interests they serve.[1] But, whatever be the precise limits of piracy *jure gentium*, it is at least clear that anything that does not fall within them would not be regarded as a piracy at common law.

EXTENSION OF COMMON LAW BY STATUTE

¶ 479. But by statute it has further been made piracy:

(*a*) for any British subject to commit hostilities at sea under the commission of any foreign Power, against *other British subjects*;[2]

(*b*) for any British subject, or any resident in the British dominions, to take part in the slave trade.[3]

Every piracy, whether of the common law form or of the statutory, is a felony,[4] and punishable with imprisonment for life. It is an offence now almost unknown in our criminal courts, five persons having been charged in 1894 and none since.[5]

SECTION 2. BREACH OF NEUTRALITY

¶ 480. Previous to the nineteenth century, there was no hindrance in the way of an Englishman's following the profession of a soldier of fortune wheresoever he chose, saving only the claim of the King of England to his continued loyalty, and perhaps to his services if they should be needed.[6] The former right of the King was considered to be in jeopardy in James I's reign, and an Act (3 Jac. I, c. 4) was passed with the object of preventing subjects of the Crown from being contaminated in religion or loyalty by the Jesuits whom they might meet in Continental armies.[7] The second right appears to have been in the mind of the framers of the statute passed in 1736,[8] now repealed, which made it felony, without benefit of clergy, to enlist in the service of any foreign prince, an enactment which seems, however, to have remained a dead letter. But the modern development of international law created a new reason for similar prohibitions; and in the nineteenth century Foreign Enlistment Acts were passed with the object of preserving England's neutrality, by forbidding her subjects to give any assistance to foreign belligerents. In treatises on international law the student will find narrated the growth of the principle of neutrality, as determining the course of conduct to which nations are now bound to adhere, whenever a condition of war exists between Powers with whom they themselves are at peace. The ancient powers of the Crown in England being insufficient to enable it to prevent its subjects from committing acts which

[1] *In re Tivnan* (1864) 5 B. and S. at p. 680. Cf. *Republic of Bolivia* v. *Indemnity Co.*, *supra*.

[2] 11 and 12 Will. III, c. 7, s. 7.

[3] 5 Geo. IV, c. 113, s. 9.

[4] Piracy Acts of 1698, 1721 and 1837 as amended by the Criminal Justice Act, 1948, sect. 1 (1).

[5] *Criminal Statistics of England and Wales* (issue of 1901), 29.

[6] See Stephen, *Hist. Crim. Law*, III, 257–62.

[7] See the preamble to the Act.

[8] 9 Geo. II, c. 30.

might be at variance with the modern conceptions of the obligations of neutrality, Parliament found it necessary to make participation in foreign hostilities a criminal offence. The first Foreign Enlistment Act was passed in 1819,[1] to restrain outbursts of sympathy with the revolt of Spain's South American colonies against her. During the American Civil War, it proved insufficient to prevent the traffic between English ship-builders and the Confederate Government, and was accordingly replaced in 1870 by a more stringent enactment.[2]

THE FOREIGN ENLISTMENT ACT, 1870

¶ 481. Under this Act, the chief offences forbidden are:

(1) To enlist oneself or others—without a licence from the Crown—for service under a foreign State which is at war with a State that is at peace with us.[3]

(2) To equip, build,[4] despatch, or even agree to build within British dominions—without a licence from the Crown—a ship, with reasonable cause to believe that it will be employed in such service as aforesaid.[5]

(3) To fit out, within the British dominions—without a licence from the Crown—any naval or military expedition to proceed against the dominions of any State that is at peace with us.[6]

Each of these offences is a misdemeanour, punishable with a fine and with imprisonment for a period not exceeding two years. All ships or munitions of war in respect of which the offence is committed are to be forfeited to the Crown.

SECTION 3. OFFENCES AGAINST AMBASSADORS

¶ 482. As regards offences against the privileges of ambassadors, it is unnecessary to add to the brief mention that has already been made of the statute of 1708,[7] which made it a misdemeanour (with remarkable peculiarities of procedure) to execute even a judicial civil process against the person or goods of any ambassador or his registered servant.

The student must bear in mind that, though it is sometimes said that 'international law is part of the laws of England', this is true only in that loose historical sense in which the same is also said of Christianity. But an indictment will not lie in English law for not loving your neighbour as yourself. Equally little will it lie for trading in contraband of war, or for the running of a blockade in a war between two other countries. Both these acts are visited by international law with the

[1] 59 Geo. III, c. 69. [2] 33 and 34 Vict. c. 90.

[3] Sect. 4. This is an offence whether committed within *or even without* the British dominions.

[4] The previous Act (of 1819) forbade nothing short of the ultimate 'equipping, fitting-out, or arming' of a ship. See the case of *The Alexandra* (1864) 2 H. and C. 431.

[5] Sect. 58.

[6] Sect. 11; see *R.* v. *Jameson* [1896] 2 Q.B. 425.

[7] 7 Anne, c. 12; *ante*, ¶ 74.

penalties of confiscation; but neither of them constitutes any offence against the laws of England, and it has been held that it is not sufficiently unlawful to render void a contract connected with it.[1] But difficult questions may arise in civil law.[2]

[1] See *Ex parte Chavasse* (1864) 4 De G. J. and S. 655. To trade with persons domiciled in a country with which *our own* country is at war seems to have been regarded in William III's time as an indictable misdemeanour at common law. Cf. a case in 1319 of trading with Scotland during our war with her (Rolle's Abr. *tit.* Prerogative). But in 1817 Sir Samuel Romilly repudiated this doctrine as one which 'no one' would now hold (*Life of Robert Aspland*, 383). In 1914 it was made a statutory misdemeanour, punishable with seven years' penal servitude, for any one thus to trade with the enemy 'during *the present war*', except in such transactions as might be permitted by royal proclamation (4 and 5 Geo. V, c. 87). See the Trading with the Enemy Act, 1939.

[2] See *Foster* v. *Driscoll* [1929] 1 K.B. 470, at pp. 510, 520–2.

Chapter XXV

OFFENCES OF VAGRANCY

SECTION I. HISTORY

¶ 483. The historical interest and the juridical anomalies of the Vagrancy Act are such as to justify a fuller reference to it here than the importance of the offences created by it might seem to call for. An experienced observer of criminal proceedings has pronounced it, somewhat sweepingly, to be 'the most unconstitutional law yet lingering on the statute book'.[1] It is a survival from a long series of penal enactments—enforced by imprisonment, flogging, enslavement, and death—whereby the legislature strove to grapple with the difficulties created by the steady increase in the numbers of the migratory population. Legislation for this purpose began as far back as 1388, when the dearth of labourers, caused by the devastations of the Black Death in the period 1348–69, had produced competition amongst employers and, consequently, many migrations of labourers towards the districts where they could profit by this competition. The legislature interposed in order to check both the rise of wages consequent upon all such free exchange between labour and capital, and also some more genuine evils, arising from the mendicancy of such of the wanderers as did not obtain employment, and the dishonesty of many of them who did not even seek for it. To this latter class of vagrants an addition was made in the reign of Henry VIII by the arrival of the first gypsies. The establishment under Elizabeth I of a compulsory parochial assessment, for the relief of the destitute, naturally led to the imposition of further penalties to protect parishes from the arrival of strangers who might become a burden on the local assessment. The modern reform of our industrial legislation and of our former system of poor relief has now swept away almost the whole of the long series of enactments which four centuries had accumulated.[2] But there still remain some parts of the Vagrancy Act, 1824, which might be unintelligible if we did not regard them as a supplement to the old Poor Law, intended to prevent indigent persons from wandering out of their parishes, and to restrain the offences likely to be committed by such wanderers. Offenders against the Act (5 Geo. IV, c. 83) were of three classes, according to the maximum punishment to be inflicted upon them. Every case is tried at petty sessions, though in cases of the third class, as will be seen, the sentence is not pronounced there.

[1] Serjeant Cox's *Principles of Punishment*, 212.

[2] See, in particular, the National Assistance Act, 1948.

SECTION 2. IDLE AND DISORDERLY PERSONS

¶ 484. The first class consisted[1] of the persons guilty of the more trivial offences of vagrancy. Typical instances are:

[(1) A person whose wilful neglect to work causes him or her, or any of his or her family, to become chargeable to the parish.[2]]

(2) A person wandering abroad to hawk goods without a pedlar's licence.

(3) A person begging[3] in any public place,[4] or encouraging any child to do so.

(4) A common prostitute wandering in the public streets and behaving riotously or indecently.[5]

(5) Persons committing various offences in connexion with poor relief, e.g. refusing to work when in receipt of relief.[6]

All these were technically denominated by the Act 'idle and disorderly persons'. They are liable to a punishment of imprisonment for not more than a month, or a fine not exceeding £5.

SECTION 3. ROGUES AND VAGABONDS

¶ 485. The second class consists[7] of the persons who are guilty of the graver forms of vagrancy. The following instances may be cited (see also ¶ 217, notes 5 and 6 *ante*):

(1) A person convicted for a second time of any of the offences of the former series. The two need not be both of the same species.

[(2) A person running away and leaving his wife (or her husband) or child chargeable to the parish.[2]]

(3) A person endeavouring to procure alms by exposing wounds or deformities or by making fraudulent pretences.

(4) A person found in a building, or inside an inclosed yard, garden or area, for any unlawful (i.e. criminal[8]) purpose.

[1] Sect. 3.

[2] By virtue of the National Assistance Act, 1948, sched. 7, such offenders are no longer to be called by any of the opprobrious epithets which stand as the titles to sections 2, 3 and 4 in the Act of 1824 (¶¶ 484, 485, 486); they are now dealt with by sections 42 and 51 of this Act, and are liable to a fine up to £50 and/or imprisonment up to three months.

[3] For any able-bodied man to beg was made an offence by 12 Ric. II, c. 7; but a university student might beg if the chancellor of the university had given him a certificate. At Bridgwater such a certificate is still preserved.

[4] Metropolitan magistrates have held that a street box-collector can be convicted of begging, if he receives *any* share of the money collected.

[5] The Town Police Clauses Act, 1847, makes it an offence for her simply to 'loiter and importune' in a street. But within the precincts of the Universities of Oxford (6 Geo. IV, c. 97, s. 3) and of Cambridge (57 and 58 Vict. c. 60) she commits an offence by merely wandering in a public street and not giving a satisfactory account of herself. And note the Street Offences Act, 1959; *Smith* v. *Hughes* [1960] 2 All E.R. 859.

[6] See now the National Assistance Act, 1948, s. 51.

[7] Sect. 4.

[8] Not immorality. There must be unmistakable evidence that the accused had been found in the building, *R.* v. *Lumsden* [1951] 1 All E.R. 1101. In *Knott* v. *Blackburn* [1943] K.B. 77 a divisional court held that the words 'inclosed area' denote the open space below

(5) A person gaming[1] in an open and public place (even a railway compartment in transit)[2] at some game of *chance*,[3] with cards, coins, or other devices.

(6) A person telling fortunes, or using any subtle craft, by palmistry or otherwise, to deceive,[4] e.g. casting astrological nativities. It must now be noted that the Fraudulent Mediums Act, 1951, repeals this provision 'so far as it extends to persons purporting to act as spiritualistic mediums or to exercise any powers of telepathy, clairvoyance or other similar powers, or to persons who, purporting so to act, or to exercise such powers, use fraudulent devices'. See ¶ 369 *ante*.

(7) A suspected person, or reputed thief, frequenting any river, dock, quay, etc., or any street or any place of public resort, etc. or place adjacent thereto, or loitering[5] about or in any of the said places with intent to commit a felony.[6] It is not necessary to prove any particular acts tending to show intent, but there may be a conviction if from the circumstances of the case and the known character of the suspect as proved it appears that the intent of the accused was to commit felony.[7] For the purpose of this crime, however, a man is not 'a suspected person' merely because on the occasion in question the constable who arrested him (without a warrant)[8] reasonably suspected that he was then about to commit a felony. 'A man is not a reputed thief merely because a constable thinks he is a thief and I cannot see how a man can be said to be a suspected person merely because a constable suspects him.'[9] A suspected person is one who has acquired that character by reason of antecedent conduct and previous record apart from his

the level of the ground which has been excavated for the purpose of building a house on the site, leaving open the question whether the words might apply to an enclosure not connected with a house and whether an area must always be an excavation.

[1] I.e. for stakes contributed, even in part, by the *players* themselves, not for a prize given entirely by someone else. See Vagrant Law Amendment Act, 1873 (36 and 37 Vict. c. 38, s. 3). Cf. *R.* v. *Governor of Brixton Prison* [1912] 3 K.B. 568, *ante*, ¶ 367.

[2] *Langrish* v. *Archer* (1882) 10 Q.B.D. 44.

[3] But a *publican* commits an offence by permitting gaming at *any* game, even one of skill, on his licensed premises; e.g. bowls played for beer.

[4] A *fortune-teller* who believes in his skill is nevertheless guilty, *Stonehouse* v. *Mason* [1921] 2 K.B. 818. But an avowed juggler is not, *Johnson* v. *Fenner* (1869) 33 J.P. 740. The view has been expressed that to come within the mischief of the Act there must be exploitation of the public by an impostor for the purposes of gain, and that to prove an offence, under s. 4, of using any subtle craft etc. (as distinct from fortune-telling) there must be evidence that the accused is an impostor and is pretending to have powers which he is conscious of not having.

[5] Penal Servitude Act, 1891 (54 and 55 Vict. c. 69) s. 7. Loitering means acting in such a way as to indicate that the person in question is idling in the street for some unlawful purpose.

[6] The evidence must show that the accused was then and there about to commit an offence, *R.* v. *Goodwin* [1944] 1 All E.R. 506.

[7] Prevention of Crimes Act, 1871, s. 15.

[8] *Post*, ¶ 697.

[9] *Per* Greene, L.J., in *Ledwith* v. *Roberts* [1937] 1 K.B. at p. 254; notwithstanding *Hartley* v. *Ellnor* (1917) 117 L.T. 304, with which Greene, L.J., expressed his disagreement (at p. 255).

behaviour on the particular occasion in question. However, it was held in *Rawlings* v. *Smith*[1] that so long as there are two separate elements, first, antecedent acts occasioning suspicion and bringing the accused into the class of suspected persons, and secondly, an act which was the culminating point of a long series of acts, namely the act which caused him to be arrested, the interval of time between the two is only a matter of degree, and it is not, for example, necessary that he should have got into the class of suspected persons on a day earlier than that of the loitering.[2]

(8) A person wandering abroad and lodging in unoccupied buildings or under a tent or in a cart,[3] and not giving a good account of himself. It must be proved (*a*) that he has been directed to a reasonably accessible place of shelter and has failed to apply there or refused accommodation there or (*b*) that he is a person who persistently wanders abroad or lodges as aforesaid or (*c*) that while lodging as aforesaid he has caused damage to property or infection with vermin or other offensive consequence, or lodged as aforesaid in circumstances likely to cause such damage or infection.[4]

(9) A male person (*a*) knowingly living, wholly or in part, on the earnings of prostitution; or (*b*) persistently soliciting, in public, for immoral purposes. A man may be living on the earnings of prostitution notwithstanding that he receives payment direct from a person for whom he provides, or whom he assists to meet, the prostitute and not from her.[5] This prohibition of the calling of a *souteneur* was added by the Vagrancy Act, 1898 (61 and 62 Vict. c. 39), as amended by the Criminal Law Amendment Act, 1912.[6] Prosecution for it may also be by indictment.

(10) A person (*a*) who wilfully exposes to view in any street or other public place or in a window situate in any such public place, any obscene picture or other indecent exhibition, or (*b*) who, with intent to insult any female, wilfully and obscenely exposes his person (whether in a public place or not).

All these were styled 'rogues and vagabonds'. (Both words originally meant simply 'wanderers', the 'rogues forlorn' of *King Lear*; from the Latin *rotare* and *vagari*.) They may be punished with imprisonment up to three months, or with a fine not exceeding £25.

[1] [1938] 1 K.B. 675. And see *Cohen* v. *Black* [1942] 2 All E.R. 299; *R.* v. *Fairbairn* (1949) 65 T.L.R. 559. But a person can be properly described as a 'suspected person' within the section, although the police officers who arrested him were at the time unaware of his previous convictions, *R.* v. *Clarke* [1950] 1 All E.R. 546.

[2] Loitering may be carried on in a moving vehicle; *Bridge* v. *Campbell* (1947) 177 L.T. 444.

[3] Other than that with or in which he travels.

[4] Vagrancy Act, 1935 (25 and 26 Geo. V, c. 20). This act is criticized in 180 *L.T.Jo.* 56.

[5] *Calvert* v. *Mayes* [1954] 1 All E.R. 41. And note *R.* v. *Silver* [1956] 1 All E.R. 716, a case adversely criticized in *R.* v. *Thomas* [1957] 1 W.L.R. 747; *ante*, ¶ 149. And see *Shaw* v. *D.P.P.* [1961] 2 W.L.R. 897.

[6] Now repealed by the Sexual Offences Act, 1956.

SECTION 4. INCORRIGIBLE ROGUES

¶ 486. The third class consists chiefly of those who have been twice[1] convicted—or who have resisted arrest when apprehended on even a first charge—of any offence of the second series.[2] Such a person is technically an 'incorrigible rogue'. The procedure is curious. The offender, as in the two previous classes, is convicted at a court of petty sessions as a member of this class,[3] but this court can only commit him to imprisonment until the next court of quarter sessions. That court will receive the conviction and without further accusation can inquire and pass the sentence upon it, which may extend to a year's further imprisonment. It has been stated[4] that the number of incorrigible rogues committed to quarter sessions in London alone probably now exceeds that of the whole country in 1930 (when it was 58).

[1] The two convictions need not be for offences of the same species.

[2] Other than the ninth, the *souteneur*, 2 and 3 Geo. V, c. 20, s. 7 (2).

[3] *R.* v. *Evans* [1915] 2 K.B. 762.

[4] 226 *L.T.Jo.* 74.

BOOK III

MODES OF JUDICIAL PROOF

Chapter XXVI

THE NATURE OF PRESUMPTIONS AND OF EVIDENCE

SECTION 1. STRICTNESS OF ENGLISH RULES OF EVIDENCE

¶ 487. A ready knowledge of the law of evidence is essential to all who are engaged in forensic practice. The occasions for its use arise suddenly; and the rules must be applied forthwith, before the witness has had time to break them.

The restrictions imposed by the English rules of evidence appear in marked contrast to the laxity[1] of proof allowed in some foreign tribunals.[2] But the constitutional value of our stringency is great. For it has done much towards producing that general confidence in our criminal courts which has kept popular feeling in full sympathy with the administration of the criminal law, and has thereby facilitated the task of government to an extent surprising to some foreign observers.

The student may be assisted in marshalling in his mind the somewhat complicated details of this branch of law if he realizes at the outset that, at any rate so far as the administration of justice in the criminal courts is concerned, the fabric of our evidential system has been gradually built up to give effect to three main ethical axioms. The first is that any person who makes a positive assertion of fact in legal proceedings should be compelled to establish the truth of his allegations to the satisfaction of the tribunal before which he makes them; this is what is known as the burden of proof, or *onus probandi*.[3] The second is that in endeavouring to discharge the burden of proof no one may be allowed to bring in matters which are not logically relevant to the fact or the facts in issue;[4] there are two fundamental reasons for this principle, (i) lest untrained minds might thereby be led to a false conclusion,

[1] The danger of laxity is illustrated by the fact that, about 1750, to serve a client indicted at the Old Bailey for robbery, an attorney named Brecknock forged an almanac to show that there had been no moon that night (Burke's *Connaught Circuit*, 129).

[2] France permits (*a*) leading questions, (*b*) hearsay evidence, (*c*) evidence of matters only remotely relevant.

[3] E.g. *post*, ¶¶ 525, 526.

[4] E.g. *post*, ¶ 541.

and (ii) lest the time of the court should be wasted. The third is that an accused person must be treated fairly and equitably[1] at all stages of the proceedings.[2]

A SAFEGUARD AGAINST MISTAKES BY THE JURY

¶ 488. Bearing the above axioms in mind it will be seen that many of our rules of evidence were created in consequence of a peculiarity of English procedure in taking away from the trained judges the determination of questions of fact, and entrusting it to untrained laymen. The Romans had no law of evidence as we understand it; for, with them, questions of fact were tried in civil cases by a *judex* who was a citizen of standing; and in criminal cases by a court actually forbidden to check a witness.[3] But in England jurymen's inexpertness led the courts to establish many rules for the exclusion of certain kinds of evidence that seemed likely to mislead minds not accustomed to logical processes of thought.

SECTION 2. THE CONTRAST OF PROOF BY EVIDENCE AND PROOF BY PRESUMPTIONS

¶ 489. Whenever, in any country, a tribunal is called upon to decide any question of fact, it must do so either by obtaining actual evidence, or by the easier yet less precise method of employing, instead, some *a priori* presumption. Before commencing a detailed account of evidence, it may be convenient to explain the technical substitutes which thus sometimes replace it.

Upon analysis it will be seen that the difference between reaching a conclusion upon evidence and reaching a conclusion on a presumption is only one of degree. In the former case the mind is easily led to the conclusion by habitual experience and by a long-accustomed process of thought. Thus, to take an extravagant example, when evidence has been given that the prisoner had plunged a dagger into the breast of a man who was also proved to have been alive a few minutes before, it would seem to most people that they would not be making any very doubtful conjecture if they should conclude that it was proved that the prisoner had killed the deceased. In fact, however, they are taking it for granted (doubtless quite reasonably) that it was the dagger thrust that killed the man.[4] And if medical evidence be given that the stabbing

[1] E.g. *post*, ¶¶ 595, 596, and 609–629.

[2] See *R.* v. *Christie* [1914] A.C. 545 (*T.A.C.*), *per* Lord Reading at p. 564: 'Judges are aware from their experience that in order to ensure a fair trial for the accused...it is desirable in certain circumstances to relax the strict application of the law of evidence....' e.g. by the exclusion of admissible evidence where the prejudice it would raise greatly exceeds its probative value, *R.* v. *Coombes* [1961] Crim. L.R. 54, *post*, ¶ 547*a*. And see *R.* v. *Collister and Warhurst* (1955) 39 Cr.App.R. 100, as to the duty of the police to disclose to the defence actual convictions of crime standing on the record of the prosecutor.

[3] Mommsen, *Strafr.*, 422; Strachan-Davidson's *Problems*, II, 119.

[4] See *R.* v. *White* [1910] 2 K.B. 124, in which it appeared that those who framed the charge of murder against the prisoner had made a mistaken assumption of this character.

had been the cause of the death, even then there is the assumption that the witness really carried out the examination as he stated and that his conclusions (as an expert witness) are to be relied upon. Over the years, however, the courts have found by experience that there are certain factual situations from which it is safe to make a wider leap to a conclusion than a cautious juryman might, unguided, be disposed to take; and it is in such cases that the judge decides and advises the jury that the conclusion is one which is to be presumed. Yet in this latter case, where it is realized that a presumption is being employed, the only difference really is that there is a wider gap between the last fact deposed to in evidence and the conclusion which the jury are advised they may reach: as will be seen in the following paragraphs. Presumptions are traditionally classed as: (*a*) *praesumptiones juris et de jure*, (*b*) *praesumptiones juris sed non de jure*, and (*c*) *praesumptiones hominis* (or *praesumptiones facti*).

(*a*) *Praesumptiones juris et de jure*[1]

¶ 490. These are inferences of fact which the law will not permit evidence to be called to contradict. Such is the presumption (*ante*, ¶ 51) that an infant under eight cannot have a guilty intention. Such presumptions,[2] though in form connected with the law of proof, are in truth rules of substantive law disguised in the language of adjective rules.

(*b*) *Praesumptiones juris sed non de jure*

¶ 491. These are inferences of fact which only hold good until evidence has been given which contradicts them. They consequently afford merely a *prima facie* proof of the fact presumed, a proof which may be overthrown by evidence which negatives it,[3] or by collision with some other and still stronger presumption which suggests a contrary inference. Thus, in the United States, when slavery existed, there was, in the slave-holding States, a *prima facie* presumption that every man of black or mulatto skin was a slave, unless he proved himself to be a freeman.

(*c*) *Praesumptiones hominis* (or *praesumptiones facti*)

¶ 492. These perhaps should not be classed amongst legal presumptions; for though, like the two preceding classes, they are inferences of fact, the law does not (as in those two cases) command juries to draw them, but only advises their doing so. They properly illustrate the nature of a presumption as such, since they are instances that when fact x is 'proved', then the jury are left to conclude that fact y followed,

[1] I.e. drawn by the law and in an obligatory manner.

[2] For other examples see Phipson on Evidence, 9th ed., 698.

[3] Note that in *R.* v. *White*, *supra*, ¶ 489 n. 4, what could have passed for proof was in like manner upset by unexpected evidence. The skilled scientific investigations of the police laboratory in modern times have perhaps as frequently (and as surprisingly) established the innocence of a suspected person as they have established the guilt.

a task which is always theirs when any case is finally left to them.[1] A good instance of this class is the presumption that arises from possession of goods recently stolen (see ¶ 500).

The presumptions important enough to call for detailed notice belong mainly to class (*b*), the *praesumptiones iuris sed non de jure.*

PRESUMPTION OF INNOCENCE

¶ 493. There is a presumption of this kind against the commission of any crime.[2] This holds good, not merely in criminal trials, but probably also in every civil case where any allegation is made that a criminal act has been committed.[3] Thus in an action on a life-insurance policy, the presumption is against suicide. So strong is this presumption that, in order to rebut it, the crime must be brought home to a prisoner 'beyond reasonable doubt';[4] and the graver the crime, the greater will be the degree of doubt that is reasonable. Hence (*a*) the commission of the crime—that the horse actually was stolen, or the man killed—must be clearly proved, so clearly indeed, that circumstantial evidence will rarely suffice to prove it.[5] Thus on a charge of murder the fact of death must be fully proved, which can rarely be done unless the body be found, circumstantial evidence of death thus being usually insufficient.[6] Moreover (*b*) after proving that the crime was committed, the prosecution must also prove distinctly that it was committed by the very person accused, so that when two men are charged with a crime, and it is made clear that one of them committed it, but it cannot be shown which one, both must be acquitted.[7] If, too, the defence suggests an alternative theory which is possible and consistent with the evidence, the accused must be acquitted.[8]

Even where, either by statute or by common law, some matter is presumed against an accused person 'unless the contrary is proved', still the burden of proof to be carried by the accused is less than that which is required of the prosecution in proving their case beyond reasonable doubt, and is no more than that which rests upon a party in a *civil* action; it is therefore enough if he satisfies the jury of the *probability* of that which he is called upon to establish.[9]

[1] The student must remember the rule (*post*, ¶ 596) that the jury must be satisfied beyond reasonable doubt that they are right in drawing the inference suggested by counsel for the prosecution.

[2] *R.* v. *Manning* (1849) *The Times*, 27 Oct. (*T.A.C.*). It must be remembered that there is no similar *general* presumption of innocence of all crimes, alleged or unknown. So if a prisoner assert his good character, he must give some proof of it. Study 'The presumption of innocence', C. K. Allen, *Legal Duties*, 253.

[3] But as to whether the presumption is *equally* strong against a defendant who in a *civil* action is charged with crime, see ¶ 595 *post*.

[4] See ¶ 596 *post*.

[5] *Post*, ¶ 516.

[6] 1 Hale P.C. c. 39; 3 Co. *Inst.* 104 (*T.A.C.*). See ¶¶ 508 and 517 *post*.

[7] *R.* v. *Richardson* (1785) 1 Leach 387 (*T.A.C.*).

[8] *R.* v. *Turkington* (1930) 22 Cr.App.R. 91; *R.* v. *Johnson* [1961] 3 All E.R. 969.

[9] *R.* v. *Carr-Briant* [1943] K.B. 607 (*T.A.C.*); *Sodeman* v. *R.* [1936] 2 All E.R. 1138 (*T.A.C.*); *R.* v. *Patterson* [1962] 1 All E.R. 340. And see [1959] *Crim. L.R.* 27.

¶ 494. *When it conflicts with an assumption of continuance of life.* The presumption of innocence is very strong and this means that the burden is always upon the prosecution to establish, beyond reasonable doubt, the guilt of the prisoner.[1] Therefore, although there is in civil cases a *praesumptio facti* (but not *juris*) of continuance of life,[2] it does not prevail against the presumption of innocence in a case of bigamy so as to cause the prisoner to call legal evidence to raise a doubt as to his guilt; for there is no presumption either way as to the continuance of life of the first spouse and the matter is entirely one of fact for the jury,[3] who must look at all the facts. Accordingly if for example it were proved that the first spouse was in good health a day or two before the day of the second marriage the jury could reasonably, and would probably, infer that the person was alive on the later day; plainly, they would not be likely to draw that conclusion if there was further evidence that the spouse was in a dying condition when last seen.[4]

But the effect of the proviso in the relevant statute[5] must be remembered, so that if the evidence goes no further than to show that the spouse was living at a date which is more than seven years prior to the second marriage, then there can be no question to be left to the jury, since the legislature has sanctioned a presumption that a spouse not heard of for seven years is dead.[6]

Students should note that the question whether a person continued to *live* is not the same as the question whether, if proved to have lived, that person continued in any particular relationship to another person so that the latter knew of the continuance of that life. Thus in *R.* v. *Jones*,[7] in the absence of evidence to the contrary, it was presumed that a husband and wife continued to live together, i.e. that an existing state of things continued (*post*, ¶ 498).

The rule of criminal law that the prosecution must make out its case is not, of course, confined to cases of bigamy; for in all criminal charges the prisoner is entitled to plead not guilty and, if he wishes, to offer no evidence, but to submit merely that the evidence of the prosecution is

[1] *Mancini* v. *D.P.P.* [1942] A.C. 1 (*T.A.C.*); explaining *Woolmington* v, *D.P.P.* [1935] A.C. 462 (*T.A.C.*); *ante*, ¶ 25. See Russ. 38.

[2] *R.* v. *Harborne* (1835) 2 A. and E. 540, a pauper's settlement case; *R.* v. *Jones* (1883) 11 Q.B.D. 118; *post*, ¶ 498. See Phipson on Evidence, 9th ed. 108. As to *commorientes* (persons who die together in some disaster) see the Law of Property Act, 1925, s. 184, as modified by the Intestates' Estates Act, 1952, s. 1 (4).

[3] *R.* v. *Lumley* (1869) L.R. 1 C.C.R. 196; and see *R.* v. *Willshire* (1881) 6 Q.B.D. 366 (*T.A.C.*).

[4] Or in a position of great danger (e.g. on a raft, after a shipwreck), or in a house which a little later was demolished by an enemy bomb.

[5] Offences against the Person Act, 1861, s. 57; *ante*, ¶ 175.

[6] This is for criminal law a statutory recognition of a long established presumption at common law for civil proceedings; see *Hopewell* v. *De Pinna* (1809) 2 Camp. 113. But the *converse* does not arise; for the Act does not create a presumption that a spouse known to be alive within seven years past is still living.

[7] (1883) 11 Q.B.D. 118.

not sufficient.[1] However, in certain special circumstances to be described below[2] the judge may direct the jury that the prosecution have done enough to make it possible (although not obligatory) for them to convict unless the prisoner offers, even by an unsworn statement, some explanation.[3] If he remain silent and leave this hostile testimony unexplained, his silence can be regarded as sufficient to justify his conviction. The position when a person accused of a theft is shown to have been in possession of the goods *shortly after* the stealing is considered later.[4]

PRESUMPTION AGAINST THE COMMISSION OF AN IMMORAL ACT

¶ 495. There is a presumption against the commission of an immoral act. This presumption is scarcely to be distinguished from the one mentioned in the next paragraph. Cohabitation, with the general reputation of being husband and wife, is in most cases sufficient *prima facie* evidence of marriage.[5] And birth is presumed to be legitimate. But the presumption against moral wrongdoing is not so strong as the presumption against criminal wrongdoing. Hence *A*'s cohabitation with *B* does not constitute such strong evidence of his being married to her as will justify his being convicted of bigamy if he proceeds to marry *C*.[6]

OMNIA PRAESUMUNTUR RITE AC SOLENNITER ESSE ACTA[7]

¶ 496. All things are presumed to have been done in the due and wonted manner. This presumption acquires increased weight as the event recedes in time. It is one of great force, especially when applied to public or official acts.[8] Thus from the fact that a church has been frequently used for the celebration of marriage services the court will infer that it had been duly licensed for that purpose.[9] Similarly the fact of a person's acting in a public office (e.g. as sheriff, justice of the peace, or constable), is sufficient *prima facie* evidence of his having been duly appointed to it.[10] And there is a presumption that in any government office the regular course of business has been followed (e.g. that the particulars on a postmark represent the time and place at which the letter was handled in the post). Even in a private establishment the course of dealing may become so systematic and regular as to justify a similar employment of this presumption.[11] Thus a letter left in the

[1] E.g. *R.* v. *Walker* (1854) Dearsly 280; *R.* v. *Slingsby* (1864) 4 F. and F. 61. Contrast *R.* v. *Hobson* (1854) Dearsly 400.

[2] *Post*, ¶ 501.

[3] *R.* v. *Frost* (1839) 4 St. Tr. (n.s.) 85 (*T.A.C.*); *R.* v. *Wood* (1911) 7 Cr.App.R. 58.

[4] *Post*, ¶ 500.

[5] *Doe dem. Fleming* v. *Fleming* (1827) 4 Bingham 266 (*T.A.C.*); *In re Taylor* [1961] 1 W.L.R. 9.

[6] *Morris* v. *Miller* (1767) 1 W.Bl. 632 (*T.A.C.*).

[7] See *Neal* v. *Denston* (1932) 48 T.L.R. 637.

[8] See *Re Crippen* [1911] P. 108; *Knowles* v. *R.* [1930] A.C. 366.

[9] *R.* v. *Cresswell* (1876) 1 Q.B.D. 446.

[10] *R.* v. *Borrett* (1833) 6 C. and P. 124.

[11] *Macgregor* v. *Kelly* (1894) 3 Exch. 794.

ordinary course with a servant for delivery to his master may be presumed to have reached the master's hands; or a letter, duly addressed and posted, and not returned soon afterwards by the Dead Letter Office, to have been duly delivered; or a postcard, duly posted, to have been read during its transmission.[1] Again, a deed will be presumed to have been executed on the day whose date it bears.[2] And the holder of a bill of exchange is deemed *prima facie* to be a 'holder in due course'. And anyone who has entered into a contract is presumed to be of sufficient age to be legally competent to contract.[3]

PRESUMPTION OF OWNERSHIP

¶ 497. The possessor of property, real or personal, is presumed *prima facie* to be full owner of it.[4] In the case of real property, accordingly, the presumption is that he is seised in fee simple.

PRESUMPTION AGAINST CHANGE OF *STATUS QUO*

¶ 498. There is a presumption that any existing state of things will continue for some time further. Accordingly if a partnership or agency is shown to have once existed, those who allege it to have been subsequently dissolved will have the burden of proving the dissolution. And the speed of a train or of a motor vehicle is presumed to remain the same for *some* time.[5] When the charge is one of dangerous driving, evidence may be given of the manner of driving just before the spot in relation to which the charge is made.[6] Again, Mr Bradlaugh, an atheist in 1882, was taken still to be one in 1884 (*infra*, ¶ 529).

PRESUMPTIONS AS TO STATE OF MIND

¶ 499. Every man is presumed to be sane, until the contrary is proved.[7] And every sane adult is *presumed*[8] to intend all the *consequences* likely to flow directly from his intentional conduct. But the prosecution must *prove* that his *conduct* was intentional[9] before this presumption as to the consequences of it can arise.[10] As previously mentioned[11] this presumption is not a proposition of law but a deduction from common

[1] *Huth* v. *Huth* [1915] 3 K.B. 32; *Powell* v. *Gelston* [1916] 2 K.B. 615.

[2] *Malpas* v. *Clements* (1850) 19 L.J., Q.B. 435; and see *Re Peete, Peete* v. *Crompton* [1952] 2 All E.R. 599, as to the effect of the description of a woman as 'widow' in a certificate of marriage.

[3] *Borthwick* v. *Carruthers* (1787) 1 T.R. 648.

[4] *Jayne* v. *Price* (1814) 5 Taunt. 326; *Hall* v. *Penfold* (1838) 8 C. and P. at p. 537.

[5] *R.* v. *Dalloz* (1908) 1 Cr.App.R. 258.

[6] *Hallett* v. *Warren* (1929) 93 J.P. 225.

[7] The position is not too clear in criminal cases as to whether it is enough for the defence to raise a *doubt* about the prisoner's sanity; on a strict application of the M'Naghten rules (*ante*, ¶ 53) it would seem that it is not. And see *Woolmington* v. *D.P.P.* [1935] A.C. 462 (*T.A.C.*); *ante*, ¶¶ 25, 494, as explained in *Mancini* v. *D.P.P.* [1942] A.C. 1 (*T.A.C.*). In *Sodeman* v. *R.* [1936] 2 All E.R. 1138 (*T.A.C.*) it was said that the burden in cases in which the accused has to prove insanity is not greater than the burden which rests upon a plaintiff or defendant in civil proceedings.

[8] *R.* v. *Sheppard* (1810) R. and R. 169; *ante*, ¶ 25.

[9] See ¶ 18 *ante*.

[10] *R.* v. *Davies* (1913) 8 Cr.App.R. 211.

[11] ¶ 25 *ante*. *Hosegood* v. *Hosegood* [1950] 66 T.L.R. 735, *per* Denning, L.J.; *Wilson* v. *Inyang* [1951] 2 All E.R. 237. See [1959] *Crim. L.R.* 557, article by G. H. L. Fridman.

experience in everyday life; all it means is that since the accused may be presumed to have the brain of an ordinary man it is reasonable for the jury to infer that he did in fact foresee such consequences as the jury themselves in the like situation would have foreseen, and that since he went on to bring them about he must have intended them. It is, however, not an inference which *must* be drawn, for all the facts of the case must be taken into consideration, and when they are, an element of doubt may arise.

If, however, the prosecution prove an act, the natural consequences of which would be a certain result, and no evidence or explanation is given by the defence on the point, then the jury may, on a proper direction by the judge, find that the prisoner is guilty of doing the act with the intent that has been alleged; but, if on the totality of the evidence there is room for more than one view as to the intent of the prisoner, the jury should be directed that it is for the prosecution to prove the intent to the jury's satisfaction; and, unless on receiving the whole of the evidence the jury are so satisfied, they should acquit the prisoner.[1]

Yet it must be noted that where a particular intent is made a necessary element in the crime, then that intent must be proved by the Crown just as thoroughly as any other fact legally necessary to constitute the offence, and the burden of proving such intent remains throughout on the prosecution.[2]

Students should note that even a presumption of law does not need *sworn* evidence to rebut it; see *ante*, ¶ 493.

PRESUMPTION ARISING FROM POSSESSION OF RECENTLY STOLEN GOODS: *PRAESUMPTIO HOMINIS VEL FACTI*

¶ 500. Besides these presumptions of law, there is one discretionary presumption of fact which deserves careful attention—viz. that the possessor of goods recently[3] stolen may fairly be regarded as either the actual thief or else a guilty receiver.[4] His possession raises also—but less strongly—a presumption of his guilty connexion with any further crime that accompanied the theft, e.g. a burglary, an arson, or a murder.

We have said that this presumption arises in the case of goods which had been stolen recently.[5] It therefore does not arise until proof has been given that the goods in question have actually been stolen.[6] Thus

[1] *Woolmington* v. *D.P.P.* [1935] A.C. 462 (*T.A.C.*).

[2] *R.* v. *Steane* [1947] K.B. 997 (*T.A.C.*); *R.* v. *Foley* [1959] Crim. L.R. 286. For other presumptions of law (e.g. under statutes) see Phipson on Evidence, 9th ed., 699 *et seq.*

[3] I.e. recently before he obtained possession, though long before he was arrested.

[4] See *R.* v. *Langmead* (1864) L. and C. 427 (*T.A.C.*). In a case in 1918 the goods stolen in a burglary were found in the prisoner's possession two days after it. Avory, J., said: 'Possession so long afterwards is not sufficient evidence of stealing; you had better convict of receiving.' Possession even so early as twenty minutes after the theft may support a verdict of receiving; *R.* v. *Proctor* (1923) 17 Cr.App.R. 124; *R.* v. *Townsend* (1924) 18 Cr.App.R. 118.

[5] *R.* v. *Loughlin* (1951) 35 Cr.App.R. 69.

[6] 1 Hale P.C. c. 39; *R.* v. *Yend* (1833) 6 C. and P. 176 (*T.A.C.*); *R.* v. *Young* [1953] 1 All E.R. 21.

it is not sufficient that a tramp is carrying three gold watches and gives quite contradictory accounts as to how he got possession of them.[1] As to what time is near enough to be 'recent', no general rule can be given; for the period within which the presumption can operate will vary according to the nature of the article stolen. Three months has been held sufficiently recent for a motor car, and four months for a debenture bond.[2] But for such articles as pass from hand to hand readily, two months would be a long time, particularly in the case of money. In regard to a horse, it has been held that six months is too long.[3] Eight months is too long to be 'recent' for a bale of silk.[4] And it would seem that, whatever the article were, sixteen months would be too long a period.[5]

¶ **501.** *How rebutted.* This presumption does not displace the presumption of innocence so far as to throw upon the accused the burden of producing legal proof of the innocent origin of his possession. He merely has to state how it did originate. If his account is given at, or before, the preliminary examination, and is minute and reasonably probable, then he must not be convicted unless the prosecution can prove the story to be untrue. It has been declared[6] that a proper direction to the jury would be: 'If the prisoner's account raises a doubt in your minds, then, of course, you ought not to say that the case has been proved to your satisfaction.' But if he has put forward two inconsistent accounts, his explanation cannot be regarded as satisfactory; and the prosecution need not call evidence to rebut these varying stories. Even if he give an explanation which the jury disbelieve, or give none at all, they are not bound to convict him,[7] though they probably will do so. For, if his story *might* reasonably be true, the Crown has not given proof 'beyond reasonable doubt'.[8] The position has been stated in the following general terms by the Court of Criminal Appeal in a recent case:[9] 'Where the only evidence is that an accused person is in possession of property recently stolen, a jury may infer guilty knowledge (*a*) if he offers no explanation to account for his possession, or (*b*) if the jury are satisfied that the explanation he does offer is untrue.[10] If, however, the explanation offered is one which leaves the jury in doubt as to whether he knew the property was stolen, they should be told that the

[1] Cf. ¶ 516 *post*; but if it occurred in London see ¶ 531 (iv).

[2] *R.* v. *Livock* (1914) 10 Cr.App.R. 264.

[3] *R.* v. *Cooper* (1852) 3 C. and K. 318.

[4] *R.* v. *Marcus* (1923) 17 Cr.App.R. 191.

[5] *Anon* (1826) 2 C. and P. 459 (*T.A.C.*), *per* Bayley, J.

[6] *R.* v. *Garth* [1949] 1 All E.R. 773.

[7] The absence of satisfactory explanation does not *compel* a jury to convict, *R.* v. *Schama and Abramovitch* (1915), 11 Cr.App.R. 45; 31 T.L.R. 88. Cf. *R.* v. *Badash* (1917) 13 Cr.App.R. 17; *R.* v. *Ketteringham* (1926) 19 Cr.App.R. 159; *R.* v. *Garth* [1949] 1 All E.R. 773.

[8] *R.* v. *Crowhurst* (1844) 1 C. and K. 370. See ¶ 493 *ante*.

[9] *R.* v. *Aves* [1950] 2 All E.R. 330; 34 Cr.App.R. 159 (*T.A.C.*).

[10] E.g. *R.* v. *Young* [1953] 1 All E.R. 21.

case has not been proved, and therefore the verdict should be Not Guilty.'

A kindred presumption of guilt may arise when a murdered body is found in the possession of someone who is concealing it.[1]

RULES OF EVIDENCE AND PRESUMPTIONS DECIDE WHERE THE BURDEN OF PROOF LIES

¶ 502. Students should note that the rules as to presumptions and as to evidence generally relate to a forensic question of the greatest practical importance, namely, which party to the proceedings bears the burden of proof,[2] as the following statement indeed indicates:

> Presumptions of guilt and *prima facie* cases of guilt, in the trial of a party charged with a crime, mean no more than that from the proof of certain facts the jury will be warranted in convicting the accused of the offence with which he is charged.[3]

If this be remembered, it will be easier to avoid the common mistake of confusing *what has to be proved* (which is a requirement of *law* in each case) with the *evidence* by which it may be proved. These two matters must always be kept quite distinct in the lawyer's mind.

SECTION 3. EVIDENCE

¶ 503. *Classification.* No action or prosecution can succeed by the use of presumptions alone, and therefore a party who initiates proceedings (and in most cases also the party who defends them) must be prepared to convince the tribunal by producing evidence. Evidence coming before our courts can be classified according to differences in its intrinsic nature as (*a*) oral evidence, (*b*) documentary evidence,[4] (*c*) material (meaning thereby not 'relevant' but 'physical') non-documentary evidence.[5]

¶ 504. *Non-documentary evidence.* This class will include particulars as to the condition of physical matter (even of a human body, living or dead, such as an involuntary blush, a limp, a tattoo mark, a scar,[6] or an assailant's bitten finger or scratched face). The examples are innumer-

[1] See the charge to the jury by Cockburn, C.J., reproduced in *The Trial of the Wainwrights*, Notable British Trials series (1920), at p. 226.

[2] *Post*, ¶ 525.

[3] *Woolmington* v. *D.P.P.* [1935] A.C. 462 (*T.A.C.*). The jury will not be so warranted, unless they feel satisfied that the prosecution has made out the case against the accused. If they have any reasonable doubt about this, they must acquit. *R.* v. *Blackburn* (1955) 39 Cr.App.R. 84. See *post*, ¶ 596.

[4] So early as 1292 we find a writing used as evidence to a jury; Thayer, *Evidence*, pt. 1, 106, n. 5.

[5] So classified in the Indian Evidence Act, 1872.

[6] The lion-bitten shoulder which identified Dr Livingstone's corpse. And see *R.* v. *Crippen*, *post*, ¶ 518.

able, e.g. bloodstains on clothing or on a knife, the smell of prussic acid, finger-prints, footmarks, noises, smears of paint, fragments of hair or wool.[1]

¶ 505. *Evidence classified as direct or indirect.* But the best known, and usual, classification of evidence is one which turns upon differences in its logical bearing upon the question before the court. Considered from this point of view all evidence is commonly said to be either *direct* or *indirect* (*circumstantial*[2]).

Evidence is oral testimony given by a witness in court after having been duly sworn. 'Direct evidence' has been traditionally described as testimonial evidence to one or more of the *facta probanda* (or 'facts in issue'), the essential elements of the question under trial, i.e. those facts which, if all of them be proved, render legally necessary a decision favourable to the party who bases his case upon them; whereas the term 'circumstantial evidence' has been described as 'all other evidence' and therefore comprising not only all 'documentary' and 'non-documentary' evidence (within the classification given in ¶¶ 503, 504 *ante*) but also such oral evidence as concerns only one or more *facta probantia*, i.e. such elements as are not *in themselves* essential in the case, but which help to prove, or to disprove, one or more of the *facta probanda* (which are essential). Students may be somewhat puzzled by this, since they know quite well that no point either of 'documentary' or of 'non-documentary' evidence can come before the court unless its existence and its circumstances have been deposed to by some witness who gives this testimony on oath; he knows also that many pieces of circumstantial evidence could point to a *factum probandum* with even greater cogency than could the direct evidence of a witness who swears he saw that '*factum*' occur.[3]

It would seem, therefore, a more sound description to say that the term '*direct evidence*' indicates the testimony of a witness who speaks to his own personal perception of a *factum probandum* whereas the term *indirect*, or *circumstantial*, *evidence* indicates the testimony of a witness who speaks to his personal perception of a *factum probans*.

Thus in a prosecution for libel the act of publication by the defendant is a *factum probandum*, whereas the similarity of the defendant's proved handwriting (or of the peculiarities of his own typewriting machine) to that on the envelope, is a *factum probans*, i.e. a fact that *tends* to prove the publication by him.

[1] Bentham's classification of evidence into 'real and personal' is no longer regarded as helpful.

[2] The student must distinguish between this technical use of the word and a more popular one, in which it is also applied to evidence, but means simply 'full of detail', 'circumstanti*ated*' (e.g. 'his tedious and circumstantial description'), and in which it consequently may be as applicable to a witness's direct as to his indirect evidence.

[3] E.g. a fingerprint contrasted with direct evidence of identity in the case of a prisoner who pleads an alibi.

A. *Indirect or circumstantial evidence*

¶ **506.** The following are instances of some of the principal forms of circumstantial evidence familiar in criminal cases: the rank of the defendant, his disposition, his motives, his threats, his opportunities, his preparations, his attempts, his false statements, his silence, his fabrication or destruction of evidence, his flight, his possession of stolen property. But circumstantial evidence is just as applicable in civil cases as in criminal. Thus, in an action on a loan, the defendant may call evidence of the poverty of the plaintiff in order to help to prove that the money was not lent. Yet the controversies with regard to its value have arisen almost entirely in connexion with criminal offences. For the much greater severity of the penalties that may be inflicted for them has caused many persons to challenge the probative force of *facta probantia* as being logically inadequate to support a conviction for (at any rate) any capital crime.

DEFECTS OF CIRCUMSTANTIAL EVIDENCE

¶ **507.** The question thus raised is so fundamental as to need careful consideration. It is clear that in dealing with any testimonial evidence whatever, whether 'circumstantial' or 'direct', a jury may be misled. For they have to depend upon:

(1) the accuracy of the witness's original observation of the events he describes;

(2) the correctness of his memory; and

(3) his veracity.

But in addition to the risks of mistake, forgetfulness and falsehood, which thus arise when direct evidence is given, there are additional risks to run in dealing with circumstantial evidence. For here the jury have also to depend upon:

(4) the cohesion of each circumstance in the evidence with the rest of that chain of circumstances of which it forms a part;

(5) their own logical accuracy in deducing inferences from this chain of facts. 'The more ingenious the juryman the more likely is he to strain his facts to fit his theory' (Alderson, B.). For 'every fact has two faces'. Readiness in detecting them and seizing on the favourable aspect is an important qualification in an advocate. Thus excitement on being accused may be due either to consciousness of guilt or to indignant innocence. Lord Jeffrey,[1] in defending Paterson for poisoning his wife, was met by proof of his having once contemplated that murder; but this very fact he claimed as exculpative, urging that contemplation of so horrible a purpose must have made a husband ultimately recoil from it.

CIRCUMSTANTIAL EVIDENCE IN CAPITAL OFFENCES

¶ **508.** These fourth and fifth hazards have impressed some writers so deeply as to make them urge that no conviction for any capital offence

[1] Lord Cockburn's *Life of Lord Jeffrey*, I, 359.

should be allowed to take place upon circumstantial evidence alone. But those who so contend have not always realized that in every criminal case the *mens rea* must necessarily be proved by circumstantial evidence alone[1] (except when the prisoner actually confesses). Nor have they realized how extremely obvious may often be the inference to be drawn from circumstantial evidence, as, for instance, in a case where the evidence is of an 'alibi'.

SCIENTIFIC AIDS IN CIRCUMSTANTIAL EVIDENCE

¶ 509. The machinery of modern science is increasingly operated in the investigation of crime with startlingly convincing results.[2] For this the best known illustration is that of identification by finger-prints.[3] Indeed the circumstantial element often plays a large part in what would pass, at first sight, as excellent 'direct evidence'. Thus a witness may depose that he saw *A* point a rifle at *B* and fire it, saw the smoke, heard the crack, and saw *B* fall; and then, on going up to him, he saw a bullet-hole in his leg. But still he did not see *A*'s bullet strike *B*; so this fact (the really essential one) depends entirely upon circumstantial evidence, i.e. it has to be merely inferred from these other facts which he actually did see.[4]

CIRCUMSTANTIAL EVIDENCE ACCEPTED IN ENGLISH LAW

¶ 510. No distrust of circumstantial evidence has been shown by English law. It does not even require that direct evidence shall receive any preference over circumstantial. Memorable instances of important capital convictions,[5] whose correctness is unquestioned, that were based solely on indirect evidence are found in the trials of Courvoisier for

[1] Aided by legal presumptions, e.g. that 'a man intends the natural consequences of his act'; *ante*, ¶ 499.

[2] Establishing innocence as well as guilt, as the records of the police laboratory show.

[3] See the very interesting article, 'Finger-prints', by Chief Superintendent Cherrill of New Scotland Yard, in the *Journal of Criminal Science*, II, 160. Of the first million finger-prints recorded by the London police, no two corresponded in more than seven out of the eleven 'characteristics' by which they are classified. An important extension of these records has been 'poroscopy', the examination of the pores (instead of merely the ridges) in the finger-prints. By the telestereograph, finger-prints can now be wired by our police to those of foreign countries. Finger-prints are admissible evidence of identity (*R.* v. *Castleton* (1909) 3 Cr.App.R. 74), and there is no necessity for corroboration, but *quaere* whether such evidence is conclusive (*R.* v. *Parker* [1912] V.L.R. 152 and 14 C.L.R. 681 and *R.* v. *Krausch* (1913) 32 N.Z.L.R. 1229). Finger-prints of an arrested person may be taken without a warrant, *R.* v. *M'Garry* [1933] S.C. (J.) 72. And see ss. 39 and 40 of the Criminal Justice Act, 1948.

[4] Accordingly, in an old case under unpopular game laws, a friendly jury accepted the hypothesis of the poacher's counsel, that the gun fired by his client was not loaded with shot, and that the pheasant died of fright. And the superior court did not set aside this verdict (though, it being a civil case, they had full jurisdiction to do so); *R.* v. *Payne* (1791) 4 T.R. 468.

[5] Whenever an inquiry has to be made into the cause of death of a person and, there being no direct evidence, recourse must be had to circumstantial evidence, any evidence as to the habits and ordinary doings of the deceased which may contribute to the circumstances by throwing light upon the probable cause of death is admissible, *Joy* v. *Phillips Mills & Co. Ltd.* [1916] 1 K.B. 849, 854.

the murder of Lord William Russell in 1840,[1] and of Crippen in 1911 for the murder of his wife.[2]

Indeed some experienced English and American lawyers have even gone so far as to prefer circumstantial evidence to direct. 'Witnesses', say they, 'can lie; circumstances cannot.' Moreover, perfectly honest witnesses may give quite inaccurate accounts of events which they have observed. Undoubtedly many famous cases may be cited where great masses of direct evidence have proved to be utterly misleading.[3] Such cases have shown that the direct and explicit assertions of scores of witnesses, by being given on *opposite* sides, may create a far greater uncertainty than circumstantial evidence.[4] Three such cases may be briefly referred to.

B. *Direct evidence of witnesses*

¶ 511. *The Leigh Peerage Case.* In this case[5] the claimant of a title based his claim on his alleged descent from one Christopher Leigh. The proof of such descent was the alleged inscription on a monument, which was said to have formerly stood inside Stoneleigh Church. Thirty witnesses appeared before a committee of the House of Lords, and swore orally to their recollection of the monument; and affidavits to the same effect were made by about thirty others. But these sixty witnesses were contradicted (*a*) by twenty-one other witnesses, who denied altogether that any such monument had existed; and also (*b*) by the fact that their own descriptions of its shape, its colour, and the inscription carved on it were utterly irreconcilable.[6] Accordingly the committee refused to accept the evidence of these sixty persons.

¶ 512. *Elizabeth Canning's Case.* In this case[7] thirty-five witnesses swore that a gypsy (of peculiarly unmistakable features) who had been

[1] *The Times*, 19 June 1840; Townsend's *Modern State Trials*, I, 267, where an account will be found of the grave question raised by this case as to the duties of an advocate to a client who tells him that he is guilty.

[2] [1911] 1 K.B. 149, *post*, ¶ 518. Reference may also be made to *R.* v. *Nash* (1911) 6 Cr.App.R. 225; and *R.* v. *Robertson* (1913) 9 Cr.App.R. 189.

[3] There was a remarkable error in 'direct' evidence of identity in *Adolf Beck's* case in 1904; see '*The Trial of Adolf Beck*', Notable British Trials series. Similarly, twenty-one witnesses mistakenly identified a man in *R.* v. *Thompson* (1912) 7 Cr.App.R. 203.

[4] On the general controversy see pp. 36–51 of Wills, *Circumstantial Evidence* (7th ed.).

[5] *Parl. Papers* (1828), Reports, Min. of evidence.

[6] To take, for instance, only some seven out of the first thirty, they thus differed as to the colour of the monument: 'nearly black'; 'a kind of dove colour'; 'black with white letters'; 'had been originally white'; 'black'; 'light marble with dark introduced into it'; 'bluish grey'. As to its shape: 'oblong'; 'square at top, but narrowed to a point at bottom'; 'square at bottom, but narrowed to a point at top'; 'square at top and square at bottom'. And as to the inscription on it: 'all Latin'; 'a great deal of it English'; 'all English except *anno domini*'.

[7] (1754) 19 St. Tr. 283. See *Cornhill Magazine*, 1904. A full account of this extraordinary case will be found in an article in *Blackwood's Magazine* (1860), 581, written by a well-known metropolitan magistrate, who considered it 'perhaps the most inexplicable judicial puzzle on record'; and also in one contributed by Professor Kenny to the *Law Quarterly Review* in 1897.

convicted of a robbery in Middlesex, was in Dorset at the time of the robbery; but they were contradicted by twenty-five other witnesses, who swore to having seen her then in Middlesex. Besides showing by this contradiction how untrustworthy even the most direct testimonial evidence may be, the case further emphasizes the same lesson by the instance of Canning's own narrative of abduction and robbery, which was discredited by its sheer improbability, without being contradicted at all.

¶ 513. *R.* v. *Castro.* This remarkable case,[1] the longest reported trial in our legal history, affords a vivid illustration of the untrustworthiness of direct evidence. A butcher, named Orton, or Castro, came forward in 1866 claiming to be Sir Roger Tichborne, a young baronet who was believed to have perished in 1854 in a shipwreck. On Orton's being ultimately tried for perjury, 212 witnesses were examined for the Crown, and 256 for the defence. These included four large groups of people who respectively gave the following items of direct evidence:

(1) the claimant is not Roger Tichborne;
(2) he is Arthur Orton;
(3) he is not Arthur Orton;
(4) he is Tichborne.

These four groups, accordingly, served only to prove each other to be untrustworthy; and the case had therefore to be decided by circumstantial evidence, such as the claimant's degree of education, his ignorance of the affairs of the Tichborne family, and his conduct towards them and towards the Orton family.

TESTIMONY CAN BE CONFLICTING; CIRCUMSTANCES CAN MISLEAD

¶ 514. All these cases go to show that testimony, even when a large number of witnesses corroborate each other, may be quite untrustworthy; and therefore that direct evidence is not necessarily to be believed. It may even be less trustworthy than circumstantial evidence,[2] if the latter happens to consist of a great number of detached facts, which are severally proved by different witnesses. For, in such a case, each witness's contribution may well appear to him too trivial for it to be worth while to commit perjury about it (though, on the other hand, the same triviality which thus diminishes the chance of mendacity, increases somewhat the chances of mistake and of forgetfulness). But in all other cases circumstantial evidence should probably be pronounced to be less reliable than direct evidence, since a dangerous source of error is introduced by the difficulty of reasoning from the fragmentary items of proof to the conclusion to be proved. For, though

[1] *Annual Register*, vols. for 1871, 1872, 1873, 1874; (1874) L.R. 9 Q.B. 350.

[2] Especially in oriental countries, where 'truthfulness is an eccentricity, and evidence on oath a marketable commodity'; Sydney Smith's *Forensic Medicine*, 472.

'circumstances cannot lie', they can mislead.[1] They may even have been brought about for the very purpose of misleading, as when Joseph's silver cup was placed in Benjamin's sack, or when Lady Macbeth 'smeared the sleeping grooms with blood'.

CIRCUMSTANTIAL EVIDENCE USUALLY IMPORTANT IN CRIMES OF GRAVITY

¶ 515. It is in the graver rather than the lesser crimes that circumstantial evidence has the most frequently to be relied upon, because in such crimes an offender is the more careful to avoid eye-witnesses. Just as adultery can seldom be proved by direct evidence,[2] so no deliberately planned murder is likely to be carried out when any third person is at hand.[3] Hence comes it that if a child has died just about the time of birth, though the question whether it was born alive or dead can usually be settled easily in civil actions (friends of the mother, who were present at the birth, being called), yet its determination on a criminal trial for killing the child is usually most difficult.[4] It ordinarily has to depend wholly on circumstantial evidence, and this has to be drawn from post-mortem appearances of an ambiguous character. Hence has arisen a widespread impression that the evidence *requisite* to prove live birth is different in civil and in criminal cases, the only difference being, in reality, in the evidence usually *available* in the one and in the other.

SAFEGUARDS AGAINST ITS MISUSE. (*a*) In larceny

¶ 516. These various considerations point to the conclusion that circumstantial evidence must be admitted, but admitted only with watchful caution.[5] The hesitation of English law in regard to circumstantial evidence has found expression in some familiar restrictions upon its employment. Two of these are of special importance.

No conviction for larceny is to be allowed unless the fact that a larceny has actually taken place be proved fully.[6] It is not enough that a penniless tramp has been found to be wearing two diamond rings. To convict him of larceny, it must further be proved that these rings had somewhere been stolen; and this must be proved either by direct evidence or at least by exceptionally strong circumstantial evidence. Usually therefore it will be necessary to bring the owner

[1] 'For the woman not to weep when accused is one of the strongest presumptive proofs of witchcraft that Grillard and other Inquisitors had observed, after having tried and executed very many witches' (Bodin, *Démonomanie*, ed. 1598, IV, ch. IV).

[2] Lord St Helier said that if direct evidence of adultery be given, this very fact should inspire doubts as to the truth of the accusation. But the combination of guilty passion with opportunity affords some circumstantial evidence of it.

[3] See the remarks of Holt, C.J., in *Bath and Montague's Case* (1693) 3 Cas. in Chancery 55 at p. 105.

[4] 'Almost impracticable' (Ogston's *Medical Jurisprudence*, 220); 'almost impossible' (T. F. Smith's *Medical Jurisprudence*, 224).

[5] See Stephen, *General View of Criminal Law*, 2nd ed., 179–207.

[6] Cf. ¶ 493 *ante*.

himself, to prove his loss of some article and its identity with the article which is the subject-matter of the indictment.[1] But it is possible that even circumstantial evidence may be so peculiarly strong as to justify a conviction without any such direct proof; as where a person, on coming out of a warehouse, is found to have pepper (or one coming out of a cellar is found to have wine) concealed in his pockets.[2]

(*b*) In homicide

¶ 517. Similarly no conviction for homicide is allowed unless the fact that there has been a death be proved fully. This again must be done either by direct evidence (e.g. the finding of the body), or by circumstantial evidence of an exceptionally strong character.[3] Hale and Coke illustrate the importance of this rule by actual instances in which persons were executed for murder, and yet their supposed victims subsequently reappeared alive.[4] Hence in a case where the father and mother of a bastard child were seen to strip it and throw it into the Liverpool docks, and the body could not afterwards be found, Gould, J., nevertheless advised that, as there was a bare chance that the child might have been carried out to sea by the tide and picked up alive, the parents ought not to be convicted of its murder.[5] It thus is usually necessary that the body, or some identifiable portion of it, should be found.[6]

¶ 518. *Onus of proof.* In the absence of evidence either of the killing or of the death of the person alleged to have been killed, there is no

[1] *R.* v. *Joiner* (1910) 4 Cr.App.R. 64. Hence the former impunity of many of those who make a trade of picking up stray balls on golf-links; but now see *Hibbert* v. *McKiernan* [1948] 1 All E.R. 860 (*T.A.C.*).

[2] *R.* v. *Burton* (1854) Dearsly 282; and as to receiving see *R.* v. *Fuschillo* [1940] 2 All E.R. 489.

[3] *R.* v. *Hindmarsh* (1792) 2 Leach 569; *R.* v. *Onufrejczyk* [1955] 2 W.L.R. 273.

[4] 2 Hale P.C. c. 39; 3 Co. *Inst.* 232 (*T.A.C.*).

[5] Cited in *R.* v. *Hindmarsh, supra*. Doubt has been thrown on this ruling as overcautious. But *R.* v. *Farquharson* (Suss. Ass., 29 June 1908) is similar. The prisoner confessed to having thrown her baby into a tidal stream. It was proved that on the next morning the body of a baby of the same sex and age was found on the shore, a mile away, in the line of current. Jelf, J., told the jury not to convict unless satisfied that the body was that of the prisoner's child. In *R.* v. *Armstrong* (1875) 13 Cox 184, a man had been thrown overboard in a Gold Coast river, rife with sharks, and his body was never seen again. Archibald, J., left the case to the jury, saying (according to *The Times*, 18 Aug. 1875): 'The rule only requires the jury to act with caution.' See *The Trial of James Cam*, Notable British Trials series (1949). For a discussion of a remarkable case in New Zealand, *R.* v. *Horry* [1952] N.Z.L.R. 111, see Morris, '*Corpus delicti* and circumstantial evidence' (1952) 68 *L.Q.R.* 391.

[6] The phrase *corpus delicti*, though often applied to the body of a murdered man, or the stolen goods, or any other thing which is the subject-matter of criminal conduct, more properly means the criminal conduct itself, e.g. the act of killing the man, or of stealing the goods. See the phrase discussed by Wills (*Circumstantial Evidence*, 324).

onus upon the prisoner to account for the disappearance or non-production of such person.[1] A memorable instance of identification by a small fragment occurred in a famous American trial of 1850, that of Professor Webster, of Harvard University, for the murder of Dr Parkman.[2] The body had been burnt in a furnace in the professor's laboratory and the only identifiable portion left was the victim's false teeth; but it happened that they were of a peculiar character.

[1] See *R.* v. *Davidson* (1934) 25 Cr.App.R. 21.

[2] 5 Cushing 295. Compare, too, *Crippen's Case* in England in 1910; where no head and no bones were found and no organs that indicated sex, but only pieces of flesh, on one of which was an identificatory scar. And in *R.* v. *Peacock* (1911), an Australian case (13 C.L.R. 619), the murderer had burned the whole of the corpse, yet was convicted. Cf. *R.* v. *McNicholl* [1917] 2 I.R. 557, and *R.* v. *Rouse*, *The Times*, 27 Jan. 1931. See *R.* v. *Haigh* (1950) in 18 *Medico-legal Journal*, pt. 2, 38.

Chapter XXVII

THE GENERAL RULES OF EVIDENCE

SECTION I. INTRODUCTORY

SOME TESTIMONY, THOUGH RELEVANT, IS EXCLUDED

¶ 519. The chief general rules of evidence consist, as we have seen (*ante*, ¶ 488), mainly of rules of exclusion. And they are not limited to excluding such matters as are irrelevant to the issue to be tried. For even of relevant testimony there are two kinds which it has been found desirable to exclude.[1]

(*a*) Evidence of matters so slightly relevant as not to be worth the time occupied in proving them. If every circumstance which might tend to throw light on the matters in issue were let in, trials would be protracted to an intolerable length, especially (Maine says) in India, where extraordinary ingenuity is exhibited in discovering every fact which has the remotest bearing on a question under litigation.

(*b*) Evidence which, though relating to facts that are not only relevant but even important, is itself of such a character that experience shows it to be likely to impress persons of ordinary intelligence as being a more cogent proof of those facts than it really is. 'Hearsay' affords a conspicuous example of this kind of evidence.

ORIGIN OF RULES OF EVIDENCE

¶ 520. The development of the legal rules of evidence seems, as we have already noted, to have been influenced by the gradual discovery by judges that certain kinds of proof were apt to be thus accepted, by inexperienced jurymen, with a degree of respect which was undeserved. Hence an adherence to the rules was insisted upon chiefly in cases where it was by jurymen that the evidence was to be weighed. Accordingly where the functions of the court alone are concerned (as in determining the sentence for a convicted prisoner), facts are often taken into account which have not been established in accordance with the strict rules of evidence.[2] The law of evidence was not reduced to definite form until long after our forensic procedure had come to include the practice of producing witnesses to give evidence to juries. It was in civil courts in the seventeenth century that the rules of evidence first arose; and

[1] 'Experienced citizens, and judges of the highest eminence, reach conclusions in their own private affairs by reference to a more relaxed standard than the courts allow. But the issues pronounced upon by courts are attended with such grave consequences that in matters of evidence a standard of admissibility so cautious as to be meticulous is in fact essential' (Lord Birkenhead, L.C.).

[2] But the fact that the prisoner is present, and does not deny them, often gives ground for receiving them, even technically, as admissions.

they thence passed to criminal courts, where, however, they came to assume an even greater importance than was accorded to them in civil ones.[1]

STRICT RULES ADOPTED IN CRIMINAL COURTS

¶ 521. A marked distinction between the civil and the criminal views of the law of evidence is that its rules may in civil cases be waived, either by consent or by an order made on a summons for directions; but in criminal cases the rules of evidence are matters *publici juris*, and cannot be dispensed with by consent of the parties.[2] For, here, others than they have an interest at stake. Not merely the single person accused, but also every other inhabitant of the realm, has an interest in seeing that the prisoner's liberty or life is not taken away except under the whole of the safeguards which the law has prescribed. Thus a photograph, unverified by oath, cannot be given in evidence even if both parties are willing that it should be.

IMPROPER ADMISSION OF EVIDENCE MAY BE FATAL

¶ 522. And till recently there was a further distinction. For in civil cases, a new trial is not allowed merely because of an improper admission or rejection of evidence at the original trial, unless this error had occasioned 'some substantial wrong or miscarriage'.[3] But in criminal cases a jury's verdict of guilty used to be liable to be quashed if *any* inadmissible evidence for the Crown had gone in, even though that evidence was trivial, and though the rest of the evidence was amply sufficient to warrant a conviction. Now, however, the Criminal Appeal Act, 1907,[4] has abolished this scrupulosity. For it provides that 'the court may, notwithstanding that they are of opinion that the point raised in the appeal might be decided in favour of the appellant, dismiss the appeal if they consider that no substantial miscarriage of justice has actually occurred'.[5] A similarly wide power of dismissal had already been adopted by the High Court in dealing with appeals from rulings given about evidence in courts of petty sessions.[6]

WHEN OBJECTIONS SHOULD BE TAKEN

¶ 523. So, now, a small slip in the evidence will not entitle a prisoner to appeal successfully if (even had an opposite ruling been given) the only reasonable and proper verdict for the jury to return would still have been the same, one of guilty; in other words, if in the opinion of

[1] 'In criminal courts the rules of evidence are strictly observed; and in six months you learn more of practical advocacy there than in ten years elsewhere' (Lord Brampton).

[2] *R.* v. *Bateman* (1845) 1 Cox 186 (*T.A.C.*); cf. *R.* v. *Bertrand* (1867) L.R. 1 P.C. 520, at p. 534; *R.* v. *Lee Kun* (1915) 11 Cr.App.R. 292, at p. 300. But the quasi-civil character which the early law attached to misdemeanours (*ante*, ¶ 77) has occasionally led, in their case, to slight relaxations of this rule; see e.g. ¶ 608 *post*.

[3] Rules of the Supreme Court, Order XXXIX, rule 6.

[4] *Post*, ¶ 654. See *R.* v. *McVitie* [1960] 2 All E.R. 498.

[5] See *post*, ¶ 778 n. 2.

[6] *Shortt* v. *Robinson* (1899) 63 J.P. 295.

the judges in the Court of Criminal Appeal a reasonable jury not only might, but would, have convicted. Yet there may be a sufficient 'miscarriage of justice' to warrant setting aside a conviction,[1] even though the Court of Appeal itself thinks the conviction justifiable. It is sufficient that it would have been 'fairly and reasonably' *possible* for the jury to have refused to convict, had the rules of evidence been strictly observed. For the prisoner has lost that chance of acquittal.[2] Hence a prosecutor should not press for the admission of any evidence which is at all of doubtful admissibility. But, on the other hand, a prisoner's counsel should not be too eager to take objections to evidence; for the jury resent any technicality which closes the avenues to truth, and therefore a successful objection often creates in their minds a prejudice more injurious than the excluded evidence itself would be. American lawyers are often surprised at the rarity, in English trials, of objections to evidence.

If any improper evidence is given, the judge should strike it out of his notes and should bid the jury pay no attention to it. Where an inadmissible statement has been made with regard to the prisoner's record[3] or a point of similar importance, and the statement is to the prejudice[4] of the prisoner, an application for a fresh jury should be made forthwith by counsel for the defence and the judge should then discharge the jury and re-try the prisoner before a fresh jury.[5] It is advisable that such application be made at once,[6] although it is not fatal to an appeal founded on the admission of an improper question that counsel failed at the time to raise the matter.[7] And it is the duty of the judge to stop improper questions without waiting for objection to be taken by counsel.[8] The ordinary practice is, if counsel knows that there may be evidence to which he will object, that he should inform the prosecution beforehand so that the prosecution should not open that piece of evidence to the jury, who at a later stage should be told to retire during the argument as to the admissibility of a certain point.[9]

SECTION 2. RULES COMMON TO CIVIL AND CRIMINAL CASES

¶ 524. In the discussion of the rules of evidence it will be convenient to begin with an account of the main principles of fundamental importance which are applicable in all courts whether civil or criminal, and

[1] Wrongful rejection: *R.* v. *Watkins* (1909) 2 Cr.App.R. 119. Wrongful admission: *R.* v. *Green* (1908) 1 Cr.App.R. 124 at p. 128; *R.* v. *Joyce* (1908) 1 Cr.App.R. 83; *R.* v. *Atherton* (1910) 5 Cr.App.R. 233; *R.* v. *Mullins* (1910) 5 Cr.App.R. 13.

[2] *R.* v. *Fisher* (1910) 3 Cr.App.R. 176. Cf. *R.* v. *Hilliard* (1913) 9 Cr.App.R. 171; *R.* v. *Harrison-Owen* [1951] 2 All E.R. 726.

[3] *Post*, ¶ 609.

[4] *R.* v. *Wattam* [1942] 1 All E.R. 178; *R.* v. *Ellis* [1961] 1 W.L.R. 1064.

[5] *R.* v. *Peckham* (1935) 25 Cr.App.R. 125.

[6] *R.* v. *Firth* [1938] 3 All E.R. 783.

[7] E.g. *R.* v. *Biggin* (1920) 14 Cr.App.R. 87.

[8] *Stirland* v. *D.P.P.* [1944] A.C. 315; 2 All E.R. 13 (*T.A.C.*).

[9] *R.* v. *Cole* (1941) 165 L.T. 125; *R.* v. *Hammond* [1941] 3 All E.R. 318.

then to pass to the rules peculiar to courts of criminal jurisdiction. These basic conceptions are twelve in number.

(I) GENERAL BURDEN OF PROOF

¶ 525. The 'burden of proof', or *onus probandi*, is an expression which is used to indicate at any given moment which party to legal proceedings must lose if no further evidence be adduced.[1] It has always been held, in every judicial system worthy of the name, to be a requirement so fundamental as to be beyond argument, that any person who makes a positive assertion of fact in legal proceedings should be compelled to establish the truth of his allegations to the satisfaction of the tribunal before which he makes them. Therefore a plaintiff in civil proceedings and a prosecutor in a criminal case must establish by evidence (with the aid of legal presumptions, if need be) that, *prima facie* at least, there exist the essential facts of the kind which the law requires to constitute the right (or the crime) which he claims to exist.[2] Unless he does so much as this, it is plain that he has not discharged the burden of proof which lies upon him at the outset, and accordingly the defendant (or the accused person in a criminal case) has no need to speak (he 'has no case to answer') and the tribunal's decision must therefore be given in his favour. This general situation is usually expressed in the Latin maxim, *omnia praesumuntur pro negante.*

Omnia praesumuntur pro negante

¶ 526. The rule is also stated by the Roman jurist, Paulus,[3] as '*ei incumbit probatio qui dicit, non qui negat*'.

Thus the creditor who claims a debt has the burden of proving it to be owed.[4] Similarly, in any criminal accusation,[5] the burden of proof almost always lies upon the accuser as regards the *actus reus*,[6] and usually also as regards the *mens rea*, while the accused, on the other hand, is entitled to maintain 'a sullen silence'. And this duty of every affirmant to make out his case is so clearly imposed by law that, although the judge is not a judge of fact, yet he is a judge as to the absence of fact, and so must not allow the jury to pronounce a verdict in the affirmant's favour if the only evidence he has produced be so slight that no reasonable man would accept it as establishing the fact which is to be proved. Thus if it is necessary to show that a transaction took place on a Monday, and the evidence only shows that it took place 'either on a Monday or else on a Tuesday', there would be no case which the judge could submit to the jury, unless indeed this evidence were eked out by some

[1] See Phipson on Evidence, 9th ed. 1952, 32.

[2] This burden of proof of the main issue is heavier in a criminal case than it is in a civil action, see *post*, ¶¶ 594–596.

[3] *Dig.* XXII, 3. 2.

[4] And even in civil cases the defendant's refusal to give information does not satisfy the plaintiff's burden of proof; *Smith* v. *G.W. Rly Co.* [1922] 1 A.C. 178, at p. 185.

[5] *R.* v. *Hazy* (1826) 2 C. and P. 458 (*T.A.C.*); *Williams* v. *East India Co.* (1802) 3 East 192 (*T.A.C.*).

[6] But as to negative averments see ¶¶ 527, 531 *post*.

presumption, as for instance, *omnia rite esse acta*.[1] So, again, if a prisoner be identified only by footmarks, but many similar pairs of boots have been sold in his village, there would be no case.

Negative averments

¶ 527. A little thought will show that by an appropriate alteration of the wording, a statement may be changed from the form of a positive allegation into the negative form of a denial. The true burden of proof cannot be shifted by any such device and care must be taken to observe the substance of the matter.[2] The presumption of innocence is fundamental, and cannot be evaded by a use of words. Thus where a party to proceedings sets up a *denial* that the other party has performed some active duty, this really amounts to a positive allegation of misconduct, and must be proved.[3]

¶ 528. *Require affirmative counter-evidence.* But difficulty has arisen in some cases of 'negative averments' where the affirmative fact, which would disprove guilt, is one which (if it exists) lies peculiarly within the knowledge of the litigant in whose interest it is that this guilt should be disproved. For in these special cases, so soon as the accuser has given so much evidence as a reasonable man might consider to be sufficient to establish the positive elements of the offence, there then is cast upon the accused person the burden of disproving the negative element by producing affirmative counter-evidence. So if he fail to produce that evidence, this failure may be taken as proving that no such affirmative evidence exists, and accordingly as establishing the accuser's negative allegation. Thus on an indictment for misprision of treason, though it is for the Crown to prove that the prisoner knew of the treason, it yet may legally leave the prisoner to prove (if he can) that he discharged his consequent duty of disclosing it to some magistrate.[4] And similarly in proceedings for practising medicine without a qualification, or selling game without a licence, or producing a play without the author's consent, so soon as the active conduct alleged has been proved, it has often been left to the defendant to prove that he possessed the qualification or licence or consent.[5] In most of the statutory cases the point

[1] *Ante*, ¶ 496.

[2] To take an imaginary and, of course, absurd example, the affirmative allegation, that the prisoner is guilty of a particular crime, could be converted into a denial that he is innocent of it, an example of the logicians' 'obversion'.

[3] E.g. in cases of indecent assault the prosecution must negative consent, *R.* v. *Horn* (1912) 7 Cr.App.R. 200; *R.* v. *Donovan* [1934] 2 K.B. 498 (*T.A.C.*). So in civil actions for malicious prosecution the plaintiff must prove the negative fact that there was 'no reasonable cause' for prosecuting (*Abrath* v. *N.E. Rly Co.* (1883) 11 Q.B.D. 440). So also in ejectment for *non*-insurance (*Doe* v. *Whitehead* (1838) 8 A. and E. 571). Cf. *Williams* v. *East India Co.* (1802), 3 East 192 (*T.A.C.*), *post*, ¶ 537.

[4] *R.* v. *Thistlewood* (1820) 33 St. Tr. at p. 691. Cf. *R.* v. *Ahlers* [1915] 1 K.B. 618.

[5] *R.* v. *Turner* (1816) 5 M. and S. 206 (*T.A.C.*); *R.* v. *Scott* (1921) 86 J.P. 69, supplying cocaine without licence; *R.* v. *Oliver* [1943] 2 All E.R. 800, selling sugar without a licence; *Williams* v. *Russell* (1933) 49 T.L.R. 315. Cf. *Larkin* v. *Belfast Harbour Cmrs*

seems to be that, where the statute prohibits a deed, it cannot have been intended by the legislature that its prohibition should be stultified by a requirement that the prosecution must prove that of which it is impossible or very difficult to obtain evidence of a negative character. Yet in some at least of the cases it would seem that the prosecution ought to have put in some evidence, e.g. that the official records (if any) did not show that any licence had been issued to the accused, or that he had been asked to produce his licence, and had refused or neglected to do so.[1]

The prosecution need not negative a proviso in a statute, and a distinction must be drawn between the enacting part of a law which the prosecution must normally negative and exceptions in a proviso within which the accused must bring himself; *R.* v. *Audley* [1907] 1 K.B. 383.

Silence rarely proves guilt

¶ **529.** But it is only in this unusual class of cases, viz. accusations of omission, where, moreover, the act omitted is such that its performance could easily be proved by the accused and hardly disproved by the prosecution, that a defendant's mere silence can suffice to prove any element of his guilt.[2] Usually, the utmost hostile inference that can be drawn from his silence does not amount to proof but merely to confirmation. It is not sufficient to rebut so strong a presumption as that of innocence; but it is capable of being taken into account to corroborate other evidence which, even uncorroborated, was already legally adequate to effect that rebuttal.[3] Of course the value of this fact of silence increases in proportion as the ground of defence, about which the defendant is silent, lies the more particularly within his own knowledge. In *Att.-Gen.* v. *Bradlaugh*,[4] an action for penalties for acting as a member of parliament without having taken the oath, the informant alleged that the defendant's religious views made him incompetent to take an oath; and this assertion was supported by evidence. As the defendant could himself have disproved the assertion if it were not true, the jury were directed to take into account the fact that he had not done so. And in divorce proceedings, if the co-respondent is present in court, and yet does not go into the witness-box to assert his innocence, this corroborates (though only slightly) the evidence given against him. So, in the

[1908] 2 I.R. 214. A prisoner setting up, in answer to a charge of bigamy, a marriage valid by foreign law must prove the foreign law as strictly as it must be proved if a foreign marriage is relied upon by the prosecution; *R.* v. *Naguib* [1917] 1 K.B. 359. In *John* v. *Humphries* [1955] 1 All E.R. 793 it was held that the words 'unless he is the holder of a licence' in s. 4 (1) of the Road Traffic Act, 1930 (see now the Road Traffic Act, 1960, sect. 98 (1)), place on the driver of a motor car the onus of proving that he has a licence.

[1] E.g. *R.* v. *Putland and Sorrell* [1946] 1 All E.R. 85 (*T.A.C.*).

[2] *R.* v. *Davis* (1959) 43 Cr.App.R. 215.

[3] Cf. *McQueen* v. *G.W. Rly Co.* (1875) L.R. 10 Q.B. 569 at p. 574. See also *M'Kewen* v. *Cotching* (1857) 27 L.J. Ex. 41.

[4] *The Times*, 1 July 1884; and on appeal, 14 Q.B.D. 667.

proceedings in 1820, on the allegation of adultery against Queen Caroline, great stress was laid upon her failure to bring her devoted attendant Bergami, the alleged adulterer, as a witness to her innocence.[1]

Defendant allowed to give evidence

¶ 530. The importance of this rule as to a defendant's silence is very great, ever since the Criminal Evidence Act, 1898,[2] allowed all accused persons to give evidence for themselves on oath. For, though this Act forbids counsel (see ¶ 625 *post*) to comment on the prisoner's not giving evidence, no such restriction is imposed upon the judge; and indeed jurymen themselves are usually quick to notice the prisoner's abstention.

Cases when the *onus probandi* is on the prisoner

¶ 531. It should be noted, in conclusion, that there are a few exceptional criminal cases in which the legislature has thrown upon the prisoner the *onus probandi* of a part of the issue. The following are instances:

(i) By the Obscene Publications Act, 1857, s. 1, the onus is on the accused to show why the publications should not be destroyed.[3]

(ii) By the Explosive Substances Act, 1883,[4] it is a felony, punishable with imprisonment for fourteen years, knowingly to have in his possession or under his control any explosive substance under suspicious circumstances, unless the prisoner can show that his possession was for a lawful purpose.

(iii) By the Larceny Act, 1916, s. 28 (2) it is made a misdemeanour for a person to be found by night in possession of housebreaking implements, 'without lawful excuse (the proof whereof shall lie on such person[5])'; see ¶ 217 *ante*.

(iv) By 2 and 3 Vict. c. 71, s. 24 it is made an offence to be in unlawful possession, in any street or public place, in the *metropolitan* police district, of goods which may reasonably be suspected of being stolen, unless the prisoner gives a good account of how he came by them (punishable by two months' imprisonment).

(v) By s. 2 of the Prevention of Corruption Act, 1916, on a charge of corruption made under the Prevention of Corruption Act, 1906, a consideration shall be deemed to be given corruptly unless the contrary is proved. This goes no further than to put upon the accused person the

[1] Lord Eldon, for instance, in his speech in the House of Lords (2 Nov. 1820) treats this failure as 'amounting to a tacit admission'.

[2] See ¶ 621 *post*. Cf. *R.* v. *Mudge* (1908) 1 Cr.App.R. 62; *R.* v. *Corrie* (1904) 20 T.L.R. 365; *R.* v. *Boyd* (1908) 1 Cr.App.R. 64; *R.* v. *Bernard* (1908) 1 Cr.App.R. 218. *Ward* v. *Mauritius (Bishop)* (1906) 23 T.L.R. 52.

[3] *Cox* v. *Stinton* [1951] 2 K.B. 1021; *Thomson* v. *Chain Libraries Ltd* [1954] 2 All E.R. 616; *ante*, ¶ 184.

[4] As amended by the Criminal Justice Act, 1948; mere knowledge that the explosive was there was held not to be enough in *R.* v. *Rutter and White* [1959] Crim. L.R. 288.

[5] Yet it has been held that it is enough for the accused to raise 'reasonable doubt'; *R.* v. *Ward* [1915] 3 K.B. 696, *ante* ¶ 217; *R.* v. *Patterson* [1962] 1 All E.R. 340.

onus to satisfy the jury that the *probability* was that the gift was made innocently, and if he does so the statutory presumption is rebutted.[1]

(II) THE MODE IN WHICH TESTIMONIAL EVIDENCE IS GIVEN

¶ 532. The method adopted is one which was gradually developed by the common law courts. Towards the end they went far in excluding evidence, but they elicited in an exemplary manner all that was not excluded. In Chancery far more evidence was always admissible, but the mode of elicitation was such as to render all of it far less trustworthy. In common law courts the witness must give his testimony not 'spontaneously' but 'responsively', i.e. not in a consecutive narrative, but by brief answers to brief successive questions. This method affords the opposing party an opportunity of objecting, before it is too late, to any question which tends to elicit an answer that would not be legally admissible as evidence. The questions moreover are put by counsel and not by the judge.[2]

Examination-in-chief. Cross-examination

¶ 533. The questions proposed to a witness may occur in as many as three successive series.

(1) He is first 'examined in chief' by the party that has called him, with the object of eliciting from him evidence in support of that party's view of the question at issue.[3] The counsel ought to control his witness, and check him from tendering any inadmissible evidence.

(2) He is then cross-examined by the opposite party, in order to diminish the effect of the evidence which he has thus given, and perhaps also to obtain evidence in support of the case of the party cross-examining. For a cross-examination is not, as is sometimes imagined, limited to the scope of the examination-in-chief. But it should be limited to matters relevant to the issue (indirectly relevant at least, if not directly).[4] Yet irrelevant questions are sometimes asked quite properly, simply to test a witness's intelligence, or to throw a dishonest

[1] *R.* v. *Carr-Briant* [1943] K.B. 607 (*T.A.C.*).

[2] Yet so late as *Lilburne's Case* (1649) a strong court told the prisoner that he might not cross-examine the Crown witnesses, but only suggest questions for the court to put (4 St. Tr. at p. 1334). However, in French criminal trials they are put through the medium of the presiding judge. For though the prisoner's counsel may now carry on an examination or cross-examination, he usually can only do so by getting the leave of the judge for each question; 'with the result that his cross-examination becomes comparatively ineffective', wrote Lord Russell of Killowen (*Life*, 320), after attending the trial of Capt. Dreyfus at Rennes. The French Code of Criminal Procedure provides that a witness must not be interrupted in his answer. Hence, upon the trial of M. Zola (in connexion with the *Dreyfus Case*) in 1898, more than one of the military witnesses made a continuous speech that occupied over a quarter of an hour; and General de Pellieux was called as a witness expressly on account of his extreme eloquence.

[3] 'Far and away the most important function of an advocate is the examination-in-chief; to think it is the cross-examination is a great mistake' (Atkin, L.J.).

[4] See *R.* v. *Banks* (1916) 12 Cr.App.R. 74 at p. 76.

witness off his guard. Hence judges are slow to interfere with a cross-examiner. Cross-examination may reduce the effect of the evidence given in examination-in-chief either simply by eliciting further facts which tend to harmonize that evidence with the case set up by the cross-examiners,[1] or by shaking that evidence itself. This latter effect may, for instance, be produced by bringing the witness to admit that his opportunities of observing the facts narrated were inadequate, or that his character or bias is such as to make it unwise to rely on his veracity, or again, by involving him in such inconsistencies of statement as to make all such reliance impossible on (at any rate) this particular occasion.[2] If on a crucial point of the case it is proposed to ask a jury to disbelieve a witness, the witness should be cross-examined on that point.[3] Cross-examination should be directed to facts not arguments. It is objectionable to begin a question to a witness: 'Do you ask the jury to believe' or 'Is your evidence to be taken as suggesting that'.[4]

¶ 534. *Cross-examination to be used with care.* Students should note the danger of an indiscriminate cross-examination. Counsel who puts an ill-considered question in cross-examination may elicit evidence highly damaging to his own case, which the opposing counsel could not obtain from the witness by the examination-in-chief (in which of course leading questions may not be asked[5]) or has overlooked.[6] It would indeed be wise to adhere to a rule never to ask a question unless you know (i) what the *true* answer to it really is and (ii) that the true answer will assist your case. To put a question on the chance[7] of extracting some useful answer is to take an unjustifiable risk.

Re-examination

¶ 535. Finally, (3) a witness who has undergone cross-examination may be re-examined by the party who originally called him; in order to show the real meaning of the evidence elicited by the cross-examination.[8] A re-examiner may, for instance, get the witness to explain any ambiguous expressions which he may have used on cross-examination, or his motives (e.g. provocation) for any conduct which he may have

[1] A prisoner's evidence, in 1911, 'I am an industrious man and recently worked for seven years in Devonshire', was cancelled by the cross-examiner's well-founded question, 'Was it not at Dartmoor?'

[2] Quintilian's instructions on the cross-examination of witnesses are still noteworthy; *Inst. Orat.* v. 7.

[3] *R.* v. *Baldwin* (1925) 133 L.T. 191; 18 Cr.App.R. 175.

[4] *R.* v. *Hart* (1932) 23 Cr.App.R. 202; cf. ¶ 540 *post.*

[5] See ¶ 537.

[6] An example of deadly mistakes made by counsel for the defence in cross-examination of a witness for the Crown is to be seen in the case of *John Donellan* in 1781, as described by Stephen in his *General View of the Criminal Law of England* (1863), pp. 346, 347.

[7] Often called a 'fishing' question.

[8] Re-examination is so difficult that the leading counsel rarely trusts it to his junior. A great advocate said that 'unless conducted irregularly, it is useless'.

admitted when under cross-examination.[1] Thus, if the cross-examiner has asked, 'Didn't you once assault a neighbour?' the re-examiner may ask 'What did this neighbour do to make you assault him?' Or if the witness has been asked in cross-examination, 'What are you to receive for coming here to-day?' the re-examiner may ask, 'And what have your journey here and your loss of time cost you?' But re-examinations are limited strictly to the matters that have been elicited in the cross-examination.

¶ 536. *Questions about conversations or documents.* It should be added that if either an examiner-in-chief or a cross-examiner has elicited from a witness some portion of a conversation or of a document (even though he may have brought out all that it was legally permissible for *him* to ask for), his opponent becomes entitled to elicit (in his subsequent cross-examination or re-examination) all the rest of that conversation or document, so far as it concerns the same subject. Thus if the examiner-in-chief asks, 'Why did you go to that house?' and receives for answer, 'Because of a remark my brother made to me', *he* cannot go on to ask what this remark was (for that would be to adduce hearsay evidence); but the opposite party, when he comes to cross-examine, will be fully entitled to ask (see ¶ 577).

(III) LEADING QUESTIONS

¶ 537. Questions put to a witness by the counsel who produces him (whether in examination-in-chief or in re-examination) must not be 'leading' ones.[2] A question 'leads' if, though it admits of several answers, it suggests that a particular answer is desired by the questioner. Thus an examiner-in-chief must not ask 'Wasn't it a wet day?' but, 'What sort of weather was it?'; not, 'Was it eleven o'clock?' but, 'What time was it?'; not, 'Was he drunk?' but, 'What was his state as to sobriety?'; not, 'When he was leaving did he offer you £5?' but, 'When he was leaving what did he do?' Leading questions are objectionable because (1) to a false witness they suggest what particular lie would be desirable; and (2) even an honest witness is prone to give an assenting answer from mere mental laziness.[3] But these

[1] Mr Richard R. Harris had an apt story of a witness who had sworn to the sanity of a testator and being asked in cross-examination, 'What will you get as a legatee if the will be found valid?' answered '£10,000'. But the re-examiner asked, 'And what, as next of kin, if it be found invalid?' '£50,000.' Professor Kenny recorded that he had heard a cross-examiner's question 'Have you been prosecuted for theft' (which the witness admitted) followed by the re-examiner's 'With what result?' and the answer 'Acquittal'.

[2] But in the examination before justices previous to committal for trial, the taking of depositions by leading questions, although undesirable, is not a breach of the Indictable Offences Act, 1948, s. 17; *R.* v. *Walker* [1950] 2 All E.R. 911.

[3] Leading questions were objected to even as early as the trial of Lilburne in 1649, The Attorney-General having asked a witness such a question, Lilburne interposed, 'I pray, Sir, do not direct him what to say, but leave him to his own conscience and memory' (4 St. Tr. at p. 1337).

objections are not likely to apply to a cross-examination, so leading questions are freely permitted there.[1]

Allowed in five cases

¶ 538. To certain portions, also, of the examination-in-chief the objections are inapplicable; and therefore even here, as leading questions save much time, they are allowed in the following cases.

(1) As to undisputed matter, e.g. the name, address, and occupation of a witness. If a fact has been deposed to by a witness, and he has not been cross-examined about it, this may *prima facie* be taken to imply that the fact is undisputed, and accordingly that subsequent witnesses may be 'led' with respect to it.

(2) As to the identity of persons or things, e.g. 'Is this the watch that you missed?' Thus an examiner may ask, 'Is the prisoner the man you saw?' Yet a jury would be more fully impressed if counsel asked first, 'Would you recognize the man?' and then bade the witness point him out. A photograph is admissible as evidence of identity when put to a witness, because it is only a visible representation of the image or impression made upon the minds of the witnesses of the sight of the person or the object it represents; and therefore it is, in reality, only another species of the evidence which persons give of identity when they speak merely from memory.[2] Photographs may be shown to persons who can identify a criminal if the police are seeking for information as to the person or persons who may have committed a crime, but after identification the police should not try to corroborate the evidence of a witness by showing him the photograph of a person whom he has already identified.[3] Photographs of a person under arrest should not be shown to witnesses who are just about to attend an identification parade.[4]

(3) For the purpose of contradicting the account which some previous witness, *A*, has given of his own utterances, a subsequent witness, *B*, may be asked a leading question, such as, 'Did *A* say so-and-so?' But, *before* this is asked, *B* should be asked to give his own version of what *A* said.

(4) Sometimes a witness, in the course of his examination-in-chief, shows himself to be hostile to the party producing him—meaning thereby, not that he merely gives evidence which is at variance with that party's case, but that he shows an evident unwillingness to disclose what he knows in favour of it. Thereupon the judge may, if he think fit, permit the examiner to contend with this unwillingness by asking leading questions.[5]

[1] Hence there is often a struggle as to which party shall call a witness; for it must affect the right to cross-examine, and may affect the right to make the last speech to the jury; see ¶ 752 *post*. It would seem that neither side dared call the most important witness in *Williams* v. *East India Co.* (1802) 3 East 192 (*T.A.C.*).

[2] *Per* Willes, J., in *R.* v. *Tolson* (1864) 4 F. and F. 104.

[3] R. v. *Hinds* [1932] 2 K.B. 644. Contrast *R.* v. *Dwyer and Ferguson* [1925] 2 K.B. 799.

[4] R. v. *Haslam* (1925) 134 L.T. 158; 19 Cr.App.R. 59.

[5] *Parkin* v. *Moon* (1836) 7 C. and P. 408 (*T.A.C.*).

(5) If the witness merely proves to be forgetful, no such permission will be given to ask questions that are strictly leading ones; yet after an examiner-in-chief has thoroughly tested and exhausted his witness's memory, he will usually be allowed to suggest points for recollection,[1] e.g. even to ask, 'Was nothing said on the subject of the...?'

(IV) A WITNESS SPEAKS TO HIS MEMORY, AND NOT TO HIS REASONING OR HIS OPINION

¶ 539. What a witness remembers will be admissible in evidence even though his recollection of the facts is only weak, e.g. 'my impression' (but, of course, its value may consequently be trifling). Lord Eldon admitted testimony to the genuineness of handwriting although it was twenty years since the testifier had seen the alleged writer.[2] And a letter has been admitted[3] as evidence though the witness to its authorship could go no further than to say, 'It is in a disguised hand; I believe it to be his writing, but I would not like to swear positively to it'.[4]

¶ 540. *He must not state his inferences.* A witness should not be asked to answer a question as to a consequence of law.[5] And it is only for his memory that a witness is brought into court, not for his powers of judgment (unless he be called as a scientific expert, e.g. a chemist in a case of poisoning). Hence an ordinary witness must not be asked, either in examination-in-chief or in cross-examination, to draw inferences. 'As *A* and *B* occupied the same cabin, would *A* have put this message into writing if he meant it for *B* only?' is an argument, not a question. Thus, similarly, on reminding a witness that his answer is a contradiction of the evidence which some previous witness has given, even the common question, 'If *A* says the contrary to what you have just told us, is what he says untrue?' is, strictly speaking, one which he need not answer.[6] Similarly a cross-examiner has no right to ask, 'Did you go to the prisoner's house as a spy?'[7] for this is a matter not merely of facts but of the view to be taken of those facts. Yet he may ask under what directions the witness went there, for what purpose he went, what he

[1] Cf. *Courteen* v. *Touse* (1807) 1 Camp. 43.

[2] *Eagleton* v. *Kingston*, 8 Vesey 438 at p. 474. The permission has been carried in America even to sixty years; 63 S.W. 194.

[3] *R.* v. *Bernard* (1858) 8 St. Tr. (n.s.) 887 at pp. 927, 981; cf. *R.* v. *Melville* (1806) 29 St. Tr. 549 at p. 740.

[4] Lord Tenterden refused to withdraw from the jury the question as to a defendant's signature, although the only evidence of its genuineness was that of a witness who stated, after much hesitation, that he believed the signature was the defendant's; yet upon cross-examination, after again hesitating several minutes, said he believed it was *not*; but upon re-examination stated, though again hesitatingly, that he believed it was; *Beauchamp* v. *Cash* (1822) D. and R. (N.P.) 3.

[5] *Whitehorn Bros.* v. *Davison* [1911] 1 K.B. 463 at p. 484.

[6] 'If you had known this fact, would you have taken the shares?' is similarly inadmissible; *R.* v. *Gurney* (1869) 11 Cox 414 at p. 435.

[7] *R.* v. *Bernard* (1858) 8 St. Tr. (n.s.) at p. 935; 1 F. and F. 240.

did when there, what report he afterwards made to those who employed him; and then, on the strength of the answers, he may urge to the jury that the conduct of the witness was that of a spy.

(V) EVIDENCE MUST BE RELEVANT

¶ 541. This means that the evidence must be confined to the question at issue.

A party may prove all circumstances that are relevant to the facts in issue, but no others.[1] The circumstances thus relevant consist not only of those which form part of the facts in issue themselves (the *facta probanda*, *ante*, ¶ 505), but also of all such further circumstances (the *facta probantia*) as may be necessary to identify or to explain these. This, for instance, will include in a criminal case not only the prisoner's commission of the crime and his guilty knowledge, but also—as facilitating a belief in these—his opportunities,[2] motives,[3] and subsequent conduct,[4] and the credibility of the witnesses produced at his trial.

Thus, where a prisoner, accused of murder, bore the somewhat unusual surname of Lamson, evidence was admitted that luggage had been deposited in that name on the day of the murder at a railway station near the scene of the crime, because it was proof of opportunity, though very slight proof.[5]

The conduct of the prisoner and of his accomplices may be relevant

¶ 542. Not only is the prisoner's own conduct relevant, but so soon as it has been shown that others were combined with him in carrying out a joint criminal purpose, evidence may be given of any conduct of theirs which forwarded this joint purpose, even though such conduct took place in the prisoner's absence and though they are not indicted along with him.[6] This rule is of specially frequent application in trials for conspiracy (¶ 454 *ante*), but is by no means confined to them. Thus if *A* be indicted for uttering counterfeit coin, evidence may be given of his accomplice *B* going into a market and passing it there, though *A* himself did not go. Similarly, if *A* and *B* have agreed that *B* shall obtain

[1] *Boldron* v. *Widdows* (1824) 1 C. and P. 65 (*T.A.C.*).

[2] Evidence that skeleton-keys were found at the house of a person accused of burglary will thus be admissible if the burglary were effected by keys, but not if effected by a crowbar; *R.* v. *Manning* (1923) 17 Cr.App.R. 88.

[3] Thus if a man be charged with the murder of his *wife*, evidence may be given of his being in love with another woman. So, in a case of theft, evidence of poverty may be given.

[4] Thus in *R.* v. *Hobday* (*The Times*, 12 Dec. 1933), the Court of Criminal Appeal allowed evidence that the prisoner, after committing a murder, broke into a house to remove the traces of the crime from his person, and then stole a motor bicycle on which to escape. But statements made by a prisoner *after* commission of the alleged crime, in which he has explained or stated what his defence will be, are not admissible, *R.* v. *Roberts* [1942] 1 All E.R. 187 at p. 191. For statements which are part of the *res gestae* see ¶ 570 *post*.

[5] *R.* v. *Lamson* (1882) C.C.C. Sess. Pap. xcv, 547 at p. 572.

[6] *R.* v. *Stone* (1796) 6 T.R. 527; *R.* v. *Winkworth* (1830) 4 C. and P. 444.

goods at a shop by a false pretence, what *B* says in the shop may be given in evidence against *A*, though he was not there, and even though *B* is not indicted along with him.

¶ 543. *But is limited to conduct shown on the particular occasion.* The legal limits of relevancy exclude much evidence which, in non-legal matters, would be thought very cogent. Thus if the question at issue be as to how a man acted on one occasion, evidence of the way in which he acted on some other similar occasion is not considered sufficiently relevant to be admissible. Accordingly in civil courts, in a dispute as to what the terms of a contract were, a litigant cannot corroborate his account of them by giving proof of the terms of other contracts which his opponent made on the same subject-matter with other persons.[1] Yet evidence of these other contracts would have been quite admissible had the dispute related—not, as here, to what the opponent actually said when making the present contract, but—to what was his state of mind when making it, e.g. whether or not it was with a fraudulent intent that he introduced into it some ambiguous terms.[2]

Past offences excluded

¶ 544. And in criminal courts the same principle serves to exclude evidence of the prisoner's past offences.[3] It is true that evidence of his *good* character is always regarded as relevant (*post*, ¶ 609), illogically, but from historical causes. Yet his *bad* character is not regarded as similarly relevant to the question whether he committed the *actus reus*. Consequently evidence of other (even similar) offences of which he has been guilty cannot be given[4] in order to corroborate the proof of his having committed this one; nor may a prisoner's witness be asked a question in cross-examination which would ordinarily be admissible to discredit *him*, if the question indirectly suggests that the prisoner has previously committed a crime.[5]

[1] *Hollingham* v. *Head* (1858) 4 C.B. (n.s.) 388. Cf. *Holcombe* v. *Hewson* (1810) 2 Camp. 391, where the fact that the beer which *A* had sold to *C*, *D*, and *E* was good was held to be irrelevant to the question whether that which he had sold to *B* was also good.

[2] *Barnes* v. *Merritt* (1898) 15 T.L.R. 419.

[3] 'Are you going to arraign his whole life? Away, away; that is nothing to the matter', protested Chief Justice Holt, two centuries ago; *R.* v. *Harrison* (1692) 12 St. Tr. 833 at p. 864. See a useful essay in 39 *L.Q.R.* 212. Experience shows that jurors give highly exaggerated weight to evidence of bad character. Even the publication in newspapers of evidence of previous convictions may be a ground for quashing a conviction. *R.* v. *Dyson* (1943) 169 L.T. 237 as explained in *R.* v. *Armstrong* [1951] 2 All E.R. 219.

[4] *R.* v. *Birdseye* (1830) 4 C. and P. 386 (*T.A.C.*). Or suggested; see *R.* v. *Wattam* [1942] 1 All E.R. 178. But see ¶ 550 and Appendix II *post*, where exceptions to this general rule, allowed in special circumstances, are discussed. If the judge considers that the prejudicial effect of the question is greater than its evidential value, it is his duty to exclude the question; see ¶ 547*a*, *post*.

[5] *R.* v. *McCraig* (1925) 90 J.P. 64. Yet in French criminal procedure such evidence plays a most important part. In the famous trial of Landru at Paris in 1921, for ten murders, the president began by saying '*It is my duty* to enlighten the jury as to the ante-

¶ 545. *But evidence of relevant facts is not excluded by this rule.* Nor is there any intrinsic objection to giving evidence of the prisoner's having committed other crimes, if there be any special circumstance[1] in the case to render those crimes legally relevant. Thus burglary may be brought home to a man by showing that a cigar case, which the burglar left behind in the house, had that day been stolen from its owner by *him*. Or, to show the motive of the present offence, some other crime may be disclosed;[2] as where a murder is accounted for by proving that the deceased had been an accomplice with the prisoner in some previous crime, and consequently was a person to be got rid of, or where an earlier act of sexual passion between *the same two* persons renders probable the further existence of their passion.[3] And the conduct of a prisoner, even subsequently to his offence, may throw light upon it; as where a thief, on being arrested, shoots his arrester.[4]

Similar offences may be relevant

¶ 546. Moreover, a distinction similar to that which we have already noticed in civil courts (*ante*, ¶ 543) holds good in criminal ones. Though a prisoner's bad character is not in itself relevant to show his guilt, yet the fact that he has committed offences *similar* to the offence with which he is charged may be relevant in order to show either *mens rea*[5] or *actus reus*, especially where the offences are so closely connected as to form one continuous course of action;[6] and evidence of similar facts will then be admissible and a prisoner witness may be cross-examined about them.[7] 'Similar' in this connexion means similar in points significant for the purpose of the inquiry in hand.[8]

¶ 547. *Limits of admissible similarity.* Thus the use of drugs to procure abortion is similar to the use of instruments by the same person for the same purpose,[9] but the uttering of notes not proved to be forged is not similar to the uttering of forged notes.[10] Such evidence is sometimes admissible to establish *mens rea*. Where a man was charged with obtaining money by falsely pretending that certain cheques were good and valid, evidence was admitted that in another case he had given another prosecutor a cheque which was dishonoured on presentation,[11]

cedents of the accused'. The Roman *quæstiones* paid more attention to those antecedents than to the testimony about the crime which was being tried.

[1] See App. II. Cf. *Charnock* v. *Merchant* [1900] 1 Q.B. 474.

[2] *R.* v. *Neill* (1892) C.C.C. Sess. Pap. CXVI, 1417 (*T.A.C.*).

[3] *R.* v. *Ball* [1911] A.C. 47 (*T.A.C.*).

[4] Cf. *R.* v. *Armstrong* [1922] 2 K.B. 555; 16 Cr.App.R. 149.

[5] *R.* v. *Francis* (1874) 2 C.C.R. 128; *R.* v. *Ollis* [1900] 2 Q.B. 758. Even acts done *after* the offence charged, *R.* v. *Rhodes* [1899] 1 Q.B. 77.

[6] *R.* v. *Ellis* (1826) 6 B. and C. 145 (*T.A.C.*); *R.* v. *Rearden* (1864) 4 F. and F. 76.

[7] See Appendix, II, B, 2, *post.*

[8] See article by Stone in 46 *Harvard L.R.* 954; and by Logan in 50 *L.Q.R.* 386; *R.* v. *Jones* [1961] 3 W.L.R. 668.

[9] *R.* v. *Starkie* [1922] 2 K.B. 275 (admissible evidence even where the women were different, in order to rebut the contention that the acts were done innocently).

[10] *R.* v. *Millard* (1813) R. and R. 245.

[11] *R.* v. *Ollis* [1900] 2 Q.B. 758.

but on a charge of obtaining a pony and cart by false pretences evidence was rejected that the accused had obtained provender by *different* false pretences.[1]

¶ 547*a*. *Judicial discretion exercised in fairness to the accused.* It has many times been emphasized that in criminal cases, where evidence of previous conduct, of offences (and sometimes of confessions[2]) and of other discreditable matters is held by the judge to be admissible, yet even then it is right for him to exclude it if in his considered opinion the prejudice which it will raise against the accused man clearly outweighs its probative value.[3]

Evidence of criminal tendency is inadmissible

¶ 548. It is a fundamental rule that evidence is not admissible merely to prove that the person accused has a general propensity to commit a crime similar in character to that with which he is charged.[4] Yet frequently evidence that will have this effect is admissible because relevant upon other grounds.[5] It has been said that evidence of similar facts is only admissible where it can be brought under the head of some specific exception to the general rule excluding it, but the tendency of recent decisions is to admit such evidence wherever relevant,[6] provided that it is not admitted merely to show the bad disposition of the accused.[7]

¶ 549. *Save when relevant on other grounds.* It has been suggested that this class of evidence is admitted not because it shows that other offences have been committed, but notwithstanding that in a particular case it

[1] *R.* v. *Fisher* [1910] 1 K.B. 149 (*T.A.C.*); *R.* v. *Slender* (1938) 26 Cr.App.R. 155.

[2] *Post,* ¶ 614.

[3] *R.* v. *Christie* [1914] A.C. 545 (*T.A.C.*); *Noor Mohamed* v. *R.* [1949] A.C. 182 at p. 192; *Harris* v. *D.P.P.* [1952] A.C. 694 at p. 707; *R.* v. *Miller* [1952] 2 All E.R. 667; *R.* v. *Cook* [1959] 2 All E.R. 97; *R.* v. *Coombes* [1961] Crim. L.R. 54; *R.* v. *Flynn* [1961] 3 All E.R. 58. But see *R.* v. *Pike* [1961] 11 Curr.L. 323.

[4] *R.* v. *Cole* (1810) Russ. 823; *Thompson* v. *The King* [1918] A.C. 221, 237; *Noor Mohamed* v. *R.* [1949] A.C. 182.

[5] *Noor Mohamed* v. *R.* [1949] A.C. 182; *Harris* v. *D.P.P.* [1952] A.C. 694. And see *post*, Appendix II, B (2) and D.

[6] A learned writer in the *Harvard Law Review* (cited in ¶ 546 *ante*) considers that there never was at common law a general rule excluding evidence of similar facts, but that such evidence was always admissible where relevant apart from merely showing evil disposition, and that it was not until the nineteenth century that judges began to lay down a general rule excluding such evidence save in certain specific cases. The tendency towards admission shown in some modern decisions (but halted by *Harris* v. *D.P.P.*, *supra*) is well illustrated by two articles in the *Law Quarterly Review*, 23 *L.Q.R.* 28 and 39 *L.Q.R.* 212. See also C. K. Allen, *Legal Duties*, 290–4.

[7] Even this rule would appear to have been disregarded in *R.* v. *Chesshire and others* (1927) 20 Cr.App.R. 47, where, on a charge against two police officers for corruptly accepting a gift and against a third person for corruptly making it, evidence was admitted against all three defendants that there was found upon the third person a piece of paper which bore words alleged by the prosecution, but denied by the defence, to relate to other acts of corruption.

may happen to do so;[1] and the likelihood of such evidence giving rise to undue prejudice has led to its admission being jealously regarded. It was at one time thought that before evidence of similar facts can be admitted there must first be some evidence of the doing by the accused of the act charged, and that evidence of similar facts is only admissible e.g. to show intent or guilty knowledge or to rebut a defence of innocent mistake.[2] The basis of admission is, however, today wider than this. See the conspectus of this topic contained in Appendix II *post*.

Statutory exceptions to the basic rule

¶ 550. In one instance the legislature has even extended this principle to evidence of offences that are not of a precisely similar kind. For under the Larceny Act, 1916, s. 43 (1) (*b*), on indictments for receiving stolen goods, so soon as it has been established that the prisoner did have possession of the stolen property, the fact of his having been convicted,[3] within five years previous to the receiving, of '*any* offence involving fraud or dishonesty' is admissible to show guilty knowledge.[4] It has, however, been declared that evidence of a previous conviction cannot be admitted where there is another charge on which a verdict is sought and the prosecution feel that they cannot confine their case to one of receiving, but must also rely on some other count, be it of stealing or of being an accessory after the fact to stealing.[5] Again, on indictments for receiving stolen goods the same section, section 43 (1) (*a*), also admits evidence of the fact that other property,[6] stolen within a year before this offence, has been or is found in the defendant's possession. Such evidence may include evidence as to the circumstances and any statements made in explanation, and evidence of possession may be given even before evidence that it is stolen property.[7] Finally, in certain circumstances, an accused person, who testifies under the Criminal Evidence Act, 1898 (*post*, ¶ 621), may be cross-examined as to character. Where the accused so conducts his defence as to render such cross-examination admissible (see ¶ 623 *post*) he may

[1] *R.* v. *Ollis* [1900] 2 Q.B. 758.

[2] *R.* v. *Hall* (1887) 5 N.Z.L.R. 93.

[3] Provided the case is substantially one of receiving and is presented to the jury on that footing, so that they are not asked to find a verdict on some other count (e.g. larceny of the goods); *R.* v. *Davies* [1953] 2 W.L.R. 304 at p. 306, differing from a dictum in *R.* v. *Jones* [1948] 2 All E.R. 964; 33 Cr.App.R. 33 (*T.A.C.*). Both these cases related to the admissibility of previous *convictions* under s. 43 (1) (*b*).

[4] If prisoner has had seven days' notice of this evidence.

[5] *R.* v. *Davies, ubi supra.*

[6] This evidence is admitted to show guilty knowledge. Distinguish carefully the rule that, in the case of the goods which are the subject-matter of the charge, possession of them, if recently stolen, raises a presumption of fact that the possessor is either the thief or a guilty receiver; see ¶ 500 *ante*. But in *R.* v. *Jackson* [1953] 1 W.L.R. 591, Lord Goddard, C.J., said of *R.* v. *Davies* that 'in some respects that case may require at the proper time some further consideration as to the extent of the decision and how far it was intended to go'; *Jackson's* case related to the discovery of stolen property under s. 43 (1) (*a*).

[7] *R.* v. *Smith* [1918] 2 K.B. 415.

be cross-examined as to his past offences though their only relevance is to attack his credibility and probably even to show his disposition.

Evidence of the character of a witness is admissible

¶ 551. By a distinction precisely the converse of that which is thus applied in the case of a prisoner's character, the badness of a *witness's*[1] character is always relevant, but its goodness is not. For the party by whom witnesses are produced cannot (in the first instance) corroborate their evidence by proof of their good character or even of their having on former occasions told the same tale they now tell.[2] But the party hostile to these witnesses may discredit their characters, in order to throw doubt on the veracity of their story.

Discrediting a witness

¶ 552. (*a*) *His mendacity*. This is done by evidence[3] to show that the witness has a general reputation for mendacity. This course is now rare; for it was decided in *R.* v. *Watson* (1817)[4] that no evidence can be given of any particular misconduct of his, and the question to be asked is the vague general one, 'Is he to be believed on his oath?'—as if mendacity were a fixed habit that did not vary with subject-matter and with personal interests.[5] The party who has produced the witness can never discredit him thus, even if he turn out utterly hostile. When such evidence is given it entitles the other party to contradict it by proof of his witness's good character for veracity.[6]

¶ 553. (*b*) *His bias*. Bias may, for instance, be shown by evidence that the witness has received money, or has offered money to other witnesses, or that he has threatened revenge.[7] And even relationship to the litigant who produces him is some evidence of bias.[8] But no proof of bias can be given unless the witness has, by cross-examination, been given an opportunity of explaining the circumstances.

[1] In *R.* v. *Hammond* [1941] 3 All E.R. 318 (at p. 320) a question, in cross-examination, to the *prisoner* as to whether a confession by him was true, was treated as admissible because 'it went to the credit of the person who was giving the evidence'.

[2] Evidence to corroborate a prisoner's defence by showing that he told his present story before he was accused is not relevant. A far-seeing offender might tell a lie. But see *Crouch* v. *Drury* (1661) 1 Keble 27 (*T.A.C.*) and *R.* v. *Benjamin* (1913) 8 Cr.App.R. 146 (*T.A.C.*); *post*, ¶¶ 572, 573.

[3] Or by cross-examination, *post*, ¶ 556. A witness so deposing can be cross-examined as to what means he had of ascertaining this general reputation, *Mawson* v. *Hartsink* (1802) 4 Esp. 102.

[4] 32 St. Tr. 1 at p. 486; *R.* v. *Brown* (1867) 1 C.C.R. 70.

[5] A witness may say 'From my knowledge of the witness *X*, I would not believe him on his oath'; but, save under cross-examination, he is *not* allowed to give his reasons for that opinion; *R.* v. *Gunewardene* [1951] 2 All E.R. 290.

[6] *R.* v. *Canning* (1754) 19 St. Tr. 283 at pp. 588, 595. General good conduct of witness held not admissible in *R.* v. *Wood* [1951] 2 All E.R. 111; 35 Cr.App.R. 61.

[7] *R.* v. *Yewin* (1811) 2 Camp. 637 (*T.A.C.*).

[8] *Thomas* v. *David* (1836) 7 C. and P. 350 (*T.A.C.*).

¶ 554. (*c*) *His previous inconsistent statement.* On some relevant fact, to which he now deposes, he may have previously made a statement inconsistent with what he now says. Here, again, before proof can be given of the discrediting statement, the witness's attention must be specifically drawn to it in cross-examination, in order that he may, if possible, explain it. In criminal cases this mode of discrediting is very common,[1] because most of the witnesses at the trial have already given evidence, viz. at the preliminary examination before the justice of the peace who committed the prisoner for trial. At common law, if the previous statement were in writing (e.g. a deposition[2] at this examination for commitment), the cross-examiner had to put it in as part of his own evidence (thereby giving the other party a right to a speech in reply), before even asking the witness about it. But now by the Criminal Procedure Act, 1865,[3] s. 5, he need not put it in, unless he desires actually to contradict what the witness says in cross-examination. He must, however, be able to produce it if required to do so by the court.[4] Yet the judge may use it for such a contradiction, although the cross-examiner has not put it in. Even if put in, it merely cancels the evidence previously given, and must be allowed no probative effect beyond this.[5] Its effect is to make the witness a negligible one. If, however, the accused heard the previous statement and by his conduct admitted it (see ¶ 575 *post*) a jury is entitled to believe the previous statement even though unsworn as opposed to a subsequent sworn statement.[6] But unsworn, unwritten statements made on a previous occasion, although they may be put in to discredit the person who made them when he now gives discordant evidence on oath, may *not* be treated as evidence against the accused person.[7] Depositions, though they may be used to impeach the credit of a witness, do not thereby become evidence at the trial so as to provide corroboration of a witness. So where a witness, whose evidence on deposition incriminated the accused, subsequently at the trial repudiated that statement and was then treated as hostile by the prosecution but still refused to admit that her deposition was true, it was declared by the Court of Criminal Appeal that the proper direction to

[1] Even in civil cases, the opposite party occasionally calls for any signed 'proof' of his intended evidence, which the witness may have given to the solicitor; cf. ¶ 588 *post*. But there is no obligation to produce it.

[2] See ¶ 709 *post*. But word for word agreement with a deposition looks like learning by heart, and so is far more suspicious than slight variances.

[3] This Act, by s. 4, provides in effect that, if a witness gives evidence of a *relevant* fact (not, e.g., going merely to his *credit*), it can be put to him that on a previous occasion (not necessarily in writing or on oath) he made a contradictory statement to another person, *X*, and if he denies it then *X* can be called to give affirmative evidence of that statement.

[4] *R.* v. *Anderson* (1929) 142 L.T. 580; 21 Cr.App.R. 178.

[5] See *R.* v. *Dibble* (1908) 1 Cr.App.R. 155; *R.* v. *White* (1922) 17 Cr.App.R. 64; *R.* v. *Harris* (1927) 20 Cr.App.R. 144.

[6] See 99 J.P. 386.

[7] *R.* v. *Allpress* [1956] Crim. L.R. 622.

the jury was (*a*) that her evidence at the trial should be treated as unreliable and (*b*) that her previous statements, inconsistent with the present ones, whether sworn or not, did not constitute evidence on which the jury could act.[1]

¶ 555. *Discrediting a witness who becomes hostile.* Even the party who produces a witness is allowed to discredit him by thus proving a previous inconsistent statement of his, should he turn out to be (in the opinion of the judge) hostile to that party, i.e. not doing his best to answer frankly (cf. ¶ 538 (4) *ante*).[2] And, even without any such recognition of his hostility, the assertion which he now makes may be contradicted by the subsequent witnesses, called on the same side, if it be a fact which is intrinsically relevant to the issue. For clearly those witnesses, who could have spoken to this fact if they had been examined before he was, cannot be excluded by the accident of his having been called first.[3]

¶ 556. *Witness may be cross-examined as to his discreditable conduct.* Besides these three modes of discrediting a witness by the evidence of other persons, his credit may, as we have said, be shaken by his own[4] cross-examination, and shaken in a manner much more extensive.[5] For he may be cross-examined not only on the matters already mentioned—his mendacity, his bias, his former inconsistent statements—but on any past conduct of his of a discreditable character.[6] This rule is often made use of to elicit facts which are admissible for this purpose, with the real purpose of employing them to bear upon the main issue in the case; though that bearing is too remote to render them legally admissible on the ground of relevancy to it. Thus on an indictment for ravishing *A*, a letter written to the prisoner immediately afterwards by *A*'s father, demanding a pecuniary compensation, cannot be put in

[1] *R.* v. *Golder* [1960] 1 W.L.R. 1169, applying *R.* v. *Birch* (1924) 18 Cr.App.R. 26; *R.* v. *Harris* (1927) *ubi supra*; *R.* v. *Hart* (1958) 42 Cr.App.R. 47.

[2] It has been said to be the duty of prosecuting counsel to ask leave to treat the prosecutor as a hostile witness when counsel knows that he is giving evidence contrary to statements of identification which he had previously made; see *R.* v. *Frazer and Warren* (1956) 40 Cr.App.R. 160. Students should remember that the 'prosecutor in a criminal case is *not* a party' but a witness for the prosecution, the true parties to the proceedings being the Crown and the accused person.

[3] *Greenough* v. *Eccles* (1859) 5 C.B. (n.s.) 803; cf. 8 Bing. 50.

[4] But not by cross-examining *another* witness about him.

[5] But the party *producing* a witness cannot put to him discrediting questions, though he may, if the witness prove hostile, obtain leave to cross-examine him as to relevant facts.

[6] See the cross-examination of the spy, Castles, in *R.* v. *Watson* (1817) 32 St. Tr. 1 at p. 284. This power of putting painful questions, which may revive even long-forgotten frailties, would be intolerable but for the high sense of responsibility traditional to the English bar. It has been stated that although the police are not to be expected to see whether possibly there exists somewhere any matter which may affect the character of a witness, yet it is their duty to disclose to the defence actual convictions of crime standing on the record of the prosecutor; *R.* v. *Collister and Warhurst* (1955) 39 Cr.App.R. 100.

evidence to discredit *A* herself (unless there be legal proof that she authorized its being written). But, if her father be called as a witness he can be asked about it, to discredit him; and it will thus effect, indirectly, the more important result of discrediting her.

It must always be remembered that in certain circumstances (see *post*, ¶¶ 621 *et seq.*) an attack on the character of the prosecutor or of any other witness for the prosecution may entitle the prosecution to disclose the character and previous record of the accused person.

¶ 557. *But his answers are final.* It must be noted that the answers which a witness gives to questions that are put merely to discredit him, are 'final'; i.e. the cross-examiner cannot call evidence to disprove them, for thus to digress into the determination of side-issues might render a trial interminable.[1] (The legislature has, however, created an exception in one case, in which the disproof is peculiarly simple and peculiarly important. For by the Criminal Procedure Act, 1865, s. 6, if a witness denies having been convicted of a crime, or refuses to answer the question, evidence of that conviction may be given). If, however, the discreditable act were relevant not merely to credit but also directly to the actual issue in the litigation, evidence might of course be given, in regard to it, in contradiction of the witness; for such evidence would have been intrinsically admissible even if he had never been examined.[2] For instance, on an indictment for rape, if the prosecutrix be cross-examined as to her unchastity with third persons, and deny it, she cannot be contradicted; and, consequently, witnesses to her good character cannot be called by the prosecution to confirm her denial. But if the question had related to her previous unchastity with the prisoner himself, or to her being a common prostitute, her denial might be contradicted. For these facts, if true, would not merely affect her credit but would be relevant to an essential part of the issue, viz. whether the act now complained of took place against her will.[3] Similarly, if in cross-examination a witness denies having been drunk at the time when he watched the events that are in issue, he may be contradicted on this point by direct evidence, since it is not a question of his character, but of his power of accurate observation and memory.

Thus evidence cannot be called to contradict a witness on his answers

[1] Hence if to a cross-examiner's question 'Did you once seduce a woman?' the witness *A* has answered 'No', a subsequent witness *cannot* be asked, even in cross-examination, 'Did *A* once tell you that he had seduced *B*?'

[2] *R.* v. *Jackson* (1936) 182 L.T.Jo. 343. Cf. R. v. *Phillips* (1936) 26 Cr.App.R. 17 where children who had given evidence against their father, who was charged with incest, denied in cross-examination that they were repeating what their mother had told them to say; the conviction was quashed because the judge had refused to allow the defence to call witnesses who, it was alleged, could state that the children had previously admitted to them that they had been so instructed by their mother.

[3] *R.* v. *Greatbanks* [1959] Crim. L.R. 450, where evidence of witnesses was admitted to the effect that the prosecutrix, who denied her alleged consent, was a woman of notoriously bad character for want of chastity and common decency.

as to character, except as to his answers about (1) his bias,[1] or (2) his own previous inconsistent statements, or (3) his previous conviction or (4) facts which the opposite party could have proved as part of his own case. Nor, conversely, can the party who called the witness whose character has been impugned in cross-examination, call further evidence in order to refute the suggestion and to re-establish that witness's good character.[2]

(VI) THE 'BEST EVIDENCE' RULE

¶ 558. The best evidence must be given or its absence must be accounted for. The rule is still usually stated in this traditional and general form; but its actual application[3] is nowadays limited to one particular case, viz. the proof of the contents of a written document. The fact that the document has actually been drawn up, or the condition of it, may be proved by secondary evidence; that is, by the production, not of the document itself, but of remoter evidence derived from it through some intermediate channel (the recollections, for instance, of a witness who has seen it). But if, on the other hand, it is desired to prove what the actual contents of the document were, then the rule now under discussion excludes—even in cross-examination—all secondary evidence. A witness must not be asked on what day an unproduced letter was dated; but he can be asked on what day he received it. So where it is sought to give the contents of a message sent by telegram in evidence against the sender of it (e.g. when the surgeon whom it summoned, sues for his fee), the original paper handed in by him at the post office must be produced. The subsequent paper, which the telegraph boy delivered, cannot be given in evidence for this purpose (unless it be proved that the first-mentioned paper has been destroyed or lost). It, however, would be otherwise if the object were to prove not what message was sent, but what message was in fact received (e.g. when the surgeon summoned is sued for negligence); for then the positions would be reversed, and the paper brought by the boy would be the necessary 'best evidence'.

Rule as to evidence of written statements

¶ 559. Accordingly when, in any litigation, a witness is asked, 'Was any bargain made on this subject?' the opposing counsel will probably interpose by asking, 'Was it made in writing?' For if it were embodied in written words, the witness must not give parol evidence about them. Thus a witness, as Lord Eldon said, 'may be asked whether a particular house was purchased and conveyed; but, if he states that it was conveyed by a written instrument, then the examination must stop there'. Similarly it would not be permissible to ask, 'Did you write a note to

[1] E.g. if he has denied having expressed hostility to the prisoner; or was biased in his favour, *Thomas* v. *David* (1836) 7 C. and P. 350 (*T.A.C.*).

[2] *R.* v. *Wood* [1951] 35 Cr.App.R. 61.

[3] *Jolley* v. *Taylor* (1807) 1 Camp. 143 (*T.A.C.*); *R.* v. *Francis* (1874) 2 C.C.R. 128 (*T.A.C.*). See Wigmore, *Evidence*, ss. 1173, 1287; Chamberlayne, *Evidence*, s. 480. The rule used to be much wider; an example can be seen in *Williams* v. *East India Co.* (1802) 3 East 192 (*T.A.C.*); for the history see Phipson on Evidence, 9th ed., 6 *et seq.*

your master asking to be taken back into service?' for that would be to elicit the contents of the note without producing it. The utmost that the examiner can do will be to ask, 'After leaving your master's service did you write to him?' and, on getting an affirmative answer, to proceed: 'After so writing were you taken back into his service?'

¶ 560. *Limits of the rule.* But the rule only applies where the object desired is to prove what actually were the contents of a document. Hence where words have been uttered orally, by a person who apparently read them out from a paper, if the object be to show, not what the words of the document itself were, but what he actually did utter, any persons who heard him may narrate what they heard, and his paper need not be produced. For the words he uttered may have varied from the written ones.[1] Similarly, such a question as, 'What did you tell your clerk to state in the letter?' would be quite permissible, if the point to be proved be not the actual contents of the letter, but merely what the witness intended those contents to be (as, for instance, where the only object is to show his knowledge of the matters thus mentioned by him to the clerk).

When secondary evidence of documents is admissible

¶ 561. It will, however, sometimes happen that no primary evidence is available. In that case the production of the document will be dispensed with, and secondary evidence may take its place. The following are the most frequent instances in which this occurs:[2]

(1) When the writing has been destroyed, or where, after proper search having been made for it, it cannot be found.[3] Thus on a trial for forgery the contents of the note, which was alleged to have been forged, were allowed to be proved by parol evidence, because the prisoner had himself swallowed the note.[4]

(2) When its nature is such that it is physically impossible to produce it, as in the case of a placard posted on a wall,[5] or of a tombstone. This has at times been extended to cases where it was not absolutely impossible, but only extremely inconvenient, to produce the writing; as when, in *R.* v. *Hunt*,[6] parol evidence was admitted of the inscriptions on the banners and flags that had been displayed at a meeting. Similarly, if the

[1] *R.* v. *Sheridan* (1811) 31 St. Tr. 673–4; cf. *Bishop Gardiner's Case* (1551) 1 St. Tr. 551 at p. 558.

[2] See also Evidence Act 1851, s. 13; Criminal Procedure Act, 1865, s. 6; Prevention of Crimes Act, 1871, s. 18; Bankers' Books Evidence Act, 1879, ss. 3–7; Perjury Act, 1911, s. 14; Criminal Justice Act, 1925, s. 34.

[3] See the remarkable case of Lord St Leonards's lost will; *Sugden* v. *St Leonards* (1876) 1 P.D. 154.

[4] *How* v. *Hall* (1811) 14 East 274 at p. 276. Similarly when the ledgers, which a witness was about to produce, were stolen from him at the porch of the Central Criminal Court (*ante*, p. 299 n. 2), oral testimony became admissible instead.

[5] *R.* v. *Fursey* (1833) 6 C. and P. at p. 84 (*T.A.C.*).

[6] (1820) 3 B. and Ald. 566.

possessor of the document has, and insists on, a legal privilege to withhold it (cf. ¶¶ 585 *et seq. post*).

(3) When the writing is in the possession of the opposite party[1] and, though notice[2] has been given to him to produce it, he fails to do so. Sometimes the very nature of the litigation (e.g. an indictment for stealing this very document) is of itself a sufficient notice to him that he is expected to produce it.[3]

(4) When the secondary evidence which is tendered consists of an admission, by the opposite party himself, as to what the contents of the document were.[4]

(5) When the original is a 'public'[5] document, it is provided by statute that it may be proved by means of an examined copy.[6]

(6) When the original is an entry in a banker's book it is now provided by statute that it may be proved by a copy of the entry, if verified by some officer of the bank, either orally or even by affidavit.[7]

¶ 562. *The rule only applies to written documents.* The rule of best evidence goes no further than simply to postpone all secondary evidence whatever of the contents of documents to the primary evidence of them. It takes no heed of the different degrees of value of various kinds of secondary evidence. For instance, it will allow a witness to give his recollections of the contents of a document, even when some attested copy of it is available. And the rule ceases to have any operation at all where the thing under discussion is not a written document. For where, in any litigation, the quality or condition of some chattel is in dispute, the law does not similarly require the chattel itself to be produced in

[1] A private prosecutor is not a 'party'.

[2] The student must distinguish (1) this notice to produce, given by one party to the other, to secure the right to tender secondary evidence, from (2) the notice to admit, given similarly, to save the expense of proving the genuineness of documents, and (3) a subpœna *duces tecum*, issued by the court, to compel a witness to bring a document to the trial.

[3] Where a motorist is required to show his licence to a police officer it is not necessary to give notice to produce the licence in order to give evidence in subsequent proceedings of its contents, *Marshall* v. *Ford* (1908) 72 J.P. 480; cf. *Williams* v. *Russell* (1933) 49 T.L.R. 315 (certificate of insurance). The production of a licence by a driver is evidence that the driver is the person named in the licence, *Martin* v. *White* [1910] 1 K.B. 665. See ¶ 574 *post.*

[4] *Earle* v. *Picken* (1833) 5 C. and P. 542.

[5] 'Public' document means one that is made for the use of anyone who wishes to refer to it; it must be made for the purpose of being kept public, so that persons concerned may have access to it afterwards; *Sturla* v. *Freccia* (1880) 5 App. Cas. 623, confirmed in *Pettit* v. *Lilley* [1946] 1 All E.R. 593 in which it was held that regimental records, although official, were not 'public'. See *Irish Society* v. *Derry* (1846) 12 Cl. and Fin. 641.

[6] Evidence Act, 1851 (14 and 15 Vict. c. 99), s. 14. Copies are of various kinds: 'exemplified', under the seal of a tribunal; 'official', signed by the custodian-officer; 'attested', bearing a certificate from someone who has checked it; 'plain' (but perhaps examined with the original by a witness who can swear to it).

[7] Bankers' Books Evidence Act, 1879.

court for actual inspection.[1] If the purchaser of a horse, or of a diamond ring, or of corn, refuses payment of the price because the animal is unsound, or the jewel is false, or the grain does not come up to sample, he need not produce the horse, or the ring, or the sample (though he will arouse suspicion by not producing it). Similarly, in an action to recover compensation for the damage sustained by a bicycle which a cart has run down, it will not be technically necessary at the trial to produce the bicycle. Equally little is any principle of best evidence applied to the proof of handwriting; for it is not essential that the party, who is alleged to have signed a document, should himself be called to prove, or (as at a trial for forgery) to disprove his handwriting. And to prove that a person holds a public office (e.g. that of a justice of the peace or of a solicitor), it is sufficient to show that he is in the habit of acting as a holder of it, without producing his written commission which conferred the office (*ante*, ¶ 496).

Primary evidence is not graded

¶ 563. Finally it may be noted, as a further illustration of the limited application of the 'best evidence' principle, that the law does not prescribe any preference between different species of primary evidence. Thus the testimony of a witness, who had watched through a telescope an assault which took place a mile away, would not be postponed to the testimony of the actual victim of the attack.

The Evidence Act, 1938.[2] Relaxation of rules

¶ 564. The former strictness of the rules of evidence has in one matter been relaxed by the legislature in order to facilitate the administration of justice in civil actions. For where, in civil proceedings, direct oral evidence of a fact would be admissible, and a document is produced which contains any statement which tends to establish that fact, the statement so contained in the document is admissible in evidence, provided (i) that the maker of the statement had personal knowledge of the matter dealt with by the statement, or the document is, or forms part of, a record purporting to be a continuous record and the person made the statement in the performance of a duty to record information supplied to him by one who had (or might reasonably be supposed to

[1] So difficulty may arise if a 'document' be offered in evidence, not as a statement, but merely as an identificatory mark on a thing. In *R.* v. *Pierce* (C.C.C. Sess. Pap. XLV at p. 377) Willes, J., and Martin, B., allowed a witness to identify two debentures by stating their numbers, without producing them; just as oral evidence of the brand on an ox or the number of a cab would be similarly receivable. For identification Martin, B., had allowed a witness to describe even the indorsement on a deed, and his ruling had been approved by the Queen's Bench. Cf. *Dew* v. *Clark* (1826) 3 Adam 143 (Scottish case); contrast *R.* v. *Truman* (1850) C.C.C. Sess. Pap. XXXIII, 251 at p. 253. But even ticks in a stockbook, against items sold, need production if tendered as statements; *R.* v. *Bruck* (1853) C.C.C. Sess. Pap. XXXVIII, 125.

[2] 1 and 2 Geo. VI, c. 28. This Act is not a modification of the best evidence rule in the strict sense, since it allows the production of documents in the place of parol evidence.

have had) personal knowledge of the matter; and provided (ii) that the maker of the statement (unless he be not available)[1] is called as a witness in the proceedings. Even these conditions may be relaxed by the court if it is satisfied that undue delay or expense would otherwise be caused.[2] There seems to be no authority either way as to the effect of the Act on the principle embodied in such cases as *Crouch* v. *Drury*.[3]

¶ 565. *Safeguards.* The Act imposes[4] the safeguards, (*a*) that no such statement is admissible if it was made by a person interested[5] at a time when proceedings were pending or anticipated involving a dispute as to any fact which the statement might tend to establish; and (*b*) that the document, or the material part of it, was written or made by him with his own hand, or at least was signed or initialled or otherwise recognized by him in writing as one for the accuracy of which he is responsible.

(VII) HEARSAY EVIDENCE

¶ 566. It is submitted that the analysis of 'hearsay' and '*res gestae*', and the principles propounded thereon in this and the succeeding paragraphs can be legitimately drawn from the decided cases, although they have not so far been expressly enunciated in any judgment of the court. The decisions, superficially at least, appear to be conflicting and difficult to reconcile;[6] and the courts have more than once declined to attempt to arrive at a general formula.[7] When, however, a condition of doubt exists in the law, it has long been recognized that it is the duty of academic writers to offer such solution as they are able to produce. Especially is this so where the lawyer is confronted with a number of associated legal situations and it is desired to extract from the mass some clear general principle, hitherto undetected, by which they are really governed.

The word 'hearsay', as used in the law of evidence, is a term of art. It is a compound noun, of which for legal purposes the meaning is brought out by placing the emphasis on 'say' rather than 'hear'. It consists in words uttered by a spectator (=said) for the purpose of conveying information to the hearer concerning what the speaker had himself observed; it thus constitutes a testimonial, or evidential, statement which, if given by that speaker under oath in court, would be *his direct evidence* tending to establish the facts to which he thus deposes *at first hand.* But if another person who had heard that speaker's statement were now to repeat his words, in order to establish these same facts,

[1] I.e. if he is dead, or unfit by reason of his bodily or mental condition to be a witness, or beyond the seas, or not to be found.

[2] See s. 1 (2) for the extent of the relaxation.

[3] (1661) 1 Keble 27 (*T.A.C.*); *ante*, ¶ 551.

[4] Sect. 1 (3) and (4).

[5] *Kelleher* v. *Wall* [1958[3 W.L.R. 236.

[6] See *per* Lord Normand in *Teper* v. *R.* [1952] A.C. 480 at p. 487; and as R. N. Gooderson has revealed in his articles, '*Res gesta* in criminal cases', [1956] and [1957] *Cambridge. L.J.*

[7] E.g. *per* Lord Normand, *Teper* v. *R.* (*supra*).

this would be 'hearsay' evidence, by which is meant 'direct evidence at *second-hand*'.[1] It is a fundamental rule of English law (with a few carefully safeguarded and limited exceptions, to be discussed later[2]) that such second-hand direct evidence is not permitted to be given in court for the purpose of establishing the facts alleged by the person who uttered it at first hand.[3] The rule can be expressed thus: *A witness in court is not allowed to give another person's direct evidence for him.* Thus where a Maltese who could neither speak nor understand English was questioned, through an interpreter, by a police officer who could neither speak nor understand Maltese, it was held that the officer could not be allowed to give in evidence what the accused had said, since such evidence would be a repetition of what the interpreter had told him and therefore hearsay; nor could he give in evidence what he himself had said since it had not been said 'in the presence and hearing of the accused' (*post*, ¶ 575).[4]

¶ 567. *History of the rule of exclusion.* The untrustworthiness of hearsay was recognized in England as early as 1202, and in the same century Bracton repeatedly disapproved of all such 'testimonium de auditu alieno'.[5] Yet when the procedure of trial by jury and witnesses became established, hearsay evidence was at first freely admitted. Thus, in 1603, on the trial of Sir Walter Raleigh, a witness was allowed to narrate that 'Mr Brooke told me he had heard of a most dangerous plot'. But in 1660, we find hearsay only received after direct evidence had been given, and merely to corroborate it; and thus not admissible of itself.[6] And within another generation the full modern principle of exclusion had become accepted—probably before any other rule of evidence. For in 1683 the one caution which Algernon Sidney's counsel could furnish him with was to bid him, 'Desire that evidence of hearsay from witnesses may not be given; and *suffer it not* to be given'. Accordingly in 1684[7] Lord Jeffreys, C.J., ruled that what a witness heard from a woman was no evidence. 'If she were here herself, if she did say it,

[1] For example, if *A*, secretly listening to *X* and *Y* who were engaged in a burglary, heard *X* tell *Y* that he had seen *Z* on some former occasion stab *B*, then *A* would not be permitted to repeat *X*'s statement at the trial of *Z* on a charge of attacking *B*.

[2] *Post*, ¶ 578.

[3] *Samson* v. *Yardley and Tottill* (1667) 2 Keble 223 (*T.A.C.*); *R.* v. *The Inhabitants of Eriswell* (1790) 3 T.R. 707 (*T.A.C.*).

[4] *R.* v. *Attard* (1959) 43 Cr.App.R. 90. See also *R.* v. *Gordon and Spencer* (1958) 42 Cr.App.R. 177, where the evidence of employees of a shipping line, who read out bills of lading to prove the arrival and off-loading at the docks, and the evidence of 'counters-off' who stated what amounts were written on slips of paper handed to them by checkers, were held inadmissible in order to establish an unexplained deficiency of merchandise.

[5] Pollock and Maitland, II, 622. The Romans recognized its defects even in the time of Plautus: 'Pluris est oculatus testis unus quam auriti decem: qui audiunt, audita dicunt; qui vident, plane sciunt'; *Trucul.* II, 6. Yet in 1598 Bodin said, 'In cases of witchcraft, common repute is almost infallible' (*Démonomanie*, ed. 1598, IV, ch. IV).

[6] *R.* v. *Hulet* (1660) 5 St. Tr. 1185 at p. 1195.

[7] *R.* v. *Braddon and Speke* (1684) 9 St. Tr. 1127 at p. 1189.

and would not swear to it, we could not hear her; how then can her saying be an evidence before us? I wonder to hear any man that wears a gown, to make a doubt of it.' Hence it is that a witness cannot prove the date of his own birth,[1] though the American courts, sacrificing logic to convenience, permit this. Yet he may prove that his birthday has always been kept on the date mentioned in the birth certificate of a person of his name.

¶ 568. *Hearsay forbidden for unreliability, not for irrelevancy.* Students should note at the outset that hearsay is not excluded on the ground that it is irrelevant; for it may be in the highest degree relevant.[2] Its emphatic exclusion in England[3] is mainly due to its untrustworthiness, but there is the additional reason that its admission would tend to prolong the proceedings in many trials. Its dangers are grave. It is peculiarly liable to be distorted by mistake[4] and by deceit. It is ultimately derived from an absent witness who was not on oath and did not undergo cross-examination,[5] so that his credibility cannot be tested; moreover the light which his demeanour, if he were efficiently questioned, would throw on his testimony is lost.[6] The above description of hearsay has, for initial simplicity of exposition, been confined to spoken words; but, for the purposes of the rule of exclusion, hearsay is a term used to cover also words written; further, the same principle of exclusion has been applied to evidence of another man's conduct, if it be adduced for the purpose of constituting a representation by him of the existence of some fact which, in the particular trial before the court, it is sought thereby to prove. As was said by Baron Parke,[7] the conduct of some deceased sea-captain, who examined every part of a vessel and then deliberately embarked on her with his family, cannot be given in evidence to show that she must have been seaworthy.

[1] *R.* v. *Rishworth* (1842) 2 Q.B. 476; 9 C. and P. 722. But see 98 *J.P.Jo.* 698. [2] See *R.* v. *Parker* (1960) 110 L.J. 720; *post*, ¶ 779.

[3] But in Continental countries, hearsay evidence remains acceptable. In the *Dreyfus Case* the great bulk of the evidence given was pure hearsay. For on the Continent, as in Scotland, trial by jury was not introduced until so late an epoch that the admission of hearsay had become a practice too inveterate to be shaken. Before that introduction it was comparatively innocent, because when trained judges are to determine the facts in dispute they can trust themselves to give hearsay evidence only its due weight. In a famous Belgian trial (1901) the following fifth-hand evidence was received, 'He told me that Mme Lagasse had heard from a lady that van Steen told her he knew the prisoners were guilty'. In the great French case of *Calas*, 1762 (*Encyc. Britannica*, art. Calas), his threat to murder was only proved at *sixth*-hand. See *The Case of Jean Calas* by Lord Maugham (Heinemann, 1928).

[4] Everyone knows how rumour passing even from one honest man to another can develop into a story entirely without truth.

[5] Hence, 'Did you find, *as a result of your inquiries*, that he had done much business?' is not a lawful question.

[6] See Lord Normand's remarks in *Teper* v. *R.* [1952] A.C. 480 at p. 486. As to the need for the opportunity of an adequate cross-examination, see 'Hearsay and non-hearsay', E. M. Morgan, *Harvard L.R.* XLVIII, 1138.

[7] *Wright* v. *Doe* (1837) 7 A. and E. 313 at p. 388.

¶ 569. *Evidence of another's words admissible if they were not a piece of testimony.* As explained above hearsay is not excluded because it repeats another person's words but because it repeats another person's direct evidence. Where the words overheard are not in the nature of testimony[1] as to *facta probanda* in the case before the court,[2] they are as admissible as any other relevant noise which the witness may have heard. Thus the 'hearsay' (evidence by *A* of what he had heard *B* say) although *not* admissible as evidence of *the truth of its contents*, yet *is* admissible to establish, when relevant, e.g. that *B* did speak, or to establish what was the state of mind of some person who heard *B*'s remarks, whether adduced by the defence,[3] or by the prosecution.[4] In *R.* v. *Gibson*[5] it was held that on a charge of unlawful wounding brought against G. it was inadmissible evidence for a witness (the prosecutor) to state: 'Immediately after I was struck by the said stone, a lady going past,[6] pointing to the prisoner's door, said "The person who threw the stone went in there".' Such a statement was clearly 'testimonial', for as Lord Normand has said:[7] 'The words ... were prompted by the sight of a man quitting the scene of the assault and they were spoken for the purpose of helping to bring him to justice.' If, however, the woman had been heard to say, as a man approached her, 'Hello, Mr Gibson, where are you going?' it would clearly have been permissible for the witness to have repeated this remark, just as he could have deposed that he heard the woman scream,[8] or shout 'Shame',[9] or saw her run away or the like; for any of these things would be circumstantial evidence, since they would be the phenomena created by the appearance of the man and by what he was doing; and therefore evidence of the reaction of the woman, as Lord Normand put it[10] 'spontaneously forced from the woman' by what she had seen. Even where an established legal principle lays down a clear line there must from time to time arise a set of facts so near the line that it is difficult to say on which side the case falls, and then the court's decision will not satisfy everyone. Much greater therefore is the chance of such differences of opinion about decisions when there is no clearly enunciated

[1] They may, of course, be the very *factum probandum* themselves, as in slander, see ¶ 571 *post*.

[2] Take again the imaginary case of the two burglars mentioned *ante*, p. 483 n. 1. Although the statement by *X* about the stabbing of *B* by *Z* could not be repeated by *A* at the trial of *Z*, for the purpose of proving *Z*'s guilt, it could be repeated by *A* at the trial of either *X* or *Y* for the purpose, e.g., of identifying one or other of them.

[3] *Subramaniam* v. *D.P.P.* [1956] 1 W.L.R. 965.

[4] *R.* v. *Willis* [1960] Crim. L.R. 56.

[5] (1887) 18 Q.B.D. 537.

[6] There was no evidence as to who the woman was, and she could not be called as a witness.

[7] In *Teper* v. *R.* [1952] A.C. 480 (*T.A.C.*), at p. 488.

[8] See *R.* v. *Goddard* (1882) 15 Cox 7.

[9] *Milne* v. *Leisler* (1862) 7 H. and N. 786, *per* Pollock, C.B., at p. 796.

[10] In *Teper* v. *R.*, *supra*.

principle upon which the courts can rely; so that it is not surprising that different views are held about many of the decisions on the present topic.[1]

Res gestae

¶ 570. It is unfortunate that owing to the lack of a clear formulation of the nature of hearsay, and of the principles which govern its exclusion, there has arisen a confusion of that topic with what is fundamentally a different one, namely the law relating to that which has for a long time been called *res gestae*, two Latin words which are mostly used without any attempt to explain precisely what their meaning is. The Latin words may be translated simply 'the events which happened', and for legal purposes they are a term of art restricted to *events which happened in the affair which is now being considered by the court*. It is obvious that, in and during the continuance of any factual situation which has been selected for the consideration of a court of law in a trial (i.e. a fact 'in issue'), there are an infinite number of other events or facts which existed contemporaneously with this alleged fact in issue which has to be proved. Only a few of these will be found to help to establish the existence or non-existence of the fact in issue, and the rules (to which we have already adverted, *ante*, ¶ 541) as to relevance adequately restrict the admissible evidence to these few.[2] *Res gestae* therefore comprise all relevant facts or events which are either in issue, or which, though not themselves in issue, yet accompany some fact which is in issue so as to constitute circumstantial evidence which goes to explain or establish that fact. It is easy to understand that sounds of all kinds may be a part (and only a part) of the total *res gestae*; and also that of all these sounds only such as constitute or are relevant to a fact in issue may be deposed to by a witness in the trial. So long, however, as it is so relevant any sound, even spoken words, can be repeated or described in evidence.

Now it will be difficult to find spoken words which can be relevant to a fact in issue unless they were either (*a*) of a testimonial character (in which case, whenever they may have been uttered, they cannot be given at second hand, since they would then be hearsay) or (*b*) not testimonial, but were uttered close to the fact in issue in time, place or circumstances, and thus are admissible as circumstantial evidence (being noises which were part of the *res gestae*). From this point of view the question of admissibility is really quite a simple one, namely, whether the evidence offered is circumstantial or direct, i.e. whether it goes to establish a *factum probans* or a *factum probandum* (*ante*, ¶ 505). Lord

[1] E.g. *R.* v. *Fowkes* (1856) Leicester Spring Assizes, cited by Stephen, *Digest of the Law of Evidence*, 12th ed., p. 8, where the disputed words were 'There's butcher' uttered by a boy through a window; *R.* v. *Foster* (1834) 6 C. and P. 325.

[2] Thus, if it were desired to prove that A was in a certain place at a certain specified time of day, it is not likely to be relevant that the sun was or was not shining or that birds were or were not singing at the moment in question: but if that moment were alleged to be midnight the presence or absence of such contemporaneous matters might well be of great importance.

Normand, again in *Teper* v. *R.* (*ubi supra*), came very near to enunciating this principle when he said (at p. 587):

the words sought to be proved *by hearsay* should be *if not absolutely contemporaneous with the action or event, at least so clearly associated with it, in time, place and circumstances, that they are part of the thing done, and so* an item or part of real evidence and not merely a reported statement.

If the words printed above in italic had been excluded, it is respectfully submitted that what remained would point towards the true principle which has so long lain buried; their presence, however, renders the whole passage indecisive.

It may be well at this point to warn students that, *if spoken words are themselves a fact in issue*, then they are admissible *whatever their character*; for example, in an action for slander a witness can of course narrate the defamatory words which he heard the defendant utter (even though they be a statement at third hand).[1] For in such cases as these the question for decision is 'What did that man say?'

As stated above *res gestae* comprise every sort of relevant event or fact associated with the fact in issue; unhappily both in the books and in the judgments the expression '*res gestae*' is seldom used except when there is a dispute as to the admissibility of evidence purporting to state words spoken by some other person than the present witness; then because of the failure to grasp clearly what are the basic principles of exclusion or admission there has been engendered an erroneous proposition to the effect that if the words are part of the *res gestae* they are admissible and therefore are an exception to the rule against hearsay; from what has been stated above it will be seen that such a proposition contains a double non-sequitur.[2]

¶ 571. *Exclamations distinguished from testimonial utterances.* An example of words admissible as relevant and yet not testimonial would be where a person listening outside a closed door happened to hear a woman cry out 'Don't, don't, you'll kill me';[3] he could be allowed to repeat these words in evidence at the trial (for her murder) of the man in the room with her. Contrast the case of *Bedingfield*[4] in which it was very properly

[1] For it is equally defamatory to say about a man 'I have been told he is a thief' as to say 'He is a thief'.

[2] An article by G. D. Nokes, '*Res gestae* as hearsay' in 70 *L.Q.R.* 370, gives examples of the confusion resulting from the indiscriminate use of the phrase *res gestae* in many different situations.

[3] See the remarks of Cockburn, C.J., in *R.* v. *Bedingfield* (1879) 14 Cox 341 (*T.A.C.*) at p. 342; and *R.* v. *Osman* (1881) 15 Cox 1 at p. 2, where the words were 'Oh, Will, don't'; *R.* v. *Curley* (1909) C.C.C. Sess. Pap. CL, 703 at pp. 705, 706, 'You are murdering me; let me out'.

[4] *Ubi supra*, at p. 345. In *R.* v. *Foster* (1834), 6 C. and P. 325, a statement made by the deceased, just after he had been knocked down, as to how the accident happened, was admitted, but this ruling was questioned by Cockburn, C.J., in *R.* v. *Bedingfield*. Cf. *R.* v. *Christie* [1914] A.C. at pp. 556, 566. A dumb man's fingered narrative is 'hearsay'; *R.* v. *Guy* (1839) C.C.C. Sess. Pap. x, 979. See also *R.* v. *Goddard* (1882) 15 Cox 7.

held that, where a woman with her throat cut came suddenly out of a house towards some women who were standing in the yard and pointing back to the house said: 'See what Harry has done', her words could not be given in evidence. This was clearly a testimonial statement,[1] and an instance of inadmissible hearsay. Another example of relevant exclamations was the evidence admitted against Lord George Gordon of the various seditious cries uttered by the rioters whom he led.[2] Similarly not only the remarks made by persons engaged in drilling, but also those made by persons who were watching them have been allowed to be given in evidence against the former to show the illegal purpose of the drilling.[3] And when a libellous picture was exhibited in public, remarks uttered by the spectators were admitted to show whom the figures in it were meant to represent.[4]

But in many cases the task, not always an easy one, is to decide whether words uttered were of a testimonial character (and therefore not admissible) or were really no more than exclamatory[5] (and therefore admissible). Thus in one case[6] evidence was admitted that a gas-fitter, while rushing excitedly off a landing-stage, exclaimed 'My God the landing-stage is on fire. I did it.'[7] Again in a running-down case a witness would be allowed to say that he had heard cries of 'Shame' uttered by persons on the spot.[8] The contents of documents found near the body of a murdered man have been held admissible as part of the circumstances[9] of the murder.

Again where a workman had fallen into a bath of acid and when rescued repeated, within a period of two minutes after his rescue, 'I shouldn't have done it', these words were admitted 'as part of the *res gestae*'.[10] This shows the fallacy of regarding the admissibility as due

[1] The reason given for the exclusion by the Chief Justice was that 'here it was something stated by her after it was all over, whatever it was, and after the act was completed'. This is seeking for a principle based upon a time factor, which has been many times attempted but has always failed to yield a satisfactory general principle. In the present case it has led to much adverse criticism of the Chief Justice's ruling—an instructive example of a correct decision being vitiated by its being based upon an unsound reason.

[2] (1780) 21 St. Tr. at p. 535. But *not* seditious statements made by members of the crowd, upon their dispersing, when about half a mile from the spot.

[3] *Redford* v. *Birley* (1822) 1 St. Tr. (n.s.), 1071.

[4] *Du Bost* v. *Beresford* (1810) 2 Camp. 511 (*T.A.C.*); cf. *R.* v. *Podmore* (1930) 22 Cr.App.R. 36 (*T.A.C.*).

[5] Like a groan, or a more lengthy expletive on the receipt of a sudden pain.

[6] *Mersey Docks Board* v. *Liverpool Gas Co.* (*The Times*, 23 August 1875). This utterance secured a verdict for £200,000 against the gas company.

[7] Similarly an exclamation by a pilot, on a collision at sea, 'The damned helm is still a-starboard!' was held admissible; *The Schwalbe* (1859) Swab. 521.

[8] *Milne* v. *Leisler* (1862) 7 H. and N. 786, *per* Pollock, C.B., at p. 796.

[9] *R.* v. *Podmore* (1930) 22 Cr.App.R. 36 (*T.A.C.*).

[10] *Davies* v. *Fortior* [1952] 1 All E.R. 1359. Mr N. N. McKinnon, Q.C., has pointed out that the admission of the evidence in this case could be justified on either of two other reasons, not, apparently, submitted to the court, (*a*) that the words were an admission by a deceased person against his pecuniary interest, and (*b*) that they were an admission by a predecessor in title to the plaintiff, who was the deceased's personal representative suing

to the words being part of the *res gestae* in the sense of the phrase as used in *R.* v. *Bedingfield*; for on that view of the rule *Davies* v. *Fortior* would clearly be in conflict with *Bedingfield*. The true test shows no conflict between the two cases since clearly in *Bedingfield* the woman's words were testimonial, whereas in *Davies's* case the man's words were exclamatory.

Of course, from the point of *relevance*, it will be found that admissible utterances are almost always simultaneous, or nearly so, with the fact or facts in issue.

¶ 571a. *The admission of evidence of* res gestae *is not an exception to the rule against hearsay*. From the previous paragraphs it will be seen that it is wrong, and misleading, to treat the admission of evidence of relevant facts among the *res gestae* (whether spoken words or anything else) which constitute circumstantial evidence, as though they were exceptions to the rule against the admission of hearsay, which is second-hand direct evidence. Certain other instances of admissible evidence which superficially appear to be, but which really are not, exceptions to the hearsay rule will be discussed in the paragraphs which now follow, before the true exceptions are dealt with.

¶ 572. *Expression of feelings is admissible evidence*. It must now be mentioned that where the bodily or mental *feelings*, or state of mind, of a person are relevant to the issue, that person's expression of such feelings when made in words may be properly given in evidence[1] in the same way as may evidence as to his appearance on that occasion or as to his groans or breathing. Thus, for example, it may be stated that he said 'I have a dreadful pain' or 'I feel sick, as though I were poisoned'. But in statements such as 'I feel pain where *A* kicked me', or 'This pain came on after I took the drink that *A* sent me' the words 'where *A* kicked me' and 'that *A* sent me' would be inadmissible;[2] so also Lord St Leonards's declaration as to legacies he *meant to insert* in his will,[3] but perhaps not his subsequent statements as to what he *had* inserted.[4]

Complaints

¶ 573. In some criminal cases a complaint, not uttered till some time after the conduct complained of, is admitted in evidence. But this is only allowed after the person complaining has given testimony as a

(*inter alia*) for the benefit of the deceased's estate; *Woolway* v. *Rowe* (1834) 1 A. and E. 114. Contrast the facts in *R.* v. *Parker* (1961) 45 Cr.App.R. 1.

[1] *Aveson* v. *Lord Kinnaird* (1805) 6 East 188 *per* Ellenborough, L.C.J., at p. 193; *R.* v. *Blandy* (1752) 18 St.Tr. 1135. In *Tracey* v. *Kelly* (1930) W.C. and Ins. Rep. 214, a workman's statement to his mates on leaving a shed was admitted as evidence that he had left the shed for the purpose of relieving nature. And see *R.* v. *Black* (1921) 16 Cr.App.R. 118.

[2] *R.* v. *Horsford* (1898) *The Times*, 2 and 6 June. And see *R.* v. *Nicholas* (1846) 2 C. and K. 246.

[3] *Sugden* v. *St Leonards* (1876) 1 P.D. 154.

[4] See *Re Jessop* [1924] P. 221. For an analogous case see *R.* v. *Crutchley* (1831) 5 C. and P. 133, note 3 on p. 134.

witness in the case,[1] and, even then, only for the purpose of supporting that testimony (by showing the complainant's consistency of conduct), and not as being intrinsically any evidence[2] of the alleged act complained of. For a complaint is not a *corroboration* of the complainant's evidence.[3] A witness, as we have seen, is not allowed to repeat what he has said on a previous occasion, so as to bolster up what he now says on oath.[4] Neither the admission of a complaint nor the admission (in order to rebut an allegation of recent fabrication of false evidence[5]) of a statement previously made is a true exception to the hearsay rule, since in both these cases the maker of the complaint or the previous statement must himself have first given the evidence on oath in the witness box. In a wife's suit for judicial separation on the ground of cruelty, the question 'Did the petitioner complain to you of her husband's cruelty?' is always allowed to be put, even by the examiner-in-chief, to such of her witnesses as are examined subsequently to herself. Thus, in cases of sexual assault on a female, evidence that she complained about it, on the first reasonable opportunity,[6] will be admitted in criminal (but not in civil) proceedings if she has been examined as a witness.[7] And, besides the fact of the complaint's having been made, even the details[8] uttered in it are now held admissible. The whole rule is extended to sexual offences against males.[9] But in non-sexual crimes the details of a complaint certainly cannot be admitted; and the more recent authorities deny that even the bare fact that a complaint has been made can be admitted. In ordinary civil cases the rule is strict.[10]

Admissions

¶ 574. Admissions also have often been discussed as exceptions to the hearsay rule, but again this is not quite accurate since they can only be produced against a party to the proceedings who himself can, and

[1] Hence not at all, if he die before giving evidence.

[2] Hence any details in it, not repeated by him at the trial, are not evidence at all. And see *R.* v. *Wallwork* (1958) 42 Cr.App.R. 153 where, on a charge of incest with a child of five, who was incapable of giving evidence, the grandmother's evidence of the child's complaint to her was held inadmissible.

[3] *R.* v. *Evans* (1924) 18 Cr.App.R. 123; cf. ¶ 599 *post.*

[4] If such were allowed a cunning man might make evidence for himself for future use. See *ante*, ¶ 551; *Crouch* v. *Drury* (1661) 1 Keble 27 (*T.A.C.*); *Smyth* v. *Anderson* (1849) 7 C.B. 21; and contrast the position in *R.* v. *Benjamin* (1913) 8 Cr.App.R. 146 (*T.A.C.*) and *O'Gorman* v. *O'Gorman* (1912) 56 S.J. 634, explained in Phipson on Evidence, 9th ed. 84. And see the strange case *R.* v. *Rouse* [1957] Crim.L.R. 112.

[5] As in *R.* v. *Benjamin, supra.*

[6] It is for the judge to decide whether the complaint was made as speedily as possible; *R.* v. *Cummings* [1948] 1 All E.R. 551 (*T.A.C.*).

[7] This apparently lax criminal rule is a survival from the old 'appeals' of rape, before the law of evidence arose, great importance being attached in them to prompt complaint.

[8] *R.* v. *Lillyman* [1896] 2 K.B. 167 (*T.A.C.*). The complaint must not be caused by *leading* questions. *R.* v. *Osborne* [1905] 1 K.B. 551 (*T.A.C.*) shows that the admissibility of details is *not* limited to those sexual crimes in which consent would be a defence.

[9] *R.* v. *Camelleri* [1922] 2 K.B. 122.

[10] *Beatty* v. *Cullingworth* (1896) 60 J.P. 740; (C.A.) *The Times*, 17 Jan. 1897.

usually does, give evidence; in which case any previous admission made by him is relevant to the question of the reliability of his present allegations and he has an opportunity of explaining it; it cannot therefore properly be held to be a case of direct evidence at second hand. The rule is that admissions made by, or by the authority of, the party against whom they are produced[1] can be repeated in evidence. The term 'admission' is here used in the wide sense which it always bears in civil cases; though in criminal cases it is usually applied only to those individual details of fact which do not involve the guilty intent, an admission of full guilt being styled a 'confession'. The authority to make an admission need not expressly relate to the particular statement; so a man will be responsible for admissions made on his behalf in the ordinary course of business by his partner or his agent, or even by some one to whom he has referred a third person for information on the topic.[2]

An admission may be made either expressly, in words (either spoken or written), or tacitly, by mere silent conduct. An instance of an express admission is furnished by the case of *Maltby* v. *Christie* (1795).[3] One party to the case, who was an auctioneer, had issued a catalogue in which he described certain goods as being the property of a bankrupt; and this fact was held to render it unnecessary for the other party to produce any further proof that the person to whom they belonged had really become bankrupt. A tacit admission arises when, at a policeman's demand, a motorist produces a licence, thereby implying that he is the person named in it.[4]

¶ 575. *Admission by silence.*[5] A less simple but more frequent illustration is afforded whenever a statement is uttered in the presence of someone who would naturally contradict it if it were not true, and who nevertheless remains silent. *Qui tacet consentire videtur*; he impliedly admits its truth. In this way, hearsay is often rendered admissible by the question, 'Was the other party [to this litigation] present, within hearing, when you heard that man say this?' Thus in an action for breach of promise of marriage, if the plaintiff was heard to say to the defendant 'You always promised to marry me', his silence is sufficient corroboration of her statement.[6] Yet the fact of the other party's having been present will not let in this evidence, if the circumstances were such

[1] The admission is, of course, evidence only against the party and not against others whom he may accuse in it. E.g. an adulterous wife's diary is evidence against herself but not against her adulterer; a landlord's notice to quit on a day named is evidence against him that the years of tenancy end on *that* day, but not against the tenant.

[2] *Williams* v. *Innes* (1808) 1 Camp. 364.

[3] 1 Esp. 340 (*T.A.C.*).

[4] See *ante*, p. 480 n. 3. Hearsay evidence of the prisoner's character is admissible *after* conviction; *R.* v. *Marquis* (1951) 115 J.P. 329.

[5] See *post*, 'Confessions', ¶ 613.

[6] *Bessela* v. *Stern* (1877) 2 C.P.D. 265. Similarly on being accused of crime; *R.* v. *Feigenbaum* (1919) 14 Cr.App.R. 1; contrast *R.* v. *Whitehead* (1928) 21 Cr.App.R. 23. Cf. ¶ 529 *ante*.

as to make it unlikely that he would have contradicted the statement even if he had known it to be false. The basic criterion for admissibility is relevance, but it is also governed in criminal cases by the oft-repeated principle that in deciding whether to admit the evidence the judge should weigh the possible prejudice to the prisoner against the value of the evidence itself, in order to secure a fair trial. In these situations very much depends upon the demeanour of the accused, and there is no rule of law that any particular form of response, whether of a positive or negative character, is such that it cannot in some circumstances have an evidential value.[1] Thus when a magistrate brought a prisoner into the presence of his dying victim, who then made a statement to the magistrate about the crime, which the prisoner did not contradict, this statement was nevertheless held to be inadmissible.[2] For the prisoner might well have been kept silent by his respect for the magistrate, and his silence therefore raised no fair inference of his assent. In the same way, if a person, after having received a letter asserting that he had made a promise of marriage or accusing him of having committed a crime, should never send any reply to the letter, this inaction will be no proof that he admitted the promise or the accusation, and consequently will not enable his opponent to put in the letter as evidence against him.[3] Yet it would be different in the case of any letter—such as a mercantile one—which it would be the ordinary course of business to contradict at once, if the recipient dissented from the statements it contained. So the fact that to a letter which contained a statement of accounts no reply was sent is some evidence of the correctness of those accounts, though weaker than silence when *spoken to* about them.[4] In like manner, when papers are found in a person's possession, even though they were not written *by* but *to* him, they may be evidence against him. For his conduct in having preserved them affords some evidence that the contents of them had reached his knowledge, and also some (though weaker) evidence that he approved of them.[5]

When it is alleged that the man remained silent when a spoken accusation against him was made, the question arises whether the prosecution must prove that he heard the accusation or whether it is enough to prove that he was present when it was made. The latter seems to have been suggested by the Court of Criminal Appeal in a recent case.[6]

[1] See *R.* v. *Christie* [1914] A.C. 545 (*T.A.C.*); contrast *R.* v. *Feigenbaum* (1919) 14 Cr. App.R. 1 and *R.* v. *Marsh* (1925) 19 Cr.App.R. 27 and cf. *Chanter* v. *Bromley* (1921) 14 B.W.C.C. 14. See *R.* v. *Leckey* [1944] 1 K.B. 80 (*T.A.C.*), *post*, p. 542 n. 8, and *R.* v. *Keeling* [1942] 1 All E.R. 507 (*T.A.C.*) *post*, ¶ 603.

[2] *R.* v. *Gilligan* (1844) 3 Craw. and D. 175; cf. *Child* v. *Grace* (1826) 2 C. and P. 193. See ¶ 606 *post* as to its admissibility as a 'dying declaration'.

[3] *Wiedemann* v. *Walpole* [1891] 2 Q.B. 534. Cf. *Thomas* v. *Jones* [1921] 1 K.B. 22 (a letter taxing the recipient with paternity of a child).

[4] *Gaskill* v. *Skene* (1850) 14 Q.B. 664.

[5] *Cotton* v. *James* (1829) M. and M. 273 (*T.A.C.*).

[6] *R.* v. *Spencer* [1959] Crim. L.R. 284, with comment on p. 285.

¶ 576. *The admission may be explained.* It must be remembered (see ¶ 536) that when an admission is given in evidence against a party, he can demand that the whole statement, and not merely the inculpating part, shall be brought out. And if this statement was qualified or explained by any other statement made at the same time, or if it referred expressly or impliedly to any previous statement, such statements may be incorporated with the inculpating statement.

¶ 577. *In cross-examination.* An instance which is more akin to a true exception to the rule against hearsay is when in examination-in-chief a witness has said 'In consequence of what I heard or read, I did so and so'; the cross-examiner will be entitled (though the party calling the witness was not) to ask what the witness heard, or to call for the document which he read. For otherwise the witness's evidence would be left incomplete. A re-examiner may similarly supplement a cross-examination (cf. ¶ 536).

TRUE EXCEPTIONS TO THE HEARSAY RULE

¶ 578. There are, however, some well ascertained and much more important cases in which hearsay is freely and fully admitted as evidence. Of these exceptions we may now discuss such as are accepted equally in civil and criminal tribunals (postponing for the present some others which only concern the latter, see *post* ¶¶ 605 *et seq.*). The following deserve careful attention.

(*a*) *In pedigree and legitimacy suits.* Four exceptions arise in cases of death. Thus, one exception is that, in questions of pedigree or in legitimacy suits,[1] evidence is allowed to be given of statements that were made, before any dispute arose, by deceased members of the family,[2] as to births, marriages or deaths (or the dates when these events occurred), or as to relationships. The deceased person must have been an actual member of the family, not a mere servant or friend.[3] And he must have made this statement before any dispute on the matter had arisen, as that might have tainted him with some bias. But he need not have spoken from personal knowledge of the fact he narrated; family tradition is sufficient.

The introduction of this exception is due to the difficulty of obtaining any first-hand evidence of events after intervals of time so long as those over which disputed genealogies often extend. It is, however, for no very obvious reason restricted to cases strictly genealogical; so that if a defendant, sued for the price of jewellery, sets up a plea of infancy, he cannot support it by merely proving what his deceased mother said as to the date when he was born.[4]

[1] *In the matter of A. H. Davy* [1935] P. 1.

[2] Including the reputed father of an illegitimate child, *In the matter of A. H. Davy, supra.*

[3] But, in *conveyancing*, the statutory declaration of a stranger is readily accepted, even in his lifetime, to establish matters of pedigree.

[4] *Figg* v. *Wedderburne* (1841) 6 Jur. 218.

¶ 579. (*b*) *In disputes about public rights.* A similar exception is recognized in regard to disputes as to public rights, which may concern all the King's subjects (e.g. the existence of a highway), and even as to general rights, which concern only some large class of people (e.g. the customs of a manor, or the boundaries of a parish). For in all such cases—unlike disputes as to a private right of way or the boundaries of a private person's estate—evidence of repute is admissible. And it may be given even by narrating statements that were made (whether orally or in writing) before any dispute arose, by deceased persons who were likely to have a competent knowledge of the subject.[1] But such statements can only be given in evidence so far as they do relate to current repute. They cannot be adduced to show any particular facts that would bear on the question,[2] e.g. the fact of the deceased person's having seen boys whipped or cakes distributed at a particular place, by some person who wished thereby to commemorate its being a parish boundary.

¶ 580. (*c*) *Declarations against interest made by a person since deceased.* Declarations made by a person, since deceased, against his pecuniary or proprietary interest are admissible. Thus a declaration of a deceased person as to the terms of his tenancy of a house has been admitted as sufficient both to rebut the presumption of law (*ante*, ¶ 497) that the person in possession of real property holds it in fee simple, and also to establish the actual amount of rent which the deceased paid.[3] And when any such declaration is admitted, all details which form part of the same statement will be admitted, even though they were in no way against the deceased man's interests.[4] Thus the fact of a life estate having been surrendered has been proved by the entry in a deceased solicitor's ledger of his having been paid for carrying out the surrender; and the date of a child's birth by a similar entry, in the accoucheur's accounts, of the payment of his fee for his attendance.[5] This class of evidence usually takes the form of written entries made by the deceased; but it is none the less admissible if the declaration were oral.[6]

Since this principle only admits declarations against the pecuniary or proprietary interests of the deceased man, his declaration that he—and not the suspected persons—committed a crime would not be admissible, on behalf of those persons should they be indicted for that crime.[7] So statements made by a deceased woman that she had operated upon

[1] E.g. '*X*, who died twenty years ago, used to say that no one dared lock the gate of that road.'

[2] *R.* v. *Bliss* (1837) 7 A. and E. 550. The Royal Commission on the Despatch of Business at Common Law (1936, Cmd. 5065, 78) suggested that in civil cases the judge should have discretion to admit any documents coming into existence before a dispute arose.

[3] *R.* v. *Birmingham* (*Churchwardens of*) (1861) 1 B. and S. 763 (*T.A.C.*).

[4] *Warren* v. *Greenville* (1740) 2 Strange 1129; *Homes* v. *Newman* [1931] 2 Ch. 112.

[5] *Higham* v. *Ridgway* (1808) 1 East 109.

[6] *Fawke* v. *Miles* (1911) 27 T.L.R. 202.

[7] *Sussex Peerage Case* (1844) 11 Cl. and F. 85 at p. 112.

herself were held not admissible in favour of a person accused of operating illegally upon her.[1]

¶ 581. (*d*) *Declarations in course of duty made by a person since deceased.* A similar privilege is extended to statements (whether written or oral) made by a person, since deceased, in the discharge of a *duty* (mere habit does not suffice) which he owed to an employer, in the ordinary course of his employment,[2] even though they may be actually in favour of his own interests. Thus the fact that a man was served with a writ may be proved by the endorsement made on it by the deceased clerk who served it,[3] and the note entered by a deceased drayman, in a book kept for that purpose, of having made delivery of certain goods is evidence that those goods were so delivered.[4] But, as the routine of business affords a less effective guarantee for accuracy than does self-interest, this privilege is restricted by limitations that were not imposed upon the one which we last explained. Thus a statement is not rendered admissible by having been made in the course of employment, unless it was made at the time of the occurrence to which it relates—i.e. within so few hours of it as to be practically a part of the transaction.[5] Moreover the admission of such a statement will be limited strictly to its mention of those circumstances which were essential to the performance of the duty, and will not, as in the case of a statement made against interest, cover the collateral details which may have been added. A third limitation is that it must record, not mere hearsay, but the personal knowledge of the person recording.[6] As previously mentioned the rule has been extended, for civil cases, by the Evidence Act, 1938.[7]

For some further exceptions to the hearsay rule of great importance but peculiar to criminal law, see *post*, ¶¶ 605 *et seq.*

(VIII) BIAS

¶ 582. The judges of the eighteenth century went far in excluding the testimony of witnesses who seemed to them to be likely, from personal interest in the case or other causes, to give but untrustworthy evidence. But a reaction was initiated by Jeremy Bentham. He pointed out that even the stupidest jurymen are on the alert to suspect bias in a witness; and moreover that from every witness's evidence, whether true or

[1] *R.* v. *Thomson* [1912] 3 K.B. 19.

[2] *R.* v. *Buckley* (1873) 13 Cox 293; a case of *oral* statement.

[3] *Poole* v. *Dicas* (1835) 1 Bing. (N.C.) 649.

[4] *Price* v. *Torrington (Earl)* (1703) 1 Salk. 283 (*T.A.C.*).

[5] *Djambi (Sumatra) Rubber Estates, In re* (1912) 29 T.L.R. 28.

[6] Cf. *Ryan* v. *Ring* (1889) 25 Ir. Ch. 185. Here a deceased Irish priest had had—unlike Anglican clergymen—the duty, when registering a baptism, of stating if the child had been born in wedlock. He had therefore recorded it as a child of 'J.H. and H.F. *his wife*'. The register, though evidence of the baptism, was held not to be evidence of the wifehood; for it was not shown that he had 'personal knowledge' of the wedding ceremony.

[7] *Ante*, ¶ 563.

false, instructive inferences may be drawn—the very fact that he thinks it worth while to lie being itself a suggestive one. The influence of Bentham has brought about legislative reforms which have removed almost all objections to the competency of witnesses on the ground of bias[1] or of character; it being left to the jury to take account of these considerations when deciding upon the value of their testimony.

(IX) UNDERSTANDING

¶ 583. An adequate degree of *understanding* is, of course, necessary in a witness; and, on the ground of want of understanding, children or insane persons may be excluded if the judge finds, on investigation,[2] that they are incapable of comprehending the facts about which they are to testify. Yet a lunatic is not necessarily incompetent to give evidence.[3] The arbitrary rule treating children under eight years of age as necessarily too young for criminal liability has, however, no counterpart in the law of evidence, it being now settled that competency depends not upon the precise age but upon the actual intelligence of the witness.[4]

(X) OATHS

¶ 584. The value added to testimony by its being given under supernatural sanctions is frequently so great that the law formerly made it essential to the competency of every witness that he should know and accept the religious obligation of an oath. Increased intercourse with the East led in the seventeenth century to the recognition of Mohammedans, and in the eighteenth to that of Hindus, as satisfying this condition, and being entitled to be sworn with their own sacred ceremonies. But now, even in the case of adult witnesses, the requirement of an oath is no longer universal; for, by the Oaths Act, 1888, 'every person objecting to be sworn, on the ground either that he has no religious belief or that the taking of an oath is contrary to his religious belief, shall be permitted to make his solemn affirmation in all places and for all purposes where an oath shall be required by law'. And now by virtue of the Oaths Act, 1961, a person may be required, as well as permitted,

[1] In 1843, Lord Denman's Act made mere interest cease to be a disqualification; and in 1846 and 1851 Lord Brougham's Acts qualified even the parties to a suit to give evidence.

[2] In the presence of the jury, *R.* v. *Reynolds* [1950] 1 K.B. 606; 1 All E.R. 335 (*T.A.C.*).

[3] *R.* v. *Hill* (1851) 2 Den. 254. At Leeds Assizes on 2 Dec. 1914, in *R.* v. *Firth*, before Shearman, J., an asylum attendant was convicted, on a lunatic's evidence, of assaulting her. It was ruled by the Supreme Court of the United States (107 U.S. 419), that it is for the judge, after hearing evidence as to the mental condition of the witness, to decide whether or not his insanity extends so far as to prevent 'his giving a perfectly accurate and lucid statement as to what he has seen and heard'. Cf. *R.* v. *Slater* (1860) C.C.C. Sess. Pap. LII, 612 at p. 617.

[4] *R.* v. *Brasier* (1777) 1 Leach 199. Five is usually too young; *R.* v. *George* (1909) 2 Cr.App.R. 282. In old days the minimum age was twelve; it now seems to be about six. But even at twelve corroboration is desirable; *R.* v. *Hatton* (1925) 19 Cr.App.R. 29.

to affirm when it is not reasonably practicable, without inconvenience or delay, to administer an oath in the manner required by his religious belief.[1] A 'child of tender years', who has not yet learned the nature of an oath, may in criminal cases give evidence unsworn,[2] if it is of sufficient intelligence and 'understands the duty of speaking the truth'.[3] But the accused is not to be convicted on such evidence unless it be corroborated by material evidence which implicates him[4] (cf. ¶ 600). Although it is for the judge alone to determine whether a child of tender years is capable of giving evidence, it has been held that any questions put by the judge for this purpose must be put in open court in the presence of the jury.[5] And since it should be regarded as most exceptional that any evidence should be given in a criminal trial in the absence of the jury, any evidence as to the child's fitness to give evidence on oath must be given in the presence of the jury (although the child itself need not be present while this question is being discussed).[6]

(XI) EXCLUSIONS AND PRIVILEGES. WITNESS'S PRIVILEGES OF REFUSAL

¶ 585. (*a*) *Criminating questions.* There are some questions which it is quite legal to ask, but which a witness may, if he thinks fit, equally legally refuse to answer. Such a privilege arises, for instance, in the following cases.

A witness cannot be compelled to answer any question, or produce any document,[7] which tends to criminate him.[8] He must pledge his oath that his answer would have this effect; and it will then be for the court to decide whether the question seems to be one which, under all the circumstances of the case, it would really endanger the witness to answer. For a merely remote possibility of criminal prosecution[9] will not be regarded as sufficient to entitle a witness to withhold information.[10] Yet

[1] This obviates the difficulty experienced in *R.* v. *Singh* (1958) 42 Cr.App.R. 44. And see *R.* v. *Clark* [1962] 1 W.L.R. 180.

[2] Children and Young Persons Act, 1933, s. 38. In *R.* v. *Wilson* (1924) the C.C.A. (18 Cr.App.R. 108) recognized that the judge has still a right to question a boy of thirteen as to his religious belief and practice, even at the end of his evidence.

[3] E.g. under the Criminal Law Amendment Act, 1885, s. 4 (rep.) and the Children and Young Persons Act, 1933, s. 38.

[4] Prisoner's silence or inadequate answers are not a sufficient corroboration, *R.* v. *Whitehead* [1929] 1 K.B. 99; *R.* v. *Keeling* [1942] 1 All E.R. 507.

[5] *R.* v. *Dunne* (1929) 21 Cr.App.R. 176; 143 L.T. 120; but see 46 *L.Q.R.* 137.

[6] *R.* v. *Reynolds* [1950] 1 K.B. 606; 34 Cr.App.R. 60 (*T.A.C.*).

[7] E.g. the bill of sale whereby he disposed of an armed ship to a belligerent. But his refusal lets in secondary evidence; *Inhabitants of Llanfaethly* (1853) 2 E. and B. 940; *ante*, ¶ 562.

[8] 'One of the most sacred principles of the law of this country'; Lord Eldon (Buck 540). But a prisoner *giving evidence* on his own trial has no privilege against criminating himself as to *that* accusation; ¶ 621.

[9] *R.* v. *Boyes* (1861) 1 B. and S. 311 (*T.A.C.*).

[10] By 24 and 25 Vict. c. 96, s. 85, in a few peculiar offences of misappropriation, e.g. by agents, custodians, directors, etc. (*ante*, ¶ 333), a witness has no privilege in any *civil*

even a man who has already been tried for an offence and been acquitted may still be in risk of criminating himself in connexion with the very same crime, e.g. by admitting his having been an accessory after the fact.

¶ 586. (*b*) *Title deeds.* A witness cannot be compelled to produce his title deeds for inspection. If, however, he is himself a party to the particular litigation, he does not enjoy this privilege, except for deeds that are irrelevant to his opponent's case.

¶ 587. (*c*) *Marital communications.* A husband or wife cannot be compelled to disclose any communications made to him or her, during the coverture, by the other spouse. This rule is based on the principle of preserving the confidences of married life.

¶ 588. (*d*) *Professional privilege.* Counsel and solicitors cannot be compelled—and indeed are not even permitted—to disclose facts confided to them by[1] or on behalf[2] of a client, or to produce any documents received by them from a client in their professional capacity, unless the client consents to waive this privilege; for it is his, and not theirs. No such protection, however, exists if the adviser was being consulted, not merely in order to protect his client against the results of a past criminal act, but to facilitate the commission of some future one. Nor does the privilege cover facts merely collateral to the confidence, e.g. that he saw his client sign the perjured affidavit.[3]

There is no similar privilege[4] for confidences entrusted to a medical[5] or even to a clerical adviser,[6] nor for business secrets (e.g. the secret marks upon bank-notes).

¶ 589. (*e*) *Disclosures against public policy.* By a still stricter rule, one of exclusion rather than of privilege, a witness cannot be compelled, and indeed will not be permitted,[7] to answer any question which involves a disclosure of any official communications (whether written or oral)

court against criminating himself in respect of such an offence; but he is exempted from prosecution for it if he 'first disclosed' it when thus under compulsory examination. See also Larceny Act, 1916, s. 43 (2); *R.* v. *Maywhort* [1955] 1 W.L.R. 848. Cf. 4 and 5 Geo. V, c. 59, s. 166, as to compulsory admissions in bankruptcy.

1 *R.* v. *Withers* (1811) 2 Camp. 578. But a third party, who overheard the confidence, has no such privilege. On professional privilege generally, see Nokes, 'Professional privilege', 66 *L.Q.R.* 88.

2 E.g. the statements made to them by a witness as to what evidence he can give in a litigation contemplated, even though not yet commenced. Such statements are taken down in writing (his 'proof'), and often then signed by the witness.

3 *Doe* v. *Andrews* (1778) Cowper 845.

4 Nor even an exemption from the (theoretical) law of misprision (*ante*, ¶ 421).

5 But any other disclosure of those confidences would be an actionable breach of the doctor's obligation to secrecy.

6 *R.* v. *Gibbons* (1823) 1 C. and P. 97; cf. *Wheeler* v. *Le Marchant* (1881) 17 Ch.D. 675 at p. 681. Yet see Phillimore's *Ecclesiastical Law*, 2nd ed., 543.

7 *R.* v. *Hardy* (1794) 24 St.Tr. at pp. 818, 820. The exclusion will not let secondary evidence in, as it does in other cases of privilege.

which are such that, in the opinion of the judge, disclosure of them would be contrary to public policy.[1] Hence in the case of prosecutions so important as to have been (not nominally but actually) instituted by the executive government, the name of the informer need not be disclosed by a witness, nor can he be asked if he were himself the informer.[2] But it would seem that this rule does not extend to the case of communications made to a private prosecutor, even where the prosecution is practically in the hands of the police; all that can be done is to postpone the question until the course of the trial may make manifest its importance.

Waiver of privilege

¶ 590. Where any of these privileges is waived by a person who is at liberty to waive it, the answer he gives will be perfectly good evidence, even against himself, both in the proceedings in which it is given and in any subsequent litigation. But if, on the other hand, he claims his privilege, and yet is illegally compelled to answer, his answer will not be evidence against him as an admission, either then or in any subsequent litigation. Yet against other parties it is evidence (since the privilege is only his and not theirs); and consequently, if he were not himself a party to the particular litigation, the validity of the trial will not be affected by the reception of his answer.

(XII) PROOF OF GENUINENESS: DOCUMENTS

¶ 591. (*a*) *Documents less than twenty years old.* Where a document is tendered as evidence the necessary proof of its genuineness varies with its age. If the document be less than twenty[3] years old, express evidence of its genuineness must be adduced.[4] In ordinary cases, it is not necessary to do more than to show that the document or the signature to it is in the handwriting of the person by whom it purports to have been executed. Handwriting may be proved by any witness who from knowing the person's handwriting can swear to the genuineness of the document, or, under a modern statute,[5] even by merely letting the jury compare the document in question 'with any writing proved, to the satisfaction of the judge, to be genuine', e.g. a signature made by the person whilst actually in the witness-box before them. The function of a handwriting expert is to point out similarities and differences and to leave the jury to draw their own conclusions.[6]

[1] E.g. a captain's report to the Admiralty about a naval collision. See *Duncan* v. *Cammell Laird* [1942] A.C. 624. And see *Auten* v. *Rayner* [1958] 3 All E.R. 566.

[2] *Marks* v. *Beyfus* (1890) 25 Q.B.D. 494. As to reports made to a superintendent of police by his constables, see an article in 65 *J.P.* 209.

[3] Evidence Act, 1938, s. 4. *Ante*, ¶ 564.

[4] But conveyancers do not require any such proof on a sale of real property, even for recent documents, the genuineness being sufficiently corroborated by the fact that the vendor is in possession of the property.

[5] 17 and 18 Vict. c. 125, s. 27; extended to criminal cases by 28 and 29 Vict. c. 18, s. 8.

[6] *Wakeford* v. *Lincoln* (*Bishop*) [1921] 90 L.J.P.C. 174.

¶ 592. *Genuineness of attestation and of seal.* But there are some instruments to whose validity some further circumstance is essential; and in such cases, that circumstance must also be proved. Thus where attestation by witnesses is essential to the document (as in the case of a bill of sale) it must be shown to have been duly attested. To establish this fact one of those witnesses must, if possible, be produced. But if none of the attesting witnesses can be found the handwriting of one of them must be proved; and some evidence must be given as to the identity of the person who actually executed the instrument with the person who is under discussion in the litigation, unless the attestation clause itself sufficiently identifies him. Again, in the case of deeds the further ceremony of sealing[1] is necessary; but where there is an attestation clause the courts will, if the signature be proved, accept this clause as sufficient evidence of the sealing and delivery.[2]

¶ 593. (*b*) *Documents more than twenty years old.* In the case of documents more than twenty years old, just as in questions of pedigree (*ante* ¶ 577), the law of evidence is relaxed to meet the difficulties produced by the lapse of time.[3] Such documents, if produced from a proper custody, 'prove themselves', i.e. no express evidence of their genuineness need be adduced. Nor is it necessary that the custody from which such instruments come should be the most proper custody for them to be in. It is sufficient that the custody, though not the best, is a natural one, i.e. one which, under the circumstances of the particular case, appears to the judge to be one naturally consistent with the genuineness of the document. Thus, although papers relating to an episcopal see properly pass on the death of one bishop to his successor in office, yet an ancient document would be allowed to 'prove itself', if it were produced from the custody of a deceased bishop's descendants.[4]

[1] Any act suffices by which the party adopts the affixed seal.

[2] *In re Sandilands* (1871) 6 C.P. 411. Cf. *Talbot* v. *Hodson* (1816) 7 Taunt. 253.

[3] Evidence Act, 1938, s. 4.

[4] *Meath* v. *Winchester* (1836) 3 Bing. (N.C.) 183.

Chapter XXVIII

RULES OF EVIDENCE PECULIAR TO CRIMINAL LAW

SECTION I. A HIGHER MINIMUM OF PROOF REQUIRED

¶ 594. In criminal cases the general principles of evidence are supplemented by some rules, and modified by others, which do not hold good in civil litigation. Of these the following deserve explanation here.

A higher minimum of proof is necessary to support an accusation of crime than will suffice when the charge is only of a civil nature. For in the latter it is sufficient that there be a *preponderance* of evidence in favour of the successful party, whereas in criminal cases the burden rests upon the prosecution to prove that the accused is guilty 'beyond reasonable doubt' (*infra*, ¶ 596). When therefore the case for the prosecution is closed after sufficient evidence has been adduced to necessitate an answer from the defence, the defence need do no more than show that there is *a reasonable doubt* as to the guilt of the accused.[1]

Thus, for example, it has been stated:[2]

> If two people are jointly indicted for the commission of a crime and the evidence does not point to one rather than the other, and there is no evidence that they were acting in concert, the jury ought to return a verdict of not guilty against both because the prosecution have not proved the case. If, in these circumstances, it is left to the accused persons to get out of it if they can, that would put the onus upon them to prove themselves not guilty.

Even in civil proceedings, e.g. in actions of debt, a mere scintilla of evidence would not warrant the jury in finding a verdict for the plaintiff; for there must (as we have seen[3]) be so much evidence that a reasonable man might accept it as establishing the issue. But in criminal cases the presumption of innocence is still stronger,[4] and accordingly a still higher minimum of evidence is required; and the more heinous the crime the higher will be this minimum of necessary proof.[5] The progressive raising of the standard of proof, as the gravity of the accusation to be proved increases, is illustrated in an extract from Lord Brougham's speech in defence of Queen Caroline: 'The evidence before us', he said, 'is inadequate even to prove a debt—impotent to deprive of a civil right—ridiculous for convicting of the pettiest offence—scandalous if

[1] R. v. *Stoddart* (1909) 2 Cr.App.R. 217 at p. 242.

[2] R. v. *Abbott* [1955] A.C. 497 at p. 503, *per* Lord Goddard, C.J., a case in which R. v. *Cohen and Bateman* (1909) 2 Cr.App.R. 197 was applied and R. v. *Power* [1919] 1 K.B. 572 explained. See *King* v. R. [1962] 2 W.L.R. 301.

[3] *Ante*, ¶ 526.

[4] *Ante*, ¶ 493.

[5] See 'Burden of proof in criminal cases', 116 *J.P.Jo.* 498; '*Res ipsa loquitur* in criminal cases', 119 *J.P.Jo.* 616; Norval Morris, 'Burden of proof in bigamy', 18 *Mod.L.R.* 452.

brought forward to support a charge of any grave character—monstrous if to ruin the honour of an English Queen.'[1]

As to the charge of murder it has been said:[2]

> In cases where the evidence discloses a possible defence of self-defence the onus remains throughout on the prosecution to establish that the accused is guilty of the crime of murder, and the onus is never on the accused to establish this defence any more than it is for him to establish provocation or any other defence apart from insanity[3]...; it is clear that the rule with regard to the onus of proof in cases of murder and manslaughter is of general application, and permits of no exceptions save only in cases of insanity, which is not strictly a defence.[4]

THE RULE APPLIES TO ALL CRIMES IN ENGLISH LAW

¶ 595. It was formerly considered that this higher minimum was required on account of the peculiarities of criminal procedure, such, for instance, as the impossibility of a new trial, and (in those times) the refusal to allow felons to be defended by counsel and to allow any prisoners to give evidence; and consequently that it was required only in criminal tribunals. This view is still taken in America; but in England it was and is more usually considered that the rule is founded on the very nature of the issue, and therefore applies without distinction of tribunal;[5] e.g. if arson be the defence to an action on a fire-policy, or forgery to one on a promissory note; see Stephen's *Digest of Evidence*, art. 94, Taylor's *Evidence*, 12th ed., s. 112. But the American view was taken by Lush, J., in *Hurst* v. *Evans* [1917] 1 K.B. at p. 357, and is taken by Phipson (*Evidence*, 9th ed., p. 8).[6]

History shows how necessary is some such rule, emphatic and universal, in order to protect prisoners from the credulity which the shifting currents of prejudice will inspire about any offence, or class of offences, that may for the moment have aroused popular indignation. No less enlightened a jurist than Bodin maintained, in an elaborate treatise,[7] that persons accused of witchcraft ought to be convicted without further proof, unless they could demonstrate themselves to be innocent—'for to adhere, in a trial for witchcraft, to ordinary rules of procedure, would result in defeating the law of both God and man'.[8]

[1] *Speeches*, I, 227.

[2] *Chan Kau* v. *R.* [1955] A.C. 206, *per* Lord Tucker at p. 211.

[3] For the burden of proof see *ante*, ¶ 53.

[4] Citing *H.M. Advocate* v. *Doherty* [1954] S.C. (J.) 1; *Latour* v. *R.* [1951] 1 D.L.R. 834; and, disapproving, *R.* v. *Smith* (1837) 8 C. and P. 160, a disapproval confirmed in *R.* v. *Lobell* [1957] 2 W.L.R. 524, where the defence on a charge of wounding with intent to inflict grievous bodily harm was self-defence. See *R.* v. *McPherson* (1957) 41 Cr.App.R. 213; *Bullock* v. *R.* [1957] 3 W.L.R. 656 at p. 661.

[5] *Statham* v. *Statham* [1929] P. 131. But see ¶ 493 *ante*.

[6] Cf. *Devine* v. *Wilson* (1855) 10 Moore P.C. 502.

[7] *Démonomanie* (ed. 1598), IV, ch. IV.

[8] Similarly when in 1899 Esterházy confessed in the *Observer* newspaper that he had forged the famous 'bordereau' in order that the suspicions against Capt. Dreyfus might

'REASONABLE DOUBT'

¶ 596. Whenever, therefore, an allegation of crime is made, it is the duty of the jury—to quote Lord Kenyon's advice—'if the scales of evidence hang anything like even, to throw into them some grains of mercy'; or, as it is more commonly put, to give the prisoner the benefit of any reasonable doubt.[1] Not, be it noted, of every doubt, but only of a doubt for which reasons can be given; for everything relative to human affairs and dependent on human evidence is open to some possible or imaginary doubts. 'It is the condition of mind which exists when the jurors cannot say that they feel an abiding conviction, a moral certainty, of the truth of the charge. For it is not sufficient for the prosecutor to establish a probability, even though a strong one according to the doctrine of chances; he must establish the fact to a moral certainty[2]—a certainty that convinces the understanding, satisfies the reason, and directs the judgment.[3] But were the law to go further than this, and require absolute certainty, it would exclude circumstantial evidence altogether.'[4] As was said by a great Irish judge, 'To warrant an acquittal the doubt must not be light or capricious, such as timidity or passion prompts, and weakness or corruption readily adopts. It must be such a doubt as, upon a calm view of the whole evidence, a rational understanding will suggest to an honest heart; the conscientious hesitation of minds that are not influenced by party, preoccupied by prejudice, or subdued by fear.'[5]

MEANING OF A VERDICT OF ACQUITTAL

¶ 597. Accordingly, a verdict of acquittal does not necessarily mean that the jury are satisfied of the prisoner's innocence; it states no more than that they do not regard the evidence as legally sufficient to establish his guilt.[6] There was therefore a gross fallacy in the old forensic argument of prosecutors, 'you must convict the prisoner

be eked out by some item of actual evidence, he justified himself by the plea that 'on the trial of spies, it is always necessary to forge some documentary evidence [fabriquer des preuves matérielles], or no spy would ever be convicted'.

[1] *R.* v. *Puddick* (1865) 4 F. and F. 497 at p. 499; *Lawrence* v. *R.* [1933] A.C. 699 at p. 706; *Woolmington* v. *D.P.P.* (1935) A.C. 462; *R.* v. *Blackburn* (1955) 39 Cr.App.R. 84. 'A doubt may be regarded as reasonable in the criminal courts which would not be so in the civil courts', *Bater* v. *Bater* [1950] 2 All E.R. 458. The same strictness is required in the case of a matrimonial offence, *Ginesi* v. *Ginesi* [1948] 1 All E.R. 373. And see *R.* v. *Dunbar* [1957] 2 All E.R. 737, *ante*, ¶ 54. Cp. *R.* v. *Patterson* [1962] 1 All E.R. 340.

[2] See *R.* v. *White* (1918) 13 Cr.App.R. 211, for a case of 'the very gravest suspicion' yet not beyond reasonable doubt.

[3] For a case which illustrates the lighter task which confronts the accused person when called upon to answer the prosecution's case, see *R.* v. *Willshire* (1881) 6 Q.B.D. 366.

[4] *Per* Shaw, C.J., on the trial of Prof. Webster (*ante*, ¶ 518), 5 Cushing 295.

[5] Kendal Bushe, C.J., *Dublin Univ. Mag.* XVIII, 85.

[6] Moreover 'the acquittal of the whole offence is not an acquittal of every part of it, but only an acquittal of it as a *whole*'; Pollock, L.C.B. (*R.* v. *De Salvi* (1857) C.C.C. Sess. Pap. XLVI, 884).

unless you think my witnesses ought to be convicted of perjury'. For the jury may well be in utter doubt as to the soundness of either alternative.

This abstract, and therefore necessarily vague, direction—that they must be satisfied 'beyond reasonable doubt'—is the only restriction which, in ordinary cases, English criminal law imposes upon the discretion of juries in pronouncing upon the sufficiency of evidence.[1] The civil and the canon law, on the other hand (like the Mosaic,[2] the Roman,[3] and the modern Scottish[4]), required at least two witnesses,[5] and, from the frequent difficulty of obtaining these, had to fall back upon confessions extorted by torture. The English common law, by avoiding the unreasonable rule, escaped such cruel expedients.[6]

In recent years, however, there developed some judicial antipathy to the hallowed expression 'beyond reasonable doubt', from a feeling that it tended to lead juries into too great a hesitation to commit. This culminated in a declaration that instead of it the jury should be told that their duty was to regard the evidence and make sure that it satisfied them so that they felt sure in giving their verdict that it was the right one.[7] This doctrine came under considerable criticism,[8] and was, in effect, withdrawn in *R.* v. *Hepworth and Fearnley*,[9] so that for practical purposes the direction 'beyond reasonable doubt' has been reinstated.[10]

The cases are rare in which English law exacts any defined minimum of proof for even a criminal charge.[11] But the following are important ones.

[1] *R.* v. *Nash* (1911) 6 Cr.App.R. 225, deserves study as a case where there was just enough circumstantial evidence to support a conviction for murder. Contrast *R.* v. *Wallace* (1931) 23 Cr.App.R. 32.

[2] Deut. xix. 15. [3] *Testis unus, testis nullus.* [4] 6 Justiciary Rep. 128.

[5] See Ayliffe's *Parergon*, 541. In some cases indeed (see Best, *Evidence*, 11th ed., 37) the canon law exacted far higher degrees of proof; as when it provided that no cardinal was to be convicted of unchastity unless there were at least seven—or in Fortescue's time, according to him (*De Laudibus*, c. 32), twelve—witnesses. This requirement was rendered harder to comply with by the further rule of canon law, that in criminal cases a woman could not be a witness. The result may well have been the same as was produced by the similar rule of the Koran, requiring all accusations of adultery to be supported by four eye-witnesses, so that (according to Sir William Muir) 'the threat of punishment became almost inoperative'. For by introducing artificial rules of proof into the law of evidence it is easy to effect a modification of the substantive law, whilst appearing to modify merely the adjective law, the disguise being closely akin to that under which the *praetores urbani* succeeded in reforming the laws of Rome (Maine's *Ancient Law*, ch. III).

[6] Pollock and Maitland, II, 660.

[7] *R.* v. *Summers* [1952] 1 All E.R. 1059; W.N. 185.

[8] E.g. see 68 *L.Q.R.* pp. 314, 315; *R.* v. *Murtagh and Kennedy* [1955] Crim.L.R. 506; 39 Cr.App.R. 72, at p. 78, *per* counsel, *arguendo*; G. Williams, 'Directions to the jury on the burden of proof' [1955] *Crim. L.R.* 464.

[9] [1955] 3 W.L.R. 331; 2 All E.R. 913.

[10] See *R.* v. *Harnett* [1955] Crim. L.R. 793; *R.* v. *O'Connor* [1955] Crim. L.R. 794; *R.* v. *Young* [1955] Crim. L.R. 795. For the danger of abandoning the doctrine of 'reasonable doubt', see Cannon, '*Beyond reasonable doubt*' [1961] *Crim. L.R.* 235.

[11] Only in two instances is corroboration required by statute in *civil* courts; viz. in bastardy proceedings and in actions for breach of promise of marriage. As to divorce, see *Getty* v. *Getty* [1907] P. 334; and ¶ 602 *post*. Claims against a dead man's estate are viewed jealously if the claimant is not corroborated; *Gandy* v. *Macaulay* (1885) 31 Ch.D. 1.

CORROBORATION NEEDED: (*a*) In charges of perjury

¶ 598. Upon an indictment for perjury or subornation of perjury, or for any of the cognate offences created by the Perjury Act, 1911 (though the taking of the oath, or the giving of the false evidence, may be proved by one witness), the falsity of that evidence itself cannot be legally established merely by the testimony of one witness;[1] for that would be only oath against oath. On each 'assignment' of perjury the contradicting witness must be corroborated, and on some material point. The question whether a point is sufficiently material is for the judge, not the jury, to decide. It is not necessary that the corroborating fact should be so important that from it, standing alone, the falsity of the perjured statement could have been inferred. The corroboration may be by a second witness, or documentary evidence, or an admission by the prisoner,[2] or some other similar circumstance.[3] But merely to show that the supposed perjurer has made statements directly contradictory of each other (even though both of them were made on oath)[4] will not suffice. For this leaves it still utterly uncertain which of the two statements was the false one; and the indictment cannot be framed in a merely alternative form.

(*b*) In charges of certain sexual offences

¶ 599. Under the Sexual Offences Act, 1956, sections 2, 3 and 4,[5] it is provided in regard to certain sexual offences[6] against women and children that no person shall be convicted of these upon the evidence of one witness alone, unless such witness be corroborated in some material particular,[7] and by evidence which implicates the accused. But a complaint by the victim is not sufficient corroboration (*ante*, ¶ 573).[8]

(*c*) Of unsworn evidence of children

¶ 600. Similar corroboration is required in those cases in which under the Children and Young Persons Act, 1933 (*ante*, ¶ 584), a very young child is allowed to give evidence without being sworn.[9] The precaution

[1] 1 and 2 Geo. V, c. 6, s. 13. See ¶ 471 *ante*.

[2] *R.* v. *Hook* (1858), D. and B. 606 (*T.A.C.*). In some American cases, perjury has been proved without any witness, by a combination of two evidentiary documents; e.g. where both a letter written by the prisoner *and* an invoice written to and preserved by him, contradicted him as to the ownership of property. Whether such proof would be held sufficient in England also is not certain.

[3] *R.* v. *Parker* (1842) C. and M. 639.

[4] *R.* v. *Harris* (1822) 5 B. and Ald. 926.

[5] Which repealed and replaced the Criminal Law Amendment Act, 1885.

[6] Rape is not included, and therefore corroboration is not required as a matter of law; but it is an offence where corroboration is looked for as a matter of practice and precaution, *R.* v. *Hughes* [1955] Crim.L.R. 508.

[7] *R.* v. *Thomas* (1959) 43 Cr.App.R. 210; *R.* v. *Halligan* [1960] Crim. L.R. 422.

[8] *R.* v. *Evans* (1924) 18 Cr.App.R. 123. A lie as to the circumstances told by the accused to the police when they are investigating the case is not necessarily, but may be, corroboration; *Credland* v. *Knowler* (1951) 35 Cr.App.R. 48.

[9] Cf. *R.* v. *Davies* (1916) 85 L.J.K.B. 208. Moreover a child who thus gives evidence without being sworn is not adequately corroborated by the *unsworn* evidence given by

is wise; for a tribunal of adults may place undue reliance upon such evidence forgetting that, though children are less fraudulent than adults, they are often more imaginative. Hence the judge should caution the jury. On the other hand intelligent children are very often acutely observant of facts and events external to themselves and remember them with great accuracy.

(*d*) Of sworn evidence in certain cases

¶ 601. Moreover even in those sexual offences (whether against children or adult women[1]) in which corroboration is not legally necessary it has become the established practice that the judge should warn the jury of accepting evidence which is not corroborated;[2] and if such warning be not given a conviction will probably be quashed on appeal[3] (unless there is in fact obvious and adequate corroboration[4]). And although the warning be given yet a conviction may be quashed on the ground that the jury's verdict was unreasonable.[5] Anything which amounts to a confession by the prisoner will of course constitute corroboration.[6] But if the judge warns the jury as to the desirability of corroboration and explains to them what is meant in law by corroboration he is not under the further duty of pointing out to them pieces of evidence which could amount to corroboration. To point to evidence as corroborative when it is not so would be a misdirection.[7] But evidence of previous similar acts (when admissible) not at present charged needs no corroboration.[8]

(*e*) Of the evidence of accomplices

¶ 602. An accomplice in the crime[9] to which the indictment relates is and has always been a competent witness, and a conviction based upon

other similar children, *R.* v. *Coyle* [1926] N.I. 208; *R.* v. *Manser* (1934) 25 Cr.App.R. 18. Nor is any complaint, which this child has made, an adequate corroboration. For a complaint is (see ¶ 573 *ante*) proof merely of the complainant's consistency of conduct; and not evidence at all of the facts alleged in it. See *R.* v. *Chandor* [1959] 1 Q.B. 545 which, in effect, overrules *R.* v. *Campbell* [1956] 2 Q.B. 432.

[1] *R.* v. *Jones* (1925) 19 Cr.App.R. 40; *R.* v. *Freebody* (1935) 25 Cr.App.R. 69.

[2] 'Corroboration, though not essential in law, is always required in practice'; *R.* v. *Killick* (1924) 18 Cr.App.R. 120; *R.* v. *Winfield* (1939) 27 Cr.App.R. 139 (*T.A.C.*); *R.* v. *Gammon* (1959) 43 Cr.App.R. 155 (cited on another point, *ante*, ¶ 63). Even where mistake of identity is the sole defence the rule is the same, *R.* v. *Sawyer* (1959) 43 Cr.App. R. 187. If, however, corroboration is required by *statute* then, if there be none, the case must be withdrawn from the jury. For the position in court-martial cases see *R.* v. *Linzee and O'Driscoll* (1956) 40 Cr.App.R. 177.

[3] See *R.* v. *Brown* (1910) 6 Cr.App.R. 24; *R.* v. *Graham* (1910) 4 Cr.App.R. 218; *R.* v. *Pitts* (1912) 8 Cr.App.R. 126; *R.* v. *Cratchley* (1913) 9 Cr.App.R. 232; *R.* v. *Dossi* (1918) 13 Cr.App.R. 158.

[4] *R.* v. *Gregg* (1932) 102 L.J.K.B. 120; 24 Cr.App.R. 13; *R.* v. *Mitchell* (1952) 36 Cr.App.R. 79.

[5] *R.* v. *Dent* [1943] 2 All E.R. 596.

[6] *R.* v. *Arnold* [1949] W.N. 184; 93 S.J. 220.

[7] *R.* v. *Zielinski* [1950] 2 All E.R. 1114; *R.* v. *Jackson* [1953] 1 W.L.R. 591.

[8] *R.* v. *Sanders* [1961] 11 Curr.L. 325.

[9] But if *A* and *B* steal a horse, and *B* sells it to *C*, and *C* is tried for receiving, *A* would not need corroboration at *C*'s trial.

his evidence, though uncorroborated, could and can still today be supported: so that a judge may properly direct the jury that they are entitled, if they choose, to act on such uncorroborated evidence. But a practice has been built up during the past century and a half that the judges should warn the jury[1] that it is dangerous to convict on such evidence, free though they are to do so. This practice has steadily stiffened and it has been stated in the House of Lords[2] in three propositions:

(i) In a criminal trial, where a person who is an accomplice[3] gives evidence on behalf of the prosecution, it is the duty of the judge to warn the jury that, although they may commit upon his evidence, it is dangerous to do so unless it is corroborated.

(ii) This rule, although a rule of practice, has now the force of a rule of law.[4]

(iii) Where the judge fails to warn the jury in accordance with this rule, the conviction will be quashed,[5] even if in fact there be ample corroboration of the evidence of the accomplice, unless the appellate court can apply the proviso to section 4 (1) of the Criminal Appeal Act, 1907.

This rule, of course, only applies to witnesses for the prosecution. The House of Lords further declared[6] that for the purpose of this rule the following persons, if called as witnesses for the prosecution, are within the category:

(i) Persons who are *participes criminis* in respect of the actual crime charged whether as principals or accessories before or after the fact (in felonies) or persons committing, procuring or aiding and abetting (in cases of misdemeanours).... But in two cases, persons falling strictly outside the ambit of this category have been held to be accomplices...viz. (ii) receivers have been held to be accomplices of the thieves from whom they receive goods on a trial of the latter for larceny,[7] and (iii) when *X* has been charged with a

[1] As in the case of sexual offences mentioned above, ¶ 601; *R.* v. *Lewis* [1937] 4 All E.R. 360. But if the judge has given the due caution, a conviction will be upheld; *R.* v. *Crocker* (1922) 17 Cr.App.R. 45.

[2] In *Davies* v. *D.P.P.* [1954] A.C. 378 at p. 399, *per* Lord Tucker (*T.A.C.*).

[3] *R.* v. *Chrimes* (1959) 43 Cr.App.R. 149. In *R.* v. *Prater* (1960) 44 Cr.App.R. 83, the practice seems to have been extended beyond accomplices in the strict sense (and to apply to evidence by co-prisoners also, *post*, ¶ 629) by the words: 'It is desirable that, in cases where a person may be regarded as having some purpose of his own to serve, the warning against uncorroborated evidence should be given.' See *R.* v. *Heaps* [1961] Crim. L.R. 254.

[4] *R.* v. *Roma* [1956] Crim. L.R. 46.

[5] This seems to overrule *R.* v. *Gregg* (1932) 24 Cr.App.R. 13.

[6] At p. 400.

[7] *R.* v. *Jennings* (1912) 7 Cr.App.R. 242; *R.* v. *Dixon* (1925) 19 Cr.App.R. 36. A receiver was formerly declared an accessory after the fact by statute (e.g. Larceny Act, 1827 (rep.)); hence the rule as to corroboration was established and has been retained. In *R.* v. *Norris* (1916) 12 Cr.App.R. 156, it was the thief who gave evidence against the receiver Norris, so that it was the thief who was the accessory of the receiver and *not* vice versa.

specific offence on a particular occasion and evidence is admissible[1] and has been admitted of his having committed crimes of this identical type on other occasions, as proving system and intent and negativing accident; in such cases ...in relation to such other similar offences if evidence of them were given by parties to them, the evidence of such other parties should not be left to the jury without a warning that it is dangerous to accept it without corroboration.[2]

¶ 603. The corroboration must confirm not just any[3] material particular of the witness's story, but *some particular which connects the prisoner himself*[4] *with it.*[5] For, as the accomplice knows the whole history of the crime, he may tell a true tale, capable of thorough corroboration, and yet may easily insert in it the name of an innocent man, in place of one of the actual offenders. Hence it is not enough that an accomplice is corroborated as to the weather on the night of the burglary and the number of windows broken through.[6] And if there are two prisoners, and the accomplice's evidence is corroborated as regards one of them only, this will not suffice to dispense with the warning as regards the other. Opportunity alone is not corroboration, but opportunity coupled with suspicious circumstances may be.[7] So too in bastardy proceedings the fact that the alleged father has made a false statement is not corroboration of the mother's evidence unless the statement is of such a nature and made in such circumstances as to lead to an inference in support of the mother's evidence.[7] But the fact that a prisoner chooses not to give evidence to rebut the charge against him is not, by itself, corroboration of evidence given by an accomplice in support of the charge.[8]

Corroboration by another accomplice, or even by several accomplices,[9] does not suffice. But a spy, since his complicity extends only

[1] See *ante*, ¶ 546, and *post*, Appendix II.

[2] *R.* v. *Farid* (1945) 30 Cr.App.R. 168; see Appendix II *post*.

[3] Nor *every* material particular; for were it so there would never be any need for the accomplice's evidence.

[4] Hence in affiliation proceedings the mere fact of parturition is not corroboration enough.

[5] *R.* v. *Baskerville* [1916] 2 K.B. 658 (*T.A.C.*). E.g. that at the prisoner's house a knife was found, stamped with the same private house-address as was stamped on one which the burglar had dropped; *R.* v. *Morris* (1907) C.C.C. Sess. Pap. CXLVII, 677 at p. 683. Or the prisoner's silence when accused may corroborate (*R.* v. *Feigenbaum* [1919] 1 K.B. 431, a decision doubted in *R.* v. *Keeling* [1942] 1 All E.R. 507); and contrast *R.* v. *Marsh* (1925) 19 Cr.App.R. 27. Cf. ¶ 574 *ante*.

[6] So in the divorce court (where this sort of corroboration is always required for the evidence of private detectives) if such a detective says 'I saw respondent and co-respondent enter the hotel together, and I called this policeman's attention to it', it is not sufficient corroboration for the policeman to say merely 'He showed me *a* man and *a* woman entering that hotel'.

[7] *Jones* v. *Thomas* [1934] 1 K.B. 323.

[8] *R.* v. *Jackson* [1953] 1 All E.R. 872 at p. 873.

[9] *R.* v. *Boyes* (1861) 1 B. and S. 311 (*T.A.C.*); *R.* v. *Gay* (1909) 2 Cr.App.R. 327. 'A jury is no more bound to believe two informers than one', said Whiteside, C.J. Cf. *R.* v. *Howard* (1921) 15 Cr.App.R. 177. It is doubtful how far an accomplice may be

to the *actus reus* and not to the *mens rea*, is not truly an accomplice, and so does not need corroboration.[1]

It seems that confessions made by accomplices who have been charged and have pleaded guilty are not admissible as evidence against the principal offender and they should not be handed to the jury.[2] If two prisoners are charged jointly the question may arise whether one can give evidence against the other (on this see *post*, ¶ 629). But a person who is jointly charged with another person has full rights to defend himself even if in so doing he gives evidence which inculpates the other.[3]

(*f*) Under the Road Traffic Act, 1930

¶ 604. Section 10, in making it an offence for certain vehicles to exceed speed limits on any public highway, provides that no conviction for it is to take place 'solely on the evidence of one witness' in whose opinion the person prosecuted was exceeding the speed limit. But a single witness[4] suffices if he speaks, not to his mere 'opinion', but to a fact which he has ascertained by stop-watch and measured distance.[5]

SECTION 2. SPECIAL EXCEPTIONS TO THE HEARSAY RULE

¶ 605. To the doctrine which excludes hearsay evidence there are, besides the general exceptions which we mentioned along with it, further ones which are peculiar to criminal cases. Three of these deserve careful consideration.

(*a*) Dying declarations

¶ 606. Upon an indictment for homicide,[6] the *dying declarations* of the slain man respecting the cause of his death are admitted in certain circumstances. This exception seems to have been fully recognized as early as 1697. At the Old Bailey, in that year, whilst it was held in one trial for murder that evidence could not be received as to the murdered man's having said beforehand that he and the prisoner were going to fight a duel, yet in another, where a painter in Lincoln's Inn Fields was indicted for having killed two bailiffs, their 'dying words' were admitted as evidence against him.[7] The admission of such declarations is

corroborated by his wife; *R.* v. *Payne* (1913) 8 Cr.App.R. 171. A witness whose husband *X* has been jointly indicted with *Y* is not an accomplice of *Y* for purposes of corroboration; *R.* v. *Willis* (1916) 12 Cr.App.R. 44.

[1] *R.* v. *Bickley* (1909) 2 Cr.App.R. 53; *R.* v. *Mullins* (1848) 3 Cox 526. Yet a man who has thus taken up falsehood as his trade must be peculiarly untrustworthy.

[2] *R.* v. *Cook* [1955] Crim. L.R. 792.

[3] See *R.* v. *Armstrong* [1957] Crim. L.R. 198; *post*, ¶ 630.

[4] The evidence of one police officer, checked by the speedometer of the car which he himself was driving, is sufficient; *Russell* v. *Beesley* [1937] 1 All E.R. 527.

[5] *Plancq* v. *Marks* (1906) 70 J.P. 216.

[6] *R.* v. *Mead* (1824) 2 B. and C. 605 (*T.A.C.*). For this is the one crime where it is certain that the victim will be unable to be a witness at the trial of the man who wronged him.

[7] Hargrave MSS. in British Museum, no. 146, f. 162.

usually justified on the ground that the religious awe inspired by the approach of death is deemed fully equal to the sanction of any judicial oath.[1] Hence the rule has been held to be inapplicable to declarations made by a child of the age of four.[2] And, similarly, it will not apply unless the deceased thought his death quite imminent. It is not sufficient that he was 'in fear of death'[3] or 'thought he was going to die'.[4] He must have felt nothing short of 'a settled, hopeless expectation of death'.[5] If, however, he had thus abandoned all hope of recovery when he made the declaration, the fact that his medical attendants were not equally hopeless, or that he actually survived for several days after making it, will not render the declaration inadmissible. The present tendency, however, is to reject dying declarations except in the clearest cases, testing them (as Byles, J., put it) with 'scrupulous, and I had almost said with superstitious, care'.[6] The declaration may even exculpate the prisoner, e.g. be a confession of suicide, intentional or accidental.

¶ 607. *Dying declarations only admitted in trials for homicide.* It should be carefully remembered that the rule is limited, not merely to trials for crime, but to trials for homicide; and thus will not apply when the person who caused a death is under trial, not for it, but only for some earlier crime (perhaps an abortion or a violent robbery) of which the death was a result.[7] Moreover the dying declaration is only admissible in relation to the immediate circumstances of the death.[8]

Since dying declarations usually produce a strong effect upon juries, the judge must be careful to draw the jury's attention to any point in which the declaration is incomplete, and especially to warn them in every case that it has not been liable to cross-examination.[9] It is a question for the judge, and not for the jury, whether the declaration was made by a dying person in the belief of his impending death. What that declaration is, is a distinct question, and that is for the jury.[10]

(*b*) Depositions

¶ 608. When a witness (whether for the prosecution or the defence) has made a deposition before the justice who sent the case for trial,[11] it may

[1] *R.* v. *Woodcock* (1789) 1 Leach 500. 'They are an exception to all rule; but they always produce the greatest effect'; Coleridge, J., in 1845.

[2] Cf. *R.* v. *Jenkins* (1869) 1 C.C.R. 187 (*T.A.C.*).

[3] *R.* v. *Farmer* (1897) C.C.C. Sess. Pap. cxxvi, 841.

[4] *R.* v. *Neill* (1892) C.C.C. Sess. Pap. cxvi, 1417 (*T.A.C.*).

[5] *R.* v. *Peele* (1860) 2 F. and F. 21; *R.* v. *Gloster* (1888) C.C.C. Sess. Pap. cviii, 647 (*T.A.C.*). 'I think I am dying' was, after objection, held sufficient by Lush, J., in *R.* v. *Klaproth* (C.C.C., 21 Feb. 1921). See also *R.* v. *Perry* [1909] 2 K.B. 697 (*T.A.C.*).

R. v. *Jenkins* (1869) 1 C.C.R. 187, 193 (*T.A.C.*).

R. v. *Hind* (1860) Bell 253. [8] See 1 *Toronto L.J.* 379.

Waugh v. *R.* (1950) 66 T.L.R. 554, in which the declaration was held inadmissible on the additional ground that it was incomplete.

[10] *R.* v. *Smith* (1865) 10 Cox 82, *per* Channell, B., at p. 95.

[11] Criminal Justice Act, 1925, s. 13. See also ¶ 709 *post*.

be read[1] at the trial, instead of calling the witness himself, if he has died in the interval, or has become insane, or is too ill to travel, or is being kept away by, or on behalf of, the prisoner.[2] But if the witness has gone abroad, it cannot be used, except perhaps in misdemeanours, and then only by consent of the opposite party.

A deposition must bear the signatures both of the witness and of at least one of the committing magistrates; but it is not necessary to call any evidence to prove their genuineness. If the witness refuse or be physically unable to sign, it would appear that this signature may be dispensed with.[3] When a deposition is put in as evidence, it must be proved (i) that the absence of the witness is due to one of the grave causes which we have mentioned, and (ii) that the prisoner[4] was present when the witness gave the evidence which it embodies, and (iii) that the prisoner had an opportunity of cross-examining him.[5]

A witness's deposition will not be thus available as evidence at a trial, unless the offence for which the prisoner is being tried is substantially the same as, or arises out of the same set of circumstances as,[6] that for which he was committed.

(*c*) Certificates and statutory declarations

¶ 608*a*. For the purposes of the present volume it must suffice to mention that there are certain statutory provisions[7] for the admission of certificates and declarations purporting to be given by persons having specified qualifications, as evidence of the facts stated therein.

Section 3. The Prisoner's Character

¶ 609. Evidence of the prisoner's *good character* is always admissible on his behalf in criminal courts.[8] Yet evidence of his *bad* character is usually excluded there (¶ 544 *ante*); and in civil proceedings all evidence of

[1] In *R.* v. *Linley* [1959] Crim. L.R. 123, it seems to have been accepted that the words of the section, 'may... be read', indicate that the court has discretion to refuse permission.

[2] *R.* v. *Harrison* (1692) 12 St.Tr. 833. Cf. *The Times*, 7 March 1855; and *R.* v. *Ivimy* (1888) C.C.C. Sess. Pap. CVII, 570 at p. 581. As to children or young persons see 23 Geo. V, c. 12, s. 38. See also ¶ 713 *post*. Depositions of a witness who is dangerously ill may be taken out of court under the provisions of the Crim. Law Amend. Act, 1867 ('Russell Gurney's Act').

[3] *R.* v. *Holloway* (1901) 65 J.P. 712.

[4] Facts (ii) and (iii) are often proved by a policeman whom the committing justice has bound over to prosecute. The Criminal Justice Act, 1925, s. 13 (3), allows them to be proved by a certificate from the committing justice or his clerk.

[5] A deposition has been known to be excluded in the trial of a foreigner, because the witness to its admissibility, being ignorant of the foreign language, could not prove that the interpreter's words had really informed the prisoner of this opportunity.

[6] E.g. a murder, and a wounding with intent to murder; *R.* v. *Edmunds* (1909) 2 Cr.App.R. 257.

[7] Carriage of Goods by Sea Act, 1924; Criminal Justice Act, 1948, sect. 41. See *R.* v. *Marley* (1958) 42 Cr.App.R. 218.

[8] *R.* v. *Turner* (1664) 6 St.Tr. 565 (see *Stirland* v. *D.P.P.* [1944] 2 All E.R. at p. 17); *A.-G.* v. *Bowman* (1791) 2 Bos. and P. 532 n.; *O'Connor's Case* (1798) 27 St.Tr. 31.

character is excluded.[1] Hence this exceptional admissibility is only intelligible as a relic of the Anglo-Saxon exculpation by the oaths of compurgators.[2]

But, ancient and well-established as is this rule, opinion has been considerably divided as to its exact scope. Is the 'character', which the witnesses are thus allowed to describe, the disposition or the reputation of the accused person? In *R.* v. *Rowton* (1865) the Court for Crown Cases Reserved adopted, by a majority of eleven to two, the latter alternative.[3] Accordingly, in strictness, no evidence ought to be given about the prisoner's disposition, and still less about any particular acts of his. The witness, therefore, to borrow Erskine's words,[4] is not to say 'what *A*, *B*, or *C* told him about the man's character, but what is the *general* opinion concerning him. For "character" is the slow-spreading influence of opinion, arising from a man's deportment in society, and extending itself in one circle beyond another till it unites in one general opinion. That general opinion is allowed to be given in evidence.'

HIS GENERAL REPUTATION

¶ 610. But, as Lord Ellenborough long ago said, 'No branch of evidence is so little attended to';[5] and this strict rule of law is still constantly and humanely disregarded in practice. For the present conditions of busy life in crowded cities often render it impossible for a man's conduct to have been under the continuous observation of many persons for so long a time as would enable any 'general opinion' about it to grow up. Even neighbours and customers of his know nothing about him beyond their personal experience. Yet a departure from the strict rule opens out an inconveniently wide field of inquiry. For a witness's individual opinion of his neighbour's disposition may have to be supported or tested by protracted consideration of the innumerable facts which led him to form it. But evidence of a man's general reputation affords terse and summary proof of his disposition. On the other hand, this briefer and more technically correct mode of proof has the disadvantage of excluding all evidence (such as perhaps might have been obtained from the very same witness who proves the good reputation) of a deep-rooted evil disposition that rendered the man utterly unworthy of the good reputation which he enjoyed.

Either method of proof, however, would admit that negative evidence which in practice is so frequent, 'I never heard anything against him'. Such negative testimony may be the best of all tributes to a man's

[1] Except where directly relevant, e.g. in actions of defamation. The character of th e prosecutor is similarly generally irrelevant in criminal cases, but evidence of the general bad character of the prosecutrix may be given in defence in cases of rape or indecent assault. Cf. ¶ 557 *ante*. *R.* v. *Clarke* (1817) 2 Starkie 241. Cf. *R.* v. *Jenkins* (1945) 31 Cr.App.R. 1.

[2] See Pollock and Maitland, II, 634.

[3] L. and C. 520 (*T.A.C.*); American courts also adopt it.

[4] In his speech in defence of Hardy; (1794) 24 St.Tr. 199.

[5] *R.* v. *Jones* (1809) 31 St.Tr. at p. 310.

disposition; for most men are little talked of until fault is found with them.[1]

PECULIARITIES OF SUCH EVIDENCE

¶ 611. Evidence of good character is thus peculiar in its nature, as being a case in which the witness speaks as to other people's knowledge, instead of as to his own. And the forensic procedure in regard to it is also peculiar. For the opposite party has no right to make a speech in reply upon it; nor ought he even to cross-examine upon it, unless he knows that he can thereby elicit a definite charge against the prisoner, e.g. his having committed other similar offences. But evidence of good character even though obtained only by cross-examination of the Crown witnesses, or given by himself alone, can be rebutted by evidence of a bad reputation,[2] but not by evidence of bad disposition, still less of particular bad acts (except that it sometimes may be rebutted by evidence of previous convictions).[3]

A defendant's counsel must not assert his client's good character unless he is going to call evidence of it. On the other hand, if he do not call any, the prosecution ought never to make any comment upon this omission.

VALUE OF EVIDENCE OF CHARACTER

¶ 612. The probative value of evidence of character must not be overrated.[4] It is not sufficient ground for disbelieving solid evidence of facts. Were it so, no one would be convicted; for every criminal had a good character until he lost it. But it may be of great importance where mistaken identity is the defence, or again in determining which of two inferences should be drawn from a fact, and consequently in all questions of *mens rea*, since they must always be matters of mere inference. It thus is very useful in cases where a man is found in possession of recently stolen goods. At a charity bazaar at Lincoln, about 1900, when an alarm was raised that a purse had been stolen, the thief slipped it into the coat-pocket of a bishop who was present; but any suspicions that might have been aroused by its being found in this pocket were effectually rebutted by the episcopal character of the wearer. Yet, even for such purposes, evidence of good character is, by a curious paradox, of least avail where it is most needed, namely in offences of great heinousness. For 'in any case of atrocious criminality the act is so much out of the ordinary course of things, that, if perpetrated, it must have been produced by motives not frequently operating on the human mind. Therefore evidence to the character of a man's

[1] Cf. Cockburn, C.J., in *R.* v. *Rowton* (1865) L. and C. 520 (*T.A.C.*).

[2] But such evidence is so rare that neither Cockburn, C.J., nor Coleridge, L.C.J., had ever seen it given; *R.* v. *Griffith Jones* (1891) C.C.C. Sess. Pap. cxv, 162 at p. 170.

[3] See Appendix II, C, *post*.

[4] 'If you feel a doubt, you are entitled to take character into account. But only if the evidence has left your mind in doubt should you give any weight to testimonies to character' (Avory, J., at C.C.C., 1922).

habitual conduct in common circumstances will here become far inferior in efficacy to what it is in the case of accusations of a slighter guilt.'[1]

After conviction, however, evidence of character will always be of great importance in determining what punishment should be inflicted on an offender; and even before conviction evidence of other discreditable conduct may be admissible in certain circumstances (*ante*, ¶ 545, and *post*, Appendix II, B and C).

SECTION 4. CONFESSIONS

¶ 613. In criminal proceedings admissions[2] made by (or on behalf of) a party to the litigation are received in evidence less readily than in civil cases.

In civil tribunals, any admissions which have been made by the plaintiff, or the defendant, or the duly authorized agent of either, can be given in evidence quite freely. But in criminal cases, the admissions of the prosecutor cannot, as such, be given in evidence; for, technically speaking, he is no party at all to the proceedings, since they are brought in the name of the Crown itself. And even the admissions, or—to use the term commonly applied to full admissions of criminal guilt—the confessions (*ante*, ¶ 574), made by the person accused are not allowed to be given in evidence unless it appears that they were quite voluntary.[3] Whether or not they were so is a question for the judge, not the jury, to decide.[4] Even though no circumstances raise any doubt as to the character of the confession, it is now held to be the duty of the prosecutor to bring evidence of its having been given voluntarily. Hence confessions extorted by any form of violence or threats of violence are inadmissible.

EXCLUDED IF IMPROPERLY INDUCED[5]

¶ 614. The words 'induced' and 'inducement' are used here in their ordinary sense of *persuasion*, aimed at producing some willing action, as opposed to compulsion by force or fear of force to produce some un-

[1] *Per* Shaw, C.J., at the trial of Prof. Webster; *ante*, ¶ 518. See a good review of the effect of evidence of character in *R.* v. *Broadhurst* (1918) 13 Cr.App.R. 125.

[2] See 'Admission by silence', *ante*, ¶ 575.

[3] A similar doctrine prevails in the United States. Yet many scandals arise there from the police putting arrested persons through the 'third degree' by protracted questioning (e.g. 9 p.m. to 4 a.m.), or withholding of water, or even blows; cf. the 'Sweat-box Case', *The State* v. *Ammons* (1901) 80 Mississippi 592. The Supreme Court rebuked these practices in December, 1924. Yet in 1925, in New Jersey, Harrison Noel, arrested for murder, was questioned by the police for eleven hours, and then, after two hours of sleep, for ten hours, i.e. for twenty-one hours out of twenty-three. He then made a confession. Of what value?

[4] *R.* v. *Warringham* (1851) 2 Den. at p. 448.

[5] It must be noted that this rule of exclusion applies only to confessions. *Other* material evidence of guilt is not excluded however unfairly it may have been obtained; see *R.* v. *Nowell* [1948] 1 All E.R. 794, *post*, ¶ 617.

willing action.[1] Though a litigant's own admissions might well at first sight appear to be the most satisfactory of all forms of evidence—and indeed were so regarded in the civil and the canon law[2]—experience has now shown them to be open, especially in serious criminal charges, to three serious hazards of error. For (i) eagerness to secure the punishment of a hateful offence may lead a witness to exaggerate, even unconsciously, what was said to him by the person accused; and (ii) eagerness to propitiate those in authority may lead the accused person himself to make untrue admissions;[3] and (iii) he often means guilty only of the act, not of the evil intent. Hence English criminal lawyers have long[4] recognized that 'hasty confessions are the weakest and most suspicious of all evidence'.[5]

The rule may be stated thus: a confession must be excluded if it was made (i) in consequence of (ii) any inducement (iii) that was of a temporal character and (iv) connected with this accusation, and (v) that was held out to the accused by a person who had some authority over the accusation.[6]

It must be noticed that this rule applies in its strictness only to confessions. It has no application to relevant evidence of other kinds, as to which it has been declared[7] that if the evidence is relevant to the matters in issue the court is not concerned with how that evidence was obtained.

ANALYSIS OF THE RULE OF EXCLUSION

¶ 615. (i) *In consequence of.* The confession will only be inadmissible if it was due to the inducement. Where therefore the inducement has been

[1] This distinction seems to have been overlooked in [1959] Crim. L.R. at p. 443.

[2] But now the divorce court will not act upon an uncorroborated confession except 'with the utmost circumspection and caution'. It may be due to morbid self-deception, or to a desire for divorce, or even to mere craving for notoriety. Cf. *Getty* v. *Getty* [1907] P. 334; and *Weinberg* v. *Weinberg* (1910) 27 T.L.R. 9.

[3] A desire to shield an accused friend sometimes leads convicts under sentence for some other offence, knowing that they are not likely to be again prosecuted, to make false confessions of having committed the crime which he is accused of.

[4] The (now) indubitable falsity of the confessions made by many persons who suffered death for witchcraft has done much to bring about this change in the legal estimate of the probative value of such evidence. Mr Inderwick (*Side-Lights on the Stuarts*, 164) cites two instances of women who confessed, although they declared privately that their confessions were false, their motive being an actual desire to be put to death, in order to escape the obloquy under which they lived.

[5] Foster, 234. Yet in French law, great importance is still attached to them. Thus on the prosecution of the Abbé Auriol, in 1881, for the murder of two of his parishioners, when the questions of the examining magistrate failed to elicit from him any incriminating admission, the abbé was shut up in complete isolation for thirty-seven days. On the thirty-seventh he at last made a full confession. See H. B. Irving's *Studies of French Criminals.*

[6] The confession must of course relate to the charge now before the court: but it *may* be so relevant although it be a confession of another crime; *R.* v. *Evans* [1950] 1 All E.R. 610; 34 Cr.App.R. 72.

[7] *R.* v. *Bate* (1871) 11 Cox 686.

deprived of influence, as by lapse of time[1] or by some intervening warning (e.g. a magistrate's statutory caution), the confession will stand.

(ii) *Any inducement.* It is not necessary that the prisoner should have been pressed to confess guilt; it is sufficient if he were pressed to say anything whatever. Thus, 'It might be better for you to tell the truth and not a lie'[2] will suffice to exclude a confession; although 'Speak the truth *if you speak at all*' is harmless.

It is immaterial whether the inducement consisted in a menace of evil or in a promise of good.[3] Thus the admonitions, 'Tell the truth, or I'll send for the police' and 'Tell the truth and it will be better for you',[4] are equally objectionable; and either inducement will be fatal to the admissibility of any confession which it may elicit. Although at one time the courts were ingenious[5] in so construing colourless words as to detect a hint of some improper inducement, it is now clear that the words of any alleged inducement must be construed only in their natural and obvious meaning.[6]

(iii) *Temporal.* An inducement will not exclude confessions produced by it, unless it were of a temporal character. To urge that it is a moral or religious duty to speak out is not likely to cause a man to say what is untrue; and therefore will not affect the admissibility of what he says. Hence where a prisoner had been urged by the prosecutor to tell the truth 'so that, if you have committed a fault, you may not add to it by stating what is untrue',[7] and similarly where the mother of one of two boys said to them, 'You had better, *as good boys*, tell the truth',[8] the confessions which ensued were received as legal evidence.

(iv) *Connected with the accusation.* If the inducement had no bearing upon the legal proceedings connected with the accusation, it will not exclude the confession. Thus a confession was admitted in spite of its having been obtained by the promise, 'If you will tell where the property is, you shall see your wife'.[9] And if even an objectionable

[1] *R.* v. *Smith, T.* (1959) 43 Cr.App.R. 121, where a statement originally secured by threats of continuing constraint (and therefore inadmissible), but repeated after an interval of time to, and after caution by, another official interrogator was held admissible.

[2] By the Judicial Committee of the P.C. in *Kuruma* v. *R.* [1955] A.C. 197, approving a dictum of Crompton, J., in *R.* v. *Leatham* (1861) 8 Cox 498 at p. 501. See *post*, App. II.

[3] *R.* v. *Jarvis* (1867) 1 C.C.R. 96 (*T.A.C.*).

[4] *R.* v. *Sutherland and Johnston* [1959] Crim. L.R. 440.

[5] Cf. *R.* v. *Drew* (1837) 8 C. and P. 140.

[6] *R.* v. *Baldry* (1852) 2 Den. 430.

[7] *R.* v. *Jarvis* (1867) 1 C.C.R. 96 (*T.A.C.*).

[8] *R.* v. *Reeve* (1872) 1 C.C.R. 362. Similarly the exhortation, 'With the profession you make [of being a Christian], it is only right for you to clear the innocent ones', has been held not to exclude the consequent confession; *R.* v. *Peters* (1898) C.C.C. Sess. Pap. CXXVII, 209. Cf. *R.* v. *Stanton* (1911) 6 Cr.App.R. 198.

[9] *R.* v. *Lloyd* (1834) 6 C. and P. 393; *R.* v. *Cowell* [1940] 2 All E.R. 599. The decision, that 'Tell and you shall have some gin' will exclude a confession, is a ruling of very little authority; see Russ., 8th ed., 2021 n. And see *R.* v. *Joyce* (1957) 42 Cr.App.R. 19, where the police officer's words, 'I need to take a statement from you', were held not to be an inducement relating to the charge or accusation.

inducement to confess one crime should produce also a confession of some second and unsuspected offence, such confession will be admissible at a trial that is only for the latter crime.

(v) *By a person in authority*. A person in authority means one who has some opportunity of influencing the course of the prosecution,[1] e.g. a magistrate or a constable,[2] or even a private person if he is prosecuting or is likely to prosecute. Thus if an accusation be made against a servant, and she make a confession to her master or mistress in consequence of some inducement held out by him or her, it would be excluded if the charge were one of stealing their property; whilst if it were a charge of killing her own child, they would have no such 'authority' in the matter as to give any disabling effect to the inducement.[3] It is sufficient if the person in authority is present, silently acquiescing, when some third party spontaneously holds out the inducement.

THE JUDGES' RULES

¶ 616. But the fact that it was to a constable (or other person in official authority) that a confession was made, will not cause it to be rejected, when no inducement was held out. And this will be so even if no preliminary warning had been given to the accused who made it, and even though he made it in answer to questions put to him by this person in authority. But questions thus asked are viewed jealously by the judges; and in 1918 they formulated instructions about them.[4] These lay it down that 'when a police-officer is endeavouring to discover the author of a crime, there is no objection to his putting questions in respect thereof to any person, *whether suspected or not*, from whom he thinks that useful information can be obtained'. Yet this questioning must not be hostile or oppressive. But 'whenever a police-officer has made up his mind[5] to charge a person with a crime, he should first caution such person before asking any (or any further) questions'. Hence persons 'in custody' should not be questioned nor be allowed to volunteer a statement until they have been cautioned. And when a voluntary statement is made, no questions must follow it 'except for the purpose of removing ambiguity in what he has actually said'.[6] The usual caution (*post*, ¶ 702) should be ended with 'be given in evidence', omitting the deterrent words 'against you'. Neither should the police suggest to a person in custody that they have evidence of his guilt. Answers

[1] *R.* v. *Gibbons* (1823) 1 C. and P. 97 (*T.A.C.*).

[2] A person who has the prisoner in custody, even though not a constable, is 'in authority', e.g. a searcher of female prisoners, *R.* v. *Windsor* (1864) 4 F. and F. 361; but, apparently, not a police doctor, *R.* v. *Nowell* [1948] 1 All E.R. 794.

[3] *R.* v. *Moore* (1852) 2 Den. 522.

[4] *R.* v. *Voisin* [1918] 1 K.B. 531 at p. 539 (*T.A.C.*). For details of the Judges' Rules see Turner and Armitage, *Cases on Criminal Law*, 549. *R.* v. *Bass* (1953) 37 Cr.App.R. 51 illustrates the importance and effect of these rules. And see Brownlie, 'Police questioning, custody and caution' [1960] *Crim. L.R.* 298.

[5] Cf. *R.* v. *Booker* (1924) 18 Cr.App.R. 47.

[6] *R.* v. *Mills* (1936) 25 Cr.App.R. 138 at p. 139.

to such a suggestion are not admissible in evidence.[1] Prisoners should not be confronted with one another in order to obtain admissions, nor with that object should the statement of one prisoner be read to another.[2]

The Judges' Rules are not rules of law, but are intended only for guidance.[3] They are a code laid down for the purpose of ensuring so far as possible that statements are not obtained from the prisoner by improper means. But if statements are made voluntarily it is open to the court to accept them even if the rules have not been complied with in all strictness; and it is equally open to the court to reject the evidence.[4] Where an admission is obtained by objectionable means the Court of Criminal Appeal will quash a conviction unless they think that without the admission the jury must have convicted.[5]

RIGHT OF THE DEFENCE TO CHALLENGE THE CONFESSION WHEN ADMITTED

¶ 616a. Students should note once again that the question of *admissibility* of evidence is quite different from the question of its *cogency* once it is admitted. It is for the judge to decide whether a confession is admissible in evidence, hearing the arguments on either side. The established practice of the courts is (*a*) that the argument as to admissibility must be heard in the absence of the jury, (*b*) that the judge should give his ruling one way or the other, (*c*) that, if the judge does admit the evidence, even then 'the weight and value of a confession remain matters for the jury'.[6] But, even when the judge has decided to admit it, counsel for the defence still has the right once more to cross-examine in the presence of the jury the witnesses who have already given evidence of the confession, and to elicit statements from his own witnesses, in an endeavour to show that the confession has been obtained by threat or promise, since the weight of the evidence, and its value, is always for the jury.[7]

CONFESSIONS OBTAINED BY ARTIFICE

¶ 617. Even, however, when English law regards a confession as being rendered inadmissible by some inducement, it does not exclude evidence of any *acts* that may have been performed along with, or in consequence of, the giving of this excluded confession; e.g. the surrender, or the discovery, of stolen property. Moreover it does not exclude confessions themselves when not obtained by an inducement, even though they may have been obtained by some underhand means; e.g. by intoxicating

[1] *R.* v. *Brown and Bruce* (1931) 23 Cr.App.R. 56. And see *R.* v. *Treacy* (1944) 88 S.J. 367.

[2] The police should furnish the prisoner with a written copy of the statement made by the other prisoner, without saying or doing anything to invite a reply; *R.* v. *Mills* and *R.* v. *Lemon* [1946] 2 All E.R. 776.

[3] *R.* v. *Voisin supra.*

[4] *Ibid.* And see *R.* v. *Wattam* (1952) 36 Cr.App.R. 72; *R.* v. *Wilson* [1954] Crim. L.R. 56, a court-martial appeal case.

[5] *R.* v. *Pilley* (1922) 16 Cr.App.R. 138.

[6] *R.* v. *Murray* [1951] 1 K.B. 391 at p. 393.

[7] *R.* v. *Francis* (1959) 43 Cr.App.R. 174.

the prisoner,[1] or by abusing his confidence (as by a gaoler appropriating a letter which he had promised the prisoner to put into the post[2]), or by artifice (as by falsely asserting that some of the prisoner's accomplices are already in custody[3]). In such cases, however, the judge should warn the jury not to attach to the confession too much weight.

CONFESSIONS BY AGENTS OR ACCOMPLICES

¶ 618. A further difference between civil and criminal courts, in their treatment of admissions, concerns such admissions as are made by agents. In civil proceedings, wherever the acts of an agent will bind the principal his admissions will also bind him, if made in the same affair and at the same time, so as to constitute a part of the transaction.[4] But criminal law does not adopt this wide rule; it never holds a principal liable for admissions made by his agents except when he has authorized them expressly. Accordingly an admission made by a prisoner will not be evidence against his accomplices in the crime unless it had been expressly authorized by them.[5] Yet, as we have seen (*ante*, ¶ 454), so soon as a common criminal purpose has been shown, evidence of the *acts* of one accomplice, though done in the absence of the others, will be admissible against all of them.

SECTION 5. COMPETENCY OF WITNESSES

¶ 619. The principles relating to the competency of witnesses are not identical in civil and in criminal courts. We have already mentioned (*ante*, ¶ 584) the cases in which recent statutes have permitted evidence to be given in criminal proceedings by children who do not understand the nature of an oath, if they be sufficiently intelligent and be aware of the duty of speaking the truth. A converse and far more important peculiarity in the criminal rules of evidence is that by which (A) accused persons, and (B) the wives or husbands of accused persons, are entitled to refuse to give evidence. (In fact, until comparatively recently, they were entirely incompetent to give it.)

A. *INCOMPETENCY OF INTERESTED PERSONS AT COMMON LAW: STATUTORY CHANGES*

¶ 620. The common law disqualified every person who had an interest in the result of any legal proceeding—whether civil or criminal—from

[1] *R.* v. *Spilsbury* (1835) 7 C. and P. 187; and compare *R.* v. *Nowell* [1948] 1 All E.R. 794 and *R.* v. *Garside* [1959] Crim. L.R. 778, where *not* confessions but other evidence was obtained by pressure.

[2] *R.* v. *Derrington* (1826) 2 C. and P. 418.

[3] *R.* v. *Burley* (1818). Cf. the case where evidence has been illegally obtained; see the Scottish case, *Lawrie* v. *Muir* (1950) S.L.T. 37.

[4] Thus, in an action against a railway company by a passenger for the loss of his luggage, the admissions of the station-master as to the way in which the loss took place, made by him the next day after the loss, in answer to inquiries for the luggage, are good evidence against the company, *Morse* v. *C.R. Railroad* (1856) 6 Gray 450.

[5] *R.* v. *Swinnerton* (1842) C. and M. 593; *R.* v. *Moore* (1956) 40 Cr.App.R. 50.

giving evidence in it. Hence, of course, the actual parties to that proceeding, since they had the strongest interest of all, were disqualified: plaintiffs and defendants in civil cases, and prisoners in criminal ones. (But the prosecutor in a criminal case could give evidence; for, technically, he is no party to the proceedings, the Crown being the *dominus litis.*) Prisoners, however, until early in the eighteenth century, were usually questioned (though not upon oath) by the judge himself, at the conclusion of the Crown evidence, in order to elicit their defences.[1] And this often was of great assistance to them, especially as no felon could then be defended by counsel. On the other hand, it gave wide scope for judicial cruelty, as was often shown by Lord Jeffreys and other judges in the Stuart period.[2]

In civil cases the evidence of the parties was rendered admissible in 1851.[3] Subsequently in 1872 there began a series of legislative enactments which enabled prisoners to give evidence in the case of a few particular crimes. The judicial experience of the working of these exceptional privileges proved so favourable that ultimately a general enactment was passed,[4] the Criminal Evidence Act, 1898.

THE CRIMINAL EVIDENCE ACT, 1898

(i) The prisoner a competent witness

¶ 621. By this statute the person charged is made a competent (but not compellable) witness for the defence[5] at every stage of the proceedings,[6] whether he be charged solely, or jointly with some other person. The judge should inform him of his right to give evidence. It is to be given from the box and not from the dock.

(ii) Stage in trial at which his evidence is given

¶ 622. (*a*) On committal for trial, he gives his evidence immediately after the magistrate has delivered the usual statutory caution as to the ultimate use that may be made at trial of anything he may say.

(*b*) At trial, he gives it immediately after the Crown witnesses, unless he is going to call some witness[7] of his own (other than a witness who

[1] See *Harrison's Case* in 1692, 12 St.Tr. at p. 859.

[2] And by Page, J., even as late as 1741. See in *Tom Jones*, bk. VIII, ch. XI, Fielding's vivid picture of Page's satirical questioning of a prisoner until 'everybody fell a-laughing. It is indeed charming sport to hear trials upon life and death! But I own I thought it hard that there should be so many of them—my lord and the jury and the counsellors and the witnesses—all upon one poor man, and he too in chains. He was hanged; as, to be sure, it could be no otherwise.'

[3] Lord Brougham's Act; 14 and 15 Vict. c. 99.

[4] 61 and 62 Vict. c. 36.

[5] Not merely of himself, but of fellow-prisoners also.

[6] This includes evidence given between a plea of guilty and sentence, *R.* v. *Wheeler* [1917] 1 K.B. 283. If co-prisoners wish to give evidence, they give it in the order in which their names stand in the indictment.

[7] If he call witnesses, his counsel appears to have discretion as to the order in which he and they should be called; but see *R.* v. *Morrison* (1911) 6 Cr.App.R. 159 at p. 165.

speaks solely to character). When he thus does not call a witness, the fact of his having himself given evidence creates no right of reply; so that, if he be undefended by counsel, the Crown counsel will have no opportunity at all of commenting upon the evidence he gives.

(iii) Cross-examination as to previous offences and character

¶ 623. A prisoner witness must not in general be asked any question tending to show that he has committed or been convicted of or been charged with any offence other than that wherewith he is then charged, or that he is of bad character.[1] In certain circumstances, however, as we have mentioned (*ante*, ¶ 545; see also App. II), evidence of other similar offences is relevant to show guilt, and where such evidence could be given a prisoner witness may, under the Criminal Evidence Act, 1898, in exactly the same circumstances, be cross-examined to show that he has committed or been convicted of other offences which (¶546 *ante*) would have been admissible as evidence-in-chief as tending to reveal his guilt of the crime charged.[2] In three cases the cross-examination may be even wider:[3] (i) where the prisoner or his counsel has asked questions of the witnesses for the prosecution in order to establish his good character, or has given evidence of his good character;[4] (ii) where the nature or conduct[5] of the defence is such as to involve imputations on the character of the prosecutor[6] or of the witnesses for the prosecution;[7]

[1] *R.* v. *Cohen* [1938] 3 All E.R. 380. Thus a prisoner must not in general be cross-examined to show that he is a person likely to have committed the offence charged, e.g. a man charged with a sexual offence must not be asked whether he is a single man; *R.* v. *Coulman* (1927) 20 Cr.App.R. 106. According to a dictum of Hewart, L.C.J., to elicit from such a prisoner in examination-in-chief that he is a married man puts his character in issue and renders him liable to be cross-examined *to credit*, *R.* v. *Baldwin* (1925) 133 L.T. 191; 18 Cr.App.R. 175; but Mr P. M. Wright, Q.C., in 11 *Cam. L.J.* (1953) at p. 460 expressed the opinion that, despite Lord Hewart's dictum in *Baldwin*, the courts would not hold that a person accused of sexual crime puts in issue either his character or his credit by merely giving in chief his status as a married man.

[2] *Jones* v. *D.P.P.* [1962[2 W.L.R. 575; Crim. L.R. 244; [1961] 3 All E.R. 668 (at p. 675) in which *Charnock* v. *Merchant* [1900] 1 Q.B. 474 was not discussed.

[3] Sect. 1 (*f*).

[4] But not where one of his witnesses has merely volunteered a eulogy of him unasked; *R.* v. *Reid* (1923) 17 Cr.App.R. 36. But even if the prisoner sets up his own good character this does not render admissible the evidence that a former employer had *suspected* him of a crime; *Stirland* v. *D.P.P.* [1944] 2 All E.R. 13 (*T.A.C.*).

[5] These words must receive 'their ordinary and natural interpretation', *R.* v. *Hudson* [1912] 2 K.B. 465, affirmed in *R.* v. *Jenkins* (1945) 31 Cr.App.R. 1; *R.* v. *Cook* [1959] 2 All E.R. 97; *R.* v. *Flynn* [1961] 3 All E.R. 58.

[6] A living prosecutor; e.g. not the murdered victim, *R.* v. *Biggin* (1920) 14 Cr.App.R. 87.

[7] *R.* v. *Clark* [1955] 3 W.L.R. 313 (see 105 *L.J.* 821). But not by merely denying, even violently, the truth of the evidence against him, *R.* v. *Jones* (1923) 39 T.L.R. 457. Study *R.* v. *Preston* [1909] 1 K.B. 568 and *R.* v. *Hudson* [1912] 2 K.B. 465. The imputations need not be as to general character. It is sufficient if the defence suggests e.g. that a witness is committing perjury for the sake of revenge, *R.* v. *Dunkley* [1927] 1 K.B. 323. In such cases it is the established practice for prosecuting counsel to indicate in advance that he is going to claim his rights under the subsection, or for the judge to give the defence a

(iii) where he has given evidence against another person charged with the same offence.[1]

But even when the trial judge has decided that questions by the advocate for the prosecution as to, and evidence of, the prisoner's convictions and bad character are legally permissible, he must still exercise his discretion with all due consideration[2] as to whether in the circumstances of the case it would be unfair to the prisoner to admit them (*ante*, ¶ 547*a*). This discretion however does not exist in cases within (iii) above where the question is to be put by, or on behalf of, a co-prisoner, for *this* cross-examination is a matter of right.

It has been declared that a person who, in any of the cases provided for in the Statute, thus exposes his character puts the *whole* of his character in issue and may be asked questions as to anything of a discreditable character which he may have done.[3]

¶ 624. *Purpose of such cross-examination.* In these three cases a prisoner may be asked questions relating to matters which would not be admissible as evidence-in-chief against him at common law. Thus he may be asked questions as to previous offences, convictions or (in special circumstances, *infra*) charges, or to show that he is of bad character, provided that the questions are relevant. A question may in those cases be relevant because it relates to his credibility as a witness, and probably also because it tends to show that he is of bad character and so likely to have committed the offence with which he is charged.[4] The fact that a prisoner has previously been charged and acquitted of an offence is

caution; *R.* v. *Cook* (1959) 43 Cr.App.R. 138, confirmed in *R.* v. *Morris* (1959) 43 Cr. App.R. 206. But it is not sufficient if the prisoner is cross-examined so as to involve him inadvertently in an attack upon Crown witnesses, *R.* v. *Eidinow* (1932) 23 Cr.App.R. 145. And it must be noted that so long as the prisoner neither (*a*) sets up his own good character, nor (*b*) gives evidence on his own behalf under the Criminal Evidence Act, 1898, s. 1 (*f*), any attack made by the defence upon the character of a witness for the prosecution does *not* expose the prisoner's character to attack, nor render admissible any evidence of the prisoner's previous convictions; *R.* v. *Butterwasser* [1948] 1 K.B. 4 (*T.A.C.*).

[1] The offence charged must be *the same*, *R.* v. *Roberts* (1936) 52 T.L.R. 234; 25 Cr.App.R. 158. He is liable to be cross-examined by or on behalf of any co-defendant whom he has prejudiced by his evidence. But if questions be put to him for a co-defendant whom his evidence has *not* prejudiced, this will give the Crown a right to a speech in reply as against that prisoner; *R.* v. *Paget* (1900) 64 J.P. 281. Cross-examination by or for a co-defendant which should precede the Crown's cross-examination, is a matter of right, *R.* v. *Miller* (1952) 36 Cr.App.R. 169; *R.* v. *Ellis* [1961] 1 W.L.R. at p. 1066.

[2] *R.* v. *Flynn* [1961] 3 All E.R. 58 at pp. 62 and 63.

[3] *R.* v. *Winfield* (1939) 27 Cr.App.R. 139 (*T.A.C.*), where a man who, on a charge of indecent assault, had set up his good character with regard to sexual morality was questioned as to previous convictions for offences of dishonesty.

[4] It is arguable that such cross-examination ought only go to attack credibility and not to show a bad disposition. The distinction is not, however, one that can be easily drawn in practice. See, on the whole question, Julius Stone, 'Cross-examination by the prosecution', 51 *L.Q.R.* 443. See also *R.* v. *Wood* (1920) 84 J.P. 92.

normally,[1] however, not relevant evidence against him. Thus in *Maxwell* v. *Director of Public Prosecutions*,[2] the House of Lords quashed a conviction where a prisoner charged with performing an illegal operation had been asked about an occasion seven years before when he had been charged with a similar offence and acquitted. The judge's leave must be asked for cross-examination as to credit.[3] Where a previous conviction is lawfully put to an accused in cross-examination and denied, evidence of the conviction may be given.[4]

It may also be mentioned here that general evidence relating to the accused person's character and previous convictions can be given *after* he has been found guilty of the crime with which he has been charged, in order that the court may decide upon the proper sentence.[5]

(iv) Comment on a prisoner's refusal to give evidence

¶ 625. The prosecutor must not comment on the fact of a prisoner's having refused to give evidence.[6] But the court is not placed (as in the United States[7] it is) under any such restriction.[8] Experience, however, seems to show that juries now, without the help of any comment, readily draw for themselves a hostile inference from the prisoner's refusal.[9] But since the prosecution are not permitted to comment on that fact it is incumbent upon the judge to be restrained in commenting upon it, and he should point out to the jury that the prisoner is not bound to give evidence, and that it is for the prosecution to make out their case beyond reasonable doubt.[10]

[1] A previous charge may be relevant apart from its result in some circumstances, e.g. a previous charge of receiving stolen goods might be relevant to show that the accused must have been put on inquiry in the case now charged as to goods received out of the ordinary course of business, *R.* v. *Waldman* (1934) 24 Cr.App.R. 204. Or, on a charge of obtaining by false pretences, to show that the accused knew his statement to be false; *R.* v. *Ollis* [1900] 2 Q.B. 758. See the explanation of certain dicta of Lord Sankey in *Maxwell* v. *D.P.P.* (*infra*) by the C.C.A. in *R.* v. *Cokar* (1960) 44 Cr.App.R. 165 at pp. 168, 169.

[2] (1934) 50 T.L.R. 499; 24 Cr.App.R. 152 (*T.A.C.*). Followed and affirmed in *R.* v. *Nicoloudis* (1954) 38 Cr.App.R. 118; and in *R.* v. *Cokar* [1960] 2 All E.R. 175.

[3] *R.* v. *McLean* (1926) 134 L.T. 640.

[4] The Prevention of Crimes Act, 1871 (34 and 35 Vict. c. 112, s. 18), contains provisions as to the method of proving previous convictions. And see *Martin* v. *White* [1910] 1 K.B. 665. And now, under s. 39 of the Criminal Justice Act, 1948, previous convictions may be proved by certificates of identity of the accused person's fingerprints.

[5] *R.* v. *Campbell* (1911) 6 Cr.App.R. 131. And see now the Criminal Justice Act, 1948, ss. 3, 17, 20, 21, 22 and 23.

[6] Criminal Evidence Act, 1898, s. 1 (*b*).

[7] Mr C. H. Tuttle described this rule as the result of 'a fetish all too superstitiously worshipped'; *Records of American Bar Association*, 1934.

[8] Such comment by the court is 'in some cases unwise, in others absolutely necessary'; *R.* v. *Rhodes* [1899] 1 Q.B. 77; *R.* v. *Smith* (1915) 84 L.J.K.B. 2153; 11 Cr.App.R. 229; *R.* v. *Voisin* [1918] 1 K.B. 531 (*T.A.C.*).

[9] Cf. *R.* v. *Kelson* (1909) 3 Cr.App.R. 230.

[10] *Waugh* v. *R.* (1950) 66 T.L.R. 554, a case which seems to go somewhat against the earlier authorities.

(v) Admissibility of evidence relating to his previous conduct

¶ 626. Owing to the importance and the complexity of the various rules as to the admissibility of evidence relating to a prisoner's previous conduct, character and convictions, a detailed summary has been provided in Appendix II *post*.

OBJECTION TO IMPROPER QUESTIONS

¶ 627. The convicted man may appeal to the Court of Criminal Appeal even though his counsel did not take objection[1] to the improper question at the trial; but the failure of counsel to object may have a bearing upon the question whether the accused was really prejudiced.[2] It is not a proper use of counsel's discretion to raise no objection at the time in order to preserve a ground for a possible appeal.[3] But his failure to do so is not necessarily fatal to an appeal on the ground that the question was improper.[4] Yet apart from any duty of counsel for the defence the judge when trying a case should not wait for objection to be taken but should himself stop any such question.[5]

Even if an improper question has been put the question which the Court of Criminal Appeal must consider is whether the case was not such that no other verdict than that which was given could have been given by a reasonable jury; and the court will not quash the conviction merely because something has been said at the trial which it was irregular to say.[6]

COMMON LAW RIGHT OF UNSWORN STATEMENT PRESERVED

¶ 628. The prisoner had at common law a right (at any rate when undefended by counsel[7]) to make a statement in his own defence without being sworn. And the Criminal Evidence Act, 1898, expressly provides[8] that 'nothing in this Act shall affect... any right of the person charged to make a statement without being sworn'. This proviso seems intended to operate even in the case of a prisoner who gives evidence on oath, enabling him to add to it an argumentative unsworn statement.[9] If the prisoner is defended, his unsworn statement should be made before the speech of prosecuting counsel summing up the evidence.[10]

[1] As to the moment when the objection should be argued see *R.* v. *Zielinski* [1950] 2 All E.R. 1114, and *R.* v. *Patel* [1951] 2 All E.R. 29. [2] See *post*, ¶ 778.

[3] *Stirland* v. *D.P.P.* [1944] 2 All E.R. 13 at p. 18 (*T.A.C.*); *R.* v. *Cutter* [1944] 2 All E.R. 337.

[4] *Stirland* v. *D.P.P.* (*supra*) at p. 18 overruling on that point the interpretation of *R.* v. *Firth* [1938] 3 All E.R. 783 given in *R.* v. *Wattam* [1942] 1 All E.R. 178.

[5] *R.* v. *Ellis* [1910] 2 K.B. 746, at p. 764; *Stirland* v. *D.P.P.* (*supra*) at p. 19; *R.* v. *Jones*, *ante*, p. 521, n. 2.

[6] *R.* v. *Hateley* [1949] 65 T.L.R. 204; 93 S.J. 221.

[7] And probably even when defended, *R.* v. *Shimmin* (1882) 15 Cox 122; *R.* v. *Bernay*, *The Times*, 3 June 1907. [8] Sect. 1 (*h*).

[9] Allegations of fact made by him in it are, of course, not 'evidence', as they would be if he took the option of swearing to them and facing cross-examination. Hence as against co-prisoners, they must be disregarded; but as regards himself the jury are allowed to give them whatever weight they may think fit. [10] *R.* v. *Sheriff* (1903) 20 Cox 334.

Experience has shown that the Criminal Evidence Act, 1898, though so great a departure from what had been a fundamental principle in English criminal procedure, has worked admirably. Lord Brampton[1] found it 'a danger to the guilty, but of the utmost importance to the innocent'. We may add that there is also in force another statute which departs even further from the ancient principles, viz. the Evidence Act, 1877.[2] Under this, whenever criminal proceedings are taken merely to test or to enforce some *civil* right, e.g. the repair of a highway or the abatement of a nuisance, the party charged is not only competent but even compellable to give evidence, either for the defence or even for the prosecution.

CO-PRISONERS

¶ 629. If any persons who took part with the prisoner in his crime should be indicted along with him for it, they would nevertheless, even at common law, be competent (and indeed compellable) to give evidence, either for him or for the prosecution, unless they were put up for actual *trial* along with him.[3] Accordingly, a prisoner who desired to call any co-prisoners as witnesses would request a separate trial; if he obtained it, he then could call them although their own trial had not yet taken place. Sometimes the Crown calls one of a group of prisoners as 'King's evidence'; but it often takes a formal verdict of acquittal before calling him, to enhance the weight of his evidence. To render co-prisoners, or their consorts (except as provided by statute, see ¶ 634 *post*), competent to be called by the prosecution, they must have been acquitted, or have obtained a *nolle prosequi*, or have pleaded guilty, or must be tried separately.[4]

Even since the Act which rendered accused persons competent to give evidence, a prisoner will still sometimes apply thus to be tried apart from those indicted along with him. For some fellow-prisoner, whom he wishes to give evidence on his behalf, may—perhaps from the dread of cross-examination—be unwilling (although now compe-

[1] *Reminiscences*, ch. 46. See the testimony of Sir H. B. Poland, in *A Century of Law Reform* (ed. 1901), 54. But it has no doubt led to much perjury; Grantham, J., thought by nine in every ten, Rowlatt, J. (in 1920), by three in every four, of prisoner witnesses.

[2] 40 and 41 Vict. c. 14.

[3] *R.* v. *Grant and others* [1944] 2 All E.R. 311; and see *Att.-Gen.* v. *Egan* (Eire) [1948] Ir. R. 433. For a longer survey of this topic see Gooderson, 'The evidence of co-prisoners', 11 *Curr. L.J.*, no. 3, 209; and see *R.* v. *Rhodes* (1960) 44 Cr.App.R. 23.

[4] If one co-prisoner pleads guilty and the others not guilty, then if the first one is going to give evidence against the others he should be sentenced forthwith so that his evidence may not be biased by some hope that he may be treated leniently. But if he be not going to give evidence then his sentence should be postponed until the others have been tried so that all may be sentenced together; *R.* v. *Payne* [1950] 1 All E.R. 102. And a prisoner may, at the discretion of the judge, withdraw his plea of guilty at any time before he is sentenced, *R.* v. *Plummer* [1902] 2 K.B. 339; but not after sentence has been pronounced, *R.* v. *McNally* (1954) 38 Cr.App.R. 90, following *R.* v. *Plummer* and dissenting from *R.* v. *Blakemore* (1948) 33 Cr.App.R. 49.

tent) to do so at his own trial.[1] Or the applicant may desire to avoid the danger of the jury's taking into account against himself some evidence which, legally, is only admissible against some fellow-prisoner. Any doubts as to whether the evidence of one co-prisoner against another requires corroboration[2] seem to have been removed by *R.* v. *Prater*[3] and *R.* v. *Heaps.*[4]

B. *SPOUSES AS WITNESSES, MOSTLY INCOMPETENT AT COMMON LAW*

¶ 630. The common law imposed an incompetency to give evidence, not only upon the person under accusation, but also upon that person's wife or husband.[5] Thus, if several prisoners were tried together, not only all of them but also all their spouses were thus disqualified from giving evidence (even though each one of them was charged in an entirely separate count). The rule produced strange results. Serjeant Ballantine, in his *Some Experiences of a Barrister's Life*, mentions having once prosecuted a man who obtained an acquittal by calling his mistress to prove an alibi, viz. his having been away at the races with her. Had he, instead, taken his wife, she could not have thus given evidence for him. On the other hand, Rush (the Norfolk murderer of 1848) was hanged on the testimony of his mistress. He had promised to marry her; and, had he kept his word, it might perhaps have saved his life.

A wife's incompetency remains even if she has been *divorced* before the husband's trial, but not so if the marriage has been annulled as *void*;[6] but the incompetency does still attach after a decree of nullity when the marriage annulled was merely *voidable.*[7] See *R.* v. *Alger* (or *Algar*)[8] for a general account of this topic.

SOME EXCEPTIONS

¶ 631. An exceptional competency was, however, almost of necessity conceded in those cases where the crime consisted in some act of personal violence committed by the prisoner upon the wife or husband. In recent years, a few statutes created further exceptions in the case of those crimes in which prisoners themselves were being rendered com-

[1] Even though *A* may have been bound over, by the magistrate who committed *B*, to give evidence for *B*'s defence, he cannot be compelled to give such evidence if he be himself indicted *and tried* along with *B*.

[2] *Ante*, ¶ 602. [3] (1960) 44 Cr.App.R. 83. [4] (1961) Crim. L.R. 254.

[5] For a case in which this well-known rule was inexplicably overlooked, see *R.* v. *Boucher* (1952) 36 Cr.App.R. 152. No other relationship, not even that of parent and child, was regarded as producing sufficient community of interest with a prisoner to create any incompetency. Professor Kenny saw, in 1909, a woman tried for murder on the evidence of her two brothers and her mother.

[6] E.g. for bigamy, consanguinity, non-age or breach of the requirements of law.

[7] E.g. on grounds of impotence.

[8] [1953] 3 W.L.R. 1007. The difference between a marriage void *ab initio* and a marriage *annulled* as void was considered in *Wiggins* v. *Wiggins and Ingram* [1958] 1 W.L.R. 1013.

petent. But the whole doctrine was thrown into a new form by the Criminal Evidence Act, 1898.[1]

The changes thus effected may be summarized as follows:

CHANGES MADE BY THE CRIMINAL EVIDENCE ACT, 1898

(i) In ordinary criminal cases

¶ 632. (1) The husband or wife of the party charged is now competent to give evidence, but only for the defence,[2] and only on the application of the party charged[3] (and is not compellable[4] to give evidence).

(2) And this husband or wife has the full liability of an ordinary witness to be cross-examined as to credit; not merely the (very limited) liability of a prisoner who becomes a witness under this Act.[5]

(3) A prisoner's omission to call the husband or wife is not to be commented upon by the prosecution.[6]

(4) To call the husband or wife has the same effect as calling any ordinary witness for the defence, in giving the Crown the right of reply.

(ii) In special cases

¶ 633. In the following instances, the husband or wife of the party charged is a competent witness for either the defence or even the prosecution, and quite irrespectively of the consent of the party charged.[7]

(1) Cases where the common law itself recognized an exception to the general rule,[8] viz. upon charges of personal violence committed against the husband or wife in question.[9] This covers assault or attempt to murder, but not crimes that involve no actual violence, like bigamy or libel; and it has lately been decided[10] that at common law the wife's evidence is not admissible against her husband on a charge[11] that he sent a letter to her in which he threatened to murder her, since a threat to murder is not a 'personal injury' to the wife;[12] nor is it admissible under the Criminal Evidence Act, 1898, s. 4,[13] since the Offences against the

[1] 61 and 62 Vict. 36.

[2] Note how the prosecution can get round this rule if husband and wife are charged *jointly* with murder; for then the wife, giving evidence on *her own behalf* may put the blame on the husband (or vice versa) and thus in fact give evidence against him; *R.* v. *Armstrong and Wife* [1957] Crim.L.R. 198.

[3] Sect. 1 (*a*).

[4] *Leach* v. *D.P.P.* [1912] A.C. 305. Not even for the defence. As to polygamously married spouses see 48 *L.Q.R.* 341 and cases cited there.

[5] *Ante*, ¶ 623.

[6] Sect. 1 (*b*).

[7] Sect. 4.

[8] *Ante*, ¶ 631.

[9] Sect. 4 (1). *R.* v. *Moore* (1954) 38 Cr.App.R. 95; arson by husband of wife's property, wife held competent under s. 12 of the Married Women's Property Act, 1882.

[10] *R.* v. *Yeo* [1951] 1 All E.R. 864.

[11] Under s. 16 of the Offences against the Person Act, 1861.

[12] But in *R.* v. *Blanchard* (1952) 35 Cr.App.R. 183, it was held that an unnatural sexual treatment of the wife was an offence against her person so as to render her a competent witness for the prosecution.

[13] See above, ¶ 632.

Person Act, 1861, s. 16, was not mentioned in the schedule to the former.

(2) Cases where, under the Married Women's Property Act, 1882,[1] the husband or wife is taking criminal proceedings for an offence committed against his or her property by the prisoner.

(3) Cases of the sexual offences dealt with by sections 48–55 of the Offences against the Person Act, 1861, or by the Criminal Law Amendment Act, 1885 (repealed and replaced by the Sexual Offences Act, 1956); incest;[2] bigamy.[3]

(4) Cases specified in Part I of the Children and Young Persons Act, 1933,[4] e.g. offences involving bodily injury to a person under seventeen.

(5) Cases of persons charged under the Vagrancy Act[5] with neglecting to maintain (or with deserting) their families, or with being *souteneurs*.

(6) Cases where criminal proceedings are taken to test or to enforce a *civil* right.[6]

WHEN COMPELLABLE

¶ 634. Even before the Act of 1898 the husband or wife was already *compellable* to give evidence in (2) and (6), but it was doubtful whether they were compellable in (1). It was decided in *R.* v. *Lapworth*[7] that they were in such cases both competent and compellable at common law. In the other three cases, (3), (4) and (5), the husband or wife is, though a competent witness, not a compellable one, *Leach* v. *Director of Public Prosecutions*.[8] Where the husband or wife of a prisoner is not competent to give evidence for the prosecution the exclusion applies also to the husband or wife of a co-defendant, unless the co-defendant would himself be competent[9] (see ¶ 629 *ante*).

SECTION 6. UNSTAMPED DOCUMENTS

¶ 635. Documents which require to be stamped are treated differently in civil and in criminal courts.

For purposes of revenue an artificial restriction upon the admissibility of documents as evidence has been created by the imposition of stamp duties upon certain classes of them. Familiar instances are the stamp upon receipts for the amount of £2 or over, the sixpenny stamp upon a written agreement whose subject is worth £5 or over, and the *ad*

[1] 45 and 46 Vict. c. 75, ss. 12, 16; *ante*, ¶ 254. See *R.* v. *Moore* (1954), *supra*.

[2] Sexual Offences Act, 1956, ss. 10 and 11.

[3] Criminal Justice Administration Act, 1914.

[4] 23 Geo. V, c. 12, s. 15. Discussed in *R.* v. *Moore* (1954) *ubi supra*.

[5] *Ante*, ¶¶ 484, 485, subject to the provisions of sect. 51 of the National Assistance Act, 1948. See part II of the schedule to the Statutory Instrument, no. 1334 of 1952.

[6] Evidence Act, 1877, s. 6 (1); *ante*, ¶ 628.

[7] [1931] 1 K.B. 117 (*T.A.C.*). From which it would seem that the wife in *R.* v. *Blanchard*, *ubi supra*, would have been a compellable witness.

[8] [1912] A.C. 305.

[9] *R.* v. *Mount and Metcalfe* (1934) 24 Cr.App.R. 135.

valorem stamp on mortgages and bonds. Under the earlier Stamp Acts, an unstamped document that ought to have borne a stamp was incapable of being used as evidence in any court whatever, whether civil or criminal. Thus on the trial of a man for having burned down his shop, with intent to defraud the insurance company of the sum for which he had insured it, it was held that the absence of any stamp on the policy of insurance rendered it inadmissible in evidence, even though it was tendered for the mere purpose of proving the particular intent alleged in the indictment.[1]

Hence such duties formed a conspicuous example of taxes on litigation, which Bentham condemned as 'the worst of all taxes, being denials of justice, co-operating with every injury and with every crime, and directly violating that first of statutes, Magna Carta—"Justice shall be sold to no man".'[2] But the severity of their operation was greatly mitigated in 1854, when an enactment (now replaced by the Stamp Act, 1891) established with respect to them an important difference between civil and criminal courts. For whilst in civil proceedings unstamped documents are still incapable of being given in evidence, without at least the payment of penalties,[3] the absence of a stamp no longer prevents any document from being given in evidence in criminal proceedings.

SECTION 7. EVIDENCE TAKEN ABROAD

¶ 636. The testimony of witnesses who are abroad can be made available much more easily in civil than in criminal courts.

The fundamental principle which, as we have seen, excludes hearsay evidence rendered it impossible for such persons to give their testimony by merely sending letters or affidavits, without coming to England to appear in court in person. Even an official telegram from the Madras Government in answer to an inquiry addressed to it by the India Office has been held inadmissible.[4] But in civil courts this difficulty has now been overcome by making a general provision for taking the evidence of such witnesses upon oath, with full formalities, in the foreign country where they reside,[5] or by granting a commission or appointing a special examiner.[6]

SELDOM ADMITTED IN CRIMINAL CASES

¶ 637. But in criminal courts no such general rule prevails.[7] In some exceptional instances, however, statutes have sanctioned the taking of

[1] *R.* v. *Gilson* (1807) 2 Leach 1007; R. and R. 138.

[2] *Works*, IV, 582.

[3] And some instruments (e.g. bills of exchange and bills of lading) can only be stamped at the time of execution, so that, if not stamped then, they cannot be rendered admissible as evidence even by payment of penalty.

[4] *R.* v. *O'Flynn* (1894) C.C.C. Sess. Pap. CXX, at p. 916.

[5] Rules of the Supreme Court, Order XXXVII, rule 5.

[6] And see also the Evidence Act, 1938, s. 1 (1) (ii).

[7] Accordingly in the Tichborne proceedings, the witnesses from Chile, whose evidence had been taken in that country for the civil action, had to come to England to give evidence in person at the criminal trial.

evidence abroad for use in criminal cases. The most important of these provisions is one, contained in the Merchant Shipping Act, 1894, which provides for all cases in which an accused person is himself in the foreign country where the witness is (as may well happen if the crime be committed at sea, or abroad). For it permits any deposition on oath made outside the United Kingdom before a proper official—a magistrate if in a British possession, or a British consular officer if in a foreign country—*in the presence of the accused* to be given in evidence in any criminal proceedings here to whose subject-matter it relates, if, at the time of using it, the witness is not in the United Kingdom.[1]

[1] The other statutes are of a less general character. In extradition proceedings, the Extradition Act, 1870, allows written depositions taken abroad to be given in evidence.

BOOK IV

CRIMINAL PROCEDURE

Chapter XXIX

LIMITATIONS ON CRIMINAL JURISDICTION

SECTION 1. INTRODUCTORY

¶ 638. *Procedure is a part of adjective law.* We have now discussed the substantive law of crime, and also that portion of the adjective law which regulates the evidence by which crimes are to be proved. Finally, we have to consider the remaining portion of adjective law, that which regulates the procedure by which offenders who have committed crime are brought to punishment. We may begin by mentioning some limitations upon the exercise of this procedure, and then go on to describe the various courts in which it is exercised.

SECTION 2. LIMITATION BY TIME

NONE AT COMMON LAW

¶ 639. To civil actions, lapse of time may often operate as a bar: *vigilantibus, non dormientibus, jura subveniunt.* But it can rarely affect a criminal prosecution. For the King could do no wrong; and consequently it was impossible that his delay in pressing his claims, whether civil or criminal, could be due to any blamable negligence. Accordingly at common law it was a rule that those claims remained unaffected by lapse of time: *nullum tempus occurrit regi.* And though, as regards civil claims, this kingly privilege has now been subjected to limitations by 9 Geo. III, c. 16, it still operates almost unimpaired in criminal prosecutions. Hence, in several noteworthy cases, offenders have been brought to justice many years after the commission of their crimes. In 1905 John Appleton received sentence of death (afterwards commuted) on his own confession of a murder committed in 1882 (*The Times*, 15 July 1905). The trial of Governor Wall (1802)[1] took place nineteen years, that of Edward Shippey (1871)[2] thirty years, and that of William Horne[3] thirty-five years, after the respective murders of which they were accused. Stephen,[4] indeed, mentions a prosecution in 1863 for the theft of a leaf from a parish register no less than sixty years previously.

[1] 28 St.Tr. 51; *ante*, ¶ 13 (iv). [2] 12 Cox 161.

[3] *Annual Register*, II, 368; *Gentleman's Magazine* (1759), 604, 627.

[4] *Hist. Crim. Law*, II, 2.

STATUTORY CHANGES

¶ 640. But this rule, that lapse of time is no bar to criminal justice, is subject to a few statutory exceptions. Of these the following are the chief:[1]

(i) A prosecution for treason or misprision of treason must be brought within three years from the commission of the crime; unless the treason either consists in an actual plot to assassinate the Sovereign, or was committed abroad.[2]

(ii) Offenders against the Riot Act[3] must be prosecuted within twelve months.

(iii) A prosecution for the misdemeanour of unlawful sexual intercourse (or attempting the same) with a girl between the ages of thirteen and sixteen must be brought within twelve months.[4]

(iv) A prosecution by indictment under the Perjury Act, 1911 (s. 4), for making a false statement in registering a birth or death, must be brought within three years.

(v) And for the innumerable offences which are punishable on summary conviction the prosecution must be within six months.[5] For the rare exceptions, see Stone's *Justice's Manual*, Index, 'Limitation'.

SECTION 3. LIMITATION BY TERRITORY

¶ 641. According to international law, a State ought only to exercise jurisdiction over such persons and property as are within its territory.[6] And in criminal matters it does not always exercise jurisdiction over an offender even though he actually be within its territory. For many States hold the view that a State may not try foreigners for offences committed outside its territorial jurisdiction.[7] One unique exception is, indeed, universally allowed. For persons guilty of any act of 'piracy *jure gentium*'[8] are treated as the common enemies of all mankind, and any nation that can arrest them may exercise jurisdiction over them,[9] whatsoever their nationality, and wheresoever their crime may have

[1] Others are mentioned in Stephen, *op. cit.* II, 2.

[2] 7 and 8 Will. III, c. 3, ss. 5, 6; *ante*, ¶ 417.

[3] 1 Geo. I, st. 2, c. 5; *ante*, ¶ 439.

[4] Sexual Offences Act, 1956, Sch. 2.

[5] Magistrates' Courts Act, 1952, s. 104.

[6] For the claim of Italy to try persons not in the State territory for political offences committed abroad, and to try foreigners found in the State territory for any crimes committed abroad on the request of the Ministry of Justice or the complaint of the injured party, see *Journal of Comparative Legislation and International Law*, XV, 185–7. On the whole question see W. E. Beckett in *British Year Book of International Law*, vol. VI. As to an offence committed in a British aircraft flying over foreign land, see *R.* v. *Martin* [1956] 2 W.L.R. 975. Cf. *Cox* v. *Army Council* [1962] 1 All E. R. 880.

[7] See Oppenheim's *International Law*, 8th ed., pt. 1, 331 *et seq.*

[8] *Ante*, ¶ 478.

[9] As to conspiracy here for piracy on the high seas, see *R.* v. *Kohn* (1864) 4 F. and F. 68. Conspiracy abroad to kill here is not triable here.

been committed, even within the territorial waters of some other nation.[1]

Hence the activity of a nation's criminal courts is mostly confined to those persons[2] who have committed offences on its own soil[3] or in one of its own ships.

IMMUNITY ACQUIRED BY CHANGE OF TERRITORY

¶ 642. Accordingly, persons who come into a State's territory, after having committed a crime elsewhere, usually incur no risk of being punished by the courts of their new home for what they did in their old one. In modern times, however, to counterbalance this immunity, almost all civilized countries have concluded extradition treaties: mutual arrangements whereby any person who betakes himself abroad after he has perpetrated a serious offence may be arrested, and then sent back to take his trial in the country where his offence was committed, if it were not a 'political' crime.[4] Since 1870 England has made such treaties with almost all foreign countries. Most of them provide at option for the mutual extradition of nationals.[5] The foreign offender is surrendered under a warrant from the Home Secretary, after an investigation (under an order from him) by a magistrate at Bow Street.

EXTRADITION

¶ 643. Extradition transmits an offender from the territory of one nation to that of another. But even within a nation's own territory, if her constitution be a federated or quasi-federated one, some similar provision may be necessary, in order to transmit offenders from one of the component local jurisdictions to another. Thus within the British sphere, the Fugitive Offenders Act, 1881,[6] provides for a surrender, akin

[1] *The Marianna Flora* (1826) 11 Wheaton at p. 41; *In re Tivnan* (1864) 5 B. and S. at p. 677. But this would not cover acts which, like trading in slaves, are made piracy by local laws alone. For one country—or even several countries—cannot add to international law. The right to exercise extra-territorial jurisdiction in criminal matters may be conceded to one State by another, e.g. conventions relating to white slave traffic.

[2] But it covers such persons even though they be aliens, *Courteen's Case* (1618) Hobart 270; *Re Barronet* (1853) 1 E. and B. 1.

[3] As to 'territorial waters', see the Territorial Waters Jurisdiction Act, 1878. In our Atlantic island of Ascension a manslaughter was committed in 1851 but no competent tribunal existed there. Hence a special commission was issued for a trial at Winchester (cf. ¶ 137*a ante*); thirteen witnesses were brought from Ascension (*The Times*, 5 March 1852). English law claims concurrent jurisdiction with the flag State over foreign merchant ships in British ports; so too, probably, in the case of aircraft; as to crimes connected with air navigation see the Civil Aviation Act, 1949, and *R.* v. *Naylor* [1961] 2 All E.R. 932.

[4] See *Re Castioni* [1891] 1 Q.B. 149. The crime must be incidental to and form part of a political disturbance. See Oppenheim's *International Law*, 8th ed., 704 *et seq.*

[5] Italy, which normally will not extradite its own nationals, is prepared to try them in its own courts for offences committed abroad; see *Journal of Comparative Legislation and International Law*, xv, 62.

[6] 44 and 45 Vict. c. 69. As to protectorates, see Fugitive Offenders (Protected States) Act, 1915.

to an extradition by a foreign nation, where a person who has committed an offence in one part of the Queen's dominions has fled to another part of them. The range of crimes for which such a person may be thus surrendered is naturally much wider than in the case of extradition to a foreign country. It comprises all offences that are punishable (in the territory where they are committed) with not less than twelve months' imprisonment (formerly with hard labour). The statute moreover applies even though the conduct with which the fugitive is charged would have constituted no offence at all if committed in that part of the British dominions to which he has fled.

CRIMES IN GENERAL ARE LOCAL MATTERS

¶ 644. International law, whatever view be taken of the right to exercise criminal jurisdiction over foreigners for offences committed by them outside the territorial jurisdiction, nevertheless leaves unlimited a State's power to punish its own subjects. Yet nations vary in their readiness to exercise this power in respect of crimes which their subjects have committed whilst away from their native soil. Great Britain (like France and the United States) prefers, in nearly all cases, to adhere to the principle that crimes are local matters, to be dealt with where they are committed. But to this general rule she has by modern statutes made a few exceptions, empowering her courts to exercise jurisdiction over British subjects who commit certain specified offences even upon foreign soil.[1]

CONSPIRACY TO COMMIT A CRIME ABROAD

¶ 645. Doubt has arisen whether, even when a man is in England, he would commit any offence against English law by conspiring to commit (or by being accessory to the commission of) a crime in some country abroad.[2] For as English courts have no official knowledge of foreign

[1] Examples are homicide (Offences against the Person Act, 1861, s. 9; *ante*, ¶ 137), bigamy (*ibid.* s. 57; *ante*, ¶ 172 (2)), piracy (*ante*, ¶ 641), treason and misprision of treason (35 Hen. VIII, c. 2, s. 1), offences by colonial governors (11 Will. III, c. 12; see *R.* v. *Eyre, Governor* (1868) L.R. 3 Q.B. 487), foreign enlistment (33 and 34 Vict. c. 90, s. 4; *ante*, ¶ 481), offences under the Representation of the People Act, 1949, the Corrupt Practices Act, 1883, the Official Secrets Acts, 1911 and 1920, and the Explosive Substances Act, 1883. Under the Criminal Justice Act, 1948, s. 31, a servant of the Crown who, when acting or purporting to act in the course of his employment, commits an offence in a foreign country, is subject to the same punishment in an English court as if the offence had been committed in England. The only statute which gives (as it seems) to English courts jurisdiction over foreigners for offences committed in foreign territory is the Merchant Shipping Act, 1894, which, by s. 687, in effect gives jurisdiction to try in England, for any offence committed abroad against property or person, any master, seaman or apprentice who at the time when it was committed was, or within three months previously had been, employed in a British ship; see Stallybrass, in *J. Comp. Leg. and Inter. Law*, XV, 81.

[2] This doubt was debated hotly in 1858, when various persons had conspired in London to assist Orsini in his project of assassinating Napoleon III in Paris. Orsini's attempt was made on 14 January 1858, the emperor escaping unhurt, but ten of the spectators being killed, and a hundred and fifty-six wounded. The three bombs inflicted 516 wounds.

law they cannot be sure that the act, however wicked, is actually a crime by the law of the particular foreign country concerned. Similarly, if a thing stolen abroad were brought to this country by a man who had knowingly received it abroad, and persons knowingly received it from him here, it formerly appeared to lawyers to be doubtful whether they could be punished here.[1] This point, however, was settled by the Larceny Act, 1916, *infra*. Conspiracy (or incitement) here to commit a *murder* abroad has been made indictable.[2] And now the House of Lords has laid down a more general rule in *Board of Trade* v. *Owen* [1957] 2 W.L.R. 351, a case already discussed, *ante*, p. 415.

GOODS STOLEN ABROAD

¶ 646. The offence of handling in this country goods stolen abroad has been dealt with by the Larceny Act, 1916;[3] which provides that it shall be an offence, punishable with seven years' imprisonment, to receive, or to have[4] in possession, in this country, without lawful excuse, any property stolen outside the United Kingdom, knowing such property to have been stolen. Property is to be deemed to be 'stolen' whenever it has been obtained under such circumstances that if the act had been committed in the United Kingdom it would have constituted an indictable offence, even though not a larceny. The Act applies not only to cases of receiving in England goods stolen abroad by other persons, but also to cases where the thief himself is found in possession of the goods in England.

CRIMES COMMITTED THROUGH THE AGENCY OF THE POST

¶ 647. A person, although himself abroad, may by the hands of an innocent agent commit a crime in England, e.g. by posting in France a libellous letter or a forged telegram, which the postman will deliver for him in London. If the Frenchman come to England, he may be tried here. Similarly,[5] if money be sent in a letter from England to Holland, in consequence of a false pretence made in London, there is an 'obtaining' here, sufficient to give jurisdiction to our courts; for the Dutch criminal has made the English postmaster his agent[6] to receive the missive. It is, however, necessary, before the English courts can claim jurisdiction, either that the direct results of the crime take place in England, or that an overt act be committed in England.

[1] Cf. *R.* v. *Nadal* (1876) C.C.C. Sess. Pap. LXXXIV, 295; *R.* v. *Fitzgerald* (1878) LXXXVIII, 635.

[2] Offences against the Person Act, 1861, s. 4; *R.* v. *Most* (1881) 7 Q.B.D. 244.

[3] Sect. 33 (4).

[4] Thus covering cases in which not only the act of stealing, but even that of receiving, took place abroad.

[5] *R.* v. *Stoddart* (1909) 2 Cr.App.R. 217.

[6] Conversely, a man who without quitting England posts forged bills from here to a foreign country may be held guilty of uttering them *there*. And the very wide definition of 'fugitive' in the Extradition Act renders it possible to extradite him, as a 'fugitive criminal', for trial there; *R.* v. *Godfrey* [1923] 1 K.B. 24.

HOMICIDE IS COMMITTED IN THE PLACE WHERE THE ATTACK TAKES EFFECT

¶ 648. Consistently with the principle first mentioned above it would seem the better opinion that a homicide is committed in the place where the deceased was when the attack took physical effect upon him. So that if a man, being in a boat on the water, be shot at and fatally hit by another who stands on the shore the murder (or manslaughter as the case may be) is committed in the boat on the water,[1] and vice versa. Similarly where a man in Paris by false returns caused incorrect figures to be entered in the account books of his firm in London it was held that the offence of false accounting was committed by him in London.[2]

[1] *R.* v. *Coombes* (1785) 1 Leach 388. Notwithstanding the declaration in *R.* v. *Keyn* (1876) 2 Ex. D. 63, with which contrast the '*Lotus*' *Case* (1926), discussed in 44 *L.Q.R.* 154, and see Stallybrass, in *J. Comp. Leg. and Inter. Law*, xv, 83, and W. E. Beckett in *British Y.B. of International Law*, VIII. It should be noted that *R.* v. *Lewis* (1857) 7 Cox 277 was a case decided solely on the interpretation of the statutes 2 Geo. II, c. 21, s. 1 and 9 Geo. IV, c. 31, s. 8; *R.* v. *Depardo* (1807) R. and R. 134, and *R.* v. *De Mattos* (1836) 7 C. and P. 458 were also cases which depended on the interpretation of relevant statutory provisions. See Offences against the Person Act, 1861, s. 10.

[2] *R.* v. *Oliphant* [1905] 2 K.B. 67; *R.* v. *Harden* [1962] 1 All E.R. 286 (false pretences).

Chapter XXX

CRIMINAL COURTS

SECTION I. THE HIGH COURT OF THE QUEEN IN PARLIAMENT

¶ **649.** The various courts that possess a general criminal jurisdiction will now be considered in the order of their dignity, beginning with the highest court in the realm. Its title must not mislead the student into supposing either that the Queen sits there in person, or that the word 'Parliament' is used in the usual modern sense, as including the House of Commons. But a Parliament, sitting without the Sovereign or the Commons, becomes simply the House of Lords, by which, accordingly, the jurisdiction of this court is exercised. That jurisdiction is twofold: (*a*) as a court of appeal, and (*b*) as a court of first instance.

(*a*) AS A COURT OF APPEAL

¶ **650.** In civil matters the House of Lords is the only final court of appeal on all questions of law from English secular tribunals. But in criminal causes it is only one, and far the less active, of two such courts. Until 1907 its functions of appeal were limited to those extremely rare cases of error of law apparent on the record itself.[1] Such an error would appear in any indictment that disclosed no crime. But the Act of 1907[2] which created the new Court of Criminal Appeal provided that from it there might be an appeal to the House of Lords by either the prosecution or the defence on any point of law which the Attorney-General should certify to be of such exceptional *public* importance that it would be desirable 'in the public interest' to have the highest decision on it. But now the Administration of Justice Act, 1960, in effect provides by section 1 (1) that an appeal lies to the House of Lords, at the instance of the plaintiff or the prosecutor, from any decision (*a*) of a Divisional Court of the Queen's Bench in a criminal cause or matter; (*b*) of the Court of Criminal Appeal, on an appeal to that court. But by virtue of subsection (2) no appeal lies under this section except with the leave of the court below, or of the House of Lords; and such leave is not to be granted unless it is certified by the court below that a point of law 'of general public importance' is involved in the decision, and it appears to that court or to the House of Lords, as the case may be, that the point is one which ought to be considered by that House. By subsection (4) it is provided that for the purpose of disposing of an appeal under this section the House of Lords may exercise any powers of the court below

[1] Chitty says that the record contains (*inter alia*) the judge's commission, the indictment by the grand jury, the arraignment, plea, issue, award of jury, verdict, judgment (*Practical Treatise on Criminal Law*, I, 720). But it never shows the evidence, or the rulings of the judge as to admission or rejection of evidence, or his statements in his summing-up to the jury.

[2] 7 Edw. VII, c. 23. *Post*, ¶ 655.

or may remit the case to that court. It should be noted that the words 'of general public importance'[1] in the new statute replace the words 'of exceptional public importance' of section 1 (6) of the Act of 1907, and that the words 'desirable in the public interest' have been omitted. It will also be observed that no application for leave to appeal can be made directly to the House of Lords, who can only hear an appeal if the lower court has granted the statutory certificate.

A sitting of 'Parliament' for legal appeals differs very greatly from an ordinary sitting of the House of Lords. For, by the Appellate Jurisdiction Act, 1876, there must be present at least three 'Lords of Appeal';[2] and, on the other hand, by a rule of constitutional etiquette which has prevailed since *O'Connell's Case* in 1844,[3] all peers who are not lawyers abstain from casting a vote. Moreover, under the Act of 1876, the lords of appeal may be allowed by the House of Lords to hold these sittings after the prorogation of Parliament; and the Crown may authorize them to sit even after Parliament has been dissolved.

(*b*) AS A COURT OF FIRST INSTANCE

¶ 651. The House of Lords is also a court of first instance. In this capacity, unlike that already mentioned, it can try questions of fact as well as of law;[4] and the modern rule of etiquette excluding non-legal peers has no application here. But as the early Chancellors, being ecclesiastics, could take no part in capital trials, it became the practice for the Crown to appoint some peer (it will now probably be the Lord Chancellor himself) as Lord High Steward, to preside. Criminal cases formerly could be tried before this august tribunal, on account of the dignity of either (i) the accused or (ii) the accusers.

(i) Trial by peers

¶ 652. Until the Criminal Justice Act, 1948, s. 30, abolished privilege of peerage in relation to criminal proceedings, peers, when accused of treason, or felony, or the misprision of either, had to be tried by their noble peers.[5] This privilege depended upon nobility of blood, not upon the right to a seat in the House of Lords, and accordingly was possessed by peeresses in their own right, wives of peers, infant peers, and non-representative Scottish or Irish peers. The weight of authority was decidedly in favour of the view that a peer could not waive the privilege,[6]

[1] But see *R.* v. *Gnipyuk* (1961) *The Times*, 11 Jan.: where the Court of Criminal Appeal, *per* Hilbery, J., is reported to have used the phrase 'of real public importance'.

[2] 39 and 40 Vict. c. 59. These may be either lords of appeal 'in ordinary' (i.e. salaried life peers appointed by virtue of the Appellate Jurisdiction Act, 1876), or peers of the realm who have held high judicial office.

[3] Wade and Phillips, *Constitutional Law*, 5th ed., 229.

[4] It thus forms the nearest surviving approach 'to the old *judicium parium*' (Holdsworth, *Hist. Eng. Law*, I, 389).

[5] Pollock and Maitland, I, 140. But for misdemeanours a peer was, and still is, tried by an ordinary jury of commoners.

[6] See *Hansard*, CCCX, 245 (31 Jan. 1887).

cumbrous and inconvenient though the form of procedure was,[1] as was shown by the trial of Earl Russell for bigamy.[2] All prosecutions of peers were, however, commenced in one of the ordinary courts, by an indictment, this indictment being subsequently removed into the House of Lords (or into the Lord High Steward's Court)[3] by a writ of certiorari.

Bishops could not be tried by the House of Lords. No bishop has ever been so tried; and Archbishop Cranmer and Bishop Fisher were tried by ordinary juries.[4] Bishops could, however, sit at the trial of a secular peer, until the final moment when the lords came to the vote of 'guilty' or 'not guilty'. This disqualification for pronouncing judgment doubtless arose from the rule of canon law which forbade clerks to take part in any sentence of death, though it also has been explained by the doctrine of 'ennobled blood'.

(ii) Impeachment

¶ 653. Any person, whether peer or commoner, who is impeached by the House of Commons must be tried by the House of Lords. A peer may be thus impeached for any crime, and so may a commoner for, at any rate, any high misdemeanour.[5] But as the House of Commons is itself now able to exercise directly an effective political control over the proceedings of the great officers of state, judicial procedure by impeachment has fallen into desuetude. Its inconveniences were manifested in the tedious proceedings against Warren Hastings, which lasted from 1786 until 1795. Since Lord Melville's impeachment in 1805[6] there has been no instance of it, and none is likely to arise. For impeachment, as Lord Macaulay says, 'is a fine ceremony, which may have been useful in the seventeenth century, but not one from which much good can be expected now'.

SECTION 2. THE COURT OF CRIMINAL APPEAL

¶ 654. Except for those rare errors of law which are actually (in technical phrase) 'apparent on the record', the common law provided no court of appeal in criminal cases, although it made abundant provision

[1] It will be found described in *Blackwood's Magazine*, Dec. 1850, in an account of the trial of Lord Cardigan in 1841 (4 St.Tr. (n.s.) 601) for firing at Capt. Tuckett in a duel; and see C. Woodham-Smith's *The Reason Why* (1953), ch. v.

[2] [1901] A.C. 446.

[3] The Court of the Lord High Steward was the substitute for the House of Lords when the recess or the dissolution of Parliament made it impossible to have recourse to the House of Lords. It consisted of such temporal peers as the Lord High Steward might summon, and it had some special rules of procedure. It has not sat since 1686.

[4] Yet the resolution of the House of Lords, excluding bishops from trial by the peers (Lords' S.O., no. 61), depends upon the doctrine of 'ennobled blood', which Bishop Stubbs regarded as historically an absurdity.

[5] On the controversy whether a commoner can also be impeached for felony and for treason, or may for these crimes insist on being tried by 'his peers', the conflicting cases from 1330 to 1689 are collected in Hatsell's *Precedents* (IV, 397). It is now generally thought that he *is* impeachable even for these graver crimes.

[6] 29 St.Tr. 550. It was described by a lawyer as 'not an impeachment of waste, but a waste of impeachment'.

for civil appeals. Hence the judges had recourse to the wise practice of holding informal meetings to discuss questions of difficulty which had arisen before any of them at criminal trials. By 11 and 12 Vict. c. 78 these informal meetings were superseded by the establishment of a formal tribunal, the 'Court for Crown Cases Reserved',[1] with power to determine points of law that arose upon the trial of any prisoner at either the assizes or the quarter sessions. By the Judicature Act, this jurisdiction was transferred to the High Court of Justice, i.e. the lower section of the Supreme Court of Judicature. Such appeals could be made by the prisoner only, not by the Crown. But he could not make them as of right; for he could not compel the judge to reserve a point. And only questions of law could be reserved, never questions of fact. The annual number of such appeals averaged only eight.

ITS CONSTITUTION

¶ 655. A more comprehensive principle was established by the Criminal Appeal Act, 1907, which created a general 'Court of Criminal Appeal',[2] that can review any question whether of law or of fact. This court now consists of the Lord Chief Justice of England along with the judges of the Queen's Bench Division. It may sit in several divisions; but a sitting requires a quorum of at least three judges.[3] To render impossible an equal balance of opinion, it is enacted that the number of judges present must always be an uneven one. And, further to secure certainty in the law, only a single judgment—as in the Judicial Committee of the Privy Council—is usually delivered.

WRIT OF ERROR ABOLISHED

¶ 656. This Act of 1907 abolished (s. 20) a very rare form of appeal—the writ of error. By this, a decision of the Queen's Bench Division upon a point of law that was 'apparent on the record' of a criminal case might be brought before Her Majesty's Court of Appeal (i.e. the upper section of the Supreme Court of Judicature), though that court was debarred, by section 47 of the Judicature Act, from receiving any other form of appeal in *criminal* matters. Thence the case might be carried up to the House of Lords.

Thus, since 1907, both Her Majesty's Court of Appeal[4] and (in its *collective* form) the High Court of Justice have ceased to exercise any jurisdiction as courts of criminal law.

[1] This court was often called the 'Court of Criminal Appeal', see Cox, *Reports of Cases in Criminal Law* (e.g. vol. 7).

[2] For an account of its working, see ¶ 774 *post*.

[3] In *R.* v. *Norman* [1924] 2 K.B. 315, *thirteen* sat.

[4] Except that, in the quasi-criminal offences of obstructing (or not repairing) a highway or bridge or river, the Supreme Court of Judicature Act, 1925, s. 29 confers on the convicted offender the same full rights of appeal as if he were a defendant in a civil action at assizes, apparently including the right of resort to Her Majesty's Court of Appeal.

SECTION 3. THE QUEEN'S BENCH DIVISION OF THE HIGH COURT OF JUSTICE

¶ **657.** This tribunal exercises the criminal jurisdiction of the ancient *Curia Regis*. Hence, though the Lord Chancellor is the highest of the judicial functionaries of the realm, not he but the Lord Chief Justice (who presides in this division) is the head of our criminal judicature. And it is now usual to select the judges of assize from it alone, not from any of the other divisions of the High Court.

(*a*) As a court of first instance

¶ **658.** Like the House of Lords, the Queen's Bench Division has cognizance both of matters of first instance and of matters of appeal. As a court of first instance it possesses an original jurisdiction in three classes of offence. It can try (1) any misdemeanour for which an information has been filed by the Queen's Attorney-General[1] (see ¶ 716 *post*), and (2) any indictable crime that has been committed in the county of London and the county of Middlesex.[2] (No such indictments have been preferred in the Queen's Bench Division for some years past.) It can also try (3) any indictable crime, an indictment for which has been found in some other court (e.g. at assizes) and has since been removed by *order* into the Queen's Bench Division for trial.[3] Such a removal may be ordered (i) for the purpose of bringing to the Central Criminal Court or some other court a case which owing to e.g. local prejudice is unlikely to receive a fair trial; (ii) because some question of law of unusual difficulty or importance makes desirable a trial at bar; (iii) because a view of premises by the jury is desirable. The Business of Courts Committee[4] had in 1936 recommended that removal to secure fair trial should be direct from one venue to another; that the power to order trial at bar in suitable cases should be preserved; that it should be possible for a jury, without any practical difficulty, to view premises where desirable.

(*b*) As a court of appeal

¶ **659.** In its appellate functions the Queen's Bench Division is much more active. They are usually exercised through two (or three) of its judges sitting as a divisional court. The appeals are of two kinds.

(1) By *order* (granted upon an application)[5] the proceedings of quarter sessions or of any still lower tribunal—but not of assizes or of

[1] *R.* v. *Mylius*, *The Times*, 2 Feb. 1911.

[2] Trial is at bar before three judges usually with a special jury. The Administration of Justice Act, 1938, s. 11 gives the High Court power to direct in suitable cases trial at the Central Criminal Court before three judges or a single judge.

[3] See the Administration of Justice (Misc. Provisions) Act, 1938, s. 11 and S.R. and O., 1938, no. 1576/L. 29.

[4] Cmd. 5066.

[5] Formerly by writ of certiorari (¶ 686 *post* and ¶ 652 *ante*); see Administration of Justice (Misc. Provisions) Act, 1938, s. 11.

the Central Criminal Court—may be brought before it, at the instance of either the prosecutor or the defendant, to be reviewed and, if necessary, quashed for absence of jurisdiction.

(2) By a case being stated by justices of the peace at a magistrates' court (at the instance of either prosecutor or defendant), any question of law[1] that has arisen before them may be submitted to the Queen's Bench Division. Courts of quarter sessions also may state a case for the consideration of the Queen's Bench Division, but only in regard to some matter that has come to them on appeal from a magistrates' court.[2]

SECTION 4. THE COURTS OF THE COMMISSIONERS OF ASSIZE

¶ 660. These ancient itinerant criminal tribunals are created by two commissions,[3] issued two, three, or four times a year (according to the county) to judges of the High Court and some eminent members of the bar, authorizing them to try the prisoners presented for trial in the several counties for which the assize is to be held. One criminal commission is that of Oyer and Terminer ('to hear and to determine'), giving authority to try all prisoners committed to a particular assize. The other is that of General Gaol Delivery, giving authority to try all prisoners who are in gaol or have been released on bail, whatever may have been the assize at which the bills against them were preferred. There is, in practice, little difference between the lists of prisoners triable under the two commissions; and the two commissions form only one document. The courts thus held are now, by the Supreme Court of Judicature (Consolidation) Act, 1925, s. 18, to be regarded as branches of the High Court of Justice. They can try any indictable offence whatever, and are the most important of our criminal courts of first instance. But they have no appellate jurisdiction.

THE CENTRAL CRIMINAL COURT

¶ 661. In London and its suburbs, for a population of over eight millions, the function of the assizes is discharged by the Central Criminal Court—a special tribunal created by 4 and 5 Will. IV, c. 36, the commissions of oyer and terminer and of general gaol delivery for the metropolitan district being addressed to the Lord Mayor and aldermen of the City of London, along with all the judges of the High Court, the recorder, the common serjeant, and others. The Lord Mayor is, titularly, the head of the commission. The sittings under these com-

[1] Occasionally the divisional court does overrule the justices in findings of fact; properly so if the court finds, e.g., that there was no evidence justifying the finding; and sometimes, it seems, without giving any reason. See the case of *Hill* v. *Baxter* [1958] 2 W.L.R. 76.

[2] Criminal Justice Act, 1925, s. 20. For military offences see the Courts Martial (Appeals) Act, 1951. But cp. *Greenly* v. *Lawrence* [1949] 1 All E.R. 241.

[3] See Stephen, *Hist. Crim. Law*, I, 75–144.

missions are held monthly. They sometimes proceed in as many as four courts simultaneously (once, in 1911, in five), one or another legal member of the commission presiding in each of these.[1]

Section 5. General Quarter Sessions[2]

¶ 662. These, in their oldest form, are meetings of the justices of the peace[3] of a particular county; and two at least of such justices must be present. They are held once a quarter,[4] or, by adjournment,[5] oftener. A large number of cities and boroughs have also obtained the privilege of a local court of quarter sessions, presided over, however, not by justices of the peace, but by a recorder, who is the sole judge. He must be a barrister of at least five years' standing.[6] Every court of quarter sessions, whether for a county, a city or a borough, has both an original and an appellate jurisdiction.

(*a*) As a court of first instance

¶ 663. This court can try all indictable offences with certain exceptions, the chief of which are:[7]

Treason.

Murder.

Felonies punishable with penal servitude (now imprisonment) for life on a first conviction (other than burglary[8] and offences relating to the stealing or receiving of mail bags and postal packets, which may be tried at quarter sessions).

Perjury (though quarter sessions may try offences under section 5 of the Perjury Act, 1911, in relation to statutory declarations).[9]

Bigamy.

Offences against the Sexual Offences Act, 1956 (except brothel-keeping, which may be tried at quarter sessions).

Concealment of birth.

Libel.

[1] And see the Criminal Justice Administration Act, 1956, which established a Crown court in Liverpool and in Manchester, in substitution for the criminal assizes in each of these two cities, with various consequential changes.

[2] Technically, 'the courts of the sessions of the peace', quarterly *or other*. Those for London try one-fifth of all the persons indicted in England and Wales and are held twice a month. But the quarter sessions of the *City* of London, though sitting to hear appeals, try no jury cases. These, however trivial, go to the Central Criminal Court.

[3] The title 'justice of the peace' occurs as early as 1378; Rot. Parl.

[4] Within three weeks before, or after, quarter-day; Criminal Justice Act, 1925, s. 22. See ¶ 666 *post*.

[5] Administration of Justice (Misc. Provisions) Act, 1938, s. 3.

[6] Sect. 1 (2) (*f*). In the quarter sessions of counties the chairman is elected and need have no professional qualification. And see the Criminal Justice Administration (Amendment) Act, 1959.

[7] See the Quarter Sessions Act, 1842, the Criminal Justice Act, 1925, s. 18, and sch. I, and the Administration of Justice Act, 1938, s. 2, sch. I. Arch. 255–66.

[8] Larceny Act, 1916, s. 38.

[9] ¶ 467 *ante*.

Conspiracy (other than conspiracies to defraud or cheat or to commit an offence triable, when committed by one person, at quarter sessions).

Forgery (though quarter sessions may try offences relating to the obtaining of property of not more than £20 value).[1]

If, however, the court has a 'legally qualified chairman'[2] it can try some of the above offences[3] such as concealment of birth,[4] damage to machinery and goods in process of manufacture[5] and various perjuries[6] and forgeries.[7]

For indictable crimes not specifically excepted, courts of quarter sessions have a jurisdiction concurrent with that of the assizes.[8]

(*b*) As a court of appeal

¶ 664. All courts of quarter sessions have also an appellate[9] jurisdiction (extending to questions not only of law but even of fact) over convictions that have taken place at magistrates' courts. But its details can more conveniently be considered in connexion with the latter tribunals (see ¶ 687).

SECTION 6. THE CORONER'S COURT

¶ 665. The coroner's court, which has a history stretching back for seven hundred years,[10] is held as a court of record for inquests upon cases of homicide or sudden death. But its criminal function is only to accuse and not to try. The finding of a coroner's inquest, accusing a prisoner of murder or manslaughter or infanticide, is equivalent to an indictment[11] and the coroner has the same powers of committing for trial as might be exercised by examining justices if the accused was charged before them.[12] It is the practice however in such cases also to prefer a bill of indictment. Where a person is charged before examining justices with murder, manslaughter or infanticide, the coroner in the absence of reason to the contrary adjourns the inquest of the deceased person until after the conclusion of the criminal proceedings.[13] He may resume

[1] See Criminal Justice Act, 1925, sch. I.

[2] As defined by the Administration of Justice (Misc. Provisions) Act, 1938, s. 2.

[3] Specified in schedule I of the Act.

[4] Offences against the Person Act, 1861, s. 60.

[5] Malicious Damage Act, 1861, s. 14.

[6] Perjury Act, 1911, ss. 2–6. [7] Forgery Act, 1913, s. 2 (2) (*a*), s. 4, etc.

[8] Quarter sessions of counties and boroughs have in the past tried more prisoners than the assizes and the Central Criminal Court combined.

[9] The quarter sessions for the City of London, as we have seen (*ante*, ¶ 662 n. 2), sit only for this appellate work and for civil business.

[10] See Pollock and Maitland, I, 534; and the introduction to the Selden Society's *Select Coroners' Rolls*. [11] *Post*, ¶ 717.

[12] Coroners (Amendment) Act, 1926 (16 and 17 Geo. V, c. 59), s. 25; for examining justices see ¶ 701 *post*.

[13] The strict rules as to judicial evidence are habitually relaxed at coroners' inquests. For their proceedings are investigations rather than trials. The coroner 'is bound to collect, as far as he can, all information and knowledge from neighbours and others who can throw any light upon the cause of death' (Wills, J.). So hearsay evidence

the inquest if he is of opinion that there is cause to do so after the conclusion of the criminal proceedings.[1] But if a bill be signed the accused can be tried upon both the indictment and the inquisition together.

SECTION 7. MAGISTRATES' COURTS (PETTY SESSIONS[2])

¶ **666.** These constitute a noteworthy survival of the medieval idea of a popular justice (now generally superseded by the royal justice, which acts only as Magna Carta provides (s. 45) through professional experts '*qui sciunt leges regni*'). For they are composed of justices of the peace, men or women, not necessarily of legal experience, nominated to their office by the Lord Chancellor,[3] who acts on the advice of the Lord Lieutenant assisted by an advisory committee in the case of the county justices, and on the advice of separate advisory committees in the case of borough[4] justices. Their jurisdiction, powers and duties are now regulated by the Magistrates' Courts Act, 1952.

LAY MAGISTRATES

¶ **667.** By being held in every locality, and with great frequency, magistrates' courts effectively secure public order and tranquillity. By them mainly is the popular standard of justice educated. In the scale of dignity such sittings of justices of the peace are the lowest of our criminal courts; but the amount of work done by them is so vast that they play a far more important part in our penal system than some tribunals of much greater dignity. 'They have to deal with a wider range of subjects and a greater variety of cases than even a judge of the High Court.'[5] The vast majority—say, about two-thirds of a million

is freely taken; but the jury, before finding a verdict that accuses any person of *crime*, should disregard everything except strictly legal evidence; see Jervis on Coroners, 9th ed., 160. A departmental committee on coroners (1936, Cmd. 5070) recommended that the strict rules of evidence should be observed in cases involving criminality and that persons suspected of homicide should only be called at their own desire and should not be cross-examined. They further recommended that a coroner's inquest should be in no way concerned with civil liability.

[1] Coroners (Amendment) Act, 1926 (16 and 17 Geo. V, c. 59), s. 20. The committee on coroners (*supra*) recommended that coroners should no longer have power to commit for trial, and that an inquisition should not name any person as guilty of murder, manslaughter or infanticide.

[2] 'Petty sessions' is a relatively modern term, of somewhat uncertain origin and meaning. 'There is some difficulty', said Patteson, J., 'in saying what is a Petty Session' (*R.* v. *Rawlins* (1838) 8 C. and P. 440). The current definitions limited it to cases where *two or more* justices were present. Previous doubts as to the correct definition of these courts were settled by the Justices of the Peace Act, 1949 (12, 13 and 14 Geo. VI, c. 101), which adopted the name 'magistrates' courts'. The term 'magistrates' court' means a court of summary jurisdiction or of examining justices, and includes a single examining justice; s. 44 (1).

[3] See Justices of the Peace Act, 1949, ss. 1–9.

[4] For now the Crown may, on the petition of any borough, grant it a separate commission of the peace. But the persons appointed to act as justices under this are not thereby authorized to act in any quarter sessions.

[5] Troup's *Home Office*, 79.

annually—of our criminal cases are entirely disposed of by justices in their courts, and the remainder are usually commenced before them. There is an obvious advantage in the association of laymen with the administration of justice, and the State is a gainer from the services performed unpaid by lay magistrates. Moreover the majority of questions falling to be decided by these courts turn on points of fact not points of law and in handling such cases justices discharge their duties in the main with success.

¶ 668. *Their limitations.* It has been the view, however, of many people that it is an anomaly that persons without any legal training should be called upon to interpret Acts of Parliament and decide points of law,[1] and the Act of 1949 makes provision for improving the standard of the bench of magistrates, e.g. by the institution of courses of instruction (s. 17). Moreover they may not try any case which involves a decision of a question of title to land.[2] It has been suggested that more stipendiary magistrates[3] should be appointed to deal with major matters and cases involving difficult questions of law.

¶ 669. *Their functions not solely judicial.* In exercising some of their many functions the justices do not constitute a court of law (although they may have to sit in public, and to take evidence and act on it), e.g. in some of their licensing duties.[4] In others, although they constitute a court, it is not one of summary jurisdiction, e.g. when conducting a merely preliminary examination into some grave charge, which they will send to be tried by a jury.[5] And even when sitting as a court of summary jurisdiction to try a charge and adjudicate upon it finally, they do not always constitute a 'petty sessional court', as when sitting in a building which they only occasionally use.[6]

JUVENILE COURTS

¶ 670. By the Children and Young Persons Act, 1933,[7] a court of summary jurisdiction, when dealing with any case that concerns a person under seventeen, with no adult co-defendant, is called a 'juvenile court'. It must sit either in a different room, or else on a different day,

[1] For a statement of this point of view see a paper read to the Law Society by J. S. Walsh, reprinted in 180 *L.T. Jo.* atp. 239. It must be remembered, however, that the justices can rely upon their clerk for advice as to the law; and that the Justices of the Peace Act, 1949, provided that in future all justices' clerks will be either barristers or solicitors of at least five years' standing.

[2] *Ante,* ¶ 188; see Russ., app. 2.

[3] See ¶ 671 *post,* n. 5.

[4] See s. 12 of the Act of 1949. The decision in *Boulter* v. *Justices of Kent* [1897] A.C. at pp. 563, 573, narrows the wide definition of 'court of summary jurisdiction' given in the Interpretation Act, 1889. When sitting thus (i.e. not 'judicially' but 'administratively'), they may act on *un*sworn testimony or on their own knowledge.

[5] *Post,* ¶ 701.

[6] *Post,* ¶ 672. Yet they still are a 'petty *session*'.

[7] Sects. 45–49 (as amended by the Justices of the Peace Act, 1949, seventh schedule). Juvenile courts were first established by the Children Act, 1908.

from its ordinary one; and it must exclude all persons, except those directly concerned in the proceedings and the newspaper reporters. Juvenile courts consist of special panels of suitably qualified justices appointed by the justices of each (petty sessional) division from their own number. The juvenile court justices are required to appoint from amongst their number by secret ballot a chairman and so many deputy chairmen as will ensure that the court will always be presided over by a chairman so qualified.[1] In the metropolitan police area a juvenile court consists of a metropolitan magistrate specially nominated for the purpose, and two justices, one a woman, chosen from a panel of justices nominated by the Home Secretary. When an offence has been proved or the grounds of an application have been established, evidence with certain safeguards may be taken in writing, and the parent or guardian, or the child or young person, may be required to withdraw from the court.[2] The words 'conviction' and 'sentence' may not be used in relation to children or young persons dealt with summarily.[3]

[1] Juvenile Courts (Constitution) Rules, 1954.

[2] Summary Jurisdiction (Children and Young Persons) Rules, 1933.

[3] Sect. 59.

Chapter XXXI

SUMMARY PROCEDURE

Section I. Courts of Summary Jurisdiction

¶ 671. The summary jurisdiction of justices of the peace is the creation of statutes. Parliament has thus immeasurably extended the common law powers of justices, whilst at the same time reducing to a minimum[1] their legal responsibility; and the steady tendency of modern legislation is towards giving enhanced importance to these courts of summary jurisdiction. It is advisable, therefore, to consider their procedure somewhat fully.[2] It is regulated by the Magistrates' Courts Act, 1952,[3] and references in this chapter are to that Act unless otherwise stated.

This summary jurisdiction is not exclusively criminal, but extends also to a few civil cases. It may in some matters be exercised (though even in them only to a limited extent) by a single justice; but in most it is necessary to have either two ordinary justices[4] or a stipendiary magistrate or a metropolitan stipendiary magistrate.[5] It is subjected to a limitation of time; for the proceedings must be begun within the six months following 'the time when the offence was committed, or the matter of complaint arose'.[6] And for its exercise a prescribed place of meeting is now made essential, in order to secure ready access for the public. Two kinds of place are recognized.

PLACE OF MEETING

¶ 672. (1) The habitual place of meeting of the justices of the locality is their 'petty-sessional court-house'.[7] *Two* justices, by sitting here, constitute themselves a 'magistrates' court'; and such a court alone can

[1] Justices' Protection Act, 1848. But see *ante*, ¶ 188.

[2] For a review of the general effect on previous law of the Criminal Justice Act, 1948, see Jolly, 'Changes in criminal procedure', *Journal of Criminal Science*, II, 126.

[3] Which must be construed as one with the Magistrates' Courts Act, 1957.

[4] If several justices sit, the majority decide; the chairman has no casting vote. Accordingly if the votes be equal, the matter must either drop in order to be renewed before a different court, or else one justice must withdraw his vote—perhaps the junior, or one whose vote is opposed to that of the chairman.

[5] The metropolitan stipendiary magistrate was formerly known as 'metropolitan police magistrate'; Justices of the Peace Act, 1949, s. 44 (1). The latter two classes of magistrate must be barristers of several years' standing; each accordingly is empowered to exercise all the power that a full petty sessional court of two justices would possess. 'Stipendiaries' are appointed in some provincial towns; if one sits with other justices, he has only a single vote. But a 'metropolitan stipendiary magistrate'—there are many of these—is the sole judge, even though other justices be on the bench with him.

[6] Sect. 104. Save where *indictable* offences are tried summarily (*post*, ¶ 679), or where statute has otherwise provided (e.g. the Customs and Excise Act, 1952, sect. 283; the National Insurance Act, 1946, sect. 53 (3)). Cf. ¶ 640 *ante*.

[7] See sect. 98. As to 'juvenile courts', see ¶ 670 *ante*.

exercise the summary jurisdiction to the full. For a single justice, wherever sitting, can only hear certain classes[1] of case; and in them he can pass only a sentence of imprisonment of not more than fourteen days, or a fine (including costs) of not more than twenty shillings.[2]

(2) In counties, even the area of a single petty sessional division may be so wide as to make it convenient to provide in it subsidiary places of meeting for use in case of emergency. Such a place is called an 'occasional court-house'.[3] When sitting in it, even a bench of two or more justices can inflict no greater sentence than that which a single justice could, though they are not limited to his range of cases.[4]

INFORMATIONS

¶ 673. (*a*) In the normal case where both the prosecutor and the accused are present in court the hearing of any matter within the summary jurisdiction is commenced by stating to the defendant the substance of the information or complaint.[5] If he denies its truth, the case proceeds. Justices can compel the attendance of any witness in any case before them (alike in their summary jurisdiction, both civil and criminal, and also in their preliminary hearings of indictable offences), by issuing a summons to him to come,[6] or even, in case of need, a warrant to bring him. The prosecutor, or complainant, opens his case by a speech; and then calls his witnesses, who are examined in chief, cross-examined, and re-examined. The defendant may then similarly open his case, and his witnesses are similarly heard. The other party may then, if necessary,

[1] E.g. 'Found drunk' in a public place; vagrancy offences.

[2] Sect. 98 (5).

[3] Sect. 98 (3) (*b*).

[4] Sect. 98 (5).

[5] Students must be careful not to confuse these informal informations with the formal information which may be filed *ex officio* by the Attorney-General (¶ 658 *ante* and ¶ 716 *post*). The 'information' (or, similarly, the 'complaint') is at once the foundation of the justices' jurisdiction and the definition of the charge (*R.* v. *Hughes* (1879) 4 Q.B.D. 614); it is in the nature of an indictment. (The summons or warrant is, on the other hand, a mere process to secure the defendant's presence; its absence or its illegality does not affect the jurisdiction of the court, so long as he is in fact present before it to answer to the accusation.) But the charge so defined need not be adhered to with such strictness as an indictment is. For, as Lord Russell said, the hearing is not 'of', but only 'based on', the information. By section 100, the justices may disregard any small variance between the information (or complaint) and the evidence adduced in support of it, and give judgment against the defendant accordingly, unless he has been so far misled by the variance that it is right to adjourn the proceedings to enable him to meet the charge in the shape it has now assumed. But they are not authorized actually to 'amend' the summons or information or complaint (unless the defendant agrees; for the procedure then open to the court, see *Meek* v. *Powell* [1952] 1 All E.R. 347). This provision, however, only applies to variances in the mere circumstances of the charge, not to evidence which discloses some charge legally different from that alleged in the information or complaint, even though the difference be only that between being 'drunk and riotous' and being 'drunk', *Martin* v. *Pridgeon* (1859) 1 E. and E. 778. In *R.* v. *Southampton Justices, ex p. Tweedie* (1932) 48 T.L.R. 636, a conviction was quashed where justices convicted of careless driving where the charge was one of dangerous driving; but see now Road Traffic Act, 1960, s. 3 (2), or where the wrong Act is mentioned, *Meek* v. *Powell, ubi supra.* See also ¶ 443 *ante.*

[6] Or to produce documents or things; sect. 77.

call rebutting evidence.[1] The defendant or his solicitor or his counsel is entitled, at his discretion, to address the court either at the conclusion of the case for the prosecution or at the conclusion of the evidence for the defence; and, where oral evidence is given by witnesses for the defence in addition to the evidence of the defendant himself, the court may allow him, or his legal representative, to address the court both at the conclusion of the case for the prosecution and at the conclusion of the evidence for the defence, but in that event the prosecutor is entitled to the right of reply.[2] The decision of the justices is then given. If it be against the defendant, they have power, both in civil and in criminal cases, to adjudge him to pay to his opponent such costs as they shall think fit. If, on the other hand, they dismiss the case, they can similarly direct costs to be paid to the defendant, or by him, if the charge was proved (see ¶ 678). There is now[3] power, as in the case of indictable offences (see ¶ 683 *post*), to order the payment of the costs of the prosecution or defence out of public funds.

(*b*) But now, by virtue of section 1 (2) of the Act of 1957, the court may proceed to hear and dispose of a case in the absence of the accused[4] (and even in the absence of the prosecutor also) provided (i) that the offence charged is not indictable; and (ii) that the maximum term of imprisonment allowed to be imposed is three months; and (iii) that the prosecutor has in writing informed the accused both of the effect of the section and also of the facts, concisely stated, to be placed before the court in support of the charge; and (iv) that the accused has given written notice to the court that he desires to plead guilty to such charge. If, however, in the above situation, the prosecutor does elect to appear, then neither he nor anyone on his behalf may make to the court any statement as to the facts other than the aforementioned statement.[5] The main purpose of the above acceptance of a written plea of guilty is to save unnecessary expenditure of time by the court and by police witnesses attending in case they might be called to give evidence.

CIVIL JURISDICTION

¶ 674. The summary jurisdiction of magistrates' courts covers, as we have said, both civil and criminal cases.

[1] But see Stone, *Justice's Manual*, 1958, p. 2659 note (1), which suggests that the prosecution should only exercise this power where, during the defendant's case, some matter has arisen *ex improviso* (*post*, ¶ 751) which no human ingenuity could foresee.

[2] Criminal Justice Act, 1948, s. 42 (2). Contrast the rule where a preliminary examination is being held, see *post*, ¶ 703. The difference seems to be that in this latter case the accused himself cannot address the court, i.e. advance arguments, although he can make a statement as to facts.

[3] Criminal Justice Act, 1948, s. 44 (1).

[4] But if they do so they may not sentence the accused to any term of imprisonment or to any other form of detention or order him to be subject to any disqualification, save where the trial is resumed after an adjournment under sect. 14 (3) of the Act of 1952. The submission of the accused must be read out in open court before he may be convicted in his absence. *R.* v. *Oldham J.J. ex parte Morrissey* [1958] 3 All E.R. 559.

[5] Except on a resumption of the trial after an adjournment under sec. 14 (3) of the Act of 1952.

The civil jurisdiction is the less important. Amongst the matters coming within it are bastardy proceedings; disputes between employers and workmen; matrimonial separations; claims for district rates, or for contributions due under Public Health Acts from the owners of house property, for making streets or repairing sewers (contributions which are sometimes of large amount).[1] These civil proceedings are commenced by a 'complaint'. It can be, and in some cases[2] must be, made on oath, but need not be made in writing.[3] Only a summons can in the first instance be issued, though, should the defendant fail to appear in obedience to the summons, a warrant for his arrest may then be issued, if the complainant substantiates his claim upon oath.[4] As in all other civil proceedings, the defendant can be compelled to give evidence on oath. If the case be decided in favour of the plaintiff, there can only be made an order to pay money, which creates a mere 'civil debt'. Hence payment of it cannot be enforced by imprisonment, except in case of wilful non-payment[5] when the defendant has it in his power to pay; and even then it is only a civil and not a criminal imprisonment.

CRIMINAL JURISDICTION

¶ 675. But in criminal cases the summary jurisdiction covers some hundreds of offences; e.g. many forms of dishonesty or of malicious damage, acts of cruelty to animals, transgressions against the by-laws that secure order in streets and highways, numerous motoring offences, and violations of the laws relating to game, intoxicating liquors, adulteration of food, revenue, gambling, public health and education.[6]

POLICE CHARGES AND INFORMATIONS

¶ 676. A large number of offenders are brought before justices upon a charge preferred by the police or other prosecutor after an arrest under powers of arrest without warrant. But very many proceedings (amongst them nearly all motoring offences) commence with an 'information', laid before a justice of the county where the offence was committed,[7] which (unlike a 'complaint') is usually in writing,[8]

[1] E.g. £546 from one estate, *Corbett* v. *Badger* [1901] 2 K.B. 278.

[2] E.g. for an affiliation order made before, or twelve months after, the birth of the child.

[3] Sect. 43.

[4] Sect. 47.

[5] As to bastardy and maintenance orders see sects. 43 *et seq.*, and sect. 74 of the Magistrates' Courts Act, 1952.

[6] Occasionally a severe pecuniary penalty is possible; e.g. that for keeping a gaming-house may amount to £500 (17 and 18 Vict. c. 38, s. 4); and so may that upon a railway company which provides any special facilities for conveyance to a prize fight (31 and 32 Vict. c. 119, s. 21).

[7] A justice in whose district there resides or is a person suspected of having committed an offence punishable summarily may issue a warrant, as if the offence had been committed within his jurisdiction; but the warrant should direct that the offender be taken before a court having jurisdiction to deal with the offence. Where a joint trial of two offenders (whether charged with indictable or summary offences) is desirable, a justice within whose jurisdiction one of the offenders is in custody or is being tried may issue a warrant against the other offender; sect. 1.

[8] Magistrates' Courts Rules, 1952. You 'lay' an information, but 'make' a complaint.

and may (though it need not) be on oath. Any information or complaint is sufficient if it contains a statement of the specific offence with which the accused is charged together with such particulars as are necessary for giving reasonable information as to the nature of the charge. Technical terms are not required, and the offence is to be described in ordinary language. If it be on oath a warrant may, even in the first instance, be issued for the arrest of the defendant.[1] If it be not on oath, only a summons can be issued in the first instance;[2] though if the defendant fails to appear in answer to the summons, a warrant can then be issued.[3]

PUNISHMENTS

¶ 677. At the hearing, as the proceedings are criminal, the defendant cannot be compelled to give evidence, though since the Act of 1898 (*ante*, ¶ 621) he now can do so if he desires. If the hearing results in a conviction the sentence may impose imprisonment (which can only very rarely[4] exceed six months) or a fine;[5] and payment of the fine is enforceable by (criminal) imprisonment.[6] Imprisonment may not be for less than five days. In lieu thereof there may be ordered police custody for a period not exceeding four days or detention for one day in the precincts of the court.[7] Imprisonment for non-payment of a fine may not be ordered forthwith unless the court is satisfied that the person sentenced has means to pay, or unless upon being asked he expresses no desire for time to pay, or has no fixed abode, or unless for some special reason the court expressly directs that no time shall be allowed.[8] When time is allowed the court must not on that occasion impose a period of imprisonment in default of payment unless there are special circumstances, e.g. the gravity of the offence or the character of the defendant.[9] On a subsequent occasion imprisonment in default may be imposed but only after an inquiry as to the defendant's means made

[1] Sect. 1.

[2] For the comparative statistics see ¶ 701 *post*. In London police courts, it is the courteous practice that defendants who appear on a summons stand outside the 'dock', and only those who have been arrested have the humiliation of going inside it.

[3] By the common law anyone accused of crime must appear in person at the bar of the criminal court. But by statute, courts of summary jurisdiction, as the offences are trivial, may try an offender in his absence; see s. 15 of the Act of 1952 now somewhat restricted by the provisions of s. 1 (3) and s. 4 of the Act of 1957. Thus if a defendant who has been served with a summons does not appear at the appointed time, the justices may either issue a warrant to bring him up, or they may instead proceed to hear and determine the case without him.

[4] E.g. under the Prevention of Crimes Act, 1871, s. 12.

[5] Any court before which an offender is convicted on indictment of felony (not being one for which the sentence is fixed by law) has power to fine the offender in lieu of or in addition to dealing with him in any other manner in which the court has power to deal with him; Criminal Justice Act, 1948, s. 13.

[6] If the offender is not less than sixteen but under twenty-one he may be sent to quarter sessions where he may be sentenced to Borstal training; Criminal Justice Act, 1948, s. 20 (5). See ¶ 682 *post*.

[7] Sect. 109.

[8] Sect. 69 (1) and (2).

[9] Sect. 69 (3).

in his presence.[1] Instead of ordering imprisonment in default of payment the court may order one day's police custody.[2]

POWER TO DISCHARGE AND TO AWARD DAMAGES

¶ 678. The justices are invested in these criminal cases with a statutory power of showing mercy. For if, though the charge is proved, they think that having regard to the circumstances[3] it is inexpedient actually to punish, or to put the offender on probation,[4] they may discharge him, either absolutely or subject to the condition that he commits no offence during a period not exceeding twelve months from the date of his discharge.[5] But, in taking either course, they may, if they like, order the defendant to pay as damages to the prosecutor (or to such other person as may have suffered the damage) any sum up to £100[6] (cf. ¶ 75 (2) *ante*), and to pay costs.

SECTION 2. SUMMARY TRIAL OF INDICTABLE OFFENCES

THREE CLASSES OF OFFENDER

¶ 679. The summary criminal jurisdiction was originally concerned only with non-indictable offences; but it has since been extended to many cases of indictable ones. Thus, as already mentioned,[7] assaults (not so grave as to be of a felonious character[8]) may be thus tried, provided that the person assaulted be himself the prosecutor. And, by consent of the accused, charges of libel when brought against the publishers of a *newspaper*[9] may also be tried summarily. And even cases of felony may be thus tried.

Power has been given to magistrates' courts to deal summarily with three large classes of offender, whom previously they could only have committed for trial by a jury in a higher court.[10] In the case of adults and young persons the power is only to be exercised if the court thinks it expedient, having regard to any representation made by the prosecutor, the character and antecedents of the accused, the nature of the

[1] *Ibid.* [2] Sects. 110, 111.

[3] E.g. from the nature of the offence and the character of the offender.

[4] Criminal Justice Act, 1948, s. 7.

[5] *Ibid.* s. 7 (i). [6] *Ibid.* s. 11. As to costs see *R.* v. *Davis* [1962] 1 All E.R. 490.

[7] *Ante*, ¶ 168; also as to magisterial orders for matrimonial separation after an *aggravated* assault.

[8] Offences against the Person Act, 1861, ss. 39, etc. And when not charged as an 'affray', i.e. fighting in a public place, so as to cause general affright.

[9] Newspaper Libel Act, 1881, s. 5. But the libel must be only of a trivial character and the only punishment that can be inflicted is a fine (which must not exceed £50).

[10] Summary Jurisdiction Act, 1879; Magistrates' Courts Act, 1952. By s. 19 of the last mentioned Act a court which has begun to deal summarily with an offence which is punishable on conviction on indictment may, at any time before the conclusion of the case for the prosecution, discontinue the summary trial and proceed to hear the charge as for an indictable offence; but except as aforesaid the court cannot, after beginning to deal summarily with the offence, change and proceed to hear the charge as for an indictable offence.

offence and the absence of circumstances rendering the offence one of a grave or serious character. If at any time during the hearing of a charge against an adult or young person the court becomes satisfied that it is expedient to deal with the case summarily the consent of the accused must be obtained.[1] The charge must be reduced into writing and read to the accused who must then be asked: Do you desire to be tried by a jury, or do you consent to the case being dealt with summarily? If the court thinks it desirable, the meaning of summary trial should be explained and the accused should be informed of the assizes or quarter sessions at which he would be tried.[2] Where a case affects the property or affairs of Her Majesty or a public body, or where the prosecution is being carried on by the Director of Public Prosecutions, the consent of the prosecution is also necessary if the accused is an adult.[3] The three classes who may thus be dealt with are the following:

(*a*) Children under fourteen

¶ 680. Children can be tried summarily when charged with any indictable offence whatever, except homicide. But the punishment must not exceed one month in a remand home[4] or a fine of forty shillings. Children charged with offences other than homicide must be dealt with summarily, unless some person other than a child is charged jointly with a child and is committed for trial, in which case, if the interests of justice demand it, the child also may be committed for trial.[5]

(*b*) Young persons

¶ 681. Offenders aged from fourteen up to seventeen years of age,[6] when charged with any indictable offence whatever, except homicide, may be tried summarily. But a court of summary jurisdiction may not impose imprisonment on a person under seventeen years of age,[7] and may only fine him a maximum of £10.

(*c*) Adults

¶ 682. Those who have reached seventeen can be tried summarily but only when charged with certain particular offences (First Schedule), the chief ones being:

Simple larceny, thefts punishable like larceny, stealing from the person, stealing fixtures, stealing electricity, stealing by lodgers, stealing in a port or dock, stealing trees or shrubs in private grounds, stealing by a clerk or servant; embezzlement, obtaining by false pretences, ob-

[1] Such consent is usually given readily, in order to avoid the risk of imprisonment while awaiting trial, and of receiving a severer sentence than it is possible for the petty sessions to inflict. See ¶ 682 *post*. [2] Sect. 19 (3). [3] Sect. 19 (7).

[4] Children and Young Persons Act, 1933, s. 54.

[5] Sects. 21, 32.

[6] Sect. 20 (as modified by the Magistrates' Courts Act, 1952, sched. 5). See also, as to punishment of young persons, ¶¶ 758, 763 *post*.

[7] Sect. 20 (5). A court of assize or quarter sessions may not impose imprisonment on any person under fifteen years of age; s. 17 (2).

taining credit by fraud, receiving stolen goods, falsification of accounts; arson of crops, malicious damage (even when over £5); false statutory declarations; assaults occasioning actual bodily harm, inflicting grievous bodily harm, indecent assaults on persons under sixteen, attempts at suicide; aiding, abetting, counselling or procuring the commission of any offence which can be dealt with summarily, or attempting to commit any such offence.

But the punishment must not exceed six months'[1] imprisonment, or a fine of £100, or both.[2] And for merely inciting to commit an offence punishable summarily the maximum punishment must be no greater than for actually committing that offence.

Where a person not less than seventeen years of age is tried summarily for an indictable offence, and is convicted of that offence by a court of summary jurisdiction, then, if on obtaining information as to his character and antecedents the court is of opinion that they are such as to deserve a greater punishment than that which the court has power to inflict, the court may commit him in custody to quarter sessions for sentence.[3] But quarter sessions can only inflict such punishment as they could have inflicted if the offender had been tried and convicted by them.[4] Furthermore a court of summary jurisdiction has power,[5] after a person has been convicted, and before he has been sentenced or otherwise dealt with, to adjourn the case[6] to enable inquiries to be made or to determine the most suitable method of dealing with his case; these inquiries can extend to an investigation of his physical or mental condition.[7] And now the First Offenders Act, 1958, by sect. 1, in effect provides that a magistrates' court shall not pass sentence of imprisonment on a first offender of or over the age of twenty-one unless the court is of opinion that no other method of dealing with him is appropriate.[8]

Section 3. Trial by Jury of Non-indictable Offences

¶ 683. By a converse innovation, the Magistrates' Courts Act, 1952, repealing and replacing the Summary Jurisdiction Act, 1879, makes it possible for the graver of the non-indictable offences to be dealt with,

[1] But now no court may impose imprisonment on a person under twenty-one years of age unless the court is of opinion that no other method of dealing with him is appropriate; Criminal Justice Act, 1948, s. 17 (2).

[2] Sect. 19 (6).

[3] Sect. 29.

[4] And if the case is one which could not have been tried at quarter sessions (e.g. a charge under the Prevention of Corruption Act, 1906, s. 1), then that court cannot sentence the offender at all; *R.* v. *Middlesex Quarter Sessions and another, ex p. D.P.P.* [1950] 1 All E.R. 916; 34 Cr.App.R. 112. In this case it was declared that justices should not try summarily indictable offences of a grave nature merely because they have power to do so (even though the offenders can be sent to quarter sessions for sentence). Such serious cases should be sent for trial to quarter sessions or to the assizes.

[5] Sect. 14.

[6] Not for any single period longer than three weeks.

[7] Sect. 26.

[8] The Act also applies sect. 17 (2) of the Criminal Justice Act, 1948, to such cases to determine what punishment is appropriate, see *post*, ¶ 758.

instead, by indictment. For it enacts (s. 19) that (except in the case of children) any offence (except assault) for which, on summary conviction, a sentence of imprisonment for more than three months can be imposed shall be dealt with by indictment if at the hearing the defendant, in person and before he pleads to the charge, claims to be tried by a jury.[1] Accordingly when any person appears before justices upon a charge of any such offence, they must—before taking any evidence—inform him of his right to be tried by a jury.[2] Their consecutive sentences, for his two or more *indictable* offences, must not exceed in the aggregate twelve (for *non*-indictable, six) months.[3]

When dealing summarily with indictable offences the justices may now order the convicted defendant to pay the costs of the prosecution, or may order the costs of the prosecution or defence to be paid out of public funds.[4]

NO SUMMARY TRIAL IF A QUESTION OF REAL PROPERTY RIGHTS IS INVOLVED

¶ 684. An important restriction upon *all* exercise of summary jurisdiction by justices must be noticed. In consequence of the difficulties of the English law of land, they have immemorially been debarred from dealing with any question which involves the decision of a *bona fide* and legally possible claim to real property or to some right therein. Hence if a riotous crowd pull down the fences enclosing a private estate, which they reasonably, even though erroneously, believe to be common land, the justices cannot try them.[5]

SECTION 4. ADVANTAGES AND ANOMALIES OF SUMMARY JURISDICTION

¶ 685. An American observer has described the policy of enlarging the power of the courts of summary jurisdiction to hear and determine indictable offences as the most important development in the administration of English criminal justice during the last half century.[6] It has resulted undoubtedly in more expeditious trials and a material saving in expense. But many cases are dealt with summarily which, owing to their importance or difficulty, should be tried before a jury. Moreover, in order to bring cases within the jurisdiction of justices, there is a tendency to ignore the more serious elements and to deal with cases on a less serious basis, e.g. housebreaking is treated as larceny.[7] The police are more interested in conviction than punishment. The result of this tendency, in his view, is that the criminal jury is becoming obsolescent. High Court judges have indicated that the practice of dealing sum-

[1] Sect. 25. [2] Sect. 19. [3] Sect. 108.

[4] Costs in Criminal Cases Act, 1952, sections 5 and 6.

[5] On this subject see Russ. App. 2.

[6] *Criminal Justice in England*, by Pendleton Howard (New York, Macmillan Co., 1931), an invaluable description and criticism of English procedure.

[7] For a strong animadversion on this practice see *R.* v. *Bennett* (1928) 20 Cr.App.R. 188.

marily with indictable offences of a serious nature is becoming far too common.[1] The power should only be exercised when there is an absence of circumstances which lend to the offence a grave or serious character. The importance attached to these criticisms depends upon the value attached to trial by jury. As the same learned writer points out, the antiquity of an institution is no adequate proof of its utility. Trial by a judge or a legally qualified chairman, with a jury, probably leads to many guilty persons being acquitted, but undoubtedly provides a greater safeguard for an innocent defendant than trial before a bench of lay magistrates. There are, however, many anomalies in the present system which are pointed out by those who advocate the extension of summary jurisdiction. Thus a man who steals jewellery worth a hundred pounds from an open house may be tried summarily, while a man who opens a closed door and steals a packet of cigarettes may not. Similarly a man who steals a valuable motor car can be dealt with summarily, while a man who fails to account for £5 of his fellow-workmen's money entrusted to him to save must be tried at assizes or sessions.[2]

SECTION 5. APPEALS FROM MAGISTRATES' COURTS

(*a*) To the Queen's Bench Division

¶ 686. There are, as we have already seen (¶¶ 660, 662), two tribunals by which the summary proceedings of justices may be reviewed, the Queen's Bench Division and the Quarter Sessions.

The control of the Queen's Bench Division is exercised in two ways:

(i) It may issue an order[3] to bring up a conviction, and quash it, if necessary, for some defect of jurisdiction which vitiates it; e.g. if the justices have convicted on an 'information' that was not laid within the six months.[4]

(ii) It may determine any case which justices have themselves stated for its decision, as to any point of law that has been determined by them[5] (whether apparent on the face of the proceedings, or not); e.g. where they have overruled a defendant's objection that the evidence against him was not legally sufficient to support a conviction. They may state such a case at the instance of either party, unlike appeals from trials before jury, which can only be initiated (¶ 774 *post*) at the instance of the defendant.[6]

[1] Howard, *op. cit.*

[2] See a paper read to the Law Society by J. S. Walsh, reprinted in 180 *L.T.Jo.* at p. 239.

[3] Formerly by a writ of certiorari: see Administration of Justice Act, 1938, s. 11.

[4] *Ante*, ¶ 676. This division may also intervene to compel justices to perform duties devolving upon them; e.g. by issuing an order of mandamus, or rule, requiring them to issue a summons or to hear and determine a charge; see Administration of Justice Act, 1938, s. 8.

[5] Magistrates' Courts Act, 1952, part v, ss. 87–90. And see the Magistrates' Courts Rules, s. 1 (1952), no. 2190.

[6] Even when justices have refused to state a case, the Queen's Bench Division may order them to do so; sect. 87 (6).

(*b*) To quarter sessions

¶ 687. The appellate jurisdiction of quarter sessions is not, like that of the Queen's Bench, coextensive with the whole range of the summary jurisdiction of justices. It arose first in the case of particular offences to which it was expressly attached by the respective statutes that prohibited them. And for most of the non-indictable offences such an appeal came to be thus allowed to the defendant, and occasionally even to the prosecutor. But, now, the Magistrates' Courts Act, 1952, has made a general provision that any person aggrieved by any conviction of a court of summary jurisdiction for any offence[1] may appeal to quarter sessions against conviction or sentence (unless in the lower court he admitted his guilt, when he may only appeal against sentence). On the other hand, these appeals are not—like those to the Queen's Bench Division—limited to questions of law; for the quarter sessions hear the whole case again[2] (even new witnesses, who were not heard at the magistrates' court, being admissible).

SUMMARY JURISDICTION APPEALS

¶ 688. The number of appeals to quarter sessions from justices was very small. Considerations of expense had much to do with this and in 1933 there was passed the Summary Jurisdiction (Appeals) Act, 1933,[3] to amend the law relating to appeals from courts of summary jurisdiction. Under this Act the powers and duties of county quarter sessions[4] in respect of such appeals from courts of summary jurisdiction were delegated to a committee of the justices of the county to be known as the appeals committee.[5] The committee acts by a court consisting of not less than three, nor more than twelve members, who sit without a jury. The appeals committee is chosen as far as is practicable from justices having special qualifications for the hearing of appeals.[6] Appellants may no longer be compelled to enter into recognizances[7] to pay costs, but only to present their appeal with diligence, and in fixing the amount of recognizances, justices must have regard to the appellant's means.[8] Free legal aid may be given to appellants.[9] In awarding costs to be paid by any party to an appeal regard must be had to his means,[10] and where

[1] Sect. 83. But there is no similar *general* right of appeal from magistrates' courts in civil cases.

[2] Accordingly it is not here, as in appeals in higher courts, for the appellant to show that the decision of which he complains was wrong, but for the respondent to show that it was right. Hence, if the prosecutor does not appear, the quarter sessions will have to quash the conviction, *R.* v. *Surrey Justices* [1892] 2 Q.B. 719; unless the appeal is against sentence only, *R.* v. *Kent Justices* (1935) 52 T.L.R. 78.

[3] 23 and 24 Geo. V, c. 38.

[4] Other than the County of London, as to which see *ibid.* s. 8.

[5] *Ibid.* s. 7.

[6] Criminal Justice Act, 1948, s. 34. See the Magistrates' Courts Act, 1952, ss. 83–5 for rules as to the right of appeal, procedure on appeal and abandonment of appeal.

[7] See ¶ 770 *post.*

[8] *Ibid.* s. 1.

[9] *Ibid.* s. 2.

[10] *Ibid.* s. 5 (1).

an appeal is allowed there may be included in the costs to be paid to the appellant the costs properly incurred before the magistrates' court.[1] A case may be stated by the appeal committee for the decision of the Queen's Bench Division upon a point of law in the same way that justices in courts of summary jurisdiction may state a case.[2] The appeal committee may on an appeal award a punishment either greater or less than that awarded by the lower court.[3] The recorder, in a borough which has a separate court of quarter sessions, may hold a court for hearing appeals whenever he so decides.[4]

[1] *Ibid.*

[2] Criminal Justice Act, 1925, s. 20; and Magistrates' Courts Act, 1952, s. 87.

[3] Summary Jurisdiction (Appeals) Act, 1933. [4] *Ibid.* s. 7.

Chapter XXXII

ORDINARY PROCEDURE

I. PRELIMINARY STEPS

¶ 689. *Trial by jury. Ten possible stages.* From the modern and purely statutory form of procedure which prevails in courts of summary jurisdiction, we now pass to the more ancient form which prevails in those courts where offenders are tried in the common law manner, that is to say, by a jury. In this procedure—still styled 'ordinary', though now far rarer than the summary—there are ten possible stages which call for explanation. These are (1) information; (2) arrest; (3) commitment for trial; (4) prosecution, i.e. accusation; (5) arraignment; (6) plea and issue; (7) trial and verdict; (8) judgment; (9) reversal of judgment; (10) reprieve or pardon.[1]

¶ 690. *Early methods of detection and arrest.* During the greater portion of the history of English criminal law its provisions for the detection and arrest of offenders were very defective.[2] In the earliest times, indeed, excellent provision had been made by the system of frankpledge.[3] A frankpledge was a group of adult males—sometimes all those within a particular township, sometimes only a 'tithing' or group of ten, selected individually—who were liable to amercement if they did not surrender to justice any one of their number who committed a crime (each individual in the group is sometimes also called a 'frankpledge'). This institution apparently only existed south of the Humber; but probably arose there as far back as the Anglo-Saxon period. From at least the time of Henry I a 'view of frankpledge' was taken by the sheriff periodically, at which the above-mentioned amercements were collected. After the frankpledges fell into decay in the fourteenth century, England possessed no effective machinery for arresting criminals or for preventing the commission of crime, until the creation, by Sir Robert Peel's energy, of the modern police force. Even in London, as stated in the preamble to his Act,[4] 'the local establishments of nightly watch and nightly police have been found inadequate to the prevention and detection of crime, by reason of the frequent unfitness of the individuals employed, the insufficiency of their number, the limited sphere of their authority, and their want of connexion and co-operation with each other'. But since the successive establishment

[1] For a review of the changes in procedure made by the Criminal Justice Act, 1948, see Jolly, 'Changes in criminal procedure', *Journal of Criminal Science*, II, 126.

[2] 'In 1800, in no department of English government was inefficiency so pronounced as in that of police'; W. L. M. Lee's *History of Police*, 214. For a full study of the development of the police system see Radzinowicz, *History of English Criminal Law*, vols. II and III.

[3] Pollock and Maitland, I, 568.

[4] Metropolitan Police Act, 1829.

of metropolitan, borough, and county police forces, the detection of offenders has become extremely efficient. Rewards are no longer offered officially for information; they are now discredited as creative of false, and as impairing the weight of true, testimony.

SECTION 1. INFORMATION

¶ 691. Every justice of the peace[1] has by his commission the duty of 'conserving the peace' by taking active steps to exact securities from suspected persons, to suppress riots, and to apprehend offenders. These duties he still actively exercises (though the judges of the Queen's Bench Division, on whom they are also conferred, have long ceased to do so, regarding as more constitutional a differentiation of function which keeps the judicial office apart from all the strictly executive work of government).

Hence in ordinary procedure, just as in summary, the first step usually is to lay an 'information' before a justice of the peace.[2] It may be laid by *any* person[3] who is aware of the facts, whether or not he be the person aggrieved. The requirements for an information of an indictable offence are similar to those for an information of a summary offence (see ¶ 676 *ante*).

SECTION 2. ARREST

¶ 692. Where there is good ground for supposing—as, for instance, from the gravity of the charge—that a summons would not suffice to secure the attendance of an accused person, he should be arrested,[4] in order to bring him before a magistrate. On accusations of indictable offences, a warrant is sometimes obtained—only in about ten per cent of the arrests for such crimes—in order to authorize the arrest. But the cases in which arrest is legally permissible, without any such special authorization, are numerous (see ¶ 695 *post*). In the case of certain crimes, search warrants may be issued.[5] Apart too from specific crimes

[1] See Justices of the Peace Act, 1360 (34 Ed. III, c. 1); *ante*, ¶ 441.

[2] *Ante*, ¶ 676. The justice may belong either to the county where the offence was committed or to that where the offender is, Magistrates' Courts Act, 1952, s. 1 (2). Do not confuse such informations with the far rarer and more formal 'informations' (¶¶ 658, 716) by officials of the Crown, which were a substitute for indictments; these last were abolished (except those filed *ex officio* by the Attorney-General) by the Administration of Justice (Misc. Provisions) Act, 1938, s. 12. As to joint offenders see ¶ 676 n. 5 *ante*.

[3] Not confined to police officers. See *Lund* v. *Thompson* [1958] 3 W.L.R. 594, where the court stated emphatically the right of any member of the public to lay an information and to prosecute an offender. And there would seem to be, since *Sykes* v. *D.P.P.*, *ante*, ¶ 421, in certain circumstances, at least a *duty* to report an offence.

[4] See Pollock and Maitland, II, 582; Lieck, 99 *J.P.Jo.* 92.

[5] E.g. the receiving of stolen goods (for full list see Lieck, *Criminal Justice Act, 1925*, Appendix III). Where a judge of the High Court is satisfied by information on oath that there is reasonable ground for suspecting that an offence under the Incitement to Disaffection Act, 1934 (¶ 427 *ante*), has been committed, and that evidence of the commission thereof is likely to be found at any premises specified in the information, he may,

there is a general right to search arrested persons, and on arrest any property may be taken which is found in the possession of the arrested person and which would form material evidence on the prosecution of any criminal charge against *any* person. Articles or documents taken must be returned on the conclusion of the charge to which they were material.[1]

(*a*) BY WARRANT

¶ 693. Special authorization for arrest always takes in modern times the form of a written warrant.[2] This may be issued in cases of political crime by a Secretary of State or any other Privy Councillor, or, in any criminal case whatever, by a judge of the Queen's Bench Division or (as usually happens) by a justice of the peace. If issued by an ordinary justice of the peace, it formerly could only be executed within the district to which his commission extended, though it could be executed in any other district as soon as it had been 'backed'[3] by any justice commissioned there. But now by virtue of sect. 102 of the Magistrates' Courts Act, 1952, any warrant of arrest, commitment, distress, or search, can be executed anywhere in England and Wales by any person to whom it is addressed or by any constable acting within his police area.[4]

¶ 694. *The execution of a warrant.* Whenever, in such a manner, a warrant is executed outside the district of the justice who issued it, the accused is usually taken back to be examined in that district. But it is permissible, in the case of indictable offences, for him to be instead brought before some justice of the place of his arrest (Criminal Justice Act, 1925, s. 11). A warrant authorizes the person executing it to arrest the person therein described.[5] When executing the warrant, he (by the Criminal Justice Act, 1925, s. 44) need not now have it with him,[6] but

on the application of a police inspector, grant a warrant to search the premises, by force if necessary, and to seize anything found on the premises or on any person found therein which there is reasonable ground for suspecting to be evidence of the commission of such an offence; Incitement to Disaffection Act, 1934, s. 2.

[1] *Elias* v. *Pasmore* (1934) 50 T.L.R. 196. This case is criticized by E. C. S. Wade, 'Police search', 50 *L.Q.R.* 354. It is pointed out that there was previously no authority for seizing articles material to a charge against any person other than the person arrested, and that there is no authority for the search of premises not in the occupation of the person arrested. Professor Wade stresses the need for legislation and suggests that the police should be given power to remove documents for sorting in cases where seizure is sanctioned.

[2] In early times (Pollock and Maitland, II, 578) it was the duty of anyone who discovered that a grave crime had been committed to raise orally a 'hue and cry' (*hue* is an exclamation of pursuit, akin to *hoot*). This gave to all taking part in it the same powers of arrest as a written warrant nowadays would.

[3] This still applies to Scotland, the Isle of Man and the Channel Islands.

[4] And see Magistrates' Courts Rules, 1952, rule 74 (2).

[5] Magistrates' Courts Act, 1952, s. 1.

[6] This section does not justify arrest under an invalid warrant, *Horsfield* v. *Brown* [1932] 1 K.B. 355.

it must, if demanded, be shown to the person arrested as soon as is practicable. Since the charge is not a civil but a criminal one, he is allowed to break open even the outer doors of a house if he cannot otherwise seize the person who is to be arrested (e.g. if those in the house will not give him up). If the charge be one of treason, violent felony, or dangerous wounding, he may, moreover, use any degree of force that may be necessary to effect the arrest, or prevent the escape,[1] of the accused; even to the infliction of wounds or death upon him. If, on the other hand, the accused, knowing the authority or intent of the arrester, should kill the arrester he may be guilty of murder even if innocent of the charge. But if a constable attempts to arrest offenders illegally (e.g. on a void warrant) they may be guilty only of manslaughter if, in resisting such an arrest, they kill the constable.[1]

(*b*) WITHOUT WARRANT: (i) By a private person

¶ 695. *At common law.* Even when no warrant has been issued, the common law often permits an arrest to be effected, a permission accorded not only to a constable but even to private persons.[2]

Firstly, at common law a private person, without any warrant, may arrest any person who, *in his presence*, commits a treason or felony or dangerous wounding. The law does not merely permit, but requires, the citizen to do his best to arrest such a criminal.[3] And as he is thus acting not only by a right but under an imperative duty, he may break outer doors in pursuit of the criminal. And for a treason or a violent felony he may use whatever force is necessary for capturing the offender, as, for instance, shooting at him, if he cannot otherwise be prevented from escaping; so that if the felon's death results, the case will be one of justifiable homicide. Besides this power to arrest, with a view to permanent detention, a person who has actually committed a grave crime, every private citizen has also the right to prevent such crimes, by seizing any man who is *about* to commit a treason or felony or even a breach of the peace, and detaining him *temporarily*, until the danger is over.[4] Strangely enough what constitutes a 'breach of the peace' has not been authoritatively laid down. But, as it seems to mean a 'breach of the Queen's peace', it should include every crime. It has been held in Scotland that a person who peered into lighted windows after nightfall had properly been found guilty of a breach of the peace.[5]

[1] The old cases frequently cited in this connexion should now be read with caution, since the law of felonious homicide is nowadays not the same as it was in the time of Hale and of Foster. See *ante*, ¶¶ 96 and 99, and Russ. 504 *et seq*.

[2] See Williams, 'Arrest for felony at common law' [1954] *Crim.L.R.* 408. The power has been further extended by modern statutes, especially in the case of constables.

[3] 2 Hawk. P.C. c. 12, s. 1.

[4] *Timothy* v. *Simpson* (1835) 1 C.M. and R. 757. See Williams, 'Arrest for breach of the peace' [1954] *Crim.L.R.* 578. To prevent the commission of a felony doors may be broken open, *Handcock* v. *Baker* (1800) 2 Bos. and P. 260.

[5] *Raffaelli* v. *Heatly* (1949) S.L.T. 284, in the High Court of Justiciary. For the offence of 'eavesdropping', see Russ., 11th ed., ch. 92; *R.* v. *County of London Quarter Sess. A.C.* [1948] 1 K.B. 670. See also 231 *L.T.* 115.

Secondly, at common law a private person may arrest without warrant any person whom he reasonably suspects of having[1] committed a treason or felony or dangerous wounding, provided[2] that this very crime[3] has been actually committed by someone (whether by the arrested person or not). But in this case, as also in all the statutory ones about to be mentioned, the law, though permitting a private person to make an arrest (and so making it a felonious homicide for a guilty man to kill him by resisting it), does not command him to do so, and hence confers no *general* right to effect it by breaking into a house or by using blows or other violence.[4]

¶ 696. *Statutory powers of arrest.* In addition to these two common law powers, modern statutes permit any private person to arrest anyone whom he 'finds'[5] signalling to a smuggling vessel;[6] or committing any offence under the Vagrancy Act,[7] the Larceny Act, 1916,[8] or the Coinage Offences Act, 1936; or committing *by night* any indictable offence whatever;[9] or, if the arrest be authorized by the owner of the property concerned, anyone whom he finds committing any offence against the Malicious Damage Act, 1861, the Night Poaching Act, 1828,[10] the Town Police Clauses Act, 1847, or the Metropolitan Police Act, 1839.

(ii) By a police constable

¶ 697. A police constable, even when acting without a warrant, has powers still more extensive than those of a private person. Moreover, as his official position renders it in all these cases a duty[11] for him to make the arrest, it will, in any of them, be a duty, even for an innocent person, to submit to him and not resist arrest.[12] He is entitled to call for the assistance of any able-bodied bystander if necessary, *R.* v. *Brown* (1841),[13]

[1] A felony *unknown* to him will not justify arrest; *R.* v. *Dadson* (1850) 3 C. and K. 149.

[2] This proviso is mentioned as early as Y.B. 9 Edw. IV, fo. 26*b*. But note Larceny Act, 1916, s. 41 (2).

[3] See an interesting case, *Walters* v. *Smith* [1914] 1 K.B. 595. Though the mistake does not justify the arrest, it may defeat any action for malicious prosecution.

[4] I.e. the private person will be justified in arresting the suspected felon, even by fatal violence, if the suspicion be correct; but an *innocent* man is not bound to submit to a private arrester, so a killing, by either of them, would be a manslaughter.

[5] Accordingly, if the offender has completed the offence, even though he has gone 'but a single yard' away before detection or even before apprehension, it is too late to arrest him. But see *ante*, p. 563 n. 1.

[6] Customs and Excise Act, 1952, s. 71 (1).

[7] *Ante*, ¶ 483.

[8] Sect. 41 (1) (except extortion by libelling). Or anyone offering stolen goods for sale or pawn; s. 41 (2).

[9] 14 and 15 Vict. c. 19, s. 11.

[10] Where the offender is found on the land.

[11] See *Gelberg* v. *Miller* [1961] 1 W.L.R. 153, applying the Prevention of Crimes Amendment Act, 1885, s. 3, and the Metropolitan Police Act, 1839, s. 54 (6). But for him to assist a householder in ejecting an intruder, though a kindly act, is no part of his duty; for a mere trespass is no crime. Hence if the intruder resist him, it will be only a common assault, not an assault 'on a constable in the execution of his duty'.

[12] But as to *needless* handcuffing, see *Wright* v. *Court* (1825) 3 D. and R. (M.C.) 299, *ante*, ¶ 152.

[13] C. and M. 314.

and it is an offence at common law for a person so called upon to refuse to assist when reasonably able to do so. It is doubtful whether in the case of all crimes for which arrest without warrant is permissible a police officer may enter premises in search of material evidence.[1] In *Thomas* v. *Sawkins* (1935), it was held that a police officer may enter private premises to prevent a breach of the peace, and *per* Lord Hewart, C.J., to prevent the commission of any offence that he believes to be imminent or likely to be committed.[2]

¶ 698. *Constable's wide powers of arrest at common law.* Like a private person he may arrest anyone who commits, in his presence, a treason, or felony, or dangerous wounding, and may break doors or use fatal violence if necessary.[3]

Unlike a private person[4] he probably may arrest, for *permanent* detention, anyone who, in his presence, commits even a mere breach of the peace.[5]

He may arrest anyone whom he reasonably suspects[6] of treason, or felony, or dangerous wounding, whether (unlike the restriction on such arrest by a private person) the crime has *actually* taken place or not;[7] e.g. because he finds a man hurrying away and carrying house-breaking tools. It would seem that in these arrests also he may use any *necessary* violence even though fatal,[8] and may break outer doors; but some authorities limit these powers to cases where the crime has actually taken place.[9]

¶ 699. *Statutory extensions.* Like a private person, he may arrest in the first five cases set out in ¶ 696; and, even *without* any authorization

[1] See 'Police search', E. C. S. Wade, 50 *L.Q.R.* 351, and *Shepherd* v. *Menzies* (1903) 37 S.L.R. 355.

[2] 51 T.L.R. 514. For a strong criticism of this case see A. L. Goodhart, '*Thomas* v. *Sawkins*: a constitutional innovation', (1936) 6 *Cambridge L.J.* 22.

[3] And (nowadays) reasonable in the circumstances of the particular case.

[4] *Ante*, ¶ 695.

[5] 1 Hale P.C. 587; 2 Hale P.C. 90. But see 1 East P.C. c. 5, s. 71; as to 'breach of the peace' see *ante*, ¶ 695.

[6] *McArdle* v. *Egan* (1933) 150 L.T. 412. Probably the fact that a man has been guilty of previous offences of a similar kind may be given some, though not decisive, weight.

[7] *Lawrence* v. *Hedger* (1810) 3 Taunton 14; *Beckwith* v. *Philby* (1827) 6 B. and C. 635. These cases show that the constable's privilege, where the supposed crime has not in fact taken place, extends to cases where he acts merely on his own suspicion, without any third person's having made the charge. As to its being murder for the supposed felon to kill the constable, even where no felony has actually taken place, see *R.* v. *Woolmer* (1832) 1 Moo. 334.

[8] This power to use violence in arresting felons extends also to the preventing of their escape. Hence convicted prisoners who are felons can be employed, under armed supervision, over a wide range of land (as at Dartmoor) in out-door labour, a coveted advantage not so open to misdemeanants, since the risk of their successful flight would be great. See ¶ 694 *ante*.

[9] See the Children and Young Persons Act, 1933, s. 13, for a constable's power to arrest persons reasonably suspected of certain offences against persons *under seventeen*.

of the owner of the property, in the last four[1] cases enumerated there.

He may arrest any person loitering at night in a highway or yard, whom he reasonably suspects of having committed, or even of being about to commit, a felony against the Larceny Act, 1916, the Malicious Damage Act, 1861, or the Offences against the Person Act, 1861.[2]

In *London*[3] a constable may also arrest any person reasonably suspected of having committed, or even of being about to commit, *any* indictable offence, and even anyone loitering at night who cannot give a satisfactory account of himself.[4] It seems doubtful if a constable, without warrant, has power to arrest a person who (without committing any assault or other specific crime) is obstructing him in the exercise of his duty, save in London.[5]

As a person who arrests another without waiting to obtain a warrant usually does so because he must act instantly, if he is to act at all, the law on the subject ought to be clear and simple. But, as the foregoing summary sufficiently shows, modern legislation has rendered it highly complicated, and (in the words of a very learned writer) 'most unsatisfactory and—to private persons—almost a snare'.[6]

¶ 700. *Arrested persons should be informed of the charge.* An arrest without warrant, either by a police officer, or by a private person, can be justified only if it is an arrest on a charge which is made known to the person arrested (unless the circumstances are such that he must know the substance of the alleged offence). A citizen is entitled to know on what charge or on suspicion of what crime he is seized. If the citizen is not so informed, but is nevertheless seized, the police officer (or private person), apart from certain exceptions, is liable for false imprisonment. However, the person arrested cannot complain that he has not been informed as above if he himself makes it practically impossible to inform him, e.g. by immediate counter-attack, or by running away.[7]

¶ 700 *a*. *Power to demand name and address.* There are many offences for which the law does not allow the offender to be arrested on the spot, and if a stranger is found committing one of these it must often happen that he can never be brought to book unless there is some power to compel him to give his name and address. Power of this kind is given

[1] There is a doubt as to s. 2 of the Night Poaching Act, 1828 (when no assault upon the arrester is committed), since a police officer is not included among the persons specified. But he may arrest an offender against s. 9 since that offence is indictable and covered by s. 11 of the Prevention of Offences Act, 1851.

[2] Sects. 41 (3), 57, and 66 of these Acts.

[3] Metropolitan Police Act, 1839, s. 64.

[4] This does not exhaust the list; see *Isaacs* v. *Keech* [1925] 2 K.B. 354.

[5] Under the Metropolitan Police Act, 1839; see *Gelberg* v. *Miller*, *ubi supra*.

[6] Mr C. S. Greaves, Q.C., *Criminal Law Consolidation Acts* (p. 188).

[7] *Christie* v. *Leachinsky* [1947] A.C. 573; 1 All E.R. 567.

by certain statutes but in many instances in terms so badly chosen that the provision is ineffective. The law of this matter is so confused and unsatisfactory that it cannot be discussed in a book of this size, but some general enactment to improve the position is urgently needed.[1]

SECTION 3. COMMITMENT FOR TRIAL[2]

¶ 701. Of the persons who appear before justices of the peace, for preliminary examination upon charges of indictable crime, about thirty per cent come in obedience to a summons.[3] The others are brought up in custody, about ten per cent under warrants, and about ninety per cent after being arrested without a warrant.[4]

As the summons or warrant is merely a process to secure appearance, the justice must take cognizance of *any* information laid against the defendant when before him (even upon an illegal arrest), and may commit him for trial thereon.[5]

A preliminary examination (unlike most of the summary hearings) never requires the presence of more than a single justice.[6] There is full power of compelling the attendance of witnesses,[7] either by summons or (if necessary) by warrant; and if, on appearing, they refuse to give evidence, the justice may commit them to prison for a week or until earlier submission. At common law the accused could not, as a right, demand the assistance of an advocate, nor could the public insist upon admission. And it would seem[8] that this rule still holds good. The practice, followed in some rare cases, of communicating only in writing the names and addresses of particular witnesses, and of forbidding the accused to put any questions about them openly is justifiable only in this view of the proceedings as not being necessarily public.

It must be noted that at these preliminary inquiries the presence of the accused is absolutely essential.[9]

[1] See Glanville Williams, 'Power to demand name and address', 66 *L.Q.R.* 465.

[2] See ss. 12, 13, 14 of the Criminal Justice Act, 1925, as amended by the Magistrates' Courts Act, 1952, part I.

[3] But of persons tried for non-indictable offences, nearly eighty per cent appear on summons, about twenty per cent on arrest without warrant, and only two per cent under warrants.

[4] A person arrested without a warrant may be—and, if it is impracticable to bring him before a justice within twenty-four hours, *must* be—released on bail by the officer in charge of the police station, unless he thinks the offence serious; Magistrates' Courts Act, 1952, s. 38.

[5] *R.* v. *Hughes* (1879) 4 Q.B.D. 614.

[6] And even if there be two or more they are not a 'petty sessional court', since *it* sits only for summary jurisdiction. The six months' limit (¶ 640) does not apply to these examinations.

[7] And production of documents etc. But until an actual prosecution has begun, a justice has no power to summon anyone to come and afford information. The police have to pursue their inquiries as best they can.

[8] *Boulter* v. *Justices of Kent* [1897] A.C. 556. And see now Magistrates' Courts Act, 1952, s. 4 (2), s. 98 (4).

[9] Sect. 4 (3). Contrast the power given to justices in their summary proceedings to try a defendant in his absence for petty offences, if he fails to appear when summoned; *ante*, p. 552 n. 3.

PRELIMINARY EXAMINATION. PROSECUTOR'S CASE

¶ 702. The preliminary examination is conducted as follows. The prosecutor 'opens his case' by any necessary explanation. Then his witnesses are examined in chief, cross-examined and re-examined, their evidence being taken down in writing at the time by the clerk to the justices. The Crown witnesses having been heard, and their evidence summed up[1] by the prosecutor (if he wishes), the examining justice (or his clerk for him) then reads the charge to the accused,[2] explaining its nature in ordinary language. The magistrate next asks him if he has anything to say, telling him that he need not say anything unless he likes, that he has nothing to hope or fear from any promise or threat, and that whatever he says will be taken down and may be used at his trial.[3] The defendant may either remain silent (a frequent but generally unwise course for an *innocent* man) or make a statement, or leave it for his advocate to make one.[4] After this the magistrate asks the accused whether he wishes to be sworn and give evidence, and whether he wishes to call witnesses.

CASE FOR THE DEFENCE

¶ 703. If he does so wish the justices must proceed to take such evidence, and if he is represented by counsel or a solicitor this advocate must be heard on his behalf either before or after (at his discretion) such evidence is given; and if the accused himself gives evidence and calls witnesses his advocate may (with leave of the justices) be heard on his behalf both before and after such evidence is taken. But when his advocate is so heard both before and after the evidence is taken then counsel or the solicitor for the prosecution is entitled to be heard in reply.[5]

Hostile comments should not be made by the trial judge on a prisoner's failure to disclose his defence at the preliminary examination,[6] unless such comment is necessary in the interest of other defendants.[7]

[1] Oke's *Magisterial Synopsis*, 887 (contrast ¶ 673 *ante*). Any adjournment of the proceedings must be for not more than eight clear days, unless both prosecutor and accused consent to a longer one; and in some other special circumstances; see sect. 105 (4).

[2] The accused should be warned not to plead *at this stage*, and he should *not be asked* whether he intends to plead guilty at his trial: see *post*, ¶ 713.

[3] The old final words 'against you' are omitted. But it is only *against* him that this statement is evidence; so it is for the Crown to determine whether or not to put it in at the trial. But it is prudent to put it in, for it may become important to the Crown as contradicting evidence given subsequently for the prisoner; and it is also kind, since to make the prisoner put it in would give the Crown the final speech. What the prisoner said before the magistrates is not evidence unless the prosecutor make it so.

[4] The defendant himself may not *address* (i.e. advance arguments to) the court at all, but only make a statement as to facts, and if he does so that statement is, as he was warned, taken down and may be used at his trial.

[5] Criminal Justice Act, 1948, sched. 9, amending s. 12 (5) of the Criminal Justice Act, 1925; *ante*, ¶ 673.

[6] *R.* v. *Naylor* [1932] 1 K.B. 685; *R.* v. *Davis* (1959) 43 Cr.App.R. 215.

[7] *R.* v. *Parker* [1933] 1 K.B. 850.

The defence of an alibi is, of course, of little value unless disclosed in sufficient time for it to be tested[1] and at one time it was thought that there was no objection to a judge's pointing this out in summing up.[2] If the defendant make a statement it is taken down in writing and afterwards read over to him and signed by one of the examining justices. The prisoner's witnesses,[3] if any, are examined, cross-examined, and re-examined, and their evidence is taken down in writing.[4] The 'deposition' of each witness, on either side, is read over to the witness himself, and to the accused, at the end of *his* examination; and it is signed by him and by the justice.[5] Subject to what has been said above even if the accused call witnesses the prosecutor's advocate has no second speech. The prisoner's advocate speaks after the prisoner's own evidence (if he gives any) in the case where he does not call any witnesses.

DECISION OF THE JUSTICE

¶ 704. The examining justice (or, if there be more than one, the majority) must then determine whether or not there is a strong enough case[6] to justify committing the accused for trial,[7] and if so, where that trial is to be. If the offence is one which quarter sessions are competent to try,[8] the case must be sent thither, unless there are special reasons for preferring a trial at the assizes.[9] All the proceedings in the magistrates' court must be strictly regular.[10]

VENUE

¶ 705. At common law an offence could only be tried by the court within whose jurisdiction it (or a part of it) was committed, but by section 11 of the Criminal Justice Act, 1925, as modified by the Magistrates' Courts Act, 1952, s. 2 (4), it is provided that a person charged

[1] *R.* v. *Brown and Bruce* (1931) 23 Cr.App.R. 56.

[2] *R.* v. *Littleboy* [1934] 2 K.B. 408. But *R.* v. *Littleboy* was unfair to the accused and would seem in effect to be overruled by *R.* v. *Leckey* [1944] 1 K.B. 80. See 60 *L.Q.R.* 130 criticizing a previous note, *ibid.* p. 33. For a criticism see 179 *L.T.Jo.* 212. He has not to *prove* his alibi, *R. v. Johnson* [1961] 3 All E.R. 969.

[3] Sect. 4 (3).

[4] It must not be taken down in advance, *R.* v. *Gee and others* [1936] 2 K.B. 442; 2 All E.R. 89.

[5] It should be noted that depositions *may* be taken by leading questions although it is declared undesirable to do so; *R.* v. *Walker* [1950] 2 All E.R. 911 (¶ 537 *ante*).

[6] See ¶ 711 *post.*

[7] If they refuse to commit for trial, this does not bar a subsequent accusation before some other justice. Should they think the charge not merely groundless but malicious, sect. 55 empowers them to make the prosecutor pay costs, *R.* v. *Essex Justices, ex p. Churchill* (1933) 49 T.L.R. 283.

[8] *Ante*, ¶ 662.

[9] Assizes Relief Act, 1889 (52 and 53 Vict. c. 12). Under s. 10 of the Magistrates' Courts Act, 1952, this power to send the case to the assizes is not to be exercised unless the justices are satisfied that there are circumstances which make the case an unusually grave or difficult one, or that serious delay or inconvenience would be occasioned by committal to quarter sessions.

[10] *R.* v. *Gee and others* [1936] 2 K.B. 442; *R.* v. *Phillips and Quayle* [1939] 1 K.B. 63; *R.* v. *Grant and others* [1944] 2 All E.R. 311.

with any indictable offence may be proceeded against, indicted, tried and punished in any place in which he was apprehended, or is in custody, or has appeared to a summons, on that same charge, just as if the offence had been committed there; unless it appears to the examining justices that the accused would suffer hardship if he were indicted and tried in such place.[1] If the accused raises the issue of hardship, he may appeal to the High Court against the justices' decision on this point. Where an accused is charged with more than one indictable offence all may be dealt with where any one of them could be dealt with.[2] By virtue of sections 9 and 10 of the Magistrates' Courts Act, 1952, instead of being committed to the assizes or quarter sessions of the locality where he would normally be committed (i.e. where the offence was committed or, under sections 1 and 2 of the Act, where the accused was apprehended or charged), an accused person may be committed to the assizes or sessions of some other place if, having regard to the date and place of such other sessions, it appears more convenient to commit to them either to expedite trial or save expense. This power is not to be exercised unless it appears to the examining justices to be unlikely that the next[3] assizes, or quarter sessions,[4] as the case may be, will be held within one month from the date of the committal; nor is it to be exercised in any case in which the accused satisfies the justices that he would, if the power were exercised, suffer hardship.[5] Where any person who is to be committed for trial to a particular sessions is to be admitted to bail, he may, if the next date of such sessions falls within five days, be committed to the next sessions but one provided that such next sessions but one are to be held within eight weeks of the date of committal.[6]

RELEASE ON BAIL

¶ 706. Again, if the accused ask to be released on bail[7] the court must determine whether this is to be allowed, and, if it be, on what terms. In cases of treason, however, bail cannot be granted by a justice, but only by a Secretary of State or a judge of the Queen's Bench Division. But in cases of felony the matter is in the justice's discretion.[8] In

[1] And see Criminal Justice Act, 1948, s. 31 (2).

[2] Criminal Justice Act, 1925, s. 11 (1), in conjunction with s. 1 (2) (*b*) of the Magistrates' Courts Act, 1952; see *R.* v. *Blandford and Freestone* [1955] 1 All E.R. 681.

[3] 'Next' means 'next after the date of committal' and the term does not include assizes or sessions already begun at the time of committa ; *R.* v. *Murray* (1935) 52 T.L.T. 141.

[4] If the offence is within the jurisdiction of quarter sessions, see ¶ 662 *ante*.

[5] There is no appeal to the High Court as under s. 11 of the Criminal Justice Act, 1925, *supra*.

[6] Sect. 10 (2).

[7] This word means properly (1) the contract whereby the man is 'bailed' (i.e. delivered) to his surety, but is also applied to (2) that surety himself. Even nowadays the surety, if he should desire to discharge himself, is allowed to arrest the defendant (and even to break into his house for the purpose) that he may give him back again into the custody of the court by which he was bailed.

[8] As to the matters which ought to be taken into consideration for the exercise of the discretion see *R.* v. *Phillips* (1947) 32 Cr.App.R. 47; 111 J.P. 333.

misdemeanours he had not, at common law, even a discretion (when once the preliminary examination was over) but was bound[1] to release the accused on his finding adequate bail.[2] But now, as the result of statutory changes,[3] the discretion seems to be equally universal.[4]

RELEASE BEFORE EXAMINATION

¶ 707. In certain circumstances persons may be released on bail from custody by the police before the case is examined. Thus if a person is arrested without a warrant the Act of 1952[5] authorizes (and *requires*, where the prisoner cannot be brought before the court within twenty-four hours after his arrest) the officer in charge of any police station to discharge him upon his entering into a recognizance, with or without sureties, to appear before the court; moreover, under the Act,[6] if the police investigation cannot be completed forthwith the police officer may discharge the prisoner under the like conditions requiring him to appear at the police station at a stated date. In the case of offences against children and young persons which are included in the first schedule of the Act of 1933[7] bail must be granted to any person arrested without warrant unless to do so would tend to defeat the ends of justice or expose to injury or danger the victim of the alleged offence. And under section 32 of the same Act where a person apparently under the age of seventeen is arrested the police officer in charge, after inquiring into the case, has a like power and duty to release him on bail.[8]

AMOUNT OF BAIL

¶ 708. The Bill of Rights forbids the requiring of 'excessive' bail; but justices must use their own judgment as to what sum is adequate without being excessive.[9] Here, as also in exercising their discretion about admitting to bail at all, they have simply to consider what likelihood there is of the defendant's failing to appear for trial.[10] That likelihood

[1] The current but anomalous view that the judges of the Queen's Bench Division are *still* so bound was negatived in *R.* v. *Phillips* (1922) 38 T.L.R. 897.

[2] *Ante*, ¶ 76.

[3] E.g. Indictable Offences Act, 1848 (rep.), Costs in Criminal Cases Act, 1908 (rep.).

[4] By Criminal Justice Administration Act, 1914, s. 23 (rep.), justices who did not grant bail to a misdemeanant after committal had to tell him of his right to apply to the Queen's Bench Division for it. Until committal the justices have discretion. The Criminal Justice Act, 1948, s. 37 (1) (*a*) gives power to the High Court to grant bail to a person committed to quarter sessions for sentence; *Re Whitehouse* [1951] 1 All E.R. 353.

[5] Sect 38 (1).

[6] Sect. 38 (2).

[7] Children and Young Persons Act, 1933, s. 13 (2).

[8] If not he must be detained in a remand home (if possible) until the hearing.

[9] *Ex p. Thomas* [1956] Crim.L.R. 119. Bail is not usually allowed on charges of murder save where the facts point to a verdict of justifiable homicide. It has been declared undesirable to grant bail in cases of housebreaking where there is likelihood of a repetition of the offence, *R.* v. *Phillips* (1947) 32 Cr.App.R. 47; or to a person with a long criminal record, Practice Note [1949] W.N. 123; *R.* v. *Wharton* [1955] Crim.L.R. 565.

[10] *R.* v. *Rose* (1898) 18 Cox 717; *R.* v. *Phillips*, n. 9 *supra*. The importance of release on bail was great even as late as the seventeenth century. There was no provision of adequate food for prisoners awaiting trial. Hence, 19 Car. II, c. 4 recites that 'they many times perish before their trial'.

will be affected by (1) the gravity of the charge, (2) the cogency of the evidence, (3) the wealth of the offender (which renders him both more willing to bear the forfeiture of bail and less willing to bear the disgrace of a conviction), (4) the consideration whether the proposed sureties are independent or are likely to have been indemnified by the accused,[1] and (5) the probability of the accused's tampering with the Crown witnesses, if he be at large.[2] But experience shows that, on the whole, very few persons admitted to bail fail to appear for trial. Hence in modern times the judges have urged[3] magistrates to grant bail very readily, and (especially if the offence is a small one and the day of trial is distant) to accept the recognizances of the accused himself, even without any sureties, unless they see grave reason to think that he will not appear for trial if left at large.[4]

DEPOSITIONS

¶ 709. It will be the duty of the justices to transmit to the court where the trial is to take place the depositions of the witnesses and the prisoner's statement.[5] The depositions are important for several purposes. (*a*) They enable the opposite party to check the evidence given at the trial, and to cross-examine or contradict a witness whose evidence there varies from that which he gave at the commitment. (*b*) They form a substitute[6] for the witness in the event of his being, at the time of the trial, either dead or too ill to travel[7] or give evidence,[8] or kept out of the way by, or on behalf of, the prisoner.[9] But his absence abroad does not

[1] *R.* v. *Butler* (1881) 14 Cox 530. All arrangements, between a person bailed and his sureties, that if he abscond he shall indemnify them for the bail forfeited, are so contrary to public policy that they are void as agreements, and moreover are indictable as conspiracies to pervert the course of justice, even though no intention to pervert it be alleged (*R.* v. *Porter* [1910] 1 K.B. 369).

[2] Bail is less readily granted during a preliminary inquiry, when the depositions have not yet been completed, than after its conclusion. During the preliminary inquiry a magistrate has power to remand the accused in custody for a period not exceeding eight days (ss. 6 and 105 (4)) or commit him to the custody of a constable for three days (s. 105 (5)). And under sect. 26 (1) where the offence is punishable on summary conviction with imprisonment, and the court is satisfied that the accused has committed it, they may remand him in custody or on bail (but not for any single period exceeding three weeks) to enable a medical examination and report to be made as to his physical or mental condition.

[3] The need of such injunctions is shown by the fact that many persons sent to prison to await trial are ultimately acquitted (yet not necessarily *innocent*).

[4] The Criminal Justice Act, 1948, s. 37, makes provisions whereby the High Court may release from custody on bail persons who are appealing against conviction or sentence, or by way of case stated; *ante*, p. 545 n. 3.

[5] ¶ 608 *ante*.

[6] Being a legally required official record they are the 'best evidence' (*ante*, ¶ 558) of what passed at the committal, and cannot be altered by oral evidence. Indeed oral evidence is probably not admissible even to supplement their omissions, when they are used as 'substantive evidence' (i.e. as a substitute for an absent witness), though it is admissible when they are used to contradict a witness who appears. *R.* v. *Brooks* (1857) C.C.C. Sess. Pap. XLVI, 912.

[7] Sect. 41 and Criminal Justice Act, 1925, s. 13; ¶ 608 *ante*.

[8] *R.* v. *Wicker* (1854) 18 Jur. 252.

[9] *R.* v. *Harrison* (1692) 12 St.Tr. 833.

suffice to render them admissible.[1] (*c*) They assist the draftsman who has to frame the indictment. (*d*) They enable the judge to learn the difficulties of the case before the trial. And (*e*) they inform the defendant as to the precise case which he has to meet.[2] To him[3] this is obviously an advantage, and it is often an advantage to the public, for if the case thus disclosed be a strong one, the defendant is the more likely to plead guilty.

¶ **710.** *No power to secure disclosure of the defence.* It is, however, to be noted that our law does not take measures for securing a reciprocal disclosure of the intended defence. At present it is possible to raise at the trial some speculative defence, which there is then no opportunity of contradicting, and to support it by witnesses about whom it is too late to make inquiries. The facility has become greater since the prisoner himself has been allowed to come forward as a witness.[4]

¶ **711.** *Disadvantages of depositions.* As has been stated (¶ 704 *ante*) the duty of magistrates at a preliminary inquiry is to determine not whether the accused is guilty, but whether there is a *prima facie* case against him which requires investigation. The advantages of depositions have been pointed out, but there are disadvantages too in the system. Delay and expense are caused by the necessity of what is really a double hearing. It is not often that a magistrate will take the responsibility of deciding that there is not a *prima facie* case for trial. In the opinion of many the number of cases where a prisoner is not committed is so small that, even if a committal without a full preliminary hearing were to be a hardship in a few cases, such hardship would be far outweighed by the advantage to the majority. It would of course be necessary for the magistrate to investigate the statements of the principal witnesses before deciding to commit, but such investigation could be brief and private.[5] Another

[1] Except by consent, in cases of misdemeanour, perhaps.

[2] Hence *he* has, after commitment, a statutory right to purchase copies of them at 1½*d.* per ninety words (Magistrates' Courts Rules, 1952, Rule 13); before commitment 6*d.* is charged. But the witness has no such right, and indeed ought not to be supplied with a copy.

[3] It was said by Jessel, M.R., in *Benbow* v. *Low* (1880) 16 Ch.D. 95: 'If you give one side the opportunity of knowing the particulars of the evidence that is to be brought against him, then you can give a rogue an enormous advantage.' But in civil proceedings, the defendant, though entitled to know the nature of the claim against him, is not entitled to know by what evidence it will be supported (*Lever* v. *Associated Newspapers Ltd* [1907] 2 K.B. 626).

[4] ¶ 621 *ante*; ¶ 703 *ante* as to defence of alibi.

[5] For a criticism of the existing system and proposals for reform, see a paper read to the Law Society by J. S. Walsh, reprinted in 180 *L.T.Jo.* at p. 249. Mr Walsh suggested that the magistrate before deciding whether to commit should scrutinize the statements of material witnesses, or interrogate them briefly in his room. Where the offence is one triable summarily by consent (see ¶ 679 *ante*) he suggested that the accused should be asked directly he appears whether he wishes to be dealt with summarily, in which case the court should proceed to try the case. Some courts take depositions in every indictable case until a *prima facie* case is disclosed, before asking the accused to elect whether he wishes to be tried summarily.

danger of the present system is the prejudice aroused in the minds of those who may be jurors by press reports of a preliminary examination.

RECOGNIZANCES

¶ 712. The justice, having already bound over each witness (on signing his deposition) to appear at the trial, now binds over someone, usually a policeman, to prosecute, i.e. to prefer a bill of indictment. He may commit to prison anyone who refuses to be thus bound over to give evidence at the trial.[1] Witnesses and prosecutors are only bound over in their own recognizances, though defendants, as we have seen, are usually required to find one or two sureties also. 'A recognizance', says Blackstone,[2] 'is an obligation of record, which a man enters into before some court of record, or magistrate duly authorized, with condition to do some particular act, as, to keep the peace.' Although the magistrate's court is not a court of record yet its records are, in this respect, on the same footing as those of the higher courts.[3] A recognizance is a contract not by parol nor by deed, but of record,[4] since, so soon as it is actually enrolled, the record of the court is conclusive evidence as to its existence and terms, and often is the only evidence of them. For the party bound need not sign anything (though in some courts he does), but may merely assent orally to the court's oral question. His assent consists in an admission of his owing to the Crown some specified sum of money to be payable unless a specified condition be fulfilled, e.g. unless he appear at the next assizes. Unlike other contracts (which have to be sued upon) recognizances admit of direct enforcement. For, if the condition be not fulfilled, the recognizance may at once be 'estreated', i.e. an extract (Norman-French, *estrait*) showing the terms of the obligation is copied from the court's record, and is sent to the clerk of the peace, who thereupon directs the sheriff to levy the amount upon the defendant's goods.[5]

¶ 713. *Conditional recognizances.* By virtue of section 5 (2) of the Act of 1952, witnesses whose evidence seems likely to be unnecessary at the trial, either because the accused has pleaded guilty or because their evidence is merely of a formal nature, may only be bound to attend the trial conditionally, i.e. if they receive from the prosecutor or the accused a notice to attend. Their depositions may be read at the trial, if notice to attend has *not* been given (s. 13 (3) and (5)).[6] As we have seen (*ante*, ¶ 702) the accused should not be asked if he intends to plead guilty at his trial, but if he clearly intimates that such is his intention then the witnesses should be bound over conditionally.[7]

[1] Sect. 5 (1) and (4).

[2] 4 Bl. *Comm.* 341.

[3] See Brooke's Abridgment, *tit.* Recognizance, pl. 8.

[4] Halsbury, *Laws of England*, 3rd ed. v. 8, p. 56.

[5] Levy of Fines Act, 1822, s. 2. See *R.* v. *Smith* (1892) 17 Cox 601, as to the difficulty of effectually binding an infant by recognizances, because of his incapacity to contract.

[6] As to the desirability of making use of this procedure see 'Practice note' [1952] W.N. 245.

[7] *R.* v. *Collins* [1938] 3 All E.R. 130.

LEGAL AID

¶ 714. The Legal Aid and Advice Act, 1949 (12 and 13 Geo. VI, c. 51),[1] in Part II applies and in some respects modifies provisions contained in the Criminal Appeal Act, 1907, the Poor Prisoner's Defence Act, 1930, and the Summary Jurisdiction (Appeals) Act, 1933. The general effect of these enactments is that justices of the peace, upon committing a prisoner for trial (or a single justice in response to a letter applying for aid addressed to the clerk to the justices, sent by a person arrested or summoned for an offence), are authorized to certify that a solicitor and, where necessary, a counsel should be assigned to him and the expenses of his defence ultimately defrayed out of the legal aid fund established under the provisions of the Act of 1949. A similar certificate may be given at any time by a judge of the assize or chairman of the quarter sessions at which he is to be tried.[2]

This power is only to be exercised where (1) the prisoner is too poor to pay for his own defence, and (2) it appears, having regard to all the circumstances of the case (including the nature of such defence, if any, as may have been set up), that it is desirable in the interests of justice that legal aid should be granted. There may be mitigating circumstances which should be brought before the court even though no defence is disclosed. Legal aid may be granted by justices so that a prisoner may be defended before them, whether on summary proceedings or on a preliminary examination, but except where the charge is one of murder only a solicitor is assigned in such cases. If legal aid is not given for the preliminary examination unnecessary expense may result through the committal of persons who are subsequently acquitted.

[1] See S.I., 1952, no. 390. This for civil matters prescribes general principles to be applied under regulations made by the Lord Chancellor whereby to persons of limited means there may be assigned, at the cost of a special fund (the Legal Aid Fund), a solicitor and, so far as necessary, a counsel to give the usual assistance in steps connected with legal proceedings. The Act also provides (sect. 5) for giving free legal advice to persons contemplating taking steps to assert or dispute a claim where proceedings have not yet arisen.

[2] The Act repeals sect. 18 (6), sect. 20 (5) (*b*) and sect. 29 (3) (*b*) of the Criminal Justice Act, 1948.

Chapter XXXIII

ORDINARY PROCEDURE

II. FROM ACCUSATION TO SENTENCE

SECTION 1. PROSECUTION

¶ 715. The process of commitment by a justice of the peace which we have described, though in actual practice it is adopted in almost every instance, is not legally essential for bringing an accused person to trial before a jury.[1] All that is truly essential is some mode of 'prosecution', i.e. of formal accusation. Such an accusation may be made either by a Crown official's information, or by an indictment or in the case of murder, manslaughter or infanticide by a coroner's inquisition.

BY INFORMATION

¶ 716. An information is a written complaint made on behalf of the Crown by one of its officers and filed in the Queen's Bench Division. Since such a mode of accusation dispenses with any accusing jury, and with any examination before a justice of the peace, it is only allowed in cases of misdemeanour. Since 1938[2] the Attorney-General is the only officer who has this right, *ex officio*, which he may exercise at his own discretion (but seldom does so).[3]

BY INDICTMENT

¶ 717. A bill of indictment is a written accusation of crime.[4] Practically every case that comes to a petty jury for trial comes on indictment. A bill of indictment may be preferred (i) when the person charged has been committed for trial[5] or (ii) under the direction or with the consent of a judge of the High Court,[6] or (iii) in the case of perjury by order of a judge or magistrate who is of opinion that in the course of any pro-

[1] Thus occasionally when a coroner's inquest has occupied an unusually protracted time, the magisterial inquiry is omitted; as in the case of Paine (*The Times*, 25 Feb. 1880), who was indicted for a remarkable manslaughter (by plying with intoxicating liquor) without being taken before a magistrate, the coroner's inquest having lasted five days. See ¶ 665 *ante*. A Departmental Committee on Coroners (1936, Cmd. 5070) recommended that coroners should no longer have the power to commit for trial.

[2] Administration of Justice (Misc. Provisions) Act, 1938, s. 12.

[3] In 1911 one was filed against Mylius for libelling the King; see ¶ 658 *ante*.

[4] Usually drawn on circuit by the clerk of assize or the clerk of indictments, at quarter sessions by the clerk of the peace; see forms in Appendix III *post*, p. 639.

[5] See ¶¶ 703 *et seq. ante* and ¶ 715 *ante*. The committal must be regular, see *R.* v. *Gee*, *ante*, p. 569.

[6] Administration of Justice (Misc. Provisions) Act, 1933 (23 and 24 Geo. V, c. 36), s. 2. When no judge is present at assizes, a commissioner of assize may act. The Court of Criminal Appeal will not inquire into the exercise of the judge's discretion; *R.* v. *Rothfield* [1937] 4 All E.R. 320.

ceeding before himself any person has been guilty of perjury.[1] A bill of indictment may be preferred by any person and, if satisfied that any of the above three requirements has been fulfilled, the proper officer[2] of the court before which the bill is preferred signs the bill which thereupon becomes an indictment.[3] The judge or chairman[4] of the court, if satisfied that any of the above three requirements has been fulfilled, may of his own motion or on the application of the prosecution direct the bill to be signed. If none of the three requirements has been fulfilled and yet a bill of indictment is signed, the indictment is liable to be quashed,[5] but, if the requirements have been fulfilled in respect of any count[6] of the indictment, only the counts wrongly included can be quashed on this ground. Where a prisoner is committed for trial by a magistrate, the bill of indictment may include any counts founded on facts or evidence disclosed in any examination or deposition taken before a justice in his presence,[7] being counts which lawfully may be joined in the same indictment.[8] It is permissible for the prosecution to insert, without previous application to the judge (unless the defence object), a count in the indictment upon which the justices have refused to commit.[9] An indictment may not be quashed on appeal on the ground that the requirements for preferment have not been fulfilled, unless application to quash it was made at the trial.[10]

GRAND JURY

¶ 718. Until 1933 a bill of indictment had to be laid before a grand jury of from twelve to twenty-three persons. If the grand jury[11] found a true bill, the bill became an indictment and was presented to the petty jury. If the grand jury 'ignored' the bill, the accused was discharged.[12] The origin of the grand jury can be found in the Assize of Clarendon of 1166,[13] when Henry II[14] required twelve knights, or other freemen, of every hundred, and four men (who would probably be unfree) of every township, to send in accusations of murder, robbery, larceny and

[1] *Ibid.* and Perjury Act, 1911 (1 and 2 Geo. V, c. 6), s. 9.

[2] The clerk of assize or the clerk of the peace.

[3] The finding of a coroner's inquest may be equivalent to an indictment; *ante*, ¶ 665.

[4] Including a deputy chairman or assistant chairman.

[5] See ¶ 738 *post*.

[6] See ¶ 720 *post*.

[7] See ¶ 703 *ante*.

[8] See ¶ 728 *post*.

[9] See *R.* v. *Morry* [1946] K.B. 153.

[10] Administration of Justice Act, 1933, s. 2.

[11] Twelve grand jurors had to agree.

[12] In cases of murder or manslaughter the accused could be tried on a coroner's inquisition (see ¶ 665 *ante*), but where a grand jury ignored a bill in such cases it was customary to offer no evidence upon the coroner's inquisition.

[13] In Saxon times Ethelred the Unready enacted the law of wantage: 'Let a moot be held in every Wapentake, let the twelve senior thegns go out, and the reeve with them, and let them swear on a relic that they will accuse no innocent man nor conceal any guilty one', Stubbs, *Select Charters*, 9th ed. by H. W. C. Davis, 85; *Constitutional History*, I, 611.

[14] Henry II probably adopted the precedents not of Anglo-Saxon times but of Frankish inquests customary in Normandy, see Pollock and Maitland, II, 642; Holdsworth, *Hist. Eng. Law*, I, 12.

harbouring of criminals. In 1176 arson and forgery were added.[1] The grand jury was established in order to multiply accusations of crime, but its function by a curious inversion became that of revising and thereby diminishing such accusations. Hence it was enacted by the Administration of Justice (Miscellaneous Provisions) Act, 1933,[2] that grand juries should be abolished except grand juries of the county of London and county of Middlesex[3] for the purpose of certain trials. But now this last vestige of the grand jury has been eliminated by the Criminal Justice Act, 1948, s. 31 (3).

AN INDICTMENT CONSISTS OF THREE PARTS

¶ 719. Sir Matthew Hale, under Charles II, described an indictment as 'a plain, brief, and certain narrative of an offence committed'.[4] The growth of technicalities soon destroyed both the brevity and the plainness. But the sweeping alterations introduced by the Indictments Act, 1915, have reduced this portion of criminal procedure to a simple and rational system, making it easier for the accused to defend himself, and harder for him to escape by mere technical objections. An indictment now consists of three parts: (*a*) the commencement, (*b*) the statement of offence, (*c*) the particulars of offence. For examples, see Appendix III *post*. The Act abolishes the rhetorical 'conclusion' which previously, in some shape or other—e.g. 'against the peace of our Lord the King, his crown and dignity'—usually terminated indictments, although rendered superfluous by an Act of 1851.

(*a*) The commencement

¶ 720. This states the place of the court's jurisdiction, usually a particular county or borough.[5]

The form of commencement prescribed by the Act of 1915 (schedule I, rule 2)[6] is as follows:

The Queen *v.* *A. B.*

Court of Trial [e.g. Central Criminal Court, *or* (Kent) Assizes held at (Maidstone) *or* (Hants) Quarter Sessions held at (Winchester)[7]] *A. B.* is charged with the following offence *or* offences.

[1] Stubbs, *Select Charters*, 9th ed. by H. W. C. Davis, pt. 4. These ordinances came to fix a line between felonies and 'trespasses', i.e. misdemeanours (*ante*, ¶ 75).

[2] Sect. 1.

[3] *Ibid.* s. 1 (4) and schedule I.

[4] 2 Hale P.C. 169. Yet in charges of treason, conspiracy or fraud, indictments were often of remarkable length. Thus the indictment in *O'Connell's Case*, in 1844 (5 St.Tr. (n.s.), 1), was a hundred yards long. In France the indictment of Landru in Nov. 1921, for murder, took two hours to read aloud.

[5] I.e. the 'venue'. The Criminal Justice Act, 1925, s. 11 (1), as modified by ss. 1 and 2 of the Magistrates' Courts Act, 1952, in effect provides that a person charged with any indictable offence may be indicted, tried, and punished in any county or place in which he was apprehended, or is in custody on that charge or has appeared in answer to a summons. And see the Criminal Justice Act, 1948, s. 31 (2), for the case of offences committed abroad by servants of the Crown; and the Civil Aviation Act, 1949, s. 62, for the cases of offences committed in a British aircraft.

[6] Amended by the Administration of Justice Act, 1933.

[7] Or whatever other tribunal is the 'court of trial'.

Then comes one or more paragraphs, each of which is called a 'count' and describes an offence whereof the prisoner is accused. If there be more than one paragraph, they must be consecutively numbered. Each count is in effect a separate indictment.[1]

(*b*) The statement of offence

¶ 721. The statement of offence, with which every count must begin, merely names the crime charged, e.g. 'murder', 'manslaughter', 'cruelty to a child, contrary to sect. 1 of the Children and Young Persons Act, 1933'. Under the Act of 1915 it must use ordinary language, avoiding technical terms as far as possible, and need not set out all the essential elements of the offence. If the offence be a statutory one, the statute and the particular section must be specified in the statement (schedule I, rule 4 (3)).

(*c*) The particulars of offence

¶ 722. The particulars of offence follow, in order to inform the accused as to the circumstances—e.g. time, place, conduct, subject-matter—of the crime which has thus been alleged against him, in fact, such particulars as may be necessary for giving reasonable information as to the nature of the charge. Here, again, ordinary language is to be employed, and the use of technical terms is not to be necessary (schedule I, rule 4 (4)). The particulars may, too, be very brief, e.g. '*A. B.* on the first day of July 1951, in the county of Cambridge, murdered *Y. Z.*' But they must be sufficient to indicate to the accused 'with reasonable clearness' (schedule I, rule 9) the occasion and the circumstances of his crime. This is necessary in order that he may be able to know what defence to offer and, moreover, may be able, should he be prosecuted a second time for this same misdeed, to protect himselt by showing—see ¶ 743 *post*—that the identical charge has already been dealt with.[2]

GENERAL COUNTS

¶ 723. Hence if a count be not detailed enough, but too 'general', the judge may quash it; for 'generality of accusation is difficulty of defence'. A count, for instance, would be too general if it merely alleged the act of 'inciting *A* to commit an indictable offence', or of 'attempting to induce *A* to contravene the law of the land', without specifying what the particular offence or contravention was. Formerly it was also required that no count should run in the alternative (as by alleging that the prisoner murdered *A or* wounded him), the result being to purchase precision at the cost of prolixity; for a further count was added in order to allege the second of the alternatives.

[1] There were twenty-four counts in the indictment in 1922 of Horatio Bottomley, M.P., for fraudulent conversion. As to the limitation on plurality of counts, see ¶ 728 *post*.

[2] Hence, e.g., an indictment should not charge a theft of a coat 'and other articles'.

¶ **724.** *Alternative counts permitted by statute.* But by the Act of 1915 (schedule I, rule 5 (1)) in the case of any *statutory* offence which is defined by alternatives—as, for instance, conduct performed with any one of different intentions, or in any one of different capacities, or consisting of doing or omitting any one of different acts—a count may now allege the different alternatives which the defining statute sets out. A good instance is afforded in the Act of 1915 itself: 'ill-treated *or* neglected the said child, *or* caused *or* procured the said child to be ill-treated *or* neglected, in a manner likely to cause the said child unnecessary suffering *or* injury to its health' (form 6).

¶ **725.** *Duplicity.* A count may, however, still be held bad for duplicity. Thus a conviction was quashed where a prisoner was charged that he 'by night unlawfully took or destroyed game or rabbits on land at *C* or was on the said land by night with a gun, net or other instrument for the purpose of unlawfully taking or destroying game'. The count was held bad as charging the appellant in one count with two different offences.[1] The section under which the prisoner was charged did not deal with one act in alternative ways but with two different offences. Thus, under the Larceny Act, 1916, a prisoner may be charged with 'ripping or cutting or severing or breaking fixtures with intent to steal' but not with 'stealing or with intent to steal, ripping, severing or breaking fixtures'.[2] Again, under the Debtors Act, 1869, s. 13 (1) a count alleging that the accused obtained credit 'under false pretences or by means of other fraud' is not bad for duplicity.[3] A count is bad which charges a man with driving 'recklessly or in a manner which was dangerous to the public having regard to all the circumstances of the case including the nature, condition and use of the road and the amount of the traffic'.[4] The courts disapprove of any semblance of duplicity even when the irregularity is not enough to warrant the quashing of a conviction.[5] It is possible, however, to comprise the whole of any *single* transaction in one count, however complex, e.g. when *A*, *B*, *C* and *D* have set upon *E* and *F* together and robbed them.[6]

WHAT A COUNT SHOULD STATE

¶ **726.** To be good, a count should state in the particulars of offence (i) the party indicted; (ii) the party injured; and (iii) the facts and the intent that are necessary ingredients of the offence. But the Act of 1915

[1] *R.* v. *Disney* [1933] 2 K.B. 138.

[2] *R.* v. *Molloy* [1921] 2 K.B. 334. And *R.* v. *Nicholls* [1960] 2 All E.R. 449, where the appellant had been indicted on one count of 'warehouse-breaking contrary to s. 26 (1) and s. 27 (2) of the Larceny Act, 1916'.

[3] *R.* v. *Perry* (1945) 31 Cr.App.R. 16.

[4] *R.* v. *Wilmot* (1933) 24 Cr.App.R. 63; 49 T.L.R. 427.

[5] *R.* v. *Johnson* (1945) 30 Cr.App.R. 159.

[6] *R.* v. *Giddins* (1842) C. and M. 634. For the alternative possibility of subdividing a single but complex transaction into separate counts, see *R.* v. *Brettell* (1842) C. and M. 609. E.g. nine counts for wounding nine cows.

(schedule I, rules 7, 9) relaxes the precision formerly required in stating them.

¶ 727. *Description of the parties; elements of the offence.* (i) The party indicted should be described. But it need only be in such a manner 'as is reasonably sufficient to identify him', without necessarily stating his occupation or abode or even his correct name. And if his name is unknown, and he refuses to disclose it, he may be indicted as 'a person unknown'.

(ii) The party injured should be described, but only with the like reasonable sufficiency. And, if this be impossible, he too may be described as 'a person unknown', as in the case of the murder of some stranger found dead. And in an indictment for obtaining by false pretences it is not necessary to state the person to whom the false pretences were made.[1]

(iii) The acts, circumstances, and state of mind constituting the offence should be set out. Here, again, certainty was formerly required.[2] And in some offences the due degree of legal certainty could only be obtained by employing particular technical expressions; e.g. in indictments for any treason by saying 'traitorously', for any felony, 'feloniously', for burglary, 'feloniously and burglariously'. But now, by the Act of 1915 (schedule I, rule 9), it will usually 'be sufficient to describe any place, time, thing, matter, act, or omission whatsoever (to which it is necessary to refer in any indictment) in ordinary language, in such a manner as to indicate with reasonable clearness the place, time, thing, matter, act or omission referred to'. In Appendix III the student will find actual forms of indictments, which may make these rules clearer to him.

PLURALITY OF COUNTS

¶ 728. In early days no indictment could contain more than one count. This simplicity of statement made inevitable a miscarriage of justice, if the facts proved at the trial happened to deviate even slightly from those alleged in the indictment. To avoid this danger, a plurality of counts was soon allowed, describing the same crime in many forms, as if there had been so many distinct occurrences.[3] Later practice came to permit even entirely different crimes to be charged in the same indictment, of course in different counts. But all of them had to be of the same grade, i.e. *all* had to be treasons or all felonies or all misdemeanours.

¶ 729. *Statutory restriction of plurality.* The Act of 1915 (s. 4, schedule I, rule 3) forbids the joinder of several charges in the same indictment,

[1] *R.* v. *Johnstone* [1950] 1 All E.R. 830; 34 Cr.App.R. 107.

[2] No 'variance' was allowed, especially in capital offences. For an interesting account, with examples, of this strictness which was often applied from a humane desire to relax the extreme severity of the criminal law see Radzinowicz, *Hist. Eng. Crim. Law*, I, 98 *et seq.*

[3] Thus (*R.* v. *Good* (1842) C.C.C. Sess. Pap. XVI, 233), in a case of murder where only the headless trunk of the victim was found, there were thirty-five counts alleging different modes of death.

except when[1] all the charges either 'are founded on the same facts', or else 'form, or are a part of, a series[2] of offences of the same or a similar character'. Section 5 (3) of the Act confers on the judge a discretion to order a separate trial on any count or counts, a discretion with which the Court of Appeal will not interfere unless justice has not been done.[3] The mere fact that evidence was admissible on one count and inadmissible on another is not, by itself, a ground for separate trials.[4] On the other hand, wherever a joinder becomes permissible, the old prohibition against joining felonies and misdemeanours together is removed.[5] That prohibition was due to the fact that the procedure at a trial for felony is slightly different from that at trials for misdemeanour. But the Act (s. 4) gets over this difficulty by enacting that 'where a felony is tried together with any misdemeanour, the jury shall be sworn, and the person accused shall have the same right of challenging jurors, as if *all* the offences charged in the indictment were felonies'. On general principles of fairness an accused person should not be put to answer an array of counts containing several distinct charges.[6] And it has been declared that it is undesirable to join two murders in one indictment.[7] Where the indictment does contain more than one count, each count should be put separately to the accused and his plea should be taken separately to each count.[8]

AMENDMENT OF INDICTMENT

¶ 730. By section 5 of the Act of 1915:

> Where, before trial, or at any stage[9] of a trial, it appears to the court that the indictment is defective, the court shall make such order for the

[1] Nor even then if embarrassing; e.g. adding to *murder* another crime. But when possible it is desirable to multiply counts rather than to multiply indictments, as it saves costs. Two indictments cannot, even by consent, be tried together (*Crane* v. *D.P.P.* [1921] 2 A.C. 299; 15 Cr.App.R. 23).

[2] E.g. sixteen separate assaults on sixteen persons, *R.* v. *Bailey* (1924) 18 Cr.App.R. 42; cf. *R.* v. *Lyle* (1924) 18 Cr.App.R. 59; seventeen makings of *the same* false pretence to seventeen persons, all counts tried at once (C.C.C. February 1924). The prosecution will usually be required to select certain counts on which to proceed. A separate trial of any count or counts will be ordered where the accused would be embarrassed by their being tried together. And see *R.* v. *Chandor* [1959] 1 Q.B. 545.

[3] *R.* v. *Sims* [1946] K.B. 531; 1 All E.R. 697.

[4] *Ibid.* Of course the judge should direct the jury to ignore the evidence where it is inadmissible.

[5] Thus to a count for a woman's felonious bigamy there may be added one for her misdemeanour in obtaining a separation allowance by the false pretence of being the wife of a soldier (the 'second husband').

[6] *R.* v. *Carless* (1934) 25 Cr.App.R. 43.

[7] *R.* v. *Davis* [1937] 3 All E.R. 537.

[8] *R.* v. *Boyle* (1954) 38 Cr.App.R. 111.

[9] In *R.* v. *Martin* [1961] 2 All E.R. 747 the C.C.A. intimated that *after arraignment* it is doubtful whether a new count can be added at all, as the defendant will not have pleaded to it nor, if the trial has started, will he have been put in charge of the jury on it, so that injustice would almost certainly be caused. On the effect of the arraignment see ¶¶ 735, 738 *post*.

amendment[1] of the indictment as the court thinks necessary to meet the circumstances of the case unless having regard to the merits of the case the required amendments cannot be made without injustice; and may make such order as to the payment of any costs incurred owing to the necessity for amendment as the court thinks fit.[2]

AVERMENTS DIVISIBLE AT COMMON LAW

¶ 731. As a logical rule, the evidence should of course establish, and the conviction also be for, the actual offence stated in the count which it concerns. But even by common law, 'averments are divisible'; so that if the words in which a count states an offence involve the statement of some minor offence, the petty jury can reject part of the averment and convict of the minor offence alone, though it was not stated separately. Thus a statement of murder will be a statement of manslaughter if the words 'of malice aforethought' be omitted, whilst similarly every statement of aggravated larceny includes one of simple larceny.

CONVICTION OF A CRIME DIFFERENT FROM THAT CHARGED

¶ 732. And the legislature has gone still further, in two ways. For in some cases it has enabled juries to convict of the crime which has in fact been proved, although it is not the crime charged in the indictment.[3] Thus on an indictment for any crime the jury may convict of an attempt to commit it;[4] and on one for robbery, of an assault with intent to rob;[5] on one for embezzlement, of either stealing as servant or simple stealing; on one for stealing, of embezzlement or false pretences[6] but not of fraudulent conversion;[7] on one for murder, of concealment of birth;[8] and on one for rape, or for several other felonies under the Sexual Offences Act, 1956 (e.g. having unlawful sexual intercourse with a girl under thirteen), the jury may instead convict of an indecent assault, or of procuring connexion by threats or by false

[1] E.g. by adding 'with intent to defraud' where accidentally omitted, *R.* v. *Fraser* (1923) 17 Cr.App.R. 182; 40 T.L.R. 81; but not by adding a new false pretence, *R.* v. *Errington* (1922), 16 Cr.App.R. 148; nor by substituting a representation of an existing fact where the false pretence charged was consistent with futurity, *R.* v. *Hughes* (1927) 20 Cr.App.R. 4. And see *R.* v. *Smith and others* [1950] 2 All E.R. 679; 66 T.L.R. 319 (*sub nom. R.* v. *Pople*), which *inter alia* lays down that the responsibility for the correctness of an indictment lies in every case on counsel for the prosecution and not on the court.

[2] Within the conditions indicated in the section, the decision to allow the amendment is within the judge's discretion; *R.* v. *Tuttle* (1929) 140 L.T. 701, as explained in *Meek* v. *Powell* [1952] 1 All E.R. 347. But if the indictment mentions the wrong Act and conviction be obtained thereunder it is too late to ask the Court of Criminal Appeal for amendment and they must quash the conviction: for the same rule where an information is before justices, see *ante*, ¶ 673.

[3] In one instance, that of incest, they are allowed to convict of a specified crime even *graver* than that charged; see Sexual Offences Act, 1956, s. 10, sch. 2, 14 (*a*).

[4] Criminal Procedure Act, 1851, s. 9. Yet the crime may be a felony, whilst the attempt is only a misdemeanour.

[5] Larceny Act, 1916, s. 44 (1).

[6] *Ibid.* s. 44 (2) and (3).

[7] *R.* v. *Stevens* (1933) 24 Cr.App.R. 85.

[8] Offences against the Person Act, 1861.

pretences, or of having unlawful sexual intercourse with a girl between thirteen and sixteen.[1]

Again, the legislature has in other cases permitted juries to convict of the crime alleged in an indictment, even though a different (but a graver one) has been disclosed by the evidence. Thus on a trial of any person for misdemeanour, if it appears that the facts given in evidence amount in law to a felony, such person shall not by reason thereof be entitled to be acquitted of such misdemeanour.[2] Moreover if, on an indictment for obtaining by false pretences, the defendant is proved to have obtained the property by means amounting to stealing, he may be convicted as indicted.[3] A further similar provision is that an accessory before the fact to any felony may be indicted, tried, convicted, and punished as if he were a principal felon.[4]

Moreover, in all these three groups of substitutions, a prisoner, on being arraigned, may now plead guilty to the substitutable offence, instead of to the one charged in the indictment (Criminal Justice Administration Act, 1914, s. 39 (1)).

ENGLISH PRACTICE IN PROSECUTION

¶ 733. It has been said that 'the fundamental and outstanding procedural difference between the administration of criminal justice in England and the United States lies in the management of prosecutions'.[5] In the United States, though the original complaint is, of course, more often than not made by a private person, the 'prosecuting attorney' supersedes the private complainant immediately a formal information has been laid.[6] In Scotland prosecutions are conducted by procurators-fiscal working under the supervision of the Lord Advocate. In England in theory the institution of the bulk of criminal proceedings is left to private individuals,[7] who are not compelled to prosecute and are only repaid their costs on a most inadequate scale.[8] Such may be the theory, but the great majority of prosecutions in England are instituted and carried on by the police and are referred to as 'police' as opposed to 'private' prosecutions. Private individuals may, and in the case of e.g. commercial frauds do, institute and carry through prosecutions, employing their own solicitors and counsel; but in the ordinary run of

[1] I.e. where the girl, instead of being under thirteen, is found to be between thirteen and sixteen. By the Children and Young Persons Act, 1933, s. 1 (4), on an indictment of a person over sixteen for infanticide or the manslaughter of a person *under* sixteen who was in his charge, the jury may instead convict of any of the numerous offences of cruelty set out in the section. Hence any such indictment will tacitly involve several distinct issues.

[2] Criminal Procedure Act, 1851, s. 12. The effect of this section is discussed in Russ. 208.

[3] Larceny Act, 1916, s. 44 (4).

[4] 24 and 25 Vict. c. 94, s. 1. *Ante*, ¶ 69.

[5] *Criminal Justice in England*, by Pendleton Howard (New York, Macmillan Co. 1931).

[6] Howard, *ibid.* 3.

[7] See Atkinson, 'The department of the Director of Public Prosecutions' (1944), 22 *Can. Bar Review*, 412.

[8] See ¶ 769 *post.*

criminal cases it is the police who institute proceedings in the public interest, and, even where a prosecution is started on the initiative of a private person, e.g. for theft or burglary, it is normally carried on by the police. In courts of summary jurisdiction a police officer will frequently himself conduct the case and examine witnesses.[1] If the case is sent to quarter sessions or assizes, a solicitor will be instructed by the police to brief counsel and prepare for trial.[2] Only barristers have a right of audience at assizes and at most quarter sessions, and they must be instructed by a solicitor. At assizes and quarter sessions only those barristers may appear who are members of the particular circuit or sessions unless a special fee is paid them. This rule of the bar, while restricting freedom of choice, ensures the attendance of a reasonably strong bar.

DIRECTOR OF PUBLIC PROSECUTIONS

¶ 734. Cases of exceptional gravity and importance are conducted by the Director of Public Prosecutions, who will instruct counsel where necessary.[3] This office was created by the Prosecution of Offences Act, 1879.[4] In 1884 the office was merged with that of the Treasury Solicitor, but in 1908 the two offices were separated by the Prosecution of Offences Act, 1908. The Director of Public Prosecutions is appointed by the Home Secretary, but acts under the supervision of the Attorney-General. It is his duty to prosecute in all cases where the offence is punishable with death, in the case of offences such as coinage offences where the prosecutions were formerly undertaken by the Treasury Solicitor, and in all cases where it appears that the public interest requires prosecution and where there are special difficulties in the way of securing due prosecution. In cases of incest only the Director can prosecute unless the Attorney-General gives his consent. The Director may take over any prosecution at any stage of the proceedings.[5] The Director has a special duty to prosecute offences against election laws. Further the Director is responsible for the defence of criminal appeals. The power to intervene at any stage of a prosecution prevents the wrongful abandonment of a prosecution by a private person.

[1] The practice of police advocacy is confined in the main to country districts and has been strongly condemned (see Howard, *op. cit.* 183). Large cities usually employ an official prosecuting solicitor, while in some counties or districts the police in cases of difficulty instruct local solicitors to prosecute.

[2] The procedure varies from county to county and borough to borough. Where there is an official solicitor, he will prepare the case and instruct counsel. Where there is no official solicitor, there is an infinite variety in the procedure adopted (Howard, *op. cit.* ch. v).

[3] See Atkinson, *loc. cit.* Where a particular government department is concerned, e.g. the Post Office, the solicitor to that department will conduct the prosecution and instruct counsel where necessary.

[4] Bentham had urged the appointment of a public prosecutor as early as 1802.

[5] 8 Edw. VII, c. 3, s. 2 (3).

SECTION 2. ARRAIGNMENT

¶ 735. An *indicted* defendant (contrast ¶ 676, n. 7), must personally appear[1] at the bar of the court in order to be 'arraigned', i.e. called to a reckoning (*ad rationem*), by hearing the indictment read, and to plead to it. (The only exception is that, if the trial be in the Queen's Bench Division and be for misdemeanour, the defendant may, by leave of the court, appear by attorney. When he appears he is 'put up to plead', and he pleads either 'guilty' or 'not guilty';[2] the jury are sworn and then the defendant is 'put in charge of the jury', the clerk of the court addressing the jury in formal words, stating what the charge is, and ending: 'To this indictment he has pleaded "not guilty"; it is your charge to listen to the evidence and to say whether he be guilty or not guilty.' If, however, he do not appear, the court will issue a bench-warrant for his arrest and 'estreat' (¶ 712) his recognizances, and will 'enlarge' *sine die* the recognizances of the prosecutor and the witnesses. As a general rule, too, the defendant must remain in court during all the proceedings[3] including the passing of sentence.[4] But in cases of misdemeanours the court may (perhaps) give him leave of absence so soon as he has pleaded.[5] A corporation may by its representative enter in writing a plea of guilty or not guilty. If no appearance is made by a representative, or there is a failure to enter a plea, the court will order a plea of not guilty to be entered.[6]

SECTION 3. PLEA AND ISSUE

(*a*) Confession

¶ 736. When the indictment has been read[7] to the accused he has several courses open. He may either (*a*) confess, or (*b*) stand mute, or (*c*) take some legal objection to the indictment, or (*d*) plead to it.

If he confesses, i.e. 'pleads guilty',[8] he may be at once sentenced.

[1] Hence corporations, since they were incapable of appearing in person, were originally outside the criminal law (*ante*, ¶ 50).

[2] See *post*, ¶ 737, for the procedure if he 'stands mute'.

[3] Cf. *R.* v. *Hales* (1924) 17 Cr.App.R. 193; see *post*, ¶ 748. And he must be capable of understanding the proceedings. Hence the trial of a deaf person or a foreigner may have to be delayed until a competent interpreter is found. For an African prisoner who spoke Fanti alone, only two competent interpreters could be found in all England (*The Times*, 9 Dec. 1908).

[4] *Lawrence* v. *The King* [1933] A.C. 699.

[5] Thus the Tichborne claimant was absent on a few of the 188 days of his trial for perjury.

[6] Criminal Justice Act, 1925, s. 33.

[7] Under the Indictments Act, 1915, it is the duty of the clerk of the court to supply to the accused person, on request, a copy of the indictment free of charge. Formerly a felon could not even *buy* one, for fear of his basing on it an action for malicious prosecution.

[8] The prisoner must himself plead; it is not enough for his counsel to state that he wishes to plead guilty; *R.* v. *Heyes* [1950] 2 All E.R. 587. Very many of the prisoners

But in serious cases, lest he should be confessing under some misapprehension as to the law or even as to the facts of his case, the court often advises him to withdraw his plea of guilty, and so let the matter be fully investigated.[1] If to a plea of guilty the accused happens to add some statement which seems so to qualify the plea as to raise doubts whether it is not, in substance, a plea of not guilty, the justices (or quarter sessions on appeal) may take all into account in order to decide which plea it is.[2]

(*b*) Standing mute

¶ 737. If he 'stands mute', i.e. says nothing at all, a jury must be impanelled to try whether he is thus mute 'of malice', or 'by the visitation of God'. In the latter case, the question will arise whether or not he can be made to understand by signs.[3] But if he is mute merely from malice, a plea of not guilty will at once be entered.[4] In treason and misdemeanour at common law, standing mute used to amount, on the other hand, to a confession of guilt. But in felony the matter was less simple. It was preferred to try him; yet he could not be tried by jury (instead of by ordeal) without his own consent. To extort that consent he was (until 12 Geo. III, c. 20) subjected to the *peine forte et dure*, by being laid under a heavy mass of iron, and deprived almost entirely of food. Many prisoners deliberately preferred to die under this torture rather than be tried, because, by dying unconvicted, they saved their families from that forfeiture of property which a conviction would have brought about. In 1772 however, it was provided[5] that a

indicted at assizes or quarter sessions plead guilty. They may plead guilty to some only of the counts, or even to only a part of the count, e.g. 'I admit the jewels but not the money', or to a substitutable offence, not mentioned in the indictment (see ¶ 732 *ante*). The prosecution will frequently abandon a major charge if the accused offers to plead guilty to a minor charge, e.g. to common assault instead of to unlawful wounding.

[1] A plea of guilty may, at the discretion of the judge, be withdrawn at any time before sentence, *R.* v. *McNally* (1954) 38 Cr.App.R. 90, following *R.* v. *Plummer* [1902] 2 K.B. 339; but not after sentence, *R.* v. *McNally* again, dissenting from *R.* v. *Blakemore* (1948) 33 Cr.App.R. 49. In the remarkable case, however, of Constance Kent who, to clear her father's memory, pleaded guilty in 1865 to the Road murder of 1860, Willes, J., at once pronounced sentence of death (*The Times*, 22 July 1865). For procedure when a plea of guilty was made on a charge of murder, see also *R.* v. *Vent* (1935) 25 Cr.App.R. 55.

[2] *R.* v. *Ingleson* [1915] 1 K.B. 512, explained in *R.* v. *Durham Qr. Sess., ex p. Virgo* [1952] W.N. 108.

[3] In *R.* v. *Roberts* [1953] 1 W.L.R. 178, where the jury had found the prisoner to be mute by the visitation of God, Devlin, J., held that the defence might elect to have the general issue tried first, while preserving the right of also setting up unfitness to plead, on the ground that if and when the accused were found unfit to plead the court would be compelled to order his detention as a Broadmoor patient, and yet he might be innocent of the crime charged. But from this ruling Byrne, J., dissented in *R.* v. *Beynon* [1957] 2 W.L.R. 956 (a case in which the prisoner was alleged to be insane) and directed the preliminary question of insanity to be proceeded with and left to the jury.

[4] Criminal Law Act, 1827, s. 2. For an instance in 1912 of a verdict of mute of malice, see *R.* v. *Titus* (1912) C.C.C. Sess. Pap. CLVIII, 46.

[5] Felony and Piracy Act, 12 Geo. III, c. 20 (rep.).

prisoner mute of malice should be treated as guilty and convicted; and now, as above stated, a plea of not guilty is entered.

¶ 737a. *Fitness to plead.* The cases seem to establish that the question whether the accused is fit to plead opens up an inquiry into his sanity or insanity within the M'Naghten Rules (*ante*, ¶ 53), since the Criminal Lunatics Act, 1800, s. 2, provided that, 'if any person indicted for any offence shall be insane . . . so that such person cannot be tried upon such indictment, it shall be lawful for the court . . . to order such person to be kept in strict custody until His Majesty's pleasure be known.' In *R.* v. *Sharp*[1] it was held that the issue whether the prisoner is capable of pleading to and of taking his trial on an indictment is one issue only, and that if the jury find he is unable to communicate with his legal advisers he should be found unfit to plead, and that the onus is on the Crown to prove fitness when the defence raise this issue.[2] However, in *R.* v. *Podola*[3] the Court of Criminal Appeal[4] declared that *R.* v. *Sharp*[5] was wrongly decided, and, in effect, that the question was to be decided on the rules as to the defence of insanity.[6]

(*c*) Objection to indictment

¶ 738. He may show that the indictment is, on the face of it, open to some legal objection, e.g. that a count is too general in its language, or that the court has no jurisdiction to try the offence. Legal objections may be raised by a demurrer[7] or by a motion to quash the indictment (which for technical reasons is the far more common course), e.g. if the offence alleged is not an indictable one.[8] Such a motion may be made at any time before the verdict. If, after the indictment is read but before the accused is put up to plead, a successful objection to the indictment is made by the defence, and the judge quashes the indictment,[9] then there is neither conviction nor acquittal (since only a jury can acquit) but the accused is merely released.[10]

(*d*) Pleas to indictment

¶ 739. He may put in a 'plea' to the indictment. The most important pleas are:

(i) *To the jurisdiction.* This plea is very rarely made. For an objection

[1] (1957) 41 Cr.App.R. 197. [2] Following *R.* v. *Davies* (1853) 6 Cox 326.

[3] [1959] 3 All E.R. 418.

[4] Referring to the Trial of Lunatics Act, 1883, s. 2, which replaces s. 2 of the Act of 1880. [5] Together with *Ley's Case* (1828) 1 Lew. 239 and *R.* v. *Davies, supra.*

[6] *Ante*, ¶ 53. The entirely different point as to whether injustice would be done should a prisoner be convicted where, for instance, the sole witness of the actual shooting is unable to give evidence, was not, it would seem, either decided or discussed.

[7] The Crown may demur to a prisoner's 'plea'.

[8] *R.* v. *Philpotts* (1843) 1 C. and K. 112.

[9] As in *R.* v. *Martin* [1956] 2 All E.R. 86.

[10] Sometimes a jury is sworn solely for the purpose of an acquittal, e.g. where the prosecution have decided to offer no evidence against that one of two co-prisoners who has pleaded not guilty.

to the jurisdiction of the particular court (as when a man is indicted at the quarter sessions for perjury), being a legal objection, may also be raised in the manner just now explained. And if the offence is one over which no English court at all has jurisdiction (e.g. an offence committed on board a foreign ship on the high seas), this defence can clearly be raised not only as a legal objection but even under 'not guilty'.[1]

¶ 740. (ii) *In abatement.* This is an objection alleging some fact which shows that there is in the indictment some error of form, as formerly when a peer was arraigned before assizes or quarter sessions.[2] Such pleas, however, have been rendered obsolete by the powers given to amend indictments.[3]

¶ 741. (iii) *In bar; general.* A plea in bar means a substantial defence (e.g. that the indictment shows no offence known to the law). A *general* plea in bar raises the 'general issue', and traverses (i.e. denies) the whole indictment by alleging that the defendant is 'not guilty'.

¶ 742. (iv) *In bar; special. Justification.* A special plea in bar[4] is rare, as almost any matter of defence can be raised under 'not guilty'. The only ones which require any notice are justification, a pardon from the Crown, autrefois acquit and autrefois convict.

Justification in cases of libel is where the defendant pleads, under Lord Campbell's Act,[5] that the matter charged as libellous is true, and that it was for the public benefit that it should be published. But on this plea costs may be given against the defendant if he fails to establish it. Along with this defence he may (contrary to the general rule, ¶ 744) plead at the same time 'not guilty'.

PARDON FROM THE CROWN

¶ 742a. At common law the Sovereign as the fountain of all justice necessarily possessed the prerogative of pardoning offenders whether before[6] or after the conviction by a court of law. The existence of such

[1] *R.* v. *Johnson* (1805) 6 East 583. Cf. *R.* v. *Jameson* [1896] 2 Q.B. 425.

[2] In *R.* v. *Bray* (Old Bailey Sess. Pap. for 1819, 460) a thief had to be acquitted because the indictment styled the prosecutor as Augustus Stanley, whereas his name was Augustine.

[3] Indictments Act, 1914, s. 5. See ¶ 730 *ante*.

[4] To any special plea the Crown may put in either a 'demurrer' on grounds of law, or a 'special replication' on grounds of fact. E.g. to a plea of 'autrefois acquit' the Crown may reply 'not acquit of arson but only of murder by arson' (*R.* v. *Serné*, *ante*, ¶ 111; *post*, ¶ 744).

[5] 6 and 7 Vict. c. 96; *ante*, ¶ 181. Such a plea may show how peculiar to prisoners is the privilege of tendering evidence of good character (*ante*, ¶ 609). If *A*, being indicted for libellously accusing *B* of theft, should plead the truth of the accusation, *B* (being not a prisoner but a prosecutor) cannot call evidence of his own good character to disprove its truth, though he could do so, if he were *indicted* for the theft.

[6] In addition to pardon there is the possibility of an order staying proceedings on an indictment at any time after the bill of indictment is signed and before judgment. This is effected by the entry of a *nolle prosequi* (*post*, ¶ 773 (iv)) under the authority of the

a power and the limits within which it should be exercised have formed the subjects of much difference of opinion.[1] This topic is mentioned again below (¶ 784).

AUTREFOIS ACQUIT; AUTREFOIS CONVICT

¶ 743. The general principle of common law is *nemo debet bis vexari*—a man must not be put twice in peril for the same offence. Hence, it he be indicted again, he can plead as a complete defence his former acquittal or conviction.[2] Even though it were in a foreign country that the acquittal or conviction took place, it will none the less constitute a defence in our courts.[3] The effect of a verdict of acquittal pronounced by a competent court, indeed, means rather more than that the person acquitted cannot be tried again for the same offence; for to this must be added that the verdict is binding and conclusive in all subsequent proceedings between the parties to the adjudication.[4] The maxim *res judicata pro veritate accipitur* is no less applicable to criminal than to civil proceedings.[5] To determine in any particular case whether such a plea is available, it is necessary to ask:

Was the prisoner 'in jeopardy' on the first indictment?
Was there a final verdict?
Was the previous charge substantially the same as the present one?

A prisoner cannot have been in jeopardy if the indictment was legally invalid; for no conviction upon it would have been effectual. If therefore he defeats it by some plea to the jurisdiction (e.g. where he has been indicted in the wrong county), or by getting it quashed,[6] he will still remain liable to be again indicted on the same charge.

It is necessary that a final verdict should actually have been given. If the petty jury be discharged without a verdict (e.g. on their being unable to agree), this will no more prevent a second trial than would formerly the fact of a former bill's having been ignored by a grand jury.[7]

Attorney-General. Thereupon all proceedings on the indictment are terminated and the accused, if in custody, is released. This is not a pardon, since the accused *may* be indicted once more on the same charge.

[1] The prerogative of mercy is discussed by Radzinowicz, *op. cit.* I, 107 *et seq.*

[2] *R.* v. *Burnham JJ. ex p. Anorge* [1959] 3 All E.R. 505. And a similar plea is allowed by the Magistrates' Courts Act, 1952, in cases where an indictable offence has been dealt with summarily (the ordinary forms of plea being confined to acquittal or conviction by a jury). As to assaults, see also 24 and 25 Vict. c. 100, s. 44.

[3] *Sambasivam* v. *Public Prosecutor, Federation of Malaya* [1950] 66 T.L.R. 254.

[4] *R.* v. *Roche* (1775) I Leach 134 (acquittal by Dutch court). Contrast the law of Italy, see *Jour. Comp. Leg. and Inter. Law*, XV, 87.

[5] A verdict of 'guilty but insane' (*ante*, ¶ 54) has been held by the House of Lords in *Felstead* v. *R.* [1914] A.C. 534. to be a verdict of acquittal against which no appeal lies. But see *R.* v. *Duke* [1961] 3 All E.R. 737 where it was indicated that legislation is needed to improve this unsatisfactory position.

[6] Before he has been put up to plead; *ante*, ¶ 738. But a conviction quashed *on appeal* becomes an acquittal.

[7] See ¶ 718 *ante*.

¶ 744. *Difficulties involved in these pleas.* To determine whether the two charges are 'substantially' identical is often a subtle problem. The test is not whether the facts relied upon are the same in the two trials, but whether there has been an acquittal of an offence which is the same, or practically the same, as that charged in the subsequent indictment.[1] The two indictments must refer to the same transaction.[2] Yet the intent or the circumstances alleged in the one may be more aggravated than those alleged in the other. Thus an acquittal (or similarly a conviction) for a common assault bars a subsequent indictment for an unlawful wounding,[3] and an acquittal for manslaughter bars a subsequent indictment for murder,[4] and vice versa. But neither an acquittal nor a conviction for wounding with intent to murder bars a subsequent indictment for murder;[5] and an acquittal on an indictment for murdering *A* by burning a house in which he was asleep does not bar a subsequent indictment for the arson of the house.[6] For in each of these two pairs of charges, members of the pair are so dissimilar that proof of the allegations made in the second indictment would not necessarily call for some conviction under the first one.[7] An acquittal on a charge of conspiracy is not a bar to a subsequent prosecution of the accused as a principal in the second degree in the same transaction,[8] since a conspirator is not necessarily an aider and abettor, nor vice versa.

In misdemeanours, by a harsh rule, judgment on a plea of autrefois acquit or convict is final, so that if the accused be defeated on it he cannot proceed to establish his innocence, but must be sentenced. Yet

[1] *R.* v. *Kendrick and Smith* (1931) 23 Cr.App.R. 1; 144 L.T. 748. And see *R.* v. *Thomas* [1950] K.B. 26; [1949] 2 All E.R. 662.

[2] They may do this even though they have stated some of the immaterial circumstances in contradictory ways. Thus if *A* has been indicted for murdering *B* on Monday in one parish, and has been acquitted, he can plead autrefois acquit if he be subsequently indicted for murdering him on Tuesday in the adjoining parish, provided he can show by evidence that, though the averments thus differ, the two charges relate to the same transaction.

[3] In *R.* v. *Grimwood* (1896) 60 J.P. 809, a man was indicted on four counts, the first three charging the infliction of grievous bodily harm, etc., but the fourth merely a common assault. On the first three counts the jury disagreed, but they convicted him of the common assault. He was sent to the assizes, to be tried again on the first three counts. At the assizes, however, he pleaded autrefois convict (by the verdict as to the common assault) and was accordingly discharged.

[4] 2 Hale P.C. 246. Similarly an acquittal for any crime bars a second indictment for an attempt to commit that crime, now that (by the Criminal Procedure Act, 1851, s. 9) a jury, on an indictment for any completed offence, can convict of an attempt of it. And, since by the Larceny Act, 1916, s. 44 (2) a jury may convict of embezzlement upon an indictment for larceny or vice versa, an acquittal for either of these felonies bars a subsequent indictment for the other on the same facts.

[5] *R.* v. *De Salvi* (1857) C.C.C. Sess. Pap. XLVI, 884; *R.* v. *Thomas* [1950] K.B. 26; [1949] 2 All E.R. 662; but see *R.* v. *Hogan* (1960) 44 Cr.App.R. 255.

[6] *R.* v. *Serné* (1887) C.C.C. Sess. Pap. CVII, 418.

[7] *Flatman* v. *Light* [1946] 1 K.B. 144. Similarly an acquittal for burglary with intent to commit larceny will not bar a subsequent indictment for the larceny, though it would be otherwise if the first indictment had charged burglary with an actual larceny.

[8] *R.* v. *Kupferberg* (1918) 13 Cr.App.R. 166; 34 T.L.R. 587; *ante*, ¶ 454.

in felony or treason he is allowed to 'plead over', i.e. to put in a further plea of 'not guilty'.

SECTION 4. TRIAL AND VERDICT

¶ 745. 'Justice', said Lord Bacon, 'is sweetest when it is freshest.' Hence the Habeas Corpus Act makes definite provision to secure this freshness, by providing that if any man, who has been committed on a charge of either treason or felony, be not indicted at the next assizes after his commitment, he must be released on bail;[1] and if at the next subsequent assizes he be not both indicted and tried, he must be discharged altogether. And see now the Administration of Justice Act, 1960, sections 14 and 15.[2] The Assizes Relief Act, 1889, ensures the speedy trial of all persons committed to quarter sessions, whether charged with felony or misdemeanour, but there appears to be no statutory provision ensuring the speedy trial of misdemeanants committed to assizes.

HISTORY OF TRIAL BY JURY

¶ 746. When a person indicted pleads 'not guilty' to the accusation he thereby 'joins issue' with the Crown. This issue must be decided by a trial.[3] His indictment will be tried *per patriam*—by a petty jury composed of twelve representatives of his countrymen.[4] The history of such

[1] Unless the witnesses for the Crown cannot appear.

[2] These sections are discussed in [1961] *Crim. L.R.* at pp. 103, 104.

[3] Modern practice concedes to every accused person the right to know, before his trial, what evidence will be given against him. Hence if anyone who was not produced before the committing justice is to be called as a witness, full information should be furnished to the accused, both as to his name and as to the evidence he will give. If this has not been done, his evidence should not be pressed at the trial if the accused objects (*per* Hawkins, J., in *R.* v. *Harris* (1882) C.C.C. Sess. Pap. xcv, 525). The same principle applies to letters or other documents. And every witness whose depositions have been taken before examining justices must be made to attend (unless he has been conditionally bound over to attend as stated in ¶ 713 *ante*) at the trial in order that, if the Crown do not call him, the prisoner may be able to do so. For the prosecuting counsel is not bound to call all his witnesses (*R.* v. *Woodhead* (1847) 2 C. and K. 520), though it is the usual practice to call any witnesses whom the prisoner desires called, so that the defence may cross-examine them. But should the prisoner elect to call a Crown witness who has been thus passed over, he thereby makes him his own witness; and the Crown can accordingly cross-examine the witness, and can reply on his evidence (*R.* v. *Cassidy* (1858) 1 F. and F. 79).

[4] See Pollock and Maitland, I, 138, II, 617; Holdsworth, *Hist. Eng. Law*, I, 312–50; Stubbs, *Constitutional History*, I, s. 164; Stephen, *Hist. Crim. Law*, I, 254. 'It is the most transcendent privilege which any subject can enjoy or wish for, that he cannot be affected either in his property, his liberty or his person but by the unanimous consent of twelve of his neighbours and equals' (3 Bl. *Comm.* 379). And see *Trial by Jury* by Sir Patrick Devlin, Hamlyn Lecture, no. 8. It is true that, as an instrument of accurate inquiry, the value of the jury may sometimes be small. In matters of complicated mercantile accounts, or in scientific disputes about a prisoner's insanity or the results of a poison, or in any very protracted investigation, trial by a common jury—'that bizarre creation' as Garofalo calls it—would have little superiority over trial by ordeal or by compurgation,

trials is noteworthy. Originally, accusations made by the grand jury were tried by ordeal. After the abolition of ordeals in 1215, every accusation had to be referred back to the grand jury, sometimes with the addition of some further colleagues.[1] In the course of a century, it came to be the practice for these new jurors alone to undertake this duty of revision, without the presence of the original accusers; and at last the latter were definitely excluded by a statute of 1352. This produced the system of two juries. But both juries proceeded upon common repute, or upon their personal knowledge, men who knew the circumstances of the crime being often put on as additional or 'afforcing' jurors. About 1500, however, such persons ceased to be added to the jury itself, and instead were sent to give evidence before it. This differentiation of the functions of the witness from those of the juror was intensified, two centuries later, by allowing witnesses to be called expressly on behalf of the prisoner. Documentary evidence became common before that of witnesses; and it seems probable that even the evidence of witnesses was at first usually received in a written form. At any rate the practice of producing the witnesses themselves at the trial, to give their evidence orally in open court—though well-established in non-political cases at least as early as Elizabeth I's reign[2]—did not become usual in trials for treason until the Commonwealth.[3] Under James I and Charles I the evidence produced to the jury in political trials usually consisted only in 'examinations', i.e. reports of what had been said by witnesses when interrogated by royal commissioners, in the absence of the prisoner and in private—perhaps in prison or even on the rack. Often the accused himself was thus interrogated, as when Peacham, in 1615, was examined 'before torture, in torture, between torture, and after torture'.[4] But from the time of the Commonwealth onwards the modern course of trial has prevailed, in political as well as in non-political cases.[4]

were it not for the guidance afforded in the judge's summing up. Hence, ever since the Rules of 1883 (Order XXXVI), trial by a judge, with no jury, has been recognized as the normal *civil* method. But in criminal cases it is not so important that the verdict should be accurate as that it should be humane and, moreover, be supported by public sentiment: to let some guilty men escape is a lesser evil than to punish any innocent man.

[1] Pollock and Maitland, II, 628, 647; Holdsworth, *Hist. Eng. Law*, I, 323, 334.

[2] Sir T. Smith's *Commonwealth of England.*

[3] The provision made (*ante*, ¶ 417) by 1 Edw. VI, c. 12 to secure the production of at least two witnesses in open court in all cases of treason was regarded as having been impliedly repealed by 1 and 2 Ph. and Mary, c. 10.

[4] *Ante*, ¶ 404; 2 St.Tr. at p. 871. On the trial of Lord Essex in 1600 (1 St.Tr. 1333), in which many of these 'examinations' were used, Coke, then Attorney-General, blamed the 'overmuch clemency' of Elizabeth I in having had no witness racked or tortured whilst being examined.

[5] An inroad upon the dignity of trials was checked by the Criminal Justice Act, 1925, which makes it an offence, punishable by a fine of £50, to sketch for publication, or to photograph, in any court whether criminal or civil, any of the persons concerned in a judicial proceeding (s. 41).

JURY SERVICE

¶ 747. To serve as a petty juror in criminal cases (or as a common juror in civil ones) a person[1] must be over twenty-one years of age,[2] and must be the owner, in fee or for life, of lands or tenements worth £10 a year or of long leaseholds worth £20 a year, or else be the occupier of a house rated at £20 a year, or if in Middlesex at £30.[3] In each county the sheriff returns a 'panel',[4] or list, at every assize, of persons thus qualified whom he has summoned. There is no fixed number; but forty-eight is a frequent number at assizes, and thirty-six at sessions. From this panel the clerk calls twelve names, and the prisoner then has the opportunity of challenging any of these jurors. Jury service can be a real burden.

This will now not be so serious as in the past, since the Juries Act, 1949, has made provision for the payment to jurors of travelling and subsistence allowances and compensation for loss of earnings which they would otherwise have made, and for additional expenses (other than those on account of travelling and subsistence) which they would not otherwise have incurred.

RIGHT OF CHALLENGE

¶ 748. Challenges are now rare in England,[5] but less rare in Ireland.[6] They may be either to the 'array' (i.e. the whole panel), where the sheriff has composed it in an unfair manner, e.g. by choosing men on

[1] Of either sex. For the Sex Disqualification (Removal) Act, 1919, 9 and 10 Geo. V, c. 71, provides that 'A person shall not be disqualified by sex or marriage from the exercise of any public function, or from...holding any civil or judicial office;...and a person shall not be exempted by sex or marriage from the liability to serve as a juror'. But the judge who tries a case, criminal or civil, may—on application of either side or at his own instance—make an order 'that the jury shall be composed of men only or of women only'. It has since been provided, by Rules, that every jury panel shall include women in the same proportion as they hold in the local list of persons qualified to be jurors, and, if possible, not fewer than fourteen women. But husband and wife are not to be on the same panel.

[2] If over sixty he may claim exemption.

[3] In boroughs that have a court of quarter sessions the persons whose names are included in so much of the county jurors' book as covers the borough are the jurors qualified and liable to serve.

[4] I.e. a strip (Latin, *pannus*); hence names written on a strip of parchment. The preparation of this list is governed by the Juries Act, 1922, and the Representation of the People Act, 1949, s. 6. In Scots law, however, the person or persons accused are called 'the panel', i.e. the *list* named in the indictment.

[5] This rarity makes it easy to arraign together before one jury prisoners concerned in different indictments, thus saving time.

[6] In the United States, from the diversities of race and language, they are employed freely, sometimes occupying two or more days of a trial. Hence, 'experience in the selection of a jury is one of the fine arts of an [American] advocate'. A like cause may lead to a like result in East London. In one case there, eight of the twelve jurors were Polish Jews who could not write. Maître Lachaud, that most successful defender of prisoners in France, made it his rule, 'I challenge every man who looks intelligent'. In Ireland a kindred rule was at one time current: 'Challenge every juror who wears a neck-tie.'

the ground of their religion, or to the polls (i.e. to individual jurors). Felons jointly indicted sometimes challenge *different* groups of jurors, so as to secure being tried separately, e.g. when one prisoner has made admissions, or been found in possession of papers, that would not be legal evidence against the other man. An individual may be thus challenged either for cause shown, or even 'peremptorily' (i.e. without showing cause). A challenge for cause may be made *propter respectum*, e.g. to a peer; *propter affectum*, e.g. for being near of kin to the defendant; *propter defectum*, e.g. for infancy or alienage; *propter delictum*, i.e. on the ground of the juror's having been convicted of some infamous offence, e.g. perjury. These objections may be raised either by the Crown or by the accused. But a 'peremptory' challenge can be made only by the accused. And now he can exercise this right in all indictments under which he is arraigned for treason,[1] felony, or misdemeanour.[2] But he may not challenge more than seven jurors without cause.[3] The jury are then sworn.[4] If the case be one of felony or treason, the indictment is read over to the jury; this is called 'charging' them[5] with the inquiry concerning the prisoner. It is not so read in cases of misdemeanour, because there the defendant has always been entitled to a copy. The prisoner has a right to be present in court throughout the trial for felony.[6]

OPENING THE INDICTMENT

¶ 749. The indictment is then 'opened'[7]; that is to say, the counsel for the prosecution[8] addresses the jury, in order to direct their minds to the main questions in dispute, to tell them what evidence he proposes to adduce, and to explain its bearings upon the case.[9] A prosecuting counsel stands in a position quite different from that of an advocate who represents the person accused or represents a plaintiff or defendant in a civil litigation. For this latter advocate has a private duty—that of

[1] Treason Act, 1945, s. 1.

[2] Criminal Justice Act, 1948, s. 35 (1).

[3] *Ibid.*

[4] See the Oaths Act, 1909 (9 Edw. VII, c. 39). The Criminal Justice Act, 1925, s. 15, provides against death or illness of a juror, or of *two*, during a trial, allowing the remainder to act, if prosecutor and accused consent in writing.

[5] Until they had performed this charge, by completing the inquiry, the common law did not permit them, in cases of treason or felony, to depart from the custody of the court, however protracted the trial might be. In 1873, in *R.* v. *Moore*, an Irish trial for murder (114 witnesses), the jury were thus secluded for more than six weeks (*The Times*, 11 Sept. 1873). But now the court may, if it thinks fit, at any time before the jury consider their verdict, permit them to separate; Criminal Justice Act, 1948, s. 35 (4).

[6] *Ante*, ¶ 735; *R.* v. *St George* (1840) 9 C. and P. 483; *R.* v. *Hales* [1924] 1 K.B. 602. Unless he creates a disturbance, *R.* v. *Berry* (1897) 104 L.T.Jo. 110. And see [1954] *Crim.L.R.* 279 concerning *R.* v. *Vernell* (1953) Vict.L.R. 590.

[7] A table of the order of speeches will be found in Arch. ¶ 560.

[8] A prosecutor who employs no counsel is not allowed (as he is in summary proceedings) to make any such opening speech or to examine the witnesses.

[9] In Scotland there is no such speech; its absence makes the work of the jury harder.

doing everything that he honourably can to protect the interests of his client. He is entitled to 'fight for a verdict'. But the Crown counsel is a representative of the State, 'a minister of justice';[1] his function is to assist the jury in arriving at the truth. He must not urge any argument that does not carry weight in his own mind, or try to shut out any legal evidence that would be important to the interests of the person accused.[2] 'It is not his duty to obtain a conviction by all means; but simply to lay before the jury the whole of the facts which compose his case, and to make these perfectly intelligible, and to see that the jury are instructed with regard to the law and are able to apply the law to the facts.'[3] 'It cannot be too often made plain that the business of counsel for the Crown is fairly and impartially to exhibit all the facts to the jury. The Crown has no interest in procuring a conviction. Its only interest is that the right person should be convicted, that the truth should be known, and that justice should be done.'[4] Thus it has been declared that witnesses essential to the unfolding of the narratives, on which the prosecution is based, must, of course, be called by the prosecution, whether in the result the effect of their testimony is for or against the case for the prosecution.[5] But there is no rule or principle of practice that the prosecution must call witnesses irrespective of considerations of number and of reliability, or that the prosecution should discharge the functions both of prosecution and defence.[6] It is regarded as proper, and enough, for the prosecution to acquaint the defence with any relevant information which has come into their hands so that the defence may have the opportunity to use it if they desire, and so that no unfairness should be visited upon a defendant.[7]

PROSECUTOR'S WITNESSES

¶ 750. On concluding his address, the prosecuting counsel calls his witnesses, one after another; and each is examined in chief, cross-examined, and re-examined, successively.[8] Then, the Crown evidence

[1] R. v. *Puddick* (1865) 4 F. and F. 497 at p. 499; R. v. *Rudland* (1865) 4 F. and F. 495; R. v. *Banks* [1916] 2 K.B. 621 at p. 623.

[2] E.g. if the prisoner has written one letter confessing the crime, and another retracting this confession, the Crown must not put the former in evidence without producing the latter also. Similarly, if the victim of an alleged assault has been examined by the police surgeon, this surgeon should be called by the Crown, even if he negative the assault.

[3] Sir J. Holker, Att.-Gen. (*The Times*, 25 Feb. 1880).

[4] R. v. *Sugarman* (1935) 25 Cr.App.R. 109 at p. 115.

[5] *Seneviratne* v. R. [1936] 3 All E.R. 36.

[6] Notwithstanding the remarks of Lord Hewart, C.J., *arguendo*, in R. v. *Harris* [1927] 2 K.B. 587 at p. 590, which were clearly not intended to be understood as a general statement for all cases.

[7] The question was discussed in R. v. *Nicholson* (1936) Notts Summer Assizes, before Hawke, J.; see 100 *J.P.Jo.* 553. And see R. v. *Collier* [1958] Crim. L.R. 544; [1958] Curr. Law 8, no. 95.

[8] *Ante*, ¶ 533. And the prisoner's statement to the committing justice is usually read now; cf. ¶ 702 *ante*.

being thus completed, the prisoner's counsel sometimes submits that it is not such as could reasonably satisfy any jury that the accusation is established; and he therefore asks the judge to withdraw the case from the jury. If the request be refused or not made, then comes the defence of the person accused. If the judge refuses to withdraw the case from the jury the defence must proceed, and if evidence for the defence is called and it happens that this evidence in fact incriminates the prisoner, then this will be taken into account against him, so as to defeat a subsequent appeal by him on the ground that the judge's ruling was wrong.[1]

¶ 751. *New matter arising* ex improviso *after the case for the prosecution is closed.* The general rule is that the prosecution must close their case before the defence begins, and that they must stand or fall by the evidence which they have given, and cannot afterwards support their case by calling fresh witnesses, because they have been met by evidence on behalf of the defence which contradicts the evidence which the prosecution had previously given.[2]

Yet if any new matter arises *ex improviso* which the prosecution could not have foreseen, and, as it has been stated, 'which no human ingenuity can foresee',[3] then the judge, at his discretion, may himself call a witness or witnesses, notwithstanding that the case for the prosecution has closed.[4] So also the judge has power to call a new witness after the case for the defence has closed, but here also it has been declared that it should be limited to the occasion when matter has arisen *ex improviso*, in order to avoid injustice.[5] Two other exceptions arise in circumstances where the question of the prisoner's previous convictions becomes relevant,[6] and when the defence has given evidence of the prisoner's good character.[7]

[1] *R.* v. *Power* [1919] 1 K.B. 572, explained in *R.* v. *Abbott* [1955] A.C. 497.

[2] *R.* v. *Frost* (1839) 4 St.Tr. (n.s.) 85; 9 C. and P. 159, *per* Tindal, C.J.; *R.* v. *Browne* (1943) 29 Cr.App.R. 106, 126.

[3] *R.* v. *Harris* [1927] 2 K.B. 587 at p. 595 *per* Avory, J. See *R.* v. *Day* [1940] 1 All E.R. 402.

[4] This power is rarely exercised, e.g. Baron Bramwell refused to exercise it, in *R.* v. *Haynes* (1859) 1 F. and F. 666. And not after the judge has summed up, *R.* v. *Owen* [1952] 2 Q.B. 362 at p. 368; save in very special circumstances, *R.* v. *Sanderson* (1953) 37 Cr.App.R. 32 (where the summing-up was not concluded, but interrupted). In *R.* v. *Wilson* (1957) 41 Cr.App.R. 226, it was stated, following *R.* v. *Owen*, that once the summing-up is concluded no further evidence will be admitted, a rule which must be maintained in every case.

[5] *R.* v. *Harris*, *supra*; *R.* v. *Jordan* (1956) 40 Cr.App.R. 152, where the C.C.A. admitted fresh evidence; *post*, ¶ 777. And see *R.* v. *Silverman* [1961] 11 Curr. Law 326*a*.

[6] See *post*, App. II, C; *R.* v. *Hughes* (1843) 1 Cox 44.

[7] *R.* v. *Rowton* (1865) L. and C. 520; *post*, App. II. It should be noted that in a *civil* case the judge is not allowed to call a witness whom he thinks might throw some light on the facts; he must rest content with the witnesses called by the parties; *In re Enoch and Zaretzky, Bock & Co.* [1910] 1 K.B. 327, cited in *Jones* v. *N.C.B.* [1957] 2 W.L.R. 760.

THE CASE FOR THE DEFENCE

¶ 752. If the accused has no witnesses to call (except witnesses merely to character), he may nevertheless himself give evidence on oath (should he desire to do so) and be cross-examined upon it.[1] After doing this (or declining to do it), and calling any witnesses to *character*, then if he have no counsel, he may address the jury in his own defence; if he have counsel,[2] the prosecuting counsel may, should there actually be adequate cause,[3] make a second speech, summing up the Crown evidence and commenting on the prisoner's own evidence[4] (if any). Then the counsel for the accused addresses the jury.[5]

But if the accused has witnesses to facts then, so soon as the Crown witnesses have finished, his counsel[6] (or he[7]) 'opens' his case. Then his witnesses (including himself, if he desire to give evidence on oath) are examined, cross-examined, and re-examined.[8] His counsel (or he) makes a second speech, summing up the defence. Finally the prosecuting counsel makes a speech in reply.

It must be noted that the accused person has the right (for himself or his advisers) to hear all the evidence given to the jury upon which their verdict is to depend, even though the particular evidence be elicited in his favour.[9] And further, the judge must be present during the whole of the trial (which includes any inspection of the scene of the alleged offence, at which witnesses point out particular places which

[1] See ¶ 621 *ante*.

[2] For an account of the traditional institution known as 'dock briefs' see 226 *Law Times* 74, 8 Aug. 1958; and ¶ 785 n. 5, *post*.

[3] E.g. if the evidence has proved to be other than was indicated in his opening speech; *R.* v. *Holchester* (1866) 10 Cox 226.

[4] *R.* v. *Gardner* [1899] 1 Q.B. 150.

[5] By a somewhat harsh privilege, the Attorney-General or Solicitor-General, *if present in person*, may in both cases make a final speech in reply. Otherwise a prisoner, by calling no witnesses, secures the right to the last word. The law officers in 1930 announced that they would not exercise the right of reply.

[6] Where several prisoners, who are being tried together, take the same course as to calling (or not calling) witnesses, their respective counsel usually make their speeches (not in order of professional seniority but) in the order in which their several clients' names occur in the indictment (*R.* v. *Barber* (1844) 1 C. and K. 434). Where, again, some prisoners call witnesses but others do not, the counsel for the latter will have the right to the last word, and so will not speak until after the Crown counsel has replied upon the evidence tendered by the other prisoners (*R.* v. *Burns* (1887) 16 Cox 195; cf. *R.* v. *Vass and Baldock* (1883) C.C.C. Sess. Pap. XCVIII, 357 at p. 363; *R.* v. *Serné and Goldfinch* (1887) C.C.C. Sess. Pap. CVII, 122 at p. 147; *R.* v. *Wilson* (1904) C.C.C. Sess. Pap. CXL, 597 at p. 602).

[7] To statements of fact in his address 'the jury may, as regards *himself*, pay any degree of credence that they may think fit' though they are not uttered upon oath (Channell, J.).

[8] In the rare cases where the witnesses for the defence introduce new matter of importance which the prosecution could not have foreseen (e.g. an alibi, or insanity), rebutting evidence to contradict them may be called even at this late stage, *R.* v. *Frost* (1839) 4 St.Tr. (n.s.) 85; *R.* v. *Stimpson* (1863) 2 C. and P. 415; *ante*, ¶ 751.

[9] *R.* v. *Bodmin Justices, ex p. McEwen* [1947] K.B. 321.

had been mentioned in their evidence and demonstrate what had happened).[1]

The judge's part during the course of any trial has been expressed to be:[2]

> to hearken to the evidence, only himself asking questions of witnesses when it is necessary to clear up any point that has been overlooked or left obscure; to see that the advocates behave themselves seemly and keep to the rules laid down by law; to exclude irrelevancies and discourage repetition; to make sure by wise intervention that he follows the points that the advocates are making and can assess their worth; and at the end to make up his mind where the truth lies. If he goes beyond this, he drops the mantle of a judge and assumes the robe of an advocate; and the change does not become him well. Lord Bacon spoke right when he said that:[3] 'Patience and gravity of hearing is an essential part of justice; and an over-speaking judge is no well-tuned cymbal.'

THE JUDGE SUMS UP

¶ 753. When both cases have thus been fully stated it becomes the duty of the judge to sum up the case to the jury, a security for justice unknown to the tribunals of classical antiquity.[4] He not only directs them as to any points of law that are involved in the case, but also advises[5] them, though not imperatively, as to the bearing and value of the evidence. There was no enforceable standard for summings up until the creation of the Court of Criminal Appeal. But now it requires every summing up to be not only accurate but also adequate. The judge may ask the jury to answer definite questions of fact; but they are entitled to refuse to do so, if they prefer to give a general verdict.

It is the duty of the judge to draw the attention of the jury to points in the evidence which may establish a defence for the accused (e.g. provocation, *ante*, ¶ 126) even though his counsel has not done so.

[1] *Tameshwar* v. *R.* [1957] 3 W.L.R. 157 in which *R.* v. *Martin and Webb* (1872) 1 C.C.R. 378 was distinguished.

[2] *Jones* v. *N.C.B.* [1957] 2 W.L.R. at p. 767.

[3] *Essays or Counsels Civil and Moral*, 'Of Judicature'.

[4] Yet in England it is found as early as 1348; Holdsworth, *Hist. Eng. Law*, III, 614. But in France the judges were deprived in 1881 of the power of summing up, as they were thought to exercise it too exclusively in the interests of the prosecution. American lawyers complain of the restrictions whereby some of their States limit or abolish the judge's power to express an opinion on questions of fact, and to control trials 'and hold the jury to its province' (see Prof. Roscoe Pound's *Spirit of the Common Law*, 123). They attribute to this lack of guidance many undeserved acquittals.

[5] Cf. *R.* v. *Mason* (1924) 18 Cr.App.R. 132; and *Clouston* v. *Corry* [1906] A.C. 122 at p. 130. See *R.* v. *Tillman* [1962] Crim. L.R. 261.

VERDICT

¶ 754. The jury then have to consider their verdict,[1] and may, if necessary, retire for that purpose.[2] In *R.* v. *McKenna and Busby*[3] the court stated a 'cardinal principle of our common law':

> A jury shall deliberate in complete freedom, uninfluenced by any promise, unintimidated by any threat.... A jury should be free to take such time [to consider their verdict] as they feel they need, subject always, of course, to the right of a judge to discharge them if protracted consideration still produces disagreement.[3]

The jury may, at their discretion, return either a 'special' verdict, i.e. one on the facts alone,[4] or a 'general' verdict pronouncing on both the facts and the law,[5] i.e. 'guilty', or 'not guilty'.[6] The verdict may dispose of the whole indictment in the same way, or may pronounce the prisoner guilty on some counts but not on others, or even on one part of a divisible count but not on the residue. We have already seen (¶ 732) that, in a few exceptional cases, juries are empowered by modern statutes to convict of an offence other than that which the evidence has established. The first delivery of the verdict is not final; for the court may direct the jury to reconsider it. If they find it hopeless to agree, the judge may discharge them; cases have been tried even four times; e.g. *Tease*, at Belfast, in 1909.

In the interests of justice it has been held that any communication between a jury, after their retirement, and the presiding judge, even though it may be quite immaterial, must be read out in open court and the answer given in the presence and hearing of the prosecution and of the accused person,[7] unless the point be one upon which no argument

[1] A verdict must be the utterance of twelve jurors, so that in the petty jury, as there are but twelve, unanimity is essential; see *R.* v. *Davey* [1960] 3 All E.R. 533. But in any larger jury, such as a jury on an inquisition of lunacy, a majority suffices, if it consist of twelve. In Scotland (the jury there consisting of as many as fifteen) the verdict of a majority suffices. As to illness, see ¶ 748, p. 595 n. 4.

[2] They are no longer debarred from 'food, drink, and fire' after retiring; the Juries Act, 1870, permits them to have 'reasonable refreshment'.

[3] *R.* v. *McKenna and Busby* (1960) 44 Cr.App.R. 63. See *Shoukatallie* v. *R.* [1961] 3 W.L.R. 1021.

[4] Rare; a modern instance is *R.* v. *Dudley* (1884) 14 Q.B.D. 273 (*T.A.C.*); *ante*, ¶ 47.

[5] It has sometimes been suggested that the jury are thus 'made judges of the law as well as of the facts'. But this is not so; for it is their duty to adopt the law as laid down to them by the judge. See *R.* v. *Shipley* (1783) 21 St.Tr. 847 at p. 1039. True there is *now* (contrast *Wharton's Case* (1602) Yelv. 24 and Noy 48; *R.* v. *Penn* (1670) 6 St.Tr. 951 at p. 967) no legal redress if they violate this duty, e.g. if they declare a homicide to have been a murder although by law it was justifiable. But this legal impunity only shows that their duty of making their verdict accord with the law, is—like their duty of making it accord with the evidence—not a jural but an ethical obligation.

[6] Meaning that there is not full legal proof of guilt, but not necessarily that they think him *innocent*. Scotland, by a third alternative verdict ('not proven', like Rome's 'non liquet'), avoids this ambiguity, and so renders 'not guilty' a clearly definite exculpation.

[7] *R.* v. *Green* [1950] 1 All E.R. 38; *R.* v. *Ion* (1950) 34 Cr.App.R. 152.

could possibly take place.[1] After verdict the court will hear evidence for the Crown, or for the prisoner, for the purpose of deciding upon the appropriate sentence.[2] If the verdict is incomprehensible, ambiguous,[3] or contradictory,[4] or defective in the sense that it is one which, on the evidence, is not within the jury's competence to give,[5] then the judge may direct them to reconsider it.

MOTION IN ARREST OF JUDGMENT

¶ 755. On being convicted of felony or treason the prisoner is asked if he has anything to say why the court should not pronounce judgment against him. This inquiry contemplates only objections of *law*, i.e. grounds for a motion in arrest of judgment[6] (now practically unknown). Since the establishment of the Court of Criminal Appeal the question might well be abandoned, as it serves no purpose and tends to elicit irrelevant and mendacious protestations of innocence.[7]

SECTION 5. JUDGMENT

¶ 756. Sentences are not final or complete until the document delivered to the gaoler as recording the sentences is finally signed.[8] In times past sentence was sometimes postponed, in order to give the prisoner an opportunity of mitigating it by making restitution or giving information, or in order to inflict on him *some* punishment without any obvious disgrace, when it was intended merely to discharge him on recognizances; but such a course is now regarded as improper.[9]

A criminal decision, whether of conviction or of acquittal, constitutes a conclusive estoppel as between the Crown and the prisoner. But in any subsequent civil proceedings between either of them and a third party, that decision is no estoppel. It is, however, admissible evidence to rebut a claim to property made by or through the convict.[10]

PUNISHMENTS

¶ 757. Already, in our successive accounts of the various kinds of criminal offences, we have mentioned, in connexion with each one, the character of the punishments which the law prescribes for it. All that now remains, therefore, is to state some provisions which affect punishment in general. Thus the Bill of Rights provides that 'excessive

[1] *R.* v. *Furlong* [1950] 1 All E.R. 636; 34 Cr.App.R. 79. And see *R.* v. *Thompson* [1962] 1 All E.R. 65.
[2] See App. II A (5), C (2) and (7), *post.*
[3] *R.* v. *Gibbs* [1960] Crim. L.R. 197, n.; *R.* v. *Cowdell* [1962] Crim. L.R. 262.
[4] *R.* v. *Crisp* (1912) 7 Cr.App.R. 173; *R.* v. *White* [1961] Crim. L.R. 59; *R.* v. *O'Brien* [1961] Crim. L.R. 490.
[5] *R.* v. *Meany* (1862) 9 Cox 231.
[6] See Arch. 612. A motion may be made in arrest of judgment in misdemeanours.
[7] A salient instance of the untrustworthiness of such protestations is that of Alvin, sentenced to death at York for murder in 1712. During the 'condemned sermon' he made a loud protest of his innocence, which so startled the preacher, the Rev. Mr Mace, that he fell dead in the pulpit. Alvin claimed this as a divine vindication of himself. Yet, at his execution, he confessed his guilt. (Poulson's *History of Holderness*, II, 407.)
[8] *R.* v. *Batchelor* (1952) 36 Cr.App.R. 64, *per* Lord Goddard, C.J.
[9] See Arch. 612.
[10] *Re Crippen* [1911] P. 108

fines ought not to be imposed, or cruel and unusual punishments inflicted'. Hence judges cannot create new punishments.[1]

The forms of punishment now permitted by law are death, imprisonment, fine, and, chiefly in the case of juvenile offenders, detention (in approved schools, etc.[2]).

The penalty of death[3] is now practically restricted to cases of capital murder.[4]

¶ 758. *Imprisonment.* The Criminal Justice Act, 1948, s. 1 (1) abolished the punishment of penal servitude, which had been created in 1853[5] to take the place of transportation. The Act also abolished the punishment of imprisonment *with hard labour*,[6] so that now there is only one form of imprisonment for crime, the distinctions between imprisonment in the first, second, or third divisions having also been removed.[7] And now by virtue of the Criminal Justice Act, 1961, ss. 2, 3 and 4, no court may impose imprisonment on a person under seventeen years of age; for those offenders within the limits of age (i.e. fifteen to twenty-one years) which qualify for a sentence of borstal training no court may exceed a sentence of six months' imprisonment (or, in certain serious cases, three years); but even so the court must not impose this punishment on a person under twenty-one unless it thinks that no other method of dealing with him is appropriate; in order to determine this question the court must obtain and consider information about the circumstances, taking into account anything relevant to his character and his physical and mental condition. Instead, the offenders aged fourteen to twenty-one who would have been eligible for imprisonment if adult, may be sent to a detention centre or to a remand home; *post*, ¶ 762*a*. And as more detention centres become available even

[1] Thus where a defendant was sentenced to be imprisoned, and also to ask the prosecutor's pardon and advertise the fact in certain newspapers, this was held bad, except as to the imprisonment; *R.* v. *Collier and Cape* (1752) 1 Wils. K.B. 332.

[2] See ¶ 763 *post.*

[3] The hanging does not operate now through suffocation, but by a 'long drop', invented by Prof. Haughton of Dublin, which dislocates the vertebrae and so produces an instantaneous and painless death. Persons under eighteen cannot now be sentenced to death, but are 'detained' during the Queen's pleasure; Homicide Act, 1957, s. 9 (3). Bishop, aged eighteen, was executed in 1925. Where a woman convicted of an offence punishable with death is found by the trial jury to be pregnant, she is sentenced to imprisonment for life instead; Sentence of Death (Expectant Mothers) Act, 1931. Until the passing of this Act pregnancy did not affect the sentence, but resulted in a stay of execution. The issue of pregnancy or not was decided by a jury of twelve matrons.

[4] Homicide Act, 1957, part II. There are, however, three other capital offences: viz. treason and certain forms of piracy and arson (*ante*, ¶¶ 419, 478, 203).

[5] 16 and 17 Vict. c. 99. [6] Sect. 1 (2). [7] Sect. 1 (3).

[8] Magistrates' Courts Act, 1952, s. 107, and Criminal Justice Act, 1948, s. 17 (1). But note the provisions whereby in very grave crimes a young offender may be sentenced to be detained during Her Majesty's pleasure, by virtue of the Children and Young Persons Act, 1933, s. 53, the Homicide Act, 1957, s. 9, and the Criminal Justice Act, 1961, s. (2) (1). On the last named Act see [1961] *Crim. L.R.* 582, an article by A. Samuels.

short terms of imprisonment may be abolished.[1] The new Acts have thus restricted the use of prison, as such, as a place for criminal sanction, and have restricted its employment to cases for which other methods have failed or are inappropriate.[2] A sentence for felony involves forfeiture of any pension unless the sentence be only one of imprisonment for not more than twelve months.[3]

At common law the punishment for misdemeanours (as distinct from felonies) was fine or imprisonment (or both), entirely at the discretion of the court as to the amount of each.[4] But in modern times the courts had formed the practice of not passing sentences of over two years' imprisonment owing to the relatively severe conditions of imprisonment as compared with penal servitude, although there was really nothing illegal in exceeding that limit, or in sentencing a person found guilty under two or more counts of an indictment to periods of imprisonment in respect of each offence to run consecutively so as to make a larger total period.[5] However, in the last fifty years the severities of prison regime have been greatly mitigated, even before the changes made by the Criminal Justice Act, 1948, so that the courts have no reason to feel so restricted as formerly in deciding on the period of sentence for a common law misdemeanour.[6]

¶ 759. *The Firearms Act, 1937.* This Act, which regulates, under pain of criminal sanctions, the manufacture, sale, purchase, and possession of firearms,[7] also makes an offender liable to imprisonment for seven years[8] in addition to any other punishment to which he may be liable, if at the time of his apprehension for any of the offences specified in the Act[9] he has in his possession any firearm[10] or imitation firearm. See also

[1] Criminal Justice Act, 1961, sect. 5 (5). By Order in Council.

[2] For an account of the effect of this legislation on the sanction of imprisonment see Fox, 'The Criminal Justice Act and prison administration', *Journal of Criminal Science*, II, 1 *et seq.*

[3] Forfeiture Act, 1870, s. 2; the Criminal Justice Act, 1948, s. 70 (2) allows the appropriate authority to restore the pension either in whole or in part.

[4] Within the general prohibitions of excessive penalties contained in Magna Carta and in the Bill of Rights, 1688.

[5] E.g. *R.* v. *Roberts and Morriss* (1926) 134 L.T. 635.

[6] See *R.* v. *Morris* [1951] 1 K.B. 394, in which the subject is fully discussed in the judgment of the court. *R.* v. *Bryan* (1951) 35 Cr.App.R. 121 (a sentence of ten years). And contrast *R.* v. *Murray* [1950] 2 All E.R. 925, an earlier case, in which it was stated by the Court of Criminal Appeal (at p. 928) that the maximum sentence for common law attempt (which is a misdemeanour) was two years' imprisonment. But now see *R.* v. *Blake* [1961] 3 All E.R. 125.

[7] See Russ. ch. 35.

[8] Sect. 23; fourteen years, if he makes any use of the firearm with intent to resist or prevent the arrest of himself or of another person.

[9] Schedule III. The offences include those under ss. 1–12, 14, 15, 26–9, 33–8, and 54 of the Malicious Damage Act, 1861; under ss. 20–2, 30, 32, 38, 47, 48, 53–6 of the Offences against the Person Act, 1861; ss. 2–4, 12–15, 24–7, 28 (paras. (2), (3), (4)), 29, 30, of the Larceny Act, 1916; s. 28 of the Road Traffic Act, 1930; certain offences under the Vagrancy Act, 1824, and the Prevention of Crimes Act, 1871; and aiding or abetting the commission of any of the above offences; and attempting any but those under ss. 8, 27, or 38 of the Malicious Damage Act, 1861.

[10] See *Moore* v. *Gooderham* [1960] 1 W.L.R. 1308.

the Prevention of Crime Act, 1953,[1] by virtue of which any person who, without lawful authority or reasonable excuse (the proof whereof shall lie on him[2]), has with him[3] in any public place[4] any offensive weapon[5] is guilty of an offence. And see the Restriction of Offensive Weapons Acts, 1959 and 1961.

¶ 760. *Borstal training.*[6] By virtue of the Criminal Justice Act, 1948, s. 20, as amended by the Criminal Justice Act, 1961, when a person has been convicted on indictment[7] of an offence punishable with imprisonment, then if he is not less than fifteen and under twenty-one the court may pass a sentence of Borstal training in place of any other sentence, provided the court is satisfied that it is expedient to do so for his reformation and for the prevention of crime, and, if he is under seventeen at conviction, that no other method is appropriate. In coming to this conclusion the court must have regard to the offender's character and previous conduct, and to the circumstances of the offence. The court is not to specify any period for this training but the Act of 1961 provides[8] that the period shall be for not less than six months[9] nor more than two years from the date of his sentence.[10]

¶ 761. *Origin of Borstal institutions.* The name Borstal is derived from Borstal, near Rochester, where the experiment of educational training for young offenders in place of the usual prison regime was tried in 1902. Its success led to the passing of section 1 of the Prevention of Crime Act, 1908,[11] under which such convicted persons could be sent

[1] Unless, if charged under the former Act, he can show that he has it in his possession for a lawful object.

[2] If the weapon is one made or adapted for causing injury (e.g. pistol, bludgeon, stiletto, etc.) the burden is on the defence to show, on balance of probabilities, lawful authority etc.; but if it is not so made or adapted the prosecution must prove that it was carried with intent to be used to cause injury, *R.* v. *Petrie* [1961] 1 All E.R. 466; and see *R.* v. *Jura* (1954) 38 Cr.App.R. 53.

[3] This means 'knowingly has with him', *R.* v. *Cugullere* [1961] 2 All E.R. 343.

[4] This includes any highway or other place to which the public have access with or without payment.

[5] This is either one made or adapted for causing injury (which includes intimidating or frightening a person), or one intended to be used to cause injury, and this last can appear from the use which the accused did make of it; see *Woodward* v. *Koessler* [1958] 1 W.L.R. 1255, distinguished in *Farrell* v. *Rennicks* [1959] 9 Curr. Law 53.

[6] See Fry, 'The Borstal system', *Penal Reform in England* (English Studies in Criminal Science, I, 1946), 143; and *idem*, 'The effect of the Criminal Justice Act on the Borstal system', *Journal of Criminal Science*, II, 60.

[7] In the case of an offence punishable on summary conviction with imprisonment, the court may commit the offender in custody to quarter sessions for sentence to Borstal training, Magistrates' Courts Act, 1952, s. 28.

[8] Sect. 11.

[9] Three months for girls, by virtue of the Act of 1948.

[10] But whatever the period of detention, each offender must, on release, pass through a course of statutory supervision for a period of not less than two years, so as to make a total of four years' detention and supervision; Criminal Justice Act, 1961, s. 11.

[11] 8 Edw. VII, c. 59, now repealed and replaced by the Criminal Justice Act, 1948.

to 'Borstal institutions'[1] instead of to prison. These institutions are classified, and accordingly those sentenced to them are themselves classified during a period of preliminary detention. In the Borstal institutions the inmates receive physical, industrial, and moral training. Good behaviour is rewarded in various ways, e.g. by a period spent in a summer camp, and there is a system of wages (of small amount) as an incentive to attention and industry. In suitable cases they are allowed to spend some free time out of the institution, and to attend technical classes at outside schools. Facilities for sports and games are provided and hobbies allowed and encouraged. The organization is on the basis of the house system traditional in the English public schools, and a close relation between the masters and the boys is maintained and stimulated.

¶ 762. *Success of the system.* On leaving the institution every young person is placed under the care of the Central After-care Association (the boys going to the Borstal division, the girls to the Women's and Girls' division). The success of the Borstal system must be accepted, especially when it is remembered that many of those subjected to it are mentally or physically below average; indeed it has attracted the interest and admiration of criminological authorities in other countries, many of which have been led to establish institutions on the English model. Of Borstalians discharged between 1949 and 1951, the records up to the end of 1955 show figures, for males, of the order of 41 per cent not reconvicted, of 28 per cent reconvicted once only, and of 31 per cent reconvicted twice or more.

¶ 763. *Special treatment of children and young persons.* The Children and Young Persons Act, 1933, made provision for special treatment for young offenders in the hope of reforming them by a system of careful and humane training. Under this legislation offenders under seventeen may be sent to an approved school[2] (Home Office school) or to custody in a remand home for a month or less.[3] A child may be sent to a Home Office school for three years or until he attains the age of fifteen, a young person for three years or, if over sixteen, until he attains the age of nineteen.

¶ 764. *Approved schools.* No responsibility lies on the court for fixing the period of detention. The order merely authorizes detention for the period. It is for the managers of the schools, under Home Office guidance, to watch the progress of the boys and girls and place them out in life when they are ready. A child under ten may not be sent to a Home Office school unless he cannot be dealt with otherwise. The training in Home Office schools has proved successful with a high

[1] 'Places in which offenders not less than sixteen but under twenty-one years of age may be detained and given such training and instruction as will conduce to their reformation and the prevention of crime', Criminal Justice Act, 1948, s. 48 (1) (*c*).

[2] See Henderson, 'Approved schools', *Penal Reform in England* (English Studies in Criminal Science, 1, 1946), 128. And see the Criminal Justice Act, 1961, ss. 14–19.

[3] Sects. 54, 57 and 71.

percentage of their pupils.[1] A fine or damages or costs may be exacted from the parent or guardian of an offender who is under seventeen unless the court is satisfied that his neglect did not conduce to the offence.[2] The Children and Young Persons Act, 1933, provides that every court in dealing with a child or young person brought before it, either as being 'in need of care or protection' (as now defined in the Children and Young Persons Act, 1952), or as an offender or otherwise, shall have regard to the welfare of the child or young person and shall in a proper case take steps to remove him from undesirable surroundings and for securing that proper provision is made for his education or training.[3] Juvenile courts are urged to co-operate with education authorities, police authorities, probation officers and other social workers. A child or young person may be committed to the care of any fit person. It is the duty of local authorities to bring before a juvenile court any child or young person needing care or protection, and the police or any authorized person[4] may take the same course.[5] A local authority may itself act as a fit person and may arrange for the boarding out of children committed to its care.

¶ 764a. (i) *Detention centres.* The Criminal Justice Act, 1948, s. 18,[6] in effect provided that when a court has power to sentence to imprisonment a person aged from fourteen to twenty-one it may, instead, order him to be detained in a detention centre (if available) for a period varying according to circumstances specified in the statute, up to a maximum of six months. This is considered to be particularly suitable for offenders who have been previously sentenced to at least six months' imprisonment or to a period of Borstal training.

(ii) The notion of a punishment for juveniles in the form of deprivation of leisure on the lines of detention in school without complete removal into an institution was publicly allowed from about 1927, and we hear of benches of magistrates who formed a practice, which they found highly successful, of binding certain young offenders over on condition that they should spend a prescribed number of Saturday afternoons sitting in the local police station where they had to remain, although if they wished they could read or write. Eventually this method of treatment was adopted by the legislature, which authorized the establishment of attendance centres for this purpose.[7] The scheme,

[1] In the Report of the Departmental Committee on Persistent Offenders, [Cmd. 4090] 1932, p. 6, the percentage given was ninety.

[2] Children and Young Persons Act, 1933, s. 55, extended to payment of compensation by Criminal Justice Act, 1961, s. 8; see ¶ 35a *ante*.

[3] *Ibid.* s. 44.

[4] The N.S.P.C.C. has been so authorized.

[5] 23 Geo. V, c. 12, s. 62.

[6] As amended by the Magistrates' Courts Act, 1952, and the Criminal Justice Act, 1961, ss. 4–7. See *ante*, ¶ 758; *Prisons and Borstals*, 4th ed. 1960, p. 52, H.M. Stationery Office; S.I. 1952, no. 1432, Detention Centre Rules, 1952.

[7] Criminal Justice Act, 1948, s. 19, since amended by the Justice of the Peace Act, 1949, ss. 15 and 16; the Magistrates' Courts Act, 1952, s. 131; the Criminal Justice Act, 1961, s. 10. For a full account and report on its effects see McClintock, *Attendance Centres*, Cambridge Studies in Criminology, vol. XIII.

originally conceived as a short and telling punishment, admitted the idea of reformative treatment and this was recognized in the Attendance Centre Rules, 1950, which in rule 2 provided for arrangements to be made so as to occupy the boys, while at the centre, in a manner conducive to health of mind and body. It applies only to males who are not less than ten and under seventeen years, and who have not previously been sentenced to prison, Borstal, detention centre or approved school. So far the scheme has been found beneficial and the number of attendance centres has been steadily increased.

¶ 765. *Whipping abolished.* Whipping was abolished by the Criminal Justice Act, 1948, s. 2, which allows corporal punishment[1] in prisons or institutions only for mutiny, incitement to mutiny or gross personal violence to an officer of a prison, when committed by a male person serving a sentence of imprisonment, corrective training or preventive detention.[2]

¶ 766. *Fines.* Fining[3] was a punishment rarely resorted to in the higher criminal courts. But now section 13 of the Criminal Justice Act, 1948, provides in effect that any court may fine an offender convicted on indictment of any felony (not being a felony for which the sentence is fixed by law) in lieu of or in addition to dealing with him in any other manner in which the court has power to deal with him.[4]

REMISSION AND TAKING OFFENCES INTO CONSIDERATION

¶ 767. By the modern repeal of all the statutes which for certain offences prescribed minimum punishments, English criminal courts have obtained, at the present day, a complete power of remitting punishment—a discretion very rarely entrusted to judges under the Continental codes.[5]

It has become a practice[6] for judges, when determining the sentence

[1] Under rules made by the Secretary of State (s. 52).

[2] Sect. 54 (1) and (2).

[3] See the *Journal of Criminal Science*, II, 46, 'Fines and their enforcement', by E. Cordes. A fine must be distinguished from the (now vanished) amercement, which was a pecuniary penalty fixed by the jurors, a fine being fixed by the court. The earliest fines were compositions agreed upon between the judge and the prisoner, to avoid imprisonment, at a time when the judges had no power to impose pecuniary punishments (Pollock and Maitland, II, 517).

[4] And see the Magistrates' Courts Act, 1952, s. 32. If the fine is not paid the court has power to fix a term of imprisonment (even in addition to any term already imposed together with the fine), *R.* v. *Carver* [1955] 1 W.L.R. 181.

[5] The effect of minimum punishments in creating in the minds of juries an exaggerated reluctance to convict is illustrated by the fact that on the final abolition of the minimum limit of punishment (ten years' penal servitude) for unnatural offences, the percentage of trials for such crimes which ended in convictions rose at once from the low rate of 35 to 47. *Criminal Judicial Statistics* (issue of 1896), 26.

[6] 'A convention of fairly respectable antiquity', *per* Lord Goddard, C.J., in *R.* v. *Batchelor* (1952) 36 Cr.App.R. 64. See Margrave-Jones, 'Taking other offences into consideration' in [1959] *Crim. L.R.* 18.

on a prisoner, to be asked to 'take into consideration' other charges of the same *kind* of offence, on which warrants have been issued against him, and which he now admits to be true,[1] and desires to be now dealt with. Cases so dealt with should then be endorsed on the indictment.[2] Such taking into consideration of offences at the request of an accused person does not mean that there has been a conviction in respect of each offence. It is true that in the normal case no proceedings follow on any one of them but this is not because there have been convictions of them but because they have been taken into consideration. It usually means a longer sentence, but the total punishment does not usually exceed what would be the maximum for *one* offence of that class. In one case, in 1925, fifty-two such other charges were thus taken into account. Under this practice the offender secures a free start on coming out of prison, instead of being rearrested, but technically the practice does not afford the plea of 'autrefois convict'.[3] But charges of offences of a different kind (e.g. false pretences as against burglary) are less readily taken into account.[4]

PREVENTIVE MEASURES

¶ 768. Besides these punitive measures, a court may also make orders whose effect is of a preventive character. Thus, as has been seen, with the object of removing the young from criminal surroundings, a juvenile court may order children needing care or protection to be sent to an approved school or to be committed to the care of a fit person.[5] Another preventive measure is the order, issued by a court[6] which sentences an offender to not less than twelve months' imprisonment (upon conviction of any offence punishable with imprisonment for two or more years), that he shall be under the supervision of a society (appointed by the Prison Commissioners) for twelve months from his discharge from prison.[7] (As to the preventive detention of persistent offenders, see ¶ 787 *post*.) At the other extreme, even a person who has not actually committed any offence at all may be required to find

[1] See *R.* v. *Berkofsky* (1935) 25 Cr.App.R. 66.

[2] *R.* v. *Nicholson* [1947] 2 All E.R. 535, disapproving *R.* v. *McMinn* (1945) 109 J.P. 130; even where the substantive conviction has afterwards been set aside, *R.* v. *Neal* [1949] 2 All E.R. 438.

[3] *R.* v. *Batchelor, ubi supra.* There is, perhaps, a danger that under this practice there may grow up a class of serial offenders. In 1929 John Donnelly, sentenced at Chester County Sessions, admitted 315 offences in addition to those charged in the indictment. *Criminal Statistics of 1928* [Cmd. 3581].

[4] Offences under the Road Traffic Act, 1930, rep., now Road Traffic Act 1960, are not proper cases to be taken into consideration when sentencing a person convicted of another class of offence; *R.* v. *Collins* [1947] K.B. 560.

[5] Children and Young Persons Act, 1933. See ¶ 763 *ante*.

[6] Unless, having regard to the circumstances and to the offender's character, it otherwise determines.

[7] Criminal Justice Act, 1948, s. 22, ¶ 791 *post*. And at the opposite extreme, an offender who deserves *no* actual punishment may be supervised, but by a probation officer (Criminal Justice Act, 1948, s. 3 (1)).

sureties[1] for good behaviour or to keep the peace, if there be reasonable grounds to fear that he may commit some offence, or may incite others to do so, or may act in some manner which would naturally tend to induce other people (even against his desire) to commit one.[2]

ORDER FOR RESTITUTION; ORDER FOR COSTS

¶ 769. After the judgment itself has been given there are further orders which the judge may have cause to make.

Of one such we have already spoken[3]—the order which, after any trial for theft, the court may make for restitution, to the true owner, of stolen property which has been identified at the trial.

Another, of much more frequent application, may be made in respect of costs. In criminal law costs do not 'follow the event'. The common law knew nothing of costs. And the statutes which introduced them did not mention the Crown—an omission which Blackstone elevates into rules, that it is the prerogative of the Crown not to pay costs, and that it would be beneath its dignity to receive them.[4] Hence, as criminal proceedings are technically at the suit of the Crown, no judgment for costs could be given in them. Even if the prosecution were in fact brought by a private individual, the law in no way reimbursed him for the outlay he had incurred in discharging this public duty. But criminal courts are now empowered[5]—the comprehensive statute being the Costs in Criminal Cases Act, 1952[6]—to order the reasonable costs of the prosecution and of the witnesses for the defence, or of either of them, and of the accused, if acquitted, to be repaid out of public funds, in the case of any indictable offence.[7] (The merely quasi-criminal offence of obstructing a road or river is excepted.) The power is given, not only to assizes and quarter sessions, but also to justices of the peace when dealing summarily (*ante*, ¶ 679) with an indictable offence, or when holding (*ante*, ¶ 701) a preliminary examination about one. Neither side, usually, will receive an allowance for witnesses who speak only to character. Even now the costs awarded may not adequately recompense a private prosecutor or an innocent defendant.[8]

[1] It is not certain whether this power is derived from common law or from statute 34 Edw. III, c. 1.

[2] *Lansbury* v. *Riley* [1914] 3 K.B. 229; *R.* v. *Sandbach* (1935), 153 L.T. 63. See ¶ 431 *ante*; and *R.* v. *County of London Q.S. Appeals Committee* [1948] 1 K.B. 670 for a discussion of the power of justices under the Justices of the Peace Act, 1360, to bind over to be of good behaviour a person who has acted in a manner whereby the peace may be blemished; *ante*, ¶ 695.

[3] *Ante*, ¶ 313.

[4] III, 400; cf. *R.* v. *Canterbury, Abp. of* [1902] 2 K.B. 503. By the Administration of Justice (Misc. Provisions) Act, 1933 (23 and 24 Geo. V, c. 36), s. 7, costs may be awarded to and against the Crown in civil proceedings.

[5] For the exercise of discretion see *R.* v. *Sansbury* (1959) 44 Cr.App.R. 14.

[6] The costs payable under the Act are taxed by the proper officer of the court, s. 1 (3). The money is paid *locally*, out of the rates of the county or county-borough where the offence was committed, s. 1 (1) (*a*) and (*b*).

[7] This includes cases dealt with summarily, s. 5.

[8] See 98 *J.P. Jo.* 472 and 664.

¶ 770. *Costs against individuals.* Besides these orders upon public funds, orders for costs may now also be made upon individuals concerned in the criminal proceedings. For under section 2 of the Act a court of assize or of quarter sessions may award the whole or any part of the costs incurred to a successful prosecution[1] or defence (as the case may be) against the unsuccessful defendant or prosecutor; and the like power is given to a magistrates' court under section 6, subject to the conditions laid down in the section [2]

ORDER FOR DAMAGES

¶ 771. The common law knew nothing of orders for damages in criminal proceedings, as they are instituted for punitive and not compensatory purposes. But a great economy of time and money is effected whenever a single judicial investigation into any wrongful transaction can be made to cover all its consequences, reparative as well as penal. Hence the French code freely permits the addition, at criminal trials, of a civil action to claim damages against the prisoner.[3] An experimental, and therefore very limited, step in this direction was taken by the Forfeiture Act, 1870, which by section 4 in cases of felony empowers the court to order a convicted prisoner to pay a sum not exceeding £100, by way of compensation for any loss of property suffered by any person 'through[4] or by means of' the felony. Thus a prisoner convicted of forging a bill of exchange may be made to repay to the prosecutor money which he has lost by discounting it. But the clause, being limited to 'losses of property', does not extend to injuries as such to the person.[5] And now, by section 34 of the Magistrates' Courts Act, 1952, a magistrates' court, on convicting a person of felony, is given the same power to award a sum of money to any person aggrieved, as a court of assize or quarter sessions has under section 4 of the Forfeiture Act, 1870.

[1] Even though it inflict no punishment beyond binding over; *R.* v. *Yeatman* (1912) C.C.C. Sess. Pap. CLVII, 453. And see *R.* v. *Davis* [1962] 1 All E.R. 490.

[2] For *felonies* an order to pay the taxed costs of the prosecution had been permitted by the Act of 1870 (*ante*, ¶ 75), before which a conviction for treason or felony caused a forfeiture of the prisoner's goods. And a sentence of death for treason or felony involved, as a necessary consequence, an 'attainder' (4 Bl. *Comm.* 374). A person attainted (*attinctus*, 'blackened') became dead to civil rights; his lands were forfeited, and his blood was 'corrupted', so that descent could not be traced through him. These consequences were abolished by the Forfeiture Act. An attainder could formerly be produced by a judgment of outlawry; outlawry, however, was abolished by s. 12 of the Administration of Justice (Misc. Provisions) Act, 1938.

[3] 'L'action civile peut être poursuivie en même temps et devant les mêmes juges que l'action publique' (Code d'Instruction Criminelle, art. 3).

[4] It does not appear to be certain whether this would extend to such consequences as medical expenses or loss of earnings 'through' a felonious attack on the person.

[5] For the power to award compensation (*a*) when dismissing trifling charges—if in summary proceedings, up to £25 only—see ¶ 678 *ante*; (*b*) on convicting for malicious injuries to property, see ¶ 193 *ante*.

SECTION 6. DEFENCE AGAINST ERRORS OF LAW

¶ 772. Along with the steps which may be taken at this stage to secure a revision of any supposed error in the judgment, it may be convenient to recall those other modes and occasions of appealing to higher tribunals which we have already noticed at earlier stages of the ordinary criminal procedure, as the student will thus obtain a general view of the subject. The following are the prisoner's opportunities, at the various successive stages, of defending himself against errors of law.

(*a*) Before trial

¶ 773. (i) A motion to quash the indictment alleges insufficiency apparent on the face of it. As the court has a discretion to refuse to quash an indictment, even for a valid objection, there is no appeal from the refusal; and the prisoner, if he wishes to press his objection, must do it by demurrer, or else wait till after trial.

(ii) A demurrer[1] alleges similarly that the indictment is on the face of it insufficient. The court has no discretionary power of refusing to hear objections raised thus; but demurrers involve such disadvantages that they are unfamiliar now.

(iii) Of course any contract to suppress or withdraw from a prosecution for any offence is both illegal and unenforceable, even if it were entered into with the approval of a court.[2] But it is not unusual for counsel for the prosecution, when the indictment is opened, to ask the leave of the court to offer no evidence on the charge for reasons stated, e.g. that the prosecution is not provided with sufficient evidence upon which the case could properly be left to the jury.[3] If the court accedes to this[4] the jury are directed to find a verdict of not guilty.

(iv) *Nolle prosequi*. It is a prerogative power of the Crown to intervene to stop a prosecution after a bill of indictment has been signed, or proceedings on information *ex officio*[5] have been instituted, and before judgment;[6] this power is exercised only on the direction of the Attorney-General[7] on the application either of the prosecution or of the defence.[8]

(*b*) After trial. Reversal of judgment

¶ 774. (i) A motion in arrest of judgment raises an objection in *law* that appears on the face of the record (unless it be merely formal).

[1] *Ante*, ¶ 738.

[2] See *Windhill L.B.* v. *Vint* (1890) 45 Ch.D. 351.

[3] See *Elworthy* v. *Bird* (1824) 2 Bing. 258. A similar application can be made to a magistrates' court, which may accede to it, under s. 7 (1) of the Magistrates' Courts Act, 1952, if it is of opinion that the evidence is not sufficient. For a discussion of an interesting case involving technical difficulties, see [1956] *Crim.L.R.* 725, 'Nina Ponomareva'.

[4] *R.* v. *Comptroller of Patents* [1899] 1 Q.B. 909 at p. 914.

[5] See ¶¶ 658 and 716, *ante*.

[6] *R.* v. *Dunn* (1843) 1 C. and K. 730; *R.* v. *Colling* (1847) 2 Cox 184.

[7] *R.* v. *Rowlands* (1851) 17 Q.B. 671. His discretion is not subject to the control of the courts.

[8] E.g. *R.* v. *Teal* (1809) 11 East 307; *R.* v. *Beresford* (1952) 36 Cr.App.R. 1. Cf. *Poole* v. *R.* [1960] 3 W.L.R. 770 (Crim. Procedure Code, Laws of Kenya, 1948, c. 27, s. 82).

A felon as we have seen (*ante*, ¶ 755) is *asked* if he raises such objection.

(ii) An application can be made to the Court of Criminal Appeal.

The creation of a general Court of Criminal Appeal,[1] by the Criminal Appeal Act of 1907,[2] constituted a revolution in the administration of our penal justice. Previously (except[3] for cases tried in courts of summary jurisdiction) the general principle had been that in criminal cases—unlike civil ones—no appeal was allowed to either party upon any question of fact. And even on questions of law the Crown had little opportunity of appeal and the prisoner a not unlimited one.[4] If a jury wrongfully acquitted a man, the Crown had, as it still has, no redress. If it wrongfully convicted him, his only resource was to apply to the Home Secretary for a pardon—a derogatory form of redress for an innocent man. The Act of 1907 does not enlarge the Crown's opportunities of appeal; but it greatly extends those of every prisoner convicted[5] upon a trial by jury. (To convictions at magistrates' courts[6] or on impeachments, it does not apply.)

RIGHT OF APPEAL

¶ 775. (*a*) In the rare cases where his offence is the merely quasi-criminal one of obstructing a highway or bridge or navigable river, he has the full right of appeal as in a civil action; section 20 (3). (See ¶ 656 *ante.*)

(*b*) And even when the offence charged is a truly criminal one—as in almost all cases it will be—he nevertheless has (s. 3):

(i) an unconditional right to appeal on any question of pure law;[7]

(ii) a right, *in case of* his obtaining leave either from the judge who tried him or from the Court of Criminal Appeal itself or from one of its judges,[8] to appeal on any question of fact, or of mixed fact and law;

(iii) a right, *in case of* his obtaining leave from the Court of Criminal Appeal or from one of its judges, to appeal against the sentence passed on him unless the sentence is one fixed definitely by the law.[9]

A prisoner who desires to appeal should give notice of his desire within ten days after his conviction (s. 7 (1)); but the court may[10] grant

[1] *Ante*, ¶ 654.

[2] 7 Edw. VII, c. 23.

[3] *Ante*, ¶ 686.

[4] *Ante*, ¶ 654.

[5] Or pleading guilty. But *not* if found 'guilty but insane'; *Felstead* v. *R.* [1914] A.C. 534; a rule which the court in *R.* v. *Duke* [1961] C.C.A. 3 All E.R. 737 regarded as unsatisfactory and worthy of legislative amendment.

[6] Except as to the *sentences* on 'incorrigible rogues' (*ante*, ¶ 486), or on 'juvenile adults', sent to quarter sessions.

[7] But the registrar of the court—s. 15 (2)—may bring before it promptly any appeal on a purely legal point that seems to him untenable; and the court may deal with it at once, without hearing arguments.

[8] From his refusal an appeal lies to the full court.

[9] But in the case of conviction of murder the Homicide Act, 1957, 1st sched. 1 (2), 2 (3), 3 (1) and 4 (1) make special provisions for appeals against sentence.

[10] Except in the case of an offence punishable with death.

him an enlarged time. Accordingly (s. 7 (2)) any sentence of death, or even of corporal punishment, is not to be carried out until the ten days or the enlarged time, be over, nor until the appeal, if then instituted, be disposed of. If the prisoner be poor, the court may assign him, at the public expense, a solicitor and a counsel. Applications for leave to appeal are usually made in writing; the appellant has no right to be present. He has, however, a right to be present at the hearing of the actual appeal, unless it be on a matter of pure law. At actual appeals the Director of Public Prosecutions must see that the prosecutor is duly represented (s. 12).

For appeals to the House of Lords see *ante*, ¶ 650.

¶ 776. *Procedure.* On every appeal, or application for leave to appeal, the judge who tried the appellant must furnish to the court his notes of the trial and a report giving his opinion upon any points arising in the case (s. 8). (Or, if the appeal involves only a question of pure law, the court may require the judge to 'state a case' as in the old practice of the Court for Crown Cases Reserved; s. 20.) And in view of the possibility of an appeal, shorthand notes are to be taken, at the public expense, of every criminal trial before a jury[1] (s. 16), thus rendering universal a practice which, by the sedulous caution of the City of London, had been in force at the Old Bailey for nearly two centuries.

POWER TO ORDER AND RECEIVE EVIDENCE

¶ 777. Moreover the court, when dealing with the appeal, are empowered (s. 9) to order the production of documentary or circumstantial evidence, and to receive direct evidence from witnesses, whether they were called at the trial or not, either in open court or by depositions for the purpose.[2] In a recent case[3] the Court of Criminal Appeal has stated that fresh evidence will be heard provided that (*a*) it was not available at the trial, (*b*) it is relevant, (*c*) it is credible, and (*d*) that it is sufficient to raise a reasonable doubt as to the appellant's guilt. (But new evidence not given at the original trial is never to be made a ground for *increasing* the sentence.) The court may also, if necessary, appoint some expert, e.g. a chemist or a specialist in lunacy, to act with them as an assessor, or appoint a special commissioner to report to them on any question which involves such a scientific or local investigation, or such a prolonged examination of documents or accounts (e.g. in cases of embezzlement) as cannot conveniently be conducted before themselves. Provision is made (ss. 12, 13) out of public funds for all the expenses connected with an appeal, including even those of the appellant's own attendance.

[1] These do not include the speeches of counsel (unless the judge order it, so as to make clear what issues are actually raised).

[2] *R.* v. *Jordan* (1956) 40 Cr.App.R. 152; *R.* v. *Foley* [1959] Crim. L.R. 286. In *R.* v. *Robinson* [1917] 2 K.B. 108, it was held that on an appeal the prosecution might give in evidence a letter written by the prisoner from prison. See article in (1952) 214 L.T. 85.

[3] *R.* v. *Parks* 1961, *The Times*, 5 October.

¶ 778. *Groundless appeals.* Groundless appeals, such as impede so greatly the administration of justice in the United States, are discouraged by various provisions.[1] There is, for instance, the necessity of obtaining leave to appeal, whenever the point is not one of mere law. There is also a provision, section 4 (1), that, even where the appellant is technically in the right, his appeal may be dismissed if 'no substantial miscarriage of justice has actually occurred', and if no reasonable jury, properly directed, would or could have given any other verdict than that which was in fact given, and no substantial injustice has been done.[2] A fact, for instance, has been elicited by an improper leading question; but the fact was of no moment. The existence of this provision makes for no little uncertainty in the result of appeals.[3] There is, further, in the case of appeals against a sentence, a power (s. 4 (3)) for the court to alter that sentence by increasing instead of diminishing it. Moreover although, between the institution of an appeal and the decision of it, the appellant escapes the treatment of an ordinary prisoner[4] (being merely detained in a very lenient custody or in rare cases admitted to bail), yet this period will not count (except by special order of the court)[5] as any part of the punishment. So any man who appeals on untenable grounds postpones thereby the time of his final return to liberty.

QUASHING THE CONVICTION

¶ 779. But if (s. 4) a substantial miscarriage of justice has occurred (whether from the judge's wrong decision of a question of law, or from the jury's having returned a verdict incapable of being supported when regard is had to the evidence[6] or from any other cause[7]), then the

[1] Nevertheless, in 1924, Avory, J., declared the court to be habitually 'burdened with frivolous appeals'. A number of successful appeals release, on a technicality, men who are really guilty.

[2] *R.* v. *Garland* (1943) 29 Cr.App.R. 41 n.; *R.* v. *Haddy* [1944] K.B. 442; 1 All E.R. 319, confirmed in *Stirland* v. *D.P.P.* [1944] 2 All E.R. 13 (*T.A.C.*); and *R.* v. *Farid* (1945) 30 Cr.App.R. 168; in *R.* v. *Collins* (1950) 34 Cr.App.R. 146.

[3] E.g. in sexual cases where the point is absence of corroboration. Cf. *R.* v. *Murray* (1913) 9 Cr.App.R. 248, *R.* v. *Southern* (1930) 22 Cr.App.R. 6; 142 L.T. 383, *R.* v. *Coulthread* (1933) 148 L.T. 480; 24 Cr.App.R. 44 and *R.* v. *Bramhill* (1933) 24 Cr.App.R. 79

[4] Even if he be under two concurrent convictions and appeal against only one.

[5] Which has never been made in any case where the grounds of appeal are so slight that leave to appeal was originally refused; *R.* v. *Gott* (1922) 16 Cr.App.R. 87 at p. 90. And see now the Criminal Justice Act, 1948, s. 38.

[6] If the verdict be *unreasonable* (cases merely weak are not retried), e.g. where the conviction was obtained on a defective information (*ante*, ¶ 673) or a defective indictment (*ante*, ¶ 730); *Meek* v. *Powell* [1952] 1 All E.R. 347. Or where there has been a denial of natural justice, *R.* v. *Wandsworth JJ.* [1942] 1 K.B. 281. Or if the justices relied upon evidence given in another case and not in the case which they were trying, *Roper* v. *Taylor's Central Garage* [1951] 2 T.L.R. 284 (*T.A.C.*). And see *R.* v. *Rowley* [1948] 1 All E.R. 570 where the court quashed the conviction of an appellant who had pleaded guilty to being an accessory, the alleged principals having been subsequently acquitted.

[7] In *R.* v. *Parker* (1961) 45 Cr.App.R. 1, where a witness had blurted out a piece of inadmissible hearsay the C.C.A. refused to apply s. 4 (1) since, despite the trial judge's strong direction to the jury to disregard it, the statement was still likely to have influenced them.

appeal will be allowed, the conviction quashed, and a judgment of acquittal entered. If the conviction were for theft, the court can review not only the conviction but also (s. 6 (2)) any order that may have been made for the restitution of the property alleged to have been stolen.

NEW TRIAL; *VENIRE DE NOVO*

¶ 780. Strictly speaking a new trial cannot be ordered[1] (except after a merely abortive one) even though the prisoner be clearly guilty. Although there have been cases in which the court has ordered a *venire de novo* because of a mistrial, this has never been done after a verdict of not guilty, whether by a court of summary jurisdiction or by a jury on indictment, however improperly that verdict may have been obtained. To constitute a mistrial the proceedings must have been abortive from beginning to end, so that had the record been drawn up the error would have been apparent.[2] In *R.* v. *Hancock* (1931),[3] the prisoner during the course of the trial confessed his guilt and was sentenced without the verdict of the jury being taken. The Court of Criminal Appeal ordered a new trial on the ground that the trial had been a nullity.[4] Avory, J., stated: 'Once a prisoner is in charge of the jury his statement that he is guilty is merely evidence on which the jury may act.' Similarly a new trial was ordered where two prisoners separately indicted were tried together.[5] A similar order was made where an unqualified juryman sat on the jury,[6] and would be made should a juryman after the trial be found not to have understood English.[7] Though evidence may not be given on appeal by a juror as to discussions in the jury room, evidence may be given as to the competence of a juror.[8]

QUASHING THE SENTENCE

¶ 781. If the appellant appeals against his sentence, the court may quash that sentence, and pass instead 'such other sentence (whether

[1] The writ of *venire facias de novo juratores* is an order of the court to summon and swear a fresh jury to try the case again.

[2] *R.* v. *Chairman of Middlesex Q.S.* [1952] 2 Q.B. 758 citing *R.* v. *Neal* [1949] 2 K.B. 590.

[3] 23 Cr.App.R. 16.

[4] *R.* v. *Heyes* [1950] 2 All E.R. 587, in which the court refrained from ordering a new trial.

[5] *Crane* v. *D.P.P.* [1921] 2 A.C. 299. See also *R.* v. *Gee* [1936] 2 All E.R. 89 (depositions improperly taken). Other instances are *R.* v. *Baker* (1911) 7 Cr.App.R. 217 (no proper plea of guilty or not guilty), and see *R.* v. *Heyes* [1950] 2 All E.R. 587; 34 Cr.App.R. 161; *R.* v. *Dennis* and *R.* v. *Parker* [1924] 1 K.B. 867 (two separate indictments heard together); *R.* v. *Williams* (1925) 19 Cr.App.R. 67 (jury not properly constituted). For a general discussion see *R.* v. *Neal* [1949] 2 K.B. 590; and Cooke 'Venire de novo' (1955), *L.Q.R.* 100.

[6] *R.* v. *Wakefield* [1918] 1 K.B. 216. But note *R.* v. *Kelly* [1950] 1 All E.R. 806; 34 Cr.App.R. 95.

[7] *Ras Bahari Lal* v. *King Emperor* (1933) 50 T.L.R. 1.

[8] *Ibid.*, disapproving *R.* v. *Thomas* [1933] 2 K.B. 489.

more or less severe) as they think ought to have been passed'; section 4 (3). It will not quash a sentence unless it be so excessive as to show an error of principle. If, on *any* appeal, the court finds that, though the appellant did commit the crime, he did so in a condition of irresponsible insanity, they may quash the conviction, and commit him to custody as a criminal lunatic.

The decision pronounced by the court will usually be final.[1] But by virtue of the Administration of Justice Act, 1960, in cases where a point of law is raised which is of general public importance, a certificate may be obtained which will enable either the prosecution or the defence to take the case from this court directly to the House of Lords. See ¶ 650, *ante*.

THE PREROGATIVE OF MERCY

¶ 782. The Act leaves untouched the Crown's prerogative of mercy; and the Home Secretary will thus still be able to institute inquiries of his own, in which he will be free from the technical rules of evidence, and also will be able to consider pleas for mercy based upon grounds which a court of law cannot accept. Or he may instead (s. 19) refer to the Court of Criminal Appeal either the whole case, or any special point in it.[2]

The Act has conferred great benefits, by remedying miscarriages of justice and (still more) by removing the former public anxiety as to the possibility of such miscarriages. It has also raised the level of summings up, and has done something towards standardizing sentences. And it does not seem to have weakened that sense of responsibility in the minds of jurymen which is the great safeguard of accused persons. Countless are the acquittals that have been secured by the influence of those impressive words—still used, though now unjustifiable—'Remember that your verdict is final'.

SECTION 7. REPRIEVE AND PARDON

¶ 783. The execution of the sentence may be postponed by a respite of it, i.e. a reprieve of the offender, or be altogether remitted by a pardon.

Postponements may be granted not only by the Crown but even by the judge. For except in cases of murder, a judge of assize may not only delay[3] the delivery of his judgment, but may, even after delivering

[1] But its decisions (like those of the Judicial Committee and unlike those of the House of Lords) are *not* absolutely binding on itself; cf. the effect of *Ettridge* (1909) 2 Cr.App.R. 62, on *Davidson* (1909) *ib.* at p. 51; of *Baskerville* (1916) 12 Cr.App.R. 81 on *Willis* (1916) *ib.* at p. 44; of *Power* (1919) 14 Cr.App.R. 17 on *Joiner* (1910) 4 Cr.App.R. 64; and of *Norman* (1924) 18 Cr.App.R. 81 on *Stanley* (1920) 14 Cr.App.R. 141. In *R.* v. *Taylor* [1950] 2 K.B. at p. 370 a full Court of Criminal Appeal declared that if in the opinion of a full court assembled for that purpose the law had been misapplied, or misunderstood in a decision which it had previously given, on the strength of which an accused person had been sentenced and imprisoned, it was the duty of the court to reconsider the earlier decision.

[2] See *R.* v. *McGrath* [1949] 2 All E.R. 495.

[3] See ¶ 756 *ante*.

it, delay its execution. And, in the case of capital sentences, it is his imperative duty thus to respite it if the prisoner be proved to be insane. But a pardon lies beyond all judicial discretion, and can be granted by no authority below that of the Crown itself.[1] It may be absolute, or be subject to some condition,[2] or may only 'remit' a portion of the punishment, or 'commute' it to a milder form. Pardons may be granted by the Crown for all crimes, except two. Firstly under the Habeas Corpus Act the Crown cannot pardon the offence of sending a prisoner out of England to evade the protection of the writ of habeas corpus;[3] and secondly, even at common law, pardon cannot be granted to one convicted of a common nuisance until the nuisance has been abated, for such a pardon might prejudice the rights of the private persons injured by the nuisance.[4] Moreover upon an impeachment by the House of Commons, a pardon by the Crown cannot be pleaded as a defence so as to prevent the trial,[5] though it saves from punishment. A breach of the statutes of a corporation (e.g. a university or a college) is not a 'crime', and so is not within the Crown's power of pardon.[6]

¶ 784. *Power of pardon needed.* It has often been maintained that a perfect code would remove all necessity for a power of pardon. 'Happy that nation,' says Beccaria, 'in which clemency shall come to be considered dangerous.' But long experience has shown that human foresight is incompetent to frame, and human language to express, a faultless scheme of legislation. The power of pardon therefore is one which is indispensable to the wise administration of penal justice. In their Report of 1879[7] the Royal Commissioners who prepared the Draft Criminal Code and recommended the establishment of a Court of Criminal Appeal stated:[8]

> Cases in which, under some peculiar state of facts, a miscarriage of justice takes place, may sometimes though rarely occur; but when they occur it is under circumstances for which fixed rules of procedure cannot provide.
>
> Experience has shown that the Secretary of State is a better judge of the existence of such circumstances than a court of justice can be. He has every facility for inquiring into the special circumstances; he can and does, if

[1] Wade and Phillips, *Constitutional Law*, 5th ed., 245. The Crown can review the whole history and condition of the offender, and even take into account popular emotion, as when in *Lee's Case*, at Exeter, the damp gallows had thrice failed to act.

[2] E.g. the pardons which introduced transportation. Or the pardon granted, about 1730, to a condemned criminal on condition that he would allow the great surgeon Cheselden to perforate the drum of his ear, that the consequent effect upon hearing might be ascertained.

[3] 31 Car. II, c. 2, s. 11.

[4] Contrast the former rule that it was only *before* any informer had commenced an action that the Crown could grant a pardon in the case of conduct forbidden under some penalty recoverable in a civil action by a common informer. For 'common informer' see *ante*, ¶ 364, n. 2.

[5] By the Act of Settlement (12 and 13 Will. III, c. 2).

[6] *Dr Bentley's Case* (1731) 2 Str. 912.

[7] [C. 2345].

[8] On p. 39.

necessary, avail himself of the assistance of the judge who tried the case, and of the law officers.... He is fettered by no rule, and his decision does not form a precedent for subsequent cases. We do not see how a better means could be provided for inquiry into the circumstances of the exceptional cases in question.

¶ 785. *The accusatorial system.* The accusatorial system of English criminal procedure is in strong contrast with the inquisitorial system of continental Europe.[1] In France a searching preliminary inquiry is made by a *juge d'instruction* who investigates the circumstances of the crime and rigorously examines the accused in private.[2] If the accused is sent to trial he is again examined by the presiding judge, although there is a *procureur-général* to conduct the prosecution. There is no cross-examination as in England but questions may be put through the presiding judge.

English criminal procedure is based upon the presumption of innocence. The judge is dispassionate and tends to assist the accused rather than the prosecution. Prosecuting counsel are restrained by strict convention from acting oppressively or unfairly.[3] From the beginning criminal proceedings take place in public and may be fully reported. A prisoner is rarely refused free legal aid,[4] and always has the right to a dock defence.[5] The rules of evidence are stringent against the prosecution, but are frequently relaxed in favour of the accused.[6] The verdict of a jury must be unanimous. Undoubtedly there is more risk in England of the acquittal of a guilty man than the conviction of an innocent man.[7] It must, however, be remembered that, though there is a presumption of innocence upon which the rules of evidence are based, yet there is a natural tendency to assume that an accused person committed for trial after an examination before a magistrate is probably guilty.[8] One distinguished French writer considers that in some points

[1] *Criminal Justice in England*, by Pendleton Howard, 384.

[2] The accused may be represented by counsel.

[3] See ¶ 749 *ante*. [4] See ¶ 714 *ante*.

[5] The right to call upon any counsel present in court to conduct the defence at a very low fee.

[6] 'If a point of evidence is a near thing, I never decide it against the prisoner'; Lord Darling. Cf. *R.* v. *Shellaker* (1913) 9 Cr.App.R. 240 at p. 244.

[7] Whether this is advantageous probably varies with variations in social security. Writing a good many years ago, J. D. Lewis stated that, after a study of English criminal trials from the time of James II, he found only three cases in which any person had been actually executed who had afterwards been proved quite innocent; viz. the clear cases of Shaw (executed at Edinburgh for the supposed murder of a daughter who had committed suicide), of Jennings (executed at Hull in 1762 for theft by a mistake of identity), and the much more doubtful case of Eliza Fenning (executed in London in 1815 for an alleged attempt at poisoning). That of the inn-keeper, Jonathan Bradford (executed in 1736 for the murder of a traveller), though a case of innocence, was one of moral guilt, as he had entered the traveller's room to kill him but found him already slain by his own valet (*Causes célèbres de l'Angleterre*).

[8] Study 'The presumption of innocence' in C. K. Allen's *Legal Duties*.

the French system is more favourable to the accused than the English.[1] An innocent man will gain advantage from the thorough preliminary sifting of evidence. An accused person who defends himself is in England perplexed by the necessity of distinguishing, when cross-examining witnesses, between statements and questions.

[1] *Les principes directeurs de la procédure criminelle de l'Angleterre*, by Emile Seitz.

Chapter XXXIV

ORDINARY PROCEDURE

III. DETENTION AND PROBATION

Section 1. Detention

TREATMENT OF PERSISTENT OFFENDERS

¶ 786. Our review of the long-accustomed forms of punishment, all of them instituted mainly for *deterrence*, must be supplemented by consideration of the methods of dealing with convicted offenders which aim instead at *seclusion* or at *reformation*. They are intended, not for the average criminal, but for those who are either worse or better—less capable or more capable of reclamation—than he.

In the reaction of the nineteenth century against penal severities, a theory arose that punishments should be solely directed to the reformation of the offender. But protracted experience has shown that noble aim to be far more difficult of achievement than this theory presupposed.[1] The great number of recidivists, a number now increasing in almost every country, sufficiently attests this. The great object of criminal law is to prevent crime; hence, if any particular offender has been convicted so frequently as to make it clear that he cannot be kept from crime through the medium of either reformation or deterrence, it remains only to effect that prevention in a direct way, by placing him in a seclusion where it will be impossible for him to repeat his offences. Unless so secluded, he will not only continue his offences, but will also train others to offend, and will moreover transmit his aptitudes to a tainted posterity. At the same time it has to be remembered that not all 'persistent' offenders are incorrigible; it has been well said that so-called incorrigible offenders are very often offenders whom no attempt has been made to correct.

PREVENTION OF CRIME ACT, 1908

¶ 787. For social safety, an attempt was made, by the Inebriates Act, 1898 (61 and 62 Vict. c. 60), to provide State reformatories for the seclusion for three years of those offenders whose cravings for alcohol had proved to be incorrigible, but the experiment was a failure and the reformatories are now closed.[2] Seclusion is still more advisable in the case of those with similarly incorrigible cravings for crime, on the principle that if they cannot be deterred they should be debarred the

[1] See Radzinowicz, 'The persistent offender', *Mod. App. Crim. Law*, 162 *et seq.* And the Report of the Departmental Committee on Persistent Offenders [Cmd. 4090], 1932.

[2] Against the once notorious Jane Cakebread, who died in 1898, 281 convictions for drunkenness stood recorded; Eleanor Larkin underwent her 228th in 1920. Lord Herschell mentions a woman who underwent 404 imprisonments for drunkenness.

opportunity. Hence in France, a criminal whose record shows him to be thus hopeless must be placed in perpetual *relégation*, in a penal colony. Accordingly the Prevention of Crime Act, 1908 (8 Edw. VII, c. 59), part II, enabled the court which sentenced to penal servitude a person whom a jury had convicted of felony,[1] and had also pronounced to be an 'habitual criminal',[2] with at least three previous serious convictions since the age of sixteen, to add a further[3] sentence of merely 'preventive detention' after the end of the penal servitude. This detention could be for any period between five years and ten (but not, as the Bill at first proposed, for life). It went on under treatment less rigorous than in prisons; e.g. as to hours, food, visits, recreation, and earnings.[4]

FAILURE AND REPEAL OF THE ACT OF 1908

¶ 788. Amongst other criticisms of this measure it was pointed out that in effect it amounted to no more than a system of increasing the period of imprisonment; and as it was provided that the preventive detention should last at least five years but not exceed ten there were some classes of persistent offender for whom the increase of sentence was inadequate, while on the other hand tribunals[5] were in many cases disinclined to subject the delinquents to a double punishment. In practice the powers which were thus given to the courts were seldom exercised, and the statute failed to justify the hopes of its supporters. This unsatisfactory position was discussed, and suggestions for its improvement were made, in the Report of the Departmental Committee on Persistent Offenders which was issued in 1932.[6] The recommendations of this committee were largely followed in the Criminal Justice Bill of 1938, which, after the long interruption caused by the war, was revived and in a slightly altered form passed into law as the Criminal Justice Act, 1948. This Act repealed the Act of 1908, and replaced its provisions relating to the persistent offender by sections 21–3.[7]

[1] Or of coining, false pretences, conspiracy to defraud, or being found by night about to commit burglary.

[2] If the indictment had charged him with this 'habitualism'; this it could only do by consent of the Director of Public Prosecutions. Consent was not given unless the man had already undergone penal servitude once, and was over thirty, and the offence for which he was then on trial was grave. A previous finding that a man was a habitual criminal did not mean that he would always continue to be an habitual criminal; *R.* v. *Norman* [1924] 2 K.B. 315.

[3] The offender could (*ante*, ¶ 775), without leave, appeal against this.

[4] The average number of persons serving this sentence was 128.

[5] Not only in England, but in other countries which have tried a similar system. It is often called a 'dual system' since it consists of a period of imprisonment followed by what, in effect, is a second period of the like kind of incarceration, although given the name of 'preventive detention'.

[6] [Cmd. 4090] 1932. Of the existing system the report said: 'The present system not only fails to provide adequate protection for society; it fails also to provide the treatment of which so many persistent offenders stand in need' (p. 4, para. 8).

[7] As modified by the Prison Act, 1952. For a more detailed account of the provisions of the Criminal Justice Act see Grünhut, 'The treatment of persistent offenders', *Journal of Criminal Science*, II, 65 *et seq.*

CORRECTIVE TRAINING AND PREVENTIVE DETENTION UNDER THE CRIMINAL JUSTICE ACT, 1948

¶ 789. The Act of 1948 adopts in section 21 a 'single system' of detention, of which it offers two kinds. First there is a period of *corrective training* (for not less than two nor more than four years) for a person not less than twenty-one who (*a*) is convicted on indictment of an offence punishable with two years' imprisonment or more, and who (*b*) has been convicted on at least two previous occasions of offences of the like gravity since he was seventeen.[1] Secondly there is a period of *preventive detention* (for not less than five nor more than fourteen years)[2] for a person not less than thirty (at the date when he appears for sentence[3]) who (*a*) is convicted on indictment of an offence punishable with two years' imprisonment or more, and who (*b*) has been convicted on indictment on at least three previous occasions[4] of offences of the like gravity and on at least two of these occasions was sentenced to Borstal training, imprisonment, or corrective training.

FEATURES OF THE PRESENT SYSTEM

¶ 790. A notable feature of the system now established is that in deciding to adopt the former the court must be satisfied that it is expedient to do so with a view to the reformation of the offender as well as to the prevention of crime, whereas the latter course offered for the older and more hardened offenders is to be adopted when the courts are satisfied that it is expedient merely for the prevention of crime. But in both cases the courts are to take into account any reports made by the prison commissioners as to the offender's physical and mental condition and suitability for such a sentence. In either case if he be released on licence before the expiration of his sentence there is provision for him to be placed under supervision for the remainder of the sentence (sch. III). The Court of Criminal Appeal has declared that the object of preventive detention is to protect the public from those who have shown themselves to be a menace to society while at large: it is not a question of punishment, which has proved to be of no use.[5]

[1] A sentence of corrective training should not be ordered to run concurrently with a sentence of imprisonment; *R.* v. *Heritage* [1951] 1 All E.R. 1013.

[2] The Court of Criminal Appeal has declared with emphasis that the irreducible minimum sentence of preventive detention should be seven years save in the case of an old man whom a court does not desire to die in prison or spend his last days in prison, for whom, therefore, five years' detention might be a proper sentence; *R.* v. *Sedgwick* [1950] 2 All E.R. 397; 34 Cr.App.R. 156; *R.* v. *Hewitt* (1950) 34 Cr.App.R. 163; *R.* v. *Churchill* [1952] 2 Q.B. 637.

[3] *R.* v. *Fallows* (1954) 38 Cr.App.R. 52.

[4] 'Occasion' means *different* sessions or assizes, and not a *conviction* merely at the same sessions or assizes, *R.* v. *Rogers* [1953] 1 Q.B. 311.

[5] *R.* v. *Churchill, ubi supra.* And see *R.* v. *Askew* [1949] 2 All E.R. 687; *R.* v. *Powell* [1953] 1 W.L.R. 1351.

SUPERVISION AFTER DISCHARGE

¶ 791. In addition to the above there is provision[1] for subjecting an offender to a period of twelve months' supervision[2] from his next discharge from prison. This is to apply[3] when a person is convicted of an offence as stated above (¶ 789), and is sentenced by the court to at least twelve months' imprisonment, provided (*a*) that he has been at least twice previously convicted and sentenced to Borstal training or imprisonment, or (*b*) that he has been previously convicted and sentenced to corrective training.

SECTION 2. PROBATION AND DISCHARGE

¶ 792. The probation system[4] was inaugurated by the Probation of Offenders Act, 1907.[5] Under the system so established a court by or before which a person is convicted of an offence[6] may take into account the circumstances, including the nature of the offence and the character of the offender, and, if it thinks it expedient to do so, instead of sentencing him may make an order requiring him to be under the supervision of a probation officer[7] for a period to be specified in the order, of not less than one nor more than three years.[8]

PROBATION ORDER MAY IMPOSE CONDITIONS

¶ 793. Such order may also require the offender to comply with conditions which the court considers necessary for securing his good conduct or for preventing his repeating the offence or committing others. The court may thus require him to reside in some specified place or institution,[9] and, on the evidence of an appropriately qualified and experienced medical practitioner, require him to submit for a period not exceeding twelve months to treatment with a view to the improvement of his mental condition. But none of the above mentioned requirements is to be imposed on a person who is fourteen years of age or older unless he expresses his willingness to comply with them.

[1] Sect. 22.

[2] Under conditions contained in s. 22 (2) (*a*) and sched. IV.

[3] Unless the court 'having regard to the circumstances, including the character of the offender, otherwise determines'.

[4] See Rackham, 'The probation system', *Penal Reform in England* (English Studies in Criminal Science, I, 1946), 118; Coddington, 'The probation system under the Criminal Justice Act', *Journal of Criminal Science*, II, 23.

[5] Now repealed, and replaced by ss. 3–12 and sch. I of the Criminal Justice Act, 1948.

[6] Not being an offence the sentence of which is fixed by law.

[7] Comprehensive provisions for the creation of administrative machinery, including the appointment of probation officers, are contained in ss. 45–7 and sched. V of the Act.

[8] If a court makes a probation order it cannot also impose a fine, although it can award compensation (up to £100, *post*, ¶ 797) under s. 3 (3), (5), and s. 11 (2), (3) of the Act. Sect. 13 does not permit a fine as well as probation, *R.* v. *Parry* [1950] 2 All E.R. 1189. And see *R.* v. *Evans* [1961] 1 All E.R. 313.

[9] See s. 46 and rules made thereunder by way of s. 1.

DISOBEDIENCE TO PROBATION ORDER

¶ 794. If the probationer fails to comply with the requirements of the order he may be brought before the court again; and then, without prejudice to the continuance of the order, the court may extend the order (but not so as to exceed three years in all) or may impose new conditions, or may fine[1] the probationer or order him (if between twelve and twenty-one years of age) to attend at an attendance centre,[2] or to be dealt with for the offence in respect of which the order was originally made.

DISCHARGE ON CONVICTION

¶ 795. Where, however, the court by or before whom a person is convicted thinks (on the same considerations as stated above in ¶ 792) that it is inexpedient to inflict punishment, and that a probation order is *inappropriate* in his case, the court may discharge him absolutely, or conditionally on his not committing any offence during a further period, not exceeding twelve months.

PROBATION ORDER NOT A PARDON

¶ 796. If a probationer or person 'conditionally discharged' should be convicted of an offence, then he may be brought before the court which made the original order, to be dealt with for the offence in respect of which that original order was made.[3]

ORDER TO PAY DAMAGES

¶ 797. The Act gives power to the court, when making a probation order, or an order for conditional discharge or on discharging an offender absolutely, to order the offender to pay reasonable damages for injury, or compensation for loss[4] caused by him.

CONVICTION NOT TO INVOLVE DISQUALIFICATIONS

¶ 798. In order to encourage a person discharged on probation or conditionally, to observe the conditions of the order and to abstain from other offences, the Act provides[5] that his conviction shall be deemed not to be a conviction for any purpose other than that of the proceedings in respect of which the order was made and shall be disregarded for the purposes of any enactment imposing disqualification or disability upon convicted persons.

Although it is thus provided that the *conviction* shall not be used

[1] Not exceeding £10; Criminal Justice Act, 1948, s. 6.

[2] Sect. 19. So far these centres have only been set up for males aged from twelve to sixteen (inclusive).

[3] Criminal Justice Act, 1948, s. 8.

[4] Not exceeding £100 in all, in the case of an order made by a court of summary jurisdiction. This order does not affect any power the court may have to award *costs* against the offender. See Compensation for Crimes of Violence, Cmnd. 1406 (1961). As to fines and compensation payable by parents or guardians of young offenders, see *ante*, ¶ 764

[5] Sect. 12.

against the discharged person, yet any relevant matters which arose during the proceedings which ended in his discharge can (subject to the established rules as to admissibility of evidence) be given in evidence in later proceedings against him. Thus a confession which led to his former conviction (and conditional discharge) may, in the later proceedings, be disclosed by a witness who was present in court when it was made in the former trial, although the conviction may not be disclosed.[1]

[1] *R.* v. *Harris* [1950] 2 All E.R. 816, in which it was stated that in order to establish a person's known 'character' for the purposes of the Prevention of Crimes Act, 1871, s. 15 (*post*, App. II, C (4)), it would have been proper for a witness to have stated that he had heard the accused confess to the offence with which he had been charged in the former trial and had heard the court discharge him subject to the condition.

Appendix I

THE MEANING OF 'CREDIT'

Some difficulty has been caused in recent years by judicial dicta and decisions as to the meaning of the word 'credit' for the purposes of the three statutory offences created by (i) section 13 of the Debtors Act, 1869; (ii) section 155 of the Bankruptcy Act, 1914; and (iii) section 156 of the same Act. The material words are:

in (i), 'If in incurring a debt or liability...he has obtained credit[1] under false pretences, or by means of any other fraud...';

in (ii), 'Where an undischarged bankrupt (*a*) ...obtains credit to the extent of £10 or upwards from any person without informing that person that he is an undischarged bankrupt...';

in (iii), 'If any person who has been adjudged bankrupt or in respect of whose estate a receiving order has been made (*a*) in incurring any debt or liability has obtained credit under false pretences or by means of any other fraud...'.

It will be observed that in (ii) the gist of the offence lies in failing to inform of the bankruptcy, and it is *not* necessary for the prosecution (as it is in (i) and (iii)) to allege or to prove 'false pretences' or 'any other fraud'.

The expression 'to give (or obtain) credit', in the ordinary economic acceptance of the words, signifies that a person is entrusted with money or goods on the faith of future payment for them.[2] 'Credit' does not appear to be a term of art, and therefore when it occurs in a statute it should be interpreted to accord with the tenor and purpose of the statute as a whole. Credit is a different and separate thing from any economic or other advantage which the possession of credit may produce. Thus a vendor who makes a complete transfer of the goods sold and allows the purchaser time in which to pay for them clearly gives to the purchaser not only the goods, but also credit.

The converse must also be true, so that if the purchaser pays the purchase money in advance and allows the vendor time in which to deliver the goods he gives not only the money but also credit to the vendor. Again, when a bank allows a customer to overdraw his account it gives him credit and also the cash which he draws out, just as in the ordinary case of a money loan by one man to another both credit and the coins or bank-notes are given by the lender and received by the borrower.

Provided that ownership and possession in the goods or money (as

[1] See *R.* v. *Garlick* (1958) 42 Cr.App.R. 141.

[2] *O.E.D. s.v.* And see Jevons, *Primitive Political Economy* (1878), 110: 'Thus anyone who lends a thing gives credit, and he who borrows it receives credit.'

the case may be) are completely transferred by the one party, credit must inevitably be given to the other, if he is allowed time in which to discharge his side of the obligation. In such a situation it is difficult, on principle, to see that it can make the slightest difference whether the time allowed be long or short.[1] The vendor who transfers his goods completely to the purchaser before payment reposes his confidence in the purchaser. If, however, the vendor insists upon payment *before* despatch or delivery[2] this shows that he is not prepared to give a purchaser any credit; conversely therefore, when in such a case a would-be purchaser pays in advance, he does repose his confidence in the vendor. In the case of a sale in a street or a market it is unusual for credit to be given on either side: money and goods are handed over as nearly as possible simultaneously, and the transfer of ownership of each is only completed by the delivery of both.

Now to examine some of the cases.

R. v. *Crosby*.[3] The accused Crosby was charged with obtaining money by false pretences.[4] It appeared that he was in the employment of the prosecutors as captain of a vessel, being remunerated on a profit-sharing basis. He had caused certain repairs to be done for which he had paid, and on returning to the prosecutor's office he presented a statement showing more money to have been expended than in truth he had paid; he thus was allowed a greater set-off than that to which he was entitled in the calculation of profits. The judge, Manisty, J., directed the jury to acquit the accused on the ground that it was essential for the prosecution to prove, as alleged in the indictment, that he had obtained *money*, whereas the evidence showed that he had *not* obtained money but only 'credit in account', which means that the entry in the firm's books would be to his advantage, shown there to his credit, in the sense that he had disbursed the sum on behalf of the firm and was entitled to be reimbursed. He *received* no actual money from the firm but he paid in less than he ought to have paid in.[5] Moreover, even if Crosby had in fact been paid money in respect of his false account, he would still have caused the false entry to be made in the first place,[6] although this, of course, could not have been an obtaining of credit in the present meaning of the word.

R. v. *Salomon*.[7] The defendant Salomon was charged[8] in the Lord Mayor's court with obtaining credit to the extent of over £20 from the prosecutor without informing the prosecutor that he was an undischarged bankrupt. It

[1] In *R.* v. *Jones* [1898] 1 Q.B. 119 (*T.A.C.*) (a case of obtaining credit by fraud contrary to s. 13 of the Debtors Act, 1869) the L.C.J. said: 'It does not seem to matter that the period of credit was a short period.'

[2] As, for example, in the case where the articles are in an automatic machine and the purchaser must drop in it his money before he can obtain one of them.

[3] (1843) 1 Cox 10.

[4] Contrary to the Larceny Act, 1861, s. 88, now s. 32 of Larceny Act, 1916.

[5] It must be remembered that in 1843 the crime of fraudulent conversion (now a misdemeanour under s. 20 of the Larceny Act, 1916) did not exist.

[6] See, e.g., *R.* v. *Carpenter* (1911) 22 Cox 618 *per* Channell, J., at p. 622.

[7] (1893) 28 L.J. 879.

[8] Under s. 31 of the Bankruptcy Act, 1883, now s. 155 of the Act of 1914.

appeared that he had obtained a loan of £50 upon his promissory note. The Lord Mayor, considering that borrowing money was not an obtaining of credit within the section, which in his view merely applied to obtaining goods on credit, and not to cash transactions of a money-lending nature, held that the prosecutor was not entitled to be bound over to prosecute.[1] On a rule to show cause the Queen's Bench Divisional Court held that borrowing money was clearly a credit within the section, and remitted the case to the Lord Mayor's court to be dealt with upon the merits.

R. v. *Coyne*.[2] It appeared that the accused man Coyne, without revealing that he was an undischarged bankrupt, had taken apprentices on payment of a premium of £25 in each case. The premiums were not to be returnable by him. But in two cases the money had been advanced on the boy's behalf by a charitable society, and in respect of these he had entered into a separate undertaking with the society to collect the money from the boy (by deducting from his earnings as apprentice) and transmit it to the society on behalf of the boy, whose debt it was thus recognized to be. He was charged[3] with obtaining credit from the society without disclosing that he was an undischarged bankrupt; however, on the argument that the prisoner had incurred no personal liability for the repayment, but had merely undertaken 'to become the channel by which the instalments should reach the society', the recorder directed his acquittal, stating that it was quite clear that he had obtained money, but not credit. It is plain that in so far as any credit was given by the society it was given to the apprentices and not to the prisoner;[4] if the apprentices had died or had earned nothing the society could have claimed nothing from the prisoner.

R. v. *Laker*.[5] This was an appeal against conviction of obtaining credit contrary to section 156(*a*) of the Bankruptcy Act, 1914. In this case it was necessary to allege and prove that the credit had been obtained by false pretences or other fraud. It appeared that Laker had represented to the prosecutrix that he could get a certain engine for her and that it would cost £125. Later he said that he had ordered the engine and asked her to pay the price in advance of delivery, which she did. But Laker had neither delivered the engine nor returned the money which in fact he had used to pay his own rent, which it appeared was what he always intended to do with it. Without referring to any decided case or expressing any *ratio decidendi* the court stated that while it was abundantly clear that the appellant had defrauded the prosecutrix 'he did not obtain credit' and that therefore his conviction of the offence charged must be quashed. The report of this case therefore sheds no judicial light upon the meaning to be given to the word 'credit'. Since, however, the money was paid in advance upon the faith of the man's undertaking to provide the engine it would seem that credit was obtained by him and that his conviction ought to have been affirmed.

[1] Under the Vexatious Indictments Act, 1859.

[2] (1905) 69 J.P. 151.

[3] Under s. 31 of the Bankruptcy Act, 1883.

[4] So far as can be seen from the report, this point was not mentioned by the Court of Criminal Appeal in *R.* v. *Pryce* (1949) 34 Cr.App.R. 21, at p. 23, when referring to *R.* v. *Coyne*.

[5] (1949) 34 Cr.App.R. 36.

Osborn v. *Barton*.[1] The respondent (in an appeal by the prosecutor on a case stated) had been acquitted by the justices on a charge under section 155 of the Bankruptcy Act, 1914 (in which an allegation of false pretences or fraud is neither necessary nor relevant). He had advertised, in a newspaper, parcels of goods for sale with the request 'cash with order'. A firm, whom he did not inform of his bankruptcy, ordered some goods enclosing a money order for £25, and duly received the goods ordered. Then they sent a cheque for £100 for more goods; this cheque the bankrupt cleared through his own bank but he did not send the goods. The case for the respondent was that the operative word in section 155 was 'credit' and, that the difference between 'credit' and 'property' was recognized by law;[2] and that, in everyday business purchasing, obtaining credit was the opposite of paying immediately (by either cash or cheque) and that what Barton had obtained was money and not credit. The prosecution on the other hand contended that a cheque was neither money nor a valuable security but was a bill of exchange, and that obtaining a cheque was obtaining credit at the bank of the drawer, and that for the period between receipt of the cheque and delivery of the goods the defendant had obtained credit from the purchaser, so that on failure to deliver the goods he was under personal liability to return to the purchasers, as his creditors, any money obtained on the authority of the cheque. All this contention was true enough, but, on basic principle, hardly necessary since the simple point was that Barton obtained the money first, and thus was trusted by the purchaser to deliver the goods. The appeal was, however, dismissed, Lord Goddard, C.J., saying: 'So far as we can see he did not obtain credit at all. Obtaining credit means obtaining something on a promise to do something in the future. This defendant was to send the goods at once.'

As to the arguments for the prosecution and as to the judgment it must respectfully be objected (*a*) that *R.* v. *Crosby* was not relevant, since the charge against Crosby was that of *obtaining money by false pretences* and the evidence failed to disclose that he had obtained any money; all that it did disclose was that he had been allowed a set-off, the falsely alleged payment by him being 'entered to his credit' in the firm's books; (*b*) that *R.* v. *Coyne* was not in point at all since it was held that there was no personal liability in Coyne for the repayment of the money; and (*c*) that, if the above dictum of the divisional court that 'obtaining credit means obtaining something on a promise to do something in the future' be accepted, then, it is submitted, that is exactly what Barton did. 'Cash' with order does not mean 'cheque' with order, and it is obvious that a would-be vendor in such a case intends to be secure before parting with his goods: he does not know that a stranger's cheque will be honoured, and he therefore puts it through his bank before he commits himself by dispatching the goods. Secondly, if the sending of the cheque be an offer to purchase, the cashing of the cheque must, it is submitted, amount to an acceptance which completes

[1] (1950) 66 T.L.R. pt. 1, 115.

[2] Citing *R.* v. *Crosby* and *R.* v. *Coyne*, *ubi supra*; *R.* v. *Salomon* was not mentioned.

a contract. Barton's stipulation for cash with order plainly showed that he was taking no risks, even with a firm with whom he had already had one successful transaction, and that accordingly he was not willing to give them any credit. It was they who must repose their confidence and credit in him by paying in advance, which they did. The vendor cashed the cheque and thereby, as suggested above, not only took credit from the purchasers, but also so acted as to accept their offer and conclude a contract with them. The accused lived in Cornwall and the purchasers in Yorkshire; the goods were unascertained, and after the payment for them had been made they still had to be appropriated to the contract, packed, and dispatched, and notice to the purchaser given before the ownership would pass. During this time the vendor held the payment. It is to be noted that the decision in *Osborn* v. *Barton* does no more than decide that on the evidence in this particular case it did not appear to the court that the purchasers did give any credit to the defendant; it does not lay down that, when money is paid in advance for goods by a purchaser who gives the vendor time for delivery, credit is not thereby given to the vendor.

But none the less the decision hardly seems consonant with the general purpose of the Bankruptcy Act which, it might be supposed, was aimed at preventing the kind of transaction which took place in this case, as the result of which unsuspecting purchasers were induced to part with their money to an undischarged bankrupt in reliance upon his ability to discharge his obligation in full.

R. v. *Mitchell.*[1] This is a case which must be read with care. M., the appellant, had pleaded guilty to a charge of obtaining credit to the amount of £65. It appeared that the appellant had possession of a motorcycle on a hire purchase agreement from *X*. Before he had fully paid for it he feloniously converted it to his own use by handing it over to another firm by way of part consideration (to the agreed amount of £65) for another motorcycle which he also bought on hire-purchase terms. This clearly did not constitute a giving of credit to the appellant to the amount of £65, since on any view of that part of the whole transaction M. was not thereby regarded as owing, or being trusted to pay, £65, but was entered in the firm's books as having himself paid it to them.[2] It could not, therefore, be properly regarded as an obtaining of credit by M. of £65 contrary to section 13 of the Debtors Act, 1869, as was pointed out by the Court of Criminal Appeal. It may be suggested, however, that what M. in fact did obtain was credit as to the *unpaid* instalments of his debt on the hire-purchase of the second motorcycle. But he was not charged with this.

The difficulties created by *Osborn* v. *Barton* seem now to have been removed by *R.* v. *Ingram.*[3]

[1] [1955] 3 All E.R. 263.

[2] 'Credited' only in the sense of having it recorded to his favour on the 'debit' side of the firm's ledger.

[3] [1956] 2 Q.B. 424.

This was an appeal against conviction of obtaining credit contrary to section 13 of the Debtors Act, 1869 (an offence in which false pretences or other fraud must be alleged and proved). The appellant had contracted with certain shopkeepers to erect or renovate electric signs. He obtained from each shopkeeper part of the agreed price in advance, but failed to carry out the work or to return the money paid to him. The jury as a fact found that at the time when he received the money he never intended to do the stipulated work. Counsel for the appellant cited *R.* v. *Laker* and *Osborn* v. *Barton*, relying upon both cases. Counsel for the Crown, and members of the court, sought to distinguish *Osborn* v. *Barton*, firstly, on the ground that there was no time stipulated for the supply of the goods and that therefore there was no credit;[1] this, it is submitted, was an unsound point since the facts clearly showed that the vendor B. was paid in advance on his promise to provide goods afterwards, which definitely is 'in the future' as defined in *R.* v. *Jones*;[2] it is submitted that it cannot be put as 'a matter of degree' but that the true principle is to be found in the fact that the *obligation of the one party was fully discharged against the promise of the other party to perform his side of the obligation thereafter*. In the *Barton* case it was plain that B. was to have time to clear the cheque and thereafter was trusted to perform his part and to set about the delivery of the goods. Secondly it was suggested that the *Barton* case was distinguished because there the jury did not find that the defendant never intended to send the goods;[3] this overlooked the fact that Barton was charged under section 155 of the Bankruptcy Act, 1914, an offence in which the question of false pretences or fraud is irrelevant. Further arguments were based on the meaning of the words, 'debt', 'liability' and 'money's worth' in the relevant statutes, all of which pointed to the same result, that credit is obtained in incurring any liability to pay not only money but money's worth, which may consist of commodities or services.[4] The appeal was dismissed.

The conclusion is inescapable that counsel for the Crown was right in saying[5] that 'getting money on a promise to repay in the future is obtaining credit and incurring a debt',[6] and that 'it equally follows that credit can be obtained by getting money on a promise to provide goods or services in the future'. The result is that the only way in which the decision in *Osborn* v. *Barton* can now be supported is by taking a very special view of the facts in that case.[7]

[1] At pp. 427 (Donovan, J.) and 428 (counsel).

[2] [1898] 1 Q.B. 119, 'it does not seem to matter that the period of credit was a short period'; *R.* v. *Jones* was alluded to in the judgment of *Ingram* (at p. 431) as 'in many respects the converse of the present case'.

[3] *Per curiam* at p. 427.

[4] Pp. 430, 431.

[5] At p. 428.

[6] See *R.* v. *Pryce* (1949) 34 Cr.App.R. 21.

[7] See [1956] *C.L.J.* 164. In *R.* v. *Goodall* (1959) 43 Cr.App.R. 24 (a case under s. 155 of the Bankruptcy Act) Parker, L.C.J., in referring to *Osborn* v. *Barton* and *R.* v. *Ingram* said: 'The court is of opinion that at some time these cases will have to be looked at with very great care.' Goodall's conviction was quashed on the ground that the issue whether any credit at all was given to *him* or to another person was not left to the jury.

Appendix II

RULES AS TO ADMISSION OF EVIDENCE WHICH REVEALS TO THE JURY FACTS DISCREDITABLE TO THE PERSON ACCUSED

Students should be careful to distinguish

(i) the case when the *character* of the accused is a *matter which is in issue*, i.e. when the purpose of the evidence is to establish what is the character of the accused, from

(ii) the case in which a fact in issue is not the accused's character, but *some fact* (e.g. his identity, or his *mens rea*) to prove which evidence of *his conduct* (*whether discreditable or not*) *on other occasions*, or even his *previous conviction* may be *relevant*; and from

(iii) the case in which a fact in issue is whether or not the accused has been *previously convicted* of crime. Thus

(i) the accused's character is in issue in A, B (1) and (4), C (1) and (5) below;

(ii) his conduct on other occasions is relevant in B (2) and (3), and his previous conviction is relevant in C (4) and (6) below;

(iii) his previous conviction is in issue in C (2) and (3) below.[1]

A. Evidence of general bad reputation is only admissible:

(1) Under the Criminal Evidence Act, 1898, s. 1 (*f*). If a prisoner has exposed himself to cross-examination as to his reputation and denies that it is bad, he may (apparently) be contradicted by independent evidence under the Criminal Procedure Act, 1865, s. 6.

(2) To rebut evidence of *good* reputation either set up by the defence or extracted by the defence in cross-examination (*R.* v. *Farrington* (1908) 1 Cr.App.R. 113; *R.* v. *Redd* [1923] 1 K.B. 104; *R.* v. *Samuel* (1956) 40 Cr.App.R. 8, where the prisoner, accused of larceny on finding, was held to have put the whole of his character in issue by giving evidence of his having, on other occasions, given back lost goods which he had found). But where the defence has merely attacked the character of witnesses for the prosecution (i.e. the defence has *not* set up the *prisoner's* good character, *nor* has he elected to give evidence) and has suggested that they are unreliable, this does not put the prisoner's character in issue (*R.* v. *Butterwasser* [1947] 2 All E.R. 415 (*T.A.C.*)).

[1] The judges of the Queen's Bench Division have issued a Practice Direction ([1955] 1 All E.R. 386) concerning the supplying of lists of previous convictions by the police, when requested, to the solicitor and counsel for the defence, so that they may know whether they can safely put the prisoner's character in issue.

(3) Under the Prevention of Crimes Act, 1871, s. 15, intent to commit a felony under section 4 of the Vagrancy Act, 1824 (as since amended) may be inferred from 'his known character as proved to the justices'.

(4) Under the Official Secrets Act, 1911, s. 1 (2). It may be inferred from the accused's 'known character as proved' that his purpose was 'prejudicial to the safety or interests of the State'.

(5) After verdict in order that the judge may determine the amount of punishment.

B. EVIDENCE OF OTHER WRONGFUL ACTS is only admissible:

(1) Under the Criminal Evidence Act, 1898, s. 1 (*f*). If a prisoner has exposed himself to cross-examination as to his previous wrongful acts and denies them he may be contradicted as in A (1) above.

(2) When relevant to the issue. The question of admissibility under this head is one of the most difficult in the whole law of evidence.[1] The general principles are stated in the quotations below, followed by examples. But the interpretation of the general principles has been a matter of some controversy in the courts, and the chief points are given in D below.

> ...if, as is plain, we have to recognize the existence of certain circumstances in which justice cannot be attained at the trial without a disclosure of prior offences, the utmost vigilance at least should be maintained in restricting the number of such cases, and in seeing that the general rule of the criminal law of England, which (to the credit, in my opinion, of English justice) excludes evidence of prior offences, is not broken or frittered away by the creation of novel and anomalous exceptions. (Kennedy, J., in *R.* v. *Bond* [1906] 2 K.B. 389.)

> It is undoubtedly not competent for the prosecution to adduce evidence tending to show that the accused has been guilty of criminal acts other than those covered by the indictment, for the purpose of leading to the conclusion that the accused is a person likely from his criminal conduct or character to have committed the offence for which he is being tried. On the other hand the mere fact that the evidence adduced tends to show the commission of other crimes does not render it inadmissible if it be relevant to an issue before the jury; and it may be so relevant if it bears upon the question whether the acts alleged to constitute the crime charged in the indictment were designed or accidental, or to rebut a defence which would otherwise be open to the accused. (Lord Herschell, L.C., in *Makin* v. *Att.-Gen. for N.S. Wales* [1894] A.C. 57 (*T.A.C.*).)

(i) *To establish* mens rea. Arson, to show intention to burn (*R.* v. *Dossett* (1864) 2 C. and K. 306; *R.* v. *Gray* (1866) 4 F. and F. 1102). False pretences, to show knowledge of falsity (*R.* v. *Francis* (1874) L.R. 2 C.C.R. 128 (*T.A.C.*); *R.* v. *Rhodes* [1899] 1 Q.B. 77; *R.* v. *Ollis* [1900] 2 Q.B. 758). Larceny, to negative innocent mistake (*R.* v. *Hill* (1908) 1 Cr.App.R. 158; *R.* v.

[1] E.g. *R.* v. *Chandor* [1959] 1 Q.B. 545.

Bleasdale (1848) 2 C. and K. 765). Obtaining credit by fraud, to show intent (*R.* v. *Wyatt* [1904] 1 K.B. 88; *R.* v. *Baird* (1915) 11 Cr.App.R. 186). Uttering base coin, to show knowledge (*R.* v. *Wylie* (1804) 1 B. and P. N.R. 92). Indecency, to rebut the defence of accident (*Perkins* v. *Jeffery* [1915] 2 K.B. 702). Intentional killing by driving a motor vehicle (*R.* v. *Mortimer* (1936) 25 Cr.App.R. 150). To rebut defence of innocent possession (*R.* v. *Hodges* [1957] Crim. L.R. 682).

(ii) *To connect the accused with specific features of the crime and thus to establish the* actus reus. Poisoning (*R.* v. *Geering* (1849) 18 L.J.M.C. 215; *R.* v. *Armstrong* [1922] 2 K.B. 555). Burglary, possession of housebreaking implements. Sodomy, possession of indecent photographs, to show a propensity to unnatural practices (*R.* v. *Twiss* [1918] 2 K.B. 853; *R.* v. *Gillingham* [1939] 4 All E.R. 122). Murder of children by baby farmers, discovery of bodies in other gardens occupied by the accused (*Makin* v. *Att.-Gen.* [1894] A.C. 54); deaths of other women married to the prisoner all by drowning in a bath (*R.* v. *Smith* (1915) 11 Cr.App.R. 229). Incest, to negative defence of innocent association (*R.* v. *Ball* [1911] A.C. 47 (*T.A.C.*)). *R.* v. *Shellaker* [1914] 1 K.B. 414; *R.* v. *Marsh* (1949) 33 Cr.App.R. 185, to prove carnal knowledge of the same girl. *R.* v. *Lovegrove* [1920] 3 K.B. 643, to corroborate evidence given of an operation to procure abortion. False pretences, to show the representation, *R.* v. *Murphy* (1876) I.R. 10 C.L. 508 (*T.A.C.*), sending half banknotes to different people.

(iii) *To establish identity.* (*R.* v. *Rickman* (1789) 2 East P.C. 1035; *Thompson* v. *R.* [1918] A.C. 221; *Perkins* v. *Jeffery* [1915] 2 K.B. 702; *R.* v. *Giovannone* [1961] Crim. L.R. 53.)[1]

(iv) *To show purpose.* (*R.* v. *Egerton* (1819) R. and R. 375; *R.* v. *Winkworth* (1830) 4 C. and P. 444; *R.* v. *Neill* (1892) C.C.C. Sess. Pap. CXVI, 1417.)

(3) Under the Larceny Act, 1916, s. 43 (*a*). On a charge of receiving stolen property evidence may be given at any stage in the proceedings of prisoner's possession of property stolen within the previous twelve months.

(4) Under the Official Secrets Act, 1911, s. 1 (2). The accused's 'known character' may be proved by evidence of other wrongful acts.

C. EVIDENCE OF PREVIOUS CONVICTIONS is only admissible:

(1) Under the Criminal Evidence Act, 1898, s. 1 (*f*). If prisoner has exposed himself to cross-examination as to his previous convictions and denies them, he may be contradicted by independent evidence as provided by the Prevention of Crimes Act, 1871, s. 18; and see s. 6 of the Criminal Procedure Act, 1865.

[1] See *R.* v. *Robinson* (1953) 37 Cr.App.R. 95 at p. 101, and comment thereon in [1959] Crim. L.R. 52.

R. v. *Hudson* [1912] 2 K.B. 465; suggestion by defendant's counsel in cross-examination that witnesses for prosecution had themselves stolen the money. *R.* v. *Pollinger* (1930) 22 Cr.App.R. 75; prisoner in evidence suggested that witnesses for prosecution had received stolen property. *R.* v. *Jenkins* (1945) 31 Cr.App.R. 1; prisoner alleged indecency by the prosecutrix.

(2) After conviction of a crime in those cases where there is a special statutory *punishment* to be inflicted in consequence of previous convictions: felonies (except those punishable by death, and simple larceny), Criminal Law Act, 1827, s. 11 (*R.* v. *Willshire* (1881) 6 Q.B.D. 366); simple larceny and offences similarly punishable (but perhaps not false pretences, *R.* v. *Horn* (1883) 15 Cox 205 (C.C.R.); *R.* v. *Marquis* (1951) 115 J.P. 329), Larceny Act, 1916, s. 37 (1) and (2).

In these cases the prisoner is in the first instance to be arraigned only to so much of the indictment as states the crime with which he is now charged, and until the question of his guilt has been determined the jury are to hear nothing of the existence of his previous conviction unless the defence sets up the prisoner's good character, in which case evidence of the previous conviction may thereupon be given, and the jury shall inquire concerning such previous conviction at the same time as they inquire concerning the crime with which he is now charged (Previous Conviction Act, 1836; Larceny Act, 1861, s. 116; Indictments Act, 1915, rule 11).

(3) When the *offence* depends upon there having been a previous conviction, e.g.

- (i) Stealing, etc., a dog, after previous summary conviction for any such offence (Larceny Act, 1916, s. 5 (1) and (2));
- (ii) Uttering base coin after previous conviction for a coinage offence (Coinage Offences Act, 1936, s. 5 (5)).

In the above two cases the jury are only to hear of the previous conviction under the same conditions as in C (2) above.

- (iii) Being a habitual drunkard. Where a person is charged on indictment with a crime and in addition is charged with being a habitual drunkard (Inebriates Act, 1898, s. 1 (2)), the charge of being a habitual drunkard must be made in a separate statement, and the jury are not to hear of it unless the crime charged is first established. Then the latter charge is inquired into, and for purposes of its decision evidence may be given of previous convictions as provided in the Act.
- (iv) Being a persistent offender, under the Criminal Justice Act, 1948, ss. 21, 22, and 23. In the circumstances stated in the sections a person convicted on indictment may be sentenced to corrective training or to preventive detention, provided that he has been given at least three days' notice before the trial that it is intended to give his previous convictions. In these cases either the indictment should include an averment as to the previous convictions (*R.* v. *Allen* [1949] 2 All E.R. 808), or the notice of intention to

prove them should be attached to the indictment (*R.* v. *Dickenson* [1949] 2 All E.R. 810). In such cases it would seem that the previous convictions should not be revealed to the jury until after the accused has pleaded or been found guilty of the offence with which he is charged (see section 10 (5) of the repealed Prevention of Crimes Act, 1908).

(v) Under the Prevention of Crimes Act, 1871, s. 7. A person commits an offence, if after two previous convictions and within seven years of the last (*a*) he gets his living by dishonest means, or (*b*) when charged with an offence he refuses, or falsely gives, his name and address, or (*c*) he is found about to commit or aid an offence, or (*d*) he is found on premises without being able to give a good account of his presence.

In cases under this section of the Act the previous convictions are *essential ingredients in the offence charged* and therefore must be proved to the jury before verdict and irrespective of any rebuttal of good character etc. (*R.* v. *Penfold* [1902] 1 K.B. 547; *Faulkner* v. *R.* [1905] 2 K.B. 76).

(4) Under the Prevention of Crimes Act, 1871, s. 15. Intent to commit a felony under the Vagrancy Act, 1824 (as since amended), may be proved by evidence of previous convictions.

(5) Under the Official Secrets Act, 1911, s. 1 (2). The accused's 'known character' may be proved by evidence of previous convictions.

(6) Receiving. On a charge of receiving stolen property, after proof of possession, evidence may be given of previous conviction within the past five years of any offence involving fraud or dishonesty, if seven days' notice has been given to the offender (Larceny Act, 1916, s. 43 (1) (*b*)).

(7) After conviction of the crime with which he is now charged, in order to guide the court as to sentence. For this purpose the previous record of the prisoner must be stated accurately and with precision. Strict proof need not be given unless the evidence is challenged or contested (*R.* v. *Campbell* (1911) 27 T.L.R. 256; 6 Cr.App.R. 131; *R.* v. *Butterwasser* [1947] 2 All E.R. 415 (*T.A.C.*) at p. 417). See the Criminal Justice Act, 1948, ss. 3, 17, 20–3, and the Magistrates' Courts Act, 1957, s. 3.

D. Note on admissibility of evidence relating to previous offences

(*a*) The controversy mentioned in Section B (2) above as to the principles for the admission of evidence of the prisoner's previous offences is illustrated in the following quotations.

Before an issue can be said to be raised, which would permit the introduction of such evidence so obviously prejudicial to the accused, it must have been raised in substance if not in so many words, and the issue so raised must be one to which the prejudicial evidence is relevant. The mere theory that a plea of Not Guilty puts everything material in issue is not enough for this purpose. The prosecution cannot credit the accused with fancy defences in order to rebut them at the outset with some damning piece of prejudice. (Lord Sumner in *Thompson* v. *R.* [1918] A.C. 221.)

...Their Lordships think that one qualification of the rule laid down by Lord Sumner must be admitted. An accused person need set up no defence other than a general denial of the crime alleged. The plea of Not Guilty may be equivalent to saying: 'Let the prosecution prove its case, if it can', and, having said so much, the accused may take refuge in silence. In such a case it may appear (for instance) that the facts and circumstances of the particular offence charged are consistent with innocent intention, whereas further evidence, which incidentally shows that the accused has committed one or more other offences, may tend to prove that they are consistent only with a guilty intent. The prosecution could not be said, in their Lordships' opinion, to be 'crediting the accused with a fancy defence' if they sought to adduce such evidence. (Lord du Parcq in *Noor Mohamed* v. *R.* [1949] A.C. 182.)

In 1946 some perplexity was created by dicta in a judgment of the Court of Criminal Appeal[1] which raised doubts whether the principle in *Makin's Case* was being extended. Fortunately, however, the doubts and perplexity have been dispersed by the House of Lords[2] in a judgment delivered by Viscount Simon in 1952. In this judgment the principle laid down by Lord Herschell (which is cited *ante*, p. 633) in *Makin's Case* was repeated,[3] confirmed, and explained. The judgment went on to add a second proposition, not as a rule of law but as a rule of judicial practice, cited from *Noor Mohamed* v. *R.*[4] which is as follows:

...In all such cases the judge ought to consider whether the evidence which it is proposed to adduce is sufficiently substantial, having regard to the purpose to which it is professedly directed, to make it desirable in the interest of justice that it should be admitted. If, so far as that purpose is concerned, it can in the circumstances of the case have only trifling weight, the judge will be right to exclude it. To say this is not to confuse weight with admissibility. The distinction is plain, but cases must occur in which it would be unjust to admit evidence of a character gravely prejudicial to the accused even though there may be some tenuous ground for holding it technically admissible. The decision must then be left to the discretion and the sense of fairness of the judge.[5]

(*b*) On the same principle as that in B (2) above, evidence which is relevant to the prisoner's defence does not expose his own character

[1] *R.* v. *Sims* [1946] K.B. 531; the dicta were criticized in *Noor Mohamed's Case.*

[2] *Harris* v. *D.P.P.* [1952] A.C. 694 (*T.A.C.*).

[3] At pp. 705, 706; the student should read these pages carefully.

[4] [1949] A.C. 182 at p. 192.

[5] The judgment added that this last proposition flows from the duty of the judge when trying a charge of crime to set the essentials of justice above the technical rule of the strict application if the latter would operate unfairly against the accused, *ante*, ¶ 547*a*. See *R.* v. *Bartlett* [1959] Crim. L.R. 285; *R.* v. *Cook* (1959) 43 Cr.App.R. 138.

even though it tends to discredit the character of the prosecutor or one of the witnesses for the prosecution.

(i) The prisoner is not to be prejudiced by evidence which is 'logically probative' of facts which are material to his defence, even though that evidence incidentally discloses facts discreditable to the prosecutor or his witnesses.

R. v. *Eidinow* (1932) 23 Cr.App.R. 145. (Prisoner in cross-examination stated that property had not come into his possession but into that of a witness for the prosecution.)

R. v. *Sheean* (1908) 72 J.P. 232. (Allegation of consent by the prosecutrix on a charge of rape.)

R. v. *Turner* [1944] 1 All E.R. 599. (Allegation of gross indecency by prosecutrix with prisoner on charge of rape held to be directed to proof of consent.)

And see R. v. *Harrison-Owen* [1951] 2 All E.R. 726, in which it was held that a prisoner could not be cross-examined as to his previous *convictions* in order to negative his defence that, since he was in a state of automatism and did not know what he was doing, his act was involuntary.

(ii) Mere abuse of the prosecutor or his witnesses is not an attack upon their character. R. v. *Rouse* [1904] 1 K.B. 184. (Prisoner called witness a liar.)

(iii) The character of the prisoner is not exposed to attack as the result of a reference to his good character which he did not make or intend. R. v. *Reid* (1923) 17 Cr.App.R. 36. (Witness for the defence volunteered the statement that the prisoner was 'all right so far as I know'.)

See also R. v. *Biggin* (1920) 14 Cr.App.R. 87 (a prisoner charged with murder who made allegations against the character of the deceased did not expose his own character since deceased was not the prosecutor); R. v. *Roberts* (1936) 25 Cr.App.R. 158 (evidence against a fellow prisoner who was not charged with the same offence); R. v. *Preston* [1909] 1 K.B. 568 (evidence by a prisoner suggesting that the identification parade was not properly conducted).

Appendix III

FORMS OF INDICTMENT

After studying the rules for the drafting of an indictment, the student may obtain a better understanding of them from the following illustrations, taken from the Indictment Rules.

(I) COMMENCEMENT

The Queen *v.* A.B.
[Durham County Assizes] held at [Durham]
A.B. is charged with the following offence [*or* offences]

(II) COUNTS. The commencement will be followed by one or more counts,[1] as in the following various examples.

A

STATEMENT OF OFFENCE

Capital Murder.[2]

PARTICULARS OF OFFENCE

A.B., on the day of , in the county of , murdered J.S. by shooting[3]

Capital Murder by A.B. and C.D. Murder by E.F.

PARTICULARS OF OFFENCE

A.B., C.D. and E.F., on the day of , in the county of , murdered J.S.

A.B. and C.D. murdered J.S. as aforesaid, he being a police officer acting in the execution of his duty, for the purpose of effecting an escape from legal custody (or as the case may be). A.B. by his own act caused the death of the said J.S. or attempted to inflict grievous bodily harm on the said J.S. C.D. by his own act caused the death of the said J.S. or attempted to inflict grievous bodily harm on the said J.S.

B

STATEMENT OF OFFENCE

Manslaughter.

PARTICULARS OF OFFENCE

A.B., on the day of , in the county of , unlawfully killed J.S.

[1] See § 279 *ante*. [2] See S.I. 669 for 1957.

[3] Or 'in the course or furtherance of theft' (or as the case may be).

C

STATEMENT OF OFFENCE

Accessory after the Fact to Murder.

PARTICULARS OF OFFENCE

A.B., well knowing that H.C. had murdered C.C. did on the day of and on other days afterwards, in the county of , receive, comfort, harbour, assist and maintain the said H.C.

D

First Count

STATEMENT OF OFFENCE

Arson contrary to section 2 of the Malicious Damage Act, 1861.

PARTICULARS OF OFFENCE

A.B., on the day of , in the county of , maliciously set fire to a dwelling-house, one F.G. being therein.

Second Count

STATEMENT OF OFFENCE

Arson contrary to section 3 of the Malicious Damage Act, 1861.

PARTICULARS OF OFFENCE

A.B., on the day of , in the county of , maliciously set fire to a house with intent to injure or defraud.

E

First Count

STATEMENT OF OFFENCE

Larceny.[1]

PARTICULARS OF OFFENCE

A.B., on the day of , in the county of , stole a bag, the property of C.D.

Second Count

STATEMENT OF OFFENCE

Receiving stolen goods contrary to section 33 (1) of the Larceny Act, 1916.

[1] It would seem that this Statement of Offence is still sufficient, notwithstanding *R.* v. *Bryant* (no. 1) 39 Cr.App.R. 59 and *R.* v. *Bryant* (no. 2) 40 Cr.App.R. 6.

PARTICULARS OF OFFENCE

A.B., on the day of , in the county of , did receive a bag, the property of C.D., knowing the same to have been stolen.

A.B. has been previously convicted of felony, to wit, burglary, on the day of , at the Assizes held at Reading.

Contrast a form in use before the Act of 1915, for larceny and receiving:

Cambridgeshire, to wit.

The jurors for our Lord the King upon their oath present that John Doe, on the 1st day of January in the year of our Lord 1903, at the parish of and in the county of Cambridge, an umbrella and a gun, of the goods and chattels of Richard Doe, feloniously did steal take and carry away; against the peace of our Lord the King, his crown and dignity.

And the jurors aforesaid, upon their oath aforesaid, do further present that the said John Doe afterwards, to wit, on the day and year aforesaid, the goods and chattels aforesaid, before then feloniously stolen taken and carried away, feloniously did receive and have, he the said John Doe (at the time when he so received the said goods and chattels as aforesaid) then well knowing the same to have been feloniously stolen taken and carried away; against the form of the statute in such case made and provided, and against the peace of our said Lord the King, his crown and dignity.

INDEX

[The references are given by paragraph number with the page number in parentheses beside it.]

www.ingramcontent.com/pod-product-compliance
Lightning Source LLC
LaVergne TN
LVHW082003200926
848481LV00010B/2796

* 9 7 8 1 1 0 7 6 7 5 9 1 9 *